EASTERN & CENTRAL EUROPE

21st Edition

Where to Stay and Eat for All Budgets

Must-See Sights and Local Secrets

Ratings You Can Trust

Fodor's Travel Publications   New York, Toronto, London, Sydney, Auckland
www.fodors.com

FODOR'S EASTERN & CENTRAL EUROPE

Editor: Douglas Stallings, Paula Margulies, Julie Tomasz

Editorial Production: Linda K. Schmidt
Editorial Contributors: Mark Baker, Lee A. Evans, Jane Foster, Betsy Maury, Diane Naar-Elphee, Paul Olchváry, Evan Rail, Dorota Wasik
Maps & Illustrations: David Lindroth, *cartographer*; Bob Blake and Rebecca Baer, *map editors*
Design: Fabrizio LaRocca, *creative director*; Guido Caroti, Siobhan O'Hare, *art directors*; Tina Malaney, Chie Ushio, Ann McBride, *designers*; Melanie Marin, *senior picture editor;* Moon Sun Kim, *cover designer*
Cover Photo (Rila Monastery in Sofia, Bulgaria): Chris Sanders/Workbook Stock/Jupiter Images
Production/Manufacturing: Angela L. McLean

21st Edition

ISBN 978-1-4000-1910-6

ISSN 1074-1216

SPECIAL SALES

This book is available at special discounts for bulk purchases for sales promotions or premiums. Special editions, including personalized covers, excerpts of existing books, and corporate imprints, can be created in large quantities for special needs. For more information, write to Special Markets/Premium Sales, 1745 Broadway, MD 6-2, New York, New York 10019, or e-mail specialmarkets@randomhouse.com.

AN IMPORTANT TIP & AN INVITATION

Although all prices, opening times, and other details in this book are based on information supplied to us at press time, changes occur all the time in the travel world, and Fodor's cannot accept responsibility for facts that become outdated or for inadvertent errors or omissions. So **always confirm information when it matters,** especially if you're making a detour to visit a specific place. Your experiences—positive and negative—matter to us. If we have missed or misstated something, **please write to us.** We follow up on all suggestions. Contact the Eastern & Central Europe editor at editors@fodors.com or c/o Fodor's at 1745 Broadway, New York, NY 10019.

PRINTED IN THE UNITED STATES OF AMERICA
10 9 8 7 6 5 4 3 2 1

Be a Fodor's Correspondent

Your opinion matters. It matters to us. It matters to your fellow Fodor's travelers, too. And we'd like to hear it. In fact, we need to hear it.

When you share your experiences and opinions, you become an active member of the Fodor's community. That means we'll not only use your feedback to make our books better, but we'll publish your names and comments whenever possible. Throughout our guides, look for "Word of Mouth," excerpts of your unvarnished feedback.

Here's how you can help improve Fodor's for all of us.

Tell us when we're right. We rely on local writers to give you an insider's perspective. But our writers and staff editors—who are the best in the business—depend on you. Your positive feedback is a vote to renew our recommendations for the next edition.

Tell us when we're wrong. We're proud that we update most of our guides every year. But we're not perfect. Things change. Hotels cut services. Museums change hours. Charming cafés lose charm. If our writer didn't quite capture the essence of a place, tell us how you'd do it differently. If any of our descriptions are inaccurate or inadequate, we'll incorporate your changes in the next edition and will correct factual errors at fodors.com immediately.

Tell us what to include. You probably have had fantastic travel experiences that aren't yet in Fodor's. Why not share them with a community of like-minded travelers? Maybe you chanced upon a beach or bistro or B&B that you don't want to keep to yourself. Tell us why we should include it. And share your discoveries and experiences with everyone directly at fodors.com. Your input may lead us to add a new listing or highlight a place we cover with a "Highly Recommended" star or with our highest rating, "Fodor's Choice."

Give us your opinion instantly at our feedback center at www.fodors.com/feedback. You may also e-mail editors@fodors.com with the subject line "Eastern & Central Europe Editor." Or send your nominations, comments, and complaints by mail to Eastern & Central Europe Editor, Fodor's, 1745 Broadway, New York, NY 10019.

You and travelers like you are the heart of the Fodor's community. Make our community richer by sharing your experiences. Be a Fodor's correspondent.

Happy traveling!

Tim Jarrell, Publisher

CONTENTS

MAPS

CONTENTS

CLOSE UPS

ABOUT
THIS BOOK

Our Ratings

Sometimes you find terrific travel experiences and sometimes they just find you. But usually the burden is on you to select the right combination of experiences. That's where our ratings come in.

As travelers we've all discovered a place so wonderful that its worthiness is obvious. And sometimes that place is so experiential that superlatives don't do it justice: you just have to be there to know. These sights, properties, and experiences get our highest rating, **Fodor's Choice,** indicated by orange stars throughout this book.

Black stars highlight sights and properties we deem **Highly Recommended,** places that our writers, editors, and readers praise again and again for consistency and excellence.

By default, there's another category: any place we include in this book is by definition worth your time, unless we say otherwise. And we will.

Disagree with any of our choices? Care to nominate a place or suggest that we rate one more highly? Visit our feedback center at www.fodors.com/feedback.

Budget Well

Hotel and restaurant price categories from ¢ to $$$$ are defined in the opening pages of each chapter. For attractions, we always give standard adult admission fees; reductions are usually available for children, students, and senior citizens. Want to pay with plastic? **AE, D, DC, MC, V** following restaurant and hotel listings indicate whether American Express, Discover, Diners Club, MasterCard, and Visa are accepted.

Restaurants

Unless we state otherwise, restaurants are open for lunch and dinner daily. We mention dress only when there's a specific requirement and reservations only when they're essential or not accepted—it's always best to book ahead.

Hotels

Hotels have private bath, phone, TV, and air-conditioning and operate on the European Plan (aka EP, meaning without meals), unless we specify that they use the Continental Plan (CP, with a Continental breakfast), Breakfast Plan (BP, with a full breakfast), Modified American Plan (MAP, with breakfast and dinner), Full American Plan (FAP, with all meals), or are all-inclusive (AI, including all meals and most activities). We always list facilities but not whether you'll be charged an extra fee to use them.

Many Listings
★ Fodor's Choice
★ Highly recommended
⊠ Physical address
✛ Directions
⌖ Mailing address
☎ Telephone
🖷 Fax
⊕ On the Web
✎ E-mail
🖃 Admission fee
☉ Open/closed times
Ⓜ Metro stations
☐ Credit cards

Hotels & Restaurants
🏨 Hotel
🛏 Number of rooms
⌂ Facilities
🍴 Meal plans
✗ Restaurant
⌂ Reservations
↘ Smoking
🍷 BYOB
✗🏨 Hotel with restaurant that warrants a visit

Outdoors
🏌 Golf
⛺ Camping

Other
🄲 Family-friendly
⇨ See also
⊠ Branch address
☞ Take note

Eastern & Central Europe

Rail lines

Black Sea

| 0 | | 200 mi |
| 0 | | 200 km |

WHAT'S WHERE

AUSTRIA	Vienna is a popular air gateway to Eastern and Central Europe, and with its well-preserved Old Town, there is plenty of flavor, art, and music to keep the typical tourist occupied for a few days before moving on to other parts of the region. Just outside of Vienna, the Lower Danube Valley is easily accessible to those travelers looking to see a bit more of the country before moving on.
BOSNIA & HERZEGOVINA	The destruction of Sarajevo was one of many tragedies in the aftermath of the dissolution of Yugoslavia in the early 1990s. But the city has come back and is ready to accept visitors once again. In Sarajevo today you'll find one of the most vibrant cities in Central Europe, chock-full of first-class historic sights, dramatic mountains, affordable meals, homey accommodations, and friendly people. And if you are willing to venture a few hours south, you'll be able to see Mostar or the popular Catholic pilgrimage site Medđugorje.
BULGARIA	The southernmost frontier of Eastern and Central Europe, Bulgaria borders Greece and Turkey to the south and the Black Sea to the east. Although still somewhat off the beaten tourist path, Sofia is one of Eastern Europe's up-and-coming capitals. The sunny, sandy beaches of Bulgaria's Black Sea coast attract visitors from all over Europe, and ski resorts in Bansko are increasingly popular.
CROATIA	Presiding over the eastern shore of the Adriatic Sea, Croatia stretches all the way from Slovenia to Montenegro at its southern tip. Once the meeting point for three great empires, you'll find influences from Venice, Habsburg Austria-Hungry, and the Ottoman Turks. Most tourists are drawn to the many islands and inviting towns of the coast, but Zagreb is an approachable and strollable capital, and the relatively unexplored reaches of Slavonia are just now starting to draw tourists.
CZECH REPUBLIC	Planted firmly in the heart of Central Europe, the Czech Republic is culturally and historically more closely linked to Western, particularly Germanic, culture than any of its former Eastern-bloc brethren. The most popular tourist destination in the region, Prague was discovered shortly after the fall of the Iron Curtain. But the stunning medieval towns in southern Bohemia and the famous spa resorts of the west are just as approachable. Travelers looking to get off the beaten path may wish to head for Moravia, the lesser-visited region in the eastern Czech Republic.

GERMANY	Eastern Germany is as much a part of Central Europe as Austria (and as a part of the Soviet-dominated bloc, was literally a part of Central Europe until the Berlin Wall fell in the late 1980s). It's relatively easy to include Europe's newest capital, Berlin, on your Central European itinerary. And nearby are two Saxon cities, Leipzig and Dresden, that have always been at the forefront of the German cultural landscape.
HUNGARY	Sandwiched between Slovakia and Romania, Hungary was the Austro-Hungarian Empire's eastern frontier. The heart of the nation is the capital, Budapest, just three hours from Vienna. Go there if you want a big-city vacation, but don't neglect the rest of the country: beautifully rural stretches in the north, the vineyards of the Danube Bend, and the verdant, rolling countryside of Transdanubia, including some beautifully restored smaller towns like Sopron and Pécs.
MONTENEGRO	Tiny Montenegro is one of the newest members of the United Nations, having been a recognized independent country only since 2006. Montenegro's relatively unspoiled natural landscape, with sand-and-pebble beaches along the coast—is dotted with delightful Venetian-era fortified port towns and is home to some excellent seafood restaurants. The country offers ample opportunities for a quick getaway into a country that is only starting to find its footing on the tourist path.
POLAND	The northernmost country in Central Europe, Poland is a vast nation made up primarily of a great plain in the north and central region and a small but dramatic stretch of mountainous territory to the south (on its border with Slovakia and the Czech Republic). Although its capital, Warsaw, is a major draw (particularly for business travelers), vacationers may be more enchanted with Kraków in the south. Other important Polish destinations include Gdańsk, the country's major Baltic port. Fans of castles and mountains will have plenty to keep them busy in Poland.
ROMANIA	Generally considered one of the most beautiful countries on the continent, Romania is bordered by Bulgaria, the Black Sea, the Republic of Moldova, Ukraine, Hungary, and Serbia. Its 238,000 square km (92,000 square mi) encompass cities with intact medieval districts and villages where traditional culture thrives. From Bucharest, the capital, you can explore the province of Transylvania, where cities such as Braşov,

WHAT'S WHERE

	Sighișoara, and Sibiu have preserved their historic core. Or you can explore the monasteries of Bucovina or frolic on the country's famous Black Sea coast.
SLOVAKIA	Deep-rooted traditions and folklore continue to flourish in the heart of the largely agrarian Slovak countryside. After ending a 74-year union with the Czech Republic in 1993, Slovakia's road to a free-market economy was a bit bumpy at first, but the country is now a member of the European Union. Bratislava, the capital, lies on the Danube in the southwestern corner of the country and offers a viable alternative to Vienna as an airline hub. But the beauty of the country lies to the east: from hilly Central Slovakia to the High Tatras, Slovakia's great outdoors waits to be discovered.
SLOVENIA	Geographically, politically, and culturally, Slovenia lies in a fascinating corner of Europe: here the former Yugoslavia meets the former Soviet bloc meets the gradually expanding European Union. The refined yet progressive capital, Ljubljana, lies in the center of the country. In less than three hours you can reach the border with Italy to the west, Austria to the north, Hungary to the northeast, Croatia to the southeast, and the Adriatic coast to the southwest. The country's dramatic alpine landscape is perfect for skiing in winter and hiking in summer. The coast, though short, is a popular draw for summer seaside excursions.

WHEN TO GO

The Eastern and Central European tourist season generally runs from April or May through October; spring and fall combine good weather with a more bearable level of tourism. The ski season lasts from mid-December through March. Outside the mountain resorts you will encounter few other visitors during the winter. You'll have the opportunity to see the region covered in snow, but many of the sights are closed, and it can get very, very cold in much of the region. If you're not a skier, try visiting the Giant Mountain of Bohemia, the High Tatras in Slovakia and Poland, and the Romanian Carpathians in late spring or fall; the colors are dazzling, and you'll have the hotels and restaurants pretty much to yourself. Bear in mind that many attractions are closed from November through March. Although the major cities can be visited year-round, midsummer (especially July and August) and the Christmas and Easter holidays are especially busy periods in much of the region, though Prague and Budapest are among the busiest cities, and Croatia's Dalmatian coast is among the busiest resort areas in the summer.

Climate

Much of Eastern and Central Europe has a standard Continental climate, with late spring and autumn having the nicest weather almost everywhere. It's not too hot or too cool to enjoy the outdoors, and the level of tourism is bearable in the busiest places. Summers can be hot and stifling throughout the region, even in much of Poland, and the farther south you travel, the hotter the weather gets (and the more Mediterranean the climate). The dividing line seems to be around Hungary. The Balkan countries, Croatia, and Bulgaria enjoy significantly milder winters, but temperatures in the summer can be stifling unless you are on the coast.

Information Weather Channel Connection (☎ 900/932–8437 95¢ *per minute from a Touch-Tone phone* ⊕ *www.weather. com*).

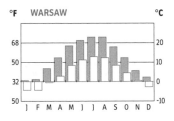

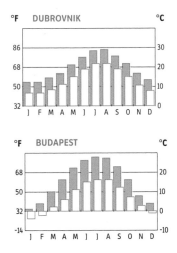

SIMPLE PLEASURES

Beer

Every discussion about the Czech Republic begins and ends with beer: Czechs are the world's largest consumers of beer per capita, they invented modern pilsner (named after the town, Plzen), and Czech beer is still considered among the best in the world. Pilsner Urquell and Gambrinus are among the more popular Czech beers. But beer doesn't stop at the Czech border. Whether you are talking about Żywiec or Okocim in Poland, Kelt and Topvar in Slovakia, Gosser or Augustiner in Austria, Laško and Union in Slovenia, Karlovačko in Croatia, Niksic in Montenegro, and Berliner Weisse or Leipzig Gose in Germany, each country and, indeed, each city, has its own special brew. Look especially for brewpubs that make their own beer for a very authentic local experience, and ask about popular beers in cafés and pubs.

Café Culture

The Ottoman Empire's many attempted incursions and invasions left countless relics around Eastern and Central Europe, but none has been more enduring or widely adopted than coffee. The café tradition dates from the 19th century and has been the center of towns both small and large all around the region. Anywhere the Habsburg's mighty empire touched was left with a café tradition. Whether sipping a coffee in Kraków, Sarajevo, Budapest, Vienna, or Bucharest, you'll find a favorite place where locals stop, read the newspaper, converse, or just kick back to relax and people-watch. Most cities of Eastern and Central Europe are filled with streetside cafés, and many of these also serve simple, wholesome food or pastries, making them good spots for a meal as well as a break from sightseeing.

Eastern and Central Europe is a remarkably varied place, and though each country has its own distinct cultural traditions, there are a few aspects of daily life that are constant across the region.

Wine & Spirits

Whether you are talking about vodka in Poland; plum brandy (called *rakija* in Croatia, Bulgaria, Montenegro, and Slovenia, *slivova* or slivovitz in Poland, Bosnia and Herzegovina, and Slovakia, *ţuică* in Romania); and herbal digestifs like Bekerovka in the Czech Republic or Unicum in Hungary, don't be surprised if your meal begins or ends with a small glass of these spirits, which are still a part of everyday life. Wine also plays a prominent role in Eastern and Central Europe. Hungary—with its famous sweet Tokaj and hearty Egri Bikavér (Bull's Blood)—and Croatia—where the Zinfandel grape originated—may be among the more famous wine-producing countries in Central Europe, but don't discount up-and-coming countries such as Austria, Bulgaria, Montenegro, or even the Czech Republic (more famous, admittedly, for its beer).

Christmas Markets

Central Europe comes alive during the holidays, when cobblestone squares are transformed with decorations and a dusting of snow into colorful Christmas markets. The markets, which originated in northern Europe, are especially popular in Central Europe, less so in the Balkans. You can shop for cakes and other sweets, not to mention locally made crafts and toys. Performances are always on hand to entertain and enchant. Nearly every city has a Christmas market in December, often in a main square near a church. Among the better ones are those in Prague, Budapest, Vienna, Kraków, Berlin, and Bratislava, and there are countless others in smaller towns in Austria, Germany, Hungary, Poland, Slovakia, and the Czech Republic. More southerly countries like Croatia, Montenegro, Romania, and Bulgaria have their own Christmas traditions.

IF YOU LIKE

To Eat Well

For many vacationers, it just wouldn't be a vacation without a few great meals. Great food needn't be extravagant or even fancy; sometimes, the best food is the most down to earth. Happily, prices in Eastern and Central Europe won't generally hit your wallet as hard as those in the euro-zone.

Inat Kuća, Sarajevo, Bosnia and Herzegovina. You won't find a more charming spot for traditional Bosnian meal *begova corba* (beg's soup), a rich stew chock-full of veal and vegetables. **Hebros, Plovdiv, Bulgaria.** The rabbit confit with a glaze of plums and figs may be the best dish you'll have in all of Bulgaria.

Kampa Park, Prague, Czech Republic. Prague's legendary restaurant at the foot of the Charles Bridge is both a celebrity magnet and a memorable dining experience.

Kádár Étkezde, Budapest, Hungary. Reasonably priced, tasty, traditional Hungarian Jewish food has been served here for decades.

Bąkowo Zohylina, Zakopane, Poland. Hearty, regional dishes are guaranteed to keep you warm in the chilly mountain air.

Slovenská reštaurácia, Bratislava, Slovakia. One of Bratislava's best restaurants serves Slovak specialties such as moufflon (a kind of sheep) with bilberry–wild cherry sauce.

Castles & Palaces

Castles dot the landscape of Eastern and Central Europe, reminding you of a time when secure walls were a necessary means of survival.

Diocletian's Palace, Split, Croatia. This massive 3rd-century AD Roman edifice now shelters Split's Old Town within its walls.

Eger Vár, Eger, Hungary. This imposing fortress was built in the 13th century and expanded over the ages.

Sveti Stefan, Montenegro. Not a castle per se, this tiny island is protected by 600-year-old defensive walls; it's been restored and turned into a luxury resort hotel.

Zámek Konopiště, Benešov, Czech Republic. Although it dates from around 1300, Habsburg Duke Franz Ferdinand's extravagant taste and lifestyle are on full display in several of the rooms.

Zamek Królewski, Kraków, Poland. Stroll the courtyards and chambers of Kraków's 14th-century Royal Castle to get a compact lesson in the trials and tribulations of Polish history and to view fine collections of artwork, arms and armor, and tapestries.

Peleş Castle, Sinaia, Romania. This 19th-century castle, summer home of Romania's former royalty, is one of the best-preserved palaces in Europe.

Cathedrals & Churches

Although neglected under the Communist regimes after World War II, the many beautiful churches of Eastern and Central Europe are once again a part of everyday life.

Bazilika, Esztergom. The imposing neoclassical dome of Hungary's largest church looming over the village and river below is one of the Danube Bend's best sights.

Chrám svaté Barbory, Kutná Hora, Czech Republic. Arguably the best example of the Gothic impulse in Bohemia, St. Barbara's Cathedral lifts the spirit and gives the town of Kutná Hora its unmistakable skyline.

Hram-pametnik Alexander Nevski, Sofia, Bulgaria. A modern, neo-Byzantine structure with glittering interlocking domes, this memorial to Bulgaria's Russian neighbor-liberators can hold some 5,000 worshippers.

Klasztor Paulinów, Częstochowa, Poland. The 14th-century church in this monastic complex holds Poland's holiest religious image, the famous Black Madonna of Częstochowa, a destination for pilgrims from around the world.

Pleterje Samostan (Pleterje Monastery), Sentjernej, Slovenia. You can't go inside the monastery, but you can visit the beautiful Gothic church and watch an enlightening audiovisual presentation about the way the monks live.

Voroneţ Monastery, Bucovina, Romania. The most famous of Bucovina's "painted monasteries," Voroneţ has exterior walls that are covered with vivid frescoes depicting scenes from the Bible. The unusually penetrating shade of blue that predominates is known to art historians and artists as Voroneţ blue.

Natural Wonders

Eastern and Central Europe are not all churches and castles. There is some beautiful scenery, and there are natural wonders to explore.

Jelení skok, Karlovy Vary, Czech Republic. The "Stag's Leap" offers a mythical panorama of Karlovy Vary.

Krutynia River, Poland. Kayaking through the ancient forest of Puszcza Piska as well as through numerous lakes is one of the great water-borne experiences in Poland.

Sinaia, Romania. A lovely turn-of-the-20th-century Carpathian resort makes for a good base for hiking in summer and skiing in winter and has the added lure of Castle Bran looming in the distance.

Škocjanske Jama, Slovenia. The breathtaking, enormous underground cavern is so deep it looks as if it could hold the skyscrapers of Manhattan.

Nacionalni Park Plitvička **Jezera, Croatia.** Sixteen cascading lakes are nestled in a protected forest.

Austria

VIENNA, BADEN, AND THE LOWER
DANUBE VALLEY

WORD OF MOUTH

"We drove to Krems, rented a bike, biked to Spitz,
and then hopped on a boat and rode it back to
Krems. Afterwards we drove to Melk to visit the
spectacular abbey. What a wonderful day!"

—tcreath

"One of our favorite evenings [in Vienna] was at
the Kunsthistoriches Museum. On Thursday nights
you can reserve a table for dinner on the second
floor of the museum. It's a candlelit evening catered
by Gerstner, and the food is excellent."

—malka

Updated by
Diane Naar-
Elphee

AN OFT-TOLD STORY CONCERNS AN airline pilot whose prelanding announcement advised, "Ladies and gentlemen, we are on the final approach to Vienna Airport. Please make sure your seat belts are fastened, please refrain from smoking until you are inside the terminal, and please set your watches back 100 years."

Apocryphal or not, the pilot's observation suggests the allure of a country where visitors can sense something of what Europe was like before the pulse of the 20th century quickened to a beat that would have dizzied our great-grandparents. Today, the occasional gentleman will kiss a lady's hand just as in the days of the Habsburgs, and Lipizzan stallions still dance to Mozart minuets—in other words, Austria is a country that has not forgotten the elegance of its past.

Look beyond the postcard clichés of dancing white horses, the zither strains, and the singing of the Vienna Boys Choir, however, and you'll find a conservative-mannered yet modern country, one of Europe's richest, in which the juxtaposition of old and new often creates excitement—even controversy. Vienna has its sumptuous palaces, but it is also home to an assemblage of UN organizations housed in a wholly modern complex. Tucked away between storybook villages are giant industrial plants, one of which turns out millions of compact discs for Sony. The world's largest penicillin producer is hidden away in a Tyrolean valley. By no means is the country frozen in a time warp: rather, it is the contrast between the old and the new that makes Austria such a fascinating place to visit.

Poised as it is on the northeastern edge of the Alps, Austria shares a culture with Europe but has deep roots as well in the lands that lie beyond to the east. It was Prince Klemens Wenzel von Metternich who declared that "Asia begins at the Landstrasse," referring to Vienna's role as a meeting place of East and West. In recent years, Austria's unique position as a crossroads has shown shaky resilience in the face of the meteoric rise and precipitous fall of the anti-immigrant and extremist Freedom Party. In fact, the success of the euro came as a bit of a surprise in Austria. The Austrian schilling was considered to be a symbol of national identity, like the national flag, and thus hard to surrender. The Austrians' quick acceptance of the euro could be a corroboration of a decline in national sentiment, a sign of willingness to be part of the new European community, or simply an acceptance of basic economic interest.

Vienna's spectacular historical and artistic heritage—exemplified by the legacies of Beethoven, Freud, Klimt, and Mahler—remains to lure travelers. A fascinating mélange of Apfelstrudel and psychoanalysis, Schubert and sausages, Vienna possesses a definite old-world charm that natives would be the last to underplay. But as with most countries, the capital is only a small part of what Austria has to offer. Nevertheless, since it is often an entry-point for travel to Central Europe, Vienna and the scenic Wachau stretch of the Danube Valley can easily be combined with a trip to Prague or Budapest or Kraków or any number of destinations in the region.

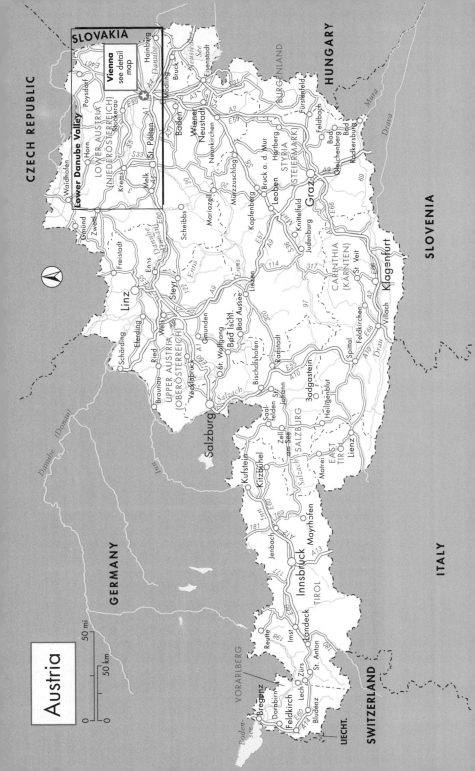

EXPLORING VIENNA & THE DANUBE VALLEY

AUSTRIA TOP 5

■ Delight your eyes and ears with a night out at the Vienna's State Opera or Musikverein.

■ Enjoy the best of Breughel and Titian at the Kunst Historisches Museum.

■ Step back in time when you visit the Habsburgs' former summer home, Schönbrunn Palace.

■ Visit Melk Abbey, a magnificent, baroque-era masterpiece.

■ Spend the night in Dürnstein; once all the day-trippers depart, you can really understand the town's storybook spell.

Vienna has been characterized as an "old dowager of a town"—an Austro-Hungarian empress widowed in 1918 by the Great War. Well, yes and no. A love of music; a discreet weakness for rich food (especially cakes); an adherence to old-fashioned and formal forms of address; a high regard for the arts; and a gentle mourning for lost glories have all helped to maintain Vienna's enchanting elegance and dignity. If you wish to get out of the city, then you will find that some of the most beautiful stretches of the Danube (Donau) extend about 88 km (55 mi) west of Vienna. This is also a region of legend: the Danube shares with the Rhine the story of the mythical Nibelungen, defenders of Siegfried, hero of German myth.

ABOUT THE HOTELS

Austrian hotels and pensions are officially classified using from one to five stars. These grades broadly coincide with our own four-point rating system. No matter what the category, standards for service and cleanliness are high. All hotels in the upper three categories have either a bath or shower in the room; even the most inexpensive accommodations provide hot and cold water. Accommodations include castles and palaces, conventional hotels, *Gasthöfe* (country inns), and the more modest pensions. In summer, student dormitories offer a reasonably priced option to guests of all ages.

Although exact rates vary, a single room generally costs more than half the price of a comparable double. Breakfast at the roll-and-coffee level is often included in the room rate; full and sumptuous breakfast buffets, however, can involve a supplementary charge. Keep in mind that hotels outside Vienna may offer comprehensive rates that include breakfast *and* dinner; these are often excellent values.

ABOUT THE RESTAURANTS

Take your choice among full-fledged restaurants in every price category, plus sidewalk *Würstel* (sausage) stands, *Imbissstuben* (quick-lunch stops), cafés, *Heurigen* (wine taverns), self-service restaurants, and modest *Gasthäuser* (neighborhood establishments serving local specialties). Most places post their menus outside. Shops (such as Eduscho) that sell coffee beans also offer coffee by the cup at prices considerably lower than those in cafés, though you can't sit down. Many Anker bakery shops also offer tasty *Schmankerl* (snacks) and coffee, and some offer a full breakfast. Würstel stands offer a tempting selection of grilled sausages, including *Käsekrainer* (beef and melted cheese), served with a roll and mustard. A growing number of shops and snack bars offer pizza by the slice.

WHAT IT COSTS IN EUROS (€)			
	$$$$	**$$$**	**$$**	**$**
RESTAURANTS	over €20	€12–€20	€8–€12	under €8
HOTELS	over €225	€175–€225	€125–€175	under €125

Restaurant prices are for a main course at dinner. Hotel prices are for two people in a double room in high season, excluding taxes and service charges.

TIMING

Austria has two tourist seasons. The summer season technically starts around Easter, reaches its peak in July, and winds down in September. In summer, Vienna moves outdoors. May, June, September, and October are the most temperate months, and the most affordable. The winter cultural season starts in October and runs into June; winter sports get under way in December and last until the end of April, although you can ski in certain areas well into June and on some of the highest glaciers year-round. Some events—the Salzburg Festival is a prime example—occasion a substantial increase in hotel and other prices.

Summer can be warm; winter, bitterly cold. The southern region is usually several degrees warmer in summer, several degrees colder in winter. Winters north of the Alps can be overcast and dreary, whereas the south basks in winter sunshine.

VIENNA

Most of Vienna lies roughly within an arc of a circle with the straight line of the Danube Canal as its chord. The most prestigious address of city's 23 *Bezirke*, or districts, is its heart, the **Innere Stadt** ("Inner City"), or 1st District, bounded by the Ringstrasse (Ring). The fabled 1st District holds the vast majority of sightseeing attractions and once encompassed the entire city. In 1857 Emperor Franz Josef decided to demolish the ancient wall surrounding the city to create the more cosmopolitan Ringstrasse, the multilane avenue that still encircles the expansive heart of Vienna. At that time several small villages bordering the inner city were given district numbers and incorporated into Vienna. Today, the former villages go by their official district number, but they are sometimes referred to by their old village or neighborhood name, too.

The circular 1st District is bordered on its northeastern section by the Danube Canal and 2nd District, and clockwise from there along the Ringstrasse by the 3rd, 4th, 6th, 7th, 8th, and 9th districts. The 2nd District—Leopoldstadt—is home to the venerable Prater amusement park with its famous *Riesenrad* (Ferris wheel), as well as a huge park used for horseback riding and jogging. Along the southeastern edge of the 1st District is the 3rd District—Landstrasse—containing a number

IF YOU LIKE

WINE

Although not as well known as regional varieties in France and Italy, Austrian wines, particularly whites, are now recognized by wine experts around the world for their excellent quality. The center of wine production in Austria is found in northern and eastern Lower Austria, in Burgenland, in Styria, and on the hilly terraces overlooking Vienna. Whites account for nearly seventy percent of production, but the quality of Austrian reds continues to improve. The most popular white variety is grüner veltliner, followed by Riesling, sauvignon blanc, and pinot blanc (often labeled as weissburgunder). The major red varieties are zweigelt and blaufränkisch.

MUSIC

What closer association to Vienna is there than music? Saturated with musical history and boasting one of the world's greatest concert venues (the Musikverein), two of the world's greatest symphony orchestras (Vienna Philharmonic and Vienna Symphony), and one of the top opera houses (the Staatsoper), it's no wonder that music and the related politics are subjects of daily conversation. If you are looking for inspirational tourism, you can visit homes associated with Schubert, Strauss, Haydn, Beethoven, and, of course, Mozart.

CASTLES, PALACES & ABBEYS

It seems that if you travel a few miles in any direction in Austria, you are confronted with a fairytale castle, an ostentatious palace, or an ornate Baroque abbey. It's easy to be overwhelmed by all of the architectural splendor, the fanciful decorations, and the often impossibly intricate mythical lore attached to these sites. From the Schönbrunn Palace in Vienna to the giant abbey of Melk, with its imposing architecture, lovely gardens, and one of Europe's most resplendent Baroque libraries, there is always another great building to see.

of embassies and the famed Belvedere Palace. Extending from its southern tip, the 4th District—Wieden—is fast becoming Vienna's new hip area, with trendy restaurants, art galleries, and shops, plus Vienna's biggest outdoor market, the Naschmarkt, which is lined with dazzling Jugendstil buildings.

The southwestern 6th District—Mariahilf—includes the biggest shopping street, Mariahilferstrasse, where small, old-fashioned shops compete with smart restaurants, movie theaters, bookstores, and department stores. Directly west of the 1st District is the 7th District—Neubau. Besides the celebrated Kunsthistorisches Museum and headline-making MuseumsQuartier, the 7th District also houses the charming Spittelberg quarter, its cobblestone streets lined with beautifully preserved 18th-century houses. Moving up the western side you come to the 8th District—Josefstadt—which is known for its theaters, good restaurants, and antiques shops. And completing the circle surrounding the Innere Stadt on its northwest side is the 9th District—Alsergrund—once Sigmund Freud's neighborhood and today a nice residential area with lots of outdoor restaurants, curio shops, and lovely early-20th-century apartment buildings.

The other districts—the 5th, and the 10th through the 23rd—form a concentric second circle around the 2nd through 9th districts. These are mainly suburbs and only a few hold sights of interest for tourists. The 11th District—Simmering—contains one of Vienna's architectural wonders, Gasometer, a former gas works that has been remodeled into a housing and shopping complex. The 13th District—Hietzing—whose centerpiece is the fabulous Schönbrunn Palace, is also a coveted residential area, including the neighborhood Hütteldorf. The 19th District—Döbling—is Vienna's poshest neighborhood and also bears the nickname the "Noble District" because of all the embassy residences on its chestnut-tree-lined streets. The 19th District also incorporates several other neighborhoods within its borders, in particular, the wine villages of Grinzing, Sievering, Nussdorf, and Neustift am Walde. The 22nd District—Donaustadt—now headlines Donau City, a modern business and shopping complex that has grown around the United Nations center. The 22nd also has several grassy spots for swimming and sailboat watching along the Alte Donau (Old Danube).

EXPLORING VIENNA

Vienna is a city to explore and discover on foot. When you explore the architectural riches of central Vienna, be sure to set aside enough time to visit the Schönbrunn Palace and its gardens. Above all, *look up* as you tour Vienna: some of the most fascinating architectural and ornamental bits are on upper stories or atop the city's buildings.

THE MEDIEVAL HEART OF THE INNER CITY

For more than eight centuries, the enormous bulk of the Stephansdom has remained the nucleus around which the city has grown. Vienna of the Middle Ages is encapsulated behind the cathedral. You could easily spend half a day or more just prowling the narrow streets and passageways—Wollzeile, Bäckerstrasse, Blutgasse—typical remnants of an early era. Stephansplatz is the logical starting point from which to track down Vienna's past and present, as well as any acquaintance (natives believe that if you wait long enough at this intersection of eight streets, you'll run into anyone you're searching for).

2 **Belvedere Palace.** One of the most splendid pieces of Baroque architecture anywhere, the Belvedere Palace—actually two imposing palaces separated by a 17th-century French-style garden parterre—is one of the masterpieces of architect Lucas von Hildebrandt. Built outside the city fortifications between 1714 and 1722, the complex originally served as the summer palace of Prince Eugene of Savoy; much later it became the home of Archduke Franz Ferdinand, whose assassination in 1914 precipitated World War I. Though the lower palace is impressive in its own right, it is the much larger upper palace, used for state receptions, banquets, and balls, that is acknowledged as Hildebrandt's masterpiece. The main attraction is the legendary collection of 19th- and 20th-century Austrian paintings, centering on the work of Vienna's three preeminent early-20th-century artists: Gustav Klimt, Egon Schiele, and Oskar Kokoschka. Modern music, too, has roots in the

Fodor's Choice
★

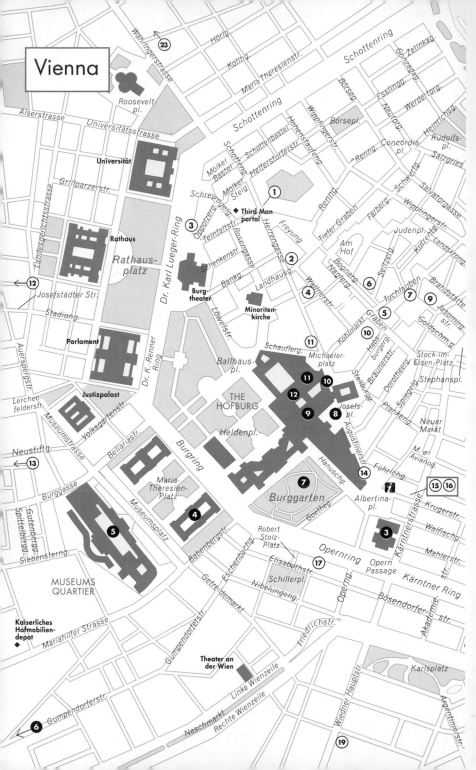

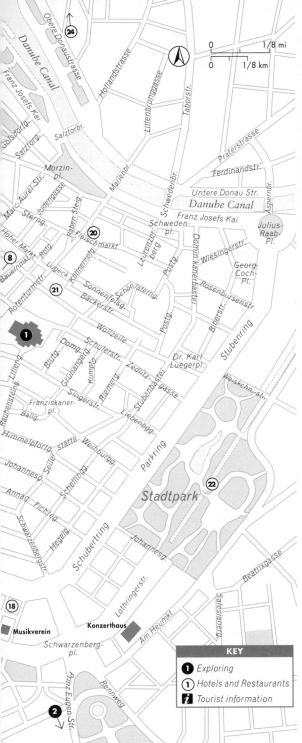

KEY

❶ *Exploring*
① *Hotels and Restaurants*
𝑖 *Tourist information*

CLOSE UP

Walking Tours

Guided walking tours (in English) are a great way to see the city highlights. The city tourist office offers around 40 tour topics, ranging from "Unknown Underground Vienna" to "Hollywood in Vienna," "For Lovers of Music and Opera," "Old World Vienna–Off the Beaten Track," "Jewish Families and Their Past in Vienna," and many more. Vienna Walks and Talks offers informative walks through the old Jewish Quarter and a *Third Man* tour from the classic film starring Orson Welles, among other subjects. Tours take about 1½ hours, are held in any weather provided at least three people turn up, and cost €11, plus any entry fees. No reservations are needed for the city-sponsored tours. Get a full list of the guided-tour possibilities at the city information office. Ask for the monthly brochure "Walks in Vienna," which details the tours, days, times, and starting points. You can also arrange to have your own privately guided tour for €120 for a half day.

Belvedere complex: the composer Anton Bruckner lived and died here in 1896 in a small garden house now marked by a commemorative plaque. ⊠ *Prinz-Eugen-Strasse 27, 3rd District/Landstrasse* ☎ *01/795–57–134* ⊕ *www.belvedere.at* ☜ *€9* ⊗ *Tues.–Sun. 10–6, Thurs. until 8* Ⓜ *U1, U2, or U4 Karlsplatz, then Tram D/Belvederegasse.*

❻ **Schönbrunn Palace.** The glories of imperial Austria are nowhere brought
Fodor's Choice together more convincingly than in the Schönbrunn Palace (Schloss
★ Schönbrunn) complex. This is one of Austria's primary tourist sites, and although the assorted outbuildings might seem eclectic, they served as centers of entertainment when the court moved to Schönbrunn in summer, accounting for the zoo, the priceless theater, the fake Roman ruins, the greenhouses, and the walkways. In Schönbrunn you step back 300 years into the heart of a powerful and growing empire and follow it through to defeat and demise in 1917. Within the palace, the magisterial state salons are quite up to the splendor of the gardens, but note the contrast between these chambers and the far more modest rooms in which the rulers—particularly Franz Josef—lived and spent most of their time. Of the 1,400 rooms, 40 are open to the public on the regular tour. ⊠ *Schönbrunner-Schloss-Strasse, 13th District/Hietzing* ☎ *01/81113–239* ⊕ *www.schoenbrunn.at* ☜ *Guided grand tour of palace interior (40 rooms) €14, self-guided tour €11.50* ⊗ *Apr.–June, Sept., and Oct., daily 8:30–5; July and Aug., daily 8:30–6; Nov.–Mar., daily 8:30–4:30. Park Apr.–Oct., daily 6 AM–dusk; Nov.–Mar., daily 6:30 AM–dusk* Ⓜ *U4/Schönbrunn.*

★ **❸** **Staatsoper** *(State Opera House).* The famous Vienna Staatsoper on the Ring vies with the cathedral for the honor of marking the emotional heart of the city—it is a focus for Viennese life and one of the chief symbols of resurgence after the cataclysm of World War II. The first of the Ringstrasse projects to be completed (in 1869), the opera house suffered disastrous bomb damage in the last days of World War II (only the outer walls, the front facade, and the main staircase area behind it survived). The auditorium is plain when compared to the red-and-gold

GREAT ITINERARIES

Like a well-bred grande dame, Vienna doesn't rush about, and neither should you. Saunter through its stately streets—and rub elbows with its creative spirits—and marvel at its Baroque palaces. Then dream an afternoon away at a cozy *Kaffeehaus*. Depending on how much time you have, you can explore a bit of the Danube Valley as well.

IF YOU HAVE 3 DAYS

There's plenty to keep you busy in Vienna for two very full days. On Day 3 take a trip to **Baden** or spend some additional time exploring Vienna's sights; there's plenty to see.

You might want to begin with an organized sightseeing tour, which will describe the highlights. Plan to spend time at the **Stephansdom** and a full afternoon at **Schönbrunn Palace.** Reserve the second day for art, tackling the exciting **KunsthistorIches Museum** before lunch, and after you're refreshed, the dazzling **MuseumsQuartier,** which comprises several major modern art collections. If your tastes tend to the grand and royal, visit instead the magnificent collection of Old Master drawings at the **Albertina**

Museum and the impressive **Belvedere Palace.** Do as the Viennese do, and fill in any gaps with stops at cafés, reserving evenings for relaxing over music or wine. On the third day, head for the world-famous **Spanische Reitschule** and watch the Lipizzaners prance through morning training. While you're in the neighborhood, view the sparkling court jewels in the Imperial Treasury, the **Schatzkammer,** and the glitzy **Silberkammer,** the museum of court silver and tableware, and take in one of Vienna's most spectacular Baroque settings, the glorious Grand Hall of the **Hofbibliothek.**

IF YOU HAVE 5 DAYS

You can spend your first three days touring Vienna and seeing some of the secondary sights, or take that trip to Baden. On Day 4, head to **Melk** to see the magnificent abbey. Instead of coming back to Vienna, head to **Dürnstein** and spend the night, so you can appreciate some of the beautiful town's storybook charm. Begin the morning of Day 5 in Dürnstein, and then stop at **Krems** or **Weissenkirchen** (or both) on your way back to Vienna.

eruptions of London's Covent Garden or some of the Italian opera houses, but it has an elegant individuality that shows to best advantage when the stage and auditorium are turned into a ballroom for the great Opera Ball. Tours of the Opera House are given regularly, but starting times vary according to opera rehearsals; the current schedule is posted at the east-side entrance under the arcade on the Kärntnerstrasse marked GUIDED TOURS, where the tours begin. The ticket office is there as well. ⊠ *Opernring 2, 1st District* ☎ *01/514–44–2613* ⊕ *www.staatsoper.at* ☜ *€4* ☉ *Tours year-round when there are no rehearsals, but call for times* Ⓜ *U1, U2, or U4 Karlsplatz.*

★ ❶ **Stephansdom** *(St. Stephen's Cathedral).* Vienna's soaring centerpiece, this beloved cathedral enshrines the heart of the city—although it is curious to note that when first built in 1144–47, it actually stood outside the city walls. Vienna can thank a period of hard times for the Catholic

Church for the cathedral's distinctive silhouette. Originally the structure was to have had matching 445-foot-high spires, a standard design of the era, but funds ran out, and the north tower to this day remains a happy reminder of what gloriously is not. The lack of symmetry creates an imbalance that makes the cathedral instantly identifiable from its profile alone. The cathedral, like the Staatsoper and some other major buildings, was very heavily damaged in World War II. Since then it has risen from the fires of destruction like a phoenix. The bird's-eye views from the cathedral's beloved **Alter Steffl** (Old Stephen Tower) will be a highlight for some. The south tower is 450 feet high and was built between 1359 and 1433. The climb up the 343 steps is rewarded with vistas that extend to the rising slopes of the Wienerwald, although until restoration is completed the view is somewhat limited. The north steeple houses the big Pummerin bell and a lookout terrace (access by elevator). ■TIP→ The wealth of decorative sculpture in St. Stephen's can be intimidating to the nonspecialist, so if you wish to explore the cathedral in detail, buy the admirably complete English-language description sold in the small room marked DOM SHOP. ⊠ *Stephansplatz, 1st District* ☎ *01/515–5237–67* 🎟 *Guided tour €4; catacombs €4; stairs to south tower €3; elevator to Pummerin bell €4* ⊘ *Daily 6 AM–10 PM. Guided tours in English daily Apr.–Oct. at 3:45; catacombs tour (minimum 5 people) Mon.–Sat. every half hr 10–11:30 and 1:30–4:30, Sun. every half hr 1:30–4:30; North Tower elevator to Pummerin bell, Apr.–Oct., daily 8:30–5:30; July and Aug., daily 8:30–6; Nov.–Mar., daily 8:30–5* Ⓜ *U1 or U3/Stephansplatz.*

AN IMPERIAL CITY: THE HOFBURG

A walk through the Imperial Palace, called the Hofburg, brings you back to the days when Vienna was the capital of a mighty empire. You can still find in Viennese shops vintage postcards and prints that show the revered and bewhiskered Emperor Franz Josef leaving his Hofburg palace for a drive in his carriage. Today you can walk in his very footsteps, gaze at the old tin bath the emperor kept under his simple iron bedstead, marvel at his bejeweled christening robe, and, along the way, feast your eyes on great works of art, impressive armor, and some of the finest Baroque interiors in Europe.

❼ **Burggarten.** The intimate Burggarten in back of the Neue Burg is a quiet oasis that includes a statue of a contemplative Franz Josef and an elegant statue of Mozart, moved here from the Albertinaplatz after the war, when the city's charred ruins were being rebuilt. Today the park is one of the most favored time-out spots for the Viennese; the alluring backdrop is formed by the striking former greenhouses that are now the gorgeous Palmenhaus restaurant and the **Schmetterlinghaus.** Total enchantment awaits you here at Vienna's unique Butterfly House. Inside are towering tropical trees, waterfalls, a butterfly nursery, and more than 150 species on display (usually 400 winged jewels are in residence). ⊠ *Access from Opernring and Hanuschgasse/Goethegasse, 1st District* 🎟 *€5* ⊘ *Apr.–Oct., weekdays 10–4:45, weekends 10–6:15; Nov.–Mar., daily 10–3:45* ⊕ *www.schmetterlinghaus.at* Ⓜ *U2/MuseumsQuartier; Tram: 1, 2, and D/Burgring.*

9 Hofburgkapelle *(Chapel of the Imperial Palace)*. Fittingly, this is the main venue for the beloved Vienna Boys' Choir (Wiener Sängerknaben), since they actually have their earliest roots in the Hofmusikkapelle choir founded by Emperor Maximilian I five centuries ago (Haydn and Schubert were both participants as young boys). Today the choir sings mass here at 9:15 on Sunday from mid-September to June (even though this is a mass, tickets are sold to hear the choir, ranging from €5 to €35). In case you miss out on tickets to the Sunday performance, note that just to the right of the chapel entrance a door leads into a small foyer. Here a television screen shows the whole mass for free. *For ticket information, see Nightlife and the Arts, below.* ⊠*Hofburg, Schweizer Hof, 1st District* ☎*01/533–9927* ⊕*www.wsk.at* 🖶*01/533–9927–75* Ⓜ*U3/Herrengasse.*

8 Josefsplatz. Many consider this Vienna's loveliest courtyard. Indeed, the beautifully restored imperial decor adorning the roof of the buildings forming Josefsplatz is one of the few visual demonstrations of Austria's onetime widespread power and influence. The square's namesake is represented in the equestrian **statue of Emperor Joseph II** (1807) in the center. ⊠*Herrengasse, 1st District* Ⓜ*U3/Herrengasse.*

11 Kaiserappartements *(Imperial Apartments)*. From the spectacular portal gate of the Michaelertor—you can't miss the four gigantic statues of Hercules and his Labors—you enter and climb the marble Kaiserstiege (Emperor's Staircase) to begin a tour of a long, repetitive suite of 18 conventionally luxurious state rooms. ⊠*Hofburg, Schweizer Hof, 1st District* ⊕*www.hofburg-wien.at* ☎*01/533–7570* 💶*€8.90* ☽*Daily 9–5; July and Aug., daily 9–5:30* Ⓜ*U3/Herrengasse.*

12 Schatzkammer *(Imperial Treasury)*. The entrance to the Schatzkammer, with its 1,000 years of treasures, is tucked away at ground level behind the staircase to the Hofburgkapelle. The elegant display is a welcome antidote to the monotony of the Imperial Apartments, for the entire Treasury was completely renovated in 1983–87, and the crowns and relics and vestments fairly glow in their surroundings. Here you'll find such marvels as the Holy Lance—reputedly the lance that pierced Jesus's side—the Imperial Crown (a sacred symbol of sovereignty once stolen on Hitler's orders), and the Saber of Charlemagne. Don't miss the Burgundian Treasure, connected with that most romantic of medieval orders of chivalry, the Order of the Golden Fleece. ⊠*Schweizer Hof, 1st District* ☎*01/525240* 💶*€8* ☽*Wed.–Mon. 10–6* Ⓜ*U3/Herrengasse.*

FodorśChoice ★

★ 10 Spanische Reitschule *(Spanish Riding School)*. Between Augustinerstrasse and the Josefsplatz is the world-famous Spanish Riding School, a favorite for centuries, and no wonder: who can resist the sight of the stark-white Lipizzaner horses going through their masterful paces? For the last 300 years they have been perfecting their *haute école* riding demonstrations to the sound of Baroque music in a ballroom that seems to be a crystal-chandeliered stable. The interior of the riding school, the 1735 work of Fischer von Erlach the Younger, is itself an attraction—surely Europe's most elegant sports arena—and if the prancing horses begin to pall, move up to the top balcony and examine the ceiling. Information offices have a brochure with the detailed schedule (performances are usually March–December, except July and August). Generally the full, 80-minute show takes place Sunday at 11 AM plus selected Fridays at 6 PM. Morning training sessions with music are held Tuesday–Saturday 10–noon. Tickets are available at the visitor center, Michaelerplatz 1, Tuesday to Saturday (except holidays) 9–5, and at Josefsplatz, Gate 2 on the day of the morning exercise 9–12:30. It's best to get there early to get a place in line. For performance ticket orders, write to **Spanische Reitschule** (⊠*Hofburg, A-1010, Vienna*). Pick up reserved tickets at the office under the Michaelerplatz rotunda dome. ⊠*Michaelerplatz 1, Hofburg, A-1010, 1st District* ☎*01/533–9031-0* 🖷*01/535–0186* ⊕*www.srs.com* 🖅*€35–€160; standing room €22–€28, morning training sessions €12. Sat. classical dressage final rehearsal, €20* ☉*Mar.– June and late Aug.–mid-Dec. Closed tour wks* Ⓜ*U3/Herrengasse.*

THE RINGSTRASSE: GEMS OF THE "RING"

Late in 1857 Emperor Franz Josef issued a decree announcing the most ambitious piece of urban redevelopment Vienna had ever seen. The inner city's centuries-old walls were to be torn down, and the *glacis*— the wide expanse of open field that acted as a protective buffer between inner city and outer suburbs—was to be filled in. In their place was to rise a wide, tree-lined, circular boulevard, upon which would stand an imposing collection of new buildings reflecting Vienna's special status as the political, economic, and cultural heart of the Austro-Hungarian Empire. As an ensemble, the collection is astonishing in its architectural presumption: it is nothing less than an attempt to assimilate and summarize the entire architectural history of Europe.

❹ Kunsthistorisches Museum *(Museum of Fine Art).* However short your
Fodor'sChoice stay in Vienna, you will surely want to pay a visit to one of the great-
★ est art collections in the world, that of the Kunsthistorisches Museum. The collection stands in the same class with those of the Louvre, the Prado, and the Vatican. It is most famous for the largest collection of paintings under one roof by the Netherlandish 16th-century master Pieter Brueghel the Elder—just seeing his sublime *Hunters in the Snow* is worth a trip to Vienna, many art historians will tell you. The large-scale works concentrated in the main galleries shouldn't distract you from the equal share of masterworks in the more intimate side wings. ⊠*Maria-Theresien-Platz, 7th District/Neubau* ☎*01/525240* ⊕*www. khm.at* 🖅*€10* ☉*Tues.–Sun. 10–6; extended hrs for picture galleries, Thurs. until 9* PM Ⓜ*U2/MuseumsQuartier, U2, or U3/Volkstheater.*

★ ☕ ❺ MuseumsQuartier *(Museum Quarter).* New and old, past and present, Baroque and Modernism dazzlingly collide in this headline-making, vast culture center that opened in 2001. Claiming to be the largest of its kind in the world, the MuseumsQuartier—or **MQ** as many now call it—is housed in what was once the Imperial Court Stables, the 250-year-old Baroque complex designed by Fischer von Erlach, and is ideally situated between the great old master treasures of the Kunsthistorisches Museum and the Spittelberg neighborhood, today one of Vienna's hippest enclaves. The original structure (fetchingly adorned with pastry-white stuccoed ceilings and rococo flourishes) was retained, although ultramodern wings were added to house five museums, most of which showcase modern art at its best.

Once ensconced in the Palais Liechtenstein, the **Leopold Museum** (⊕ *www. leopoldmuseum.org* ⊞ €9 ⊘ *Wed.–Mon. 10–6*) comprises the holdings amassed by Rudolf and Elizabeth Leopold and famously contains one of the greatest collections of Egon Schiele in the world, as well as impressive works by Gustav Klimt and Oskar Kokoschka. Other artists worth noting are Josef Dobrowsky, Anton Faistauer, and Richard Gerstl. Emil Jakob Schindler's landscapes are well represented, as are those by Biedermeier artist Ferdinand Georg Waldmüller. Center stage is held by Schiele (1890–1918), who died young, along with his wife and young baby, in the Spanish flu pandemic of 1918. His colorful, appealing landscapes are here, but all eyes are invariably drawn to the artist's tortured and racked depictions of nude mistresses, orgiastic self-portraits, and provocatively sexual couples, all elbows and organs.

WHERE TO EAT

To appreciate how far the restaurant scene in Vienna has come in recent years, it helps to recall the way things used to be. Up until 2000, Austria was still dining in the 19th century. Most dinners were a *mitteleuropäisch* sloshfest of *Schweinebraten, Knödeln,* and *Kraut* (pork, dumplings, and cabbage). Today Vienna's dining scene is as lively, experimental, and as good as it is thanks in part to changing epicurean tastes and a rising generation of chefs dedicated to taking the culinary heritage of the nation to a new phase of *Neu Wiener Küche* (New Vienna Cuisine).

Be aware that the basket of bread put on your table is not free. Most of the older-style Viennese restaurants charge €.80–€1.50 for each roll that is eaten, but more and more establishments are beginning to charge a per person cover charge—anywhere from €1.50 to €4—which includes all the bread you want, plus usually an herb spread and butter.

$$$$ ✗ **Anna Sacher.** Complete renovation and a new foyer has brought the Hotel Sacher into the 21st century. What remains traditional is the restaurant Anna Sacher, a name that has almost as many reverberations as Strauss's. The legendary Sachertorte cake is the crown of a family saga that began with Franz Sacher, Prince von Metternich's pastry chef. Franz's son and his wife, Anna, Vienna's "hostess with the mostest," opened the famed 19th-century hotel. A showcase for "internationale und typische Wiener Küche," it seeps the monarchical magic of former glory: wainscotted oak walls, beige silk fabrics, gilt-frame oil paintings, and sparkling chandeliers create a suitably aristo ambience. Sacher offers some of the city's best Tafelspitz (boiled beef), garnished with creamed spinach and hash-brown potatoes, with chive cream sauce and apple horseradish adding extra flavor to this favorite dish of Emperor Franz Josef. Angus beef served with chanterelles and quail eggs is another good choice. ⊠ *Philharmonikerstrasse*

4, 1st District ☎01/5145–6840 ⊕www.sacher.com ⌖Reservations essential Jacket and tie ⊟AE, DC, MC, V ⊗No lunch Ⓜ U1, U2, or U4/Karlsplatz/Opera.

$$$$ ✕**Julius Meinl am Graben.** A few doors down from the Hofburg Pal-

Fodor's Choice ace, Meinl opened as a caterer to the Habsburgs in 1862, and has

★ remained Vienna's poshest grocery store and ranks among the city's best restaurants. Take a left at the door, walk through the coffee and tea sections, head upstairs past the cheese bar, and then, turning the corner, you'll find a cozy salon, all deep orange banquettes and dark wood. The window tables have stunning views over the pedestrian crossroads of Graben/Kohlmarkt. The maestro in command is Joachim Gradwohl, whose young sous-chef, Thomas Göls, is a past winner of the "Newcomer of the Year" award at the international Bocuse d'Or competition. The staff is tremendous with advice. The lobster terrine and its side of lobster bisque (adorably served in an espresso cup) is always a winner, and the sizzling duck, carved tableside and served with roasted chestnuts and apple-studded *Rotkraut* (red cabbage) is delicious. ⊠*Graben 19 (entrance after 7* PM *from outdoor elevator on Naglergasse), 1st District* ☎01/532–3334–99 ⌖*Reservations essential* ⊟AE, DC, MC, V ⊗*Closed Sun.* Ⓜ*U3/Herrengasse.*

$$$$ ✕**Steirereck.** Possibly the most raved-about restaurant in Austria is

Fodor's Choice Steirereck, in the former Milchhauspavilion, a grand Jugendstil-vintage

★ "drinking hall" overlooking the Wienfluss promenade in the Stadtpark, the main city park on the Ringstrasse. At the entrance is a 20-foot-long rococo banqueting table topped by a video screen that allows a peek into the kitchen that achieves perfection in all its creations. Winners include delicate smoked catfish, turbot in an avocado crust, or char on a bed of white garlic sauce. At the end of the meal, an outstanding selection of more than 60 cheeses from Steirereck's own cheese cellar await the palate. If you don't want the gala Steirereck experience, opt for a bite in the lower-floor "Meierei," which is strikingly stylish with a hand-painted floor and furniture in shades of milky white. ⊠*Im Stadtpark, 3rd District/Landstrasse* ☎01/713–3168 ⊕*www.steirereck.at* ⌖*Reservations essential* ⊟AE, DC, MC, V Ⓜ*U4/Stadtpark.*

★ $$$–$$$$ ✕**Fabios.** The easiest way for Viennese to visit sleek, suave, power-dining New York—short of paying $800 for a round-trip ticket—is to book a table at this cool hot spot. If they can, that is. Exceedingly popular and wait-listed weeks in advance, this modernist extravaganza has brought a touch of big-city glamour to Alt Wien, and foodies to fashionistas love it. Chef Christoph Brunnhuber has a truly sophisticated touch, as you'll see with his octopus carpaccio with paprika, crispy pork with orange pesto on fennel, or duckling breast on kumquat-cassis sauce with potato-olive puree. ⊠*Tuchlauben 6, 1st District* ☎01/532–2222 ⊕*www.fabios.at* ⌖*Reservations essential* ⊟AE, DC, MC, V ⊗*Closed Sun.*

★ $$$–$$$$ ✕**Griechenbeisl.** Mozart, Beethoven, and Schubert all dined here—so how can you resist? Neatly tucked away in a quiet and quaint area of the Old City, this ancient inn goes back half a millennium. You can hear its age in the creaking floorboards when you walk through some of the small dark wood–paneled rooms. Yes, it's historic and touristy, yet the food, including all the classic hearty dishes like goulash soup, Wiener schnitzel, and *Apfelstrudel*, is as good as in many other Beisln. The Mark Twain room has walls and ceiling covered with signatures of the famed who have been served here—ask the waiter to point out the most famous. ⊠ *Fleischmarkt 11, 1st District* ☎ *01/533–1941* ⊕ *www. griechenbeisl.at* ⊟ *AE, DC, MC, V* Ⓜ *U1 or U4/Schwedenplatz.*

$$$–$$$$
Fodor'sChoice
★
✕ **Zum Schwarzen Kameel.** The ladies who lunch love to shop and dine at "the Black Camel," a foodie landmark already 200 years ago, back when Beethoven used to send his manservant here to buy wine and ham. In timeless Viennese fashion, this provisioner split into both a *Delikatessen* and a restaurant. You can use the former if you're in a hurry—the fabulously fresh sandwiches are served at the counter. If time is not an issue, dine in the elegant Art Nouveau dining area. Let the headwaiter do his number—he's the one with the Emperor Franz Josef beard who, in almost perfect English, will rattle off the specials of the day. He recently won the award "Best Waiter of the Year." ⊠ *Bognergasse 5, 1st District* ☎ *01/533–8125* ⊿ *Reservations essential* ⊟ *AE, DC, MC, V* ☾ *Closed Sun.* Ⓜ *U3/Herrengasse.*

★ $$–$$$
✕ **Figlmüller.** This Wiener schnitzel institution is known for its gargantuan breaded veal and pork cutlets so large they overflow the plate, and is always packed. The cutlet is so large because it has been hammered into a two-fisted portion (you can hear the kitchen's pounding mallets from a block away). They wind up wafer-thin but delicious, because the quality, as well as the size, is unrivaled (a quarter kilo of quality meat for each schnitzel). As the Viennese are fond of saying, "A Schnitzel should swim," so don't forget the lemon juice. ⊠ *Wollzeile 5, 1st District* ☎ *01/512–6177* ⊟ *AE, DC, MC, V* ☾ *Closed first 2 wks Aug.* Ⓜ *U1 or U3/Stephansplatz.*

$$–$$$
✕ **Wrenkh.** Once Vienna's vegetarian pioneer extraordinaire, Christian Wrenkh now prefers a mixed cuisine in his house (over in the 15th District his ex-wife keeps up with the healthy kitchen). Happily, those delightful dishes like the wild-rice risotto with mushrooms or the Greek fried rice with vegetables, sheep's cheese, and olives, or the tofu and tomato and basil-pesto tarts still carry his signature. Now, however, you can also be tempted by steak, fish, and fowl. The minimalist-style café section offers inexpensive lunch specials, and the more elegant adjacent dining room is perfect for a relaxed lunch or dinner. Fortunately, Christian hasn't changed the no-smoking policy in his restaurant. ⊠ *Bauernmarkt 10, 1st District* ☎ *01/533–1526* ⊕ *www.wrenkh. at* ⊟ *AE, DC, MC, V* Ⓜ *U1 or U3/Stephansplatz.*

WINE TAVERNS

In the city center, wine taverns are known as *Weinkeller*. Hundreds of years ago Vienna's vintners started taking advantage of the cavernous spaces found below ancient monasteries and old houses by converting them into underground wine cellars. The fact that these subterranean cellars were some of the coolest spots in summertime Vienna has always proved a big drawing card.

Heurigen

The city's light and slightly fizzy "new wine"—the *Heurige,* harvested every September and October in hills around the city—has been served up for centuries in suburban taverns known as "Heurigen." These are charmingly set in the picturesque wine villages that dot Vienna's outskirts: Stammersdorf, Grinzing, Sievering, Nussdorf, and Neustift (tram lines to take from the city center are listed under the reviews below). Grinzing is a particularly enchanting destination. Although colonized by faux-Heurigen and tour buses, it has enough winding streets, antique lanterns, stained-glass windows, and oh-so-cozy taverns that you may feel you're wandering through a stage set for an "Old Austria" operetta (don't forget to look

for the town organ-grinder). The best times to visit the Heurigen are in summer and fall, when many of these places famously hang a pine branch over their doorway to show they are open, though often the more elegant and expensive establishments, called *Noble-Heurigen,* stay open year-round. Begin by ordering the classic *Viertel*—a quarter liter of wine—then check out the buffet. In the old days the *Salamutschi* (sausage seller) would trot his wares from one tavern to another. Today, increasingly, full dinners are available. If you go to a Heurige in the fall, be sure to order a glass of *Sturm,* a cloudy drink halfway between grape juice and wine, with a delicious yeasty fizz.

$–$$$ ✗**Augustinerkeller.** Built into the old brick vaults of the 16th-century historic fortifications surrounding the old city, this is one of the last monastic wine cellars in central Vienna. The atmosphere is very *gemütlich* (cozy)—vaulted brick ceiling, wooden "cow-stall" booths, street lanterns, Austrian bric-a-brac, and a troupe of roaming musicians (dig that accordion!) in the evening. The spit-roasted chicken is excellent, as is the filling *Stelze* (roast knuckle of pork). ⊠ *Augustinerstrasse 1, Albertinaplatz, 1st District* ☎01/533–1026 ▤*DC, MC, V* Ⓜ *U3/Herrengasse.*

$–$$$ ✗**Schreiberhaus.** In Neustift am Walde, the Schreiberhaus has one of the prettiest terraced gardens in the city, with picnic tables stretching straight up into the vineyards. The buffet offers delicious treats such as spit-roasted chicken, salmon pasta, and a huge selection of tempting grilled vegetables and salads. The golden traminer wine is excellent. ⊠ *Rathstrasse 54, 19th District/Neustift am Walde* ☎01/440–3844 ▤*AE, DC, MC, V* Ⓜ *U4, U6/Spittelau; Bus 35A/Neustift am Walde.*

$–$$$ ✗**Wieninger.** Heurige wine and food are both top-notch here, and the charming, tree-shaded inner courtyard and series of typical vintner's rooms are perfect for whiling away an evening. Wieninger's bottled wines are ranked among the country's best. It's across the Danube in Stammersdorf, one of Vienna's oldest Heurige areas. ⊠ *Stammersdorferstrasse 78, 21st District/Floridsdorf* ☎01/292–4106 ▤*V* ⊘*Closed late Dec.–Feb. No lunch except Sun.* Ⓜ *U2, U4/Schottenring; Tram: 31/Stammersdorf.*

CAFÉS & COFFEEHOUSES

To best savor the traditional coffeehouse experience, set aside a morning or an afternoon, or at least a couple of hours, and settle down in the one you've chosen. Read a while, or catch up on your letter writing, or plan tomorrow's itinerary: there is no need to worry about overstaying one's welcome, even over a single small cup of coffee, though don't expect refills. (Of course, in some of the more opulent coffeehouses your one cup of coffee may cost as much as a meal somewhere else.) As for the actual *Speisekarte* (menu), most places offer hot food, starting with breakfast, from early morning until around 11 AM, lunch menus in some, and many offer a great variety of meals until about an hour before closing time.

$–$$$ ✗**Café Central.** The coffeehouse *supreme*. Made famous by its illustrious guests, the Café Central is probably the world's most famous coffeehouse—outside of Florian's in Venice. Although recently somewhat over-restored (by its Donald Trump–like new owner), its old vibes remain attached to it as though by suction pad. Don't expect a cozy hole in the wall Kaffeehaus. With soaring ceiling and gigantic columns giving it the look of an apse strayed from St. Stephen's cathedral, it provided a rather sumptuous home away from home for Leon Trotsky, who mapped out the Russian Revolution here beneath portraits of the imperial family. It's just across from the Spanish Riding School. Piano music fills the marble pillared hall in the afternoon and although it will never again be all that it used to be, Central should be on the "must see" list. ⊠*Herrengasse 14, corner Strauchgasse 1st District* ☎*01/5333–76424* ⊕*www.palaisevents.at/* Ⓜ*U3/Herrengasse.*

$–$$$ ✗**Café Griensteidl.** Once the site of one of Vienna's oldest coffeehouses and named after the pharmacist Heinrich Griensteidl—the original dated back to 1847 but was demolished in 1897—this café was resurrected in 1990. Here Karl Kraus, the sardonic critic, spent many hours writing his feared articles, and here Hugo von Hofmannsthal took time out from writing libretti for Richard Strauss. Although this establishment is still looking for the patina needed to give it back its real flair, locals are pleased by the attempt to re-create the former atmosphere that exuded history. The daily, reasonably priced midday menu is a winner. Numerous newspapers and magazines hang on the rack (a goodly number of them in English). ⊠*Michaelerplatz 2, 1st District* ☎*01/533–2692* Ⓜ*U3/Herrengasse.*

$–$$$ ✗**Café Landtmann.** A recent $500,000 government-sponsored renovation has brought new luster to the chandeliers of Landtmann, a century-old favorite of politicians, theater stars (the Burg is next door), and celeb-watchers. Sigmund Freud, Burt Lancaster, Hillary Rodham Clinton, and Sir Paul McCartney are just a few of the famous folk who have patronized this vaguely Secession-ish-looking café, whose glass-and-brass doors have been open since 1873. If you want a great meal at almost any time of the day, there are few places that can beat this one. If you just want coffee and cake, then choose the right-hand seating area (just beyond the door). But if it is bustle and star-sightings, head for the elongated salon that runs parallel with the Ring avenue, just opposite the main university building. At night lots of theatergoers turn up after the Burg has turned out. ⊠*Dr.-Karl-Lueger-Ring 4, 1st District* ☎*01/532–0621* Ⓜ*U2/Schottenring.*

WHERE TO STAY

When you have only a short time to spend in Vienna, you will probably choose to stay in the inner city (the 1st District, or 1010 postal code), to be within walking distance of the most important sights, restaurants, and shops.

$$$$
Fodor's Choice
★

Das Triest. An ultrasleek ocean-liner look is Sir Terrence Conran's nod to the past of this former postal coach station on the route between Vienna and the port city of Trieste. The original cross vaulting remains in the lounges and some suites, but otherwise the interior and furnishings are Conran. In rooms, beige-on-beige fabrics are offset by glowing pine headboards the size of walls. Decor is delightful—linen-fresh, with accents of blue carpeting and honey-hue woods, and high-style as only a Conran hotel can be; even doorknobs feel nice to the touch. The hotel also allures with an excellent Austro-Italian restaurant, Collio. Das Triest may be a little off the beaten track, but is still within easy walking distance of the city center. ⊠ *Wiedner Hauptstrasse 12, A-1040, 4th District/Wieden* ☎ *01/589–180* 🖷 *01/589–1818* ⊕ *www. dastriest.at* ⟳ *72 rooms* ⟐ *In-room: no a/c (some), safe, DVD, Wi-Fi. In-hotel: restaurant, room service, bar, gym, laundry service, concierge, public Wi-Fi* ▭ *AE, DC, MC, V* ⦿*BP.*

$$$$
Fodor's Choice
★

Imperial. One of the great landmarks of the Ringstrasse, this hotel has exemplified the grandeur of imperial Vienna ever since Emperor Franz Josef formally opened its doors in 1873. Adjacent to the famed Musikverein concert hall and two blocks from the Staatsoper, the emphasis here is on Old Vienna elegance and privacy, which accounts for a guest book littered with names like Elizabeth Taylor, José Carreras, and Bruce Springsteen. Originally the home of Philipp Duke of Württemberg, this remains a symphony of potted-palm luxe. Don't overlook, as if you could, the grand marble staircase, a wonder in colored marbles modeled on the one in Munich's court library. The main lobby looks as opulent as a Hofburg ballroom. On the ground floor is the true showpiece: the Marmorsaal, or Marble Hall, where you can now dine amid Corinthian columns. Upstairs, the reception floor is filled with rooms done in whipped-cream neo-rococo. As for the beautiful guest rooms, they are furnished with sparkling chandeliers, gorgeously swagged fabrics, and original 19th-century paintings. The larger suites are found on the lower floor; as you ascend, guest rooms get smaller, but those on the top floor (the former attic) are done in an enchanting Biedermeier style, and several have small terraces offering amazing views of the city. Suites come with a personal butler. ⊠ *Kärntnerring 16, A-1010, 1st District* ☎ *01/501–10–0* 🖷 *01/501–10–410* ⊕ *www.luxurycollection.com/imperial* ⟳ *138 rooms* ⟐ *In-room: safe, refrigerator (some), dial-up. In-hotel: 2 restaurants, room service, bar, gym, laundry service, concierge, public Internet, parking (fee), no-smoking rooms* ▭ *AE, DC, MC, V* ⦿*EP.*

★ **$$$$**
Le Méridien. One of Le Méridien's super-cool "art and tech" ventures, their Vienna outpost occupies three former 19th-century Ringstrasse palaces, but you'd never know it after one step inside the front door. The lobby is minimalist, but adorned with Mies van der Rohe–style

sofas and ottomans, acres of nouvelle fluorescent-light panels, and contemporary art renditions of Austrian actors Oskar Werner and Romy Schneider. Ideally located two minutes from the Staatsoper, the hotel is also home to Shambala, the luxe restaurant masterminded by Michel Rostang, the Parisian chef-guru, so you can enjoy the latest in Austrian/Asian fusion cuisine. Adjacent is a hip bar with a DJ. Guest rooms are white and strikingly decorated with glass headboards, contempo vases, and other cutting-edge items. Cloudlike mattresses, flat-screen plasma TVs, and roomy "tower of power" showers with three massaging jets pour on the luxe. Outside, visual excitements continue, as the tranquil, soundproofed rooms offer views of the Hofburg, Burggarten, and Ring. Add to this a complimentary minibar and Internet service, and you have the makings for a truly pampered stay, which you can enjoy from the get-go: the buffet breakfast is arguably the best in the country. ⊠*Opernring 13, A-1010, 1st District* ☎*01/588–900* 🖷*01/588–9090–90* ⊕*www.starwoodhotels.com* 🗘*294 rooms* ♿*In-room: safe, Ethernet, dial-up. In-hotel: 2 restaurants, room service, bar, pool, gym, laundry service, public Internet, parking (fee), no-smoking rooms* ⊟*AE, DC, MC, V* ⊙*EP.*

$$$$
Fodor's Choice
★
🖼 **Sacher.** The legendary Sacher dates from 1876. Adding two extra floors and a spa on the fifth floor, the hotel has augmented its historic aura with luxurious, modern-day comfort. It hardly comes as a surprise to learn that the spa's top billing is "Hot Chocolate Treatments." The corridors serve as a veritable art gallery, and guest rooms are exquisitely furnished with antiques, heavy fabrics, and original artwork. The location directly behind the Opera House could hardly be more central, and the ratio of staff to guests is more than two to one. Meals in the Anna Sacher Room are first-rate, and the Rote Bar restaurant has garnered culinary awards. The Café Sacher, of course, is legendary. Then there's the Sacher Eck, a new, elegant, and airy snack bar where the ultrafashionable meet. ⊠*Philharmonikerstrasse 4, A-1010, 1st District* ☎*01/514–56–0* 🖷*01/514–56–810* ⊕*www.sacher.com* 🗘*152 rooms* ♿*In-room: safe, Ethernet, dial-up, Wi-Fi (some). In-hotel: 2 restaurants, room service, bar, gym, spa, laundry service, concierge, parking (fee), no-smoking rooms* ⊟*AE, DC, MC, V* ⊙*EP.*

$$$$
Fodor's Choice
★
🖼 **Style Hotel Vienna.** Within the hotel's Art Nouveau shell London interior designer Maria Vafiadis has paid tribute to Viennese Art Deco. Quite an eye-catcher is the tremendous glass-enclosed vault, smack bang in the middle of the lobby. You would never have guessed the edifice was previously a bank and the big bucks were stashed right here. Today this wonderful feature serves as a wine cellar. Have your favorite vintage served up at the push of a button. Enjoy your glass of wine in the elegant marble-and-wood wine bar, which has an enormous open fire and the dreamiest of contemporary music playing. Rooms are full of streamlined, sedate furnishings. Step out of the hotel and you're in the venerable Café Central in a flash, and just down the cobbled street is the Hofburg palace. ⊠*Herrengasse 12, A-1010, 1st District* ☎*01/22–780–0* 🖷*01/22–780–77* ⊕*www.stylehotel.at* 🗘*78 rooms* ♿*In-room: safe, DVD, Ethernet, Wi-Fi. In-hotel: restaurant, room service, bar, gym, concierge, public Internet* ⊟*AE, DC, MC, V* ⊙*BP.*

★ $–$$$ ⊞**Wandl.** The restored facade identifies a 300-year-old house that has been in family hands as a hotel since 1854. You couldn't find a better location, tucked behind St. Peter's Church, just off the Graben. The hallways are punctuated by cheerful, bright openings along the glassed-in inner court. The rooms are modern, but some are a bit plain and charmless, despite parquet flooring and red accents. If you can, ask for one of the rooms done in period furniture, with decorated ceilings and gilt mirrors; they're rather palatial, with plush Victorian chairs, carved-wood trim, and velvet throws. ⊠*Petersplatz 9, A-1010, 1st District* ☎*01/534–55–0* 🖷*01/534–55–77* ⊕*www.hotel-wandl.com* ⤶*138 rooms* ♿*In-room: no a/c. In-hotel: bar, concierge, public Internet* ▭*AE, DC, MC, V* ⦿|*BP.*

$$ ⊞**Altstadt.** A cognoscenti favorite, this small hotel was once a patrician home, and is in one of Vienna's most pampered neighborhoods—and we mean neighborhood: a plus here is being able to really interact with real Viennese, their stores (hey, supermarkets!), and residential streets. In fact, you are lucky enough to be in the chic and quaint Spittelberg quarter. The Altstadt is blessed with a personable and helpful management. Palm trees, a Secession-style wrought-iron staircase, modernist fabrics, and halogen lighting make for a very design-y interior. Guest rooms are large with all the modern comforts, though they retain an antique feel. The English-style lounge has a fireplace and plump floral sofas. Upper rooms have lovely views out over the city roofline. Last but not least, you are one streetcar stop or a pleasant walk from the main museums. ⊠*Kirchengasse 41, 7th District/Neubau* ☎*01/526–3399–0* 🖷*01/523–4901* ⊕*www.altstadt.at* ⤶*25 rooms* ♿*In-room: no a/c. In-hotel: bar* ▭*AE, DC, MC, V* ⦿|*BP.*

$$ ⊞**Pension Pertschy.** Housed in the former Palais Cavriani, just off the Graben, this pension is as central as you can get—just behind the Hofburg and down the street from the Spanish Riding School. One of those typical Viennese mansion-turned-apartment houses, the structure is still graced with a massive arched portal and yellow-stone courtyard, around which the 18th-century edifice was built. A few guest rooms contain lovely old ceramic stoves (just for show). Most rooms are spacious, and each one is comfortable. Some rooms are sweet, with bed canopies and chandeliers, although others are decorated with "repro"–antique furniture that verges on the kitsch. As for noise, the street outside gets a lot of horse-drawn fiacre carriages (and street sweepers at night), so opt for a courtyard room if you need complete peace and quiet. Use the elevator, but don't miss the palatial grand staircase. ⊠*Habsburgergasse 5, A-1010, 1st District* ☎*01/534–49–0* 🖷*01/534–49–49* ⊕*www.pertschy.com* ⤶*43 rooms* ♿*In-room: no a/c. In-hotel: no-smoking rooms* ▭*AE, DC, MC, V* ⦿|*BP.*

★ $$ ⊞**Rathaus Wine & Design.** The friendliest staff and the most salutiferous breakfast buffet in town—see to it that your schedule allows you to savor the spread—make this abode a worthwhile choice. The brainchild of entrepreneurs Petra und Klaus Fleischhaker of Salzburg, this exclusive boutique hotel pays homage to the winemakers of Austria. The spacious, high-ceiling, ultramodern guest rooms have polished wooden floors and accent wood walls, with warm orange, yellow, ochre, and cream colors. On each door is the name of a different winemaker, with a bottle of the vintner's wine inside (sorry, it's not included in the room price), and some of the greatest Austrian winemakers are represented, such as Bründelmayer, Gesellmann, Sattlerhof, and Markowitsch. Guests can take a grape escape in the chic, minimalist lounge, where vintages and snacks are served. ⊠*Langegasse 13, A-1080* ☏*01/400–1122* 📠*01/400–1122–88* ⊕*www.hotel-rathaus-wien.at* ⮂*33 rooms* ♿*In-room: safe, Ethernet. In-hotel: bar, concierge, laundry service* ▤*AE, DC, MC, V* ⷮ❙*BP.*

$ ⊞**Benediktushaus.** You can stay in this guesthouse of a monastery without following the dictum *ora et labora* (pray and work). Stay in the Benedictine house and see how the monks live, pray, and work. It's guaranteed to be one of the most tranquil stays you've ever had. The rooms are simply furnished and without frills—no TV set either—so switch on to relax mode and go chant with the fratres in the Freyung. The picturesque square is but a minute from Café Central if you think you're missing out on some of the fun. ⊠*Freyung 6a, A-1010, 1st District* ☏*01/534–98–900* 📠*01/534–98–905* ⊕*www.schottenstift.at* ⮂*21 rooms* ♿*In-room: no a/c* ▤*AE, DC, MC, V* ⷮ❙*BP.*

NIGHTLIFE & THE ARTS

Vienna's nightlife and arts scenes present you with myriad tantalizing choices, so only by combining Admiral Byrd–ish foresight with a movie editor's ruthless selectivity can you hope to ride herd on it all.

THE ARTS

TICKETS

With a city as music mad and opera crazy as Vienna, it is not surprising to learn that the bulk of major performances are sold out in advance. The State Theater Booking Office, or **Österreichischer Bundestheaterkassen** (⊠*Theaterkassen, back of Opera, Hanuschgasse 3, in courtyard* ☏*01/513–1513* ⊕*www.bundestheater.at*), sells tickets for the Akademietheater, Schauspielhaus, Staatsoper, Volksoper, and Burgtheater. To purchase tickets at the box office, the above address also operates as a central clearinghouse, open weekdays 8–6, weekends from 9 AM to noon. Tickets for the Staatsoper and Volksoper go on sale one month before the date of performance; credit-card reservations are taken up to six days before the performance.

You can purchase tickets online from **Culturall** (⊕*www.culturall.at*)

The most trusted ticket agency is **Liener Brünn** (☏*01/533–0961* ⊕*www.ims.at/lienerbruenn*)—charging a minimum 22% markup and generally dealing in the more expensive seats. Tickets to musicals and some events, including the Vienna Festival, are available at the **"Salettl" gazebo** kiosk alongside the Opera House on Kärntnerstrasse, open daily 10 AM to 7 PM. Tickets to that night's musicals are reduced by half after 2 PM.

MUSIC

Vienna is one of the main music centers of the world. Contemporary music gets its due, but it's the hometown standards—the works of Beethoven, Brahms, Haydn, Mozart, and Schubert—that draw the Viennese public and make tickets to the Wiener Philharmoniker the hottest of commodities. A monthly printed program, the *Wien-Programm,* gives a general overview of what's going on in the worlds of opera, concerts, jazz, theater, and galleries. Vienna is home to four full symphony orchestras: the great Wiener Philharmoniker (Vienna Philharmonic), the outstanding Wiener Symphoniker (Vienna Symphony), the broadcasting service's ORF Symphony Orchestra, and the Niederösterreichische Tonkünstler. There are also hundreds of smaller groups, from world-renowned trios to chamber orchestras.

★ The most important concert halls are in the buildings of the Gesellschaft der Musikfreunde, called the **Musikverein** (✉ *Dumbastrasse 3, ticket office at Karlsplatz 6* ☎ *01/505–8190* 🖷 *01/505–8190–94* ⊕ *www.musikverein.at*). There are actually six halls in this magnificent theater, but the one that everyone knows is the venue for the annually televised New Year's Day Concert—the Goldene Saal, the Gold Hall, officially called the Grosser Musikvereinssaal. Possibly the most beautiful in the world, this Parthenon of a music hall was designed by the Danish 19th-century architect Theophil Hansen, a passionate admirer of ancient Greece. But the surprise is that his smaller Kleine Saal is even more sumptuous—a veritable Greek temple with more caryatids and lots of gilding and green malachite. What Hansen would have made of the four newly constructed (2004) subsidiary halls, set below the main theater, must remain a mystery. A three-minute walk from the Musikverein, crossing Schwarzenbergplatz, is the **Konzerthaus** (✉ *Lothringerstrasse 20, 1st District* ☎ *01/242002* 🖷 *01/242–0011–0* ⊕ *www. konzerthaus.at*), home to the Grosser Konzerthaussaal, Mozartsaal, and Schubertsaal. The first is a room of magnificent size, with red-velvet and gold accents. The calendar of Grosser Konzerthaussaal is packed with goodies, including the fabulous early-music group Concentus Musicus Wien, headed by Nicolaus Harnoncourt, and concerts of the Wiener Philharmoniker and the Wiener Symphoniker.

The beloved Vienna Boys' Choir, the **Wiener Sängerknaben** (✉ *Hofburg, Schweizer Hof, 1st District* ☎ *01/533–9927* 🖷 *01/533–9927–75* ⊕ *www.wsk.at*), are far from just being living "dolls" out of a Walt Disney film. Their professionalism is such that they regularly appear with the best orchestras around the world. The troupe originated as a choir founded by Emperor Maximilian I in 1498. When the troupe lost its imperial patronage in 1918, they traded in their court costume for these charming costumes, then the height of fashion (a look even sported by Donald Duck, who was also born in that era).

From mid-September to late June, the apple-cheeked lads sing mass at 9:15 AM Sunday in the **Hofburgkapelle** (✉ *Verwaltung der Hofmusikkapelle, Hofburg, A-1010 Vienna*). Written requests for seats should be made at least eight weeks in advance. You will be sent a reservation card, which you exchange at the box office (in the Hofburg courtyard) for your tickets. Tickets are also sold at ticket agencies and at the box office (open Friday 11–1 and 3–5; any remaining seats may be available Sunday morning, 8:15–8:45). General seating costs €5, prime seats in the front of the church nave €29. It's important to note that only the 10 side balcony seats allow a view of the actual choir; those who purchase floor seats, standing room, or center balcony will not have a view of the boys. On Sunday at 8:45 AM any unclaimed, preordered tickets are sold. You can also opt for standing room, which is free.

OPERA & OPERETTA

★ The **Staatsoper** (*State Opera House* ⊠*Opernring 2, 1st District* ☎*01/514–440* ⊕*www.wiener-staatsoper.at*), one of the world's great opera houses, has been the scene of countless musical triumphs and a center of unending controversies over how it should be run and by whom. (When Lorin Maazel was unceremoniously dumped as head of the opera not many years ago, he pointed out that the house had done the same thing to Gustav Mahler almost a century earlier.) A performance takes place virtually every night September–June, drawing on the vast repertoire of the house, with emphasis on Mozart and Verdi works. Guided tours of the opera house are given year-round.

★ Opera and operetta are also performed at the **Volksoper** (⊠ *Währinger-strasse 78* ☎*01/514–440* ⊕*www.volksoper.at*), outside the city center at Währingerstrasse and Währinger Gürtel (third stop on Streetcars 41, 42, or 43, which run from "downstairs" at Schottentor, U2, on the Ring). Prices here are significantly lower than at the Staatsoper, and performances can be every bit as rewarding. This theater has a fully packed calendar, with offerings ranging from the grandest opera, such as Mozart's *Don Giovanni,* to an array of famous Viennese operettas, such as Johann Strauss's *Wiener Blut* and *Die Fledermaus,* to modern Broadway musicals (during 2004, Rodgers and Hammerstein's *Sound of Music* finally received its first Austrian staging here ever). Most operas are sung here in German.

For decades the **Theater an der Wien** (⊠ *Linke Wienszeile 6* ☎*01/588—30–660* ⊕*www.theater-wien.at*), a historic theater dating to 1801, was misused as a contemporary musical venue. Now this building closely linked to Beethoven—who lived here—and to Schikaneder, the librettist who wrote *The Magic Flute* for Mozart, has renewed its role as a opera house. It will be open year-round with a premiere every month. Each opera is to be performed by the same cast, to guarantee the highest standard possible. Also on the schedule will be concerts, dance performances, and the occasional operetta—such as Johann Strauss's *Die Fledermaus,* which premiered here. The Vienna Summer of Music is held here in July and August.

THEATER

For theater in English (mainly standard plays), head for **Vienna's English Theater** (⊠*Josefsgasse 12, 8th District/Josefstadt* ☎*01/402–1260*). Another option is the equally good **International Theater** (⊠*Porzellangasse 8, 9th District/Alsergrund* ☎*01/319–6272*).

NIGHTLIFE

BARS, LOUNGES & NIGHTCLUBS

Where once night owls had to head to Vienna's *Bermuda Dreieck* (Bermuda Triangle, around St. Ruprecht's church on the Ruprechtsplatz, two blocks south of the Danube Canal), today's nightclub scene has blossomed with a profusion of delightful and sophisticated bars, clubs, and lounges. Many of the trendoisie like to head to the clubs around the Naschmarkt area, then move on to nearby Mariahilferstrasse to shake their groove thing. The Freihaus Quarter sizzles with cafés and shops. For the rundown of options, log on to ⊕*www.freihausviertel.at*.

Chic, chic, and once again chic, the designer café-bar **Shultz** (⊠*Siebensterngasse 31, 7th District/Neubau* ☎*01/522–9120* ⊕*www.schultz. at* Ⓜ*U4/Kettenbrückengasse*) seduces fashionable folk with its long drinks, retro cocktails, and Vienna Moderne setting. Back in 1870, Viennese used to come to the **Volksgarten** (⊠*Burgring 2, 1st District* ☎*01/532–0907* ⊕*www.volksgarten.at* Ⓜ*U2/3 MuseumsQuartier*) to waltz, share champagne, and enjoy the night in a candlelit garden. Today they come to the same site to *diskothek* the night away under pink strobes, enjoy some boogie-woogie or tango dancing in the Tanzcafe (Dance Café), and sip a beer against the greenery. A best bet when you don't know where else to head, this one-in-all club complex is set within a lush garden and has a pretty, vaguely Jugendstil dining salon with a vast curved wall of windows overlooking a terrace set with tables. Beyond lies the Pavilion, a 1950s jewel that looks airlifted from California and serves brews and nibbles.

DANCE CLUBS

In the MuseumsQuartier, **Café Leopold** (⊠*Museumsplatz 1, MuseumsQuartier, 1st District* ☎*01/523–6732* ⊕*www.cafe-leopold.at/* Ⓜ*U2 or 3/MuseumsQuartier*) is in the big modern white cube that is the Leopold Museum. After enough house and electro music, you can escape to a table outdoors in the plaza. In the middle of the Freihaus Quarter, **Club Schikaneder** (⊠*Margaretenstrasse 22–24, 4th District/Wieden* ☎*01/585–2867* ⊕*www.schikaneder.at* Ⓜ*U1, U2, or U4/Karlsplatz*) is a former movie theater that has become a multimedia art and dance center. It still screens three to five art films daily, and has exhibitions and first-class DJ lineups. **Flex** (⊠*Donaukanal/Augartenbrücke, 1st District* ☎*01/533–7525* ⊕*www.flex.at* Ⓜ*U1, U2, or U4/Karlsplatz*) is an alternative rock venue set in a dark, dungeonlike cave—with a famous sound system.

JAZZ CLUBS

★ The jazz scene in Vienna is one of the hottest in Europe. The stage might be small at **Birdland** (⊠*Am Stadtpark 3 [enter Landstrasser Hauptstrasse 2], 3rd District* ☎*01/2196–39315* ⊕*www.birdland.at*), but the stars are major. The club under the Hilton Hotel Stadtpark hosts some of the best in the world of jazz. Jazz legend Joe Zawinul named it after one of his most renowned compositions and New York City's legendary temple of jazz. Set in a cellar under St. Ruprecht's church and the granddaddy of Vienna's jazz clubs, **Jazzland** (✉ *Franz-Josefs-Kai 29, 1st District* ☎*01/533–2575* ⊕*www.jazzland.at*) opened more than 30 years ago when there was just a small local jazz scene. But thanks to the pioneering work of the club's founder, Axel Melhardt, Austrian jazz musicians have vibed with the best American stars. The club also serves excellent and authentic Viennese cuisine. In the course of a few years, **Porgy & Bess** (✉ *Riemergasse 11, 1st District* ☎*01/512–8811* ⊕*www.porgy.at*) has become a fixed point in the native and international jazz scene.

SHOPPING

SHOPPING DISTRICTS

The Kärntnerstrasse, Graben, and Kohlmarkt pedestrian areas in the 1st District, **Inner City,** claim to have the best shops in Vienna, and for some items, such as jewelry, some of the best anywhere, and prices are appropriately steep. The side streets within this area have developed their own character, with shops offering antiques, art, clocks, jewelry, and period furniture. **Ringstrasse Galerie,** the indoor shopping plaza at Kärntner Ring 5–7, brings a number of shops together in a modern complex, although many of these stores have other, larger outlets elsewhere in the city. Outside the center, concentrations of stores are on **Mariahilferstrasse,** straddling the 6th and 7th districts; **Landstrasser Hauptstrasse** in the 3rd District; and, still farther out, **Favoritenstrasse** in the 10th District.

A collection of attractive small boutiques can be found in the **Palais Ferstel** passage at Freyung 2 in the 1st District. A modest group of smaller shops has sprung up in the **Sonnhof** passage between Landstrasser Hauptstrasse 28 and Ungargasse 13 in the 3rd District. The **Spittelberg** market, on the Spittelberggasse between Burggasse and Siebensterngasse in the 7th District, has drawn small galleries and handicrafts shops and is particularly popular in the weeks before Christmas and Easter. Christmas is the time also for the tinselly **Christkindlmarkt** on Rathausplatz in front of City Hall; in protest over its commercialization, smaller markets specializing in handicrafts have sprung up on such traditional spots as Am Hof and the Freyung (1st District), also the venue for other seasonal markets.

Vienna's **Naschmarkt** (between Linke and Rechte Wienzeile, starting at Getreidemarkt) is one of Europe's great and most colorful food and produce markets. Stalls open at 5 or 6 AM, and the pace is lively until 5 or 6 PM. Saturday is the big day, when farmers come into the city to sell at the back end of the market, but shops close around 3 PM. Also Saturday there's a huge flea market at the Kettenbrückengasse end. It is closed Sunday.

FLEA MARKETS

Every Saturday (except holidays), rain or shine, from about 7:30 AM to 4 or 5, the **Flohmarkt** in back of the Naschmarkt, stretching along the Linke Wienzeile from the Kettenbrückengasse U4 subway station, offers a staggering collection of stuff ranging from serious antiques to plain junk. ■**TIP→Haggle over prices**. On Thursday and Friday from late spring to mid-fall, an outdoor combination arts-and-crafts, collectibles, and flea market takes place on **Am Hof**. On weekends in summer from about 10 to 6, an outdoor **art and antiques market** springs up along the Danube Canal, stretching from the Schwedenbrücke to beyond the Salztorbrücke. Lots of books are sold, some in English, plus generally better goods and collectibles than at the Saturday flea market. Bargain over prices.

DEPARTMENT STORES

Steffl (⊠ *Kärntnerstrasse 19, 1st District*) is moderately upscale without being overly expensive. The larger department stores are concentrated in Mariahilferstrasse. By far the best is **Peek & Cloppenburg** (⊠ *Mariahilferstrasse 26–30, 6th District*). Farther up the street you will find slightly cheaper goods at **Gerngross** (⊠ *Mariahilferstrasse and Kirchengasse, 6th District*).

SPECIALTY STORES

BOOKS

★ If you are planning a hiking holiday in Austria, stock up on the necessary maps at **Freytag & Berndt** (⊠ *Kohlmarkt 9* ☎ *01/533–8685* ⊕ *www. freytagberndt.at*), the best place for maps and travel books in Vienna. If you're an art-book lover, **Wolfrum** (⊠ *Augustinerstrasse 10* ☎ *01/512–5398*) will be your home away from home. If you have money to burn, you can also spring for a Schiele print or special art edition to take home.

CERAMICS, GLASS & PORCELAIN

★ The best porcelain in town can be found at **Augarten** (⊠ *Graben/Stock-im-Eisen-Platz 3* ☎ *01/512–1494–0* ⊕ *www.augarten.at*). The Lipizzaner stallion balancing on two hind hoofs is an expensive piece but an eye-catcher. The manufactory in the 2nd District in Vienna offers tours of the palais Augarten is housed in, and you can study the steps involved in making these precious pieces. Is it a "Maria-Theresia," ornately cut diamanté chandelier with a 30%–34% lead content you're looking for? If it is, head and hunt here at **Lobmeyr** (⊠ *Kärntnerstrasse 26* ☎ *01/512–0508–0* ⊕ *www.lobmeyr.at*), one of the world's finest addresses for the best in glass and crystal. Ireland has its Waterford, France its Baccarat, and Austria has **Swarovski** (⊠ *Kärntnerstrasse 8* ☎ *01/5129032* ⊕ *www.swarovski.com*), purveyors of some of the finest cut crystal in the world and, thanks to the newer generation of Swarovskis, trinkets increasingly fashionable in style and outlook. There are your typical collector items and gifts here, but also high-style fashion accessories (Paris couturiers now festoon their gowns with Swarovski crystals the way they used to with ostrich feathers), crystal figurines, jewelry, and home accessories. This flagship store is a cave of coruscating crystals that gleam and glitter.

VIENNA ESSENTIALS

AIR TRAVEL

For information about reaching Vienna by air, see ⇨ *By Air in Austria Essentials, below.*

AIRPORT TRANSFERS

The fastest way into Vienna from Schwechat Airport is the sleek, double-decker **CAT, or City Airport Train.** The journey from the airport to Wien–Mitte (the center of the city) takes only 16 minutes, and trains operate daily every 30 minutes between 5:30 AM and midnight. The cost is €8 one-way and €15 round-trip.

The cheapest way to get to Vienna from the airport is the **S7 train,** called the *Schnellbahn,* which shuttles twice an hour between the station beneath the airport and the Landstrasse/Wien–Mitte (city center) and Wien–Nord (north Vienna) stations; the fare is €3, and it takes about 35 minutes (19 minutes longer than the CAT). Your ticket is also good for an immediate transfer to your destination within the city on streetcar, bus, or U-Bahn.

Another option is the **bus,** which has two separate lines. One line goes to Schwedenplatz/Postgasse (1st District, city center) every 30 minutes between 5 AM and 12:30 AM; traveling time is 20 minutes. The second line goes to the South and West train stations (Südbahnhof and Westbahnhof) in 20 and 35 minutes, respectively. Departure times are every 30 minutes from 5:30 AM to 11:10 PM. Fare is €6 one-way, €11 for a round-trip.

Taxis Airport Driver (☏ *01/22822–0* 🖷 *01/22822–8* ⊕ *www.airportdriver.at*).

BOAT & FERRY TRAVEL

When you arrive in Vienna via the Danube, the Blue Danube Steamship Company/DDSG will leave you at Praterlände near Mexikoplatz. The Praterlände stop is a two-block taxi ride or walk from the Vorgartenstrasse U1/subway station, or you can take a taxi directly into town. The Twin City Liner (a comfortable 102-seat catamaran) travels to and from Bratislava, departing from Schwedenplatz in the center of Vienna daily from June until late October. The round-trip costs €30, and a one-way journey costs between €15 and €23, depending on the day, direction (upstream or down), and departure time. The one-way downriver trip takes 75 minutes; the trip back is a little longer.

Boat & Ferry Information Blue Danube Schiffahrt (Steamship Company)/DDSG (✉ *Friedrichstrasse 7, A-1010, Vienna* ☏ *01/588–80* 🖷 *01/588–8044–0* ⊕ *www.ddsg-blue-danube.at*). **Twin City Liner** (☏ *01/588–80* 🖷 *01/588–8044–0* ⊕ *www.twincityliner.com*).

CAR TRAVEL

Vienna is 300 km (187 mi) east of Salzburg, 200 km (125 mi) north of Graz. Main routes leading into the city are the A1 Westautobahn from Germany, Salzburg, and Linz and the A2 Südautobahn from Graz and points south. Rental cars can be arranged at the airport or in town. Buchbinder is a local firm with particularly favorable rates and clean cars.

PARKING

Parking in Vienna is difficult and expensive. You can park free in the 1st District on weekend days, but not overnight. Overnight street parking in the 1st and 6th through 9th districts is restricted to residents with special permits, so in these districts be sure you have off-street, garage parking.

PUBLIC TRANSIT: BUS, TRAM & U-BAHN

Vienna's public transportation system is fast, clean, safe, and easy to use. Get public transport maps at a tourist office or at the transport-information offices (*Wiener Verkehrsbetriebe*), underground at Karlsplatz, Stephansplatz, and Praterstern. You can transfer on the same ticket between subway (*U-Bahn* runs until 12:30 AM), streetcar (runs from 5:15 AM to midnight), bus, and long stretches of the fast suburban railway, or *Schnellbahn* (*S-Bahn*).

Within the heart of the city, bus lines 1A, 2A, and 3A are useful cross-town routes. Special night buses with an N designation operate at half-hour intervals over several key routes after midnight; the starting (and transfer) points are the Opera House and Schwedenplatz.

Tickets for public transportation are valid for all public transportation—buses, trams, and the subway. They are cheaper if you buy them at a U-Bahn stop. Individual tickets cost €2.20; blocks of five tickets or one-, three-, and eight-day tickets make each individual ride much cheaper. You must validate your ticket before boarding the U-Bahn or after boarding a bus or tram. Otherwise, you will pay a hefty fine.

Contacts Tabak-Trafik Almassy (⊠ *Stephansplatz 4, to right behind cathedral* ☎ *01/512–5909*). **VOR, or Vorverkaufsstellen der Wiener Linien** (☎ *7909/105* ⊕ *www.wienerlinien.at*).

TAXIS

Taxis have an initial charge of €2.50 for as many as four people daytime, and about 5% more from 11 PM until 6 AM. Radio cabs ordered by phone have an initial charge of €6. They also may charge for each piece of luggage that must go into the trunk, and a charge is added for waiting. It's customary to round up the fare to cover the tip. You can't flag a cab down in the street in Vienna. Look for a taxi stand. Service is usually prompt, but when you hit rush hour, the weather is bad, or you need to keep to an exact schedule, call ahead and order a taxi for a specific time. If your destination is the airport, ask for a reduced-rate taxi. There are several companies that offer chauffeured limousines, which are listed below.

Taxi Companies Göth (☎ *01/713–7196*). **Mazur** (☎ *01/604–2530*). **Peter Urban** (☎ *01/713–5255*).

TRAIN TRAVEL

For information about train travel to Vienna, see ⇨ *By Train in Austria Essentials, at the end of this chapter.*

VISITOR INFORMATION

The main center for information (walk-ins only) is the Vienna City Tourist Office, open daily 9–7 and centrally located between the Hofburg and Kärntnerstrasse.

The Vienna-Card, which costs € 18.50, combines 72 hours' use of public transportation and more than 200 discounts.

Tourist Information Vienna City Tourist Office (⊠ *Am Albertinaplatz 1, 1st District* ☎ *01/24–555* 🖷 *01/216–84–92 or 01/24555–666*).

BADEN

★ *7 km (4½ mi) south of Gumpoldskirchen, 32 km (20 mi) southwest of Vienna.*

The Weinstrasse brings you to the serenely elegant spa town of Baden. Since antiquity, Baden's sulfuric thermal baths have attracted the ailing and the fashionable from all over the world. When the Romans came across the springs, they dubbed the town Aquae; the Babenbergs revived it in the 10th century; and with the visit of the Russian czar Peter the Great in 1698, Baden's golden age began. Austria's Emperor Franz II spent 31 successive summers here. Every year for 12 years before his death in 1835 the royal entourage moved here from Vienna for the season. Later in the century Emperor Franz Josef was a regular visitor, his presence inspiring many of the regal trappings the city still displays. In Baden Mozart composed his "Ave Verum"; Beethoven spent 15 summers here and wrote large sections of his Ninth Symphony and *Missa Solemnis* when he lived at Frauengasse 10; Franz Grillparzer wrote his historical dramas here; and Josef Lanner, both Johann Strausses (father and son), Carl Michael Ziehrer, and Karl Millöcker composed and directed many of their waltzes, marches, and operettas here.

A streetcar was built in the 19th century for the sole purpose of ferrying the rich Viennese from their summerhouses in Baden to the opera in Vienna—the last stop is directly in front of the opera house. The streetcar (the cars now are modern) still winds its way through Vienna's suburbs on its 50-minute journey to Baden. It's the traditional way to go, but the outlet stores and suburban shopping malls along its route are not exactly the picturesque stretch of 100 years ago. Things only start to get scenic about 25 minutes before Baden, as the car passes through the wine villages.

Music lovers will want to visit the **Beethoven Haus,** just one of several addresses Beethoven called his own hereabouts—the great man was always on the run from his creditors and moved frequently. ⊠ *Rathausgasse 10* ☎ *02252/86800–231* 🖾 *€3* ☉ *Tues.–Fri. 4–6, weekends 10–noon and 4–6*. North of the Danube, and east of the Kamp River, are the undulating hills of the agricultural Weinviertel (Wine District), bordering on the Czech Republic and on Slovakia, where the March River flows into the Danube.

WHERE TO EAT

$–$$$ ✕ **Rudolfshof.** A 19th-century hunting lodge above the Kurpark is now a restaurant serving traditional dishes from the region, with an excellent wine list highlighting local wines. Stop for lunch or just *Kaffee und Kuchen*. The grand vistas of the Baden basin from the restaurant's terrace ensure the Rudolfshof's popularity with locals and with Viennese on weekends. ⊠ *Am Gamingerberg 5, BadenA-2500* ☎ *02252/209-203* ⊕ *www.rudolfshof.at* ▤ *DC, MC, V* ⊘ *Closed Tues. May–Sept.; closed Tues. and Wed. Oct.–Apr.*

BADEN ESSENTIALS

BUS TRAVEL

The bus is a good way to reach Baden. Frequent scheduled service runs from across from Vienna's Opera House to the center of Baden.

TRAIN TRAVEL

Trains leave Vienna's Südbahnhof regularly for Baden, making this an easy way to travel.

THE LOWER DANUBE VALLEY

A trip along the Austrian Danube unfolds like a treasured picture book. Roman ruins (some dating to Emperor Claudius), remains of medieval castles-in-air, and Baroque monasteries with "candle-snuffer" cupolas perching precariously above the river stimulate the imagination with their historic legends and myths. This is where Isa—cousin of the Lorelei—lured sailors onto the shoals; where the Nibelungs—later immortalized by Wagner—caroused operatically in battlemented forts; and where Richard the Lion-Hearted was locked in a dungeon for a spell. Here is where Roman sailors threw coins into the perilous whirlpools near Grein in hopes of placating Danubius, the river's tutelary god. Today, thanks to the technology of modern dams, travelers have the luxury of tamely observing this part of Austria from the deck of a comfortable river steamer. In clement weather the nine-hour trip upriver from Vienna to Linz is highly rewarding. If your schedule allows, continuing onward to Passau may be less dramatic but gives more time to take in the picturesque vineyards and the castles perched on crags overlooking the river.

Even more of the region's attractions can be discovered if you travel by car or bus. Climb Romanesque towers, explore plunging Gothic streets, then linger over a glass of wine in a Weinkeller. River and countryside form an inspired unity here, with fortress-topped outcroppings giving way to broad pastures that end only at the riverbanks. Many visitors classify this as one of Europe's great trips: you feel you can almost reach out and touch the passing towns and soak up the intimacy unique to this stretch of the valley. This section follows the course of the Danube upstream from Vienna as it winds through Lower Austria (Niederösterreich) and a bit of Upper Austria (Oberösterreich) to Linz, on the way passing monasteries and industrial towns, the riverside vineyards of the lower Weinviertel, and fragrant expanses of apricot and apple orchards.

This glorious landscape becomes fairy-tale–like when apricot and apple trees are in bursting blossom, late April to mid-May. One of the best ways to discover the region is to take a bike ride alongside the blossoming orchards and the bright orange poppy fields. Others might prefer the chilly early- to mid-autumn days, when a blue haze curtains the vineyards. Throughout the region, winter can be drab. Seasons notwithstanding, crowds jam the celebrated abbey at Melk; you're best off going first thing in the morning, before the tour buses arrive, or at midday, when the throngs have receded.

KREMS

★ *80 km (50 mi) northwest of Vienna.*

Krems marks the beginning (when traveling upstream) of the Wachau section of the Danube. The town is closely tied to Austrian history; here the ruling Babenbergs set up a dukedom in 1120, and the earliest Austrian coin was struck in 1130. In the Middle Ages Krems looked after the iron trade, while neighboring Stein traded in salt and wine, and over the years Krems became a center of culture and art. Today the area is the heart of a thriving wine production, and Krems is most famed for the cobbled streets of its Altstadt (Old Town), which is virtually unchanged since the 18th century. The lower Old Town is an attractive pedestrian zone, although up a steep hill (a car can be handy) you'll find the upper Old Town, with its Renaissance Rathaus and a parish church that is one of the oldest in Lower Austria.

The **Karikaturmuseum** *(Caricature Museum)* houses more than 250 works of cartoon art from the 20th century to the present, including a large collection of English-language political satire and caricature. ⊠*Steiner Landstrasse 3a* ☎*02732/908020* ⊕*www.karikaturmuseum. at* ⊴*€8* ⊙*Daily 10–6.*

A 14th-century former Dominican cloister now serves as the **Weinstadt Museum Krems,** a wine museum that holds occasional tastings. ⊠*Körnermarkt 14* ☎*02732/801–567* ⊕*www.weinstadtmuseum.at* ⊴*€4* ⊙*Mar.–Nov., Tues.–Sun. 10–6.*

WHERE TO STAY & EAT

$$–$$$ ✕**Jell.** In the heart of Krems's medieval Altstadt, this storybook stone cottage run by Ulli Amon-Jell (pronounced "Yell") is a cluster of cozy rooms with lace curtains, dark-wood banquettes, candlelight, and Biedermeier knickknacks on the walls, making it seem like you've stepped into an early-20th-century grandmother's house. Your meal begins with tantalizing breads and dips, fine starters like cream of asparagus soup, then proceeds to delicious main courses like the pheasant breast wrapped in their own home-cured bacon. For vegetarians there's a superb dish of peppers stuffed with smoked tofu in a sweet, organic tomato sauce. And for that warm glow at the end of your

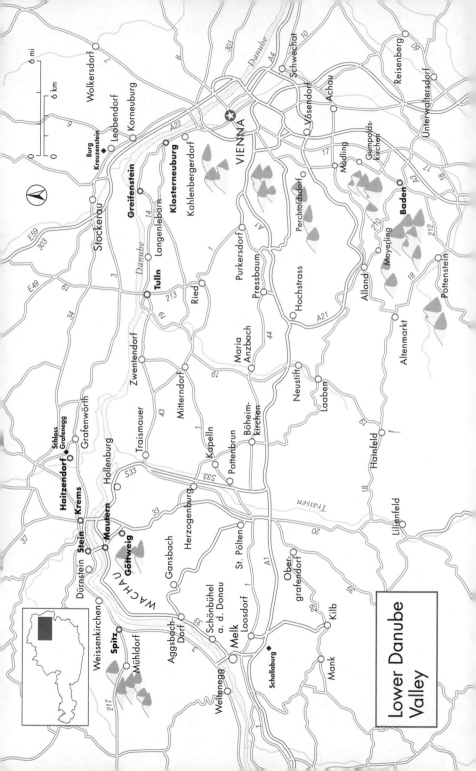

Lower Danube Valley

repast, have a glass of homemade apricot schnapps. In summer book ahead for a table under the grape arbor in the small, secluded outdoor dining area. ⊠*Hoher Markt 8–9* ☎*02732/82345* 📠*02732/82345–4* 🍴*Reservations essential* ☰*AE, DC, MC, V* ⊗*Closed Mon. No dinner weekends.*

★ $ ✕🏨**Alte Post.** The oldest inn in Krems, for centuries the mail-route post-house for the region, this hostelry is centered around an adorable Renaissance-style courtyard, which is topped with a flower-bedecked arcaded balcony and storybook mansard roof. If you're a guest here, you'll be able to drive into the pedestrian zone of the Old Town and pull up next to the Steinener Tor (Stone Gate) to find this inn. The rooms are in comfortable yet elegant country style (full baths are scarce), but the real draw here is dining ($$) on regional specialties or sipping a glass of the local wine in the courtyard. The staff is friendly (though English is a struggle), and cyclists are welcome. ⊠*Obere Landstrasse 32, A-3500Krems* ☎*02732/82276–0* 📠*02732/84396* 🌐*www. altepost krems.at* 🛏*23 rooms, 4 with bath* 🛎*In-room: no a/c. In-hotel: restaurant* ☰*No credit cards* ⊗*Closed Dec.–Mar.* 🍴*BP.*

DÜRNSTEIN

90 km (56 mi) northwest of Vienna.

If a beauty contest were held among the towns along the Wachau Danube, chances are Dürnstein would be the winner hands down—as you'll see when you arrive along with droves of tourists. The town is small; leave the car at one end and walk the narrow streets. The main street, Hauptstrasse, is lined with picturesque 16th-century residences. The top night to be here is the summer solstice, when hundreds of boats bearing torches and candles sail down the river at twilight to honor the longest day of the year—a breathtaking sight best enjoyed from the town and hotel terraces over the Danube. In October or November the grapes from the surrounding hills are harvested by volunteers from villages throughout the valley—locals garnish their front doors with straw wreaths if they can offer tastes of the new wine, as members of the local wine cooperative, the Winzergenossenschaft Wachau.

Set among terraced vineyards, the town is landmarked by its gloriously Baroque **Stiftskirche,** dating from the early 1700s, which sits on a cliff overlooking the river—this cloister church's combination of luminous blue facade and stylish Baroque tower is considered the most beautiful of its kind in Austria.

After taking in the Stiftskirche, head up the hill, climbing 500 feet above the town, to the famous **Richard the Lion-Hearted Castle,** where Leopold V held Richard the Lion-Hearted of England, captured on his way back home from the Crusades. Leopold had been insulted, so the story goes, by Richard while they were in the Holy Land, and when the English nobleman was shipwrecked and had to head back home through Austria, word got out—even though Richard was disguised as a peasant—and Leopold pounced. In the tower of this castle, the Lion-Hearted was imprisoned (1192–93) until he was located by Blondel, the faithful minnesinger. It's said that Blondel was able to locate his imprisoned king when he heard his master's voice completing the verse of a song Blondel was singing aloud—a bit famously recycled in Sir Walter Scott's *Ivanhoe* (and the Robert Taylor MGM film). Leopold turned his prisoner over to the emperor, Henry VI, who held him for months longer until ransom was paid by Richard's mother, Eleanor of Aquitaine. ■TIP→ **The rather steep 30-minute climb to the ruins will earn you a breathtaking view up and down the Danube Valley and over the hills to the south.**

WEISSENKIRCHEN

5 km (3 mi) west of Dürnstein, 95 km (59 mi) northwest of Vienna.

Tucked among vineyards, just around a bend in the Danube, is Weissenkirchen, a picturesque town that was fortified against the Turks in 1531.

On the Marktplatz, check out the 15th-century **Wachaumuseum,** which has a charming Renaissance arcaded courtyard. The building now contains many paintings by Kremser Schmidt. ⊠ *Marktplatz* ☎ *02715/2268* ⊕ *www.weissenkirchen.at/museum.php* ☜ *€4* ⊗ *Apr.–Oct., Tues.–Sun. 10–5.*

WHERE TO STAY & EAT

$$$–$$$$ ✕ **Jamek.** The Jamek family's country inn on the Danube is well known throughout Austria, and though Josef and Edeltraud have handed over the management to their daughter, the quality remains the same. You dine either in one of several rooms tastefully decorated with 19th-century touches or outdoors in the shady garden. Start with the vegetable torte gratin, then go on to lightly fried Zanderfilet (pike perch) on a bed of garlicky spinach, or pork cutlet with fried dumplings. Don't miss the house specialty, the surprisingly light chocolate cake with whipped cream and chocolate sauce. Wines are from the nearby family vineyards. Jamek is just west of Weissenkirchen in Joching. ⊠ *Joching 45* ☎ *02715/2235* 🖷 *02715/2235–22* ⊰ *Reservations essential* ⊟ *DC, MC, V* ⊗ *Closed weekends, and mid-Dec.–mid-Jan.*

EN ROUTE   The vistas are mainly of the other side of the Danube, looking across at Schönbühel and Melk, as you follow a back road via Jauerling and Maria Laach to Route 3 at Aggsbach. Shortly after Weitenegg the Wachau ends, and you come into the part of the Danube Valley known as the **Nibelungengau,** where the Nibelungs—who inspired the great saga *Das Nibelungenlied,* source of Wagner's *Ring*—are supposed to have settled for a spell. If you have always thought of the Nibelungs as a mythical race of dwarfs known only to old German legends and Wagner, dismiss that idea. The Nibelungs actually existed, though not as Wagner describes them, and this area was one of their stomping grounds.

1

Danube River Cruises

A cruise up the Danube to the Wachau valley is a tonic in any season. A parade of storybook-worthy sights—fairy-tale castles-in-air, medieval villages, and Baroque abbeys crowned with "candle-snuffer" cupolas—unfolds before your eyes. Remember that it takes longer to travel north: the trip upstream to Krems, Dürnstein, and Melk will be longer than the return to Vienna, which is why many travelers opt to return to the city by train, not boat. Keep your fingers crossed: rumor has it that on the proper summer day the river takes on an authentic shade of Johann Strauss blue.

Blue Danube Schiffahrt/DDSG. The main company offering these sightseeing cruises is based in Vienna. Their boats leave from the company's piers at Handelskai 265 every Sunday between May 11 and September 28 at 8:45 AM. Departing from the Reichsbrücke (Vienna piers) on the city's Danube Canal, they arrive in Krems at 1:55 PM, Dürnstein at 2:30 PM, returning from Dürnstein at 4:30 PM, Krems at 4:50 PM, and get back to Vienna by 8:45 PM. One-way is €19.50—the ticket office is at the Vienna piers (take the U-Bahn line U1 to Vorgartenstrasse). ⊠ *Friedrichstrasse 7, A-1043 Vienna* ☎ *01/588-800* 🖷 *01/58880-440* ⊕ *www.ddsg-blue-danube.at.*

MELK

★ *33 km (21 mi) southwest of Krems, approximately 87 km (54 mi) west of Vienna.*

Unquestionably one of the most impressive sights in all Austria, the abbey of Melk is best approached in mid- to late afternoon, when the setting sun ignites the abbey's ornate Baroque yellow facade. As one heads eastward paralleling the Danube, the abbey, shining on its promontory above the river, comes into view. It easily overshadows the town—located along Route 1—but remember that the riverside village of Melk itself is worth exploring. A self-guided tour (in English, from the tourist office) will head you toward the highlights and the best spots from which to photograph the abbey.

Fodor's Choice
★ By any standard, **Stift Melk** *(Melk Abbey)* is a Baroque-era masterpiece. Part palace, part monastery, part opera set, Melk is a magnificent vision thanks greatly to the upward-reaching twin towers capped with Baroque helmets and cradling a 208-foot-high dome, and a roof bristling with Baroque statuary. A tour of the building includes the main public rooms: a magnificent library, with more than 90,000 books, nearly 2,000 manuscripts, and a superb ceiling fresco by the master Paul Troger; the **Marmorsaal,** whose windows on three sides enhance the ceiling frescoes; the glorious spiral staircase; and the **Stiftskirche** (abbey church) of Saints Peter and Paul, an exquisite example of the Baroque style. Call to find out if tours in English will be offered on a specific day. The **Stiftsrestaurant** (closed November–April) offers standard fare, but the abbey's excellent wines elevate a simple meal to a

lofty experience—particularly on a sunny day on the terrace. ⊠*Abt Berthold Dietmayr-Strasse 1* ☎*02752/555–232* 📠*02752/555–249* ⊕*www.stiftmelk.at* 🎫*€7; with tour €8.60* ⊙*End of Mar.–Apr. and Oct., daily 9–5, ticket office closes at 4; May–Sept., daily 9–6, ticket office closes at 5.*

WHERE TO STAY & EAT

★ $$–$$$ ✕▥ **Tom's.** The Wallner family has given son Tom full creative control of the kitchen in this Melk landmark, and to show their approval they even changed the name from Stadt Melk to Tom's. Nestled below the golden abbey in the center of the village square, the elegant outpost (whose guest roster includes the Duke and Duchess of Windsor) maintains its high standards, and the decidedly Biedermeier atmosphere remains unchanged. The seasonal menu may include zucchini Parmesan lasagne with truffles or fresh grilled crayfish dribbled with butter and lemon. The fried chicken is excellent. Desserts are irresistible, such as chocolate pudding with a Grand Marnier parfait or cheese curd soufflé with homemade pistachio ice cream. Upstairs are 13 (rather plain) bedrooms in the $ category, a good bet if you wish to overnight in magical Melk. ⊠*Hauptplatz 1, A-3390* ☎*02752/52475* 📠*02752/52475–19* ⇆*16 rooms* ⊟*AE, DC, MC, V* ⊙*Closed variable wks in winter* ⊠*BP.*

DANUBE VALLEY ESSENTIALS

To research prices, get advice from other travelers, and book travel arrangements, visit www.fodors.com.

BOAT & FERRY TRAVEL

You can take a day trip from Vienna or Krems and explore one of the stops, such as Dürnstein or Melk. Boats run from May to late September. There are two boat companies that ply the Danube. *For full information on cruises offered by the Blue Danube Schiffahrt/DDSG (Vienna to Dürnstein) and Brandner Schifffahrt (Krems to Melk), see Danube River Cruises earlier in this chapter.*

Bridges across the river are few along this stretch, so boats provide essential transportation. There are a number of independent tow ferries that are attached to cables that stretch across the river. Service across the river for people, cars, and bikes is available upon request for a small fee.

BUS TRAVEL

The main bus route links Krems and Melk, or you can take a direct bus to Melk from Vienna. You can book bus tours in Vienna or Linz by calling central bus information, listed below.

Bus Information Central bus information (☎*01/71101*).

CAR TRAVEL

Driving is certainly the most comfortable way to see this region, as it conveniently enables you to pursue the byways. The main route along the north bank of the Danube is Route 3; along the south bank, there's

CLOSE UP

Grape Expectations

The epitome of Austrian viticulture is found in the Wachau, those few precious kilometers of terraced vineyards along the north bank of the Danube River. There are few pleasanter ways to spend an afternoon than to travel to the fabled wineries of the valley and sample the golden nectar coaxed from their vines. It is usually possible to stop in and meet the winemaker, who will be happy to pour you a taste from the latest vintage and share some of the secrets of the trade. A late spring drive through the charming villages of Weissenkirchen and Dürnstein, when the apricots are in blossom, is an experience not easily forgotten.

Here you can discover some of the finest white wines in Europe. The elegant, long-lived Rieslings are world-renowned, but the special glory of Austria is the grüner veltliner, an indigenous grape that can produce anything from simple Heurigen thirst quenchers to wines of a nobility that rivals the best of Burgundy.

The area has its own unique three-tiered classification system, ranging from the young, fresh Steinfeder and medium-bodied Federspiel to the rich, ripe smaragd. Some of the already legendary vintners include F.X. Pichler, Prager, Knoll, and Hirtzberger, as well as the exemplary cooperative of the Freie Weingärtner Wachau. For a fine Web site on Wachau wineries, log on to ⊕ www.vinea-wachau.at/. Straddling both sides of the Danube is the Kremstal, centering on the medieval town of Krems, the hub of the area's wine trade. Here, you can get a good idea of the regional wines with a visit to the Vinotek Und's eponymous Kloster. The range of grape varieties expands here to include intensely fragrant traminer, grauburgunder (more familiar as pinot gris), and even some full-bodied reds from cabernet sauvignon and pinot noir. To sample some of these wines, you may be tempted to make an excursion to one of the nearby wineries like Nigl, Salomon, and Malat.

Venturing farther from the Danube takes you through lush, rolling hills to the Kamptal, the valley that follows the winding course of the gentle Kamp River. Here is another premium wine region, this one dominated by Langenlois, the country's largest wine-producing town. The **Loisium** (✉ *Kornplatz A-3550, Langenlois* ⊕ *www.loisium.at*), a sleek, ultramodern emporium, provides a comprehensive selection of wines and other delectables from the area. Top producers include Hirsch, Loimer, and Bründlmayer, who makes one of Austria's best sparkling wines as well as chardonnay and *Alte Reben* (old-vine) grüner veltliner and Riesling of exceptional character.

a choice between the autobahn Route A1 and a collection of lesser but good roads. Roads are good and well marked, and you can switch over to the A1 autobahn, which parallels the general east–west course of the Danube Valley route.

TRAIN TRAVEL

All the larger towns and cities in the region can be reached by train. The rail line on the north side of the river clings to the bank in places; service is infrequent. You can combine rail and boat transportation along this route, taking the train upstream and crisscrossing your way back on the river.

Train Information **ÖBB—Österreichisches Bundesbahn** (☎ *05/1717*).

AUSTRIA ESSENTIALS

TRANSPORTATION

BY AIR

Austria is easily reached on a nonstop flight from JFK and Washington–Dulles on Austrian Airlines. Flying time is eight hours to Vienna from New York, nine hours from Washington, D.C. Austrian Airlines is a member of the Star Alliance. Most other American and European airlines offer connecting service, with the most convenient connections through London, Amsterdam, or Frankfurt. The airport at nearby Bratislava in Slovakia is an easy hour-long bus ride away from Vienna and offers the same advantages for travel to eastern Austria. Some budget airlines fly to Bratislava via London–Stansted.

Major Airlines **Air France** (☎ *01/5022–2240 within Austria* ⊕ *www.airfrance. fr*). **American Airlines** (☎ *800/433–7300* ⊕ *www.aa.com*). **Austrian Airlines** (☎ *800/843–0002, 01/051–789 within Austria* ⊕ *www.aua.com*). **British Airways** (☎ *800/247–9297, 020/8897–4000 London, 0345/222–111 outside London, 01/7956–7567 within Austria* ⊕ *britishairways.com*). **Continental Airlines** (☎ *800/523–3273 for U.S. and Mexico reservations, 800/231–0856 for international reservations* ⊕ *www.continental.com*). **Delta Airlines** (☎ *800/221–1212 for U.S. reservations, 800/241–4141 for international reservations* ⊕ *www.delta.com*). **KLM** (☎ *0900/359–556 within Austria* ⊕ *www.klm.at*). **Lufthansa** (☎ *800/645–3880, 0810/1025–8080 within Austria* ⊕ *www.lufthansa.com*). **Northwest Airlines** (☎ *800/225–2525* ⊕ *www.nwa.com*). **Swiss** (☎ *0810/810–840 within Austria* ⊕ *www.swiss.com*). **United Airlines** (☎ *800/864–8331 for U.S. reservations, 800/538–2929 for international reservations* ⊕ *www.united.com*).

Other Airlines **Air Berlin** (☎ *0870/738–8880 in London and international inquiries* ⊕ *www.airberlin.com*). **German Wings** (☎ *0870/252–1250 in London and for international inquiries* ⊕ *www.germanwings.com*). **Ryanair** (⊕ *www.ryanair.com*). **SkyEurope** (⊕ *www.skyeurope.com*).

AIRPORTS

Austria's major air gateway is Vienna's **Schwechat Airport,** about 19 km (12 mi) southeast of the city. Bratislava's M. R. Stefanik international airport in neighboring Slovakia is about 60 km (36 mi) east of Vienna and is the hub for SkyEurope, a relatively new budget carrier with low-cost connections to several European cities. Frequent buses can take you from Bratislava airport to central Vienna in about an hour.

Airport Information **M. R. Stefanik Airport (Bratislava, BTS)** (☎ *00421–2–4857–3353 from outside of Slovakia).* **Salzburg Airport (SZG)** (☎ *0662/8580).* **Schwechat Airport (Vienna, VIE)** (☎ *01/7007–0).*

BUS TRAVEL

Austria features extensive national networks of buses run by post offices and railroads. Where Austrian trains don't go, buses do. You can get tickets on the bus, and in the off-season there is no problem getting a seat, but on routes to favored ski areas during holiday periods reservations are essential. Bookings can be handled at the ticket office (there's one in most towns with bus service) or by travel agents. Most buses stop at the local rail station.

Information **Columbus** (☎ *01/534–110).* **Blaguss Reisen** (☎ *01/5018–0150).* **Post und Bahn** (☎ *01/71101).* **Dr. Richard** (☎ *01/33100–0).*

CAR TRAVEL

Because of the cost of a car rental, tolls, and gasoline, renting a car in Austria is generally much more expensive than taking the train. It's inadvisable if you are just touring Vienna. On the other hand, if you have the time and your plan is a more leisurely tour of the country, including back roads and off-the-beaten-track destinations, then car rental is certainly an option. You'll have more freedom and be able to reach places where public transportation is scarce.

GASOLINE

Gasoline and diesel are readily available, but on Sunday stations in the more out-of-the-way areas may be closed. Gasoline prices are expensive relative to the U.S. but consistent throughout the country. Make sure you ask whether your rental car uses gasoline or diesel.

ROAD CONDITIONS

Roads in Austria are excellent and well maintained—perhaps a bit too well maintained, judging by the frequently encountered construction zones on the autobahns. Secondary roads may be narrow and winding. Remember that in winter you will need snow tires and often chains, even on well-traveled roads. It's wise to check with the automobile clubs for weather conditions, since mountain roads are often blocked, and ice and fog are hazards.

ROADSIDE EMERGENCIES

You'll find emergency (orange-color) phones along all highways. If you break down along the autobahn, a small arrow on the guardrail will direct you to the nearest phone. Otherwise, if you have problems, call

ARBÖ or ÖAMTC from anywhere in the country. Both clubs charge nonmembers for emergency service.

Emergency Services ARBÖ (☎123). **ÖAMTC** (☎120). No area or other code is needed for either number.

RULES OF THE ROAD

The minimum driving age in Austria is 18, and children under 12 must ride in the backseat; smaller children require a restraining seat. Note that all passengers must use seat belts.

Drive on the right side of the road in Austria. Unmarked crossings, particularly in residential areas, are common, so exercise caution at intersections. In general at unmarked intersections, vehicles coming from the right have the right of way; the only obvious exception is for trams, which always have the right of way. No turns are allowed on red.

The maximum blood-alcohol content allowed is 0.5 parts per thousand, which in real terms means very little to drink. Remember when driving in Europe that the police can stop you anywhere at any time for no particular reason.

Unless otherwise marked, the speed limit on autobahns is 130 kph (80 mph), although this is not always strictly enforced. But if you're pulled over for speeding, fines are payable on the spot, and can be heavy. On other highways and roads the limit is 100 kph (62 mph), 50 kph (31 mph) in most urban areas, though limits can be lower.

■ TIP➔ If you're going to travel Austria's highways, make absolutely sure your car is equipped with the *Autobahnvignette,* a little sticker with a highway icon and the Austrian eagle, or with a calendar marked with an M or a W. Rental cars should already have them. If you are caught without a sticker you may be subjected to extremely high fines.

Tolls are very expensive in Austria, and you should not be surprised to find tunnel tolls of €10 or more.

CAR RENTALS

Rates in Vienna begin at about €50 a day and €132 a weekend for an economy car with manual transmission and unlimited mileage. This includes a 21% tax on car rentals. Rates are more expensive in winter months, when a surcharge for winter tires may be added. Renting a car may be cheaper in Germany, but make sure the rental agency knows you are driving into Austria and that the car is equipped with the *Autobahnvignette,* an autobahn sticker for Austria. Get your sticker, also known as a Pickerl, before driving to Austria.

The age requirement for renting a car in Austria is generally 19, and you must have had a valid driver's license for one year. For some of the more expensive car models, drivers must be at least 25 years of age. There may be some restrictions for taking a rental into Slovakia, Slovenia, Hungary, the Czech Republic, or Poland, so be sure to ask beforehand.

An International Driver's Permit (IDP), while not strictly necessary, is a good idea; these international permits are universally recognized, and having one in your wallet may save you a problem if you are ever stopped by local authorities.

BY TRAIN

Austrian train service is excellent: it's fast and, for Western Europe, relatively inexpensive, particularly if you take advantage of discount fares.

The difference between *erste Klasse* (first class), and *zweite Klasse* (second class) on Austrian trains is mainly a matter of space. First- and second-class sleepers and couchettes (six to a compartment) are available on international runs, as well as on long trips within Austria.

If you purchase your ticket on board the train, you must pay a surcharge, which is around €7 or more, depending on how far you're going. Make certain that you inquire about possible supplements payable on board trains traveling to destinations outside Austria when you are purchasing your ticket. Austrians are not generally forthcoming with information, and you might be required to pay a supplement in cash to the conductor while you are on the train. You can reserve a seat for €3.40 until a few hours before departure. Be sure to do this at peak holiday times.

Information ÖBB (Österreichische Bundesbahnen) (⊕ *www.oebb.at*).

CONTACTS & RESOURCES

BANKS & EXCHANGE SERVICES

The euro is used in Austria. You'll get the best exchange rate if you take money directly out of an ATM, even when you figure in the fee for the withdrawal and cost for currency exchange. ATMs are very common in Austria. Otherwise, you'll get the best exchange by changing your money at a bank. You won't do as well at exchange booths in airports or rail and bus stations, in hotels, in restaurants, or in stores, although you may find their hours more convenient than at a bank.

ATM Locations Cirrus (☎ *800/424-7787*). **Plus** (☎ *800/843-7587*).

ELECTRICITY

The electrical current in Austria is 220 volts, 50 cycles alternating current (AC); wall outlets take Continental-type plugs, with two round prongs.

EMERGENCIES

Embassies & Consulates Embassy of the United States (✉ *Boltzmanngasse 16, A-1090, 9th District, Vienna* ☎ *31339-0*). **Consulate of the U.S./Passport Division** (✉ *Gartenbaupromenade 2-4, A-1010, 1st District, Vienna* ☎ *31339-7580*).

General Emergency Contacts Ambulance (☎ *144*). **Fire** (☎ *122*). **Police** (☎ *133*).

INTERNET, MAIL & SHIPPING

Austria generally lags behind much of Europe in its use and avail-ability of the Internet, especially Wi-Fi. Free Internet service is rare in Austria. Outside of hotels it's usually not hard to find an Internet café somewhere nearby (ask at your hotel). The standard rate is about €2 an hour. Occasionally, especially in large cities, you'll find cafés that offer Wi-Fi to customers. The charge for this is usually around €2 an hour.

All mail goes by air, so there's no supplement on letters or postcards. Within Europe a letter or postcard of up to 20 grams (about ¾ ounce) costs €0.65. To the United States or Canada, a letter of up to 20 grams takes postage of €1.25. The Austrian post office also adheres strictly to a size standard; if your letter or card is outside the norm, you'll have to pay a surcharge. Postcards via airmail to the United States or Canada need €1.25. Shipping packages is expensive.

Contacts Cybercafés (⊕ *www.cybercafes.com*) lists more than 4,000 Internet cafés worldwide.

OPEN HOURS

In most cities banks are open weekdays 8–3, Thursday until 5:30 PM. Lunch hour is from 12:30 to 1:30. All banks are closed on Saturday, but you can change money at various locations (such as American Express offices on Saturday morning and major railroad stations around the clock).

Gas stations on the major autobahns are open 24 hours a day, but in smaller towns and villages you can expect them to close early in the evening and on Sunday. You can usually count on at least one station to stay open on Sunday and holidays in most medium-size towns, and buying gas in larger cities is usually not a problem.

PASSPORTS & VISAS

U.S. citizens need a valid passport to enter Austria for stays of up to three months.

PHONES

When calling Austria, the country code is 43. When dialing an Austrian number from abroad, drop the initial 0 from the local Austrian area code. All numbers given in this guide include the city or town area code.

CALLING WITHIN AUSTRIA

A local call from a pay phone costs €.20 for the first minute and €.20 for every three minutes thereafter. Most pay phones have instructions in English, but they are becoming increasingly rare because of the prevalence of mobile phones.

You can buy a calling card at any post office for about €7, which allows you to use the card at any SOS or credit-card phone booth. You simply insert the card and dial; the cost of the call is automatically deducted from the card, and a digital window on the phone tells you how many units you have left (these are not minutes).

When placing a long-distance call to a destination within Austria, dial the local area codes with the initial zero (for instance, 0662 for Salzburg).

For information concerning numbers within the EU and neighboring countries, dial 01/118–877; for information outside Europe, dial 0900/118–877. Most operators speak some English.

CALLING OUTSIDE AUSTRIA

Calls from post offices are usually the least expensive way to go, and you can get helpful assistance in placing a long-distance call; in large cities these centers at main post offices are open around the clock.

Access Codes AT&T Direct (☎ *01/0800–200–288, 800/435–0812 for other areas*). **MCI WorldPhone** (☎ *0800–200–235, 800/444–4141 for other areas*).

MOBILE PHONES

In Austria a cell phone is called a *Handy*. Most tri- and quad-band GSM phones will work in Austria (confirm with your own cell phone company). If your phone is unlocked, you can buy an inexpensive SIM card in Austria for local calls. You can also buy a prepaid cell phone if you are staying in Austria for a while and plan to use it often.

SAFETY

Austrians are remarkably honest in their everyday dealings, and Vienna, given its size, is a refreshingly safe and secure city. It's one of the world's few big cities where lost wallets routinely turn up found (and sometimes even with the money and credit cards still intact). That said, be sure to watch your purses and wallets in crowded spaces like subways and trams, and to take the standard precautions when walking at night along empty streets. Be particularly careful if you're traveling with a bicycle. Here, as everywhere else, bikes routinely go missing. Always lock your bike firmly, and never leave it outside unattended for more than a few minutes.

TAXES

The Value Added Tax (V.A.T.) in Austria is 20%, but this is reduced to 10% on food and clothing. If you are planning to take your purchases with you when you leave Austria (export them), you can get a refund. Wine and spirits are heavily taxed—nearly half of the sale price goes to taxes. For every contract signed in Austria (for example, car-rental agreements), you pay an extra 1% tax to the government, so tax on a rental car is 21%.

TIME

The time difference between New York and Austria is 6 hours (so when it's 1 PM in New York, it's 7 PM in Vienna). The time difference between London and Vienna is 1 hour; between Sydney and Vienna, 14 hours; and between Auckland and Vienna, 13 hours.

TIPPING

Although virtually all hotels and restaurants include service charges in their rates, tipping is still customary, but at a level lower than in the United States. In very small country inns such tips are not expected but are appreciated. In family-run establishments, tips are generally not given to immediate family members, only to employees. Tip the hotel concierge only for special services or in response to special requests. Maids normally get no tip unless your stay is a week or more or service has been special. Big tips are not usual in Austrian restaurants, since 10% has already been included in the prices.

VISITOR INFORMATION

Austrian National Tourist Office (☎ *212/944–6880* ⊕ *www.austria.info*).

Bosnia & Herzegovina

SARAJEVO, MOSTAR & MEĐUGORJE

WORD OF MOUTH

"During my recent week in Croatia on the Dalmatian coast, I spent 24 hours in Mostar. I was blown away by this incredible place. Cradled by a ring of mountains, the city nestles in a green valley, with grey stone buildings and white minaret towers piercing the incredibly blue sky."

—julia_t

By Betsy
Maury

BOSNIA'S HISTORY, LIKE THAT OF many of the countries in Eastern and Central Europe, is punctuated with conquest and assimilation. The Romans defeated Illyrian tribes to make Bosnia an outpost of the empire around 9 BC, bringing roads and aqueducts, Latin and Christianity. The Slavs migrated east to settle Bosnian lands in the 6th and 7th century AD, and by the 10th century they had formed their own church and were the predominant ethnic group living in Bosnia. Conflicts between Catholic Rome and Orthodox Byzantium plagued medieval Bosnia until Islam began its great march north in the 14th century. As the capital of Bosnia, Sarajevo was at the crossroads of Ottoman Turkey and Habsburg Europe for the next four centuries. Bosnia became fully Ottoman in 1463 and was under firm control of the Sublime Porte (the court that set policy for the Ottoman Empire) until 1878, when Austria conquered Bosnia.

The tragic assassination of Habsburg heir-apparent Franz Ferdinand in Sarajevo in 1914 brought a swift demise to the Austro-Hungarian empire in Europe and left Bosnia struggling to keep its borders intact among expansionist neighbors Serbia and Croatia. The Nazi threat brought all three quarreling neighbors together under the leadership of strongman Josip Broz Tito, whose guerrilla Partisans defended Yugoslavian territory in World War II. For much of the 20th century, an uneasy alliance prevailed among Bosnians and other South Slavs, who had been united into one country under Tito's iron fist. The dismantling of Yugoslavia in the 1990s brought lingering divisions to the fore, and the bloody breakup that ensued was most acute in Bosnia, a country where ethnically mixed people had lived for centuries. The Dayton Peace Accord signed in 1995 brought an end to the fighting and gave the country a framework for a modern, independent state. Today, visitors to Bosnia will find a country showing its battle scars but once again peaceful, multiethnic, and optimistic about the future.

The city of Sarajevo sits gracefully on the Miljacka River in a basin surrounded by mountains in central Bosnia. Jahorina Mountain to the east of Sarajevo and Bjelašnica (and Igman) to the west formed the backbone of the 1984 winter Olympics skiing competition. The drive out of the city toward Jahorina takes you through rambling Ottoman neighborhoods and up a steep, pine-covered mountain. The trip to Bjelašnica is equally dramatic, taking you through recently war-torn villages that once were home to medieval highland communities. Ski centers are up and running at both Jahorina and Bjelašnica, so if your trip to Sarajevo is in winter, don't miss a chance to ski on these world-class slopes.

Mostar is southeast of Sarajevo on the Neretva River in the heart of Herzegovina. This ancient city is famous for its Ottoman architecture and the *Stari Most* (Old Bridge) that was tragically destroyed in 1993 (although rebuilt in 2004). Mostar is the gateway to Medđugorje, known throughout the Catholic world as a place where the Virgin Mother appeared. It is today the most visited site in Bosnia and Herzegovina.

EXPLORING BOSNIA & HERZEGOVINA

Bosnia is a mountainous country surrounded by Croatia, Serbia, and Montenegro. Two entities govern the country: the Federation of Bosnia and Herzegovina and the Republika Srpska. The Federation is divided into 10 cantons, or districts. Sarajevo is in Sarajevo Canton. Travel between the two entities is fluid, and there are no border crossings. You'll know you've entered Republika Srpska when the road signs appear in Cyrillic. Reaching Bosnia from abroad is easiest by air to Sarajevo's modern airport. Mostar is about a two-hour drive from Sarajevo as well as from Dubrovnik in neighboring Croatia. Mostar's airport serves mostly charter flights from abroad, offering a convenient location where groups can meet up with bus operators for excursions to Medđjugorje. Sarajevo is well connected to Europe by train. Cities within Bosnia are well connected by bus routes, but travel is slow, as many of the two-lane roads cut through mountainous terrain.

WHAT IT COSTS IN BOSNIAN CONVERTIBLE MARKS (KM OR BAM)			
	$$$$	$$$	$$	$
RESTAURANTS	over 20 KM	12–20 KM	5–12 KM	under 5 KM
HOTELS In euros	over €100	€75–€100	€50–€75	under €50
HOTELS in KM	over 200 KM	150 KM–200 KM	100 KM–150 KM	under 150 KM

Restaurant prices are per person for a main course at dinner. Hotel prices are for a double room in high season and include breakfast and taxes.

ABOUT THE RESTAURANTS

Bosnia's food is similar to that of neighboring countries. Carnivores will have no trouble finding tasty veal, beef, and lamb dishes on most menus in Sarajevo. Meat-based stews and soups are popular, as are sausages. *Ćevapi* are tasty sausages made of ground beef and lamb and can be eaten at the numerous *ćevabdžinica* throughout Sarajevo. They are usually served with warm pita bread, onion, and yogurt on the side. Savory pies wrapped in filo dough are another popular Bosnian dish. A *burek* is a meat pie, *sirnica* a cheese pie, and *zeljanica* a spinach pie; these savory pies are fresh, filling, and cheap and are available any time of the day. They can be purchased at the many buregdžnica (pie shops) in the Baščaršija. Within Sarajevo you'll find international dishes served mostly at high-end restaurants or hotels. In general, vegetarians will have to look long and hard for innovative vegetarian dishes. Outside the capital you'll find very few variations on the traditional meat-based cuisine.

ABOUT THE HOTELS

Sarajevo isn't a city of four-star luxury hotels but good accommodation can be had in many price ranges. The star rating system is somewhat arbitrary, so ask a lot of questions about specifics when booking. For example, a "four-star" hotel in Sarajevo may not have an elevator or air-conditioning. Prices, in general, are high for the level of service you get. It's possible to book a room online either from the hotel directly or through a service, but insist on a confirmation for any reservation. Family-run pensions are plentiful but vary greatly in quality. Renting a room in someone's home is a good budget option, but is best arranged on arrival. Hotels are priced in euros and Bosnian convertible marks (KM), but hotels accept only KM as payment.

SARAJEVO

Mention a trip to Sarajevo—even to a group of well-traveled friends— and you're still likely to get a raised eyebrow or two. Isn't that a war zone? Is it safe? The truth is that the conflict in Bosnia ended in 1995, and Sarajevo has been safe for travel almost since then. The country on the whole is safe for travel as well, although land mines are still an issue in remote parts of the country. (Consult the Sarajevo Tourist Association for the most up-to-date information.) In Sarajevo today you'll find one of the most vibrant cities in Central Europe, chock full of first-class historic sights, dramatic mountains, affordable meals, homey accommodations, and friendly people. The city itself is small and easily walkable, and the mountains are within easy striking distance of the downtown center. Although the tourism engine is up and running and things like ATMs and taxis are widely available, other expected infrastructure, including such simple details as road signs and local maps, are virtually nonexistent. Internet connectivity is patchy and many, many things don't run on time. But that's half the fun of a trip to Sarajevo; there's still a little adventure and unpredictability to the place. Locals are happy to show visitors their city and are often very willing to help you get around. This welcoming atmosphere offers a good opportunity to experience the thrill of discovering a new city on your own before package tours and low-cost airlines take the thrill away.

EXPLORING SARAJEVO

Numbers in the margin correspond to points of interest on the Sarajevo map.

⑫ **Alipašina Mosque.** Built in 1561 on the burial site of Bosnian governor Ali Paša, the Alipašina mosque is considered by many to be the most architecturally beautiful mosque in Sarajevo. The classical lines, arched facade, and multiple cupolas evoke the influence of Sinan, the great Ottoman architect. The massive building stands on the corner of Mašala Tita and Alipašina streets, in an open square that was vulnerable to sniper fire in Sarajevo's recent war. ⊠ *Maršala Tita* ☎ *033– 222–315 for information* ☉ *Open by appointment only (call 48 hours in advance).*

⑤ **Baščaršija.** The construction of this Oriental marketplace began in **Fodor's**Choice 1462, and by the middle of the 16th century it was the central com- ★ mercial district in the Balkans. From here the city grew up and over the river to accommodate its continuing population expansion. Some of the important architectural features of the Baščaršija include the **Sebilj** (Pigeon Fountain), the beautiful domed fountain of Moorish design

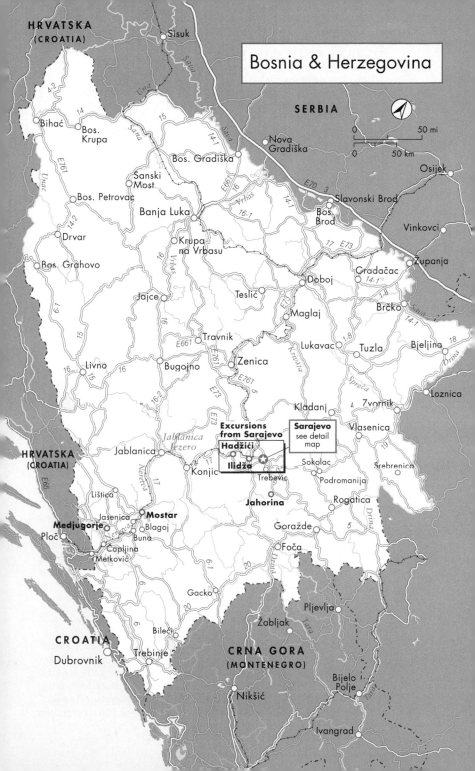

GREAT ITINERARIES

If your trip to Bosnia is limited to a day or two, stick to Sarajevo, where you will find a rich assortment of historic sights. A drive out to Jahorina or Bjelašnica for hiking and lunch in a mountain lodge is an easy day trip; plan on a full day if you want to ski. Mostar is about a two-hour drive; Medđugorje is an hour farther, so tackle that trip only if you have five days or more.

IF YOU HAVE 3 DAYS
Use all three days to concentrate on **Sarajevo,** which is best seen on foot. Meander through the **Baščaršija** and take in the 15th-century winding streets and Ottoman architecture. Have at least one coffee in this area and observe the hustle and bustle. Stroll along the Miljacka River, and cross one of the bridges, taking in the view of the hills surrounding the city. Strike out of the old town to museums farther afield, like the National Museum and the Tunnel Museum.

IF YOU HAVE 5 DAYS
Spend two and a half days in downtown Sarajevo and a half day at outlying museums. Use the remaining time to explore **Jahorina** and **Bjelašnica**. It takes less than an hour to reach either mountain, and along the way you'll get a sensational view of Sarajevo nestled in the valley below. Renting a car will allow you to cover more territory as well as see the scope of the Olympic Mountains. Check out the medieval tombstones in some of the mountain villages near Bjelašnica. Stop for lunch in one of the rustic restaurants on the slopes.

IF YOU HAVE 7 DAYS
Add an excursion to **Mostar** and **Medđugorje** to your tour of Sarajevo. The trip south will be a full day, so if you can afford the time, spend the night in either Mostar or Medđugorje. As you drive down, notice how the geography changes from hilly to mountainous to fertile plain. Mostar is a jewel of Ottoman architecture but also a sad testament to Bosnia's recent conflict. Medđugorje, a Catholic pilgrimage site, is the most visited destination in Bosnia.

built during the Austrian period (although a similar fountain had been in the Baščaršija since 1753). **Kazandžiluk** (Coppersmith Street), just off the square, with its narrow cobblestone street and souk-like shops, best captures the feel of the old Ottoman trading post. It, like all of the streets in the Baščaršija, was named after the craftsmen who worked there. **Morića Han,** just off the main square, is an old caravanserai (inn) built to house visiting traders, their goods, and pack animals. This is the only remaining caravanserai left in Sarajevo.

⑥ **Brusa Bezistan & Sarajevo Historical Museum.** The Brusa Bezistan was built in 1551 by Grand Vizier Rustem-paša as a marketplace for silk trading. Named after Bursa, a main silk production city in the Eastern Mediterranean, the besistan housed merchants' stalls. The six-domed building is used as a marketplace today as well and has been completely restored after suffering damage in the recent war. Don't miss a quick look at the **Clock Tower** tucked behind the complex. Steering the population toward timely daily ablutions at the mosque was the driving force behind its

IF YOU LIKE

HISTORY

Few places in Europe leave you with so palpable an impression of history as the streets of Sarajevo. Well-preserved Ottoman ruins are one of the citys richest treasures. If you stand on a corner in the Baščaršija area, you can squint your eyes and imagine you're in the back streets of old Constantinople. It isn't just Ottoman history you can see in Sarajevo; the Habsburgs left their mark on the city as well. The 1889 neo-Gothic Catholic Cathedral would feel at home in Vienna. Then there's the corner of Princip's Bridge, where Serbian nationalist Gavrilo Princip assassinated Franz Ferdinand and his wife, Sofia, in 1914, sparking World War I. On Ferhadija you'll find an eternal flame honoring Tito's Partisans' sacrifice in liberating the city from the Germans in World War II. Among all this, you'll see delicate drops of red wax randomly embedded in the pavement. These reminders are known as "Sarajevo Roses" and mark sites where victims of sniper fire died in Sarajevo's most recent war.

MOUNTAINS

Bosnia and Herzegovina is a rich country for mountain enthusiasts. The Dinaric Alps spread from northern Croatia through central Bosnia, south through Herzegovina and down to Montenegro. Two peaks, Jahorina and Bjelašnica—practically in the suburbs of Sarajevo—were the main locations for the 1984 Winter Olympic Games. Unspoiled mountain villages dot the area around Bjelašnica, and a trip to some of the highland cemeteries around this area is an easy day trip. Jahorina Mountain is within Republika Srpska, easily reached from Pale on the outskirts of Sarajevo. It's covered with tall pine trees and makes for excellent walking. The slopes of both Jahorina and Bjelašnica are reliably covered with snow from October to May.

MOSQUES

If hearing the call to prayer is music to your ears, a visit to Sarajevo will be a symphony of the sounds of the Orient. The city is home to 80 mosques, and in the Old Town alone there are four, many from as early as the 16th century. Gazi Husrev-begova Mosque on Ferhadija was designed by a Persian architect in 1530. Not a stone's throw from there is the Havadže Duraka Mosque (Marketplace Mosque), where the imam sings the call to prayer live. The Careva Mosque, just over the river, is a sprawling complex built in 1547 for Sultan Mehmed II and then improved in 1566 by Suleiman the Magnificent. During Sarajevos heyday as an Ottoman city, each street had its own neighborhood mosque. Walk up the hilly streets behind the Baščaršija and see tiny crumbling mosques wedged in between old

construction in the 17th century. The internal ground and first floors of the Brusa Bezistan are dedicated to the **Sarajevo Historical Museum.** There's a small but authentic collection of traditional costumes, earthenware, and framed postcards of old Sarajevo. The centerpiece of the museum is a large model of Sarajevo's Old Town. ⊠*Abadžiluk 10* ☏*033–239–590* 💶*2 KM* ⊘*Tues.–Sat. 10–5, Sun. 10–1.*

NEED A BREAK?

Željo (✉ *Corner of Kazandžiluk and Bravadžiluk* ☎ *033–447–000*) is a *ćevabdžnica* in the heart of the Baščaršija, where you can get a cheap plate of tasty grilled *ćevapi* with yogurt. The place is such a local favorite there's a Željo II across the street!

❽ Careva Džamija (*Emperor's Mosque*). A mosque complex including a court, a hamam (Turkish bath), and a caravanserai was built on this site in 1457 by Isa Beg Ishaković to honor Sultan Mehmed II. The present-day mosque dates back to 1566, when Suleiman the Magnificent ordered the expansion of the mosque and prayer area to accommodate Sarajevo's growing Muslim population. The mosque complex itself today includes a cloister and a library and a cemetery. The simple style of the mosque is augmented by beautifully carved green wooden balconies. ✉*Obala Isa-bega Isakovića* ☎*033–241–353 for information* ☽ *Open by appointment only (call 48 hours in advance)*.

BOSNIA & HERZEGOVINA TOP 5

- Settle into one of the low wooden tables in Baščaršija, and order a short, black, and sweet *Bosanska kafa.*

- Head out of town and up the mountain for a breathtaking hike and lunch at a rustic mountain lodge in the Bjelašnica.

- Visit Medđugorje, one of the holiest Catholic pilgrimage sites in Europe.

- Experience a piece of living history, the tunnel that was the main supply route during the siege of Sarajevo; it's now a museum.

- Imagine the open carriage, the shots, and the aftermath of one of the single-most important events in modern European history while standing on the corner of Princip's Bridge.

---

❷ Gazi Husrev-begova Džamija (*Gazi Husrev-beg Mosque*). This sprawling complex is one of the most active mosques in the city, located as it is on Ferhadija right smack in the middle of Sarajevo's main pedestrian street. The stucco Oriental design of the mosque was a popular style in 1530, when the original structure was built by Persian architect Adžem Esir Ali. The interior light-filled prayer room showcases a ceiling decorated with azure blue and gold-leaf geometric designs. Check out the intricate birdcage fountain in the marble enclosed front courtyard. The mosque was constructed at the behest of Gazi Husrev-beg, the philanthropic governor of the Bosnian *sandžak* (military district) from 1521 through 1541. Directly across the street is the **Gazi Husrev-beg Medressa,** an Islamic school founded in 1537 for religious education. The medressa is located on Sarač I Street (which is actually a continuation of Ferhadija). ✉*Veliki Mudželeti 21, Sarači* ☎*033–532–144* ⊕*www.vakuf-gazi.ba* ▤*2 KM* ☽*Daily 10–noon, 2:30–4, and 5:30–7, except during Ramadan.*

❾ Kozja Ćuprija (*Goat's Bridge*). Built in 1550, the single-arch stone Goat's Bridge was the first to cross leaving Sarajevo on a sojourn east to Constantinople or a pilgrimage to Mecca. Visiting Ottoman notables were welcomed to the city here with great ceremony. ✉*Follow the Miljacka*

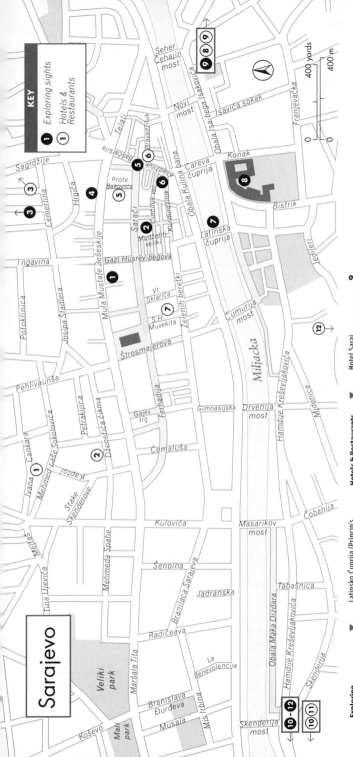

Sarajevo

KEY

- ① Exploring sights
- ① Hotels & Restaurants

Exploring ▶

Alipašina Mosque	**12**
Baščaršija	**5**
Brusa Besistan	**6**
Careva Džamija	**8**
Gazi Husrev-begova Džamija	**2**
Kozja Ćuprija	**9**
Latinsko Ćuprija (Princip's Bridge)	**7**
National Museum	**10**
Old Orthodox Church and Museum	**4**
Stari Hram (Old Temple)	**1**
Svrzina kuća	**3**
Tunnel Museum	**11**

Hotels & Restaurants ▶

Ćevabdžinica Hodžić	**6**
Dveri	**5**
Halvat Guest House	**4**
Hotel Astra	**7**
Hotel Hecco	**3**
Hotel Michele Sarajevo	**1**
Hotel Šaraj	**9**
Inat Kuća	**8**
Karuzo	**2**
Konoba Gusar	**12**
Radon Plaza	**11**
Vinoteka	**10**

2

River east out of the city through Bentbaša. A footpath along the river will take you to the Goat's Bridge.

❼ Latinsko Ćuprija *(Princip's Bridge)*. A wooden bridge was first built here
★ in 1541 and later crafted from stone in 1565. Its official name comes
from Latinluk, the Christian neighborhood the bridge linked to the
city where Catholics from Dubrovnik lived during Ottoman times. The
bridge is most famous as the site of the assassination of Archduke Francis Ferdinand and his wife on June 28, 1914, by Bosnian Serb Gavrilo Princip. It's still known as **Principov Most** among many Bosnians.
✉ *Links Obala Kulina Bana and Obala Isa-bega Isakovića.*

❿ National Museum. Right across the street from the Holiday Inn, the
National Museum is one of the few sights outside the Old Town that is
well worth a trip. Built in 1885 and in need of renovation, the museum
houses the national and cultural treasures of Bosnia and Herzegovina. One of the highlights of the museum is the botanical garden in
back, where unique *stećci* (carved medieval tombstones) are gracefully
placed among indigenous flora. There are good examples of traditional
weaponry and costumes as well as a room dedicated to the Sarajevo
Hagaddah, brought from Spain with migrating Sephardic Jews in 1492.
Sadly, most of the exhibits have descriptions written only in Bosnian.
✉ *Zmaja od Bosne 7* 🕿 *033–668–027* ⊕ *www.zemaljskimuzej.ba* 💵 *5
KM* 🕙 *Tues.–Fri. 10–5, weekends 10–2.*

❹ Old Orthodox Church and Museum. From the simple brick facade, it's hard
to see this small church and museum that chronicles the history of the
Orthodox Christians in Sarajevo just outside the Baščaršija. There's evidence of a Christian sacred site here as early as the 6th century, but the
current building dates back to 1730. The iconostasis (wall of icons and
religious paintings) inside the church is one of the best collections in the
Balkans. ✉ *Mula Mustafe Bašeskije 59* 🕿 *033–571–761* 💵 *Church 1
KM, museum 3 KM* 🕙 *Church daily 8–6; museum Tues.–Sun. 9–3.*

❸ Svrzina Kuća *(Svrzo's House)*. Step back in time with a visit to an 18th-
century Ottoman house, home of the wealthy Beg Srvzo, which is now
owned by the museum of Sarajevo. The perfectly preserved house captures unique Sarajevan architectural design during the Ottoman period.
A high wall separated the house from the street to create a harmonious,
inward-looking space for reflection. A spacious courtyard then led into
a central sitting room, and from there the house was divided into male
and female living quarters. ✉ *Gloddina 8* 🕿 *033–535–264* ⊕ *www.
muzejsarajeva.ba* 💵 *2 KM* 🕙 *Tues.–Sat. 10–6, Sun. 10–1.*

❶ Stari Hram *(Old Temple)*. Tucked behind Ferhadija is the **Velika Avlija**
(Great Courtyard) that makes up the old Jewish Quarter of Sarajevo.
The *Old Temple* was built by Sephardic Jews in 1581 and was expanded
in 1821 as the city's Jewish population increased. It is now home to
the Jewish Museum. Nearby is the site of the old synagogue, or *Il
Kal Grandi,* which was destroyed in 1788. ✉ *Mula Mustafe Bašeskije*
🕿 *033–535–688* 💵 *2 KM* 🕙 *Weekdays 10–6, Sun. 10–1.*

History You Can See

Just up the road from the restaurant Inat Kuća on Alifakovac street is an Ottoman-era cemetery dotted with gravestones of Muslim dignitaries. Many of the elaborate 16th- and 17th-century tombs have intricately carved headstones with long Arabic inscriptions. The cemetery is perched above the city in what obviously was an esteemed resting place for wealthy believers. Most of the graves are aslant now after five centuries, and the overgrown grass and disorder of the stones gives the place a sense of the final days of the mighty Ottoman Empire.

A sad truth about any trip to Sarajevo today is the number of new cemeteries. Mosques all over Sarajevo made makeshift burial places during the siege since no one could leave the city. Almost every neighborhood has a patch of land where row after row of white headstones mark the 12,000 residents lost in the Siege of Sarajevo. Seeing the road up to the Olympic Stadium lined with either side with a sea of new gravestones makes one pause over the tragedy and loss this city suffered in our own time.

⑪ **Tunnel Museum.** Seeing what's left of the hand-dug 770-foot Sarajevo
Fodor'sChoice tunnel will send chills down your spine to remember the city under
★ siege from 1993 to 1995. The tunnel began in the garage of a suburban Butmir neighborhood, ran under the airport, and came up in Dobrinja, another suburb west of the city. This supply line was vital to sustaining life in Sarajevo during the siege, and brave people carried food, medical supplies, and arms on their backs through the 5-foot-high tunnel for more than two years. Seeing the makeshift museum (actually located in the Kolar family house) brings the heroism of the tunnel to life. The easiest way to reach the Tunnel Museum is by taxi. You can take Tram 3 to Ildža as well, and take a shorter taxi ride from the tram stop to the museum. ⊠ *Tuneli 1 (Donji Kotorac 34)* ☎ *033–628–591 or 061–213–760* ⤳ *5 KM* ⊘ *Daily 10–6.*

OFF THE BEATEN PATH

Ilidža. This leafy suburb 12 km (7 mi) southwest of Sarajevo sits near a thermal spring of the Bosna River called **Vrelo Bosna.** The spring area, now a national park, has been a popular retreat for city dwellers since the turn of the century. Ilidža is linked to Vrelo Bosna by a 3-km (2-mi) alley lined with plane and chestnut trees planted in the 1890s. Follow directions to the airport and after the turnoff, continue straight (veering left) toward Ilidža. There are regular buses and trams (numbers 3 and 6) from Ilidža to the city center.

WHERE TO EAT

Sarajevo restaurants are relaxed, and few have any serious dress code. That said, dining out for most Bosnians is a special occasion, so they tend to look polished in restaurants. International restaurants as well as buregdžnica are strangled by cigarette smoke, so if a restaurant has outside seating, plan to sit there to avoid it, and pack a scarf or light jacket. Prices here, even at the higher-end international restaurants, are inexpensive by the standard of other major European capitals. Fresh, high-quality traditional dishes like *burek* and *ćevapi* can be found all over the city (and the country), and a big filling plate will rarely set you back more than US$10.

$$$–$$$$ ✕**Konoba Gusar.** Fishnets and lobster traps are strewn over pillars
★ and trellises in this leafy neighborhood restaurant above Bistrik. The relaxed, well-heeled crowd comes for the fresh St. Peter's fish or branzino, brought in daily from the Croatian coast. The outside terrace evokes seaside towns in Dalmatia and seafood specialties like *skampi na zaru ili buzara* (shrimp with a buzara sauce of tomatoes, garlic, and lemons) and big plates of razor clams may remind you of your last vacation by the sea. Try for a table outside; the slightly dreary dining room has seen better days. ✉*Mladih muslimana 12* ☎*033–655–589* ▭*AE, DC, MC, V.*

$$$–$$$$ ✕**Vinoteka.** The casual downstairs wine bar at this stylish restaurant is filled with an upmarket professional crowd in the early evenings sipping glasses of crisp *Sivi Pinot* and earthy *Nero D'Avola*. The elegant upstairs looks like your favorite Tuscan osteria, with Italian dishes like *tagliata* (steak with arugula and balsamic vinegar) and stuffed calamari taking center stage at tables laid with simple white tablecloths. Uncomplicated dishes showcase the restaurant's well-chosen wine list, which focuses on regional vintages, including Croatian *pošip* or Herzegovinian *gangaš.* ✉*Skenderija 12* ☎*033–214–996* ▭*AE, MC, V.*

$$–$$$ ✕**Karuzo.** Locals swear by this tiny, hard-to-find fish restaurant not far from the cathedral for its sushi, fresh fish, and charming owner/ waiter/cook. Sasha prepares everything himself and chats with you about travel, film, and what's fresh today. The fish is first-rate, and even sashimi aficionados will be surprised by the sushi options, given that this is Bosnia. Vegetables are expertly prepared and include more options than most Sarajevo restaurants. The pace here is leisurely, but that may not be such a bad thing since it's one of the few no-smoking places in town. ✉*Ulica DĐenetica čikma* ☎*033–444–647* ▭*No credit cards* ⊘*Closed Sun.*

$$ ✕**Dveri.** Blink and you'll miss this little gem of a restaurant on a side street in the Baščaršija. Rustic wooden farm tools, potted plants, and a beat-up license plate decorate the tiny patio where low kilim-covered chairs are set at wooden tables. Traditional Bosnian food like fresh-from-the-oven *pogača* (soft white bread) and *kajmak* (mild, soft white cheese) served on ceramic plates trump such nontraditional standbys as tuna salad. The polenta, served with cheese, sour cream, and bacon, isn't your usual northern Italian mainstay, but it's delicious nonetheless. ✉*Prote Bakovića 12* ☎*033–537–020* ▭*No credit cards.*

$$ ✕**Inat Kuća.** Whether you sit outside at a wrought-iron table under the
Fodor's Choice white birch trees or on a kilim-covered banquette inside, you won't
★ find a more charming spot for a traditional Bosnian meal than this restaurant overlooking the Miljacka River. *Begova čorba* (beg's soup) is the specialty here; it's a rich stew chock full of veal and vegetables. The structure itself was moved in 1892, brick by brick, from the other side of the river to make room for the Town Hall, thereby earning it the name the "Spite House." There's no bad will left on the menu, though, just good solid traditional food including *zeljanica*, a great

sahan (grilled mixed meat plate), and a long list of homemade spirits. ✉ *Veliki Alifakovac 1* ☎ *033–447–867* ▭ *MC, V.*

$ ✕ **Ćevabdžinica Hodžić.** *Ćevapi,* the tiny veal sausages popular throughout the Balkans, are the highlight of the menu here. Made fresh all day, they can be ordered in plates of 5, 10, or 15 and are served with soft, warmed pita bread, onions, and yogurt. This is a popular local meal for breakfast, lunch, or dinner. Hodžić is smack in the center of the Baščaršija and is pretty much crowded day or night. Popular demand created Hodžić II just around the corner at Bravadžilik 4. ✉ *Bravadžilik 34* ☎ *033–532–866* ▭ *No credit cards.*

WHERE TO STAY

Many medium-size hotels are clustered around the Old Town with good access to the city's main tourist sights. A few of the bigger business hotels are on the road out to the airport. There are many family-run pensions around the Baščaršija area. Hotel prices include breakfast and local taxes.

$$$$ ▥ **Hotel Astra.** Wedged somewhat awkwardly in a corner building
★   behind Ferhadija, the upscale Astra couldn't be better located for those who like to be near the pulse of a city. All of the major sights in Sarajevo (except the Tunnel Museum) are within walking distance, and hip cafés and bars are just a stone's throw away on Štrossmajerova. Rooms can be a bit bland, but most have gauzy curtains on the windows with good views over the red rooftops of the city. The pleasant café on the street side of the lobby is a prime spot for people-watching. Pros: central location, bustling café. Cons: Noisy at night, an awkwardly shaped building means some rooms are small with odd dimensions. ✉ *Ulica Zelenih beretki 9, 71000* ☎ *033–252–100* ⊕ *www.hotel-astra.com.ba* ⬦ *18 rooms* ⬥ *In-room: refrigerator. In-hotel: restaurant, bar* ▭ *AE, DC, MC, V* ❢❘ *BP.*

$$$$ ▥ **Radon Plaza.** You can't miss the two glass towers of this swanky hotel as you approach the city from the airport; the Radon is the splashiest thing going on in Sarajevo. First-class business services and luxurious rooms with plasma TVs make up for the somewhat imposing exterior. Once inside, you'll enjoy peak comfort levels with discreet service and a top-notch spa and pool area. Check out the views from the rotating restaurant on the top floor, where breakfast is served. The location's a bit far from the Old Town, but it's a short taxi ride away, and there's regular bus service to town nearby. Pros: modern rooms, best business facilities in the city, good a/c. Cons: most tourist sights not walkable from here, spa has a smoking section. ✉ *Džemala Bijedića 185, 71000* ☎ *033–752–900* ⊕ *www.radonplazahotel.ba* ⬦ *112 rooms* ⬥ *In-room: safe, refrigerator, Ethernet. In-hotel: restaurant, room service, bar, pool, spa, parking (no fee), no-smoking rooms* ▭ *AE, DC, MC, V* ❢❘ *BP.*

$$$–$$$$ ▥ **Hotel Michele Sarajevo.** Six apartments with parquet floors and big
☾   windows are tastefully fitted out with handwoven carpets, brass lamps, and antique ceramics in Sarajevo's first boutique hotel. Rooms are so spacious they make you feel as if you're in a villa far from the city (you're not). All apartments include modern kitchens, Wi-Fi, and state-

of-the-art bathrooms. Families can do especially well here because of the space, but business travelers like the Michele for its long-term rental options. Pictures of celebrity guests—including Bono and Richard Gere—relaxing in the sitting room make you wonder whom you'll brush up against on your visit. Pros: attentive service, peace and quiet in quarters that don't feel like a hotel. Cons: can be tricky to find because of one-way narrow streets near the hotel. ⊠ *Ivana Cankara 27, 71000* ☏ *033–560–310* ⊕ *www.hotelmichele.ba* 📞 *2 rooms, 6 apartments* ⚷ *In-room: safe, kitchen (some), refrigerator, Wi-Fi. In-hotel: laundry service, parking (free)* ⊟ *AE, DC, MC, V* ⍟⎮*BP.*

$$$ 🏨 **Hotel Saraj.** Perched high above the Miljacka River, with spectacular vistas of the red-tiled roofs of the Baščaršija below, this old standby has the best views in all of Sarajevo. Enjoy a drink on the leafy terrace around dusk, when you can hear a symphony of prayer calls from mosques in the city below. Friendly staff make up for lopsided interior design; some of the rooms have Commie-era details like ugly bedspreads and bad lighting, but some are tastefully modern. Request a room with a view in the new wing. The pool is inviting, but the hotel charges for its use. Pros: dramatic views and a bar/terrace on which to enjoy them, new rooms with luxurious Asian touches. Cons: too many facility usage fees, safes not available in every room. ⊠ *Nevjestina 5, 71000* ☏ *033–237–810* ⊕ *www.hotelsaraj.com* 📞 *140 rooms* ⚷ *In-room: no a/c (some), Ehternet, Wi-Fi, refrigerator, safe (some). In-hotel: restaurant, room service, pool, spa, parking (no fee)* ⊟ *AE, DC, MC, V* ⍟⎮*BP.*

$$ 🏨 **Hotel Hecco.** The lobby of this comfortable favorite has playful Cubist elements and lots of potted plants. The brightly decorated rooms are outfitted with free broadband and flat-screen TVs. It's no wonder the place books up quickly; guests enjoy lots of perks like large Jacuzzis and free parking that are not usually found in this price category. Conveniently located a short walk uphill) from the Baščaršija, the Hecco is on a quiet street next to a fruit-and-vegetable stand, but it's still close to the action in the Old Town. Travel light for the trip, though, because your walk up to the hotel is steep, and there's no elevator once you get there. Pros: parking garage in attached building, Wi-Fi and flat-screen TVs in rooms. Cons: no a/c, limited fans on hot nights. ⊠ *Medresa br. 1, 71000* ☏ *033–273–730* ⊕ *www.hotel-hecco.net* 📞 *20 rooms, 2 apartments* ⚷ *In-room: Ethernet, Wi-Fi. In-hotel: parking (no fee)* ⊟ *MC, V* ⍟⎮*BP.*

$–$$ 🏨 **Halvat Guest House.** Fans of the Halvat sing the praises of the friendly
Fodor's Choice   owners for welcoming guests like family. The small, centrally located
★   pension is a short walk up from the Baščaršija on a busy street close to lots of restaurants. The rooms are basic, but warm colors and soft lighting help them feel cozy instead of cramped. Hearty breakfasts are made to order in the cheery breakfast room, where the owners have been known to linger with guests over coffee all morning. Pros: friendly and attentive staff, hearty breakfast. Cons: rooms book up fast, hotel on a busy street, some say bathrooms are small and not very private. ⊠ *Kasima effendije. Dobrače do 5, 71000* ☏ *033–237–714* ⊕ *www. halvat.com.ba* 📞 *5 rooms* ⚷ *In-room: no a/c, Ethernet* ⊟ *No credit cards* ⍟⎮*BP.*

NIGHTLIFE & THE ARTS

NIGHTLIFE

Sarajevo buzzes at night along Ferhadija and Zelenih Beretki streets. The *Štrossmajerova* (pedestrian walkway) between the two is packed cheek to jowl with hipsters smoking cigarettes and drinking trendy cocktails. A quieter crowd hangs in the Morića Han sipping tea and beer in a leafy courtyard. The Baščaršija area is popular with families and nondrinkers in the evenings.

Zlatna Ribica (⊠ *Kaptol 5* ☎ *033–215–369*), tucked off on a side street near Titova square, is decorated in Euro-kitsch. The early evening sees a relaxed crowd enjoying big Sarajevsko beers. There's a cool music scene after hours.

Hacienda (⊠ *Bazerdžani 3* ☎ *033–441–918*) offers hit-or-miss Mexican food in a relaxed, cantina atmosphere, but the easygoing vibe makes it popular with locals. A DJ spins a good mix of American and Balkan pop at the bar. It's on a tiny side street lined with bars behind the Baščaršija.

★ **City Pub** (⊠ *Hadžiristića* ☎ *033–209–789*) may host hometown divas or visiting underground blues acts on its tiny stage on any given night, but this is a favorite Sarajevo institution. The mixed local/international bar scene is groovy but low-key.

THE ARTS

Each August, the **Sarajevo Film Festival** (⊕ *www.sff.ba*), a weeklong celebration of regional films, is the highlight of the summer season. Begun as a modest affair in the last year of the war, the festival is now a major European film event. Tickets go on sale the week before the festival and get snapped up quickly.

SHOPPING

Sarajevo's Baščaršija neighborhood is the city's main shopping area for souvenirs. Tiny shops selling *stari zanati* (old crafts) are worth stopping into for unique Bosnian gifts. Coppersmiths, goldsmiths, silversmiths, and other craftsmen continue to make their living here selling tea sets, copper pots, saddlebags, and gold jewelry. When you are shopping, definitely look at several stores before buying to judge quality and relative asking prices, and don't hesitate to bargain with vendors.

Buttery leather slippers with curly toes fit for a pasha are popular souvenirs. There's interesting postwar bric-a-brac fashioned from things like bullets and mortar shells for sale, too. Homemade local spirits made from pear, plum, and apple are for sale at the outdoor *markale* (market). Check out ⊕ *www.starizanati.co.ba* for a history of Bosnian crafts and list of artisans' addresses.

JAHORINA & BJELAŠNICA

Bjelašnica is 30 km (19 mi) southwest of Sarajevo; Jahorina is 25 km (16 mi) southeast of Sarajevo.

The Olympic Mountains of Jahorina and Bjelašnica are popular weekend destinations for Sarajevans all year long. Jahorina to the southeast and Bjelašnica (and Mt. Igman) to the southwest are best reached by car, as bus service from the city center is irregular. The vistas are spectacular, and winding roads take you through pine forests and unspoiled highland villages where you may have to give way to herds of sheep. In winter, you'll find both places crowded with ski enthusiasts (although nowhere near as crowded as resorts in Austria or Switzerland). Either mountain can be reached in about 45 minutes, depending on the snow.

Both Jahorina and Bjelašnica have ski centers with lifts, equipment-rental shops, instructors, food service, and accommodations. Accommodation ranges from hotels (many in Jahorina), to pensions to mountain huts. In general, services are basic, but the quality of the skiing is high. A daily pass to ski on either mountain will run around 25 KM.

To reach Jahorina, travel east toward Pale and from there drive through Bistrica up the mountain. The road is not well marked but locals will point and make hand gestures to help you get there.

To reach Bjelašnica, follow the road toward the airport, and look for signs for the Hotel Maršal. When you reach a quarry, take a right and follow signs for Hadžić I, and continue looking for the Hotel Maršal, which is at the base of the Bjelašnica slopes. (You have to watch for the quarry, but it's hard to miss since it looks like the entire side of a mountain is missing just off the road.)

Buses to ski areas leave from the National Museum during the winter months, but schedules are irregular and based entirely on demand and the amount of snow. Check with the Sarajevo tourism office for updated information. The **Sarajevo Tourism Association** (⊠ *Zelenih beretki 22a* ☎ *033–220–724* ⊕ *www.sarajevo-tourism.com*) can give you the most up-to-date information on buses to both ski areas and can also help reserve accommodations.

WHERE TO EAT

$$
Fodor's Choice
★

✕ **Planinska Kuća.** *Zeljanica* is served steaming hot in a giant cast-iron pan at this rustic mountain lodge at the base of the Bjelašnica slopes. Big wooden tables cover the sunny deck and face the mountain, so you get a view of skiers swishing down the hill while you lunch. Cowhides and carpets decorate the cozy one-room hut, and hearty dishes like *sirnica* and veal stew are authentic versions of traditional fare. All this and a choice of several homemade *rakijas* (fruit spirits) make this modest restaurant ooze Bosnian alpine charm. ▭ *No credit cards.*

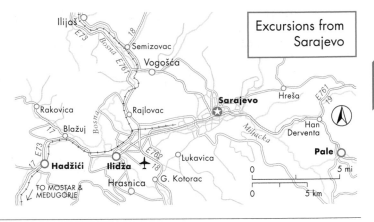

Excursions from Sarajevo

2

WHERE TO STAY

$$$$ ⊞**Hotel Termag.** Swish by any standard, the Termag would not seem out of place in Vail or Verbier. A tree springs from the stone floor in the lobby and is encased by a cowhide-covered banquette. The massive fireplace in the bar area is a work of art with a chimney made of corrugated iron. Boxy, modern wood furniture and neutral tones decorate comfortable rooms and dining areas. The design seems a bit out of step with Bosnia's rustic charm, but the facilities are first-rate. Pros: cozy touches like fluffy duvets, deluxe après-ski relaxation facilities. Con: use of solarium and Jacuzzi not included in the room rate. ✉*Jahorina, Poljice* ☎*057–270–422* ⊕*www.termaghotel.com* ⊸*18 rooms, 13 apartments* ⌂*In-room: safe, Ethernet. In-hotel: restaurant, bar, pool, parking (free)* ▤*AE, MC, V* ⏐◯⏐*BP.*

$$$ ⊞**Hotel Maršal.** You couldn't ask for a better location for this hotel and ski chalet complex; it's right at the base of the ski lift up to Bjelašnica. That said, there are no other hotels here, so the Maršal may be your best (and only) choice. The apartments have wooden shutters and alpine touches, but the hotel itself is a bit generic. Pros: modern amenities in rooms, a location that can't be beat. Con: somewhat charmless interior design. ✉*Babib do, Bjelašnica* ☎*033–279–100* ⊕*www. hotel-marsal.ba* ⊸*70 rooms* ⌂*In-hotel: restaurant, bar, parking (free)* ▤*AE, MC, V* ⏐◯⏐*BP.*

MOSTAR

100 km (62 mi) south of Sarajevo.

Anchored on the raging Neretva River, Mostar is a dramatic city surrounded by mountains in southern Herzegovina. If time allows, a day trip to walk around the Old City to take in the Ottoman *mahalas* (living quarters) lined with antiques shops and traditional craft workshops is a pleasant excursion from Sarajevo. Or, if combined with a trip from Sarajevo to Medđugorje, Mostar is a good stopping-off point for a meal, as the vibrant city has a national reputation for good food.

Mostar is remembered primarily for its Ottoman architecture and the symbolic *Stari Most* (Old Bridge) that was destroyed during the war in 1993 and rebuilt with great fanfare in 2004. The destruction of the 400-year-old bridge was one of the most contentious and emotional issues of the war in Bosnia and Herzegovina. Walking through the city is the best way to see the magnificent structure, now restored to its former glory.

Crossing back and forth on the bridges over the Neretva River, including the *Kriva Ćuprija* (Crooked Bridge), Europe's oldest single-arch bridge, gives spectacular views of the gurgling, emerald green river. Several 17th-century mosques and an Ottoman-era *hamam* complex are among the city's best sights. Sadly, many of the ruined buildings are a reminder of the bitter fighting that took place during the recent war. Sadder still, in Mostar you will see a city that continues to be effectively divided along religious lines since the conflict.

WHERE TO EAT

$$ ✕ **Konoba Taurus.** Traditional Herzegovinian and Dalmatian specialties
★ are what you'll find on the menu at this rustic stone restaurant at the foot of the Crooked Bridge. The tiny terrace overlooking the Radobolje River is a relaxing lunch spot; the dinner crowd warms to the cozy fireplace inside. Try the *pastrmka* (local trout), cooked whole with garlic and olive oil, and wash it down with a glass of young Žilavka. ⊠*Kriva Ćuprija* ☎*061–212–617* ▭*MC, V.*

WHERE TO STAY

$$$ 🛏 **Hotel Ero.** Rooms at this bustling hotel are well equipped, if not luxurious. The friendly staff is known for helping visitors find their way around the city and the region since there's still not much good tourist information about Herzegovina readily available. The hotel's restaurant is a popular local meeting spot. Pros: near the bus and train station, a short walk from the main Ottoman sights, has a good restaurant. Con: in a heavily war-damaged part of town. ⊠*Dr. Ante Starčevića, 88000* ☎*036–386–777* ⊕*www.ero.ba* ⟳*165 rooms* ⧖*In-room: safe, Ethernet. In-hotel: restaurant, bar, laundry service, parking (free)* ▭*AE, DC, MC, V.*

MEDĐUGORJE

29 km (18 mi) south of Mostar.

The Virgin Mary appeared to six teenagers in this small Herzegovinian town in 1981 and appears periodically to some of them to this day, or so many Catholics believe. Because of that miraculous appearance, the once small village has attracted 15 million believers since 1981, and although not officially recognized by the Vatican, the town is Catholicism's second-largest pilgrimage site. There are three principal sites in Medđugorje, all related to the pilgrimage: **Mount Krizevac** (Cross Mountain), where a 15-ton cross has been erected (the first cross was erected here in 1933, long before the Marian appearances) and where pilgrims trek up the sloping hillside; **Apparition Hill** (where Mary first appeared to the six children), a short walk outside of the main village, where several other crosses have been erected, including the famous "blue cross" not visible from the main road, which was built to commemorate the spot where the children met in secret during the Communist years; and **St. James Church,** which is in the center of town and packed with pilgrims and worshippers throughout the day. If you visit Međugorje, you will have no trouble finding each of these important sights.

Because so many groups come from abroad, there's plenty of accommodation available at every price point, not to mention shops, restaurants, and local guides. From Mostar, buses make the hour-long journey several times a day. You can also take a bus from Dubrovnik, Croatia. To arrange a pilgrimage with and meetings with clergy members and visionaries it's best to book a local guide *(see ⇨ Tours in Bosnia & Herzegovina Essentials, below)*.

WHERE TO STAY & EAT

Međugorje has many inexpensive local restaurants serving a mix of traditional and international dishes, though there are no true standouts in terms of cuisine.

$ ⌴**Hotel Ruža.** Within walking distance of Apparition Hill and Cross Mountain, the Ruža is close to all the main religious sights in Međugorje. Rooms are basic but clean, and many have balconies with views for private contemplation. The hotel also has its own chapel. The restaurant and snack bar are air-conditioned. Pros: proximity to the main religious sights in Međugorje, many rooms have balconies. Con: no a/c in the rooms. ⊠ *Bijakovići, Međugorje* ☎ *036–651–822* ⊕ *www.tel.net.ba/hotelruza* ⌁ *50 rooms* ⌂ *In-hotel: restaurant, no a/c* ⊟ *DC, MC, V.*

BOSNIA & HERZEGOVINA ESSENTIALS

TRANSPORTATION

BY AIR

There are no direct flights from the United States to Sarajevo, but many European airlines have regular service. At this writing there are daily flights from Vienna (Austrian Airlines), Munich (Lufthansa), Milan (Alitalia), Belgrade (JAT Airways), Ljubljana (Adria), Zagreb (Croatian Airlines), and Budapest (Malev) and thrice-weekly flights from Istanbul (Turkish Airlines) and Frankfurt (Lufthansa). Flights to Sarajevo are expensive, as there is little competition on routes. Air Bosna (aka BH Airlines), Bosnia's national airline, provides several daily flights to Sarajevo but is struggling economically and has unreliable service; it's worth checking out, especially if it receives a much-needed market recapitalization. At this writing, none of the European budget airlines fly to Sarajevo.

Information Air Bosna (☎*033-550-125* ⊕*www.airbosna.ba*). **Austrian Airlines** (☎*033-474-446*). **Lufthansa** (☎*033-278-590*). **Alitalia** (☎*033-556-565*). **JAT Airways** (☎*033-259-750*). **Adria Airways** (☎*033-232-125*). **Croatian Airlines** (☎*033-666-123*) **Malev** (☎*033-473-200*). **Turkish Airlines** (☎*033-666-092*).

AIRPORTS & TRANSFERS

Taxis to Sarajevo are available at the airport but are not well regulated. There's no organized shuttle service into the city, and crooked cabdrivers are working the airport beat most of the day. A journey from the airport to the city center *should* cost around 15 KM–20 KM (€7–€10) when the meter is used, so insist on that before you get into a taxi. There's an extra surcharge of 2 KM per piece of luggage. Given the difficulty of finding an honest cabdriver, the best way to get into Sarajevo from the airport is to prearrange a transfer with your hotel.

Information **Sarajevo International Airport** (✉*Kurt Schorka 36, Sarajevo* ☎*033-289-100* ⊕*www.sarajevo-airport.ba*).

BY BUS

Buses offer regular service from Croatia and Germany the most frequently, as well as other countries. Once in Bosnia and Herzegovina, the country is well linked by bus service. Buses make stops even in the most remote villages, and traveling by bus is a cheap and reliable way to see the country. Round-trip fares to Dubrovnik are 60 KM (about €30); a one-way journey to Berlin will cost around 350 KM (€125). A domestic journey will rarely cost more that 40 KM, even to the far reaches of the country. Centrotrans is the main bus company in Bosnia and Herzegovina. Travel between the entities (the Federation and Republika Srpksa) isn't well coordinated, though. If you plan to travel to an area of Republika Sprska or if you plan to travel to Belgrade and other parts of Serbia proper, buses leave from Lukavica Bus Station in eastern Sarajevo. The Sarajevo Tourism Association office will have the most up-to-date schedules.

Information **Centrotrans** (✉*Put života 8 [at the bus station], Sarajevo* ☎*033-213-100* ⊕*www.centrotrans.com*). **Lukavica Bus Station** (✉*Nikole Tesle, Sarajevo* ☎*057-317-377*). **Mostar Bus Station** (✉*Stjepana Radi 39, Mostar* ☎*036-312-286*).

BY CAR

Traveling by car is the best way to see Bosnia and Herzegovina. If your trip is limited to Sarajevo, Mostar, and Medugorje—all well linked by bus and train—a car rental is unnecessary. To get out to Jahorina and Bjelašnica, a car is extremely useful since bus service is irregular and part of the fun of a mountain excursion is seeing the rolling countryside. Roads in general are two-lane and slow going through much of the mountainous terrain. Road signs are very spotty in the countryside, and even driving to such well-known places as Jahorina and Bjelašnica it's easy to lose your way. Good maps of the country and the road network are scarce in bookshops and gas stations.

Car rentals are expensive in Bosnia. Expect to pay between 80 KM and 160 KM per day for a car rental, with slightly lower weekly rates. All major car rental companies are represented at the Sarajevo Airport.

Information **Avis** (✉ *Hamdija Cemerlica 2, Sarajevo* ☎ *033–660–180* ◷ *Closed weekends*). **Budget** (✉ *Fra Anđela Zvizdovića 1, Sarajevo* ☎ *033–268–190*). **Europcar** (*ASA-Rent* ✉ *Bulevar Meše Selimovića 16, Sarajevo* ☎ *033–450– 961* ✉ *Branilaca Sarajeva 20, Sarajevo* ☎ *033–760–360*). **F Rent a Car SA** (✉ *Kranjčevićeva 39, Sarajevo* ☎ *033–219–177* ⊕ *www.frac.co.ba*). **Hertz** (✉ *Holiday Inn, Zmaja od Bosne 5, Sarajevo* ☎ *033–204–090*). **National** (✉ *Kranjčevićeva, Sarajevo* ☎ *033–267–590*). **Sixt** (✉ *Sarajevo International Airport, Kurta Schorka 36, Sarajevo* ☎ *033–541–741*).

BY TAXI

Taxis are plentiful, inexpensive, and reliable in Sarajevo. Most taxi drivers do not speak English, so be able to pronounce your destination or have it written out before getting into your taxi. Taxi stands are well marked throughout the city. Fares start at 2 KM on flag-drop, and then increase at 1 KM per km (½ mi) thereafter.

Information **Sarajevo Taxi** (☎ *033–660–970, 033–660–666, or 1515*). **Samir & Emir** (☎ *1516*). **Yellow Taxi Cab** (☎ *033–663–555*).

BY TRAM & SUBWAY

Seven tram lines loop back and forth (east–west) on Zmaja od Bosna and out to the Sarajevo suburbs. Some of the trams are old German cars that have not been repainted, so don't panic if the oncoming tram says RINGSTRASSE. Tickets (1.5 KM) should be purchased before you board at kiosks in the city (*tisak*); they cost slightly more if you buy them on board. There are regular spot checks for validated tickets on public transport, so be sure to stamp your ticket once you get on the tram. Most trams stop at the Baščaršija or the main train station at Put Života 2.

Information **Tram info line** (☎ *033–293–333*).

BY TRAIN

Train service to Sarajevo from abroad is still somewhat limited in postwar Bosnia. There are regular connections to Budapest, Zagreb, and Ploče on the Croatian coast, and there are three train lines that operate within the country. Trains to Mostar take about 2½ hours and end in Ploče.

Information **Sarajevo Train Station** (*Željeznička stanica* ✉ *Trg žrtava Srebenice, Sarajevo* ☎ *033–655–330*).

CONTACTS & RESOURCES

BANKS & EXCHANGE SERVICES

ATMs are widely available in Sarajevo, Mostar, and Međđugorje although quite scarce in the rest of the country. Banks will exchange money but charge a commission; traveler's checks are rarely accepted, and many banks won't accept them at all. Most shops do not accept credit or debit cards. Since the KM is convertible, it's a good idea to have more cash on hand than you think you'll need, especially if you travel outside Sarajevo. Some hotels and shops will exchange euros at a 1:2 ratio to the KM on the spot. Other currencies need to be exchanged at banks. Banks are open from 8:30 AM to 8 PM on weekdays and 9 to 1 on Saturdays.

EMERGENCIES

Emergency Services Ambulance (☎124). Fire (☎123). Police (☎122).

Road Assistance (☎1282).

Doctors & Dentists Dental Clinic (✉Bolnička 4a, Sarajevo ☎033-214-254). The Institute of Emergency Medical Care (✉Kolodvorska 14, Sarajevo ☎033-611-111).

Hospitals Klinička Bolnica Mostar (✉Kardinala Stepinaca bb, Mostar ☎036-313-238 or 036-314-136). University of Sarajevo Koševo Hospital (✉Bolnička 25, Sarajevo ☎033-297-000).

24-Hour Pharmacies Baščaršija Pharmacy (✉Obal Kulina Bana 25, Sarajevo ☎033-272-300). Novo Sarajevo Pharmacy (✉Zmaja od Bosne 51, Sarajevo ☎033-713-830 or 033-653-472).

INTERNET, MAIL & SHIPPING

Broadband Internet is making its way to Bosnia, but the country is by no means fully wired. Internet cafés are in most cities now with good, cheap connectivity (about 1 KM per hour). Many newer hotels have broadband connections in rooms; some have Wi-Fi; however, Wi-Fi does not have the same penetration in Bosnia as it does in other European countries. Internet cafés are usually crowded and sometimes smoky, but usually the staff speaks some English.

The main Bosnian post office on Obala Kulina Bana in Sarajevo dates back to the 19th century and is one of the best examples of the Austro-Hungarian building boom in the city. Badly damaged during the conflict, it is now completely renovated. The postal service has an excellent Web site in English with a list of services, fees, and instructions on how to wrap packages for shipping.

Internet Cafés Internet Caffe (✉Ulica Rade Bitange, Mostar). Internet Club Bill Gates (✉Vladislava Skarića, Sarajevo ☎033-666-555). Internet Club "Click" (✉Kundurdžiluk 1, Sarajevo ☎033-236-914).

Post Offices Bosnian Post Office (✉Obala Kulina Bana 8, Sarajevo ☎033-252-500 ⊕www.bhp.ba). DHL (✉Džemala Bijedića 166a, Sarajevo ☎033-774-000).

TOUR OPTIONS

Bosnia's tourism industry is just getting off the ground, so reliable tourist information isn't always available. The Sarajevo Tourism Association *(see ⇨ Visitor Information, below)* can answer many questions and is very helpful in arranging well-trained guides to help you see the country. Consider hiring a guide for a walking tour of Sarajevo or Mostar. Several local tour companies can help organize the logistics of a ski excursion (getting there, accommodation, equipment rental). Few tour companies abroad have any comprehensive packages to Bosnia and Herzegovina, although well-organized charter trips to Medđugorje are available in almost every country. Independent travelers (those not traveling with a group) to Medđugorje often use a local tour company to organize transportation from nearby airports (most often Dubrovnik or Sarajevo).

Information Fortuna Tours (⊠ *Kujundžiluk 2, Mostar* ☎ *036–551–888* ⊕ *www. fortuna.ba*) is a reliable company in Mostar that can arrange knowledgeable guides for Mostar or Medđugorje. **Global Medđugorje** (⊠ *Bijakovići bb, Bijakovici* ☎ *036–651–489* ⊕ *www.global-medjugorje.com*) specializes in Medđugorje and can organize tours of all the religious sights in the area as well as transportation from Mostar and Sarajevo (and points in Croatia as well). The company can also arrange rental cars, accommodation, bus tickets, and meetings with visionaries. **Green Visions** (⊠ *Radnićka bb, Sarajevo* ☎ *033–717–290* ⊕ *www.greenvisions. ba*) is Bosnia's only ecotourism company, organizing walking and hiking tours in Bosnia, including tours of Bjelašnica. **Goya Tours** (⊠ *Bijakovići bb, Bijakovići* ☎ *036–651–700* ⊕ *www.goyatours.com*) are Medđugorje specialists. **Regent Holidays** (⊠ *15 St. John St., Bristol, U.K.* ☎ *0870–499–0439* ⊕ *www.regent-holidays. co.uk*), a British company, specializes in the Balkans and offers several multicity trips to Bosnia from the U.K., as well as shorter city-break trips to Sarajevo. **Sarajevo Discovery** (⊠ *Branilaca Sarajeva 17, Sarajevo* ☎ *061–190–591* ⊕ *www. sarajevo-discovery.com*) has energetic guides that give unique Sarajevo city tours. One called "Times of Misfortune" tells the story of the siege. The company also gives tours of Jewish Sarajevo.

VISITOR INFORMATION

Information Medđugorje Tourist Information Office (⊠ *Mala livada, Medđugorje* ☎ *036–651–011* ⊕ *www.tel.net.ba/tzm-medjugorje*). **Mostar Tourist Information Office** (⊠ *Rade Bitange 13, Mostar* ☎ *036–580–013*). **Sarajevo Tourism Association** (⊠ *Zelenih beretki 22a, Sarajevo* ☎ *033–220–724* ⊕ *www.sarajevo-tourism. com*). **Tourism Association of Sarajevo Canton** (⊕ *www.sarajevo.ba*). **Tourism Association of Bosnia and Herzegovina** (⊠ *Branilaca Sarajeva 21, Sarajevo* ☎ *033–252–900* ⊕ *www.bhtourism.ba*). **Tourism Association of Herzegovina Neretva Canton** (⊕ *www.hercegovina.ba*).

Bulgaria

WORD OF MOUTH

"You might want to google [Rila Monastery] as there are no words I can come up with to describe how completely cool this place was. The setting in the mountains; the colorful murals painted on the inside of the church, ceilings, pillars and more . . ."

—Toucan2

"Away from the main tourist spots are some really charming places like Nessebar, Stara Zagora, Balchik, Sozopol, and Veliko Turnovo. The scenery is often stunning, and the history of the place is all around. The infrastructure has improved, and continues to do so, although some elements still have a long way to go."

—doonhamer

www.fodors.com/forums

Updated by
Mark Baker

TO MANY FIRST-TIME VISITORS, BULGARIA retains a slightly sinister sound. Maybe it's the lingering memories of communism and the Soviet Union—Bulgaria was always portrayed, accurately, as the most pro-Soviet of the Eastern bloc satellite states. The country's relatively remote location, tucked away in the far southeastern corner of Europe, helped to contribute to this image of intrigue and mystery.

But that's already ancient history. On January 1, 2007, nearly 20 years after throwing off their communist oppressors, Bulgarians achieved their long-sought-after objective of joining the European Union. Change is in the air. EU membership has brought with it a flood of foreign investment in the form of new roads, office blocks, and apartments, along with a plethora of new hotels and resorts, particularly on the Black Sea coast and around the ski resort of Bansko.

Foreign tourists are quickly discovering the country's charms. Bulgaria (along with neighboring Romania) is one of the fastest-growing tourist destinations in Europe. Visitors are drawn first and foremost to the Black Sea resorts. The coastal towns and resorts here have always been popular with Eastern Europeans, but now are increasingly attracting visitors from Britain, Scandinavia, and Germany. And word of the mountain resorts, the secluded monasteries, and the charming, historically rich cities of Plovdiv and Veliko Târnovo is also spreading quickly.

Bulgaria is one of Europe's oldest nations, founded in AD 681 by the Bulgars, a Turkic tribe from Central Asia. But Bulgaria was a crossroads of civilization thousands of years before then. Archaeological finds in Varna, on the Black Sea coast, show evidence of inhabitance as early as 4600 BC. More recent discoveries of relatively sophisticated weapons and jewelry made by the ancient Thracian people show that a highly developed civilization thrived on the territory of modern-day Bulgaria hundreds of years before the birth of Christ.

During the Middle Ages, the Bulgarian kingdom spread far and wide, touching on three seas: the Black Sea to the east, the Aegean Sea to the south, and the Adriatic Sea to the west. This expansion came to an end in the 14th century, when the kingdom was conquered by the Ottoman Turks. Bulgaria would remain a part of the Ottoman Empire for four centuries, and the Turkish imprint on architecture, the landscape, and culture remains strong.

Modern Bulgaria was formed at the end of the 19th century, with the country's liberation from the Ottoman Empire. The 19th century was a rich period for Bulgaria as it began to emerge from the Turkish yoke. The "National Revival," as the era is known, brought with it a renaissance of Bulgarian architecture, culture, and literature.

Bulgaria weathered the two World Wars of the 20th century more or less intact, but fell within the Soviet sphere of influence at the end of World War II. During the 40 years of communism, Bulgaria became the closest ally of the Soviet Union and was largely isolated from the noncommunist world.

The communist period came to an end in 1989 with the overthrow of party leader Todor Zhivkov. The revolution was initially welcomed by Bulgarians, but its first decade was very difficult. The low point came at the end of 1996 and 1997, with massive unemployment, hyperinflation, rampant corruption, and growing breadlines. The people of Bulgaria took to the streets, surrounded the parliament building where members of the BSP (Bulgarian Socialist Party) were barricaded inside, and demanded new elections. Since then, the country has seen slow but steady progress. Incomes are growing, the currency—now tied to the euro—has stabilized, and living standards continue to rise.

EXPLORING BULGARIA

Bordered by Romania to the north (the Danube River forms much of the border), Serbia and the former Yugoslav Republic of Macedonia to the west, Greece and Turkey to the south, and the Black Sea to the east, Bulgaria is in the southeastern corner of Europe in the heart of the Balkan Peninsula. Geographically, Bulgaria can be divided into two basic regions: the Inland and the Black Sea's Golden Coast. Inland you'll find one of Bulgaria's two chief attractions, its towering mountains; and on the Black Sea you'll find the other, its glittering seacoast.

ABOUT THE RESTAURANTS

Balkan cooking revolves around lamb, pork, sheep's-milk cheese, eggplant, and other vegetables. Typical Bulgarian dishes include wonderful *shopska salata* (tomato, cucumber, and sirene cheese salad), *sarmi* (vine leaves stuffed with meat and rice), and *kiufté* (grilled meatballs). Bulgaria invented *kiselo mlyako* (yogurt), and excellent *tarator* (cold yogurt soups) are served in summer. Syrupy baklava and *palachinki* (crepes stuffed with chocolate or nuts and honey) are the favored desserts.

The national drink is *rakia* (brandy), either *slivova* (made from plums) or *grosdova* (made from grapes). Many Bulgarians make their own—or know someone who does—and claim this is the best of drinks. Cold rakia is typically drunk with the salad course. Bulgarian wines are usually full-bodied, dry, and inexpensive. Reds from the Melnik, Roussé, Suhindol, and Sliven regions and whites from the Black Sea area are worth requesting. Coffee is strong and is often drunk along with a cold beverage, such as cola.

Visitors have a choice between the familiar Western-style, sometimes-uninspired hotel dining and the more adventurous outing to a local restaurant or café, where the menu may be offered only in Cyrillic. In larger cities, international cuisine is easy to find, but in smaller towns the best bets are the small restaurants called *mehana,* which serve national dishes and local specialties. Dinner out in a mehana is considered a recreational experience. Bulgarians share tables with strangers (feel free to do this yourself—it's perfectly acceptable) and linger for hours over the smallest of salads while drinking rakia, smoking, and listening to loud music. (Restaurant turnover is practically unheard of—don't bother waiting if all the tables are full.) Calmer atmospheres

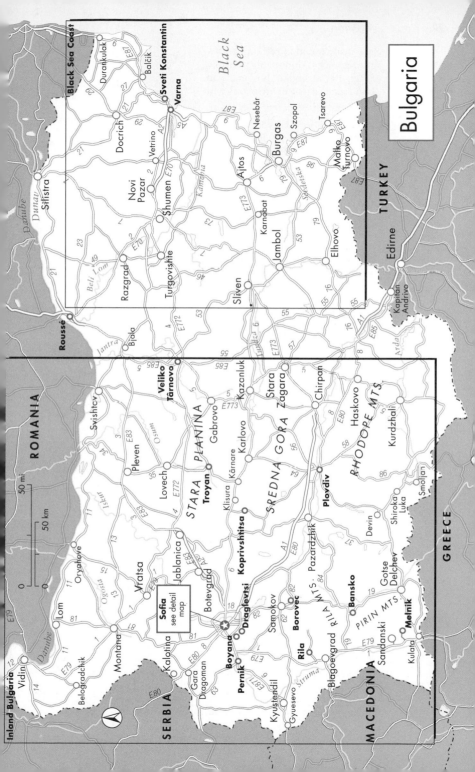

are easily found in restaurants featuring more Continental cuisine. If cigarette smoke bothers you, choose one of the many places with outdoor seating.

ABOUT THE HOTELS

The past few years have seen a building boom in the lodging industry. This is particularly true on the Black Sea and in ski resorts like Bansko, but nearly all major towns and cities have added comfortable new hotels. Be careful, though, about getting a room on the Black Sea coast during July or August, or at one of the ski resorts during ski season (December–March). During these periods, book in advance to be sure.

BULGARIA TOP 5
■ Relax on the beach at the Black Sea.
■ Ski or hike in the mountains around Bansko.
■ Tour Rila Monastery or one of the many other monasteries that dot the landscape.
■ Visit a museum town like Veliko Tãrnovo or Koprivshtitsa.
■ Sip a glass of homemade wine in Melnik.

Bulgaria hotels are graded on a scale of one to five stars, with the latter category usually reserved for the top international chains in Sofia and the Black Sea resorts. Four stars will usually mean a swimming pool (particularly on the Black Sea), as well as a fitness club or spa. In-room Internet access (Wi-Fi or Ethernet connection) and air-conditioning are pretty much standard equipment for all hotels of three stars and higher.

Hotel rates are often quoted in euros, but you can always pay your bill in leva, the Bulgarian currency. Credit cards are frequently—but not always—accepted.

WHAT IT COSTS IN LEVA AND EUROS (€)			
$$$$	**$$$**	**$$**	**$**
RESTAURANTS in leva	over 24	16–24	8–16	under 8
HOTELS in euros	over €150	€100–€150	€60–€100	under €60
HOTELS in leva	over 300	200–300	120–200	under 120

Restaurant prices in leva are per person for a main course at dinner. Hotel prices are for two people in a double room with a private bath and breakfast in high season.

TIMING

Summers are warm in Bulgaria, and winters are crisp and cold. If you're looking for sun, come in July or August. Although this is Bulgaria's "high season," the only places you'll find crowds are the Black Sea coast and Sofia. Even when the temperature climbs in summer, the Black Sea breezes and the cooler mountain air prevent the heat from being overpowering. Don't limit yourself to summer for a visit, though; the coastal areas get considerable sunshine year-round. The inland areas, however, are wet during most of March and April.

GREAT ITINERARIES

Bulgaria may be small, but its nature and landscapes are strikingly diverse. If you have more than a week to tour the country, you'll be able to see most of it (including time on the Black Sea). If you have less than a week, you'll still get to see some major sights and get an impression of the country and its people. If two or three days are all you have, you'll have to choose between the mountains and the sea.

IF YOU HAVE 3 DAYS

Begin in ◆◆Sofia and spend the day in the central part of the city—making sure to visit the magnificent Hram-pametnik Alexander Nevski (Alexander Nevski Memorial Cathedral) and some of the new art galleries. On the second day, head for ◆◆Plovdiv. Spend the morning walking around in its Old Town and have coffee on the terrace overlooking the magnificent Rimski Amfiteatur (Roman Amphitheater). On the third day, pass through the town of Karlovo to ◆◆Koprivshtitsa, where you can see some of the finest

examples of typical old Bulgarian architecture. Or, instead of heading toward Koprivshtitsa, you can go to ◆◆Borovec, the oldest and biggest mountain resort in Bulgaria, at the foot of Vrah Musala, the highest peak on the Balkan Peninsula.

IF YOU HAVE 5 DAYS

Spend a day in **Sofia**, and from there travel to ◆◆Rilski Manastir (Rila Monastery), founded in the 10th century. Spend the night here, either in the local hotel or in one of the sparse monks' rooms in the compound, and leave the next morning for ◆◆Bansko, a museum town and now hyper-modern ski resort, with charming National Revival houses. The third day, go hiking in the Pirin Mountains, and the next, visit the tiny village of **Melnik,** famous for its architecture, sandstone formations, lively taverns, and red-wine tasting in ancient caves. From Melnik, before going back to Sofia, you can visit the Rozhenski Manastir (Rozhen Monastery), most of it decorated by unknown painters.

SOFIA

Sofia is a young capital by European standards, dating only to the 1880s or so. Most of the city's historic buildings were built in the early years of the 20th century, though here and there you'll find older buildings dating back to the Ottoman presence. Sofia was bombed in Allied air raids during World War II, and many buildings were destroyed. During the post-war communist regime, parts of the city were built and rebuilt in a monolithic, undistinguished communist style. You won't notice this so much in the center, where the architecture melds in a pleasing eclectic mix. Only on the outskirts do the communist buildings really intrude.

The city's geographic position is enviable. Sofia sits on a plain just below the commanding Mt. Vitosha, a 7,600-foot peak that rises to the south of the city. If you're ever lost, simply look for the mountains to get your bearings.

IF YOU LIKE

ARCHITECTURE

Old Bulgarian architecture is best seen in the cobblestone streets, stone-vaulted bridges, and wooden houses of the country's towns and villages. Within the solid walls of houses in small mountain towns like Bansko are delicate rooms with carved ceilings and colorful hand-made rugs. Koprivshtitsa and the Old Town of Plovdiv are known for their excellent examples of National Revival architecture, a 19th-century style that helped reestablish Bulgarian artistic identity after the Turkish occupation. National Revival structures are colorfully painted, often with ornately carved wooden ceilings and second stories that extend out over the first, supported by wooden pillars.

CHURCHES, MONASTERIES & ICON PAINTINGS

Most Bulgarian churches and monasteries are from the National Revival period (18th and early 19th centuries), a time of vigorous cultural activity and increased awareness of a national identity. The famous Rila Monastery is included in the UNESCO list of World Heritage Sites. The Bachkovo and Troyan monasteries are both known for their splendid murals and icons, painted by Zahari Zograph and other great National Revival artists. Today, the biggest collections of icons are displayed in the Crypt Museum of Alexander Nevski Memorial Cathedral in Sofia and in the Museum of Art and History in Varna.

HIKING & WALKING

Mt. Vitosha and the mountains of the Rila, Pirin, and Rhodope ranges are good for walking. Nature lovers will appreciate Vitosha for its beautiful moraines, Rila and Pirin for their clear blue lakes, and the Rhodopes for their green slopes and rare plants. The Balkan Range, which crosses the entire country, has splendid rocks and caves. Two of the most interesting caves are Ledenika and Magura, with their veritable sculptures of stalactites and stalagmites. Ledenika is about 200 km (124 mi) northeast of Sofia; Magura is approximately 250 km (155 mi) north of the capital.

SPA RESORTS

Bulgaria has hundreds of mineral springs, whose healing properties were well known to the ancient Romans. The spa hotels in the resorts of Sandanski and Velingrad provide a variety of treatments, including manual therapy, acupuncture, herbal baths, phytotherapy, and slimming cures. (Sandanski is a half hour from the Greek border crossing at Kulata; Velingrad is southeast of Sofia in the Rhodopes.) The Black Sea hydrotherapy centers in Sveti Konstantin, Albena, and Pomorie are famous for their healing mud. The mineral springs along the northern

EXPLORING SOFIA

Sofia is compact and easily walkable. Its scale is comparable to Ljubljana or Bratislava—certainly not Warsaw or Bucharest. Your first view of the city coming in from the airport may not be a favorable one. The former communist government surrounded the city with unsightly—and now fully dilapidated—public housing projects. But once you clear this ring of concrete, central Sofia is surprisingly green.

You'll find parks and little cafés on seemingly every other street. The tiny residential streets that run off the main shopping boulevard, Vitosha, are covered by a canopy of trees in summer. Many streets stay cool and dark even on the hottest days.

The center of the city is laid out in a kind of grid, with the ploshtad Sveta Nedelya (St. Nedelya Square) serving as the heart of the city and the big boulevards, like Vitosha that runs south, as the axis points. Before venturing out, pick up a good map, since the streets can still be disorienting. Try to brush up a little on your Cyrillic alphabet (at least to the point where you can make out the letters). It will make navigation a lot easier.

Numbers in the text correspond to numbers in the margin and on the Sofia map.

WHAT TO SEE

★ **⑬ Banya Bashi Djamiya** *(Banya Bashi Mosque)*. A legacy of Turkish domination, this 16th-century mosque is one of the most noteworthy sights in Sofia, with its imposing dome and elegant minaret. Built in 1576 by the Turkish architect Sinan, the mosque was named for its proximity to mineral baths (*banya* means "baths"). The interior is closed to the non-Islamic public. ⊠*Bul. Maria-Luiza, across from Central Market Hall, Center.*

⑩ Borisova Gradina *(Boris's Garden)*. Though it's neglected to a certain extent, this is still a favorite spot for strolling. In summer, ice cream vendors, children riding around in battery-operated mini-cars or on skateboards, and a surprisingly pristine public pool bring the park to life. The massive statue is called the Mound of Brotherhood, and was built in the 1950s to symbolize Bulgarian-Soviet friendship. ⊠*Bul. Bulgaria between Bul. Tsar Osvoboditel and Bul. Dragan Tsankov, Center.*

⑧ **Hram-pametnik Alexander Nevski** *(Alexander Nevski Memorial Cathe-*
dral). You may recognize this neo-Byzantine structure with glittering interlocking domes from the pictures of it that appear on almost every piece of tourist literature. It was built by the Bulgarian people at the beginning of the 20th century as a sign of gratitude to their Russian liberators. Inside are alabaster and onyx, Italian marble and Venetian mosaics, magnificent frescoes, and space for a congregation of 5,000. There's a fine collection of icons and religious artifacts in the Crypt Museum, representing Byzantine influence, Ottoman rule, and the National Revival period. On Sunday morning you can attend a service and hear the superb choir. In the area near and around the church there are many women selling lace tablecloths. ⊠*Pl. Alexander Nevski, Center* ☎*02/987-76-97* ✉*Free to enter the church, crypt museum 4 leva* ☉*Church open daily 7–7, closed during services at 8* AM *and 5* PM*; crypt museum Tues.–Sun. 10–5:30.*

⑦ **Narodno Subranie** *(National Assembly)*. During the January 1997 uprising, CNN made this building famous by repeatedly broadcasting clips of protesters smashing and climbing through the windows and dragging members of the Socialist parliament out into the plaza in a demand

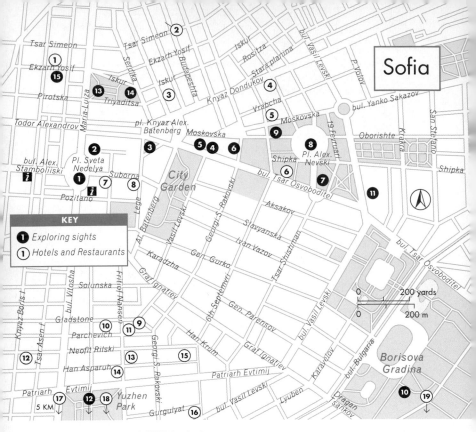

Sofia

for new elections. Topped by the Bulgarian national flag, the blocky building is adorned with an inscription reading UNITY MAKES STRENGTH, referring to the unification of the country in 1885, a few years after the defeat of the Turks. ⊠ *Bul. Tsar Osvoboditel at Pl. Narodno Subranie, Center.*

 Natzionalen Archeologicheski Musei *(National Archaeological Museum).*
Fodor's Choice   This museum is housed in the former Great Mosque. Recent renova-
★   tions make the 15th-century building as fascinating as its contents. There's an impressive set of Roman and Greek statuaries and columns on the ground floor, but be sure to head upstairs to see the amazing collection of Thracian jewels, weaponry, and burial masks unearthed in recent archaeological digs. The sophisticated designs support the assertion that the Thracians, who lived for centuries before the birth of Christ, constituted one of the earliest advanced civilizations in Europe. ⊠ *Ul. Suborna 2, behind the Sheraton hotel, Center* ☎ *02/988–24–06* ☜ *10 leva* ☉ *Tues.–Sun. 10–6.*

⑫ **Natzionalen Dvoretz na Kulturata** *(National Palace of Culture, or NDK).* This modern building, built in classic communist-era style from the late 1970s, contains the largest multipurpose conference center in southeastern Europe, designed and equipped to hold both conferences and cultural activities. Press conferences of newly elected presidents, international concerts, and trade exhibitions usually take place here. In the underpass you'll find a tourist information office, shops, restaurants, discos, and an Internet café. ⊠ *Pl. Bulgaria, 1, Center* ☎ *02/916–62–760.*

NEED A BREAK? Sofia has no shortage of inviting cafés and bars. The outdoor café behind the archaeological museum, with an enclosed dining area, is one of the best in the city. Great coffees and a full range of alcoholic and nonalcoholic drinks, plus more than decent pizzas and salads, make this a worthwhile visit. The **Art Club Museum** (⊠ *Ul. Suborna 2, behind the Sheraton hotel, Center*)is open daily from 9 AM.

 Natzionalen Etnografski Musei *(National Ethnographical Museum).* The collections of costumes, handicrafts, and tools exhibited in this former palace of the Bulgarian tsar illustrate rural life through the 19th century. ⊠ *Pl. Alexander Batenberg, 1, Center* ☎ *02/987–41–91* ⊕ *hs41. iccs.bas.bg* ☜ *3 leva* ☉ *Tues.–Sat. 10–6.*

⑤ **Natzionalna Hudozhestvena Galeria** *(National Art Gallery).* Here, in the west wing of the former royal palace, are paintings by the best Bulgarian artists of the 19th and early 20th centuries. ⊠ *Pl. Alexander Batenberg, 1, Center* ☎ *02/980–33–25* ☜ *3 leva* ☉ *Tues.–Sat. 10–6.*

 Rotonda Sveti Georgi *(Rotunda of St. George).* These ancient remains of what is billed as the oldest public building in Bulgaria are in the courtyard behind the Sheraton hotel. The rotunda, which was built in the 4th century as a Roman temple, was destroyed by the Huns, rebuilt by Justinian, and turned into a mosque by the Turks before being restored as a church. Restoration has revealed medieval frescoes. ⊠ *Pl. St. Nedelya, 2, Center* ☜ *Free* ☉ *Daily 8–5.*

★ ⑮ **Tsentralna Sofiiska Sinagoga** *(Central Sofia Synagogue)*. After decades of disrepair, the Moorish turrets and gilt domes of this 1909 synagogue have been beautifully restored. It is now one of the most spectacular buildings in downtown Sofia. The grandeur of the building reflects a time early in the 20th century when Jews made up nearly 20% of the city's population. ✉ *Ul. Ekzarh Yosif, 16, Center* ☎ *02/983–12–73* ⊕ *www.sofiasynagogue.com* 🔲 *Free* ⊙ *Weekdays 9–5, Sat. 9–1.*

⑭ **Tsentralnaya Banya** *(Central Baths)*. For years, this splendid building, once an Ottoman bathhouse, was left to disintegrate. Renovations began several years ago; at this writing the baths were not yet open to the public. Plans are to transform the space into an exhibition room for the Museum of Sofia. ✉ *Bul. Mariya Luiza, Center.*

★ ❶ **Tzarkva Sveta Nedelya** *(St. Nedelya Church)*. This impressive church was constructed from 1856 to 1863 and later altered by a Russian architect. In 1925, it was destroyed by left-wing radicals in an attempt to assassinate the Bulgarian royal family. It was rebuilt in 1931. Today it's open to visitors, and services are held each Sunday. You may even get a peek at a bride—this is one of the most popular wedding spots in the city. ✉ *Pl. Sveta Nedelya, Center* ☎ *02/987–57–48* 🔲 *Free* ⊙ *Daily 7–7.*

❾ **Tzarkva Sveta Sofia** *(Church of St. Sofia)*. One of the oldest churches in the city, it dates back to the 6th century, though excavations have uncovered the remains of even older structures on the site. Because of its great age and its simplicity, the church provides a dramatic contrast to the showy Alexander Nevski Memorial Cathedral nearby. While the church undergoes seemingly endless renovation, it's open to visitors, and services are held daily at 9:30 AM. ✉ *Ul. Parizh 2 Center* ☎ *02/987–09–71* 🔲 *Free* ⊙ *Daily 9–6.*

⑪ **Sofiiski Universitet Sv. Kliment Ochridski** *(Sofia University St. Kliment Ohridskik)*. This respected Bulgarian university was built in 1888, just after Ottoman liberation, with the financial aid of the brothers Georgievi, merchants and passionate supporters of Bulgarian culture and spirit. Stone, wood, marble, and stained glass make the university one of the most impressive architectural sites of the capital. ✉ *Bul. Tsar Osvoboditel, 15, Center* ☎ *02/9308 (within Sofia)* ⊕ *www.uni-sofia.bg.*

❻ **Tzarkva Sveti Nikolai** *(Church of St. Nicholas)*. This small and very ornate Russian church—it has five gold-plate domes and a green spire—was erected between 1912 and 1914. Inside, mosaics depict Russian saints and tsars. It's commonly called (surprise) the Russian Church. ✉ *Bul. Tsar Osvoboditel, 3, Center* ☎ *02/986–27–15* 🔲 *Free* ⊙ *Daily 8–6:30.*

WHERE TO EAT

Sofia is a great city for eating out, with a range of excellent dining options, from countless decent Bulgarian and Balkan-style restaurants to very good French, Italian, and even Indian food. By far the most authentic and enjoyable experience is to be had in a *mehana* (tavern), where the music is loud and diners can relax for hours over rakia and traditional meals such as grilled pork sausages and french fries smothered in sirene, a delicious variant of feta cheese.

Most restaurants open around 11 AM and operate until at least 11 PM—often later. Bulgarians tend to eat dinners late, so try not to show up at 8 PM or 9 PM without a reservation or you may not get a table. Note that some restaurants may not open on Sundays, or may serve only dinner. A note on dress: Bulgarians often dress smartly when going out in the evening to more expensive places. No need to overdo it, but in practice this means a nice shirt or sport coat for men and a dress for women. You may not get seated in jeans or short pants.

$$$–$$$$ ✕**Da Vidi.** This trendy eatery with a sleek, smart modern interior of dark woods and muted colors could pass for a Japanese restaurant. The cuisine could be described as fusion, with beef, chicken, and fish entrées prepared with a nod toward Asia. The exquisite grilled salmon is prepared glazed in sweet-and-sour sauce and served with polenta. The veal escalope also comes recommended. With just 10 tables, the service is friendly and attentive. There are an additional two tables outside, but they're more suited to cocktail drinking and people-watching. Da Vidi draws a mix of tourists and resident expats. ⊠*Ul. Han Asparuh, 36, Center* ☎*02/980–67–46* ▤*DC, MC, V.*

$$$–$$$$ ✕**Kushtata s Chasovnika.** The "House with the Clock" is an elegant space on a quiet street just down from the Alexander Nevski Memorial Cathedral. The refined dining room, in a lovely early-20th-century villa (yes, with a clock), is the perfect spot for a romantic meal for two or for impressing a business partner. The menu features standard international beef, pork, and chicken entrées. It's popular with local businessmen, embassy staff, and well-off Bulgarians. ⊠*Ul. Moskovska, 15, Center* ☎*02/987–56–56* ⚐*Reservations essential* ▤*DC, MC, V.*

★ $$$ ✕**Nad Aleyata, Zad Shkafa.** The name means "Beyond the Alley, Behind the Cupboard," something that sounds quirky and inviting even in Bulgarian. You will have to search out this small villa restaurant on a quiet, tree-lined street just northwest of the city center, but it's worth the effort. The menu features mostly traditional meals with a slight Middle Eastern influence, including excellent roast lamb and Turkish meatballs, served in a tomato sauce with mashed potatoes. The staff is English-speaking and accustomed to serving foreigners. There's a quiet patio for warm-weather dining. You'll also find what many consider to be the nicest toilets in town. ⊠*Ul. Budapeshta, 31, Center* ☎*02/983–55–45* ⚐*Reservations essential* ▤*DC, MC, V.*

$$ ✕**Annette.** If you've been traveling through Eastern Europe for a while, you might just have a taste for something completely different. Annette serves near-authentic tagines and couscous dishes in a refined, upscale, all-white space at prices that students could afford. Tagines are slow-cooked stews; the gold standard is chicken cooked in a lemon and black olive sauce. ⊠*Ul. Angel Kanchev, 27, Center* ☎*02/980–40–98* ▤*MC, V.*

$$ ✕**Divaka.** A good spot for a quick lunch or dinner on the go, this restaurant serves excellent Bulgarian food in a casual setting. Although popular with students because of its low prices, customers include

people from all walks of life. The terrace is the place to be in summer. In the colder months, there are indoor tables on several levels in a comfortable, modern setting. At peak meal times, staff can get a bit frazzled from the constant rush of new diners. ⊠ *Ul. Gladston, 54, Center* ☏ *02/989–95–43* ⊟ *No credit cards.*

$$ ✕ **Pod Lipite.** An intimate tavern-style restaurant done up in traditional
Fodor's Choice themes, this is an absolute must during your stay. Take a taxi to get
★   here, since the walk (about 15 minutes from the center in the direction of Boris Gardens) can be confusing. Everything is homemade, from the breads to the grilled flat sausages and meats. In summer, sit on the back terrace under the apple trees (the name means "Under the Linden Trees"—but no matter). The food, especially the salads and grilled meats, is excellent and a great value. The staff is friendly. Reservations are a must. ⊠ *Ul. Elin Pelin, 1, Center* ☏ *02/866–50–53* ⊟ *MC, V.*

$$ ✕ **Taj Mahal.** This is easily one of the best Indian restaurants in Eastern Europe. The curry dishes are perfectly spiced. Several types of rice are on offer, and the naan has a nice balance of being crispy and yet still a little doughy. The Lamb Rogan Josh is one of the high points, a moderately spicy lamb curry with plenty of pieces of tender meat. Popular during the evenings, it's nearly empty at lunch, when you'll feel you have the entire three-story place to yourself. The atmosphere is casual and the restaurant is deservedly popular with resident expats. ⊠ *Ul. 11-ti Avgust, 11, Center* ☏ *02/987–36–32* ⊟ *MC, V.*

$$ ✕ **Victoria.** Arguably the best pizza place in town, Victoria serves authentic pies cooked in a wood-fired oven. The location, just down from the Nevski Cathedral, makes it a perfect lunch spot during a hectic day of sightseeing. Pies come in "small" and "large"—with the smalls being big enough for two to share. Pizzas come topped with Bulgarian-style yellow cheese, but you can order Italian mozzarella for a couple of leva more (this is a good idea). Victoria is popular for lunch during weekdays and for dinner most nights, so try to time your arrival for off-hours or reserve in advance. ⊠ *Bul. Tsar Osvoboditel, 7, Center* ☏ *02/986–32–00* ⊟ *MC, V.*

WHERE TO STAY

Sofia has a nice range of lodging options at all price points. Many of the big international chains are represented here, and standards are the same as or higher than you would find anywhere. The past couple of years have seen newer, lower-priced properties come onto the market. Sofia is one of the few European capitals left where you can still find good, clean doubles, close to the center, for around €50–€60 a night. Rack rates are listed below, but many of the hotels can be booked much more cheaply in advance through the hotel's Web site or through an online travel service. Many hotels also offer special weekend and summer rates.

$$$$ ⊡ **Downtown Hotel.** A locally operated alternative to the big chains, this hotel has many of the latter's upscale amenities at a slightly lower price. The location is excellent, along a major boulevard just at the edge of the central core, meaning it's relatively easy to reach by car and has

ample on-site parking. Request a room away from the road, though reinforced modern windows should shield against much of the street noise. The lobby and public areas are clean and cheerful, but impersonal in keeping with the chainlike ambience. The rooms themselves are special and elegant, with cream-colored walls and blue carpets. Pros: within easy walking distance of the sights, more personalized service than the chains, handsome rooms. Cons: expensive for what you get, some street noise, small lobby. ☒*Bul. Vassil Levski, 27, Center, 1040* ☏*02/930–52–00* 🖷*02/930–53–00* ⊕*www.hotel-downtown.net* ⤵*62 rooms* ♿*In-room: safe, refrigerator, Ethernet. In-hotel: restaurant, bar, gym, spa, laundry service, public Wi-Fi, parking (no fee), no-smoking rooms* ▤*AE, DC, MC, V.*

$$$$ 🏨 **Hilton Sofia.** A better choice for business travelers than for tourists because of the hefty price tag and the hotel's location—slightly outside the center (15–20 minutes by foot), but close to exhibition venues like the National Palace of Culture—the hotel, which opened in 2000, still looks relatively new. As with any Hilton, the lobby is immaculate and the service standards are high. The rooms are enormous, and feature unique amenities like ergonomic chairs. The hotel sometimes offers discounted weekend packages. Pros: good business location, large rooms, parking. Cons: slightly outside of the center, impersonal, undistinguished-looking building. ☒*Bul. Bulgaria, 1, Ivan Vazov, 1421* ☏*02/933–50–00* 🖷*02/933–51–11* ⊕*www.sofia.hilton. com* ⤵*245 rooms* ♿*In-room: safe, refrigerator, Ethernet. In-hotel: restaurant, room service, bar, pool, gym, spa, laundry service, concierge, executive floor, public Wi-Fi, airport shuttle, parking (no fee), some pets allowed, no-smoking rooms* ▤*AE, DC, MC, V.*

★ **$$$$** 🏨 **Sheraton Sofia Hotel Balkan.** If you're going to splurge on a five-star international chain, make it this one. It's special in many ways. First, the hotel occupies a palatial, Socialist-Realist style building dating from the 1950s, with marble lobbies, beautifully polished staircases, and big, elegant rooms. Then there's the location—just in the center of town, so close to the main tourist sights that it itself is considered a sight. There are two types of rooms: "classic" rooms come with modern furniture; "executive" rooms are done up more in period style. Ask to see a few of both before choosing. The hotel is part of Sheraton's "luxury collection" of upmarket locations. Pros: "the" place in town to stay, stylish "executive" rooms, unique architecture. Cons: no pool, expensive, impersonal feel. ☒*Pl. St. Nedelya, 5, Center, 1000* ☏*02/981–65–41* 🖷*02/980–64–64* ⊕*www.luxurycollection.com/sofia* ⤵*188 rooms* ♿*In-room: safe, refrigerator, Ethernet. In-hotel: restaurant, room service, bar, pool, gym, spa, laundry service, concierge, executive floor, public Wi-Fi, airport shuttle, parking (no fee), some pets allowed, no-smoking rooms* ▤*AE, DC, MC, V.*

$$$ 🏨 **Art'otel.** Slick, high-concept boutique hotel that's a nice midway point between a smaller, more intimate hotel and a five-star chain. The rooms are beautifully designed in bold colors and fresh flowers. Room 403 has a drop-dead gorgeous view of the Sofia skyline. The public areas are muted brushed metal and dark woods, with comfy leather armchairs. Pros: dramatic rooms, friendly staff, beautiful lobby and public areas. Cons: expensive, few facilities, cramped hallways. ⊠ *Ul. Gladston, 44, Center* ☎*02/980–60–00* 🖨*02/981–19–09* ⊕*www. artotel.biz* ⬐*22 rooms* ⟐*In-room: safe, refrigerator, Wi-Fi. In-hotel: restaurant, room service, laundry service, parking (fee), no-smoking rooms* ⊟*AE, DC, MC, V.*

$$ ⊡**Arte.** This smart, boutique-style hotel occupies a slender modern building in the heart of the city. There are not many facilities here and the lobby and public areas are tiny, but the rooms are furnished in a tasteful modern style, with free Wi-Fi throughout the hotel. More central than the similarly priced Diter, but perhaps not as quiet. Within easy walking distance of the best restaurants, clubs, and sights. Pros: central location, clean rooms, attractive design. Cons: few facilities, no parking, unhelpful Web site. ⊠ *Bul. Kniaz Dondukov, 5, Center, 1000* ☎*02/402–71–00* 🖨*02/402–71–09* ⊕*www.artehotelbg.com* ⬐*25 rooms* ⟐*In-room: safe, refrigerator, Wi-Fi. In-hotel: restaurant, gym, spa, laundry service, public Wi-Fi, no parking, no-smoking rooms* ⊟*AE, DC, MC, V* ⥄*BP.*

★ $$ ⊡**Diter.** A solid business or leisure choice, the Diter offers excellent value and upscale rooms at rates a fraction of the major international chains. The lobby and public areas are spare but clean. The rooms are in a tasteful, modern style, with high-end amenities like hair dryers, bathtubs, and Internet. If you're just looking for a good room, and can do without pool and fitness club, this is an excellent choice. The location is within easy walking distance of the center and major tourist sights. You'll easily recognize the Diter by its bright blue exterior, like a hotel at a Greek island resort. Pros: well-managed hotel, helpful reception, good restaurant next door. Cons: limited parking, tends to book up fast, on the sterile side. ⊠ *Ul. Han Asparuh, 68, Center, 1000* ☎*02/989–89–98* 🖨*02/989–89–98* ⊕*www.diterhotel.com* ⬐*21 rooms* ⟐*In-room: safe, refrigerator, Wi-Fi. In-hotel: restaurant, bar, laundry service, limited parking, no-smoking rooms* ⊟*AE, DC, MC, V.*

$$ ⊡**Scotty's Boutique Hotel.** This funky, boutique hotel is situated north of the city center, just across the street from the central synagogue. The rooms are nicely done up in hardwood floors and cool colors. Each room is named after a city. The "San Francisco" is a well-proportioned double deluxe with nice street views. The baths are tiny, and the showers are nothing more than showerheads above the sink. Still, that's part of the charm. It attracts students and young professionals. Pros: great central location, attractive rooms, hip feel. Cons: some rooms opposite the reception desk lack privacy, tiny baths, few facilities. ⊠ *Ekzarh Yosif, 11, Center, 1000* ☎*02/983–67–77* 🖨*02/983–32–29* ⊕*www. geocities.com/scottysboutiquehotel* ⬐*16 rooms* ⟐*In-room: refrigerator, Wi-Fi. In-hotel: no elevator, laundry service, no-smoking rooms* ⊟*AE, DC, MC, V.*

$ ⊡**Brod.** A decent budget option, Brod is situated about 5 km (3 mi) south of the town center. The rooms are bare bones, but are clean and well proportioned, each with a large bed, table, desk, and wardrobe. It is an excellent value since each of the rooms comes with air-conditioning and free Wi-Fi. The location is convenient to the airport, but not within walking distance of town—nor is there much public transportation around. You'll end up cabbing in and out; taxis to the center run about €2 a ride. Pros: great value, clean, large rooms, friendly staff. Cons: no public transportation, some street noise (ask for a room away from the road), hard mattresses. ⊠*Simeonovsko, 66, Center, 1000* ☎*02/968–19–80* 🖷*02/968–19–84* ⊕*www.hotelbrod.com* ⇖*44 rooms* ♿*In-room: refrigerator, Wi-Fi. In-hotel: restaurant, bar, laundry service, parking (no fee), no-smoking rooms* ▤*MC, V.*

★ $ 🖾**Niky.** Every city should have a Niky. This family-run, budget hotel has a bunch of pluses, including basic but clean rooms and a nice central location, in a leafy neighborhood that's a couple of blocks from Bul. Vitosha. It's similarly priced to the Brod, but with a better location. Most hotels at this price point would have worn carpets or a generally depressing look—not so here. The lobby, public areas, stairways, and tiled hallways are cheerful and very clean. The rate listed is for a double room, but a few more euros bags you a small apartment with a kitchen. The garden restaurant out back, specializing in traditional Bulgarian cooking, is highly popular and worth a visit in its own right. Pros: clean, close to the center, cheap. Cons: no parking, small rooms, tiny bathrooms. ⊠*Ul. Neofit Rilski, 16, Center, 1000* ☎*02/952–30–58* 🖷*02/951–60–91* ⊕*www.hotel-niky.com* ⇖*22 rooms* ♿*In-room: refrigerator, Ethernet. In-hotel: restaurant, bar, laundry service, no-smoking rooms* ▤*MC, V.*

$ 🖾**Sofia Gardens.** The Sofia Gardens bills itself as a "bed-and-breakfast," but don't come here looking for scones at breakfast and daft old ladies. It's more of a Berlin-style squat, filled with hipsters and thrift-store furniture. That said, it's pretty cool for what it is and the rooms are a great value, given their central location. The three rooms share a common bath and shower. Ask for the top room, with great views and direct access to the bath. The reception desk couldn't be friendlier, and there's a nice garden out back. The hotel shares space and staff with the Art Hostel Sofia. Pros: very central, hip, cheap. Cons: no facilities, basic accommodation, shared baths. ⊠*Ul. Angel Kanchev, 21A, Center* ☎*02/987–05–45* ⊕*www.art-hostel.com* ⇖*3 rooms* ♿*In-room: no a/c, no TV. In-hotel: no elevator* ▤*MC, V.*

NIGHTLIFE & THE ARTS

NIGHTLIFE

Sofia is a good town to go out in at night, whether you're searching for something highbrow like a classical music concert, or just looking for a place to dance or throw back a few beers. The scene changes rapidly, so before venturing out, take a look at one of the following local guides (usually stacked up in piles on hotel reception desks): *Sofia City Guide, Sofia In Your Pocket,* or *The Insider's Guide.* Things don't get going at clubs or live music venues until about 11 PM, though drinking spots usually start filling up from early evening on.

BARS & NIGHTCLUBS

J.J. Murphy's (⊠*Ul. Karnigradska, 6* ☎*02/980–28–70)* is a genuine Irish pub popular with Bulgarians and the expat community alike. **Toba**

& Co (✉ *Ul. Moskovska, 6a* ☎ *02/989–46–96*) is a quieter, more civilized spot for drinks, with a nice terrace in summer, and usually a DJ on board for later in the evening. For live music, **Swingin' Hall** (✉ *Bul. Dragan Tsankov, 8* ☎ *02/963–06–96*) was one of the first "Western" clubs to open after the fall of communism and remains one of the best venues to catch live rock and blues.

DISCOS

One of the city's chicest and most expensive discos, **Chervilo** (✉ *Bul. Tsar Osvoboditel, 5, off ploshtad Narodno Subranie* ☎ *02/981–66–33*), or "Lipstick," draws Sofia's well-to-do twenty- and thirtysomethings. When taking a cab, just tell the driver the disco's name. **My Mojito** (✉ *Ul. Ivan Vazov, 12* ☎ *0889/529–001*) is a small club with different DJs every night. **Yalta** (✉ *Bul. Tsar Osvoboditel, 20* ☎ *02/987–34–81*) is another institution of the city's late-night scene. It's a good spot to catch visiting DJs from abroad. **Life House** (✉ *Bul. Vitosha, 12* ☎ *0888/241–016*) has an easy-to-find central location and is a good spot for house music. It's open nightly Thursday to Sunday.

THE ARTS

MUSIC & DANCE

Sofia maintains a rich calendar of music, opera, and dance, with performances throughout the year. To see what's on, pick up a copy of the *Sofia Echo,* available at many city-center newsstands or hotel reception desks, or the *Sofia City Guide.*

Bulgaria Hall (✉ *Ul. Aksakov, 1* ☎ *02/987–76–56*) is home to the excellent Sofia Philharmonic Orchestra. The box office is open daily 10–1:30 and 3:30–6:30. **Sofiska Durjhavna Opera** (*Sofia National Opera and Ballet* ✉ *Ul. Vrabcha, 1* ☎ *02/987–1366 [to phone for tickets]* ⊕ *www. operasofia.com [Bulgarian only]*) is the center for opera and dance, with a mix of international classics sung in Italian or Bulgarian. Tickets run from 5 leva to 30 leva.

FILM

Sofia has a good selection of multiplexes and movie houses that feature more obscure and offbeat films. Movies are usually shown in the original language with Bulgarian subtitles.

Cineplex (✉ *Bul. Arsenalski, 2* ☎ *02/964–30–07*) is a multiplex on the top floor of the City Center Sofia shopping center. **Euro Cinema** (✉ *Bul. Alexander Stamboliiski, 17* ☎ *02/980–41–61*) is more for film buffs. **House of Cinema (Dom na kinoto)** (✉ *Ul. Ekzarh Yosif, 37* ☎ *02/980–39–11*) usually shows interesting films outside of the mainstream. **Odeon** (✉ *Bul. Patriarh Evtimii, 1* ☎ *02/989–24–69*) is the place to see old movies.

SHOPPING

GIFT & SOUVENIR SHOPS

The shop at the **National Ethnographic Museum** (⊠ *Pl. Alexander Batenberg, 1, Center*) sells genuine crafts, including a selection of carpets, as well as cheap imitations. Prices may not be competitive, but it is one-stop shopping. For recordings of Bulgarian music, go to the basement labyrinth market underneath the **National Palace of Culture** (⊠ *Pl. Bulgaria, 1, Center*).

MARKETS

The quintessential shopping excursion in Sofia is to its outdoor produce and crafts markets. A little less touristy and slightly less pricey are the stalls in the underpass that runs beneath bulevard Vitosha, just north of ploshtad Sveta Nedelya at ulitsa Trapezitsa, between the Sheraton and Central Department Store. Here the shopkeepers sell handmade lace, knitted sweaters and caps, and a variety of both new and old jewelry. One of the most popular crafts and souvenir-stall markets is **Nevski Pazaar,** just west of the Nevski Cathedral, where you can find everything from antique Greek coins to original icon paintings and old Soviet whiskey flasks. The most exotic and entertaining of Sofia's markets is the **Zhenski Pazaar** (*Women's Market* ⊠ *Ul. Stefan Stambolov, between Ul. Tsar Simeon and Bul. Slivnitsa*), named for the swarms of women from neighboring villages who commute daily to hawk everything from homemade brooms and lace to produce and used electronic equipment. With all the sights and sounds of bartering—sometimes a little overwhelming—the Zhenski Pazaar can give you a feel of the Middle East.

SHOPPING MALLS

Tsentralni Hali (*Central Market Halls* ⊠ *Bul. Maria-Luiza*) specializes in food, with more than 100 different pavilion shops offering all kinds of fresh food. These shops are on three levels, with an indoor bar, a little area for children, and a change bureau. Stalls are open daily 7 AM–midnight.

What used to be Sofia's monolithic state-run department store, **Tsentralen Universalen Magazin** (*Central Department Store* ⊠ *Bul. Maria-Luiza, 2*), reopened in April 2000 as a mixed retail and office space—the closest thing central Sofia has to a Western-style shopping mall.

SOFIA ESSENTIALS

AIR TRAVEL

Sofia is the main international gateway for flights to Bulgaria. Currently, there are no direct flights between Bulgaria and North America, but the country's flagship carrier Bulgaria Air, as well as several major European carriers, offers regular service from major European hubs.

AIRPORTS & TRANSFERS

Most international flights to Bulgaria arrive at Sofia International Airport, which is 10 km (6 mi) from the city center. The airport has two terminals, 1 and 2, with most regularly scheduled passenger service now using the new terminal, 2. Check your ticket carefully to see which terminal your flight is using. Both terminals have small restaurants, as well as ATMs and taxi service into town.

Airports Sofia International Airport (Letishte Sofia) (☎ 02/937–22–11 ⊕ www. sofia-airport.bg).

AIRPORT TRANSFERS

Taxis are the easiest way into the center. The 15- to 20-minute ride should cost about 12 leva. As for public transportation, from terminal 1, take Bus 84 into the center. From terminal 2, take Bus 284.

BUS TRAVEL

Sofia's Central Bus Station (Tsentralna Avtogara) is the main point of arrival and departure for intercity bus service within Bulgaria. The station is clean and relatively new, dating from 2004. The only problem you might have is that with dozens of private companies offering services, it's not always clear where to buy a ticket. There's a main ticketing window that handles most sales, as well as an information booth. Etap is one of several large companies that operate nationwide service. It has a helpful Web site with departure times and fares.

Information Etap Adress (✉ Bul. Evlogi Georgiev, 161, Sofia ☎ 02/945–39–39 ⊕ www.etapgroup.com). **Tsentralna Avtogara Sofia (Sofia Central Bus Station)** (✉ Bul. Maria Luiza 100, Sofia ☎ 0900/210–00 ⊕ www.centralbusstation-sofia. com).

BUS AND TRAM TRAVEL WITHIN SOFIA

Buses, trolleys, and trams run quite frequently—between every 5 and 20 minutes. Buy a ticket (a single fare is 70 stotinki) from kiosks and newspaper stands near the tram or trolley car stop and punch it into the machine as you board. Persons traveling with baggage or large backpacks are required by law to have both a ticket for themselves *and* a ticket for their baggage. If you or your bag is caught without a ticket, an on-the-spot fine of 7 leva will be issued. Trams and trolleys tend to get crowded, so keep an eye on your belongings and be alert at all times.

CAR RENTALS

You'll find a bank of rental car agencies on arrival at Sofia Airport. Most of the major international companies are represented, including Avis and Hertz. On-the-spot rental fees are high, and you'll save a lot of money booking a car in advance over the Internet. All rentals at Sofia airport carry a onetime €20 service fee. For more information, see Car Rentals *in* Bulgaria Essentials, *below.*

CAR TRAVEL

If you're staying in or near the city center, there's no need for a car. Driving in Sofia is not enjoyable—traffic is heavy and potholes abound. Parking is also difficult in the city center.

INTERNET

You'll find Internet cafés sprinkled here and there throughout central Sofia. Rates typically run about 2 leva an hour. Site, in the center of town, is open 24 hours.

Internet Cafés **Site** (✉ *Bul. Vitosha, 45, Center* ☎ *02/986–08–96*).

TAXIS

Taxi rip-offs are no longer as common as they used to be, but you may still occasionally run into a dishonest driver. Your best defense is to first look at the rate posted on the passenger side of the windshield. This should be an amount somewhere between 0.45 lev and 0.60 lev per kilometer. If the rate is higher, don't get into the cab. Choose taxis run by the OK Supertrans company or Radio CB Taxi. These companies are reliable and employ honest drivers. To tip, round up the fare to the nearest full lev (i.e., if the fare is 6.5 leva, give the driver 7 leva). Drivers have surprisingly poor knowledge of the city. If you're staying at an out-of-town hotel like the Brod, for example, be sure to have the address handy to show it to the driver if necessary. Otherwise, they may not know where the hotel is.

Taxi Companies **OK Supertrans** (☎ *973–21–21*). **Radio CB Taxi** (☎ *91–263*).

TOUR OPTIONS

Balkantourist organizes all kinds of tours, from guided Sofia orientation tours to various evening tours, such as a night out to eat local food or to watch folk dances. Zig Zag is more adventure-oriented, but offers day trips and walking trips of Sofia.

Information **Balkantourist** (✉ *Ul. Enos, 2, Sofia* ☎ *02/981–98–06* ⊕ *www. balkantourist.bg*). **Zig Zag** (✉ *Bul. Alexander Stamboliiski, 20-V, Center, Sofia* ☎ *02/980–51–02* ⊕ *www.zigzagbg.com*).

TRAIN TRAVEL

All trains coming to the city arrive at Tsentralna Gara (Central Station), a depressing station at the northern edge of the central city. Apart from the station, tickets are sold downtown in the underpass of the Natzionalen Dvoretz na Kulturata (National Palace of Culture). Rila International Travel Agency sells train tickets.

Information **Natzionalen Dvoretz na Kulturata** (*National Palace of Culture* ✉ *Pl. Bulgaria, 1, Center* ☎ *02/932–42–80*). **Rila International Travel Agency** (✉ *Ul. Gen. Gurko, 5, Center* ☎ *02/987–07–77*). **Tsentralna Gara** (*Central Station* ✉ *Bul. Maria-Luiza, 112* ☎ *02/931–11–11 or 02/932–33–33* ⊕ *www.bdz.bg* [*timetable information*]).

VISITOR INFORMATION

The Bulgaria National Tourist Information Center is an excellent source of information on Sofia. It also has a good Web site to consult before you leave home. It's located in the center of the city near the Sheraton Hotel.

Three English-language publications are worth special mention: The *Sofia Echo* is a highly regarded weekly newspaper available throughout the country and has an excellent Web site. The *Sofia City Guide* is a nice overview on everything from hotels and shops to exchange rates and driving law requirements.

Information **Bulgaria National Tourist Information Center** (✉ *ul. Sveta Nedelya, 1, Center, Sofia* ☎ *02/987-97-78* ⊕ *www.bulgariatravel.org*). *Sofia City Guide* (⊕ *www.sofiacityguide.com*). *Sofia Echo* (⊕ *www.sofiaecho.com*).

SIDE TRIPS FROM SOFIA

BOYANA

10 km (6 mi) south of the city center. Hire a taxi or take Bus 64 or 107. The trip takes less than an hour.

At the foot of Mt. Vitosha, this settlement was a medieval fortress in the 10th and 11th centuries. Today it is one of Sofia's wealthiest residential neighborhoods.

The tiny, medieval **Tzarkvata Boyana** *(Boyana Church)* is one of Bulgaria's most precious monuments. Part of the church dates to the 10th century; it is a historical treasure on UNESCO's World Heritage list. The highlights here are the medieval frescoes, the work of masters from the 13th century. This is usually a tour destination, but if you're coming by car, follow ul. Alexander Pushkin uphill until you can turn uphill again onto ul. Sveti Kaloian, which branches out to ul. Brezovitsa. This will take you to ul. Boyansko Ezero, where you'll have to hike up to the church from the trailhead. ✉ *Boyansko Ezero* ☎ *02/959-09-39* ⊕ *www.boyanachurch.org* 🎟 *10 leva, 12 leva includes National History Museum* ◷ *Daily 9–5.*

Natzionalen Istoricheski Musei *(The National History Museum).* This is considered one of Bulgaria's most important museums and occupies the former residence of the country's communist leaders. The oldest holdings go back several thousand years BC. The highlights include priceless Thracian treasures, Roman mosaics, enamel jewelry from the First Bulgarian Kingdom, and glowing religious art that survived the years of Ottoman oppression. ✉ *Residence Boyana, Palace No. 1* ☎ *02/955-76-04 (to book tours)* ⊕ *www.historymuseum.org* 🎟 *10 leva, 12 leva combined admission with the Boyana Church, guided tour 20 leva* ◷ *Daily 9:30–5:30.*

OFF THE BEATEN PATH

Pernik. Less than half an hour by car southwest of Sofia is this coal-mining town, and though it has (difficult-to-find) hilltop ruins of a medieval fortress and a mining museum, the principal attraction is the *kukeri,* or mummers, festival in early February. The kukeri rites are intended to ward off evil spirits and promote fertility. Groups of men, analogous to Mardi Gras krewes, don elaborate masks and parade through the streets, making as much noise as possible. Many Bulgarian villages have kukeri events of one form or another, but Pernik has an international reputation. Sofia-based tour companies can provide information about kukeri events throughout the country.

DRAGALEVCI

Take a taxi or Tram 19 from ul. Graf Ignatievto in central Sofia to the last stop, and switch to Bus 64.

Picturesquely sprawled across the lower part of Mt. Vitosha, this was a slow-paced village just a few years ago. Today, it has been built up with modern homes and absorbed by the city, making it more or less a quiet suburb of Sofia.

In the woods above Dragalevci is the nearby **Dragalevski Manastir** *(Dragalevci Monastery)*. It's currently a convent, but you can visit the 14th-century church with its outdoor frescoes. Hike to the church from the Dragalevci bus stop (about 1½ km [1 mi]), or take Bus 64 or 93 from the Hladilnika bus station. ⌧*Dragalevci* ⊗*Thurs.–Sun. 10–6.*

A **chairlift** ride or two will give you stunning views of the area. The lift on ulitsa Panorama in Dragalevci takes you up to the Aleko resort. From the terminus, walk over to the next chairlift to head farther up to the top of Malak Rezen. There are well-marked walking and ski trails in the area. ⌧*Ul. Panorama* ☷*6 leva* ⊗*Daily 8–5.*

WHERE TO EAT

$$ ✗**Chichovtsi.** This unassuming pizza place at the top of the main square in Dragalevci has a cozy fireplace in winter and patio seating in summer. It's almost always busy with hordes of weekend Mt. Vitosha pilgrims. Try a "golyam" Zagorka (a big, frosty beer) and any of the tasty pizzas—but be aware that they may not conform to your expectations: pickles are a topping option, and mayonnaise and ketchup come on the side. ⌧*Pl. Tsar Ivan Alexander, 5* ☎*02/967–39–67* ⊟*No credit cards.*

$$ ✗**Vodenitsata.** Appropriately enough, the Miller's Tavern is made up of three old mills linked together. A folklore show and a menu of Bulgarian specialties give the tavern a tourist-friendly but authentic atmosphere. Try the *gyuveché* (potatoes, tomatoes, peas, and onions baked in an earthenware pot). ⌧*Ul. Panorama, at the southern end of town next to the chairlift* ☎*02/967–10–58* ⊟*MC, V.*

THE BLACK SEA COAST

Ask any Bulgarian what their favorite part of the country is and they will inevitably answer "the Black Sea." Indeed, Bulgaria has been blessed with miles and miles of wide, sandy beaches, a warm, calm sea, and a summer swimming season that lasts from May until well into September. The main destinations are clustered around Varna in the north and Burgas in the south. The resorts run the gamut from full-on, party-'til-you-drop spots like Golden Sands and Sunny Beach to smaller, historic towns like Nesebâr and Sozopol. Where you go depends on what you're looking for.

But be forewarned. The Black Sea's charms are well known, both in Bulgaria and abroad, and the hot summer days of July and August lure thousands and thousands of tourists from around Europe. Resorts

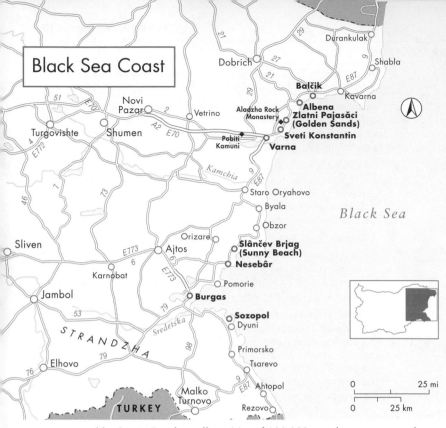

like Sunny Beach swell to cities of 100,000 people or more—and restaurants proudly tout offerings like "Authentic English Breakfasts" to draw in the crowds. The Black Sea may very well be the only place in the country where you'll get mediocre food. Even smaller resorts like Sozopol, in season, are wall-to-wall beach blankets. Consider traveling off-season if you want to avoid the crowds. If you're traveling during high season, you're best advised to book well in advance and look into a package deal, which will usually include accommodations, a major meal, and possibly travel. You'll get a much better price, and the big four- and five-star resorts are ill-prepared to handle walk-ins anyway.

If you're just passing through for a couple of days and want to get in a good day of swimming, consider the port city of Varna. Although it's a big city, it's got a pretty beachfront that's easy to get to and stretches for miles. There is ample lodging; you should always be able to find a place to stay. Other options around Varna include Sveti Konstantin and Albena—both of which are relatively quiet, have pretty beaches, and are easy to navigate. In the south, try Sozopol and the little towns farther to the south. For short-term stays, avoid mega-resorts like Sunny Beach and Golden Sands, which have major access restrictions if you don't have hotel reservations and are simply too big and busy to really enjoy.

VARNA

470 km (282 mi) east of Sofia.

Varna, Bulgaria's third-largest city and most important harbor on the Black Sea, combines the best elements of a cosmopolitan port city and a relaxed beach town. Much of the center of the city has been closed to cars, leaving a pedestrian paradise of lively cafés, bars, shops, and restaurants. The city's beaches stretch out nearly 4 km (about 3 mi), defining a long, sweeping arc of Varna Bay. The beach and the coastline form part of a unique urban park known as the Morska Gradina (Seaside Gardens), and you can stroll the coastline for miles heading north in the direction of Sveti Konstantin. The beach is just a short walk from the center, across a wide, pedestrian-only bridge and then down through a lovely park.

Varna is one of the oldest settlements in Europe, with a history that goes back at least several thousand years. Excavations of ancient burial grounds here show evidence of advanced human settlement dating from around 4,000 BC. It's not entirely clear why this civilization suddenly disappeared, but the Varna archaeological museum has an extensive collection of the gold artifacts they left behind. Much later (around 500 BC), the Greeks established a trading colony here and called it Odyssos. Later, the town was occupied by the Romans. The remains of the Roman baths, near the center of the modern city, are the most extensive Roman ruins in Bulgaria.

Varna was an important city during the crusades of the Middle Ages. It finally fell under the domination of the Ottoman Turks around the 15th century and became an important Turkish defense post. The city was liberated from the Turks in the 19th century, and became one of the leading cities of the new Bulgarian state. Today, Varna is an attractive port city with a large student population, and one of the country's most popular tourist destinations.

★ The **Natzionalen Arheologicheski Musei** *(National Archaeological Museum)* is one of the great, if lesser-known, museums of Europe. The splendid collection includes the world's oldest gold treasures, from the Varna burial grounds of the 4th millennium BC, discovered in 1972, as well as Thracian, Greek, and Roman treasures and richly painted icons. ⊠ *Bul. Maria-Luisa, 41* ☏ *052/68–10–11* 🎫 *8 leva* ⊗ *Tues.–Sat. 10–5.*

The imposing **Tsentralnata Tzarkva** *(Cathedral of the Assumption)* was built during the period 1880–86. Take a look inside at the lavish murals. ⊠ *Bul. Maria-Luiza at pl. Metropolit Simeon* 🎫 *Free* ⊗ *Daily 7–6.*

Opposite the cathedral, in the Gradska Gradina (City Gardens), is the 19th-century **Starata Chasovnikova Kula** *(Old Clock Tower)* ⊠ *Bul. Maria-Luiza.*

In the city center on the south side of the City Gardens stands **Natzionalen Teatur Stoyan Buchvarov** *(Stoyan Buchvarov National Theater*

⊠*Pl. Nezavisimost*), a magnificent baroque building. The theater was founded in 1921 and showcased some of Bulgaria's greatest actors.

You can see what remains of the **Rimskata Stena** (*Roman Fortress Wall* ⊠*Corner of Bul. Knyaz Boris I and ul. Shipka*) of the original city, Odyssos.

If you walk south along ulitsa Odessos to ulitsa Han Krum you will find the remains of the **Roman Thermae.** These public baths date from the 2nd to the 3rd century AD and constitute the most substantial Roman ruins in Bulgaria. ⊠*Ul. Han Krum, 1* ☎*052/68–10–30* 🎫*3 leva* ⏱*Tues.–Sun. 10–5.*

If you follow bulevard Primorski with the sea on your right, you will reach the **Voennomorski Musei** *(Naval Museum),* with its displays of the early days of navigation on the Black Sea and the Danube. ⊠*Corner of Graf Ignatiev and Bul. Primorski, inside park entrance* ☎*052/63–20–18* 🎫*2 leva* ⏱*Weekdays 10–6.*

☺ One of Varna's greatest treasures is its long, narrow urban park, known as the **Morska Gradina** *(Seaside Gardens),* that stretches north along the seacoast for about 4 km (3 mi). The park was planned and built at the end of the 19th and early 20th centuries, and still functions as a green oasis for city residents to stroll, skateboard, ride a bike, or simply relax on a bench with a good book. You can walk along the ridge for commanding views over the bay, or walk down to the beaches, with the usual assortment of shaggy seaside restaurants, bars, cafés, and discos. The grounds hold a variety of attractions, including an open-air theater, aquarium, observatory, planetarium, and even a dolphinarium near the park's northern end. ⊠*Off Graf Ignatiev, inside Primorski Park, outside entrance to municipal beach.*

OFF THE BEATEN PATH

Pobiti Kammani. If you plan to drive from Sofia to Varna, allow time to see the so-called "Stone Forest" just off the Sofia–Varna road between Devnya and Varna, about 20 km (13 mi) west of Varna. The unexpected groups of sandstone pillars are thought to have been formed when the area was the bed of the Lutsian Sea.

WHERE TO STAY & EAT

$$$ ✗**Paraklisa.** Half hidden behind an old chapel and surrounded by a green hedge, this is one of the coziest and most timeless little restaurants in town. A rich menu available in English describes all the traditional Bulgarian dishes in detail. Friendly waitresses wearing carnations behind their ears, wine from the best regions in the country, and a genuinely homey feeling guarantee a perfect evening. ⊠*Ul. Ioan Ekzarh, 8* ☎*052/63–97–35* ▭*MC, V.*

$$ ✗**Bistro Europe.** Standing on the busiest point of the main street, this restaurant is one of the best combinations of location and delicious food. You can sit outside under the trees and order a large portion of fresh mussels—a rarity even here on the seacoast—brought in every day from a small village nearby. The soups and salads are excellent. For dessert, the friendly, English-speaking waitresses will offer you a rich list of ice

3

creams with fruits and syrups. ✉ *Bul. Slivnitsa, 11* ☎ *052/60–39–50* ⊟ *No credit cards.*

$$ 🏨 **Grand Hotel Musala Palace.** Varna's nicest hotel is a 19th-century boutique affair in the center of town. The rooms are done up in antiques and hardwood floors. Take a look at a couple of rooms before choosing, since they are all different. The on-site wellness spa is the best around, and the restaurant comes highly recommended. The location is ideal, close to the sights and to the beach. ✉ *Pl. Musala, 3* ☎ *052/66–41–00* 🖷 *052/66–41–96* ⊕ *www.musalapalace.bg* ↗ *18 rooms* ♿ *In-room: safe, refrigerator, Ethernet. In-hotel: restaurant, room service, bar, gym, spa, laundry service, public Wi-Fi, parking (no fee), no-smoking rooms* ⊟ *MC, V.*

$ 🏨 **Černo Moré.** The only reason to recommend this communist-era high-rise is that it's so large, it's almost always likely to have a free room. Don't be put off by the gloomy, empty-looking lobby—the rooms themselves are clean and bright (if small). Ask for one with a view toward the sea. Also be sure to request one of the reconstructed rooms on the fourth, fifth, or sixth floor. They are a little more expensive, but worth it because of the updated bathrooms and air-conditioning (essential in July and August). The location is perfect, close to the cultural sights and just a 10-minute walk from the beach. ✉ *Bul. Slivnitza, 33* ☎ *052/61–22–35* 🖷 *052/61–22–20* ↗ *200 rooms* ♿ *In-room: no a/c (some), refrigerator (some), Ethernet (some). In-hotel: restaurant, bar, laundry service, parking (no fee), no-smoking rooms* ⊟ *MC, V.*

★ $ 🏨 **White House.** One of the better of several small, family-run villa-hotels in the north end of the city, the house, which dates from the early 20th century, is low on high-end amenities but big on charm. Rooms are small, but have bright yellow walls and big windows. The location, away from the beach across a four-lane road, will seem remote at first, but the beach is just a 15-minute walk away. The center of Varna is about 30 minutes by foot through the Morska Gradina. The upscale garden restaurant ($$) is one of the best in town. To find it by car, follow signs to the Best Western Park Hotel, which is located next door. Pros: friendly owners, excellent restaurant, charming house. Cons: few amenities, hard to reach without a car. ✉ *Bul. Chaika, 108* ☎ *052/30–00–21* ⊕ *www.white-house-varna.com* ↗ *10 rooms* ♿ *In-room: Wi-Fi (some). In-hotel: restaurant, no elevator, public Wi-Fi, parking (no fee), some pets allowed* ⊟ *MC, V.*

SVETI KONSTANTIN

8 km (5 mi) north along the coast from Varna.

Sveti Konstantin is Bulgaria's oldest Black Sea resort, dating from the early 20th century. Out of season, it feels small and intimate, spreading through a wooded park near a series of sandy coves. In July and August, it's close enough to Varna to bring in the crowds, and on weekends, it's simply an extension of the big city. That said, it's easy to navigate if you just want to stop by for the day to swim. Sveti Konstantin is easily reached by bus or taxi from Varna. If you're driving, you can park fairly close to the beach and walk from there. If you're planning on a long-term stay, Sveti Konstantin is home to one of the country's nicest hotels on the Black Sea coast.

WHERE TO STAY & EAT

$$ ✕ **Korab–Restorant Sirius** *(Ship–Restaurant Sirius).* This real World War I–era *korab* (ship) is now an attractive restaurant with a grand view. Choose a table on the top deck and enjoy the sunset and the meal. ✉*Sveti Konstantin* ☎*052/36–19–32 or 052/36–20–07* ▤*No credit cards.*

$$$ ⌂ **Grand Hotel Varna.** If you decide to splurge for one big, ritzy seacoast
FodorsChoice resort, make it this one. Everything about the hotel feels special, from
★ the beautiful, minimalist, white marble interiors, to the exclusive pools, with beautiful wood and linen daybeds, fashioned with canopies. The hotel complex is all-inclusive, with several on-site clubs, bars, cafés, and even an upmarket ice cream restaurant. The hotel is about 150 yards from the beach and offers a wide range of hydrotherapeutic treatments featuring the area's natural warm mineral springs. Check the hotel Web site for special deals. Pros: beautiful public areas, well-run spa, full facilities. Cons: expensive, impersonal, can be noisy on the weekends in season. ✉*Sveti Konstantin* ☎*052/36–10–89* ▤*052/36–19–20* ⊕*www.grandhotelvarna.bg* ⬦*325 rooms* ⌂*In-room: safe, refrigerator, Ethernet. In-hotel: 3 restaurants, room service, bars, tennis courts, pools, gym, spa, beachfront, water sports, laundry service, public Internet, parking (fee), no-smoking rooms* ▤*AE, DC, MC, V.*

$$ ⌂ **Čajka.** Čajka means "sea gull" in Bulgarian, and this hotel has a bird's-eye view of the entire resort from its perch above the northern end of the beach. It's not nearly as nice as the nearby Grand Hotel Varna, and the public areas feel a little dated. Nevertheless, the rooms are clean, and a nice sandy beach is just 100 yards away. Pros: excellent value, nice pool, decent chance of finding an available room in season. Cons: lingering communist-era feel, below-average food, plain rooms. ✉*Sveti Konstantin* ☎*052/36–12–57* ⬦*102 rooms* ⌂*In-room: no a/c (some). In-hotel: restaurant, pool, laundry service, parking (no fee), some pets allowed* ▤*MC, V.*

ZLATNI PJASÂCI

8 km (5 mi) north of Sveti Konstantin.

Zlatni Pjasâci (Golden Sands) shares much in common with the similar Slânčev Brjag (Sunny Beach) to the south. Both have beautiful long beaches, tons of amusements, and row upon row of big four- and five-star resort hotels. If you had to compare the two, Golden Sands is nicer. It's smaller, with a narrower strip of beach and a more intimate feel. It's also quieter in the evening and tends to draw a more upscale clientele. But like Sunny Beach, Golden Sands caters almost exclusively to the package vacation trade, making prebooking essential.

Although Golden Sands is a good place to spend a week lying on the beach, it's not ideal for day-trippers just looking for an afternoon in the sun. For one thing, if you are arriving by car and don't have confirmed hotel reservations, you won't be allowed to park. If you're coming by public transportation, buses from Varna are plentiful, but the bus drops you at a remote end of the resort—a good 30- to 45-minute walk from the beach.

Just over 4 km (2½ mi) inland from Zlatni Pjasâci is **Aladja Manastir** (*Aladja Rock Monastery* ⊠*Zlatni Pjasâci*), one of Bulgaria's oldest, dating from around the 9th or 10th century. The monastery is cut out of the cliff face and accessible to visitors by sturdy iron stairways. To get there, take a taxi from the entrance of Zlatni Pjasâci Resort. It costs 5 leva and is open daily 10–6.

3

ALBENA

10 km (6 mi) north of Zlatni Pjasâci.

Albena, a 1970s resort, is built into a forest and feels much quieter and less frenetic than either Zlatni Pjasâci (Golden Sands) or Slânčev Brjag (Sunny Beach). Albena tends to draw an older clientele and lots of families, so it's good for relaxing (but not really a great place to party if that's what you're looking for). Albena is also much smaller and more manageable than either Zlatni Pjasâci or Slânčev Brjag, making it a good choice for a simple day trip. There's ample public transportation from Varna. If you're coming by car, Albena has a sensible parking plan. You take a ticket when you enter the resort and are free to park where you choose. The beach is nearby and is wide and clean. There are plenty of surfside restaurants for lunch.

WHERE TO STAY & EAT

$$ ✕ **Rai.** This open-air restaurant offering traditional Bulgarian decor and cuisine is right on the beach. In the evenings, live entertainment includes folk music. The bar is open all day long, and the staff is used to Western standards of service. ⊠*Albena* ☎*0579/629–60* ▤*No credit cards.*

$$ ⊡ **Laguna Beach.** This attractive beachfront hotel draws a mix of Bulgarians and foreigners traveling on packages. This is a great choice for families traveling with kids, since the pool and beach are both right there. Room standards are higher here than most, but the rooms themselves are pretty small. Be sure to request a room with a sea view. Pros: right on the beach, excellent pool, attractive modern building. Cons: draws package tours, food is only so-so, noisy on weekends. ⊠*Albena* ☎*0579/629–59* ⇥*190 rooms* ♺*In-room: safe, refrigerator. In-hotel: restaurant, bar, pools, gym, beachfront, water sports, laundry service, public Internet, parking (fee), no-smoking rooms* ▤*MC, V.*

BALČIK

35 km (22 mi) north of Sveti Konstantin, 8 km (5 mi) north of Albena.

Part of Romania until just before World War II, Balčik is now a relaxed haven for Bulgaria's writers, artists, and scientists. On its white cliffs are crescent-shape tiers of vacation homes. The main attractions here are the Balčik palace and the surrounding botanical gardens. There's also a small beach area where you can swim, but the water is not as clean as the nearby resorts of Albena and Zlatni Pjasâci.

Among Balčik's many summer retreats is **Dvoretsa Balčik** *Balčik Palace)*, once the grand summer getaway for Romania's Queen Marie and her six children. Surrounding the palace are the beautiful **Botanicheska Gradina v Balčik** (Botanical Gardens), dotted with curious buildings, terraces overlooking the sea, and a small Byzantine-style **church** where the late Marie's heart was encased in a jewel-encrusted box. Her remains were returned to Romania when Bulgaria reclaimed the region. ⊠*Balïk* 🖾 *Garden 5 leva, palace 5 leva* ⊙ *Gardens and palace daily 8–8, church Tues.–Sun. 9–5.*

SLÂNČEV BRJAG

95 km 60 mi) south of Varna, 140 km 87 mi) south of Balčik.

Slânčev Brjag (Sunny Beach) is Bulgaria's take on a brash, no-holds-barred beach resort. During high season in July and August, Slânčev Brjag swells to the size of a medium-size city of nearly 100,000 people. Most of these are tourists from around Europe—especially Scandinavians, who seem to have adopted it as their home beach. The main promenade stretches a full 4 km (nearly 3 mi) and is stuffed with countless numbers of hotels, restaurants, cocktail bars, souvenir shops, fast food stands, and all manner of beach amusements—like giant slides, mini golf, and trampolines. The atmosphere is akin to a state fair. The air even seems filled with the smell of fried food.

The beach itself is nice and kid-friendly. It's a wide band of soft sand that follows the curve of a large inlet. The only disadvantage is that the area closest to the shore has been designated a "pay zone," meaning you have to rent a chair and/or an umbrella to stay there (6 leva for each). You can still unfurl a blanket for free, but you'll have to do that away from the shore and closer to the promenade.

If you're traveling with children or just like this type of lively seaside resort, then you might consider an extended stay here. On the other hand, if you're simply looking for a place to swim or enjoy the seaside for a few days, you're better advised giving Sunny Beach a miss and concentrating on somewhere smaller and less developed. If you plan on coming in July and August, advance reservations through a travel agency are an absolute must. The hotels, mostly four- and five-star resorts, are geared nearly 100 percent to package tours, and are ill-prepared to handle walk-ins. You'll also get a much better room rate, with many packages including transportation and half board.

WHERE TO STAY & EAT

Hotels in Sunny Beach run the gamut from ordinary high-rise blocks dating from the communist period to the newer and much more exclusive four- and five-star resorts. If you decide to prebook through an agency, be sure the hotel you're offered lies on or near the main promenade (many don't). As for dining, forget for the moment you're in Bul-

"I'LL HAVE THE SHOPSKA SALATA, PLEASE"

If you're like most visitors to Bulgaria, you'll probably find yourself saying that over and over again at restaurant meals. There's something about that agreeable mix of salty sirene cheese (a briny white cheese similar to feta) and fresh tomatoes, cucumbers, and onions. And it's a perfect fallback choice. Even at the simplest roadside restaurant, rest assured at least the salad course will be sublime.

There's surprisingly little variation across the country in the classic shopska. In addition to the main ingredients, you may find some roasted peppers resting in the bottom of the bowl, or perhaps some light oil or vinegar as dressing, but that's about it. And that's a good thing. Bulgaria is one of those few remaining countries where a tomato still tastes like a tomato. The cucum-

bers are pretty good, too. And then there's that cheese....

The origins of Bulgaria's signature salad remain obscure. The name "shopska" refers to the Shopi, a traditional folk group living in the west of the country. In Bulgarian lore, the Shopi play a role similar to American hillbillies—having a reputation (often unjustified) for being a little thick and very stubborn. They're the butt of lots of jokes—and not the kind of group you'd expect to create the salad of a nation.

In fact, the shopska salata is probably a relatively recent creation, dating not much farther back than the 1950s or so. At least there are apparently not many references to it in older, classic cookbooks. The name "shopska" was probably chosen to reflect the salad's simplicity. It is after all just a mix of tomatoes, cucumbers, onions, and cheese.

garia. The *shopska salata* appears on menus almost as an afterthought, alongside steaks, hamburgers, pizza, Mexican food, Indian food, and just about anything else the owners think will draw in the crowds. As for quality, it's uniformly mediocre.

$$ ✕**Hanska Šatra.** In the coastal hills behind the sea, this combination restaurant and nightclub has been built to resemble the tents of the Bulgarian rulers of old. It has entertainment well into the night and a magnificent view of half of the southern seacoast. ⊠*5 km 3 mi) west of Slânčev Brjag* ☎*0554/228–11* ▭*No credit cards* ⌂*Reservations essential.*

$$$ ▦**Čajka Beach Hotel.** The Čajka offers one of the best locations—it's directly across from the best stretch of beach. Renovated in 2002, it has been turned into an imposing and expensive mixture of ancient Greek-style marble lounges and corridors and comfortable, colorful modern rooms. It has a "Pizza Castle" (which really looks like a castle) in its garden and a glass elevator. Pros: good central location, upmarket feel, beautiful pool. Cons: mediocre food (even the pizza is not very good), impersonal, expensive walk-in rate. ⊠*Ul. Slânčev Brjag, 8* ☎*0554/223–08* ▭*415 rooms* ⌂*In-room: refrigerator. In-hotel: restaurant, bar, pools, laundry service, parking (fee), some pets allowed* ▭*MC, V.*

$$$ ⊡ **Grand Hotel Sunny Beach.** In the center of the resort, this large, pink hotel is just a short stroll from the beach. Built in 2001, it is modern, comfortable, and clean. The rooms are nicely proportioned, and there is an attractive swimming pool. The hotel draws mostly package tourists from Britain and Scandinavia, who stay for a week or two. The reception desk will handle walk-ins if there are available rooms. Pros: big rooms, great central location near the beach, nice pool. Cons: crowded in season, average food, generic vacation experience. ⊠ *Slânčev Brjag* ☎ *0554/280–00* 🖶 *0554/25–24 or 0554/29–21* ⤖ *192 rooms* ⬧ *In-room: refrigerator. In-hotel: restaurant, bar, pool, laundry facilities, parking (fee), some pets allowed* ▤ *MC, V.*

$$ ⊡ **Globus.** Once considered the best hotel in the resort area, Globus is still good. It draws a mostly package-tour crowd from the United Kingdom and northern Europe. The rooms are large and spotless. Try to book one of the larger apartments with a seaside terrace. The lobby area is plain but serviceable. The location is good, not far from the beach and near the major attractions. Pros: super clean, friendly staff, good location. Cons: poor food (don't opt for any meal plans), small fitness room, noisy at night. ⊠ *Ul. Slânčev Brjag 22* ☎ *0554/22–45 or 0554/20–18* ⤖ *110 rooms* ⬧ *In-room: refrigerator. In-hotel: restaurant, bar, pool, gym, parking (fee), no-smoking rooms* ▤ *MC, V.*

NESEBÂR

5 km 3 mi) south of Slânčev Brjag (Sunny Beach) and accessible by regular excursion buses.

Nesebâr, a rocky peninsula jutting into the coast, is one of the Black Sea region's most popular tourist destinations. It's a UNESCO World Heritage Site owing to an amazing mix of historic architecture, including Greek and Roman remains, and some beautiful stone churches dating to the early Middle Ages. The town was originally known as Messambria, and was colonized by the Greeks in the 6th century BC. In the Middle Ages, the town for a time became a stronghold of the Byzantine Empire, ruled from Constantinople. The 19th century saw another building boom—this one of evocative stone-and-wooden houses in the style known as Bulgarian National Revival.

Atmospheric—though not undiscovered—Nesebâr is densely packed with outdoor markets, galleries, and seaside cafés, where fried seafood is served in heaping portions. Small hotels, both on the peninsula and the mainland, have popped up in recent years, offering a welcome alternative to the dated resorts nearby. If you want to stay in the Old Town, make your reservations well in advance.

WHERE TO STAY

$$ ⊡ **Monte Cristo.** This small, stylish hotel tucked between National Revival homes and the ruins of Byzantine churches is pricey by Bulgarian standards, but the location and quality of the furnishings are worth it. It's also one of the few Nesebâr hotels open year-round. It's popular, and reservations are difficult to come by during high season. Pros: Old

Town location, attractive rooms, good restaurant. Cons: noisy in season, often filled up, little English spoken. ⊠ *Ul. Venera, 4* ☎*0554/420–55* 🖷*0554/455–55* ⊕*www.montecristo-bg.com* ☞*5 rooms, 4 suites* 🛆*In-room: refrigerator, Wi-Fi. In-hotel: restaurant, laundry service, no-smoking rooms* ⊟*MC, V.*

$ 🖼 **Mistral Hotel.** On the mainland in the newer part of town, a short walk north of the causeway leading to the Old Town, are several small hotels and restaurants that were built in the 1990s. Mistral is one of the better of the hotels. It's pleasant, affordable, and busy all year. The rooms are small but clean. The proprietor is a good source for information about the region. Pros: good value, convenient location to banks and shops, reachable by car. Cons: some street noise, away from the beach (15 minutes' walk), away from the Old Town (15 minutes' walk). ⊠*Ul. Han Krum, 22* ☎*0554/430–48* 🖷*0554/429–33* ☞*16 rooms, 2 suites* 🛆*In-room: refrigerator (some), Ethernet (some). In-hotel: restaurant, bar, gym, spa, laundry service, some pets allowed* ⊟*MC, V.*

BURGAS

38 km (24 mi) south of Nesebâr.

The next place of any size south along the coast from Nesebâr is the city of Burgas, Bulgaria's second main port after Varna on the Black Sea. Burgas itself is industrial and chaotic, and you're not likely to want to linger long. Nevertheless, the city's airport is a main international gateway to the Black Sea coast, so you might find yourself here for an overnight. If that's the case, be sure to take a stroll along the Primorska Gradina (Seaside Park) and enjoy the little streets of the lively city center.

WHERE TO STAY

$$$ 🖼 **Bulgaria.** This high-rise hotel bears the unmistakable look of its communist-era past. Nevertheless, it's still considered the best hotel in Burgas and is a nice place to recoup or take a day's respite from the beach. The location is away from the seashore, but in a lively part of the Old Town with lots of little bars and restaurants around. The lobby is filled with travel agencies that can help you with things like renting a car or arranging day trips. The rooms are relatively small for the price, but have been given an attractive makeover and have everything you'd need for a short stay. Pros: full facilities, nice pool, central location. Cons: unattractive high-rise building, plain rooms, away from the beach. ⊠*Ul. Aleksandrovska, 21* ☎*056/84–26–10* 🖷*056/84–15–01* ⊕*www.bulgaria-hotel.com* ☞*200 rooms* 🛆*In-room: refrigerator, Ethernet. In-hotel: restaurants, room service, bar, pool, gym, laundry service, public Internet, airport shuttle, parking (fee), no-smoking rooms* ⊟*MC, V.*

SOZOPOL

32 km (20 mi) south of Burgas.

Built on and around numerous Byzantine ruins, this fishing port was once Apollonia, the oldest of the Greek colonies in Bulgaria. With narrow, cobbled streets leading down to the harbor, it's known in Bulgaria as a popular artists' haunt, and in August and September plays host to the very popular **Apollonia Arts Festival.** The modern, upper part of Sozopol and the beach areas are developing rapidly, but the older harbor area retains a pleasant, old-world feel. Like Nesebâr to the north, Sozopol is a nice place to combine a beach vacation with cultural outings and pleasant meandering in the evenings.

Most of the hotels and tourist facilities are situated in the upper, modern part of the town, a bustling, touristy type of beach resort that's recognizable around the world. The Old Town is about a 10-minute walk downhill, along a parkway promenade. Here you'll find little shops, cafés, and taverns. The main beach is just off the parkway connecting the modern and older parts of town. If you are arriving by car, note that driving is prohibited in the Old Town. You'll have to leave your car in the public parking area just as you arrive in town. Cars are allowed in the modern part of town—meaning you can get to your hotel—but try to arrange a parking spot as part of your accommodation because street parking is tight.

Sozopol is a good base for exploring the coast south to the Turkish border, where unspoiled rivers pour out of the forested Strandja Mountains.

WHERE TO STAY & EAT

The modern part of town is home to dozens of kebab stands, pizza places, and fast food joints of all description. These are fine for a quick bite, but you'll find more interesting dining options along the parkway connecting the modern and older parts of town, and in and around the old harbor.

As for lodging, most of the better hotels are in the newer part of town. Try to arrange accommodation in advance, but don't worry if you turn up without a room. Sozopol has lots of smaller, private hotels and except in the peak weeks of August, you're unlikely to be turned away. Just keep asking and you'll find something.

$$ ✕**Mehana Sozopol.** This touristy spot on a street with several *mehani* and bars serves typical Bulgarian and seasonal fish dishes. During the summer there is folk music and patio dining. Replenish yourself with a few cups of sturdy red wine and a *sirene po shopski* (white cheese baked with tomato, herbs, and egg) after touring the cobbled streets. ⊠ *Ul. Apollonia, 46* ☎ *05514/23–84* ▭ *No credit cards.*

$ ▦**Kavaler.** You'll find this small, year-round hotel on a quiet street off the main drag in the new part of town, but it's a short walk from the beach and the Old Town. It's clean, with pleasant service, but the desk clerks keep random hours—look for help in the busy restaurant. The two apartments on the top floor have terraces with sweeping views.

Pros: quiet, some street parking, friendly staff. Cons: few facilities (no laundry service), away from the main drag (but this means it's quieter), no English spoken. ✉ *Ul. Yani Popov, 21* ☎*0888/72–44–50* ⇆*12 rooms, 2 suites* ⚐*In-room: refrigerator. In-hotel: restaurant, no elevator* ▭*No credit cards.*

THE BLACK SEA COAST ESSENTIALS

AIR TRAVEL

Both main Black Sea port cities, Varna and Burgas, have international airports with regular passenger air service to several cities around Europe. Varna Airport, situated about 10 km (6 mi) west of the city, is the preferred gateway to resorts on the northern part of the coast, with the southern resorts best served by Burgas Airport. Bulgaria Air maintains daily service from Sofia to both cities. Taxis are inexpensive and the best way to get from the airport to your hotel.

Information Bulgaria Air (☎*02/402–04–00 in Sofia, 056/90–01–55 in Burgas, 052/57–33–21 in Varna* ⊕*www.air.bg*). **Burgas Airport** (☎*056/87–02–48 [departures], 056/87–02–72 [arrivals]* ⊕*www.bourgas-airport.com*). **Varna Airport** (☎*052/57–33–23 (24-hr flight information)* ⊕*www.varna-airport.bg [Bulgarian only]*).

BOAT TRAVEL

It's possible to travel from resort to resort by boat, but most of these excursions are arranged on the spot at local ports. The harbor at Nesebâr is a good place to catch frequent boats to nearby Sunny Beach, as well as regular—though less frequent—excursions to Sozopol and destinations farther afield. Regular boat service also travels the Varna–Sveti Konstantin–Golden Sands–Albena–Balčik route. The local tourist information office at Varna can provide details.

Black Sea cruises regularly dock at the passenger terminal at Nesebâr. The terminal is located in the older part of the city, about a five-minute walk to the main sights. The port is lined with decent fish restaurants. From here, you can also catch taxis, buses, or boats to inland destinations and nearby beach resorts.

BUS TRAVEL

Buses run regularly to Varna and Burgas from Sofia and other major cities and towns around the country. The journey from Sofia will take about seven to eight hours.

It's also possible to travel between the Black Sea resorts by bus, with frequent runs between Burgas and Varna, making several stops in between. Buy your ticket in advance from the kiosks near the bus stops.

INTERNET

Internet cafés are plentiful along the Black Sea coast, catering mainly to visitors. You'll find good ones in Sozopol, Varna, and Nesebâr, among other cities. Rates average about 2 leva an hour. Ask at your hotel or tourist information to locate the nearest one.

Internet Cafés Escape (⊠ *Ul. Ropotamo, 1B, Sozopol* ☏ *No phone*). **White House Hotel** (⊠ *Ul. Tsar Simeon, 2, Nesebâr* ☏ *0554/424–88*). **Doom** (⊠ *Ul. Tsar Osvoboditel, 20, Varna* ☏ *052/61–20–43*).

TOUR OPTIONS
The various towns and resorts along the coast are filled with small, private travel companies offering a similar mix of day trips to nearby towns and resorts, as well as excursions farther afield to places like Plovdiv and the Rila Monastery. The trips change according to the season and local demand. Inquire at your hotel or simply walk down the main street to see what kinds of excursions are on offer during the time you are there. In Varna, the tourist information office can provide guidance on excursions (*see below*).

TRAIN TRAVEL
Regular train service links Sofia to the main Black Sea cities of Varna and Burgas. The trip takes six to eight hours, depending on the route and train. It's possible to book overnight sleeping carriages between Sofia and the Black Sea.

Note that trains don't run along the coast, so once you're on the Black Sea, use cars, buses, or ferries to move between the cities and resorts.

VISITOR INFORMATION
Official tourist information offices have been slow to come to the Black Sea coast, probably because most visitors are here on package tours with information included. The exception is Varna, which has a brand new, fully stocked tourist information office in the center of the city.

Information Varna Tourist Information (⊠ *Pl. Nezavisimost, Varna* ☏ *052/65–45–18*).

INLAND BULGARIA

Inland Bulgaria is less known to tourists than the capital and the coast. Adventurous travelers willing to put up with rustic hotel facilities and unreliable transportation will be rewarded with sincere hospitality and scenic beauty. Wooded and mountainous, the interior is dotted with attractive "museum" villages (entire settlements listed for preservation because of their historical value) and ancient ruins. The region's folk culture, often pagan in nature, is a strong survivor from the past, not a tourist-inspired re-creation, and spending a few nights in a secluded mountain village can feel like journeying into medieval times. The foothills of the Balkan range, marked Stara Planina (Old Mountains) on most maps, lie parallel to the lower Sredna Gora Mountains, with the verdant Valley of Roses between them. In the Balkan range is the ancient capital of Veliko Târnovo. North of Târnovo, on the Danube River, lies the town of Roussé, an old Roman port. South of the Sredna Gora stretches the fertile Thracian Plain and Bulgaria's second-largest and most progressive city, Plovdiv. Farther south and west in the mountains is the up-and-coming ski resort of Bansko and the wine-making town of Melnik.

For many people around the world, Bulgaria remains something of a mystery—a small country tucked away in a corner of Europe and isolated for decades under communism. But for an increasing number of property buyers in the United Kingdom, Bulgaria is starting to feel more and more like home. Thousands—in fact, tens of thousands—of U.K. residents are buying apartments, condos, homes, and time-shares all over Bulgaria. The most popular areas are the resort towns on the Black Sea and rapidly developing ski areas like Bansko, but there are also significant British colonies around Veliko Târnovo, Sofia, and Plovdiv. A trip to Bansko, these days, can feel like a trip to Brighton.

For visitors to Bulgaria, this new British invasion has brought some positive benefits. Namely, low-cost flights, better restaurants and hotels, and generally more cash to repair Bulgaria's long-neglected infrastructure. But the unfettered development—in fact, a new land rush—has caused its share of problems as well. As more and more condos clog the coast and cover the mountains, it's hard not to feel that something has been lost as well.

The relatively low prices of Bulgarian real estate are what's fueling the boom. Just a few years ago, a seafront home could be had for a fraction of the price of a similar place on the Italian or Spanish coasts. Prices are rising fast, but are still perceived—by the buyers at least—as good value. Don't be surprised as you walk the streets of places like Nesebâr, Sozopol, Varna, and Veliko Târnovo to see dozens of British real estate agencies nosed in and among the more traditional storefront bakeries and shoe shops. Feel free to stop in. Who knows? If you like what you see, maybe a Bulgarian home is in your future as well.

KOPRIVSHTITSA

★ *105 km (65 mi) east of Sofia.*

One of Bulgaria's showplace villages, Koprivshtitsa is set amid mountain pastures and pine forests, about 3,000 feet up in the Sredna Gora range. Founded in the 14th century, it became a prosperous trading center with close ties to Venice during the National Revival period 400 years later. The architecture of this period, also called the Bulgarian Renaissance, features carved woodwork on broad verandas and overhanging eaves, brilliant colors, and courtyards with studded wooden gates. Throughout the centuries, artists, poets, and wealthy merchants have made their homes here; many of the historic houses once inhabited by Ottoman landowners are open to visitors. The town has been well preserved and is revered by Bulgarians as a symbol of freedom, for it was here in April 1876 that the first shots were fired in the rebellion that led to the end of Turkish occupation.

WHERE TO STAY & EAT

$ ✕⌖ **Trayanova Kushta.** This charming inn uphill from the town square offers rustic rooms furnished in the traditional National Revival style, with woven rugs and low beds. One room has a fireplace; all have shared baths. An intimate restaurant offers traditional Bulgarian dishes, but no breakfast is included in the rates. Pros: lots of charm, good value, colorful rooms. Cons: small, no facilities, shared baths. ⌂ *Ul. Generilo, 5* ☎*07184/30–57* ⌂*6 rooms with shared bath* ⌂*In-room: no a/c. In-hotel: restaurant, no elevator* ⊟*No credit cards.*

$ ⌖ **Family Hotel Kalina.** This small, very pretty hotel is in the central part of the town, surrounded by a beautiful garden. All rooms have private baths, telephones, and TVs. The restaurant is good, but breakfast is not included in the rates. Pros: excellent central location, family-friendly atmosphere, nicest place in town. Cons: small, few facilities, tends to book up in summer. ⌂ *Ul. Hadji Nencho Palaveev, 35* ☎*07184/20–32* ⌂*6 rooms* ⌂*In-room: no a/c. In-hotel: restaurant, room service, bar, laundry service, parking (no fee)* ⊟*No credit cards.*

TROYAN

At the village of Karnare, 17 km (11 mi) east of Klisura, take the winding scenic road north over the Balkan range to Troyan, 93 km (58 mi) northeast of Koprivshtitsa.

The **Troyan Monastir** *(Troyan Monastery)*, built during the 1600s, is in the heart of the mountains. The church was painstakingly remodeled during the 19th century, and its icons, woodcarvings, and frescoes are classic examples of National Revival art. ⌂*Troyan* ☎*06952/28–66.*

VELIKO TÂRNOVO

Travel north on the mountain road from Troyan until it meets Hwy. E772, where you turn right for Veliko Târnovo, 82 km (50 mi) northeast of Karnare, 240 km (144 mi) northeast of Sofia.

From the 12th to the 14th century, Veliko Târnovo was the capital of the Second Bulgarian Kingdom and was often referred to at that time as the second Constantinople. Damaged by Ottoman attacks and again by an earthquake in 1913, it has been reconstructed and is now a popular museum city with panoramic vistas of steep mountain slopes through which the idyllic Jantra (or Yantra) River runs its jagged course. The town warrants one or two days of exploration. Try to begin at a vantage point above the town to get a sense of its layout, and be sure to visit the three important churches on Tsaravec and Trapezitsa hills, all of which are open daily from June to September and Tuesday through Sunday from October to May.

Tsarevec (*Carevec on some maps*), protected by a river loop, is the hill where medieval tsars and patriarchs had their palaces. Steep paths provide opportunities to view the extensive ruins of the Patriarchate and the royal palace. On summer nights, a spectacular sound-and-light show presented here can be seen from the surrounding pubs. **Tzarkvata Cheteridesette Machenika** (Church of the Forty Martyrs) is a 13th-century structure with frescoes of the Târnovo school and two inscribed columns, one dating from the 9th century. The **Tserkvata Sveti Dimitar** (Church of St. Dimitrius), from the 12th century, is built on the spot where the Second Bulgarian Kingdom was proclaimed in 1185. The 14th-century **Tzarkvata Sveti Peter y Pavel** (*Church of Sts. Peter and Paul* ⊠ *Trapezitsa*) has colorful murals both inside and out.

In the Old Town, **Samovodene Street,** lined with restored crafts workshops, is a good place to find souvenirs, Turkish candy, or a charming café.

WHERE TO STAY & EAT

$$ ✕ **Ego.** This trendy pizza and grill restaurant has amazing views over the valley from the back terrace. Try timing your arrival at dusk and snag a table in the back where the best views are (in season you'll probably have to book in advance). The salads are big and fresh, the pizzas better than average, and the pork and chicken shish kebabs some of the best around. Instead of french fries, try the house potatoes—sliced and grilled and then baked with cream. One portion is big enough for two, with potatoes to spare. ⊠ *Ul. Nezavisimost, 17* ☎ *062/601–804* ▭ *No credit cards.*

$ ✕ **Art Club Restaurant.** The Little Terrace restaurant is actually part of the local art club, though it draws a mix of residents and visitors. The emphasis here is Greek food, but what that means in practice is the typical array of Bulgarian grilled meats and kebabs with the occasional addition of Greek items like moussaka. The view from the terrace toward the valley is beautiful, and the mood here is relaxed and nontouristy. The waitstaff will treat you like one of the family. If you can't find a free table, try looking at the "Tavern" restaurant next door, which also has decent food and possibly even better views, but isn't quite as homey. ⊠*Ul. Velcho Djambdjiata, 16* ☎*0884/741–548* ▭*No credit cards.*

$ ✕**City Pub.** This faux British-style pub is popular day and night with locals and visitors alike. It's a nice spot to relax with a beer or light meal, or to start off an evening pub or club crawl. The menu—in Cyrillic only—is heavy on Bulgarian dishes like salads and grilled meats. The staff and clientele are friendly and can help you get your bearings. ⊠*Ul. Hristo Botev, 15* ☎*062/637–824* ▭*No credit cards.*

$ ✕▣**Hotel-Mehana Gurko.** Homey and modern, this hotel overlooks the river and has a great view. The rooms are clean and very comfortable, with simple modern furniture and wooden floors. Some of the baths have tubs. On the ground floor is the restaurant, which offers a good example of traditional Bulgarian cuisine, with a beautiful view over the valley below. Reserve a table in advance. Pros: perfect location, comfortable rooms, traditional setting. Cons: limited street parking, small and sometimes difficult to book, limited facilities. ⊠*Ul. Gurko, 33* ☎*062/62–78–38* ⊕*www.hotel-gurko.com* ⟿*11 rooms* ⌂*In-room: refrigerator, Wi-Fi. In-hotel: restaurant, laundry service, some pets allowed* ▭*No credit cards.*

$$$ ▣**Grand Hotel Yantra.** This modern upscale hotel is in the middle of town and offers a highly regarded wellness spa where guests can get no less than a "cosmic journey" massage with energizing crystals. The lobby is immaculate and done up in a spare minimalist decor. The rooms are on the small side for the price and are furnished like an upmarket international chain. Many baths have tubs. Try to get a room overlooking the valley, since the view out the back is not nearly as nice. Pros: wellness spa, chic decor, professional staff. Cons: limited parking, some street noise, not all the rooms come with a view. ⊠*Ul. Opalchenska, 2* ☎*062/60–06–07* ⊕*www.yantrabg.com* ⟿*60 rooms, 11 suites* ⌂*In-room: safe, refrigerator, Ethernet. In-hotel: restaurants, room service, bar, gym, spa, laundry service, parking (fee), no-smoking rooms* ▭*No credit cards* ⦿*BP.*

$$ ▣**Hotel Central.** This small, modern, family-run hotel is not far from Gurko street and the historic heart of the city. It's a nice choice, offering the in-room style and comfort of a more expensive hotel, but without amenities that can boost the room rate. The lobby is tiny and no place to linger; the rooms are large and tastefully decorated in contemporary style. The big bathrooms—no tubs—come stocked with a nice range of complimentary toiletries. The in-room Wi-Fi doesn't work quite as well as advertised. Pros: high-quality furnishings in the rooms, big bathrooms, central location with parking. Cons: few facilities, limited English language skills, sporadic Wi-Fi connection. ⊠*Ul. Haji Dimitar, 17A* ☎*062/606–096* ⊕*www.hotelcentral-bg.com* ⟿*15 rooms* ⌂*In-room: refrigerator, Wi-Fi (some). In-hotel: restaurant, room service, bar, no elevator, no-smoking rooms* ▭*MC, V.*

EN ROUTE If you leave Veliko Târnovo by E85 and head south toward Plovdiv, you'll go through the Shipka Pass, with its mighty monument on the peak to the 200,000 Russian soldiers and Bulgarian volunteers who died during the Russian-Turkish Wars. Continuing along N6, between the towns of Karlovo and Kazanluk, is the area called the Valley of Roses, hotbed of the flower industry. Although most of the crop is harvested in early June, several fields of roses are left for the benefit of passing tourists.

ROUSSÉ

110 km (65 mi) northeast of Veliko Tûrnovo, along E85, 305 km (182 mi) northeast of Sofia, along A2 and then E83.

Regrettably, Roussé is one of Bulgaria's least-visited towns, primarily due to its distance from any other major tourist spots. But the town and the surrounding area are rich in historical sites—from Roman castles to medieval monasteries to world-class nature reserves. Consider flying to nearby Bucharest, Romania—only 55 km (35 mi) away.

Since the Romans built an important castle here as part of a line of fortifications along the Danube, which formed the northern edge of the Roman Empire, Roussé has been a major military and commercial center. Under the Ottoman Empire, it was a key trading post with Christian Europe. After the 1878 liberation from Ottoman rule, Italian and Austrian architects created the historic center, which you can still see today. In summer, the town square is the site of numerous outdoor concerts, beer festivals, and constant street entertainment. The historic center, laid out in squares and connected with pedestrian-only streets, is well signposted in English.

Ploshtad na Svobodata *(Freedom Square)* is the town's central square, surrounded by open cafés and lush greenery. It connects with the main street Alexandrovska, a favorite of Roussé residents for their daily stroll.

On the west end of ulitsa Alexandrovska stands the **Dvoretsa Batenberg** *(Batenberg Palace),* newly renovated to be used for the city's **Istoricheski Muzei** (Historical Museum). The palace was built as a residence in the 1880s for Prince Batenberg, the first Bulgarian monarch after the Liberation. ⊠ *Ul. Alexandrovska.*

Northeast of the Batenberg Palace is the **Sexaginta Prista,** the ruins of a Roman fort on a landscaped riverwalk. ⊠ *Ul. Slavianska (enter from river end of street)* ☎ *No phone* 🎫 *4 leva* ⊘ *Weekdays 10–5.*

Roussé was the childhood home of Elias Canetti, who won the Nobel Prize in literature. One of the family's former homes is now the **Kushtata na Elias Canetti** *(Canetti's House).* His books include *Tongues Set Free,* which recounts his childhood in Roussé. ⊠ *Ul. Slavianska.*

If you prefer a good walk along the Danube, follow the **Pridunavski Bulevard** *(Danube Boulevard)* eastward until you reach a large staircase leading down to the riverbank. Stop for a drink or a bite to eat on one of the restaurant-boats that sometimes make two-hour cruises to the Dunav Most (the border bridge with Romania) and back.

**OFF THE
BEATEN
PATH**

Skalen Manastir v Ivanovo. The world-famous rock monasteries of Iva-novo, both of which are on UNESCO's list of World Heritage Sites, are a network of small churches perched in cliff faces of the Lom River, a tributary of the Danube. Located 21 km (8 mi) southwest of Roussé, the monastery was founded in the 5th or 6th century AD and was a cen-ter of religion and art in the Middle Ages. Its setting within the **Rusen-ski Lom Nature Park** makes it worth a whole day's exploration for hikers and those in search of a bit of untouched nature. It's possible to book private accommodations in the park office in Ivanovo. Hours for the rock monasteries are erratic, and they are often closed during lunch. ⊠*Ivanovo* ☎*082/27–23–97* ☜*Free* ☉ *Usually Wed.–Sun. 10–5.*

Trakijs ka Grobnitsa v Sveshtari. The Thracian tombs, dating from the 3rd century BC, are about 50 km (33 mi) from Roussé near the village of Sveshtari. The tombs themselves appear throughout the fields, vis-ible as house-size earthen mounds, built for the rich and powerful of a Thracian civilization long since gone. Some are open to the public. From inside, the tombs are richly decorated with impressive murals. The most famous has 10 statues of women, supposedly goddesses. They can be visited on a day trip from Roussé or en route to the Black Sea. ⊠*Sveshtari* ☜*5 leva* ☉ *Weekdays 9–4.*

WHERE TO STAY & EAT

$$ ✕ **Chiflika.** This popular, traditional restaurant on two levels has nightly live folk music and a dance floor, so it's definitely not a quiet place for dinner. However, it is recommended. Order the *Meshana skara Vulchi glad* (mixed grill, also known as "wolf's hunger") or *Pileshka kavarma* (a thick stew of meat, onions, and vegetables). Food is served on iron platters and in clay pots. Try the wine from the Roussé region. ⊠*Ul. Otets Paisiy, 2* ☎*082/82–82–22* ☐*No credit cards.*

$$$ ⌂ **Danube Plaza Hotel.** Since its renovation in 2000, this hotel—perfectly located on the main square—has been the best choice in town. The modern rooms are comfortable and well furnished. Rack rates are for a "deluxe" room, which includes a/c and in-room Internet access. A garden restaurant offers excellent local and Continental cuisine. The hotel's tourist office can assist in travel arrangements, including local sightseeing and transfers to the Bucharest Airport. Pros: decent facili-ties, perfect central location, experienced staff. Cons: sterile, limited parking, expensive for what you get. ⊠*Pl. Svoboda, 5* ☎*082/82–29–29* ☐*082/82–29–52* ⊕*www.danubeplaza.com* ☜*74 rooms, 5 suites* ☐*In-room: a/c (some), refrigerator, Ethernet (some). In-hotel: 2 res-taurants, room service, bar, gym, laundry service, parking (fee), some pets allowed* ☐*MC, V.*

PLOVDIV

174 km (104 mi) southeast of Sofia, 197 km (123 mi) southwest of Veliko Târnovo.

Bulgaria's second-biggest city is a wonderful surprise, with cultural sights, hotels, and restaurants to justify at least a day or two of sight-seeing. The city's history goes back several thousand years—and local residents are fond of pointing out that it has a longer and more impressive history than the capital, Sofia. The city was conquered by Philip II of Macedon (the father of Alexander the Great) and even for a time bore the name "Philippopolis" (city of Philip). It was also a Thracian stronghold and had a long and prosperous period under the Romans in the early years of the first millennium AD, when the city was known as "Trimontium."

Not much is known about the Roman occupation, but in the 1960s construction work for a highway through the city unearthed a spectacular Roman amphitheater dating from the 2nd century AD. The amphitheater has been carefully excavated and restored, and is now used for concerts, opera performances, and outdoor film screenings.

The city later joined the emerging Bulgarian state in the Middle Ages, and then like the rest of Bulgaria was conquered by the Ottoman Turks toward the end of the 14th century. The Turks presided over the city for some five centuries, and you can still see the Turkish imprint in the form of former mosques and baths dotted around town. Toward the end of the Ottoman occupation, in the 19th century, the city prospered as a trading point between Western Europe and the Middle East. In the Old Town (Stariya grad) you can see the fruits of this wealth in a number of beautifully preserved National Revival mansions dating from the mid- and late 19th century.

Today, Plovdiv is divided into a lively modern section, spanning both sides of the Maritsa River, and a smaller Old Town, including the amphitheater, which occupies a hill overlooking the modern city. Most of the stores, travel agencies, restaurants, and hotels are in the modern part of town, but you'll want to spend at least a few hours traipsing around the hilly, atmospheric streets of the Old Town. Be sure to wear sturdy shoes. The lanes and alleys of the Old Town are paved (if that's the right word!) with rocks the size of small boulders.

The **Natzionalen Etnografski Muzei** *(National Ethnographic Museum)* is in the much-photographed former home of a Greek merchant. It is an elegant example of the 19th-century National Revival style, which made its first impact in Plovdiv. The museum is filled with artifacts from that fertile period. ⊠ *Ul. Chomakov, 2* ☎ *032/62–42–61* 🎟*4 leva* ⊗ *Tues.–Sun. 9–noon, 2–5 (closed Fri. morning).*

Below the medieval gateway of Hisar Kapiya, the **Georgiadieva Kushta** *(Georgiadi House)* is a grandiose example of National Revival–style architecture, with its overhanging upper story, carved pillars, and intricate, painted floral decoration. It has a small museum dedicated to the 1876 uprising against the Turks. ⊠ *Ul. Tsanko Lavrenov 1* ☎ *032/62–33–78* ⊕ *www.historymuseumplovdiv.com* 🎟*4 leva* ⊗ *Tues.–Sun. 9–4.*

Steep, narrow **Strumna Street** is lined with workshops and boutiques, some reached through little courtyards.

Beyond the jewelry and leather vendors in ploshtad Stamboliiski are the remains of a **Rimski stadion** (*Roman stadium* ⊠ *Ul. Saborna and Bul. Kniaz Alexander Batenberg*) that dates from the 2nd century.

The old **Kapana District** (⊠*Northwest of Pl. Stamboliiski*) has narrow, winding streets and restored shops and cafés.

★ The exquisite hilltop **Rimski amfiteatur** (*Roman amphitheater* ⊠ *Ul. Tsar Ivailo*), discovered only in 1965 and fully excavated in 1981, has been renovated and is open for exploration. In summer, this timeless setting is frequently used for dramatic and musical performances. Admission is 3 leva, and it is usually open daily 10–5.

NEED A BREAK?   **Janet** (⊠ *Ul. 4th January, 3* ☎ *032/62–60–44*), in a traditional National Revival house just a short walk up from the Roman Amphitheater, has a secluded back garden where you can have a cold drink and light, refreshing salad. It's a full-service restaurant and also offers a good range of moderately priced Bulgarian and international specialties like grilled meats and fish.

The **Natzionalen Archeologicheski Muzei** *(National Archaeological Museum)* has a wealth of ancient Thracian artifacts from Plovdiv and the surrounding area. ⊠*Pl. Suedinenie, 1* ☎*032/62–43–39* ⊕*www.archaeologicalmuseumplovdiv.org* ⊠*3 leva* ☉*Tues.–Sun. 10–5:30.*

WHERE TO STAY & EAT

New restaurants are opening up all the time, and you'll find plenty of cafés, pizza places, and fast food outlets along Bul. Kniaz Alexander Batenberg in the modern part of town. In the Old Town, there are a couple of nice restaurants and one highly recommendable hotel. A note on hotel rates: be careful to avoid arriving during the Plovdiv International Trade Fair, held twice a year in the spring and fall. Hotels uniformly jack up rates by as much as 50 percent, sometimes more, during fair times—if you're lucky enough to find a room.

$$$ ✕**Hebros.** Inside the hotel of the same name, this may be the most
Fodor'sChoice delicious meal you'll have in Bulgaria. Hebros won a coveted "Best in
★ Bulgaria" award in 2003 and has been trying hard since to repeat. It's just a matter of time. The daily specials menu reflects what's fresh, but go for the rabbit confit that's offered on the permanent menu, served in a glaze of plums and figs. The service is leisurely (to put it mildly), so this is no place to rush. Instead, order a couple of salads to start and linger over a glass of rakia, taking each course in turn. Try to reserve the garden terrace in nice weather. Locals consider the prices too high for a regular outing, but with entrées in the 15–20 leva range, you'll be surprised at how good a value it is. Reservations recommended. ⊠*Ul. K. Stoilov, 51* ☎*032/26–01–80* ▭*MC, V.*

$$ ✕**Hemingway.** Ernest Hemingway apparently spent some time in Bulgaria, and it's a good bet he'd like this convivial, very popular grill tavern just off Bul. Kniaz Alexander Batenberg. The salads here are some of the best in town. Be sure to try the breaded zucchini, served stuffed with feta and tomato sauce, or the grilled vegetables (sliced zucchini, eggplant, and onion, served with a slice of mozzarella and a drizzle of olive oil). After dinner wander over to the little piano bar in the next room. Reservations are a must. ✉ *Ul. Gen. Gurko, 10* ☎*032/26–73–50* 🞸*MC, V.*

$$$ 🏨**Novotel Plovdiv.** This enormous chain hotel is considered the best business hotel in town. The lobby and public areas are sleek, but dimly lighted. The rooms are on the small side, but plush and comfortable. The amenities, including a highly regarded wellness spa, tennis courts, and large outdoor pool, are the best in the city. The piano bar in the lobby draws a good local crowd in the evenings. Pros: full facilities, excellent wellness spa, good location. Cons: boxy, communist-era architecture, dark public areas, expensive for what you get. ✉ *Ul. Zlatyu Boyadzhiev, 2,* ☎*032/93–45–67* 🖷*032/93–43–46* ⊕*www.novotelpdv.bg* 🛏*322 rooms, 9 suites* ⚒*In-room: safe, refrigerator, Wi-Fi. In-hotel: 2 restaurants, room service, bar(s), pool, gym, spa, laundry service, concierge, public Wi-Fi, parking (fee), some pets allowed* 🞸*MC, V.*

$$ 🏨**Hotel Hebros.** The most romantic, picture-perfect hotel in Plovdiv,

Fodor's Choice this 19th-century National Revival house in Plovdiv's Old Town was

★ apparently once the hotel of choice for Bulgaria's communist leaders— now anyone can enjoy the beautifully evocative rooms, furnished with antiques (some replicas) and goose-down duvets. Every room is exquisite, with Oriental rugs and wood-carved ceilings—be sure to look at a few before choosing, since they're all different. The in-house restaurant has been named one of the best in the country, so even if you are not staying here, try to book a table in the garden terrace for lunch or dinner. Pros: unforgettable rooms, Old Town location, fabulous restaurant. Cons: hard to reach by car, no parking, some rooms are small. ✉ *Ul. A. K. Stoilov, 51* ☎*032/26–01–80* 🖷*032/26–02–52* ⊕*www. hebros-hotel.com* 🛏*10 rooms* ⚒*In-room: refrigerator, Wi-Fi (some), Ethernet (some). In-hotel: restaurant, room service, bar, spa, no elevator, laundry service, public Wi-Fi, limited street parking* 🞸*MC, V.*

$ 🏨**Light House Aparthotel.** This is actually a block of short-term apartment rentals, offering a cheap and convenient alternative to traditional hotels. Each unit is spotless and has a bedroom with two twin beds, an efficiency-style kitchenette, and a spacious living room with sofa and TV. Balconies look out to the front and back of the building. The location—midway between the Old Town and the modern core (and five minutes' walk from each)—is ideal. There's no reception desk, so you'll have to book in advance over the telephone or Internet. Stop by the tanning salon next door to pick and drop off the keys. Pros: great location, in-unit kitchens, super clean. Cons: limited facilities, only twin beds, some street noise on weekdays. ✉ *Ul. Benkovski, 21* ☎*032/65–08–00* ⊕*www.lighthouse-pl.com* 🛏*10 rooms* ⚒*In-room: kitchen, refrigerator, Ethernet. In-hotel: no elevator* 🞸*MC, V.*

$ 🏨**Royal.** Cheaper than the Novotel next door, the Royal offers many of the same amenities, including a small fitness center and even use of the Novotel's tennis courts. The lobby and public areas are tastefully furnished in big, comfy easy chairs and hardwood floors. The rooms have a kind of upmarket chain feel, with thick carpets and heavy drapes and bedspreads. An excellent value for the money. Pros: convenient location if arriving by car, unexpected amenities at this price point, like tennis courts. Cons: no in-room Internet, not in the Old Town, no English at the reception desk. ⊠ *Ul. Belgrad, 6* ☎*032/96–07–04* 🖨*032/96–07–04* 💤*36 rooms* ♨*In-room: refrigerator. In-hotel: restaurant, room service, laundry service, public Wi-Fi, parking (no fee)* ⊟*MC, V.*

NIGHTLIFE

In the tradition of university towns, Plovdiv has scores of bars, music venues, and discos. Almost all the most popular places are clustered around the central pedestrian walkway that winds through the center, **Bul. Kniaz Alexander Batenberg.**

BOROVEC

Travel west along the E80 Sofia Rd. At Dolna Banja, turn off to Borovec, about 4,300 feet up the northern slopes of the Rila Mountains, 109 km (68 mi) from Plovdiv.

This is an excellent walking center and winter sports resort, well equipped with hotels, taverns, and ski schools. A winding mountain road leads to Sofia, 70 km (44 mi) from here, past Lake Iskar, the largest lake in the country. For information on resorts, hotels, and winter sports facilities, contact the National Tourist Information Center (⇨ *Visitor Information in Bulgaria Essentials*).

■ **EN ROUTE** On the road between Borovec and Sofia is the **Rilski Manastir** *(Rila Monastery)*, founded in the 10th century by St. Ivan of Rila, a prophet and healer. Cut across to E79, travel south to Kočerinovo, and turn east to follow the steep forested valley past the village of Rila. The monastery has suffered so frequently from fire that most of it is now a grand National Revival reconstruction, although a rugged 14th-century tower has survived. The atmosphere carries a strong sense of the past—monks are still in residence, although some of the monks' cells are now guest rooms. You can see 14 small chapels with frescoes from the 15th and 17th centuries, a lavishly carved altarpiece in the new Assumption Church, the sarcophagus of Ivan of Rila, icons, and ancient manuscripts—a reminder that the monastery was a stronghold of art and learning during the centuries of Ottoman rule. ⊠*Rila* ☎*0754/22–08* 💤*Free* ⊙*Gates open daily dawn–dusk.*

BANSKO

150 km (93 mi) south of Sofia via Blagoevgrad.

In recent years, Bansko has emerged as Bulgaria's largest and most popular ski resort, and one of the leading ski centers in the Balkans. In high season, from late December through March, the hotels, taverns, and ski lifts are packed with vacationers, and advanced planning is a must. Outside of ski season, Bansko slows down considerably, but is still an enjoyable place to spend time. In summer, several outfitters run hiking and biking outings (the Tourist Information Center is the first point of contact for these), and the area is one of the nicest in the country for mountain walks.

Banko's enviable position in a lovely valley between three mountain ranges—the Pirin, Rila, and Rhodope—has fostered considerable investment in new hotels, condos, and apartment complexes. Not everyone is completely happy with this, and Bansko has become something of a poster child for insensitive development and commercialization. But don't let that deter you. Most of the new hotels are located outside of the picturesque core (about a 15- to 20-minute walk from the older part of town), and if you're here just to ski, the newer places (with modern facilities close to the slopes) might just be what you're looking for. Much of older Bansko, with its traditional stone houses and tavern restaurants, remains intact.

Aside from the main outdoor activities—skiing, hiking, and biking—there's not much to do in Bansko aside from walk around the Old Town and take in the many unique 19th-century stone and timber homes. The Bansko region is known throughout Bulgaria as a bastion of traditional Macedonian culture. In the evening, the Old Town comes alive as the taverns open their doors and welcome you to an evening of wine, grilled meats, and—if you're lucky—festive Macedonian folk music.

The **Tzarkvata Sveta Troitsa** *(Holy Trinity Church)*, built in 1835, along with the tower and the town clock, is part of the architectural complex in the center of the town. ⊠*Pl. Vuzrazhdane, 2.*

WHERE TO STAY & EAT

Where you base yourself depends on what you want to do. If you're here just to ski, you're best off finding a place in the newer resort part of town near the ski lift. If you're here out of ski season, choose one of the more atmospheric inns or small hotels of old Bansko. Hotels raise rates sharply in season (mid-December–mid-March) and reservations are necessary. As for dining, the older part of Bansko has dozens of traditional-style taverns, all offering similar menus at similar prices.

$ ✕⊞ **Dedo Pene.** A string of cowbells clangs as you open the heavy wooden door of this traditional *krutchma* (tavern). A waitress will pour you a glass of homemade red wine before you've hung your coat on the rack. The walls are adorned with furs, stuffed bobcats, and handwoven rugs. The rooms are in a similar rustic style, many with traditional wood-burning stoves. The sinks in the bathrooms are fashioned from old metal buckets. Pros: lots of atmosphere, good restaurant, friendly, English-speaking staff. Cons: few facilities, noise carries over from the other rooms, small and hard to book in season. ⊠*Ul. Bujnov, 1* ☎*0749/883–48* ⊕*www.dedopene.com* ↗*8 rooms* ⌂*In-room: no a/c. In-hotel: restaurant, laundry service* ⊟*No credit cards.*

★ $$$ ⊞ **Kempinski Hotel Grand Arena Bansko.** Situated in the ski resort part of Bansko, this relatively new Kempinski property—opened in 2005—is one of the nicest hotels in the country. The beautiful, sweeping public areas, with stone tiles on the floor and gracious hallways, set an elegant tone. The rooms themselves are small, but well laid out and furnished in a tasteful, modern style. Be sure to request a room with a mountain view—but these book up pretty fast. The main ski lift is just outside the door. In summer, there's an outdoor pool and tennis courts. The wellness center is the best of its kind for miles around. Pros: number one address in town, close to the ski lift, unequaled facilities. Cons: outside the historic core, pricey (though rates drop in summer), rooms are small for the price. ⊠*Ul. Pirin, 96* ☎*0749/88–566* 🖷*0749/88–560* 🛏*132 rooms, 27 suites* ⚿*In-room: safe, refrigerator, Ethernet. In-hotel: 2 restaurants, room service, bar, tennis courts, pools, spa, bicycles, laundry service, concierge, public Wi-Fi, parking (no fee), no-smoking* ☰*AE, DC, MC, V.*

$$ 🔣**Hotel Sofia.** This small, modern family-run hotel with an excellent location is on the edge of Bansko's Old Town yet fairly close to the ski lifts and mountain paths of the resort area. In the winter you can rent skis from the hotel, and you get free transportation to the slopes. Pros: good location, modern facilities, excellent value. Cons: not located in a historic house, small, can be loud in the busy season. ⊠*Ul. Radon Todev, 16* ☎*07443/85–02* 🖷*07443/83–62* 🛏*10 rooms, 2 suites* ⚿*In-room: refrigerator, Ethernet. In-hotel: restaurant, laundry service, gym, spa, bicycles, parking (no fee), no-smoking rooms* ☰*MC, V.*

MELNIK

From Sandanski, head south down E79 about 8 km (5 mi). Melnik is east of E79.

"The village that slept for a century from drinking too much wine," according to local legend, Melnik is famous for its grape orchards, its wine aged in deep cellars, and its historic ambience. Just north of the Greek border, this area was an important Byzantine stronghold from the 12th through 14th century. It developed rapidly again during the 1700s due to wine and tobacco trade, but declined by the end of the following century. The town was devastated by the 1912 Balkan War and its population reduced to near zero.

Today, Melnik is making a comeback, buoyed by its pretty, desertlike location, amid an outcropping of sandstone hills, and the region's rising reputation for good wine. Truth be told, there's not much to do here except stroll the main street and admire the massive foundations of the stone-and-wood National Revival houses. After that, scale the steps at the edge of town, following the signs, to have a glass of wine in a cave. Melnik is far less commercial than Bansko and makes a good base for exploring the southwest of the country. Note, though, that it's remote, with few facilities for tourists and no banks. Be sure to stock up on maps, gasoline, and leva before you get here.

Rozhenski Manastir *(Rozhen Monastery)*, rising above Melnik, dates to the 12th century but was rebuilt in the 16th century after being ravaged by fire. Within its walls is a church dating from 1600. To reach it, you can either hike up the footpath for about 6 km (4 mi) or take the bus that goes through Melnik roughly every couple of hours (no fixed schedule) and get off at the first stop. A caretaker is normally around and will let you in. Although there's no admission charge, it's a nice gesture to buy a few candles in the church. ⊠*Rozhen.*

WHERE TO STAY & EAT

Melnik is a popular weekend getaway for Sofia residents and has a couple of nice, basic hotels and several good traditional tavern-style restaurants. Try to reserve a room in advance, but don't panic if you turn up without something in hand. Most of the town's 500 residents seem to be offering a room to rent. Just stroll down the main street and ask around.

$$ ✗**Mencheva Kushta.** This decent tavern is next door to the Despot Slav. The menu here, like everywhere else in town, runs to the traditional, featuring salads, grilled meats, and slow-cooked pork and chicken stews. The elevated terrace out front is a nice place for people-watching. ⊠*Melnik* ☎*07437/339* ▬*No credit cards.*

$ ☎**Despot Slav.** A rustic, romantic getaway kind of place, Despot Slav is pitched on a hill overlooking the dusty main road. The rooms are snug, with hardwood floors and wrought-iron beds—in harmony with Melnik's remote mountain feel. To find it, walk along the main road to the near end of the village; it's one of the last properties on the left-hand side. In summer, ask for one of the cooler rooms toward the back of the hotel. There's a good in-house tavern. Pros: charming rooms, friendly reception, central location. Cons: no a/c, hard to reach without a car, small baths. ⊠*Melnik* ☎*07437/248* ☎*07437/271* ⌨*24 rooms* ⌂*In-room: no a/c, refrigerator. In-hotel: restaurant, bar, no elevator, laundry service, some parking (no fee), some pets allowed, no-smoking rooms* ▬*No credit cards.*

INLAND BULGARIA ESSENTIALS

AIR TRAVEL

Plovdiv, the largest city in central Bulgaria, has no passenger air service, and no other airports serve the region. It's possible to reach Roussé from Bucharest, Romania, just 55 km (35 mi) away. A taxi from the airport will run about €100. S.C. Gitour, based in the Romanian city of Giurgiu, operates regular bus service between the center of Bucharest (bus stop near Piaţa Unirii) and Roussé for about €10 each way. *For airport and airline information, see Air Travel in Bucharest Essentials in Chapter 10.*

Information S.C. Gitour (⊠*Autogara Giurgiu, Giurgiu, Romania* ☎*0040-246/21–33–21*).

BUS TRAVEL

Daily bus service connects Sofia with Bansko, Plovdiv, Roussé, and Veliko Târnovo, among other destinations in inland Bulgaria. Bus service to smaller cities like Melnik is less frequent. Book tickets through a local travel agency or purchase them at the bus station.

Information Tsentralna Avtogara Sofia (Sofia Central Bus Station) (⊠*Bul. Maria-Luiza 100, Sofia* ☎*0900/210–00* ⊕*www.centralbusstation-sofia.com*).

CAR TRAVEL

Though expensive by Western standards and accompanied by its own set of problems (poor road conditions, absence of road signs), renting a car is the best way to see Bulgaria's interior. This is especially true if you plan on seeing Melnik or some of the smaller villages and monasteries in the region. Avoid night driving if possible since the roads are poorly lighted. Always carry a good road atlas.

INTERNET

Internet cafés in the interior are not as popular as they once were as more and more people buy computers for their homes. Still, here and there, you may be able to find one. To make matters worse, Wi-Fi has become much more popular. This is great if you happen to be carrying around a laptop, but less useful if you're simply looking for a computer to use for a few minutes to check e-mail. In Plovdiv, the tourist information center (*see below*) has a couple of computers that visitors can use free of charge. Otherwise, ask if you can use your hotel's computer, or better yet, if they can point you in the direction of a nearby Internet café.

Internet Café Net Cafe (⊠ *Ul. Aleksandrovska, 37, Roussé* ☎ *No phone*).

TRAIN TRAVEL

You can get direct trains from Sofia to most cities inland, including Roussé (seven hours), Plovdiv (two to three hours), and Veliko Târnovo (five hours). Less important destinations may not be reachable by train. The central station at Gorna Oriahovitsa, 10 km (6 mi) from Veliko Târnovo, offers the best interchange for smaller train lines in all directions.

VISITOR INFORMATION

Unusual for Bulgaria, many of the major destinations in the interior have full-fledged tourist information offices. These can help you with maps, make sightseeing recommendations, advise on travel or tours, and suggest hotels. Most will not be able to book rooms for you. The new Plovdiv tourist information office has a couple of computers where you can check e-mail.

Information Bansko Tourist Information (⊠ *Pl. N. Vaptsarov, 1, Bansko* ☎ *0749/885–80*). **Plovdiv Tourist Information** (⊠ *Pl. Tsentralen, 1, Plovdiv* ☎ *032/65–67–94*). **Roussé Tourist Information Center** (⊠ *ul. Aleksandrovska, 61, Roussé* ☎ *082/82–47–04*). **Veliko Târnovo Tourist Information Center** (⊠ *ul. Hristo Botev, 5, Veliko Târnovo* ☎ *062/62–21–48* ⊕ *www.velikotarnovo.info*).

BULGARIA ESSENTIALS

TRANSPORTATION

AIR TRAVEL

There are currently no nonstop flights between the United States and Bulgaria, but it's relatively easy to connect to a Sofia flight from European hubs like Frankfurt, Paris, and Amsterdam, and a few European budget carriers fly to Sofia. The Black Sea cities of Varna and Burgas also have international airports with direct connections to major European cities (⇨ *Air Travel in Black Sea Coast Essentials*).

Airlines Air France (✉ *Ul. Suborna, 2, Center* ☎ *02/939-70-10* ⊕ *www.airfrance. com*). **Alitalia** (✉ *Ul. Angel Kanchev, 5, Center* ☎ *02/981-67-02* ⊕ *www.alitalia. com*). **Austrian Airlines** (✉ *Bul. Vitosha, 41, Center* ☎ *02/980-23-23* ✉ *Sofia International Airport* ☎ *02/937-31-33*). **British Airways** (✉ *Bul. Patriarh Evtimii, 49, Center* ☎ *02/954-70-00* ⊕ *www.britishairways.com* ✉ *Sofia International Airport* ☎ *02/937-31-11*). **Bulgaria Air** (✉ *Transport Service Center, National Palace of Culture* ☎ *02/402-04-06* ⊕ *www.air.bg* ✉ *Sofia International Airport* ☎ *02/937-33-70*). **Czech Airlines** (✉ *Ul. Suborna, 9, Center* ☎ *02/981-54-08* ⊕ *www.czechairlines.com*). **Lufthansa** (✉ *Ul. Bacho Kiro, 26-30, Center* ☎ *02/930-42-42* ⊕ *www.lufthansa.com* ✉ *Sofia International Airport* ☎ *02/937-31-41*). **Malev Hungarian Airlines** (✉ *Bul. Patriarh Evtimii, 19, Center* ☎ *02/981-50-91* ⊕ *www.malev.com*). **Sky Europe** (☎ *02/489-48-98* ⊕ *www.skyeurope.com*). **Wizz Air** (☎ *02/960-38-88* ⊕ *www.wizzair.com*).

BUS TRAVEL WITHIN BULGARIA

Bus travel within Bulgaria is cheap and relatively easy to organize. Dozens of private bus companies operate services that connect cities across the country. Buses are often quicker than trains, and provide access to many towns and cities that trains don't reach. Several buses leave Sofia each day for Burgas, Plovdiv, Roussé, Varna, and Veliko Târnovo, among other destinations. Buses also run regularly between the Black Sea coastal resorts. Since most of the lines are operated by private companies, gathering central information is difficult. The best bet is to go to the bus station of the town you're in and ask whether there's bus service to the town you want to go to. On many runs, minibuses have replaced larger, standard buses. Minibuses often hold to a less rigorous schedules and depart when they fill up. Etap Adress operates modern buses in good condition and has offices in more than 25 cities.

Information Etap Adress (✉ *Bul. Evlogi Georgiev, 161, Sofia* ☎ *02/945-39-39* ⊕ *www.etapgroup.com*). **Tsentralna Avtogara Sofia (Sofia Central Bus Station)** (✉ *Bul. Maria Luiza 100, Sofia* ☎ *0900/210-00* ⊕ *www.centralbusstation-sofia. com*).

CAR TRAVEL

You don't need a car if you plan to stay in Sofia, Plovdiv, or one of the big coastal towns on the Black Sea, but a car affords greater flexibility if you want to explore Inland Bulgaria where trains and buses don't offer convenient connections. Besides the generally high rates for rental cars (including a €20 per rental surcharge if you rent at Sofia Airport), you'll have to factor in gasoline prices of about €4 per gallon, nearly double the cost in the United States. You'll also have to deal with generally overcrowded highways, aggressive drivers, and the near constant aggravation of trying to find a place to park.

You'll find gasoline stations spaced at regular intervals on main roads. Many modern filling stations come equipped with clean restrooms and small grocery stores, and will have roadmaps for sale. If you plan on setting out for some remote areas, be sure to fill up beforehand since gas stations are harder to find off the main roads. Bulgarian gas stations are "full serve" and you're expected to provide a small tip (1 or 2 leva) to the attendant for filling your car and cleaning your windshield.

If you have car trouble, call the nationwide 24-hour road assistance number. If you're renting, ask if the car company offers any special breakdown assistance. Some rental agencies do.

Information 24-Hour Road Assistance (☎ *91–146*).

CAR RENTALS

You can rent a car from one of the major agencies either in Sofia or at the airport. Note that many rental agencies will not allow you to take the vehicle outside of Bulgaria. Ask in advance whether this is a problem.

Information Avis (✉ *Ul. Orion, 84, Center* ☎ *02/826–11–00* ✉ *Sofia International Airport* ☎ *02/945–92–24*). **Car Rental Bulgaria** (✉ *Bul. Iskarsko shose, 13, Center* ☎ *02/960–14–08* ⊕ *www.carrent.bg*). **Europcar** (✉ *Ul. Kozloduy, 4, Center* ☎ *02/931–60–00* ✉ *Sofia International Airport* ☎ *0887/503–030*). **Hertz** (✉ *Ul. Rakovski, 135A, Center* ☎ *02/980–24–67* ✉ *Sofia International Airport* ☎ *02/945–92–17*).

ROAD CONDITIONS

Road conditions vary. In cities, particularly in Sofia, you'll find lots of potholes and rough stretches. Major highways between towns are generally fine, though many highways are still only two-lane and often crowded. The authorities continue to build four-lane highways, and good four-lane stretches link Sofia to the Serbian border and run between Sofia and Plovdiv and shorter stretches in other areas.

RULES OF THE ROAD

Bulgarian drivers are aggressive, so drive defensively. The speed limit is 60 kph (36 mph) in built-up areas and 90 kph (55 mph) elsewhere, except on highways, where it is 120 kph (70 mph). Speed limits are rigorously enforced, and speed traps are frequent. You are required to carry with you a first-aid kit, fire extinguisher, and breakdown triangle (rental cars should already have these in the trunk). It's mandatory for drivers and front seat passengers to wear seat belts. It's also forbidden to drive while smoking or talking on a mobile phone (if the police actually enforced this, they would have to lock up practically the entire country). The blood alcohol limit is one drink (0.5%). Police are authorized to issue spot fines of an amount determined by the officer. Expect to pay about 20 leva for minor speeding infractions. Always have your passport and driver's license ready to show if asked.

To drive on highways, cars must also have a vignette—a small sticker—attached to the windshield. Rental cars should already come with this, but you may be assessed a "vignette" tax of €1 per day, depending on the rental agency. If you're driving your own car, you can buy short-term vignettes for 30 days (25 leva) or one week (10 leva). Buy the vignettes at large gas stations, border crossings, or post offices.

TRAIN TRAVEL

Most international trains arrive at Sofia's Tsentralna Gara *(⇨ Train Travel in Sofia Essentials)*. You can book tickets for just about any destination in Europe, though certain routes are covered infrequently.

Within Bulgaria, trains cost about the same as buses but are often overcrowded and slow. There are three classifications of trains: *expresni* (express), *burzi* (fast), and *puticheski* (slow). If possible, always take the fastest train and pay a few dollars more for a seat reservation in first class. Timetables are posted in every station listing *pristigashti* (arrivals) and *zaminavashti* (departures).

From Sofia there are six main routes—to Varna and Burgas on the Black Sea coast (overnight trains between Sofia and Black Sea resorts have first- and second-class sleeping cars and second-class *couchettes,* which are cheaper but less comfortable); to Plovdiv and on to the Turkish border; to Dragoman and the Serbian border; to Kulata and the Greek border; and to Roussé on the Romanian border.

Bulgaria is not included in the Eurail network, but it is included in the Balkan Flexipass, sold through Rail Europe in the United States. This allows you to pay a set price in advance for rail travel in several Balkan countries (Bulgaria, Greece, Macedonia, Montenegro, Romania, Serbia, and Turkey). A Bulgaria-only Flexipass is also available, as is a student version. However, train tickets are still so cheap that you should estimate your costs to decide if a pass is practical or necessary.

Information **Rail Europe** (⊠ *44 South Broadway, White Plains, NY 10601* 🖷 *888/382–7245, 800/361–7245 [Canada]* ⊕ *www.raileurope.com*).

CONTACTS & RESOURCES

ADDRESSES

In Bulgaria the street names are in the reverse order of Western Europe and the United States. The first part is the abbreviation for the word street/square/boulevard (ulitsa [ul.]/ploshtad [pl.]/bulevard [bul.]), then comes the name of the street, and finally the number. Addresses in this chapter are given in this format.

BANKS & EXCHANGE SERVICES

Bulgaria is a relatively inexpensive country by European standards. The prices for things like hotel accommodation, restaurant meals, and train and bus travel are lower than in Western Europe and even below prices in fellow formerly communist countries like Hungary and the Czech Republic. The exceptions are five-star accommodations in Sofia, hotel rentals on the Black Sea in season, and rental cars. Here the prices are equal to or higher than the international norm.

ATMs are plentiful, and you can easily obtain local currency with your debit or credit card, provided it has a four-digit PIN (personal identification number) and your card has been approved for international transactions. If in doubt, inquire with the bank issuing the card.

Large hotels, restaurants, and retail stores usually accept major credit cards, though smaller establishments may not. The most common credit cards are MasterCard and Visa (abbreviated here as MC and V). American Express and Diners Club are also widely accepted, but not as frequently.

CURRENCY EXCHANGE

The unit of currency in Bulgaria is the lev (plural leva), abbreviated BGN. Although Bulgaria is a member of the European Union, the euro has not been adopted in the country, though some hotels quote prices and accept payment in euro for convenience sake. You can always opt to pay bills in leva. You can exchange foreign currency at nearly any bank or at special currency exchange offices. Rates at banks will be uniform, but rates may differ at currency exchanges, so it pays to shop around. Currency exchanges are no longer permitted to charge a commission for exchanging, so the rate you see on the sign outside should be the rate you get.

The lev is tied to the euro at a rate of 2 leva per one euro. It fluctuates with respect to other currencies. At this writing, 1 U.S. dollar is equal to about 1.45 leva. Changing traveler's checks is always problematic. Though changing them is theoretically possible at a few select locations, such as the airport and some major hotels, commissions are high. In small towns, traveler's checks are worthless.

EMBASSIES

Information U.S. Embassy (✉ *Ul. Kozyak, 16* ☎ *02/937–5100* ⊕ *bulgaria. usembassy.gov).*

EMERGENCIES

Ambulance (☎ *150*). **Emergency Roadside Assistance** (☎ *91–146, or from a mobile phone: 146*). **Fire** (☎ *160*). **Police** (☎ *166*).

LANGUAGE

Bulgarian is a Slavic language. It's nearly identical to Macedonian, and shares similarities with Russian, Serbian, Ukrainian, and other Slavic languages. Unfortunately for visitors accustomed to the Latin alphabet, Bulgarian is written in Cyrillic. You'll have no problem if you happen to have studied some Russian in college; otherwise, you'll need to sit down for a few minutes and memorize the letters. Many visitors come and go without a clue as to what they are reading, but basic knowledge of the Cyrillic alphabet will make your trip much more enjoyable. This is especially true if you will be driving, since many road signs are written in Cyrillic only.

Bulgarian body language will also present a challenge. In Bulgaria, nodding the head up and down means "no," and shaking the head from side to side means "yes." It can be very confusing in practice.

INTERNET, MAIL & SHIPPING

The number of Internet cafés has fallen in recent years as more and more people buy their own home computers. Still, you'll have no problem finding Internet cafés in Sofia and along the Black Sea coast. Ask at your hotel or at a tourist information office for the nearest location.

Rates vary but are usually around 2 leva per hour. Just because an Internet café has the word "café" in it, don't expect to get any coffee.

Wireless Internet access, Wi-Fi, has become much more popular and most three-star hotels and up—as well as many restaurants and cafés—offer free Wi-Fi access.

Postcards and small letters to the United States cost 1.40 leva to send. Postcards and letters within the EU, including to the United Kingdom, cost 1 lev. Letters generally take from 10 days to two weeks to reach the United States, and about one week within Europe. You can use DHL or UPS to send parcels.

Post Offices Sofia Central Post Office (✉ *Ul. Gurko, 6, Center* ☎ *02/980-12-25*).

Shipping Companies DHL (✉ *Ul. Prodan Tarakchiev, 10, Sofia* ☎ *02/930-94* ⊕ *www.dhl.bg*). **In Time/United Parcel Service** (✉ *Ul. Nedelcho Bonchev, 41, Center, Sofia* ☎ *02/960-99* ⊕ *www.intime.bg*).

TAXES
Bulgaria's value-added tax (VAT) of 20% is included in the prices of all goods and services. Hotel rooms and tourist packages are assessed a VAT rate of 7%.

PASSPORTS & VISAS
Visitors from the United States do not need visas to enter Bulgaria for stays of less than 90 days. Citizens of other countries should contact the Bulgarian embassy in their home country. Visas cannot be purchased at the border.

TELEPHONES
Phone numbers in Bulgaria can be anywhere from four to eight digits, depending on whether the number is on old line or a new digital one. Public phones are usually easy to find, though with the popularity of mobile phones, public pay phones are not as well maintained as they used to be. Public phones do not take coins, but operate from phone cards that you buy at magazine and tobacco kiosks.

CALLING BULGARIA FROM ABROAD
Bulgaria's country code is "359." To call a Bulgarian number from North America, dial the international access number 011, and then 359, and then the local area code (omitting the zero) and number. To call a number in Sofia, for example, with an area code of 02, dial 011-359-2-xxx-xxxx.

To call a Bulgarian number from most other countries outside of North America, simply dial 00 to reach an international line and then 359 and the Bulgarian area code (omitting the zero) and the number. To call a number in Sofia, for example, with an area code of 02, dial 00-359-2-xxx-xxxx.

Mobile telephones in Bulgaria do not have individual area codes. Instead, they are assigned nationwide prefixes (usually a three- or four-digit number starting with 08xx). To call a Bulgarian mobile phone from abroad, simply dial 011 (from North America) or 00 (from most other countries) plus 359 and then the mobile prefix (omitting the zero) and the six-digit number. To dial a mobile phone with prefix 0888 from the United States, for example, dial 011-359-888-xxx-xxx.

MAKING LOCAL CALLS

To call a fixed-line number within the same city, simply dial the local number. To call a number in another city with a different code, first dial the city code (retaining the zero) and then the number. City codes to some of the largest cities are Sofia 02, Varna 052, Burgas 056, Plovdiv 032, Roussé 082, and Veliko Târnovo 062.

To call a Bulgarian mobile phone number from a fixed-line phone in Bulgaria, dial the full four-digit prefix (retaining the zero) plus the six-digit number.

MAKING INTERNATIONAL CALLS FROM BULGARIA

To call abroad from Bulgaria, first dial "00" to get an international line and then dial the code of the country you are calling, plus the area code and number. The country code for the United States and Canada is "1." Large post offices will have phones for dialing abroad. If you have service with AT&T, you can place a call by dialing the access number below.

Access Codes AT&T (☎ *00–800–0010*).

MOBILE PHONES

If you're planning on making a lot of calls in Bulgaria, you might consider bringing your own cell phone from home. Bulgarian mobile phones operate on a GSM band of 900/1800 MHz. This is a common band across Europe, but is different from the GSM band used in the United States. U.S. mobile phones should work provided they are a "tri-band" phone (not all phones are) and you've arranged with your service provider for international roaming. European mobiles should function without any problem, provided you have international roaming switched on.

Watch your calls since international roaming fees can add up quickly. One alternative to roaming would be to bring your own phone and then buy a "pay as you go" SIM card and prepaid phone credits. That way you are assigned a local telephone number, and calls and text messages within Bulgaria are billed according to local rates. The major mobile telephone operators offer this type of service.

Mobile Telephone Operators Globul (⊠ *Sofia* ☎ *02/942–80–00* ⊕ *www.globul. bg*). **MTel** (⊠ *Sofia* ☎ *0888/088–088* ⊕ *www.mtel.bg*).

TIPPING

Tips are appreciated but not automatically expected. Tip around 10% of the bill in restaurants to reward good service. Round up taxi fares to the nearest full lev. At gas stations, give the station attendant 1 or 2 leva for filling your tank and washing your windows. Leave a small bill or some lev coins in your hotel room upon leaving for the chambermaid who cleaned your room.

TOUR OPTIONS

There are several companies operating short- or long-term tours centered around destinations, or cultural or sporting activities. Odysseia-In and nearby Zig Zag offer a broad range of adventure and outdoor recreation tours with experienced guides, including skiing/snowboarding, kayaking, mountain biking, and hiking. SunShineTours offers special-interest tours for all ages. Balkantourist is the former state-owned tourist company and offers a range of special interest tours, including a seven-day trip that visits the UNESCO World Heritage Sites. Li Tours specializes in cultural tours and operates an eight-day monastery tour.

Information Balkantourist (✉ *Ul. Enos, 2, Sofia* ☎ *02/981–98–06* ⊕ *www. balkantourist.bg*). **Odysseia-In** (✉ *Bul. Alexander Stamboliiski, 20-V, Center, Sofia* ☎ *02/989–05–38* ⊕ *www.odysseia-in.com*). **Li Tour** (✉ *Bul. Vassil Levski, 68, Center, Sofia* ☎ *02/989–15–55* ⊕ *www.li-tour.com*). **SunShineTours** (✉ *Bul. Shipchenski prohod, 47, Sofia* ☎ *02/971–34–20* ⊕ *www.sunshinetours.net*). **Zig Zag** (✉ *Bul. Alexander Stamboliiski, 20-V, Center, Sofia* ☎ *02/980–51–02* ⊕ *www. zigzagbg.com*).

VISITOR INFORMATION

The Bulgaria National Tourist Information Center is the official tourist assistance office. It maintains an excellent Web site to consult before you leave home. The center's Sofia office near the Sheraton Hotel is a great place to pick up maps and find out what's on.

Information Bulgaria National Tourist Information Center (✉ *Ul. Sveta Nedelya, 1, Center, Sofia* ☎ *02/987–97–78* ⊕ *www.bulgariatravel.org*).

Croatia

www.fodors.com/forums

By Jane Foster

CROATIA'S CALM BLUE SEA, MAJESTIC mountains, and lovingly preserved historical buildings belie a checkered past. Like its Balkan neighbors, the country has a history shadowed by conflict and political strife.

The region's earliest inhabitants were the Illyrians, and two principal tribes, the Delmata and the Histri, gave their names to Dalmatia and Istria, respectively. The Greeks arrived in the 4th century BC, setting up various colonies along the coast, notably Issa on the island of Vis and Pharos on Hvar. In the 2nd century BC, feeling threatened by the Illyrians, the Greeks called for Roman assistance, and a period of Roman expansion began.

The Romans set up military outposts and administration centers, the most important being Pola (Pula) in Istria and Salona (Solin) in Dalmatia, while inland Croatia became the Roman province of Pannonia. In 395 Roman territory was divided into the western and eastern empires, a decisive event in Balkan history, as this same border was later to divide Catholics and Orthodox, Croats and Serbs. The 7th century saw the arrival of Slavic tribes, among them the Croats. Relations with the Latin-speaking Roman population were initially fraught, but with time the two groups assimilated.

In 910, the Croatian leader Tomislav united Dalmatia and Pannonia and with the pope's consent took the title of king. When the Christian church split between Rome and Constantinople in 1054, Croatian royalty sided with Rome. In 1091, King Zvonimir died without heirs, and the Croatian crown was ceded to Hungary. Thus from the late 11th century to the mid-19th century, much of inland Croatia was governed by a local *ban* (viceroy), answerable to the Habsburgs.

Meanwhile the coast, Istria, and Dalmatia (excluding Dubrovnik, which remained an independent republic) came under the rule of Venice. Lying on the trade route to the Orient, port towns such as Split, Hvar, and Korčula flourished, and many of the regions' finest buildings date from this period.

However, by the 16th century the threat of a third Balkan presence, the Ottoman Turks, was looming on the horizon. The Venetian port towns enclosed themselves within sturdy fortifications against attack from the sea, while the Habsburgs, fearing Turkish expansion overland, created the Vojna Krajina (Military Frontier) and employed mercenaries to guard this buffer zone between Austria and the Turkish-occupied territory to the southeast. These recruits were predominantly Orthodox Christians fleeing the Turks in Serbia, and they enjoyed a certain autonomy until the Vojna Krajina was united with the rest of Croatia in the late 19th century. The creation of the Krajina explains the presence of the Serb communities within Croatia that became a major force during the war of the 1990s.

Venice fell in 1797, and by the 19th century all of Croatia was under Austria-Hungary. A pan-Slavic movement was born, calling for Croats and Serbs to unite, and with the demise of the Habsburgs at the end of

WWI, Croatia became part of the Kingdom of the Serbs, Croats, and Slovenes. However, Croatian nationalists soon objected to being ruled by Serbian royalty, and when the country was renamed Yugoslavia (Land of the Southern Slavs) in 1929, Ante Pavelić founded the Ustaše Croatian Liberation Movement. In 1934, Croatian and Macedonian extremists assassinated the Yugoslav king Alexander.

After Germany declared war on Yugoslavia in 1941, Pavelić set up the Independent State of Croatia (NDH), notorious for the mass murder of Jews, Serbs, and Gypsies in the concentration camps within its borders. Out of retaliation, Josip Broz Tito founded the Partizan movement, aimed at pushing Fascist forces out of Yugoslavia. When the war ended, Tito created the Socialist Federal Republic of Yugoslavia with Croatia as one of six constituent republics. The Tito years saw a period of peace and prosperity, and during the 1960s Croatia became a popular international tourist destination.

But following Tito's death in 1980, an economic crisis set in, and relations between Croatia and the Serb-dominated Yugoslav government deteriorated. In 1989 Franjo Tudjman founded the Croatian Democratic Union (HDZ), calling for an independent Croatia, while in Serbia the nationalist leader Slobodan Milošević rose to power. The events that followed led to civil war.

In 1991, incited by Belgrade media reports that Croatia was returning to the days of the Ustaše, Croatian Serbs proclaimed the Republic of Serbian Krajina, arguing that if Croatia took autonomy from Belgrade, they would demand autonomy from Zagreb. Thanks to backing from the Serb-dominated federal Yugoslav People's Army (JNA), by the end of the year Krajina, which represented nearly one-third of Croatia, was under Serb control.

In January 1992, Croatia was recognized by the European Union, and United Nations peacekeeping troops were sent in to oversee a cease-fire. After a period of relative calm, Croat forces crossed UN lines in May 1995 and took back a Serb-held enclave in western Slavonia. Encouraged by their success, they launched the surprise *Oluja* (Operation Storm) that August, overrunning the Krajina and causing 200,000 Serbs to flee the country.

Meanwhile, there was evidence of growing corruption within the HDZ, and Croatia faced increasing international isolation for failing to respect human rights. President Tudjman's death in December 1999 saw the demise of his party. In January 2000, a new center-left alliance was voted into power, with Ivica Račan as prime minister and Stjepan Mesić as president. Mesić immediately announced that all refugees who had fled Croatia should be allowed to return to their homes, and his victory was widely welcomed in the West.

Croatia is now back on the map as a desirable vacation destination, tourism having bounced back to prewar levels. As Croatia primes itself for entry into the EU (it will likely get a formal invitation in 2008), foreign visitors can expect more than comfortable accommodations, excellent restaurants serving fresh seasonal produce, and a truly stunning coastline, still as beautiful as it ever was. Although prices in Croatia are on the rise, they are still below those in Western Europe.

EXPLORING CROATIA

Along the eastern shore of the Adriatic, Croatia is Eastern and Central Europe's prime seaside destination. Although the capital, Zagreb, lies inland, all the other main attractions are found along the coast, from the regions of Istria and Kvarner in the north to Dalmatia in the south.

ABOUT THE RESTAURANTS

In Dalmatia, the menu tends to be quite basic, featuring *rižot* (risotto) followed by fresh fish prepared *na žaru* (barbecue-style) served with *blitva sa krumpirom* (swiss chard and potatoes in olive oil and garlic). In Istria, the choice is wider and more refined: besides fish and seafood, the specialties are *tartufi* (truffles) served with either pasta (the local variation is *fuži*) or steak; the salads are exceptionally colorful, containing mixed leaves such as *rukola* (rocket) and radicchio.

Wherever you go, fish are priced by weight (Kn/kg) rather than by portion and can be divided into two categories: Class I, which encompasses quality white fish like *zubatac* (dentex), *šampier* (John Dory), and *orada* (gilthead bream); and the cheaper Class II bluefish, including *skuše* (mackerel) and *srdele* (sardines).

Inland, meat dishes are more popular. Balkan favorites such as *janjetina* (spit-roast lamb), *kobasica* (sausage), *gulaš* (goulash), and *čevapčiči* (kebabs) are widespread, and the Zagreb area is noted for *purica* (roast turkey).

Popular desserts are *palačinke* (pancakes) and baklava (just like in Greece).

ABOUT THE HOTELS

Croatia offers a wide choice of lodgings: hotels, apartments, rooms in private homes, campsites, and agrotourism (working farms offering accommodation). Hotel prices tend to be on a par with those in Western Europe. Although you can find some excellent low-season offers, prices skyrocket through July and August with an influx of German and Italian visitors.

CROATIA TOP 5

■ Plitvice Lakes, a UNESCO World Heritage site, is Croatia's most visited park, with 16 crystal-clear lakes connected by waterfalls.

■ Roman ruins can be found all over Croatia. The Roman Arena in Pula is one of the world's biggest and best-preserved amphitheaters.

■ The Dalmatian Coast's inviting beaches include one of the finest, Zlatni Rat, on the island of Brač.

■ Explore the massive 3rd-century AD Diocletian's Palace, which shelters Split's Old Town within its walls.

■ Attend a tasting in an old-fashioned stone *konoba* at a vineyard in Hvar or Korčula.

4

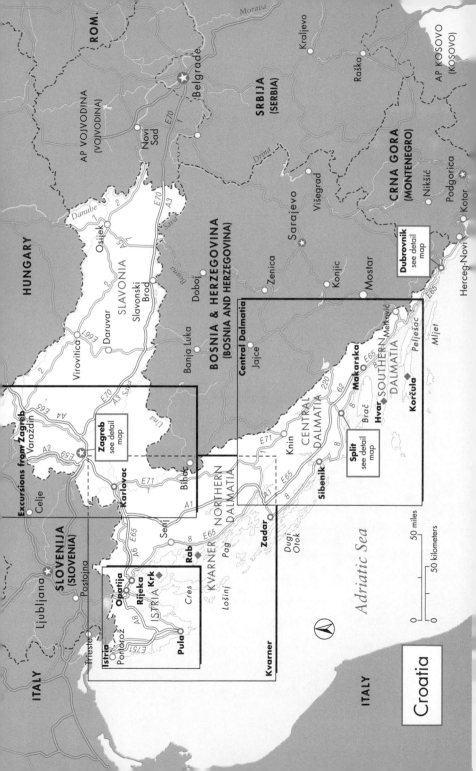

Tourism started here in the late 1800s under the Habsburgs, and along the coast you'll find a number of grand hotels built for the Central European aristocracy of the time. The second stage of tourist development took place between the 1960s and 1980s in Tito's Yugoslavia. The resulting Socialist-era hotels tend to be vast, modern structures slightly lacking in soul but endowed with truly excellent sport and recreational facilities. During the war years of the 1990s, some hotels were used to house refugees. Most of these establishments have since been fully refurbished, but in certain areas (notably Split) several are still closed or undergoing renovation. In addition, a number of small, luxurious private hotels have popped up, notably in Istria.

Along the coast, tourist agencies can help you find rooms in private homes. Standards are high, en-suite bathrooms and self-catering facilities being the norm. Host families are generally friendly and hospitable, and many visitors find a place they like, then return year after year. Agrotourism is a great option for families with kids. The idea has already taken off in Istria and will probably soon develop in other parts of the country, too. If you stay on a farm, you can expect pleasant rural surroundings, delicious home cooking, and a warm family welcome.

WHAT IT COSTS IN KUNA AND EUROS			
$	$$	$$$	$$$$
RESTAURANTS in kuna under 35 Kn	35 Kn–60 Kn	60 Kn–80 Kn	over 80 Kn
HOTELS in euros under €125	€125–€175	€175–€225	over €225
HOTELS in kuna under 550 Kn	550 Kn–800 Kn	800 Kn–1,200 Kn	over 1,200 Kn

All restaurant prices are for a main course at dinner. All hotel prices are for two people in a double room with breakfast.

TIMING

During peak season (July and August) the coast is crowded and expensive. You'll need to book a place to stay well in advance, and some people will find the temperatures unbearably hot. On the plus side, all restaurants, beachside bars, and sports facilities will be open, and you'll find a wide range of open-air cultural events and a vibrant nightlife. For a more peaceful vacation by the sea, try to tour in early summer (June) or late summer (September), when the water is still warm enough to swim in but the resorts are not too busy. The inland areas are particularly attractive in autumn, when the trees take on golden and russet hues and the grape harvest is in full swing.

The sea and islands are undoubtedly Croatia's most alluring feature. The ancient cities of Split and Dubrovnik are the main centers on the coast, offering regular ferry connections to neighboring islands. The capital, Zagreb, provides good air, road, and rail links to other countries included in this book.

IF YOU LIKE

BEACHES

With crystal-clear, emerald-green waters, the coast and islands are a haven for beachgoers, the water being warm enough to swim from mid-May to late September. Most beaches are of pebble (not sand), so if you have sensitive feet you'll need to invest in a pair of water shoes or flip-flops. Away from the larger, more commercial beaches (equipped with showers, beach chairs, and umbrellas), you'll probably find a number of small, secluded coves where you can escape the crowds. Naturism has a long tradition in Croatia. Naked bathing first became popular in Istria and Dalmatia in the 1930s and has carried on to this day. *Nudističke Plaže* (Nudist Beaches) tend to be isolated and are marked "FKK" (from the German, *Freie Kunst und Kultur*).

SAILING

With an indented coastline abounding in natural harbors, countless islands, emerald-green seas, and unspoiled nature, Croatia is a sailor's dream destination. The main company for nautical tourism is Adriatic Croatia International (ACI), which runs 21 fully equipped marinas, extending from Umag in the north to Dubrovnik in the south. There are dozens registered charter companies dealing with thousands of yachts and motorboats. To rent a yacht without a skipper, you need to have a license plus two years' sailing experience.

SCUBA DIVING

Along the mainland coast and on the islands you'll find numerous scuba-diving centers offering diving instruction, rental equipment, and organized diving expeditions to wrecks, caves, and reefs. To dive to the depth of 59 feet, you need to have a diving license (valid for one year) issued by the Croatian Divers' Association through recognized scuba-diving centers.

WINE & SPIRITS

Croatia produces some excellent wines, which have finally gained recognition abroad. The best Istrian wines are the white *Malvazija* and the red *Teran,* both of which are similar to the wines of the same names from neighboring Slovenia. Dalmatian wines have a higher alcohol content, thanks to the southwest-facing slopes, which take full advantage of the sun. The best reds are the full-bodied *Dingač,* from Pelješac peninsula, and *Plavac,* from the islands of Hvar and Vis. Among whites, *Pošip Čara,* from Hvar, and *Grk,* from Korčula, are equally respectable. The national spirit, as in Slovenia, is *rakija,* a potent brew made from a grape base, which is distilled and flavored with herbs.

ZAGREB

The capital of Croatia, Zagreb, with a population of roughly 1 million, is situated at the extreme edge of the Pannonian Plain, between the north bank of the Sava River and the southern slopes of Mt. Medvednica. Its early years are shrouded in mystery, though there are indications of a neolithic settlement on this site. The Romans are said to have established a municipality of sorts, destroyed around AD 600, when Croatian tribes moved in.

GREAT ITINERARIES

IF YOU HAVE 3 DAYS

With just three days at your disposal, concentrate on Dalmatia. Fly into **Split** to explore Diocletian's Palace. The following morning, take a boat to one of the nearby islands, either **Hvar** or **Korčula**. Devote your final day to the walled city of **Dubrovnik**.

IF YOU HAVE 5 DAYS

With five days, expand the above itinerary to begin with the capital, **Zagreb**. The following morning, transfer to Rijeka and spend the

day in **Opatija**. Take the overnight coastal ferry from Rijeka to Dalmatia, and spend your final three days following the three-day itinerary.

IF YOU HAVE 1 WEEK

If you have a couple of extra days, it would be best to do the same tour at a more leisurely pace. Another day in one of the islands as well as Dubrovnik would be most welcome.

4

Like so many other notable European cities, Zagreb started out as a strategic crossroads along an international river route, which was followed much later by north–south and east–west passage by road and then rail. For much of its history the city also served as a bastion on a defensive frontier, pounded for half a millennium by thundering hordes of invaders, among them Hungarians, Mongols, and Turks.

From the late Middle Ages until the 19th century, Zagreb was composed of two adjoining but separate towns situated on the high ground (Gornji Grad), one town secular, the other religious. In 1242 the secular town, named Gradec (Fortress), was burned to the ground in a wave of destruction by the Tartars, after which it locked itself up behind protective walls and towers. It is from this time that the real Zagreb (Behind the Hill) began to evolve; it was accorded the status of a free royal city in the same year by the Hungarian king Bela IV. In the 15th century, the ecclesiastical center, named Kaptol (Chapter House), also enclosed itself in defensive walls in response to the threat of a Turkish invasion.

When Zagreb became the capital of Croatia in 1557, the country's parliament began meeting alternately in Gradec and at the Bishop's Palace in Kaptol. When Kaptol and Gradec were finally put under a single city administration in 1850, urban development accelerated. The railway reached Zagreb in 1862, linking the city to Vienna, Trieste, and the Adriatic. It was at this time that Donji Grad (Lower Town) came into being. Lying between Gornji Grad and the main train station, it was designed to accommodate new public buildings—the National Theater, the university, and various museums. Built in grandiose style and interspersed by wide tree-lined boulevards, parks, and gardens, it makes a fitting monument to the Habsburg era.

The Tito years brought a period of increasing industrialization coupled with urban expansion, as the new high-rise residential suburb of Novi Zagreb was constructed south of the Sava. In 1991, the city escaped the war of independence relatively unscathed, but for an attempted rocket attack on the Croatian Parliament building in Gradec. Zagreb did, however, suffer severe economic hardship as the country's industries collapsed, post-Communist corruption set in, and an influx of refugees—mainly Croats from Herzegovina—arrived in search of a better life.

Since 2000, public morale has picked up considerably: trendy street cafés are thriving, numerous smart new stores have opened, and the public gardens are once again carefully tended. However, underlying this apparent affluence, unemployment remains a lingering problem. That said, unlike in Budapest, the much larger capital of neighboring Hungary, obvious signs of economic distress—such as panhandlers and homeless people—are relatively rare, and the casual observer will probably notice a general atmosphere of prosperity (fueled in part by coastal tourism).

EXPLORING ZAGREB

The city is clearly divided into two distinct districts: **Gornji Grad** (Upper Town) and **Donji Grad** (Lower Town). Whereas hilltop Gornji Grad is made up of winding cobbled streets and terra-cotta rooftops sheltering the cathedral and the Croatian Parliament building, Donji Grad is where you'll find the city's most important 19th-century cultural institutions, including the National Theater, the university, and a number of museums, all in an organized grid.

Numbers in the text correspond to numbers in the margin and on the Zagreb map.

GORNJI GRAD (UPPER TOWN)

The romantic hilltop area of Gornji Grad dates back to medieval times and is undoubtedly the loveliest part of Zagreb.

WHAT TO SEE

❿ **Crkva Svete Katerine** *(St. Catherine's Church)*. Built for the Jesuit order ★ between 1620 and 1632, this church was modeled on Giacomo da Vignola's Il Gesù in Rome. Inside, the vaults are decorated with pink and white stucco and 18th-century illusionist paintings, and the altars are the work of Francesco Robba and 17th-century Croatian artists. ⊠*Katerinin trg, Gornji Grad* 🎫*Free* ⊙*Daily 8–8.*

❻ **Crkva Svetog Marka** *(St. Mark's Church)*. The original building was ★ erected in the 13th century and was once the parish church of Gradec. The baroque bell tower was added in the 17th century, and the steeply pitched roof—decorated in brilliant, multicolored tiles arranged to depict the coats of arms of Zagreb on the right and the Kingdom of Croatia, Dalmatia, and Slavonia on the left—was added during reconstruction in the 19th century. ⊠*Markov trg, Gornji Grad* 🎫*Free* ⊙*Daily 8–8.*

❷ **Dolac** *(Market)*. Farmers from the surrounding countryside set up their stalls here daily, though the market is at its busiest on Friday and Saturday mornings. On the upper level, brightly colored umbrellas shade fresh fruit and vegetables on an open-air piazza, and dairy products and meats are sold in an indoor market below. ⊠*Trg Bana Jelačića, Gornji Grad* ⊙ *Weekdays 7–4, weekends 7–noon.*

⑨ Hrvatski Muzej Naivne Umjetnosti *(Croatian Museum of Naive Art)*. This unusual school of painting dates back to the 1930s and features more than 1,600 works of untutored peasant artists, primarily from the village of Hlebine in Slavonia. Canvases by the highly esteemed Ivan Generalić dominate here, though there are also paintings, drawings, sculptures, and prints by other noted members of the movement, plus a section devoted to foreigners working along similar lines. ⊠*Ćirilometodska 3, Gornji Grad* ☎*01/485–1911* ⊕*www.hmnu.org* 🖃*20 Kn* ⊙ *Tues.–Fri. 10–6, weekends 10–1.*

⑤ Kamenita Vrata *(Stone Gate)*. The original 13th-century city walls had four gates, of which only Kamenita Vrata remains. Deep inside the dark passageway, locals stop to pray before a small shrine adorned with flickering candles. In 1731 a devastating fire consumed all the wooden elements of the gate, except for a painting of the Virgin and Child, which was found in the ashes, remarkably undamaged. Kamenita Vrata has since become a pilgrimage site, as can be seen from the numerous stone plaques saying *hvala* (thank you). ⊠*Kamenita, Gornji Grad.*

③ Katedrala Marijina uznesenja i Svetog Stjepana *(Cathedral of the Assumption of the Blessed Virgin and St. Stephen)*. Built on the site of a former 12th-century cathedral destroyed by the Tartars in 1242, the present structure was constructed between the 13th and 16th century. The striking neo-Gothic facade was added by architect Herman Bolle following the earthquake of 1880, its twin steeples being the identifying feature of the city's skyline. Behind the impressive main altar are crypts of Zagreb's archbishops and of Croatian national heroes. The interior is otherwise relatively bare, the main point of interest being the north wall, which bears an inscription of the Ten Commandments in 12th-century Glagolithic script. ⊠*Kaptol 31, Gornji Grad* 🖃*Free* ⊙ *Daily 8–8.*

⑪ Kula Lotrščak *(Lotrščak Tower)*. Formerly the entrance to the fortified medieval Gradec, Kula Lotrščak now houses a multilevel gallery with occasional exhibits of contemporary art. Each day at noon, a small cannon is fired from the top of the tower in memory of the times when it was used to warn of the possibility of an Ottoman attack. You can climb the tower partway via a spiral wooden staircase for a look into the gallery rooms (which occupy several floors) or all the way to the observation deck up top for splendid views of Zagreb and environs. ⊠*Strossmayer Šetalište, Gornji Grad* ☎*01/485–1926* 🖃*Observation deck 10 Kn; gallery free* ⊙ *Tues.–Fri. 11–7, weekends 2–7.*

⑦ Meštrović Atelier *(Meštrović Atelier)*. This 17th-century building, with its ★ interior courtyard, served as home and studio to Ivan Meštrović from 1922 until his emigration to the United States in 1942. The building was extensively remodeled according to plans devised by the artist and was turned into a memorial museum with a permanent exhibition of

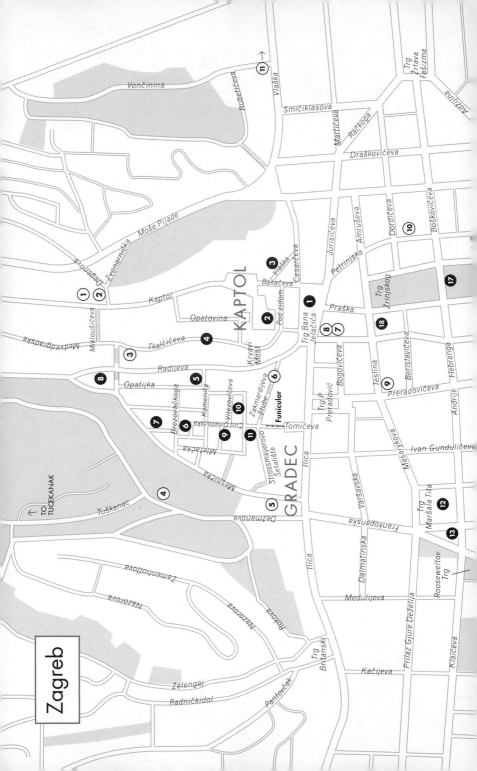

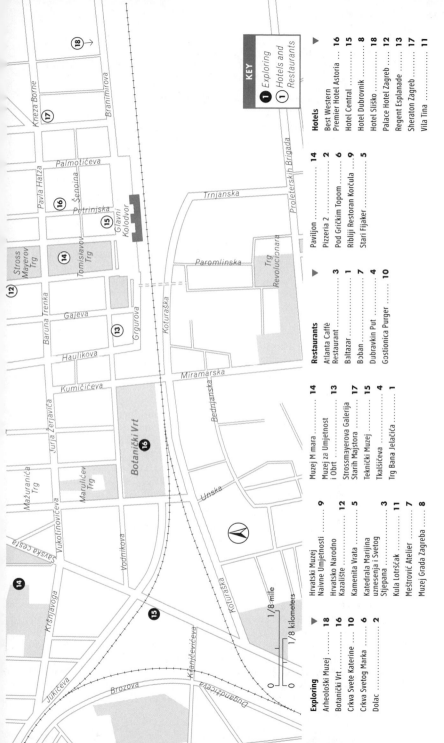

KEY

1 Exploring

1 Hotels and Restaurants

Exploring ▶

Arheološki Muzej	**18**
Botanički Vrt	**16**
Crkva Svete Katerine	**10**
Crkva Svetog Marka	**6**
Dolac	**2**
Hrvatski Muzej Naivne Umjetnosti	**9**
Hrvatsko Narodno Kazalište	**12**
Kamenita Vrata	**5**
Katedrala Marijina uznesenja i Svetog Stjepana	**3**
Kula Lotršćak	**11**
Meštrović Atelier	**7**
Muzej Grada Zagreba	**8**
Muzej M mara	**14**
Muzej za Umjetnost i Obrt	**13**
Strossmayerova Galerija Starih Majstora	**17**
Teknički Muzej	**15**
Tkalšićeva	**4**
Trg Bana Jelačića	**1**

Restaurants ▶

Atlanta Caffè Restaurant	**3**
Baltazar	**1**
B-ban	**7**
Dubravkin Put	**4**
Gostionica Purger	**10**
Paviljon	**14**
Pizzeria 2	**2**
Pod Gričkim Topom	**6**
Riblji Restoran Korčula	**9**
Stari Fijaker	**5**

Hotels ▶

Best Western Premier Hotel Astoria	**16**
Hotel Central	**15**
Hotel Dubrovnik	**8**
Hotel Sliško	**18**
Palace Hotel Zagreb	**12**
Regent Esplanade	**13**
Sheraton Zagreb	**17**
Vila Tina	**11**

0   1/8 mile

0   1/8 kilometers

4

his sculptures and drawings after his death in 1962. (There is a larger collection of his works in the Meštrović Gallery in Split.) ✉ *Mletačka 8, Gornji Grad* ☎ *01/485–1123* 💲 *20 Kn* ⊙ *Tues., Wed., and Fri. 10– 6, Thurs. 10–10, weekends 10–2.*

8 **Muzej Grada Zagreba** *(Zagreb City Museum)*. Well worth a visit for anyone interested in urban design, this museum traces the city's most important historical, economic, political, social, and cultural events from medieval times up to the present day. Exhibits include detailed scale models of how the city has evolved, as well as sections devoted to the old trade guilds, domestic life, and sacral art. ✉ *Opatička 20, Gornji Grad* ☎ *01/485–1361 or 01/485–1362* ⊕ *www.mdc.hr/mgz* 💲 *20 Kn; free guided tours at 11* AM *weekends* ⊙ *Tues.–Fri. 10–6, weekends 10–1.*

4 **Tkalčićeva.** This street was once a channel forming the boundary between Kaptol and Gradec, then known as Potok (the brook). Today it is a pretty pedestrian zone lined with 19th-century town houses, many of which have been converted into popular café-bars at street level—attracting a huge cross section of Croatian and international youth from morning until late at night. ✉ *Tkalčićeva north of Krvavi Most, Gornji Grad.*

NEED A BREAK?

For morning coffee or an early evening aperitif, stop at **Sunčani Sat** (✉ *Tkalčićeva 27, Gornji Grad*). Take a comfy wicker chair on the open-air summer terrace and enjoy watching the comings and goings of Zagreb café life. In the evening this space transforms, as with so many others along Tkalčićeva, into a trendy, crowded watering hole.

1 **Trg Bana Jelačića** *(Ban Jelačić Square)*. Buildings lining the square date from 1827 onward and include several fine examples of Viennese Secessionist architecture. The centerpiece is an equestrian statue of Ban Jelačić, the first Croatian viceroy, erected in 1866. After World War II the Communist government ordered the dismantling and removal of the statue, but it was put back in place in 1991. ✉ *Between Ilica to the west, Praška to the south, and Jurišićeva to the east, Gornji Grad.*

DONJI GRAD (LOWER TOWN)

Donji Grad came into being during the late 19th century. The urban plan, which follows a grid pattern, was drawn up by Milan Lenuci and combines a succession of squares and parks laid out in a U shape (known as the Green Horseshoe), all overlooked by the city's main public buildings and cultural institutions.

WHAT TO SEE

18 **Arheološki Muzej** *(Archaeological Museum)*. Museum exhibits focus on prehistoric times to the Tartar invasion. Pride of place is given to the Vučedol Dove, a three-legged ceramic vessel in the form of a bird, dating back to the 4th millennium BC, and a piece of linen bearing the longest known text in ancient Etruscan writing. The courtyard features a collection of stone relics from Roman times. ✉ *Trg N. Zrinjskog 19, Donji Grad* ☎ *01/487–3101* ⊕ *www.amz.hr* 💲 *20 Kn* ⊙ *Tues.–Fri. 10–5, weekends 10–1.*

16 **Botanički Vrt** *(Botanical Garden)*. Founded in 1889 as research grounds for the faculty of botany at Zagreb University, the garden includes an arboretum with English-style landscaping, a small artificial lake, and an ornamental Japanese bridge. ✉ *Marulićeva trg 9a, Donji Grad* 🎟 *Free* 🕐 *Mon. and Tues. 9–2:30, Wed.–Sun. 9–6.*

12 **Hrvatsko Narodno Kazalište** *(Croatian National Theater)*. The building dates from 1895, designed by the Viennese firm Hellmer and Fellner as part of the preparations for a state visit by Emperor Franz Josef. In front of the theater, set deep in a round concrete basin, is Meštrović's little, eerily lifelike sculpture *Zdenac Života (Fountain of Life)*, from 1912, which depicts four naked couples writhing uncomfortably in each other's arms around a small pool of water while one lone, likewise naked gentleman stares meditatively into the pool. The only way to see the inside of the theater is to attend a performance. ✉ *Trg Maršala Tita 15, Donji Grad* ☎ *01/488–8415* ⊕ *www.hnk.hr.*

14 **Muzej Mimara** *(Mimara Museum)*. In a huge gray building that's dull compared with some of those nearby, this vast private collection, including paintings, sculpture, ceramics, textiles, and rugs, was donated by Ante Topić-Mimara (1898–1987), a Croatian who spent many years abroad where he made his fortune, supposedly as a merchant. On display are canvases attributed to such old masters as Raphael, Rembrandt, and Rubens, as well as more modern works by the likes of Manet, Degas, and Renoir, and ancient artifacts including Egyptian glassware and Chinese porcelain. ✉ *Rooseveltov trg 5, Donji Grad* ☎ *01/482–8100* 🎟 *40 Kn* 🕐 *Tues., Wed., Fri., and Sat. 10–5, Thurs. 10–7, Sun. 10–2.*

13 **Muzej za Umjetnost i Obrt** *(Arts & Crafts Museum)*. Designed in 1888 by Herman Bolle, the architect responsible for the Katedrala Marijina uznesenja i Svetog Stjepana facade, this pleasant museum traces the development of the applied arts from the baroque period up to the 20th century. Exhibits are displayed in chronological order, and although furniture design predominates, there are also sections devoted to sacral art, clocks, and clothing. ✉ *Trg Maršala Tita 10, Donji Grad* ☎ *01/488–2111* ⊕ *www.muo.hr* 🎟 *20 Kn* 🕐 *Tues.–Sat. 10–7, Sun. 10–2.*

17 **Strossmayerova Galerija Starih Majstora** *(Strossmayer Gallery of Old Masters)*. Now under the custody of the Croatian Academy of Sciences and Arts, this impressive gallery was founded in 1884 by Bishop Strossmayer and later expanded to include many private donations. Works by Venetian Renaissance and baroque artists such as Bellini and Carpaccio predominate, but there are also masterpieces by Dutch painters Brueghel and Van Dyck, as well as a delightful Mary Magdalene by El Greco. ✉ *Trg Zrinjskog 11, Donji Grad* ☎ *01/481–3344* ⊕ *www.mdc. hr/strossmayer* 🎟 *10 Kn* 🕐 *Tues. 10–1 and 5–7, Wed.–Sun. 10–1.*

NEED A BREAK? The green expanse of Strossmayerov trg with its carefully tended flower beds makes an ideal stopping place for weary feet. At the terrace of the Viennese-style café of the **Palace Hotel** (✉ *Strossmayerov trg 10*), you can sip a cappuccino on a vine-enveloped sidewalk terrace across from this leafy square while sampling from a range of tempting cakes and pastries.

15 **Teknički Muzej** *(Technical Museum)*. It may be in a drab box of a building, but this museum is guaranteed to appeal to children and civil engineers alike; try to see it in the afternoon on a weekday or in the late
morning on the weekend, when a series of guided visits are offered. The
highlight here is the demonstration of some of Nikola Tesla's inven-
tions, which takes place weekdays at 3:30 and weekends at 11:30,
but there's also the tour of a lifelike reconstruction of a coal mine at
3 on weekdays and 11 on weekends, and a planetarium visit at 4 on
weekdays, noon on weekends. That's not to mention all the various
engines on display, as well as a fascinating historical exhibit of firefighting equipment including trucks, ladders, and hoses aplenty. ⊠ *Savska c
18, Donji Grad* ☎ *01/484–4050* ⊕ *www.mdc.hr/tehnicki* 🏛 *Museum
15 Kn, planetarium 10 Kn extra* ⊙ *Tues.–Fri. 9–5, weekends 9–1.*

WHERE TO EAT

For budget fare, go up the steps from the main square, Trg Bana
Jelačića, and just off the right before you reach the top is a row of
bistros where you can get everything from *bureks* (a savory cheese- or
meat-filled pastry) to simple pizzas to Balkan-style grilled meats for
around half what you'd pay at a modestly priced restaurant. And do
remember, though Zagreb is not exactly overflowing with budget sand-
wich shops, traditional bakeries have long fulfilled that role for locals;
at such places, which are on practically every street corner, you can pick
up a burek for as little as 10 Kn apiece.

$$$$ ✕ **Atlanta Caffè Restaurant.** One of the first restaurants to open among
the myriad thriving cafés that line Tkalčićeva, Atlanta boasts a stylish
interior with warm terra-cotta walls hung with enormous gilt-framed
mirrors. You might begin with the risotto with arugula and prosciutto,
followed by steak with truffles, rounded off with tiramisu. ⊠ *Tkalčićeva
65, Gornji Grad* ☎ *01/481–3848* ▭ *AE, DC, MC, V.*

$$$–$$$$ ✕ **Dubravkin Put.** Nestled in a verdant dale in Tuškanac Park, a 15-min-
Fodor's Choice ute walk from the center in a low-rise building that might be mistaken
★ for a ranch-style house, this prestigious fish restaurant specializes in
dishes from the Dubrovnik area, with the house favorites including
buzara (stew prepared with shellfish and scampi and/or fish) and sea
bass fillets in saffron and scampi sauce as well as appetizers like avo-
cado with scampi, not to mention a few meat delicacies. The dining
room is light and airy, with candlelit tables, a wooden floor, palmlike
little trees, and colorful abstract art. In the warm weather there's out-
door seating on a spacious, leafy terrace, and a playground just outside
invites children to scamper about while parents rest on benches. Res-
ervations are recommended, but only on weekdays, as the Dubravkin
Put is a popular venue for business dinners. ⊠ *Dubravkin put 2, Gornji
Grad* ☎ *01/483–4975 or 01/483–4970* ▭ *AE, DC, MC, V* ⊙ *Closed
July 20–Aug. 20.*

$$$–$$$$ ✕ **Gostionica Purger.** A flashing neon sign out front seems to suggest you
★ are passing by a diner. Not so. Wildly popular with locals but with
a faded, elegant air, this is the sort of restaurant that reminds you of
what Zagreb must have been like before the Communists. The food is

top-notch, and with animated conversations all around you (at snugly fitting tables—but then this is part of the appeal) and bright yellow walls adorned with historical sketches of Zagreb, this is one fine restaurant. The menu includes everything from goulash with white-wine sauce, on the low end of the price scale, to *domaće krvavice* (black pudding) at the middle, to suckling pig on the spit at the top. ⊠ *Petrinjska 33, Donji Grad* ☎ *01/481–0713 or 01/481–8631* ⊟ *AE, DC, MC, V* ⊘ *Closed Sun.*

$$$–$$$$ ✗ **Paviljon.** This chic restaurant—with its round, colonnaded dining
Fodor's Choice room and grand piano—occupies the ground floor of the charming
★ 19th-century Art Pavilion, which faces the train station from across a wide, green mall. The Italian-inspired menu includes dishes such as tagliatelle with zucchini and saffron sauce; lamb cutlets with basmati rice and almonds; and grilled swordfish. The wine list is equally impressive, with a choice of Croatian, Italian, and French vintages. ⊠ *Tomislavov trg 22, Donji Grad* ☎ *01/481–3066* ⊟ *AE, DC, MC, V* ⊘ *Closed Sun.*

$$$–$$$$ ✗ **Pod Gričkim Topom.** This cozy, endearingly rustic yet elegant restau-
★ rant, built into a stone wall on the hillside up a modest flight of steps from the Pansion Jägerhorn, on Ilica, and close to the funicular station in Gornji Grad, affords stunning views over the city rooftops. Dalmatian cooking predominates, with dishes such as *Jadanske lignje na žaru* (grilled Adriatic squid) and *crni rižoto od sipe* (cuttlefish-ink risotto) appreciated by locals and visitors alike. ⊠ *Zakmardijeve stube 5, Gornji Grad* ☎ *01/483–3607* ⚭ *Reservations essential* ⊟ *AE, DC, MC, V.*

$$$–$$$$ ✗ **Riblji Restoran Korčula.** As suggested by the *riblji* fish) in its full name, the Korčula is a reliable choice for fresh seafood, including Dalmatian-style cod and tuna with mangold (i.e., swiss chard). The menu also has a sprinkling of meat dishes, such as stewed beef in wine sauce with dumplings. A five-minute walk from the main square and popular with locals, this cozy restaurant is a moderately appealing place to sit back and fuel up for an hour or two, adorned as it is with black-and-white photos and fishnets hanging from the ceiling. ⊠ *Nikole Tesle 17, Donji Grad* ☎ *01/487–2159* ⊟ *AE, DC, MC, V* ⊘ *Closed first 3 wks of Aug.*

$$–$$$ ✗ **Baltazar.** In a courtyard a 10-minute walk uphill beyond the cathe-
★ dral, just beyond Pizzeria 2, Baltazar is best known for classic Balkan dishes such as *ražnjići* (pork on the spit), *čevapčići* (spiced, ground-meat kebabs), and *zapečeni grah* (oven-baked beans). The interior is elegant albeit slightly smoky, and the spacious courtyard has leaf-shaded seating. ⊠ *Nova Ves 4, Gornji Grad* ☎ *01/424–127* ⊟ *AE, DC, MC, V* ⊘ *Closed Sun.*

$$–$$$ ✗ **Stari Fijaker.** In this old-fashioned restaurant with vaulted ceilings, wood-paneled walls, and crisp white table linens, the only thing that sometimes mars the ambience is the loud TV turned to a pop-music channel. The restaurant is just off Ilica, a five-minute walk from the main square on a cobblestone side street. The menu features carefully presented traditional Croatian dishes such as *zagorskajuha* (Zagorje-style potato soup with ham and mushrooms), *pečena teletina* (roast

veal), *punjene paprike* (stuffed peppers), and even ostrich steak. ✉*Mesnička 6, Donji Grad* ☎*01/483–3829* ▱*AE, DC, MC, V.*

$–$$$ ✗ **Boban.** Just down the road from the Hotel Dubrovnik, Boban is not
★   only a street-level bar but also a restaurant in the large vaulted cellar space below. Specializing in pasta dishes, it is extremely popular with locals, so be prepared to line up for a table since reservations are not accepted. The owner, Zvonimir Boban, was captain of the Croatian national football team during the 1998 World Cup. ✉*Gajeva 9, Donji Grad* ☎*01/481–1549* ▱*AE, DC, MC, V.*

$–$$ ✗ **Pizzeria 2.** One of Zagreb's best pizzeria and pasta joints, this place is popular with the young crowd looking for a budget meal. Wooden tables, vaulted ceilings, and creamy peach walls give you the impression you're in a decked-out cellar even though it's on the ground floor. The restaurant is near the start of Nova Ves, just beyond Kaptol. ✉*Nova Ves 2, Gornji Grad* ☎*01/466–8888* ▱*AE, DC, MC, V.*

WHERE TO STAY

Zagreb offers a good choice of large, expensive hotels well geared to the needs of business travelers. This may be in part because tourists tend to frequent the coast, whereas the corporate crowd sticks to the city. However, for summertime vacationers who choose to check out the capital, this is good news: since so much of the country and indeed Europe are on the coast, Zagreb's "low season," when rates are lowest at many hotels, is from early July through late August. Since 2000 several of the capital's major hotels have come under new ownership and been given complete makeovers, guaranteed to appeal to those seeking mid- to upper-range accommodations.

$$$$ 🏨 **Sheraton Zagreb.** High standards make this modern, six-story hotel, on a small side street but just a 10-minute walk from the city center, a relative bargain. The main draw for tourists will be the luxurious look and feel; at least you can see what you're paying for here, which isn't always the case when you're down on the coast. Rooms are furnished in classical style with muted colors and en-suite marble bathrooms. Behind the glass facade are excellent sports, business, and entertainment facilities. Pros: Top-notch facilities and services, indoor pool, superb dining options. Cons: 30-minute walk from the main square, pricey, not exactly cozy. ✉*Kneza Borne 2, Donji Grad, 10000* ☎*01/455–3535* 🖷*01/455–3035* ⊕*www.sheraton.com/zagreb* ⬳*312 rooms, 29 suites* ⚫*In-room: kitchen (some), refrigerator (some), DVD, Wi-Fi. In-hotel: 2 restaurants, room service, bar, café, pool, gym, some pets allowed, public Internet, parking (fee), no-smoking rooms* ▱*AE, DC, MC, V* ⑩*BP.*

$$$–$$$$ 🏨 **Regent Esplanade.** This beautiful hotel, diagonally across from the
Fodor's Choice   train station, was built in 1925 for travelers on the original *Orient*
★   *Express.* Louis Armstrong, Elizabeth Taylor, Charles Lindbergh, Orson Welles, Woody Allen, Queen Elizabeth II, and Richard Nixon have all stayed here, among other famous names, many of whom left photos for the celebrity wall downstairs. Regular renovations, the last one in 2004, have only enhanced the hotel's luxury and elegance. From

its immaculate, Habsburg-era lobby to its dining room replete with huge, resplendent chandeliers; from its domed ballroom to its spacious outdoor terrace with sweeping views, the Esplanade remains adored by business travelers and tourists alike. The spacious, high-ceilinged rooms and marble bathrooms won't disappoint, and you'll love the special touches like a glass of champagne on check-in and classical music playing in the hallways. Rates for the smallest doubles during Zagreb's low season (early July to late August) are surprisingly affordable. Pros: Unmitigated luxury, right by the train station, great fitness center. Cons: Pricey and formal (i.e., not a place to shuffle around in your cutoffs), smallish lobby. ⊠*Mihanovićeva 1, Donji Grad, 10000* ☎*01/456–6666* ᖴ*01/456–6050* ⊕*www.regenthotels.com* ᖴ*209 rooms, 12 suites* ♿*In-room: safe, DVD (on request), Wi-Fi, Ethernet, refrigerator. In-hotel: 2 restaurants, room service, gym, Wi-Fi, public Internet, parking (fee)* ☰*AE, DC, MC, V* ⦿*EP.*

$$ ⊡ **Best Western Premier Hotel Astoria.** The Hotel Astoria reopened with a new name and a luxurious new look in March 2005 after a six-month makeover. Less than 5 minutes by foot from the train station and 10 minutes from downtown, it offers bright, modern rooms with the silky bedspreads and partly marble bathrooms that meet the requirements of its Premier category. It may be Zagreb's first hotel in which the shutters roll up automatically when you enter your room—do remember that before tearing your clothes off in a fit of passion. The standard rooms are on the small side; the executive rooms, which have king-size beds, are more spacious but also quite a bit more expensive. Pros: Good location on a quiet side street midway between the train station and the main square; marble bathrooms with excellent amenities; top-notch 24-hour business center. Cons: Smallish rooms, no health facilities or pool. ⊠*Petrinjska 71, Donji Grad, 10000* ☎*01/480–8900 or 01/480–8910* ᖴ*01/480–8908 or 01/481–7053* ⊕*www.bestwestern. com* ᖴ*100 rooms, 2 suites* ♿*In-room: safe, Ethernet, Wi-Fi, refrigerator. In-hotel: restaurant, bar, room service, laundry service, meeting rooms, Wi-Fi, public Internet, some pets allowed, no-smoking rooms* ☰*AE, DC, MC, V* ⦿*BP.*

$$ ⊡ **Hotel Dubrovnik.** Claiming the most central location in the city, just
★ off Trg Bana Jelačića, Hotel Dubrovnik has been popular with business travelers and tourists alike since opening back in 1929. The garish mirrored-glass facade conceals bright, modern, smallish but perfectly acceptable rooms. Beyond its other amenities, the hotel is also home to one of Zagreb's most popular hangouts, the Cafe Dubrovnik, which has a great view of the main square. Pros: Right off the main square, near shops and restaurants, numerous amenities. Cons: Smallish rooms, low on historic grandeur. ⊠*Gajeva 1, Donji Grad, 10000* ☎*01/486–3500 or 01/486–3555* ᖴ*01/486–3550* ⊕*www.hotel-dubrovnik.hr* ᖴ*266 rooms, 8 suites* ♿*In-room: safe, refrigerator, dial-up, room service. In-hotel: restaurant, room service, bar, Wi-Fi, public Internet, parking (fee), laundry facilities, laundry service, some pets allowed, no-smoking rooms* ☰*AE, DC, MC, V* ⦿*BP.*

$$ ⊡ **Palace Hotel Zagreb.** Built in 1891 as the Schlessinger Palace and con-
★ verted in 1907 to become the city's first hotel, the Palace Hotel offers

romantic, old-fashioned comfort. The spacious rooms, which were all completely renovated in 2005 and 2006, have modern beds and furnishings but retain their original Art Nouveau look with moldings and long drapes. Golden hues predominate. Overlooking a green square between the train station and the city center—and only a five-minute walk from either—the Palace is best known by locals for the street-level, Viennese-style café. Pros: Great location across from parklike Strossmayerov trg and close to Trg bana J. Jelačića; historical ambience; excellent café; 60% of rooms no-smoking. Cons: No health facilities or pool. ✉*Strossmayerov trg 10, Donji Grad, 10000* ☎*01/489–9618 or 01/492–0530* 📠*01/481–1358* 🌐*www.palace.hr* *123 rooms, 5 suites* *In-room: safe, Ethernet, Wi-Fi, refrigerator. In-hotel: restaurant, room service, laundry service, Wi-Fi, public Internet, some pets allowed, no-smoking rooms* 💳*AE, DC, MC, V* *BP.*

$ **Hotel Central.** On the opposite side of the train station from the Regent Esplanade—and in one boring, concrete block of a building—the Central is convenient rather than quaint. The spacious rooms are simply furnished in shades of blue, and the staff is friendly and efficient. Pros: Close to the train station, spacious rooms, friendly service. Cons: Rooms facing the street get noise from passing trams, a tad pricey for what you get, few frills, dull-looking building. ✉*Branimirova 3, Donji Grad, 10000* ☎*01/484–1122 or 01/484–0555* 📠*01/484–1304* 🌐*www.hotel-central.hr* *76 rooms, 3 suites* *In-room: Wi-Fi, refrigerator (some). In-hotel: meeting room, public Internet, bar, laundry service* 💳*AE, DC, MC, V* *BP.*

$ **Vila Tina.** If you prefer a quiet environment and don't mind the somewhat tacky look of the lobby (pseudo-classical statuettes, anyone?), then this family-run hotel may be just for you. It's well outside the center of town on a peaceful side street near Maksimir Park and a short walk from forested hills. Each room is individually furnished with surprising taste, considering the lobby, and personal touches like fresh fruit and flowers. There's a good restaurant with a summer garden. Pros: Cozier than big hotels downtown, near Maksimim Park and hiking opportunities in the hills. Cons: A 90-minute hike from the main square, few amenities. ✉*Bukovačka c 213, Donji Grad, 10000* ☎*01/244–5138* 📠*01/244–5204* 🌐*www.vilatina.com* *14 rooms* *In-room: \ Wi-Fi, refrigerator. In-hotel: restaurant, Wi-Fi, public Internet, parking (no fee)* 💳*AE, DC, MC, V* *BP.*

¢ **Hotel Sliško.** This small hotel is just a 5-minute walk from the bus station and a 15-minute walk from the center. Rooms are smart and functional, and there's a bar and breakfast room. It's normally fully booked during trade fairs (and rates are 20% more then), so check for dates well in advance. Cash payments yield a 10% discount. Pros: Reasonably priced, near the bus station, cozier than big downtown hotels. Cons: A 45-minute walk (or 15-minute tram ride) from the main square, small bathrooms, few frills. ✉*Bunićeva 7, Donji Grad, 10000* ☎*01/619–4210 or 01/618–4777* 📠*01/619–4223* 🌐*www.slisko.hr* *15 rooms, 3 apartments* *In-room: refrigerator, Wi-Fi. In-hotel: restaurant, bar, public Internet, no elevator* 💳*AE, DC, MC, V* *BP.*

NIGHTLIFE & THE ARTS

Climbing full-steam ahead out of the economic depression caused by the war, Zagreb now has a lively entertainment scene. Bars, clubs, and cinemas are predominantly frequented by the city's student population, whereas the concert hall and theater remain the domain of the older generation. For information about what's on, pick up a free copy of the monthly *Events and Performances,* published by the city tourist board.

NIGHTLIFE

BARS AND NIGHTCLUBS **BP Jazz Club** (⊠*Teslina 4, Donji Grad* ☎*01/481–4444* ⊕*www.bpclub. hr*), the capital's top venue for live jazz, is a smoky basement bar. **Bulldog** (⊠*Bogovićeva 6, Donji Grad* ☎*01/481–7393*) is a popular split-level café-cum-wine-bar with a large summer terrace. **Maraschino** (⊠*Margaretska 1, Donji Grad* ☎*01/481–2612*), named after Zadar's distinguished cherry liqueur, is a sleek and extremely popular club that's usually filled to the gills (especially on weekends) with young people come to listen, and smoke, to loud and funky tunes by live bands or DJs. **Old Pharmacy** (⊠*Andrije Hebranga 11a, Donji Grad* ☎*01/492– 1912*), a peaceful pub with CNN on television and a selection of English-language newspapers, also has a nonsmoking side room. **Pivnica Medvedgrad** (⊠*Savska 56, Donji Grad* ☎*01/617–7110*) is a beer hall and microbrewery serving the best ale in town.

DISCOS **Aquarius** (⊠*Aleja Mateja Ljubeka bb, Jarun* ☎*01/364–0231* ⊕*www. aquarius.hr*) is Zagreb's top club for dancing, especially for disco and techno music. It overlooks the beach at *Malo jezero,* the smaller of the two interconnected lakes that make up Lake Jarun, 4 km (2½ mi) from the city center. **Saloon** (⊠*Tuškanac 1a, Gornji Grad* ☎*01/483–4835*) is the city's most glamorous club, where you can rub shoulders with the stars and dance not only to commercial as well as Croatian techno but also, once a week, to classic rock.

THE ARTS

Broadway Tkalča (⊠*Nova Ves 11, Gornji Grad* ☎*01/466–7686*) is Croatia's first multiplex cinema, in the Centar Kaptol shopping complex, wedged in a serene, parklike atmosphere a 10-minute walk north of the main cathedral, first along Kaptol and then onto Nova Ves. Most foreign films (including those from the United States) are shown in their original language with Croatian subtitles. The **Hrvatsko Narodno Kazalište** (*Croatian National Theater* ⊠*Trg Maršala Tita 15, Donji Grad* ☎*01/488–8417* ⊕*www.hnk.hr*), a beautiful 19th-century building, hosts classical and contemporary dramas, opera, and ballet performances. **Koncertna Dvorana Vatroslav Lisinski** (*Vatroslav Lisinski Concert Hall* ⊠*Stjepana Radića 4, Donji Grad* ☎*01/612–1166* ⊕*www.lisinski.hr*), a large, modern complex with two auditoriums, is Zagreb's top venue for orchestral- and classical-music concerts.

SHOPPING

Although Zagreb, for all its other attractions, might not be a shopping mecca, a walk down the bustling Ilica or other nearby streets will reveal plenty of stores chock-full of the latest fashions. Frankopanska particularly is turning into something of a fashion avenue, with labels like Lacoste, Cacharel, and the British design duo Gharari Štrok. Don't pass up the chance to stroll through the beautiful Oktogon shopping arcade. Its long, bright yellow, spacious hall, with elaborate wrought-iron gates at each end and lovely glass ceilings from 1901, connects Ilica 5 with Trg Petra Preradovića and offers more than a few high-class shops along the way.

Several blocks north of the the cathedral, in a parklike setting between Nova Ves and Tkalčićeva, is the **Centar Kaptol** (⊠*Nova Ves 11, Gornji Grad*), whose stores include Marks & Spencer, Kenzo, and Max & Co. For an authentic Croatian shopping experience, visit the **Dolac open-air market** (⊠*Trg Bana Jelačića, Gornji Grad*), where besides fresh fruit and vegetables there are also a number of arts-and-crafts stalls. It's open weekdays 7 to 4 and weekends until noon.

Ties may not be the most original of gifts, but they are uniquely Croatian. During the 17th century, Croatian mercenaries who fought in France sported narrow, silk neck scarfs, which soon became known to the French as *cravat* (from the Croatian *hrvat*). At **Croata** (⊠*Ilica 5 [within the Oktogon arcade], Donji Grad* ☎*01/481–4600* ⊕*www.croata.hr* ⊠*Kaptol 13, Gornji Grad*) you can buy "original Croatian ties" in presentation boxes, accompanied by a brief history of the tie. Housed in a tastefully arranged, vaulted brick cellar, **Vinoteka Bornstein** (⊠*Kaptol 19, Gornji Grad* ☎*01/481–2361*) stocks a wide range of quality Croatian wines, olive oils, and truffle products.

ZAGREB ESSENTIALS

AIR TRAVEL

There are no direct flights between the United States and Zagreb, but Croatia Airlines and several major European carriers fly to Zagreb from Amsterdam, Brussels, Frankfurt, London, Paris, Vienna, and other cities. Croatia Airlines operates at least two flights daily to Split (45 minutes) and three flights daily to Dubrovnik (55 minutes). Through summer, there is also daily service to Prague (1 hour, 30 minutes) and flights several times a week to Warsaw (1 hour, 40 minutes). For airline contact information, see ⇨By Air *in* Croatia Essentials, at the end of this chapter.

AIRPORTS & TRANSFERS

Zagreb Pleso Airport (ZAG) is in Pleso, 17 km (10 mi) southeast of the city. A regular shuttle bus runs from the airport to the main bus station every 30 minutes from 7 AM to 8 PM and from the main bus station to the airport from 6 AM to 7:30 PM. A one-way ticket costs 30 Kn, and the trip takes 30 minutes. By taxi, expect to pay 150 Kn to 200 Kn to make the same journey; the trip will be slightly faster, about 20 minutes.

Information Airport bus (☎ *01/615–7992*). **Zagreb Pleso Airport** (☎ *01/626–5222 general information, 01/456–2229 lost and found* ⊕ *www.zagreb-airport. hr*).

BUS TRAVEL

Regular coach service to destinations all over mainland Croatia departs from the capital. The traveling time is 6 hours from Zagreb to Split, 10½ hours from Zagreb to Dubrovnik. There are also daily international bus lines to Slovenia (Ljubljana), Hungary (Barcs and Nagykanisza), Yugoslavia (Belgrade), Austria (Graz), Germany (Munich, Stuttgart, Frankfurt, Dortmund, Cologne, and Dusseldorf), and Switzerland (Zurich). Timetable information is available from the main bus station, a 20-minute walk from the center.

Bus Information **Zagreb Bus Station** (✉ *Av M Držića, Donji Grad* ☎ *060/313–333, 01/600–8607, or 01/600–8605* ⊕ *www.akz.hr*).

BUS & TRAM TRAVEL WITHIN ZAGREB

An extensive network of city buses and trams—in the center of town, almost exclusively trams—runs both during the day (4 AM–11:45 PM) and at night (11:35 PM to 3:45 AM). Tickets cost 6.50 Kn if you buy them from a newspaper kiosk, or 8 Kn from the driver. A full-day ticket (18 Kn) available at some kiosks is valid until 4 AM the next morning. As an alternative, for 90 Kn you can buy the Zagreb Card, which covers public transport within the city limits for three days and offers substantial discounts at various museums and other cultural venues. After you board the bus or tram, you must validate your ticket with a time stamp; tickets are good for 1½ hours and are transferable in the same direction. If you are caught without a valid ticket, you will be fined 150 Kn, payable on the spot.

Bus Information **ZET** (*Zagreb Transport Authority* ☎ *01/660–0442* ⊕ *www.zet.hr*).

CAR RENTALS

Prices vary, and you will probably pay less if you rent from a local company that's not part of an international chain; it's best to shop around. A small car (e.g., Opel Corsa or Fiat Uno) costs at least 400 Kn per day or 2,100 Kn per week. A slightly larger car (e.g., Opel Astra or Fiat Punto) costs more like 550 Kn per day or 2,700 Kn per week. A large car (e.g., Opal Astra Automatic) costs closer to 800 Kn per day or 4,200 Kn per week; automatic transmission is rarely available on smaller cars. These prices include CDW (collision damage waiver) and TP (theft protection) but not PAI (personal accident insurance) and allow for unlimited mileage. If you drive one-way (say, from Zagreb to Dubrovnik), there is an additional drop-off charge, but it depends on the type of car and the number of days you are renting.

Agencies **An Nova** (✉ *Prilaz Rudolfa Frizira bbDonji Grad, Zagreb* ☎ *01/456–2531* ⊕ *www.an-nova.hr*). **Avis** (✉ *Sheraton Zagreb, Kneza Borne 2, Donji Grad, Zagreb* ☎ *062/222–226 central reservations line, or 01/467–6111* ⊕ *www.avis.com.hr* ✉ *Zagreb Airport, Pleso* ☎ *01/626–5840*). **Budget** (✉ *Sheraton Zagreb, Kneza Borne 2, Donji Grad, Zagreb* ☎ *01/455–6936* ⊕ *www.budget.hr* ✉ *Zagreb Airport, Pleso* ☎ *01/626–5854*). **Dollar Rent A Car & Thrifty Car Rental** (✉ *Sub*

Rosa, Donji Grad, Zagreb ☎ *01/483–6466 or 021/399–000* ⊕ *www.subrosa.hr* ✉ *Zagreb Airport, Pleso* ☎ *01/626–5333).* **Europcar** (✉ *Pierottijeva 5, Donji Grad, Zagreb* ☎ *01/483–6045* ⊕ *www.europcar.com* ✉ *Zagreb Airport, Pleso* ☎ *01/626–5333).* **Hertz** (✉ *Ulica grada Vukovara 274, Donji Grad, Zagreb* ☎ *062/727–277 central reservations line, or 01/618–8500 main office in Zagreb* ⊕ *www.hertz.hr* ✉ *Zagreb Airport, Pleso* ☎ *01/456–2635).* **National** (✉ *Westin Zagreb, Kršnjavoja 1, Donji Grad, Zagreb* ☎ *0800/443–322 central reservations line, or 01/481–1764 (desk at the Westin Zagreb hotel)* ⊕ *www.nationalcar.hr* ✉ *Zagreb Airport, Pleso* ☎ *0800/443–322 or 01/621–5924).* **Sixt** (✉ *Trg Krešimira Ćosića 9, Donji Grad, Zagreb* ☎ *01/301–5303* ⊕ *www.e-sixt.com* ✉ *Zagreb Airport, Pleso* ☎ *01/621–9900).*

CAR TRAVEL

While staying in the capital you are certainly better off without a car. But if you wish to visit the nearby hills of Zagorje, or go farther afield to the Međimurje region, a vehicle is helpful unless you want to be riding to a different attraction by bus each day.

INTERNET

Zagreb has about half a dozen Internet cafés within a short walk of the main square. Our favorite is the reasonably priced and spacious Sublink Internet Centar, set far back in a courtyard in a onetime apartment and with plenty of machines. Here you can surf the Net for 0.245 Kn per minute, which adds up to 14.70 Kn per hour. There are a couple of log-on venues along Tkalčića, but prices tend to be higher.

Information **Art Internet Caffee** (✉ *Tkalčića 18, Gornji Grad, Zagreb* ☎ *1/481–1050).* **Surf Internet Point** (✉ *Tkalčića 13/II, 2nd floor, Gornji Grad, Zagreb* ☎ *01/169–8586).* **Sublink Internet Centar** (✉ *Teslina 12, Donji Grad, Zagreb* ☎ *01/481–1329).*

TAXIS

You can find taxi ranks in front of the bus and train stations, near the main square, and in front of the larger hotels. It is also possible to order a radio taxi. All drivers are bound by law to run a meter, starting at 19 Kn and increasing by 7 Kn per kilometer (half mile). Each piece of luggage incurs a further 3 Kn. The night tariff is 20% more and is in effect from 10 PM to 5 AM; the same tariff applies to Sunday and holidays.

Contacts **Radio Taxi** (☎ *01/660–0671 or 01/660–1235* ⊕ *www.radio-taksi-zagreb.hr).*

TOUR OPTIONS

The tourist-information center closest to the Zagreb train station organizes amusing and informative guided tours of the city. Every day of the week the Ibus travel agency offers combination bus-and-walking guided tours of the city center for between 165 Kn and 225 Kn a person (minimum five people); call a day in advance to reserve. It also provides tours of attractions farther afield, including Veliki Tabor, Trakošćan and Varaždin, and Plitvice Lakes National Park. For a state-of-the-art experience you can try the Segway CityTour from mid-April through mid-October. The 80-minute "Welcome Tour" takes place daily at 11 AM and costs 233 Kn per person; the 130-minute "All Around Tour" takes place daily at 5 PM and costs 333 Kn per person (minimum two people for all tours). Show up 15 minutes before departure at the main entrance of the Regent Esplanade Hotel *(⇨Where to Stay)*.

Contacts Ibus (✉ *Kranjčevićeva 29 [in the Hotel Laguna], Donji Grad, Zagreb* ☎ *01/369–4333 or 01/364–8633* ⊕ *www.ibus.hr).* **Segway CityTour** (✉ *Antuna Štrbana 6 (Segway dealer and main office; tours meet in front of the Regent Esplanade Hotel), Donji Grad, Zagreb* ☎ *01/301–0390* ⊕ *www.segway.hr).* **Zagreb Tourist Information** (✉ *Trg Nikole Šubića Zrinskoga 14, Donji Grad, Zagreb* ☎ *01/492–1645).*

TRAIN TRAVEL

Zagreb's main train station lies in Donji Grad, a 10-minute walk from the center. There are daily international lines to and from Budapest (Hungary), Belgrade (Yugoslavia), Munich (Germany), Vienna (Austria), and Venice (Italy).

From Zagreb, there are four trains daily to Split in Dalmatia (8 hours) and five trains daily to Rijeka in Kvarner (3½ hours). The easiest way to get to Varaždin from Zagreb is by rail, with some 15 trains daily. Travel time is about 2½ hours and costs 53 Kn each way. About 10 trains run daily between Zagreb and Karlovac (with a like number of buses), in just under an hour and for a one-way fare of 28 Kn. If you don't have wheels, your best bet reaching Sisak is by rail, with 15 trains daily from Zagreb that take just over an hour.

Train Stations Zagreb Train Station (✉ *Trg Kralja Tomislava, Donji Grad, Zagreb* ☎ *060/333–444 domestic train information [nationwide number], 01/481–1892 international train information [nationwide number]* ⊕ *www.hznet.hr).* **Čakovec Train Station** (✉ *Kolodvorska 2).* **Karlovac Train Station** (✉ *Vilima Reinera 3).* **Varaždin Train Station** (✉ *Frana Supila).*

VISITOR INFORMATION

Zagreb's main tourist-information center overlooks the main square, Trg Bana Jelačića. It's open weekdays 8:30 AM to 8 PM, Saturday 9 to 5, and Sunday 10 to 2. A smaller office is a tad closer to the train station and open weekdays 9 to 5. The Croatian Angels information hotline, sponsored by the Croatian National Tourist Board, can be called from anywhere in the country for any advice at all.

Contacts Croatian Angels (☎ *062/999–999* ⊕ *www.croatia.hr).* **Zagreb Tourist Information** (✉ *Trg Bana Jelačića 11, Donji Grad, Zagreb* ☎ *01/481–4051 or 01/481–4052* ⊕ *www.zagreb-touristinfo.hr* ✉ *Trg Nikole Šubića Zrinskog 14, Donji Grad, Zagreb* ☎ *01/492–1645).*

SIDE TRIPS FROM ZAGREB

The observatory at Sljeme is the easiest excursion from Zagreb. Northwest of Zagreb, beyond the Medvednica hills, lies a pastoral region known as Zagorje. The scenery is calm and enchanting: redbrick villages, such as Kumrovec, are animated with ducks and chickens, and the hillsides are inlaid with vineyards and orchards. Medieval hilltop castles, including Veliki Tabor and Dvor Trakoščan, survey the surrounding valleys. To the northeast of Zagreb is the charming medieval town of Varaždin.

SLJEME

5 km (3 mi) north of Zagreb by tram and cable car.

A favorite excursion to the outskirts of Zagreb is to the heights of Sljeme, the peak of **Mt. Medvednica,** at 3,363 feet. You can reach it taking Tram 14 (direction Mihaljevac), all the way to the terminal stop, where you should change to Tram 15 (direction Dolje), also to its terminal stop. From there a cable car operates hourly for the 20-minute journey to the top of the mountain for breathtaking views over the surrounding countryside. It's an ideal place for picnicking, but you may wish to save your appetite for dinner at one of the excellent restaurants on the road home.

On the southwest flank of the summit is a reconstructed fortress called **Medvegrad.** The original was built in the 13th century by Bishop Filip of Zagreb, and after a succession of distinguished owners over the next two centuries, was destroyed in an earthquake in 1590. You can wander around the outside (for free) and take in great views of Zagreb. It's a one-hour trek to the fortress from the cable car, or you can reach it more directly by taking Bus 102 from Britansk trg in central Zagreb (just off Ilica, a 20-minute walk west of Trg Bana Josipa Jelačića) to the "Blue Church" in Šestine, and hiking some 40 minutes uphill from there. Take Trail 12, which is off the paved road past the church cemetery. ✉*Dolje* ☎*01/458–0394* 💵*Cable car 17 Kn round-trip* ⊗*Daily 8–8.*

WHERE TO EAT

$$$ ✕**Stari Puntijar.** On the road between Zagreb and Sljeme, Stari Puntijar is renowned for game and traditional 19th-century Zagreb dishes such as *podolac* (ox medallions in cream and saffron), *orehnjaca* (walnut loaf), and *makovnjaca* (poppy-seed cake). The wine list is excellent, and the interior design is marked by trophies, hunting weapons, old paintings, and big chandeliers. ✉*Gračanka c 65, Medveščak, Zagreb* ☎*01/467–5500* ▤*AE, DC, MC, V.*

STUBIČKE TOPLICE

37 km (23 mi) north of Zagreb.

Established in 1805 on the foundations of a Roman-era thermal bath and expanded into a full-fledged complex in 1930, this peaceful spa at the northern edge of the Medvednica hills is where the capital's residents go to soak away those nerves and ailments in temps ranging from 45°C to 65°C (113°F to 149°F). Set at the edge of a large park replete with tall spruce trees, the **Matija Gubec** hotel is the place to go to give it a try yourself—though you needn't stay overnight at this complex of six beige, concrete, interconnected ranch-house-like buildings. After paying a small admission fee, you get access to the complex's eight outdoor

Excursions
from Zagreb

HUNGARY

Titovo
Velenje

Slov.
Bistrice

Maribor

Drava

Ormož

A1

2

Ptuj

2

Varaždin

Drava

E71

A4

Dravinja

1

2

Rogaška
Slatina

◆ Trakošćan

2

Krapina

Celje

A1

Veliki Tabor ◆

Krapinske
Toplice

5

Sava

Kumrovec

24

A2 E59

Marija Bistrica

Tuheljske
Toplice

**Stubičke
Toplice**

29

**SLOVENIJA
(SLOVENIA)**

5

Krško

A2

E71

A4

Novo
Mesto

H1

Zaprešić

Sljeme

★ **ZAGREB**

Sesvete

Samobor

A3

Dugo Selo

Ivanić
Grad

A3 E70

Velika
Gorića

**HRAVATSKA
(CROATIA)**

Kupa

A1

Karlovac

9

6

Petrinja

Sisak

Čigoč

Sava

A6

Duga
Resa

1

6

Korana

6

Glina

TO
JASÉNOVAC

Una

E71

1

Velika
Kladuša

6

Bosanski
Novi

4

**Nacionalni
Park Plitvice
Jezero**

Plitvice

1

**BOSNA I HERCEGOVINA
(BOSNIA-HERCEGOVINA)**

0   20 mi

0   20 km

Plitvička
Ljeskovac

Bihać

6

pools as well as the hotel's indoor pool, sauna, and fitness facility. The rooms (€72) are decent, with cable TV and phones but otherwise have no frills and no air-conditioning. If you are looking for a bite to eat, Restaurant Bilikum, across the street from the hotel, is a good choice. ⊠ *Viktora Šipeka 31, Stubičke Toplice* ☎ *049/282–501* ⊕ *www.hotelmgubec.com* ⊠ *45 Kn (40 Kn after 3* PM*); sauna only, 20 Kn for 20 mins* ⊙ *Weekdays 7* AM*–10* PM*, weekends 7* AM*–midnight.*

KUMROVEC

★ *40 km (25 mi) northwest of Zagreb.*

The former Yugoslavia's late president Josip Broz Tito was born here in 1892, and his childhood home has been turned into a small memorial museum. In the courtyard of his birthplace stands an imposing bronze likeness of him by Antun Augustinčić.

☾ The old quarter of Kumrovec, known as **Kumrovec Staro Selo** (*Kumrovec Old Village*), is an open-air museum with beautifully restored thatched cottages and wooden farm buildings, orchards, and a stream giving a lifelike reconstruction of 19th-century rural life. On weekends craftsmen, including a blacksmith, a candle maker, and others, demonstrate their skills. ⊠ *Kumrovec* ☎ *049/225–830* ⊕ *www.mdc.hr/kumrovec* ⊠ *20 Kn* ⊙ *Apr.–Sept., daily 9–7; Oct.–Mar., daily 9–4.*

VELIKI TABOR

★ *15 km (9 mi) north of Kumrovec.*

On a lofty hilltop stands the massive fortress of Veliki Tabor. The main pentagonal core of the building dates back to the 12th century, whereas the side towers were added in the 15th century as protection against the Turks. The colonnaded galleries of the interior cast sublime shadows in moonlight. Nine buses daily will get you here from Zagreb's main bus station in 2½ hours for 69 Kn one-way; but after getting off you have a 3-km (2-mi) walk still ahead of you. Hence, as true more generally of site-hopping in the Zagorje region, a rental car may come in handy. ⊠ *Desinić* ☎ *049/343–052* ⊕ *www.veliki-tabor.hr* ⊠ *20 Kn* ⊙ *Daily 10–6.*

WHERE TO EAT

$$–$$$ ✗ **Grešna Gorica.** Visiting this rustic tavern is like stepping into a friend's
★ home. That said, your friend's home is unlikely to have a stuffed fawn and a pair of *kuna* (martens, the national currency's namesake) on the wall (this monetary history of kuna dates from the days when the fur of this large, weasel-like creature was in fact a currency). All produce used here is supplied by local farmers, and the menu features typical Zagorje dishes, including *zagorski štrukli* (baked cheese dumplings) and *pura s mlincima* (turkey with savory pastries). The garden affords sublime views down onto Veliki Tabor fortress. ⊠ *Desinić* ☎ *049/343– 001* ▤ *No credit cards.*

WHERE TO STAY

$ ⌨ **Dvorac Bežanec.** There's a lovely old manor house waiting for you—a
Fodor'sChoice   15-minute drive east of Veliki Tabor—where you can have your spa-
★   cious room with period furniture and breakfast, too, for less than €100
a night. Owned by various barons since Count Keglević built it in
the 17th century, Bežanec castle got a new lease on life as a luxury
hotel in 1990. Part of its charm is its authenticity, and the furnishings,
while in tip-top, dust-free shape, actually feel like the real, 17th-cen-
tury McCoys. Splendid works by various Croatian artists, including a
whole series of superb naive paintings by Slauko Stolmik, line the halls.
With advance notice, the hotel will pick up guests who arrive by bus in
Veliki Tabor. Any activity, from hot-air balloon rides and horseback-
riding instruction to tennis and archery, can be yours, too, for reasonable fees. Sure, there's no air-conditioning—but was there any in the
18th century? Pros: Historical ambience, spacious rooms, reasonable
rate. Cons: Far from major tourist areas and towns, restaurants, and
shopping; no a/c. ⊠ *Valentinovo 55, 49218, Pregrada* 🕾*049/376–800*
🖷*049/376–810* ⊕*www.bezanec.hr* ⟿*20 rooms, 5 suites* ⚙*In-room:
no a/c, DVD (on request), refrigerator, Wi-Fi, Ethernet. In-hotel: restaurant, room service, tennis court, no elevator, laundry facilities, laundry service, Wi-Fi, public Internet, parking (no fee), some pets allowed,
no-smoking rooms* ▤*AE, DC, MC, V* ⦿*EP.*

VARAŽDIN

70 km (48 mi) northeast of Zagreb.

Situated on a plain just south of the River Drava, Varaždin is the most
harmonious and beautifully preserved baroque town in this corner of
the continent. A vibrant commercial and cultural center, especially in
the 18th century, Varaždin (pop. 50,000) is richly adorned by extraordinary churches and the palaces of the aristocratic families that once
lived here. It was Croatia's capital from 1756 until a devastating fire
in 1776 prompted a move to Zagreb. First mentioned under the name
Garestin in a document by the Hungarian-Croatian king Bela III from
1181, it was declared a free royal town by King Andrew II of Hungary's
Arpad dynasty in 1209 and went on to become an important economic,
social, administrative, and military center. Near the heart of the city, in
a park surrounded by grassy ramparts, the well-preserved castle is the
main attraction. A short walk from the castle, on the outskirts of town,
is one of Europe's loveliest cemeteries, with immense hedges trimmed
and shaped around ornate memorials.

Note that Varaždin's main churches are open only around an hour
before and after mass, which is generally held several times daily, more
often on weekends; the tourist information office can help you contact
individual churches to arrange a look inside at other times.

WHAT TO SEE

Fodor'sChoice   Today a historical museum, Varaždin's main attraction is the massive
★   **Stari Grad** *(Castle),* which assumed its present form in the 16th century
as a state-of-the-art defense fortification against the Turks, complete

with moats, dikes, and bastions with low, round defense towers connected by galleries with openings for firearms. In the ensuing centuries it was often reconstructed by the families that owned it; for more than three centuries, until its 1925 purchase by the city, it belonged to the Erdödy clan. From the 12th century up until 1925, the castle served as the seat of the county prefect. You enter through the 16th-century tower gatehouse, which has a wooden drawbridge, to arrive in the internal courtyard with three levels of open-arched galleries. Indoors, there's an extensive display of antique furniture, with pieces laid out in chronological order and each room representing a specific period. Even if you don't go inside, do take a stroll around the perimeter, along a path that takes you between the outer wall and a ditch that used to be the moat. ⊠*Strossmayerovo Šetalište 7* 🕾*042/210–399* ⊕*www. varazdin.hr* 🎫*15 Kn* ⊗*Oct.–Apr., Tues.–Fri. 10–3, weekends 10–1.*

Consecrated to Varaždin's patron saint in 1761 on the site of an older church, the **Župna Crkva Sv. Nikole** *(Parish Church of St. Nicholas)* is a baroque structure that is more attractive on the outside than the inside. Note the false yet imposing white columns in the facade; the red-tiled, conical steeple; and the sculpture at the foot of the steeple of a firefighting Saint Florian pouring a bucket of water onto a church, presumably an allusion to the fire that devastated Varaždin in 1776. ⊠*Trg slobode 11.*

🌣 Housed in the Herzer Palace, the **Entomološka Zbirka** *(Entomological Collection)* museum has a fascinating presentation of some 1,000 different insects. ⊠*Franjevački trg 6* 🕾*042/210–474* 🎫*20 Kn* ⊗*May–Sept., Tues.–Sun. 10–6; Oct.–Apr., Tues.–Fri. 10–5, weekends 10–1.*

The 16th-century **Lisakova kula** *(Lisak Tower)* is the only part of Varaždin's northern town wall that has been preserved. The wall formed part of the onetime city fortress, but most of it was razed in the early 19th century. Unfortunately, you can't enter the tower. ⊠*Trg Bana Jelačića.*

Gradska Vijećnica *(City Hall)*, one of Europe's oldest city halls, is still in use. This imposing landmark has been the seat of Varaždin's public administration since December 14, 1523. Restored after the great fire of 1776, it received a thorough external makeover in 1793. From April through October you can stop by on a Saturday morning between 11 and noon to watch the changing of the guard, a 250-year tradition that lives on. ⊠*Trg Krajla Tomislava.*

★ Built in 1773 and thoroughly re-landscaped in 1905 by Hermann Haller, a self-taught landscape architect who revolutionized traditional notions of what graveyards should look like, Varaždin's **Gradsko Groblje** *(Town Cemetery)* is as pleasant a place for a restful stroll as it may be, when the time comes, to be laid to rest. Replete with flower beds and rows of tall cedars and linden trees flanking ornate memorials and laid out in geometric patterns, the cemetery sublimely manifests Haller's conviction that each plot should be a "serene, hidden place only hinting at its true purpose, with no clue as to whether its occupant is rich or poor, since all are tended equally, surrounded by every kind of flower...producing perfect harmony for the visitor." Haller himself, who ran the cemetery from 1905 to 1946, is buried here in a rather conspicuous mausoleum. You can reach the cemetery by walking about 10 minutes east of the Castle along Hallerova aleja. ⊠*Hercega* ⊙*May–Sept., daily 7 AM–9 PM; Oct. and Mar.–Apr., daily 7 AM–8 PM, Nov.–Feb., daily 7 AM–5 PM.*

WHERE TO EAT

$$-$$$ ✕**Restoran Zlatna Guska.** In a lovely, vaulted brick cellar with walls orna-
★ mented by coats of arms, the Golden Goose Restaurant makes a good stopping-off point for a quick lunch or a relaxed dinner over a bottle of local wine. Here you'll find not only a whole array of soups hard to get elsewhere, such as cream of nettle, but an impressive salad bar and vegetarian fare such as fried cauliflower in mushroom sauce with sesame seeds. They also serve plenty of seafood and meat. The wood-covered menu has helpful photos of imaginatively named main dishes—"Last Meal of Inquisition Victims" (a soup, actually), "Daggers of Count Brandenburg" (skewered meat with pasta and vegetables), and "Countess Juliana Draškovic's Flower" (a pair of crêpes filled with fruit and topped with powdered sugar and whipped cream)—itself almost worth the trip. ⊠*J. Habdelića 4* ☏*042/213–393* ▭*AE, MC, V.*

$–$$ ✕**Gostionica Grenadir.** Fish is king in this elegant, spacious, red-carpeted cellar restaurant near Trg M. Stančića. Well-prepared dishes include sea bass and trout, but also a good selection of meats and poultry. ⊠*Kranjčevićeva 12* ☏*042/211–131* ▭*AE, DC, MC, V.*

$ ✕**Pizzeria Angelus.** Whether Varaždin's best pizza is here is debatable,
★ but here you can have your pie by candlelight, with soothing background music under brick-arched ceilings to boot. Across the street from a peaceful shaded park, a five-minute walk from the center of town, the Angelus has a huge menu that also includes plenty of pastas and other, more meaty (and pricey) fare, not to mention a half dozen creative salads and lots of beer (including Guinness and Kilkeny). The desserts may sound scrumptious, by the way, but the peaches capelleti, for one, is in the plural only because the single peach at its center—in a bath of cherry sauce and soft, sweet curd and ice cream—has been sparingly sliced in half. ⊠*Alojzija Stepinca 3* ☏*042/303–868* ▭*AE, DC, MC, V.*

NACIONALNI PARK PLITVIČKA JEZERA

Fodor's Choice *135 km (84 mi) southwest of Zagreb.*
★
Triple America's five Great Lakes, shrink them each to manageable size (i.e., 536 acres), give them a good cleaning until they look virtually blue, envelop them in lush green forest with steep hillsides and cliffs all around, and link not just two but all of them with a pint-size Niagara Falls. The result? **Nacionalni Park Plitvička Jezera** *(Plitvice Lakes National Park)*, a UNESCO World Heritage Site and Croatia's top inland natural wonder. And it's not even out of the way. The park is right on the main highway (E71) from Zagreb to Split, but it's certainly worth the three-hour trip from the capital regardless.

This 8,000-acre park is home to 16 beautiful, emerald lakes connected by a series of cascading waterfalls, stretching 8 km (5 mi) through a valley flanked by high, forested hills home to deer, bears, wolves, wild boar, and lots of pretty fish. Thousands of years of sedimentation of calcium, magnesium carbonate, algae, and moss have yielded the natural barriers between the lakes; and since the process is ongoing, new barriers, curtains, stalactites, channels, and cascades are constantly forming and the existing ones changing. The deposited sedimentation, or tufa, also coats the beds and edges of the lakes, yielding their sparkling, azure look. Today, a series of wooden bridges and waterside paths leads through the park. The only downside: as lovely as it is, all of Europe wants to see it, so the trails can get crowded from June through September. That said, there's not a bit of litter along the way—a testament either to respectful visitors or to a conscientious park staff, or both. No camping, no bushwhacking, no picking plants. And no swimming! This is a place to visit, for a day or two, but not to touch. It is, however, well worth the 110 Kn entrance fee.

There are two entrances just off the main road about an hour's walk apart, aptly named entrances 1 and 2. The park's pricey hotels are near Entrance 2, the first entrance you'll encounter if arriving by bus from the coast. However, Entrance 1—the first entrance if you arrive from Zagreb—is typically the start of most one-day excursions, if only because it's within a 20-minute walk of Veliki slap, the big waterfall (256 feet high). Hiking the entire loop that winds its way around the lakes takes six to eight hours, but there are other hikes, ranging from two to four hours. All involve a combination of hiking and being ferried across the larger of the park's lakes by national-park-service boats.

There are cafés near both entrances, but avoid them for anything but coffee, as the sandwiches and strudels leave much to be desired. Instead, buy some of the huge, heavenly strudels sold by locals at nearby stands, where great big blocks of cheese are also on sale. At the boat landing near Entrance 2, by the way, you can rent gorgeous wooden rowboats for 50 Kn per hour. ⊠ *Velika Poljana* 🕾 *053/751–014 or 053/751–015* 🌐 *www.np-plitvicka-jezera.hr* 🖃 *110 Kn for a one-day pass* 🕙 *May–Sept., daily 8–7; Oct.–Apr., daily 9–4.*

ISTRIA

The Istrian peninsula lies in the northwest corner of the country, bordering Slovenia. There's a sizable Italian minority here, and Italian influence is apparent in the architecture, the cuisine, and the local dialect.

The region's principal city and port, Pula, is on the tip of the peninsula and is best known for its remarkably preserved 1,900-year-old Roman amphitheater. Close by, the beautifully nurtured island retreat of Brijuni National Park can be visited in a day. Towns along the west coast have an unmistakable Venetian flavor left by more than 500 years of Venetian occupation (1238–1797). Poreč and Rovinj, Croatia's two most popular seaside resorts, are both endowed with graceful campa-

nili, loggias, and reliefs of the winged lion of St. Mark, patron saint of Venice.

If you're in Istria during autumn, a side trip to the romantic hill towns of Motovun and Grožnjan is recommended. This inland area is particularly rich in truffles and mushrooms, and from mid-September to late October these local delicacies are celebrated with a series of gastronomic festivals.

PULA

292 km (182½ mi) southwest of Zagreb.

Today an industrial port town and Istria's chief administrative center, Pula was founded by the Romans in 177 BC. Remains from its ancient past have survived up to the present day: as you drive in on the coastal route, the monumental Arena, an enormous Roman amphitheater, blocks out the sky on your left. Under Venetian rule (1331–1797), Pula was sadly neglected. Many structures from the Roman era were pulled down, and stones and columns were carted off across the sea to Italy to be used for new buildings there. Pula's second great period of development took place in the late 19th century, under the Habsburgs, when it served as the chief base for the Imperial Austrian Navy. Today it's more of a working city than a tourist destination, but there are a few outstandingly good restaurants and a number of pleasant family-run hotels.

Fodor'sChoice Designed to accommodate 22,000 spectators, Pula's **Arena** *(Roman*
★ *Amphitheater)* is the sixth-largest building of its type in the world (after the Colosseum in Rome and similar arenas in Verona, Catania, Capua, and Arles). Construction was completed in the 1st century AD under the reign of Emperor Vespasian, and the Romans staged gladiator games here until such bloodthirsty sports were forbidden during the 5th century. During the 16th century, the Venetians planned to move the Arena stone by stone to Venice, where it was to be reconstructed in its original form. The plan failed, and it has remained more or less intact, except for the original tiers of stone seats and numerous columns that were hauled away for other buildings. Today it is used for summer concerts (by musicians including Sting, James Brown, and José Carreras), opera performances, and the annual film festival in late July. The underground halls house a museum with large wooden oil presses and amphorae. ⊠*Amfiteaterska ul* ☎*052 219 028* 🖃*30 Kn* ⊙*May–Sept., daily 8 AM–9 PM; Oct.–Apr., daily 9–5.*

Still Pula's most important public meeting place after 2,000 years, the ancient Roman **Forum** is today a spacious paved piazza ringed with cafés. There were once three temples here, of which only one remains. The perfectly preserved **Augustov Hram** *(Temple of Augustus* 🖃*8 Kn* ⊙*Weekdays 9–8:30, Sat. 2:30–8:30)* was built in the 1st century AD on the north side of the square. Next to it stands the **Gradska Palača** (Town Hall), which was erected during the 13th century using part of the Roman Temple of Diana as the back wall. The Renaissance arcade was added later.

NEED A BREAK? Stop at the chic but unpretentious **Café Galerija Cvajner** (⊠*Forum 2*) for morning coffee or an evening aperitif. Inside, contemporary art and minimalist furniture play off against frescoes uncovered during restoration, and outdoor tables offer great views onto the Forum square.

WHERE TO STAY & EAT

$$$$ ✕🏨**Valsabbion.** This superb restaurant and hotel is 3 km (2 mi) from
Fodor'sChoice the city center, overlooking the sea. It was one of the first restaurants in
★ Croatia to specialize in what has come to be known as "slow food" (the owner prefers the term "creative cuisine"). Many consider it the best restaurant in Istria, if not all of Croatia. The menu changes regularly depending on available produce, but you can expect goodies such as frogfish in vine leaves or tagliatelle with aromatic herbs and pine nuts. The lavender *semifreddo*—vanilla ice cream, pine nuts, and warm fig sauce complemented by two long, delicate sticks of dark chocolate, all served artistically on several plates arranged on a large mirror—is simply divine. For all its unimpeachable elegance, the interior also feels open and friendly. The small hotel is likewise top-notch, with 10 rooms (at around €175) furnished in pine with cheerful colored linens, fresh fruit, and flowers. There's a small swimming pool on the top floor and a range of beauty treatments and aerobics courses. ⊠*Pješčana uvala*

IX/26, 52100 🖃⛁*052/218–033* ⊕*www.valsabbion.net* ⚭*Reservations essential* ▤*AE, DC, MC, V* ☉*Closed Jan.*

$$$–$$$$ ✕**Vela Nera.** In hot competition with Valsabbion—only a few hundred
★ yards away—Vela Nera is likewise located 3 km (2 mi) from the city
center, just above a yacht marina. Favorite dishes include pasta with
lobster and truffles, fish baked in a salt crust, and an ever-changing
range of creative seafood specialties. The quality of the wines matches
that of the cuisine, and the spacious, light-filled dining room makes
for a pleasant atmosphere in which to savor it all. ⊠*Pješčana uvala*
🖃*052/219–209* ⊕*www.velanera.hr* ⚭*Reservations essential* ▤*AE,
DC, MC, V.*

$ 🍴**Hotel & Restaurant Scaletta.** Ideally situated close to the Arena, this
★ small, family-run hotel occupies a tastefully refurbished old town
house. The interior is decorated in cheerful yellows and greens, with
simple modern furniture. The restaurant offers a small but select menu
with exquisite dishes such as filet mignon in bread crumbs with dates
and croquettes, and the Scaletta Pavilion, across the road, serves pizza,
grilled meats, and fish dishes. Pros: Friendly bed-and-breakfast atmo-
sphere, good restaurant. Cons: Popular but small, so books up early.
⊠*Flavijevska 26, 52100* 🖃*052/541–599 or 052/541–025* ⛁*052/540–
285* ⊕*www.hotel-scaletta.com* 🛏*12 rooms* ⚭*In-room: safe, refrig-
erator. In-hotel: restaurant, no elevator* ▤*AE, DC, MC, V* ⋈*BP.*

¢–$ 🍴**Hotel Galija.** Expanded from a restaurant into a hotel in 2002, this
family-run establishment is centrally located in a bright yellow building
on a quiet street just two blocks from Giardini and the Sergian Gate.
The rooms are bright, spacious, and clean; nine are in the main build-
ing, with another seven plus five suites in a building right across the
street. Pros: Prime downtown location, parking garage nearby. Cons:
Some say hotel's hot water isn't sufficient. ⊠*Epulonova 3, 52100*
🖃*052/383–802* ⛁*052/383–804* ⊕*www.hotel-galija-pula.com* 🛏*16
rooms, 6 suites* ⚭*In-room: safe, refrigerator. In-hotel: restaurant, no
elevator, parking (fee)* ▤*AE, DC, MC, V* ⋈*BP.*

NACIONALNI PARK BRIJUNI

Fodor's Choice *Ferry from Fažana, which is 15 km (9 mi) northwest of Pula.*
★
The Brijuni archipelago is made up of 14 islands and islets. Under Aus-
tria-Hungary, Brijuni was a vacation haven for Vienna's nobility and
high society. Archduke Franz Ferdinand summered here, as did such
literary lights as Thomas Mann and Arthur Schnitzler. From 1949 to
1979, the largest island, Veliki Brijuni, was the official summer resi-
dence of Marshal Josip Broz Tito, Yugoslavia's "president for life."
Here he retreated to work, rest, and pursue his hobbies. World lead-
ers, film and opera stars, artists, and writers were frequent guests, and
together with Nasser of Egypt and Nehru of India, Tito forged the "Bri-
oni Declaration" uniting the so-called nonaligned nations (countries
adhering to neither NATO nor the Warsaw Pact). The archipelago was
designated a national park in 1983 and opened to the public. To get
here, call or e-mail the Brijuni National Park office in Fažana at least
one day in advance to make a reservation; you can also do so in person,

but especially in midsummer, there is a substantial risk that there won't be space. (Though various private tourist agencies in Fažana and Pula offer excursions, they do not generally measure up, either cost-wise or quality-wise, to making your arrangements directly with the National Park. Indeed, some of the tourist agencies simply reserve you a spot on the "official" tour, adding their own commission when doing so.) To get here, take the National Park ferry from Fažana, which takes about 15 minutes. The entire tour of the park takes about four hours.

Your first view of the park is of a low-lying island with a dense canopy of evergreens over blue waters. Ashore on Veli Brijun, the largest island, a **tourist train** takes you past villas in the seaside forest and relics from the Roman and Byzantine eras. The network of roads on this 6½-km-long (4-mi-long) island was laid down by the Romans, and stretches of original Roman stonework remain. Rows of cypresses shade herds of deer, and peacocks strut along pathways. The train stops at the **Safari Park,** a piece of Africa transplanted to the Adriatic, its zebras, antelopes, llamas, and elephants all gifts from visitors from faraway lands. In the **museum,** an archaeological exhibition traces life on Brijuni through the centuries, and a photography exhibition, "Tito on Brijuni," focuses on Tito and his guests. ⊠ *Brijunska 10, Fažana* ☎ *052/525–883 or 052/525–882   izleti@brijuni.htnet.hr* ⊕ *www.brijuni.hr* 📷 *180 Kn* ☉ *Apr.–Oct., 8 tours daily; Nov.–Mar., 4 tours daily; reservations required.*

ROVINJ

Fodor's Choice   *35 km (22 mi) northwest of Pula.*
★

It is hard to imagine how Rovinj could be more beautiful than it is. In a fantastic setting, with centuries-old red-roofed houses clustered around the hill of a former island, Istria's cultural mecca is crowned by the monumental baroque Crkva Sv Eufemije (Church of St. Euphemia), which has a typical Venetian bell tower topped by a gleaming bronze figure of St. Euphemia. Far below, a wide harbor crowded with pleasure boats is rimmed with bright awnings and colorful café umbrellas. Artists, writers, musicians, and actors have long gravitated to this ravishing place to carve out apartments in historic houses. Throughout the summer, the winding cobbled streets are crowded with vacationers from all reaches of Europe who are more often than not staying in nearby resort developments. South of the harbor lies the beautiful landscaped park of Zlatni Rt, planted with avenues of cedars, oaks, and cypresses and offering numerous secluded coves for swimming.

Fodor's Choice   Inside the 18th-century baroque **Crkva Sv Eufemije** *(Church of St. Euphe-*
★   *mia)*, the remains of Rovinj's patron saint are said to lie within a 6th-century sarcophagus. Born near Constantinople, Euphemia was martyred in her youth, on September 16 in AD 304, under the reign of Emperor Diocletian. The marble sarcophagus containing her remains mysteriously vanished in AD 800 when it was at risk of destruction by iconoclasts—and, legend has it, it somehow floated out to sea and washed up

in faraway Rovinj! ⊠ *Grisia* ☎ *052/815–615* ⛪ *Church and sarcophagus room free, campanile 10 Kn* ☉ *Daily 10–noon and 4–7.*

☺ The Rovinj **Akvarij** *(Aquarium)* displays tanks of Adriatic marine fauna and flora. It opened in 1891, making it one of the oldest institutions of its type in Europe. It's housed within the Ruđer Bošković Institute's Center for Maritime Research. ⊠ *Obala Giordana Paliage 5* ☎ *052/804–702* 💰 *10 Kn* ☉ *May–Sept., daily 9–9; Oct.–Apr., by appointment only.*

WHERE TO STAY & EAT

$$$$
Fodor's Choice
★

✕ **Blu.** Three kilometers (2 mi) north of Rovinj's Old Town, perched on the sea in the Borik section of town, Blu is the epitome of Istrian seaside elegance. The cozy dining room has a wall of windows to the sea, a couple of stone terraces, tables on an ivy-covered patio, and a spectacular canopied table at the breakwater's edge. There's simply no bad table here. One terrace juts out into the sea where you're so close you can look at the crustaceans on the sea floor in between courses. Expect refined seafood dishes that showcase the bounty of the Adriatic waters; for example, tagliatelle with crayfish and baby zucchini, or monkfish carpaccio. It's hard to beat this class act for a quiet, romantic dinner. ⊠ *Val de Lesso 952210* ☎ *052/511–265* ⊕ *www.blu.hr* 🗏 *Reservations essential* ▤ *AE, DC, MC, V* ☉ *Closed Nov.–Easter.*

$$–$$$

✕ **Veli Jože.** This popular *konoba* lies close to the seafront, at the foot of the Old Town. Specialties include *bakalar na bijelo* (dried cod in white wine with onion and potatoes), *fuži* with goulash, and roast lamb with potatoes. The house wine is excellent, but the rock music doesn't quite match the traditional decor that includes antlers, old photos, and nautical instruments. ⊠ *Sv Križa 1* ☎ *052/816–337* ▤ *AE, DC, MC, V.*

$$$

🏨 **Villa Angelo d'Oro.** Rovinj's first boutique hotel is housed in a beautifully restored 16th-century building in the heart of the Old Town. The smallish rooms are individually furnished with antiques, and a few have balconies with breathtaking vistas. The sometimes indifferent service and dated rooms don't quite meet the aspirations of the place, but breakfast is served on a glorious roof terrace, and there's a well-regarded restaurant on the ground floor. Pros: Beautiful Venetian building with wrought-iron and stone details. Cons: Rooms are old-fashioned and service is sporadic. ⊠ *V Švalbe 38–42, 52210* ☎ *052/840–502* 🖶 *052/840–112* ⊕ *www.rovinj.at* 🛏 *22 rooms, 1 suite* ⚘ *In-hotel: restaurant, room service* ▤ *AE, DC, MC, V* ▥ *BP.*

$$
★

🏨 **Hotel Adriatic.** Founded in 1912, this harborside hotel is the oldest (still-functioning) one in town, and its attractive, Habsburg-era facade shows its age. A comprehensive renovation in the late 1980s yielded bright, clean, and fairly spacious rooms with soft blue hues. The harborside rooms offer not only a spectacular, soothing view of the sea but also an oh-so-pleasant Adriatic aroma. The service is friendly, but as at many a hotel in Croatia's resort areas, there is a 20% surcharge for stays of fewer than four nights. Pros: First-class view of Old Town square and harbor; breakfast is served on the terrace. Cons: No elevator, parking garage is a short walk away, rooms facing the square are noisy. ⊠ *P. Budicin, 52210* ☎ *0800–8858 toll-free within Croatia,*

052/815–088 ⓐ*052/813–573* ⓦ*www.maistra.hr* ⓡ*27 rooms* ⓘ*In-room: safe, refrigerator. In-hotel: 2 restaurants, no elevator* ⓔ*AE, DC, MC, V* ⓘⓞⓘ*BP.*

POREČ

55 km (34 mi) northwest of Pula.

A pretty, tile-roofed town on a peninsula jutting out to sea, Poreč was founded as a Roman castrum (fort) in the 2nd century BC. Within the historic center, the network of streets still follow the original urban layout, and Dekumanova, the Roman decumanus (the main traverse street), has maintained its character as the principal thoroughfare. Today it is a worn flagstone passage lined with Romanesque and Gothic mansions and patrician palaces, some of which host cafés and restaurants. Close by lies the magnificent UNESCO-listed Eufrazijeva Basilica (St. Euphrasius Basilica), Istria's prime attraction and one of the coast's major artistic showpieces. Although the town itself is small, Poreč has an ample capacity for overnight stays, thanks to the vast hotel complexes of Plava and Zelena Lagun, situated along the pine-rimmed shoreline, a short distance from the center.

Fodor'sChoice
★
The magnificent **Eufrazijeva Basilica** *(St. Euphrasius Basilica)* is among the most perfectly preserved early Christian churches in Europe and one of the most important monuments of Byzantine art on the Adriatic. It was built by Bishop Euphrasius in the middle of the 6th century and consists of a delightful atrium, a church decorated with stunning mosaics, an octagonal baptistery, a 16th-century bell tower you can climb (for a modest fee), and a 17th-century Bishop's Palace whose foundations date to the 5th century and whose basement contains an exhibit of stone monuments and of mosaics previously on the basilica floor. The church interior is dominated by biblical mosaics above, behind, and around the main apse. In the apsidal semidome, the Virgin holding the Christ child is seated in a celestial sphere on a golden throne, flanked by angels in flowing white robes. On the right side there are three martyrs, the patrons of Poreč; the mosaic on the left shows Bishop Euphrasius holding a model of the church, slightly askew. High above the main apse, just below the beamed ceiling, Christ holds an open book in his hands while apostles approach on both sides. Other luminous, shimmering intense mosaics portray further ecclesiastical themes. ⓜ*Eufrazijeva* ⓢ*Basilica free; bell tower 10 Kn; Bishop's Palace 12 Kn* ⓣ*Basilica daily 7–7; bell tower daily 7–6:30; Bishop's Palace daily 7–6:30.*

WHERE TO STAY & EAT

$$$$
★
✕ **Sv Nikola Restaurant.** Those with a discriminating palate and a not-so-discriminating pocketbook should try this restaurant, opened in 2004. Service is included in the price, which is a good thing, since the price is nothing to sneeze at in this sparkling, air-conditioned venue right across from the harbor. The menu offers such delicacies as fish fillet in *malvazija-* (white-) wine sauce; meat carpaccio with truffles, Parmesan, and wild arugula; and beefsteak Decumanus (with pine nuts, goose liver

pâté, and black truffles). You can set forth on this culinary adventure with a plate of raw clams and oysters from Istria's west coast or Istrian prosciutto. As good as the food may be, though, the elegant, spotless interior isn't exactly brimming with character. ⊠*Obala maršala Tita 23* ☎*052/451–018* ⚑*Reservations essential* ▭*AE, DC, MC, V.*

$$–$$$ ✕**Peterokutna Kula.** A 15th-century pentagonal tower in the heart of the Old Town has been cleverly renovated to accommodate this sophisti-cated restaurant on a series of floors and terraces, including the roof. House specialties include spaghetti with lobster and steak with truffles. Finish your meal with a glass of *šlivovica* (plum rakija). When decid-ing on your tip, do remember that the waitstaff must trudge up and down all those steps all day. ⊠*Decumanus 1* ☎*052/451–378* ▭*No credit cards.*

$$ 🏨**Hotel Laguna Galijot.** This large, modern hotel sits on a small penin-
sula surrounded by pines in the Plava Laguna resort complex, 2 km (1 mi) south of the Old Town. Most rooms have balconies and sea views. Excellent sports facilities make this ideal for families on a longer stay and those in search of an active vacation. You'll pay extra for a room with a sea view. Pros: Activities and entertainment for families. Cons: No sandy beaches nearby; Poreč is a 20-minute walk away. ⊠*Plava Laguna, 52440* ☎*052/451–877* 🖷*052/452–399* ⊕*www.plavalaguna. hr* ⚓*103 rooms* △*In room: refrigerator. In-hotel: 2 restaurants, bar, tennis court, pool, diving, bicycles, parking (fee), some pets allowed* ▭*AE, MC, V* ☽*Closed Oct.–Apr.* ⎹◉⎸*MAP.*

$ 🏨**Hotel Neptun.** On the seafront promenade, where Poreč's oldest hotels are found, the Neptune was renovated in 2000 to provide smart, func-tional accommodations right in the center of town. Still, the rooms—most of which have a sea view—are smallish and somber-hued, and the mattresses are hard. The chic, air-conditioned restaurant includes one *big* salad bar. Stays of fewer than three nights yield a 20% surcharge, and there's a small premium on rooms with a view. Pros: Easy access to the Old Town and the sea; parking in front of hotel. Cons: No air-conditioning in the rooms, noise from the promenade reaches the rooms. ⊠*Obala M Tita 15, 52440* ☎*052/400–800 or 052/408–000* 🖷*052/451–440* ⊕*www.riviera.hr* ⚓*145 rooms* △*In-room: no a/c. In-hotel: restaurant, room service, bar, parking (no fee)* ▭*AE, DC, MC, V* ⎹◉⎸*MAP.*

MOTOVUN

Fodor's Choice
★ *30 km 19 mi) east of Poreč.*

It is an understatement to say that a day exploring the undulating green countryside and medieval hill towns of inland Istria makes a pleasant contrast to life on the coast. Motovun, for one, is a ravishing place. The king of Istria's medieval hill towns, with a double ring of defen-sive walls as well as towers and gates, may even evoke a scene straight from *Lord of the Rings*. Motovun is *the* place to visit if you opt to travel inland for a day or two from the sea. Be warned, though: the town sees lots of tour buses. That said, a walk around the ramparts offers views across the oak forests and vineyards of the Mirna Valley.

Just outside the village wall stands a church built according to plans by Palladio. In late July, Motovun transforms for about five days into one of Croatia's liveliest (and most crowded) destinations—for the famed **Motovun Film Festival.**

WHERE TO STAY & EAT

$$–$$$ ✕ **Restaurant Mčotić.** If you love truffles, whether with pasta or steak, this is a fine place to eat. Unquestionably an acquired taste, these earthy delicacies are gathered each autumn in the nearby Mirna Valley. Mčotić has a large summer terrace and occupies one of the most prominent buildings of the new Motovun, at the main intersection just below the Old Town. ⊠ *Zadrugarska 19* ☎ *052/681–758* ⊟ *AE, DC, MC, V.*

$ 🏠 **Hotel Kaštel.** Just outside the Motovun town walls—but nonetheless nestled in a cloistered niche atop the hill—this peaceful, old-fashioned hotel makes an ideal retreat if you prefer green hills to sea and islands. Out front there's a small garden and pretty summer terrace. For just €10 more, dinner is also included. Pros: Breathtaking panoramic views. Cons: Uphill walk to the hotel. ⊠ *Šetalište V. Nazora 7, Motovun52424* ☎ *052/681–607 or 052/681–735* 🖷 *052/681–652* ⊕ *www.hotel-kastel-m, otovun.hr* ⏎ *30 rooms* ⚬ *In-hotel: restaurant, some pets allowed* ⊟ *AE, DC, MC, V* ⊙*BP.*

GROŽNJAN

★   *10 km (7 mi) east of Motovun.*

In 1358, after at least 250 years in existence as a walled city, Grožnjan came under Venetian rule and remained so for more than 400 years. Though most of its population left after World War II, when decades of Italian rule came to an end and it officially became part of Yugoslavia, from the mid-1960s the government encouraged artists and musicians to settle here. This explains the number of painting and sculpture galleries you will encounter in this otherwise unassuming village. During the summer, an international federation of young musicians meets for training and workshops, presenting concerts beneath the stars through July and August.

ISTRIA ESSENTIALS

AIR TRAVEL

Croatia Airlines operates flights to Pula from Zagreb. Ryanair has service three times a week from Dublin and London Stansted to Pula, and daily service from London Stansted to Trieste, Italy. EasyJet flies from Bristol and London Luton to nearby Rijeka from May until mid-September. For airline contact information, see ⇨By Air *in* Croatia Essentials, at the end of this chapter.

BOAT & FERRY TRAVEL

In summer, the Italian company Adriatica runs a catamaran service from Trieste and Grado (in Italy) to Rovinj and Brijuni. In Rovinj, tickets for the catamaran are available from Eurostar Travel. The Adriatica agent in Trieste is Samer & Co.

Information Adriatica (⊕ *www.adriatica.it*). **Eurostar Travel** (⊠ *Obala P. Budičina 1, Rovinj* ☏ *052/813–144*). **Samer & Co.** (⊠ *Piazza dell'Unità d'Italia 7, Trieste, Italy* ☏ *040/6702–7211*).

BUS TRAVEL

There are domestic connections all over mainland Croatia to and from Pula, Poreč, and Rovinj, and local services between these towns and smaller inland destinations such as Motovun and Vodnjan. International buses offer daily connections to Italy (Trieste) and Slovenia (Ljubljana, Koper, Piran, and Portorož). Timetables are available at all bus stations. However, as elsewhere in Croatia, the sheer number of different companies offering bus service out of each station can be confusing, so it's best to confirm at the information window what you might find posted on the wall.

Bus Information Poreč Bus Station (⊠ *Rade Končara 1, Poreč* ☏ *052/432–153*). **Pula Bus Station** (⊠ *Trg 1 Istarske Brigade, Pula* ☏ *052/500–040*). **Rovinj Bus Station** (⊠ *Mattea Benussia, by trg na Lokvi, Rovinj* ☏ *052/811 453*).

CAR TRAVEL

While visiting Pula, Rovinj, and Poreč a car is not really necessary: all three towns are served by good bus connections, and having your own vehicle only causes parking problems. However, you may wish to hire a car to move on to other regions of the country. Major agencies have offices in Pula. Bear in mind that finding an available car on short notice in midsummer can be tricky regardless of the agency involved.

Car Rental Agencies Europcar (⊠ *Pula Airport, Pula* ☏ *052/530–351*). **Avis** (⊠ *S Dobrića 1, Pula* ☏ *052/223–739*). **Budget** (⊠ *ACI marina, Riva 1, Pula* ☏ *052/218–252*). **Hertz** (⊠ *Hotel Histria, Verudela, Pula* ☏ *052/210–868*). **Manuel** (⊠ *Giardini 10, Pula* ☏ *052/211–858 or 098/367–637*). **Vetura** (⊠ *Verudela, Pula* ☏ *091/535–8755, 091/535–8755 for airport office*).

INTERNET

All the major towns along the Istrian coast have a few Internet cafés, some with WiFi. Expect to pay at least 10 Kn for 20 minutes, or 30 Kn per hour. The Tourist Information Office in Poreč offers 15 minutes of free Internet use, more if no one is waiting in line *(⇨Visitor Information, below)*.

Information Enigma Internet Center (⊠ *Kandlerova 19, Pula* ☏ *052/381–615*). **Planet Tourist Agency** (⊠ *Sv Križ 1, Rovinj* ☏ *052/840–494*).

TRAIN TRAVEL

Istria is not well connected to the rest of Croatia by rail. To get to Zagreb or Split you need to transit through Rijeka. However, there is a line running north from Pula to Ljubljana in Slovenia.

Train Information Pula Train Station (⊠ *Kolodvorksa, Pula* ☏ *052/541–733*).

VISITOR INFORMATION

Contacts Brijuni Tourist Information (⊠ *Fažana* ☏ *052/525–888* ⊕ *www. brijuni.hr*). **Grožnjan Tourist Information** (⊠ *Umberto Gorjan 3, Grožnjan* ☏ *052/776–131*). **Istria Tourist Board** (⊕ *www.istra.hr*). **Motovun Tourist Information** (⊠ *Šetalište V. Nazora 1, Motovun* ☏ *052/681–642*). **Poreč Tourist**

Information (⊠ *Zagrebačka 9, Poreč* ☎ *052/451–293* ⊕ *www.istra.com/porec).*
Pula Tourist Information (⊠ *Forum 3, Pula* ☎ *052/219–197* ⊕ *www.pulainfo.hr).*
Rovinj Tourist Information (⊠ *Pino Budičin 12, Rovinj* ☎ *052/811–566* ⊕ *www.*
istra.com/rovinj).

KVARNER

Separating the Istrian peninsula from Dalmatia to the south, the Kvarner Gulf is a large, deep bay backed by mountains. The principal city, Rijeka, is a busy port with good road and rail connections to Zagreb. Gentile Opatija was founded by the Habsburgs in the mid-19th century as Croatia's first seaside resort, and Rab is probably the region's most beautiful island, not to mention the birthplace of nudist bathing on the Adriatic.

RIJEKA

182 km (114 mi) west of Zagreb.

Water is the essence of Kvarner, and the region's largest city expresses this simply. Whether in Croatian or Italian (*Fiume*) the translation of the name to English is the same: "*river.*" Although the history of Croatia's third city goes back to the days of Imperial Rome, modern Rijeka evolved under the rule of Austria-Hungary. The historic core retains vestiges of the old Habsburg monarchy from the time when Rijeka served as the empire's outlet to the Adriatic. During the 1960s, under Yugoslavia, the suburbs expanded rapidly. Rijeka is the country's largest port, with a huge shipyard, massive dry-dock facilities, refineries, and other heavy industries offering large-scale employment. Since the breakup of Yugoslavia, however, Rijeka's role as a shipping town has declined significantly. Much business shifted north to the smaller Slovene ports during the crippling wars of the 1990s, and although some has returned, the volume remains less than half that seen in 1980.

Rijeka is the home port of Jadrolinija, the coast's major ferry company. Local ferries connect with all the Kvarner islands and will take you farther afield as well. If you're planning on heading south and would rather dodge the slow and dangerous roads that head that way, then let the boat take the strain. Ferries leaving Rijeka weave through islands all the way down to Dubrovnik, stopping at most major points on the way. Sunsets, sunrises, plus a mingling of stars and shore-anchored town lights in between, help transport one farther than just the few hundred kilometers to the other end of the country. Most visitors stay in the nearby seaside resort of Opatija.

Fodor'sChoice ★ The medieval **Trsat** *(Trsat Castle)* was built on the foundations of a prehistoric fort. In the early 1800s, it was bought by an Austrian general of Irish descent, who converted it into a kind of pre-Disneyland confection that even includes a Greek temple with Doric columns. Today it hosts a popular café, offering some stunning views of the Kvarner Bay; throughout the summer, open-air theater performances and concerts

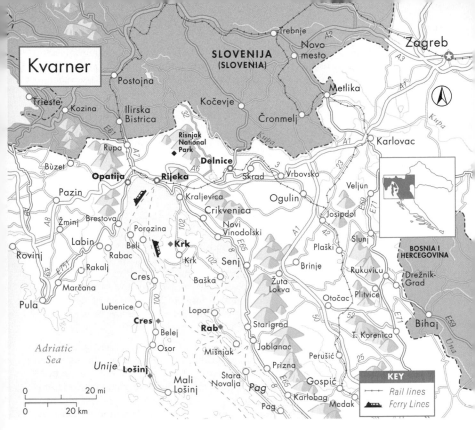

take place here. Across the street, the pilgrimage church of **Sveta Marija** (St. Mary) was constructed in 1453 to commemorate the Miracle of Trsat, when angels carrying the humble house of the Virgin Mary are said to have landed here. Although the angels later moved the house to Loreto in Italy, Trsat has remained a place of pilgrimage. The pilgrimage path up to Trsat begins in the city center, close to Titov trg, at a bridge across the Rječina. It passes through a stone gateway, then makes a long, steep climb up 538 steps. Local Bus 1 will get you here, too. ⊠ *Frankopanski trg* ☎ *No phone* ⊠ *10 Kn* ⊙ *Apr.–Oct., Tues.– Sun. 9 AM–11 PM; Feb., Mar., Nov., and Dec., Tues.–Sun. 9 AM–3 PM.*

WHERE TO STAY & EAT

$$$–$$$$ ⚫ ✕**Municipium.** Classic dining in a fine old house, this is Croatian cuisine, both fish and meat, at its finest. An extensive wine list concentrates on home produce with a good range of Istrian and Dalmatian vintages available. Tried-and-true coastal specialties such as octopus salad and *črni rižot* (black cuttlefish risotto) are expertly prepared. It's perhaps as upmarket as one can get in Rijeka. ⊠ *Trg riječke rezolucije 5* ☎ *051/213–000* ▭ *AE, DC, MC, V* ⊙ *Closed Sun.*

$–$$ ⚫ ▦**Hotel Bonavia.** In the city center, one block back from the Korzo, this modern, luxury high-rise has comfortable rooms with specially designed furnishings and original oil paintings. Rooms on the top two floors have balconies and views of Kvarner Bay. The restaurant has a sophisticated dining room with tables in the garden throughout summer. A limousine and chauffeur are at guests' disposal. Pros: Spacious rooms, top-notch service, excellent pastries in café. Cons: Parking is in a garage a short walk away instead of on-site. ⊠ *Dolac 4, 51000* 🕿 *051/357–100* 🖷 *051/335–969* ⊕ *www.bonavia.hr* ⌨ *114 rooms, 7 suites* ⅋ *In-room: safe, refrigerator, Ethernet. In-hotel: restaurant, room service, bars, gym, parking (fee)* ▤ *AE, DC, MC, V* 🍽 *BP.*

OPATIJA

15 km (9 mi) west of Rijeka.

In the late 19th century, Opatija (Abbazia in Italian) was among the most elegant and fashionable resorts in Europe. Its history dates from the 1840s, when villas were built for members of minor royalty. In 1882 the start of rail service from Vienna and Budapest, along with an aggressive publicity campaign, put Abbazia on the tourist map as a spa of the first magnitude. With the high mineral content of the seawater, iodine in the air, and an annual average of 2,230 hours of sunshine, it qualified as a top-rated climatic health resort and emerged as a favorite wintering spot for Central European nobility and high society.

A hint of the formality that shrouded Opatija in its heyday still survives; the narrow pines and grand buildings remind one of the Italian lakes. This means that many visitors from all over Europe continue to head to the Opatija Riviera in the summer. At the same time, this stretch of coast has not gone unnoticed by the locals. Until recent years, the town was a weekend haunt for some younger, motorized Rijeka citizens. Thanks to these driving forces, the upmarket hotel guests still share the resort with some of the region's more upwardly mobile restaurants. However, their number is dwindling, and the town's once admirable nightlife has packed up and headed back to the cooler parts of Rijeka, leaving Opatija to wealthy and more elderly visitors from the surrounding countries. These guests seem more eager to sip the waters than wine and spirits.

The main street, ulica Maršala Tita, runs parallel to the coast for the length of town, and you can go from one end of town to the other on foot in about a half hour, passing numerous terrace cafés along the way. The best seafood restaurants are in the neighboring fishing village of Volosko, a 15-minute walk along the seafront.

The mild climate year-round and resulting subtropical vegetation, frequently sunny skies, and shelter from cold north winds provided by Mt. Učka give Opatija pleasant weather for much of the year. In summer, fresh sea breezes tend to dispel any oppressive heat, making the city an ideal seaside resort.

★ If you enjoy walking by the sea, set off along the magnificent paved, waterfront **Lungomare.** Built in 1889, this 12-km (7½-mi) path leads from the fishing village of Volosko, through Opatija—passing in front of old hotels, parks, and gardens and around yacht basins—and all the way past the villages of Ičići and Ika to Lovran in the south. In the midst you'll find the popular town beach that fronts the center of Opatija. Close to many cafés, ice-cream shops, and other essentials, the beach also has a couple of protected sections of water for safe swimming. These would be handy for kids if it wasn't for the fact that the concrete sides and underwater steps feature extremely sharp stones that can slice skin quite nastily if met with sufficient force. ✉ *Obalno Šetalište Franza Josefa.*

From gentle hiking to mountain biking, climbing and paragliding, all are available in the 160 square km (64 square mi) of **Mount Učka Nature Park,** a series of peaks that help shelter the Liburnia Riviera (which is actually the official name for the stretch of coast centered on Opatija) and the islands from weather systems to the north. Paths toward the summit of the range start in all the resorts along the coast. A climb up to the highest peak, Vojak (4,596 feet), with a fine stone lookout tower at its summit, can be well worth it, particularly on a clear day. The view offers a cheap (but somewhat distant) tour of the islands of Kvarner Bay, the Italian Alps, and perhaps even an indistinct version of Venice. Most routes up to the heights lead through forest, so you can make the trek in summer without overheating. Along the way you'll find natural springs from which to quench your thirst, along with lakes, ponds, tumbling waterfalls (in the wetter months), impressive natural stone columns, and several hundred caves. The local inhabitants include deer, wild boar and, in the northernmost sections of the park, bears. Humans have been living in these hills for centuries also, rearing cattle, farming, and working the forest; you'll come across numerous tiny villages and historic sites if you roam far enough. ✉ *Liganj 12, Lovran* ☎ *051/293–753* ⊕ *www.pp-ucka.hr.*

WHERE TO STAY & EAT

$$$$
Fodor'sChoice
★
✕**Le Mandrac.** This upscale seafood restaurant has a glassed-in terrace for winter dining, something of a novelty here by the sea. The splashy menu—somewhere between traditional and avant-garde—changes with the seasons and the whims of the proprietors. Voted the second-best restaurant in the country by a national newspaper, Le Mandrac is Kvarner's bid to put itself on the gastronomical map. Expect dishes like prawn ravioli in tomato and cardamom sauce and octopus salad with pumpkin pesto. ✉ *Supilova obala 12, Volosko* ☎ *051/701–357* ⊟ *AE, DC, MC, V.*

$–$$$
✕**Istranka.** With a delightful covered terrace flanked by a twisting tree, this small restaurant is the best option for those who are not the greatest fans of seafood (although if that's you, what you're doing in Kvarner is a mystery). Taking its influence from the neighboring region of Istria, the menu concentrates more on landlubber food: hams, cheeses, and of course, the famous Istrian truffle! ✉ *Bože Milanoviča 2, Opatija* ☎ *051/271–835.*

$–$$
▦**Grand Hotel Kvarner-Amalia.** The former summer residence of European royalty, Kvarner's oldest hotel first opened its doors to guests in 1884. More suited to sedentary tourists than business travelers, it's a grand neoclassical-style building with peaceful gardens and a terrace

overlooking the sea, close to Villa Angelina. The Crystal Ballroom is used for the annual Miss Croatia contest. Pros: Habsburg-era grandeur, spacious patio overlooking the sea. Cons: Outdated furnishings and spotty air-conditioning in some rooms. ⊠*Park Tomašica 1–4, 51410* ☎*051/271–233* 🖷*051/271–202* ⊕*www.liburnia.hr* ➾*86 rooms* ⚘*In room: refrigerator. In-hotel: restaurant, room service, bar, pool, beachfront, parking (fee)* ☰*AE, DC, MC, V* ⧆|*BP.*

¢–$ 🎏 **Hotel Opatija.** A prime location, elegant surroundings, and helpful
★   service are rare at this price level; to have them all, along with something left over in your wallet, is extraordinary. Part of the Vienna International chain, this huge villa at the top of a park in the center of town is perfectly located. It was originally a spa and sanatorium when it was built in the late 19th century. Now, guests relax on the terrace, which, with almost comfortable, post-modern sofas, is a delight. There is a €10 per-night supplement for the use of air-conditioning. Pros: Close to the train station, well-maintained garden in front of hotel. Cons: Hilltop location makes it challenging to get there on foot. ⊠*Gortanov trg 2/1, 51410* ☎*051/271–388* 🖷*051/271–317* ⊕*www.hotel-opatija. com* ➾*216 rooms* ⚘*In-room: refrigerator, no a/c (some). In-hotel: restaurant, room service, bar, pool, parking (fee), public Internet* ☰*AE, DC, MC, V.*

RAB

Jablanac is 100 km (62½ mi) south of Rijeka; then take the ferry 1½ nautical mi to Mišnjak, 9 km (6 mi) from the town of Rab.

Rab presents an utterly schizophrenic landscape. When you drive southward, down the Magistrala, you see that the island resembles the humped back of a diving sea monster. Once you've mounted this beast, via a short ferry ride from Jablanac to Mišnjak, you travel along the center of its back, which is almost entirely bald to the north, letting all its hair hang out to the south. The high northern coast, which bears the brunt of the northern Bora winds, is dry, rocky, and barren. Crouching below this crusty ledge, the southern half of the island could hardly differ more, and has possibly the lushest terrain found on any Croatian island. Low, green hills dip into the seas, and the ancient Dundo forest grows so voraciously that it's almost impossible to walk in.

Fodor'sChoice   **Rab Town.** Sitting on a narrow peninsula halfway up the island's southern
★   coast, the compact, well-preserved medieval village is best known for its distinctive skyline of four elegant bell towers, and its many churches. Author Rebecca West, who traveled through Yugoslavia in the 1930s, called Rab Town, "one of the most beautiful cities of the world" in her masterpiece *Black Lamb and Grey Falcon.* Closed to traffic, the narrow cobbled streets of the Old Town, which are lined with Romanesque churches and patrician palaces, can be explored in an hour's leisurely stroll. The urban layout is simple: three longitudinal streets run parallel to the waterfront promenade and are linked together by steep passages traversing the hillside. The lower street is Donja ulica, the middle street Srednja ulica, and the upper street Gornji ulica.

The oldest part of Rab Town is **Kaldanac,** the very tip of the narrow peninsula that juts into the sea. From here the ancient city grew in the 15th century to include Varoš, farther north, and later was widened and fortified by walls during a brief Venetian rule. The Romanesque **Sveta Marija Velika** *(Cathedral of St. Mary),* built in the 12th century and consecrated by the pope in 1177, is the biggest church in Rab Town and was built on the site of Roman ruins. The tallest and most beautiful of Rab's campaniles, the freestanding **Veli Zvonik** *(Great Bell Tower)* forms part of the former cathedral complex and dominates the southwest side of the peninsula. Built in the 12th century, it stands 85 feet high. A climb to the top offers breathtaking views over the town and sea. ⊠*Gornja ulica* ☎*5 Kn* ⊙*Daily 10* AM–*1* PM *and 5–8* PM. On the edge of town, the green expanse of **Komrčar Park,** laid out in the 19th century, offers avenues lined with pine trees for gentle strolling and access down to the sea. Although the Old Town and its immediate surroundings are Rab's chief treasures, the city is also a gateway to the great stretches of beach that rim the towns of Kampor, Suha Punta, Lopar, and neighboring islands.

4

WHERE TO STAY & EAT

$$–$$$ ✕**Konoba Rab.** Tucked away in a narrow side street between Srednja ulica and Gornja ulica in Rab Town, this konoba is warm and inviting, with exposed-stone walls and rustic furniture. Barbecued fish and meat are the house specialties, along with a good choice of pastas and risottos. ⊠*Kneza Branimira 3, Rab Town* ☎*051/725–666* ⊟*AE, DC, MC, V.*

$$–$$$ ✕**Zlatni Zlatag.** In Supertarska Draga, 10 km (6½ mi) from Rab Town,
★   this restaurant is frequently mentioned as the best on the island. Nestled in a small bay and backed by Mediterranean woods, the restaurant and its summer terrace offer wonderful views of the sea. *Škampi i školjke Sv. Kristofor* (scampi and shells baked in béchamel sauce) is a favorite offering. The family that run "Golden Sunset"—and with the west-facing terrace, this is exactly what you'll see at the appropriate time—are well known for supporting Rab's traditional cuisine. Tradition is met with a smart and modern air-conditioned interior. ⊠*Supertarska Draga 379, Supertarska Draga* ☎*051/775–150* ⊟*AE, DC, MC, V* ⊙*Closed Jan.*

$ 🏨**Hotel Imperial.** On the edge of the old town amid the greenery of Komrčar Park, this peaceful 1930s-era resort hotel has excellent sports facilities and a beach. Suffering a little from a lack of investment, the Imperial clearly displays its Socialist-era past. However, the setting, an admirable villa in a richly scented forest park, just a stone's throw from the center of Rab Town, atones for many sins. Certainly not glamorous, it's functional and trying hard. Rooms are modern and comfortable, offering either seaside or parkside views. Pros: Good location in a wooded park near Rab Town. Cons: A little run-down, dated furnishings. ⊠*Palit, Rab Town, 51280* ☎*051/724–184* 🖷*051/724–117* ⊕*www.imperial.hr* ⟿*134 rooms* ♻*In-room: refrigerator. In-hotel: restaurant, room service, bar, tennis courts, gym, beachfront* ⊟*AE, DC, MC, V* ⊙*Closed Jan.–Mar.* 🍽*CP.*

$$ ★ **⊡Arbiana Hotel.** It's hard to imagine a more romantic setting than this harborside inn in a perfectly restored medieval villa with balconies overlooking Rab marina and the hills of Barbat in the distance. Rooms are decorated in warm tones and rich fabrics and have squeaky clean bathrooms stocked with fluffy bathrobes. Breakfast is served in the restaurant's leafy garden partially enclosed by the Old City walls. Pros: Boutique-hotel feel, personal service. Cons: No pool or beach access, not all rooms have balconies. *⊠Obala Petra Kresimira 12, 51280* *☎051/775–900* *⊕www.arbianahotel.com* *⊲28 rooms* *⟳In room: Wi-Fi, safe, refrigerator. In hotel: restaurant, bar* *⊟AE, DC, MC, V* *⊦◎⊦BP.*

KVARNER ESSENTIALS

AIR TRAVEL
Rijeka's airport is located on Omišalj on Krk Island with regular bus service provided by Autotrans to downtown Rijeka and the beach towns on Krk island as well as to Mali Lošinj and Cres (though not to Rab). The airport is served by easyJet from the United Kingdom (Bristol and London), Norwegian Air Shuttle from Oslo, Croatian Airlines from Zagreb as well as charter flight companies from several cities in Germany. These charter companies usually sell air tickets only in combination with vacation packages and flights cannot be booked separately. For airline contact information, see ⇨By Air *in* Croatia Essentials, at the end of this chapter.

Information **Rijeka Airport** (⊠*Hamec 1, Omisalj* ☎*051/842–132* ⊕*www.rijeka-airport.hr*).

BOAT AND FERRY TRAVEL
During high season (July through August), Jadrolinija ferries travel between Dubrovnik and Rijeka (journey time approximately 20 hours), stopping at Zadar, Split, Stari Grad (island of Hvar), Korčula, and Sobra (island of Mljet) en route. During the rest of the year, the service is less frequent. The fare between Dubrovnik and Rijeka is €127 for a reclining seat in your own two-berth cabin with bathroom and TV. The cheapest way to go, with no booked seat at all, is €36. In good weather you'll find the rear decks of the ship smothered with passengers camping out beneath the stars, which lends the journey a special atmosphere. Prices vary according to the season, with rates falling as much as 30% in low season. Cars cost €92. Round-trip tickets save 20%.

A catamaran service heads out to Rab at 4 PM, drops into the northern-Dalmatian island of Pag, and then pulls into Mali Lošinj about two and a half hours later. Six times per day from 6 AM to 6 PM, ferries head out from Baška on Krk toward Lopar on Rab. The trip costs €4.18, €25.27 for a car.

Ferry Information **Jadrolinija** (☎*051/211–444* ⊕*www.jadrolinija.hr*).

BUS TRAVEL

There's daily international bus service to Rijeka from Italy (Trieste), Slovenia (Ljubljana and Nova Gorica), and Germany (Dortmund, Frankfurt, Munich, and Stuttgart). You can also reach destinations all over mainland Croatia from Rijeka and Opatija. Timetable information is available from the Rijeka Bus Terminal.

Buses travel from Rijeka to all the major towns on the mainland and the islands at least once a day. If you're traveling independently, you'll find that buses to the various islands are roughly scheduled to tie in with ferry services.

Bus Information Rijeka Bus Terminal (⊠ *Žabica 1, Rijeka* ☎ *051/211–222*).

CAR TRAVEL

A car is useful if you plan to leave the Kvarner region and head for Istria (passing through the Učka Tunnel). However, good train and bus services to Zagreb and a comfortable overnight ferry to Dalmatia mean that a vehicle is not essential for moving on to other areas.

Car Rental Agencies Avis (⊠ *Riva 22, Rijeka* ☎ *051/337–917*). **Europcar** (⊠ *Rijeka Airport, Omišalj* ☎ *051/430–3038*).

INTERNET

Internet cafés are common at the resorts on both the mainland and the islands. That said, they might not contain many terminals, so you may find yourself with plenty of time to relax, sip a coffee, and enjoy the wait to spend your 20 to 30 Kn per hour.

TRAIN TRAVEL

There are five trains daily from Rijeka to Zagreb (journey time is approximately 3½ hours), three trains daily to Split (16 hours), and two trains daily to Ljublana (2½ hours).

Information Rijeka Train Station (⊠ *Krešimirova 5, Rijeka* ☎ *051/213–333*).

Hrvatske Željeznice (Croatian Railways) (☎ *060/333–444* ⊕ *www.hznet.hr*).

VISITOR INFORMATION

Contacts Opatija Tourist Information (⊠ *Vladimira Nazora 3, Opatija* ☎ *051/271–710* ⊕ *www.opatija-tourism.hr*). **Rab Tourist Information** (⊠ *Donja ul. 2, Rab Town* ☎ *051/724–064* ⊕ *www.tzg-rab.hr*). **Rijeka Tourist Information** (⊠ *Uzarska 14, Rijeka* ☎ *051/315–710* ⊕ *www.tz-rijeka.hr*).

SPLIT & CENTRAL DALMATIA

Central Dalmatia is more mountainous, wild, and unexploited than the northern regions of Istria and Kvarner. Tourist facilities may be less sophisticated, but Dalmatia's magnificent coastal towns and rugged islands offer an unrefined Mediterranean charm all their own. The region's capital is the busy port of Split, with its historic center surrounded by the sturdy walls of an imperial Roman palace. Nearby Trogir is a gem of medieval stone architecture, on a tiny island connected to the mainland by a bridge. The island of Brač has a stunning beach.

The most exclusive destination in Central Dalmatia is Hvar, with its charming 16th-century Venetian architecture and a labyrinth of winding cobbled streets. To see Dalmatia at its most authentic, take a ferry ride to Vis, Croatia's most distant inhabited island.

SPLIT

365 km (228 mi) south of Zagreb.

Split's ancient core is so spectacular and unusual that a visit is more than worth your time. The heart of the city lies within the walls of Roman Emperor Diocletian's retirement palace, which was built in the 3rd century AD. Diocletian, born in the nearby Roman settlement of Salona in AD 245, achieved a brilliant career as a soldier and became emperor at the age of 40. In 295, he ordered this vast palace to be built in his native Dalmatia, and when it was completed, he stepped down from the throne and retired to his beloved homeland. Upon his death, he was laid to rest in an octagonal mausoleum, around which Split's magnificent cathedral was built.

In 615, when Salona was sacked by barbarian tribes, those fortunate enough to escape found refuge within the stout palace walls and divided up the vast imperial apartments into more modest living quarters. Thus, the palace developed into an urban center, and by the 11th century the settlement had expanded beyond the ancient walls.

Under the rule of Venice (1420–1797), Split—as a gateway to the Balkan interior—became one of the Adriatic's main trading ports, and the city's splendid Renaissance palaces bear witness to the affluence of those times. When the Habsburgs took control during the 19th century, an overland connection to Central Europe was established by the construction of the Split–Zagreb–Vienna railway line.

After World War II, the Tito years saw a period of rapid urban expansion: industrialization accelerated and the suburbs extended to accommodate high-rise apartment blocks. Today the historic center of Split is included on UNESCO's list of World Heritage Sites.

WHAT TO SEE
Numbers in the text correspond to numbers in the margin and on the Split map.

❶ **Dioklecijanova Palača** *(Diocletian's Palace).* The original palace was a
★ combination of a luxurious villa and a Roman garrison, based on the ground plan of an irregular rectangle. Each of the four walls bore a main gate, the largest and most important being the northern *Zlatna Vrata* (Golden Gate), opening onto the road to the Roman settlement of Salona. The entrance from the western wall was the *Željezna Vrata* (Iron Gate), and the entrance through the east wall was the *Srebrena Vrata* (Silver Gate). The *Mjedna Vrata* (Bronze Gate) in the south wall faced directly onto the sea, and during Roman times boats would have docked here. The city celebrated the palace's 1700th birthday in 2005. ✉ *Obala Hrvatskog Narodnog Preporoda, Grad.*

⑪ ★ **Galerija Meštrović** *(Mesštrović Gallery).* A modern villa surrounded by extensive gardens, this building designed by Ivan Meštrovic was his summer residence during the 1920s and '30s. Some 200 of his sculptural works in wood, marble, stone, and bronze are on display, both indoors and out. Entrance to the Galerija Meštrovića is also valid for the nearby **Kaštelet** (⊠*Šetalište Ivana Meštrovića 39*), housing a chapel containing a cycle of New Testament bas-relief wood carvings that many consider Meštrović's finest work. ⊠*Šetalište Ivana Meštrovića 46, Meje* ☎*021/340–800* ⊕*www.mdc.hr* 🎫*15 Kn* ☉*May–Sept., Tues.–Sun. 9–9; Oct.–Apr., Tues.–Sat. 9–4, Sun. 10–3.*

❻ **Gradski Muzej** *(City Museum).* Split's city museum is worth a quick look both to witness the collection of medieval weaponry and to see the interior of this splendid 15th-century town house. The dining room, on the first floor, is furnished just as it would have been when the Papalić family owned the house, giving some idea of how the aristocracy of that time lived. ⊠*Papaliceva 1, Grad* ☎*021/341–240* ⊕*www.mgst. net* 🎫*10 Kn* ☉*Nov.–May, Tues.–Fri. 10–5, weekends 10–noon; June–Oct., daily 9–noon and 5–8.*

❺ **Jupiterov Hram** *(Jupiter's Temple).* This Roman temple was converted into a baptistery during the Middle Ages. The entrance is guarded by the mate (unfortunately damaged) of the black-granite sphinx that stands in front of the cathedral. Inside, beneath the coffered barrel vault and ornamented cornice, the 11th-century baptismal font is adorned with a stone relief showing a medieval Croatian king on his throne. Directly behind it, the bronze statue of St. John the Baptist is the work of Meštrović. ⊠*Kraj Sv Ivana, Grad* 🎫*5 Kn* ☉*May–Oct., daily 8–6.*

❹ **Katedrala Sveti Dujam** *(Cathedral of St. Dominius).* The main body of the cathedral is the 3rd-century octagonal mausoleum designed as a shrine to Emperor Diocletian. During the 7th century, refugees from Salona converted it into an early Christian church, ironically dedicating it to Sv Duje (St. Domnius), after Bishop Domnius of Salona, one of the many Christians martyred during the late emperor's persecution campaign. The cathedral's monumental main door is ornamented with magnificent carved wooden reliefs, the work of Andrija Buvina of Split, portraying 28 scenes from the life of Christ and dated 1214. Inside, the hexagonal Romanesque stone pulpit, with richly carved decoration, is from the 13th century. The high altar, surmounted by a late-Gothic canopy, was executed by Bonino of Milan in 1427. Nearby is the 15th-century canopied Gothic altar of Anastasius by Juraj Dalmatinac. The elegant 200-foot Romanesque-Gothic bell tower was constructed in stages between the 12th and 16th century. ⊠*Peristil, Grad* 🎫*Cathedral free, bell tower 5 Kn* ☉*Sept.–June, daily 8–noon and 4:30–7; July and Aug., daily 8–8.*

⑫ **Marjan** *(Marjan Hill).* Situated on a hilly peninsula, this much-loved park is planted with pine trees and Mediterranean shrubs and has been a protected nature reserve since 1964. A network of paths criss-

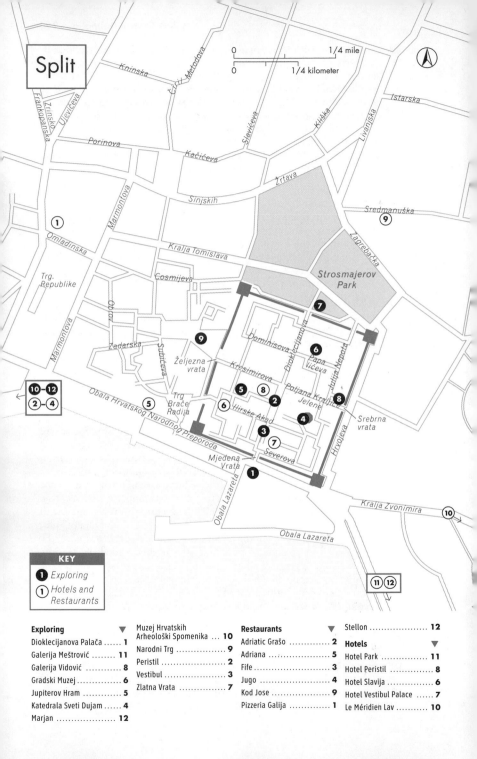

Split

0 ____ 1/4 mile

0 ____ 1/4 kilometer

Trg. Republike

Strosmajerov Park

Srebrna vrata

Željezna vrata

Trg Brače Radija

Mjedena Vrata

crosses the grounds, offering stunning views over the sea and islands. ⊠ *Marjan.*

Having reached this point you're undoubtedly in need of refreshment. Sit on a sofa at Vidilica (⊠ *Nazorov Prilaz, Marjan*), **a lounge-style café terrace, and order a long, cold drink. Then sit back and enjoy the breathtaking view.**

⓫ **Muzej Hrvatskih Arheološki Spomenika** *(Museum of Croatian Archaeological Monuments).* This modern building displays early Croatian religious art from the 7th through the 12th century. The most interesting exhibits are fine stone carvings decorated with plaitwork design, surprisingly similar to the geometric patterns typical of Celtic art. In the garden you can see several stećci, monolithic stone tombs dating back to the cult of the Bogomils (an anti-imperial sect that developed in the Balkans during the 10th century). ⊠ *Šetalište Ivana Meštrovića, Meje* ☎ *021/358–420* ⊕ *www.mhas-split.hr* 🎟 *10 Kn* ☉ *Weekdays 9:30–4, Sat. 9:30–1.*

❾ **Narodni Trg** *(People's Square).* A pedestrianized expanse paved with gleaming white marble, this is contemporary Split's main square. Although religious activity has to this day centered on Peristil, Narodni trg became the focus of civic life during the 14th century. In the 15th century, the Venetians constructed several important public buildings here: the Town Hall (housing a contemporary art gallery, with erratic opening hours), plus the Rector's Palace and a theater, the latter two sadly demolished by the Habsburgs in the 19th century. The Austrians, for their part, added a Secessionist building at the west end of the square. ⊠ *Grad.*

❷ **Peristil** *(Peristyle).* From Roman times up to the present day the main public meeting place within the palace walls, this spacious central courtyard is flanked by marble columns topped with Corinthian capitals and richly ornamented cornices linked by arches. There are six columns on both the east and west sides, and four more at the south end, which mark the monumental entrance to the Vestibul. During the Split Summer Festival, Peristil becomes an open-air stage hosting evening opera performances. ⊠ *Grad.*

The summer terrace at the Luxor Café (⊠ *Peristil, Grad*) **makes a perfect place to sit over coffee or a glass of local wine and absorb the 2,000 years of magnificent architecture that surround you. You'll even find cushions so you can sit comfortably on the stone steps if all the tables are full.**

❸ **Vestibul.** The cupola of this domed space would once have been decorated with marble and mosaics. Today there's only a round hole in the top of the dome, but it produces a stunning effect: the dark interior, the blue sky above, and the tip of the cathedral's bell tower framed in the opening. ⊠ *Peristil, Grad.*

❽ **Galerija Vidović** *(Vidović Gallery).* Emanuel Vidović (1870–1953) is acknowledged as Split's greatest painter. Here you can see 74 of his works, donated to the city by his family. Large, bold canvases depict local landmarks cast in hazy light, whereas the sketches done outdoors before returning to his studio to paint are more playful and colorful. ✉*Poljana Kraljice Jelene bb, Grad* ☎*021/360–155* 🖼*10 Kn* 🕙*June–Sept., Tues.–Fri. 9–9, weekends 10–1; Oct.–May, Tues.–Fri. 9–4, weekends 10–1.*

❼ Zlatna Vrata *(Golden Gate).* Formerly the main entrance into the palace, Zlatna Vrata, on the north side of the palace, is the most monumental of the four gates. Just outside the Zlatna Vrata stands Meštrović's gigantic bronze **statue of Grgur Ninski** (Bishop Gregory of Nin). During the 9th century, the bishop campaigned for the use of the Slav language in the Croatian Church, as opposed to Latin, thus infuriating Rome. This statue was created in 1929 and placed on Peristil to mark the 1,000th anniversary of the Split Synod, then moved here in 1957. Note the big toe on the left foot, which is considered by locals to be a good luck charm and has been worn gold through constant touching. ✉*Dioklecijanova, Grad.*

WHERE TO EAT

Split does have some good restaurants, though they're not always easy to find. As in any city of fishermen and sailors, seafood predominates here. In most restaurants, fresh fish is normally prepared over a charcoal fire and served with *blitva sa krumpirom.* For a cheaper option, bear in mind that the pizza in Split is almost as good as (and sometimes even better than) that in Italy. Last but not least, complement your meal with a bottle of Dalmatian wine.

$$$–$$$$ ✕**Adriatic Grašo.** Above the ACI marina, close to the gardens of Sveti Stipan, this seafood restaurant has a light and airy minimalist interior with a glazed frontage, and a summer terrace where you can watch the yachts sail in and out of port. In the vein of "slow food" (a reaction against fast food that started in Italy in the late 1980s), the kitchen gives great care to seasonal ingredients and presentation. The owner, Zoran Grašo, is a retired basketball player, so you may spot some well-known sporting stars from time to time among the diners. ✉*Uvala Baluni, Zvončac* ☎*021/398–560* ✐*AE, DC, MC, V.*

$$–$$$ ✕**Adriana.** Overlooking the seafront promenade, Adriana is a perfect spot for people-watching day and night. It can get a little rowdy, with loud music and large groups, but the food is remarkably good, with good grilled meat dishes such as *čevapčići, pohani sir* (fried cheese), salads, and pizzas. ✉*Obala Hrvatskog Narodnog preporoda 6, Grad* ☎*021/340–000* ✐*AE, DC, MC, V.*

$$–$$$ ✕**Jugo.** In a modern white building with floor-to-ceiling glass windows and a large roof terrace above the ACI marina, Jugo offers great views back to town across the bay, with rows of sailing boats in the foreground. The menu includes Dalmatian seafood specialties and barbecued meats, with pizza as a cheap option. ✉*Uvala Baluni bb, Zvončac* ☎*021/398–300* ✐*AE, DC, MC, V.*

$$–$$$ ✕**Kod Jose.** This typical Dalmatian *konoba* is relaxed and romantic, with exposed stone walls and heavy wooden furniture set off by candlelight. The waiters are wonderfully discreet, and the *rižot frutta di mare* (seafood risotto) is delicious. You'll find it just outside the palace walls, a five-minute walk from Zlatna Vrata (Golden Gate)—it's slightly hidden away, so many tourists miss it. ⊠*Sredmanuška 4, Manuš* ☎*021/347–397* ⊟*AE, DC, MC, V.*

$$–$$$ ✕**Stellon.** With tables on a roof terrace affording sunset views over Bačvice Bay, this restaurant-cum-pizzeria serves an eclectic array of Italian-inspired cuisine including pasta and risotto dishes, excellent steaks, fish, colorful salads, plus first-rate pizza as a cheap option. It's owned by a former Croatian national team football player, Goran Vučević, and is seriously popular with locals and visitors alike. ⊠*Kupalište Bačvice bb, Bačvica* ☎*021/489–200* ⊟*AE, DC, MC, V.*

$–$$ ✕**Pizzeria Galija.** The best pizzas in town, as well as delicious pasta dishes and a range of colorful salads, are to be found in this centrally located pizzeria, which is close to the fish market. A favorite with locals, its dining room is bustling and informal, with heavy wooden tables and benches, and a large brick oven; draft beer and wine are sold by the glass. The owner, Željko Jerkov, is a retired Olympic gold medal–winning basketball player. ⊠*Tončićeva 12, Grad* ☎*021/347– 932* ⊟*No credit cards.*

$ ✕**Fife.** With a small terrace out front overlooking the wooden fishing boats of Matejuška harbor, Fife is a firm favorite with local fishermen. Come summer, it's also popular with tourists, who come here for the reasonably priced, down-to-earth Dalmatian cooking. There's no menu, and the dishes on offer change daily depending on what the owner finds at the morning market. If it's busy, you may be asked to share a table with other guests. ⊠*Trubičeva Obala 11, Matejuška* ☎*021/345–223* ⊟*No credit cards.*

WHERE TO STAY

In the past, Split was overlooked as a sightseeing destination and considered a mere transit point to the islands. As a result, it still suffers from a shortage of good places to stay. However, there are now three recommendable hotels within the palace walls, plus several pleasant, reasonably priced hotels within walking distance from the old town.

$$$$ ▦**Hotel Vestibul Palace.** Split's first boutique hotel opened in June 2005.
Fodor'sChoice Within the palace walls and accessed through the ancient vestibule,
★ the interior of this building has been carefully renovated to expose Roman stone and brickwork, which have been cleverly combined with more modern, minimalist designer details. A bar and restaurant can be found on the ground floor, and seven rooms are upstairs, complete with subtle lighting and plasma TVs. A new Villa Dobrić annex opened near Trg Braće Radića in spring 2007, with an additional two suites, two rooms, and a bar with a terrace out front. Pros: Inside the palace walls, beautiful interior, small (so guests receive individual attention). Cons: Expensive, often fully booked, no sports facilities. ⊠*Iza Vestibula 4, Grad, 21000* ☎*021/329–329* ▤*020/329–333* ⊕*www.vestibulpalace. com* ⇨*7 rooms, 4 suites* ⵊ*In-room: safe, refrigerator, dial-up. In-hotel: restaurant, room service, bar, laundry service, no elevator* ⊟*AE, DC, MC, V* ⵏⵔ*BP.*

$$$$ ▦**Le Meridien Lav.** A world unto its own, this vast, self-contained complex lies 8 km (5 mi) south of Split. Set in landscaped gardens with a

half mile of beach, it reopened in December 2006 after a $100 million renovation, making it Split's first five-star hotel. The modern, sleek, minimalist interior was designed by Italian architect Lorenzo Bellini. The spacious guest rooms and suites have floor-to-ceiling windows and are decorated in beige with splashes of red and blue, and most of the light-wood-paneled bathrooms have a separate tub and shower. Sports facilities include a palm-lined infinity pool overlooking the sea, a private marina with berths for 60 yachts, scuba diving, water skiing, windsurfing, tennis courts, and the luxurious Diocletian Spa & Wellness Center. There is also a vast casino with 20 gaming tables and 140 slot machines. Pros: Beautifully designed modern interior, excellent sports facilities, luxurious spa. Cons: Far from the center of Split, expensive, large (so the hotel can seem somewhat impersonal). ⊠ *Grljevačka 2A, Podstrana, 21312* 🕾 *021/500–500* ⊕ *www.starwoodhotels.com* 🖘 *364 rooms, 17 suites* ⚒ *In-room: safe, refrigerator, Ethernet. In-hotel: 3 restaurants, room service, bars, tennis courts, pools, gym, spa, beachfront, diving, water sports* ⊟ *AE, DC, MC, V* ⍾❘ *BP.*

$$ ⛫ **Hotel Park.** Smart and reliable, Hotel Park reopened in 2001 after extensive renovation work. The building dates back to 1921 and lies 10 minutes east of the city walls, overlooking Bačvice Bay. The rooms are modern and neatly furnished, and a pleasant restaurant terrace with palms offers views over the sea. Pros: Close to both Old Town and beach, breakfast is served on a lovely open-air terrace. Cons: No sports facilities, rather small rooms, parking can be difficult. ⊠ *Hatzeov Perivoj 3, Bačvice, 21000* 🕾 *021/406–400* 🖶 *021/406–401* ⊕ *www.hotel-park-split.hr* 🖘 *54 rooms, 3 suites* ⚒ *In-room: dial-up, refrigerator. In-hotel: restaurant, room service, bar, laundry service, no elevator* ⊟ *AE, DC, MC, V* ⍾❘ *BP.*

$$ ⛫ **Hotel Peristil.** Offering visitors one of only three chances to wake
★   up within the palace walls, Hotel Peristil lies behind the cathedral, just inside Srebrena Vrata, the city gate leading to the open-air market. The 12 rooms are comfortable and well equipped, and most have wooden floors. The Tiffany restaurant has open-air dining on a pleasant, shady terrace out front. Many guests are impressed by the friendliness and helpfulness of the staff. Pros: Inside the palace walls, small (so guests receive individual attention), lovely open-air restaurant terrace. Cons: Small and often fully booked, nearby parking difficult, limited facilities. ⊠ *Poljana Kraljice Jelena 5, Grad, 21000* 🕾 *021/329–070* 🖶 *021/329–088* ⊕ *www.hotelperistil.com* 🖘 *12 rooms* ⚒ *In-room: safe, refrigerator, dial-up. In-hotel: restaurant, no elevator* ⊟ *AE, DC, MC, V* ⍾❘ *BP.*

$ ⛫ **Hotel Slavija.** Split's first hotel when it opened in 1900, Slavija occupies an 18th-century building within the palace walls. Fully renovated in 2004, the 25 rooms are basic but comfortable, and the ones at the top have terraces affording views over the city's terra-cotta roofs. Some travelers may find the noise from the surrounding open-air bars excessive. Breakfast is served in the bar area, but there is no restaurant as such. Pros: Inside the palace walls, nightlife nearby, several four-bed family rooms. Cons: Noise from surrounding bars can be a problem at night, basic rooms, limited facilities. ⊠ *Buvinina 2, Grad, 21000*

☎*021/323–840* 🖷*021/323–868* ⊕*www.hotelslavija.com* ↩*25 rooms* ♿*In-room: dial-up. In-hotel: bar, no elevator* ▭*AE, DC, MC, V* ♨◎*BP.*

NIGHTLIFE & THE ARTS

Split is much more lively at night during the summer season, when bars stay open late, discos hold open-air parties by the sea, and the Split Summer Festival offers a respectable program of opera and classical music concerts.

NIGHTLIFE

Through summer, many bars have extended licenses and stay open until 2 AM. In August, rock musicians from Croatia and the other countries of the former Yugoslavia perform open-air concerts. There's no particular source of information about what's on, but you'll see posters around town if anything special is planned.

BARS With a colorful, bohemian interior and a courtyard garden lighted with flaming torches, **Ghetto Klub** (✉*Dosud 10, Grad* ☎*No phone*) pulls in the cool, young artsy crowd and hosts occasional exhibitions and concerts. Hidden away on a small piazza in the Old Town, **Jazz** (✉*Poljana Grgur Ninski, Grad* ☎*No phone*) offers outdoor tables and an artsy, intellectual clientele. Close to Zlatna Vrata, **Teak** (✉*Majstora Jurja 11, Grad* ☎*No phone*) is a small café with an exposed stonework-and-wood interior plus tables outside through summer. It's popular with high-brow locals, who come here to leaf through the piles of international newspapers and magazines.

DISCOS At **Metropolis** (✉*Matice Hrvatska 1, Trstenik* ☎*021/305–110*) a program of theme nights and special performances attracts a mixed crowd of all ages. Commercial techno music predominates, with a smattering of rock and pop. Croatian singers perform at **Shakespeare** (✉*Uvala Zenta 3, Zenta* ☎*021/519–492*) on weekends, backed up by a selection of commercial techno and disco dance music played by DJs.

THE ARTS

Kino Bačvice (✉*Put Firula, Bačvice*) is an open-air summer cinema in the pine woods above Bačvice Bay. Predominantly English-language films are shown in original version with subtitles. Running from mid-July to mid-August, the **Split Summer Festival** (✉*Trg Gaje Bulata 1, Grad* ☎*021/363–014* ⊕*www.splitsko-ljeto.hr*) includes a variety of open-air opera, classical-music concerts, and theatrical performances, the highlight being *Aïda* on Peristil.

SPORTS & THE OUTDOORS

BEACHES

The best beach is **Uvala Bačvica** (Bačvice Bay), a 10-minute walk east of the Old Town, where you will find showers, beach chairs, and umbrellas to rent, plus numerous cafés and bars offering refreshments.

SAILING

Well connected to the rest of Europe by plane and ferry—and within just a few hours' sailing of several of the Adriatic's most beautiful islands—Split is the center of the yacht-charter business in Dalmatia. *For a listing of Split-based charter companies, see ⇨ Sailing & Cruising the Croatian Coast in Understanding Croatia at the end of this book.* The 364-berth **ACI marina** (✉ *Uvala Baluni, Zvončac* ☎ *021/398–548*) is southwest of the city center. It stays open all year and is a base for dozens of charter companies organizing sailing on the Adriatic.

SHOPPING

Dalmatian women—and those from Split in particular—are renowned for their elegant sense of style. Despite a poor local economy, you'll find countless exclusive little boutiques selling ladies' clothes and shoes imported from Italy. However, the city's most memorable shopping venue remains the *pazar,* the colorful open-air market held each morning just outside the palace walls. When looking for gifts, bear in mind that Dalmatia produces some excellent wines, which you can buy either in Split or while visiting the islands.

Aromatica (✉ *Dobrić 12, Grad* ☎ *021/344–061*) stocks its own brand of deliciously scented soaps, shampoos, body creams, and massage oils made from local herbs. If you buy a selection, they will also gift-wrap them for you. **Vinoteka Bouquet** (✉ *Obala Hrvatskog Narodnog Preporoda 3, Grad* ☎ *021/348–031*) is a small shop selling a select choice of Croatian regional wines, plus some truffle products and olive oils.

SIDE TRIPS FROM SPLIT

TROGIR
27 km (17 mi) west of Split.

On a small island no more than a few city blocks in length, the beautifully preserved medieval town of Trogir is connected to the mainland by one bridge and tied to the outlying island of Čiovo by a second. The settlement dates back to the 3rd century BC when it was colonized by the Greeks, who named it Tragurion. It later flourished as a Roman port. With the fall of the Western Roman Empire, it became part of Byzantium and then followed the shifting allegiances of the Adriatic. In 1420, the Venetians moved in and stayed until 1797.

Today it is a UNESCO World Heritage Site and survives principally from tourism. You can explore the city in about an hour. A labyrinth of narrow, cobbled streets centers on Narodni trg, the main square, where the most notable buildings are located: the 15th-century loggia and clock tower, the Venetian-Gothic Čipko Palace, and the splendid cathedral, with its elegant bell tower. The south-facing seafront promenade is lined with cafés, ice-cream parlors, and restaurants, and there are also several small, old-fashioned hotels that offer a reasonable alternative to accommodations in Split.

Fodor's Choice ★ The remarkable **Katedrala Sveti Lovrijenac** *(Cathedral of St. Lawrence),* completed in 1250, is a perfect example of the massiveness and power of Romanesque architecture. The most striking detail is the main (west) portal, adorned with superb Romanesque sculpture by the Croatian master Radovan. The great door, flanked by a pair of imperious lions

Central Dalmatia

KEY

🚂 Rail lines

--- Ferry Lines

that form pedestals for figures of Adam and Eve, is framed by a fascinating series illustrating the daily life of peasants in a kind of Middle Ages comic strip. In the dimly lighted Romanesque interior, the 15th-century chapel of Sveti Ivan Orsini (St. John Orsini) of Trogir features statues of saints and apostles in niches facing the sarcophagus, on which lies the figure of St. John. The bell tower, built in successive stages—the first two stories Gothic, the third Renaissance—offers stunning views across the ancient rooftops. ⊠ *Trg Ivana Pavla II* ⊠ *Cathedral free, bell tower 5 Kn* ☉ *June–Oct., daily 8–7; Nov.–May, daily 8–noon and 4:30–7.*

WHERE TO STAY & EAT

$–$$$ ✕**Restaurant Fontana.** On the seafront overlooking the Trogir Channel, this highly esteemed restaurant and pizzeria has a vast waterside terrace. Fresh fish and seafood top the menu but can be pricey, whereas pizza makes a cheap alternative. ⊠ *Obrov* ☎ *021/885–744* ▭ *AE, DC, MC, V.*

$ ▥**Hotel Fontana.** In the old town overlooking the Trogir Channel, this old building has been tastefully refurbished to form a small hotel above a popular restaurant. Most of the rooms have Jacuzzis. Pros: Location on seafront promenade in the Old Town, friendly staff, breakfast served on the seafront terrace. Cons: Some rooms rather small, furnishings basic and modern (less atmospheric than some of Trogir's more old-fashioned hotels). ✉*Obrov 121220* ☎*021/885–744* 🖷*021/885–755* 🌐*www.fontana-trogir.com* ⇄*13 rooms, 1 suite* ⌕*In-room: kitchen (some), refrigerator. In-hotel: restaurant, room service, bar, no elevator, parking (no fee)* ☰*AE, DC, MC, V* ¶◎|*BP.*

BRAČ
9 nautical mi south of Split by ferry.

Close at hand and well connected to Split by ferry and catamaran services, the island of Brač can be visited in an easy day trip, though you may want to stay a night or two. With extensive tourist development along the coast and a stark, wild interior, the island is best known for its stunning beach and is also a prime windsurfing spot. The top resort area is **Bol.**

To get there, either catch an early morning Jadrolinija ferry from Split to Supetar (9 nautical mi) and then take a bus across the island to the south coast, or catch the midafternoon Jadrolinija catamaran from Split to Bol (24 nautical mi), which then continues to Jelsa on the island of Hvar.

☽
★ A spectacular beach, **Zlatni Rat** *(Golden Cape)*, in the south-coast fishing village of Bol, is the main attraction on Brač. A tree-lined coastal promenade leads from the village to an extraordinary geographical cape composed of tiny pebbles, which juts out ¾ km (mi) to sea, moving and changing shape slightly from season to season, depending on the winds. This is Croatia's prime site for windsurfing and an ideal beach for kids, as the water is shallow and the seabed is easy on their feet. ✉*Bol* ✈*1 km (½ mi) west of town center.*

SPORTS & THE OUTDOORS
For windsurfing and scuba-diving training and equipment rentals, the best established local company is **Big Blue** (✉*Podan Glavice 2, Bol* ☎*021/635–614* 🌐*www.big-blue-sport.hr*), which also rents sea kayaks and mountain bikes, and organizes cycling trips on Vidova Gora and Blaca Monastery.

HVAR
Hvar Town is 23 nautical mi south of Split by ferry.

The island of Hvar bills itself as the "sunniest island in the Adriatic." Not only does it have the figures to back up this claim—an annual average of 2,724 hours of sunshine with a maximum of two foggy days a year—but it also makes visitors a sporting proposition, offering them a money-back guarantee if there is ever a foggy day (which has been known to happen).

Hvar is also the name of the capital, near the island's western tip. The little town rises like an amphitheater from its harbor, backed by a hilltop fortress and protected from the open sea by a scattering of small islands known as Pakleni Otoci. Along the palm-lined quay, a string of cafés and restaurants is shaded by colorful awnings and umbrellas. A few steps away, the magnificent main square, **Trg Sveti Stjepan,** the largest piazza in Dalmatia, is backed by the 16th-century Katedrala Sveti Stjepan (Cathedral of St. Stephen). Other notable sights include the kazalište (a theater) and the Franjevački Samostan (Franciscan Monastery).

The easiest way to reach Hvar Town is to catch a midafternoon Jadrolinija catamaran from Split, which stops at Hvar Town (23 nautical mi) before continuing to the South Dalmatian islands of Korčula and Lastovo. Alternatively, take an early morning Jadrolinija ferry from Split to Stari Grad (23 nautical mi) and then catch a local bus across the island.

On the upper floor of the Arsenal, the **Kazalište** *(Theater)* opened in 1612, making it the oldest institution of its kind in Croatia and one of the first in Europe. The Arsenal building, where Venetian ships en route to the Orient once docked for repairs, dates back to the 13th century but was reconstructed after damage during a Turkish invasion in 1571. It was closed for renovation in 2007 but, at this writing, was expected to reopen for summer 2008. ⊠ *Trg Sv Stjepana, Hvar Town* ⊡ *15 Kn* ⊙ *May–Oct., daily 9–1 and 5–9; Nov.–Apr., daily 10–noon.*

East of town, along the quay past the Arsenal, lies the **Franjevački Samostan** *(Franciscan Monastery).* Within its walls, a pretty 15th-century Renaissance cloister leads to the former refectory, now housing a small museum with several notable artworks. ⊠ *Obala Ivana Lučića Lavčevića, Hvar Town* ⊡ *15 Kn* ⊙ *May–Oct., daily 10–noon and 5–7.*

WHERE TO STAY & EAT

$$–$$$$ ✕ **Macondo.** This superb fish restaurant lies hidden away on a narrow,
Fodor's Choice cobbled street between the main square and the fortress—to find it,
★ follow the signs from Trg Sv Stjepana. The dining room is simply furnished with wooden tables, discreet modern art, and a large open fire. The food and service are practically faultless. Begin with the delicate scampi pâté, followed by a mixed seafood platter, and round off with a glass of homemade *orahovica* (walnut rakija). ⊠ *2 blocks north of trg Sv Stjepana, Hvar Town* ☎ *021/742–850* ▭ *AE, DC, MC, V* ⊙ *Closed Dec.–Mar.*

$–$$ ✕ **Konoba Menego.** On the steps between the main square and the castle, this authentic stone-walled konoba has candlelit tables and whole *pršut* (prosciutto) hanging from the wooden beamed ceiling. Come here to snack on small platters of locally produced, cold Dalmatian specialties such as *kožji sir* (goat cheese), pršut, *salata od hobotnice* (octopus salad), and *masline* (olives), accompanied by a carafe of homemade wine. Before leaving, round off your meal with *pijane smokve* (figs marinated in brandy), and be sure to check out the world atlas where guests sign on the pages of their hometowns. ⊠ *Groda bb, Hvar Town* ☎ *021/742–036* ▭ *No credit cards* ⊙ *Closed Dec.–Mar.*

$$$$ ⊡ **Hotel Riva.** Reopened in 2006 after total renovation, the Riva is a
★ particularly lovely small luxury hotel. Occupying a 100-year-old stone building on the palm-lined waterfront, opposite the ferry landing station, it is now considered Hvar's hippest hideaway. The rooms are rather small but funky, each decorated in pale gray with splashes of red,

and a large black-and-white portrait of a film icon such as Anita Ekberg or James Dean. The prudish may not approve of the bathrooms since the shower cubicle is visible from the bedroom through a large clear-glass window. Out front there is a delightful open-air terrace decorated with potted olive trees, where the Roots Restaurant serves innovative Mediterranean cuisine and the B.B. Club cocktail bar works into the early hours. If you object to late-night noise, forfeit the sea view and ask for a room at the back. Pros: Prime location on seafront promenade, beautifully designed interior, excellent bar and restaurant. Cons: Very expensive, rooms in front can be noisy at night (bars) and in the early morning (ferry), rooms are rather small. ⊠*Riva bb, Hvar Town, 21450* ☎*021/750–100* 🖷*021/750–101* ⊕*www.suncanihvar.hr* ⬧*46 rooms, 8 suites* ⌂*In-room: safe, refrigerator, Wi-Fi. In-hotel: restaurant, room service, bar, public Wi-Fi, some pets allowed, no-smoking rooms* ⊟*AE, DC, MC, V* ⁍⃝*BP.*

$$ ☲**Hotel Croatia.** A family-run hotel surrounded by a pine-scented garden overlooks the sea and is a lovely 10-minute seafront walk southeast of the main square. The building dates back to 1936, and the rooms are peaceful even though the furnishings are basic (but comfortable). All meals, including breakfast, can be served on a garden terrace that offers glorious views over the sea to the Pakleni Islands. Pros: Most rooms have sea views, breakfast served on open-air terrace in garden, slightly out of the town center and more peaceful (no noisy bars, no noise from ferries). Cons: Rooms rather basic, poor service (reception sometimes left unattended). ⊠*Majerovica bb, Hvar Town, 21450* ☎*021/742–400* 🖷*021/741–707* ⊕*www.hotelcroatia.net* ⬧*22 rooms* ⌂*In-hotel: restaurant, bar, beachfront, no elevator* ⊟*AE, DC, MC, V* ⊗*Closed Oct.–Mar.* ⁍⃝*BP.*

VIS

34 nautical mi southwest of Split by ferry.

Closed to foreigners until 1989, the distant island of Vis is relatively wild and unexploited. To get here from Split, you can either take the SEM Marina fast catamaran service or a 2½-hour Jadrolinija ferry ride to arrive in Vis Town. Built around a wide harbor, the town is popular with yachters, who appreciate its rugged nature, unpretentious fish restaurants, and excellent locally produced wine. The pretty fishing village of Komiža is 11 km (7 mi) from Vis Town. From here, you're just a 40-minute boat ride away from the Modra Spilja (Blue Cave), often compared to the Blue Grotto on Italy's Capri.

Throughout the summer, local fishermen will take tourists from both Vis Town and Komiža into the **Modra Spilja** *(Blue Cave)* by boat. Some of these trips are done on a regular basis. Hidden away on the small island of Biševo (5 nautical mi southwest of Komiža), the cave is 78 feet long and 39 feet wide. Sunlight enters through the water, reflects off the seabed, and casts the interior in a fantastic shade of blue. If you're lucky, you'll have time for a quick swim. Ask at the marina or at the tourist-information office to see who is offering trips. ⊠*Biševo.*

WHERE TO STAY & EAT

$$–$$$$
Fodor'sChoice
★

✗**Villa Kaliopa.** With tables set under the trees in the romantic walled garden of a 16th-century villa, dinner at this restaurant in Vis Town is an unforgettable experience. The menu changes daily, depending on what fresh fish and shellfish have come in. Your server will bring a platter to the table so you can choose your own fish before it's cooked. ⊠ *V Nazora 32, Vis Town* ☏*021/711–755* ▭*AE, DC, MC, V* ⊗*Closed Nov.–Mar.*

$$–$$$

✗**Konoba Bako.** Popular with locals and visitors alike, this excellent fish restaurant overlooks a tiny bay in Komiža. Outdoors, tables are set right up to the water's edge, and inside there's a small pool with lobsters and amphorae. The *salata od hobotnice, škampi rižot* (scampi risotto), and barbecued fish are all delicious. ⊠*Gundulićeva 1, Komiža* ☏*021/713–742* ▭*AE, DC, MC, V* ⊗*Closed mid-Nov.–mid-Feb.*

$

▤**Hotel Paula.** In Vis Town, east of the ferry quay, this friendly, family-run hotel is hidden away between stone cottages in a quiet, cobbled side street. All the rooms are smartly furnished and modern; on the top floor there's a honeymoon suite with a Jacuzzi and a large terrace with a sea view. Downstairs, there's a good fish restaurant with tables on a walled summer terrace; it stays open year-round. Pros: Nice traditional stone building in Old Town, modern and comfortable rooms, friendly staff. Cons: A couple of blocks in from the seafront (only the top-floor suite has a sea view), often fully booked, 20-minute walk from ferry landing station can be difficult for visitors with heavy luggage. ⊠*Petra Hektorovića 2, Vis Town, 21480* ☏☐*021/711–362* ⊕*www.paula-hotel.t-com.hr* ⤶*10 rooms, 1 suite* ⚏*In-room: kitchen (some). In-hotel: restaurant, bar, bicycles, no elevator* ▭*AE, DC, MC, V* ⎛⊚⎝*BP.*

$

▤**Tamaris.** Overlooking the harbor and seafront promenade in Vis Town, Tamaris occupies a late-19th-century building. The location is perfect, the rooms are basic but comfortable, and it stays open all year. Pros: On seafront promenade in center of town, most rooms have sea views, cheerful café terrace out front. Cons: Interior badly in need of refurbishment, rooms very basic, service rather indifferent. ⊠*Šetalište Apolonija Zanelle 5, Vis Town, 21480* ☏☐*021/711–350* ⤶*27 rooms* ⚏*In-hotel: restaurant, bar, no elevator* ▭*AE, DC, MC, V* ⎛⊚⎝*BP.*

SPLIT & CENTRAL DALMATIA ESSENTIALS

AIR TRAVEL

The national carrier, Croatia Airlines, operates domestic flights from Split to Zagreb, Dubrovnik, Pula, and Osijek. During the summer high season, you can fly directly to Split from Amsterdam, Bari, Brussels, Catania, Copenhagen, Frankfurt, Gothenburg, Hamburg, Helsinki, Istanbul, Lisbon, London, Lyon, Manchester, Milan, Munich, Oslo, Palermo, Paris, Prague, Rome, Sarajevo, Skopje, Stockholm, Tel Aviv, Turin, Vienna, Warsaw, and Zurich. Also through summer, Croatia Airlines flies nonstop from the island of Brač to Zagreb, Munich, and Frankfurt. Adria, British Airways, ČSA, and Malev also fly to Split. In addition, through the summer the low-cost airlines easyJet and Wizzair operate between London and Split. For airline contact information, see ⇨By Air *in* Croatia Essentials, at the end of this chapter.

AIRPORTS & TRANSFERS

Split is served by Split Airport (SPU) at Kaštela, 25 km (16 mi) northwest of the city center. The island of Brač is served by Brač Airport at Veško Polje, 14 km (8¾ mi) northeast of Bol.

Information **Split Airport** (✉ *Kaštela* ☎ *021/203–171 general information, 021/203–218 lost and found* ⊕ *www.split-airport.hr*). **Brač Airport** (✉ *Veško Polje* ☎ *021/559–711 general information* ⊕ *www.airport-brac.hr*).

AIRPORT You can take an airport bus to obala Lazereta, near the Split Bus Sta-
TRANSFERS tion. For your return, the airport bus leaves Split 90 minutes before each flight. A one-way ticket costs 30 Kn, and the travel time is 40 minutes. Brač airport is not served by bus but taxis are available.

Information **Split airport bus** (☎ *021/203–171*).

BOAT & FERRY TRAVEL

From June through September, Jadrolinija and Blue Line both run regular services to Ancona (Italy), departing 9 PM from Split and arriving in Ancona at 7 AM the following day. The same vessels depart at 9 PM from Ancona to arrive in Split at 7 AM. Journey time is approximately 10 hours either direction. In peak season only, Blue Line also runs day crossings departing from Ancona at 11 AM on Saturday, Sunday, and Monday. Through winter these services are reduced slightly.

From June to September, the Italian company SNAV runs Croazia Jet, a daily catamaran service between Ancona (Italy) and Split, departing at 5 PM from Split and arriving in Ancona at 9:30 PM. The same vessel departs at 11 AM from Ancona to arrive in Split at 3:30 PM. The journey time is 4½ hours in either direction. The same company runs Pescara Jet, a daily catamaran service between Pescara (Italy) and Split, stopping at Stari Grad (island of Hvar) en route. The vessel departs at 5 PM from Split and arrives in Pescara at 11 PM, then leaves Pescara the following morning at 10:30, arriving in Split at 4:15 PM. On Saturdays only, a corresponding catamaran connects from Stari Grad (Hvar) to Bol (Brač).

Jadrolinija operates coastal ferries that run from Rijeka to Dubrovnik. Ferries depart from Rijeka twice a week in the evening, arrive in Split in the early morning on the following day (journey time is approximately 10 hours), and then continue down the coast to Dubrovnik (journey time is approximately 9 hours), stopping at Stari Grad (island of Hvar) and Korčula en route. From Dubrovnik, they then cover an overnight stretch to Bari in Italy.

Jadrolinija runs daily ferries to Supetar (island of Brač), Stari Grad (island of Hvar), and Vis from Split.

Jadrolinija runs a daily catamaran from Split to Hvar Town (island of Hvar), which then continues to Vela Luka (island of Korčula) and Ubli (island of Lastovo). A separate service runs to Bol (island of Brač) and then continues to Jelsa (island of Hvar).

Information **Jadrolinija** (☎ 021/338–333 ⊕ www.jadrolinija.hr). **Blue Line** (☎ 021/352–533 ⊕ www.blueline-ferries.com). **SNAV** (☎ 021/322–252 ⊕ www.snav.it).

BUS TRAVEL

International buses arrive daily from Trieste (Italy), Ljubljana (Slovenia), Belgrade (Serbia), Sarajevo (Bosnia and Herzegovina), Munich, and Stuttgart (Germany). There are buses once a week from Vienna (Austria), and London (United Kingdom) via Paris (France). There are also good bus connections to destinations all over Croatia from Split.

Information **Split Bus Station** (✉ Obala Kneza Domogoja 12, Split ☎ 060/327–777 ⊕ www.ak-split.hr).

4

CAR TRAVEL

While visiting Split and the nearby islands of Brač, Hvar, and Vis, you are certainly better off without a car. However, you may wish to rent a vehicle to drive south if you are moving on to Dubrovnik or if you are driving north to Zagreb, rather than use public transport.

Information **Budget** (✉ Trubićeva Obala 12 Split ☎ 021/399–214 ✉ Split Airport, Kaštela ☎ 021/203–151). **Dollar Thrifty** (✉ Hotel Marjan, Obala K Branimira 8, Split ☎ 021/399–000 ✉ Split Airport, Kaštela ☎ 021/895–320). **Hertz** (✉ Trubićeva Obala 2, Split ☎ 021/360–455 ✉ Split Airport, Kaštela ☎ 021/895–230).

INTERNET

During the summer, small temporary Internet cafés spring up in the main resorts; some may be nothing more than a regular café with a PC in the corner. Even on the islands, you will find somewhere to check e-mail. However, very few well-established, fully equipped Internet cafés exist in the region.

TAXIS

In Split, the main taxi ranks lie at each end of the *Riva* (Obala Hrvatskog Preporoda): in front of the *pazar* (open-air market) and in front of Hotel Bellevue. You will also find taxis waiting outside the train station (Obala Kneza Domagoja). Or you can call for a taxi in Split.

Information **Radio Taxi** (☎ 970 in Split).

BY TRAIN

There are three day trains and two night trains (with sleeping cars) daily between Split and Zagreb (journey time 5½ hours daytime; 8½ hours nighttime). In addition, there are three day trains daily between Split and Šibenik (journey time approximately 3½ hours, with a change at Perković).

Information **Split Train Station** (✉ Obala Kneza Domogoja 9, Split ☎ 060/333–444 ⊕ www.hznet.hr).

VISITOR INFORMATION

Contacts **Split & Dalmatia County Tourist Board** (✉ Prilaz brace Kaliterna 10/l, Split ☎ 021/490–032 ⊕ www.dalmatia-cen.com). **Bol Tourist Information Center** (✉ Porat Bolskih Pomoraca, Bol ☎ 021/635–638 ⊕ www.bol.hr). **Hvar Town Tourist Information Center** (✉ Trg Sv Stjepana 16, Hvar Town ☎ 021/741–059 ⊕ www.

hvar.hr). **Split Tourist Information Center** (✉*Peristil, Split* ☎*021/345–606* ⊕*www.visitsplit.com)*. **Trogir Tourist Information Center** (✉*Trg Ivana Pavla II 1, Trogir* ☎*021/881–412* ⊕*www.trogir.hr)*. **Vis Tourist Information Center** (✉*Šetalište Stare Isse 5, Vis Town* ☎*021/717–017* ⊕*www.tz-vis.hr)*.

DUBROVNIK & SOUTHERN DALMATIA

The highlight of southern Dalmatia is undoubtedly the majestic walled city of Dubrovnik, which was once a rich and powerful independent republic. Overlooking the sea and backed by rugged mountains, it's an unforgettable sight and probably Croatia's most photographed city. If you're traveling to Dubrovnik by coastal ferry from either Split or Rijeka, you might choose to stop overnight in Korčula Town, on the island of Korčula, with its fine Gothic and Renaissance stone buildings laying witness to almost 800 years of Venetian rule. In contrast, the island of Mljet offers little in the way of architectural monuments but has preserved its indigenous coniferous forests, which are now contained within Mljet National Park. If you're traveling from central to southern Dalmatia by road, you'll pass through a narrow coastal strip given over to Bosnia, so have your passport at hand for the border checkpoint. The stopover is inconsequential, and you are usually off after a brief passport check. Most Croatian buses have a 20-minute stop here so people can jump off and shop, since many things—notably cigarettes—are much cheaper in Bosnia.

DUBROVNIK

Lying 216 km (135 mi) southeast of Split and commanding a splendid coastal location, Dubrovnik is one of the world's most beautiful fortified cities. Its massive stone ramparts and splendid fortress towers curve around a tiny harbor, enclosing graduated ridges of sun-bleached orange-tiled roofs, copper domes, and elegant bell towers.

In the 7th century AD, residents of the Roman city Epidaurum (now Cavtat) fled the Avars and Slavs of the north and founded a new settlement on a small rocky island, which they named Laus, and later Ragusa. On the mainland hillside opposite the island, the Slav settlement called Dubrovnik grew up. In the 12th century, the narrow channel separating the two settlements was filled in, and Ragusa and Dubrovnik became one. The city was surrounded by defensive walls during the 13th century, and these were reinforced with towers and bastions during the late 15th century.

From 1358 to 1808, the city existed as a powerful and remarkably sophisticated independent republic, reaching its Golden Age during the 16th century. In 1667, many of its splendid Gothic and Renaissance buildings were destroyed by an earthquake. The defensive walls survived the disaster, and the city was rebuilt in baroque style.

Dubrovnik lost its independence to Napoleon in 1808, and in 1815 passed to Austria-Hungary. During the 20th century, as part of Yugoslavia, the city became a popular tourist destination, and in 1979 it was listed as a UNESCO World Heritage Site. During the war for independence, it came under heavy siege, though thanks to careful restoration work, few traces of damage remain. Today, Dubrovnik is once again a fashionable, high-class destination, with

recent visitors including Tom Cruise, Sharon Stone, John Malkovich, and Sir Roger Moore.

Numbers in the margins correspond to numbers on the Dubrovnik map.

WHAT TO SEE

⑫ Akvarij *(Aquarium).* This dark, cavernous space houses several small pools and 27 well-lighted tanks containing a variety of fish from rays to small sharks, as well as other underwater denizens such as sponges and sea urchins. Children will find the octopus, in his glass tank, either very amusing or horribly scary. ⊠ *Damjana Jude 2, Stari Grad* ☎ *020/323–978* ⊑ *30 Kn* ⊙ *June–Sept., daily 9–8; Apr., May, Oct., and Nov., daily 9–6; Dec.–Mar., daily 9–1.*

❽ Crkva Svetog Vlaha *(Church of St. Blaise).* This 18th-century baroque church replaced an earlier one destroyed by fire. Of particular note is the silver statue on the high altar of St. Blaise holding a model of Dubrovnik, which is paraded around town each year on February 3, the Day of St. Blaise. ⊠ *Luža, Stari Grad* ⊑ *Free* ⊙ *Daily 8–noon and 4:30–7.*

NEED A BREAK?   **Gradska Kavarna** (⊠ *Placa, Stari Grad*) occupies the old Arsenal building and remains Dubrovnik's favorite meeting place for morning coffee with cakes or an evening aperitif. It has an ample summer terrace for when the weather is nice.

❻ Dominikanski Samostan *(Dominican Monastery).* With a splendid, late-15th-century floral Gothic cloister as its centerpiece, the monastery is best known for its museum, which houses a rich collection of religious paintings by the so-called Dubrovnik School from the 15th and 16th centuries. Look out for works by Božidarević, Hamzić, and Dobričević, as well as gold and silver ecclesiastical artifacts crafted by local goldsmiths. ⊠ *Sv Domina 4, Stari Grad* ☎ *020/321–423* ⊑ *15 Kn* ⊙ *May–Oct., daily 9–6; Nov.–Apr., daily 9–5.*

❹ Franjevačka Samostan *(Franciscan Monastery).* The monastery's chief claim to fame is its pharmacy, which was founded in 1318 and is still in existence today; it's said to be the oldest in Europe. There's also a delightful cloistered garden, framed by Romanesque arcades supported by double columns, each crowned with a set of grotesque figures. In the Treasury a painting shows what Dubrovnik looked like before the disastrous earthquake of 1667. ⊠ *Placa 2, Stari Grad* ☎ *020/321–410* ⊑ *20 Kn* ⊙ *May–Oct., daily 9–6; Nov.–Apr., daily 9–5.*

❸ Gradske Zidine *(City Walls).* Most of the original construction took place during the 13th century, though the walls were further reinforced with towers and bastions during the following 400 years. On average

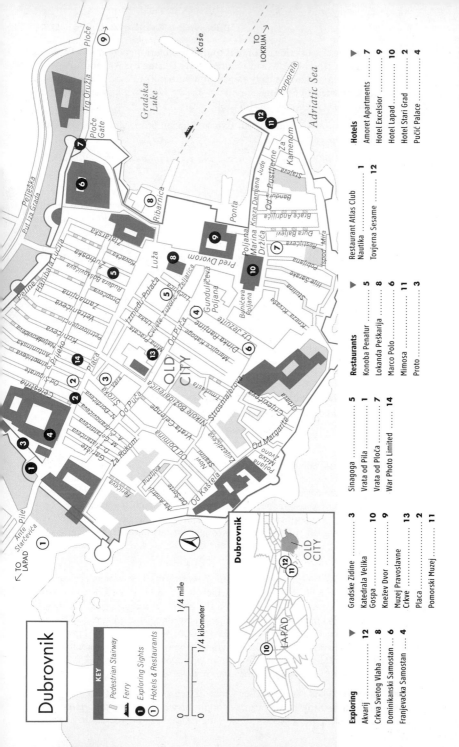

Dubrovnik

KEY

- Pedestrian Stairway
- Ferry
- ① Exploring Sights
- ① Hotels & Restaurants

0 — 1/4 mile
0 — 1/4 kilometer

Kaše

Gradska Luke

TO LOKRUM →

Adriatic Sea

Za Kamenom
Od Pustijerne
Bandura
Braće Andrijića
Đura Baljevi
Restićeva
Ilije Sarake
Kneza Krasa
Ispod Mira
Kneza Damjana Jude
Marina Kneza Držića
Poljana

Ponta
Ribarnica
Pred Dvorom
Bunićeva Poljana
Gundulićeva Poljana
Od Puča
Od Jezuite
Dinka Ranjine
Miha Pracata
Poljana Nikole Božidarevića
Strossmajerova
Od Domina

Luža
Zlatarska
Boškovićeva
Ruđera Boškovićeva
Novaka
Zamanjina
Celestina
Od Sigurate
Prijeko
Palmotićeva
Antuninska
Nalješkovićeva
Kovačka
Zlatoška
Peline
Hanibala Lucija
Veltančeva
Kunićeva
Prijeko
Plača
Zuzorićeva
Od Puča
Svetog Dominika
M. Getaldićeva
Između Polača
Garište
Za Rokom
Nikole Božidarevića
Vrata Celenge
Stulina
Zvijezdićeva
Za Rudером
Od Kaštela
Na Andriji
Od Margarite
Od Tabakarije
Miho Jvono
Poljana

OLD CITY

Trg Oružja
Ploče Gate
Pločе

⑨
Put Iza Grada
Pelješka

TO LAPAD
Ante Pile
Starčevića

⑦ ⑥ ⑧ ⑤ ⑨ ⑧ ⑤ ⑩ ⑦ ④ ⑥ ⑬ ⑭ ② ③ ③ ④ ① ⑫ ⑪ ①

Dubrovnik

LAPAD
OLD CITY
⑩ ⑪ ⑫

they are 80 feet high and up to 10 feet thick on the seaward side, 20 feet on the inland side. ✉*Placa, Stari Grad* ☎*020/324–641* 💶*50 Kn* 🕐*May–Sept., daily 8–7:30; Oct.–Apr., daily 10–3.*

🔟 **Katedrala Velika Gospa** *(Cathedral of Our Lady)*. The present structure was built in baroque style after the original was destroyed in the 1667 earthquake. The interior contains a number of notable paintings, including a large polyptych above the main altar depicting the *Assumption of Our Lady,* attributed to Titian. The Treasury displays 138 gold and silver reliquaries, including the skull of St. Blaise in the form of a bejeweled Byzantine crown and also an arm and a leg of the saint, likewise encased in decorated golden plating. ✉*Bunićeva Poljana, Stari Grad* ☎*020/323–459* 💶*Cathedral free, Treasury 10 Kn* 🕐*Mon.–Sat. 9–5:30, Sun. 11–5:30.*

4

🔟 **Knežev Dvor** *(Bishop's Palace)*. Originally created in the 15th century but reconstructed several times through the following years, this exquisite building with an arcaded loggia and an internal courtyard shows a combination of late-Gothic and early Renaissance styles. On the ground floor there are large rooms where, in the days of the Republic, the Great Council and Senate held their meetings. Over the entrance to the meeting halls a plaque reads OBLITI PRIVATORUM PUBLICA CURATE (Forget private affairs, and get on with public matters). Upstairs, the rector's living quarters now accommodate the Gradski Muzej (City Museum), containing exhibits that give a picture of life in Dubrovnik from early days until the fall of the Republic. ✉*Pred Dvorom 3, Stari Grad* ☎*020/321–497* 💶*35 Kn* 🕐*May–Oct., daily 9–6; Nov.–Apr., daily 9–2.*

🔟 **Muzej Pravoslavne Crkve** *(Orthodox Church Museum)*. Next door to the Orthodox Church, this small museum displays religious icons from the Balkan region and Russia, as well as several portraits of eminent early-20th-century Dubrovnik personalities by local artist Vlaho Bukovac. ✉*Od Puca 8, Stari Grad* ☎*020/323–283* 💶*10 Kn* 🕐*May–Oct., daily 9–2; Nov.–Apr., Mon.–Sat. 9–2.*

② **Placa.** This was once the shallow sea channel separating the island of Laus from the mainland. Although it was filled in during the 12th century, it continued to divide the city socially for several centuries, with the nobility living in the area south of Placa and the commoners living on the hillside to the north. Today it forms the venue for the *korzo,* an evening promenade where locals meet to chat, maybe have a drink, and generally size one another up. ✉*Stari Grad.*

🔟 **Pomorski Muzej** *(Maritime Museum)*. Above the Aquarium, on the first floor of St. John's Fortress, this museum's exhibits illustrate how rich and powerful Dubrovnik became as one of the world's most important seafaring nations. On display are intricately detailed models of ships as well as engine-room equipment, sailors' uniforms, paintings, and maps. ✉*Damjana Jude 2, Stari Grad* ☎*020/323–904* 💶*35 Kn* 🕐*May–Oct., daily 9–6; Nov.–Apr., Tues.–Sun. 9–2.*

NEED A BREAK? Through a small doorway (signed COLD DRINKS) in the south side of the city walls, off the narrow street of Od Margarita, **Buža** (⊠ *Od Margarita, Stari Grad*) bar serves cold drinks and coffee at tables arranged on a series of terraces set into the rocks, affording stunning views over the open sea.

⑤ Sinagoga *(Synagogue).* This tiny 15th-century synagogue, the second oldest in Europe (after Prague's) bears testament to Dubrovnik's once thriving Jewish community, made up largely of Jews who were expelled from Spain and Italy during the medieval period. ⊠ *Žudioska 5, Stari Grad* ☎ *020/321–028* ⌑ *10 Kn* ⊙ *Weekdays 10–8.*

❶ Vrata od Pila *(Pile Gate).* Built in 1537 and combining a Renaissance arch with a wooden drawbridge on chains, this has always been the main entrance to the city walls. A niche above the portal contains a statue of Sveti Vlah (St. Blaise), the city's patron saint, holding a replica of Dubrovnik in his left hand. From May to October, guards in deep-red period-costume uniforms stand vigilant by the gate through daylight hours, just as they would have done when the city was a republic. ⊠ *Pile, Stari Grad.*

❼ Vrata od Ploča *(Ploče Gate).* One of two entrances into the town walls, Ploče comprises a stone bridge and wooden drawbridge plus a 15th-century stone arch bearing a statue of Sveti Vlah (St. Blaise). As at Pile Gate, guards in period costume stand vigilant here through the summer season. ⊠ *Ploče, Stari Grad.*

⑭ War Photo Limited. Shocking but impressive, this modern gallery devotes **Fodor'sChoice** two entire floors to war photojournalism. Past exhibitions include ★ images from conflicts in Afghanistan, Iraq, former Yugoslavia, Israel, Palestine, and Lebanon. Refreshingly impartial by Croatian standards, the message—that war is physically and emotionally destructive whichever side you are on—comes through loudly and clearly. You'll find it in a narrow side street running between Placa and Prijeko. ⊠ *Antuninska 6, Stari Grad* ☎ *020/322–166* ⊕ *www.warphotoltd.com* ⌑ *30 Kn* ⊙ *May and Oct., Tues.–Sat. 10–4, Sun. 10–2; June–Sept., daily 9–9.*

WHERE TO EAT

As elsewhere along the coast, seafood dominates restaurant menus. The narrow, cobbled street Prijeko, running parallel to Placa, is packed with touristy restaurants and waiters touting for customers. Less commercial and infinitely more agreeable eateries are scattered throughout the town.

$$$–$$$$ ✕ **Proto.** A reliable choice for dinner, Proto is on a side street off Stradun, with tables arranged on a vine-covered, upper-level, open-air terrace. The menu features a good selection of traditional Dalmatian seafood dishes—including oysters from nearby Ston—and barbecued meats, notably succulent steaks. The restaurant dates back to 1886. Recent guests have included U.S. actor Richard Gere and Irish singer Bono. ⊠ *Široka 1, Stari Grad* ☎ *020/323–234* ▭ *AE, DC, MC, V.*

$$$–$$$$ ✕ **Restaurant Atlas Club Nautika.** Probably Dubrovnik's most exclusive restaurant, Nautika lies close to Pile Gate, just outside the city walls. It occupies the former Nautical Academy building, dating from 1881,

CLOSE UP

Dubrovnik under Siege

From November 1991 to May 1992, Dubrovnik was intermittently shelled by the Yugoslav army and Serb and Montenegrin irregulars, who were stationed on the rugged hills behind the city. Electricity and water supplies were cut off, and the local population took refuge in basements, surviving on a slowly diminishing quantity of foodstuffs, fuel, and medical supplies. The city's massive medieval fortifications stood up well to the assault, though none of Dubrovnik's main monuments was targeted—apparently the Yugoslav army wanted to capture the city intact. Extensive media coverage whipped up a storm of international criticism over the wanton bombing of this historic city, which effectively turned world opinion against Belgrade and in favor of granting Croatia diplomatic recognition. Once hostilities ceased, the cleanup and rebuilding began. During the second half of the 1990s, money poured in from all over the world for the restoration of the shrapnel-scarred facades and the shattered terra-cotta rooftops. Today, thanks to the work of highly skilled craftsmen, barely any traces of war damage remain.

and has two terraces overlooking the sea. Although some people feel that it is overpriced, it remains a sound choice for business lunches and formal celebrations. The restaurant serves shellfish, lobster, and fresh fish, as well as meat dishes, and has an excellent wine list. ⊠ *Brsalje 3, Pile* ☎ *020/442–526* ⊟ *AE, DC, MC, V.*

$$–$$$ ✕**Konoba Penatur.** With outdoor tables next to the Church of St. Blaise,
★ this informal restaurant offers a bargain fixed-price menu at lunchtime and romantic candlelit dining in the evening. Look out for excellent Croatian seafood specialties such as *salata od hobotnice, girice* (small fish deep fried, similar to British whitebait), and *škampi* (scampi). There's also a reasonable choice of vegetarian pasta dishes. ⊠ *Lučarica 2, Stari Grad* ☎ *020/323–700* ⊟ *AE, DC, MC, V.*

$$–$$$ ✕**Marco Polo.** This favorite haunt of actors and musicians during the Summer Festival is in the Old Town, close to Crkva Sv Vlaha. The minuscule dining room is only big enough for four tables, but there's a summer terrace in the courtyard. Choose from a range of excellent seafood dishes, including shellfish, risottos, and fresh fish. ⊠ *Lučarica 6, Stari Grad* ☎ *020/323–719* ⊟ *AE, DC, MC, V* ⊙ *Closed Nov.–Mar.*

$$–$$$ ✕**Mimosa.** Located between the old town and Lapad, Mimosa makes a perfect choice for a light lunch. The menu offers a decent selection of meat, fish, pasta, and vegetarian dishes, with pizza as a cheap option. Outside, you dine at wooden tables and benches on a large, vine-covered terrace. Indoors, the dining room is decorated in minimalist style, in white, red, and black. There's live Dalmatian klapa music on Monday, Wednesday, and Friday evenings. ⊠ *Branitelja Dubrovnika 9, Pile* ☎ *020/411–157* ⊟ *AE, DC, MC, V.*

$$–$$$ ✕**Lokanda Peškarija.** Just outside the town walls, overlooking the old
Fodor'sChoice harbor and next to the covered fish market, this seafood restaurant is a
★ particularly good value. It has a split-level interior with exposed stone walls and wooden beams, plus outdoor candlelit tables by the water.

Locals love it, so reservations are recommended, especially for dinner. ✉ *Na Ponti, Stari Grad* ☎ *020/324–750* ▭ *AE, DC, MC, V* ⊘ *Closed Jan. and Feb.*

$$–$$$ ✗ **Tovjerna Sesame.** Just outside the city walls and close to Pile Gate, this romantic eatery occupies a vaulted, candlelit space with bohemian decor. It's popular with locals, and the menu is adventurous by Dalmatian standards: beef carpaccio with Parmesan, rocket (arugula), and capers; pasta truffle dishes, and a range of beautifully presented, creative salads. It's ideal for a light supper accompanied by a good bottle of wine. ✉ *Dante Alighieria, Pile* ☎ *020/412–910* ▭ *AE, DC, MC, V.*

WHERE TO STAY ·

There are only two small but extremely desirable hotels within the city walls. The most exclusive establishments line the coastal road east of the center, offering stunning views of the Old Town and the sea, whereas modern hotels with cheaper rooms and decent sports facilities can be found in Lapad, 3 km (2 mi) west of the center. The only way to save money in Dubrovnik is to rent a private room, but, like the hotels, even these can be up to double the price of those elsewhere in Croatia.

$$$$ 🏨 **Hotel Excelsior.** On the coastal road east of the center, this prestigious, modern hotel offers well-furnished rooms with balconies overlooking the sea and Old Town. Each of the luxury suites has a jetted tub. It's slightly lacking in charm, but there are excellent sports, health and beauty, and business facilities. Of special note is the Taverna Rustica, a highly regarded restaurant with romantic nighttime views across the water to the city walls; it's popular with residents and nonresidents alike. ✉ *Put Frane Supila 12, Ploče, 20000* ☎ *020/353–300* ⊕ *www. hotel-excelsior.hr* ⤴ *146 rooms, 18 suites* ⚷ *In-room: refrigerator, dial-up. In-hotel: 2 restaurants, room service, bar, pool, gym, laundry service, public Internet* ▭ *AE, DC, MC, V* ⏀*BP.*

$$$$
Fodor's Choice
★
🏨 **Pučić Palace.** In the heart of the Old Town, occupying a beautifully restored 18th-century baroque palace, this small luxury boutique hotel offers the sort of aristocratic delights that its location suggests: rooms with dark oak parquet floors and wood-beam ceilings, antique furnishings, and Italian mosaic-tile bathrooms supplied with Bulgari toiletries. Fine wining and dining are also possible here, with the Defne restaurant serving eastern Mediterranean cuisine on a romantic upper-level terrace lined with potted lemon trees. The ground-floor Café Royal is a popular meeting point for morning coffee and pastries, with tables outside on the piazza on warm days. In the evening, head for the adjoining Razonoda wine bar, where you can sample some of Croatia's most sought-after wines and spirits. ✉ *Ul od Puča 1, Stari Grad, 20000* ☎ *020/326–200* ⊕ *www.thepucicpalace.com* ⤴ *19 rooms* ⚷ *In-room: safe, refrigerator, dial-up. In-hotel: restaurant, room service, bar, no elevator, laundry service* ▭ *AE, DC, MC, V* ⏀*BP.*

$$$ 🏨 **Hotel Stari Grad.** One of only two hotels in the Old Town, this refined and intimate establishment occupies a renovated palace that once belonged to the Drašković family, giving you some idea of how the local aristocracy once lived. The rooms are furnished with reproduction antiques, and in summer breakfast is served on a lovely roof terrace with views over the surrounding buildings. You'll find it in a quiet side street close to Pile Gate. ☒ *Od Sigurate 4, Stari Grad, 20000* ☎*020/322–244* ⊕*www.hotelstarigrad.com* ⤙*8 rooms* ☖*In-room: refrigerator, dial-up. In-hotel: bar, no elevator, laundry service* ▤*AE, DC, MC, V* ⓘⓄⒷ*BP.*

$$ ⊞**Hotel Lapad.** Occupying a 19th-century building with a garden and an outdoor pool, Hotel Lapad overlooks Gruž harbor, just a 15-minute walk west of the Old Town, making it a good midrange option. A boat service to nearby beaches is at your disposal. Rooms in the new wing are somewhat more spacious than those in the old wing and, therefore, a little more expensive. The hotel offers good discounts off-season. ☒*Lapadska obala 37, Lapad, 20000* ☎*020/432–922* ⊕*www. hotel-lapad.hr* ⤙*194 rooms* ☖*In-room: refrigerator. In-hotel: restaurant, room service, bar, pool* ▤*AE, DC, MC, V* ⊗*Closed Nov.–Mar.* ⓘⓄⒷ*BP.*

$ ⊞**Amoret Apartments.** In the heart of the Old Town, these delightful two-person studio apartments occupy two carefully restored 16th-century stone buildings, one on Restićeva (a narrow street behind the Cathedral) and the other on Dinka Ranjine (a narrow street behind the Church of St. Blaise). Each unit consists of a single room, a bathroom, and a full kitchen. All are tastefully furnished with antiques, and beds with wrought-iron bedsteads. The owner is an extremely friendly and helpful Croatian lady called Dinka. ☒*Restićeva 2, Stari Grad, 20000* ☎*020/324–005* ⊕*www.dubrovnik-amoret.com* ⤙*6 apartments* ☖*In-room: No phone, kitchen, refrigerator. In-hotel: No elevator* ▤*No credit cards.*

NIGHTLIFE & THE ARTS

Restrained through winter, aristocratic Dubrovnik wakes up with a vengeance come summer. Most nightlife takes place under the stars, as bars set up outdoor seating, discos take place by the sea, and even the cinema is open-air. The world-renowned Dubrovnik Summer Festival offers quality theatrical performances and classical-music concerts with international performers. An after-dinner drink at an outdoor table in the Old Town makes a romantic way to round out the evening. Those in search of more lively pursuits should visit one of several chic nightclubs with music and open-air bars, which cater to the city's tanned and glamorous summer visitors.

BARS **Arsenal** (☒*Pred Dvorom 1, Stari Grad* ☎*020/321–065*), a trendy wine bar, is adorned with heavy wooden furniture and much red velvet. It occupies the former arsenal, where Dubrovnik's old-fashioned galleys were once repaired. Most people come here to drink fine wine, enjoy live music, and dance, though there is also an excellent terrace restaurant affording fine views over the harbor if you need something other than liquid sustenance. **Buža** (☒*Od Margarite bb, Stari Grad* ☎*No phone*), with tables arranged on a series of terraces built into the rocks, overlooks the sea just outside the south-facing city walls. The informal bar makes a romantic venue for an evening drink. Don't expect high style—drinks are served in plastic cups—but the mellow music, crashing waves, and nighttime candles make it a memorable experience. It's open daily until 3 AM.

DISCOS **Eastwest Beach Club** (⊠*Frana Supila, Banje Beach* ☎*020/412–220*) is one of several chic establishments where you might spot well-known actors and sports celebrities. Eastwest combines a daytime café overlooking a well-equipped pebble beach and a nighttime restaurant with an Italian-inspired menu and a cocktail bar and rooftop VIP open-air lounge open until 5 AM. You'll find it a five-minute walk east of the Old Town.

THE ARTS Dubrovnik's cultural highlight is the annual **Dubrovnik Summer Festival** (⌂*Poljana P Miličevića 1* ☎*020/323–400* ⊕*www.dubrovnik-festival. hr*), which runs from early July to late August. The world-renowned festival includes a variety of open-air classical concerts and theatrical performances, notably Shakespeare's *Hamlet*, at various venues within the city walls.

SPORTS & THE OUTDOORS

BEACHES
The best beaches lie on the tiny island of **Lokrum,** a short distance south of the Old Town. Through high season boats leave regularly from the Arsenal, ferrying visitors back and forward from morning to early evening. The **Eastwest Beach Club** (⊠*Frana Supila, Banje Beach* ☎*020/412–220*), just a short distance from Ploče Gate, is a fashionable spot with a small pebble beach complete with chaise longues and parasols, waterskiing and jet-skiing facilities, and a chic café.

SAILING
The 450-berth **ACI marina** (⊠*Mokošica* ☎*020/455–020*) is 2 nautical mi from Gruž harbor and 6 km (3½ mi) from the city walls. The marina is open year-round, and a number of charter companies are based there.

SHOPPING
Despite its role as an important tourist destination, Dubrovnik offers little in the way of shopping or souvenir hunting. If you're in search of gifts, your best bet is a bottle of good Dalmatian wine or *rakija*. **Croata** (⊠*Put Frane Supila 12, Ploče* ☎*020/353–279*), a small boutique in the Hotel Excelsior, specializes in "original Croatian ties" in presentation boxes. **Dubrovačka Kuća** (⊠*Svetog Dominika, Stari Grad* ☎*020/322–092*), a tastefully decorated wine shop, stocks a fine selection of regional Croatian wines, *rakija*, olive oil, and truffle products, plus works of art by contemporary artists on the upper two levels; it's close to Ploče Gate. **Ronchi** (⊠*Lučarica 2, Stari Grad* ☎*020/323–699*), a long-standing Dubrovnik institution, is a delightful hat shop dating back to 1858, when the present owner's great-great-grandfather arrived here from Milan, Italy. Expect an amusing array of stylish, if somewhat eccentric, reasonably priced handmade bonnets.

KORČULA

Korčula island is 49 nautical mi northwest of Dubrovnik and 57 nautical mi southeast of Split by ferry.

Southern Dalmatia's largest, most sophisticated, and most visited island, Korčula was known to the ancient Greeks, who named it *Kerkyra Melaina,* or "Black Corfu." Between the 10th and 18th century it spent several periods under Venetian rule, much to the frustration of Dubrovnik, which considered the Italian city-state its archrival. Today, most Croatians know it for its traditional sword dances and its excellent white wines.

Korčula is also the name of the capital, which is near the island's eastern tip. At first view, it seems like a much smaller version of Dubrovnik: the same high walls, the circular corner fortresses, and the church tower projecting from within an expanse of red roofs. The main difference lies in the town plan, as narrow side streets run off the main thoroughfare at odd angles to form a herringbone pattern, preventing cold winter winds from whistling unimpeded through town. The eight centuries under Venetian rule bequeathed the town a treasure trove of Gothic and Renaissance churches, palaces, and piazzas, all built from fine local stone, upon which the island's early wealth was based. Korčula's main claim to fame, though one still disputed by historians, is that it was the birthplace of Marco Polo (1254–1324). The center is small and compact and can be explored in an hour.

The most impressive way to arrive in Korčula Town is by Jadrolinija coastal ferry from Dubrovnik, which stops here en route to Rijeka. Less pleasurable but faster is the daily bus service connecting Dubrovnik and Korčula Town, which follows the regional road along Pelješac Peninsula, then boards a ferry at Orebić for a short crossing to Korčula. Alternatively, the island is also served by the port of Vela Luka, close to its western tip, with daily ferry and catamaran services running between Split (Central Dalmatia) and the island of Lastovo, stopping at Vela Luka en route. From Vela Luka, a bus runs the length of the island to Korčula Town.

WHERE TO STAY & EAT

$$–$$$$ ✕**Adio Mare.** A long-standing favorite with locals and visitors alike,
Fodor'sChoice   Adio Mare occupies a Gothic-Renaissance building in the Old Town,
★   close to Kuća Marca Pola. There's a high-ceilinged dining room as well as an open-plan kitchen so you can watch the cooks while they work. The menu has not changed since the restaurant opened in 1974: expect Dalmatian classics such as *pašta-fažol* (beans with pasta) and *pašticada* (beef stewed in wine and prunes), as well as fresh fish and seafood. The local wine, *pošip,* is excellent. This restaurant is particularly popular, so reservations are strongly recommended, especially in August. ⊠*Sv. Roka 2* ☎*020/711–253* ☰*AE, DC, MC, V* ☽*Closed Nov.–Mar. No lunch.*

$$ 🖼Hotel Korčula. Built in 1871, when the area was a part of Austria-Hungary, the building was converted to become the island's first hotel in 1912. Exuding old-fashioned charm, it offers a delightful seafront café terrace, ideal for watching the sunset over the water, but no other extras. It's the only hotel in the Old Town; all the others are a short distance east of the center. ⊠*Obala Dr Franje Tudmana 5, 20260* 🕾*020/711–078* ⊕*www.korcula-hotels.com* ⇱*20 rooms, 4 suites* ⚒*In-room: no a/c. In-hotel: restaurant, room service, no elevator* ▭*AE, DC, MC, V* ⦿|*BP.*

DUBROVNIK & SOUTHERN DALMATIA ESSENTIALS

AIR TRAVEL

The national carrier, Croatia Airlines, operates year-round internal flights between Dubrovnik, Zagreb, and Split, plus summer flights to Pula. Through summer, it also flies regularly between Dubrovnik and Amsterdam, Brussels, Catania, Copenhagen, Frankfurt, Glasgow, Gothenberg, Helsinki, Istanbul, Lisbon, London, Manchester, Nottingham, Milan, Munich, Oslo, Palermo, Paris, Prague, Rome, Sarajevo, Skopje, Stockholm, Tel Aviv, Turin, Vienna, Warsaw, and Zurich.

Several other airlines, including ČSA and Malev, fly to Dubrovnik from throughout Europe, so it's often possible to connect from the United States in someplace other than Zagreb.

AIRPORTS & TRANSFERS

Dubrovnik is served by Dubrovnik Airport (DBV) at Čilipi, 18 km (11 mi) southeast of the city.

Information Dubrovnik Airport (🕾 *020/773–377 general information, 020/773–328 lost and found* ⊕ *www.airport-dubrovnik.hr*).

AIRPORT TRANSFERS   The airport bus leaves the Dubrovnik Bus Station 90 minutes before each flight and meets all incoming flights. A one-way ticket costs 25 Kn. Journey time is approximately 20 minutes.

Contacts Airport bus (🕾 *020/773–232*). **Dubrovnik Bus Station** (⊠ *Obala Pape Ivana Pavla II 44A, Gruž, Dubrovnik* 🕾 *060/305–070*).

BOAT & FERRY TRAVEL

Jadrolinija runs a twice-weekly ferry service between Dubrovnik and Bari (Italy). Ferries depart from Bari late in the evening, arriving in Dubrovnik early the next morning, with a similar schedule from Dubrovnik to Bari (journey time approximately eight hours either direction). The Italian company Azzurra Lines runs a similar service, also from June to September.

The same Jadrolinija vessel covers the coastal route, departing from Rijeka twice weekly in the evening to arrive in Dubrovnik early the following afternoon. From Dubrovnik, the ferries depart midmorning to arrive in Rijeka early the following morning (journey time approximately 20 hours in either direction). Coming and going, these ferries stop at Korčula, Stari Grad (island of Hvar), and Split.

If you are traveling as a foot passenger, a faster (but more expensive) way to reach Mljet is to take *Nona Ana*, a high-speed catamaran running daily from Dubrovnik to Sobra and Polače (island of Mljet); tickets are available through the Dubrovnik-based agency Atlantagent. It is also possible to visit Mljet as part of an organized day trip by catamaran from Dubrovnik or Korčula Town, operated by the Atlas travel agency.

Information **Atlantagent** (✉ *Stjepana Radića 26, Dubrovnik* ☎ *020/313–355*). **Jadrolinija** (✉ *Stjepana Radića 40, Dubrovnik* ☎ *020/418–000* ⊕ *www.jadrolinija.hr*).

BUS TRAVEL

There are daily bus services from Dubrovnik to Ljubljana (Slovenia); Medjugorje, Mostar, and Sarajevo (Bosnia and Herzegovina); and Trieste (Italy); plus a twice-weekly service to Frankfurt (Germany) and a once-weekly service to Zurich (Switzerland). There are regular bus routes between Dubrovnik and destinations all over mainland Croatia, with approximately 12 buses per day to Split (Central Dalmatia), 8 to Zagreb, and 3 to Rijeka (Kvarner). Within the Southern Dalmatia region, there are four buses daily to Ston and two to Orebić on Peljesac Peninsula, one of which continues to Korčula. Regular local buses run every hour up the coast to Trstenik, and every 30 minutes down the coast to Cavtat. Timetable information is available from Dubrovnik Bus Station, which moved in 2006 and now lies close to the ferry harbor in Gruž.

Bus Information **Dubrovnik Bus Station** (✉ *Obala Pape Ivana Pavla II 44A, Gruž, Dubrovnik* ☎ *060/305–070*).

CAR TRAVEL

While visiting Dubrovnik and the nearby islands of Mljet and Korčula, you are certainly better off without a car. However, as the city is not linked to the rest of Croatia by train, you may wish to rent a car if you are driving to or from Split or Zagreb, rather than taking the bus.

Car Rental Agencies **Best Buy Rent** (✉ *V Nazora 9, Pile, Dubrovnik* ☎ *020/422–043* 🚗 *Dubrovnik Airport, Čilipi* ☎ *020/773–373*). **Milenium Rent** (✉ *Put Iva Vojnovića 5, Lapad, Dubrovnik* ☎ *020/333–176* ⊕ *www.milenium-rent.com*). **Budget** (✉ *Obala Stjepana Radića 24, Gruž, Dubrovnik* ☎ *020/418–998* 🚗 *Dubrovnik Airport, Čilipi* ☎ *020/773–290*). **Hertz** (✉ *F Supila 9, Ploče, Dubrovnik* ☎ *020/425–000* 🚗 *Dubrovnik Airport, Čilipi* ☎ *020/771–568*). **Mack** (✉ *F Supila 3, Ploče, Dubrovnik* ☎ *020/423–747* ⊕ *www.mack-concord.hr*).

INTERNET

During the summer, small temporary Internet cafés spring up in the seaside resort towns, so even on the islands you will find somewhere to check e-mail. However, many are nothing more than a regular café with a PC in the corner. The one well-established, fully equipped Internet café of note in the region is Dubrovnik Internet Centar, in Dubrovnik.

Information **Dubrovnik Internet Centar** (✉ *Ante Starčevića 7, Pile, Dubrovnik,* ☎ *020/416–307*).

TAXIS

In Dubrovnik, there are taxi ranks just outside the city walls at Pile Gate and Ploče Gate, and in front of Gruž harbor.

Information Taxi Station Gruž (☎ *020/418–112*). **Taxi Station Pile** (☎ *020/424– 343*). **Taxi Station Ploče** (☎ *020/416–158*).

VISITOR INFORMATION

Contacts Dubrovnik Tourist Office (✉ *Stradun, Stari Grad, Dubrovnik* ☎ *020/323– 350* ⊕ *www.tzdubrovnik.hr*). **Korčula Tourist Office** (✉ *Obala Dr Franje Tudjmana, Korčula* ☎ *020/715–701* ⊕ *www.korcula.net*). **Mljet Tourist Office** (✉ *Polače* ☎ *020/744–086*).

CROATIA ESSENTIALS

TRANSPORTATION

BY AIR

There are no direct air connections between the United States and Croatia though some U.S.-based airlines offer code-share flights through their European travel partners. Travelers from the United States must fly into a major European hub such as Amsterdam, London, Frankfurt, Budapest, Prague, Vienna, or Warsaw and then transfer to a flight to Zagreb, Split, or Dubrovnik. Connections are on Croatia Airlines or another European-based carrier. Several European airlines offer connections to Croatia.

Traveling to Croatia using a combination of a major U.S. airline and a low-cost European airline is a good idea. If you are traveling to Istria, a budget flight to nearby Venice (2½ hours to Ljubljana by car or train) or Trieste (1½ hours to Rijeka by car or train) is an option. Most of these discount airlines sell tickets only on the Internet. Just be aware that "London"-based discount airlines rarely fly from Heathrow (most are from Gatwick or Stansted). All these airlines have stringent baggage limits and offer few free in-flight services, if any. And if you transfer from a major airline to a discounter, you may need to reclaim your bags and recheck them, so make sure you leave plenty of time between your flights.

EasyJet flies from London to Split, Rijeka, and Venice. German Wings flies to Split and Zagreb from Cologne-Bonn and Stuttgart, and to Zagreb from Hamburg. Ryanair flies from London to Zadar and Pula, Trieste and Venice in Italy. Sky Europe flies to Dubrovnik, Split, and Zadar from Bratislava or Budapest. Wizzair flies from London to Split and Zagreb.

Airlines Aer Lingus (☎ *800/474–7424* ⊕ *www.flyaerlingus.com*). **Air France** (☎ *800/237–2747* ⊕ *www.airfrance.com*). **Alitalia** (☎ *800/223–5730* ⊕ *www. alitaliausa.com*). **Austrian Airlines** (☎ *800/843–0002* ⊕ *www.aua.com*). **British Airways** (☎ *800/247–9297 in U.S.* ⊕ *www.britishairways.com*). **Croatia Airlines** (☎ *020/8563–0022 in U.K., 02/413–776 in Croatia* ⊕ *www.croatiaairlines.hr*). **Czech Airlines** (*CSA* ☎ *212/223–2365 in U.S.* ⊕ *www.csa.cz*). **EasyJet** (☎ *No phone*

⊕ *www.easyjet.com).* **German Wings** (☎*870/252–1250* ⊕ *www.germanwings.com).* **KLM Royal Dutch Airlines** (☎*800/225–2525* ⊕ *www.klm.com).* **LOT Polish Airlines** (☎*800/223–0593 in U.S.* ⊕ *www.lot.com).* **Lufthansa** (☎*800/645–3880* ⊕ *www.lufthansa.com).* **Malév Hungarian Airlines** (☎*212/566–9944* ⊕ *www.malev.hu).* **Ryanair** (☎*090/6270–5656 in U.K., 353/1–249–7791 worldwide* ⊕ *www.ryanair.com).* **Sky Europe Airlines** (☎*090/5722–2747 in U.K., 421/4850–4850 worldwide* ⊕ *www.skyeurope.com).* **Wizzair** (☎*(48) 22–351–9499 in Poland [English-language operators available]* ⊕ *www.wizzair.com)*

BY BOAT & FERRY

Several companies run ferries from Italy to Croatia. The most popular route, which is offered by all ferry services, is Ancona to Split. Jadrolinija also runs services from Bari to Dubrovnik and from Ancona to Zadar. From June to September, SNAV runs a daily high-speed catamaran service between Ancona and Split. Jadrolinija and SEM are based in Rijeka and Split, respectively. Adriatica is based in Venice, and SNAV is based in Ancona.

From early March to late October the *Prince of Venice* hydrofoil makes regularly scheduled trips between Venice and Portorož. From mid-July to mid-September, the Italian firm Adriatica runs a round-trip service from Trieste, calling at Piran and stopping at several towns on the Croatian Adriatic coast.

Information Adriatica (☎*041/781–611 in Venice, Italy* ⊕ *www.adriatica.it* ✉ *Cankarjevo nab 7, Piran, Slovenia* ☎*05/674–6508).* **Jadrolinija** (☎*051/211–444* ⊕ *www.jadrolinija.hr).* **Prince of Venice** (*Kompas Turizem,* ✉ *Obala 41, Portorož* ☎*05/617–8000).* **SEM** (☎*021/338–292* ⊕ *www.sem-marina.hr).* **SNAV** (☎*071/207–6116 in Ancona, Italy).*

BY BUS

Bus travel in Croatia is inexpensive and efficient. During the high season, the worst you'll have to put up with is crowded buses. Most buses heading out to tourist sites like Plitvice National Park will be air-conditioned, but ask before you buy your ticket, especially if it's a blistering hot day. Buses from Zagreb to the coast get booked up quickly in the summer, so once you know your travel dates you should purchase your ticket. The bus is the best option if you are traveling from Zagreb to Slavonia and don't wish to rent a car. Croatian timetables can be found online, but the Web site is mostly in Croatian.

BY CAR

In Croatia, having a car certainly gives you greater mobility in rural areas on the mainland but causes endless complications if you plan to go island-hopping. In high season, cars can wait for hours to board ferries even if you have made reservations. In addition, parking in coastal resorts is very restricted, and there are tolls on a number of highways throughout the country. Depending on where you plan to go, it might be a better idea to rent a car only on those days when you need one.

GASOLINE

In Croatia, gas stations are open daily from 7 to 7; from June through September, many stations are open until 10. In the bigger cities and on main international roads some stations offer 24-hour service. All pumps sell Eurosuper 95, Super 98, Normal, and Eurodiesel.

ROAD CONDITIONS

In Croatia, the coastal route from Rijeka to Dubrovnik is scenic but tiring; it can be notoriously slippery when wet. The new E65 highway that links Zagreb with Rijeka, Zadar, and Split is fast and has frequent, well-maintained rest stops. During winter, driving through the inland regions of Gorski Kotar and Lika is occasionally made hazardous by heavy snow. It's advisable not to take a car to the islands, but if you do decide to drive, remember that the roads are narrow, twisty, and unevenly maintained.

RULES OF THE ROAD

Croatians drive on the right and follow rules similar to those in other European countries. Speed limits are 50 kph (30 mph) in urban areas, 80 kph (50 mph) on main roads, and 130 kph (80 mph) on motorways. Seat belts are compulsory. The permitted blood alcohol limit is 0.05%; drunken driving is punishable and can lead to severe fines.

TRAIN TRAVEL

Zagreb is connected to Rijeka and Split by rail, but there is no line south of Split to Dubrovnik. International services run from Zagreb to the European cities of Ljubljana, Budapest, Belgrade, Vienna, Munich, Berlin, and Venice.

RAIL PASSES

Train Information International Train Information (☏ 01/481–1892).

The "Zone D" Interail pass is valid for Croatia, but Eurail is not.

CONTACTS & RESOURCES

BANKS & EXCHANGE SERVICES

The Croatian currency is called the kuna (Kn), which is made up of 100 lipa. The kuna is not yet fully convertible, so you cannot buy the currency outside of Croatia or exchange it once outside the country. Most hotels in Croatia are priced in euros but actually accept kuna as payment.

For the most favorable rates, change money through banks. Although ATM transaction fees may be higher abroad than at home, ATM rates are excellent because they are based on wholesale rates offered only by major banks, and ATMs are now found throughout Croatia, even on the Adriatic islands. You won't do as well at exchange booths in airports or rail and bus stations, in hotels, in restaurants, or in stores.

In Slovenia, you can exchange money and traveler's checks in a *banka* (bank) or *mjenjačnica* (exchange office). Rates for changing currency and traveler's checks are usually about the same.

EMBASSIES & CONSULATES

All the main foreign embassies are found in Zagreb.

Contacts U.S. Embassy (✉ *Hebrangova 2, Zagreb* ☏ *01/661–2200*).

EMERGENCIES

There are nationwide numbers to call to summon an ambulance, the fire brigade, and the police.

Ambulance Ambulance (☎ *94*).

Fire Fire Emergencies (☎ *93*).

Police Police Emergencies (☎ *92*).

LANGUAGE

The country's official language is Croatian, a Slavic language that uses the Latin alphabet. In Istria signs are posted in both Croatian and Italian, and many towns and villages have two names (one Croatian, one Italian), which can be confusing. Throughout the country, English is widely spoken by people working in tourism, though German and Italian are probably more widely spoken.

INTERNET, MAIL & SHIPPING

Internet cafés are a common sight along the coast in Croatia and in Zagreb. Wireless connections are being pitched as the new thing. Wireless service varies from place to place: some hotels and cafés offer it for free, although usually there's an hourly fee—anywhere from 40 Kn to 60 Kn in Croatia—to use your laptop in most places. Internet cafés charge about the same hourly rate. In Zagreb, there are a handful of Internet cafés along Preradovićeva ulica.

Airmail letters and postcards take about five days to reach other European countries and two weeks to get to Australia, Canada, and the United States. To send a postcard costs 3.5 Kn to Europe, 5 Kn to the United States. A letter costs 5 Kn to Europe, 6.5 Kn to the United States.

PASSPORTS & VISAS

U.S. citizens do not need visas to enter either country if they plan to stay for 90 days or less. A valid passport is required.

TAXES

In Croatia, foreigners who spend more than 500 Kn in one store on a single day can reclaim *PDV* (Croatia's VAT) return upon leaving the country. To do this, you need to present the receipts and the goods bought at the *carina* (customs) desk at the airport, ferry port, or border crossing on your way out of the country.

TELEPHONES

In Croatia, you can make calls from the *pošta* (post office), where you enter a kiosk and pay when you have finished, or from a public telephone booth on the street, where magnetic phone cards are necessary. Phone cards can be purchased at the post office or newsstands.

COUNTRY CODE

Area and country codes are as follows: Croatia (385), Dubrovnik (20), Split (21), Zagreb (1). When dialing a number from abroad, drop the initial 0 from the local area code.

INTERNATIONAL CALLS

To make an international call, dial "00," then the appropriate country code (the United States is 1).

Contacts Croatia International Directory Assistance (☎ 902).

LOCAL CALLS   To make a local call in Croatia, dial the area code (if you are not already in that area) followed by the number you wish to reach.

Contacts Local Directory Assistance (☎ 988).

TIPPING

When eating out, if you have enjoyed your meal and are satisfied with the service, it is customary to leave a 10% to 15% tip. It is not usual to tip in cafés or bars. Maids and taxi drivers are not usually tipped. Tour guides do receive a tip, especially if they are particularly good. For porters on trains and bellhops at hotels, 5–10 Kn per bag will be appreciated.

VISITOR INFORMATION

Before You Leave Croatian Tourist Board (✉ 350 5th Ave., Suite 4003, New York, NY 10118 ☎ 212/829–4416).

In Croatia Croatian Tourist Board (✉ Iblerov trg 10/4, Zagreb, 10000 ☎ 01/455–6455 ⊕ www.croatia.hr).

The Czech Republic

WORD OF MOUTH

"For my first morning in Prague, I got to the Charles Bridge VERY early in the morning while it was still dark, at 6 AM. . . . It was totally quiet and absolutely beautiful. Since I hadn't seen any of the city yet in daylight, my first glimpse of the city came as the sunrise slowly illuminated the Castle and the Mala Strana—it was one of the prettiest sights I've ever seen."

—Magellan_5

"Is Cesky Krumlov worth it? YES! Don't miss it and plan on spending at least one night there, two if you can spare the time. You will love it."

—Orlando_Vic

By Mark Baker
Updated by
Evan Rail

A VICTIM OF ENFORCED OBSCURITY throughout much of the 20th century, the Czech Republic, encompassing the provinces of Bohemia and Moravia, is once again in the spotlight. In 1989, in a world where revolution was synonymous with violence and in a country where truth was quashed by the tanks of Eastern-bloc socialism, Václav Havel's sonorous voice proclaimed the victory of the "Velvet Revolution" to enthusiastic crowds on Wenceslas Square and preached the value of "living in truth." Recording the dramatic events of the time, television cameras panned across Prague's glorious skyline and fired the world's imagination with images of political renewal superimposed on somber Gothic and voluptuous baroque.

Travelers have rediscovered the country, and Bohemians and Moravians have rediscovered the world. The stagnant "normalization" of the last two decades under Communist rule gave way in the 1990s to a new dynamism and international outlook. You now encounter enthusiasm and such conveniences as English-language newspapers and attentive service. Not that the Czech Republic has quite joined the ranks of "Western" countries—it remains the poor relation compared with its Central European neighbors Germany and Austria, though the economy is growing at such a rate that the countries may become economic equals within a decade. It's all happening fastest in Prague, but the pace of change is accelerating everywhere. In the small towns and villages where so many Czechs still live, however, you may struggle with a creeping sensation of melancholy and neglect—or, putting a positive spin on it, you may enjoy the slower, more relaxed tempo.

The drab remnants of socialist reality are still omnipresent on the back roads of Bohemia and Moravia. But many of the changes made by the Communists were superficial—adding ugliness but leaving the society's core more or less intact. The colors are less jarring, not designed to attract the moneyed eye; the fittings are as they always were, not adapted to the needs of a new world.

The experience of visiting the Czech Republic still involves stepping back in time. Even in Prague, now deluged by tourists two-thirds of the year, the sense of history—stretching back through centuries of wars, empires, and monuments to everyday life—remains uncluttered by the trappings of modernity. The peculiar melancholy of Central Europe still lurks in narrow streets and forgotten corners. Crumbling facades, dilapidated palaces, and treacherous cobbled streets both shock and enchant the visitor used to a world where what remains of history has been spruced up for tourist eyes.

The arrival of designer boutiques, chain restaurants, and shopping malls does mean that the country has lost some of the "feel" it had just a few years ago. Although the dark side of freedom—rising unemployment and corruption—began to hit home in the late 1990s, the Czechs continued to move toward harmonization with Western ways. The country joined the NATO alliance in 1999 and became a European Union member state in 2004.

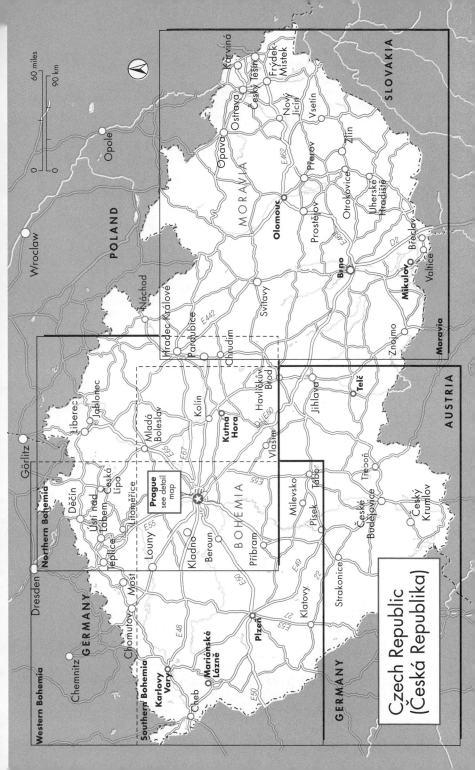

Czech Republic
(Česká Republika)

The strange, old-world, and at times frustratingly bureaucratic atmosphere of the Czech Republic is not solely a product of the Communist era. Many of the everyday rituals are actually remnants of the Habsburg Empire and can also be found, perhaps to a lesser degree, in Vienna and Budapest. The *šatna* (coat room), for example, plays a role in any visit to a restaurant or theater at any time of year other than summer. Along with a few coins, coats must be handed over to an attendant, usually an old lady with a sharp eye for ignorant or disobedient tourists.

Outside the capital, for those willing to put up with the inconveniences of shabby hotels and mediocre restaurants, the sense of rediscovering a neglected world is even stronger. And the range is startling: from imperial spas, with their graceful colonnades and dilapidated villas, to the many arcaded town squares, modestly displaying the passing of time with each splendid layer of once-contemporary style. Gothic towers, Renaissance facades, baroque interiors, and aging modern supermarkets merge. Between the man-made sights, you are rewarded with glorious mountain ranges and fertile rolling countryside laced with carp ponds and forests.

The key to enjoying the country is to relax. Although standards of service and quality are improving (particularly in upmarket establishments in Prague and Karlovy Vary), much of the Czech Republic is still relatively unchanged from its years behind the Iron Curtain, so the farther from the developed tourist infrastructure you travel, the less likely you are to experience true luxury or really good service. For the budget-conscious traveler, this is Central Europe at its most beautiful, at prices that are often much lower than those of Austria and Germany, even if there are many fewer bargains than you might have found in the mid-1990s.

CZECH REPUBLIC TOP 5

■ Admire the Prague skyline, one of the most striking collections of architecture in Europe.

■ Try a bittersweet, hoppy Czech lager (or two) in the homeland of pilsner brewing.

■ Relax in Karlovy Vary's thermal baths before star spotting at the town's international film festival.

■ Step back in time with a trip to the baroque and Renaissance streets of Český Krumlov.

■ Enjoy a slower pace and a sip of the good stuff in a traditional wine cellar in Mikulov.

EXPLORING THE CZECH REPUBLIC

The stunning silhouette of Prague is undeniably one of the country's strongest magnets, but there are plenty of beautiful vistas, spired castles, and peaceful town squares beyond the capital. Bohemia, for centuries its own kingdom, spreads around Prague to the borders of Germany, Austria, and Poland. This region is rich with spa towns in the west, walled towns and castles to the south, and moving reminders of World War II in the north. The region of Moravia, east of Bohemia, is

If You Like

CASTLES & CHÂTEAUX

More than 2,000 castles, manor houses, and châteaux form a precious and not-to-be-missed part of the country's cultural and historical heritage. Grim ruins glower from craggy hilltops, and fantastical Gothic castles guard ancient trade routes. Hundreds of noble homes—Renaissance, baroque, and Empire—dot the countryside. Their former bourgeois and aristocratic owners were expelled in the anti-German reaction of 1945–46 or were forced out by the Communists. Today, many of these valuable old houses stand in near ruin, and just as many more have been returned to the care of their original owners. Others remain in state hands as museums, homes for the elderly, or conference centers. More sights than ever are now open to the public. Picture galleries, rooms full of historic furniture, exquisite medieval stonework, and baroque chapels—all speak to a vanished way of life whose remnants survive in every town and village in Bohemia and Moravia.

HIKING

The Czech Republic has 40,000 km (25,000 mi) of well-kept, marked, and signposted trails both in the mountainous regions and leading from town to town through beautiful countryside. The most scenic areas are the Beskydy range in northern Moravia and the Krkonoše ("Giant Mountains") range in northern Bohemia. The rolling Šumava hills of southern Bohemia are also excellent hiking territory, and the environment in this region is the most pristine in the country. You'll find colored markings denoting trails on trees, fences, walls, rocks, and elsewhere. The main paths are marked in red, others are in blue and green, and the least important ones are marked in yellow. Hiking maps can be found in almost any bookstore; look for the large-scale *Soubor turistických* maps.

SHOPPING

In Prague, Karlovy Vary, and elsewhere in Bohemia, look for elegant and unusual crystal and porcelain. Bohemia is also renowned for the quality and deep-red color of its garnets; keep an eye out for beautiful rings and brooches. You can also find excellent ceramics, especially in Moravia, as well as other folk artifacts such as printed textiles, lace, hand-knit sweaters, and painted eggs. There are also crafts stores throughout the Czech Republic. In Karlovy Vary buy the strange pipelike drinking mugs used in the spas; vases left to petrify in the mineral-laden water; and Becherovka, a tasty herbal aperitif that makes a nice gift to take home.

BEER

Czechs drink more beer per capita than any other nation on Earth; small wonder, as many connoisseurs rank Bohemian lagers among the best in the world. This cool, crisp brew was invented in Plzeň in 1842, although older varieties of Czech beer had been brewed for centuries prior. Aside from the world-famous Plzeňský Prazdroj (Pilsner Urquell) and Budvar (the original Budweiser) brands, some great beers are the malty Bernard; hoppy Svijany; and the various innovative brews from Primátor, owned by the Eastern Bohemian city of Náchod. *Světlé pivo*, or golden beer, is most common, although many pubs also serve *černé* (dark), which is often slightly sweeter than the light variety.

5

anchored by Brno. This relatively modern city is surrounded by smaller, traditional towns, some tied to the wine trade. To the north, a stretch of rural hills leads into Slovakia's more rugged ranges.

ABOUT THE RESTAURANTS

The quality of restaurant cuisine and service in the Czech Republic remains uneven, though in large part it has improved dramatically in recent years. The traditional dishes—roast pork or duck with dumplings, or broiled meat with sauce—can be quite tasty when well prepared. Grilled trout appears on most menus and is often the best item available. An annoying "cover charge" (20 Kč–50 Kč in expensive eateries) usually makes its way onto restaurant bills, seemingly to subsidize the salt and pepper shakers. You should discreetly check the bill, since a few unscrupulous proprietors still overcharge foreigners.

Restaurants generally fall into three categories. A *pivnice* or *hospoda* (beer hall) usually offers a simple, inexpensive menu of goulash or pork with dumplings. The atmosphere tends to be friendly and casual, and you can expect to share a table. More attractive, and more expensive, are the *vinárna* (wine cellar) and the *restaurace* (restaurant), which serve a full menu. Wine cellars, some occupying Romanesque basements, can be a real treat.

Ignoring the familiar fast-food outlets that are now a common sight, the quickest and cheapest dining option is the *lahůdky* (snack bar or deli). In larger towns, the *kavárna* (café) and *čajovna* (teahouse) are ever more popular—and welcome—additions to the dining scene.

Lunch, usually eaten between noon and 2, is the main meal for Czechs and the best deal. Many restaurants put out a special lunch menu (*denní lístek*), with more appetizing selections at better prices. Dinner is usually served from 5 until 9 or 10, but don't wait too long to eat. Restaurant cooks frequently leave early on slow nights, and the later you arrive, the more likely it is that the kitchen will be closed. In general, dinner menus do not differ substantially from lunch offerings, with the exception of prices, which are higher.

WHERE TO STAY

The number of hotels and pensions has increased dramatically throughout the Czech Republic, in step with the influx of tourists. Finding a room should not be a problem, although it is highly recommended that you book ahead during the peak tourist season (nationwide, July and August; in Prague, April through October and the Christmas, New Year, and Easter holidays). Hotel prices, in general, remain high. This is especially true in Prague and in the spa towns of western Bohemia. Some Prague hotels reduce rates slightly in July and August, when many European travelers prefer to head for the beaches. Better value can often be found at private pensions and with individual homeowners offering rooms to let. In the outlying towns, the best strategy is to inquire at the local tourist information office or simply fan out around the town and look for room-for-rent signs on houses (usually in German: ZIMMER FREI or PRIVATZIMMER).

Most of the old-fashioned hotels away from the major tourist centers, invariably situated on a town's main square, have been modernized and now provide private bathrooms in most or all rooms and a higher comfort level throughout. Newer hotels, often impersonal concrete boxes, tend to be found on the outskirts of towns; charming, older buildings in the center of town—newly transformed into hotels and pensions—are often the best choice. Bare-bones hostels are a popular means of circumventing Prague's summer lodging crunch; many now stay open all year. In the mountains you can often find little *chaty* (chalets), where pleasant surroundings compensate for a lack of basic amenities. *Autokempink* parks (campsites) generally have a few bungalows.

At certain times, such as Easter and during festivals, prices can jump 15%–25%. As a rule, always ask the price before taking a room. Your best bet for lodging in the $ price range will usually be a private room. Unless otherwise noted, breakfast is included in the rate.

As for camping, there are hundreds of sites for tents and trailers throughout the country, but most are open only in summer (May–mid-September), although a number of campsites in and around Prague are open year-round. You can get a map from the Prague Information Service of all the sites, with addresses, opening times, and facilities. Camping outside official sites is prohibited. Campgrounds generally have hot water and toilets.

WHAT IT COSTS IN KORUNA (KČ) AND EUROS (€)			
	$$$$	$$$	$$	$
RESTAURANTS in koruna	over 500	300–500	150–300	under 150
HOTELS in euros	over €230	€140–€230	€100–€140	under €100
HOTELS in koruna	over 6,500	4,000–6,500	2,800–4,000	under 2,800

Restaurant prices are per person for a main course at dinner. Hotel prices are for two people in a double room with a private bath and breakfast in high season.

TIMING

Prague is beautiful year-round, but in summer and during the Christmas and Easter holidays the city is overrun with tourists. Spring and fall generally combine good weather with a more bearable level of tourism. In winter you'll encounter fewer tourists and have the opportunity to see Prague breathtakingly covered in snow, but it can get very cold. In much of the rest of Bohemia and Moravia, even in midsummer, the number of visitors is far smaller than in Prague. The Giant Mountains of Bohemia come into their own in winter. January and February generally bring the best skiing—and great difficulty in finding a room. If you're not a skier, try visiting the mountains in late spring (May or June) or fall, when the colors are dazzling and you'll have the hotels and restaurants nearly to yourself. The "off" season keeps shrinking as people discover the pleasures of touring the country in every season. Castles and museums now frequently stay open 9, 10, or even 12 months of the year. In midwinter, however, you may well come across

GREAT ITINERARIES

As proven by thousands of successful snapshots, Prague is a gloriously beautiful place. But by all means, consider other destinations: although the majority of tourists never leave the capital, many of the country's most interesting sights hide out in the regions, rewarding adventurous travelers. As a bonus, prices in the regions are often much lower.

IF YOU HAVE 3 DAYS

Make 🖬 **Prague** your base. This will allow you plenty of time to explore the beauty and wonder of the Old Town and Hradčany and to make a day trip to one of the country's fascinating smaller cities, such as the splendid spa town of **Karlovy Vary,** nestled in the hills of western Bohemia.

IF YOU HAVE 5 DAYS

Plan to spend three full days exploring Prague. You could easily spend a day each in the Old Town, the Lesser Quarter, and the castle and another two days visiting the well-preserved medieval mining town of **Kutná Hora** and the haunting concentration camp **Terezín.** Or you could spend a day amid the Renaissance charm of **Český Krumlov.**

this disappointing notice tacked to the door of a museum or even a hotel: CLOSED FOR TECHNICAL REASONS—which, for those in the proper frame of mind, merely adds to the charm of winter travel.

PRAGUE

It's been nearly two decades since November 17, 1989, when Prague's students took to the streets to help bring down the 40-year-old Communist regime, and in that time the city has enjoyed an exhilarating renaissance. Amid Prague's cobblestone streets and gold-tipped spires, new galleries, cafés, and clubs teem with young Czechs (the middle-aged are generally too busy trying to make a fortune) and members of the city's colony of "expatriates." New shops and—perhaps most noticeably—scads of new restaurants have opened, expanding the city's culinary reach far beyond the traditional roast pork and dumplings. Many have something to learn in the way of presentation and service, but Praguers still marvel at a variety that was unthinkable not so many years ago.

The arts and theater are also thriving in the "new" Prague. Young playwrights, a few working in English, regularly stage their own works. Classical music maintains its famous standards, and rock, jazz, and dance clubs are jammed nightly. The culture of the new era—nonverbal theater, "installation" art, world music—are as trendy in Prague as in any European capital but possess a distinctive Czech flavor.

All of this frenetic activity plays well against a stunning backdrop of towering churches and centuries-old bridges and alleyways. Prague achieved much of its present glory in the 14th century, during the long reign of Charles IV, king of Bohemia and Moravia and Holy Roman

Emperor. It was Charles who established a university in the city and laid out the New Town, charting Prague's growth.

During the 15th century, the city's development was hampered by the Hussite Wars, a series of crusades launched by the Holy Roman Empire to subdue the fiercely independent Czech noblemen. The Czechs were eventually defeated in 1620 at the Battle of White Mountain (Bílá Hora) near Prague and were ruled by the Habsburg family for the next 300 years. Under the Habsburgs, Prague became a German-speaking city and an important administrative center, but it was forced to play second fiddle to the monarchy's capital, Vienna. Much of the Lesser Quarter, on the left bank of the Vltava, was built up at this time, and there you could find the Austrian nobility and its baroque tastes.

Prague regained its status as a national capital in 1918, with the creation of the modern Czechoslovak state, and quickly asserted itself in the interwar period as a vital cultural center. Although the city escaped World War II essentially intact, Czechoslovakia fell under the political and cultural domination of the Soviet Union until the 1989 popular uprisings. The election of dissident playwright Václav Havel to the post of national president set the stage for the city's renaissance, which has since proceeded at a dizzying, quite Bohemian rate. Although Prague was beset by massive floods in 2002, most of the tourism infrastructure was only temporarily affected, and things are back to normal now.

EXPLORING PRAGUE

The spine of the city is the River Vltava (also known by its German name, Moldau), which runs through the city from south to north with a single sharp curve to the east. Prague originally comprised five independent towns, represented today by its main historic districts: Hradčany (Castle Area), Malá Strana (Lesser Quarter), Staré Město (Old Town), Nové Město (New Town), and Josefov (the Jewish Quarter).

Hradčany, the seat of Czech royalty for hundreds of years, has as its center the Pražský hrad (Prague Castle), which overlooks the city from its hilltop west of the Vltava. Steps lead down from Hradčany to the Lesser Quarter, an area dense with ornate mansions built by 17th- and 18th-century nobility.

Karlův most (Charles Bridge) connects the Lesser Quarter with the Old Town. Just a few blocks east of the bridge is the district's focal point, Staroměstské náměstí (Old Town Square). The Old Town is bounded by the curving Vltava and three large commercial avenues: Revoluční to the east, Na Příkopě to the southeast, and Národní třída to the south. North of Old Town Square, the diminutive Jewish Quarter fans out around the wide avenue called Pařížská.

Beyond the Old Town to the south is the New Town, a highly commercial area that includes the city's largest square, Karlovo náměstí (Charles Square). Roughly 1 km (½ mi) farther south is Vyšehrad, an ancient castle high above the river.

On a promontory to the east of Václavské náměstí (Wenceslas Square) stretches Vinohrady, once the favored neighborhood of well-to-do Czechs. Bordering Vinohrady are the crumbling neighborhoods of Žižkov to the north and Nusle to the south. On the west bank of the Vltava lie many older residential neighborhoods and several sprawling parks. About 3 km (2 mi) from the center in every direction, Communist-era housing projects begin their unsightly sprawl.

Numbers in the text correspond to numbers in the margin and on the Prague map.

STARÉ MĚSTO (OLD TOWN)

Prague's Old Town was spared from bombing during World War II, leaving it with one of the best-preserved centers of any major city in Europe. On a sunny summer weekend, Old Town Square can be so packed with revelers that you might think a rock concert was coming up. The 15th-century astronomical clock, which is on the side of the town hall, has a procession of 12 apostles that make their rounds when certain hours strike. From another side, the Church of Our Lady before Týn's Gothic spires and the solid gold effigy of the Virgin Mary keep watch over onlookers. You will find the streets most subdued on early weekday mornings, especially in the off-season.

WHAT TO SEE

🔟 **Betlémská kaple** *(Bethlehem Chapel).* The original church was built at the end of the 14th century, and the Czech religious reformer Jan Hus was a regular preacher here from 1402 until his exile in 1412. After the Thirty Years' War the church fell into the hands of the Jesuits and was finally demolished in 1786. Excavations carried out after World War I uncovered the original portal and three windows, and the entire church was reconstructed during the 1950s. Although little remains of the first church, some remnants of Hus's teachings can still be read on the inside walls. ✉ *Betlémské nám. 5, Staré Město* 🖭 *40 Kč* ☉ *Tues.– Sun. 10–6:30.*

🔟 **Clam-Gallas palác** *(Clam-Gallas Palace).* The beige-and-brown palace, the work of Johann Bernhard Fischer von Erlach, the famed Viennese architectural virtuoso of the day, was begun in 1713 and finally finished in 1729. Enter the building for a glimpse of the finely carved staircase, the work of the master himself, and of the Italian frescoes featuring Apollo that surround it. The building now houses the municipal archives and is rarely open to visitors (so walk in as if you have business there). Classical music concerts are sometimes held in the Great Hall in the evening, which is one way to peek inside. ✉ *Husova 20, Staré Město* ⊕ *www.ahmp.cz/eng* ☉ *Tues.–Sun. 10–6.*

🔟 **Dům U černé Matky Boží** *(House of the Black Madonna).* In the second decade of the 20th century, young Czech architects boldly applied Cubism's radical reworking of visual space to structures. Adding a decided jolt to the architectural styles along Celetná, this Cubist building, designed by Josef Gočár, is unflinchingly modern yet topped with an almost baroque tile roof. The museum interior was renovated in 2002 to better suit the permanent collection of Cubist art. A café on the second floor reopened as well. ⊠ *Celetná 34, Staré Město* ☏ *224–211–732* ⊕ *www.ngprague.cz* ▦ *100 Kč* ⊙ *Tues.–Sun. 10–6.*

⑬ Franz Kafka Exposition. Kafka came into the world on July 3, 1883, in a house next to the Kostel svatého Mikuláše (Church of St. Nicholas). For years the writer was only grudgingly acknowledged by the Communist cultural bureaucrats, reflecting the traditionally ambiguous attitude of the Czech government toward his work. As a German and a Jew, moreover, Kafka could easily be dismissed as standing outside the mainstream of Czech literature. Following the 1989 revolution, however, Kafka's popularity soared, and his works are now widely available in Czech. Though only the portal of the original house remains, inside the building is a fascinating little exhibit (mostly photographs) on Kafka's life, with commentary in English. ⊠ *Nám. Franze Kafky 3, Staré Město* ▦ *50 Kč* ⊙ *Tues.–Fri. 10–6, Sat. 10–5, Sun. 10–6.*

⑨ Jan Hus monument. Few memorials have elicited as much controversy as this one, which was dedicated in July 1915, exactly 500 years after Hus was burned at the stake in Constance, Germany. Some maintain that the monument's Secessionist style (the inscription seems to come right from turn-of-the-20th-century Vienna) clashes with the Gothic and baroque of the square. Others dispute the romantic depiction of Hus, who appears here in flowing garb as tall and bearded. The real Hus, historians maintain, was short and had a baby face. Still, no one can take issue with the influence of this fiery preacher, whose ability to transform doctrinal disputes, both literally and metaphorically, into the language of the common man made him into a religious and national symbol for the Czechs. ⊠ *Staroměstské nám., Staré Město.*

⑩ Klášter svaté Anežky České (*St. Agnes's Convent*). Situated near the river between Pařížská and Revoluční streets, this peaceful complex has Prague's first buildings in the Gothic style, built between the 1230s and the 1280s. The convent now provides a fitting home for the National Gallery's marvelous collection of Czech Gothic art, including altarpieces, portraits, and statues. ⊠ *U Milosrdných 17, Staré Město* ☏ *224–810–628* ⊕ *www.ngprague.cz* ▦ *100 Kč* ⊙ *Tues.–Sun. 10–6.*

★ ⑦ Kostel Panny Marie před Týnem (*Church of the Virgin Mary Before Týn*). The exterior of the church is one of the best examples of Prague Gothic and is in part the work of Peter Parler, architect of the Charles Bridge and Chrám svatého Víta (St. Vitus's Cathedral). Construction of its twin black-spire towers was begun later, by King Jiří of Poděbrad in 1461, during the heyday of the Hussites. Jiří had a gilded chalice, the symbol of the Hussites, proudly displayed on the front gable between the two towers. Following the defeat of the Czech Protestants by the Catholic Habsburgs, the chalice was removed and eventually replaced by a Madonna. As a final blow, the chalice was melted down and made into the Madonna's glimmering halo (you still can see it by walking into the center of the square and looking up between the spires). The entrance to the church is through the arcades on Old Town Square, under the house at No. 604.

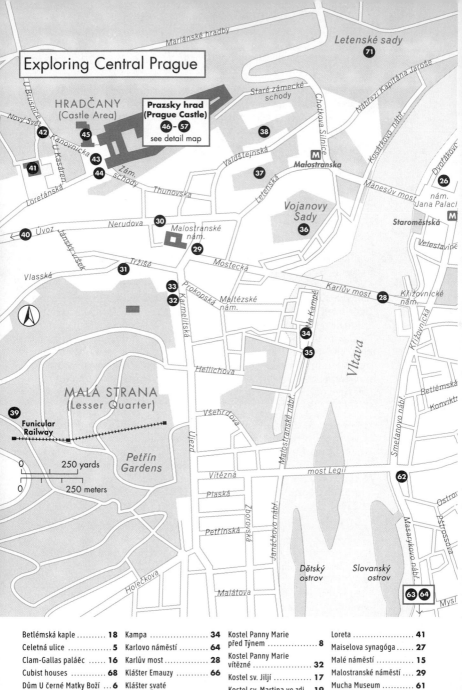

Exploring Central Prague

HRADČANY
(Castle Area)

**Prazsky hrad
(Prague Castle)**
46 – 57
see detail map

MALÁ STRANA
(Lesser Quarter)

Funicular
Railway

Petřín
Gardens

0   250 yards

0   250 meters

Letenské sady

Malostranska Ⓜ

Vojanovy
Sady

nám.
Jana Palac

Staroměstská Ⓜ

Vltava

Dětský
ostrov

Slovanský
ostrov

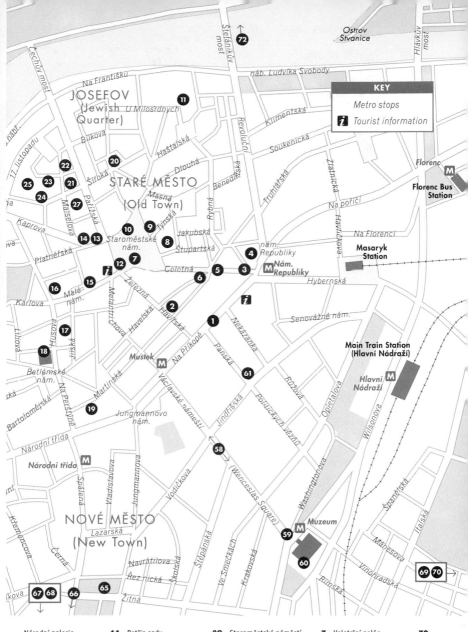

Much of the interior, including the tall nave, was rebuilt in the baroque style in the 17th century. Some Gothic pieces remain, however: look to the left of the main altar for a beautifully preserved set of early Gothic carvings. The main altar itself was painted by Karel Škréta, a luminary of the Czech baroque. Before leaving the church, look for the grave marker (tucked away to the right of the main altar) of the great Danish astronomer Tycho Brahe, who came to Prague as "Imperial Mathematicus" in 1599 under Rudolf II. As a sci-

> **CAUTION**
>
> The standards for church concerts vary massively—from world-class to rank amateur. Some of these concerts are blatant scams that depend on the nonrepeat tourist business to make their money. When purchasing tickets, always check that the performance will be played by an established chamber group, generally in the bigger and better-known churches.

entist, Tycho had a place in history that is assured: Johannes Kepler (another resident of the Prague court) used Tycho's observations to formulate his laws of planetary motion. But it is myth that has endeared Tycho to the hearts of Prague residents. The robust Dane, who was apparently fond of duels, lost part of his nose in one (take a closer look at the marker). He quickly had a wax nose fashioned for everyday use but preferred to parade around on holidays and festive occasions sporting a bright silver one. ⊠ *Staroměstské nám., between Celetná and Týnská, Staré Město.*

⓯ **Kostel svatého Jiljí** *(Church of St. Giles).* This church was an important outpost of Czech Protestantism in the 16th century. The exterior is a powerful example of Gothic architecture, including the buttresses and a characteristic portal. The interior, as in many important Czech churches, is baroque, with a design by Johann Bernhard Fischer von Erlach and sweeping frescoes by Václav Reiner. The interior can be viewed during the day from the vestibule or at the evening concerts held several times a week. ⊠ *Husova 8, Staré Město.*

⓱ **Kostel svatého Martina ve zdi** *(Church of St. Martin-in-the-Wall).* It was here in 1414 that Holy Communion was first given to the Bohemian laity in the form of both bread and wine, in defiance of the Catholic custom of the time, which dictated that only bread was to be offered to the masses, with wine reserved for the priests and clergy. From then on, the chalice came to symbolize the Hussite movement. The church is open for evening concerts, held several times each week. ⊠ *Martinská ul., Staré Město.*

⓬ **Kostel svatého Mikuláše** *(Church of St. Nicholas).* Designed in the 18th century by Prague's own master of late baroque, Kilian Ignaz Dient-zenhofer, this church is probably less successful in capturing the style's lyric exuberance than its namesake across town, the Chrám svatého Mikuláše. Still, Dientzenhofer utilized the limited space to create a well-balanced structure. The interior is compact, with a beautiful but small chandelier and an enormous black organ that seems to overwhelm the rear of the church. The church hosts almost continuous afternoon and evening tourist concerts. ⊠*Staroměstské nám., Staré Město* ⊙*Apr.– Oct., Mon. noon–4, Tues.–Sat. 10–4, Sun. noon–3; Nov.–Mar., Tues., Fri., and Sun. 10–noon, Wed. 10–4.*

❶ **Na Příkopě.** The name means "At the Moat" and harks back to the time when the street was indeed a moat separating the Old Town from the New Town. Today the pedestrian zone Na Příkopě is prime shopping territory. At No. 19 an oversize new building, one of the worst excesses of the 1990s in Prague, houses a Marks & Spencer store. Have a look at the chic, hard-edged black-and-white Černá Růže (Black Rose) arcade at No. 12. A little ways farther at No. 22, the late-18th-century neoclassical facade of Slovanský dům hides a modern mall filled with stores, restaurants, and a cinema multiplex.

❹ **Obecní dům** *(Municipal House).* The city's Art Nouveau showpiece still fills the role it had when it was completed in 1911: it's a center for concerts, rotating art exhibits, and café society. The mature Art Nouveau style recalls the lengths the Czech middle classes went to at the turn of the 20th century to imitate Paris, then the epitome of style and glamour. Much of the interior bears the work of Art Nouveau master Alfons Mucha, Max Švabinský, and other leading Czech artists. Mucha decorated the Hall of the Lord Mayor upstairs with impressive, magical frescoes depicting Czech history; unfortunately it's not open to the public. The beautiful **Smetanova síň** (Smetana Hall), which hosts concerts by the Prague Symphony Orchestra as well as international players, is on the second floor. The ground-floor café is touristy but lovely with its glimmering chandeliers and exquisite woodwork. There's also a beer hall in the cellar with passable beer, mediocre food, and superbly executed ceramic murals on the walls. ⊠*Nám. Republiky 5, Staré Město* ☎*222–002–101* ⊕*www.obecnidum.cz* ⊙*Information center and box office daily 10–7.*

5

NEED A BREAK?

If you prefer subtle elegance, head around the corner from the Obecní dům to the café at the **Hotel Paříž** (⊠ *U Obecního domu 1, Staré Město* ☎ *222–195– 816*), a Jugendstil jewel tucked away on a relatively quiet street.

❽ **Palác Kinských** *(Kinský Palace).* This exuberant building, built in 1765 from Kilian Ignaz Dientzenhofer's design, is considered one of Prague's finest late-baroque structures. With its exaggerated pink overlay and numerous statues, the facade looks extreme when contrasted with the more staid baroque elements of other nearby buildings. (The interior, however, was "modernized" under Communism.) The palace once housed a German school—where Franz Kafka was a student for nine misery-laden years—and presently contains the National Gallery's graphics collection. It was from this building that Communist leader Klement Gottwald, flanked by his Slovak comrade Vladimír Clementis, first addressed the crowds after seizing power in February 1948—an event recounted in the first chapter of Milan Kundera's novel *The Book of Laughter and Forgetting.* ⊠*Staroměstské nám. 12, Staré Město* ☎*224–210–758* ⊕*www.ngprague.cz* ⊠*100 Kč* ⊙*Tues.–Sun. 10–6.*

❸ Prašná brána *(Powder Tower)*. Construction of the tower, which replaced one of the city's 13 original gates, was begun by King Vladislav II of Jagiello in 1475. At the time, the kings of Bohemia maintained their royal residence next door, on the site of the current Obecní dům, and the tower was intended to be the grandest gate of all. But Vladislav was Polish and thus heartily disliked by the rebellious Czech citizens of Prague. Nine years after he assumed power, fearing for his life, he moved the royal court across the river to Prague Castle. Work on the tower was abandoned, and the half-finished structure was used for storing gunpowder—hence its odd name—until the end of the 17th century. The oldest part of the tower is the base. The golden spires were not added until the end of the 19th century. Climb to the top for a striking view of the Old Town and Prague Castle in the distance. ⊠ *Nám. Republiky, Staré Město* 🖃 *40 Kč* ⊙ *Apr.–Oct., daily 10–6.*

★ **⓫ Staroměstská radnice** *(Old Town Hall)*. This is one of Prague's magnets: hundreds of people gravitate to it to see the hour struck by the mechanical figures of the **astronomical clock.** Just before the hour, look to the upper part of the clock, where a skeleton begins by tolling a death knell and turning an hourglass upside down. The Twelve Apostles parade momentarily, and then a cockerel flaps its wings and crows, piercing the air as the hour finally strikes. To the right of the skeleton, the dreaded Turk nods his head, seemingly hinting at another invasion like those of the 16th and 17th centuries. This small spectacle doesn't clue viewers in to the way this 15th-century marvel indicates the time—by the season, the zodiac sign, and the positions of the sun and moon. The calendar under the clock dates from the mid-19th century.

The Old Town Hall served as the center of administration for the Old Town beginning in 1338, when King John of Luxembourg first granted the city council the right to a permanent location. The impressive 200-foot **Town Hall Tower,** where the clock is mounted, was first built in the 14th century and given its current late-Gothic appearance around 1500 by the master Matyáš Rejsek. For a rare view of the Old Town and its maze of crooked streets and alleyways, climb the ramp or ride the elevator to the top of the tower.

If you walk around the hall to the left, you'll see it's actually a series of houses jutting into the square; they were purchased over the years and successively added to the complex. On the other side, jagged stonework reveals where a large, neo-Gothic wing once adjoined the tower until it was destroyed during fighting between townspeople and Nazi troops in May 1945.

Guided tours (most guides speak English, and English texts are on hand) of the Old Town Hall depart from the main desk inside. Previously unseen parts of the tower were opened to the public in 2002, and you can now see the inside of the famous clock. ⊠ *Staroměstské nám., Staré Město* ⊙ *Apr.–Oct., Tues.–Sun. 9–6, Mon. 11–6; Nov.–Mar., Tues.–Sun. 9–5, Mon. 11–5* 🖃 *Tower 60 Kč, tours 60 Kč.*

★ **❻ Staroměstské náměstí** *(Old Town Square)*. There are places that, on first glimpse, stop you dead in your tracks in sheer wonder. Old Town

Square is one such place. Long the heart of the Old Town, the square grew to its present proportions when the city's original marketplace was moved away from the river in the 12th century. Its shape and appearance have changed little over the years. During the day the square is festive, as musicians vie for the favor of onlookers and artists display renditions of Prague street scenes. At night, the gaudily lighted towers of the Church of the Virgin Mary Before Týn rise ominously over the glowing baroque facades. The crowds thin out, and the ghosts of the square's stormy past return.

During the 15th century the square was the focal point of conflict between Czech Hussites and German Catholics. In 1422 the radical Hussite preacher Jan Želivský was executed here for his part in storming the New Town's town hall three years earlier. In the 1419 uprising, three Catholic consuls and seven German citizens were thrown out the window—the first of Prague's many famous defenestrations. Within a few years, the Hussites had taken over the town, expelled the Germans, and set up their own administration.

5

Twenty-seven white crosses set flat in the paving stones in the square, at the Old Town Hall's base, mark the spot where 27 Bohemian noblemen were killed by the Habsburgs in 1621 during the dark days following the defeat of the Czechs at the Battle of White Mountain. The grotesque spectacle, designed to quash any further national or religious opposition, took some five hours to complete, as the men were put to the sword or hanged one by one.

One of the most interesting houses on the Old Town Square juts out into the small extension leading into Malé náměstí. The house, called **U Minuty** (⊠3 Staroměstské nám., Staré Město), with its 16th-century Renaissance sgraffiti of biblical and classical motifs, was the home of the young Franz Kafka in the 1890s.

❷ **Stavovské divadlo** (Estates Theater). Built in the 1780s in the classical style, this handsome theater was for many years a beacon of Czech-language culture in a city long dominated by the German variety. It is probably best known as the site of the world premiere of Mozart's opera Don Giovanni in October 1787, with the composer himself conducting. Prague audiences were quick to acknowledge Mozart's genius: the opera was an instant hit here, though it flopped nearly everywhere else in Europe. Mozart wrote most of the opera's second act in Prague at the Villa Bertramka, where he was a frequent guest. You must attend a performance here to see inside. ⊠ Ovocný tř. 1, Staré Město ☎224–902–322 box office ⊕www.narodni-divadlo.cz.

JOSEFOV (JEWISH QUARTER)

Prague's Jews survived centuries of discrimination, but two unrelated events of modern times have left their historic ghetto little more than a collection of museums. Around 1900, city officials decided for hygienic purposes to raze the minuscule neighborhood—it had ceased to be a true ghetto with the political reforms of 1848–49, and by this time the majority of its residents were poor Gentiles—and pave over its crooked streets. Only some of the synagogues, the town hall, and the cemetery

Mozart in Prague

CLOSE UP

Considering that Wolfgang Amadeus Mozart visited Prague only four times, it's impressive how deeply he left his stamp on the city. On his first trip, in early 1787, he visited Count Thun and his wife. They lived in what is now the British Embassy in Malá Strana. Mozart stayed at an inn on Celetná Street. During this trip he conducted his *Prague Symphony* and a day later, on January 20, a performance of his opera *The Marriage of Figaro,* which had a more successful run in Prague than in Vienna. One legend from this time has the host of a party inviting him an hour before all the other guests and making him compose new dances for the evening.

His second trip is his most famous. The maestro came to visit composer F.X. Dušek and his new wife, opera singer Josephine, in 1787 at their rural villa, Bertramka (although he also kept rooms at the Uhelný třída Inn). After several missed deadlines, he conducted the world premiere of *Don Giovanni* on October 29 at Stavovské divadlo. In his spare time, he tried out a number of church organs.

His third visit was just a pass-through, but the fourth and final trip came just months before he died in 1791. He promised to write a new opera to mark the coronation of Leopold II as king of Bohemia. Unfortunately, *La Clemenza di Tito,* which premiered at the Stavovské divadlo on September 6, was written quickly and was not as well received as *Don Giovanni.* Once news of his death on December 5 reached Prague, his friends staged a memorial service that ended with church bells ringing all over town.

survived this early attempt at urban renewal. The second event was the Holocaust. Under Nazi occupation, a staggering percentage of the city's Jews were deported or murdered in concentration camps. Of the 35,000 Jews living in Prague before World War II, only about 1,200 returned to resettle the city after the war. The community is still tiny. Only a scant few Jews, mostly elderly, live in the "ghetto" today.

WHAT TO SEE

 Klausová synagóga *(Klausen Synagogue).* This baroque former synagogue was built at the end of the 17th century in the place of three small buildings (a synagogue, school, and ritual bath) that were destroyed in a fire that devastated the ghetto in 1689. Inside, displays of Czech Jewish traditions emphasize celebrations and daily life. In the neo-Romanesque **Obřadní síň** (Ceremony Hall), which adjoins the Klausen Synagogue, the focus is on rather grim subjects: Jewish funeral paraphernalia, old gravestones, and medical instruments. Special attention is paid to the activities of the Jewish Burial Society through many fine objects and paintings. ⊠*U starého hřbitova 3A, Josefov* ☎*224–819–456* ⊕*www.jewishmuseum.cz* ⊠*Combined ticket to museums and Old-New Synagogue 480 Kč; museums only, 300 Kč* ⊙*Apr.–Oct., Sun.–Fri. 9–6; Nov.–Mar., Sun.–Fri. 9–4:30.*

Maiselova synagóga *(Maisel Synagogue).* Here, the history of Czech Jews from the 10th to the 18th century is illustrated with the aid of some of the Prague Jewish Museum's most precious objects, including silver Torah shields and pointers, spice boxes, and candelabra; historic tombstones; and fine ceremonial textiles, including some donated by Mordechai Maisel to the synagogue he founded. The richest items come from the late 16th and early 17th century—a prosperous era for Prague's Jews. ✉*Maiselova 10, Josefov* ☎*224–819–456* ⊕*www. jewishmuseum.cz* ⊠*Combined ticket to museums and Old-New Synagogue 480 Kč; museums only, 300 Kč* ⊙*Apr.–Oct., Sun.–Fri. 9–6; Nov.–Mar., Sun.–Fri. 9–4:30.*

㉒ Pinkasova synagóga *(Pinkas Synagogue).* This synagogue has two particularly moving testimonies to the appalling crimes perpetrated against the Jews during World War II. One tribute astounds by sheer numbers: the inside walls are covered with nearly 80,000 names of Bohemian and Moravian Jews murdered by the Nazis. Among them are the names of the paternal grandparents of former U.S. Secretary of State Madeleine Albright, who learned of their fate only in 1997. There is also an exhibition of drawings made by children at the Nazi concentration camp Terezín. The Nazis used the camp for propaganda purposes to demonstrate their "humanity" toward the Jews, erecting fake shops and cafés to fool the Red Cross. Transports to death camps in Poland began in earnest in 1944, and many thousands of Terezín prisoners, including many of these children, eventually perished. The entrance to the old Jewish cemetery is through this synagogue. ✉*Široká 3, Josefov* ☎*224–819–456* ⊕*www.jewishmuseum.cz* ⊠*Combined ticket to museums and Old-New Synagogue 480 Kč; museums only, 300 Kč* ⊙*Apr.–Oct., Sun.–Fri. 9–6; Nov.–Mar., Sun.–Fri. 9–4:30.*

㉔ Rudolfinum. Thanks to a thorough makeover and exterior sandblasting, this neo-Renaissance monument designed by Josef Zítek and Josef Schulz presents the cleanest, brightest stonework in the city. Completed in 1884 and named for then–Habsburg Crown Prince Rudolf, the rather low-slung sandstone building was meant to be a combination concert hall and exhibition gallery. After 1918 it was converted into the parliament of the newly independent Czechoslovakia until German invaders reinstated the concert hall in 1939. Czech writer Jiří Weil's novel *Mendelssohn Is on the Roof* tells of the cruel farce that ensued when officials ordered the removal of the Jewish composer's statue from the roof balustrade. Now the Czech Philharmonic has its home base here. The 1,200-seat **Dvořákova síň** (Dvořák Hall) has superb acoustics (the box office faces 17 listopadu). To see the hall, you must attend a concert.

Behind Dvořák Hall is a set of large exhibition rooms, the **Galerie Rudolfinum** (⊕*www.galerierudolfinum.cz*), an innovative, state-supported gallery for rotating shows of contemporary art. Four or five large shows are mounted here annually, showcasing excellent Czech work along with international artists such as photographer Cindy Sherman. The gallery is open Tuesday–Sunday, 10–6; admission is 100 Kč. ✉*Alšovo nábřeží 12, Josefov* ☎*224–893–111 box office, 227–059–309 gallery* ⊕*www.czechphilharmonic.cz.*

★ ⑱ **Španělská synagóga** *(Spanish Synagogue).* A domed Moorish-style synagogue was built in 1868 on the site of the Altschul, the city's oldest synagogue. Here, the historical exposition that begins in the Maisel Synagogue continues, taking the story up to the post–World War II period. The displays are not that compelling, but the building's painstakingly restored interior definitely is. ⊠ *Vězeňská 1, Josefov* ☎*224– 819–456* ⊕*www.jewishmuseum.cz* ⊠*Combined ticket to museums and Old-New Synagogue 480 Kč; museums only, 300 Kč* ⊘*Apr.–Oct., Sun.–Fri. 9–6; Nov.–Mar., Sun.–Fri. 9–4:30.*

★ ⑳ **Staronová synagóga** *(Old-New Synagogue, or Altneuschul).* Dating from the mid-13th century, this is one of the most important early-Gothic works in Prague. The odd name recalls the legend that the synagogue was built on the site of an ancient Jewish temple and that stones from the temple were used to build the present structure. The oldest part of the synagogue is the entrance, with its vault supported by two pillars. The synagogue has not only survived fires and the razing of the ghetto at the end of the last century but also emerged from the Nazi occupation intact; it is still in active use. As the oldest synagogue in Europe that still serves its original function, it is a living storehouse of Bohemian Jewish life. Note that men are required to cover their heads inside and that during services men and women sit apart. ⊠ *Červená 2, Josefov* ☎*224–819–456* ⊕*www.jewishmuseum.cz* ⊠*Combined ticket to Old-New Synagogue and museums 480 Kč; Old-New Synagogue only, 200 Kč* ⊘*Apr.–Oct., Sun.–Fri. 9–6; Nov.–Mar., Sun.–Fri. 9–4:30.*

★ ㉓ **Starý židovský hřbitov** *(Old Jewish Cemetery).* This unforgettably melancholy sight not far from the busy city was, from the 15th century to 1787, the final resting place for all Jews living in Prague. The confined space forced graves to be piled one on top of the other. Tilted at crazy angles, the 12,000 visible tombstones are but a fraction of countless thousands more buried below. Walk the path amid the gravestones; the relief symbols you see represent the names and professions of the deceased. The oldest marked grave belongs to the poet Avigdor Kara, who died in 1439; the grave is not accessible from the pathway, but the original tombstone can be seen in the Maisel Synagogue. The best-known marker is that of Jehuda ben Bezalel, the famed Rabbi Loew (died 1609), a chief rabbi of Prague and profound scholar who is credited with creating the mythical Golem. Even today, small scraps of paper bearing wishes are stuffed into the cracks of the rabbi's tomb in the hope that he will grant them. Loew's grave lies near the exit. ⊠*Široká 3 (enter through Pinkasova synagóga), Josefov* ☎*224–819– 456* ⊕*www.jewishmuseum.cz* ⊠*Combined ticket to museums and Old-New Synagogue 480 Kč; museums only, 300 Kč* ⊘*Apr.–Oct., Sun.–Fri. 9–6; Nov.–Mar., Sun.–Fri. 9–4:30.*

⑲ **Židovská radnice** *(Jewish Town Hall).* The hall was the creation of Mordechai Maisel, an influential Jewish leader at the end of the 16th century. It was restored in the 18th century and given its clock and bell tower at that time. A second clock, with Hebrew numbers, keeps time counterclockwise. Now the Jewish Community Center, the building also houses a kosher restaurant, Shalom. ✉ *Maiselova 18, Josefov* ☎ *No telephone.*

KARLŮV MOST (CHARLES BRIDGE) & MALÁ STRANA (LESSER QUARTER)

One of Prague's most exquisite neighborhoods, the Lesser Quarter (or Little Town) was established in 1257 and for years was where the merchants and craftsmen who served the royal court lived. The Lesser Quarter is not for the methodical traveler. Its charm lies in the tiny lanes, the sudden blasts of bombastic architecture, and the soul-stirring views that emerge for a second before disappearing behind the sloping roofs.

WHAT TO SEE

★ ㉗ **Chrám svatého Mikuláše** *(Church of St. Nicholas).* With its dynamic curves, this church is one of the purest and most ambitious examples of high baroque. The celebrated architect Christoph Dientzenhofer began the Jesuit church in 1704 on the site of one of the more active Hussite churches of 15th-century Prague. Work on the building was taken over by his son Kilian Ignaz Dientzenhofer, who built the dome and presbytery. Anselmo Lurago completed the whole in 1755 by adding the bell tower. The juxtaposition of the broad, full-bodied dome with the slender bell tower is one of the many striking architectural contrasts that mark the Prague skyline. Inside, the vast pink-and-green space is impossible to take in with a single glance. Every corner bristles with movement, guiding the eye first to the dramatic statues, then to the hectic frescoes, and on to the shining faux-marble pillars. Many of the statues are the work of Ignaz Platzer, and in fact they constitute his last blaze of success. Platzer's workshop was forced to declare bankruptcy when the centralizing and secularizing reforms of Joseph II toward the end of the 18th century brought an end to the flamboyant baroque era. The tower, with an entrance on the side of the church, is open in summer. ✉ *Malostranské nám., Malá Strana* 🎟 *50 Kč* ☉ *Daily 9–4:30 for sightseeing, 8:30–9 AM for prayer only (no admission charge).*

㉜ **Kampa.** Prague's largest island is cut off from the "mainland" by the narrow Čertovka streamlet. The name Čertovka, or Devil's Stream, reputedly refers to a cranky old lady who once lived on Maltese Square (given the river's present filthy state, the name is certainly appropriate). The unusually well-kept lawns of the **Kampa Gardens** that occupy much of the island are one of the few places in Prague where sitting on the grass is openly tolerated. At night this stretch along the river is especially romantic. The spotlit jewel on Kampa Island is **Museum Kampa,** a remodeled mill house that now displays a private collection of paintings by Czech artist František Kupka and other artists, which opened in 2002. ✉ *U Sovových mlýnů 2, Malá Strana* ☎ *257–786–147* 🎟 *120 Kč* ☉ *Daily 10–6.*

★ ㉖ **Karlův most** *(Charles Bridge).* The view from the foot of the bridge on the Old Town side is nothing short of breathtaking, encompassing the towers and domes of the Lesser Quarter and the soaring spires of St. Vitus's Cathedral to the northwest. This heavenly vision changes subtly in perspective as you walk across the bridge, attended by the host of baroque saints that decorate the bridge's peaceful Gothic stones. At night its drama is spellbinding: St. Vitus's Cathedral lighted in a ghostly green, the castle in monumental yellow, and the Church of St. Nicholas in a voluptuous pink, all viewed through the menacing silhouettes of the bowed statues and the Gothic towers. If you do nothing else in Prague, you must visit the Charles Bridge at night. During the day the pedestrian bridge buzzes with activity. At night the crowds thin out a little.

When the Přemyslid princes set up residence in Prague in the 10th century, there was a ford across the Vltava at this point—a vital link along one of Europe's major trading routes. After several wooden bridges and the first stone one had washed away in floods, Charles IV appointed the 27-year-old German Peter Parler, the architect of St. Vitus's Cathedral, to build a new structure in 1357. After 1620, following the defeat of Czech Protestants by Catholic Habsburgs at the Battle of White Mountain, the bridge became a symbol of the Counter-Reformation's vigorous re-Catholicization efforts. The many baroque statues that began to appear in the late 17th century, commissioned by Catholics, eventually came to symbolize the totality of the Austrian (hence Catholic) triumph. The Czech writer Milan Kundera sees the statues from this perspective: "The thousands of saints looking out from all sides, threatening you, following you, hypnotizing you, are the raging hordes of occupiers who invaded Bohemia 350 years ago to tear the people's faith and language from their hearts."

The religious conflict is less obvious nowadays, leaving only the artistic tension between baroque and Gothic that gives the bridge its allure. Eighth on the right, the statue of St. John of Nepomuk, designed by Johann Brokoff in 1683, begins the baroque lineup of saints. On the left-hand side, sticking out from the bridge between the 9th and 10th statues (the latter has a wonderfully expressive vanquished Satan), stands a Roland (Bruncvík) statue. This knightly figure, bearing the coat of arms of the Old Town, was once a reminder that this part of the bridge belonged to the Old Town before Prague became a unified city in 1784.

In the eyes of most art historians, the most valuable statue is the 12th on the left, near the Lesser Quarter end. Mathias Braun's statue of St. Luitgarde depicts the blind saint kissing Christ's wounds. The most compelling grouping, however, is the second from the end on the left, a work of Ferdinand Maxmilian Brokoff (son of Johann) from 1714. Here the saints are incidental; the main attraction is the Turk, his face expressing extreme boredom at guarding the Christians imprisoned in the cage at his side. When the statue was erected, just 31 years after the second Turkish siege of Vienna, it scandalized the Prague public, who smeared it with mud.

Staroměstská mostecká věž (Old Town Bridge Tower), at the bridge entrance on the Old Town side, is where Peter Parler, the architect of the Charles Bridge, began his bridge building. The carved facades he designed for the sides of the tower were destroyed by Swedish soldiers in 1648, at the end of the Thirty Years' War. The sculptures facing the Old Town, however, are still intact (although some are recent copies); they depict an old and gout-ridden Charles IV with his son, who later became Wenceslas IV. Above them are two of Bohemia's patron saints, Adalbert of Prague and Sigismund. The top of the tower offers a spectacular view of the city for 60 Kč; it's open daily 10–5 (until 10 in the summer).

30 Kostel Panny Marie vítězné (*Church of Our Lady Victorious*). This comfortably ramshackle church on the Lesser Quarter's main street is the unlikely home of one of Prague's best-known religious artifacts, the *Pražské Jezulátko* (Infant Jesus of Prague). Originally brought to Prague from Spain in the 16th century, this tiny wax doll is renowned worldwide for showering miracles on anyone willing to kneel before it and pray. Nuns from a nearby convent arrive at dawn each day to change the infant's clothes; pieces of the doll's extensive wardrobe have been sent by believers from around the world. A museum in the church tower displays many of the outfits and a jewel-studded crown. ⊠ *Karmelitská 9A, Malá Strana* ⊠ *Free* ☉ *Mon.–Sat. 8:30–7, Sun. 8:30–8.*

34 Ledeburská zahrada (*Ledeburg Garden*). Rows of steeply banked baroque gardens rise behind the palaces of Valdštejnská ulice. This one makes a pleasant spot for a rest amid shady arbors and niches. The garden, with its frescoes and statuary, was restored with support from a fund headed by Czech president Václav Havel and Charles, Prince of Wales. You can also enter directly from the south gardens of Prague Castle in the summer. ⊠ *Valdštejnské nám. 3, Malá Strana* ⊠ *70 Kč* ☉ *Apr. and Oct., daily 10–6; May and Sept., daily 9–7; June and July, daily 9–9; Aug., daily 9–8.*

28 Nerudova ulice. This steep little street used to be the last leg of the Royal Way walked by the king before his coronation, and it is still the best way to get to Prague Castle. It was named for the 19th-century Czech journalist and poet Jan Neruda (after whom Chilean poet Pablo Neruda renamed himself). Until Joseph II's administrative reforms in the late 18th century, house numbering was unknown in Prague. Each house bore a name, depicted on the facade, and these are particularly prominent on Nerudova ulice. House No. 6, **U červeného orla** (At the Red Eagle), proudly displays a faded painting of a red eagle. No. 12 is known as **U tří housliček** (At the Three Fiddles). In the early 18th century, three generations of the Edlinger violin-making family lived here. Joseph II's scheme numbered each house according to its position in its "town" (here the Lesser Quarter) rather than its sequence on the street. The red plates record the original house numbers; the blue ones are the numbers used in addresses today. To confuse the tourist, many architectural guides refer to the old, red-number plates.

Two palaces break the unity of the burghers' houses on Nerudova ulice. Both were designed by the adventurous baroque architect Giovanni Santini, one of the Italian builders most in demand by wealthy nobles of the early 18th century. The **Morzin Palace,** on the left at No. 5, is now the Romanian Embassy. The fascinating facade, with an allegory of night and day, was created in 1713 and is the work of Ferdinand Brokoff of Charles Bridge statue fame. Across the street at No. 20 is the **Thun-Hohenstein Palace,** now the Italian Embassy. The gateway with two enormous eagles (the emblem of the Kolovrat family, who owned the building at the time) is the work of the other great Charles Bridge statue sculptor, Mathias Braun. Santini himself lived at No. 14, the **Valkoun House.**

The archway at Nerudova 13 hides one of the many winding passageways that give the Lesser Quarter its enchantingly ghostly character at night. Higher up the street at No. 33 is the **Bretfeld Palace,** a rococo house on the corner of Jánský vršek. This is where Mozart, his lyricist partner Lorenzo da Ponte, and the aging but still infamous philanderer and music lover Casanova stayed at the time of the world premiere of *Don Giovanni* in 1787.

㉙ Schönbornský palác *(Schönborn Palace).* Franz Kafka had an apartment in this massive baroque building at the top of Tržiště ulice in mid-1917, after moving from Zlatá ulička, or Golden Lane. The heavily guarded U.S. Embassy now occupies this prime location. If you look through the gates, you can see the beautiful formal gardens rising up to the Petřín hill. They are unfortunately not open to the public but can be glimpsed from the neighboring garden, Vrtbovská zahrada. ✉ *Tržiště at Vlašská, Malá Strana.*

★ ㉛ Vrtbovská zahrada *(Vrtba Garden).* An unobtrusive door on noisy Karmelitská hides the entranceway to a fascinating oasis that also has one of the best views of the Lesser Quarter. The street door opens onto the intimate courtyard of the Vrtbovský palác (Vrtba Palace), which is now private housing. Two Renaissance wings flank the courtyard; the left one was built in 1575, the right one in 1591. The owner of the latter house was one of the 27 Bohemian nobles executed by the Habsburgs in 1621 before the Old Town Hall. The house was given as confiscated property to Count Sezima of Vrtba, who bought the neighboring property and turned the buildings into a late-Renaissance palace. The Vrtba Garden, created a century later, reopened in summer 1998 after an excruciatingly long renovation. This is the most elegant of the Lesser Quarter's public gardens, built in five levels rising behind the courtyard in a wave of statuary-bedecked staircases and formal terraces leading up to a seashell-decorated pavilion at the top. (The fenced-off garden immediately behind and above belongs to the U.S. Embassy.) The powerful stone figure of Atlas that caps the entranceway in the courtyard and most of the other classically derived statues are from the workshop of Mathias Braun, perhaps the best of the Czech baroque sculptors. ✉ *Karmelitská 25, Malá Strana* 💷 *40 Kč* ◷ *Apr.–Oct., daily 10–6.*

OFF THE
BEATEN
PATH

Villa Bertramka. Mozart fans won't want to pass up a visit to this villa, where the great composer lived during a couple of his visits to Prague. The small, well-organized W. A. Mozart Museum is packed with memorabilia, including a flyer for a performance of *Don Giovanni* in 1788, only months after the opera's world premiere at the Estates Theater. Also on hand is one of the master's pianos. Take Tram No. 12 from Karmelitská south (or ride metro Line B) to the Anděl metro station; then transfer to Tram No. 4, 7, 9, or 10 and ride to the first stop (Bertramka). A 10-minute walk, following the signs, brings you to the villa. ✉*Mozartova ul. 169, Smíchov* ☎*257-327-732* ⊕*www.bertramka. com* 🎟*110 Kč* ☉*Apr.–Oct., daily 9:30–6; Nov.–Mar., daily 9:30–5.*

★ 33 **Valdštejnskáho zahrada** *(Wallenstein Gardens).* Albrecht von Wallenstein, onetime owner of the house and gardens, began a meteoric military career in 1622 when the Austrian emperor Ferdinand II retained him to save the empire from the Swedes and Protestants during the Thirty Years' War. Wallenstein, wealthy by marriage, offered to raise 20,000 men at his own cost and lead them personally. Ferdinand II accepted and showered Wallenstein with confiscated land and titles. Wallenstein's first acquisition was this enormous area. Having knocked down 23 houses, a brick factory, and three gardens, in 1623 he began to build his magnificent palace with its idiosyncratic high-walled gardens and superb, vaulted Renaissance *sala terrena* (room opening onto a garden). Walking around the formal paths, you'll come across numerous statues, an unusual fountain with a woman spouting water from her breasts, and a lava-stone grotto along the wall. Most of the palace itself now serves the Czech Senate as a meeting chamber and offices. The palace's cavernous former *Jízdárna,* or riding school, now hosts occasional art exhibitions. ✉*Letenská 10, Malá Strana* 🎟*Free* ☉*Apr. 1–Oct. 31, daily 10–6.*

HRADČANY (CASTLE AREA)

To the west of Prague Castle is the residential Hradčany (Castle Area), the town that during the early 14th century emerged out of a collection of monasteries and churches. The concentration of history packed into Prague Castle and Hradčany challenges those not versed in the ups and downs of Bohemian kings, religious uprisings, wars, and oppression. The picturesque area surrounding Prague Castle, with its breathtaking vistas of the Old Town and the Lesser Quarter, is ideal for just wandering. But the castle itself, with its convoluted history and architecture, is difficult to appreciate fully without investing a little more time.

WHAT TO SEE

38 **Hradčanské náměstí** *Hradčany Square).* With its fabulous mixture of baroque and Renaissance housing, topped by the castle itself, the square had a prominent role (disguised, ironically, as Vienna) in the film *Amadeus,* directed by the then-exiled Czech director Miloš Forman. The house at No. 7 was the set for Mozart's residence, where the composer was haunted by the masked figure he thought was his father. Forman used the flamboyant rococo Arcibiskupský palác (Archbishop's Palace), on the left as you face the castle, as the Viennese archbishop's palace. The plush interior, shown off in the film, is open to the public only on Maundy Thursday (the Thursday before Easter). No. 11 was home for a brief time after World War II to a little girl named Marie Jana Korbelová, who would grow up to be Madeleine Albright.

Václav Havel

One of the great men to emerge from the anti-Communist revolutions was the Czech playwright and dissident Václav Havel. The author of several anti-Communist, absurdist plays and a series of moving essays on the moral corruption of Communism, Havel captured the support of the students leading the Velvet Revolution and went on to head the country. He quickly assumed the leadership of the anti-Communist opposition and was a crucial force in negotiating the agreement that eventually led the Communists to peacefully relinquish power after 40 years of authoritarian rule.

Havel's rapid ascent from a lowly dissident to the Czech chief executive—in a matter of weeks—proves the weight of his writings. In essays like "The Power of the Powerless," Havel spoke of the power of ordinary citizens to internally and peacefully resist the Communist authorities. His voice, it's safe to say, became the country's conscience.

Prior to 1989, he was jailed several times for his writings, and when the 1989 events came around, he was one of the few public personalities who was not compromised by the previous regime.

Havel's time as president—from 1990 until 2003, with a few breaks—was a mixed affair. But if there was a success, it was in his image abroad. It's no stretch to say that much of the adoration and attention the Czechs received after 1989 was because of their universally respected president.

---

36 Loreto *(Loreto Church).* The church's seductive lines were a conscious move on the part of Counter-Reformation Jesuits in the 17th century who wanted to build up the cult of Mary and attract the largely Protestant Bohemians back to the church. According to legend, angels had carried Mary's house from Nazareth and dropped it in a patch of laurel trees in Ancona, Italy. Known as *Loreto* (from the Latin for "laurel"), it immediately became a center of pilgrimage. The Prague Loreto was one of many symbolic reenactments of this scene across Europe, and it worked: pilgrims came in droves. The graceful facade, with its voluptuous tower, was built in 1720 by Kilian Ignaz Dientzenhofer, the architect of the two St. Nicholas churches in Prague. Most spectacular of all is a small exhibition upstairs displaying the religious treasures presented to Mary in thanks for various services, including a monstrance studded with 6,500 diamonds. ⊠ *Loretánské nám. 7, Hradčany* ☎ *110 Kč* ☉ *Tues.–Sun. 9–12:15 and 1–4:30.*

★ **39 Národní galerie** *(National Gallery).* Housed in the 18th-century **Šternberský palác** (Sternberg Palace), this collection, though impressive, is limited compared with German and Austrian holdings. During the time when Berlin, Dresden, and Vienna were building up superlative old-master galleries, Prague languished, neglected by her Viennese rulers. Works by Rubens and Rembrandt are on display; other key pieces wait in the wings. Other branches of the National Gallery are scattered around town. ⊠ *Hradčanské nám. 15, Hradčany* ☎ *233–090–570* ⊕ *www.ngprague.cz* ☎ *130 Kč* ☉ *Tues.–Sun. 10–6.*

③ Nový Svět. This picturesque, winding little alley, with facades from the 17th and 18th centuries, once housed Prague's poorest residents; now many of the homes are used as artists' studios. The last house on the street, No. 1, was the home of the Danish-born astronomer Tycho Brahe. Living so close to the Loreto, so the story goes, Tycho was constantly disturbed during his nightly stargazing by the church bells. He ended up complaining to his patron, Emperor Rudolf II, who instructed the Capuchin monks to finish their services before the first star appeared in the sky.

★ ③ **Strahovský klášter** *(Strahov Monastery).* Founded by the Premonstratensian order in 1140, the monastery remained in its hands until 1952, when the Communists suppressed all religious orders and turned the entire complex into the **Památník národního písemnictví** (Museum of National Literature). The major building of interest is the **Strahov Library,** with its collection of early Czech manuscripts, the 10th-century Strahov New Testament, and the collected works of famed Danish astronomer Tycho Brahe. Also of note is the late-18th-century **Philosophical Hall.** Spread across its ceiling is a startling sky-blue fresco that depicts an unusual cast of characters, including Socrates' nagging wife, Xanthippe; Greek astronomer Thales, with his trusty telescope; and a collection of Greek philosophers mingling with Descartes, Diderot, and Voltaire. Also on the premises is the order's small art gallery, highlighted by late-Gothic altars and paintings from Rudolf II's time. ⊠*Strahovské nádvoří 1/132, Hradčany* ☎*233–107–718* ⛀*80 Kč* ☻*Gallery Tues.– Sun. 9–noon and 12:30–5; library daily 9–noon and 1–5.*

5

■ **OFF THE BEATEN PATH**

Petřín sady. For a superb view of the city—from a mostly undiscovered, tourist-free perch—stroll over from the Strahov Monastery along the paths toward Prague's own miniature version of the Eiffel Tower, which was restored in 2002. You'll find yourself in a hilltop park, laced with footpaths, with several buildings clustered together near the tower—just keep going gradually upward until you reach the tower's base. The tower and its breathtaking view, the mirror maze *(bludiště)* in a small structure near the tower's base, and the seemingly abandoned svatý Vavřinec (St. Lawrence) church are beautifully peaceful and well worth an afternoon's wandering. You can also walk up from Karmelitská ulice or Újezd down in the Lesser Quarter or ride the funicular railway from U lanové dráhy ulice, off Újezd (the line can be very long). Regular public-transportation tickets are valid. For the descent, take the funicular or meander on foot down through the stations of the cross on the pathways leading back to the Lesser Quarter.

PRAŽSKÝ HRAD (PRAGUE CASTLE)

Numbers in the text correspond to numbers in the margin and on the Prague Castle (Pražský hrad) map.

Despite its monolithic presence, the Prague Castle is not a single structure but rather a collection of buildings dating from the 10th to the 20th century, all linked by internal courtyards. The most important structures are **Chrám svatého Víta,** clearly visible soaring above the castle walls, and the **Královský palác,** the official residence of kings and presidents and still the center of political power in the Czech Republic. The castle is compact and easy to navigate. Be forewarned: in summer, the castle, especially Chrám svatého Víta, is hugely popular. **Zlatá ulička** became so crowded that in 2002 a separate admission fee was imposed for it.

WHAT TO SEE

㊽ Bazilika svatého Jiří *(St. George's Basilica)*. This church was originally built in the 10th century by Prince Vratislav I, the father of Prince (and St.) Wenceslas. It was dedicated to St. George (of dragon fame), who it was believed would be more agreeable to the still largely pagan people. The outside was remodeled during early baroque times, although the striking rusty-red color is in keeping with the look of the Romanesque edifice. The interior looks more or less as it did in the 12th century and is the best-preserved Romanesque relic in the country. The effect is at once barnlike and peaceful, the warm golden yellow of the stone walls and the small arched windows exuding a sense of enduring harmony. The house-shaped painted tomb at the front of the church holds the remains of the founder, Vratislav I. Up the steps, in a chapel to the right, is the tomb Peter Parler designed for St. Ludmila, the grandmother of St. Wenceslas. ✉*Nám. U sv. Jiří, Hradčany* ☎*224–373–368 Castle Information* ⊕*www.prague-info.cz* 💳*50 Kč. Requires castle ticket for 250 Kč or 350 Kč* ☉*Apr.–Oct., daily 9–5; Nov.–Mar., daily 9–4.*

★ **㊺ Chrám svatého Víta** *(St. Vitus's Cathedral)*. With its graceful, soaring towers, this Gothic cathedral—among the most beautiful in Europe—is the spiritual heart not only of Prague Castle but of the entire country. It has a long and complicated history, beginning in the 10th century and continuing to its completion in 1929. If you want to hear its history in depth, English-speaking guided tours of the cathedral and the Královský palác can be arranged at the information office across from the cathedral entrance.

Once you enter the cathedral, pause to take in the vast but delicate beauty of the Gothic and neo-Gothic interior glowing in the colorful light that filters through the startlingly brilliant stained-glass windows. This western third of the structure, including the facade and the two towers you can see from outside, was not completed until 1929, following the initiative of the Union for the Completion of the Cathedral, set up in the last days of the 19th century. Don't let the neo-Gothic illusion keep you from examining this new section. The six stained-glass windows to your left and right and the large rose window behind are modern masterpieces. Take a good look at the third window up on the left. The familiar Art Nouveau flamboyance, depicting the blessing of Sts. Cyril and Methodius (9th-century missionaries to the Slavs), is the work of the Czech father of the style, Alfons Mucha. He achieved the subtle coloring by painting rather than staining the glass.

If you walk halfway up the right-hand aisle, you will find the **Svato-václavská kaple** (Chapel of St. Wenceslas). With a tomb holding the saint's remains, walls covered in semiprecious stones, and paintings depicting the life of Wenceslas, this square chapel is the ancient heart of

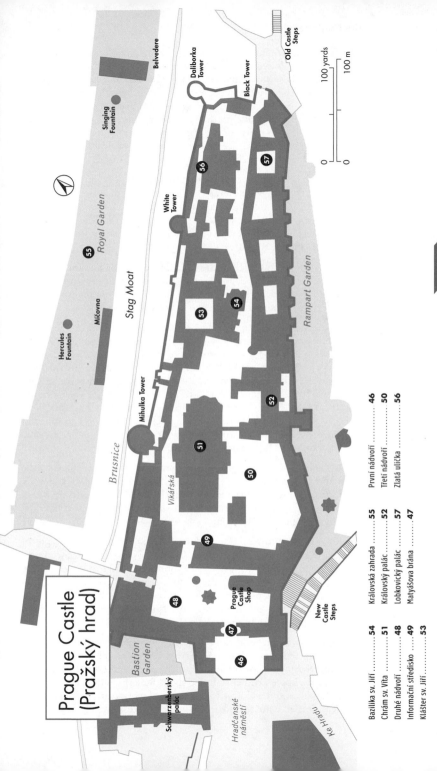

Prague Castle (Pražský hrad)

5

the cathedral. Around 925, as prince of Bohemia, Wenceslas founded a rotunda church dedicated to St. Vitus on this site. But the prince's brother, Boleslav, was impatient to take power, and he had Wenceslas killed in 929 (or 935 according to some experts) near a church at Stará Boleslav, northeast of Prague. Wenceslas was originally buried in that church, but his grave produced so many miracles that he rapidly became a symbol of piety for the common people. Boleslav was finally forced to honor his brother by reburying the body in the St. Vitus Rotunda. Shortly afterward, Wenceslas was canonized.

The rotunda was replaced by a Romanesque basilica in the late 11th century. Work was begun on the existing building in 1344. For the first few years the chief architect was the Frenchman Mathias d'Arras, but after his death in 1352 the work was continued by the 22-year-old German architect Peter Parler, who went on to build the Charles Bridge and many other Prague treasures.

The small door in the back of the chapel leads to the **Korunní komora** (Crown Chamber), the repository of the Bohemian crown jewels. It remains locked with seven keys held by seven important people (including the president) and is definitely not open to the public.

A little beyond the Chapel of St. Wenceslas on the same side, stairs lead down to the underground **royal crypt,** interesting primarily for the information it provides about the cathedral's history. As you descend the stairs, you'll see parts of the old Romanesque basilica and portions of the foundations of the rotunda. Moving around into the second room, you'll find a rather eclectic group of royal remains ensconced in new sarcophagi dating from the 1930s. In the center is Charles IV, who died in 1378. Rudolf II, patron of Renaissance Prague, is entombed at the rear in the original tin coffin. To his right is Maria Amalia, the only child of Empress Maria Theresa to reside in Prague.

The cathedral's **Kralovské oratorium** (Royal Oratory) was used by the kings and their families when attending mass. Built in 1493, the work is a perfect example of the late-Gothic style, laced on the outside with a stone network of gnarled branches very similar in pattern to the ceiling vaulting in the Královský palác.

A few more steps toward the east end, you can't fail to catch sight of the ornate silver **sarcophagus of St. John of Nepomuk.** According to legend, when Nepomuk's body was exhumed in 1721 to be reinterred, the tongue was found to be still intact and pumping with blood. This strange tale served a highly political purpose. The Catholic Church and the Habsburgs were seeking a new folk hero to replace the Protestant forerunner Jan Hus, whom they despised.

The eight chapels around the back of the cathedral are the work of the original architect, Mathias d'Arras. Opposite the wooden relief, depicting the looting of the cathedral by Protestants in 1619, is the **Valdštejnská kaple** (Wallenstein Chapel). Since the 19th century, the chapel has housed the Gothic tombstones of its two architects, d'Arras and Peter Parler, who died in 1352 and 1399, respectively. If you look up to the balcony, you can just make out the busts of these two men, designed by Parler's workshop. The other busts around the triforium depict royalty and other VIPs of the time.

The Hussite wars in the 15th century put an end to the first phase of the cathedral's construction. During the short era of illusory peace before the Thirty Years' War, the massive south tower was completed, but lack of money quashed any idea of finishing the building, and the cathedral was closed by a wall built across from the Chapel of St. Wenceslas. Not until the 20th century was the western side of the cathedral, with its two towers, completed in the spirit of Parler's conception.

⌂ *St. Vitus's Cathedral, Pražský Hrad* ☎ *224–373–368 Castle Information* ⊕ *www.katedralapraha.cz* ☒ *Western section free; chapels, crypt, and tower require 2-day castle ticket for 350 Kč* ⊘ *Mar.–Oct., Mon.–Sat. 9–5, Sun. noon–5; Nov.–Feb., Mon.–Sat. 9–4, Sun. noon–4.*

❷ **Druhé nádvoří** *(Second Courtyard).* Empress Maria Theresa's court architect, Nicolò Pacassi, received the imperial approval to remake the castle in the 1760s, as it was badly damaged by Prussian shelling during the Seven Years' War in 1757. The Second Courtyard was the main victim of Pacassi's attempts at imparting classical grandeur to what had been a picturesque collection of Gothic and Renaissance styles. Except for the view of the spires of St. Vitus's Cathedral, the exterior courtyard offers little for the eye to feast upon. This courtyard also houses the rather gaudy **Kaple svatého Kříže** (Chapel of the Holy Cross), with decorations from the 18th and 19th centuries, which now serves as a souvenir and ticket stand.

Built in the late 16th and early 17th centuries, the Second Courtyard was originally part of a reconstruction program commissioned by Rudolf II, under whom Prague enjoyed a period of unparalleled cultural development. Once the Prague court was established, the emperor gathered around him some of the world's best craftsmen, artists, and scientists, including the brilliant astronomers Johannes Kepler and Tycho Brahe.

Rudolf II amassed a large and famed collection of fine and decorative art, scientific instruments, philosophic and alchemical books, natural wonders, coins, and everything else under the sun. The bulk of the collection was looted by the Swedes during the Thirty Years' War, removed to Vienna when the imperial capital returned there after Rudolf's death, or auctioned off during the 18th century. Artworks that survived the turmoil, for the most part acquired after Rudolf's time, are displayed in the **Obrazárna** *(Picture Gallery* ☒ *100 Kč* ⊘ *Daily 10–6),* on the left side of the courtyard as you face St. Vitus's. In rooms elegantly redecorated by the official castle architect, Bořek Šípek, there are good Renaissance, mannerist, and baroque paintings that hint at the luxurious tastes of Rudolf's court. Across the passageway by the gallery entrance is the **Císařská konírna** (Imperial Stable), where temporary exhibitions are held. The passageway at the northern end of the courtyard forms the northern entrance to the castle and leads out over a luxurious ravine known as the **Jelení příkop** (Stag Moat), which can be entered (from

April through October) either here or at the lower end via the metal catwalk off Chotkova ulice, when it isn't closed for sporadic renovations. ⊠ *Obrazárna: Second Courtyard, Hradčany* ☎ *224–373–368 Castle Information* ⊕ *www.prague-info.cz* ✉ *Courtyard free; Picture Gallery 150 Kč* ☉ *Apr.–Oct., daily 9–6; Nov.–Mar., daily 9–4.*

㊽ Informační středisko *(Castle Information Office).* This is the place to come for entrance tickets, guided tours, headphones for listening to recorded tours in English, tickets to cultural events held at the castle, and money changing. Tickets are valid for one day and allow admission to the older parts of St. Vitus's Cathedral (the 20th-century sections are free), Královský palác, St. George's Basilica (but not the adjacent National Gallery exhibition, which has an additional entry fee), and a medieval bastion called Mihulka with an exhibition on alchemy. Other castle sights—including Golden Lane—require separate tickets, and you purchase these at the door. If you just want to walk through the castle grounds, note that the gates close at midnight April–October and at 11 PM the rest of the year, although the gardens are open April–October only. ⊠ *Třetí nádvoří, across from entrance to St. Vitus's Cathedral, Pražský Hrad* ☎ *224–373–368* ⊕ *www.prague-info.cz* ✉ *Castle tickets 250 Kč (short) or 350 Kč (long); Golden Lane 50 Kč; St. George's Basilica 50 Kč; English-language guided tours 400 Kč for up to 4 people, 100 Kč per additional person, advance booking recommended; grounds and gardens free* ☉ *Apr.–Oct., daily 9–5; Nov.–Mar., daily 9–4.*

㊼ Klášter svatého Jiří *(St. George's Convent).* The first convent in Bohemia was founded here in 973 next to the even older St. George's Basilica. The National Gallery collections of Czech mannerist and baroque art are housed here. The highlights include the voluptuous work of Rudolf II's court painters, the giant baroque religious statuary, and some fine paintings by Karel Škréta and Petr Brandl. Although inside Prague Castle, the museum has a separate admission. ⊠ *Nám. U sv. Jiří, Hradčany* ☎ *257–320–536* ⊕ *www.ngprague.cz* ✉ *130 Kč* ☉ *Daily 10–6.*

㊾ Královská zahrada *(Royal Garden).* This peaceful swath of greenery affords an unusually lovely view of St. Vitus's Cathedral and the castle's walls and bastions. Originally laid out in the 16th century, it endured devastation in war, neglect in times of peace, and many redesigns, reaching its present parklike form early in the 20th century. Luckily, its Renaissance treasures survive. One of these is the long, narrow **Míčovna** (Ball Game Hall), built by Bonifaz Wohlmut in 1568, its garden front completely covered by a dense tangle of allegorical sgraffiti.

The **Královský letohrádek** (Royal Summer Palace, also known as the Belvedere), at the garden's eastern end, deserves its usual description as one of the most beautiful Renaissance structures north of the Alps. Italian architects began it; Wohlmut finished it off in the 1560s with a copper roof like an upturned boat's keel riding above the graceful arcades of the ground floor. During the 18th and 19th centuries, military engineers tested artillery in the interior, which had already lost its rich furnishings to Swedish soldiers during their siege of the city in

1648. The Renaissance-style *giardinetto* (little garden) adjoining the summer palace centers on another masterwork, the Italian-designed, Czech-cast Singing Fountain, which mimics the sound of falling water. ✉ *U Prašného mostu ul. and Mariánské hradby ul. near Chotkovy Park, Hradčany* ☎ *224-373-368 Castle Information* ⊕ *www.prague-info.cz* 🎫 *Free* ⊘ *Mar.–June and Sept.–Oct., daily 10–7; July–Aug., daily 10–8.*

🐽 **Královský palác** *(Royal Palace).* The palace is an accumulation of the styles and add-ons of many centuries. The best way to grasp its size is from within the **Vladislavský sál** (Vladislav Hall), the largest secular Gothic interior space in Central Europe. The enormous hall was completed in 1493 by Benedikt Ried, who was to late-Bohemian Gothic what Peter Parler was to its earlier version. The room imparts a sense of space and light, softened by the sensuous lines of the vaulted ceilings and brought to a dignified close by the simple oblong form of the early Renaissance windows. In its heyday, the hall was the site of jousting tournaments, festive markets, banquets, and coronations. In more recent times, it has been used to inaugurate presidents, from the Communist Klement Gottwald in 1948 to Václav Havel in 1989, 1993, and 1998, and Válav Klaus in 2003.

From the front of the hall, turn right into the rooms of the **Česká kancelář** (Bohemian Chancellery). This wing was built by the same Benedikt Ried only 10 years after the hall was completed, but it shows a much stronger Renaissance influence. Pass through the Renaissance portal into the last chamber of the chancellery. This room was the site of the second defenestration of Prague, in 1618, an event that marked the beginning of the Bohemian rebellion and, ultimately, the Thirty Years' War. This peculiarly Bohemian method of expressing protest (throwing someone out a window) had first been used in 1419 in the New Town Hall, during the lead-up to the Hussite wars. Two hundred years later the same conflict was reexpressed in terms of Habsburg-backed Catholics versus Bohemian Protestants. Rudolf II had reached an uneasy agreement with the Bohemian nobles, allowing them religious freedom in exchange for financial support. But his next-but-one successor, Ferdinand II, was a rabid opponent of Protestantism and disregarded Rudolf's tolerant "Letter of Majesty." Enraged, the Protestant nobles stormed the castle and chancellery and threw two Catholic officials and their secretary, for good measure, out the window. Legend has it they landed on a mound of horse dung and escaped unharmed, an event the Jesuits interpreted as a miracle. The square window in question is on the left as you enter the room.

At the back of the Vladislav Hall, a staircase leads up to a gallery of the **Kaple všech svatých** (All Saints' Chapel). Little remains of Peter Parler's original work, but the church contains some fine works of art. The large room to the left of the staircase is the **Stará sněmovna** (council chamber), where the Bohemian nobles met with the king in a kind of prototype parliament. The descent from Vladislav Hall toward what remains of the **Romanský palác** (Romanesque Palace) is by way of a wide, shallow set of steps. This **Jezdecké schody** (Riders' Staircase) was the entranceway for knights who came for the jousting tournaments. ✉ *Royal Palace, Třetí nádvoří, Pražský Hrad* ☎ *224–373–368 Castle Information* ⊕ *www.prague-info.cz* 💳 *140 Kč or part of 2-day castle ticket, 250 Kč or 350 Kč* ⊙ *Apr.–Oct., daily 9–5; Nov.–Mar., daily 9–4.*

⑤ Lobkovický palác *(Lobkowicz Palace).* From the beginning of the 17th century until the 1940s, this building was the residence of the powerful Catholic Lobkowicz family. It was supposedly to this house that the two defenestrated officials escaped after landing on the dung hill in 1618. During the 1970s the building was restored to its early baroque appearance and now is used for the National Museum's temporary exhibitions and concerts. If you want to get a chronological understanding of Czech history from the beginnings of the Great Moravian Empire in the 9th century to the Czech national uprising in 1848, this is the place. Copies of the crown jewels are on display here, but it is the rich collection of illuminated Bibles, old musical instruments, coins, weapons, royal decrees, paintings, and statues that makes the museum well worth visiting. Detailed information on the exhibits is available in English. Although inside Prague Castle, this museum has a separate admission. ✉ *Jiřská ul., Hradčany* ⊕ *www.nm.cz* 💳 *20 Kč* ⊙ *Tues.–Sun. 10:30–6.*

④ Matyášova brána *(Matthias Gate).* Built in 1614, the stone gate once stood alone in front of the moats and bridges that surrounded the castle. Under the Habsburgs, the gate survived by being grafted as a relief onto the palace building. As you go through it, notice the ceremonial white-marble entrance halls on either side that lead up to the Czech president's reception rooms (which are only rarely open to the public).

④ První nádvoří *(First Courtyard).* The main entrance to Prague Castle from Hradčanské náměstí is a little disappointing. Going through the wrought-iron gate, guarded at ground level by Czech soldiers and from above by the ferocious *Battling Titans* (a copy of Ignaz Platzer's original 18th-century work), you'll enter this courtyard, built on the site of old moats and gates that once separated the castle from the surrounding buildings and thus protected the vulnerable western flank. The courtyard is one of the more recent additions to the castle, designed by Maria Theresa's court architect, Nicolò Pacassi, in the 1760s. Today it forms part of the presidential office complex. Pacassi's reconstruction was intended to unify the eclectic collection of buildings that made up the castle, but the effect of his work is somewhat flat.

④ Třetí nádvoří *(Third Courtyard).* The contrast between the cool, dark interior of St. Vitus's Cathedral and the brightly colored Pacassi facades of the Third Courtyard just outside is startling. The courtyard's clean lines are the work of Slovenian architect Josip Plečnik in the 1930s, but the modern look is a deception. Plečnik's paving was intended to cover an underground world of house foundations, streets, and walls dating from the 9th through 12th century and rediscovered when the cathedral was completed. (You can see a few archways through a grating in a wall of the cathedral.) Plečnik added a few eclectic features to catch the eye: a granite obelisk to commemorate the fallen of the First World War, a black-marble pedestal for the Gothic statue of St. George (a copy of the National Gallery's original statue), the inconspicuous entrance to his Bull Staircase leading down to the south garden, and the peculiar golden ball topping the eagle fountain near the eastern end of the courtyard.

☾ ⑤⓪ **Zlatá ulička** *(Golden Lane)*. An enchanting collection of tiny, ancient, brightly colored houses crouches under the fortification wall and looks remarkably like a set for *Snow White and the Seven Dwarfs*. Legend has it that these were the lodgings of the international group of alchemists whom Rudolf II brought to the court to produce gold. The truth is a little less romantic: the houses were built during the 16th century for the castle guards, who supplemented their income by practicing various crafts. By the early 20th century, Golden Lane had become the home of poor artists and writers. Franz Kafka, who lived at No. 22 in 1916 and 1917, described the house on first sight as "so small, so dirty, impossible to live in and lacking everything necessary." But he soon came to love the place. As he wrote to his fiancée: "Life here is something special . . . to close out the world not just by shutting the door to a room or apartment but to the whole house, to step out into the snow of the silent lane." The lane now houses tiny stores selling books, music, and crafts.

Within the walls above Golden Lane, a timber-roof **corridor** (enter between Nos. 23 and 24) is lined with replica suits of armor and weapons (some of it for sale), mock torture chambers, and the like. A shooting range allows you to fire five bolts from a crossbow for 50 Kč. ⊠*Pražský Hrad* ☎*224–373–368* ⊕*www.prague-info.cz* ✒*Included in combination 2-day castle tickets for 250 Kč or 350 Kč; free after 6* PM.

NOVÉ MĚSTO (NEW TOWN) & VYŠEHRAD

To this day, Charles IV's building projects are tightly woven into the daily lives of Praguers. His most extensive scheme, the New Town, is still such a lively, vibrant area you may hardly realize that its streets, Gothic churches, and squares were planned as far back as 1348. With Prague fast outstripping its Old Town parameters, Charles IV extended the city's fortifications. A high wall surrounded the newly developed 2½ square km (1½ square mi) area south and east of the Old Town, tripling the walled territory on the Vltava's right bank. The wall extended south to link with the fortifications of the citadel called Vyšehrad. In the mid-19th century, new building in the New Town boomed in a welter of Romantic and neo-Renaissance styles, particularly on Wenceslas Square and avenues such as Vodičkova, Na Poříčí, and Spálená. One of the most important structures was the Národní divadlo (National Theater), meant to symbolize in stone the revival of the Czechs' history, language, and sense of national pride. Both preceding and following Czechoslovak independence in 1918, modernist architecture entered the mix, particularly on the outer fringes of the Old Town and in the New Town. One of modernism's most unexpected products was Cubist architecture, a form unique to Prague, which produced four notable examples at the foot of ancient Vyšehrad.

SIGHTS TO SEE

63 **Cubist buildings.** Born of zealous modernism, Prague's Cubist architecture followed a great Czech tradition in that it fully embraced new ideas while adapting them to existing artistic and social contexts. Between 1912 and 1914, Josef Chochol (1880–1956) designed several of the city's dozen or so Cubist projects. His apartment house **Neklanova 30**, on the corner of Neklanova and Přemyslova, is a masterpiece in dingy concrete. The pyramidal, kaleidoscopic window moldings and roof cornices are completely novel while making an expressive link to baroque forms; the faceted corner balcony column elegantly alludes to Gothic forerunners. On the same street, at **Neklanova 2**, is another apartment house attributed to Chochol; like the building at Neklanova 30, it uses pyramidal shapes and the suggestion of Gothic columns.

Nearby, Chochol's **villa**, on the embankment at Libušina 3, has an undulating effect created by smoothly articulated forms. The wall and gate around the back of the house use triangular moldings and metal grating to create an effect of controlled energy. The **three-family house**, about 100 yards away from the villa at Rašínovo nábřeží 6–10, was completed slightly earlier, when Chochol's Cubist style was still developing. Here, the design is touched with baroque and neoclassical influence, with a mansard roof and end gables.

59 **Karlovo náměstí** *(Charles Square).* This square began life as a cattle market, a function chosen by Charles IV when he established the New Town in 1348. The horse market (now Wenceslas Square) quickly overtook it as a livestock-trading center, and an untidy collection of shacks accumulated here until the mid-1800s, when it became a green park named for its patron. ⊠*Bounded by Řeznická on the north, U Nemocnice on the south, Karlovo nám. on the west, and Vodičkova on the east, Nové Město.*

61 Another of Charles IV's gifts to the city, the Benedictine **Klášter Emauzy** *(Emmaus Monastery)* sits south of Karlovo náměstí. It is often called Na Slovanech, literally "At the Slavs'," in reference to its purpose when established in 1347: the emperor invited Croatian monks here to celebrate mass in Old Slavonic and thus cultivate religion among the Slavs in a city largely controlled by Germans. A faded but substantially complete cycle of biblical scenes by Charles's court artists lines the four cloister walls. The frescoes, and especially the abbey church, suffered heavy damage from a February 14, 1945, raid by Allied bombers that may have mistaken Prague for Dresden, 121 km (75 mi) away. The church lost its spires, and the interior remains a blackened shell. Some years after the war, two curving concrete "spires" were set atop the church. ⊠*Vyšehradská 49 (cloister entrance on left at rear of church), Vyšehrad* 🚇*30 Kč* ☉ *Weekdays 9–4.*

56 **Mucha Museum.** For decades it was almost impossible to find an Alfons Mucha original in the homeland of this famous Czech artist, until, in 1998, this private museum opened with nearly 100 works from his long career. What you'd expect to see is here—the theater posters of actress Sarah Bernhardt, the magazine covers, and the luscious, sinuous Art Nouveau designs. There are also paintings, photographs taken in Mucha's studio (one shows Paul Gauguin playing the piano in his underwear), and even Czechoslovak banknotes designed by the artist. ✉*Panská 7 (1 block off Wenceslas Square, across from Palace Hotel), Nové Město* ☎*221–451–333* ⊕*www.mucha.cz* ✉*120 Kč* ⊙*Daily 10–6.*

57 **Národní divadlo** *(National Theater)*. The idea for a Czech national theater began during the revolutionary decade of the 1840s. In a telling display of national pride, donations to fund the plan poured in from all over the country, from people of every socioeconomic stratum. The cornerstone was laid in 1868, and the "National Theater generation" who built the neo-Renaissance structure became the architectural and artistic establishment for decades to come. Its designer, Josef Zítek (1832–1909), was the leading neo-Renaissance architect in Bohemia. The nearly finished interior was gutted by a fire in 1881, and Zítek's onetime student Josef Schulz (1840–1917) saw the reconstruction through to completion two years later. Statues representing Drama and Opera rise above the riverfront side entrances; two gigantic chariots flank figures of Apollo and the nine Muses above the main facade. The performance space itself is filled with gilding, voluptuous plaster figures, and plush upholstery. Next door is the modern (1970s–80s) Nová scéna (New Stage), where the popular Magic Lantern black-light shows are staged. The Národní divadlo is one of the best places to see a performance; ticket prices start as low as 30 Kč, and you'll have to buy a ticket if you want to see inside because there are no public tours. ✉*Národní tř. 2, Nové Město* ☎*224–901–448 box office* ⊕*www.narodni-divadlo.cz.*

55 **Národní muzeum** *(National Museum)*. This imposing structure, designed by Prague architect Josef Schulz and built between 1885 and 1890, does not come into its own until it is bathed in nighttime lighting. By day the grandiose edifice seems an inappropriate venue for a musty collection of stones and bones, minerals, and coins. This museum is only for dedicated fans of the genre. ✉ *Václavské nám. 68, Nové Město* ☎*224–497–111* ⊕*www.nm.cz* ✉*120 Kč* ⊙*May–Sept., daily 10–6; Oct.–Apr., daily 9–5; except for 1st Tues. of each month, when it's closed.*

60 **Novoměstská radnice** *(New Town Hall)*. At the northern edge of Karlovo náměstí, the New Town Hall has a late-Gothic tower similar to that of the Old Town Hall, as well as three tall Renaissance gables. The first defenestration in Prague occurred here on July 30, 1419, when a mob of townspeople, followers of the martyred religious reformer Jan Hus, hurled Catholic town councillors out the windows. Historical exhibitions and contemporary art shows are held here regularly (admission prices vary), and you can climb the tower for a view of the New Town. ✉*Karlovo nám. at Vodičkova, Nové Město* ☎*224–948–225* ⊕*www.novomestskaradnice.cz* ✉*Tower 40 Kč; gallery admission varies by exhibition* ⊙*Tower May–Sept., Tues.–Sun. 10–6; gallery Tues.–Sun. 10–6.*

54 **Statue of St. Wenceslas.** Josef Václav Myslbek's huge equestrian grouping of St. Wenceslas with other Czech patron saints around him is a traditional meeting place at times of great national peril or rejoicing. In 1939, Praguers gathered to oppose Hitler's takeover of Bohemia and Moravia. It was here also, in 1969, that the student Jan Palach set himself on fire to protest the bloody invasion of his country by the Soviet Union and other Warsaw Pact countries in August of the previous year. The invasion ended the "Prague Spring," a cultural and political movement emphasizing free expression, which was supported by Alexander Dubček, the popular leader at the time. Although Dubček never intended to dismantle Communist authority completely, his political and economic reforms proved too daring for fellow comrades in the rest of Eastern Europe. In the months following the invasion, conservatives loyal to the Soviet Union were installed in all influential positions. The subsequent two decades were a period of cultural stagnation. Hundreds of thousands of Czechs and Slovaks left the country, a few became dissidents, and many more resigned themselves to lives of minimal expectations and small pleasures. ⊠ *Václavské nám., Nové Město.*

58 **Tančící dům** *(Dancing House).* This whimsical building was partnered into life in 1996 by architect Frank Gehry (of Guggenheim Museum in Bilbao fame) and his Croatian-Czech collaborator Vlado Milunic. A wasp-waisted glass-and-steel tower sways into the main structure as though they were a couple on the dance floor—a "Fred and Ginger" effect that gave the wacky, yet somehow appropriate, building its nickname. The French restaurant La Perle de Prague occupies the top floors, and there is a café at street level. ⊠ *Rašínovo nábř. 80, Nové Město.*

53 **Václavské náměstí** *(Wenceslas Square).* You may recognize this spot, for it was here that some 500,000 students and citizens gathered in the heady days of November 1989 to protest the policies of the former Communist regime. The government capitulated after a week of demonstrations, without a shot fired or the loss of a single life, bringing to power the first democratic government in 40 years (under playwright-president Václav Havel). Today this peaceful transfer of power is half ironically referred to as the "Velvet" or "Gentle" Revolution (*něžná revoluce*). It was only fitting that the 1989 revolution should take place on Wenceslas Square: throughout much of Czech history, the square has served as the focal point for popular discontent. The long "square," which is more like a broad, divided boulevard, was first laid out by Charles IV in 1348 as a horse market at the center of the New Town.

At No. 25, the **Hotel Europa** (⊠ *Vaclavske nám. 25*) is an Art Nouveau gem, with elegant stained glass and mosaics in the café and restaurant. The terrace is an excellent spot for people-watching. Note in particular the ornate sculpture work of two figures supporting a glass egg on top of the building and the ornate exterior mural. In 1906, when the hotel opened, this was a place for the elite; now the rooms reflect a sense of sadly faded grandeur.

⟲ ⓺ **Vyšehrad.** Bedřich Smetana's symphonic poem *Vyšehrad* opens with four bardic harp chords that seem to echo the legends surrounding this ancient fortress. Today, the flat-topped bluff standing over the right bank of the Vltava is a green, tree-dotted expanse showing few signs that splendid medieval monuments once made it a landmark to rival Prague Castle.

The historical father of Vyšehrad, the "High Castle," is Vratislav II (ruled 1061–92), a Přemyslid duke who became first king of Bohemia. He made the fortified hilltop his capital, but under subsequent rulers, it fell into disuse until the 14th century, when Charles IV transformed the site into an ensemble of palaces, the Gothicized main church, battlements, and a massive gatehouse called *Špička,* whose scant remains are on V Pevnosti ulice. By the 17th century, royalty had long since departed, and most of the structures they built were crumbling. Vyšehrad was turned into a fortress.

Vyšehrad's place in the modern Czech imagination is largely thanks to the National Revivalists of the 19th century, particularly writer Alois Jirásek (1851–1930), who mined medieval chronicles for legends and facts to glorify the early Czechs. The military history of the fortress and the city is covered in a small exposition inside the **Cihelná brána** (*Brick Gate* ✉10 Kč military exhibit*). The gate is also the entrance to the **casemates** (✉*20 Kč tour*), a long, dark passageway within the walls that ends at a dank hall used to store several original, pollution-scarred Charles Bridge sculptures. A guided tour into the casemates and the statue storage room starts at the military history exhibit. With its neo-Gothic spires, **Kapitulní kostel svatých Petra a Pavla** (*Chapter Church of Sts. Peter and Paul* ⊠*K rotundi 10, Vyšehrad* ☎*224–911–353*) dominates the plateau as it has since the 11th century. Next to the church lies the burial ground of the nation's revered cultural figures. Most of the buildings still standing are from the 19th century, but scattered among them are a few older structures and some foundation stones of the medieval palaces. Surrounding the ruins are gargantuan, excellently preserved brick fortifications built from the 17th to the mid-19th century; their broad tops allow strollers to take in sweeping vistas up- and downriver. A concrete result of the National Revival was the establishment of the **Hřbitov** (*cemetery* ⊠*Vinohradská 294/212, Vyšehrad* ☎*224–919–815*) in the 1860s, adjacent to the Church of Sts. Peter and Paul—it peopled the fortress with the remains of luminaries from the arts and sciences. The grave of Smetana faces the Slavín, a mausoleum for more than 50 honored men and women, including Alfons Mucha, sculptor Jan Štursa, inventor František Křižík, and the opera diva Ema Destinnová. All are guarded by a winged genius who hovers above the inscription AČ ZEMŘELI, JEŠTĚ MLUVÍ ("Although they have died, they yet speak"). Antonín Dvořák (1841–1904) rests in the arcade along the north wall of the cemetery. Among the many writers buried here are Jan Neruda, Božena Němcová, Karel Čapek, and the Romantic poet Karel Hynek Mácha, whose grave was visited by students on their momentous November 17, 1989, protest march. ⊠*V Pevnosti 159/5b, Vyšehrad* ☎*241–410–348* ⊕*www.praha-vysehrad.cz* ☉*Grounds* *daily. Casemates, military history exhibit, and St. Lawrence Basilica Apr.–Oct., daily 9:30–6; Nov.–Mar., daily 9:30–5. Cemetery Jan. and Feb., daily 8–5; Mar. and Apr., daily 8–6; May–Sept., daily 8–7; Oct., daily 8–6; Nov. and Dec., daily 8–5* Ⓜ *Line C: Vyšehrad.*

VINOHRADY

From Riegrovy Park and its sweeping view of the city from above the National Museum, the eclectic apartment houses and villas of the elegant residential neighborhood called Vinohrady extend eastward and southward. The pastel-tint ranks of turn-of-the-20th-century apartment houses—many crumbling after years of neglect—are slowly but unstoppably being transformed into upscale flats, slick offices, eternally packed new restaurants, and all manner of shops unthinkable only a half decade ago. Much of the development lies on or near Vinohradská, the main street, which extends from the top of Wenceslas Square to a belt of enormous cemeteries about 3 km (2 mi) eastward. Yet the flavor of daily life persists: smoky old pubs still ply their trade on the quiet side streets; the stately theater, Divadlo na Vinohradech, keeps putting on excellent shows as it has for decades; and on the squares and in the parks nearly everyone still practices Prague's favorite form of outdoor exercise—walking the dog.

64 **Kostel Nejsvětějšího Srdce Páně** *(Church of the Most Sacred Heart).* If you've had your fill of Romanesque, Gothic, and baroque, this church will give you a look at a startling art deco edifice. Designed in 1927 by Slovenian architect Josip Plečnik (the same architect commissioned to update Prague Castle) the church resembles a luxury ocean liner more than a place of worship. The effect was conscious: during the 1920s and '30s, the avant-garde imitated mammoth objects of modern technology. Plečnik used many modern elements on the inside. Notice the hanging speakers, seemingly designed to bring the word of God directly to the ears of each worshipper. You may be able to find someone at the back entrance of the church who will let you walk up the long ramp into the fascinating glass clock tower. ⊠ *Nám. Jiřího z Poděbrad, Vinohrady* 🎟️ *Free* 🕙 *Daily 10–5* Ⓜ *Line A: Jiřího z Poděbrad.*

65 **Nový židovský hřbitov** *(New Jewish Cemetery).* Tens of thousands of Czechs find eternal rest in Vinohrady's cemeteries. In this, the newest of the city's half-dozen Jewish burial grounds, you'll find the modest **tombstone of Franz Kafka,** which seems grossly inadequate to Kafka's stature but oddly in proportion to his own modest ambitions. The cemetery is usually open, although guards sometimes inexplicably seal off the grounds. Men may be required to wear a yarmulke (you can buy one here). Turn right at the main cemetery gate and follow the wall for about 100 yards. Kafka's thin, white tombstone lies at the front of section 21. City maps may label the cemetery *Židovské hřbitovy.* ⊠ *Vinohradská at Jana Želivského, Vinohrady* 🎟️ *Free* 🕙 *Apr.–Sept., Sun.–Thurs. 9–4:30, Fri. 9–2:30; Oct.–Mar., Sun.–Thurs. 9–3:30, Fri. 9–1:30* Ⓜ *Line A: Želivského.*

LETNÁ & HOLEŠOVICE

From above the Vltava's left bank, the large, grassy plateau called Letná gives you one of the classic views of the Old Town and the many bridges crossing the river. (To get to Letná from the Old Town, take Pařížská Street north, cross the Čechův Bridge, and climb the stairs.) Beer gardens, tennis, and Frisbee attract people of all ages, and amateur soccer players emulate the professionals of Prague's top team, Sparta, which plays in the stadium just across the road. A 10-minute walk from Letná, down into the residential neighborhood of Holešovice, brings you to a massive, gray-blue building whose cool exterior gives no hint of the treasures of Czech and French modern art that line its corridors. Just north along Dukelských hrdinů Street is Stromovka—a royal hunting preserve turned gracious park.

Numbers in the margin correspond to numbers on the Exploring Prague map.

5

67 **Letenské sady** *(Letna Park).* Come to this large, shady park for an unforgettable view of Prague's bridges. From the enormous concrete pedestal at the center of the park, the largest statue of Stalin in Eastern Europe once beckoned to citizens on the Old Town Square far below. The statue was ripped down in the 1960s, when Stalinism was finally discredited. On sunny Sundays expatriates often meet up here to play ultimate Frisbee. Head east on Milady Horáové street after exiting the metro. ⊠ *Letná* Ⓜ *Line A: Hradčanská.*

68 **Veletržní palác** *(Trade Fair Palace).* The National Gallery's **Sbírka moderního a soucasného umění** (Collection of Modern and Contemporary Art) has become a keystone in the city's visual-arts scene since its opening in 1995. Touring the vast spaces of this 1920s Constructivist exposition hall and its comprehensive collection of 20th-century Czech art is the best way to see how Czechs surfed the forefront of the avant-garde wave until the cultural freeze following the Communist takeover in 1948. Also on display are works by Western European—mostly French—artists from Delacroix to the present. Especially noteworthy are the early Cubist paintings by Picasso and Braque. The 19th-century Czech art collection of the National Gallery was installed in the palace in the summer of 2000. Watch the papers and posters for information on traveling shows and temporary exhibits. ⊠ *Dukelských hrdinů 47, Holešovice* ☎ *224–301–111* ⊕ *www.ngprague.cz* 🏷 *160 Kč* ☉ *Daily 10–6* Ⓜ *Line C: Vltavská.*

WHERE TO EAT

Dining choices in Prague have increased greatly in the past two decades as hundreds of new places have opened to meet the soaring demand from tourists and locals alike. These days, most out-and-out rip-offs have almost disappeared, but before paying up at the end of a meal it's a good idea to take a close look at the added cover charge on your bill. Also keep an eye out for extra-large fees tacked onto credit-card bills. In pubs and neighborhood restaurants, ask if there is a *denní lístek* (daily menu) of cheaper and often fresher selections, but note

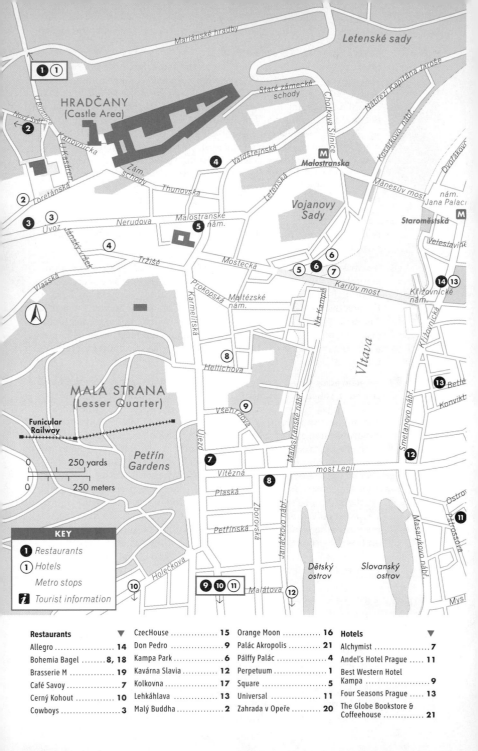

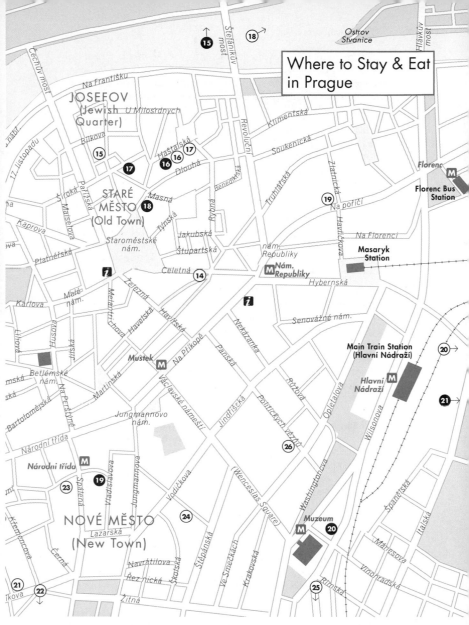

Where to Stay & Eat in Prague

that many places provide daily menus for the midday meal only. Special local dishes worth making a beeline for include *cibulačka* (onion soup), *kulajda* (potato soup with sour cream), *svíčková* (beef sirloin in cream sauce), and *ovocné knedlíky* (fruit dumplings, often listed under "meatless dishes").

The crush of tourists has placed tremendous strain on the more popular restaurants. The upshot: reservations are an excellent idea, especially for dinner during peak tourist periods. If you don't have reservations, try arriving a little before standard meal times: 11:30 AM for lunch or 5:30 PM for dinner.

For a cheaper and quicker alternative to the sit-down establishments listed below, try a light meal at one of the city's growing number of street stands or fast-food places. Look for stands offering *párky* (hot dogs) or the fattier *klobásy* (grilled sausages served with bread and mustard). Also, chic new cafés and bakeries spring up all the time, so it may pay to keep an eye out.

STARÉ MĚSTO (OLD TOWN)

ASIAN
$–$$$

✕**Orange Moon.** Excellent Burmese, Thai, and Indian dishes draw tourists and locals alike to this reasonably priced spot a short walk from Old Town Square. The two levels are slightly dim and atmospheric, with blond-wood fixtures, orange walls, and photographs of Asian scenes providing a mood-boosting effect. Burmese curried noodles, chicken soup with coconut milk and lemongrass, and beef kebabs with Madras curry represent just three outstanding items from a consistently good menu. ⊠*Rámova 5, Staré Město* ☏*222–325–119* ▭*AE, DC, MC, V* Ⓜ*Line B: Náěstí Republiky.*

CZECH
★ $–$$$

✕**Kolkovna.** For Czechs and expatriates living in Prague, this is one of the most popular spots to take visitors for a taste of local cuisine without the stress of tourist rip-offs and dingy neighborhoods. The wood-and-copper decor gives off an appropriate air of a brewery taproom, and you can wash down traditional meals—such as *svíčkova*, roast duck, and fried pork cutlets, or upgrades of traditional food, such as turkey steak with Roquefort sauce and walnuts—with a mug of unpasteurized Pilsner Urquell. ⊠*V Kolkovně, Staré Město* ☏*224–818–701* ▭*AE, MC, V* Ⓜ*Line A: Staroměstská.*

$–$$
Fodor's Choice
★

✕**Kavárna Slavia.** Easily the city's best-known café, Slavia serves good coffee, drinks, and light snacks, as well as the standards of Czech cuisine: roast duck with potato dumplings and sauerkraut, beef goulash, and roast smoked pork with white cabbage and potato pancakes. Sandwiches and quotidian pasta plates offer lighter, less-expensive options, though aesthetes can make a full meal out of the rich views of the National Theater, the Vltava, and Prague Castle. This spectacular location has a historic air that winds from the days of Viktor Oliva's painting The Absinth Drinker (which hangs in the main room), through the era of the playwright and regular patron Václav Havel, and continues into the modern day. ⊠*Smetanovo nábř. 1012/2, Staré Město* ☏*224–218–493* ▭*AE, MC, V* Ⓜ*Line B: Národní Třida.*

DELICATESSENS
$–$$

✕**Bohemia Bagel.** This Czech cousin of a college-town bagel shop, despite its thick accent, wouldn't feel out of place in Berkeley or Boston. This branch of Bohemia Bagel has a boisterous, morning-after feel. Though they've got nothing on those from the Big Apple, the bagels are a favorite for homesick expats, as are the bottomless cups of filter coffee and the free bulletin board postings, making this place not just a deli but a community center. Offerings include a classic BLT and lox with cream cheese and capers, as well as eggs, pancakes, hash browns, and other usual breakfast staples. ⊠*Masná 2, Staré Město* ☎*224–812–560* ⊟*No credit cards* Ⓜ*Line A: Staromětska.*

ITALIAN
$$$$
Fodor's Choice
★

✕**Allegro.** At the house restaurant of the Four Seasons hotel, the chef Vito Mollica raised the bar for Prague dining to heights other restaurants have never even dreamed of—and that's to say nothing of the outstanding service, elegant riverside atmosphere, and world-class wine list. Main courses have included such rare fare as monkfish saltimbocca, yellowfin tuna carpaccio, and house-made gnocchi with rabbit. Regularly recognized as one of the best Italian kitchens in Central Europe, Allegro is a treat for those who indulge in the top of the line. ⊠*Four Seasons Prague, Veleslavinova 21, Staré Město* ☎*221–427–000* ⌖*Reservations essential* ⊟*AE, DC, MC, V* Ⓜ*Line A: Staroměstska.*

VEGETARIAN
$

✕**Lehkáhlava.** Welcome to the new Czech Republic: Lehká hlava ("Clear head") serves clever vegetarian dishes at bargain-basement prices in a wacky, tripped-out dreamscape that includes an arched blue ceiling with thousands of tiny "stars" and tables that glow from inside. Appetizers like the rich spinach dip and creamy red-lentil soup lead to great veggie stir-fries and a better-than-decent burrito with smoky ratatouille. Attentive service and unusual, extremely affordable wines from Spain make it one of the city's recent favorites. ⊠*Boršov 2/280, Staré Město* ☎*222–220–665* ⊟*No credit cards* Ⓜ*Line B: Národní Třída.*

MALÁ STRANA (LESSER QUARTER)

$$$–$$$$
Fodor's Choice
★

✕**Kampa Park.** The apex of Vltava riverside dining is offered at this legendary restaurant just off Charles Bridge, known almost as much for its chic decor and celebrity guests as it is for elegant Continental cuisine and great wines—it's the kind of place where European royals and heads-of-state mingle with their head-of-studio counterparts from Hollywood. But the real star power arrives on the plate, courtesy of chef Marek Raditsch, whose sophisticated cooking blends seasonal ingredients with worldly culinary technique: halibut and foie gras with bean ragout, monkfish with port-glazed sweetbreads, venison with turnip fondant and figs. Incredible foods, incredible views. ⊠*Na Kampě 8/b, Malá Strana* ☎*257–532–685* ⊟*AE, DC, MC, V* Ⓜ*Line A: Malostranská.*

★ **$$$–$$$$**

✕**Pálffy Palác.** Tucked inside an establishment that's literally palatial, age-old elegance and artful Continental cuisine combine on the second story of a baroque palazzo just below Prague Castle. A favorite for special occasions, magical evenings, and affairs to remember, Pálffy is one of the few ancient locations in Prague to maintain a feel for the past without seeming stuffy, kitschy, or fake. Instead, it's all high ceilings, candlelight, and haute cuisine: baked yellowfin with udon, veal T-bone with onion skewer, fallow deer with rosehip-orange sauce. The overall effect is elegant, yet lighthearted. ⊠*Valdštejnská 14, Malá Strana* ☎*257–530–522* ⊟*AE, MC, V* Ⓜ*Line A: Malostranská.*

$$–$$$$ ✕**Cowboys.** This new steak house, part of the Kampa group of restaurants, occupies a unique location just below the Prague Castle ramparts, and the sound track here is as hip and smooth as the restored interior. But don't get stuck inside: in fair weather head up the labyrinthine staircases to the rooftop garden, which displays great views of Old Town and Malá Strana. The kitchen sends out the town's best cuts of beef, expertly prepared, including a killer double-cut T-bone. Even vegetarians have solid options, such as the faux burger, made of grilled portobello mushrooms. An excellent wine list includes top-shelf selections from four continents, as well as a special collection of single-barrel Bourbons. ⊠*Nerudova 40, Malá Strana* ☎*257–535–050* ⊟*AE, DC, MC, V* Ⓜ*Line A: Malostranská.*

★ $$–$$$ ✕**Square.** Once the site of a glimmering café, beloved by artists and writers from the mid-19th-century onward, this space is now a prime meeting spot for power players in Malá Strana. Excellent bistro foods and tapas as well as an exceptional selection of wines by the glass make this a favorite place for the beautiful people and their friends. Dinner kicks it up a notch with tiger prawns and avocado ceviche, lamb steak with saffron risotto, duck breast with seared foie gras, and a coy interpretation of fish-and-chips. Seeing and being seen is, naturally, part of the show, and the terrace overlooking the tram stop plays center stage on long, late summer afternoons. ⊠*Malostranské nám., Malá Strana* ☎*257–532–109* ⊟*AE, DC, MC, V* Ⓜ*Line A: Malostranská.*

★ $–$$$ ✕**Café Savoy.** Stellar service and elegant meals of high quality at moderate prices are de rigueur here. Oh, and killer sweets. This restored café, a onetime favorite of the city's fin-de-siècle Jewish community, serves everything from meal-size split-pea and cream of cauliflower soups to Wiener schnitzel, with huge salads complemented by fresh breads from the in-house bakery. The house cake, topped with marzipan, makes a properly sweet finish. But if you can't handle too much more, consider the bite-size chocolate truffles, sold individually, with fillings like Irish cream, rum, green pepper, and chili. ⊠*Vitězná 1, Smíchov* ☎*257–311–562* ⊟*AE, DC, MC, V* Ⓜ*Line A: Malostranská.*

HRADČANY

ASIAN ✕**Malý Buddha.** Bamboo, wood, paper, incense—and the random creepy
$–$$ mask on the wall—are all part of the decor at this earthy hilltop hideaway near Prague Castle. Spring rolls, vegetable and mixed stir-fries, fish, and shark steaks come in generous portions. The drink list is unusual, with ginseng wine, herbal drinks, and mystery shots of exotic alcoholic concoctions. The restaurant has a no-smoking policy—a rarity in Prague—so the aromas are pure. If the decorations interest you, you can buy much of what you see, including the colorful Asian ceramics. ⊠*Úvoz 46, Hradčany* ☎*220–513–894* ⊟*No credit cards* ⊘*Closed Mon.* Ⓜ*Line A: Hradčanská.*

CZECH ✕**Perpetuum.** The country's greatest culinary resources—wild duck and
$$ goose—get a makeover here with improved culinary techniques from France and Italy. Starters include one of the city's best duck *rillettes*, a deliciously greasy spread of slow-cooked duck meat, as well as gratifying salads and soups using seasonal ingredients. But that merely sets the stage for the main courses, such as goose breast with ginger and

the stir-fry-like duck fricassee. As if they were competing for a medal in hedonism, Perpetuum also includes one of the city's best wine lists, featuring Czech's best vintages, like the crisp whites from cult producer Dobrá vinice. If you want to see how good Czech food and drink can get, this is it. ⊠*Na hutích 9, Dejvice* ☎*222–522–784* ⊟*MC, V* ⊘*Closed Mon.* Ⓜ*Line A: Dejvická.*

NOVÉ MĚSTO (NEW TOWN) & VYŠEHRAD

COLOMBIAN

★ $–$$$

✕**Don Pedro.** Right on the riverfront, yet overlooked by most tourists, this hip bistro serves authentic dishes from Bogotá, courtesy of the Colombian-Czech couple who own the place. In large part that means beef: clear beef broth with stewed beef rib known as *caldo de costilla*; white-corn empanadas stuffed with ground beef and rice; and arepas, thick corn pancakes filled with gooey white cheese. Both the 300-gram (10-ounce) beefsteak and the grilled beef liver are excellent meals for hearty appetites. ⊠*Masarykovo nábř. 2, Nové Město* ☎*224–923–505* ⊟*MC, V* Ⓜ*Line B: Národní Třída.*

CONTINENTAL

$$–$$$

✕**Universal.** Prices here have doggedly remained unchanged since it opened in the late 1990s. Universal is a Continental cornucopia of excellent salads, classically European main courses, titanic side orders of scalloped potatoes, luscious lemon tarts, and sweet profiteroles. An affordable midday menu makes it even more alluring at lunchtime, and the cheap house wine draws out after-dinner conversations. Reservations are advisable. ⊠*V Jirchářích 6, Nové Město* ☎*224–934–416* ⊟*MC, V* Ⓜ*Line B: Národní Třída.*

CZECH

$$$–$$$$

✕**Černý Kohout.** Cozy, comfortable, and full of European charm, "the Black Rooster" serves classic Czech cuisine in a Continental context, bringing a strong French touch to such traditional fare as Czech lamb from the Šumava national forest and roasted Slovak peppers, as well as adding an Italian influence to the risotto with Czech forest mushrooms. Graceful service in upscale surroundings gives the impression of something from a bygone era. Thrifty diners, take note: midweek brings a three-course business lunch of the same high quality for a much lower price. ⊠*Vojtěšská 9, Nové Město* ☎*251–681–191* ⊟*AE, DC, MC, V* Ⓜ*Line B: Národní Třída.*

$$$–$$$$

Fodor'sChoice

★

✕**CzecHouse.** On the ground floor of the capacious Hilton Hotel, this renewed restaurant reopened in late 2005 to rave reviews for its upscale interpretations of Czech recipes, including one of the few versions of svíčková *na smetaně* in town to be made from tenderloin, resulting in a radically different version from that at your average corner pub. Czech wines are similarly of a higher standard, though beer goes very well with most recipes. Excellent service provides another reason to make the trip to metro station Florenc. ⊠*Pobřežní 1, Karlín 186 00* ☎*224–842–125* ⊟*AE, DC, MC, V* Ⓜ*Line B or C: Florenc.*

ECLECTIC

★ $$–$$$

✕**Zahrada v opeře.** Don't be put off by appearances: despite the external harshness of this Communist-era building, it contains an airy, open restaurant inside, with the most innovative and surprising menus in the city. A perfect balance of creativity and price, the "Garden in the Opera" is an epicurean bull's-eye. Dishes include grilled and roasted fresh fish and regional specialties like the tender rabbit fricassee with mustard sauce. Special events bring in chefs from countries like Nepal and South

5

Africa, making frequent visits a must. It's an exceptional value for the price, and a favorite of many discerning diners. ⊠ *Legerova 75, Nové Město* ☏ *224–239–685* ▭ *AE, DC, MC, V* Ⓜ *Line C: Muzeum.*

FRENCH
★ $$–$$$$

✕ **Brasserie M.** When chef Jean-Paul Manzac left the Prague Marriott to open his own shiny bistro, he changed the very definition of local French food. Brasserie M. is a spacious restaurant with all the classics, from simple *croque* sandwiches to elegant grilled turbot, alongside true Alsatian fare, like *choucroute garnie* (a sort of sauerkraut with meat) and a traditional chocolate mousse (the recipe was passed down from the chef's father). It's all excellent and generally about half the price of fancier French places around town. ⊠ *Vladislavova 17, Nové Město* ☏ *224–054–070* ▭ *AE, MC, V* Ⓜ *Line B: Národní Třída.*

ŽIŽKOV

ECLECTIC
$–$$

✕ **Palác Akropolis.** Though the concert venue/club downstairs is pulsing at night, this restaurant is a draw in its own right, in part due to the loopy interior by Czech artist František Skála. Steel-covered menus offer large portions of traditional Czech fare such as pork cutlets and potato pancakes, as well as Mexican-style soups and Buffalo wings, all at reasonable prices. Aquariums containing Skála's industrial sculptures provide something to look at while the food arrives, though sometimes the hipster staff is even more captivating. The music, which ranges from hip-hop to Czech rock, can be quite loud. ⊠ *Kubelíková 27, Žižkov* ☏ *296–330–990* ▭ *No credit cards* Ⓜ *Line A: Jiřího z Poděbrad.*

WHERE TO STAY

The rise in lodging standards continues, though the standards at all but the most expensive hotels lag behind those of Germany and Austria—as do prices. During the peak season reservations are absolutely imperative; for the remainder of the year they are highly recommended. Many hotels in Prague go by a three-season system: the lowest rates are charged from December through February, excluding Christmas (at some hotels) and New Year's (at all hotels), when high-season rates are charged; the middle season includes March, November, and often July and August; and spring and fall bring the highest rates. Easter sees higher-than-high-season rates, and some hotels up the price for other holidays and trade fairs. It always pays to ask first. Standard room rates almost always include breakfast. Only the top-end hotels have air-conditioning.

A private room or apartment can be a cheaper and more interesting alternative to a hotel. You'll find agencies offering such accommodations all over Prague, including at the main train station (Hlavní nádraží), Holešovice station (Nádraží Holešovice), and at Ruzyně Airport. These bureaus normally are staffed with people who can speak some English, and most can book rooms in hotels and pensions as well as private accommodations. Rates for private rooms start at around $15 per person per night and can go much higher for better-quality rooms. In general, there is no fee, but you may need to try several bureaus to find the accommodation you want. Ask to see a photo of the room before accepting it, and be sure to pinpoint its location on a map—you don't want to wind up in an inconveniently distant location. You may be approached by (usually) men in the stations hawking rooms, and although these deals aren't always rip-offs, you should be wary of them. **Prague Information Service** arranges lodging from all of its central offices, including the branch in the main train station, which is in the booth marked TURISTICKÉ INFORMACE on the left side of the main hall as you exit the station.

For a short-term stay, **Mary's Accommodation Service** (⊠ *Italská 31, Vinohrady* ☎ *222–254–007* ⊕ *www.marys.cz*) can help you find a reasonably priced apartment in the center of town. **Stop In** (⊠ *V Holešovičhách 15, Libeň* ☎ *284–680–115* ⊕ *www.stopin.cz*) offers private apartments and rooms, some in the more residential areas.

STARÉ MĚSTO (OLD TOWN)

$$$$ **Four Seasons Prague.** If you love hotels with every small luxury—morning newspapers with your breakfast, in-room massages, and twice-daily maid service—the expense of these rooms will be easier to justify. Sean Connery and Owen Wilson could only agree, having stayed here while they worked in Prague. A baroque house from 1737 and a renovated neoclassical former factory from 1846 were joined together through a contemporary building to form this large luxury hotel with an unbeatable riverside location. Room 234 is the proverbial "room with a view" offering a sweeping vista of the Charles Bridge. Service is consistently excellent and the friendliness of the staff is unbeatable. The in-house restaurant could serve your best meal in Prague. ⊠ *Veleslavinova 21, Staré Město, 110 00* ☎ *221–427–000* ⊟ *221–426–977* ⊕ *www.fourseasons.com* ⇆ *141 rooms, 20 suites* ⚐ *In-room: safe, dial-up. In-hotel: restaurant, bar, gym, concierge, parking (fee), no-smoking rooms, some pets allowed* ⊟ *AE, DC, MC, V* ⛌ *EP* Ⓜ *Line A: Staroměstská.*

$$–$$$ **Haštal.** The price is great for the location—on a quiet square just a few minutes from the Old Town Square. The building was used as a brewery until the turn of the 20th century. It's low on glamour, but nicely appointed. ⊠ *Haštalská 16, Staré Město, 110 00* ☎ *222–314–335* ⊟ *222–314–336* ⊕ *www.hastal.com* ⇆ *24 rooms* ⚐ *In-room: no a/c. In-hotel: restaurant, parking (fee), some pets allowed* ⊟ *AE, DC, MC, V* ⛌ *BP* Ⓜ *Line A: Staroměstská.*

$$–$$$ **Maximilian.** If hotels could be featured on an Oprah makeover show, this would be the result. The transformation is so lovely, it practically brings a tear to the eye. After a renovation in 2005, the Maximilian has become completely modern in the most tasteful way, with classic cherrywood furniture. Comfortable and intimate, it's quiet enough for even the lightest of sleepers and close enough to Old Town Square for the laziest of travelers. ⊠ *Haštalská 14, Staré Město, 110 00* ☎ *225–303–118* ⊟ *225–303–110* ⊕ *www.maximilianhotel.com* ⇆ *72 rooms* ⚐ *In-room: safe, dial-up. In-hotel: restaurant, room service, laundry service, parking (fee), no-smoking rooms, some pets allowed* ⊟ *AE, DC, MC, V* ⛌ *BP* Ⓜ *Line A: Staroměstská.*

$$–$$$ **U Zlatého Jelena.** The simple furnishings may skirt the line on being frumpy, but a killer location, just down from Old Town Square, makes

this a nice "budget" choice. If you're curious what most standard Prague apartments are like, this is probably a good example—high ceilings, parquet floors, and brass furniture. And these are probably the largest rooms you will find in the city center without spending a fortune at a four-star hotel. The staff is honest and helpful. ⊠*Celetná 11, Staré Město, 110 00* ☎*222-317-237* 🖷*222-318-693* ⊕*www. beetle-tour.cz* ⇥*10 rooms* ⌂*In-room: no a/c, safe, VCR. In-hotel: restaurant, some pets allowed, no elevator* ⊟*AE, DC, MC, V* ⑩*CP* Ⓜ*Line A: Staroměstská.*

$$ 🏨 **Hotel Ibis Praha Old Town.** Two words: flower power. That's the design vision for this chain hotel, which opened in 2006. The location is one of the best, putting you right across the street from Obecní dům. Reasonable rates, clean rooms with a modern touch, and Wi-Fi available in public areas and some rooms give this hotel its appeal. ⊠*Na Poříčí 5, Staré Město, 110 00* ☎*266-000-999* 🖷*266-000-666* ⊕*www.ibishotel.com* ⇥*271 rooms* ⌂*In-room: safe, dial-up. In-hotel: restaurant, bar, parking (fee), no-smoking rooms, some pets allowed* ⊟*AE, DC, MC, V* ⑩*BP* Ⓜ*Line B: Nám. Republiky.*

MALÁ STRANA (LESSER QUARTER)

With a bewitching storybook suite of baroque palaces and Renaissance facades, the Lesser Quarter—at the other end of the Charles Bridge from the Old Town—is the darling of Prague. Mostly a quiet area, removed from the bustle across the river, it's also filled with great restaurants and music clubs. Malá Strana provides an excellent location for visiting Prague Castle just up the hill, but may not be the best choice for people with mobility problems. Other cons: access to cars on the narrow cobblestone streets is restricted, parking is difficult, and you'll spend a lot of your time walking on the Charles Bridge to get to the Old Town.

$$$$ 🏨 **Hotel Neruda.** Built in 1348, this landmark—now a small and modern hotel—is where the author Jan Neruda and his mother lived in 1860. As a tribute, lines from Neruda's *Povidky malostranske* (*Malá Strana Stories*) are painted in the stone hallways. The building supposedly has a ghost—you might hear her and her jingling keys in the hallway. Then again, many of the buildings on this street are said to have their own—friendly—ghosts. Try to see a couple of rooms before choosing one, as some rooms look out onto a wall. ⊠*Nerudova 44, Malá Strana, 110 00* ☎*257-535-558* 🖷*257-531-492* ⊕*www.hotel-neruda-praha.cz* ⇥*20 rooms* ⌂*In-room: safe. In-hotel: restaurant, parking (fee), some pets allowed* ⊟*AE, DC, MC, V* ⑩*BP* Ⓜ*Line A: Malostranská.*

$$$$
Fodor's Choice
★
🏨 **Mandarin Oriental Prague.** The picture of understated taste, this outpost of the Mandarin Oriental opened in late 2006. Appropriately built in a former monastery, the vaulted ceilings and original 14th-century staircases now offer luxurious serenity to guests. Contemporary Asian touches work into a harmonious blend of beige, red, black, and navy. Silk tassels in red or gold indicate to the staff "do not disturb" or "please make up my room." An underground passageway leads to the spa, where a glass floor displays the ruins of a Gothic church uncov-

ered during construction. Here you can receive a Czech specialty, the Linden Blossom scrub, using blossoms long believed to be medicinal in Czech culture. ⊠*Nebovidská 459, Malá Strana, 118 00* ☎*233–088–888* 🖷*233–088–668* ⊕*www.mandarinoriental.com* 🛏*99 rooms, 22 suites* ⚓*In-room: safe, DVD, dial-up, Wi-Fi. In-hotel: restaurant, bars, gym, spa, laundry service, parking* ▭*AE, DC, MC, V* ⦿❙*EP* Ⓜ*Line A: Malostranská.*

$$$$
Fodor's Choice
★

🏨 **Residence Hotel Alchymist.** When dreaming of Prague, this is the hotel that comes to mind. Both the front of the hotel (which is UNESCO-protected) and the squished lobby disguise how large this building actually is. It brings together four Renaissance and baroque houses from the late 15th century. Owned by an Italian and possessing that signature Italian flair, this hotel not only features a 500-year-old staircase, but the imported tiki wood creates a bridge (over a fish-filled pond) linking the massage rooms and the sushi bar in the basement. It's truly an embarrassment of riches. ⊠*Tržiště 19, Malá Strana, 118 00* ☎*257–286–011* 🖷*257–286–017* ⊕*www.alchymisthotel.com* 🛏*26 rooms, 20 suites* ⚓*In-room: safe, DVD, dial-up. In-hotel: restaurant, gym, spa, laundry service* ▭*AE, DC, MC, V* ⦿❙*BP* Ⓜ*Line A: Malostranská.*

$$$

🏨 **Best Western Hotel Kampa.** This early-baroque armory-turned-hotel is tucked away on an abundantly picturesque street at the southern end of Malá Strana, just off Kampa Island. Note the late-Gothic vaulting in the massive dining room. At one time the bucolic setting and proximity to the city center made this lodging option a comparative bargain; now hotels within blocks offer the same, if not better, services and can be a few euros cheaper. But it's a good fallback option if you can't get a room anywhere else in this location. ⊠*Všehrdova 16, Malá Strana, 118 00* ☎*257–404–444 or 257–404–333* 🖷*257–404–333* ⊕*www. bestwestern-ce.com* 🛏*85 rooms* ⚓*In-room: refrigerator, no a/c. In-hotel: restaurant* ▭*AE, MC, V* ⦿❙*BP* Ⓜ*Line A: Malostranská.*

$$

🏨 **U Tří Pštrosů.** This inviting inn has taken a couple of licks—first it was flooded, then burned to the ground, and then rebuilt, only to be taken by the Communists. Now it's been restituted to the family owners. But there is beauty in triumph, and the location is so close to the Charles Bridge that you could barter with one of the street vendors from your window. The rooms are spacious and feature a beautifully ornate ceiling. Sadly, there is no air-conditioning, but the rooms do have Wi-Fi, so it's behind the times in some ways and ahead in others. ⊠*Dražického nám. 12, Malá Strana, 118 00* ☎*257–288–888* 🖷*257–533–217* ⊕*www.utripstrosu.cz* 🛏*14 rooms, 4 suites* ⚓*In-room: refrigerator, no a/c, dial-up, Wi-Fi. In-hotel: restaurant, laundry service, no elevator* ▭*AE, DC, MC, V* ⦿❙*BP* Ⓜ*Line A: Malostranská.*

HRADČANY

For some, Prague Castle is the romantic capital in this city. Though it is a hectic spot during the day with a lot of foot traffic, it is quiet and even spacious in the evening, when the starlighted castle grounds open onto hilly parks perfect for long strolls and drinking in a breathtaking panoramic view of the city.

★ **$$$$** ⚇ **Savoy.** A modest yellow Jugendstil facade conceals one of the city's most luxurious small hotels. Once a budget hotel, the building was gutted and lavishly refurbished in the mid-1990s. A harmonious maroon-and-mahogany color scheme carries through the public spaces; some rooms are furnished in purely modern style, whereas others have a 19th-century period look. A tram stop is practically at the front door, making trips into the center quick and easy. ⊠ *Keplerova 6, Hradčany, 118 00* ☎ *224–302–430* 🖷 *224–302–128* ⊕ *www.hotel-savoy.cz* ⇔ *55 rooms, 6 suites* ⚅ *In-room: safe, DVD, dial-up. In-hotel: restaurant, gym, concierge, no-smoking rooms, some pets allowed* ⊟ *AE, DC, MC, V* Ⓞ| *BP.*

NOVÉ MĚSTO (NEW TOWN)

Not exactly "new," this district dates back to the 14th century and includes the bustling Wenceslas Square. New Town isn't as clean and architecturally fragile as Old Town, but what it loses in baroque curls it makes up for in good location, variety, nightlife, and slightly cheaper prices.

$$$–$$$$ ⚇ **Hotel Yasmin.** Opened in 2006, the Hotel Yasmin has brought a funky flavor to what, until now, has been a conservative approach to modern in the city's hotels. A confluence of classy Asian design and splashy modernism, this hotel is for those who crave über-trendy surroundings in common areas but prefer clean, breathable, and less flamboyant sleeping rooms. The views are nothing to write home about, but the location—one street over from Václavské náměstí—is. A white lily motif is splashed from floor to ceiling, and the decorations—mirrored balls like water drops—add fresh accents. ⊠ *Politickych Veznu 12/913, Nové Město, 110 00* ☎ *234–100–100* 🖷 *221–426–977* ⊕ *www.hotel-yasmin.cz* ⇔ *187 rooms, 11 suites* ⚅ *In-room: safe, dial-up. In-hotel: restaurant, bar, gym, concierge, parking (fee), no-smoking rooms, some pets allowed* ⊟ *AE, DC, MC, V* Ⓞ| *CP* Ⓜ *Line A: Můstek.*

$$$ ⚇ **Hotel Élite Prague.** A 14th-century Gothic facade and many poetic architectural details have been preserved, thanks to an extensive renovation. Rooms are furnished with antiques, and many have decorated Renaissance-style wooden ceilings. One of the suites is even adorned with a mural ceiling. But rest assured that they did not forsake modern comforts: this is also a Wi-Fi hot spot. ⊠ *Ostrovní 32, Nové Město, 110 00* ☎ *224–932–250* 🖷 *224–930–787* ⊕ *www.hotelelite.cz* ⇔ *77 rooms, 2 suites* ⚅ *In-room: safe, dial-up, Wi-Fi. In-hotel: restaurant, room service, bar, laundry service, parking (fee), some pets allowed* ⊟ *AE, DC, MC, V* Ⓞ| *BP* Ⓜ *Line B: Narodní Třida.*

$$$ ⚇ **Hotel Icon.** Stylish and ultramodern, Icon makes up for its central-but-still-slightly-nowhere location south of Wenceslas Square with an array of high-end creature comforts, including in-house GPS rentals, biometric laptop safes, Skype phones, plasma TVs, hypoallergenic linens from Belgium, and Hästens beds from Sweden. If you're looking for tradition and formality, the Icon is probably not for you: the staff here wears uniforms from Diesel and the in-house restaurant serves breakfast until 11 PM, making it an ideal destination for night owls and other late risers. ⊠ *V Jamě 6, Nové Město, 120 00* ☎ *221–634–100* 🖷 *221–634–105*

⊕*www.hotelicon.eu* ⟳*31 rooms* ⟳*In-room: safe, Ethernet, refrigerator. In-hotel: bar, laundry service, restaurant* ☰*AE, DC, MC, V* ⓘ⊙ⓒP Ⓜ*Line A: Můstek.*

VINOHRADY

Literally translated to mean "vineyards," as this area was many centuries ago, you can still find vestiges of grapevines in parks like Havlíčkovy sady in Prague 10. Today it's home to some of the city's wealthiest residents, and the values of the town houses here have tripled in value over the last decade. For visitors, the wealth means excellent restaurants and pleasant tree-lined streets, perfect for meandering after an exhausting day in the center.

SAVING ON SUDS

Little extras on your hotel bill—the hot chocolate from room service, that in-house laundry service—can add up. Take your dirty clothes to the local Laundromat and surf the Web at the same time. **Prague Laundromat** (✉*Korunniæ 14, Vinohrady* ☎*222–510–180* ⊕*www.volny.cz/laundromat/english.htm*) has magazines, snacks, and a staff that speaks English if you need to buy soap.

$$$$ ⓧ**Hotel Le Palais.** Built in 1841, this venerable building served as the home and shop of Prague's main butcher (one of the front rooms was used to produce and sell sausage until 1991). Today you will find sausage only in the distinctive hotel's restaurant. Rooms have original frescoes painted by Bohemian artist Ludek Marold, and a hallway has an original mosaic floor from 1897. Some rooms have fireplaces, making them especially cozy in winter, and all rooms are air-conditioned. Service is personal and welcoming, and the outstanding gym is a big plus. Public areas and suites are equipped with Wi-Fi. ✉*U Zvonařky 1, Vinohrady, 120 00* ☎*234–634–111* 📠*222–634–635* ⊕*www.palaishotel.cz* ⟳*60 rooms, 12 suites* ⟳*In-room: DVD, dial-up. In-hotel: restaurant, bar, gym, parking (fee), no-smoking rooms, some pets allowed* ☰*AE, DC, MC, V* ⓘ⊙BP Ⓜ*Line A: Nám. Miru.*

SMÍCHOV

Smíchov means "mixed neighborhood." When the city had walls, the neighborhood was on the outside and all manner of people could live there. Although it's still a colorful, working-class area, lots of new construction has made it a shopping and entertainment hub as well, with relatively easy access—via tram, metro, or foot—to the city's historical center.

$$$$
Fodor's Choice
★

ⓧ**Andel's Hotel Prague.** Simply and modernly minimalist, this is where many of the young, up-and-coming British trendsetters stay. And they should feel right at home, considering the hotel was designed by Britain's Jestico + Whiles. It quickly rose to being the most popular business hotel in the city, offering not only rooms for the in-and-out businessperson, but luxury apartments for those who feel the pull to stay in Prague longer. With a nod to the Czech glass industry, glass is used liberally for the walls of conference rooms and in the rooms. One of the city's best shopping malls is next door. ✉*Stroupežnického 21, Smíchov, 150 00* ☎*296–889–688* 📠*296–889–999* ⊕*www.andelsho-*

tel.com ↻*231 rooms, 8 suites* ♿*In-room: safe, DVD, dial-up. In-hotel: restaurant, room service, bar, gym, laundry service, parking (fee), no-smoking rooms* ☰*AE, DC, MC, V* ¶◎|*BP* Ⓜ*Line B: Anděl.*

$–$$ 🖾 **Kinsky Garden.** You could walk the mile from this hotel to Prague Castle entirely on the tree-lined paths of Petřín, the hilly park that starts across the street. Opened in 1997, this Best Western hotel takes its name from a garden established by Count Rudolf Kinsky in 1825. The public spaces and rooms are small, but everything is tasteful and comfortable. Aim for a room on one of the upper floors for a view of the park. ✉*Holečkova 7, Smíchov, 150 00* ☎*257–311–173* 🖨*257–311–184* ⊕*www.hotelkinskygarden.cz* ↻*60 rooms* ♿*In-room: dial-up. In-hotel: restaurant, bar, parking (fee), no-smoking rooms, some pets allowed* ☰*AE, DC, MC, V* ¶◎|*BP* Ⓜ*Line B: Anděl.*

EASTERN SUBURBS

$ 🖾 **Hotel Ibis Karlín.** Minutes from the city center in a peaceful neighborhood with cheap restaurants—not to mention a great wine bar—this hotel offers an excellent way to save money, without sacrificing location or cleanliness. ✉*Šaldova 54, Karlín, 186 00 Prague 8* ☎*222–332–800* 🖨*224–812–681* ↻*226 rooms* ♿*In-room: safe. In-hotel: restaurant, some pets allowed, parking (fee)* ☰*AE, DC, MC, V* ¶◎|*BP* Ⓜ*Line B: Křižíkova.*

NIGHTLIFE & THE ARTS

The fraternal twins of the performing arts and nightlife continue to enjoy an exhilarating growth spurt in Prague, and the number of concerts, plays, musicals, and clubs keeps rising. Some venues in the city center pitch themselves to tourists, but there are dozens of places where you can join the local crowds for music, dancing, or the rituals of beer and conversation. For details of cultural and nightlife events, look for the English-language newspaper the *Prague Post* or one of the multilingual monthly guides available at hotels, tourist offices, and newsstands.

NIGHTLIFE

DISCOS

Dance clubs come and go regularly. **Valentino** (✉*Vinohradská 40, Vinohrady* ☎*222–313–491* ⊕*www.club-valentino.com*) is one of the few gay discos to emerge on the scene in Prague. **Karlovy Lázně** (✉*Novotného lávka, Staré Město*), near the Charles Bridge, is a four-story dance palace with everything from Czech oldies to ambient chill-out sounds. A longtime favorite is **Radost FX** (✉*Bělehradská 120, Nové Město* ☎*222–513–144*), with imported and homegrown DJs playing the latest house, hip-hop, and dance music.

JAZZ CLUBS

Jazz gained notoriety under the Communists as a subtle form of protest, and the city still has some great jazz clubs, featuring everything from swing to blues and modern. All listed clubs have a cover charge. **AghaRTA** (✉, *Železná 16, Staré Město* ☎*222–211–275*) presents jazz acts in an intimate space. Music starts around 9 PM, but come earlier to get a seat. **Jazz Club U staré paní** (⊠*Michalská 9, Staré Město* ☎*224–228–090* ⊕*www.jazzinprague.com*) has a rotating list of tried-and-true Czech bands. **Reduta** (⊠*Národní 20, Nové Město* ☎*224–933–487* ⊕*www.redutajazzclub.cz*) has a full program of local and international musicians.

PUBS & BARS

Bars and lounges are not traditional Prague fixtures, but bars catering to a young crowd have elbowed their way in over the past few years. Still, most social life of the drinking variety takes place in pubs (*pivnice* or *hospody*), which are liberally sprinkled throughout the city's neighborhoods. Tourists are welcome to join in the evening ritual of sitting around large tables and talking, smoking, and drinking beer. Before venturing in, however, it's best to familiarize yourself with a few points of pub etiquette: always ask if a chair is free before sitting down (*Je tu volno?*). To order a beer (*pivo*), do not wave the waiter down or shout across the room; he will usually assume you want beer—most pubs serve one brand—and bring it over to you without asking. He will also bring subsequent rounds to the table without asking. To refuse, just shake your head or say no thanks (*ne, děkuju*). At the end of the evening, usually around 10:30 or 11, the waiter will come to tally the bill. There are plenty of popular pubs in the city center, all of which can get impossibly crowded.

The oldest brewpub in Europe, **U Fleků** (⊠*Křemencova 11, Nové Město* ☎*224–930–831* ⊕*www.ufleku.cz*), has been open since 1499 and makes a tasty, if overpriced, dark beer. **U Medvídků** (⊠*Na Perštýně 7, Staré Město* ☎*224–211–916* ⊕*www.umedkidku.cz*) was a brewery at least as long ago as the 15th century. Beer is once again made on the premises; downstairs, they serve draft Budvar shipped from České Budějovice. **U Zlatého Tygra** (⊠*Husova 17, Staré Město* ☎*222–221–111*) is famed as one of the three best Prague pubs for Pilsner Urquell, the original and perhaps the greatest of the pilsners. It also used to be a hangout for such raffish types as the writer Bohumil Hrabal, who died in 1997.

U Malého Glena (⊠*Karmelitská 23, Malá Strana* ☎*257–531–717* ⊕*www.malyglen.cz*) offers a popular bar and a stage for local and expat jazz, blues, and folk music.

ROCK CLUBS

Prague's rock, alternative, and world-music scene is thriving. The younger crowd flocks to **Lucerna Music Bar** (⊠*Vodičkova 36, Nové Město* ☎*224–217–108* ⊕*www.musicbar.cz*) to catch popular Czech rock and funk bands and visiting acts. The cavernous **Palác Akropolis** (⊠*Kubelíkova 27, Žižkov* ☎*299–330–913* ⊕*www.palacakropolis.cz*) has top Czech acts and major international world-music performers; as the name suggests, the space has an Acropolis theme. Hard-rock enthusiasts should check out the **Rock Café** (⊠*Národní 20, Nové Město* ☎*224–933–947* ⊕*www.rockcafe.cz*). For dance tracks, hip locals congregate at **Roxy** (⊠*Dlouhá 33, Staré Město* ☎*224–826–296* ⊕*www.roxy.cz*).

THE ARTS

Prague's cultural flair is legendary, and performances are often booked far in advance by all sorts of Praguers. The concierge at your hotel may be able to reserve tickets for you. Otherwise, for the cheapest tickets, go directly to the theater box office a few days in advance or immediately before a performance. Ticket agencies may charge higher prices than box offices do. American Express offices sell tickets to many concerts. **Bohemia Ticket International** (⊠ *Na Příkopě 16, Nové Město* ☎ *224–215–031* ⊕ *www.ticketsbti.cz* ⊠ *Malé nám. 13, Staré Město* ☎ *224–227–832*) specializes in mostly classical music. **Ticketpro** (⊠ *Václavské náměstí 10, Nové Město* ☎ *224–814–020* ⊕ *www.ticketpro.cz*), with outlets all over town, accepts major credit cards. Tickets for some club and live music events are handled by **Ticketstream** (⊠ *Koubkova 8, Nové Město* ☎ *224–263–049* ⊕ *www.ticketstream.cz*), which also has outlets at some hotels and restaurants.

CLASSICAL MUSIC

Classical concerts are held all over the city throughout the year. In addition to Prague's two major professional orchestras, classical ensembles are the most common finds, and the standard of performance ranges from adequate to superb, though the programs tend to take few risks. Serious fans of baroque music may have the opportunity to hear works of little-known Bohemian composers at these concerts. Some of the best chamber ensembles are the Martinů Ensemble, the Prague Chamber Philharmonic (also known as the Prague Philharmonia), the Wihan Quartet, the Czech Trio, and the Agon contemporary music group.

Performances are held regularly at many of the city's palaces and churches, including the Garden on the Ramparts below Prague Castle (where the music comes with a view); both Churches of St. Nicholas; the Church of Sts. Simon and Jude on Dušní in the Old Town; the Church of St. James on Malá Štupartská, near Old Town Square; the Zrcadlová kaple (Mirror Chapel) in the Klementinum on Mariánské náměstí in the Old Town; and the Lobkowicz Palace at Prague Castle. If you're an organ-music buff, you'll most likely have your pick of recitals held in Prague's historic halls and churches. Popular programs are offered at the Church of St. Nicholas in the Lesser Quarter and the Church of St. James, where the organ plays amid a complement of baroque statuary.

Dvořák Hall (⊠ *Rudolfinum, nám. Jana Palacha, Staré Město* ☎ *224–893–111* ⊕ *www.czechphilharmonic.cz*) is home to one of Central Europe's best orchestras, the Czech Philharmonic. Frequent guest conductor Sir Charles Mackerras is a leading proponent of modern Czech music. One of the best orchestral venues is the resplendent Art Nouveau **Smetana Hall** (⊠ *Obecní dům, nám. Republiky 5, Staré Město* ☎ *222–002–100* ⊕ *www.obecnidum.cz*), home of the excellent Prague Symphony Orchestra and major venue for the annual Prague Spring music festival. Concerts at the **Villa Bertramka** (⊠ *Mozartova 169, Smíchov* ☎ *257–318–461* ⊕ *www.bertramka.cz*) emphasize the music of Mozart and his contemporaries.

OPERA

The Czech Republic has a strong operatic tradition. Unlike during the Communist period, operas are almost always sung in their original tongue, and the repertoire offers plenty of Italian favorites as well as the Czech national composers Janaček, Dvořák, and Smetana. (Czech operas are supertitled in English.) The major opera houses also often stage ballets. Appropriate attire is recommended for all venues; the National and Estates theaters instituted a "no jeans" rule in 1998. Ticket prices are still quite reasonable, at 40 Kč–900 Kč.

A great venue for a night at the opera is the plush **Národní divadlo** (*National Theater* ⊠*Národní tř. 2, Nové Město* ☎*224–901–448* ⊕*www.narodni-divadlo.cz*). Performances at the **Statní opera Praha** (*State Opera House* ⊠*Wilsonova 4, Nové Město* ☎*224–227–266* ⊕*www.opera.cz*), near the top of Wenceslas Square, can also be excellent. The historic **Stavovské divadlo** (*Estates Theater* ⊠*Ovocný tř. 1, Staré Město* ☎*224–215–001* ⊕*www.narodni-divadlo.cz*), where Mozart's *Don Giovanni* premiered in the 18th century, plays host to a mix of operas and dramatic works.

PUPPET SHOWS

This traditional form of Czech popular entertainment has been given new life thanks to the productions mounted at the **Národní divadlo marionet** (*National Marionette Theater* ⊠*Žatecká 1* ☎*224–819–322*). In season, shows are also performed at Celetná 13. Children and adults alike can enjoy the hilarity and pathos of famous operas adapted for nonhuman "singers." The company's bread and butter is a production of Mozart's *Don Giovanni*.

THEATER

A dozen or so professional theater companies play in Prague to ever-packed houses. Visiting the theater is a vital activity in Czech society, and the language barrier can't obscure the players' artistry. Nonverbal theater also abounds: not only tourist-friendly mime and "Black Light Theater"—a melding of live acting, mime, video, and stage trickery—but also serious (or incomprehensible) productions by top local and foreign troupes. A few English-language theater groups operate sporadically. For complete listings, pick up a copy of the *Prague Post*. The famous **Laterna Magika** *(Magic Lantern)* puts on a multimedia extravaganza in the National Theater's glass-encased modern hall (⊠*Národní tř. 4, Nové Město* ☎*224–914–129*). The popular **Archa Theater** (⊠*Na Poříčí 26, Nové Město* ☎*221–716–333*) offers avant-garde and experimental theater, music, and dance and has hosted world-class visiting ensembles such as the Royal Shakespeare Company.

SHOPPING

Although Prague has a long way to go before it can match such great European shopping cities as Paris and Rome, the Czech Republic capital is a great place to pick up gifts and souvenirs. Bohemian crystal and porcelain deservedly enjoy a worldwide reputation for quality, and plenty of shops offer excellent bargains. The local market for antiques and art is still relatively undeveloped, although dozens of antiquarian bookstores harbor some excellent finds, particularly German and Czech books and graphics.

SHOPPING DISTRICTS

The major shopping areas are **Na Příkopě**, which runs from the foot of Wenceslas Square to náměstí Republiky (Republic Square), and the area around **Old Town Square**. The Old Town **Pařížská ulice** and **Karlova ulice** are streets dotted with boutiques and antiques shops. In the Lesser Quarter, try **Nerudova ulice,** the street that runs up to Hradčany. An artistically designed modern glass shopping mall, **Nový Smíchov** (⊠ *Corner of Plzeňská and Nádražní, Smíchov* ⊕ *www.novysmichovoc.cz* Ⓜ *Anděl*), covers an entire city block. It opened in 2001 and includes a multiplex cinema and bowling alley plus clothing, perfume, electronics, and book stores.

DEPARTMENT STORES

Prague's department stores are catching up quickly to their Western counterparts. **Bílá Labuť** (⊠ *Na Poříčí 23, Nové Město* ☎ *224–811–364*) has a decent selection, but the overall shabbiness harks back to socialist times. **Kotva** (⊠ *Nám. Republiky 8, Nové Město* ☎ *224–801–111*) is comparatively upscale, with a nice stationery section and a basement supermarket with wine and cheese aisles. The centrally located **Tesco** (⊠ *Národní tř. 26* ☎ *222–003–111*) is generally the best place for one-stop shopping and a supermarket with peanut butter and other hard-to-find items.

STREET MARKETS

For fruits, vegetables, and souvenirs, the best street market in central Prague is on **Havelská ulice** in the Old Town. The biggest market is the one in **Holešovice,** north of the city center; it offers food, jewelry, electronic goods, clothes, and imported liquor. Take the metro (Line C) to the Vltavská station and then catch any tram heading east (running to the left as you exit the metro station). Exit at the first stop and follow the crowds. It's better to shop in the week, as both are closed Saturday afternoon and all day on Sunday.

SPECIALTY STORES

ANTIQUES

Rumor has it that once the Communists were out, antiques dealers from Germany and Austria came swarming in, rummaging through the country for every stick of furniture and knickknack. This could explain why the supply of interesting items seems to have leveled off, despite the rising prices in recent years. Nevertheless, there's enough here to keep any magpie interested. Just look for the word *starožitnosti* ("antiques shop"), which tend to be small, one-room jumbles of old glass and bric-a-brac.

Art Deco Gallery Shop. This shoe-box-size shop has a great selection of art deco tea sets from the 1930s, bearing a "Made in Czechoslovakia" stamp on the bottom. The owner has English-language art books on hand so that you can read what other collectors have written about her wares. The shop is open only from 2 PM to 7 PM most days, so plan on hitting it after lunch. ⊠ *Jánský vršek 8, Malá Strana* ☎ *257–535–801* Ⓜ *Line A: Malostranská.*

Fodor'sChoice
★ **Bric a Brac.** If you're a believer in the equation "more clutter = better," you might be inclined to think of this as the best shop in Prague. The tiny shop is really two stores next door to each other in a tiny space as big as a child's bedroom, but it's packed with antique treasures, like candleholders and tobacco tins. The owner speaks perfect English in order to answer any questions. ⊠ *Týnská 7, Staré Město* ☎ *222–326–484* Ⓜ *Line A: Staroměstská.*

Dorotheum. A local branch of the fabled 300-year-old Austrian auction house, the Dorotheum is synonymous with class when it comes to buying clocks, jewelry, porcelain knickknacks, and standing clocks. Expect prices to reflect its upscale roots. ⊠ *Ovocný trh 2, Nové Město* ☎ *224–222–001* Ⓜ *Line B: Nám. Republiky.*

Starožitnosti Ungelt. The house specialty here is Art Nouveau and art deco furniture, paintings, and glass objects that are practically museum quality. One of the best antiques dealers, this store is perfectly situated in the elaborate courtyard behind the Old Town Square's Týn church and holds some colorful goblets by Moser and wonderful Loetz vases. ⊠ *Týn 1, Staré Město* ☎ *224–895–454* Ⓜ *Line A: Staroměstská.*

ART GALLERIES

Galerie JBK. Carefully selected Czech artists are on display at this breathable, yet intimate, gallery. The selections never disappoint. In the basement you can find a nice ensemble of antique wooden furniture. ⊠ *Betlémské nám. 8, Staré Město* ☎ *222–220–689* Ⓜ *Line B: Národní třída.*

Galerie NoD. Above the Roxy, the most popular dance club in the city, NoD consistently exhibits young and eclectic work. Funds from the club support the gallery's mission of finding the next generation of up-and-coming artists. Try to predict which Bohemian expat or local artist might be the next Picasso. ⊠ *Dlouhá 33, Staré Město* ☎ *No phone* Ⓜ *Line A: Staroměstská.*

★ **Galerie Peithner-Lichtenfels.** The crowded feel of this gallery is like a glimpse into a tormented artist's head. There are enough paintings, prints, and drawings to please even the most critical art admirer. ⊠ *Michalská 12, Staré Město* ☎ *224–227–680* Ⓜ *Line A: Staroměstská.*

FOOD AND WINE

Cellarius. This inviting shop stocks the best Moravian and Bohemian wines and spirits, as well as excellent wines from around the world. ⊠ *Lucerna pasáž, Václavské nám., between Vodičkova and Štěpánská, Nové Město* ☎ *224–210–979* Ⓜ *Line A or B: Můstek.*

Fruits de France (⊠ *Jindřišská 9, Nové Město* ☎ *224–220–304*) charges Western prices for fruits and vegetables imported directly from France.

GLASS

Glass has traditionally been Bohemia's biggest export, and it was one of the few products manufactured during Communist times that managed to retain an artistically innovative spirit. Today Prague has plenty of shops selling Bohemian glass, though much of it is tourist kitsch.

Fodor'sChoice **Artěl.** Luxury glass that's "funky" might seem like an oxymoron, but
★ that's exactly what you'll find here. The store's U.S.-born creator, Karen Feldman, has married a modern-American style with a Czech tradition of crystal in a winning combination. Feldman is perfectly proud to say, "Everything is functional." By appointment only. ✉ *Celetná 29, Staré Město* Ⓜ *Line A or B: Můstek* ✉ *Vinohradská 164, Vinohrady* ☎ *271–732–161* Ⓜ *Line A: Jiřího z Poděbrad.*

Galerie Tesař. This shop gives you that euphoric feeling of walking into a silent room after a loud concert. After seeing the loud, vibrant colors and shapes of blown glass, this is where you will find stunning simplicity. Minimalist clear glass on silver shelves gives the store a crisp, modern feel. ✉ *Skořepká 4, Staré Město* ☎ *572–695–476* Ⓜ *Line B: Národní třída.*

Galerie 'Z.' This gallery specializes in limited-edition mold-melted and blown glass. ✉ *Michalská pasáž, Malé nám. 11, Staré Město* ☎ *No phone* Ⓜ *Line A or B: Můstek.*

★ **Material.** Even the door handle for this store is an artistically crafted vase, demonstrating this store's devotion to the craft. The eye-catching shop below the Charles Bridge sells glass that is crafted from the Czech company Ajeto. Rare pieces include long-stem candlesticks with glass leaves. ✉ *U Lužického semináře 7, Malá Strana* ☎ *257–533–663* Ⓜ *Line A: Malostranská.*

Moser. An opulent flagship store of the world-famous Karlovy Vary glassmaker (started in 1857) offers the finest top-quality traditional Bohemian glass. Even if you're not in the market to buy, stop by simply to look at the elegant wood-panel display rooms on the second floor. The staff will gladly pack goods for traveling. ✉ *Na Příkopě 12, Nové Město* ☎ *224–211–293* Ⓜ *Line B: Nám. Republiky.*

HOME DESIGN

Czech design is wonderfully rich both in quality and imagination, emphasizing old-fashioned craftsmanship while often taking an offbeat, even humorous approach. Strained relations between Czech designers and producers have reined in the potential selection, but there are nevertheless a handful of places showcasing Czech work. **Arzenal** (✉ *Valentinská 11, Staré Město* ☎ *224–814–099*) is a design shop that offers Japanese and Thai food in addition to vases and chairs; it exclusively sells work by Bořek Šípek, the official designer during Havel's presidency.

Fodor'sChoice **Modernista.** A celebration of forward-thinking design, this store moved
★ to an expanded location on Celetná, creating something of a 20th-century-design museum in 2006, selling Cubist, modernist, and midcentury furniture and housewares. Ruby-red armchairs and Cubist tea sets

can give you the coolest home on the block. ⊠*Celetná 12, Staré Město* ☎*224–241–300* Ⓜ*Line B: Nám. Republiky.*

★ **Qubus Design.** An IKEA-free fun house of home design. Moose-head coat racks and galosh-shape vases prove childhood is the new black. ⊠*Rámová 3, Staré Město* ☎*222–313–151* Ⓜ*Line B: Nám. Republiky.*

JEWELRY

Alfons Mucha is perhaps most famous for his whiplash Art Nouveau posters, but he also designed furniture, lamps, clothing, and jewelry. **Art Décoratif** (⊠*Michalska 19, Staré Město* ☎*225–777–156* Ⓜ*Line A or B: Můstek*), right next door to the Art Nouveau Obecní Dům, sells Mucha-inspired designs—the jewelry is especially remarkable. Other locations are at (⊠*Melantrichova 5, Staré Město* ☎*224–222–283*), and (⊠*U Obecního domu 2, Staré Město* ☎*222–002–350*).

Český Granát (⊠*Celetná 4, Staré Město* ☎*224–228–281*) has a comprehensive selection of garnet jewelry, plus contemporary and traditional pieces set in gold and silver. **Halada** (⊠*Karlova 25, Nové Město* ☎*224–228–938*) sells sleek, Czech-designed silver jewelry; an affiliate shop at Na Příkopě 16 specializes in gold, diamonds, and pearls.

Fodor'sChoice
★ Nicole Kidman donned a **Swarovksi** crystal dress, Yves Saint Laurent sported a crystal heart on a celebrated cover of *Vogue*—and both came from this world-renowned crystal designer. Crystal jewelry with a brilliant glimmer and midrange prices make this a must. ⊠*Celetná 7, Staré Město* ☎*222–315–585* Ⓜ*Line A or B: Můstek.*

MARIONETTES

Marionettes have a long tradition in Bohemia, going back to the times when traveling troupes used to entertain children with morality plays on town squares. Now, although the art form survives, it has become yet another tourist lure, and you'll continually stumble across stalls selling almost identical marionettes. Secondhand and antique marionettes are surprisingly hard to find, but several genuine puppet makers still carry on the craft with integrity.

Galerie Marionette. Czech and French-style marionettes dangle from the rafters as angels and devils. The local artists who peddle their creations here see marionettes as an art form, not a toy, and put detailed work into the facial features. This is where former President Bill Clinton picked up one for himself. ⊠*U Lužického semináře 7, Malá Strana* ☎*257–535–091* Ⓜ*Line A: Malostranská.*

★ **Obchod Pod lampou.** Wall-to-wall hanging puppets can be a joy or a fright, depending on taste, with handcrafted versions of Frankenstein's monster or princess puppets. Prices vary for those less serious about the art and simply seeking a high-quality souvenir. ⊠*U Lužického semináře 5, Malá Strana* ☎*No phone* Ⓜ*Line A: Malostranská.*

Marionety. The owner of this shop has a discerning collection of new and antique marionettes. Find a modern devil or, if you prefer, an antique devil from 1910, with twice the painted eeriness at twice the price. ⊠*Nerudova 51, Malá Strana* ☎*257–533–035* Ⓜ*Line A: Malostranská.*

Pohádka. Harry Potter, devils, and angels can all be found in marionette form hanging from the ceiling or sitting on shelves. Right there among the tourist shops, this seller of marionettes offers puppets at reasonable prices. ⊠*Celetná 32, Nové Město* ☎*No phone* Ⓜ*Line B: Nám. Republiky.*

TOYS & GIFTS FOR CHILDREN

Nearly every stationery store has beautiful watercolor and colored-chalk sets available at rock-bottom prices. The Czechs are also master illustrators, and the books they've made for young "pre-readers" are some of the world's loveliest. For the child with a theatrical bent, a marionette—they range from finger-size to nearly child-size—can be a wonder. For delightful and reasonably priced Czech-made wooden toys and wind-up trains, cars, and animals, look in at **Hračky** (⊠*Pohořelec 24, Hradčany* ☎*0/603–515–745*).

PRAGUE ESSENTIALS

AIR TRAVEL

Prague has the busiest international airport in the Czech Republic, and it's the only airport where trans-Atlantic flights land. For contact information on airlines that fly to Prague, see Air Travel *in* Czech Republic Essentials, *below.*

AIRPORTS & TRANSFERS

Ruzyně Airport is 20 km (12 mi) northwest of the downtown area. It's small but easily negotiated. An expanded main terminal has eased traffic flow. The trip to downtown is a straight shot down Evropská Boulevard and takes approximately 20 minutes. The road is not usually busy, but anticipate an additional 20 minutes during rush hour (7 AM–9 AM and 3 PM–6 PM).

Airport Information Ruzyně Airport (☎*220–111–111* ⊕*www.prg.aero*).

TRANSFERS

There are several options for getting into town from the airport, depending on the amount of time you have, your budget, and the amount of luggage. The cheapest is Prague's municipal bus No. 119, which leaves from just outside the arrivals area and makes the run to Dejvická metro station (on the green line, aka Line A) every 15 minutes or so during weekdays. The 20 Kč ticket—plus an extra 10 Kč ticket if you have a large bag—can be purchased from the yellow vending machine at the bus stop and includes a transfer to the metro. To reach Wenceslas Square, get off at the Můstek station.

The Cedaz minibus shuttle links the airport with náměstí Republiky (Republic Square, just off the Old Town). It runs hourly, more often at peak periods, between 5:30 AM and 9:30 PM daily and makes an intermediate stop at the Dejvická metro station. The one-way fare is 90 Kč. The minibus also serves many hotels for 370 Kč–650 Kč, which is sometimes less than the taxi fare.

A taxi ride to the center will set you back about 500 Kč–700 Kč; the fare will be higher for destinations outside the center and away from the airport. Most crooked cabs have been cleaned up since the country's European Union entry in 2004, but beware of dishonest drivers and stick with a reputable service like AAA.

Information Cedaz (☎ *220–114–296* ⊕ *www.aas.cz/cedaz*). **AAA Radiotaxi** (☎ *222–333–222* ⊕ *www.aaa.radiotaxi.cz*).

BUS TRAVEL TO & FROM PRAGUE

The Czech complex of regional bus lines known collectively as ČSAD operates its dense network from the sprawling Florenc station. For information about routes and schedules, call, consult the confusingly displayed timetables posted at the station, or visit the information window in the lower level lobby, which is open daily 6 AM–9 PM. The company's Web site will give you bus and train information in English (click on the British flag).

Bus Lines ČSAD (✉ *Florenc station, Křižíkova, Karl'n* ☎ *12999, 224–214–990 route and schedule information* ⊕ *www.jizdnirady.cz* Ⓜ *Florenc [Line B or C]*).

BUS & TRAM TRAVEL WITHIN PRAGUE

Prague's extensive bus and streetcar network allows for fast, efficient travel throughout the city. Tickets are the same as those used for the metro, although you validate them at machines inside the bus or tram. Tickets (*jízdenky*) can be bought at hotels, some newsstands, and from dispensing machines in the metro stations. The basic, transferrable ticket costs 12 Kč. It permits one hour's travel throughout the metro, tram, and bus network between 5 AM and 8 PM on weekdays, or 90 minutes' travel at other times. Single-ride tickets cost 8 Kč and allow one 15-minute ride on a tram or bus, without transfer, or a metro journey of up to four stations lasting less than 30 minutes (transfer between lines is allowed). You can also buy a 1-day pass allowing unlimited use of the system for 80 Kč, a 3-day pass for 220 Kč, a 7-day pass for 280 Kč, or a 15-day pass for 320 Kč. The passes can be purchased at the main metro stations, from ticket machines, and at some newsstands in the center. A pass is not valid until stamped in the orange machines in metro stations or aboard trams *and* the required information is entered on the back (there are instructions in English). A refurbished old tram, No. 91, travels through the Old Town and Lesser Quarter on summer weekends. The metro shuts down at midnight, but Trams 50–59 and Buses 500 and above run all night. Night trams run at 40-minute intervals, and all routes intersect at the corner of Lazarská and Spálená streets in the New Town near the Národní třída metro station. Schedules and regulations in English are on the transportation department's official Web site.

Information Dopravní Podnik (⊕ *www.dp-praha.cz*).

CAR RENTALS

Several major agencies have offices at the Prague airport and also in the city. It's usually cheaper if you make a reservation for your rental car before you leave home. For a list of car-rental agencies, see Car Rentals *in* Czech Republic Essentials, *below.*

CAR TRAVEL

If your visit is restricted to the Czech capital, you'll do better not to rent a car. The capital is congested, and you'll save yourself a lot of hassle if you rely on public transportation. If you are planning to take excursions into the country, then a car will be useful, but don't pick it up until you are ready to depart. If you are arriving by car, you'll find that Prague is well served by major roads and highways from anywhere in the country. On arriving in the city, simply follow the signs to CENTRUM (city center).

ENGLISH-LANGUAGE MEDIA

In the city center nearly every bookstore carries a few guidebooks and paperbacks in English. Street vendors on Wenceslas Square and Na Příkopě carry leading foreign newspapers and periodicals. To find out what's on, consult the entertainment listings in Prague's weekly English-language newspaper, the *Prague Post* (⊕*www.praguepost.com*), available at many downtown newsstands as well as in major North American and European cities. For the best Web listings of concerts and events, try PragueTV (⊕*www.prague.tv*), a favorite choice for long-term expatriates.

INTERNET, MAIL & SHIPPING

As the country has gotten more and more wired, the once-ubiquitous Internet café has become much less common: you're far more likely to come across a wireless hot spot for laptop connections than an actual Internet bar with terminals, though a few still exist. Prague has offices for many of the regular international shipping services, though the options really dry up outside of the capital.

Internet Cafés Bohemia Bagel (⊠ *Masná 1, Old Town* ☎ *224–812–603*). **Planeta** (⊠ *Vinohradská 102, Vinohrady* ☎ *267–311–182*).

Shipping Companies FedEx (⊠ *Na Radosti 399, Zličín* ☎ *800–133–339*). **DHL** (⊠ *Václavské nám. 47, Nové Město* ☎ *800–103–000*). **UPS** (⊠ *K letišti 57, Airport Ruzyně* ☎ *800–181–111*).

SUBWAY TRAVEL

Prague's subway system, the metro, is clean and reliable; the stations are marked with an inconspicuous M sign. Trains run daily 5 AM–midnight. Validate your ticket at an orange machine before descending the escalator. Trains are patrolled often; the fine for riding without a valid ticket is 800 Kč. Beware of pickpockets, who often operate in large groups on crowded trams and metro cars.

TAXIS

Though far less common than before, dishonest taxi drivers remain a problem. Luckily, you probably won't need to rely on taxis for trips within the city center (it's usually easier to walk or take the subway).

Typical scams include drivers doctoring the meter or simply failing to turn the meter on and then demanding an exorbitant sum at the end of the ride. In an honest cab, the meter starts at 30 Kč and increases by 25 Kč per km (½ mi) or 4 Kč per minute at rest. Most rides within town should cost no more than 200 Kč–300 Kč. To minimize the chances of getting ripped off, avoid taxi stands in Wenceslas Square, Old Town Square, and other heavily touristed areas. The best alternative is to phone for a taxi in advance. Many radio-taxi firms have English-speaking operators.

Information **AAA Taxi** (☎ *222–333–222* ⊕ *www.aaa.radiotaxi.cz*). **Profitaxi** (☎ *844–700–800* ⊕ *www.profitaxi.cz*).

TOUR OPTIONS

Čedok offers a 3½-hour "Grand City Tour," a combination bus and walking venture that covers all the major sights with commentary in English. It departs daily at 9:30 AM and 2 PM, year-round, from opposite the Obecní dům (Municipal House), on Republic Square, near the main Čedok office. The price is about 660 Kč. "Historic Prague on Foot" is a slower-paced, three-hour walking tour for 400 Kč. From April through October, it departs Republic Square on Wednesday, Friday, and Sunday at 9:30 AM; in the off-season, it departs Friday and Sunday at 9:30 AM. More tours are offered, especially in summer, and the schedules may well vary according to demand. You can also contact Čedok's main office to arrange a personalized walking tour. Times and itineraries are negotiable; prices start at around 1,100 Kč per hour.

Very similar tours by other operators also depart daily from Republic Square, Národní třída near Jungmannovo náměstí, and Wenceslas Square. Prices are generally a couple hundred crowns less than for Čedok's tours. Themed walking tours are very popular as well. You can choose medieval architecture, "Velvet Revolution walks," visits to Communist monuments, and any number of pub crawls. Each year, four or five small operators do these tours, which generally last a couple of hours and cost 200 Kč–300 Kč. Inquire at Prague Information Service or a major ticket agency for the current season's offerings.

TRAIN TRAVEL

International trains arrive at and depart from either of two stations: the main station, Hlavní nádraží, is about 500 yards east of Wenceslas Square on Opletalova or Washingtonova street. Then there's the suburban Nádraží Holešovice, about 2 km (1 mi) north of the city center. This is an unending source of confusion—always make certain you know which station your train is using. Note also that trains arriving from the west usually stop at Smíchov station, on the west bank of the Vltava, before continuing to the main station. Prague's other central train station, Masarykovo nádraží, serves mostly local trains but has an international ticket window that is often much less crowded than those at the main station.

For train times, consult timetables in a station or get in line at the information office upstairs at the main station (for domestic trains, open daily 3 AM–11:45 PM) or downstairs near the exits under the ČD

Centrum sign (open daily 6 AM–7:30 PM). The main Čedok office also provides train information and issues tickets.

Wenceslas Square is a convenient five-minute walk from the main station (best not undertaken late at night), or you can take the subway (Line C) one stop in the Háje direction to Muzeum. A taxi ride from the main station to the center should cost about 100 Kč, but the station cabbies are known for overcharging. To reach the city center from Nádraží Holešovice, take the metro (Line C) four stops to Muzeum; a taxi ride should cost roughly 200 Kč–250 Kč.

Information Čedok (⊠ *Na Příkopě 18, Staré Město* ☎ *224–197–111* ⊕ *www. cedok.cz*).

Train Stations Hlavní nádraží (⊠ *Wilsonova ul., Nové Město* ☎ *224–224–200 schedules and fares*). **Masarykovo nádraží** (⊠ *Hybernská 13, Nové Město*). **Nádraží Holešovice** (⊠ *Vrbenskéoo, Holešovice*).

VISITOR INFORMATION

The Czech Tourist Authority office on Old Town Square can provide information on tourism outside Prague but does not sell tickets or book accommodations. The Prague Information Service has four central offices. The Town Hall branch is open weekdays 9–6, weekends 9–5. The Na Příkopě office, just a few doors down from Čedok's main office, is open weekdays 9–6 and Saturday 9–3. The Hlavní nádraží branch is open April–October, weekdays 9–7 and weekends 9–4, and November–March, weekdays 9–6 and Saturday 9–3. The Charles Bridge tower office on the Malá Strana end of Charles Bridge is open April–October, daily 10–6.

Information Czech Tourist Authority (⊠ *Staroměstské nám. 6, Staré Město* ☎ *227–158–111*).

There are four central offices of the municipal **Prague Information Service** (*PIS* ⊠ *Staroměstská radnice [Old Town Hall], Staré Město* ☎ *224–482–562* ⊕ *www.pis. cz* ⊠ *Na Příkopě 20, Nové Město* ☎ *No phone* ⊠ *Hlavní nádraží, lower hall, Staré Město* ☎ *No phone* ⊠ *Malostranská mostecká věž, Malá Strana* ☎ *No phone*).

SOUTHERN BOHEMIA

With Prague at its heart and Germany and the former Austro-Hungarian Empire on its mountainous borders, the kingdom of Bohemia was for centuries buffeted by religious and national conflicts, invasions, and wars. But its position also meant that Bohemia benefited from the cultural wealth and diversity of Central Europe. The result is a glorious array of history-laden castles, walled cities, and spa towns set in a gentle, rolling landscape.

Southern Bohemia (separate sections on the northern and western areas follow) is particularly famous for its involvement in the Hussite religious wars of the 15th century, which revolved around the fortress town of Tábor. But the area also has more than its fair share of well-preserved and stunning walled towns, built up by generations of noble

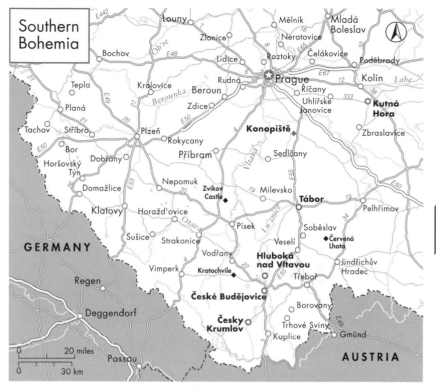

families, who left behind layers of Gothic, Renaissance, and baroque architecture (particularly notable in Český Krumlov). Farther north and an easy drive east of Prague is the old silver-mining town of Kutná Hora, once a rival to Prague for the royal residence.

Český Krumlov (along with the spas of western Bohemia) offers some of the best accommodations in the Czech Republic outside the capital.

KUTNÁ HORA

70 km (44 mi) east of Prague.

The approach to Kutná Hora looks much as it has for centuries. The long economic decline of this town, once Prague's chief rival in Bohemia for wealth and beauty, spared it the postwar construction that has blighted the outskirts of so many other Czech cities. Though it is undeniably beautiful, with an intact Gothic and baroque townscape, Kutná Hora feels a bit melancholy. The town owes its illustrious past to silver, discovered here during the 12th century. For some 400 years the mines were worked with consummate efficiency, the wealth going to support grand projects to rival those of Prague and the nearby Cistercian monastery of Sedlec. As the silver began to run out during the 16th and 17th centuries, however, Kutná Hora's importance faded.

Since the early 1990s, the town has beautified itself to a degree, but despite a significant tourist industry, modern Kutná Hora is dwarfed by the splendors of the Middle Ages. The city became a UNESCO World Heritage Site in 1995.

Fodor'sChoice ★ Approaching the **Chrám svaté Barbory** *(St. Barbara's Cathedral)*, overlooking the river, you pass through a magnificent landscape. The 10-minute stroll from the main Palackého náměstí along Barborská ulice is lined with baroque statues in front of a vast former Jesuit college as you near St. Barbara's. From a distance, the three-peak roof of the church gives the impression of a large, magnificently peaked tent more than a religious center. St. Barbara's is undoubtedly Kutná Hora's masterpiece and a high point of the Gothic style in Bohemia. Begun in the 1380s, it drew on the talents of the Peter Parler workshop as well as two luminaries of the late-Gothic of the late 15th century, Matyáš Rejsek and Benedikt Ried. The soaring roof was added as late as 1558, replaced in the 18th century, and finally restored in the late 1800s; the western facade also dates from the end of the 19th century. From here you can see the romantic view over the town, marked by the visibly tilting 260-foot-tower of St. James's Church.

St. Barbara is the patron saint of miners, and silver-mining themes dominate the interior of the church. Gothic frescoes depict angels carrying shields with mining symbols. The town's other major occupation, minting, can be seen in frescoes in the **Mintner's Chapel.** A statue of a miner, donning the characteristic smock, stands proudly in the nave and dates from 1700. But the main attraction of the interior is the vaulting itself, which carries the eye effortlessly upward. ⊠ *Barborská ul.* ☏ *327–515–797* 🎫 *40 Kč* ⊘ *Apr.–Oct., Tues.–Sun. 9–5:30, Mon. 10–4:30; Nov.–Mar., Tues.–Sun. 10–4:30.*

The **České Muzeum Stříbra** *(Czech Museum of Silver)*, housed in the Hrádek (Little Castle) that was once part of the town's fortifications, is a museum of mining and coin production. In the 16th century, Kutná Hora boasted the deepest mines in the world, some going down as far as 1,650 feet. It's somewhat fitting, then, that the highlight of the Hrádek—and the focal point of the longer museum tours—is a hike down into a claustrophobic medieval mine tunnel. The small trek (you're inside for about 30 minutes) is more titillating than scary, though you may be happy you weren't a medieval miner. The cheapest tour, which doesn't include the mine, is dull, unless you're a fan of ore samples and archaeology. If it's available, go for the 1½-hour tour, which includes a portion of the displays from the museum proper, plus the mine. ⊠ *Barborská ul. 28* ☏ *327–512–159* ⊕ *www.cms-kh.cz* 🎫 *60 Kč–110 Kč* ⊘ *Apr. and Oct., Tues.–Sun. 9–5; May, June, and Sept., Tues.–Sun. 9–6; July and Aug., Tues.–Sun. 10–6.*

Coins were first minted at the **Vlašský dvůr** *(Italian Court)* in 1300, made by Italian artisans brought in from Florence—hence the mint's odd name. It was here that the Prague groschen, one of the most widely circulated coins of the Middle Ages, was minted until 1726. There's a **coin museum,** where you can see the small, silvery groschen being struck and buy replicas. ⊠*Havlíčkovo nám.* ☎*327–512–873* 🎫*80 Kč* ☉*Apr.–Sept., daily 9–6; Oct. and Mar., daily 10–5; Nov.–Feb., daily 10–4.*

If the door to the **Chrám svatého Jakuba** *(St. James's Church)*—next door to the old mint—is open, peek inside. Originally a Gothic church dating from the 1300s, it was almost entirely transformed into baroque during the 17th and 18th centuries. A characteristic onion dome on the tower was added in 1737. Paintings on the wall include works from the best baroque Czech masters; the pietà is by the 17th-century painter Karel Škréta. The church is open only sporadically during the week and for Sunday mass. ⊠*Havlíčkovo nám.* ☎*No phone.*

Fodor'sChoice
★ No trip to Kutná Hora is complete without a visit to the nearby suburb of Sedlec (about 2 km [1 mi] from the center of the city), where you can find one of Europe's most chilling sights: a chapel decorated with the bones of some 40,000 people. The Kaple všech svatých (All Saints' Chapel), commonly known as the **Kostnice** *([ossuary]* or "Bone Church"), is just up the road from the former Sedlec Monastery. The church came into being in the 16th century, when development forced the clearing of a nearby graveyard. Monks of the Cistercian order came up with the bright idea of using the bones to decorate the chapel; the most recent creations date from the end of the 19th century. The run-down **Church of the Assumption of the Virgin** at the former Sedlec monastery exemplifies the work of Giovanni Santini (1667–1723). A master of expressive line and delicate proportion, this one-of-a-kind architect fathered a bravura hybrid of Gothic and baroque. ⊠*Zămecka 127, Sedlec* ☎*728–125–488* ⊕*www.kostnice.cz* 🎫*40 Kč* ☉*Apr.–Sept., daily 8–6; Oct. and Mar., daily 9–noon and 1–5; Nov.–Feb., daily 9–noon and 1–4. Church closed Sun. and Mon.*

WHERE TO STAY

$ 🏨**Medínek.** A modern hotel situated on the main square, Medínek has clean, quiet rooms and basic services. The ground-floor restaurant serves decent Czech cooking in an atmosphere more pleasant than that found in the local beer halls. Although the hotel's 1960s architecture is a little jarring, it does offer the advantages of larger windows and more spacious rooms than those found in many older hotels. ⊠*Palackého nám. 316, 284 01* ☎*327–512–741* 📠*327–512–743* ⊕*www.medinek. cz* ⛱*50 rooms* ♿*In-room: no a/c. In-hotel: restaurant, gym, some pets allowed* ▭*AE, MC, V* ⊪*BP.*

¢ 🏨**U Hrnčíře.** Sitting next to a potter's shop, this quaint inn is right next to the town center. Rooms are plain and the stairs are steep, but the friendly staff gives the hotel a decidedly homey feel. The restaurant in the back garden is strongly recommended for decent Czech food and a beautiful view overlooking St. James's Church. ⊠*Barborská 24, 284 01* ☎*327–512–113* ⛱*5 rooms* ♿*In-room: no a/c. In-hotel: restaurant, some pets allowed, no elevator* ▭*MC, V* ⊪*BP.*

KONOPIŠTĚ

45 km (27 mi) southeast of Prague.

History buffs of World War I take note: Konopiště Castle could be the highlight of your trip. It was the home of none other than Franz Ferdinand d'Este, the ill-fated heir to the Austrian throne whose assassination in Sarajevo in 1914 is credited with unleashing the "Great War" that same year. Franz Ferdinand's castle and surrounding gardens, lakes, and woodland paths make for a blissfully peaceful half-day excursion from Prague. The neo-Gothic castle dates from the 14th century and was passed down through several noble families before the Habsburg heir made it his residence in the late 19th century. Franz Ferdinand—Austrian emperor Franz Josef's oldest nephew and first in line for the Habsburg crown—is described in history books as a bit thick, dour, and highly unpopular in Vienna. This may explain why he took up residence in what was considered at the time a remote location. He certainly spared no expense in restoring the castle and filling its 82 rooms with outlandish paintings, statues, and curiosities.

OUT OF AUSTRIA

Visiting Konopiště Castle, you may find yourself wondering about Franz Ferdinand. He clearly loved travel and hunting. The numbers speak for themselves—his home is covered with almost 100,000 hunting trophies. His other great love was his wife, whom he courted in secret for two years. Against the wishes of Emperor Franz Joseph and the criticism of the court, he married his secret sweetheart. The slander that followed drove them out of Austria to Konopiště until he and his wife were assassinated on a trip to Sarajevo in 1914, triggering World War I.

Fodor'sChoice
★ Getting to **Zámek Konopiště** *Konopiště Castle)* generally involves at least a ½-km (mi) walk through the woods. At first glimpse the castle makes a strong impression; the rounded, neo-Gothic towers appear through the trees, and then you reach the formal garden with its mystical circle of classical statues. The castle dates from around 1300 and for centuries served as a bastion of the nobility in their struggle for power with the king. Franz Ferdinand's extravagant taste and lifestyle are on full display in several of the rooms, which are open to the public during the high season. A valuable collection of weapons from the 16th through 18th century can be seen in the Weapons Hall on the third floor. As an avid hunter, the archduke covered every surface with stuffed animals. At times the walls almost feel like a tribute to taxidermy. The interior is open only to tours; guides may not speak English, but there are English texts available. ✉ *Zámek Konopiště, Benešov* ☎ *317–721–366* ⊕ *www.zamek-konopiste.cz* ✇ *Tours 190 Kč–300 Kč* ☉ *Apr. and Oct., Tues.–Fri. 9–3, weekends 9–4; May–Aug., Tues.–Sun. 9–5; Sept., Tues.–Fri. 9–4, weekends 9–5; Nov., weekends 9–3.*

WHERE TO STAY & EAT

$ ✕🏨 **Amber Hotel Konopiště.** A popular weekend getaway for well-heeled Prague residents who come for the fresh air and the excellent on-site tennis courts, this modern but well-maintained motel is about a 15-

minute walk through the woods from the castle. Rooms are small but nicely appointed (ask for one away from the main road). Its lodgelike restaurant, Stodola ($$–$$$; open for lunch and dinner), has a fine selection of grilled meats and fish dishes. Live folk music is occasionally offered during busy weekends in season. ⊠ *Benešov, 256 01* ☎ *317–722–732* 🖷 *317–722–053* 🛏 *40 rooms* ⚤ *In-room: no a/c. In-hotel: 2 restaurants, tennis court, pool, gym, some pets allowed, no elevator (and no steps)* ▤ *AE, DC, MC, V* ⍾ *BP.*

TÁBOR

90 km (54 mi) south of Prague.

Looking at Tábor now, it's hard to believe that this was once a counter-culture utopia and fortress. In the 15th century the town began as an encampment for religious reformers centered around the teachings of the anti-Catholic firebrand preacher Jan Hus. After Hus was burned at the stake at Lake Constanz, his followers came here by the thousands to build a society opposed to the excesses of Rome and modeled on the primitive communities of the early Christians. Tábor quickly evolved into the symbolic and spiritual center of the Hussites and, along with Prague, served as the bulwark of the religious reform movement.

The 1420s in Tábor were heady days for the reformers. Private property was denounced, and the many poor who made the pilgrimage to Tábor were required to leave their possessions at the town gates. Some sects rejected the doctrine of transubstantiation (the belief that the Eucharistic elements become the body and blood of Christ), turning Holy Communion into a bawdy, secular feast of bread and wine. Other reformers considered themselves superior to Christ—who by dying had shown himself to be merely mortal.

War fever in Tábor ran high, and the town became one of the focal points of the Hussite Wars (1419–34), which pitted reformers against an array of foreign crusaders, Catholics, and noblemen. Under the brilliant military leadership of the one-eyed general Jan Žižka, the Taborites enjoyed early successes, but the forces of the established church and the nobility proved too mighty in the end. Žižka died in 1424, and the Hussite uprising ended 10 years later. Still, many of the town's citizens resisted recatholicization. Fittingly, following the Battle of White Mountain in 1620 (the final defeat for the Czech Protestants), Tábor was the last city to succumb to the conquering Habsburgs.

Many of Tabor's original fortifications can still be seen today, including parts of the town walls and the elaborate system of underground tunnels running below the main square. The original purpose of the tunnels is disputed. Some sources say the townspeople used the tunnels for hiding in and storing ammunition during the religious wars; others say they were used only as cellars for storing food. Nevertheless, their scope is amazing. The tunnels run to some 16 km (10 mi) in length. Tábor is also blessed with several nice places to stay. If you're in the neighborhood and it's getting late, consider a stopover.

5

Žižkovo náměstí *(Žižka Square)* is dominated by a large, 19th-century bronze statue of the gifted—and partly blind—Hussite military leader Jan Žižka. The stone tables in front of the Gothic town hall and the house at No. 6 date from the 15th century and were used by the Hussites to give daily communion to the faithful. Many fine houses that line the square bear plaques describing their architectural style and original purpose. Be sure to stroll the tiny streets around the square, as they curve around, branch off, and then stop; few lead back to the main square. This bemusing layout, created in the 15th century, was done purposely to thwart incoming invasions.

> **MOM WAS RIGHT**
>
> Echoing the advice of moms everywhere, be sure to bring a sweater when you walk through the tunnels. Even on hot summer days, the temperature never exceeds 10°C (50°F).

The **Husitské muzeum** *(Hussite Museum)*, just behind the town hall, documents the history of the religious reformers. This is also where you can enter part of the extensive labyrinth of tunnels below the Old Town. The tour of the tunnels takes about 20 minutes. ⊠ *Žižkovo nám. 2* 🕾 *381–252–242* ⊕ *www.husmuzeum.cz* 🖾 *Museum and tunnel tours 40 Kč–80 Kč* ☉ *Apr.–Oct., daily 8:30–5; Nov.–Mar., weekdays 8:30–5.*

Pražská ulice is a main route to the newer part of town, delightfully lined with beautiful Renaissance facades. If you turn right at Divadelní and head to the Lužnice river, you can see the remaining walls and fortifications of the 15th century, evidence of the town's vital function as a stronghold.

Hrad Kotnov *(Kotnov Castle)*, rising above the river in the distance, dates from the 13th century and was part of Tábor's earliest fortifications. The large pond to the northeast of the Old Town was created as a reservoir in 1492. ⊠ *Klokotská* 🕾 *381–252–242* ⊕ *www.husmuzeum. cz* 🖾 *Castle 40 Kč, tower 20 Kč* ☉ *May–Sept. 8:30–5; other times by appointment.*

WHERE TO STAY

$ 🏨 **Nautilus.** A real find, this tiny boutique hotel, right on the edge of

Fodor's Choice   Tabor's charming central square, exhibits touches of Bohemian crafts-

★   manship in the architecture, beautiful antiques in the rooms, and elegant, original art on the walls. The hotel's restaurant—"Goldie"—is, bar none, the best place to eat in the city. Very few central squares in the Czech Republic are blessed with such an elegant and comfortable place to stay. Don't pass this up. ⊠ *Žižkovo nám. 20, 390 01* 🕾 *380–900– 900* 🖷 *380–900–999* ⊕ *www.hotelnautilus.cz* 🛏 *22 rooms* ⚒ *In-hotel: restaurant, bar* ☰ *AE, DC, MC, V* ⏸ *BP.*

★ $ 🏨 **Pension 189 Karel Bican.** The service couldn't be nicer at this lovely family-run pension, nor could the soothing view of the river from some rooms. The building dates from the 14th century, and the Bicans will gladly show you the house's own catacombs, which once linked up to the medieval tunnel network. When it's hot outside, you can chill out in the cool basement lounge. Some rooms have cooking facilities. The level of comfort exceeds that found in many a Czech "luxury" hotel. ⊠*Hradební 189, 390 01* 🕮381–252–109 ⊕*www.globalnet. cz/bican* ⇆*6 rooms* ♿*In-room: no a/c, kitchen (some). In-hotel: bicycles, some pets allowed, no elevator* ☰*AE, MC, V* ⏏*BP.*

ČESKÝ KRUMLOV

★ *22 km (13 mi) north of Rožmberk nad Vltavou.*

Český Krumlov, the official residence of the Rosenbergs for some 300 years, is an eye-opener. None of the surrounding towns or villages, with their open squares and mixtures of old and new buildings, will prepare you for the beauty of the Old Town. Here the Vltava works its wonders as nowhere else but in Prague itself, swirling in a nearly complete circle around the town. Across the river stands the proud castle, rivaling any in the country in size and splendor.

For the moment, Český Krumlov's beauty is still intact, even though the dilapidated buildings that lend the town its unique atmosphere are slowly metamorphosing into boutiques and pensions. Visitor facilities are improving but can become overburdened during peak months. Overlook any minor inconveniences, however, and enjoy a rare, unspoiled trip in time back to the Bohemian Renaissance. Greenways trails lead to and from the town; for details, contact the tourist office.

The town's main square, **náměstí Svornosti** *(Unity Square)*, is home base for an exploration of the Old Town. Tiny alleys fan out in all directions—there's no point in trying to plan an orderly walk. Simply choose a direction and go. Each turn seems to bring a new drop-dead gorgeous vista of the castle or a charming café or shop that begs for a stop. On the main square itself, the **town hall,** at No. 1, built in 1580, is memorable for its Renaissance friezes and Gothic arcades. You'll also find the main tourist information office here.

From the main square, a street called Horní ulice leads off toward the **Městské muzeum** *(City Museum).* A quick visit gets you acquainted with the rise and fall of the Rožmberk dynasty. ⊠*Horní 152* 🕮*380–711–674* 💶*50 Kč* ☉*May, June, and Sept., daily 10–5; July and Aug., daily 10–6; Oct.–Apr., Tues.–Fri. 9–4, weekends 1–4.*

Just opposite the City Museum are the lively *sgraffiti* facades of the former Jesuitská škola (Jesuit school)—now the luxurious **Hotel Růže.** Abundant Renaissance flourishes like these are due to the town's history as a trading route to Italy and Bavaria—making it a prime position to absorb incoming fashions. The view over the Old Town and castle is most spectacular from the hotel parking area. ⊠*Horní 154.*

The tower of the Gothic **Kostel svatého Víta** *(St. Vitus's Church),* built in the early 1400s, offsets the castle's larger, older tower across the river. Within the church, a marble-column baldachin shelters an elaborate baptismal font. At one time it covered the tomb of Vilém von Rozmberk (1535–92), who was one of his line's most august heads and a great patron of the town. ✉ *Kostelní ul.*

⌕ To get to **Hrad Krumlov** *(Krumlov Castle)* , cross the Vltava on the main street, Radniční, and enter via the staircase leading up from Latrán Street, or continue a little farther up the street to the massive main gateway on the left (walking away from the main square). The oldest and most striking part of the castle is the round, 13th-century **tower,** renovated in the 16th century to look something like a minaret, with its delicately arcaded Renaissance balcony. Part of the old border fortifications, the tower guarded Bohemian frontiers from the threat of Austrian incursion. Now repainted in something like its former Renaissance finery, from various perspectives it appears pompous, absurd, astonishingly lovely—or all of these at once. From dungeon to bells, its inner secrets can be seen climbing the interior staircase.

Vilém von Rožmberk oversaw a major refurbishment of the castle, adding buildings, heightening the tower, and adding rich decorations—generally making the place suitable for one of the grandest Bohemians of the day. The castle passed out of the Rožmberks' hands, however, when Vilém's brother and last of the line, the dissolute Petr Vok, sold both castle and town to Emperor Rudolf II in 1602 to pay off his debts. Under the succeeding Eggenberg and Schwarzenberg dynasties, the castle continued to transform into an opulent palace. The Eggenbergs' prime addition was a **theater,** which was begun in the 1680s and completed in 1766 by Josef Adam of Schwarzenberg. Much of the theater and its accoutrements—sets, props, costumes, stage machinery—survive intact as a rare working display of period stagecraft.

As you enter the castle area, look into the old moats, where two playful brown bears now reside—not really much help in protecting the castle from attack. In season, the castle rooms are open to the public. Be sure to ask at the ticket office about newly accessible areas of this enormous monument, as renovations and additional openings are ongoing. One sightseeing tour focuses on the Renaissance, baroque, and rococo rooms, taking in the delightful **Maškarní Sál** (Masquerade Hall), with its richly detailed 18th-century frescoes. A second tour highlights the seigneurial apartments of the Schwarzenbergs, who owned the castle until the Gestapo seized it in 1940. (The castle became state property in 1947.)

The courtyards and passageways of the castle are open to the public year-round. After proceeding through the Renaissance-era third and fourth courtyards, you come to a wonderfully romantic elevated passageway with spectacular views of the huddled houses of the Old Town. The Austrian Expressionist painter Egon Schiele often stayed in Český Krumlov in the early 1900s and liked to paint this particular view over the river; he titled his Krumlov series *Dead City.* From the river below, the elevated passageway is revealed as the middle level of **most Na plášti** (Cloaked Bridge), a massive construction spanning a deep ravine. Below the passageway are three levels of high arches, looking like a particularly elaborate Roman viaduct. On top runs a narrow three-story block of enclosed passages dressed in light blue and white. At the end of the passageway you come to the theater, then to the nicely appointed **castle garden,** rather formal at the near end, leafy and contemplative on the other. In the middle is an 18th-century summerhouse with a modern, revolving open-air stage in front. Performances are held here in summer. ⊠ *Český Krumlov* ☎ *380–711–687* ✉ *Garden free, castle tours 160 Kč, tower 35 Kč, theater tours 180 Kč* ☉ *Garden Apr. and Oct., Tues.–Sun. 9–5:30; May–Sept., Tues.–Sun. 9–7. Castle interior Apr. and Oct., Tues.–Sun. 9–5:30; May and June, Tues.–Sun. 9–6; July and Aug., daily 9–6; Sept., Tues.–Sun. 9–5:30. Tower May–Sept., Tues.–Sun. 9–7; Apr. and Oct., Tues.–Sun. 9–4:30. Theater May–Oct., Tues.–Sun. 10–4.*

The **Egon Schiele Center** exhibits the work of Schiele and other 20th-century and contemporary European and Czech artists in a rambling Renaissance building near the river. The museum closes occasionally during the winter season. ⊠ *Široká 70–72* ☎ *380–704–011* ⊕ *www. schieleartcentrum.cz* ✉ *120 Kč* ☉ *Daily 10–6.*

WHERE TO EAT

$ ✕ **Na Louži.** Lovingly preserved wood furniture and paneling lends a
Fodor's Choice traditional touch to this warm, inviting, family-run pub. The food is
★ unfussy and satisfying; look for the *pstruh* (trout) with potatoes. Finish off with *ovocné knedlíky,* delicious, traditional Czech fruit dumplings that are frustratingly hard to find on menus around the country. The five country-style rooms upstairs (¢) are small but comfortable enough for an overnight stay; breakfast is included. ⊠ *Kájovská 66* ☎☎ *380–711–280* ▤ *No credit cards.*

WHERE TO STAY

Český Krumlov is crammed with pensions and private rooms for rent. Prices have risen in recent years, but a good double room in a pension can still be found for around 800 Kč a person per night. The best place to look is along the tiny Parkán ulice, which parallels the river just off the main street. A safe bet is the house at **Parkán No. 107** (☎ *380–716–396*), containing several nice rooms and friendly management to boot.

$$$–$$$$ ⊡ **Hotel Růže.** Converted from a Renaissance monastery, this excellent
Fodor's Choice hotel is only a two-minute walk from the main square. The decor is Ye
★ Olde Bohemian but tastefully done, even extending to the bathroom "thrones." The rooms are spacious, and a few have drop-dead views of the castle, so ask to see several before choosing. Note that some double rooms have two narrow single beds, whereas some singles have beds large enough for two. The restaurant offers top-notch dining in a setting that's formal but not stuffy. ⊠ *Horní 154, 381 01* ☎ *380–772–100* 🖷 *380–713–146* ⊕ *www.hotelruze.cz* ⇆ *71 rooms* ⚒ *In-room: no a/c. In-hotel: 2 restaurants, pool, gym, bicycles, laundry service, some pets allowed* ▤ *AE, MC, V* ⦿ *BP.*

★ $ ⊡ **Hotýlek & Hospoda u malého Vítka.** Just a couple of doors up from the Dvořák Hotel toward the central square, this charming hotel has been thoughtfully renovated with a tasteful touch. The rooms are minimal with traditional wooden furniture and fittings. The most highly decorative feature must be the names of the rooms themselves. They are all based on titles of Czech fairy tales. The eye for traditional details extends to the hotel restaurant, complete with a "wine room." ⊠*Radniční 27, 381 01* ☎*380–711–925* 🖷*380–711–937* ⊕*www.vitekhotel.cz* ☎*45 rooms* ♿*In-room: no a/c. In-hotel: restaurant, bar, bicycles, some pets allowed, no elevator* ☐*AE, MC, V* ❖❘*BP.*

NIGHTLIFE & THE ARTS

Český Krumlov hosts numerous summertime cultural events, including Renaissance fairs, a chamber-music festival (in June and July), organ and piano festivals (July), and the top-notch International Music Festival in the castle (August), with performances by leading Czech and foreign classical ensembles. Theater and opera companies from České Budějovice perform in the castle garden in the summer.

ČESKÉ BUDĚJOVICE

26 km (16 mi) southwest of Trébon; 164 km (99 mi) south of Prague.

České Budějovice is the largest city in Southern Bohemia and the community's center and transportation hub. Not nearly as charming as its smaller neighbors, the town still merits a few hours of exploration if you happen to have a stopover. The major attraction is the enormously proportioned main square named after King Přemysl Otakar II and lined with arcaded houses. The well-preserved Gothic Dominican monastery and Church of the Virgin on Piaristické náměstí make for interesting sightseeing. But the town's real claim to fame is its beer—the slightly sweetish *Budvar,* which can be found across the country and around the world. Unfortunately, you can't tour the Budvar brewery itself, but the beer is easily found at pubs around town—simply look for the "Budvar" sign.

To get a good view over the city, climb the 360 steps up to the Renaissance gallery of the **Černá věž** *(Black Tower),* at the northeast corner of the square next to St. Nicholas's Cathedral. ⊠*Nám. Přemysla Otakara II* 🖷*25 Kč* ⊗*Apr.–June, Sept., and Oct., Tues.–Sun. 10–6; July and Aug., daily 10–6.*

A source of pride for České Budějovice, **Koněspřežka** is the oldest railway station on the continent. Designed to transport salt to Bohemia from Linz in Austria, a horse-driven railway was built between 1825 and 1832. One of the first major industrial developments in Europe, it reduced the journey between Linz and České Budějovice from two weeks to four days. Public transport was introduced soon afterward. The station is now a part of the city museum. ⊠*Mánesova 10* ☎*386–354–820* ⊕*www.jiznicechy.org* 🖷*25 Kč* ⊗*July–Sept., daily 9–noon and 12:30–5.*

Founded in 1877, the **Jihočeské Museum** started with a couple of hundred donated items in three rooms in the town hall on the main square. Nowadays, the large collections are held and displayed in the main building and at four other locations outside the town. The major exhibits include theme collections portraying the history of the town and the region through an extensive variety of artifacts that include metalwork, ceramics, glass, and furniture. A fascinating large-scale model shows the Old Town and its picturesque medieval walls and towers. A regular series of temporary exhibitions also runs alongside the permanent ones. ✉ *Dukelská 1* ☎ *386–356–447* 🎫 *80 Kč* ⏲ *Tues.–Sun. 9–12:30 and 1–5.*

WHERE TO STAY

★ $$–$$$ **Grand Hotel Zvon.** Old-fashioned, well kept, and comfortable, this historic hotel has a winning list of attributes, including an ideal location right on the main square. A room with a view costs extra, but these rooms are considerably larger and brighter and include large period bathtubs. ✉ *Nám. Přemysla Otakara II 28, 307 01* ☎ *387–311–384* 📠 *387–311–385* 🌐 *www.hotel-zvon.cz* *75 rooms* *In-room: refrigerator (some), no a/c. In-hotel: 2 restaurants, bar, parking (fee), some pets allowed* 💳 *AE, DC, MC, V* 🍴 *BP.*

$ Fodor'sChoice ★ **Hotel Bohemia.** The combination of two old burgher houses formed this hotel. The building, listed as a monument, has been modernized but still retains its centuries-old ceilings. Refurbishment resulted in a pleasant design in a quiet part of the old town. The adjoining winebar restaurant serves excellent local dishes. ✉ *Hradební 20, 370 01* ☎ *386–360–691* 📠 *386–360–691* 🌐 *www.bohemiacb.cz* *18 rooms* *In-room: no a/c. In-hotel: restaurant, laundry service, parking (no fee), some pets allowed, no elevator* 💳 *AE, MC, V* 🍴 *BP.*

NIGHTLIFE & THE ARTS

As a regional capital, **České Budějovice** has its own theater, ballet, orchestra, and opera companies. Unlike theater, music knows no language barriers, and the local opera company is regularly praised for the quality of its productions. Summer performances are held in Český Krumlov Castle Park. It's worth noting that these tickets are very popular and are often sold out a month in advance. They can be obtained from the theater box office in České Budějovice. ✉ *Dr. Stejskala 19* ☎ *386–356–925* 🌐 *www.jihoceskedivadlo.cz.*

HLUBOKÁ NAD VLTAVOU

Fodor'sChoice ★ *17 km (10½ mi) southwest of Trébon; 155 km (93½ mi) south of Prague.*

With a cluster of white rooks flanking its walls, this is one of the Czech Republic's most curious châteaux. Although the structure dates from the 13th century, what you see is pure 19th-century excess, perpetrated by the wealthy Schwarzenberg family attempting to prove their good taste. If you think you've seen this castle somewhere before, you're probably thinking of Windsor Castle, near London, which served as the template. Take a tour; the pompous interior reflects the no-holds-barred tastes of the time, and many individual pieces are interesting. The wooden Renaissance ceiling in the large dining room was removed by the Schwarzenbergs from the castle at Český Krumlov and brought here. Also look for the beautiful late-baroque bookshelves in the library.

If your curiosity in Czech painting wasn't satisfied in Prague, have a look at the **Galerie Mikoláše Alše** (*Aleš Art Gallery* ☎387–967–041) in the Riding Hall, which displays a major collection of Gothic art and an exhibition of modern Czech works. The gallery is also a popular spot for chamber concerts. ✉*Zamék 142, off Rte. 105 or 146, Hluboká nad Vltavou* ☎387–967–045 ⊕*www.zamekhluboka.cz* ✉*180 Kč castle, 40 Kč Aleš Art Gallery* ⊙*Castle: Apr.–June, Sept., and Oct., Tues.–Sun. 9–4:30; July and Aug., daily 9–5. Aleš Art Gallery: May–Sept., daily 9–5; Oct.–Apr., Tues.–Sun. 9–3:30.*

SOUTHERN BOHEMIA ESSENTIALS

BUS TRAVEL
All the major destinations in the region are reachable from Prague and České Budějovice on the ČSAD bus network (⇨ *Bus Travel to and from Prague in Prague Essentials, above*).

CAR TRAVEL
Car travel affords the greatest ease and flexibility in this region. The main artery through the region, the two-lane E55 from Prague south to Tábor and České Budějovice, though often crowded, is in relatively good shape. If you are driving from Vienna, take the E49 toward Gmünd.

TOURS
Čedok offers several specialized tours from Prague that include visits to České Budějovice, Hluboká Castle, Český Krumlov, Kutná Hora, and Konopiště. The main Prague departure point is náměstí Republiky (Republic Square) in central Prague, opposite the Prašná brána (Powder Tower). Most tours need to be booked a day in advance.

Information Čedok (☎*800–112–112* ⊕*www.cedok.cz*).

TRAIN TRAVEL
Benešov (Konopiště), Tábor, and České Budějovice lie along the major southern line in the direction of Linz, and train service to these cities from Prague is frequent and comfortable. Most Vienna–Prague trains travel through Moravia, but a few stop at Třeboň and Tábor (with a change at Gmünd).

VISITOR INFORMATION
Information České Budějovice Tourist Center (✉*Nám. Přemysla Otakára II 1* ☎*386–359–480* ⊕*www.c-budejovice.cz*). **Český Krumlov Tourist Information** (✉*Nám. Svornosti 1* ☎*380–711–183* ⊕*www.ckrumlov.cz*). **Kutná Hora Tourist Information** (✉*Palackého nám. 377* ☎*327–512–378* ⊕*www.kutnahora.cz*). **Tábor Tourist Information** (✉*Žižkovo nám. 2* ☎*381–486–230* ⊕*www.tabor.cz*).

WESTERN BOHEMIA

Until World War II, western Bohemia was the playground of Central Europe's rich and famous. Its three well-known spas, Karlovy Vary, Mariánské Lázně, and Františkovy Lázně (better known by their German names, Karlsbad, Marienbad, and Franzensbad, respectively), were the annual haunts of everybody who was anybody: Johann Wolfgang von Goethe, Ludwig van Beethoven, Karl Marx, and England's King Edward VII, to name but a few. Although strictly "proletarianized" in the Communist era, the spas still exude a nostalgic aura of a more elegant past and, unlike most of Bohemia, offer a basic tourist infrastructure that makes dining and lodging a pleasure.

KARLOVY VARY

★ *132 km (79 mi) due west of Prague on Rte. 6 (E48).*

Karlovy Vary, better known outside the Czech Republic by its German name, Karlsbad, is the most famous Bohemian spa. It is named for Emperor Charles IV, who allegedly happened upon the springs in 1358 while on a hunting expedition. As the story goes, the emperor's hound—chasing a harried stag—fell into a boiling spring and was scalded. Charles had the water tested and, familiar with spas in Italy, ordered baths to be established in the village of Vary. The spa reached its heyday in the 19th century, when royalty came here from all over Europe for treatment. The long list of those who "took the cure" includes Peter the Great, Goethe (no fewer than 13 times, according to a plaque on one house by the main spring), Schiller, Beethoven, and Chopin. Even Karl Marx, when he wasn't decrying wealth and privilege, spent time at the resort; he wrote some of *Das Kapital* here between 1874 and 1876.

After decades of neglect under the Communists that left many buildings crumbling behind their beautiful facades, the town leaders today face the daunting task of carving out a new role for Karlovy Vary, since few Czechs can afford to set aside weeks or months at a time for a leisurely cure. To raise some quick cash, many sanatoriums have turned to offering short-term accommodations to foreign visitors (at rather expensive rates). By the week or by the hour, "classical" spa procedures, laser treatments, acupuncture, and even plastic surgery are purveyed to German clients or to large numbers of Russians who bought property in town in the late 1990s. For most visitors, though, it's enough simply to stroll the streets and parks and allow the eyes to feast awhile on the splendors of the past.

Whether you're arriving by bus, train, or car, your first view of the town on the approach from Prague will be of the ugly new section on the banks of the Ohře River. Don't despair: continue along the main road—following the signs to the Grandhotel Pupp—until you reach the lovely main street of the older spa area, situated gently astride the banks of the little Teplá ("Warm") River. (Drivers, note that driving through or parking in the main spa area is allowed only with a permit obtainable from your hotel.) The walk from the new town to the spa area is about 20 minutes.

Shooting its scalding water to a height of some 40 feet, the Vřídlo is indeed the Karlovy Vary's hottest and most dramatic gusher, and built around it is the jarringly modern **Vřídelní kolonáda** *Vřídlo Colonnade)*. Walk inside the arcade to watch hundreds of patients take the famed Karlsbad drinking cure. They shuffle somnambulistically up and down, eyes glazed, clutching drinking glasses filled periodically at one of the five "sources." The waters, which range from -1°C to 22°C (30°F to 72°F), are said to be especially effective against diseases of the digestive and urinary tracts. They're also good for gout (which probably explains the spa's former popularity with royals). If you want to join the crowds and take a sip, you can buy your own spouted cup from vendors within the colonnade. ⊠ *Vřídelní ul., near Kosterní nám.*

★   To the right of the Vřídlo Colonnade, steps lead up to the white **Kostel Mařˇí Magdaleny** *(Church of Mary Magdalene)*. Designed by Kilian Ignaz Dientzenhofer (architect of the two churches of St. Nicholas in Prague), this is the best of the few baroque buildings still standing in Karlovy Vary. ⊠ *Moravská ul.* ☎ *No phone* ⊙ *Daily 9–6.*

The neo-Renaissance pillared hall **Mlýnská kolonáda** *(Mill Colonnade)*, along the river, is the town's centerpiece. Built from 1871 to 1881, it has four springs: Rusalka, Libussa, Prince Wenceslas, and Millpond. ⊠ *Mlýnské nábřeží.*

Delicately elegant, the **Sadová kolonáda** *(Park Colonnade)* is laced with white wrought iron. It was built in 1882 by the Viennese architectural duo Fellner and Helmer, who sprinkled the Austro-Hungarian Empire with many such edifices during the late 19th century. They also designed the town's theater, the quaint wooden Tržní kolonáda (Market Colonnade) next to the Vřídlo Colonnade, and one of the old bathhouses. ⊠ *Zahradní.*

The 20th century raises its head in the form of the huge, bunkerlike **Hotel Thermal,** across the river from the historic district. Built in the late 1960s as the Communist idea of luxury, the building is jarring to the eye. But a visit to the rooftop pool is nothing short of spectacular. Even if you don't feel like a swim, it's worth taking the winding road up to the baths for the view. ⊠ *I. P. Pavlova 11* ☎ *359–001–111* 💶 *70 Kč per hr* ☉ *Pool Tues.–Sat. 8 AM–9:30 PM; café daily 10–11.*

A five-minute walk up the steep Zámecký vrch from the Market Colonnade brings you to the redbrick Victorian **Kostel svatého Lukáše** *(St. Luke's Church)*, once a gathering point for the local English community. ⊠ *Zámecký vrch at Petra Velikého.*

Fodor'sChoice
★ From Kostel svatého Lukáše, take a sharp right uphill on a redbrick road, then turn left onto a footpath through the woods, following signs to **Jelení skok** *(Stag's Leap)*. After a while steps lead up to a bronze statue of a deer looking over the cliffs, the symbol of Karlovy Vary. From here a winding path threads toward a little red gazebo opening onto a mythical panorama. ⊠ *Sovava trail in Petrova Výšina park.*

■ NEED A BREAK? After reaching the summit of Stag's Leap, reward yourself with a light meal at the nearby restaurant **Jelení skok.** There may be an entrance fee if a live band is playing (but you'll also get the opportunity to polka). If you don't want to walk up, you can drive up a signposted road from the Victorian church.

The splendid Russian Orthodox **Kostel svatých Petra a Pavla** *(Church of Sts. Peter and Paul)* has six domes. It dates from the end of the 19th century and is decorated with paintings and icons donated by wealthy Russian visitors. ⊠ *Třída Krále Jiřího.*

Give your feet a rest. You won't need to walk to one of the best views of the town. Even higher than Stag's Leap sits an observation tower, **rozhledna Diana,** accessible by funicular from behind the Grandhotel Pupp. There's an elevator to the top of the tower. ⊠ *Výšina přátelství* 💶 *Funicular 30 Kč one-way, 50 Kč round-trip; tower 10 Kč* ☉ *June–Sept., Mon.–Thurs. and Sun. 11–9, Fri. and Sat. 11–11; May and Oct., Tues., Wed., and Sun. 11–6, Fri. and Sat. 11–7; Mar., Apr., Nov., and Dec., Wed.–Sun. 11–5.*

On one of the town's best shopping streets you can find **Elefant,** carrying the torch for a dying breed of sophisticated coffeehouses. This is

5

the spot for that mandatory apple strudel and coffee. ⊠*Stará louka 30* ☎*353–232–511.*

WHERE TO EAT

Unfortunately, the culinary scene in Prague has yet to spark off in Karlovy Vary. The variety and quality of the food generally still lags well behind the quality of the hotels and the demands of the visitors. The riverbank is lined with nondescript Czech restaurants on both sides. These are fine for a plate of pork or a schnitzel, but are unlikely to leave a lasting positive impression. Hotel food tends to be better.

> **TO YOUR HEALTH**
>
> Becherovka, herbal alcoholic liqueur, is often referred to as the "The Thirteenth Spring" in Karlovy Vary. Many Czechs believe this locally produced drink does indeed have medicinal properties, such as aiding digestion. The recommended dosage is three small cups a day: one before lunch, dinner, and bedtime.

$$–$$$
Fodor'sChoice
★
✕**Embassy.** Cozy and sophisticated, this wine restaurant, conveniently near the Grandhotel Pupp, serves an innovative menu by local standards. Tagliatelle with smoked salmon in cream sauce makes an excellent main course, as does roast duck with cabbage and dumplings. The wine list features Czech varieties like the dry whites Rulandské bílé and Ryzlink Rýnský (the latter being the domestic version of the Riesling grape) and some pricey imports. For a romantic evening, request one of the tables on the bridge over the river. ⊠*Nová louka 21* ☎*353–221– 161* ▤*AE, DC, MC, V.*

$$–$$$ ✕**Pizzeria Capri.** This riverfront pizzeria has become an institution during the annual film festival. The walls are decked out with photos of the owner smiling next to Hollywood stars. The pizza and fresh-fish dishes range from good to very good. On a warm evening in summer sit out along the sidewalk. ⊠*Stará Louka 42* ☎*353–236–090* ▤*MC, V.*

$–$$ ✕**U Švejka.** Usually when a restaurant has the name "Schweik" in it— from the novel Good Soldier Schweik—it means one thing: tourist trap. But this local Schweik incarnation is a cut above its brethren. If you're looking for a simple, decent Czech pub, with good local cooking and excellent beer, you've found it. ⊠*Stará Louka 10* ☎*353–232–276* ▤*No credit cards.*

WHERE TO STAY

★ $$$–$$$$ ▨**Carlsbad Plaza.** An eye-popping new luxury hotel, not far from the Grandhotel Pupp, Carlsbad Plaza is aimed at attracting Karlovy Vary's wealthiest visitors. Everything here speaks refinement, down to the lunchtime dress code: "jacket and tie" for men. Reserve the "Moser" suite if you've just cashed out your 401K. The staff tries hard to maintain the highest standards, but the overall effect is a little chilly. The rooms are tastefully furnished, with all modern conveniences. The "wellness center" (a small pool and sauna complex), spa, and fitness centers offer every comfort and treatment yet invented. ⊠*Mariánskolázeňská 23, 360 01* ☎*352–441–111* ☎*353–236–392* ⊕*www.carlsbadplaza. cz* ⇗*146 rooms, 14 suites* ⌂*In-hotel: 4 restaurants, gym, spa, some pets allowed* ▤*AE, MC, V* ⏇*BP.*

$$$–$$$$
Fodor'sChoice
★

Grandhotel Pupp. The grand-daddy of them all, this is one of Central Europe's most famous resorts, going back some 200 years. Standards and service slipped under the Communists, when the hotel was called "Moskva-Pupp," but the highly professional management has more than made up for the decades of neglect. The vast public rooms exude the very best

> **CAUTION**
>
> The waters from natural springs are loaded with minerals, which means they often have a sulfuric smell and taste—not necessarily the most appetizing thing. You may want to sip it at first as you get used to the flavor.

taste, circa 1913, when the building was completed. Every July, the Pupp houses international movie stars in town for the Karlovy Vary International Film Festival. (The adjacent Parkhotel Pupp, under the same management, is a more affordable alternative.) ⊠ *Mírové nám. 2, 360 91* ☎ *353–109–630* 🖷 *353–226–638* ⊕ *www.pupp.cz* 🛏 *75 rooms, 34 suites* ⟨ *In-room: no a/c (some), safe. In-hotel: 4 restaurants, bar, gym, spa, some pets allowed, public Internet* ⊟ *AE, DC, MC, V* ⟩⊙|*BP.*

$$
Fodor'sChoice
★

Hotel Embassy. On a peaceful bend of the river, this family-run hotel's spacious, well-appointed rooms usually include a sitting table and chairs or a couch with accompanying coffee table. The Embassy is more intimate and personal than the Carlsbad Plaza or Grandhotel Pupp, with the same high level of excellence in its restaurant, rooms, and staff. It also offers green-fee discounts and starting times at four local courses for the golf-obsessed, and massages and spa treatments for those who are not. ⊠ *Nová Louka 21, 360 01* ☎ *353–221–161* 🖷 *353 223 146* ⊕ *www.embassy.cz* 🛏 *18 rooms, 2 suites* ⟨ *In-room: no a/c. In-hotel: restaurant, bar, some pets allowed* ⊟ *AE, MC, V* ⟩⊙|*BP.*

$–$$

Hotel Heluan. A clean, safe bet if you've arrived in town without reservations and don't want to spend your savings on a room. Rooms are starkly furnished—and not nearly as exciting as the stately exterior and public areas. But no matter. The location, right at the center of the main spa area, couldn't be better. ⊠ *Tržíště 41, 360 01* ☎ *353–225–756* 🖷 *353–321–111* ⊕ *www.travelguide.cz/heluan* 🛏 *25 rooms* ⟨ *In-room: no a/c. In-hotel: restaurant, bar, some pets allowed* ⊟ *AE, MC, V* ⟩⊙|*BP.*

NIGHTLIFE & THE ARTS

California Club (⊠ *Tyršova 1753/2* ☎ *353–222–087*) has enough space for you and 249 of your closest friends. DJs spin "oldies" (which usually means music from the 1970s on up) or disco, depending on the night. There's no cover, and it's open from 1 PM until 5 AM.

The center of Karlovy Vary's underground music scene, **Club Propaganda** (⊠ *Jaltská 7* ☎ *353–233–792*) is in a former ballroom. It showcases DJs spinning nightly as well as the occasional live rock act. **Grandhotel Pupp** (⊠ *Mírové nám. 2* ☎ *353–109–111*) has a nightclub and the casino of the biggest hotel in town. Gamble the night away within the mirrored walls and under the glass ceiling of the Pupp Casino Club, or settle into a cocktail and some cheesy live crooning at the English-theme Becher's Bar.

5

SPORTS & THE OUTDOORS

Karlovy Vary's warm, open-air public pool on top of the **Thermal Hotel** (✉ *I. P. Pavlova*) offers the experience of swimming at a cozy bathtub temperature even in the coolest weather; the view over the town is outstanding. Even if you are not staying at the hotel, you can still take a dip in the waters for 70 Kč per hour. The **Karlovy Vary Golf Club** (✉ *Pražská 125* ☎ *353–331–001* ⊕ *www.golfresort.cz*) is just out of town on the road to Prague; green fees are 1,800 Kč for 18 holes.

SHOPPING

A cluster of exclusive stores huddles around the Grandhotel Pupp and back toward town along the river on Stará Louka. Lesser-known, high-quality makers of glass and porcelain can also be found on this street. If you're looking for an inexpensive but nonetheless singular gift from Karlovy Vary, consider a bottle of the bittersweet (and potent) Becherovka, a liqueur produced by the town's own Jan Becher distillery. Another thoughtful gift would be one of the pipe-shape ceramic drinking cups used to take the drinking cure at spas; you can find them at the colonnades. Boxes of tasty *oplatky* (wafers), sometimes covered with chocolate, can be found at shops in all of the spa towns. The challenge is stopping yourself from dipping into the box if you intend to give it as a gift.

To glass enthusiasts, Karlovy Vary is best known as the home of **Moser** (✉ *Tržíště 7* ☎ *353–235–303* ⊕ *www.moser.cz*), one of the world's leading producers of crystal and decorative glassware.

MARIÁNSKÉ LÁZNĚ

★ *30 km (18 mi) southeast of Cheb, 47 km (29 mi) south of Karlovy Vary.*

Your expectations of what a spa resort should be may come nearest to fulfillment here. It's far larger and more active than Františkovy Lázně and greener and quieter than Karlovy Vary. This was the spa favored by Britain's Edward VII. Goethe and Chopin also repaired here frequently. Mark Twain, on a visit to the spa in 1892, labeled the town a "health factory" and couldn't get over how new everything looked. Indeed, at that time everything was new. The sanatoriums, most built during the 19th century in a confident, outrageous mixture of "neo" styles, fan out impressively around a finely groomed oblong park. Cure takers and curiosity seekers alike parade through the Empire-style Cross Spring pavilion and the long colonnade near the top of the park. Buy a spouted drinking cup (available at the colonnades) and join the rest of the sippers taking the drinking cure. Be forewarned, though: the waters from the Rudolph, Ambrose, and Caroline springs, though harmless, all have a noticeable diuretic effect. For this reason they're used extensively in treating disorders of the kidney and bladder.

A stay in Mariánské Lázně can be healthful even without special treatment. Special walking trails of all difficulty levels surround the resort in all directions. The best advice is simply to put on comfortable shoes, buy a hiking map, and head out. One of the country's few golf courses lies about 3 km (2 mi) to the east of town. Hotels can also help to arrange special activities, such as tennis and horseback riding. For the less intrepid, a simple stroll around the gardens, with a few deep breaths of the town's famous air, is enough to restore a healthy sense of perspective.

For information on spa treatments, inquire at the main **spa offices** (✉*Masarykova 22* ☎*354–655–501* ⊕*www.marienbad.cz*). Walk-in treatments can be arranged at the **Nové Lázně** (*New Spa* ✉*Reitenbergerova 53* ☎*354–644–111*).

WHERE TO EAT

★ **$$–$$$** ✕**Koliba.** An excellent alternative to the hotel restaurants in town, Koliba serves grilled meats and shish kebabs, plus tankards of Moravian wine try the dry, cherry-red Rulandské červené), with traditional gusto. Occasionally fiddlers play rousing Moravian folk tunes. Exposed wooden ceiling beams add rustic charm to the inn's 15 rooms that face the surrounding nature preserve. ✉*Dusíkova 592* ☎*354–625–169* ▭*MC, V.*

$–$$ ✕**Filip.** This bustling wine bar is where locals come to find relief from the hordes of tourists. There's a nice selection of traditional Czech dishes—mainly pork, grilled meats, and steaks. ✉*Poštovní 96* ☎*354–626–161* ▭*No credit cards.*

$–$$ ✕**Paradiso.** Fast pasta and pizza dishes are all served with a welcome smile. Keep your pizza simple—ham or just cheese are recommended—or you can end up with a soggy pie. ✉*Hlavní 166* ☎*603–742–292* ▭*No credit cards.*

WHERE TO STAY

Hotel prices have risen in recent years and many properties are terribly overpriced for what is offered. Bear in mind, too, that the glorious Empire and neoclassical facades of many of the hotels and spas are rarely reflected in the disappointingly sterile rooms. Read the price list carefully—some of the spas now calculate the price of a room on a per-person basis. You can get better deals by booking packages, including spa treatments, in advance from the hotel. Check the hotel's Web site for current offers. Private accommodation can also offer a real savings. The best place to look for a private room is along Paleckého ulice and Hlavní třída, south of the main spa area, or look in the neighboring villages of Zádub and Závišín.

★ **$$$–$$$$** ⊞**Hotel Nové Lázně.** This neo-Renaissance, multitower hotel and spa—opened in 1896—lines a large part of one side of the park. In the center of the building, a cast-iron sculpture of the donor of health, Hygiea, is carried by the sea god Triton, the son of Neptune, who stands on top, stressing the importance of water in spa treatments. Inside, the complex of Roman baths is decorated with marble, and houses period frescoes. This is a serious spa, aimed at spa package devotees rather than overnight visitors. ✉*Reitenbergerova 53, 353 01* ☎*354–644–111* 🖷*354–644–044* ⊕*www.marienbad.cz* ⇗*97 rooms, 1 suite* ⌕*In-room: no a/c (some). In-hotel: restaurant, bar, gym, spa* ▭*AE, MC, V* ⦿*BP.*

$$$ ⊞**Grandhotel Pacifik.** This regal hotel, at the top of Hlavní street with commanding views of the main spa area, has been thoroughly renovated and now may be the best of the bunch. It has a full range of spa and wellness facilities. The rooms are toned down and tastefully modern in contrast to the over-exuberant balcony-studded, yellow facade. Rooms with a view over the park are worth the extra money. ⊠ *Mírové nám. 84, 353 48* ☎ *354–651–111* 📠 *354–651–200* ⊕ *www.marien-bad.cz* ⮐ *95 rooms, 7 suites* ♿ *In-hotel: restaurant, spa, public Internet* 🝙 *AE, MC, V* ⦿ *BP.*

$$ ⊞**Hotel Bohemia.** As a slightly cheaper alternative to some of the posher places in town, this late-19th-century hotel feels like a throwback. The crystal chandeliers in the lobby and the graciously proportioned rooms—some with a balcony off the front—feel like stepping into the days of Goethe. The plain furnishings, however, recall the days before 1989 when the spas were used as recuperation centers for factory workers. The helpful staff can arrange spa treatments and horseback riding. An annex, Dependence, has added 12 additional suites. ⊠ *Hlavní třída 100, 353 01* ☎ *354–610–111* 📠 *354–610–555* ⊕ *www.orea.cz/bohe-mia* ⮐ *72 rooms, 4 suites, 12 additional suites in Dependence* ♿ *In-room: no a/c. In-hotel: restaurant, bar, some pets allowed* 🝙 *AE, MC, V* ⦿ *BP.*

$ ⊞**Koliba.** This is a perfect choice if you're just here for a day or two,
Fodor's Choice   puttering around town without an interest in lavish spa treatments.
★   This hunting-style lodge is situated above and behind the main spa area, about a 15-minute walk from town. What makes this place so special are the exceptionally cute, clean, rustic rooms and the over-the-top friendliness of the staff. Some of the best grilled dishes in town are served in the highly stylized romantic restaurant. ⊠ *Dusíkova 592* ☎ *354–625–169* 📠 *354–626–310* ⊕ *koliba.xercom.cz* ⮐ *12 rooms* ♿ *In-room: no a/c. In-hotel: restaurant, some pets allowed, no elevator* 🝙 *AE, DC, MC, V* ⦿ *BP.*

NIGHTLIFE & THE ARTS

The West Bohemian Symphony Orchestra performs regularly in the New Spa (Nové Lázně). The town's annual Chopin festival each August brings in pianists from around Europe to perform the Polish composer's works. Otherwise, nightlife here can be pretty dry.

PLZEŇ

92 km (55 mi) southwest of Prague.

Plzeň—or Pilsen in German, as it's better known abroad—is the industrial heart of western Bohemia and the region's biggest city. But for visitors, the city is known as a beer mecca. Anyone who loves the stuff must pay homage to the enormous Pilsner Urquell brewery, where modern "Pils"-style beer was first developed more than 150 years ago. Brewery tours are available and highly recommended. There's even a brewing museum here for intellectual beer aficionados.

Another item of interest—particularly for Americans—is historical. Whereas most of the Czech Republic was liberated by Soviet troops

gondola.cz ⌚*12 rooms* ♿*In-room: Ethernet. In-hotel: restaurant, parking, no elevator (though many rooms don't need one)* ☰*AE, DC, MC, V* ⍩❘*BP.*

NIGHTLIFE

House of Blues (✉*Černická 10* ☎*377–224–294*), related to the American chain in name only, showcases live blues and rock acts. Ignore the mirrored disco ball on the ceiling—ashtrays on every table let you know you're in a real joint. **Jazz Rock Cafe** (✉*Sedláčkova 18* ☎*No phone*) gives you a license to party. Drop by on Wednesday to catch some live blues or jazz music. **Klec** (✉*Dřevěná 6* ☎*No phone*), with its mottled blue-and-orange walls and metal balcony, is a hangout for the teen-to-twentysomething set, with music to match. **Maxim Music Club** (✉*Martinská 8* ☎*377–221–271*) features different music every night of the week. Call first to check if that evening's performance will be jazz, rock, blues, dance music, or some other genre. Doors open at 6; closing time is around 5 AM. **Zach's Pub** (✉*Palackého nám.* ☎*377–223–176*) highlights various live acts, including Latin and blues, outdoors on its summer patio.

WESTERN BOHEMIA ESSENTIALS

BUS TRAVEL

Most major towns are easily reachable by bus service. Smaller towns, though, might have only one bus a day or even fewer. Be sure to know when the next bus comes so you won't be stranded. Frequent bus service between Prague and Karlovy Vary makes the journey only about two hours each way. Many places such as Plzeň are reachable by both bus and train. Both the price and time differences can be great *(⇨ Bus Travel to & from Prague in Prague Essentials).*

CAR TRAVEL

If you're driving, you can take the E48 directly from Prague to Karlovy Vary. Roads in the area tend to be in good condition, though they can sometimes be quite narrow.

TOURS

Most of Prague's tour operators offer excursions to Karlovy Vary. Čedok offers one-day and longer tours covering western Bohemia's major sights, as well as curative vacations at many Czech spas.

Information Čedok (☎*800–112–112* ⊕*www.cedok.cz*).

TRAIN TRAVEL

Good, if slow, train service links all the major towns west of Prague. The best stretches are from Františkovy Lázně to Plzeň and from Plzeň to Prague. The Prague–Karlovy Vary run takes far longer than it should—more than three hours by the shortest route.

VISITOR INFORMATION

Information Karlovy Vary Tourist Information (*Kur-Info* ✉*Vřídelní kolonáda [Vřídlo Colonnade], Karlovy Vary* ☎*353–322–4097* ⊕*www.karlovyvary.cz* ✉*Nám. Dr. M. Horákové 18 [near bus station], Karlovy Vary* ☎*353–222–833*). **Marián-**

ské Lázně Tourist Information (*Cultural and Information Center* ⊠*Hlavní 47, Mariánské Lázně* ☎ *354–625–892 or 354–622–474* ⊕*www.marianskelazne.cz*). **Plzeň Tourist Information** (⊠*Nám. Republiky 41, Plzeň* ☎ *378–032–750* ⊕*info. plzen-city.cz*).

NORTHERN BOHEMIA

Northern Bohemia is a paradox: much of it was despoiled by 40 years of rampant postwar industrialization, but here and there you can still find areas of great natural beauty. Along the Labe River, rolling hills, perfect for walking, guard the country's northern frontiers with Germany and Poland. Hikers and campers head for the Krkonoše range on the Polish border. As you move toward the west, the interest is more historical, in an area where the influence of Germany was felt in less pleasant ways than in the spas. You don't have to drive too far to reach the Sudetenland, the German-speaking border area that was handed over to Hitler by the British and French in 1938. The landscape here is riddled with the tragic remains of the Nazi occupation of Czech lands from 1939 to 1945. Most drastically affected was Terezín, better known as the infamous concentration camp Theresienstadt.

As tourist amenities keep improving, reasonably priced, adequately comfortable small-to-middling hotels are now not too difficult to find. Dining options still generally are standard Czech and German cooking, although Asian restaurants are now a less-than-amazing sight in the area's larger towns, thanks to the presence of sizable Chinese and Vietnamese communities in border areas. Pizzerias, which range from ghastly to quite congenial, are now ubiquitous.

LIDICE

18 km (11 mi) from Prague.

No more than a speck on the map to the northwest of Prague, this tiny village was plucked out of obscurity by the Nazis during World War II to teach Czechs not to oppose German rule. In 1942 Adolf Hitler ordered Lidice razed to the ground in retaliation for the assassination of the Nazi wartime leader in Bohemia, Reinhard Heydrich, by Czech patriots.

On the night of June 9, 1942, a Gestapo unit entered Lidice, shot the entire adult male population (192 men), and sent the 196 women to the Ravensbrück concentration camp. A handful of the 103 children in the village were sent to Germany to be "Aryanized"; the others perished in death camps. By June 10, the entire village had been destroyed.

During the war and in the years immediately after, the name Lidice was known around the world as a symbol of Nazi atrocities. A group of miners from Birmingham, England, formed a committee called "Lidice Must Live" and on their initiative a new village of Lidice was rebuilt not far from the original site.

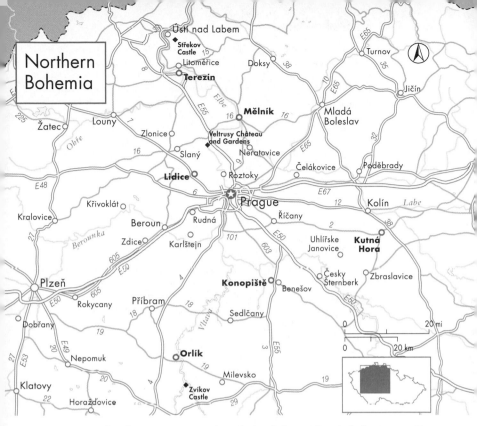

Today, however, it must be admitted that Lidice feels forgotten. For many Czechs, especially after the fall of Communism, World War II feels like part of the distant past.

That's not to say a trip here is not worth the effort. The memorial and adjoining museum are deeply moving. Pair a trip here with a visit to Terezín, farther up the road, to see how World War II has etched its mark on the Czech psyche.

The **Lidice Memorial** is a haunting sight. A tall cross next to a small stream marks where the original village once stood. The monument is graphic in its depiction of the deportation and slaughter of the inhabitants. Inside a museum there's a photograph of each person and a short description of his or her fate. You can also find reproductions of the German documents ordering the village's destruction, including the Gestapo's chillingly bureaucratic reports on how the massacre was carried out and the peculiar problems encountered in Aryanizing the deported children. Exhibits highlighting the international response hold a more heartwarming message. The staff tend to speak German rather than English, but they will helpfully play a short film (about 20 minutes) in English on request, between the other showings.

Outside, you are free to wander about. The wooden cross in the field, starkly decorated with barbed wire, marks the place where the men were executed. Remains of brick walls are visible here, left over from the Gestapo's dynamite and bulldozer rampage. There are several moving sculptures made in tribute to the horror, including a large one representing the 82 children gassed by the Nazis. It's worth walking to the far end of the meadow, where the town cemetery was. Note that the Lidice museum and grounds were undergoing extensive renovation in 2006. Plans were in place to add more films and to expand the museum and rose garden, among other changes. ⊠ *Ul. 10 června 1942* ⊕*www. lidice-memorial.cz* ⊠*80 Kč* ⊙*Apr.–Oct., daily 9–6; Nov.–Feb., daily 9–4; Mar., daily 9–5.*

TEREZÍN

48 km (30 mi) northwest of Prague.

Just the word Terezín (Theresienstadt in German) immediately recalls the horrors of the Jewish Holocaust for Czechs. As the main Nazi concentration camp in Bohemia, Terezín held much of Prague's large prewar Jewish population during the war. It wasn't a death camp in the way that Auschwitz was—though in the end, very few of the tens of thousands of Jews transported there survived the war.

Terezín was originally built by the Austrians in the 18th century to house soldiers guarding the Austrian frontier with Prussia. During World War II the Germans were quick to recognize the garrison and surrounding town as a potential concentration camp.

Terezín was an exception among the many Nazi concentration camps scattered around Central Europe. The Germans, for a time, used it as a showcase camp in order to deflect international criticism of their policy toward Jews. In the early years of the war—until as late as 1944—the detainees were permitted a semblance of normal life, with limited self-government, schools, a theater, and a library. (Pictures drawn by the children at Terezín, at their drawing lessons in school, are on display in Prague's Jewish museum.) The International Red Cross was even permitted to inspect the town in 1944. Nazis prepared for the visit by sprucing it up with a fresh coat of paint.

Through 1944 and 1945, as the Nazis' war effort soured, the masquerade of their benevolence in Terezín was dropped. Train transports to Auschwitz and other death camps to the east were stepped up to a rate of several a week. In all, some 87,000 Jews from Terezín were murdered in this way, and another 35,000 died from starvation or disease. The conductor Karel Ančerl, who died in 1973, and the novelist Ivan Klíma are among the few thousand who survived imprisonment at Terezín.

The shock in visiting Terezín today is that it's pretty much remained the same. To their credit, Czechs have done very little to dress it up for visitors. You're free to walk the town's run-down streets and imagine what it must have been like to be held prisoner there. It's dark, depressing, and at the same time, profoundly engrossing.

The enormity of Terezín's role in history is difficult to grasp at first because the Czechs have put up few signs to give you guidance, but the **Památník Terezín** *(Terezín Memorial)* encompasses all the existing buildings that are open to the public. Buildings include the **Magdeburg Barracks**, where the Jewish Council of Elders met, and the **Jewish cemetery's crematorium** just outside the town walls.

★ Told in words and pictures, the town's horrific story is depicted at the **Museum of the Terezín Ghetto** (⊠ *Komenského ul.* ☎416–782–577), just off the central park in town. A short documentary is also shown in many languages. Tell the staff that you speak English—they'll let you roam the building and flag you down when the next English-language video is being shown. The **Malá Pevnost** *(Small Fortress)*, about 1 km (½ mi) east of Terezín, functioned as a special prison camp, holding mostly POWs or political prisoners in totally abject conditions. Around 30,000 prisoners came through here during the war. Those who did not die in detention were shipped off to other concentration camps. Above the entrance to the main courtyard stands the cruelly cynical motto ARBEIT MACHT FREI (Work Brings Freedom). Take a walk around the rooms, still holding a sad collection of rusty bed frames, sinks, and shower units. At the far end of the fortress, opposite the main entrance, is the special wing built by the Nazis when space became tight. Imagining life in the windowless cells is crushing. ⊠ *Principova alej 304, Terezín* ☎416–782–225 ⊕ *www.pamatnik-terezin.cz* ⊠ *One unit 160 Kč; all units 180 Kč* ☉ *Ghetto Museum and Magdeburg Barracks Apr.–Oct., daily 9–6; Nov.–Mar., daily 9–5:30. Small Fortress Apr.–Oct., daily 8– 6; Nov.–Mar., daily 8–4:30. Crematorium Apr.–Nov., Sun.–Fri. 10–5.*

MĚLNÍK

About 40 km (23 mi) north of Prague.

The town's **Zámek,** a petite castle a few blocks from the main square, grandly hovers over the confluence of the Labe (Elbe) River and two arms of the Vltava. The view here is stunning, and the sunny hillsides are covered with vineyards. Indeed, the town is known best for its special Ludmila wines made from these grapes. As the locals tell it, Emperor Charles IV was responsible for bringing wine production to the area. Having a good eye for favorable growing conditions, he encouraged vintners from Burgundy to come here and plant their vines. Every autumn, usually in late September, Mělník celebrates what is likely the region's best *Vinobraní,* an autumn festival held when barrels of young, still fermenting wine, called *burčak,* are tapped. If you happen to come at this time, look for the rare red-wine version.

The courtyard's three dominant architectural styles jump out at you, reflecting alterations to the castle over the years. On the north side, note the typical arcaded Renaissance balconies, decorated with *sgraffiti.* To the west, a Gothic touch is still easy to make out. The southern wing is clearly baroque (although also decorated with arcades). Inside the castle at the back, you can find a *vinárna* (wine room) with decent food and excellent views overlooking the rivers. On the other side is a **museum** of paintings, furniture, and porcelain belonging to the old aristocratic Lobkowicz clan, which has recovered quite a few castles and estates from the state. For day-tripping oenophiles, tour the wine cellars under the castle and book a wine tasting. ⊠*Zámek Mělník* ☎*315–622–121* ≦*Castle 60 Kč, wine cellar tour 25 Kč, or up to 220 Kč with wine tasting* ⊙*Castle daily 10–5. Wine cellar daily 10–5.*

WHERE TO EAT

$–$$$ ✗ **Zámecká Restaurace.** Right in the castle itself, you can find the best place in town to eat. It certainly has the best view. Choose the simpler and cheaper of two buffets that the castle offers. Sipping a glass of Ludmila wine and taking in the scenery is a treat at a very reasonable price. ⊠*Inside Zámek, Nám. Míru 54* ☎*315–622–485* ⊟*No credit cards.*

WHERE TO STAY

¢   🏨 **Venezia.** Perhaps the best hotel in Mělník, if not the entire region, this recent arrival offers clean, spacious doubles and large, modern bathrooms at very moderate prices, just steps from the main attractions and the pedestrian zone. Rooms facing the street may have a bit too much noise for extremely sensitive ears, but the trade-off in proximity, comfort, and style are well worth the shouts, howls, and other sounds of Mělník's small-town nightlife. ⊠*Fibichova 1, 276 01* ☎*315–695–278* 🖷*315–695–278* ⬛*26 rooms* ⊘*In-room: no a/c (some), refrigerator* ⊟*AE, MC, V* �†⊘⁞*BP* ⊕*www.hotelvenezia.cz.*

NORTHERN BOHEMIA ESSENTIALS

BUS TRAVEL

There are direct buses from Prague to Terezín, Litoměřice, Mělník, Špindlerův Mlýn, and Pec pod Sněžkou *(⇨ Bus Travel to and from Prague in Prague Essentials).*

CAR TRAVEL

If you are driving, the E55 leads directly into the Czech Republic from Dresden and winds down to Prague via the old spa town of Teplice. The main road from Prague in the direction of the Krkonoše range is the E65, which is a four-lane highway for most of the distance. If you are driving through northern Bohemia, you'll be rewarded with a particularly picturesque drive on Route 261 along the Labe (Elbe) River on the way to Střekov Castle near Ústí nad Labem.

TOURS

Several private companies offer trips from Prague to Lidice, Mělník, Nelahozeves, Terezín, and Veltrusy Château. Wittmann Tours has a good tour to Terezín; buses leave Prague from the Inter-Continental Hotel, on Pařížská near the Staronová synagóga (Old-New Synagogue), daily from mid-March to December at 10 AM, returning around 5 PM, for a fare of 1,150 Kč.

Information Wittmann Tours (☎*222–252–472* ⊕*www.wittman-tours.com*).

TRAIN TRAVEL

Train connections in the north are spotty at best; bus is the preferred means of travel. Regular express trains connect Prague with Ústí nad Labem, but to reach other towns you'll have to take slower local trains or the bus (⇨ *Train Travel to and from Prague in Prague Essentials*).

VISITOR INFORMATION

Information Mělník Tourist Information (⊠ *Nám. Míru 30, Mělník* ☎ *315–627–503* ⊕ *www.melnik.cz*).

SOUTHERN MORAVIA

Lacking the turbulent history of Bohemia to the west or the stark natural beauty of Slovakia farther east, Moravia, the easternmost province of the Czech Republic, is frequently overlooked as a travel destination. Still, although Moravia's cities do not match Prague for beauty and its gentle mountains hardly compare with Slovakia's strikingly rugged Tatras, Moravia's colorful villages and rolling hills certainly do merit a few days of exploration. Come here for the good wine, the folk music, the friendly faces, and the languid pace.

Moravia has a bit of both Bohemia and Slovakia. It is closer culturally to Bohemia: the two were bound together as one kingdom for some 1,000 years, following the fall of the Great Moravian Empire (Moravia's last stab at Slavonic statehood) at the end of the 10th century. All the historical and cultural movements that swept through Bohemia, including the religious turbulence and long period of Austrian Habsburg rule, were felt strongly here as well. But, oddly, in many ways Moravia resembles Slovakia more than its cousin to the west. The colors come alive here in a way that is seldom seen in Bohemia. The subdued earthen pinks and yellows in towns such as Telč and Mikulov suddenly erupt into the fiery reds, greens, and purples of the traditional folk costumes farther to the east. Folk music, all but gone in Bohemia, is still very much alive in Moravia.

Southern Moravia's highlands define the "border" with Bohemia. Here, towns such as Jihlava and Telč are virtually indistinguishable from their Bohemian counterparts. The handsome squares, with their long arcades, bear witness to the prosperity enjoyed by this part of Europe during the 16th and early 17th century, until the Habsburg crackdown on the Czech lands at the outset of the Thirty Years' War. In the south along the frontier with Austria—until the late 1980s a heavily fortified expanse of the Iron Curtain—the towns and people on both sides of the border seek to reestablish ties going back centuries. One of their common traditions is wine making. Znojmo, Mikulov, and Valtice are to the Czech Republic what the small towns of the *Weinviertel* on the other side of the border are to Austria.

Don't expect gastronomic delights in Moravia. The choices—especially outside Brno—are usually limited to roast pork with sauerkraut and dumplings, ho-hum chicken dishes, and the ever-reliable trout. Hotels are getting better, and the shabby, dim, bathroom-down-the-hall places

are practically a thing of the past. In mountainous areas inquire locally about the possibility of staying in a *chata* (cabin). These are abundant, and they are often a pleasant alternative to the faceless modern hotels. Many lack modern amenities, though, so be prepared to rough it.

TELČ

30 km (19 mi) south of Jihlava; 154 km (94 mi) southeast of Prague, via Rte. 406

Don't be fooled by the dusty approach to the little town of Telč or the unpromising, unkempt countryside surrounding the place. Telč is a knockout. Its main square is even more impressive than that of Jihlava, but what strikes the eye most here is not just its size but the unified style of the buildings. On the lowest levels are beautifully vaulted Gothic halls, just above are Renaissance floors and facades, and all the buildings are crowned with rich Renaissance and baroque gables.

Fodor'sChoice
★ **Náměstí Zachariáše z Hradce,** the main square, is so perfect you feel like you've stepped into a painting, not a living town. Zacharias of Neuhaus, the square's namesake, allegedly created the architectural unity. During the 16th century, so the story goes, the wealthy Zacharias had

the castle—originally a small fort—rebuilt into a Renaissance château. But the town's dull buildings clashed so badly, Zacharias had the square rebuilt to match the castle's splendor. Luckily for architecture fans, the Neuhaus dynasty died out shortly thereafter, and succeeding nobles had no desire to outfit the town in the latest architectural fashions.

If you've come by car, park outside the main walls on the side south of town and walk through the **Great Gate,** part of the original fortifications dating to the 13th century. As you approach on Palackého ulice, the square unfolds in front of you, laced with the château at the northern end and beautiful houses, bathed in pastel, ice-cream shades. Fans of Renaissance reliefs, note the *sgraffito* corner house at No. 15, etched like fine porcelain. The house at No. 61, across from the Černý Orel Hotel, also bears intricate details.

Credit the Italians for transforming **Statní zámek Telč** *Telč château)* from a Gothic castle into a refined Renaissance château. The château, grouped in a complex with the former **Jesuit college** and **Kostel svatého Jakuba** (Church of St. James), was built during the 14th century, perhaps by King John of Luxembourg, the father of Charles IV. Renovation, overseen by Italian masters, took place between 1553 and 1568. In season you can tour the castle and admire the rich Renaissance interiors. Given the reputation of nobles for lively, lengthy banquets, the chastising *sgraffito* relief in the dining room depicting gluttony (in addition to the six other deadly sins) seems odd indeed. Other interesting rooms with *sgraffiti* include the Treasury, the Armory, and the Blue and Gold chambers. A curious counterpoint to all this Renaissance splendor is the castle's permanent exhibit of paintings by leading Czech modernist Jan Zrzavý. There are two tours: the first goes through the Renaissance chambers; the second displays the rooms that were used as recently as 1945. ⊠ *Statní zámek Telč, nám. J. Kypty* ☎ *567–243–943* 🖾 *Tours in English 140 Kč–160 Kč each, or 70Kč–80 Kč with English printed text; gallery 30 Kč* ⊘ *Apr. and Oct., Tues.–Sun. 9–noon and 1–4; May–Sept., Tues.–Sun. 9–noon and 1–5.*

■ **NEED A BREAK?**

Obey your sweet tooth and indulge in good freshly made cakes or an ice-cream cone at Cukrárna u Matěje, a little café and pastry shop at Na baště 2, on the street leading past the château to a small lake.

A tiny street leading off the main square takes you to the 160-foot Romanesque tower of the **Kostel svatého Ducha** *(Church of the Holy Spirit),* a solid tower finished off in conical gray peaks. This is the oldest standing structure in Telč, dating from the first quarter of the 13th century. The interior, however, is a confused hodgepodge, as the style was fiddled with repeatedly, first in a late-Gothic makeover and then refashioned again because of fire damage. ⊠ *Palackého ul.*

WHERE TO STAY & EAT

$ ✕🖾 **Černý Orel.** In a lemon-yellow baroque house on the square, this is a decent older hotel that nevertheless has maintained suitably high standards. The public areas mix architectural details, such as vaulted ceilings, with plush, contemporary armchairs, but the basic rooms are inviting and well balanced. Ask for a room overlooking the square. Even if you don't stay here, take a meal at the very good hotel restaurant ($–$$$$), arguably the best place in town for straightforward beef and pork dishes. ⊠*Nám. Zachariáše z Hradce 7, 588 56* ☎*567–243–220* 🖷*567–243–221* ⊕*www.hotelcernyorel.cz* ⮝*30 rooms, 25 with bath* ♿*In-room: no a/c. In-hotel: restaurant, bar, some pets allowed* ⊟*AE, MC, V* ⦿❙*BP.*

$ 🌂**Celerin.** Occupying a tiny corner of the square on the opposite side from the castle, this is the nicest hotel in town. Room No. 5 features some bright, 19th-century period furnishings and a pretty view of the square. The attic rooms are larger, with modern furnishings. ⊠*Nám. Zachariáše z Hradce 1/43, 588 56* ☎*567–213–580* 🖷*567–213–581* ⮝*10 rooms* ⊕*www.hotelcelerin.cz* ♿*In-room: no a/c, Wi-Fi. In-hotel: restaurant, some pets allowed, no elevator* ⊟*AE, DC, MC, V* ⦿❙*BP.*

MIKULOV

54 km (34 mi) east of Znojmo; 283 km (174 mi) southeast of Prague.

In many ways, Mikulov is the quintessential Moravian town, with pastel pink-and-yellow buildings and green rolling hills. For centuries it was one of the most important towns in the region—the seat of the Lichtenstein family in the late Middle Ages and then later the home to the powerful Dietrichstein family. The castle's size and splendor demonstrate Mikulov's onetime crucial position astride the traditional border between Moravia and Austria.

But Mikulov began an extended decline in the 19th century when the main railroad line from Vienna bypassed the town in favor of Břeclav. Historically, Mikulov was the center of Moravia's Jewish community, growing to a population of several thousand at one point, but many Jews left to seek their fortunes in bigger cities. The 20th century was especially cruel to Mikulov. The Nazis Aryanized many of the industries and deported remaining Jews. After the war, many local industries—including the all-important wineries—were nationalized. Mikulov stagnated as a lonely outpost at the edge of the Iron Curtain.

Recent years have seen a slow revival. Much of the wine industry is back in private hands and standards are rising. Day-trippers from Austria have spurred development of a nascent tourist industry. And after many decades of decline, the old Jewish Quarter is getting overdue attention. Although the Jewish community is still tiny—numbering just a handful of people—work is under way to try to preserve some of the remaining houses in the quarter. You can tour the quarter, where many of the houses are now marked with plaques explaining their significance. The Jewish cemetery is one of the largest in Central Europe and a must-see if you're passing through.

Grape-harvesting time in October provides an ideal moment to visit and enjoy the local pastoral delights. Head for one of the many private *sklípeks* (wine cellars) built into the hills surrounding the town. The tradition in these parts is simply to knock on the door; more often than not, you'll be invited in by the owner to taste a recent vintage. If you visit in early September, try to hit Mikulov's renowned wine-harvest festival, which is celebrated with traditional music, folk dancing, and much guzzling of local Riesling.

The arresting **Mikulov zámek** *(Mikulov Château)* looms over the tiny main square and surrounding area. Built as the Gothic-era residence of the noble Liechtenstein family in the 13th century, the château later served as the residence of the powerful Dietrichsteins. Napoléon Bonaparte also stayed here in 1805 while negotiating peace terms with the Austrians after winning the Battle of Austerlitz (Austerlitz is now known as Slavkov, near Brno). Sixty-one years later, Bismarck used the castle to sign a peace treaty with Austria. The castle's darkest days came at the end of World War II, when retreating Nazi SS units set fire to it. Much of what you see today—though it looks deceptively ancient—is relatively new, having been rebuilt after World War II. The château holds the **Regionální Muzeum** (Regional Museum), exhibiting period furniture and local wine-making items, including a remarkable wine cask made in 1643, with a capacity of more than 22,000 gallons. ✉ *Zámek 5* ☎ *519–510–255* 💶 *20 Kč–40 Kč* 🕑 *Apr.–Oct., Tues.–Sun. 9–4. Closed Nov.–Mar.*

Little of Mikulov's once-thriving Jewish Quarter, *Židovská čtvrt'*, has survived. The community once numbered several thousand people, and the town was the seat of the chief rabbi of Moravia from the 17th to the 19th century. Several respected Talmudic scholars, including rabbis Jehuda Loew and David Oppenheimer, lived and taught here. What's left can be seen on a stroll down Husova ulice, which was once the center of the quarter. An information board near the corner with Brněnská ulice explains the significance of the community and what happened to it. The most important building still standing is the 16th-century **Altschul** *(Upper Synagogue).* ✉ *Husova 11* 🕑 *May–Sept., Tues.–Sun. 1–5.*

FodorśChoice ★ Mikulov's massive and moving **Jewish Cemetery** is not far from Husova ulice, just off Brněnská. The cemetery gate is usually locked, but the key may be borrowed from the Efram Gallery at Husova 4. Out of respect for Jewish customs, the key is not given out on Saturday. ✉ *Off Brněnská ul.*

WHERE TO STAY & EAT

★ ¢ ✗🏨 **Hotel Tanzberg.** Formerly known as Rohatý Krokodýl, this prim hotel sits in the middle of the former Jewish Quarter, on Husova ulice. The doubles are on the small side, but the suites, which cost just a little more, are quite roomy. Facilities are the best in Mikulov, particularly the ground-floor restaurant ($–$$), which serves a typical but delicately prepared selection of traditional Moravian dishes. ✉ *Husova ul. 8, 692 01* ☎ *519–510–692* 🖶 *519–511–695* 🌐 *www.hotel-tanzberg.cz* 🛏 *14 rooms* ☝ *In-room: no a/c. In-hotel: restaurant, bar, some pets allowed, no elevator* ☰ *AE, MC, V* 🍽 *BP.*

OUTDOOR ACTIVITIES & SPORTS

For walking enthusiasts, the white limestone **Pavlovské vrchy** *(Pavlov Hills)*, where the Stone Age remains in Dolní Věstonice were found, is a challenging climb with views of a couple of castle ruins. From **Děvín Peak** (1,800 feet), just south of Dolní Věstonice, a series of clearly marked paths follow the ridges the 10 km (6 mi) to Mikulov.

SHOPPING

The secret of Moravian wine is only now beginning to extend beyond the country's borders. A vintage bottle from one of the smaller but excellent vineyards in Bzenec, Velké Pavlovice, or Hodonín would be appreciated by any wine connoisseur.

VALTICE

13 km (8 mi) east of Mikulov.

Palaces, obelisks, colonnades, and other exotic structures are dotted throughout Valtice and the nearby town of Lednice, which collectively form a UNESCO World Heritage Site. Bestowed on the region by the Liechtenstein family in the 18th and 19th centuries, they transformed the entire area into a massive man-made park. Admittedly, it looks a little forlorn these days. The Communists did not take kindly to the whimsical fantasies of the nobility, and filled the empty spaces with now-dilapidated public housing and collective farms. Since 1989, though, the region's fortunes have improved. The palaces are getting cleaned up, new pensions and restaurants have opened, and the towns are vigorously promoting their position at the center of the Moravian wine industry. The local tourist offices can advise on the best places to sample wines, or trek out for hiking and biking. The main Prague–Vienna bike trail crosses through the area, and excellent trails lead in all directions.

Valtice is a compact little town wholly dominated by the captivating **Zámek Valtice** *(Valtice Château)*, just off the main street. The *château* was built for the Liechtenstein family by a group of leading baroque architects, among them Fischer von Erlach. Painted ceilings, ornate woodwork, and some 365 windows provide flair for the opulent home. You can tour more than a dozen rooms, the chapel, and a picture gallery. The massive gardens out back are open to the public without having to pay a fee. The site is also home to the National Wine Center, a collection of the country's best bottles, with numerous wine-tasting programs available and a very good wine shop on the premises. ⊠ *Zámek 1* ☎ *519–352–423* 🖅 *70 Kč, guided tour in German (occasionally in English; phone or email valtice@brno.npu.cz for reservation) 140 Kč, wine tastings 120 Kč–390 Kč* ☺ *Apr. and Oct., Tues.–Sun. 9–4; May–Aug., Tues.–Sun. 9–6; Sept., Tues.–Sun. 9–5.*

WHERE TO STAY & EAT

★ $–$$ ✕ **Keltkská Restaurace Avalon.** This lovely neighborhood spot is on a small street that runs off the right-hand side of the main square. Keltkská means "Celtic," but don't ask us why. Most of the main courses run to the usual steaks, pork, and chicken dishes, albeit done with more care and flavor than the usual joint; a few inauthentic (but tasty) Mexican, Lebanese, and Indian recipes round out the bill. The real draws here are the tiny garden on a warm night and the in-house tearoom on a chilly evening. ⊠*Příční 46* ☎*519–352–252* ⊟*No credit cards.*

¢ ⊡**Hotel Hubertus.** A rare treat for the Czech Republic—you can actually spend the night in a wing of the Valtice palace. Room rates are inexpensive for the location, so don't expect palatial interiors that match the setting—but that said, the proprietors have tried to make the rooms inviting, with high ceilings and fresh flowers. ⊠*Zámek 1, 691 42* ☎*519–352–537* ⊟*519–352–538* ⊕*www.hotelhubertus.cz* ⇥*29 rooms, 22 with bath* ⅋*In-room: no a/c, no TV (some). In-hotel: restaurant, bar, some pets allowed, no elevator* ⊟*AE, MC, V* ⊺⊙⊺*BP.*

LEDNICE

7 km (4½ mi) from Valtice.

As a display of their wealth and taste, the Liechtenstein family sprinkled neoclassical temples and eclectic follies across a huge swath of parkland around Valtice and Lednice throughout the 18th and 19th centuries. The extravagantly neo-Gothic **château** at Lednice, though obviously in disrepair, has a sumptuous interior; particularly resplendent are the blue-and-green silk wall coverings embossed with the Moravian eagle in the formal dining room and bay-window drawing room. The grounds, now a pleasant park open to the public, have a 200-foot-tall minaret and a massive greenhouse filled with exotic flora. The landscaped area has been on the UNESCO World Heritage list since 1996. ⊠*Lednice* ☎*519–340–128* ⊕*www.lednice.cz* ⊡*Tours 130 Kč–150 Kč, minaret 10 Kč* ⊙*Apr. and Oct., weekends 9–3; May–Aug., Tues.–Sun. 9–5; Sept., Tues.–Sun. 9–4.*

BRNO

202 km (122 mi) southeast of Prague via Hwy. E65.

Nicknamed the "Manchester of Moravia," Brno (pronounced *burr-no*) has a different feel from other Czech or Moravian cities. Beginning with a textile industry imported from Germany, Holland, and Belgium, Brno became a leading industrial center of the Austro-Hungarian empire during the 18th and 19th centuries. Some visitors search in vain for an extensive old town, pining for the traditional arcaded storefronts that typify other historic Czech towns. But instead you'll see fine examples of the Empire and neo-Renaissance styles, their formal, geometric facades more in keeping with the conservative tastes of the 19th-century middle class.

In the 1920s and '30s, the city became home to some of the best young architects working in the early-modern, Bauhaus, and "international" styles. Experimentation wasn't restricted to architecture. Leoš Janáček, an important composer of the early-modern period, lived and worked in Brno, as did Austrian novelist Robert Musil. That artistic support continues today, and the city is considered to have some of the best theater and performing arts in the country, as well as a small but thriving café scene.

Avoid Brno at trade-fair time (the biggest are in early spring and early autumn), when hotel and restaurant facilities are strained. If the hotels are booked, the tourist information center at the town hall will help you find a room.

WHAT TO SEE

Chrám svatých Petra a Pavla (Cathedral of Sts. Peter and Paul). Best admired from a distance, the silhouette of slim neo-Gothic twin spires—added in the 20th century—give the cathedral a touch of Gothic dignity. Up close, the interior is light and tasteful but hardly mind-blowing. This is the church pictured on the face of the 10 Kč coin. ✉Petrov, at Petrská ul. 🎫Free ⊙Daily dawn–dusk; closed during services.

> ## SAVED BY THE BELL
>
> During the Thirty Years' War, Brno faced a fierce attack by Swedish troops. Brno's resistance had been determined, and the Swedish commander decided if the town couldn't be taken by noon the next day, they would give up the fight. Word of this reached the cathedral's bell ringer, and just as the Swedish troops were preparing their final assault, they rang the noon bells—an hour early. The ruse worked, and the Swedes decamped. The cathedral bells proved to be the final defensive strategy that saved the town from being taken.

★ **Kostel Nalezení svatého Kříže** (Church of the Holy Cross). If you've ever wondered what a mummy looks like without its bandages, this church will hold the answer. Formerly part of the Capuchin Monastery, the Church of the Holy Cross combines a baroque form with a rather stark facade. Enter the *krypta* (crypt) in the basement, where the mummified remains of some 200 nobles and monks from the late 17th and 18th centuries are displayed, ingeniously preserved by a natural system of air circulating through vents and chimneys. The best-known mummy is Colonel František Trenck, commander of the brutal Pandour regiment of the Austrian army, who, at least in legend, spent several years in the dungeons of Špilberk Castle before finding his final rest here in 1749. Experts have concluded that his head is real, contrary to stories of its removal by a thief. A note of caution about the crypt: the graphic displays can be frightening to children (and even some adults), so ask at the admission desk for a small brochure (20 Kč) with pictures that preview what's to come. ✉Kapucínské nám. 5 🕿542–213–232 ⊕www.kapucini.cz 🎫40 Kč ⊙May–Sept., Mon.–Sat. 9–11:45 and 2–4:30, Sun. 11–11:45 and 2–4:30; Oct.–mid-Dec. and mid-Jan.–Apr., Tues.–Sat. 9–11:45 and 2–4:30, Sun. 11–11:45 and 2–4:30.

Místodržitelský palác (Governor's Palace). Moravia's strong artistic ties to Austria can be seen in the impressive collection of Gothic, baroque, and 19th-century painting and sculpture found in this splendid palace. Particularly interesting are Austrian painter Franz Anton Maulbertsch's ethereal rococo pageants. ✉Moravské nám. 1A 🕿542–321–100 ⊕www.moravska-galerie.cz 🎫60 Kč ⊙Apr.–Sept.,

Wed. and Fri.–Sun. 10–6, Thurs. 10–7; Oct.–Mar., Wed. and Fri.–Sun.
10–5, Thurs. 10–6.

Muzeum Romské kultury *(Museum of Romani Culture).* A small but singular museum devoted to the culture of the Roma, as Gypsies prefer to be called, is halfway from Brno's historical center to the ⇨ *Villa Tugendhat.* To bridge cross-cultural understanding, as Roma people are often the victims of discrimination, this museum was dedicated to their culture and history. Exhibits deal with traditional occupations, dress, and lifestyles. A study room has documents and photographs. ✉ *Bratislavská 67* ☎ *545–571–798* ⊕ *www.rommuz.cz* 🖃 *40 Kč* ⊗ *Tues.–Fri. 10–6.*

Náměstí Svobody *(Freedom Square).* The best place to start any walking tour, this is the focal point of the city and a centerpiece for the massive effort to modernize the area. The square underwent extensive renovation in 2006, and adjoining streets feature some of the city's best shopping. Anyone who has been to Vienna might experience déjà vu here, as many of the buildings were designed by 19th-century Austrian architects. Especially noteworthy is the stolid Klein Palace at No. 15, built by Theophil Hansen and Ludwig Foerster, both prominent for their work on Vienna's Ringstrasse.

Pražákův palác *(Pražák Palace).* The largest collection of modern and contemporary Czech art outside of Prague lines the walls of this handsome, 19th-century neo-Renaissance building. If you've already seen these same artists represented in Prague's major galleries, you may be tempted to adopt a been-there-done-that attitude. But the emphasis here is on Moravian artists, who tended to prefer rural themes—their avant-garde concoctions have a certain folksy flavor. ✉ *Husova 18* ☎ *542–215–758* ⊕ *www.moravska-galerie.cz* 🖃 *60 Kč* ⊗ *Apr.–Sept., Wed. and Fri.–Sun. 10–6, Thurs. 10–7; Oct.–Mar., Wed. and Fri.–Sun. 10–5, Thurs. 10–6.*

★ **Hrad Špilberk** *(Spielberg Castle).* Once among the most feared places in the Habsburg Empire, this fortress-cum-prison still broods over Brno behind menacing walls. The castle's advantageous location brought the early lords of the city, who moved here during the 13th century from neighboring Petrov Hill. Successive rulers gradually converted the old castle into a virtually impregnable fortress. Indeed, it successfully withstood the onslaughts of Hussites, Swedes, and Prussians over the centuries; only Napoléon, in 1809, succeeded in occupying the fortress. But the castle's fame comes from its gruesome history as a prison for enemies of the Austro-Hungarian monarchy and, later for the Nazis' prisoners during World War II. Although tales of torture during the Austrian period are probably untrue (judicial torture had been prohibited prior to the first prisoners' arrival in 1784), conditions for the hardest offenders were hellish: they were shackled day and night in dank, dark catacombs and fed only bread and water. The castle complex is large, and the various parts generally require separate admissions. The **casemates** (passages within the walls of the castle) have been turned into an exhibition of the late-18th-century prison and their Nazi-era use as an air-raid shelter. You can see the entire castle grounds as well as the surrounding area from the **observation tower.** Above ground, a **museum** in the fortress starts off with more displays on the prison era with detailed English texts. Included in the tour of the museum is an exhibition on the history of Brno, including several panoramic paintings showing the city in the 17th century, and photos showing then-and-now views of 19th- and 20th-century redevelopment in the Old Town. One of the best of the permanent exhibitions, in room No. 5, focuses on the city's modern architectural heritage. You'll find room after room of sketches, drawings, and photographs of the most important buildings built in the 1920s and '30s. Unfortunately, most of the descriptions are in Czech, but if you speak the language or go with someone who does, you'll be in heaven. ✉ *Špilberk 1* ☎ *542–123–611* 🎟 *Casemates 70 Kč, museum 70 Kč; casemates, tower, and exhibitions, 120 Kč* ⊗ *Casemates and tower May, June, and Sept., Tues.–Sun. 9–6; July and Aug., daily 9–6; Oct.–Apr., Tues.–Sun. 9–5. Museum Apr.–Sept., Tues.–Sun. 9–6; Oct.–Mar., Wed.–Sun. 10–5.*

NEED A BREAK? After climbing to the Špilberk Castle and touring several museums, what could be better than a nice cold beer? The **Stopkova pivnice** (✉ *Česká 5*) will set you up with one. If you're hungry, try the house goulash, a tangy mixture of sausage, beef, rice, egg, and dumpling.

Stará radnice *(Old Town Hall).* The oldest secular building in Brno exhibits an important Gothic portal. This door is the work of Anton Pilgram, architect of Vienna's St. Stephen's Cathedral. It was completed in 1510, but the building itself is about 200 years older. Look above the door to see a badly bent pinnacle that looks as if it wilted in the afternoon sun. This isn't the work of vandals but was apparently done by Pilgram himself out of revenge against the town. According to legend, Pilgram had been promised an excellent commission for his portal, but when he finished, the mayor and city councillors reneged on their offer. Pilgram was so angered by the duplicity that he purposely bent the pinnacle and left it poised, fittingly, over the statue of justice.

Just inside the door are the remains of two other famous Brno legends, the **Brno Dragon** and the **wagon wheel.** The dragon—actually an alligator—apparently turned up at the town walls one day in the 17th century and began eating children and livestock. As the story goes, a gatekeeper came up with the idea of stuffing a freshly slaughtered goat with limestone. The dragon devoured the goat, swallowing the limestone as well, and when it drank at a nearby river, the water mixed with the limestone and burst the dragon's stomach (the scars on the preserved dragon's stomach are still clearly visible). The story of the wagon wheel, on the other hand, concerns a bet placed some 400 years ago that a young wheelwright, Jiří Birek, couldn't chop down a tree, form the wood into a wheel, and roll it from his home at Lednice (53 km [33 mi] away) to the town walls of Brno—all between sunup and sundown. The wheel stands as a lasting tribute to his achievement. (The townspeople, however, became convinced that Jiří had enlisted the help of the devil to win the bet, so they stopped frequenting his workshop; poor Jiří died penniless.)

No longer the seat of the town government, the Old Town Hall holds exhibitions and performances, and the town's tourist information office. To find out what's on, ask in the information center just inside Pilgram's portal. The view from the top of the tower is one of the best in Brno, but the climb (five flights) is strenuous. ⊠ *Radnická 8* ⊕ *www. kultura-brno.cz* ☎ *Tower 20 Kč* ⊙ *Apr.–Sept., daily 9–5.*

★ **Uměleckoprůmyslové muzeum** *(Museum of Applied Arts).* Arts and crafts shine in this museum, which is without a doubt the Czech Republic's best. It has an assemblage of artifacts far more extensive than the truncated collection in Prague's museum of the same name. The collection includes Gothic, Art Nouveau, and Secessionist pieces, as well as an excellent, comprehensive overview of Bohemian and Moravian glass. Keep an eye out for the elegant furniture from Josef Hoffmann's Wiener Werkstätte (Vienna Workshop). Milan Knížák's jagged, candy-color table provides a striking example of contemporary work. ⊠ *Husova 14* ☎ *532–169–111* ⊕ *www.moravska-galerie. cz* ☎ *70 Kč* ⊙ *Tues.–Sun. 9–5.*

Fodor'sChoice **Villa Tugendhat.** Designed by Ludwig Mies van der Rohe and completed
★ in 1930, this austere white Bauhaus villa counts among the most important works of the modern period and is now a UNESCO World Heritage Site. Function and the use of geometric forms are emphasized. The Tugendhat family fled before the Nazis, and their original furnishings vanished. Replicas of Mies's cool, functional designs have been installed in the downstairs living area. Some of the original exotic wood paneling and an eye-stopping onyx screen remain in place. The best way to get there is to take a taxi or Tram 3, 5, or 11 to the Dětská nemocnice stop and then walk up unmarked Černopolní ulice for 10 minutes or so; you'll be able to see the modernist structure up on the hill. Advance reservations for tours are highly recommended. The building is undergoing a long-term renovation, and is occasionally closed to the public; a long-term closure has been proposed several times over the past decade. ⊠ *Černopolní 15* ☎ *545–212–118* ⊕ *www.tugendhat-villa.cz* ☎ *120 Kč* ⊙ *Wed.–Sun. 10–6; last tour starts at 5.*

Zelný trh *(Cabbage Market).* Only in this Cabbage Market could Brno begin to look like a typical Czech town—not just for the many stands from which farmers still sell vegetables but also for the flamboyant **Parnassus Fountain** that adorns its center. This baroque outburst (inspiring a love-it-or-hate-it reaction) couldn't be more out of place amid the formal elegance of most of the buildings on the square. But when Johann Bernhard Fischer von Erlach created the fountain in the late 17th century, it was important for a striving town like Brno to display its understanding of the classics and of ancient Greece. Therefore, Hercules slays a three-headed dragon, and Amphitrite awaits the arrival of her lover—all incongruously surrounded by farmers hawking turnips and onions. What could be more Czech?

OFF THE BEATEN PATH

Moravský Krumlov. Admirers of Art Nouveau master Alfons Mucha may find themselves drawn 50 km (30 mi) off the main highway linking Mikulov and Brno. This town château is the unlikely home of one of Mucha's most celebrated works, his 20-canvas *Slav Epic*, which tells the story of the emergence of the Slav nation. The enormous work was not well received when it was completed in 1928; painters at the time were more interested in imitating modern movements and considered Mucha's representational art to be old-fashioned. The city of Prague owns the paintings and has from time to time said it was going to relocate them, but so far no concrete action has been taken. A music festival takes place here in June. ⊠*Zámecká 1* ☎*515–322–789* ☉*Apr.–June, Sept., and Oct., Tues.–Sun. 9–4; July and Aug., Tues.–Sun. 9–5* ⚒*70 Kč.*

WHERE TO STAY & EAT

$$–$$$$ ✕**U Královny Elišky.** With rooms named "The Musketeer" and "The Napoléon" and a menu full of wild game and fish, this 14th-century wine cellar–turned-restaurant plays on its historic roots. In summer the historic ambience gets kicked up a notch as the garden becomes an arena for fencers in historical dress crossing swords while spectators enjoy roast suckling pig or lamb. The adjacent pension (¢) offers eight reasonably comfortable rooms at a good price (rates double during major trade fairs, however). ⊠*Mendlovo nám. 1A, 603 00* ☎*543–212–578 restaurant, 543–216–898 pension* ▤*No credit cards* ☉*Restaurant closed Sun. and Mon. No lunch.*

$–$$ ✕**Restaurace Špalíček.** This homey pub with a terrific central location is right on the edge of the Zelný trh (Cabbage Market). The menu features the standard roast pork and dumplings kind of thing, but in a comfortable and merry setting. On a warm evening in summer sit outside and bask in the view on the square. ⊠*Zelný trh 12* ☎*542–211–526* ▤*No credit cards.*

$–$$ ✕**Taj.** Ethnic food in Brno is rarely attempted. This Indian eatery hidden upstairs in a Victorian house creates a nice atmosphere and delicious samosas. Once you cross the tiny bridge over a man-made indoor stream, you can sit in the Indian-theme main room and choose from the vegetarian or meat dishes. Some dishes can be prepared on a lava grill, which is brought out to your table. Lunch specials are a real value. ⊠*Běhounská 12/14* ☎*542–214–372* ▤*AE, DC, MC, V.*

$ ✕**Zemanova kavárna.** A contemporary re-creation of a landmark 1920s coffeehouse (the original was razed by the Communists to make way for a theater), this spot is high on flapper style. Everything from the light fixtures to the furniture was faithfully copied from the original interior. The lofty ceilings provide pleasant, lilting acoustics, and the food isn't bad either: the few main courses are Czech with a dash of French, such as pepper steak with fries. ⊠*Jezuitská 6, between Za Divadlem and Koliště* ☎*542–217–509* ▤*DC, MC, V.*

$$–$$$ ▣**Grandhotel Brno.** If you are traveling to Brno by train, this hotel makes a fine choice, being just across the street from the station. The hotel dates from 1870, but got a thorough face-lift in the late 1980s, making it both comfortable and convenient. High standards are maintained through the hotel's association with an Austrian chain. Service is attentive; the rooms, though small, are well appointed, with coffered ceilings and leather sofas. Ask for a room at the back, facing the town and away from the station. ⊠*Benešova 18/20, 657 83* ☎*542-518–138* 🖶*542–210–345* ⊕*www.grandhotelbrno.cz* ⇋*116 rooms* ⚘*In-room: no a/c, Ethernet. In-hotel: 3 restaurants, gym, some pets allowed, public Wi-Fi* ⊟*AE, DC, MC, V* ⦿⊫*BP.*

$$–$$$
Fodor's Choice
★

🏨**Royal Ricc.** Lovingly restored from a baroque town house, this boutique hotel retains period details, like exposed-beam ceilings. Some of the rooms even have functional stoves made with tiles. The location is central, just a short stroll up from the Zelný trh (Cabbage Market). ⊠*Starobrněnská 10, 602 00* ☎*542–219–262* 🖶*542–219–265* ⊕*www.romantichotels.cz* ⇋*30 rooms* ⚘*In-room: refrigerator, safe, Wi-Fi. In-hotel: restaurant, public Wi-Fi* ⊟*AE, DC, MC, V* ⦿⊫*BP.*

★ **$**

🏨**Hotel Pegas.** A little inn with a reasonable price and central location, Pegas has plain rooms that are snug and clean, with wood paneling and down comforters. The staff is helpful, friendly, and even speaks English. An in-house microbrewery and restaurant will have beer lovers doing their sightseeing at the bottom of a tasty mug of lager. ⊠*Jakubská 4, 602 00* ☎*542–210–104* 🖶*542–211–232* ⊕*www.hotelpegas. cz* ⇋*14 rooms* ⚘*In-room: no a/c. In-hotel: restaurant, bar, some pets allowed, refrigerator* ⊟*DC, MC, V* ⦿⊫*BP.*

$

🏨**Slavia.** The century-old Slavia, just off the main Česká ulice, feels a little dated, but the prices here are lower than at the comparable Grandhotel and the location is excellent. The rooms are spacious and clean. Ask to see a few before choosing since they are not uniform. The café, with adjacent terrace, is a good place to enjoy a cool drink on a warm afternoon. ⊠*Solniční 15/17, 622 16* ☎*542–321–249* 🖶*542–211–769* ⊕*www.slaviabrno.cz* ⇋*81 rooms* ⚘*In-room: no a/c, safe. In-hotel: restaurant, no-smoking rooms, some pets allowed* ⊟*AE, DC, MC, V* ⦿⊫*BP.*

NIGHTLIFE & THE ARTS

Brno is renowned throughout the Czech Republic for its theater and performing arts. Jacket-and-tie cultural events take place at a few main venues, both slightly northwest of the center of town, a five-minute walk from náměstí Svobody. Check the schedules at the theaters or pick up a copy of *Do města/Downtown*, Brno's free fortnightly bulletin of cultural events.

In Brno you can buy tickets for performing arts productions at individual theater box offices or at the central **Předprodej vstupenek** (*Ticket office* ⊠*Běhounská 17*).

One of the country's best-known fringe theater companies, **Divadlo Husa na provázku** (*Goose on a String Theater* ⊠*Zelný třída 9, at Petrská ulice* ☎*542–123–425*), has its home in Brno. Opera and ballet productions are held at the modern **Janáček Theater** (⊠*Rooseveltova 7* ☎*542–158–111*). The **Mahen Theater** (⊠*Rooseveltova 1* ☎*542–158–111*) is the city's principal venue for dramatic theater.

A few blocks north of the city center, **Klub Alterna** (⊠*Kounicova 48* ☎*541–212–091*) hosts good Czech jazz and folk performers.

SHOPPING

Bright red, orange, and yellow flower patterns are the signature folk pottery look in Moravia. You can find these products in stores and hotel gift shops throughout the region. For sophisticated artwork, including paintings and photography, stop by **Ambrosiana** (⊠ *Jezuitská 11* 🕾🕾 *542–214–439*). For rare books, art monographs, old prints, and a great selection of avant-garde 1920s periodicals, stop by **Antikvariát Alfa** (⊠ *Jánská 11, in arcade* 🕾 *542–211–947*). English-language paperbacks and art books are sold at **Knihkupectví Jiří Šedivý** (⊠ *Masarykova 6* 🕾 *542–215–456*). **S: Lukas** (⊠ *Kapucínské nám. 5* 🕾 *542–221–358*) stocks handmade textiles, ceramics, and glass.

SOUTHERN MORAVIA ESSENTIALS

BUS TRAVEL

Brno, a regional transport hub, is the best base from which to head off into southern Moravia. Most buses arrive at the main bus station, a 10-minute walk from the train station. Some buses stop next to the train station. There are also frequent direct bus connections from Prague to Jihlava (two hours); the bus journey to the other towns on the tour will take three to five hours from Prague.

Getting around the region is more difficult. In general, buses run sporadically, especially on weekends. If you're planning a day trip or two, Mikulov may be the best base, as there is regular bus service to Lednice, Valtice, and Brno.

Information Main bus station (ÚAN Zvonařka ⊠ *Zvonařka 1* 🕾 *543–217–733*).

CAR TRAVEL

Southern Moravia is within easy driving distance of Prague and Bratislava. Jihlava is 124 km (75 mi) southeast of Prague along the excellent D1/E65 freeway. From here, it's easy to continue to Brno, or to take the E59, which goes down to Vranov and Znojmo. Southern Moravia is also easily reached by car from Austria; there are major border crossings at Háté (below Znojmo) and Mikulov.

PUBLIC TRANSPORTATION

Trams are the best way to get around the city. Tickets cost 7 Kč–19 Kč, depending on the time and zones traveled, and are available at newsstands, yellow ticket machines, or from the driver. Single-day, three-day, and other long-term tickets are available. Most trams stop in front of the main station (Hlavní nádraží). Buses to the city periphery and nearby sights such as Moravský Kras in northern Moravia congregate at the main bus station, a 10-minute walk behind the train station. To find it, simply go to the train station and follow the signs to ČSAD.

TAXIS

The nominal taxi fare is about 18 Kč per km (½ mi). There are taxi stands at the main train station, Výstaviště exhibition grounds, and on Joštova Street at the north end of the Old Town. Dispatchers tend not to understand English.

TRAIN TRAVEL

Six comfortable EuroCity or InterCity trains daily make the three-hour run from Prague to Brno's station. They depart either from Prague's main station, Hlavní nádraží, or the suburban nádraží Holešovice. Trains leaving Prague for Bratislava, Budapest, and Vienna normally stop in Brno (check timetables to be sure).

Train Stations Hlavní nádraží (⊠ *Nádražní 1* ☎ *542–214–803* ⊕ *www.jizd-nirady.cz*).

VISITOR INFORMATION

Information Brno Tourist Information (⊠ *Radnická 8, Old Town Hall* ☎ *542–423–960* ⊕ *www.ticbrno.cz* ⊠ *Nádražní 8, across from train station* ☎ *542–211–090*).

Mikulov Tourist Information (⊠ *Nám. 1, Mikulov* ☎ *625–510–855* ⊕ *www.mikulov.cz*). **Telč Tourist Information** (⊠ *Nám. Zachariáše z Hradce 10, Telč* ☎ *567–724–3145* ⊕ *www.telc-etc.cz*). **Valtice Tourist Information** (⊠ *Nám. Svobody 4, Valtice* ☎ *519–352–977* ⊕ *www.valtice.cz*).

OLOMOUC

★ *77 km (48 mi) northeast of Brno; 275 km (165 mi) east of Prague.*

Olomouc (pronounced OH-LOH-MOATS) is a handsome district capital, with some beautifully restored baroque houses along its broad central squares and the country's largest trinity column—another UNESCO World Heritage Site. Its laid-back, small-town feel, compared with bustling Brno, and the presence of a charming, inexpensive pension right in town make it an easy choice for an overnight stay.

Olomouc owes its relative prosperity to its loyalty to the Austro-Hungarian empire. In the revolutionary days of the mid-19th century, when the rising middle classes throughout the empire were asserting their independence from the nobility, the residents of Olomouc remained true to the ruling Habsburgs. During the revolutions of 1848, the royal family even fled here from Vienna for protection. Mozart, Mahler, and other famous composers stopped by on occasion, leaving behind a musical heritage that is still alive today with an active classical music scene.

The most prominent open space in Olomouc is the triangular Horní náměstí (Upper Square). Four of the city's half-dozen renowned **baroque fountains,** depicting Hercules (1687), Caesar (1724), Neptune (1695), and Jupiter (1707), dot the square and the adjacent other large square, Dolní náměstí (Lower Square) to the south.

A discount card called the **Olomouc Region Card** is valid for most tourist sites in and around the city and is available for 160 Kč for 48 hours. Admission to the Town Hall tower, botanical gardens, zoo, Hrad Bouzov, Hrad Šternberk, and other sites is included. The card also provides discounts at some restaurants, pools, fitness centers, and hotels. You can buy the card—and get more information on discounts and deals—at the main tourist information center at Horní náměstí 1.

Fodor's Choice   The eccentric **Morový sloup** *(Trinity Column),* in the northwest corner
★   of Horní náměstí, is one of the best surviving examples of the Olomouc baroque style, which was prevalent in this region of Moravia after the Thirty Years' War in the 17th century. At 115 feet, it's the tallest column devoted to victims of the plague in the Czech Republic. The column alone (not the rest of the square) is a UNESCO World Heritage Site. Its construction began in 1717, but it was not completed until 1754, long after the death of its principal designer, Václav Render, who left all his wealth to the city of Olomouc so that the column could be finished. Inside is a small chapel that, unfortunately, is never open. ⊠*Horní nám.*

Olomouc's central square is marked by the bright, spire-bedecked Renaissance **Radnice** *(Town Hall)* with its 220-foot tower. The tower was constructed in the late 14th century. The Astronomical Clock on the outside was built in 1422 and once rivaled the one in Prague. It was mostly destroyed by an artillery shell on the last two days of World War II. The modern Socialist-Realist mosaic decorations of the current clock date from 1955. Be sure to look inside the town hall at the beautiful stairway. You can also visit a large Gothic banquet room in the main building, with scenes from the city's history, and a late-Gothic chapel. Tours of the tower and chapel are given several times daily; contact the tourist office in the town hall. ⊠*Horní nám.* ☎*585–513–385 tourist office* ✉*Tours 20 Kč* ☉*Mar.–Oct., daily 9–7; Nov.–Feb., daily 9–5.*

NEED A BREAK?   Wood paneling and floral upholstery in the **Café Mahler** (⊠*Horní nám. 11)* recall the taste of the 1880s, when Gustav Mahler briefly lived around the corner while working as a conductor at the theater on the other side of the Upper Square. It's a good spot for ice cream, cake, or coffee, or simply to sit back and take in the lovely square.

The original **Chrám svatého Mořice** *(Church of St. Maurice)* stood just north of the Horní náměstí in 1257, but nothing is left of that structure. A new church was started in 1412 on the same site and remodeled many times. Its current fierce, gray exterior dates from the middle of the 16th century. A sculpture of Christ on the Mount of Olives dates to the 15th century. The baroque organ inside, the largest in the Czech Republic, originally contained 2,311 pipes until it was expanded in the 1960s to more than 10,000 pipes. An international organ festival takes place in the church every September. ⊠*Jana Opletalova ul.* ☉*Hrs are sporadic, but church is often open during day.*

The interior of triple-dome **Kostel svatého Michala** *(St. Michael's Church)* casts a dramatic spell. The frescoes, the high and airy central dome, and the shades of rose, beige, and gray trompe-l'oeil marble on walls and arches work in concert to present a harmonious whole. The decoration followed a fire in 1709, only 30 years after the original construction. The architect and builder are not known, but it's surmised they are the same team that put up the Church of the Annunciation on Svatý Kopeček (Holy Hill), a popular Catholic pilgrimage site just outside Olomouc. ⊠ *Žerotínovo nám., 1 block uphill from Horní nám., along Školní ul.* ⊙ *Hrs are sporadic, but church is often open during day.*

Between the main square and the **Dóm svatého Václava** *(Cathedral of St. Wenceslas)* lies a peaceful neighborhood given over to huge buildings, mostly belonging either to the university or the archbishop. The church itself is impressive, but its Gothic appearance comes only from a 19th-century makeover. ⊠ *Václavské nám.* ⊙ *Daily 9–6.*

★ Next to the Cathedral of St. Wenceslas is the small entrance to the **Palác Přemyslovců** *Přemyslid Palace)*, which houses a museum where you can see early-16th-century wall paintings decorating the Gothic cloisters and, upstairs, a wonderful series of two- and three-arch Romanesque windows. This part of the building was used as a schoolroom some 700 years ago, and you can still make out drawings of animals engraved on the walls by young vandals. ⊠ *Václavské nám.* ⊠*40 Kč* ⊙ *Apr.–Oct., Tues.–Sun. 9–12:30 and 1–5.*

At the **Děkanství** *(Deacon's House)* in 1767, the young musical prodigy Wolfgang Amadeus Mozart, age 11, spent six weeks recovering from a mild attack of chicken pox. The 16-year-old King Wenceslas III suffered a much worse fate here in 1306, when he was murdered, putting an end to the Přemyslid dynasty. These two unusual claims to fame build the mystery of this house, but sadly, it isn't open to the public. ⊠ *Václavské nám.*

★ **Hrad Bouzov** *(Bouzov Castle)*. One of Moravia's most impressive castles—30 km (18 mi) west of Olomouc—has been featured in several fairy-tale films. Its present romanticized exterior comes from a remodeling at the turn of the 20th century, but the basic structure dates back to the 1300s. Owned by the Order of Teutonic Knights from the late 1600s up to the end of World War II, it was later confiscated by the state. Inside, the knights' hall has extensive carved-wood decorations and wall paintings that look old, even if many are reconstructions. Other rooms have collections of period furniture. The castle kitchen, which was used up to 1945, is one of the best-preserved examples. Four tours are available, with the grand tour offering most of the highlights. The supplementary tour (doplňková trasa) includes a secret passage. You can easily arrange a tour from the tourist information office in Olomouc; the castle is included in the Olomouc card. ⊠*Bouzov 8, Bouzov* ☎*585–346–201* ⊠*Classic tour 100 Kč, grand tour 140 Kč* ⊙ *Apr. and Oct., weekends 9–3; May–Sept., Tues.–Sun. 9–4.*

WHERE TO STAY & EAT

$–$$$ ✕**Moravská restaurace a vinárná.** Traditional Moravian dishes like roast duck with cabbage, chicken breast stuffed with almond butter, and roast piglet are served in a rustic interior. The wine cellar, open weekdays, is a bit homier than the street-level restaurant. The staff wears folk costumes, and live musicians sometimes perform folk music of the region. International wines are available alongside a large selection of Moravian wine. ✉*Horní nám. 23* ☎*585–222–868* ▭*AE, MC, V.*

$–$$ ✕**Hanácká Hospoda.** Offering a lower-key, cheaper dining alternative to the Moravská, this popular local pub serves staples like pork, chicken, and duck, but nicely turned out. A quieter, no-smoking room is available at the back. According to an inscription on the outside of the house, Mozart stayed here as a young boy on a trip with his parents. ✉*Dolní nám. 38* ☎*585–237–186* ▭*AE, MC, V.*

$–$$ ⊞**Flora.** The words "traditional Communist-era hotel" don't evoke comfort, but this one was made much more inviting with a thorough makeover of the lobby and public areas. The rooms are small but clean, and the price is reasonable. It's a 15-minute walk from the main square. ✉*Krapkova 34, 779 00* ☎*585–422–200* 🖶*585–421–211* ⊕*www.hotel-flora.cz* ⥲*140 rooms, 4 suites* &*In-room: no a/c. In-hotel: restaurant, some pets allowed, no elevator* ▭*AE, DC, MC, V* ¶⊙*BP.*

★ $ ⊞**U Dómu.** Each of the rooms in this quiet, family-run pension just off Vaclavské náměstí sleeps up to four and has a small kitchenette. Modern furnishings are somewhat dull, but the cleanliness of the rooms and the friendliness of the staff make up for it. It's an excellent value. ✉*Dómská 4, 772 00* ☎*585–220–502* 🖶*585–220–501* ⥲*6 rooms* &*In-room: no a/c, kitchen. In-hotel: no elevator* ▭*AE, MC, V* ¶⊙*BP.*

OLOMOUC ESSENTIALS

TRANSPORTATION

Olomouc lies about an hour by car or train from Brno. The drive is quick and comfortable mostly along a four-lane highway. Follow the signs to Olomouc on the D1 highway.

Traveling from Prague, in addition to driving, you can take either a train or a bus. By car, follow the D1 motorway south to Brno and then follow the signs and turnoffs to Olomouc from Brno. The trip will take about three hours in moderate traffic.

Direct train travel from Prague takes at least 3¼ hours and costs around 300 Kč for the 250-km (150-mi) trip.

Direct bus service from Prague's Florenc bus station takes between four and five hours and costs around 170 Kč for the 262-km (157-mi) trip. Bus service with a change in Brno can be faster, however, at 3½ hours; the 300-km (180-mi) trip costs about 280 Kč.

VISITOR INFORMATION

Information **Olomouc Tourist Information** (✉*Radnice, Horní nám., Olomouc* ☎*585-513-385* ⊕*www.olomouc-tourism.cz*).

CZECH REPUBLIC ESSENTIALS

TRANSPORTATION

AIR TRAVEL
Almost all international flights go into Prague, with a few budget flights now landing in Brno. Central Connect flies from Ostrava to Vienna, though it's usually more cost-effective to drive or take a bus or train. Czech Airlines, the main carrier in the country, also flies to Ostrava and Brno.

ČSA (Czech Airlines), the Czech national carrier, offers the only direct flights from New York (JFK) to Prague, with six flights a week most times (daily flights during the busiest season). It's also possible to connect through a major European airport and continue to Prague. The flight from New York to Prague takes about 8 hours; from the West Coast, including a stopover, 12 to 16 hours. Go Airways, easyJet and others offer discount flights to Prague from Britain. Another way to save money is either changing flights in Frankfurt or catching a bus from Frankfurt to Prague.

Major Carriers Air Canada (☎ *224–810–181*). **Air France** (☎ *224–227–164*). **Alitalia** (☎ *224–194–150*). **Austrian Airlines** (☎ *224–826–199*). **American Airlines** (☎ *224–234–985*). **British Airways** (☎ *222–114–444*). **British Midland** (☎ *224–810–180*). **ČSA** (☎ *220–104–310* ⊕ *www.csa.cz*). **Delta** (☎ *224–946–733*). **EasyJet** (☎ *No telephone* ⊕ *www.easyjet.com*). **Go** (☎ *296–333–333* ⊕ *www.go-fly.com*). **KLM** (☎ *233–090–933*). **Lufthansa** (☎ *224–811–007*). **SAS** (☎ *220–114–456*). **Swiss** (☎ *224–812–211*).

Small Carriers Central Connect (☎ *597–471–466* ⊕ *www.centralconnectairlines.eu*). **ČSA** (☎ *220–104–310* ⊕ *www.csa.cz*).

AIRPORTS
Almost all international flights to the Czech Republic fly into Prague's Ruzyně Airport, which is about 20 km (12 mi) northwest of downtown. Recently, Brno airport has begun offering limited direct flights to London, Barcelona, and a few other cities. Ostrava airport handles domestic flights almost exclusively.

Airports Brno-Turany Airport (☎ *545–521–136* ⊕ *www.airport-brno.cz*). **Ruzyně Airport** (☎ *220–113–314* ⊕ *www.prg.aero*).

BUS TRAVEL
Several bus companies run direct services between major Western European cities and Prague. The Czech Republic's extremely comprehensive state-run bus service, ČSAD, is usually much quicker than the normal trains and more frequent than express trains, unless you're going to the major cities. Prices are quite low—essentially the same as those for second-class rail tickets. Buy your tickets from the ticket window at the bus station or directly from the driver on the bus. Buses can be full to bursting. On long-distance trips, it's a good idea to buy advance tickets when available (indicated by an "R" in a circle on timetables); get them at the local station or at some travel agencies. The only draw-

back to traveling by bus is figuring out the timetables. They are easy to read, but beware of the small letters denoting exceptions to the times given. If in doubt, inquire at the information window or ask someone for assistance.

Bus Lines **ČSAD** (✆ 222–630–851 in Prague ⊕ www.jizdnirady.cz). **Eurolines** (✆ 224–218–680 ⊕ www.eurolines.com).

CAR RENTALS

There are no special requirements for renting a car in the Czech Republic, but be sure to shop around, as prices can differ greatly. Major firms like Avis and Hertz offer Western makes starting at around $45 per day or $300 per week, which includes insurance, damage waiver, and VAT (value-added tax); cars equipped with automatic transmission and air-conditioning are available, but it's best to reserve your rental car before you leave home, and it may be less expensive as well. Smaller local companies, on the other hand, can rent Czech cars for significantly less, but the service and insurance coverage may be inferior. A surcharge of 5%–12% applies to rental cars picked up at Prague's Ruzyně Airport.

Major Agencies **Avis** (✉ Ruzyně Airport, Ruzyně ✆ 220–114–270 ✉ Klimentská 46, Nové Město ✆ 221–851–225). **Budget** (✉ Ruzyně Airport, Ruzyně ✆ 220–113–253 ✉ Hotel Inter-Continental, Curieových nám. 5, Staré Město ✆ 224–889–995). **Europcar** (✉ Ruzyně Airport, Ruzyně ✆ 235–364–531 ✉ Pařížská 28, Staré Město ✆ 224–811–290). **Hertz** (✉ Ruzyně Airport, Ruzyně ✆ 220–114–340 ✉ Karlovo nám. 28, Nové Město ✆ 222–231–010 ✉ Diplomat hotel, Evropská 15, Dejvice ✆ 224–394–175).

CAR TRAVEL

Traveling by car is the easiest and most flexible way of seeing the Czech Republic; however, if you intend to visit only the capital, you can do without a car. The city center is congested and difficult to navigate, and you'll save yourself a lot of hassle by sticking to public transportation.

A permit is required to drive on expressways and other four-lane highways. They cost 200 Kč for one week, 300 Kč for one month, and 900 Kč for one year and are sold at border crossings, some service stations, and all post offices.

In case of an accident or breakdown, see Emergencies, below.

ROAD CONDITIONS

The Prague city center is mostly a snarl of traffic, one-way streets, and tram lines. If you plan to drive outside the capital, there are few four-lane highways, but most of the roads are in reasonably good shape, and traffic is usually light. Roads can be poorly marked, however, so before you start out, buy one of the inexpensive multilingual auto atlases available at any bookstore.

RULES OF THE ROAD

The Czech Republic follows the usual Continental rules of the road. A right turn on red is permitted only when indicated by a green arrow. Signposts with yellow diamonds indicate a main road where drivers have the right of way. The speed limit is 130 kph (78 mph) on four-lane highways, 90 kph (56 mph) on open roads, and 50 kph (30 mph) in built-up areas. Seat belts are compulsory, and drinking before driving is absolutely prohibited. Passengers under 12 years of age, or less than 150 cm (5 feet) in height, must ride in the backseat.

TRAIN TRAVEL

You can take a direct train from Paris via Frankfurt to Prague (daily) or from Berlin via Dresden to Prague (five times a day). Vienna is a good starting point for Prague, Brno, or Bratislava. There are three trains a day from Vienna's Südbahnhof (South Station) to Prague (five hours). Southern Moravia and southern Bohemia are served by trains from Vienna and Linz.

The state-run rail system is called České dráhy (ČD). On longer runs, it's not really worth taking anything less than an express (*rychlík*) train, marked in red on the timetable. Tickets are still very inexpensive: a second-class ticket from Prague to Brno cost 182 Kč at this writing. First-class is considerably more spacious and comfortable and well worth the cost (50% more than a standard ticket). A 40 Kč–60 Kč supplement is charged for the excellent international expresses, EuroCity (EC) and InterCity (IC), and for domestic SuperCity (SC) schedules. A 20 Kč supplement applies to reserved seats on domestic journeys. If you haven't bought a ticket in advance at the station (mandatory for seat reservations), you can buy one aboard the train from the conductor. On timetables, departures (*odjezd*) appear on a yellow background; arrivals (*příjezd*) are on white. It is possible to book sleepers (*lůžkový*) or the less-roomy couchettes (*lehátkový*) on most overnight trains.

Information České dráhy (*ČD* ☎ *224–224–200 information* ⊕ *www.cd.cz*).

RAIL PASSES

The Eurail Pass and the Eurail Youthpass are not valid for travel within the Czech Republic, and most rail passes, such as the Czech Flexipass, will wind up costing more than what you'd spend buying tickets on the spot, particularly if you intend to travel mainly in the Czech Republic, since international tickets normally are more expensive. The European East Pass, for example, is good for first-class travel on the national railroads of the Czech Republic, Austria, Hungary, Poland, and Slovakia. The pass allows five days of unlimited travel within a one-month period for $199, and it must be purchased from Rail Europe before your departure.

Information Rail Europe (✉ *226–230 Westchester Ave., White Plains, NY 10604* ☎ *877/257–2887* ⊕ *www.raileurope.com* ✉ *2087 Dundas E, Suite 106, Mississauga, Ontario, Canada L4X 1M2* ☎ *800/361–7245*).

CONTACTS & RESOURCES

ADDRESSES

Navigation is relatively simple once you know the basic street-sign words: *ulice* (street, abbreviated to ul., commonly dropped in printed addresses); *náměstí* (square, abbreviated to nám.); and *třída* (avenue).

In most towns, each building has two numbers, a confusing practice with historic roots. In Prague, the blue tags mark the street address (usually); in Brno, ignore the blue tags and go by the white ones.

BANKS & EXCHANGE SERVICES

The Czech Republic is still generally a bargain by Western standards. Prague remains the exception. Hotel prices in particular are often higher than the facilities would warrant, but prices at tourist resorts outside the capital are lower and, in the outlying areas and off the beaten track, very low. Unfortunately, many museums, castles, and certain clubs charge a higher entrance fee for foreigners than they charge for Czechs. A few hotels still follow this practice, too.

CREDIT CARDS

Visa, MasterCard, and American Express are widely accepted by major hotels and stores, Diners Club less so. Smaller establishments and those off the beaten track are less likely to accept a wide variety of credit cards.

Lost Credit Cards American Express (☎ *336–393–111*). **Diners Club** (☎ *267–314–485*). **MasterCard** (☎ *261–354–650*). **Visa** (☎ *224–125–353*).

CURRENCY

The unit of currency in the Czech Republic is the koruna, or crown (Kč), which is divided into 100 haléřů, or hellers. There are (little-used) coins of 50 hellers; coins of 1, 2, 5, 10, 20, and 50 Kč; and notes of 50, 100, 200, 500, 1,000, 2,000, and 5,000 Kč. Notes of 1,000 Kč and up may not always be accepted for small purchases.

CURRENCY EXCHANGE

Try to avoid exchanging money at hotels or private exchange booths, including the ubiquitous Chequepoint and Exact Change booths. They routinely take commissions of 8%–10%. The best places to exchange are at bank counters, where the commissions average 1%–3%, or at ATMs. The koruna is fully convertible, which means it can be purchased outside the country and exchanged into other currencies. Of course, never change money with people on the street. Not only is it illegal, but you will almost definitely be ripped off.

At this writing the exchange rate was around 21 Kč to the U.S. dollar, 19 Kč to the Canadian dollar, 42 Kč to the pound sterling, and 28 Kč to the euro.

EMBASSIES & CONSULATES

Information **U.S. Embassy** (✉ *Tržiště 15, Malá Strana, Prague* ☎ *257–022–000* ⊕ *www.usembassy.cz*).

EMERGENCIES

Emergency roadside assistance is offered by the Central Automobile Club and the Autoklub Bohemia Assistance unit, both of which operate 24 hours. There is also a general number to call if you have a breakdown on a highway and need assistance.

Information **Police** (☎*158*). **Ambulance** (☎*155*). **Autoklub Bohemia Assistance** (☎*1240* ⊕ *www.aba.cz*). **Fire** (☎*150*). **ÚAMK Emergency Roadside Assistance** (☎*1230* ⊕ *www.uamk.cz*).

LANGUAGE

Czech, a Slavic language closely related to Slovak and Polish, is the official language of the Czech Republic. Learning English is popular, but German is still a useful language for tourists, especially outside Prague.

INTERNET, MAIL & SHIPPING

With the recent spread of affordable, broadband Internet at home and a number of Wi-Fi hot spots, Czech Internet cafés are not nearly as popular as they were in the dark days of the nineties. However, cafés in many small towns and a few Prague neighborhoods still have a few terminals, usually marked with a sign reading "Internet" or using the @ symbol. Expect to pay 60 Kč–100 Kč per hour. Standalone Wi-Fi hot spots in cafés are often free with purchase. Nationwide hot-spot networks are available from T-Mobile (⊕ *www.t-mobile.cz*) and O2 (⊕ *www.cz.o2.com*). Mobile phone users with a GSM handset should have no trouble connecting to Czech cellular networks with high international roaming rates. But if your handset uses a removable SIM card and is "unlocked," you can buy a Czech SIM card and make calls from a new, local Czech number, using the pay-as-you-go billing method. All three Czech mobile operators offer such services: Vodafone (⊕ *www.vodafone.cz*), T-Mobile (⊕ *www.t-mobile.cz*), and O2 (⊕ *www.cz.o2.com*). Expect to pay about 400 Kč for an SIM card and enough credit for several calls.

Information **Incentives CZ** (⊠ *Vřídelní 51* ☎ *353-226-027* ⊕ *www.incentives.cz*). **Prague Main Post Office** (⊠ *Jindřišská ul. 14* ⊕ *www.cpost.cz*).

PASSPORTS

United States citizens need only a valid passport to visit the Czech Republic as tourists. U.S. citizens may stay for 90 days without a visa.

TELEPHONES

The country code for the Czech Republic is 420. The country dropped regional codes and adopted a nationwide nine-digit standard in late 2002. Prefixes 601 to 777 denote mobile phones.

Now that most people have mobile phones, working phone booths are harder to find. If you can't find a booth, the telephone office of the main post office is the best place to try. Once inside, follow signs for TELEGRAF/TELEFAX.

INTERNATIONAL CALLS

The international dialing code is 00. For calls to the United States, Canada, or the United Kingdom, dial the international operator. Otherwise, ask the receptionist at any hotel to put a call through for you, but the surcharges and rates will be tremendously high.

With the prepaid Karta X (300 Kč–1,000 Kč), rates to the United States are roughly 13 Kč per minute; a call to the United Kingdom costs about 12 Kč per minute. The cards are available at many money-changing stands and can work with any phone once you enter a 14-digit code. You do not need to find a booth with a card slot to use the cards.

You can reach an English-speaking operator from one of the major long-distance services on a toll-free number. The operator will connect your collect or credit-card call at the carrier's standard rates. In Prague, many phone booths allow direct international dialing.

Long-Distance Access Numbers AT&T (☎ *0/042–000–101*). **BT Direct** (☎ *0/042–004–401*). **CanadaDirect** (☎ *0/042–000–151*). **MCI** (☎ *0/042–000–112*). **Sprint** (☎ *0/042–087–187*).

Information International Operator (☎ *133004*). **International Directory Assistance** (☎ *1181*).

LOCAL CALLS

Coin-operated pay phones are hard to find. Most newer public phones operate only with a special telephone card, available from post offices and some newsstands in denominations of 150 Kč and up. A short call within Prague costs a minimum of 4 Kč from a coin-operated phone or the equivalent of 3.5 Kč (1 unit) from a card-operated phone. The dial tone is a series of alternating short and long buzzes.

TIPPING

Service is usually not included in restaurant bills. Round the bill up to the next multiple of 10 (if the bill comes to 83 Kč, for example, give the waiter 90 Kč); 10% is considered appropriate in all but the most expensive places. Tip porters who bring bags to your rooms 40 Kč total. For room service, a 20 Kč tip is enough. In taxis, round the bill up by 10%. Give tour guides and helpful concierges between 50 Kč and 100 Kč for services rendered.

TOUR OPTIONS

Several Prague-based companies offer tours of the capital and other regions of the country. Čedok has a wide range of offerings, including driving and cycling tours. Precious Legacy Tours arranges tours to Jewish sites. Sportturist Special has regional and local tours and is the local office for Western Union. Wittmann Tours specializes in tours to sites of Jewish interest throughout the country and Central Europe. Contact Wolff Travel for regional and capital tours and international transportation tickets.

Tour Companies Čedok (✉ *Na Příkopě 18, Prague* ☎ *800–112–112* ⊕ *www. cedok.cz*). **Precious Legacy Tours** (✉ *Maiselova 16, Prague* ☎ *222–321–951* ⊕ *www.legacytours.cz*). **Sportturist Special** (✉ *Národní tř. 33, Prague* ☎ *222–075–343* ⊕ *www.sportturistspecial.cz*). **Wittmann Tours** (✉ *Manesova 8, Prague* ☎ *222–252–472* ⊕ *www.wittmann-tours.com*). **Wolff Travel** (✉ *Dykova 31, Prague* ☎ *222–511–333* ⊕ *www.wolff-travel.com*).

VISITOR INFORMATION

Most major towns have a local information office (Infocentrum or Informační středisko), usually in the central square and identified by a green-and-white sign with a lowercase "i" on the facade. These offices are often good sources for maps and guidebooks and can usually help you book hotel and private accommodations. In season (generally April through October), most are open during normal business hours and often on Saturday morning, sometimes even Sunday. In the winter, most are closed weekends. The Czech Tourist Authority, official provider of tourist information to the Czech Republic, has offices in the United States, Canada, Great Britain, European countries, and Japan, as well as in Prague. They stock maps and brochures on tourism outside Prague and dispense advice but do not book tickets or accommodations.

Information Czech Tourist Authority (✉ *Staroměstské nám. 6, Prague* ☎ *224– 810–411* ⊕ *www.visitczech.cz*).

5

Germany

BERLIN, DRESDEN, LEIPZIG

WORD OF MOUTH

"Berlin is fabulous. It is the only city in Europe without fixed closing hours, which means the nightlife makes New York City look like a church social."
—JP

"[I loved] the vastness of the Zwinger, especially the amazing collection of masterwork paintings in the Gemäldegalerie. I recall hearing a terrific lecture on the Sistine Madonna in that collection, which made the work appealing to me . . ."
—fritzrl

"Leipzig is highly recommended for fans of Bach or if you are interested in the East German citizen movements of 1989."
—Bird

Updated by
Lee A. Evans

GERMANY'S TRADITIONAL CHARM IS MOST evident in the eastern states, including Saxony and Saxony-Anhalt. The area, one of Europe's best-kept secrets, hides some cultural gems. A comfortable "German" state of mind exists here, the likes of which you will never find in West Germany. Communism never penetrated the culture here as deeply as the American influence did in West Germany. The German Democratic Republic (GDR—commonly referred to by its German initialism, DDR) resolutely clung to its German heritage, proudly preserving connections with such national heroes as Luther, Goethe, Schiller, Bach, Handel, Wagner, and the Hungarian-born Liszt.

The former East Germany is also worth visiting precisely because it is *still* a culture in transition. Since the fall of the Iron Curtain, no city in Europe has seen more development and change. Two Berlins that had been separated for 40 years struggled to meld into one, and in the scar of barren borderland between them sprang government and commercial centers that have become the glossy spreads of travel guides and architecture journals. After successfully uniting its own east and west, Berlin, as German capital and one of the continent's great cities, now plays a pivotal role in a European Union that has undertaken the same task.

But even as the capital thinks and moves forward, history is always tugging at its sleeve. Between the wealth of neoclassical and 21st-century buildings there are constant reminders, both subtle and stark, of the events of the 20th century. For every new embassy and relocated corporate headquarters, a church stands half ruined, a synagogue is under 24-hour guard, and an empty lot remains where a building either crumbled in World War II or went up in dynamite as East Germany cleared a path for its Wall. In the chillier months, the scent of coal wafts through the trendy neighborhoods of Prenzlauer Berg and Friedrichshain, where young residents who fuel the cultural scene heat their simple apartments with coal stoves.

The revolutions of 1989 began in the Saxon city of Leipzig. The now legendary *Montagsdemonstrationen* (Monday demonstrations) began as weekly prayers for peace and ended as mass protests in the streets. The prayers and demonstrations startled the East German government so much, especially after police sent in to break up the demonstrations joined in, that the regime collapsed without a shot being fired. Riding the euphoria of 1989, the two German states became one a mere two years after the "Wall" came tumbling down. This is not the end of the story, however. Both the East and West are still struggling with problems caused by the sudden unification of their country. In the former East Germany, the closing of factories, a shrunken welfare system, and the loss of many social benefits (like guaranteed child care) have left many jobless and disillusioned. In the former West, people are burdened by additional taxes (which East Germans must also pay) imposed to help rebuild the East and the dwindling resources to renovate their own infrastructure.

Though economic woes still haunt parts of the eastern region, a class of young entrepreneurs has transformed cities such as Leipzig and Dresden with a wave of start-up businesses. This is particularly impressive when you consider that Saxony's Dresden area was once nicknamed *Tal der Ahnungslosen* (Valley of the Clueless), as residents there couldn't receive Western television or radio signals. Eastern Germany used to move very slowly, but today the pace of cities such as Leipzig and Dresden has overtaken that of their West German counterparts.

EXPLORING BERLIN, DRESDEN & LEIPZIG

The new Berlin embraces a culturally promising but financially uncertain future. "Poor but sexy," a line coined by Klaus Wowereit, the flamboyant Governing Mayor, is the city's current state of mind. But unresolved problems such as unemployment rates of up to 16%, overstretched city budgets, and the loss of thousands of industrial jobs may just be too much even for a metropolis like Berlin. Two of Germany's most important historical cities are south of the country's newly restored capital. Dresden is promoting its reputation as the "Florence on the Elbe," and Leipzig, in particular, has washed off its grime and almost completely restored its historic city center.

ABOUT THE RESTAURANTS
The cuisine of the region is hearty and seasonal. Try *Gebratene Kalbsbrust* (roast veal breast), spicy *Thüringer Bratwurst* (sausage), *Schlesische Himmelreich* (ham and pork roast smothered in baked fruit and white sauce with dumplings), *Blauer Karpfe* (blue carp, marinated in vinegar), and *Harzer Handkäse* (a strong-smelling cheese). Lamb from Saxony-Anhalt is particularly good.

ABOUT THE HOTELS
Major international chain hotels are present in all three cities, some of them in restored, historic structures. Smaller and family-run hotels often combine a good restaurant with fairly good accommodations. In an effort to further improve tourism, most big hotels offer special (weekend) or activity-oriented packages that aren't found in the western part of the country, especially in Dresden and Leipzig.

WHAT IT COSTS IN EUROS				
	¢	$	$$	$$$	$$$$
RESTAURANTS	under €9	€9–€15	€16–€20	€21–€25	over €25
HOTELS	under €50	€50–€100	€101–€175	€176–€225	over €225

Restaurant prices are per person for a main course at dinner. Hotel prices are for two people in a standard double room, including tax and service.

TIMING
Winters in this part of Germany can be cold, wet, and dismal, so it's best to visit in late spring, summer, or early autumn. Avoid Leipzig at trade-fair times, particularly in March and April.

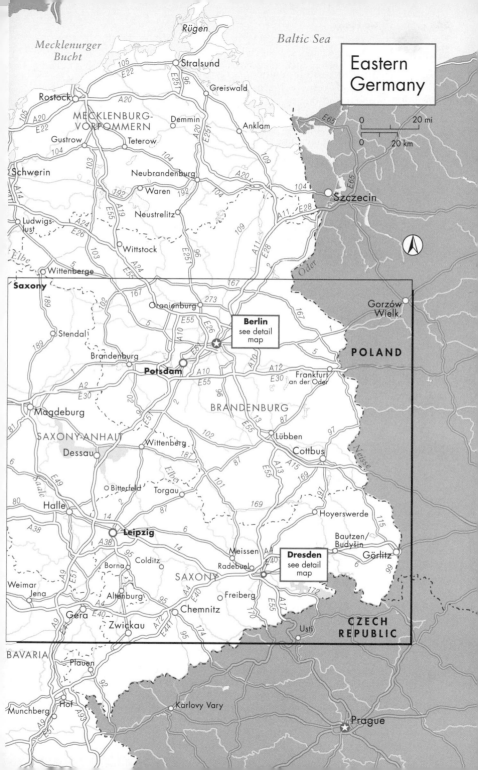

BERLIN

Updated
by Jürgen
Scheunemann

After successfully uniting its own east and west, Berlin, as German capital and one of the continent's great cities, now plays a pivotal role in a European Union that has undertaken the same task.

Compared with other German cities, Berlin is quite young and, ironically, began as two separate entities more than 770 years ago. The Spree River divided the slightly older Cölln on Museum Island from the fishing village Berlin. By the 1300s Berlin was prospering thanks to its location at the intersection of important trade routes. After the ravages of the Thirty Years' War, Berlin rose to power as the seat of the Hohenzollern dynasty. The Great Elector Friedrich Wilhelm, in the almost 50 years of his reign (1640–88), touched off a renaissance by supporting such institutions as the Academy of Arts and the Academy of Sciences. Later, Frederick the Great (1712–1786) made Berlin and Potsdam his glorious centers of the enlightened yet autocratic Prussian monarchy.

> ## GERMANY TOP 5
>
> ■ **Frauenkirche in Dresden:** The church is a worthy symbol of a city destroyed and rebuilt from its ashes.
>
> ■ **Coffee and Cake in Leipzig:** Take some time off from exploring the city to enjoy a Leipzig institution.
>
> ■ **Berlin's Museum Island:** The architectural monuments and art treasures here are well worth a day.
>
> ■ **The Reichstag's Cupola:** Spiral up the spectacular glass cupola to enjoy great views of central Berlin and the leafy Tiergarten.
>
> ■ **Trace History's Path:** Follow the cobblestone markers that remember the former Wall's path.

In 1871 Prussia, ruled by the "Iron Chancellor" Count Otto von Bismarck, unified the many independent German states into the German Empire. Berlin maintained its status as capital for the duration of the German Empire (1871–1918), through the post–World War I Weimar Republic (1919–33), and also through Hitler's so-called Third Reich (1933–45). The city's golden years were the Roaring '20s, when Berlin, the energetic, modern, and sinful counterpart to Paris, became a center for the cultural avant-garde. World-famous writers, painters, and artists met here while the impoverished bulk of its 4 million inhabitants lived in heavily overpopulated quarters. This "dance on the volcano," as those years of political and economic upheaval have been called, came to a grisly and bloody end after January 1933, when Adolf Hitler became chancellor. The Nazis made Berlin their capital but ultimately failed to remodel the city into a silent monument to their power. By World War II's end, 70% of the city lay in ruins, with more rubble than in all other German cities combined.

Along with the division of Germany after World War II, Berlin was partitioned into American, British, and French zones in the west and a Soviet zone in the east. By 1947 Berlin had become one of the Cold War's first testing grounds. The three western-occupied zones gradu-

GREAT ITINERARIES

IF YOU HAVE 2 DAYS

With only two days, limit yourself to Berlin. Begin in western, downtown Berlin by visiting the stark shell of the **Kaiser-Wilhelm-Gedächtnis-Kirche** (Kaiser Wilhelm Memorial Church). Catch the double-decker public Bus 100 (in front of the Zoo railway station) and get a seat on top. The entire scenic ride shows you the prime attractions in Berlin before doubling back again. Save a good amount of time and energy for the museums on **Museumsinsel** (Museum Island) and the **Deutsches Historisches Museum** (German History Museum). You can take a break with German cakes and coffee in the Opernpalais on Unter den Linden. On your second day visit the dome of the **Reichstag** and Potsdamer Platz, a study in urban renewal and modern architecture. Whatever order you do it in, walk along Ebertstrasse between the sights, as it takes you past the **Brandenburger Tor** (Brandenburg Gate) and the **Denkmal für die Ermordeten Juden Europas** (Memorial to the Murdered Jews of Europe). Behind the showy corporate buildings of Potsdamer Platz are the Gemäldegalerie (in the **Kulturforum**) and **Neue Nationalgalerie**, two outstanding fine-arts museums. From Potsdamer Platz it's a 10-minute walk to the **Topographie des Terrors** (Topography of Terror), a free, open-air exhibit on the organizations of the SS and the Gestapo, their crimes, and their victims. The site is bordered by a remaining stretch of the Berlin Wall, and **Mauermuseum-Museum Haus am Checkpoint Charlie** lies another 250 yards farther east. Spend one evening or some shopping hours meandering the smaller streets around Hackescher Markt in Mitte.

IF YOU HAVE 3 DAYS

Follow the two-day itinerary above. On your third day, round out the sights and eras of history you've seen by visiting the royals' apartments in **Schloss Charlottenburg** and the lovely gardens behind it. After touring the palace, hop the U-7 subway from Richard-Wagner-Platz to Adenauerplatz. Head east and browse through the most elegant of the boutiques within old city mansions along the **Kurfürstendamm**. Turn left on Bleibtreustrasse to reach the cafés and restaurants in the fashionable but casual Savignyplatz area. Spend one evening at a show, perhaps at Chämeleon Varieté or Bar Jeder Vernunft.

IF YOU HAVE 5 DAYS

Spend your fourth day and night in **Leipzig**, where Bach once resided. Continue southeast to spend a night in **Dresden**, with its impressive Zwinger complex and fine museums.

ally merged, becoming West Berlin, and the Soviet-controlled eastern zone defiantly remained separate. Peace conferences repeatedly failed to resolve the question of Germany's division, and in 1949 the Soviet Union established East Berlin as the capital of its new puppet state, the German Democratic Republic (GDR). The division of the city was cruelly finalized in concrete in August 1961, when the East German government erected the Berlin Wall, the only border fortification in history built to keep people from leaving rather than to protect them.

With the Wall relegated to the pile of history (most of it was recycled as street gravel), visitors can now appreciate the qualities that mark the city as a whole. Its particular charm has always lain in its spaciousness, its trees and greenery, and its anything-goes atmosphere. Moreover, the really stunning parts of the prewar capital are in the historic eastern part of town, which has grand avenues, monumental architecture, and museums that house world treasures.

Bristly Berliners deal with this and other challenges by resorting to their brash, witty, and often plain grumpy attitudes, coming across well with their piquant dialects. Whatever the bad press their bad moods might earn them, Berliners consider themselves a city of *"Herz mit Schnauze"* (a big heart hidden behind every big mouth).

Numbers in the text correspond to numbers in the margin and on the Berlin map.

EXPLORING BERLIN

Berlin is laid out on an epic scale—western Berlin alone is four times the size of the city of Paris. When the city-state of Berlin was incorporated in 1920, it swallowed towns and villages far beyond the downtown area. Of its 12 boroughs, the five of most interest to visitors are Charlottenburg-Wilmersdorf in the west; Tiergarten (a district of the Mitte borough) and Kreuzberg-Friedrichhain in the center; Mitte, the historic core of the city in the eastern part of town; and Prenzlauer Berg in the northeast. Southwest Berlin has lovely escapes in the secluded forests and lakes of the Grunewald area.

Many of the 17 Staatliche Museen zu Berlin (state museums of Berlin) are world-renowned and offer several ticket options (children under 17 are welcomed free of charge). A single ticket ranges €4–€8. A three-day pass (*Tageskarte*) to all state museums costs €15. The SchauLust Museen ticket (€15) allows entrance to all state museums plus many others for three consecutive days. State museums tend to cluster near one another, and usually a single entrance ticket grants admission to all museums in that area. These areas include Charlottenburg (€6), Dahlem (€6), the Kulturforum in Tiergarten, the out-of-the-way Hamburger Bahnhof in Moabit (€8), and Museum Island (€12) in Mitte. All these entrance tickets are for the permanent exhibitions and include an audio guide; special exhibits cost extra. ∎TIP➜ **State museums are free on Thursday for the last four open hours (there is a fee for the audio guide during free hours).**

KURFÜRSTENDAMM & WESTERN DOWNTOWN BERLIN

Ku'damm is the easy-to-pronounce nickname for Kurfürstendamm, a broad, tree-lined boulevard that stretches for 3 km (2 mi) through the heart of western downtown. It developed in the late 19th century as wealthy Berliners moved out to the "New West." Shoppers are the life force of the boulevard, with enough energy and euros to support the local boutiques on the quieter side streets, too. Out-of-towners take it easy at Ku'damm's sidewalk tables as Berliners bustle by with a purpose. The Ku'damm is most crowded on Saturday, and stores are not open on Sunday.

④ Kaiser-Wilhelm-Gedächtnis-Kirche *(Kaiser Wilhelm Memorial Church).* A dramatic reminder of World War II's destruction, the ruined bell tower is all that remains of the once massive church, which was completed in 1895 and dedicated to the emperor, Kaiser Wilhelm I. In stark contrast to the old bell tower (dubbed the Hollow Tooth) are the adjoining Memorial Church and Tower, designed by the noted German architect Egon Eiermann in 1959–61. These ultramodern octagonal structures, with their myriad honeycomb windows, have nicknames as well: the Lipstick and the Powder Box. Brilliant, blue stained glass from Chartres dominates the interiors. Church music and organ concerts are presented in the church regularly. ✉*Breitscheidpl., Western Downtown* ☎*030/218–5023* ⊕*www.gedaechtniskirche.de* ✆*Free* ☉*Old Tower Mon.–Sat. 10–6:30, Memorial Church daily 9–7* Ⓜ*Zoologischer Garten (U-bahn and S-bahn).*

NEED A BREAK? Forget the fast-food options at Zoo Station. Instead, follow the train tracks to the back of the taxi and bus queues, where you'll enter Tiergarten and within 100 yards come upon the best hideaway in the area: **Schleusenkrug** (✉*Tiergarten, Western Downtown* ☎*030/313–9909).* In warmer weather you can order at the window and sit in the beer garden or on the back patio, watching pleasure ships go through the lock. Inside is a casual restaurant with a changing daily menu. Between October and mid-March the Krug closes at 6 PM.

☺ ❸ The Story of Berlin. You can't miss this multimedia museum for the airplane wing exhibited outside. It was once part of a "Raisin bomber," a U.S. Air Force DC-3 that supplied Berlin during the Berlin Airlift in 1948 and 1949. Eight hundred years of the city's history, from the first settlers casting their fishing poles to Berliners heaving sledgehammers at the Wall, are conveyed through hands-on exhibits, film footage, and multimedia devices in this unusual venue. The sound of footsteps over broken glass follows your path through the exhibit on the *Kristallnacht* pogrom, and to pass through the section on the Nazis' book-burning on Bebelplatz, you must walk over book bindings. Many original artifacts are on display, such as the stretch Volvo that served as Erich Honnecker's state carriage in East Germany. ■TIP➔**The eeriest relic is the 1974 nuclear shelter, which you can visit by guided tour on the hour.** Museum placards are also in English. ✉*Ku'damm Karree, Kurfürstendamm 207–208, Western Downtown* ☎*030/8872–0100* ⊕*www.story-of-berlin.de* ✆*€9.80* ☉*Daily 10–8; last entry at 6* Ⓜ*Uhlandstrasse (U-bahn).*

★ ☺ ❺ Zoologischer Garten *(Zoological Gardens).* The little polar bear Knut, one of the few of this endangered species to be born in captivity, is a star attraction at Germany's oldest zoo; his sunny character beams from magazine covers around the globe. Home to more than 14,000 animals belonging to 1,500 different species (more than any other zoo in Europe), the zoo has been successful at breeding rare and endan-

6

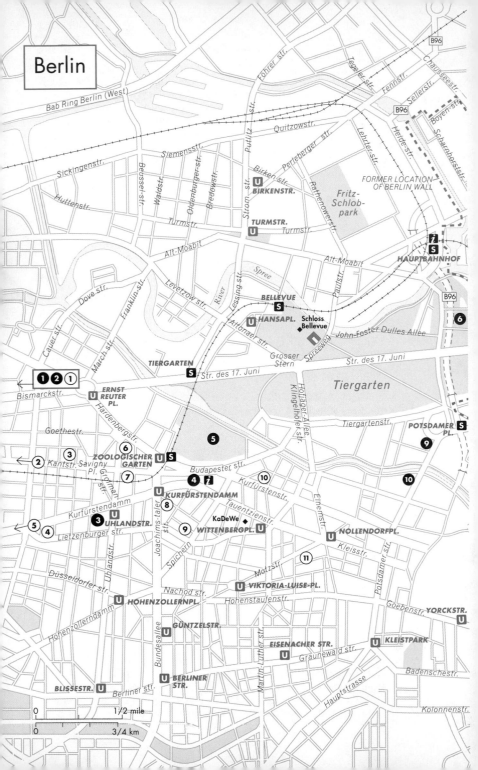

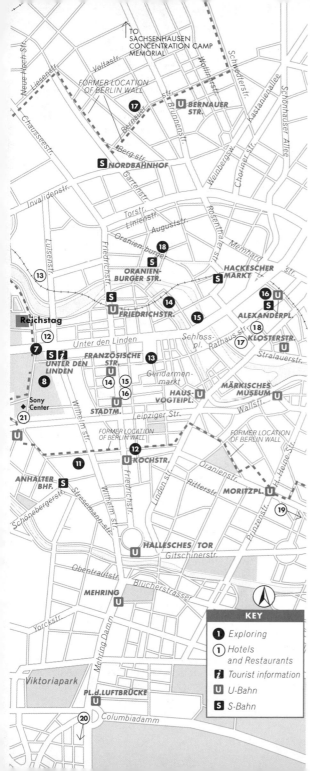

6

gered species. New arrivals in the past years include Ivo (a popular male gorilla), roadrunners, and a pair of Barbary lions. The animals' enclosures are designed to resemble their natural habitats, though some structures are ornate, such as the 1910 Arabian-style zebra house. Pythons, frogs, turtles, invertebrates, and Komodo dragons are part of the three-floor aquarium. ⊠ *Hardenbergpl. 8 and Budapester Str. 34, Western Downtown* ☎ *030/254–010* ⊕ *www.zoo-berlin.de* ☜ *Zoo or aquarium €11, combined ticket €16.50* ☉ *Zoo Nov.–mid-Mar., daily 9–5; mid-Mar.–mid-Oct., daily 9–6:30. Aquarium daily 9–6* Ⓜ *Zoologischer Garten (U-bahn and S-bahn).*

TIERGARTEN & THE GOVERNMENT DISTRICT

The Tiergarten, a bucolic 630-acre park with lakes, meadows, and wide paths, is the "green lung" of Berlin. In the 17th century it served as the hunting grounds of the Great Elector. Now it's the Berliners' backyard for sunbathing and barbecuing. Berlin's most fertile grounds for modern architecture—the government district, Potsdamer Platz, and the embassy district—ring the park from its eastern to southern edges. Many of the embassies have exhibitions open to the public, and Germany's parliament convenes beneath one of the city's most popular attractions: the glass dome of the Reichstag. Bordering Tiergarten and the government district is the meticulously restored Brandenburger Tor, the unofficial symbol of the city, and the Memorial to the Murdered Jews of Europe, whose design and scope engendered many debates.

❼ **Brandenburger Tor** *(Brandenburg Gate).* Once the pride of Prussian Ber-
Fodor'sChoice lin and the city's premier landmark, the Brandenburger Tor was left
★ in a desolate no-man's-land when the Wall was built. Since the Wall's dismantling, the sandstone gateway has become the scene of the city's Unification Day and New Year's Eve parties. This is the sole remaining gate of 14 built by Carl Langhans in 1788–91, designed as a triumphal arch for King Frederick Wilhelm II. Its virile classical style pays tribute to Athens's Acropolis. The quadriga, a chariot drawn by four horses and driven by the Goddess of Victory, was added in 1794. Troops paraded through the gate after successful campaigns—the last time in 1945, when victorious Red Army troops took Berlin. The upper part of the gate, together with its chariot and Goddess of Peace, was destroyed in the war. In 1957 the original molds were discovered in West Berlin, and a new quadriga was cast in copper and presented as a gift to the people of East Berlin. A tourist-information center is in the south part of the gate. ⊠ *Pariser Pl., Mitte* Ⓜ *Unter den Linden (S-bahn).*

❽ **Denkmal für die Ermordeten Juden Europas** *(Memorial to the Murdered Jews of Europe).* An expansive and unusual memorial dedicated to the 6 million Jews who were killed in the Holocaust, the monument was designed by American architect Peter Eisenman. The stunning place of remembrance consists of a grid of more than 2,700 concrete stelae, planted into undulating ground. The abstract memorial can be entered from all sides and offers no prescribed path. ■TIP➔**It's requested that you do not stand on any of the stelae, though you may sit on the lower ones.** An information center that goes into specifics about the Holocaust lies underground at the southeast corner. ⊠ *Cora-Berliner-Str. 1, Mitte*

☎*030/2639–4336* ⊕*www.holocaust-mahnmal.de* ✉*Free* ⊙*Daily 24 hrs; Information Center: Nov.–Feb., Tues.–Sun. 10–7; Mar.–Oct., Tues.–Sun. 10–8* Ⓜ*Unter den Linden (S-bahn).*

★ ⑥ **Reichstag** *(Parliament Building).* After last meeting here in 1933, the Bundestag, Germany's federal parliament, returned to its traditional seat in the spring of 1999. British architect Sir Norman Foster lightened up the gray monolith with a glass dome, which quickly became one of the city's main attractions: you can circle up a gently rising ramp while taking in the rooftops of Berlin and the parliamentary chamber below. At the base of the dome is an exhibit on the Reichstag's history, in German and English. ■**TIP➜ The best way to visit the Reichstag dome without waiting in line is to arrive at 8 AM, or to make a reservation for the pricey rooftop Käfer restaurant (** ☎*030/2262–9933***). Those with reservations can use the doorway to the right of the Reichstag's main staircase.** Completed in 1894, the Reichstag housed the imperial German parliament and later served a similar function during the ill-fated Weimar Republic. On the night of February 27, 1933, the Reichstag burned down in an act of arson, a pivotal event in Third Reich history. The fire led to state protection laws that gave the Nazis a pretext to arrest their political opponents. The Reichstag was rebuilt but again badly damaged in 1945. The graffiti of the victorious Russian soldiers can still be seen on some of the walls in the hallways. ✉*Pl. der Republik 1, Tiergarten* ☎*030/2273–2152, 030/2273–5908 Reichstag* ⌨*030/2273–0027 (Reichstag), 030/4000–1881 (Bundeskanzleramt)* ⊕*www.bundestag.de* ✉*Free* ⊙*Daily 8 AM–midnight; last admission 10 PM. Reichstag dome closes for 1 wk 4 times a yr* Ⓜ*Unter den Linden (S-bahn).*

POTSDAMER PLATZ & KREUZBERG

The once-divided capital is rejoined on Potsdamer Platz, which was Berlin's inner-city center and Europe's busiest plaza before World War II. Bombings and the wall system left this area a sprawling, desolate lot, where tourists in West Berlin could climb a wooden platform to peek into East Berlin's death strip. After the Wall fell, Sony, the former Daimler-Benz, Asea Brown Boveri, and other companies made a rush to build their headquarters on this prime real estate. A few narrow streets cut between the hulking modern architecture, which includes two high-rise office towers owned by DaimlerChrysler, one of which was designed by star architect Renzo Piano. The round atrium of the Sony Center comes closest to rendering a traditional square used as a public meeting point. Farther down Potsdamer Strasse are the state museums and cultural institutes of the Kulturforum.

Kreuzberg held the American side of the border-crossing Checkpoint Charlie, and is one of the liveliest districts in Berlin. A largely Turkish population shares the residential streets with a variegated assortment of political radicals and bohemians of all nationalities. There are few traditional attractions here, but it's a great place to people-watch.

★ ⑨ **Kulturforum** *(Cultural Forum).* This unique ensemble of museums, galleries, and the Philharmonic Hall was long in the making. The first designs were submitted in the 1960s and the last building completed in 1998. The **Gemäldegalerie** *(Picture Gallery)* reunites formerly separated collections from East and West Berlin. It's one of Germany's finest art galleries and has an extensive selection of European paintings from the 13th to the 18th century. Seven rooms are reserved for paintings by German masters, among them Dürer, Cranach the Elder, and Holbein. A special collection has works of the Italian masters—Botticelli, Titian, Giotto, Lippi, and Raphael—as well as paintings by Dutch and Flemish masters of the 15th and 16th centuries: Van Eyck, Bosch, Brueghel the Elder, and van der Weyden. The museum also holds the world's second-largest Rembrandt collection. ✉ *Matthäikirchpl. 4, Tiergarten* ☎ *030/266–2951* ⊕ *www.smb.museum* 💶 *€8* ⊙ *Tues., Wed., and Fri.– Sun. 10–6, Thurs. 10–10* Ⓜ *Potsdamer Platz (U-bahn and S-bahn).*

Steps away from the Gemäldegalerie are two examples of ultramodern architecture. Inside the **Kunstgewerbemuseum** *(Museum of Decorative Arts)* are European arts and crafts from the Middle Ages to the present. Among the notable exhibits are the Welfenschatz (Welfen Treasure), a collection of 16th-century gold and silver plates from Nürnberg, as well as ceramics and porcelains. ✉ *Matthäikirchpl. 4, Tiergarten* ☎ *030/266–2902* ⊕ *www.smb.museum* 💶 *€8* ⊙ *Tues.–Fri. 10–6, weekends 11–6.*

The mustard-yellow complex that resembles a great tent belongs to the **Philharmonie** (☎ *030/2548–8156*), home to the renowned Berlin Philharmonic Orchestra since 1963. The Philharmonie and the smaller Chamber Music Hall adjoining it were designed by Hans Scharoun. ■**TIP**➔ **There's a free tour of the Philharmonie daily at 1** PM. *Museum* ✉ *Tiergartenstr. 1, Tiergarten* ☎ *030/2548–1129* 💶 *€4, tour €2* ⊙ *Tues., Wed., and Fri. 9–5, Thurs. 9* AM*–10* PM*, weekends 10–5.*

★ ⑫ **Mauermuseum-Museum Haus am Checkpoint Charlie.** Just steps from the famous crossing point between the two Berlins, the Wall Museum— House at Checkpoint Charlie tells the story of the Wall and, even more riveting, the stories of those who escaped through, under, and over it. The homespun museum reviews the events leading up to the Wall's construction and, with original tools and devices, plus recordings and photographs, shows how East Germans escaped to the West (one of the most ingenious contraptions was a miniature submarine). Exhibits about human rights and paintings interpreting the Wall round out the experience. ■**TIP**➔ **Come early or late in the day to avoid the multitudes dropped off by tour buses.** Monday can be particularly crowded. ✉ *Friedrichstr. 43–45, Kreuzberg* ☎ *030/253–7250* ⊕ *www.mauermuseum.com* 💶 *€9.50* ⊙ *Daily 9* AM*–10* PM Ⓜ *Kochstrasse (U-bahn).*

NEED A BREAK? Try your best to conjure up an image of the Wall from a window seat at **Café Adler** (✉ *Friedrichstr. 206, Kreuzberg* ☎ *030/251–8965*), which once bumped right up against it. The quality fare is inexpensive and the soups are particularly delicious. Breakfast is served until 5 PM.

★ ⑩ **Neue Nationalgalerie** *(New National Gallery).* Bauhaus member Mies van der Rohe originally designed this glass-box structure for Bacardi Rum in Cuba, but Berlin became the site of its realization in 1968. The main exhibitions are below ground. Highlights of the 20th-century collection of paintings, sculptures, and drawings include works by expressionists Otto Dix, Ernst Ludwig Kirchner, and Georg Grosz. Special exhibits often take precedence over the permanent collection, however. ⊠*Potsdamer Str. 50, Tiergarten* ☎*030/266–2951* ⊕*www. smb.museum* ✆*€8* ☉*Tues., Wed., and Fri. 10–6, Thurs. 10–10, weekends 11–8* Ⓜ*Potsdamer Platz (U-bahn and S-bahn).*

★ ⑪ **Topographie des Terrors** *(Topography of Terror).* Within the cellar remains of the Nazis' Reich Security Main Office (which was composed of the SS, SD, and Gestapo), photos and documents explain the secret state police and intelligence organizations that planned and executed Nazi crimes against humanity. The fates of both perpetrators and victims are included in the free, open-air exhibit. Within a makeshift complex (a new documentation center is scheduled to be built in 2008), you can leaf through books and copies of official documents. Pick up a free audio guide here before viewing the exhibit. ⊠*Niederkirchnerstr. 8, Kreuzberg* ☎*030/2548–6703* ⊕*www.topographie.de* ✆*Free* ☉*Oct.– Apr., daily 10–5; May–Sept., daily 10–8.*

MITTE: UNTER DEN LINDEN TO ALEXANDERPLATZ

The Mitte (Middle) district is where Berlin first began as two fishing villages separated by the Spree River. Throughout its 765-year-plus history it has served as a seat of government for Prussian kings, German emperors, the Weimar Republic, Hitler's Third Reich, the communist German Democratic Republic, and, since 1999, reunited Germany. Treasures once split between East and West Berlin museums are also reunited on Museum Island, a UNESCO World Heritage site.

The historic boulevard Unter den Linden proudly rolls out Prussian architecture and world-class museums. Its major cross-street is Friedrichstrasse, which was revitalized in the mid-1990s with car showrooms (including Bentley, Bugatti, and Volkswagen) and upscale malls. At its eastern end, Unter den Linden turns into Karl-Liebknecht-Strasse, which leads to vast Alexanderplatz, where eastern Berlin's handful of skyscrapers are dwarfed beneath the city's most visible landmark, the Berlin TV tower.

⑬ **Bebelplatz.** After he became ruler in 1740, Frederick the Great personally planned the buildings surrounding this square (which has a huge parking garage cleverly hidden beneath the pavement). The area received the nickname *Forum Fridericianum,* or Frederick's Forum. On May 10, 1933, Joseph Goebbels, the Nazi minister for propaganda and "public enlightenment," organized one of the nationwide book-burnings here. The books, thrown on a pyre by Nazi officials and students, included works by Jews, pacifists, and Communists. In the center of Bebelplatz, a modern and subtle memorial marks where 20,000 books went up in flames.

6

The green patina dome belongs to **St. Hedwigskathedrale** *(St. Hedwig's Cathedral).* Begun in 1747, it was modeled after the Pantheon in Rome and was the first Catholic church built in resolutely Protestant Berlin since the 16th-century Reformation. It was Frederick the Great's effort to appease Prussia's Catholic population after his invasion of Catholic Silesia (then Poland). A treasury lies inside. ⊠*Bebelpl., Mitte* ☎*030/203–4810* ⊕*www.hedwigs-kathedrale.de* ⊠*Free* ⊙*Weekdays 10–5, Sun. 1–5* ⌨*Tours (€1.50) available in English, call ahead* Ⓜ*Französische Strasse (U-bahn).*

⑮ Berliner Dom *(Berlin Cathedral).* A church has stood here since 1536, but this enormous version dates from 1905, making it the largest 20th-century Protestant church in Germany. The royal Hohenzollerns worshipped here until 1918, when Kaiser Wilhelm II abdicated and left Berlin for Holland. The massive dome wasn't restored from World War II damage until 1982; the interior was completed in 1993. The climb to the dome's outer balcony is made easier by a wide stairwell, plenty of landings with historic photos and models, and even a couple of chairs. The more than 80 sarcophagi of Prussian royals in the crypt are significant but to less-trained eyes can seem uniformly dull. All morning services include communion. ⊠*Am Lustgarten 1, Mitte* ☎*030/2026–9136* ⊕*www.berlinerdom.de* ⊠*€5* ⊙*Mon.–Sat. 9–7, Sun. noon–6* Ⓜ*Hackescher Markt (S-bahn).*

⑯ Berliner Fernsehturm *(Berlin TV Tower).* Finding Alexanderplatz is no problem: just head toward the 1,198-foot-high tower piercing the sky. It was completed in 1969 and is not accidentally 710 feet higher than western Berlin's broadcasting tower and 98 feet higher than the Eiffel Tower. You can get the best view of Berlin from within the tower's disco-ball-like observation level; on a clear day you can see for 40 km (25 mi). One floor above, the city's highest restaurant rotates for your panoramic pleasure. ■**TIP**➡ **Make reservations in advance and stick to the German dishes.** ⊠*Panoramastr. 1a, Mitte* ☎*030/242–3333* ⊕*www. berlinerfernsehturm.de* ⊠*€8.50* ⊙*Nov.–Feb., daily 10* AM*–midnight; Mar.–Oct., daily 9* AM*–midnight; last admission ½ hr before closing* Ⓜ*Alexanderplatz (U-bahn and S-bahn).*

⑭ Museumsinsel *(Museum Island).* On the site of one of Berlin's two original settlements, this unique complex of four state museums is an absolute must.

FodorśChoice
★

The **Alte Nationalgalerie** (Old National Gallery, entrance on Bodestrasse) houses an outstanding collection of 18th-, 19th-, and early-20th-century paintings and sculptures. Works by Cézanne, Rodin, Degas, and one of Germany's most famous portrait artists, Max Liebermann, are part of the permanent exhibition. Its Galerie der Romantik (Gallery of Romanticism) collection has masterpieces from such 19th-century German painters as Karl Friedrich Schinkel and Caspar David Friedrich, the leading members of the German Romantic school. The **Altes Museum** (Old Museum), a red marble, neoclassical building abutting the green Lustgarten, was Prussia's first building purpose-built to serve as a museum. Designed by Karl Friedrich Schinkel, it was completed in 1830. Until 2009, when the collection will relocate to the Neues Museum, it serves as temporary home to the Egyptian collection, which traces Egypt's history from 4000 BC and whose prize piece is the exquisite 3,300-year-old bust of Queen Nefertiti. The permanent collection of the Altes Museum consists of everyday utensils from ancient Greece as well as vases and sculptures from the 6th to 4th century BC. Etruscan art is its highlight, and there are a few examples of Roman art. Antique sculptures, clay figurines, and bronze art of the Antikensammlung (Antiquities Collection) are also housed here; the other part of the collection is in the Pergamonmuseum. At the northern tip of Museum Island is the **Bode-Museum,** a somber-looking gray edifice graced with elegant columns. Reopened in 2006, it now presents the state museum's stunning collection of German and Italian sculptures since the Middle Ages, the Museum of Byzantine Art, and a huge coin collection. Even if you think you aren't interested in the ancient world, make an exception for the **Pergamonmuseum** (entrance on Am Kupfergraben), one of the world's greatest museums. The museum's name is derived from its principal display, the Pergamon Altar, a monumental Greek temple discovered in what is now Turkey and dating from 180 BC. The altar was shipped to Berlin in the late 19th century. Equally impressive are the gateway to the Roman town of Miletus and the Babylonian processional way. Art and culture buffs who want to enjoy as many Berlin museums as possible should consider the three-day pass for €15, which allows unlimited access to many state museums. There is also a special Mitte ticket that covers all state museums in that area for one day at a price of €14. If you get tired of antiques and paintings, drop by any of the museums' cafés. ⊠*Entrance to Museumsinsel: Am Kupfergraben, Mitte* ☎*030/2090–5577* ⊕*www.smb.museum* ⊠*All Museum Island museums €8* ☯*Pergamonmuseum Fri.–Wed. 10–6, Thurs. 10–10. Alte Nationalgalerie Tues., Wed., and Fri.–Sun. 10–6, Thurs. 10–10. Altes Museum Fri.–Wed. 10–6, Thurs. 10–10. Bode-Museum Fri.–Wed. 10–6, Thurs. 10–10* Ⓜ*Hackescher Markt (S-bahn).*

MITTE'S SCHEUNENVIERTEL & PRENZLAUER BERG

The hip scene of Mitte, the historic core of Berlin, is best experienced in the narrow streets and courtyard mazes of the Scheunenviertel (Barn Quarter), which also encompasses the former Spandauer Vorstadt (Jewish Quarter)—the streets around Oranienburger Strasse. Some streets are lined with hip shops, bars, and eateries, whereas others look empty and forlorn. Northeast of Mitte, the old working-class district of Prenzlauer Berg used to be one of the poorest sections of Berlin. In socialist East Germany, the old (and mostly run-down) tenement houses attracted the artistic avant-garde, who transformed the area into a refuge for alternative lifestyles (think punk singer Nina Hagen, stepdaughter of a folk singer expelled by the East German government). The renovated 19th-century buildings with balconies and stuccowork tend to feature unwanted graffiti, but Prenzlauer Berg is now a trendy area full of young couples with baby in tow.

 Gedenkstätte Berliner Mauer *(Berlin Wall Memorial Site).* This site combines memorials and a museum and research center on the Berlin Wall.

The division of Berlin was particularly heart-wrenching on Bernauer Strasse, where neighbors and families on opposite sides of the street were separated overnight. The Reconciliation Chapel, completed in 2000, replaced the community church dynamited by the Communists in 1985. The church had been walled into the "death strip" and was seen as a hindrance to patrolling it. A portion of the Wall remains on Bernauer Strasse, and an installation meant to serve as a memorial unfortunately only confuses those wondering what the border once looked like. For a wealth of images and information, head into the museum, where German-speakers can even hear radio broadcasts from the time the Wall was erected. ⊠*Bernauer Str. 111, Wedding* ☎*030/464–1030* ⊕*www.berliner-mauer-gedenkstaette.de* ✉*Free; tours €3* ◉ *Apr.–Oct., Tues.–Sun. 10–6; Nov.–Mar., Tues.–Sun. 10–5* Ⓜ*Bernauer Strasse (U-bahn), Nordbahnhof (S-Bahn).*

NEED A BREAK? Within the first courtyard of Hackesche Höfe, **Anatre Feinkost** (⊠*Rosenthaler Str. 40–41, Mitte* ☎*030/2838–9915*) uses top-quality ingredients for its Mediterranean sandwiches and pastas. You can also just sit with a coffee or glass of wine.

⑱ Neue Synagoge *(New Synagogue).* This meticulously restored landmark, built between 1859 and 1866, is an exotic amalgam of styles, the whole faintly Middle Eastern. Its bulbous, gilded cupola stands out in the skyline. When its doors opened, it was the largest synagogue in Europe, with 3,200 seats. The synagogue was damaged on November 9, 1938 (*Kristallnacht*—Night of the Broken Glass), when Nazi looters rampaged across Germany, burning synagogues and smashing the few Jewish shops and homes left in the country. It was destroyed by Allied bombing in 1943, and it wasn't until the mid-1980s that the East German government restored it. The effective exhibit on the history of the building and its congregants includes fragments of the original architecture and furnishings. ■**TIP➔** Sabbath services are held in a modern addition. ⊠*Oranienburger Str. 28–30, Mitte* ☎*030/8802–8316* ⊕*www. cjudaicum.de* ✉*€3, €4.60 including special exhibits; tour €1.50, German only* ◉*Nov.–Apr., Sun.–Thurs. 10–6, Fri. 10–2; May–Oct., Sun. and Mon. 10–8, Tues.–Thurs. 10–6, Fri. 10–5. Tours Wed. at 4, Sun. at 2 and 4. Cupola Apr.–Sept.* Ⓜ*Oranienburger Strasse (U-bahn), Oranienburger Tor (S-bahn).*

CHARLOTTENBURG

The city's outlying areas abound with palaces, lakes, and museums set in lush greenery. Central to the former West Berlin but now a western district of the united city, Charlottenburg was once an independent and wealthy city that became part of Berlin only in 1920. It holds the baroque Charlottenburg Palace and, across the street, a collection of Picassos in the Museum Berggruen.

★❷ Museum Berggruen. This small modern-art museum holds works by Matisse, Klee, Giacometti, and Picasso, who is particularly well represented with more than 100 works. Heinz Berggruen (1914–2007), a businessman who left Berlin in the 1930s, collected the excellent paintings. He narrates portions of the free audio guide, sharing anecdotes about how he came to acquire pieces directly from the artists, as well as his opinions of the women portrayed in Picasso's portraits. ✉*Schlossstr. 1, Charlottenburg* ☎*030/3269–5815* ⊕*www.smb. museum* 🎟*€6* ⊘*Tues.–Sun. 10–6* Ⓜ*Sophie-Charlotte-Platz (U-bahn), Richard-Wagner-Platz (U-bahn).*

❶ **Schloss Charlottenburg** *(Charlottenburg Palace).* A grand reminder of imperial days, this showplace served as a city residence for the Prussian rulers. The gorgeous palace started as a modest royal summer residence in 1695, built on the orders of King Friedrich I for his wife, Sophie-Charlotte. In the 18th century Frederick the Great made a number of additions, such as the dome and several wings designed in the rococo style. By 1790 the complex had evolved into a massive royal domain that could take a whole day to explore. Behind heavy iron gates, the Court of Honor—the front courtyard—is dominated by a baroque statue of the Great Elector on horseback. ✉*Luisenpl., Charlottenburg* ☎*030/320–911* ⊕*www.spsg.de* 🎟*A Tageskarte (day card) for €12 covers admission for all bldgs., excluding tour of Altes Schloss baroque apartments* Ⓜ*Richard-Wagner-Platz or Sophie-Charlotten-Platz (U-Bahn).*

The **Altes Schloss** *(Nering-Eosander-Bau* ☎*030/3209–1440* 🎟*€10 with tour; €2 for upper floor only* ⊘*Apr.–Oct., Tues.–Sun. 9–5; Nov.– Mar., Tues.–Sun. 9–4)* is the main building with the ground-floor suites of Friedrich I and Sophie-Charlotte. Paintings include royal portraits by Antoine Pesne, a noted court painter of the 18th century. A guided tour visits the Oak Gallery, the early-18th-century palace chapel, and the suites of Friedrich Wilhelm II and Friedrich Wilhelm III, furnished in the Biedermeier style. Tours leave every hour on the hour from 9 to 5. The upper floor has the apartments of Friedrich Wilhelm IV, a silver treasury, and Berlin and Meissen porcelain. It can be seen on its own. The **Neuer Flügel** *(New Wing* ☎*030/3209–1454* 🎟*€6* ⊘*Tues.–Sun. 9–5),* where Frederick the Great once lived, was designed by Knobbelsdorff, who also built Sanssouci. The 138-foot-long Goldene Galerie (Golden Gallery) was the palace's ballroom. West of the staircase are Frederick's rooms, in which parts of his extravagant collection of works by Watteau, Chardin, and Pesne are displayed. An audio guide is included in the admission. The park behind the palace was laid out in the French baroque style beginning in 1697, and was transformed into an English garden in the early 19th century. In it stand the Neuer Pavillon by Karl Friedrich Schinkel and Carl Langhan's **Belvedere teahouse** (☎*030/3209–1415* 🎟*€2* ⊘*Late Mar.–Oct., Tues.–Fri. noon–5, weekends 10–5; Nov.–late Mar., Tues.–Sun. noon–4),* which overlooks the lake and the Spree River and holds a collection of Berlin porcelain. The **Museum für Vor- und Frühgeschichte** *(Museum of Pre- and Early History* ☎*030/326–7480* 🎟*€3. A combination ticket for €6 is valid for this museum, the Museum Berggruen, and the Newton Collection.* ⊘*Tues.–Fri. 9–5, weekends 10–5)* traces the evolution of mankind from 1 million BC to AD 1,000. It's opposite Klausener Platz (to the left as you face the palace).

6

NEED A BREAK?

Between visits to the museums clustering around Schloss Charlottenburg, give your feet a rest in the country-kitchen room of the **Kleine Orangerie** (⊠ *Spandauer Damm 20, Charlottenburg* ☎ *030/322–2021* ◷ *Easter–Oct., daily 10* AM *–9:30* PM; *Nov.–Easter, Tues.–Sun. 9–8*), next door to the palace. The breakfast is a good deal. There's also atrium and outdoor seating.

WHERE TO EAT

Neighborhood stalwarts serve residents from morning to night with a mix of German and international cuisine. Berlin is known for curt or slow service, except at very high-end restaurants. Note that many of the top restaurants are closed on Sunday.

The most common food for meals on-the-go are *Wursts* (sausages). *Currywurst*, a pork sausage served with a mildly curried ketchup, is local to Berlin. Even more popular are Turkish *Döner* shops that sell pressed lamb or chicken in flat-bread pockets.

CHARLOTTENBURG & WESTERN DOWNTOWN

$$$–$$$$ ✗ **Alt Luxemburg.** Wrought-iron lamps, 19th-century-style furniture, and wonderfully attentive service create an intimate atmosphere. Working behind the stove since 1982, owner and chef Karl Wannemacher uses only the freshest ingredients for his modern German dishes, which change monthly. Lobster is always on the menu in some form, be it in a salad or the divine lobster lasagna. Entrée options might include rolled saddle of rabbit in coffee sauce. ⊠ *Windscheidstr. 31, Charlottenburg* ☎ *030/323–8730* ⊟ *AE, DC, MC, V* ◷ *Closed weekends. No lunch* Ⓜ *Wilmersdorfer Strasse (U-bahn), Charlottenburg (S-bahn).*

★ $–$$ ✗ **Engelbecken.** The beer coasters are trading cards of the Wittelsbach dynasty in this relaxed but high-quality restaurant serving dishes from Bavaria and the Alps. Classics like Wiener schnitzel, goulash, and grilled saddle steak are made of "bio" meat and vegetable products, meaning that even the veal, lamb, and beef are the tasty results of organic and humane upbringing. ■TIP➜ **In warm weather, reserve a sidewalk table.** With its corner position facing a park bordering Lake Lietzensee, Engelbecken is a lovely open-air dining spot. ⊠ *Witzlebenstr. 31, Charlottenburg* ☎ *030/615–2810* ⊟ *MC, V* ◷ *No lunch Mon.–Sat.* Ⓜ *Sophie-Charlotte-Platz (U-bahn).*

¢–$$ ✗ **Ottenthal.** This intimate restaurant with white tablecloths is the city cousin of the Austrian village of Ottenthal, which delivers up the wines, pumpkin-seed oil, and organic ingredients on the menu. Curious combinations might include pike perch with lobster sauce and pepper-pine-nut risotto, or venison medallions with vegetable-potato-strudel, red cabbage, and rowanberry sauce. The huge Wiener schnitzel extends past the plate's rim, and the pastas and strudel are homemade. ■TIP➜ **Offering one of the best meals for your money in Berlin, Ottenthal is a particularly good choice on Sunday evening, when many of Berlin's finer restaurants are closed.** It's just around the corner from both the Zoo and the Ku'damm. ⊠ *Kantstr. 153, Western Downtown* ☎ *030/313–3162* ⊟ *AE, MC, V* ◷ *No lunch* Ⓜ *Zoologischer Garten (U-bahn and S-bahn).*

★ ¢–$ ✕**Kuchi.** Japanese sushi, sashimi, yakitori, and dunburi dishes along with some Thai, Chinese, and Korean recipes are served in this groovy landmark restaurant, one of the finest sushi places in town. Chefs work with an almost religious devotion to quality and imagination (they even wear shirts saying SUSHI WARRIOR), and the knowledgeable Asian-German staff makes you feel at home. The spicy, fresh, and healthy ingredients and the laid-back vibe pack the restaurant in the evening, so reservations are a must. ■**TIP**➔ Try to get a seat at the sushi bar or at one of the three more-private tables at the window. ⊠*Kantstr. 30, Western Downtown* ☎*030/3150–7815* ◈*Reservations essential* ⊟*AE, MC, V* Ⓜ*Zoologischer Garten (U-bahn and S-bahn).*

SCHÖNEBERG & TIERGARTEN

★ $–$$$ ✕**Café Einstein.** The Einstein is a Berlin landmark and one of the leading coffeehouses in town. Set in the historic grand villa of silent movie star Henny Porten, it charmingly recalls the elegant days of the Austrian-Hungarian empire, complete with slightly snobbish waiters gliding across squeaking parquet floors. The Einstein's very own roasting facility produces some of Germany's best coffee, and the cakes are fabulous, particularly the fresh strawberry cake best enjoyed in the shady garden behind the villa in summer. The café also excels in preparing solid Austrian fare such as schnitzel or goulash for an artsy, high-brow clientele. ⊠*Kurfürstenstr. 58, Tiergarten* ☎*030/261–5096* ⊟*AE, DC, MC, V* Ⓜ*Kurfürstenstrasse (U-bahn).*

$ ✕**April.** The back room is dressed with white tablecloths, but most regulars pick a place in the front, where there are art-nouveau light fixtures, stuccowork, and a street view. This is a relaxed bistro, meaning the service can be sluggish, but the consistently delicious meals are very reasonably priced. The menu has a mix of Italian, French, and German cooking and a kids' section. The only lackluster items are the thin-crust Alsatian pizzas (*Flammkuchen*). The generous *Vorspeitenteller* (selection of five appetizers) might include *bresaola* (air-cured beef) over arugula, grilled vegetables, and shrimp tempura. The restaurant is near Winterfeldplatz. ⊠*Winterfeldstr. 56, Schöneberg* ☎*030/216–8869* ⊟*No credit cards* Ⓜ*Nollendorfplatz (U-bahn).*

MITTE

★ $$–$$$ ✕**Lutter & Wegner.** One of the city's oldest vintners (*Sekt*, German champagne, was first conceived here in 1811 by actor Ludwig Devrient), Lutter & Wegner has returned to its historic location across from the Konzerthaus and Gendarmenmarkt. The dark wood-paneled walls, parquet floor, and multitude of rooms take you back to 19th-century Vienna. The cuisine is mostly Austrian, with superb game dishes in winter and, of course, a Wiener schnitzel with lukewarm potato salad. The sauerbraten (marinated pot roast) with red cabbage has been a national prizewinner. ■**TIP**➔ In the Weinstube, meat and cheese plates are served until 3 AM. ⊠*Charlottenstr. 56, Mitte* ☎*030/2029–5417* ⊟*AE, MC, V* Ⓜ*Französische Strasse and Stadtmitte (U-Bahn).*

★ $$ ✕**Bocca di Bacco.** Hip Bocca di Bacco is the talk of the town, primarily because of its blend of down-to-earth atmosphere and high-quality cuisine. Homemade pasta dishes, surprisingly hearty Tuscan classics (with an emphasis on wild game and fish), and an equally delectable assortment of desserts make for authentic Italian cooking—perhaps even Berlin's finest. The three-course prix-fixe lunch is €19.50. ⊠*Friedrichstr. 167–168, Mitte* ☎*030/2067–2828* ⚒*Reservations essential* ⊟*AE, MC, V* ⊘*No lunch Sun.*

$-$$ ✕**Reinhard's.** Friends meet here in the Nikolaiviertel to enjoy the carefully prepared entrées and to sample spirits from the amply stocked bar, all served by friendly, tie-wearing waiters. The honey-glazed breast of duck, *Adlon,* is one of its specialties. There's a nice outdoor area for dining. ⊠*Poststr. 28, Mitte* ☎*030/242–5295* ⚒*Reservations essential* ⊟*AE, DC, MC, V* Ⓜ*Alexanderplatz (U-Bahn).*

¢-$ ✕**Zur Rippe.** This popular place in the Nikolaiviertel serves wholesome food in an intimate setting of oak paneling and ceramic tiles. Specialties include the platter of *Kasseler, Ribbchen, und Eisbein* (cured pork, ribs, and pig knuckle) and a herring casserole. ⊠*Poststr. 17, Mitte* ☎*030/242–3310* ⊟*AE, DC, MC, V* Ⓜ*Klosterstr. (U-bahn).*

> **TURKISH MARKET & CAFES**
>
> On Tuesday and Friday from noon to 6:30 you can find the country's best selection of Arab and Turkish foods on the Maybachufer lining the southern bank of the Landwehrkanal. The quirky student bar and café on the Kottbusser bridge, Ankerklause, or those on Paul-Lincke-Ufer, the opposite bank, are great places for a late breakfast, coffee break, and local color. The closest U-bahn stations are Kottbusser Tor and Schönlein Strasse. For Turkish fast food (a chicken or lamb kebab, or falafel), walk up Adalbertstrasse from Kottbusser Tor.

POTSDAMER PLATZ

$$$$ ✕**Facil.** One of Germany's top restaurants, the Facil is also the most

Fodor$Choice affordable and relaxed one of its class. The elegant, minimalist set-

★ ting—complete with green marble walls, exquisite wall panels, and a Giallo Reale patinato floor, all set under a glass roof (opened in summer, yet no view of the city)—and the impeccable, personal service make the six-course dinners a highlight in any gourmet's life. The food is a careful combination of French and regionally inspired first-class cuisine. Don't hesitate to ask sommelier Felix Voges for advice, as he certainly ranks among the most knowledgeable in his art. ⊠*Potsdamer Str. 3, at the Mandala Hotel, Tiergarten* ☎*030/5900–51234* ⊟*AE, DC, MC, V* ⊘*Closed weekends* Ⓜ*Potsdamer Platz (U-bahn and S-bahn).*

WHERE TO STAY

In general, even Berlin's first-class hotels are much cheaper than their counterparts in Paris, London, or Rome. And Internet services like Expedia can sometimes book a room at a five-star hotel in Berlin for half the normal price, even in summer. Hotels listed here as $$$$ often come down to a $$ level on weekends or when there is low demand. You usually have the option to decline the inclusion of breakfast, which can save you anywhere from €8 to €30 per person per day. Year-round business conventions and fairs (February and early March, early September) and tourism peak during Christmas and summer (especially from mid-June to mid-July), meaning you should make reservations well in advance.

CHARLOTTENBURG

★ $$ ⊞ **Art Nouveau Hotel.** The owners' discerning taste in antiques, color combinations, and even televisions (designed by Philippe Starck) makes this bed-and-breakfast-like pension a pleasure to live in. Each room has a prize piece, such as a hand-carved 18th-century Chinese dresser or a chandelier from the Komische Oper's set of *Don Carlos.* Several rooms are hung with a large black-and-white photo by Sabine Kačunko. The apartment building shows its age only in the antique wood elevator, high stucco ceilings, and an occasionally creaky floor. You can serve yourself tea or coffee in the breakfast room throughout the day and mix your own drinks at the honor bar. Your English-speaking hosts are Mr. and Mrs. Schlenzka. ⊠ *Leibnizstr. 59, Charlottenburg, D–10629* ☎ *030/327–7440* 🖷 *030/3277–4440* ⊕ *www.hotelartnouveau.de* ⟿ *19 rooms, 3 suites* ⚲ *In-room: no a/c, Wi-Fi. In-hotel: bar, laundry service, no-smoking rooms* ▭ *AE, MC, V* ⦿ *CP* Ⓜ *Adenauerplatz (U-bahn).*

WESTERN DOWNTOWN

★ $$$$ ⊞ **Hotel Brandenburger Hof.** The foyer of this turn-of-the-20th-century mansion is breathtaking, with soaring white Doric columns, but once past these you'll find luxurious minimalism. You can breakfast and sip afternoon tea at the sun-soaked tables in the atrium courtyard or, in the evening, sit and listen to piano music. Between courses of French cuisine in the restaurant Quadriga, diners lean back in cherrywood chairs by Frank Lloyd Wright. Guest-room furnishings include pieces by Le Corbusier and Mies van der Rohe. Complementing the timeless Bauhaus style are ikebana floral arrangements. The spa features Asian silk cosmetic treatments. The location on a very residential street makes this a quiet hideaway, but the Tauentzien and KaDeWe are just a short walk away. ⊠ *Eislebener Str. 14, Western Downtown, D–10789* ☎ *030/214–050* 🖷 *030/2140–5100* ⊕ *www.brandenburger-hof.com* ⟿ *58 rooms, 14 suites* ⚲ *In-room: no a/c (some), Ethernet, Wi-Fi. In-hotel: restaurant, bar, spa, public Internet, parking (fee), no-smoking rooms* ▭ *AE, DC, MC, V* Ⓜ *Augsburger Strasse (U-bahn).*

$$–$$$$ ⊞ **Swissôtel Berlin.** At the bustling corner of Ku'damm and Joachimsthaler Strasse, this hotel excels with its reputable Swiss hospitality—from accompanying guests to their floor after check-in to equipping each room with an iron, an umbrella, and a Lavazza espresso machine that preheats the cups. Beds are specially designed to avoid allergens and provide maximum comfort. After using the Wi-Fi, you can store and recharge your laptop in the room safe (the safe also charges cell phones). The unusual, rounded building has a sleek interior with original artwork by Marcus Lüpertz and a respected restaurant. Your room's soundproof windows give you a fantastic view of the area. ⊠ *Augsburger Str. 44, Western Downtown, D–10789* ☎ *030/220–100* 🖷 *030/2201–02222* ⊕ *www.swissotel.com* ⟿ *291 rooms, 25*

suites ♿ *In-room: safe, dial-up, Wi-Fi. In-hotel: restaurant, room service, bar, gym, concierge, laundry service, public Internet, parking (fee), no-smoking rooms, some pets allowed (fee)* ▭ *AE, DC, MC, V* Ⓜ *Kurfürstendamm (U-bahn).*

$$ 🏨**Hotel Astoria.** Each simple room in this small building dating to 1898 is different, and the family owners are diligent about making renovations every year. When making a reservation, state whether you'd like a bathtub or shower and ask about weekend specials or package deals for longer stays. The fifth- and sixth-floor rooms have air-conditioning for an extra charge. Two terraces allow you to sun yourself, and a stroll down the charming street leads to the shops along Ku'damm. Internet use at a PC station in the lobby is free; Wi-Fi services in the lobby and in your room are subject to a fee. ✉ *Fasanenstr. 2, Western Downtown, D–10623* ☎ *030/312–4067* 🖷 *030/312–5027* ⊕ *www.hotelastoria.de* 🛏 *31 rooms, 1 suite* ♿ *In-room: no a/c (some), safe, Wi-Fi. In-hotel: room service, bar, laundry service, public Wi-Fi, public Internet, parking (fee), some pets allowed* ▭ *AE, DC, MC, V* Ⓜ *Uhlandstrasse (U-bahn), Zoologsicher Garten (U-bahn and S-bahn).*

★ $–$$ 🏨**Hotel-Pension Dittberner.** For traditional Berlin accommodations, this third-floor pension (with wooden elevator) run by Frau Lange since 1958 is the place to go. Close to Olivaer Platz and next to Ku'damm, the turn-of-the-20th-century house shows its age, but the huge rooms are wonderfully furnished with antiques, plush stuffed sofas, and artwork selected by Frau Lange's husband, a gallery owner. The high ceilings have stuccowork, and some rooms have balconies. Wi-Fi Internet access is available in the foyer. ✉ *Wielandstr. 26, Western Downtown, D–10707* ☎ *030/884–6950* 🖷 *030/885–4046* ⊕ *www.hotel-dittberner. de* 🛏 *21 rooms, 1 suite* ♿ *In-room: no a/c. In-hotel: concierge, laundry service, some pets allowed, public Wi-Fi* ▭ *AE, MC, V* ⦿|CP Ⓜ *Adenauerplatz (U-bahn).*

MITTE

★ $$$$ 🏨**Hotel Adlon Berlin.** Aside from its prime setting on Pariser Platz, the allure of the government's unofficial guesthouse is its almost mythical predecessor. Until its destruction during the war, the Hotel Adlon was considered Europe's ultimate luxury resort. Rebuilt in 1997, the hotel's elegant rooms are furnished in 1920s style with cherrywood trim, myrtle-wood furnishings, and brocade silk bedspreads. The large bathrooms are done in black marble. Book a suite for a Brandenburger Tor view. Sipping coffee in the lobby of creamy marble and limestone makes for good people-watching. Meetings at the nearby Reichstag or Chancellery sometimes continue with a meal at Lorenz Adlon. ✉ *Unter den Linden 77, Mitte, D–10117* ☎ *030/22610* 🖷 *030/2261–2222* ⊕ *www.hotel-adlon.de* 🛏 *304 rooms, 78 suites* ♿ *In-room: safe, Wi-Fi. In-hotel: 3 restaurants, room service, bar, pool, gym, spa, concierge, laundry service, parking (fee), no-smoking rooms, some pets allowed (fee)* ▭ *AE, DC, MC, V* Ⓜ *Unter den Linden (S-bahn).*

★ $$$ 🏨**Dorint Sofitel am Gendarmenmarkt.** Built before the Wall came tumbling down, this luxurious lodging has maximized that era's minimalist look. In the formerly austere conference room the designers added an illuminated glass floor that made it a masterpiece. The spa tucked under the mansard roof is suffused with light, thanks to the new, angled windows. Request a room facing Gendarmenmarkt, one of the city's most impressive squares. Decorative motifs are inspired by plant photographer Karl Blossfeldt, whose models inspired wrought-iron craftsmen. Toylike bedside pull chains set off a short tinkling tune to send you off to sleep. ✉ *Charlottenstr. 50–52, Mitte, D–10117* ☎*030/203–750* 🖨*030/2037–5100* ⊕*www.sofitel.com* 🛏*70 rooms, 22 suites* ♿*In-room: safe, dial-up, Wi-Fi. In-hotel: restaurant, room service, gym, spa, laundry service, no-smoking rooms* ▤*AE, DC, MC, V* Ⓜ*Französische Strasse (U-bahn).*

★ **$$** 🏨 **Arte Luise Kunsthotel.** This hotel's name suggests a bohemian commune, but all the residents are paying guests. The Luise is one of Berlin's most original boutique hotels, with each fantastically creative room in the 1825 house or new wing—facing the Reichstag—styled by a different artist. Memorable furnishings range from a suspended bed and airplane seats to a gigantic sleigh bed and a freestanding, podlike shower with multiple nozzles. A lavish breakfast buffet in the neighboring restaurant costs €9. The hotel is a stretch from the Friedrichstrasse train station, but a convenient bus line stops just outside. ✉ *Luisenstr. 19, Mitte, D–10117* ☎*030/284–480* 🖨*030/2844–8448* ⊕*www.arteluise.com* 🛏*44 rooms, 40 with bath; 3 apartments* ♿*In-room: no a/c (some), no TV (some), Wi-Fi. In-hotel: restaurant, laundry service, no-smoking rooms, some pets allowed, no elevator in historic part* ▤*MC, V* Ⓜ*Friedrichstrasse (U-bahn and S-bahn).*

6

KREUZBERG

$$ 🏨 **Riehmers Hofgarten.** The appeal of this late-19th-century apartment house with a leafy courtyard is its location in a lively neighborhood marked by the streets Mehringdamm and Bergmannstrasse. The richly decorated facade hints that 100 years ago the aristocratic officers of Germany's imperial army lived here. Rooms with low-lying beds are spartanly modern, quiet, and functional. Downstairs is a light-filled lounge and restaurant. In less than five minutes you can reach the subway that speeds you to Mitte and the Friedrichstrasse train station. ✉*Yorckstr. 83, Kreuzberg, D–10965* ☎*030/7809–8800* 🖨*030/7809–8808* ⊕*www.riehmers-hofgarten.de* 🛏*21 rooms, 1 suite* ♿*In-room: no a/c, Ethernet, Wi-Fi. In-hotel: restaurant, room service, bar, laundry service, parking (fee), no-smoking rooms, some pets allowed (fee), no elevator* ▤*AE, MC, V* 🍽*CP* Ⓜ*Mehringdamm (U-bahn).*

$ 🏨 **Die Fabrik.** Near Kreuzberg's and Friedrichshain's alternative nightlife scene and a five-minute walk from the subway, this former factory building—solar powered—is perfect for those who place a priority on mixing with the local scene. Though this is a backpacker stop, basic double rooms and suites with carpeting and metal lockers are also available. To connect to the Internet, insert a euro into the computer at reception. Downside: there are no private bathrooms. Upside: there's a small courtyard with plants, and the café is decent. Seven doubles have a sink, and double prices drop between November and February. ✉*Schlesische Str. 18, Kreuzberg, D–10997* ☎*030/611–7116* 🖨*030/618–2974* ⊕*www.diefabrik.com* 🛏*50 rooms without bath* ♿*In-room: no a/c, no phone, no TV. In-hotel: restaurant, public Internet, no elevator* ▤*No credit cards* Ⓜ*Schlesisches Tor (U-bahn).*

NIGHTLIFE & THE ARTS

THE ARTS

Today's Berlin has a tough time living up to the reputation it gained from the film *Cabaret*. In the 1920s it was said that in Berlin, if you wanted to make a scandal in the theater, you had to have a mother committing incest with *two* sons; one wasn't enough. Political gaffes are now the prime comic material for Berlin's cabarets. Even if nightlife has toned down since the 1920s and '30s, the arts and the avantgarde still flourish. Detailed information about events is covered in the *Berlin Programm*, a monthly tourist guide to Berlin arts, museums, and theaters. The magazines *Tip* and *Zitty*, which appear every two weeks, provide full arts listings (in German), and the free *(030)* is the best source for club and music events. For listings in English, consult the monthly *Ex-Berliner*.

If your hotel can't book a seat for you or you can't make it to a box office directly, go to a ticket agency. Surcharges are 18%–23% of the ticket price. **Showtime Konzert- und Theaterkassen** (⊠ *KaDeWe, Tauentzienstr. 21, Western Downtown* ☎ *030/217–7754* ⊠ *Wertheim, Kurfürstendamm 181, Western Downtown* ☎ *030/882–2500*) has offices within the major department stores. The **Theaterkasse Centrum** (⊠ *Meinekestr. 25, Western Downtown* ☎ *030/882–7611*) is a small agency but employs a very informed and helpful staff. The **Hekticket offices** (⊠ *Karl-Liebknecht-Str. 12, off Alexanderpl., Mitte* ☎ *030/2431–2431* ⊠ *Next to Zoo-Palast, Hardenbergstr. 29d, Western Downtown* ☎ *030/230–9930*) offer discounted and last-minute tickets.

CONCERTS

Among the major symphony orchestras and orchestral ensembles in Berlin is one of the world's best, the Berlin Philharmonic Orchestra, which resides at the **Philharmonie mit Kammermusiksaal** (⊠ *Herbert-von-Karajan-Str. 1, Tiergarten* ☎ *030/2548–8999* ⊕ *www.berliner-philharmoniker.de*). The Kammermusiksaal is dedicated to chamber music. Tickets sell out in advance for the nights when Sir Simon Rattle or other star maestros conduct the Berlin Philharmonic, but other orchestras and artists appear here as well. Free guided tours take place daily at 1 PM.

The beautifully restored hall at **Konzerthaus Berlin** (⊠ *Gendarmenmarkt, Mitte* ☎ *030/2030–92101 or 030/2030–92102*) is a prime venue for classical music concerts. Its box office is open from noon to curtain time.

OPERA

Berlin's three opera houses also host guest productions and companies from around the world. Vladimir Malakhov, a principal guest dancer with New York's American Ballet Theatre, is a principal in the Staatsballett Berlin as well as its director. The company jetés its classic and modern productions between the Deutsche Oper in the west and the Staatsoper in the east. Of the 17 composers represented in the repertoire of **Deutsche Oper Berlin** (⊠ *Bismarckstr. 35, Charlottenburg* ☎ *030/343–8401* ⊕ *www.deutscheoperberlin.de*), Verdi and Wagner are the most presented. Most of the operas are sung in German at the **Komische Oper** (⊠ *Behrenstr. 55–57, Mitte* ☎ *030/4799–7400 or 01805/304–168* ⊕ *www.komische-oper-berlin.de*). On the day of the performance, discount tickets are sold at the box office on Unter den Linden 41.

Though renovated twice after bombings, the **Staatsoper Unter den Linden** (⊠ *Unter den Linden 7, Mitte* ☎ *030/2035–4555* ⊕ *www.staatsoper-berlin.de*) dates to 1743, when Frederick the Great oversaw productions. Maestro Daniel Barenboim oversees a diverse repertoire. Tickets can be as inexpensive as €7.

NIGHTLIFE

Berlin's nightspots are open to the wee hours of the morning, but if you stay out after 12:45 Monday to Thursday or Sunday, you'll have to find a night bus line or the last S-bahn to get you home. On Friday and Saturday nights all subway lines (except U4) run every 15 to 20 minutes throughout the night. Clubs often switch the music they play nightly, so their crowds and popularity can vary widely. Though club nights are driven by the DJ name, the music genres are written in English in listing magazines.

Clubs and bars in downtown western Berlin tend to be dressier and more conservative; the scene in Kreuzberg, Prenzlauer Berg, Mitte, and Friedrichshain is laid-back, alternative, grungy, and only occasionally stylish, particularly in Mitte. For the latest information on Berlin's house, electro, and hip-hop club scene, pick up *(030)*, a free weekly. Dance clubs don't get going until about 12:30 AM, but parties labeled "after-work" start as early as 8 PM for professionals looking to socialize during the week.

BARS & LOUNGES

In Germany the term *Kneipen* is used for down-to-earth bars that are comparable to English pubs. These places are pretty simple and laid-back; you probably shouldn't try to order a three-ingredient cocktail at one unless you spot a lengthy drink menu.

The cocktail menu is the size of a small guidebook at **Bar am Lützowplatz** (⊠ *Am Lützowpl. 7, Tiergarten* ☎ *030/262–6807*), where an attractive, professional crowd lines the long blond-wood bar. The Grand Hotel Esplanade's **Harry's New-York Bar** (⊠ *Am Lützowufer 15, Tiergarten* ☎ *030/2547–88633*) is the best hotel bar in town. In good weather you can sit outside and watch moneyed guests make their entrance into the hotel. A pianist entertains Monday–Saturday. Old-world **E. & M. Leydicke** (⊠ *Mansteinstr. 4, Schöneberg* ☎ *030/216–2973*) is a must for out-of-towners. The proprietors operate their own distillery and have a superb selection of sweet wines and liqueurs. Shabby **Kumpelnest 3000** (⊠ *Lützowstr. 23, Tiergarten* ☎ *030/261–6918*) has a reputation as wild as its carpeted walls. It's the traditional last stop of the evening, and both gays and heteros mingle on the tiny dance floor. There's no tap beer.

Now the oldest posh bar in Mitte, marble-lined **Newton** (✉ *Charlottenstr. 57, Mitte* ☎ *030/2029–5421*) flaunts Helmut Newton's larger-than-life photos of nude women across its walls.

CLUBS

More like a lounge than a club, **Delicious Doughnuts** (✉ *Rosenthaler Str. 9, Mitte* ☎ *030/2809–9274*) has a small dance floor, and its layout is fairly conducive for mingling. The ultra-hip and leading club in town is the over-the-top **Felix** (✉ *Behrenstr. 72 [behind the Hotel Adlon], Mitte*), where doormen and patrons tend to think rather highly of themselves. Hollywood stars drop by when shooting in town, and you have to be good-looking, rich, or—even better—both to get in. Berlin's mixed, multiculti crowd frequents the **Havanna Club** (✉ *Hauptstr. 30, Schöneberg* ☎ *030/784–8565*), where you can dance to soul, R&B, or hip-hop on four different dance floors. The week's highlights are the wild salsa and merengue nights (Wednesday, Friday, and Saturday, starting at 9 PM). If your Latin steps are weak, come an hour early for a lesson. **Sage-Club** (✉ *Köpenicker Str. 78, Mitte* ☎ *030/278–9830*) is the most popular of Berlin's venues for young professionals who dance to house and some techno music. On some nights it can be tough getting past the man with the "by invitation only" list.

JAZZ CLUBS

With no columns to obstruct your view, you can see young German artists almost every night at **B-Flat** (✉ *Rosenthaler Str. 13, Mitte* ☎ *030/283–3123*). The Wednesday jam sessions focus on free and experimental jazz. On Sunday, dancers come for tango night. Snacks are available. **Quasimodo** (✉ *Kantstr. 12a, Charlottenburg* ☎ *030/312–8086* ⊕ *www.quasimodo.de*), the most established and popular jazz venue in the city, has a college-town pub feel in its basement. Seats are few.

SHOPPING

What's fashionable in Berlin is creative, bohemian style, so designer labels have less appeal here than in Hamburg, Düsseldorf, or Munich. Young people seem to spend more money on cell-phone cards than clothing.

SHOPPING DISTRICTS

CHARLOTTENBURG

Although Ku'damm is still touted as the shopping mile of Berlin, many shops are ho-hum retailers. The best stretch for exclusive fashions, such as Bruno Magli, Hermès, and Jil Sander, are the three blocks between Leibnizstrasse and Bleibtreustrasse. For home furnishings, gift items, and unusual clothing boutiques, follow this route off Ku'damm: Leibnizstrasse to Mommsenstrasse to Bleibtreustrasse, then on to the ring around Savignyplatz. Fasanenstrasse, Knesebeckstrasse, Schlüterstrasse, and Uhlandstrasse are also fun places to browse.

Ku'damm ends at Breitscheidplatz, but the door-to-door shopping continues along Tauentzienstrasse, which, in addition to international retail stores, offers continental Europe's largest department store, the upscale Kaufhaus des Westens, or KaDeWe.

MITTE

The finest shops in historic Berlin are along Friedrichstrasse, including the French department store Galeries Lafayette. Nearby, Unter den Linden has just a few souvenir shops and a Meissen ceramic showroom. Smaller clothing and specialty stores populate the Scheunenviertel. The area between Hackescher Markt, Weinmeister Strasse, and Rosa-Luxemburg-Platz alternates pricey independent designers with groovy secondhand shops. Neue Schönhauser Strasse curves into Alte Schönhauser Strasse, and both streets are full of stylish casual wear. Galleries along Gipsstrasse and Sophienstrasse round out the mix.

DEPARTMENT STORES & ARCADES

The smallest and most luxurious department store in town, **Department Store Quartier 206** (⊠ *Friedrichstr. 71, Mitte* ☏ *030/2094–6240*) offers primarily French women's and men's designer clothes, perfumes, and home accessories. Anchoring Alexanderplatz, **Galeria Kaufhof** (⊠ *Alexanderpl. 9, Mitte* ☏ *030/247–430* ⊕ *www.kaufhof.de*) is the most successful branch of the German chain, though the wares are fairly basic.

The largest department store in continental Europe, classy **Kaufhaus des Westens** (*KaDeWe* ⊠ *Tauentzienstr. 21, Western Downtown* ☏ *030/21210* ⊕ *www.kadewe.de*) has a grand selection of goods on seven floors, as well as food and deli counters, champagne bars, beer bars, and a winter garden on its two upper floors. Its wealth of services includes fixing umbrellas and repairing leather and furs.

Similar to an American mall, the three-tiered **Potsdamer Platz Arkaden** (⊠ *Alte Potsdamer Str. 7, Tiergarten* ☏ *030/255–9270* ⊕ *www.potsdamer-platz-arkaden.de*) has shops such as Benetton, H & M, Esprit, Eddie Bauer, an Ampelmann gift store, and reputedly the best gelato café in Berlin. **Wertheim** (⊠ *Kurfürstendamm 231, Western Downtown* ☏ *030/880–030*) is neither as big nor as attractive as KaDeWe, but offers a large selection of fine wares.

BERLIN ESSENTIALS

AIR TRAVEL

Berlin has three airports: Tegel Airport (TXL); Tempelhof Airport, which will close in late 2008; and Schönefeld, about 24 km (15 mi) outside the downtown area and used principally by charter and low-budget airlines. For information on flights into Germany, see Germany Essentials.

Information Central airport service (☏ *0180/500–0186* ⊕ *www.berlin-airport.de*).

AIRPORT TRANSFERS

The X9 airport bus runs at 10-minute intervals between Tegel and Bahnhof Zoologischer Garten (Zoo Station). From here you can connect to bus, train, or subway. The trip takes 25 minutes; the fare is

€3.10, or an additional €1 if you already have a regular metro or bus ticket. Alternatively, you can take Bus 128 to Kurt Schumacher Platz or Bus 109 to Jakob-Kaiser-Platz and change to the subway, where your bus ticket is also valid. Expect to pay about €15 for a taxi from the airport to the western downtown area.

Tempelhof Airport is linked directly to the city center by the U-6 subway line. From Schönefeld Airport a free express shuttle bus leaves every 10–15 minutes for the S-bahn station (a 10-minute walk). From there, you can take the S-bahn or Airport Express train for €2.10. Bus 171 also leaves Schönefeld every 20 minutes for the Rudow subway station. A taxi ride from the Schönefeld Airport takes about 40 minutes and will cost around €35. By car, follow the signs for Stadtzentrum Berlin.

CAR TRAVEL

Since Berlin has both expensive parking and excellent public transportation, it makes little sense to rent a car if Berlin is your only destination in Germany; however, although car rentals can be expensive, they offer the most convenient mode of travel if you want to explore beyond Berlin itself.

PUBLIC TRANSIT

The city has one of the most efficient public-transportation systems in Europe, a smoothly integrated network of subway (U-bahn) and suburban (S-bahn) train lines, buses, and trams (in eastern Berlin only). Get a map from any information booth.

From Sunday through Thursday, U-bahn trains stop around 12:45 AM and S-bahn trains stop by 1:30 AM. All-night bus and tram service operates seven nights a week (indicated by the letter *N* next to route numbers). On Friday and Saturday night some S-bahn and all U-bahn lines except U4 run all night. Buses and trams marked with an *M* mostly serve destinations without S-bahn or U-bahn link.

Most visitor destinations are in the broad reach of the fare zones A and B. At this writing, both the €2.10 ticket (fare zones A and B) and the €2.60 ticket (fare zones A, B, and C) allow you to make a one-way trip with an unlimited number of changes between trains, buses, and trams. A ticket increase is expected in 2008. You can also buy short-ride tickets or one- or seven-day passes for the system. Other cards combine transport and discounts.

Tickets are sold in vending machines in all stations. After you purchase a ticket, you are responsible for validating it when you board the train or bus, or else face a hefty fine.

Contacts Berliner Verkehrsbetriebe (☎ *030/19449* ⊕ *www.bvg.de*). **S-Bahn Berlin GmbH** (☎ *030/2974–3333* ⊕ *www.s-bahn-berlin.de*). **VBB** (✉ *Hardenbergpl. 2, Western Downtown* ☎ *030/254–140* or *030/19449* ⊕ *www.vbbonline.de*).

TAXIS

The base rate is €3, after which prices vary according to a complex tariff system. Figure on paying around €8 for a ride the length of the Ku'damm. You can also get cabs at taxi stands or order one by calling; there's no additional fee if you call a cab by phone. From April through October, you can also hail *velotaxis*, rickshaw-like bicycle taxis, along Kurfürstendamm, Friedrichstrasse, and Unter den Linden and in Tiergarten.

Information Taxis (☎ *030/210–101, 030/210–202, 030/443–322, or 030/260–26)*.

TOUR OPTIONS

Bus number 100 runs between Zoo Station and Alexanderplatz, and Number 200 runs between Zoo Station, Potsdamer Platz, Alexanderplatz, and Prenzlauer Allee. The buses stop at almost all major sightseeing spots on the way.

BOAT TOURS

Tours of central Berlin's Spree and Landwehr canals give you up-close and unusual views of sights such as Charlottenburg Palace, the Reichstag, and the Berliner Dom. Tours usually depart twice a day from several bridges and piers in Berlin, such as Schlossbrücke in Charlottenburg; Hansabrücke and Haus der Kulturen der Welt in Tiergarten; Friedrichstrasse, Museum Island, and Nikolaiviertel in Mitte; and near the Jannowitzbrücke S-bahn and U-bahn station. Drinks, snacks, and wursts are available during the narrated trips. Reederei Riedel offers three inner-city trips that range from €6 to €14.

Information Reederei Bruno Winkler (☎ *030/349-9595)*. **Reederei Riedel** (☎ *030/693-4646)*. **Stern und Kreisschiffahrt** (☎ *030/536-3600* ⊕ *www. sternundkreis.de)*.

BUS TOURS

Four companies (Berliner Bären, Berolina Berlin-Service, Bus Verkehr Berlin, and Severin & Kühn) jointly offer city tours on yellow, double-decker City Circle buses, which run every 15 or 30 minutes, depending on the season. The full circuit takes two hours, as does the recorded narration listened to through headphones. For €18 you can jump on and off at the 14 stops. The bus driver sells tickets. During the warmer months, the last circuit leaves at 4 PM from the corner of Rankestrasse and Kurfürstendamm. Most companies have tours to Potsdam. Severin & Kühn also runs all-day tours to Dresden and Meissen.

Information Berliner Bären Stadtrundfahrten (*BBS* ✉ *Seeburgerstr. 19b, Charlottenburg* ☎ *030/3519-5270* ⊕ *www.sightseeing.de)*. **Berolina Berlin-Service** (✉ *Kurfürstendamm 220, at Meinekestr., Western Downtown* ☎ *030/8856-8030* ⊕ *www.berolina-berlin.com)*. **Bus Verkehr Berlin** (*BVB* ✉ *Kurfürstendamm 225, Western Downtown* ☎ *030/683-8910* ⊕ *www.bvb.net)*. **Severin & Kühn** (✉ *Kurfürstendamm 216, Western Downtown* ☎ *030/880-4190* ⊕ *www.severin-kuehn-berlin.de)*.

TRAIN TRAVEL

Since 2006 all long-distance trains stop only at the huge and glitzy central station, Hauptbahnhof–Lehrter Bahnhof, which lies at the north edge of the government district in former West Berlin. Regional trains also stop at the two former "main" stations of the past years: Bahnhof Zoo (in the West) and Ostbahnhof (in the East). Regional trains also stop at the central eastern stations Friedrichstrasse and Alexanderplatz.

VISITOR INFORMATION

Information **Berlin Infostore** (✉ *Kurfürstendamm 21, Neues Kranzler Eck, Western Downtown* ☎ *030/250–025* ⌚ *Mon.–Thurs. 9:30–8, Fri. and Sat. 9:30–9, Sun. 9:30–6* ⊕ *www.berlin-tourist-information.de).* **MD Infoline** (☎ *030/9026–99444* ⌚ *Weekdays 9–4, weekends 9–1).* **Staatliche Museen zu Berlin** (☎ *030/266–2951 operator* ⊕ *www.smb.museum).* **Tourist Information Center in Prenzlauer Berg** (✉ *Kuturbrauerei entrances on Schönhauser Allee 36–39, Knaackstr. 97, Sredzkistr. 1* ☎ *030/4431–5151* ⊕ *www.tic-prenzlauerberg.de).*

LEIPZIG

184 km (114 mi) southwest of Berlin.

With its world-renowned music, impressive art-nouveau architecture, incredibly clean city center, meandering back alleys, and the temptations of coffee and cake on every corner, the wonderfully cosmopolitan city of Leipzig is reminiscent of Vienna. Yet it is still a distinctively Saxon town.

Johann Sebastian Bach (1685–1750) was organist and choir director at the Thomaskirche, and the 19th-century composer Richard Wagner was born here in 1813. Today's Leipzig maintains this tradition with an extraordinary offering of music, theater, and opera, not to mention a fantastic nightlife.

Wartime bombs destroyed much of Leipzig's city center, but reconstruction efforts have uncovered one of Europe's most vibrant cities. Leipzig's art-nouveau flair is best discovered by exploring countless alleys, covered courtyards, and passageways. Many unattractive buildings from the postwar period remain but reinforce Leipzig's position on the line between modernity and antiquity.

With a population of about 500,000, Leipzig is the second-largest city in eastern Germany (after Berlin) and has long been a center of printing and bookselling. Astride major trade routes, it was an important market town in the Middle Ages, and it continues to be a trading center, thanks to the *Leipziger Messe* (trade and fair shows) throughout the year that bring together buyers from East and West.

TIMING   Leipzig can easily be explored in one day; it's possible to walk around the downtown area in just about three hours. The churches can be inspected in less than 20 minutes each. But if you're interested in German history and art, you'll need perhaps two full days so you can spend

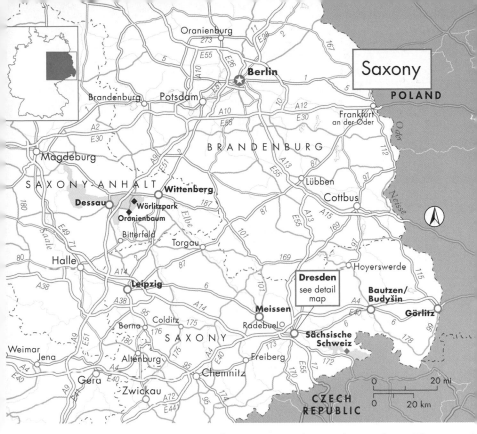

a whole day just visiting the museums and go to the symphony. The Völkerschlachtdenkmal is perfect for a half-day side trip.

EXPLORING LEIPZIG

Grassimuseum. British star architect David Chipperfield restored and modernized this fine example of German art deco in 2003–05. The building, dating to 1925–29, houses three important museums.

The **Museum für Angewandte Kunst** (*Museum of Applied Arts and Crafts* ☎0341/2229–100 ⊕*www.grassimuseum.de* 🎫*€4* 🕐*Tues. and Thurs.–Sun. 10–6, Wed. 10–8*) showcases works from Leipzig's and eastern Germany's proud tradition of handicrafts such as exquisite porcelain, fine tapestry art, and modern Bauhaus design. The **Museum für Völkerkunde** (*Ethnological Museum* ☎0341/9731–300 ⊕*www.grassimuseum.de* 🎫*€3* 🕐*Tues.–Fri. 10–6, weekends 10–5*) presents arts and crafts from all continents and various eras, including a thrilling collection of Southeast Asian antique art. The **Musikinstrumentenmuseum** (*Musical Instruments Museum* ☎0341/973–0750 ⊕mfm.uni-leipzig. de 🎫*€3* 🕐*Tues.–Sun. 11–5*) showcases musical instruments, mostly from the Renaissance, including the world's oldest clavichord, constructed in 1543 in Italy. There are also spinets, flutes, and lutes. Sample sounds of these instruments can be heard while looking at them. ✉ *Johannispl. 5–11.*

Mädlerpassage *(Mädler Mall).* The ghost of Goethe's Faust lurks in every marble corner of Leipzig's finest shopping arcade. Goethe set one of the scenes of *Faust* in the famous Auerbachs Keller restaurant, at No. 2. A bronze group of characters from the play, sculpted in 1913, beckons you down the stone staircase to the restaurant. ■TIP→**Touching the statues' feet brings good luck.** A few yards away is a delightful art-nouveau bar called Mephisto, done in devilish reds and blacks. ✉ *Grimmaische Str.*

Markt. Leipzig's showpiece is its huge, old market square. One side is occupied completely by the Renaissance town hall, the **Altes Rathaus,** which houses the **Stadtgeschichtliches Museum,** where Leipzig's past is well documented. ✉ *Markt 1* ☎ *0341/965–130* €3 ☉ *Tues.–Sun. 10–6.*

★ **Museum der Bildenden Künste** *(Museum of Fine Arts).* The city's leading art gallery is set in a new, ultramodern, cubelike complex at the exact location of the original, historic museum, which was destroyed by Allied bombing. The museum has more than 2,700 paintings representing everything from the German Middle Ages to contemporary American art; one of its finest collections focuses on Cranach the Elder. ✉ *Sachsenpl.* ☎ *0341/216–990* ⊕ *www.mdbk.de* €5, free 2nd Sun. of month ☉ *Tues. and Thurs.–Sun. 10–6, Wed. noon–8.*

★ **Nikolaikirche** *(St. Nicholas Church).* This church with its undistinguished facade was center stage during the demonstrations that helped bring down the Communist regime. Every Monday for months before the government collapsed, thousands of citizens gathered in front of the church chanting "*Wir sind das Volk*" ("We are the people"). Inside is a soaring Gothic choir and nave. Note the unusual patterned ceiling supported by classical pillars that end in palm-tree-like flourishes. Martin Luther is said to have preached from the ornate 16th-century pulpit. ■TIP→ **The prayers for peace that began the revolution in 1989 are still held on Monday at 5 PM.** ✉ *Nikolaikirchhof* ☎ *0341/960–5270* Free ☉ *Mon.–Sat. 10–6; Sun. services at 9:30, 11:15, and 5.*

Fodor'sChoice **Thomaskirche** *(St. Thomas's Church).* Bach was choirmaster at this ★ Gothic church for 27 years, and Martin Luther preached here on Whitsunday 1539, signaling the arrival of Protestantism in Leipzig. Originally the center of a 13th-century monastery, the tall church (rebuilt in the 15th century) now stands by itself. Bach wrote most of his cantatas for the church's famous boys' choir, the Thomanerchor, which was founded in the 13th century; the church continues as the choir's home as well as a center of Bach tradition.

The great music Bach wrote during his Leipzig years commanded little attention in his lifetime, and when he died he was given a simple grave, without a headstone, in the city's Johannisfriedhof (St. John Cemetery). It wasn't until 1894 that an effort was made to find where the great composer lay buried, and after a thorough, macabre search, his coffin was removed to the Johanniskirche. That church was destroyed by Allied bombs in December 1943, and Bach subsequently found his final resting place in the church he would have selected: the Thomaskirche.

■TIP➡ **You can listen to the famous boys' choir during the** *Motette,* **a service with a special emphasis on choral music.**

Bach's 12 children and the infant Richard Wagner were baptized in the early-17th-century font; Karl Marx and Friedrich Engels also stood before this same font, godfathers to Karl Liebknecht, who grew up to be a revolutionary as well. ⊠*Thomaskirchhof, off Grimmaischestr.* ☎*0341/2222 24 200* ⊕*www.thomaskirche.org* ☐*Free, Motette €1* ⊙*Daily 9–6; Motette Fri. at 6* PM*, Sat. at 3.*

WHERE TO STAY & EAT

★ **$$–$$$$** ✕**Kaiser Maximilian.** Leipzig's best Mediterranean restaurant serves inventive Italian and French dishes in a setting dominated by high, undecorated walls and black leather seats. The Maximilian is known for its pasta and fish dishes such as *Schwarze Lachstortelloni im Safransud* (black salmon tortelloni cooked in saffron juice). The gourmet set menu is the reason to visit the Kaiser: three courses for €35, five courses for €60. ⊠*Neumarkt 9–19* ☎*0341/3553–3333* ⚏*Reservations essential* ☰*AE, MC, V.*

$–$$$ ✕**Auerbachs Keller.** The most famous of Leipzig's restaurants consists
Fodor's Choice of an upscale, international gourmet restaurant and another restaurant
★ specializing in hearty Saxon fare. ■TIP➡ **It has been around since 1530, and Goethe immortalized one of the several vaulted historic rooms in his** *Faust.* The menu features regional dishes from Saxony, mostly hearty, roasted meat recipes. There's also a good wine list. ⊠*Mädlerpassage, Grimmaische Str. 2–4, D–04109* ☎*0341/216–100* ⚏*Reservations essential* ☰*AE, DC, MC, V* ⊙*Closed Mon.*

$–$$ ✕**Barthels Hof.** The English-language menu at this restaurant explains not only the cuisine but the history of Leipzig as well. Waitresses wear traditional *Trachten* dresses, but the rooms are quite modern. With a prominent location directly on the Markt, the restaurant is popular with locals, especially for the incredible breakfast buffet. ⊠*Hainstr. 1* ☎*0341/141–310* ☰*AE, DC, MC, V.*

¢–$ ✕**Thüringer Hof.** One of Germany's oldest restaurants and pubs (dating back to 1454) served its hearty Thuringian and Saxon fare to Martin Luther and the likes—who certainly had more than a mere pint of the beers on tap here. The menu in the reconstructed, cavernous, and always buzzing dining hall doesn't exactly offer gourmet cuisine but rather an impressively enormous variety of game, fish, and bratwurst dishes. The Thuringian sausages (served with either sauerkraut and potatoes or onions and mashed potatoes) and the famous Thuringian sauerbraten (beef marinated in a sour essence) are a must. ⊠*Burgstr. 19* ☎*0341/994–4999* ☰*AE, MC, V.*

$$$$ ⊟**Hotel Fürstenhof Leipzig.** The city's grandest hotel is inside the
Fodor's Choice renowned Löhr-Haus, a revered old mansion 1,650 feet from the main
★ train station on the ring road surrounding the city center. The stunning banquet section is the epitome of 19th-century grandeur, with red wall-

6

paper and black serpentine stone; the bar is a lofty meeting area under a bright glass cupola. Rooms are spacious and decorated with cherrywood designer furniture. ⌧*Tröndlinring 8, D–04105* ☎*0341/1400* 🖷*0341/140–3700* ⊕*www.luxurycollection.com* ⌧*80 rooms, 12 suites* ⌂*In-room: refrigerator, safe, dial-up, Wi-Fi (some). In-hotel: restaurant, room service, bar, pool, gym, spa, concierge, public Wi-Fi, laundry service, parking (fee), no-smoking rooms, some pets allowed (fee)* ⊟*AE, DC, MC, V.*

$ 📠**Ringhotel Adagio.** The quiet Adagio, tucked away behind the facade of a 19th-century city mansion, is centrally located between the Grassimuseum and the Neues Gewandhaus. All rooms are individually furnished; when making a reservation, ask for a "1920s room," which features the style of the Roaring '20s and bathtubs almost as large as a whirlpool. ⌧*Seeburgstr. 96, D–04103* ☎*0341/216–690* 🖷*0341/960–3078* ⊕*www.hotel-adagio.de* ⌧*30 rooms, 2 suites, 1 apartment* ⌂*In-room: no a/c, dial-up. In-hotel: laundry service, parking (fee), no-smoking rooms, some pets allowed (fee)* ⊟*AE, DC, MC, V* 🍴*CP.*

NIGHTLIFE & THE ARTS

In Faust, Goethe describes Leipzig as "Little Paris," and, with a vast assortment of restaurants, cafés, and clubs to match the city's exceptional musical and literary offerings, Leipzig is a fun city at night. The *Kneipenszene* (pub scene) is centered on the **Drallewatsch** (a Saxon slang word for "going out"), the small streets and alleys around Grosse and Kleine Fleischergasse and the Barfüsschengasse.

The **Neues Gewandhaus** (⌧*Augustuspl. 8, D–04109* ☎*0341/127–0280* ⊕*www.gewandhaus.de*), a controversial piece of architecture, is home to an undeniably splendid orchestra. Tickets to concerts are very difficult to obtain unless you reserve well in advance and in writing only. Sometimes spare tickets are available at the box office a half hour before the evening performance. Leipzig's annual music festival, **Music Days,** is in June.

One of Germany's most famous cabarets, the **Leipziger Pfeffermühle** (⌧*Thomaskirchhof 16* ☎*0341/960–3196*), has a lively bar off a courtyard opposite the Thomaskirche. On pleasant evenings the courtyard fills with benches and tables, and the scene rivals the indoor performance for entertainment.

SHOPPING

Small streets leading off the Markt attest to Leipzig's rich trading past. Tucked in among them are glass-roof arcades of surprising beauty and elegance, including the wonderfully restored **Specks Hof, Barthels Hof, Jägerhof,** and the **Passage zum Sachsenplatz.** Invent a headache and step into the *Apotheke* (pharmacy) at Hainstrasse 9—it is spectacularly art nouveau, with finely etched and stained glass and rich mahogany. For more glimpses into the past, check out the antiquarian bookstores of the nearby **Neumarkt Passage.**

The **Hauptbahnhof** (✉ *Willy-Brandt-Pl.*) offers more than 150 shops, restaurants, and cafés. All shops are open Monday through Saturday 9:30 AM–10 PM, and many shops are also open on Sunday, with the same hours. Thanks to the historic backdrop, it's one of the most beautiful and fun shopping experiences in eastern Germany.

DRESDEN

25 km (16 mi) southeast of Meissen, 140 km (87 mi) southeast of Leipzig, 193 km (120 mi) south of Berlin.

Saxony's capital city sits in baroque splendor on a wide sweep of the Elbe River, and its proponents are working with German thoroughness to recapture the city's old reputation as the "Florence on the Elbe." Its yellow and pale-green facades are enormously appealing, and their mere presence is even more overwhelming when you compare what you see today with photographs of Dresden from February 1945, after an Allied bombing raid destroyed the city overnight. Dresden was the capital of Saxony as early as the 15th century, although most of its architectural masterpieces date from the 18th century and the reigns of Augustus the Strong and his son, Frederick Augustus II.

Though some parts of the city center still look as if they're stuck halfway between demolition and construction, the present city is an enormous tribute to Dresdeners' skills and dedication. The resemblance of today's riverside to Dresden cityscapes painted by Canaletto in the mid-1700s is remarkable. Unfortunately, the war-inflicted gaps in the urban landscape in other parts of the city are too big to be closed anytime soon.

EXPLORING DRESDEN

❸ **Albertinum** *(Sculpture Collection).* The Albertinum is named after Saxony's King Albert, who between 1884 and 1887 converted a royal arsenal into a suitable setting for the treasures he and his forebears had collected. This massive, imperial-style building usually houses Dresden's leading art museum, one of the world's great galleries. However, the Albertinium will be closed for renovation until 2009. Until then selected pieces of the collection will be on display as special exhibits. The **Skulpturensammlung** will be exhibited as a constantly changing selection of pieces called *Sculpture in the Zwinger* (⇨ *Zwinger, below).* The collection contained in the **Gemäldegalerie Neue Meister** (Gallery of Modern Masters), which includes outstanding works by German masters of the 19th and 20th centuries (Caspar David Friedrich's haunting *Das Kreuz im Gebirge,* for example) and French impressionists and postimpressionists, is on a select rotating display in Dresden's other museums and galleries. Some of the paintings are on view at the Semperbau in the Zwinger. Check the Web site to see what is available for viewing at the time of your visit. ✉*Am Neumarkt, Brühlsche Terrasse* ⊕*www.skd-dresden.de.*

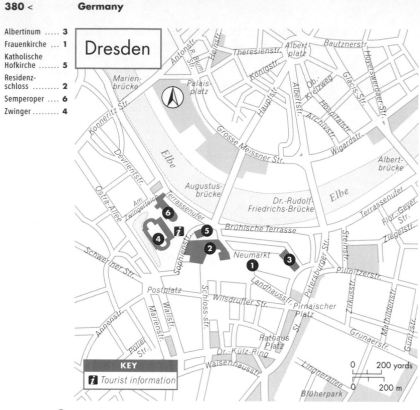

❶ **Frauenkirche** *(Church of Our Lady).* Dresden's Church of Our Lady,

Fodor'sChoice completed in 1743, was one of the masterpieces of baroque church

★ architecture. The huge dome set on a smaller square base, known as
the Stone Bell, was the inspiration of George Bähr, who designed the
church to be built "as if it was a single stone from the base to the
top." On February 15, 1945, two days after the bombing of Dresden, the burned-out shell of the magnificent Stone Bell collapsed. For
the following five decades the remains of the church, a pile of rubble,
remained a gripping memorial to the horrors of war. In a move shocking to the East German authorities, who organized all public demonstrations, a group of young people spontaneously met here on February
13, 1982, for a candlelight vigil for peace.

Although the will to rebuild the church was strong, the political and
economic situation in the GDR prevented it. It wasn't until the unification of Germany that Dresden began to seriously consider reconstruction. In the early 1990s a citizens' initiative, joined by the Lutheran
Church of Saxony and the city of Dresden, decided to rebuild the
church using the original stones. The goal of completing the church by
2006, Dresden's 800th anniversary, seemed insurmountable. Money
soon started pouring in from around the globe, however, and work
began. The rubble was cleared away, and the size and shape of each

stone were catalogued. Computer-imaging technology helped place each recovered stone in its original location.

During construction, guided tours and Frauenkirche concerts brought in donations. The biggest supporter of the project in the United Kingdom, the Dresden Trust, is centered in the city of Coventry, itself bombed mercilessly by the German *Luftwaffe* during the war. The Dresden Trust raised more than €600,000 and donated the gold pinnacle cross that now graces the church dome.

On Sunday, October 30, 2005 (almost a year ahead of schedule), Dresden's skyline became a little more complete with the consecration of the Frauenkirche. Leading the service was the bishop of Coventry. Although the church is usually open to all, it closes frequently for concerts and other events. Check the English-language schedule next to entrance D. ⊠*An der Frauenkirche* ☎*0351/498–1131* ⊕*www.frauenkirche-dresden.org* 🖰*Free. Cupola and tower €8. Audio guides in English €2.50* 🕑 *Weekdays 10–noon and 1–6. Cupola and tower daily 10–6.*

❺ Katholische Hofkirche *(Catholic Court Church).* The largest church in Saxony is also known as the Cathedral of St. Trinitatis. Frederick Augustus II (who reigned 1733–63) brought architects and builders from Italy to construct a Catholic church in a city that had been the first large center of Lutheran Protestantism (like his father, Frederick Augustus II had to convert to Catholicism to be eligible to wear the Polish crown). Inside, the treasures include a beautiful stone pulpit by the royal sculptor Balthasar Permoser and a painstakingly restored 250-year-old organ said to be one of the finest ever to come from the mountain workshops of the famous Silbermann family. In the cathedral's crypt are the tombs of 49 Saxon rulers and a reliquary containing the heart of Augustus the Strong. Owing to restoration work, the cathedral's opening hours may vary. ⊠*Schlosspl.* ☎*0351/484–4712* 🖰*Free* 🕑 *Mon.–Thurs. 9–5, Fri. 1–5, Sat. 10–5, Sun. noon–4:30.*

❷ Residenzschloss *(Dresden City Royal Palace).* Restoration work is still under way behind the Renaissance facade of this former royal palace, much of which was built between 1709 and 1722. Some of the finished rooms in the **Georgenbau** host historical exhibitions, among them an excellent one on the reconstruction of the palace itself. The palace's main gateway, the Georgentor, has an enormous statue of the fully armed Saxon count George. ■TIP➔ **From April through October, the palace's old Hausmannsturm (Hausmann Tower) offers a wonderful view of the city and the Elbe River.**

But the main attraction is the world-famous **Grünes Gewölbe** (Green Vault). Named after a green room in the palace of Augustus the Strong, the collection is divided into two sections.

Fodor'sChoice ★ The **Neues Grünes Gewölbe** *(New Green Vault)* contains an exquisite collection of unique objets d'art fashioned from gold, silver, ivory, amber, and other precious and semiprecious materials. Among the crown jewels is the world's largest "green" diamond, 41 carats in weight, and a dazzling group of tiny gem-studded figures called *Hofstaat zu Delhi* *am Geburtstag des Grossmoguls Aureng-Zeb* (the Court at Delhi during the Birthday of the Great Mogul Aureng-Zeb). The unwieldy name gives a false idea of the size of the work, dating from 1708; some parts of the tableau are so small they can be admired only through a magnifying glass. Somewhat larger and less delicate is the drinking bowl of Ivan the Terrible, perhaps the most sensational artifact in this extraordinary museum. The **Historisches Grünes Gewölbe** (*Historic Green Vault* ☎*0351/4919–2285 for tours* ⊕*www.skd-dresden.de* 🎫*€11.50* ⊙ *By appointment only*) is the section of the castle most reflective of Augustus the Strong's obsession with art as a symbol of power. The intricately restored baroque interior is not only a display that highlights the objects in the collection but also an integral part of the presentation itself. The last section of the museum houses the Jewel Room, displaying the ceremonial crown jewels of Augustus the Strong and his son. Access to the Historic Green Vault is limited to 100 visitors per hour and is by appointment only. Tickets can be reserved by phone or online. The palace also houses the **Münzkabinett** (Coin Museum) and the **Kupferstichkabinett** (Museum of Prints and Drawings), with more than 500,000 pieces of art spanning several centuries. Changing exhibits at the Kupferstichkabinett present masterworks by Albrecht Dürer, Peter Paul Rubens, and Jan van Eyck, but also 20th-century art by Otto Dix, Edvard Munch, and Ernst Ludwig Kirchner as well as East European art and some Southeast Asian prints. ✉*Schlosspl.* ☎*0351/491–4619* 🎫*All museums and collections at palace (except Historic Green Vault) €6. Historic Green Vault €11.50* ⊙ *Wed.–Mon. 10–6; Historic Green Vault by appointment only.*

★ ❻ **Semperoper** (*Semper Opera House*). One of Germany's best-known and most popular theaters, this magnificent opera house saw the premieres of Richard Wagner's *Rienzi, Der Fliegende Holländer,* and *Tannhäuser* and Richard Strauss's *Salome, Elektra,* and *Der Rosenkavalier.* The Dresden architect Gottfried Semper built the house in 1838–41 in Italian Renaissance style, then saw his work destroyed in a fire caused by a careless lamplighter. Semper had to flee Dresden after participating in a democratic uprising, so his son Manfred rebuilt the theater in the neo-Renaissance style you see today. Even Manfred Semper's version had to be rebuilt after the devastating bombing raid of February 1945. On the 40th anniversary of that raid—February 13, 1985—the Semperoper reopened with a performance of *Der Freischütz,* by Carl Maria von Weber, another artist who did much to make Dresden a leading center of German music and culture. Check the Web site for the performance schedule. Even if you're no opera buff, the Semper's lavish interior can't fail to impress. Velvet, brocade, and well-crafted imitation marble create an atmosphere of intimate luxury (it seats 1,323). Guided tours of the building are offered throughout the day, depending on the opera's rehearsal schedule. Tours begin at the entrance to your right as you face the Elbe River. ✉*Theaterpl. 2* ☎*0351/491–1496* 🎫*Tour €7* ⊙ *Tours usually weekdays at 1:30, 2, and 3; weekends at 10.*

4 **Zwinger** *(Bailey).* Dresden's magnif-
Fodor'sChoice icent baroque showpiece is entered
★ by way of the mighty Kronentor
(Crown Gate), off Ostra-Allee.
Augustus the Strong hired a small
army of artists and artisans to create a "pleasure ground" worthy
of the Saxon court on the site of
the former bailey, part of the city
fortifications. The artisans worked
under the direction of the architect
Matthäus Daniel Pöppelmann, who

UNDER CONSTRUCTION

Dresden is a work in progress and
renovations are under way at several of Dresden's top attractions,
including the Zwinger, the Residenzschloss, and the Albertinum.
Be sure to double-check avail-
ability and hours when planning
your visit.

came reluctantly out of retirement to design what would be his greatest
work, begun in 1707 and completed in 1728. Completely enclosing a
central courtyard filled with lawns, pools, and fountains, the complex
is made up of six linked pavilions, one of which boasts a carillon of
Meissen bells, hence its name: Glockenspielpavillon.

The Zwinger is quite a scene—a riot of garlands, nymphs, and other
baroque ornamentation and sculpture. Wide staircases beckon to gal-
leried walks and to the romantic Nymphenbad, a coyly hidden courtyard where statues of nude women perch in alcoves to protect them
from a fountain that spits unexpectedly. The Zwinger once had an
open view of the riverbank, but the Semper Opera House now closes in
that side. Stand in the center of this quiet oasis, where the city's roar is
kept at bay by the outer wings of the structure, and imagine the court
festivities held here.

The **Gemäldegalerie Alte Meister** (*Gallery of Old Masters* ☎*0351/491–
4679* 🎟*€6* ⊙*Tues.–Sun. 10–6*), in the northwestern corner of the
complex, was built to house portions of the royal art collections.
Among the priceless paintings are works by Dürer, Holbein, Jan van
Eyck, Rembrandt, Rubens, van Dyck, Hals, Vermeer, Raphael (*The
Sistine Madonna*), Titian, Giorgione, Veronese, Velázquez, Murillo,
Canaletto, and Watteau. On the wall of the entrance archway you'll see
an inscription in Russian, one of the few amusing reminders of World
War II in Dresden. It reads, in rhyme: MUSEUM CHECKED. NO MINES. CHA-
NUTIN DID THE CHECKING. Chanutin, presumably, was the Russian soldier responsible for checking one of Germany's greatest art galleries for
anything more explosive than a Rubens nude. The Zwinger's **Porzellans-
ammlung** (*Porcelain Collection* ☎*0351/491–4619* 🎟*€5* ⊙*Tues.–Sun.
10–6*), stretching from the curved gallery that adjoins the Glockenspielpavillon to the long gallery on the east side, is considered one of the
best of its kind in the world. The focus, naturally, is on Dresden and
Meissen china, but there are also outstanding examples of Japanese,
Chinese, and Korean porcelain. The **Rüstkammer** (*Armory* ☎*0351/491–
4619* 🎟*€3* ⊙*Tues.–Sun. 10–6*) holds medieval and Renaissance suits
of armor and weapons. The **Staatlicher Mathematisch-Physikalischer
Salon** (*State Mathematics and Physics Salon* ☎*0351/491–4660* 🎟*€3*
⊙*Tues.–Sun. 10–6*) is packed with rare and historic scientific instruments. ✉*Zwinger entrance, Ostra-Allee* ⊕*www.skd-dresden.de.*

6

WHERE TO STAY & EAT

★ $$ ✗ **Alte Meister.** Set in the historic mansion of the architect who rebuilt the Zwinger and named after the school of medieval German painters that includes Dürer, Holbein, and Rembrandt, the Alte Meister has a sophisticated old-world flair that charms locals and tourists alike. The food, however, is very current, and the light German nouvelle cuisine with careful touches of Asian spices and ingredients has earned chef Dirk Wende critical praise. In summer this is one of the city's premier dining spots, offering a grand view of the Semperoper from a shaded terrace. ✉*Braun'sches Atelier Theaterpl. 1a* ☎*0351/481–0426* ▭*AE, MC, V.*

¢–$ ✗ **Ball- und Brauhaus Watzke.** One of the city's oldest microbreweries, the Ballhaus Watzke offers a great reprieve from Dresden's mass-produced Radeberger. Several different homemade beers are on tap (you can even help brew one). Tours of the brewery cost €5 with a tasting or €12.50 with meal, and you can get your beer to go in a one- or two-liter jug called a *Siphon*. The food is hearty, contemporary Saxon. There is a fantastic panorama view of Dresden and a beer garden. ✉*Koetzschenbroderstr. 1* ☎*0351/852–920* ▭*AE, MC, V.*

★ $$$$ ▦ **Kempinski Hotel Taschenbergpalais Dresden.** Destroyed in wartime bombing but now rebuilt, the historic Taschenberg Palace—the work of the Zwinger architect Matthäus Daniel Pöppelmann—is Dresden's premier address and the last word in luxury, as befits the former residence of the Saxon crown princes. Rooms are as big as city apartments, although suites earn the adjective *palatial*; they are all furnished with bright elm-wood furniture. ✉*Taschenberg 3, D–01067* ☎*0351/49120* 🖷*0351/491–2812* ⊕*www.kempinski-dresden.de* ↗*188 rooms, 25 suites* ♿*In-room: safe, Ethernet, Wi-Fi. In-hotel: 4 restaurants, room service, bar, pool, concierge, laundry service, parking (fee), no-smoking rooms, some pets allowed (fee)* ▭*AE, DC, MC, V.*

$$ ▦ **Schlosshotel Dresden-Pillnitz.** On the grounds of Schloss Pillnitz (Pillnitz Palace), this small hotel allows you to enjoy the countryside without getting too far from the city. The beautifully restored mansion is run by the Zepp family, who extend extremely personal service. The airy rooms are decorated with bright colors and timeless, elegant country furniture. Just a few hundred yards from the hotel is a pier where Elbe River cruises depart. The spa Vitalzentrum zum goldenen Apfel is a short walk away. ✉*August-Böckstiegel-Str. 10, D–01326* ☎*0351/26140* 🖷*0351/261–4400* ⊕*www.schlosshotel-pillnitz.de* ↗*42 rooms, 3 suites* ♿*In-room: no a/c, Ethernet, dial-up. In-hotel: restaurant, bar, laundry service, parking (no fee), no-smoking rooms, some pets allowed (fee)* ▭*AE, MC, V* ⦶*BP.*

$–$$ ▦ **Rothenburger Hof.** One of Dresden's smallest and oldest luxury hotels, the historic Rothenburger Hof opened in 1865 and is only a few steps away from the city's sightseeing spots. A highlight is the dining room, which gives you some insight as to how Dresden's wealthy wined and dined 150 years ago. The rooms are not very large, but they're comfortable and nicely decorated with furniture that looks antique but, in fact, is reproduction. ⊠*Rothenburger Str. 15–17, D–01099* 🕿*0351/81260* 🖷*0351/812–6222* ⊕*www.dresden-hotel.de* ⇆*26 rooms, 13 apartments* ♿*In-room: no a/c, Ethernet.* *In-hotel: room service, public Wi-Fi, bar, pool, gym, laundry service, parking (fee), no-smoking rooms* ⊟*AE, MC, V* ⚆*BP.*

NIGHTLIFE & THE ARTS

Dresdeners are known for their industriousness and very efficient way of doing business, but they also know how to spend a night out. Most of Dresden's pubs, bars, and *Kneipen* are in the **Äussere Neustadt** district and along the buzzing **Münzgasse** (between Frauenkirche and Brühlsche Terrasse).

The opera in Dresden holds an international reputation largely due to the **Semper Opera House** (*Sächsische Staatsoper Dresden* ⊠*Theaterpl.* ⊕*www.semperoper.de* ⊠*Evening box office, Abendkasse, left of main entrance* 🕿*0351/491–1705*). Destroyed during the war, the building has been meticulously rebuilt and renovated. Tickets are reasonably priced but also hard to come by; they're often included in package tours. ■**TIP➜ Try your luck at reserving tickets at the Web site or stop by the evening box office about a half hour before the performance.** If that doesn't work, take one of the opera-house tours.

Dresden's fine **Philharmonie Dresden** (*Philharmonic Orchestra Dresden* ⊠*Kulturpalast am Altmarkt* 🕿*0351/486–6286*) takes center stage in the city's annual music festival, from mid-May to early June. In addition to the annual film festival in April, open-air **Filmnächte am Elbufer** (*Elbe Riverside Film Nights* ⊠*Am Königsufer, next to the State Ministry of Finance* 🕿*0351/899–320*) take place on the bank of the Elbe from late June to late August.

SHOPPING

Dresden is almost as famous as Meissen for its porcelain. It's manufactured outside the city in **Freital,** where there's a showroom and shop, **Sächsische Porzellan-Manufaktur Dresden** (⊠*Carl-Thieme-Str. 16, Freital* 🕿*0351/647–130*), open Monday through Saturday 9–5. Within Dresden you'll find exquisite Meissen and Freital porcelain at the department store **Karstadt** (⊠*Prager Str. 12* 🕿*0351/490–6833*). The **Kunststube am Zwinger** (⊠*Hertha-Lindner-Str. 10–12* 🕿*0351/490–4082*) sells wooden toys and the famous Saxon *Räuchermännchen* (Smoking Men) and *Weihnachtspyramiden* (Christmas Lights Pyramids) manufactured by hand in the Erzbirge Mountains.

GERMANY ESSENTIALS

TRANSPORTATION

BY AIR

Lufthansa is Germany's leading carrier and is a member of the Star Alliance. Germany's internal air network is excellent, with flights linking all major cities in little more than an hour. A handful of smaller airlines—Deutsche BA, Germanwings, and TUIfly—compete with low-fare flights within Germany and to other European cities. Most trans-Atlantic flights land in Frankfurt, but there are also flights into Munich and nonstop to Berlin. You may have to connect in another European airport to get to Berlin.

Airline Contacts Air Canada (☏ *888/247-2262* ⊕ www.aircanada.com). **American Airlines** (☏ *800/433-7300* ⊕ *www.aa.com*). **Continental Airlines** (☏ *800/523-3273 for U.S. and Mexico reservations, 800/231-0856 for international reservations* ⊕ *www.continental.com*). **Delta Airlines** (☏ *800/221-1212 for U.S. reservations, 800/241-4141 for international reservations* ⊕ *www.delta.com*). **Icelandair** (☏ *800/223-5500* ⊕ *www.icelandair.com*). **LTU** (☏ *866/266-5588* ⊕ *www.ltu.de*). **Lufthansa** (☏ *800/645-3880* ⊕ *www.lufthansa.com*). **Northwest Airlines** (☏ *800/225-2525* ⊕ *www.nwa.com*). **United Airlines** (☏ *800/864-8331 for U.S. reservations, 800/538-2929 for international reservations* ⊕ *www.united.com*). **USAirways** (☏ *800/428-4322 for U.S. and Canada reservations, 800/622-1015 for international reservations* ⊕ *www.usairways.com*).

Within Germany Air Berlin (☏ *01805/737-800, 0870/738-8880 in U.K.* ⊕ *www.airberlin.com*). **Deutsche BA** (☏ *01805/359-322* ⊕ *www.flydba.com*). **Germanwings** (☏ *0900/191-9100* ⊕ *www.germanwings.com*). **TUIfly** (☏ *01805/757-510* ⊕ *www.TUIfly.com*). **Lufthansa** (☏ *0180/380-3803 or 0180/5838-42672* ⊕ *www.lufthansa.com*).

AIRPORTS

Frankfurt is Germany's air hub. The large airport has the convenience of its own long-distance train station, but if you're transferring between flights, don't dawdle or you could miss your connection. Delta and Continental have nonstop service between New York and Tegel, the largest of the three airports in Berlin. Continental also has nonstop service between New York and Hamburg. There are a few nonstop services from North America to Munich and Düsseldorf.

Airport Information Berlin: Schönefeld (*SXF* ☏ *01805/000-186 €.12 per minute* ⊕ *www.berlin-airport.de*).

BY CAR

Entry formalities for motorists are few: all you need is proof of insurance, an international car-registration document, and your driver's license. If you or your car is from an EU country, Norway, or Switzerland, all you need is your domestic license and proof of insurance. *All* foreign cars must have a country sticker. There are no toll roads in Germany, except for a few Alpine mountain passes. In addition to the cost of a rental car, remember that gasoline is typically much more expensive anywhere in Europe than in the United States.

RULES OF THE ROAD

In Germany, road signs give distances in kilometers. There *are* posted speed limits on autobahns, and they advise drivers to keep below 130 kph (80 mph) or 110 kph (65 mph). A sign saying *Richtgeschwindigkeit* and the speed indicates this. Speed limits on country roads vary from 70 kph to 100 kph (43 mph to 62 mph) and are usually 50 kph (30 mph) through small towns.

Don't enter a street with a signpost bearing a red circle with a white horizontal stripe—it's a one-way street. Blue EINBAHNSTRASSE signs indicate you're headed the correct way down a one-way street. The blood-alcohol limit for driving in Germany is very low (.05%). Note that seat belts must be worn at all times by front- *and* back-seat passengers.

Note that German drivers tend to drive fast and aggressively. If you wish to drive comfortably on the autobahn, stay in the right lane. Speeds under 80 kph (50 mph) are not permitted. Though prohibited, tailgating is a favorite sport on German roads. Do not react by braking for no reason: this is equally prohibited. You may not use a handheld mobile phone while driving.

6

CAR RENTALS

If you need to rent a car for your travels in Germany, you can do so in Berlin, either at the airport or in the city center. All the major car-rental companies are represented. If you are going to rent a car in Germany, you will need an International Driving Permit (IDP); it's available from the American Automobile Association and the National Automobile Club. These international permits are universally recognized, and having one in your wallet may save you problems with the local authorities. In Germany you usually must be 21 to rent a car. Nearly all agencies allow you to drive into Germany's neighboring countries. It's frequently possible to return the car in another West European country, but not in Poland or the Czech Republic, for example.

Rates with the major car-rental companies begin at about €55 per day and €300 per week for an economy car with a manual transmission and unlimited mileage. Most rentals are manual, so if you want an automatic, be sure to request one in advance. If you're traveling with children, don't forget to ask for a car seat when you reserve.

Information Avis (⊠ *Tegel Airport, Reinickendorf* ☎ *030/4101–3148* ⊠ *Budapester Str. 43, at Europa Center, Western Downtown* ☎ *030/230–9370*). **Europcar** (⊠ *Tegel Airport, Reinickendorf* ☎ *030/417–8520* ⊠ *Kurfürstenstr. 101, Schöneberg* ☎ *030/235–0640* ⊠ *Zentrale Omnibusbahnhof, Messedamm 8, Charlottenburg* ☎ *030/306–9590*). **Hertz** (⊠ *Tegel Airport, Reinickendorf* ☎ *030/4170–4674* ⊠ *Budapester Str. 39, Western Downtown* ☎ *030/261–1053*). **Sixt** (⊠ *Tegel Airport, Reinickendorf* ☎ *030/4101–2886* ⊠ *Budapester Str. 45, Western Downtown* ☎ *030/4101–2886* ⊠ *Kaiserdamm 40, Charlottenburg* ☎ *030/411–7087* ⊠ *Leipziger Str. 104, Mitte* ☎ *030/4101–2886*).

BY TRAIN

Deutsche Bahn (DB—German Rail) is a very efficient, privatized railway. Its high-speed InterCity Express (ICE), InterCity (IC), and EuroCity (EC) trains make journeys between the centers of many cities—Munich–Frankfurt, for example—faster by rail than by air. City-NightLine (CNL) trains serving Austria and Switzerland and Nachtzug ("night train" or NZ) long-distance trains have sleepers. For round-trip travel you can save 25% if you book at least three days in advance, 50% if you stay over a Saturday night and book at least three to seven days in advance. Other kinds of discount tickets can also save you a great deal off the regular fares.

If Germany is your only destination in Europe, consider purchasing a German Rail Pass, which allows 4 to 10 days of unlimited first- or second-class travel within a one-month period on any DB train, up to and including the ICE. A Twin Pass saves two people traveling together 50% off one person's fare. Remember that you must still reserve seats for the ICE trains.

In order to comply with the strict rules about validating tickets before you begin travel, read the instructions carefully. Some tickets require that a train official validate your pass, whereas others require you to write in the first date of travel.

CONTACTS & RESOURCES

MONEY

The official currency in Germany is the euro (€), Most business accept credit cards—and all major U.S. credit cards are accepted in Germany—so you probably won't have to use cash for payment in high-end hotels and restaurants. Many businesses on the other end of the spectrum don't accept them, however. ATMs are common, but some German banks exact €3–€5 fees for use of their ATMs. Nevertheless, you'll usually get a better rate of exchange via an ATM than you will at a currency-exchange office or even when changing money in a bank.

EMERGENCIES

Throughout Germany call ☎110 for police, ☎112 for an ambulance or the fire department.

The German automobile clubs ADAC and AvD operate tow trucks on all autobahns. NOTRUF signs every 2 km (1 mi) on autobahns (and country roads) indicate emergency telephones. By picking up the phone, you'll be connected to an operator who can determine your exact location and get you the services you need. Help is free (with the exception of materials).

Emergency Services Roadside assistance (☎ 01802/222–222).

Foreign Embassies U.S. Embassy (✉ Neustädtische Kirchstr. 4–5, D–10117 Berlin ✉ Clayallee 170 [consular section] ☎ 030/83050, 030/832–9233 for American citizens ⊕ www.usembassy.de).

INTERNET, MAIL & SHIPPING

Nearly all hotels have in-room data ports, but you may have to purchase, or borrow from the front desk, a cable with an end that matches German phone jacks. If you're plugging into a phone line, you'll need a local access number for a connection. Wireless Internet (called WLAN in Germany) is more and more common in high-end hotels. The service is not free, however. You must purchase blocks of time from the front desk or online using a credit card. The cost is fairly high, however, usually around €4 for 30 minutes.

There are alternatives. Some hotels have an Internet room for guests needing to check their e-mail. Otherwise, Internet cafés are common, and many bars and restaurants let you surf the Web.

MAIL

A post office in Germany (*Postamt*) is recognizable by the postal symbol, a black bugle on a yellow background. In some villages you will find one in the local supermarket. Stamps (*Briefmarken*) can also be bought at some news agencies and souvenir shops. Post offices are generally open weekdays 8–6, Saturday 8–noon.

Airmail letters to the United States cost €1.55; postcards, €1. These rates apply to standard-size envelopes. Letters take approximately five to seven days to the United States.

PASSPORTS & VISAS

U.S. citizens need only a passport valid for at least four months to enter Germany for stays of up to 90 days. Border guards often don't stamp passports; if you require a stamp, you often have to request it. Children must be included in a parent's passport or have their own valid passports.

PHONES

The country code for Germany is 49. When dialing a German number from abroad, drop the initial "0" from the local area code. Many companies have service lines beginning with 0180. The cost of these calls averages €.12 per minute. Numbers that begin with 0190 can cost €1.85 per minute and more.

A local call from a telephone booth costs €.10 per minute. Dial the "0" before the area code when making a long-distance call within Germany. When dialing within a local area code, drop the "0" and the area code.

Telephone booths are not a common feature on the streets, so be prepared to walk out of your way to find one (most post offices have one). Phone booths have instructions in English as well as German. Most telephone booths in Germany are card-operated, so buy a phone card at a post office or newsstand.

International calls can be made from any telephone booth in Germany. It costs only €.13 per minute to call the United States, day or night, no matter how long the call lasts. Use a phone card. If you don't have a good deal with a calling card, there are many stores that offer international calls at rates well below what you will pay from a phone booth. At a hotel, rates will be at least double the regular charge.

Access Codes AT&T Direct (☎ *0800/225–5288*). **Sprint International Access** (☎ *0800/888–0013*). **MCI WorldPhone** (☎ *0800/888–8000*).

MOBILE PHONES

If you have a multiband phone (some countries use different frequencies from what's used in the United States) and your service provider uses the world-standard GSM network (as do T-Mobile and AT&T), you can probably use your phone abroad. Roaming fees can be steep, however: 99¢ a minute is considered reasonable. And overseas you normally pay the toll charges for incoming calls. It's almost always cheaper to send a text message than to make a call, since text messages have a very low set fee (often less than 5¢).

If you just want to make local calls, consider buying a new SIM card (note that your provider may have to unlock your phone for you to use a different SIM card) and a prepaid service plan in the destination. You'll then have a local number and can make local calls at local rates. If your trip is extensive, you could also simply buy a new cell phone in your destination, as the initial cost will be offset over time.

TAXES

Most prices you see on items already include Germany's 19% value-added tax (V.A.T.). When making a purchase, ask for a V.A.T. refund form and find out whether the merchant gives refunds—not all stores do, nor are they required to. An item must cost at least €25 to qualify for a V.A.T. refund.

Have the form stamped like any customs form by customs officials when you leave the country or, if you're visiting several European Union countries, when you leave the EU. After you're through passport control, take the form to a refund-service counter for an on-the-spot refund (which is usually the quickest and easiest option), or mail it to the address on the form (or the envelope with it) after you arrive home. You receive the total refund stated on the form, but the processing time can be long, especially if you request a credit-card adjustment.

V.A.T. REFUNDS AT THE AIRPORT

If you're departing from Terminal 1 at Frankfurt Airport, where you bring your purchases to claim your tax back depends on how you've packed the goods. If the items are in your checked luggage, check in as normal, but let the ticket counter know you have to claim your tax still. They will give you your luggage back to bring to the customs office in departure hall B, Level 2. For goods you are carrying on the plane with you, go to the customs office on the way to your gate. After you pass through passport control, there is a Global Refund office.

If you're departing from Terminal 2, bring goods in luggage to be checked to the customs office in Hall D, Level 2 (opposite the Delta Airlines check-in counters). For goods you are carrying on the plane with you, see the customs office in Hall E, Level 3 (near security control).

V.A.T. Refunds Global Refund (☎ *800/566-9828* ⊕ *www.globalrefund.com*).

TIPPING

Tipping is done at your own discretion. Theater ushers and tour guides do not necessarily expect a tip, but waiters, bartenders, and taxi drivers do. Rounding off bills to the next highest sum is customary for bills under € 10. Above that sum you should add a little more.

Service charges are included in all restaurant checks (listed as *Bedienung*), as is tax (listed as *MWST*). Nonetheless, it is customary to round up the bill to the nearest euro or to leave about 5%–10%. Give it to the waitstaff as you pay the bill; don't leave it on the table, as that's considered rude.

VISITOR INFORMATION

Information Dresden (✉ *Dresden Werbung und Tourismus GmbH, Ostraallee 11, D–01067* ☎ *0351/491–920* 🖶 *0351/4919–2244* ⊕ *www.dresden-tourist. de*). **Leipzig** (✉ *Leipzig Tourist Service e.V., Richard-Wagner-Str. 1, D–04109* ☎ *0341/710–4260* 🖶 *0341/710–4301* ⊕ *www.leipzig.de*).

6

Hungary

Updated by
Paul Olchváry

ALTHOUGH A POST–WORLD WAR I treaty left Hungary a third the size of its former self, Hungary has a wealth of cultural and geographic splendors on offer to visitors almost a century on. Immerse yourself in beautiful, bustling Budapest with its grand old boulevards, age-old baths, and celebrated views of its city-center bisected by the Danube. Take in the dramatic hills and historic towns and villages of the Danube Bend north of the capital, where the river makes its sudden, southward shift toward Budapest. Soak in the sun at Central Europe's largest body of water, Lake Balaton. Dine on traditional, spicy fare at a thatched-roof *csárda* (inn) on the sweeping Great Plain, with its almost eerie natural splendors. Explore sumptuous smaller towns like Pécs or Eger, Sopron or Szeged, Kecskemét or Debrecen, each with an appeal all its own. And, by all means, imbibe in Hungary's world-class wine regions such as that of Tokaj.

Having survived countless invasions and foreign occupations, Hungary sits at the crossroads of Central Europe. Its resilient people have a history of brave but unfortunate uprisings: against the Turks in the 17th century, the Habsburgs in 1848, and the Soviet Union in 1956. In 1990, with the Iron Curtain finally torn away, Hungary held free elections and embarked on an era of sweeping changes. The adjustment to a free-market economy has not been all smooth sailing, but with its self-determination regained, Hungary has rebuilt a political and economic system devastated by years of Communist misrule. Hungary joined NATO in 1999 and entered the European Union (EU) in 2005. And while it continues to be a country in transition, much seems possible as an entire generation of Hungarians is coming of age for whom foreign occupation and repression of free speech are a distant memory.

Ironically, despite trying to shake off its communist legacy, in 2006 Hungary voted the Socialist Party, the successor to the communist party, back into power for a second four-year term. Almost immediately, the government found itself mired in a major scandal: Prime Minister Ferenc Gyurcsány was recorded admitting that his government had been repeatedly lying—"morning, day, and night"—about the economy to win the elections. Massive street protests followed, eerily coinciding with the 50th anniversary of the 1956 revolution, but in the end, Gyurcsány's government survived.

Two rivers cross the country: the famous Duna (Danube) flows from the west through capital city Budapest on its way to the southern frontier, and the smaller Tisza flows from the northeast across the Nagyalföld (Great Plain). Western

7

GOOD TO KNOW

What not to say to a Hungarian: That Hungary is great because everything is so cheap. Hearing visitors say this sends a chill up locals' spines: it is a double reminder not only of their shaky economy but also of how folks elsewhere are relatively well off. Instead, tell Hungarians you love Hungary because it is lovely, because the people and places are bright and beautiful, because their language sounds so sumptuous, and because the food is scrumptious—likewise good reasons to love Hungary, after all.

Hungary is dominated by Lake Balaton. Notwithstanding some over-development, its shores are still lined with historic villages, relaxing spas, magnificent vineyards, and shaded garden restaurants serving the catch of the day. In eastern Hungary, the Nagyalföld (Great Plain) offers opportunities to explore the folklore and customs of the region that many consider to be the heartland of the Magyars (the Hungarians' name for themselves). It is an area of spicy food, vast dusty flatlands, and the proud *csikósok* (horsemen).

Hungarians are known for their hospitality toward visitors. Although their unique language is no quick study, English is a second language for many young Magyars. But what all Hungarians share is a deep love of music, and the calendar is studded with it, from Budapest's famous opera to its annual spring music festival. And, although you may find few locals at such "touristy" establishments, there are still plenty of restaurants where Gypsy violinists serenade you during your evening meal.

EXPLORING HUNGARY

Hungary's main geographical regions begin with the capital city and thriving urban heart of **Budapest.** Just north of Budapest, the Danube forms a gentle heart-shaped curve along which lie the romantic and historic towns of the region called the **Danube Bend.** Southwest of Budapest are the vineyards, quaint villages, and popular summer resorts around **Lake Balaton.** The verdant, rolling countryside of **Transdanubia** stretches west of the Danube to the borders of Austria, Slovenia, and Croatia; in the northern hills nestle the gemlike, beautifully restored town of Sopron and in the south, the culturally rich, beautiful city of Pécs. Given Hungary's relatively small size, all of these points are within two or three hours from Budapest by car or train. As for **eastern Hungary,** its thin northern band bordering Slovakia comprises a rural and gently mountainous landscape that includes the handsome, vibrant town of Eger and the wine village of Tokaj; the contrastingly flat and dry expanses of the Great Plain, stretching south and east, are spiced with legendary traditions of horsemanship and agriculture and anchored by the culturally vibrant cities of Szeged, Debrecen, and Kecskemét.

ABOUT THE RESTAURANTS

Through the lean postwar years the Hungarian kitchen lost none of its spice and sparkle, and although international cuisine has inspired many a chef and restaurant to explore exciting, often more nutritious new directions since the early 1990s, meats, rich sauces, and creamy desserts still predominate. In addition to the dishes most foreigners are familiar with, such as the chunky beef soup called *gulyás* (goulash) and *paprikás csirke* (chicken paprika) served with *galuska* (little pinched dumplings), Hungarian classics include hot-paprika-spiced *halászlé* (fish soup); *fogas* (pike perch) from Lake Balaton; goose liver, duck, and veal specialties; and a whole host of pork dishes. Hungarians are also fond of carp (*ponty*) and catfish (*harcsa*). And there's always *turós*

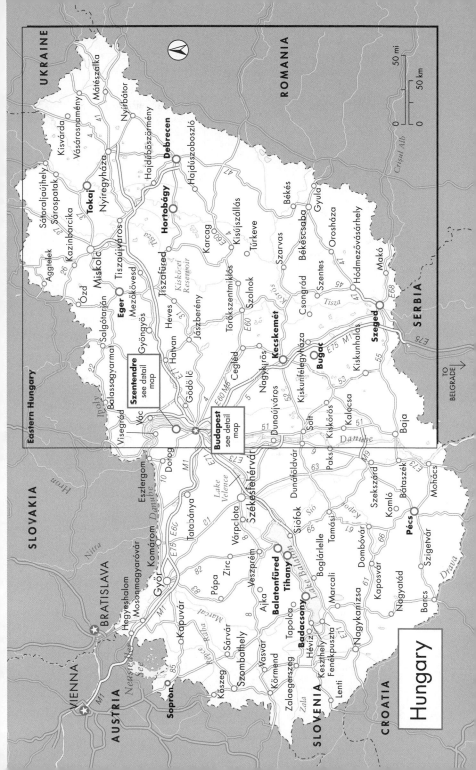

Hungary

csusza, a favorite dish of noodles covered with curded cheese topped off with bits of bacon.

As for desserts, every restaurant seems to have its house *torta* (cake), though *rétes* (strüdels), *Somlói galuska* (a steamed sponge cake soaked in chocolate sauce and whipped cream), and *palacsinta* (rolled crêpes) are ubiquitous. Traditional rétes fillings are *mák* (sugary poppy seeds), *meggy* (sour cherry), and *túró* (sweetened cottage cheese); palacsintas always come rolled with *dió* (sweet ground walnuts), túró, or *lekvár* (jam). You might also try the *zserbó,* a delicious layered cake with apricot-jam and walnut filling. Finally, don't pass up a visit to at least one *cukrászda* (pastry shop).

HUNGARY TOP 5

■ **Castle Hill.** Baroque, Gothic, and Renaissance houses and museums make this Budapest's top destination.

■ **Andrássy út.** This wide boulevard is lined with plane trees, cafés, and grand old architecture.

■ **Sopron.** Perched in Hungary's hilly northwest, Sopron has a walled historic center.

■ **Eastern Hungary and the Great Plain.** With its national parks and quiet lowland towns, this is the nation's heartland.

■ **Pécs.** Pécs is a perennial favorite for its cathedral, Turkish heritage, and lively cultural scene.

If you long for something non-Hungarian—from Italian to Indian, Middle Eastern to Asian, just plain vegetarian or, yes, American-style fast food—you can find it aplenty in Budapest. Although prices are increasing, eating out—even in pricier Budapest—can provide you with some of the best value for the money of any European capital.

A note about restaurant protocol: In most cases you will need to ask for the bill. ■TIP➔ **Except at those few restaurants where tips are automatically included (as should be made clear on the English menu), add a tip of at least 10% as you pay, rather than leaving it on the table when you go.**

ABOUT THE HOTELS

Budapest has seen a steady increase in both the quantity and quality of its accommodations since 1990, and the first years of the 21st century have seen an extraordinary number of new hotels opening their doors—with luxury (and ever higher rates) the trend. Outside Budapest there are few expensive hotels. In addition, there are numerous alternative affordable (and delightful) lodging options.

Guesthouses, also called *panziók* (pensions), provide simple budget accommodations. Like bed-and-breakfasts, most are run by couples or families and offer simple breakfast facilities and rooms that usually have private bathrooms; they're generally outside the city or town center. Another good budget option is renting a room in a private home. Look for signs reading SZOBA KIADÓ (or the German ZIMMER FREI). Reservations and referrals can also be made by any tourist office, and if you go that route, you have someone to complain to if things don't work out.

IF YOU LIKE

FOLK ART

Hungary's centuries-old traditions of folk art are still beautifully alive. Carved wooden boxes, colorful embroidered tablecloths and shirts, matte-black pottery pitchers, woven lace collars, ceramic plates splashed with painted flowers and birds, and decorative heavy leather whips are among the favorite handcrafted pieces you can purchase.

PORCELAIN

Among the most sought-after items in Hungary are the exquisite hand-painted Herend and Zsolnay porcelain. Although prices on all brands have risen in recent years, authenticity can be yours at Herend and Zsolnay shops in major cities or at the factories themselves in Herend and Pécs, respectively.

SPAS & THERMAL BATHS

Several thousand years ago, the first settlers of the area of present-day Budapest chose their home because of its hot springs. Centuries later, the Romans and the Turks built baths aplenty. Now there are more than 1,000 medicinal hot springs around the country. Budapest alone has around a dozen historic working baths, which attract patients with medical prescriptions for specific water cures as well as "recreational" bathers wanting to soak in the relaxing waters, experience the architectural beauty of the bathhouses, and perhaps get a brisk massage.

WINE

Hungary tempts wine connoisseurs with its major wine regions, especially Villány and Szekszárd, in the south; Eger and Tokaj in the north; and the northern shore of Lake Balaton. Szürkebarát (a pinot gris varietal) and especially Olaszrizling (a milder Rhine Riesling) are common white table wines, but Tokay Furmint and Hárslevelű, which come in both *száraz* (dry) and *édes* (sweet) varieties, are better quality. And, yes, there is Tokay Aszú, one of the great wines of the world; heavy, dark, and sweet, it is enjoyed as an aperitif or a dessert wine.

Although the red table wine of Hungary, Egri Bikavér (Bull's Blood of Eger), has long been ubiquitous among Hungarian offerings in liquor stores abroad, its quality can vary depending on the label; and Szekszárd also produces an excellent Bikavér. Within Hungary itself, the dry red Kékfrankos (Blaufrankisch in neighboring Austria) is the most popular red. Villány produces superb reds and the best rosés.

7

Apartments in Budapest and cottages at Lake Balaton are available for short- and long-term rental and can make the most economic lodging for families—particularly for those who prefer to cook their own meals.

At hotels, for single rooms with bath, count on paying about 80% of the double-room rate. During the off-season (in Budapest, September through March; at Lake Balaton, September through May), rates can drop considerably. Note that most large hotels set their rates in euros. Breakfast and VAT are usually—but not always—included in your quoted room rate. There is also a "tourist tax" of 3% in Budapest;

outside the capital it varies region to region but is always less than 1,000 HUF. This tax is usually not included in the quoted rates.

WHAT IT COSTS IN FORINTS (HUF) AND EUROS (€)					
	¢	$	$$	$$$	$$$$
RESTAURANTS	under 1,000 HUF	1,000 HUF–2,000 HUF	2,000 HUF–3,000 HUF	3,000 HUF–4,000 HUF	over 4,000 HUF
HOTELS In euros	under €75	€75–€125	€125–€175	€175–€225	over €225
HOTELS In forints	under 18,500 HUF	18,500 HUF–31,000 HUF	31,000 HUF–44,000 HUF	44,000 HUF–56,000 HUF	over 56,000 HUF

Restaurant prices are per person for a main course at dinner. Hotel prices are for two people in a double room with a private bath and breakfast in high season, tax included.

BUDAPEST

Situated on both banks of the Danube, amid a wealth of geographic and architectural splendor, Budapest (pronounced "*boo*-duh-pesht") unites the colorful hills of Buda and the wide, bustling boulevards of Pest. Though it was the site of a Roman outpost during the 1st century AD, the city per se was not officially created until 1873, when the towns of Óbuda, Pest, and Buda united. By the turn of the 20th century Budapest was among the world's fastest-growing cities. Its newly developing face was modeled after Paris—which meant wide boulevards; eclectic, Art Nouveau architecture; and elegant cafés. To this day many of Budapest's 2 million residents—about a fifth of the nation's population—live in an urban landscape amazingly similar to its pre–World War I "golden age."

Budapest has suffered many ravages over the centuries—but has always arisen from the ashes. It was destroyed by the Mongols in 1241; captured by the Turks in 1541; ransacked more than a century later when retaken from the Turks; pummeled by Allied bombing, retreating Germans, and advancing Soviet troops in 1944–45; and in the 1956 revolution, shot up again by Soviet tanks. But this bustling industrial and cultural center survived as the capital of the People's Republic of Hungary after the war and the revolution. Beginning in the 1960s and through the next two decades, Hungary became the economic star of the Soviet bloc, thanks to a political environment called "goulash communism" that allowed breathing room for small businesses—and thanks to foreign loans it later struggled to repay.

Budapest has undergone a radical makeover since the fall of Communism in 1990, with more and more restaurants, bars, shops, and boutiques opening their doors and with fashion-conscious youth parading the streets. But still, much of the charm of a visit to Budapest lies in unexpected glimpses into shadowy courtyards and in long vistas down sunlit cobbled streets. Although some 30,000 buildings were destroyed during World War II and in the 1956 revolution, the

GREAT ITINERARIES

You'll want to spend at least three days to get a satisfying sense of the Budapest experience, plus a side trip to the Danube Bend and perhaps Lake Balaton. A longer stay will allow you to also see one or more lovely historic towns farther afield, such as Pécs, Kecskemét, Sopron, Szeged, or Debrecen—not to mention the famed *puszta* (prairie).

TIMING

The ideal times to visit Hungary are in the spring (May–June) and end of summer into early fall (late August–September). July and August, peak vacation season for Hungarians as well as foreign tourists, can be hot and humid; Budapest is stuffy and crowded, and much of Lake Balaton is overrun with vacationers. Summer holds the unforgettable Hungarian sights of sweeping fields of swaying golden sunflowers and giant white storks summering in their bushy nests built on chimney tops.

IF YOU HAVE 3 DAYS

The must-sees include **Várhegy**, a stroll along **Andrássy út** or on the **Danube korzó**, a glimpse of **Országház**, a look at **Hősök tere** followed by a dip in the **Széchenyi Fürdő**, a hearty meal, and a night at the **Magyar Állami Operaház**. After a night's rest in Budapest, hop on an early boat to explore the time-honored artists' village of **Szentendre** and Hungary's biggest cathedral, in lovely **Esztergom**, upriver in the Danube Bend. You can spend another night in Budapest; the next morning, drive down to **Badacsony** on Lake Balaton's northern shore. Follow a refreshing swim with a lunch of fresh Balaton fish and some wine tasting in the cool cellars on Mt. Badacsony's vineyard-covered slopes. On your way back to Budapest, stop for a stroll on **Tihany**'s cobblestone streets and drink in the views from its lovely hilltop abbey.

IF YOU HAVE 6 DAYS

Spend two full days exploring ☷ **Budapest**; on your third day visit **Szentendre** and **Visegrád** or else **Esztergom**, making the trip by some mix of boat, car, rail, or bus tour. Return to Budapest for the night and head out the next morning for a day on the Great Plain, strolling among the sights of lovely ☷ **Kecskemét** before venturing out to the nearby *puszta* (prairie). Depending on how much you want to drive and how much of Budapest's nightlife you want to take in, you can either go back to Budapest (85 km [53 mi] from Kecskemét) for the night or spend it here in Kecskemét. On Day 5, drive down to ☷ **Pécs** to see its beautiful town square, cathedral, and excellent museums. After a night's rest, make your way on scenic secondary roads through southern Transdanubia to Lake Balaton, visiting ☷ **Badacsony** on the northern shore, where you can hike up the vineyard-carpeted slopes of Mount Badacsony, rewarded by generous wine tastings in the local cellars and a big fish dinner with live Gypsy music. Depending on the amount of wine you've tasted, instead of sleeping in Badacsony, you may prefer to move on along the northern shore and spend the fifth night in ☷ **Tihany** or ☷ **Balatonfüred,** both of which have good lodging possibilities with more facilities and amenities. Either way, you can spend your sixth day exploring Tihany and Balatonfüred, cooling off with a swim in the lake before heading back to Budapest.

7

past lingers on in the often crumbling architectural details of the aged structures that remain.

EXPLORING BUDAPEST

The city's principal sights fall roughly into three areas—Castle Hill and environs, central Pest (including Margaret Island), and Óbuda—each of which can be comfortably covered on foot. The Buda hills are best explored by public transportation.

Note that, by tradition, the district number—a Roman numeral designating one of Budapest's 22 districts—precedes each address. For the sake of clarity, in this book the word "District" precedes the number. Districts V, VI, and VII are in downtown Pest; District I includes Castle Hill, Buda's main tourist district.

VÁRHEGY (CASTLE HILL)

Most of Buda's major sights are on Várhegy (Castle Hill), a long, narrow plateau laced with cobblestone streets, clustered with beautifully preserved baroque, Gothic, and Renaissance houses, and crowned by the magnificent Royal Palace. The area is closed to private cars except for those of neighborhood residents and hotel guests. As in all of Budapest, thriving urban new has taken up residence in historic old; international corporate offices, diplomatic residences, restaurants, and boutiques occupy many of Castle Hill's landmark buildings.

Castle Hill's cobblestone streets are best explored on foot. The area is small enough to cover in a two- to three-hour power walk, but perusing it at a leisurely pace and visiting its major museums and several tiny exhibits will require a full day. Bear in mind that the museums will be closed on Monday.

Numbers in the text correspond to numbers in the margin and on the Castle Hill (Várhegy) map.

⓾ Bécsi kapu tér *(Vienna Gate Square).* Marking the northern entrance to Castle Hill, the stone gateway (rebuilt in 1936) called Vienna Gate opens toward Vienna—or, closer at hand, Moszkva tér a few short blocks below. The square named after it has some fine baroque and rococo houses, but is dominated by the enormous neo-Romanesque (1913–17) headquarters of the **Országos Levéltár** (Hungarian National Archives). ⊠*District I.*

➐ Budavári Labirintus *(Labyrinth of Buda Castle).* Used as a wine cellar during the 16th and 17th centuries and then as an air-raid shelter during World War II, this fascinating 16-meter (52-foot) deep, 1,200-meter (3,900-foot) long labyrinth can be explored with a tour or, if you dare, on your own. ⊠*District I Úri utca 9* ☎*1/212–0207 Ext. 34* ☜*1,500 HUF* ☉*Daily 9:30–7:30.*

➒ Hadtörténeti Múzeum *(Museum of Military History).* Fittingly lodged in a former barracks, this museum, whose exhibits range from uniforms to military regalia to old photos, traces Hungary's military history from the original Magyar conquest in the 9th century through the period of

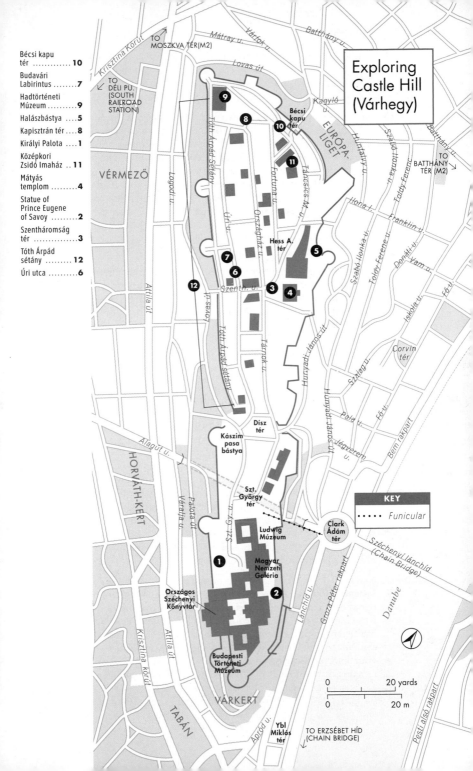

Exploring Castle Hill (Várhegy)

KEY

····· Funicular

0 — 20 yards

0 — 20 m

Ottoman rule to the mid-20th century. ⊠*District I, Tóth Árpád sétány 40* ☎*1/325–1647, 1/325–1600, or 1/344–1000* ⊕*www.militaria.hu* ⌨*Museum free, photos 600 HUF, videos 1,200 HUF* ⊙*Apr.–Sept., Tues.–Sun. 10–6; Oct.–Mar., Tues.–Sun. 10–4.*

⑤ Halászbástya *(Fishermen's Bastion).* The wondrous porch overlooking

Fodor'sChoice ★ the Danube and Pest is the neo-Romanesque Fishermen's Bastion, a cluster of white stone towers, arches, and columns above a modern bronze statue of St. Stephen, Hungary's first king. Medieval fishwives once peddled their wares here, but on the bustling space outside it you can now see merchants selling souvenirs and crafts, musicians, and—less visible but often present—pickpockets. Buy your tickets at the tiny office beside the Tourinform by the adjacent park; note that outside of official hours, you can enter for free. ⊠*District I* ☎*400 HUF May–Sept., 9 AM–10 PM daily; Mar.–Apr. and Oct. 1–15, 9–9 daily; free Oct. 15–Feb.* ⊙*Daily 24 hrs.*

⑧ Kapisztrán tér *(Capistrano Square).* Castle Hill's northernmost square was named after St. John of Capistrano, an Italian friar who in 1456 recruited a crusading army to fight the Turks who were threatening Hungary. There's a statue of this honored Franciscan on the northwest corner; also here are the Museum of Military History and the remains of the 12th-century Gothic Mária Magdolna templom (Church of St. Mary Magdalene). Its steeple, completed in 1496, is the only part left standing; the rest of the church was destroyed by air raids during World War II. ⊠*District I.*

① Királyi Palota *(Royal Palace).* A palace originally built on this spot in

Fodor'sChoice ★ the 13th century for the kings of Hungary was reconstructed in Renaissance style under the supervision of King Matthias during the 15th century. That, in turn, was demolished as Buda was recaptured from the Turks in 1686. The Habsburg empress Maria Theresa had a new palace built in the 1700s. It was damaged during an unsuccessful attack by revolutionaries in 1849, but the Habsburgs set about building again, completing work in 1905. Then, near the end of the Soviets' siege in early 1945, it was reduced to rubble. Decades passed before whatever restoration was possible was completed. Archaeologists were able to recover both the original defensive walls and royal chambers, due in part to still surviving plans and texts from the reigns of Holy Roman Emperor Sigismund and King Matthias.

Fodor'sChoice ★ The Royal Palace's baroque southern wing (Wing E) contains the **Budapesti Történeti Múzeum** *(Budapest History Museum),* displaying a permanent exhibit of modern Budapest history from Buda's liberation from the Turks in 1686 through the 1970s. Viewing vintage 19th- and 20th-century photos and videos—and seeing them as the backdrop to the horrors of World War II and the 1956 revolution—helps to put your later sightseeing in context. This is also the best place to view remains of the medieval Royal Palace and other archaeological excavations. ⊠*District I, Szent György tér 2* ☎*1/487–8801* ⊕*www.btm. hu* ☎*1,100 HUF* ⊙*Mid-May–mid-Sept., daily 10–6; Mar.–mid-May and mid-Sept.–Oct., Wed.–Mon. 10–6; Nov.–Feb., Wed.–Mon. 10–4.*

The **Magyar Nemzeti Galéria** *(Hungarian National Gallery)*, which comprises the immense center block of the Royal Palace (Wings B, C, and D), exhibits centuries of Hungarian fine art, from medieval ecclesiastical paintings and statues through Gothic, Renaissance, and baroque artworks, to a rich collection of 19th- and 20th-century works. Especially notable are the works of the romantic painter Mihály Munkácsy, the impressionist Pál Szinyei Merse, and the surrealist Mihály Tivadar Kosztka Csontváry, whom Picasso much admired. ✉ *District I, Dísz tér 17, entrance in Wing C* ☎ *1/212–7356 or 20/439–7326* ⊕ *www. mng.hu* ✉ *Museum free; special exhibits 800–1,200 HUF; photos 1,500 HUF, videos 2,000 HUF* ☉ *Tues.–Sun. 10–6.* The western wing (F) of the Royal Palace is the **Országos Széchenyi Könyvtár** *(Széchenyi National Library)*, which houses more than 2 million volumes. Its archives include well-preserved medieval codices, manuscripts, and historic correspondence. This is not a lending library, but the reading rooms are open to the public (you must show a passport); the most valuable materials can be viewed only on microfilm, however. Temporary exhibits on rare books and documents are usually on display; the hours for these special exhibits vary, and admission is sometimes free, though major exhibits usually have a charge of around 600 HUF. The entire library closes in August. ✉ *District I, Dísz tér 17* ☎ *1/224– 3700 to arrange English-language tours* ⊕ *www.oszk.hu* ✉ *Museum 600 HUF; sometimes a separate fee for special exhibits; one-day pass to the reading rooms 600 HUF* ☉ *Reading rooms Tues.–Sat. 10–8; exhibits Tues.–Fri. 10–6, Sat. 10–3.*

⑪ **Középkori Zsidó Imaház** *(Medieval Synagogue).* The excavated one-room medieval synagogue is now used as a museum. On display are objects relating to the Jewish community, including religious inscriptions, frescoes, and tombstones dating to the 15th century. ✉ *District I, Táncsics Mihály utca 26* ☎ *1/487–8801* ✉ *400 HUF* ☉ *May–Oct., Tues.–Sun. 10–6.*

NEED A BREAK? **Magyar Borok Háza** (*House of Hungarian Wines* ✉ District 1, Szentháromság tér 6 ☎ 1/212–1030 or 1/212–1031) is the best place in Budapest to sample a comprehensive selection of the country's finest wines. A ticket (4,000 HUF) is good for a two-hour, self-guided tour through a cellar, with more than 700 wines on display arranged by 22 wine regions; you may pour as you wish from some 50 open bottles, but you may not get visibly smashed. It's open daily noon–8.

④ Fodor'sChoice ★ **Mátyás templom** *(Matthias Church).* The ornate white steeple of the Matthias Church—the highest point on Castle Hill—was added in the 15th century above a 13th-century Gothic chapel. Officially the Buda Church of Our Lady, it has been known as the Matthias Church since the 15th century, in remembrance of the so-called "just king" who greatly added to and embellished it during his reign. Many of these changes were lost when the Turks converted it into a mosque. The intricate white stonework, mosaic roof decorations, and some of its geometric patterned columns seem to suggest Byzantium, yet it was rebuilt again in the neo-baroque style after the Turkish defeat in 1686.

The **Szentháromság Kápolna** (Trinity Chapel) holds an *encolpion,* an enameled casket containing a miniature copy of the Gospel to be worn on the chest; it belonged to the 12th-century king Béla III and his wife, Anne of Chatillon. Their burial crowns and a cross, scepter, and rings found in their excavated graves are also displayed here. The church's **treasury** contains Renaissance and baroque chalices, monstrances, and vestments. In summer there are usually organ recitals on Sundays at 7:30 PM. ⊠*District I, Szentháromság tér 2* ☎*1/355–5657* ⊘*Church weekdays 9–5and 7–9* PM, *Sat. 9–2:30 (often closed to the public on Sat. afternoon), Sun. 3–5; treasury daily 9–5* ☙*Church and treasury 650 HUF; church alone when treasury closed 450 HUF.*

② **Statue of Prince Eugene of Savoy.** In front of the Royal Palace, facing the Danube by the entrance to Wing C, stands an equestrian statue of Prince Eugene of Savoy, a commander of the army that liberated Hungary from the Turks at the end of the 17th century. ⊠*District I, Dísz tér 17.*

❸ **Szentháromság tér** *(Holy Trinity Square).* This square, in front of the famous Gothic Matthias Church, is named for its baroque Trinity Column, erected in 1712–13 as a gesture of thanksgiving by survivors of a plague. The column has been undergoing off-site refurbishment but is expected back on the square by spring 2008. ⊠*District I.*

NEED A BREAK?

A few yards west of Szentháromság tér is the Ruszwurm (⊠*District I, Szentháromság utca 7* ☎*1/375–5284*)**, Budapest's oldest surviving café, dating from the early 19th century and offering excellent pastries at reasonable prices.**

⑫ ★ **Tóth Árpád sétány** *(Árpád Tóth Promenade).* This romantic, tree-lined promenade along the Buda side of the hill is often overlooked by sightseers. Beginning at the Museum of Military History, the promenade takes you behind the scenes along the back sides of the matte-pastel baroque houses that face Úri utca, with their regal arched windows and wrought-iron gates, and it offers a sublime view of the quiet Buda neighborhoods below. ⊠*District I.*

❻ **Úri utca** *(Úri Street).* Running parallel to Tárnok utca, Úri utca has been less commercialized by boutiques and other shops. The longest and oldest street in the castle district, it is lined with many stately houses, all worth special attention for their delicately carved details. Both gateways of the baroque palace at Nos. 48–50—like those at Nos. 54–56—are articulated by Gothic niches from the 14th and 15th centuries.

OFF THE BEATEN PATH

Gyermek Vasút. The 12-km (7-mi) Children's Railway—so called because its train switches and ticket services are operated by (adult-supervised) children—runs from Széchenyi-hegy to Hűvösvölgy. The sweeping views make the trip well worthwhile for those of any age. To get to the departure point at Széchenyi-hegy, take Tram 56 from Moszkva tér, and change to the cog railway (public transport tickets valid) at the Fogaskereku Vasút stop. Take the cog railway uphill to the last stop and then walk a few hundred yards down a short, partly forested road to the left to the railway station. The railway terminates at

Hűvösvölgy, where you can catch Tram 56 for a lovely ride past the ivy-covered villas of Buda back to Moszkva tér. ⊠ *District XII, Szillágyi Erzsébet fasor and Pasaréti út* ☎*1/397–5394* ⊕*www.gyermekvasut.com* 💰*600 HUF one-way* ⊙*Mar. 16–Oct. 23, weekdays 9–5, weekends 9–5:30; Oct. 24–Mar. 15, Tues.–Fri. 9–4, (sometimes closed Tues.). Trains run hourly on weekdays, every 45 mins on weekends 9–5.*

DON'T MISS MÁTYÁS

Just behind Wing C on the palace's western side is one of Castle Hill's most striking sculptures—Alajos Strobl's multilevel, patina-covered work Mátyás's Kútja (Matthias's Well), complete with a little waterfall, hunting dogs, king's helpers, and a triumphant King Matthias topping off the scene—above a felled stag, that is.

TABÁN & GELLÉRT-HEGY (TABÁN & GELLÉRT HILL)

Spreading below Castle Hill is the old quarter called Tabán. A onetime suburb of Buda, it was known at the end of the 17th century as Little Serbia (*Rác*) because so many Serbian refugees settled here after fleeing from the Turks. It later became a district of vineyards and small taverns. Though most of the small houses once characteristic of this district are no more, some traditional buildings remain. As for nearby Gellért-hegy (Gellért Hill), at 761 feet high it is the most beautiful natural formation on the Buda bank. It takes its name from St. Gellért (Gerard) of Csanád, a Venetian bishop who came to Hungary in the 11th century and, legend has it, was rolled off the top of the hill in a cart by pagans.

The Citadella and Szabadság szobor are lighted in golden lights every night, but the entire Gellért-hegy is at its scenic best every year on August 20, when it forms the backdrop to the spectacular St. Stephen's Day fireworks display. A quick stroll through the area, including a hike up Gellért-hegy, will take three hours, but add at least two more hours if you stop in at a bath.

Numbers in the text correspond to numbers in the margin and on the Central Budapest map.

16 **Citadella.** The sweeping views of Budapest from this hilltop fortress ★ were once valued by the Austrian army, which used it as a lookout after the 1848–49 War of Independence. In the 1960s the Citadel was converted into a tourist site. Its outer perimeter includes a café and a beer garden. Within the walls, which you can enter for 1,200 HUF, you'll find a small graphic exhibition (with some relics) of Budapest's 2,000-year history and a life-size exhibit of bunkers used on the hill during World War II.

Visible from many parts of the city, the 130-foot-high **Szabadság szobor** *(Liberty Statue)*, just below the southern edge of the Citadella, was originally planned as a memorial to a son of Hungary's then-ruler, Miklós Horthy, whose warplane crashed in 1942. However, by the time of its completion in 1947 (three years after Horthy was ousted), it had become a memorial to the Russian soldiers who fell in the 1944–45

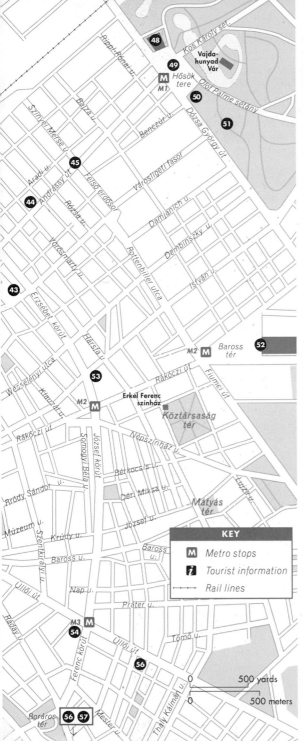

7

KEY

M Metro stops

i Tourist information

Rail lines

0   500 yards

0   500 meters

siege of Budapest. A sturdy young girl, her hair and robe swirling in the wind, holds a palm branch high above her head. During much of the communist era, she was further embellished with sculptures of giants slaying dragons, Red Army soldiers, and peasants rejoicing at the freedom that Soviet liberation supposedly meant. In 1992 the Soviet infantrymen were detached and carted away to join other evicted statues in Szoborpark in the city's 22nd district. ⊠*District XI, Citadella sétány* ☏*No phone* 💷*1,200 HUF to enter walls* ☉*Fortress grounds daily 24 hrs; interior daily 10–6.*

⑭ Erzsébet híd *(Elizabeth Bridge)*. This bridge was named for Empress Elizabeth (1837–98), nicknamed Sissi, of whom the Hungarians were fond. The beautiful but unhappy wife of Franz Joseph, she was stabbed to death in 1898 by an anarchist while boarding a boat on Lake Geneva. The bridge was built between 1897 and 1903; at the time, it was the longest single-span suspension bridge in Europe.

⑰ Gellért Szálloda és Thermál Fürdő *(Gellért Hotel and Thermal Baths)*. At
★ the foot of Gellért Hill is this beautiful Art Nouveau complex. The Danubius Hotel Gellért is the oldest spa hotel in Hungary, with hot springs that have supplied curative baths for nearly 2,000 years. There's a wealth of treatments, some of which require a doctor's prescription; prescriptions from foreign doctors are accepted, and most staff speak English. Men and women have separate steam and sauna rooms; both the indoor pool and the outdoor wave pool are coed. ⊠*District XI, Gellért tér 1* ☏*1/466–5747 baths* 💷*2,800 HUF with a locker, 3,100 HUF with a private cabin; treatments extra* ☉*Baths daily 6 AM–7 PM.*

⑮ Rudas Fürdő *(Rudas Baths)*. The thermal baths at the Rudas have been a favorite spot for Budapest men since the 16th century, when the Turks made their daily ablutions here. Since 2005, the men-only policy has been loosened to welcome women several days a week. Settle in for a soak and contemplate life as the central octagonal pool catches light from the glass-tiled cupola and casts it around the surrounding six pools. ⊠*Döbrentei tér 9, District I* ☏*1/356–1322* ⊕*www.spasbudapest.com* 💷*2,200 HUF (partial refunds if you leave within 3 hrs)* ☉*Men only Mon., Wed., and Fri. 6 AM–8 PM; women only Tues. 6 AM–8 PM; coed weekends 6–5 and Fri. and Sat. 10–4.*

⑬ Tabán plébánia-templom *(Tabán Parish Church)*. In 1736, this church was built on the site of a Turkish mosque and subsequently reconstructed several times, eventually assuming its "restrained baroque" present form—mustard-colored stone with a rotund, green clock tower. ⊠*District I, Attila u. 1.*

**OFF THE
BEATEN
PATH**

Szoborpark (Statue Park). After the collapse of the Iron Curtain, the symbols of Soviet domination that once dotted Budapest's streets and squares were moved to this open-air "Disneyland of Communism." As well as the huge figures of Lenin and Marx, there are statues of the Hungarian worker shaking hands with his Soviet army comrade, and Hungarian puppet prime minister János Kádár. Songs from the Hungarian and Russian workers' movements play on a tinny speaker system. To get there, go to Etele tér in Buda via a red-numbered bus 7 from Ferenciek tere in Pest, and then catch the yellow Volán bus from Platform 7 or 8 bound for Diósd-Érd (but ask to be sure) and get off at Szoborpark after around 15 minutes. For a whopping 3,950 HUF one-way, you can also catch a special bus (with the Szoborpark sign on it) from Deák tér at 11 AM and, in July and August, also at 3 PM; the ticket includes the park entrance fee. ⊠ *District XXII, Balatoni út, corner of Szabadkai út* ☎ *1/427–7500* ⊕ *www.szoborpark.hu* ☎ *600 HUF* ⊙ *Daily 10 AM–dusk.*

DOWNTOWN PEST & THE KIS KÖRÚT (SMALL RING ROAD)

Budapest's urban heart is full of bona fide sights plus innumerable tiny streets and grand avenues where you can wander for hours admiring the city's stately old buildings—some freshly sparkling after their first painting in decades, others silently but still gracefully crumbling.

Dominated by the Parliament building, the district surrounding Kossuth tér is the legislative, diplomatic, and administrative nexus of Budapest; most of the ministries are here, as are the National Bank and Courts of Justice. Downriver, the romantic Danube promenade, the Duna korzó, extends along the stretch of riverfront across from Castle Hill. With Vörösmarty tér and pedestrian shopping street Váci utca just inland, this area forms Pest's tourist core. Going south, the korzó ends at Március 15 tér. One block in from the river, Ferenciek tere marks the beginning of the university area, spreading south of Kossuth Lajos utca.

Another stretch of Váci utca, pedestrianized in the 1990s and rivaling the older section with a rich array of antiques stores, bookshops, cafés, and restaurants, continues on the other side of busy Szabad sajtó út all the way to the next bridge, Szabadság híd, and the indoor food market, the Vásárcsarnok. From here it's just a few blocks to yet another vibrant, Pest-side street revitalized in the 1990s, Ráday utca.

Pest is laid out in broad circular *körúts* ("ring roads" or boulevards). Vámház körút is the first sector of the 2½-km (1½-mi) Kis körút (Small Ring Road), which traces the route of the Old Town wall from Szabadság híd (Liberty Bridge) to Deák tér. Changing names as it curves, after Kálvin tér it becomes Múzeum körút (passing by the National Museum) and then Károly körút for its final stretch ending at Deák tér. Deák tér, the only place where all three subway lines converge, could be called the dead center of downtown. East of Károly körút are the weathered streets of Budapest's former Jewish ghetto.

㉕ **Belvárosi plébánia templom** *(Inner City Parish Church).* Dating to the ★ 12th century, this is the oldest—and, in terms of architectural history, the most extraordinary—ecclesiastical building in Pest. It's built on even older structures—an 11th-century Romanesque church commissioned by Hungary's first king, St. Stephen, plus the remains of the Contra Aquincum (a 3rd-century Roman fortress and tower), parts of which are visible. There is hardly any architectural style that cannot be found in some part or another, starting with a single Romanesque arch in its south tower. From 1867 to 1875 Franz Liszt lived in a town house a few steps away, where he held regular "musical Sundays" at

A GOOD WALK

This is a particularly rich part of the city; the suggested walk will take the better part of a day, including time to visit the museums, stroll on the Korzó, and browse on Váci utca—not to mention time for lunch. Keep in mind that the museums are closed on Monday.

After starting at Kossuth tér to see the **Országház** ⑱ and the **Néprajzi Múzeum** ⑲, it's worth walking a few blocks southeast to take in stately **Szabadság tér** ⑳ before heading back to the Danube and south to **Roosevelt tér** ㉑, which is at the foot of the **Széchenyi Lánchíd** (Chain Bridge) ㉒. As this tour involves a lot of walking, you may want to take Tram 2 from Kossuth tér a few stops downriver to Roosevelt tér to save your energy. At some point during your visit, a walk across the nearby Chain Bridge is a must.

From Roosevelt tér go south, across the street, and join the **Korzó** ㉓ along the river, strolling past the **Vigadó** ㉔ at Vigadó tér, all the way to the **Belvárosi plébánia templom** ㉕ at Március 15 tér, just under the Elizabeth Bridge. Double back up the korzó to Vigadó tér and walk in from the river on Vigadó utca to **Vörösmarty tér** ㉖. Follow the crowds down pedestrian-only **Váci utca** ㉗, and when you reach Régiposta utca, take a detour to the right to see the **Görög Ortodox templom** ㉘. Return to Váci utca and continue south; at Ferenciek tere, look for the grand **Párizsi udvar** ㉙ arcade. Across busy Kossuth Lajos utca, you will find the **Ferenciek templom** ㉚. From here, stroll Petőfi Sándor utca, and continue along Károlyi Mihály utca past **Egyetem**

tér ㉛. Take a right on Szerb utca until you get to Veres Pálné utca, where you will find the 17th-century **Szerb Ortodox templom** ㉜. Continuing down Szerb utca, you'll find yourself at the southern end of Váci utca, facing **Vásárcsarnok** ㉝, the huge market.

Across Vámház körút is the campus of the **Közgazdasági Egyetem** ㉞, the University of Economics. From here you can either walk or take Tram 47 or 49 to **Kálvin tér** ㉟. One block before Kálvin tér is Ráday utca, which in recent years has been transformed into a lively, largely pedestrian thoroughfare of cafés and restaurants.

Just north of Kálvin tér on Múzeum körút is the **Magyar Nemzeti Múzeum** ㊱. The **Nagy Zsinagóga and Zsidó Múzeum** ㊲, the Great Synagogue and the adjacent Jewish Museum, are about ¾ km (⅓ mi) farther north along the Kis körút (Small Ring Road)—a 10-minute walk or one stop by tram. From here, more walking along the körút, or a tram ride, brings you to Pest's main hub, Deák tér, where you'll find the **Evangélikus templom** ㊳, Budapest's main Lutheran church.

From Deák tér it's a short walk to the **Városház** ㊴, Budapest's old city hall building. The **Szent István Bazilika** ㊵ is an extra but rewarding 500-yard walk north on Bajcsy-Zsilinszky út.

which Richard and Cosima Wagner were frequent guests. Liszt's own musical Sunday mornings often began in this church. He conducted many masses here, including the first Budapest performance of his *Missa Choralis* in 1872. ⊠*Március 15 tér 2, District V* ☎*1/318–3108* 🖃*Free* ⊙ *Weekdays 9–7, weekends during services.*

 Egyetem tér *(University Square).* Budapest's University of Law sits here in the heart of the city's university neighborhood. On one corner is the cool gray-and-green marble **Egyetemi Templom** (University Church), one of Hungary's most beautiful baroque buildings. Built between 1725 and 1742, it has an especially splendid pulpit and an elaborately carved door. ⊠*District V* ⊙*Church daily 6:30* AM–6:30 PM.

NEED A BREAK? **Centrál** (⊠*District V, Károlyi Mihály utca 9,* ☎*1/266–2110*) enjoyed fame as an illustrious literary café during Budapest's late-19th- and early-20th-century golden age and, after decades of neglect, was restored to its original luster in the 1990s. Centrál's menu includes, with each main dish, a recommended wine by the glass—as well as a good selection of vegetarian dishes and desserts.

 Evangélikus templom *(Lutheran Church).* The neoclassical Lutheran Church sits in the center of it all on busy Deák tér. Classical concerts are regularly held here. The church's interior designer, János Krausz, flouted then-traditional church architecture by placing a single large interior beneath the huge vaulted roof structure. ⊠*District V, Deák Ferenc tér 4* ☎*1/317–4173.*

🔟 **Ferenciek templom** *(Franciscan Church).* This pale yellow church was built in 1743. On the wall facing Kossuth Lajos utca is a bronze relief showing a scene from the devastating flood of 1838; the detail is so vivid that it almost makes you seasick. A faded arrow below the relief indicates the high-water mark of almost 4 feet. ⊠*District V, Felszabadulás tér.*

🔟 **Görög Ortodox templom** *(Greek Orthodox Church).* Built at the end of the 18th century in late-baroque style, the Greek Orthodox Church was remodeled a century later by Miklós Ybl, who designed the Opera House and many other important Budapest landmarks. The church retains some fine woodcarvings and a dazzling collection of icons by late-18th-century Serbian master Miklós Jankovich. ⊠*District V, Petőfi tér 2/b.*

🔟 **Kálvin tér.** Calvin Square takes its name from the neoclassical Hungarian Reformed (Calvinist) church that tries to dominate this busy traffic hub. The Kecskeméti Kapu, a main gate of Pest, once stood here, as well as a cattle market that was a notorious den of thieves. At the beginning of the 19th century this was where Pest ended and the prairie began. ⊠*District V.*

 Korzó *(Promenade).* The neighborhood to the south of Roosevelt tér is ★ defined, above all, by three luxury hotels that bear the drab exteriors typical of communist-era architecture. Traversing all three and continuing well beyond them is the riverside *korzó*, a pedestrian promenade

7

lined with park benches and appealing outdoor cafés from which one can enjoy postcard-perfect views of Gellért Hill and Castle Hill directly across the Danube. ⊠*District V, from Eötvös tér to Március 15 tér.*

㉞ Közgazdasági Egyetem *(University of Economics).* Just below Szabadság híd (Liberty Bridge) on the waterfront, the monumental neo-Renaissance building was once the Customs House. Built in 1871–74 by Miklós Ybl, it is also known as *közgáz* ("econ."). ⊠*District V, Fővám tér.*

㊱ Magyar Nemzeti Múzeum *(Hungarian National Museum).* Come here
★ for a stimulating journey into the heart of the everyday Hungarian experience from the Hungarian conquest (896) to the late 20th century. Among the highlights are the 20th-century exhibit, including an early cinema replete with films of the era, an old schoolroom, a 1960s apartment interior, and a host of historical posters. Other parts of this mix include masterworks of cabinetmaking and woodcarving (e.g., church pews from Transylvania); a piano that belonged to both Beethoven and Liszt; and masterpieces of goldsmithing. ⊠*District IX, Múzeum körút 14–16* ☏*1/338–2122* ⊕*www.hnm.hu* ☞*Free* ⊙*Tues.–Sun. 10–6.*

㊲ Nagy Zsinagóga *(Great Synagogue).* Seating 3,000, Europe's largest syn-
Fodor'sChoice agogue was designed by Ludwig Förs and built between 1844 and 1859
★ in a Byzantine-Moorish style. Desecrated by German and Hungarian fascists, it was painstakingly reconstructed with donations from all over the world; its doors reopened in the fall of 1996. In the courtyard behind the synagogue a weeping willow made of metal honors the victims of the Holocaust. The four-room **Zsidó Múzeum** *(Jewish Museum),* adjoining the Great Synagogue, has priceless relics and displays explaining the effect of the Holocaust on Hungarian and Transylvanian Jews. ⊠*District VII, Dohány utca 2–8, H-1072* ☏*1/342–8949* ☞*1,400 HUF (allows entry to both the synagogue and the museum), 500 HUF videos and photos* ⊙*Synagogue: Mon.–Thurs. 10–5, Fri. 10–3, and Sun. 10–6; museum: mid-Mar.–mid-Oct., Mon.–Thurs. 10–5, Fri. and Sun. 10–2; mid-Oct.–mid-Mar., weekdays 10–3, Sun. 10–1.*

⑲ Néprajzi Múzeum *(Museum of Ethnography).* This 1890s neoclassical
Fodor'sChoice temple formerly housed the Supreme Court. Now an impressive perma-
★ nent exhibition, "The Folk Culture of the Hungarian People," explains (with labels in both English and Hungarian) all aspects of peasant life from the end of the 18th century until World War I. Besides embroideries, pottery, and carvings, there are farming tools, furniture, and traditional costumes. The central room alone is worth the entrance fee: a majestic hall with ornate marble staircases and pillars, and towering stained-glass windows. ⊠*District V, Kossuth tér 12, H-1054* ☏*1/473–2400* ⊕*www.neprajz.hu* ☞*800 HUF* ⊙*Tues.–Sun. 10–6.*

⑱ Országház *(Parliament).* The most striking symbol of Budapest's left
★ bank is the huge neo-Gothic Parliament. A fine example of historicizing, eclectic fin-de-siècle architecture, it was designed by the Hungarian architect Imre Steindl and built by a thousand workers between 1885 and 1902. The grace and dignity of its long facade and 24 slender towers, with spacious arcades and high windows balancing its vast

central dome, lend this living landmark a baroque spatial effect. The exterior is lined with 90 statues of great figures from Hungarian history; the corbels are ornamented by 242 allegorical statues. Inside are 691 rooms, 10 courtyards, and 29 staircases; some 88 pounds of gold were used for the staircases and halls. These halls are also a gallery of late-19th-century Hungarian art, with frescoes and canvases depicting Hungarian history.

Parliament's most sacred treasure is not the Hungarian legislature but the **Szent Korona** (Holy Crown), which reposes with other royal relics under the cupola. The crown sits like a golden soufflé above a Byzantine band of holy scenes in enamel and pearls and other gems. It dates from the 12th century so, despite what many believe, it could not be the crown that Pope Sylvester II presented to St. Stephen in the year 1000, when he was crowned the first king of Hungary. The crown has long been recognized as Hungary's legal symbol of statehood. In 1945 the fleeing Hungarian army handed over the crown and its accompanying regalia to the Americans rather than have them fall into Soviet hands. They were restored to Hungary in 1978. The crown can be seen in the course of daily tours of the Parliament building, which is the only way you can visit; the building is closed to the public during ceremonial events and when the legislature is in session (Monday and Tuesday from mid-September to late April). Arrive at least 30 minutes early. (Phone reservations are taken only for specially arranged group tours.) The building can also be visited as part of a four-hour city tour led by IBUSZ Travel at 10 and 11 AM daily. ⊠ *District V, Kossuth tér* ☏ *1/441–4904 or 1/441–4415 for info and tour reservations, 1/485–2765 or 1/485–2700 for IBUSZ Travel* ⛫ *1/441–4801* ⊕ *www.mkogy. hu* ☞ *Free for EU citizens, 2,520 HUF for everyone else* ⊙ *Daily tours in English at 10, 12, and 2, starting from Gate No. 10, just right of main stairs.*

㉙ Párizsi udvar *(Paris Court).* This glass-roof arcade was built in 1914 in richly ornamental neo-Gothic, Renaissance, and arabesque styles. Nowadays it's filled with touristy boutiques and an excellent little foreign-language bookshop. ⊠ *District V, corner of Petőfi Sándor utca and Kossuth Lajos utca.*

㉑ Roosevelt tér. This square opening onto the Danube has less to do with America's World War II president than with the progressive Hungarian statesman Count István Széchenyi, dubbed "the greatest Hungarian" even by his adversary, fellow statesman (and leader of the 1848 revolution) Lajos Kossuth. The neo-Renaissance palace of the **Magyar Tudományos Akadémia** (Academy of Sciences) on the north side was built between 1862 and 1864, after Széchenyi's suicide; in 1825 he had donated a year's income from all his estates to establish the academy. Another Széchenyi project, the Széchenyi Lánchíd (Chain Bridge), leads into the square. The spectacular Art Nouveau **Gresham Palota** is situated ideally on the square's east side facing the bridge. Designed by Zsigmond Quittner and completed in 1906, it reopened in 2004 as a luxury hotel. ⊠ *District V.*

7

㉚ **Szabadság tér.** The sprawling Liberty Square is dominated by the long-
★ time headquarters of **Magyar Televízió** (Hungarian Television), a former stock exchange with what look like four temples and two castles
on its roof. Across from it is a solemn-looking neoclassical shrine, the
Nemzeti Bank (National Bank). In the square's center remains a gold
hammer and sickle atop a white stone obelisk, one of the few remaining
monuments to the Russian "liberation" of Budapest in 1945. Although
its continuing presence rankles some, good relations with Russia mean
it will probably stay, as the monument marks a gravesite of fallen Soviet
troops. With the Stars and Stripes flying out in front, the **United States
Embassy** is at Szabadság tér 12. ✉*District V.*

㉒ **Széchenyi Lánchíd** *(Chain Bridge).* This is the oldest and most beautiful
Fodor'sChoice of the seven road bridges that span the Danube in Budapest. When
★ lighted up at night, it practically defines Budapest's radiance. It was
constructed at the initiative of the great Hungarian reformer and phi-
lanthropist Count István Széchenyi, using an 1839 design by the English civil engineer William Tierney Clark. This classical suspension
bridge was finished by the Scotsman Adam Clark (no relation to William Tierney Clark), who also built the 383-yard tunnel under Castle
Hill, thus connecting the Danube quay with the rest of Buda. After it
was destroyed by the Nazis, the bridge was rebuilt in its original form
(though widened for traffic) and reopened in 1949, on the centenary of
its inauguration. ✉*Districts I and V, linking Clark Ádám tér in Buda
with Roosevelt tér in Pest.*

㊵ **Szent István Bazilika** *(St. Stephen's Basilica).* Handsome and massive, this
Fodor'sChoice is one of the chief landmarks of Pest and the city's largest church—it
★ can hold 8,500 people. Its very Holy Roman front porch greets you
with a tympanum bustling with statuary. The basilica's dome and the
dome of Parliament are the most visible in the Pest skyline, and this is
no accident: with the Magyar Millennium of 1896 in mind (the lavishly
celebrated thousandth anniversary of the settling of the Carpathian
Basin in 896), both domes were planned to be 315 feet high.

The millennium was not yet in sight when architect József Hild began
building the basilica in neoclassical style in 1851. After Hild's death,
the project was taken over in 1867 by Miklós Ybl, the architect who
did the most to transform modern Pest into a monumental metropolis.
Wherever he could, Ybl shifted Hild's motifs toward the neo-Renaissance mode. Ybl died in 1891, five years before the 1,000-year celebration, and the basilica was completed in neo-Renaissance style by József
Kauser—but not until 1905.

Below the cupola is a rich collection of late-19th-century Hungarian
art: mosaics, altarpieces, and statuary. Stephen's mummified right hand
is preserved as a relic in the **Szent Jobb Kápolna** (Holy Right Chapel); for 100 HUF it will be illuminated for two minutes. You can also
climb the 364 stairs (or take the elevator) to the top of the cupola for
a spectacular view of the city. Guided tours (available in English) cost
1,500 HUF a person and, if a large-enough group has arranged this in
advance, leave three times a day on weekdays (at 11, 2, and 3:30) and
once on Saturdays (at 11); it's best to phone ahead. ✉*District V, Szt.*

István tér, H-1054 ☎*1/338–2151* ⊕*www.basilika.hu* 🔊*Church and Szt. Jobb Chapel free, cupola 500 HUF, treasury 300 HUF* ⊙*Church Mon.–Sat. 9–5:30, Sun. 1–5:30. Szt. Jobb Chapel Apr.–Oct., Mon.–Sat. 9–5, Sun. 1–5; Nov.–Mar., Mon.–Sat. 10–4, Sun. 1–4. Cupola Apr. and Sept.–Oct., daily 10–5; May–Aug., daily 9–6.*

㉜ Szerb Ortodox templom. Built in 1688, this lovely burnt-orange church, one of Budapest's oldest buildings, sits in a shaded garden surrounded by thick stone walls decorated with a large tile mosaic of St. George defeating the dragon. Its opening hours are erratic, but if the wrought-iron gates are open, wander in for a look at the beautiful hand-carved wooden pews. ⊠*District V, Szerb utca.*

㉗ Váci utca. Just north of Elizabeth Bridge is Budapest's best-known shopping street and most unabashed tourist zone, Váci utca, a pedestrian precinct with electric 19th-century lampposts and smart shops with credit-card emblems on ornate doorways. No bargain basement, Váci utca gets its special flavor from the mix of native furriers, tailors, designers, folk-craft shops, china shops, bookstores, and internationally known boutiques. ⊠*District V, from Vörösmarty tér to Fővám tér.*

㊴ Városház *(City Hall).* The monumental former city council building, which used to be a hospital for wounded soldiers and then a home for the elderly, is now Budapest's city hall. You can freely enter its courtyard. The Tuscan columns at the main entrance and the allegorical statuary of *Atlas, War,* and *Peace* are especially splendid. ⊠*District V, Városház utca 9–11,* ☎*1/327–1000* 🔊*Free* ⊙*Weekdays 6* AM–6:30 PM.

Fodor'sChoice ★ **Vásárcsarnok** *(Central Market Hall).* The magnificent hall, a 19th-century iron-frame construction near the southern end of Váci utca, reopened in late 1994 after years of renovation. The cavernous, three-story market teems with people browsing among stalls packed with salamis and red-paprika chains. Upstairs you can buy folk embroideries and souvenirs and have your fill of Hungarian-style fast food or sit down at the cafeteria-style Fakanál restaurant *see Dining.* ⊠*District IX, Vámház körút 1–3* ☎*1/366–3300* ⊕*www.basilika.hu* ⊙*Mon. 6–5, Tues.–Fri. 6–6, Sat. 6–2.*

㉔ Vigadó *(Concert Hall).* Designed in a striking romantic style by Frigyes Feszl and inaugurated in 1865 with Franz Liszt conducting his own *St. Elizabeth Oratorio,* Budapest's premier city-center concert hall—closed for renovation until sometime in 2009—is a curious mixture of Byzantine, Moorish, Romanesque, and Hungarian motifs, punctuated by dancing statues and sturdy pillars. Brahms, Debussy, and Casals are among the other phenomenal musicians who have graced its stage. Mahler's *Symphony No. 1* and many works by Bartók were first performed here. ⊠*District V, Vigadó tér 2* ☎*1/354–3755 for info.*

▌ NEED A BREAK? If you visit only one café in Budapest, stop on Vörösmarty Square at Gerbeaud (⊠*District V, Vörösmarty tér 7* ☎*1/429–9000*), a café and pastry shop founded in 1858 by Hungarian Henrik Kugler and a Swiss, Emil Gerbeaud. The decor (green-marble tables, Regency-style marble fireplaces) is as sumptuous as the tempting selection of cakes and sweets.

7

㉖ **Vörösmarty tér.** Downtown revitalization since the early 1990s has
★ decentralized things somewhat, but this large, handsome square at the
northern end of Váci utca is still the heart of Pest's tourist life in many
respects. Street musicians, sidewalk cafés, and ice-cream-toting tourists
make this one of the liveliest places in Budapest and a good spot to take
it all in. At its center is a white-marble statue of the 19th-century poet
and dramatist Mihály Vörösmarty, and nearby is an elegant former pis-
soir. Stores and businesses occupy the perimeter, and at this writing a
grand new "multifunctional" building was rising on the square's west
side. ⊠*District V.*

ANDRÁSSY ÚT

Behind St. Stephen's Basilica, at the intersection with Bajcsy-Zsilinszky
út, begins Budapest's grandest avenue, Andrássy út. Under communism
this broad boulevard bore the name Népköztársaság útja (Avenue of
the People's Republic). In 1990, it reverted to its old name honoring
Count Gyula Andrássy, a statesman who in 1867 became Hungary's
first constitutional premier. The boulevard that would eventually bear
his name was begun in 1872, as Buda and Pest (and Óbuda) were
about to be unified. Most of the mansions lining it were completed by
1884. It took another dozen years before the first underground railway
on the Continent was completed all along its length for—you guessed
it—the Magyar Millennium in 1896. Though preceded by London's
Underground (1863), Budapest's was the world's first electrified subway. Only slightly modernized but refurbished for the 1996 millecen-
tenary, this "Little Metro" is still running a 4-km (2½-mi) stretch from
Vörösmarty tér to just beyond City Park. Using tiny yellow trains with
tanklike treads, and stopping at antique stations marked FÖLDALATTI
(Underground), Line 1 is a tourist attraction in itself.

Most museums are closed Monday, so it's best to explore Andrássy út
on a weekday or early Saturday, when stores are also open for browsing. During opera season you can time your exploration to land you at
the Operaház stairs just before 7 PM to watch the spectacle of opera-
goers flowing in for the evening's performance. You may want to save
City Park for a clear day. Walking the length of the boulevard at one go
takes less than an hour, but figuring the cafés and sites into the equation, you're easily looking at four hours or more.

㊻ **Hősök tere.** Andrássy út ends in grandeur at Heroes' Square, with Buda-
★ pest's answer to Berlin's Brandenburg Gate. The **Millenniumi Emlékmű**
(Millennial Monument) is a semicircular twin colonnade with statues
of Hungary's kings and leaders between its pillars. Set back in its open
center, a 118-foot stone column is crowned by a dynamic statue of the
archangel Gabriel, his outstretched arms bearing the ancient emblems
of Hungary. At its base ride seven bronze horsemen: the Magyar chief-
tains, led by Árpád, whose tribes conquered the land in 896. Before the
column lies a simple marble slab, the **Nemzeti Háborús Emlék Tábla**
(National War Memorial), at which visiting foreign dignitaries lay ceremonial wreaths. ⊠*District VI.*

45 **Kodály körönd.** A handsome traffic circle with imposing statues of three Hungarian warriors—leavened by a fourth one of a poet—Kodály körönd is surrounded by plane and chestnut trees. Look carefully at the towered mansions on the north side of the circle—behind the soot you'll see the fading colors of ornate frescoes peeking through. The circle was named for the composer Zoltán Kodály, who lived just beyond it, at Andrássy út 89. ⊠*District VI, Andrássy út at Szinyei Merse utca.*

43 **Liszt Ferenc Zeneakadémia** *(Franz Liszt Academy of Music).* This magnificent Art Nouveau building, one of the city's main concert halls, presides over the cafés and gardens of bustling Liszt Ferenc tér. On summer days the sound of daytime rehearsals enhances this pedestrian oasis of café society, just off buzzing Andrássy út. Farther along the square is a dramatic statue of Liszt Ferenc (Franz Liszt) himself. ⊠*District VI, Liszt Ferenc tér 8* ☎*1/462–4600 Ext. 179 (box office).*

41 **Magyar Állami Operaház** *(Hungarian State Opera House).* Miklós Yhl's ★ crowning achievement is the neo-Renaissance Opera House, built between 1875 and 1884. Badly damaged during the siege of 1944–45, it was restored for its 1984 centenary. Two buxom marble sphinxes guard the driveway; the main entrance is flanked by Alajos Strobl's "romantic-realist" limestone statues of Liszt and of another 19th-century Hungarian composer, Ferenc Erkel, the father of Hungarian opera (his patriotic opera *Bánk bán* is performed for national celebrations).

Inside, the spectacle begins even before the performance does. You glide up grand staircases and through wood-paneled corridors and gilt lime-green salons into a glittering jewel box of an auditorium. Its four tiers of boxes are held up by helmeted sphinxes beneath a frescoed ceiling by Károly Lotz. Lower down there are frescoes everywhere, with intertwined motifs of Apollo and Dionysus.

The best way to experience the Opera House's interior is to see a ballet or opera; tickets are relatively affordable and easy to come by, at least for tourists. There are no performances in summer, except for the week-long BudaFest international opera and ballet festival in mid-August. You cannot view the interior on your own, but 45-minute tours in English are conducted daily; buy tickets in the Opera Shop. (Large groups should call in advance.) ⊠*District VI, Andrássy út 22* ☎*1/332–8197 for tours, 1/353–0170 box office* ⊕*www.opera.hu* ☎*Tours 2,500 HUF, photos 500 HUF* ⊙*Tours daily at 3 and 4.*

42 **Magyar Fotógráfusok Háza (Mai Manó Ház)** *(Hungarian Photographers' House [Manó Mai House]).* This ornate turn-of-the-20th-century building was built as a photography studio, where the wealthy bourgeoisie would come to be photographed by imperial and royal court photographer Manó Mai. Inside, ironwork and frescoes ornament the curving staircase leading up to the exhibition space, the largest of Budapest's three photo galleries. ⊠*District VI, Nagymező utca 20* ☎*1/473–2666* ☎*700 HUF* ⊙*Weekdays 2–7, weekends 11–7.*

47 Műcsarnok *(Palace of Exhibitions).* The city's largest hall for special exhibitions is a striking 1895 temple of culture with a colorful tympanum. Its program of events includes exhibitions of contemporary Hungarian and international art and a rich series of films, plays, and concerts. Admission is free on Tuesday. ⊠*District XIV, Hősök tere* ☎*1/460–7000* ⊕*www.mucsarnok.hu* ⊠*1,500 HUF* ◷*Tues., Wed., Fri., and Sun. 10–6, Thurs. 10–8.*

NEED A BREAK?

The Müvész Café (⊠*District VI, Andrássy út 29* ☎*1/352–1337*) is perhaps the only surviving "writer's café" where you will occasionally see an actual writer at work. The combination of low lighting and striped, dark gold-green wallpaper gives it an elegant yet chic appeal. Sit at a table outside on a warm day to watch the world passing by on Andrássy út (or to avoid the smoke inside).

48 Szépművészeti Múzeum *(Museum of Fine Arts).* Across Heroes' Square

Fodor's Choice from the Palace of Exhibitions and built by the same team of Albert
★ Schickedanz and Fülöp Herzog, the Museum of Fine Arts houses Hungary's best art collection, rich in Flemish and Dutch old masters; the collection of Spanish old masters is among the best outside Spain. The Italian school is represented by Giorgione, Bellini, Correggio, Tintoretto, and Titian masterpieces and, above all, by a couple of superb Raphael paintings. Nineteenth-century French art includes works by Delacroix, Pissarro, Cézanne, Toulouse-Lautrec, Gauguin, Renoir, and Monet. The collection also contains more than 100,000 drawings (including some by Rembrandt and by Leonardo da Vinci), and Egyptian and Greco-Roman exhibitions. A 20th-century collection comprises statues, paintings, and drawings by Chagall, Le Corbusier, and others. The special exhibits are outstanding and frequent. ⊠*District XIV, Hősök tere, H-1146* ☎*1/469–7100* ⊕*www.szepmuveszeti. hu* ⊠*Free, special exhibits each 800–2,000 HUF, entry to all special exhibits 2,400 HUF* ◷*Tues.–Sun. 10–5:30.*

44 Terror Háza *(House of Terror).* A powerful journey into the darkest
★ sides of both communism and fascism, this state-of-the-art, multimedia museum is appropriately housed in a building with a terrible history. Starting in 1939 it was headquarters of the fascist Arrow Cross party; from 1945 to 1956 the communist state security police used it as its headquarters and interrogation-cum-torture center. With everything from videos of sobbing victims telling their stories to a full-size Soviet tank, it strikes some visitors as too slick, others as just right. An English-language audio guide, available for 1,300 HUF per person above the ticket price, helps make sense of it all, as there's little English text. ⊠*District VI, Andrássy út 60* ☎*1/374–2600* ⊕*www.terrorhaza.hu* ⊠*1,500 HUF* ◷*Tues.–Fri. 10–6, weekends 10–7:30.*

49 Városliget *(City Park).* Heroes' Square is the gateway to a square kilo-
◷ meter (almost ½ square mi) of recreation, entertainment, beauty, and culture. A bridge behind the Millennial Monument leads across a boating basin that becomes an artificial ice-skating rink in winter. You can soak or swim at the lovely, turn-of-the-20th-century Széchenyi Fürdő,

jog in the park, or careen on Vidám Park's roller coaster. There's also the Petőfi Csarnok, a leisure-time youth center and major concert hall on the site of an old industrial exhibition hall. The Gundel restaurant charms diners with its turn-of-the-20th-century ambience. ⊠ *District XIV* ▣ *Park free, admission charged for attractions* ☉ *Daily.*

🌣 The **Budapesti Állat-és Növénykert** *(Budapest Zoo & Botanical Garden)* has petting opportunities aplenty, and a monkey house allows little simians to climb all over you. Don't miss the elephant pavilion, decorated with Zsolnay majolica and glazed ceramic animals; or for that matter, the tropical greenhouse and the aquarium. Note that the last tickets are sold one hour before closing, and animal houses don't open until an hour after the zoo gates. ⊠ *District XIV, Állatkerti körút 6–12* ☏ *1/273–4901* ⊕ *www.zoobudapest.com* ▣ *1,700 HUF* ☉ *May–Aug., Mon.–Thurs. 9–6, Fri.–Sun. 9–7; Mar., Apr., Sept., and Oct., daily 9–5; Nov.–Feb., daily 9–4.* At the **Fővárosi Nagycirkusz** *(Municipal Grand Circus)*, colorful performances by local acrobats, clowns, and animal trainers, as well as by international artists, are staged in a small ring. ⊠ *District XIV, Állatkerti körút 7* ☏ *1/343–8300* ⊕ *www.maciva.hu* ▣ *1,500–2,200 HUF* ☉ *Performances Apr.–mid-June, Wed.–Fri. at 3, Sat. at 10:30, 3, and 7, Sun. at 10:30 and 3; mid-June–Aug., Wed.–Fri. at 5, Sat. at 3 and 7, and Sun. at 10:30 and 3; Sept.–Mar., schedule varies.* **Széchenyi Fürdő** *(Széchenyi Baths).* More than 2 million visitors to Budapest have taken the waters at this glorious indoor and outdoor thermal bath complex, one of Europe's largest. The turn-of-the-20th-century baths in the heart of City Park have that old-world feel, with yellow-and-white Secessionist-style architecture, beautiful grounds, and lots of fountains and loggias. Outside are a big swimming pool and two thermal baths; inside are thermal pools, a cold shock pool, and the hottest steam room in Budapest. ⊠ *District XIV, Állatkerti körút 11* ☏ *1/363–3210* ⊕ *www.spasbudapest.com* ▣ *2,400 HUF (partial refunds if you leave within 3 hours, and discounted admission beginning 3 hrs before closing)* ☉ *Daily 6* AM–10 PM *(smaller thermal pools close by 7* PM *or earlier).* Beside the City Park's lake stands **Vajdahunyad Vár** (Vajdahunyad Castle), a fantastic medley of Hungary's historic and architectural past, starting with the Romanesque gateway of the cloister of Ják, in western Hungary. The Transylvanian turrets, Renaissance loggia, baroque portico, and Byzantine decorations are all guarded by a spooky modern (1903) bronze statue of the anonymous medieval "chronicler." Designed for the millennial celebration in 1896, the castle was not completed until 1908. It houses the surprisingly interesting **Mezőgazdasági Múzeum** *(Agricultural Museum)*, which touts itself as Europe's largest such museum. Twelve permanent exhibitions cover animal husbandry, forestry, horticulture, viticulture, hunting, fishing, and more. There are regular arts and crafts activities for kids. ⊠ *District XIV* ☏ *1/422–0765* ⊕ *www.mmgm.hu* ▣ *Free, 300 HUF for special exhibits* ☉ *Mar.–Nov. 15, Tues.–Sun. 10–5; Nov. 15–Feb. 15, Tues.–Fri. 10–4, weekends 10–5.* Budapest's somewhat weary amusement park, **Vidám Park,** is next to the zoo. In all, there are about 50 different attractions, including Europe's longest wooden roller coaster and a merry-go-round dating from 1906 and beautifully

7

restored in 1998. Unusually, the admission, which covers most rides, is by height. ⊠*District XIV, Állatkerti körút 14–16* ☎*1/343–8310* ⊕*www.vidampark.hu* 🖰*Those under 100 cm (3'4") free; to 140 cm (4'8") 2,100 HUF weekdays, 2,500 HUF weekends; above 140 cm (4'8") 3,100 HUF weekdays, 3,500 HUF weekends* ⊙*Apr.–Sept., daily 10–8, Oct.–Mar., daily 10–7.*

EASTERN PEST & THE NAGY KÖRÚT (LARGE RING ROAD)

Pest's Large Ring Road (Nagy körút) was laid out in the late 19th century in a wide semicircle, anchored to the Danube at both ends; an arm of the river was covered over to create this 114-foot-wide thoroughfare. The massive apartment buildings on both sides also date from this era. Along with theaters, stores, and cafés, they form a boulevard unique in Europe for its "unified eclecticism." Its entire length of almost 4½ km (2¾ mi) from the Margaret Bridge to the Petőfi Bridge is traversed by Trams 4 and 6, but strolling it in stretches is also a good way to experience the hustle and bustle of Budapest's busy, less-touristy urban thoroughfares full of people, cars, shops, and the city's unique urban flavor.

Like its smaller counterpart, the Kis körút (Small Ring Road), the Large Ring Road comprises sections of various names. Beginning with Ferenc körút at the Petőfi Bridge, it changes to József körút at the intersection marked by the Museum of Applied Arts, then to Erzsébet körút at Blaha Lujza tér. Teréz körút begins at the busy Oktogon crossing with Andrássy út and ends at the Nyugati (West) Railway Station, where Szent István takes over for the final stretch to the Margaret Bridge.

As the Large Ring Road is packed with stores, it's best to explore during business hours—weekdays until around 5 PM and Saturday until 1 PM. Saturday will be most crowded. Keep in mind that the Iparművészeti Múzeum is closed Monday. A leisurely walk from one end to the other on the Pest side takes around 90 minutes, but a thorough exploration of the area will take several hours.

⑤ **Holocaust Emlékközpont** *(Holocaust Memorial Center).* The stone facade
★ of this onetime synagogue is a high, windowless wall. Just inside the courtyard is a black wall bearing the names of all known Hungarian victims of the Holocaust, including both Jews and many Romas (Gypsies). From there you go downstairs into a cellar, where you proceed through a compelling and haunting blend of family and individual stories told through photos, films, original documents, personal objects, and touch-screen computers (with text in English). You are taken from 1938, when the Hungarian state first began depriving Jews and others of their rights; to 1944, by which time these people were being systematically deprived of their freedom and their lives; to liberation in 1945. ⊠*District IX, Páva utca 39* ☎*1/455–3333* ⊕*www.hdke.hu* 🖰*1,000 HUF, audio guide 500 HUF* ⊙*Tues.–Sun. 10–6.*

⑤ **Iparművészeti Múzeum** *(Museum of Applied and Decorative Arts).* This
★ templelike structure is a shrine to Hungarian Art Nouveau, and in front of it sits a statue of its creator, Hungarian architect Ödön Lechner. Opened in the Magyar Millennial year of 1896, it has a striking

dome of deep green and golden tiles crowned by a majolica lantern from the same source: the Zsolnay ceramic works in Pécs. Inside its central hall are playfully swirling whitewashed, double-decker, Moorish-style galleries and arcades. The museum, which collects and studies objects of interior decoration and use, has five departments: furniture, textiles, goldsmithing, ceramics, and everyday objects. ✉ *District VIII, Üllői út 33–37* ☎ *1/456–5100* ⊕ *www.imm.hu* ✉ *Permanent collection free, special exhibits 500–1,600 HUF, all exhibits 2,300 HUF* ☉ *Tues.–Sun. 10–6.*

🔵52 **Keleti pályaudvar** *(East Railway Station).* The grandiose, imperial-looking station was built in 1884. Its neo-Renaissance facade, which resembles a gateway, is flanked by statues of two British inventors and railway pioneers, James Watt and George Stephenson. ✉ *District VIII, Baross tér.*

🔵57 **Nemzeti Színház** *(National Theater).* Round and colonnaded in front and square in back, this massive building is a spectacular blend of modern and classical. The spacious square out front includes metal statues of late, great Hungarian thespians of the 20th century, each performing a legendary role. ✉ *District IX, Bajor Gizi Park 1* ☎ *1/476–6800* ⊕ *www.nemzetiszinhaz.hu.*

🔵53 **New York Palota** *(New York Palace).* Commissioned by the New York Insurance Company and designed in eclectic styles with an Italian Renaissance edge by Alajos Hausman, Flóris Korb, and Alajos Giegl, this magnificent palace first opened in 1894 and soon became famous for its New York Café. After years of renovation it reopened in 2006 as a luxury hotel *see Lodging.* It's well worth a peek (and perhaps a break for a cappuccino and pastry) even though its café is today more of a restaurant, and even if many Budapesters are pooh-poohing the new glitter and the mirror-topped tables that reflect the painfully restored ceiling frescoes above you. ✉ *District VII, Erzsébet körút 9–11* ☎ *1/886–6111* ⊕ *www.newyorkpalace.hu.*

★ **Művészetek Palotája** *(Palace of the Arts).* This monumental venue next
🔵58 to the similarly grand National Theater is glitzier than the city's older cultural halls and hosts a wide array of musical, theatrical, and dance performances. The spacious and sparkling inside, much of which you can wander around for free, contains many intimate, well-cushioned nooks where you can take a seat and ponder life and/or art. ✉ *District IX, Komor Marcell utca 1* ☎ *1/555–3000* ✉ *Free to enter, admission for events* ⊕ *www.mupa.hu.*

In addition to housing the National Concert Hall, the Festival Theatre, a stylish restaurant, and a couple of stores, the Palace is home to the **Ludwig Múzeum,** a venue of contemporary art whose permanent collection covers American Pop Art (e.g., Warhol); the German, French, and Italian trans-avant-garde; and Eastern and Central European art (including, of course, Hungarian art from the 1960s to the present day). ✉ *District IX, Komor Marcell utca 1* ☎ *1/555–3444* ✉ *Free, special exhibits 1,050 HUF* ☉ *Tues.–Sun., 10–8 (until 10 the last Sat. of each month)* ⊕ *www.ludwigmuseum.hu.*

⑤④ Nyugati pályaudvar *(West Railway Station).* The iron-laced glass hall of the West Railway Station is in complete contrast to—and much more modern than—the newer East Railway Station. Built in the 1870s, it was designed by a team of architects from Gustav Eiffel's office in Paris. ⊠*District XIII, Teréz körút.*

⑤⑤ Vígszínház *(Comedy Theater).* This neo-baroque, late-19th-century, ★ gemlike theater twinkles with just a tiny, playful anticipation of Art Nouveau and sparkles inside and out since its 1994 refurbishment. The theater hosts primarily musicals as well as dance performances and classical concerts. ⊠*District XIII, Pannónia utca 1* ☎*1/329–2340 box office* ⊕*www.vigszinhaz.hu.*

ÓBUDA & MARGIT-SZÍGET

Until its unification with Buda and Pest in 1872 to form the city of Budapest, Óbuda (meaning "Old Buda") was a separate town; now it is usually thought of as a suburb. Although a vast housing project and busy roadways are what first strike the eye, the historic core of Óbuda has been preserved in its entirety. As for Margit-szíget (Margaret Island), if you have fair weather during a stay of three days or more in Budapest, do take a stroll (or go for a swim) in this centrally located, vast expanse of green—the capital's most beloved spot for R and R.

A leisurely stroll from one end of Margaret Island to the other takes about an hour, but it's nice to spend some extra time wandering. It's best to begin touring Óbuda either on a relatively cool day or in the cooler hours of the morning, as the heat on the area's busy roads can get overbearing. Avoid Monday, when museums are closed. Exploring the core of Óbuda will take three hours or more, given the relatively large distances; add a couple of hours for a jaunt out to Aquincum.

⑥② Aquincum. This complex comprises the reconstructed remains of a Roman settlement dating from the 1st century AD and the capital of the Roman province of Pannonia. Careful excavations have unearthed a varied selection of artifacts and mosaics, giving a tantalizing inkling of what life was like in the provinces of the Roman Empire. The **Aquincum múzeum** (Aquincum Museum) displays the dig's most notable finds: ceramics, a fascinating red-marble sarcophagus, and jewelry from a Roman lady's tomb. ⊠*District III, Szentendrei út 139* ☎*1/250–1650* ⊕*www.aquincum.hu* ▦*Museum 900 HUF* ⊙*Museum mid- to late Apr. and Oct., Tues.–Sun. 10–5; May–Sept., Tues.–Sun. 10–6 (grounds open an hour earlier than museum).*

⑥⓪ Flórián tér *(Flórián Square).* The center of today's Óbuda is Flórián tér, where Roman ruins were first discovered when the foundations of a house were dug in 1778. Two centuries later, careful excavations were carried out during the reconstruction of the square, and today the restored ancient ruins lie in the center of the square in sharp contrast to the surrounding racing traffic and apartment blocks. ⊠*District III, Vörösvári út at Pacsirtamező u.*

⑥① Fő tér *(Main Square).* Óbuda's old main square is its most picturesque part, and includes several good restaurants and interesting museums in and around the baroque **Zichy Kúria** (Zichy Mansion), which has become a neighborhood cultural center. ⊠*District III, Kórház u. at Hídfő u.*

59 **Kiscelli Múzeum** *(Kiscelli Museum).* A climb up the steep sidewalks of Remetehegy (Hermit's Hill) will deposit you at this elegant, mustard-yellow baroque mansion. Built between 1744 and 1760 as a Trinitarian monastery, today it holds an eclectic mix of paintings, sculptures, engravings, and sundry items related to the history of Budapest. ⊠*District III, Kiscelli u. 108* ☏*1/250–0304* 💰*700 HUF* ⊗*Nov.–Mar., Tues.–Sun. 10–4; Apr.–Oct., Tues.–Sun. 10–6.*

56 **Margit híd** *(Margaret Bridge).* Providing gorgeous mid-river views of Castle Hill and Parliament, the Margaret Bridge is the closer of the two access points to Margaret Island for those coming from downtown Buda or Pest. The original bridge was built during the 1840s by French engineer Ernest Gouin in collaboration with Gustave Eiffel. In late 1944 it was blown up by the retreating Nazis while crowded with rush-hour traffic. It was later rebuilt in the same unusual shape—forming an obtuse angle in midstream, with a short leg leading down to the island.

57 **Margit-sziget** *(Margaret Island).* More than 2½ km (1½ mi) long and nearly 200 acres, this island park is ideal for strolling, jogging, sunbathing, or just loafing. In good weather it draws a huge cross section of the city's population to its gardens and sporting facilities. The grassy, outdoor pool complex of the Palatinus Baths (toward the northern end), built in 1921, attracts thousands on a summer day; and then there's the huge, all-year, indoor-outdoor (but concrete) swimming complex, the Hajós Alfréd Nemzeti Sportuszoda. Nearby are a tennis stadium, an athletic center, and boathouses. The island's hot springs supply baths at the Danubius Grand and Thermal hotels at the northern end of the island. Toward the island's center is a small, free game farm, and at the northern end you'll find an artificial rock garden with Japanese dwarf trees and lily ponds.

Fodor'sChoice ★

The island was first mentioned almost 2,000 years ago as the summer residence of the commander of the Roman garrison at nearby Aquincum. Later known as Rabbit Island (Insula Leporum), it was a royal hunting ground during the Árpád dynasty. King Imre, who reigned from 1196 to 1204, held court here, and several convents and monasteries were built here during the Middle Ages. (A walk around the island takes you by the ruins of some such buildings.) It takes its current name from St. Margaret (1242–71), the pious daughter of King Béla IV, who at the ripe old age of 10 retired to a Dominican nunnery situated here from the 13th to the 16th century. ⊠*District XIII, Margit-sziget.*

58 **Római amfiteátrum** *(Roman Amphitheater).* Probably dating back to the 2nd century AD, Óbuda's Roman military amphitheater once held some 16,000 people and, at 144 yards in diameter, was one of Europe's largest. Down below are the cells where prisoners and lions were held while awaiting confrontation. ⊠*District III, Pacsirtamező u. at Nagyszombat u.*

WHERE TO EAT

A far cry from the spare options available in the socialist era, Budapest's culinary scene now offers variety and quality, both in huge portions. It's possible, for instance, to eat good sushi in this landlocked nation's capital, and the range of styles encompassed by the culinary classification "Hungarian" runs to much more than just paprika and goulash served up in faux Gypsy surroundings.

A few of the city's grander dining establishments overlook the Danube and downtown from the imperious Castle Hill, and Pest has a busy restaurant scene, including bustling lunchtime bistros and late-night cafés. To be right up to the minute on the restaurant scene, you can riffle through local English-language press for ideas on where to dine.

> **WHAT'S FREE**
>
> The permanent collections of many of Budapest's museums can be visited for free, though admission is charged for special exhibits. Among many others, the museums include the **Magyar Nemzeti Galéria** and the **Hadtörténeti Múzeum** on Várhegy (Castle Hill), and the **Magyar Nemzeti Múzeum** and the **Szépművészeti Múzeum** in Pest. Note that you may feel pressured to pay something, after all, if a permanent collection seems to pale in comparison to what's there temporarily; museums with several special exhibits often have one price that covers all.

Numbers in the text correspond to numbers in the margin and on the Where to Eat and Stay in Central Budapest map.

DOWNTOWN PEST & THE KIS KÖRÚT (SMALL RING ROAD)

$$$$
Fodor'sChoice
★ ✕**Pava.** The premier restaurant of the Four Seasons Hotel Gresham Palace is everything you'd expect from this chain: discreet luxury in a unique and historic building. The international menu hardly lets you know you're in Hungary, but the food is so expertly prepared you're willing to settle for the breathtaking views of the Chain Bridge and Budapest Castle as a reminder. Service is friendly but white-glove all the way. The menu changes frequently and there's usually a five- or six-course prix-fixe option. ⊠*District V, Roosevelt tér 5–6, H-1051* ☎*1/268–5100* ⚮*Reservations essential* ▤*AE, MC, V.*

$$$–$$$$ ✕**Óceán Bar & Grill.** If you're looking for an elegant seafood dinner, you'll find it here. You'll also find rope accents in the dining room, colorful fish tanks in the atrium, crisp white-linen table settings, and shell napkin rings. The first-rate service does justice to the food, whether innovatively prepared fish dishes like roast octopus with okra or meat specialties such as duck leg or beef tenderloin. All fish can be cooked to order. ⊠*District V, Petőfi tér 3* ☎*1/266–1826* ▤*AE, MC, V.*

$–$$
★ ✕**Gerlóczy Kávéház.** The green-and-yellow cane chairs and café tables of this elegant bistro remind you of a scene out of your favorite French movie. The terrace in the summertime is about the prettiest location for lunch in Budapest, on a quiet, leafy square tucked behind Váci utca. The menu has seasonal Hungarian favorites like *sült libacomb* (crispy goose leg) with red cabbage in winter and cold fruit soup in late spring.

Breakfast draws a big crowd on weekends. ⊠*District V, Gerlóczy utca 1* ☎*1/235–0953* ⊟*MC, V.*

AROUND KÁLVIN TÉR & SZABADSÁG-HÍD

$$$ ✗**Múzeum.** Traditional cuisine served in turn-of-the-20th-century style is what you get under the elegant, if somewhat faded, grandeur of a beautifully frescoed ceiling and at tables set with sterling silver and Zsolnay porcelain. Hungarian classics here, such as *Hortobágyi palacsinta* (pancakes), and crispy goose leg with steamed cabbage, are accomplished, but the menu also includes fish. Try pork or veal paired with a good red wine from Villány. A tip of 12% is included. ⊠*District VIII, Múzeum körút 11* ☎*1/338–4221 Jacket and tie* ⊟*MC, V* ☾*Closed Sun.*

$$–$$$ ✗**Trattoria Toscana.** Visiting Italians tell us this popular trattoria feels
★ authentic, with its bustling waiters, rustic interior, and wooden tables. An antipasti bar in front overflows with marinated artichokes, white-bean salad, and other classic Tuscan treats, and there's a brick pizza oven in back. The menu boasts some of the best fish in town, with several sea bass options. Though it's not on the menu, you might ask for the mozzarella *ventigli* pasta with San Marzano tomatoes and fresh oregano—a dish to die for. ⊠*District V, Belgrád Rakpart 13* ☎*1/327–0045* ⌔*Reservations essential* ⊟*AE, DC, MC, V.*

$–$$ ✗**Soul Cafe.** Big club chairs and mustard-colored walls covered with framed textiles warm up this Mediterranean restaurant on lively Ráday utca. Grilled sandwiches and ample salads please vegetarians, and there's a good range of poultry dishes if you want to go non-veg. The desserts are heavenly. ⊠*District IX, Ráday utca 11–13,* ☎*1/217–6986* ⊟*MC, V.*

$ ✗**Fakanál.** If you find yourself getting hungry while browsing the food stands at the Central Market Hall, try the market's only sit-down restaurant as an alternative to its many stand-and-eat snack bars. Hungarian staples like stuffed peppers and goose leg with steamed cabbage are what you get at this cafeteria-style restaurant—at affordable prices, and with rustic, pinewood benches to sit on and a greenhouselike glass ceiling above you. ⊠*District IX, Vámház krt. 1–3* ☎*1/217–7860* ☾*Weekdays 10–5, Sat. 10–2* ⊟*No credit cards.*

AROUND THE NAGY KÖRÚT (LARGE RING ROAD)

$$$–$$$$ ✗**Wasabi.** If you're looking for dinner and distraction, try this Asian
☺ restaurant where the tables are set in front of a conveyer belt that whizzes by with such treats as sushi rolls, chicken satay, egg rolls, and canned peaches, of all things. The theme is a hodgepodge of Japanese, Thai, and Korean, but the conveyer-belt gimmick is the real show. Kids go wild for the place. One price gets you as many courses as you'd like: Weekdays from 11 to 5 it's 3,700 HUF; otherwise, it's 4,000 HUF. ⊠*District VI, Podmanicsky utca 21* ☎*1/374–0008* ⊟*MC, V.*

$–$$$ ✗**Kiskakukk.** The Art Deco facade of the Little Cuckoo restaurant evokes
Fodor's Choice the history of this once-fashionable residential neighborhood. The set-
★ ting is comfortable and the service is attentive; wood-paneled walls and red-velvety chairs give the place a sophisticated, albeit homey, feel. The classic Hungarian poultry dishes are well done, including duck leg with

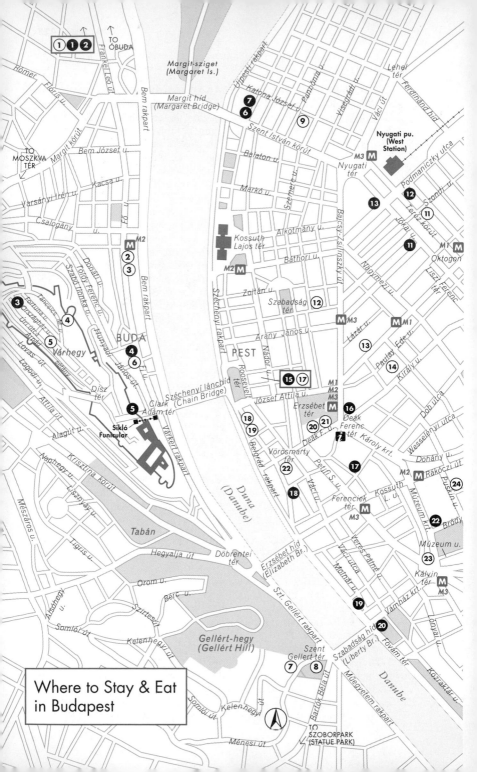

Where to Stay & Eat in Budapest

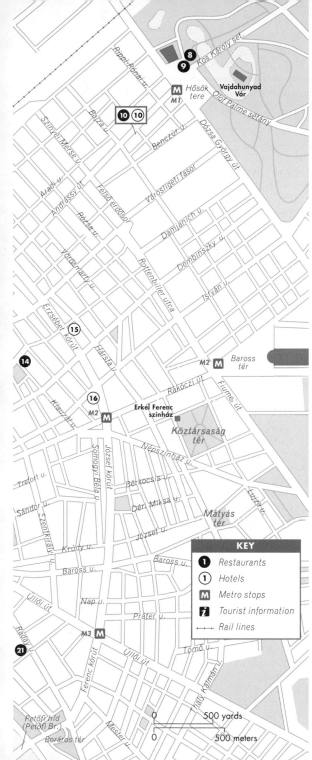

7

Paprika Is the Spice of Life

Hungarian cuisine—and, in particular, its two most famous dishes, *gulyás leves* (goulash soup) and *csirke paprikás* (chicken paprikash)—is closely identified with bright-red paprika. This rich spice comes in many forms, from light and sweet to bold and fiery, and is available in all Hungarian supermarkets. The varieties include *különleges* (special), the highest-quality version, which has a pleasantly spicy aroma and is finely ground; *édes* (sweet), which has a rich color, mild aroma, and is somewhat coarsely ground; *csipős* (hot), which is light brown with yellowish tones, has a fiery flavor, and is coarsely ground; *rózsa* (rose), bright red in color, medium spicy, and medium ground; and *csemege* (mild), which is light red in color, has a rich aroma, and is medium ground.

---

cabbage, and there are some refined dishes, too, such as veal medallions in stewed vegetables and lamb with rosemary. ⊠*District XIII, Pozsonyi utca 12, H-1137* ☎*1/450–0829* ▤*MC, V.*

$–$$ ✗**Nirvana.** What with the arched brick ceiling, it may seem like you're entering just another little Hungarian cellar pub-cum-restaurant as you descend the stairs, but this is the latest—and perhaps most affordable—among Budapest's growing number of quality Indian dining options. The food—from samosas to Punjabi lentils, tandoori chicken, and tikkas—is scrumptious. ⊠*District VI, Jókai utca 8* ☎*1/302–5468* ▤*MC, V.*

¢–$ ✗**Noa Grill.** This clean, spacious, Israeli-owned fast-food restaurant is the best choice for falafel or döner kebab near the Nyugati railway station. Open until midnight, the Noa is a favorite of partygoers fueling up for the night with tasty Middle Eastern dishes like grilled eggplant salad and hummus, as well as decent pizza. You have your choice of the take-away window or a pleasant seating area inside. In the morning there's a hearty Continental breakfast. ⊠*District VI, Terez Körút 54* ☎*1/354–1670* ▤*AE, MC, V.*

¢–$ ✗**Pozsonyi Kisvendéglő.** Rock-bottom prices ensure a crowd most days for lunch and dinner at this well-loved neighborhood *vendeglő* (restaurant serving home cooking). Big bowls of *jókai bableves* (bean soup) are sopped up with fresh bread, and classics like *marhapörkölt* (beef paprikash), *pacalpörkölt* (tripe paprikash) and, yes, *szalontüdő* (lung in cream sauce) are made the way Hungarian grandmothers used to make them. ⊠*District XIII, Radnóti Miklós utca 38, at the corner of Pozsonyi út* ☎*1/787–4877* ⚠*Reservations essential* ▤*No credit cards.*

AROUND ANDRÁSSY ÚT

$$$–$$$$
Fodor's Choice
★

✗**Baraka.** The leafy outside terrace of this celebrated restaurant, which occupies the same building as the exquisite Andrássy Hotel, looks onto majestic Andrássy út and Heroes Square; the spacious dining room thrums big-city glamour. Dimmed crystal chandeliers, sleek black tables, and massive vases filled with calla lillies suggest a sophisticated evening in store. Expect innovative seasonal dishes like caramelized Belgian endive with fresh peaches, and blue-cheese and sweet-corn bisque, as well as creative fish courses. There's a reasonable two-course lunch special daily. ⊠ *District VI, Andrássy út 111, H-1063* ☎ *1/483–1355* ⊛ *Reservations essential* ⊟ *AE, MC, V* ⊘ *Closed Sun.*

¢–$ ✕ **Kádár Étkezde.** This home-style family restaurant has been around for
Fodor'sChoice a while, as have generations of fans. The walls are decorated with pho-
★ tos of celebrities from years gone by and the tables are topped with old-fashioned spritzer bottles from which you serve yourself water. Tasty, traditional Hungarian Jewish cooking is the thing here (not kosher, though); think stuffed kohlrabi, *káposztás kocka* (cabbage pasta), and boiled beef. Everyone orders the tasty raspberry (*málna*) drink. Tell the cashier what you ate, and pay at the door. It's open only from 11:30 to 3:30. ⊠ *District VII, Klauzá tér 9, H-1061* ☎ *1/321–3622* ⊟ *No credit cards* ⊘ *Closed Sun. and Mon. No dinner.*

¢ ✕ **Duran Szendvics.** You might feel almost like a kid in a candy store standing outside the window of this take-away sandwich shop at lunchtime. Beautiful rows of canapés are delicately piled with fluffy egg salad, ham with black caviar, pickled herring salad, and spicy pepperoni, each topped with a pretty sprig of curly parsley. Buy a boxful and picnic on a nearby bench. There are several other Duran Szendvics shops in the city center, including one at Október 6 utca 15, near St. Stephen's Basilica. ⊠ *District VI, Bajcsy Zsilinszky út 7* ☎ *1/267–9624* ⊟ *No credit cards* ⊘ *No dinner.*

AROUND MOSZKVA TÉR & CASTLE HILL

$$$–$$$$ ✕ **Rivalda.** On summer nights you can choose to dine outside in an
★ 18th-century courtyard or in the restaurant's rococo interior—with poplin stage curtains, theatrical masks, and peach-colored walls. The location couldn't be more romantic, on a quiet street in the Castle District. The food is a lighter take on Hungarian cuisine, with some excellent seafood dishes, including cream of pumpkin bisque with smoked salmon, and poultry specialties such as pheasant with chestnut stuffing. Rivalda also has a small vegetarian menu. ⊠ *District I, Színház utca 5–9* ☎ *1/489–0236* ⊟ *AE, DC, MC, V.*

$$–$$$$ ✕ **Café Pierrot.** When touring Castle Hill, tuck into this elegant café for
★ a relaxing lunch. You may not want to leave once you hear the soothing live jazz piano in the evening and see the charming interior—walls covered with paintings of harlequins and fresh flowers on the tables. The menu includes updated Hungarian favorites, as well as inventive pastas and sandwiches. ⊠ *District I, Fortuna utca 14* ☎ *1/375–6971* ⊟ *AE, MC, V.*

$$–$$$$ ✕ **Le Jardin de Paris.** Across the street from the French Institute, one of Budapest's oldest French restaurants has a tranquil outdoor garden, a small dining room decorated with antique movie posters and caricatures, and scrumptious food, from wild game to poultry to a whole host of seafood specialties—and, yes, chocolate mousse. ⊠ *District II, Fő utca 20,* ☎ *1/201–0047* ⊛ *Reservations essential* ⊟ *AE, DC, MC, V.*

7

ÓBUDA

$$–$$$$ ✗**Kéhli.** This pricey but laid-back, sepia-toned neighborhood tavern is on a hard-to-find street near the Óbuda end of the Árpád Bridge. Practically all the food here arrives in huge servings, which was just the way that early-20th-century Hungarian writer Gyula Krúdy liked it when he was a regular customer. Dishes like the hot pot with marrow bone and toast, or *lecsó* (a stew with a base of onions, peppers, tomatoes, and paprika) are great comfort food on a cool day. ⊠ *District III, Mókus utca 22* ☎ *1/250–4241 or 1/368–0613* ⊟ *AE, DC, MC, V.*

$$–$$$ ✗**Kisbuda Gyöngye.** Considered by many the finest restaurant in Óbuda,
★ this intimate place is filled with antique furniture and decorated with an eclectic but elegant patchwork of carved wooden cupboard doors and panels. Meat and game dishes stand out. Try the tarragon ragout of game, or sample the goose wedding feast, a richly flavorful dish that includes a crispy goose leg with braised red cabbage, grilled goose liver, and lightly fried goose cracklings. ⊠ *District III, Kenyeres utca 34* ☎ *1/368–6402 or 1/368–9246* ⚄ *Reservations essential* ⊟ *AE, DC, MC, V* ⊘ *Closed Sun.*

CITY PARK

$$$–$$$$ ✗**Gundel.** This is Hungary's most celebrated restaurant, for its history (opened in 1894) as well as its renovation in the 1990s by Hungarian-American restaurateur George Lang. The gorgeous setting in City Park includes an Art Nouveau bar designed by Adam Tihany. Fin-de-siècle grandeur shines through in the glorious dining room, tastefully adorned with 19th- and 20th-century Hungarian paintings, and a Gypsy band adds an earnest nostalgia. Although the food is just a bit above average, some classics such as goose liver pâté and Gundel pancakes are well executed. Nevertheless, a visit is a uniquely memorable experience. ⊠ *District XIV, Állatkerti út 2* ☎ *1/468–4060* ⚄ *Reservations essential Jacket and tie* ⊟ *AE, DC, MC, V.*

$$$–$$$$ ✗**Robinson Restaurant.** Robinson can lay claim to one of the more exotic locations in Budapest dining—on wooden platforms atop an artificial lake, looking across to Vajdahunyad Castle in City Park. You can sit out on the terrace during summer or enjoy the warm pastel interior in colder months. The menu includes some Hungarian highlights such as goose liver and *becsi szelet* (Wiener schnitzel), but also has innovative dishes like giant prawns with honey-flavored tamarind and coriander-enhanced curry. ⊠ *District XIV, by the lake in City Park* ☎ *1/422–0222* ⚄ *Reservations essential* ⊟ *AE, DC, MC, V.*

WHERE TO STAY

The good news: Budapest has seen the overall quality and variety of its tourist accommodations skyrocket since the fall of communism in 1990, including numerous upscale, international-standard hotels. The bad news: finding a hotel room for less than €100 a night in the city center can be a challenge, though lower-priced alternatives—hostels, private rooms or apartments, and budget hotels (mostly outside downtown)—can be had.

All room rates are based on double occupancy in high season (mid-June–August). For luxury hotels, 12% VAT and a 3% tourist tax are usually not included in the room rate; breakfast is also often not included. Assume they are included unless the review has a note to the contrary.

In the low season it's much easier to find a hotel room, and prices are often reduced by 20%–30%. The best budget option is to book a private room or an entire apartment. A short-term room rental in Budapest will cost €30–€50 a day in high season, with apartments running a bit more. The number of rooms available can be limited in high season, so if you're booking your accommodation on the spot, it may be best to arrive to do so early in the morning.

IBUSZ Private Accommodation Service (⊠ *District V, Ferenciek tere 10* ☎ *1/485–2768, 1/485–2770, or 1/485–2700 [central switchboard]* 🖷 *1/338–4987* ⊕ *www.ibusz.hu*) rents out private apartments and rooms in Budapest. The main office, on Ferenciek tere, is closed on weekends and open only until 4 PM Monday through Thursday, until 3 PM Friday. **To-Ma Tours** (⊠ *District V, Október 6 utca 22* ☎ *1/353–0819* 🖷 *1/269–5715* ⊕ *www.tomatour.hu*) also arranges such lodging options and, unlike IBUSZ, is also open on weekends.

AROUND CASTLE HILL

$$$$ 🏨 **Budapest Hilton.** This hotel—built in 1977 around the remains of a
☾ 17th-century Gothic chapel and right next to the Matthias Church—
★ has an exterior that betrays its 1970s origins, but the modern, tasteful rooms and great views from Castle Hill more than compensate. Rooms with the best Danube vistas cost more. Children, regardless of age, stay free when sharing a room with their parents. Pros: In the heart of Castle Hill, lovely views, 24-hour business center, free airport shuttle. Cons: Far from downtown Pest, touristy neighborhood, minimal fitness facilities, only pricey restaurants nearby, taxes not included. ⊠ *District I, Hess András tér 1–3, H-1014* ☎ *1/889–6600, 800/445–8644 in U.S. and Canada* 🖷 *1/889–6644* ⊕ *www.budapest.hilton.com* ⇆ *298 rooms, 24 suites* ♿ *In-room: safe, Wi-Fi. In-hotel: restaurant, room service, bar, gym, concierge, laundry service, public Wi-Fi, public Internet, airport shuttle, parking (fee), some pets allowed (fee), no-smoking rooms* ▤ *AE, DC, MC, V* �ⓄⓁ *EP.*

$$–$$$ 🏨 **art'otel.** Travelers bored with bland, business-hotel decor might
★ appreciate this mod lodging's snazzy design. Everything—from the impressive art on the walls to the whimsical red-and-white carpeting and even the cups and saucers—is the work of one man, American artist Donald Sultan. Encompassing one new building and four 18th-century baroque houses on the Buda riverfront, the art'otel adroitly blends old and new. Pros: Lovely views, on the Danube, easy access to Pest, snazzy design. Cons: Smallish room, snazzy design not for all tastes, removed from downtown Pest. ⊠ *District I, Bem rakpart 16–19, H-1011* ☎ *1/487–9487* 🖷 *1/487–9488* ⊕ *www.artotel.de* ⇆ *156 rooms, 9 suites* ♿ *In-room: safe, Wi-Fi, refrigerator. In-hotel: restaurant, room service, bar, gym, concierge, laundry service, parking (fee), no-smoking rooms, public Wi-Fi, public Internet* ▤ *AE, DC, MC, V* ⓄⓁ *EP.*

7

$ ⛤**Burg Hotel.** You don't have to splurge on the Hilton to stay on Szen-
tháromság tér. The only downside is having the peak-season crowds
thronging under your window during the day, but then the quiet nights
are that much more magical. Rooms have green wall-to-wall carpeting,
beige wallpaper, and blue-tiled bathrooms with either tubs or shower
stalls. Pros: In the heart of Castle Hill, good price for location, cozy
size. Cons: Far from downtown Pest, touristy neighborhood, only
pricey restaurants nearby, few amenities. ⊠*District I, Szentháromság
tér 7, H-1014* ☎*1/212–0269* 🖷*1/212–3970* ⊕*www.burghotelbuda-
pest.com* ⬅*24 rooms, 2 suites* ⚲*In-room: refrigerator. In-hotel: bar,
parking (fee), no-smoking rooms, public Internet, public Wi-Fi, no
elevator* ⊟*AE, DC, MC, V* �ⓘⓂBP.

$ ⛤**Carlton Hotel.** The Carlton is further proof that you can stay on Cas-
★   tle Hill—well, nestled near its foot—without paying a fortune. Rooms
on the upper floors offer lovely views over rooftops to Castle Hill,
although the windows are smallish. Request a newly refurbished room
to avoid the adequate but stark gray furnishings of the earlier design.
With downtown just a walk across the Chain Bridge away and the
Castle Hill district rising in your backyard, it's hard to do better for
location and price. Pros: Near Castle Hill, quiet neighborhood, good
price for location. Cons: Removed from downtown Pest, smallish windows, older rooms a bit bland. ⊠*District IApor Péter utca 3, H-1011*
☎*1/224–0999* 🖷*1/224–0990* ⊕*www.carltonhotel.hu* ⬅*95 rooms*
⚲*In-room: safe, refrigerator, Wi-Fi. In-hotel: bar, laundry service,
public Internet, public Wi-Fi, parking (fee), no-smoking rooms, some
pets allowed (fee).* ⊟*AE, DC, MC, V* �ⓘⓂBP.

$ ⛤**Hotel Victoria.** This small, family-run hotel has had a loyal follow-
★   ing since it opened soon after the Iron Curtain came down. Taking
advantage of a choice Buda-side location on the Danube riverbank,
each room has a small seating area in front of floor-to-ceiling windows
looking across the river to Parliament. The reception staff is kind and
able, and can direct you to the nearby restaurants where you can charge
your meals to your room. Pros: Gorgeous views of Pest, on the Danube, easy access to Pest, cozy size, friendly staff. Cons: Removed from
downtown Pest, few amenities. ⊠*District I, Bem rakpart 11, H-1011*
☎*1/457–8080* 🖷*1/457–8088* ⊕*www.victoria.hu* ⬅*27 rooms* ⚲*In-
room: safe, refrigerator, Wi-Fi. In-hotel: bar, laundry service, public
Wi-Fi, public Internet, parking (fee), no-smoking rooms* ⊟*AE, DC,
MC, V* ⓘⓂBP.

AROUND THE KIS KÖRÚT (SMALL RING ROAD)

$$$$ ⛤**Four Seasons Hotel Gresham Palace Budapest.** It doesn't get much better
Fodor'sChoice   than this: a centrally located, super-deluxe hotel in a museum-quality
★   landmark with the prettiest views in town. No detail has been spared
in restoring this stunning 1906 Art Nouveau palace to its original majesty: delicate wrought-iron vents in the hallways, exquisite gold mosaic
tiles on the facade, stained-glass windows, and cupolas. Rooms, some
with balconies and vaulted ceilings, are large and plush. Spanish-mar-
ble bathrooms—unlike any in Budapest—have both showers and deep
soaking tubs. The lobby café is modeled after the building's original.

Pros: Luxury amid historic grandeur, near main tourist district by the famous Chain Bridge, superb restaurant, excellent views. Cons: Pricey, lots of traffic out front, taxes not included. ✉ *District V, Roosevelt tér 5–6, H-1051* ☎ *1/268–6000* 🖷 *1/268–5000* ⊕ *www.fourseasons. com/budapest* ⇌ *162 rooms, 17 suites* ♿ *In-room: safe, refrigerator, Ethernet, Wi-Fi. In-hotel: restaurant, room service, bar, pool, gym, spa, concierge, laundry service, public Internet, public Wi-Fi, parking (fee), no-smoking rooms* ☰ *AE, DC, MC, V* ⏀ *EP.*

$$$$
Fodor'sChoice
★
🖬 **Kempinski Hotel Corvinus Budapest.** Budapest's best business hotel doesn't cater only to the international CEO set. Though cold and futuristic-looking on the outside, the Kempinski has exceptionally spacious rooms and suites, with custom-made Art Deco fittings and furniture, as well as an emphasis on functional touches like three phones in every room. Large, sparkling bathrooms have tubs and separate shower stalls. Pros: Huge rooms, in the center of everything, large-hotel amenities. Cons: Pricey, bland on the outside, in heavily touristed neighborhood, taxes not included. ✉ *District V, Erzsébet tér 7–8, H-1051* ☎ *1/429–3777, 800/426–3135 in the U.S. and Canada* 🖷 *1/429–4777* ⊕ *www.kempinski-budapest.com* ⇌ *335 rooms, 31 suites* ♿ *In-room: safe, refrigerator, Ethernet, Wi-Fi. In-hotel: 3 restaurants, room service, bar, pool, gym, spa, concierge, laundry service, parking (fee), public Internet, public Wi-Fi, some pets allowed (fee), no-smoking rooms* ☰ *AE, DC, MC, V* ⏀ *EP.*

$$$$
★
🖬 **Le Méridien Budapest.** There could scarcely be more contrast between the stately Méridien and its pointedly modern neighbor, the Kempinski. The rooms of this entirely renovated, early-20th-century building are decorated in the French Empire style and are both comfortable and plush, with king-size beds in every double room and large bathrooms with separate shower stalls and bathtubs. Pros: Luxurious antique-style furnishings, in the center of everything, large-hotel amenities, substantial Internet discounts. Cons: Pricey, in heavily touristed neighborhood, smaller rooms on upper floors, taxes not included. ✉ *District V, Erzsébet tér 9–10, H-1051* ☎ *1/429–5500, 800/543–4300 in U.S. and Canada* 🖷 *1/429–5555* ⊕ *www.lemeridien.com* ⇌ *218 rooms, 26 suites* ♿ *In-room: safe, refrigerator, Ethernet, Wi-Fi. In-hotel: restaurant, room service, bar, pool, gym, concierge, laundry service, public Wi-Fi, public Internet, parking (fee), no-smoking rooms* ☰ *AE, DC, MC, V* ⏀ *EP.*

$
🖬 **Hotel Hold.** A fantastic location on a lovely street behind the American Embassy and across from the ornately mosaicked Hungarian National Bank gives this low-key little hotel its appeal. The Parliament building and the basilica are a few minutes' walk away. Converted from private apartments in a turn-of-the-20th-century building, most guest rooms are quite small, but have soaring ceilings and tall windows with translucent white curtains. Furnishings are flimsy but adequate; there's royal-blue wall-to-wall carpeting throughout. Pros: Quiet neighborhood a short walk from key sites and city center, inn-like charm, good value. Cons: Few amenities and services, rooms on ground floor open onto the courtyard restaurant, most rooms with showers only, limited Internet access. ✉ *District V, Hold utca 5, H-1054* ☎ *1/472–0480*

7

☎ *1/472–0484* ⊕ *www.hotelhold.hu* ⌁ *24 rooms, 4 suites* ⌂ *In-room: refrigerator. In-hotel: restaurant, public Internet, no elevator* ▭ *AE, DC, MC, V* ⌷ *BP.*

AROUND ANDRÁSSY ÚT

$$$–$$$$
Fodor'sChoice
★

⌸ **Andrássy Hotel.** Budapest's best boutique hotel has come a long way from its origins as a 1930s-era orphanage. Opened as a hotel in 2001, it exudes grand style. In the bright Art Deco lobby the sound of rushing water from a glass-window waterfall blends artfully into soft jazz music playing on the sound system, and hip young staff receive guests at the funky orange-lighted front desk. Done up in terra-cotta, blue, and cream, rooms are large and well appointed; most have lovely balconies overlooking the trees and mansions of Andrássy út. With colorful, coordinated tilework, bathrooms follow the room design. Pros: Superb restaurant, lovely rooms with views, a few blocks from Heroes' Square and City Park. Cons: Pricey, no on-site fitness facilities (but free access to a nearby center), taxes not included. ⌧ *District VI, Andrássy út 111, H-1063* ☎ *1/462–2118* ☎ *1/322–9445* ⊕ *www.andrassyhotel. com* ⌁ *62 rooms, 7 suites* ⌂ *In-room: safe, refrigerator, Wi-Fi. In-hotel: restaurant, room service, bar, concierge, laundry service, public Internet, parking (fee), no-smoking rooms* ▭ *AE, DC, MC, V* ⌷ *EP.*

$$
Fodor'sChoice
★

⌸ **Hotel Pest.** Echoes of old Pest are preserved in this once-crumbling— now imaginatively refurbished—18th-century apartment building. In typical Budapest style, rooms open off an inner courtyard shared with the private building next door, where thick, green ivy spills over wrought-iron railings. In the guest rooms daylight filters discreetly through sheer curtains and homey brown wood window frames. Decor is a soothing mix of dark wood and sage-colored textiles. The breakfast room's stone walls are covered by a central glass skylight. Pros: Two blocks from the Opera House and Andrássy út, lots of restaurants nearby, historic building, reasonable rates. Cons: Most rooms with showers only, fewer amenities and services than at the larger K+K Hotel Opera nearby, limited Internet access, 15-minute walk to the Danube. ⌧ *District VI, Paulay Ede utca 31, H-1061* ☎ *1/343–1198* ☎ *1/351–9164* ⊕ *www.hotelpest.hu* ⌁ *25 rooms* ⌂ *In-room: no a/c (some), refrigerator, Ethernet. In-hotel: bar, laundry service, parking (fee), no-smoking rooms* ▭ *AE, DC, MC, V* ⌷ *BP.*

$$
★

⌸ **K+K Hotel Opera.** Location, location, location: the K+K Hotel Opera has it all, around the corner from Budapest's beautiful opera house and just far enough away from busy Andrássy út to block out the noise of traffic. Sunflower-yellow walls and bamboo and wicker furniture coupled with warm-hued accents, fresh flowers, and striking rectangular lamps give the rooms—and, indeed, the entire hotel—a cheerful-cum-squarishly-modern look. Pros: Near the Opera House and Andrássy út, lots of restaurants nearby, reasonable rates. Cons: Less cozy than the smaller Hotel Pest nearby, 15-minute walk to the Danube. ⌧ *District VI, Révay utca 24, H-1065* ☎ *1/269–0222* ☎ *1/269–0230* ⊕ *www. kkhotels.com* ⌁ *203 rooms, 2 suites* ⌂ *In-room: safe, Ethernet, Wi-Fi. In-hotel: restaurant, room service, bar, gym, concierge, laundry service, parking (fee), no-smoking rooms, some pets allowed (fee)* ▭ *AE, DC, MC, V* ⌷ *BP.*

AROUND KÁLVIN TÉR & SZABADSÁG-HÍD

$$ ☷**Hotel Mercure Budapest Museum.** A more charming but often overlooked alternative to a much larger Mercure property nearby, this hotel, housed in a fin de siècle, golden-brick building, is tucked into a quiet side street near the National Museum. Sure, the facilities are fewer than at its larger counterpart, but you do get spacious, orange-and-blue-hued rooms, and a more personal touch—at a lower price. Room 301 has a balcony at no extra cost. Pros: Quiet side street, a short walk from Pest's main tourist district, reasonable rates. Cons: Not quite in the center of things, relatively few amenities and services, inner Pest neighborhood can feel claustrophobic. ⊠*District VIII, Trefort utca 2, H-1088* ☎*1/485–1080* 🖷*1/485–1081* ⊕*www.mercure. com* ⤳*54 rooms* ☖*In-room: refrigerator, Wi-Fi, no-smoking (some). In-hotel: restaurant, room service, bar, laundry service, parking (fee), public Wi-Fi, public Internet* ☰*AE, DC, MC, V* ⦿❘*EP.*

AROUND GELLÉRT HILL

$$$ ☷**Danubius Hotel Gellért.** Budapest's most renowned Art Nouveau hotel
★ is undergoing a gradual overhaul, aimed at restoring its original, World War I–era Jugendstil. Rooms are elegant and spacious. Request a refurbished room when you reserve for optimal comfort; unrenovated rooms (offered at reduced rates) are a good value if you don't mind a little Iron Curtain sternness. Regardless, ask about options—and perhaps bargains—as rooms in this quirky building come in all shapes, sizes, and prices. Everyone staying here has free access to the hotel's famous, ornate thermal baths. Pros: Famous on-site baths, historic grandeur, at foot of lovely Gellért Hill, numerous amenities and services. Cons: Rooms vary in quality and size, 15-minute walk to main tourist district in Pest, a bit pricey. ⊠*District XI, Szent Gellért tér 1, H-1111* ☎*1/889–5500* 🖷*1/889–5505* ⊕*www.danubiusgroup.com* ⤳*220 rooms, 14 suites* ☖*In-room: no a/c (some), safe, Wi-Fi. In-hotel: 2 restaurants, room service, bar, pools, spa, concierge, laundry service, parking (fee), no-smoking rooms, public Wi-Fi, public Internet* ☰*AE, DC, MC, V* ⦿❘*BP.*

$ ☷**Kalmár Bed & Breakfast.** This treasure trove of elegant, old Budapest
Fodor's Choice is in a cream-colored, 1900 stone mansion-cum-apartment-building
★ on the lower slopes of Gellért Hill, right behind the Hotel Gellért. Those who appreciate original ambience over amenities will be pleased. Although lower-priced doubles on the ground floor are smaller and darker, there are also antiques-filled suites and opulent, full-scale apartments that can accommodate two couples. Some rooms come with a kitchen, others with a terrace. Breakfast is served on delicate matching porcelain. The Kalmár family has been running this B&B since 1964; ask for Eszter (who speaks English). Pros: Excellent value, elegant and friendly inn-like atmosphere, a short walk from the Gellért baths, on lovely Gellért Hill. Cons: 20-minute walk to main tourist district in Pest, few amenities and services, rooms vary in size, (short) uphill walk to property. ⊠*District XI, Kelenhegyi út 7–9, H-1118* ☎*1/372–7531, 372–7530, 30/271–9312 English-speaking* 🖷*1/385–2804* ✉*kalmar-panzio@freemail.hu* ⤳*5 rooms, 2 suites, 2 apartments* ☖*In-hotel: refrigerator, no elevator* ☰*No credit cards* ⦿❘*BP.*

7

AROUND THE NAGY KÖRÚT (LARGE RING ROAD)

$$$$ 📺 **Corinthia Grand Hotel Royal.** One of the newer five-star properties
Fodor's Choice in Budapest—and, with 414 rooms, the biggest—the Royal is back
★   to its 1896 origins, when it opened as a luxury hotel for the Magyar
Millennium. The expansive atrium lobby is full of Italian marble and
wrought-iron ornamentation, and the hotel's luxurious Royal Spa (free
to guests, 10,000 HUF a day for others) is something to behold. Guest
rooms are stylish with dark woods and jewel-tone upholstery; bathrooms are all-Italian, from marble floors to gleaming fixtures. Some
rooms look inward onto the lobby. Pros: Luxury redolent of history,
superb spa facility, numerous amenities and services, on main tram line.
Cons: Pricey, 20-minute walk from main downtown tourist district, on
busy road. ⊠*District VII, Erzsébet körút 43–49, H-1073* 📞*1/479–
4000* 🖶*1/479–4333* ⊕*www.corinthiahotels.com* ⇆*363 rooms, 51
suites* ⇕*In-room: safe, Ethernet. In-hotel: 3 restaurants, room service,
bar, pool, spa, concierge, laundry service, parking (fee), no-smoking
rooms, public Internet* ▤*AE, DC, MC, V* ᵀᴼ❘*EP.*

$$ 📺 **NH Budapest.** Extra-thick mattresses, a pick-your-own pillow bar,
★   and free ironing service are some of the welcome extras that set this
Spanish-owned business hotel apart. In the eight-story atrium lobby
real-time flight information is streamed in from Ferihegy airport onto
the television screen behind the front desk. Dark-wood and gray-tone
rooms, though on the small side, are slick and professional, each with
a whimsical cherry-red easy chair. The NH is central to sights and
business, just behind the Vígszínház theater and near the Nyugati rail-
way station. Pros: On quiet side street near the Nyugati train station
and Margaret Island; chic, super-comfy rooms; restaurants nearby;
near main tram line. Cons: Somewhat pricey, 20-minute walk from
major tourist area of downtown Pest, smallish rooms. ⊠*District XIII,
Vígszínház utca 3, H-1137* 📞*1/814–0000* 🖶*1/814–0100* ⊕*www.
nh-hotels.com* ⇆*160 rooms* ⇕*In-room: safe, refrigerator, Ethernet,
Wi-Fi. In-hotel: restaurant, room service, bar, gym, laundry service,
parking (fee), some pets allowed (fee), public Wi-Fi* ▤*AE, DC, MC,
V* ᵀᴼ❘*EP.*

MARGARET ISLAND

$$$ 📺 **Danubius Grand Hotel Margit-sziget.** The older, more attractive next-
★   door neighbor of the Thermal Hotel Margit-sziget was built in 1873
by Opera House architect Miklós Ybl in neo-Renaissance style. Ceilings are high, and rooms are decorated in Empire style, with red- or
blue-upholstered antique-looking wood furnishings. Guests have free
admission to the Thermal's spa facilities, directly accessed by a heated,
underground walkway. Pros: On peaceful Margaret Island, excellent
bathing facilities, numerous amenities and services. Cons: Pricey, a
hefty walk or 15-minute bus ride from downtown, few restaurants
and shops on island. ⊠*District XIII, Margit-sziget, H-1138* 📞*1/889–
4700* 🖶*1/889–4988* ⊕*www.danubiusgroup.com* ⇆*154 rooms, 10
suites* ⇕*In-room: safe, refrigerator, Wi-Fi. In-hotel: restaurant, room
service, bar, laundry service, parking (fee), no-smoking rooms, some
pets allowed (fee), public Wi-Fi, public Internet* ▤*AE, DC, MC, V*
ᵀᴼ❘*BP.*

CLOSE UP

Other Hotels to Consider

Obviously, we can't include every property deserving mention without creating an encyclopedia. Our favorites receive full reviews, but you might also consider the following good accommodations.

($$$$) **New York Palace** (⊠ *Erzsébet körút 9–11, H-1073* ☎ *1/886–6111* ⊕ *www.newyorkpalace.hu or www.boscolohotels.com*) is a mostly pleasing, somewhat weird luxury hotel whose blend of tradition and high fashion confronts you right away in the cavernous atrium populated by headless mannequins as pop music carries from the adjacent New York Café.

($$$–$$$$) **Budapest Marriott** (⊠ *District V, Apáczai Csere János utca 4, H-1052* ☎ *1/266–7000, 800/228–9290 in U.S. and Canada* ⊕ *www.marriott.com*) may be in a drab building, but the prime Danube location makes for breathtaking views, and renovations under way should render its rooms slightly more spacious and sparkling by summer 2008.

($$$–$$$$) **Hotel InterContinental Budapest** (⊠ *District V, Apáczai Csere János utca 12–14, H-1052* ☎ *1/327–6333* ⊕ *www.ichotelsgroup.com*) appeals to the modern business traveler, but anyone might appreciate its location right next to the Chain Bridge in Pest. Rooms are decorated in pleasant pastels and furnished in Biedermeier style, and those with Danube views are about €50 more.

($$$–$$$$) **Hotel Mercure Korona** (⊠ *District V, Kecskeméti utca 14, H-1053* ☎ *1/486–8800* ⊕ *www.mercure-korona.hu*). The downside of a big chain hotel on one of Budapest's busiest squares is that the rooms are tiny and traffic outside is fierce. The upside: you're near all the sights and experiences of bustling downtown Pest, including the National Museum and hot nightlife.

($$$–$$$$) **Radisson SAS Béke Hotel Budapest** (⊠ *District V, Teréz körút 43, H-1051* ☎ *1/889–3900* ⊕ *www.radissonsas.com*) is just right if you are arriving in Budapest's Nyugati Train Station, within walking distance on a bustling stretch of the Nagy körút (Large Ring Road). Once you've ascended the sweeping marble staircase, you'll discover bland though comfy, modern rooms.

($$$–$$$$) **Sofitel Atrium Budapest** (⊠ *District VI, Roosevelt tér 2, H-1067* ☎ *1/266–1234* ⊕ *www.sofitel.com*) has a spectacular 10-story atrium that might not be quite representative of the city it's in, but the postcard views across the Danube to Castle Hill are quintessentially Budapest. Rooms with Danube views are €35 more.

7

NIGHTLIFE & THE ARTS

NIGHTLIFE

There is a mysterious quiet around the inner-city streets of Pest at night, even in summer: mysterious because meanwhile, behind closed doors, the nightlife is hopping on almost any night. For basic beer and wine drinking, *sörözős* (beer pubs) and *borozós* (wine bars) abound, although many such places, especially the drunk tanks among them, are unaccustomed to tourists. For quiet conversation there are *drink-bárs* in many hotels and all over town, but some are seedy and may tack on a special foreigner surcharge.

Most nightspots and clubs have bars and dance floors, and some also have pool tables. Paper, not plastic, is the usual way to pay. The venues listed below are among the most popular and seem here to stay. But for the latest on the more transient "in" spots, consult the widely available, free *Budapest Funzine,* which appears twice a month, or other local English-language publications.

■**TIP➔**Budapest also has its share of seedy go-go clubs and "cabarets." Many a hapless single man has found himself facing an exorbitant tab after accepting an invitation from a woman asking to join her for a drink. This scam is particularly prevalent around Váci utca.

Some of the most lively nightlife in Budapest hinges around the electronica scene—trance, techno, drum and bass, etc. Recreational drug use is fairly common, and travelers should be aware that penalties for possessing even small amounts of so-called soft drugs can be stiff.

A word of warning to the smoke-sensitive: although a 1999 law requiring smoke-free areas in many public establishments has already had a discernible impact in restaurants, the bar scene is a firm reminder that Budapest remains a city of smokers.

Fodor's Choice A large ship permanently moored on the Buda side of the Danube,
★ **A38** (⊠ *District XI, near the Petőfi Híd, on the Buda side of the river* ☎*1/464–3940*), has a restaurant upstairs and a large dance floor downstairs, with a different band every night, from jazz to Latin, retro to electronic. Hungary's biggest Irish pub, **Becketts** (⊠ *District V, Bajcsy-Zsilinszky út 72* ☎*1/311–1035*), is a great place for a lunch, a quiet afternoon pint, or a rollicking good time in the evening as a band comes on and the place fills up. **Café del Rio** (⊠ *District XI, Goldmann György tér 1, South Buda* ☎*06–30/297–2158*) calls itself a "fancy club for fancy people," and, indeed, it is one of Budapest's largest and hottest dance clubs. It's near the Buda side of the Petőfi Bridge. Of all the see-and-be-seen cafés in Budapest, **Cafe Vian** (⊠ *District VI, Liszt Ferenc tér 9* ☎*1/268–1154*) is the most renowned. One of the most popular gay bars in Budapest, **Club Bohemian Alibi** (⊠ *District VIII, Üllői út 45* ☎*1/219–5260*), is a cellar venue with no less than three bars, with music provided by DJs. On a fine summer evening it seems that all the under-30 brainy types this side of the Danube are in the spacious **Gödör Klub** *(Ditch Club)* (⊠ *District V, Erzsébet tér,* ☎*06–20/201–3868*), sitting around with plastic cups of wine or beer on the steps leading down into the "ditch" or inside listening to live jazz on the club's small stage. If you ever wondered what Hungarian interior design looked like under communism, look no farther than **Mélypont** (⊠ *District V, Magyar utca 23* ☎*06–30/812–4064 [mobile]*) , a carefully stylized cellar bar that transports you back into 1970s Hungary. **Oscar American Bar** (⊠ *District I, Ostrom u. 14* ☎*1/212–8017*) gets a mixed Hungarian and international crowd to venture over the Danube to perhaps Buda's most jumping neighborhood bar. **Old Man's Music Pub** (⊠ *District VII, Akácfa utca 13* ☎*1/322–7645*) is *the* (smoky) place

for live bluesy rock and jazz—while everyone squeezes onto the small dance floor. The largest outdoor bar in Budapest, **Zöld Pardon** (⊠*District XI, Goldmann György tér* ☏*1/279–1880*), is near the Buda side of the Petőfi Bridge.

THE ARTS

For the latest on arts events, from thrash band gigs in wild clubs to performances at the Opera House, consult the entertainment listings of the English-language press.

Tickets can be bought at the venues themselves, but many ticket offices sell them without an extra charge. Booking through your hotel may include a markup of up to 30%, but since ticket prices are fairly low it shouldn't dent your wallet. Just two among many ticket offices are listed below; check with Tourinform for more suggestions.

Theater and opera tickets are sold at the **Central Ticket Office** (⊠*District VI, Paulay Ede utca 3* ☏*1/322–0000 or 1/322–0001*). The biggest such agency in Budapest, **Ticket Express** (⊠*District VI, Andrássy út 18* ☏*1/312–0000 or 06–30/303–0999*), sells tickets to nearly every show or performance happening in Hungary, including theater, opera, musicals, and concerts.

Fodor's Choice
★

The tiny recital room of the **Bartók Béla Emlékház** (*Bartók Béla Memorial House* ⊠*District II, Csalán út 29* ☏*1/394–4472*) hosts intimate Friday-evening chamber music recitals by well-known ensembles from mid-March to June and September to mid-December. The homely little sister of the Opera House, the **Erkel Színház** (*Erkel Theater* ⊠*District VII, Köztársaság tér 30* ☏*1/333–0540*), is Budapest's other main opera and ballet venue, but has no regular performances in the summer. The **Liszt Ferenc Zeneakadémia** (*Franz Liszt Academy of Music* ⊠*District VI, Liszt Ferenc tér 8* ☏*1/462–4600 Ext. 179*) is the city center's premier classical concert venue. The glittering **Magyar Állami Operaház** (*Hungarian State Opera House* ⊠*District VI, Andrássy út 22* ☏*1/353–0170*), Budapest's main venue for opera and classical ballet, presents an international repertoire of classical and modern works. It is mostly closed during the summer. **Művészetek Palotája** (*Palace of the Arts* ⊠*District IX, Komor Marcell utca 1* ☏*1/555–3000* ⊕*www.mupa.hu*), one of the world's biggest and brightest cultural centers, is next to the National Theater. At its center is the Béla Bartók National Concert Hall, which has world-class acoustics and regularly hosts the celebrated Budapest Festival Orchestra. Colorful operettas are staged at their main Budapest venue, the **Operetta Theater** (⊠*District VI, Nagymező u. 19* ☏*1/312–4866*).

"SZIA!"

It may sound like it, but this most common of all friendly greetings in Hungarian neither means nor derives from "See you!" Used between people who are already on friendly terms—or who are approximately the same age and wish to be on informal terms—or by a person speaking to someone younger, *szia* (pronounced "see-ya") means both "Hi!" and "Bye," depending, of course, on the circumstances.

7

FOLKLORE   The **Hungarian State Folk Ensemble** performs regularly at the **Budai Vigadó** (⊠*District I, Corvin tér 8* ☎*1/201–3766*); shows incorporate instrumental music, dancing, and singing. The **Folklór Centrum** (⊠*District XI, Fehérvári út 47* ☎*1/203–3868*) hosts traditional folk concerts and dance performances from spring through fall.

☾   The **Budapest Bábszínház** (*Budapest Puppet Theater* ⊠*District VI,*
Fodor'sChoice *Andrássy út 69* ☎*1/321–5200*) produces colorful shows that both
★   children and adults enjoy even if they don't understand Hungarian. For English-language dramas check out the **Merlin International Theater** (⊠*District V, Gerlóczy u. 4* ☎*1/317–9338*). The **Thália Theater** (⊠*District VI, Nagymező u. 22–24* ☎*1/311–1874, 1/311–0635*) specializes in musicals. The sparkling **Vígszínház** (*Comedy Theater* ⊠*District XIII, Pannónia u. 1* ☎*1/340–4650*) hosts classical concerts and dance performances but is primarily a venue for musicals.

OUTDOOR ACTIVITIES & SPORTS

BICYCLING

Much progress has been made since the 1990s to develop bicycle paths throughout downtown and produce tourist maps with suggested routes along quiet streets. But for peace and safety, head either to Margaret Island or City Park. Rentals start around 600 HUF for two hours, 1,500 HUF for six hours, and 3,000 HUF for 24 hours. **Bringóhintó** (☎*329–2746*) is toward Margaret Island's northern end, by the Japanese garden. Right downtown, **Budapest Bike** (⊠*District VII, Wesselényi utca 18* ☎*06–30/944–5533*) is one of many center-city rental options.

THERMAL BATHS

Although they lack the charm of their older peers listed below, modern baths, which tend to offer a broader array of the latest treatments, are open to the public at hotels such as the **Danubius Grand Hotel Margitsziget** and the **Corinthia Grand Hotel Royal**. *See Exploring Budapest for more information on the baths below.* Also visit ⊕*www.spasbudapest. com* for water composition details and the most current opening hours and rates.

Gellért Thermal Baths (⊠*District XI, Gellért tér 1* ☎*1/466–5747*) are the most famous in Budapest.

Built in 1565 by the Turks, the **Király Baths** (⊠*District II, Fő u. 84* ☎*1/202–3688*) are Budapest's oldest and have long been a favorite with gay men; there are also women-only days. Closed for renovation, the Király is due to reopen in spring 2008.

The **Lukács Baths** (⊠*District II, Frankel Leó u. 25–29* ☎*1/326–1695*) were built in the 19th century but modeled on the Turkish originals and fed with waters from a source dating from the Bronze Age and Roman times.

The **Rudas Baths** (⊠ *District I, Döbrentei tér 9* ☎*1/356–1322*) were built centuries ago by the Turks. Unlike other baths with frequent men-only days, they do not have a large gay following.

In City Park, the beautiful indoor-outdoor **Széchenyi Baths** (⊠ *District XIV, Városliget, Állatkerti krt. 11* ☎*1/363–3210*) are the largest medicinal bathing facility in Europe.

SHOPPING

You'll find plenty of expensive boutiques, folk-art and souvenir shops, bookstores, and classical-record shops on or around touristy **Váci utca**, Budapest's famous, upscale pedestrian-only promenade in District V. Browsing among some of the smaller, less touristy, more typically Hungarian shops in Pest—on the **Kis körút** (Small Ring Road) and **Nagy körút** (Large Ring Road)—may prove more interesting and less pricey. Lots of arty boutiques are springing up in the section of District V **south of Ferenciek tere** and **toward the Danube**, and around **Kálvin tér**. **Falk Miksa utca**, also in District V, running south from Szent István körút, is the city's best antiques district, lined on both sides with atmospheric little shops and galleries.

MARKETS
For true bargains and an adventure, make an early morning trip to the vast **Ecseri Piac** (⊠ *District IX, Nagykőrösi út 156 [Bus 54 from Boráros tér]* ☎*1/282–9563*), on the outskirts of the city. A colorful, chaotic market that shoppers have flocked to for decades, it is an arsenal of secondhand goods, where you can find everything from frayed Russian army fatigues to Herend and Zsolnay porcelain vases to antique silver chalices. As a foreigner, you may be overcharged, so prepare to haggle. Ecseri is open weekdays 8 AM–4 PM, Saturday 6–3, and Sunday 8–1, but the best selection is on Saturday mornings. A smaller but bustling outdoor flea market is held weekends from 7 AM to 2 PM at **Petőfi Csarnok** (⊠ *District XIV, Városliget, Zichy Mihály út 14* ☎*1/251–7266*).

★ Although it's mostly a food market, you can get souvenirs at the **Vásárcsarnok** (⊠ *District IX, Vámház krt. 1–3* ☎*1/366–3300*), which is open Monday 6 AM–5 PM, Tuesday–Friday 6 AM–6 PM, and Saturday 6 AM–2 PM.

SHOPPING CENTERS & MALLS
Just below Castle Hill, a short walk from Moszkva tér, is **Mammut** (⊠ *District II, Lövőház utca 2 [main entrance on Széna tér]* ☎*1/345–8020*), Buda's most bustling mall. Hungary's biggest mall, the **West End City Center** (⊠ *District VI, Váci út 1–3* ☎*1/238–7777*), sits behind the Nyugati (West) Railway Station and teems with activity day and night, staying open weekdays until 9.

SPECIALTY STORES
Fodor's Choice **Falk Miksa utca**, lined with antiques stores, is a delightful street for
★ multiple-shop browsing. The shelves and tables at tiny **Anna Antikvitás** (⊠ *District V, Falk Miksa u. 18–20* ☎*1/302–5461*) are stacked with exquisite antique textiles—from heavily embroidered wall hangings to

dainty lace gloves. The store also carries assorted antique objets d'art. **BÁV Műtárgy** (⊠*District V, Párizsi utca 2* ☏*1/318–6217* ⊠*District V, Kossuth Lajos u. 1–3* ☏*1/318–6934* ⊠*District V, Szent István krt. 3* ☏*1/331–0513*), the State Commission Trading House, has antiques of all shapes, sizes, kinds, and prices at its several branches around the city. Porcelain is the specialty at the branch on Kossuth Lajos utca, paintings at the Szent István körút store, and jewelry at the Párizsi utca location. **Polgár Galéria és Aukciósház** (⊠*District V, Kossuth Lajos u. 3* ☏*1/318–6954*) sells everything from jewelry to furniture. **Studio Agram** (⊠*District V, Falk Miksa u. 10* ☏*1/428–0653*) specializes in urban Art Deco, from vintage club chairs to silver coffee sets exquisitely restored.

★
★ Book-selling stands, many of which sell English-language souvenir picture books, populate the streets and metro stations of the city. **Váci utca** is lined with bookstores that sell glossy coffee-table books about Hungary. **Bestsellers** (⊠*District V, Október 6 utca 11* ☏*1/312–1295*) is the city's most popular English-language bookstore. **Litea** (⊠*District I, Hess András tér 4* ☏*1/375–6987*), with a good English-language selection, has long been *the* place to browse (or have a cup of tea) while on Castle Hill.

CRYSTAL &
PORCELAIN

Hungary is famous for its Herend porcelain, which is hand-painted in the village of Herend near Lake Balaton. Almost as famous is Zsolnay porcelain, created and hand-painted in Pécs. Hungarian and Czech crystal is less expensive here than in the United States. Crystal and porcelain dealers also sell their wares at the Ecseri Piac flea market, often at discount prices, but those looking for authentic Herend and Zsolnay should beware of imitations.

Haas & Czjzek (⊠*District VI, Bajcsy-Zsilinszky út 23* ☏*1/311–4094*) has been in the business for more than 100 years, selling porcelain, glass, and ceramic pieces in traditional and contemporary styles; this is also a good place to get authentic Zsolnay porcelain, created and hand-painted in Pécs. The Herend brand's largest Budapest store, **Herendi Porcelán** (⊠*District V, József Nádor tér 11* ☏*1/317–2622*), sells the delicate (and pricey) pieces, from figurines to dinner sets. For the Herend name and quality without the steep price tag, visit **Herend Village Pottery** (⊠*District II, Bem rakpart 37* ☏*1/356–7899*), where you can choose from Herend's practical line of durable ceramic cups, dishes, and table settings. Last but not least, the certified Budapest venue of another major porcelain brand, **Hollóháza** (⊠*District VII, Dohány utca 1/C* ☏*1/787–6455*), is a short walk from Deák tér.

★ There are many folk-art vendors along Váci utca, selling hand-painted wooden eggs and embroidered fabrics at inflated prices. For tablecloths and traditional Hungarian costumes, head to the second floor of the **Vásárcsarnok** (⊠*District IX, Vámház körút 1–3*, ☏*1/366–3300*). All the best Hungarian handicrafts are on display at **Folkart Kézműveshaz** (⊠*District V, Régiposta utca 12* ☏*1/318–5143*), a two-room shop off Váci utca. **Holló Műhely** (⊠*District V, Vitkovics Mihály u. 12* ☏*1/317–8103*) sells the hand-painted hope chests, chairs, jewelry boxes, candlesticks, and more of László Holló, a master wood craftsman who has resurrected motifs of earlier centuries.

WINE The burgeoning new awareness of Hungary's wine culture since the 1990s has seen the emergence of upmarket wine stores specializing in Hungarian wines. A good place to start looking is **Budapest Bortársaság** (*Budapest Wine Society* ⊠*District I, Batthyány u. 59* ☎*1/212–2569 or 1/212–0262*), a cellar shop at the base of Castle Hill. In Pest, **Monarchia Wine Shop** (⊠*District IX, Kinizsi u. 30–36* ☎*1/456–9898*) stocks well-presented selections of Hungarian and international wines and is open until 6 PM on Saturday.

BUDAPEST ESSENTIALS

BY AIR

Budapest has the country's major international airport, Ferihegy Repülőtér; almost all flights land here.

AIRPORT Ferihegy is 24 km (15 mi) southeast of downtown Budapest. Many
TRANSFERS hotels offer their guests car or minibus transportation to and from Ferihegy, but all of them charge for the service. You should arrange for a pickup in advance. If you're taking a taxi, allow anywhere between 25 minutes during nonpeak hours and at least an hour during rush hours.

The airport's official taxi service is Zóna Taxi; its rates of 3,000 HUF–4,300 HUF to downtown Budapest are as good as you will get among the taxis queued at the exit. All rates from the airport are fixed according to the zone of your final destination, and none should cost much more than 5,000 HUF.

The Airport Minibus provides convenient door-to-door service between the airport and any address in the city between 5 AM and 1 AM. On arrival, make arrangements at the company's airport desk; to get to the airport, call **at least 24 hours ahead** to arrange a pickup. Service to or from either terminal costs 2,300 HUF per person; since it normally shuttles several people at once, allow time for other pickups or drop-offs.

A new train service runs every 30 minutes between Nyugati station and Terminal 1 (direction: Monor); the one-way trip takes 25 minutes and costs 500 HUF. This is not a good choice for those with many bags, as there is no elevator or escalator at the terminal train station and the actual terminal building is still a five-minute walk away. To go on to Terminal 2, take Bus No. 200; the trip can take up to 15 minutes.

Information Airport Minibus (☎*1/296–8555, 6* AM*–10* PM). **Zóna Taxi** (☎*1/365-5555*).

BY BOAT

Budapest is situated on a major international waterway, the Danube. From mid-April through late October, hydrofoils travel between Budapest and Vienna daily; the trip takes 5½–6½ hours. There is also regular boat service to towns in the Danube Bend.

BY CAR

Budapest, like any Western city, is plagued by traffic jams during the day, but motorists should have no problem later in the evening. Motorists not accustomed to sharing the city streets with trams should pay extra attention. You should be prepared to be flagged down numerous times by police conducting routine checks for drunk driving and stolen cars. Be sure your papers are readily accessible; the police have been known to give foreigners a hard time.

PARKING Most streets in the city center have restricted, fee-based parking; there are either parking meters that accept coins (usually for a maximum of two hours) or attendants who approach your car as you park and charge you according to how many hours you intend to stay. Hourly rates average 250 HUF. Generally, parking after 6 PM and before 8 AM is free. Budapest also has a number of parking lots and some garages; two central-Pest garages, in District V, are at Szervita tér and Aranykéz utca 4–6.

BY PUBLIC TRANSPORTATION

Trams (*villamos*) and buses (*autóbusz*) are abundant and convenient. Service on Budapest's subways is fast and frequent; stations are easily located on maps and streets by the big letter "M" (for *metro*). There are three subway lines, all of which converge at Deák tér station. A fourth line, which will run between eastern Pest and southern Buda, is in the works. Most public transport runs from around 5 AM until around 11 PM, but there is all-night bus service on certain key routes.

Regardless of what you are riding, a one-fare ticket (230 HUF) is valid for only one ride in one direction. Tickets are available in metro stations and newsstands and must be validated on board by inserting them into the little devices provided for that purpose (on board trams and buses, but at the entrances to metro stations), pulling the knob, and then—depending on the particular device—checking to be sure the correct side of the ticket has either a time stamp on it or that the checkered end has a pattern of holes punched in it.

Better yet, purchase a *napijegy* (day ticket, 1,350 HUF) or a three-day "tourist ticket" (3,100 HUF), either of which allows unlimited travel on all services within the city limits. Hold on to your ticket until the end of your journey. Spot checks by aggressive checkers are numerous and often targeted at tourists; the on-the-spot fine for traveling without a ticket is 5,000 HUF plus the fare.

BY TAXI

There are plenty of honest taxi drivers in Budapest, but a few too many dishonest ones. Fortunately, the reliable ones are easy to spot: they will have a company logo and phone number, and a working meter. If one is hailed on the street, the base daytime fare is between 250 HUF and 300 HUF and then 200 HUF–250 HUF for each kilometer thereafter; late at night the rate is at least 20% more. When possible, do as locals do and order a taxi by phone (all the companies here have English-speaking operators), even when on the street; the rate generally falls by 10% or more, and you'll know you won't get cheated.

Information **BudaTaxi** (☎*1/233-3333*). **City Taxi** (☎*1/211-1111*). **Fő Taxi** (☎*1/222-2222*). **Radio Taxi** (☎*1/377-7777*). **6x6 Taxi** (☎*1/266-6666*).

BY TRAIN

Budapest is well connected to the rest of Europe by rail. There are three main *pályaudvar* (train stations) in Budapest. Most international trains, including those to and from Vienna, operate from the Keleti station. Nyugati station has international and domestic service. Trains to the Lake Balaton region depart from the Déli.

VISITOR INFORMATION

Tourinform's main office is on bustling Liszt Ferenc tér in Pest, and there are several branch locations around town. It provides information on anything and everything to do with Budapest, and can refer you to companies such as IBUSZ that arrange private accommodations. The Tourism Office of Budapest has developed the Budapest Card, which entitles holders to unlimited travel on public transportation, free admission to many museums and sights, and discounts on various services from participating businesses. The cost is around 6,500 HUF for two days and 8,000 HUF for three days; one card is valid for an adult plus one child under 14. It can be purchased at all Tourinform offices in Budapest, the Tourism Office of Budapest, private tourist offices in the capital's train stations, and at ticket windows in metro stations.

Information **Tourinform Budapest** (✉ *District VI, Liszt Ferenc tér* ☎*1/438-8080 [24-hr hotline] or 1/322-4098* ⊕ *www.tourinform.hu or www.hungary.com* ✉ *District V, Sütő utca 2* ☎*1/438-8080 [24-hr hotline]* ✉ *District I, Szentháromság tér* ☎*1/438-8080 [24-hr hotline]*). **Tourism Office of Budapest** (✉ *District V, Március 15 tér 7* ☎*1/266-0479*).

THE DANUBE BEND

About 40 km (25 mi) north of Budapest, the Danube abandons its eastward course and turns abruptly south toward the capital, cutting through the Börzsöny and Visegrád hills. This area is called the Danube Bend and includes the baroque town of Szentendre, the hilltop castle ruins and town of Visegrád, and the cathedral town of Esztergom, all on the Danube's west bank. The most scenic part of Hungary, this region is best known for a chain of riverside spas and beaches, bare volcanic mountains, and limestone hills. Here, in the heartland, are traces of the country's history—the remains of the Roman Empire's frontier, the battlefields of the Middle Ages, and the relics of the Hungarian Renaissance.

The region can be covered by car in one day—the total round-trip is no more than 112 km (70 mi)—although this affords only a cursory look around. A day trip to Szentendre from Budapest plus two days for Visegrád and Esztergom, with a night in Esztergom, would be best. No bridges span the Danube until Esztergom, but there are several ferry crossings, making it possible to combine a visit to both sides of the Danube on the same excursion.

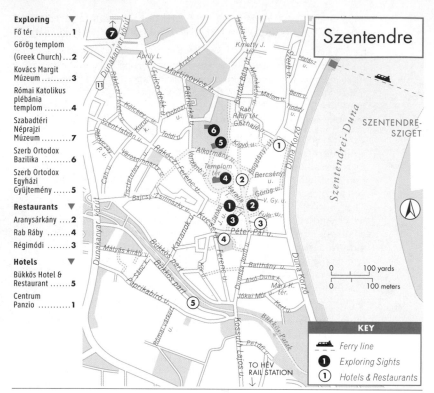

SZENTENDRE

★ *21 km (13 mi) north of Budapest.*

A romantic, lively little town with a flourishing artists' colony, this is the highlight of the Danube Bend. With its profusion of enchanting church steeples, colorful baroque houses, and winding, narrow cobblestone streets, it's no wonder Szentendre attracts swarms of visitors, tripling its population in peak season.

Szentendre was first settled by Serbs and Greeks fleeing the advancing Turks in the 16th and 17th centuries. They built houses and churches in their own style—rich in reds and blues seldom seen elsewhere in Hungary. To truly savor Szentendre, duck into any and every cobblestone side street that appeals to you. Baroque houses with shingle roofs (often with an arched eye-of-God upstairs window) and colorful stone walls abound, each more enchanting than the next.

Numbers in the margin correspond to numbers on the Szentendre map.

❶ Fő tér is Szentendre's main square, the centerpiece of which is an ornate **Memorial Cross** erected by Serbs in gratitude because the town was spared from a plague. The cross has a crucifixion painted on it and stands atop a triangular pillar adorned with a dozen icon paintings.

Every house on Fő tér is a designated landmark, and three of them are open to the public for 400 HUF each. The **Ferenczy Múzeum** (*Ferenczy Museum* ⊠*Fő tér 6* ⊙*Mid-Mar.–Sept., Tues.–Sun. 10–6; Oct.–mid-Mar., Wed.–Sun. 9–5*) displays paintings of Szentendre landscapes. The **Kmetty Múzeum** (*Kmetty Museum* ⊠*Fő út 21* ⊙*Apr.–Oct., daily 1–5*) shows the work of János Kmetty, a pioneer of Hungarian avant-garde painting. The **Szentendrei Képtár** (*Municipal Gallery* ⊠*Fő út 2–5* ⊙*Apr.–Oct., Wed.–Sun. 9–5*) has an excellent collection of local contemporary art and changing exhibits of international art.

② Gracing the corner of Görög utca (Greek Street) and Szentendre's main square, Fő tér, the so-called **Görög templom** (*Greek Church, or Blagovestenska Church*) is actually a Serbian Orthodox church that takes its name from the Greek inscription on a red-marble gravestone set in its wall. This elegant edifice was built between 1752 and 1754 by a rococo master, Andreas Mayerhoffer. Its greatest glory—a symmetrical floor-to-ceiling panoply of stunning icons—was painted between 1802 and 1804 by Mihailo Zivkovic, a Serbian painter from Buda. ⊠*Görög utca, at Fő tér* 📞*26/313–917* 💲*250 HUF* ⊙*Mar.–Oct., Tues.–Sun. 10–5.*

③ If you have time for only one of Szentendre's myriad museums, don't
★ miss the **Kovács Margit Múzeum,** which displays the collected works of Budapest ceramics artist Margit Kovács, who died in 1977. She left behind a wealth of richly textured work that ranges from ceramic figurines to life-size sculptures. ⊠*Vastagh György utca 1, off Görög utca* 📞*26/310–244 Ext. 112* ⊕*pmmi.hu/muzeumok/kovacsmargit/index.htm* 💲*700 HUF* ⊙*Apr.–Sept., daily 10–6; Oct., Tues.–Sun. 10–6; Jan. and Feb., Tues.–Sun. 9–5; Mar., daily 9–5; closed Nov. and Dec.*

④ Perched atop Vár-domb (Castle Hill) is Szentendre's oldest surviving monument, the **Római Katolikus plébánia templom** (*Roman Catholic Parish Church*). According to some sources, there was a church here dating to the 13th century, but if indeed there was one, it was apparently destroyed in some conflict in 1294. What's certain is that the new church built here in the 14th century was heavily damaged during the Turkish occupation in the 16th and 17th centuries. After many reconstructions, today the oldest visible part is a 15th-century sundial in the doorway. ⊠*Templom tér (enter from Alkotmány utca), Vár-domb* 📞*26/312–545* 💲*Free* ⊙*Mid-Mar.–Oct., daily 10–6, sometimes sporadic.*

⑦ Szentendre's farthest-flung museum is the **Szabadtéri Néprajzi Múzeum** (*Open-Air Ethnographic Museum*), the largest open-air museum in the country. It is a living re-creation of 18th- and 19th-century village life from different regions of Hungary—the sort of place where blacksmith shops and a horse-powered mill compete with wooden houses and folk handicrafts for your attention. Five kilometers (3 mi) northwest of the city center, the museum is accessible by bus from the Szentendre terminus of the HÉV suburban railway; the bus leaves from stand No.

7 (ask to be sure, and buy a ticket to the *Skanzen,* as the museum is called). ✉*Sztaravodai út* ☎*26/502–500, 26/317–965, or 26/317–966* ⊕*www.skanzen.hu* ⌖*Open-Air Exhibits: 1,000 HUF; Gallery: Apr.– Oct., free; mid-Jan.–Mar. and Nov.–mid-Dec., 300 HUF* ⊙*Apr.–Oct., Tues.–Sun. 9–5; Nov.–mid-Dec. and early Jan.–Mar., Tues.–Sun. 9–4 (special exhibition gallery only).*

❻ The crimson steeple of the handsome **Szerb Ortodox Bazilika** *(Serbian Orthodox Cathedral)* presides over a restful tree-shaded yard crowning the hill just north of Vár-domb (Castle Hill). It was built in the 1740s with a much more lavish but less beautiful iconostasis than is found in the Greek Church below it. ✉*Pátriárka utca 5* ☎*26/314– 456* ⌖*Admission with ticket to Szerb Ortodox Egyházi Gyüjtemény* ⊙*Mar.–Oct., Tues.–Sun. 10–6; Nov. and Dec., Tues.–Sun. 10–4; Jan. and Feb., Fri.–Sun. 10–4.*

❺ The **Szerb Ortodox Egyházi Gyüjtemény** *(Serbian Orthodox Collection*
★ *of Religious Art)* displays exquisite artifacts relating to the history of the Serbian Orthodox Church in Hungary, and shares a tranquil yard with the imposing Serbian Orthodox Cathedral. ✉*Pátriárka utca 5* ☎*26/312–399* ⌖*500 HUF* ⊙*Mar.–Oct., Tues.–Sun. 10–6; Nov. and Dec., Tues.–Sun. 10–4; Jan. and Feb., Fri.–Sun. 10–4.*

WHERE TO EAT & STAY

$$–$$$ ✕**Aranysárkány.** A favorite of early-20th-century Hungarian writer
Fodor'sChoice Frigyes Karinthy, the Golden Dragon has an open kitchen visible from
★ its elegant but cozy little dining room. You might begin with Dragon's Bouillon with quail eggs and move on to a main course such as trout fillets steamed in campari or venison steak in an almond crust. As for dessert, try the poppy-seed-spiked "opium" pudding or the cottage-cheese pudding with cranberries. The wine list is extensive. ✉*Alkotmány utca 1/a, H-2000* ☎*26/301–479 or 26/311–670* ▤*AE, DC, MC, V* ⌖*Reservations essential* ⊙*Closed mid-Dec.–mid-Jan.*

$–$$$ ✕**Régimódi.** This restaurant, which has an excellent wine list and specializes in fish and game dishes, is steps away from Fő tér. Lace curtains, antique knickknacks, and lovely old paintings give the small upstairs dining room—which is no-smoking—a homey intimacy and, perhaps, the restaurant its name: Old-Fashioned (in the best sense). The downstairs dining room also has a certain antiques-induced charm to it, while the comparatively colorless seating out front at least allows you to people-watch. ✉*Dumtsa Jenő utca 2* ☎*26/311–105* ▤*MC, V.*

$–$$ ✕**Rab Ráby.** Hungarian home-style cooking with an emphasis on fresh-
★ water fish is the mark of this hospitable and often busy restaurant. Old lanterns, cowbells, and musical instruments decorate the walls of this converted 18th-century blacksmith's workshop. There's live piano music every Friday and Saturday evening in summer. ✉*Kucsera Ferenc utca 1/a* ☎*26/310–819* ▤*MC, V* ⌖*Reservations essential.*

¢ ▥ **Bükkös Hotel & Restaurant.** Just west of the main square and across
★ the bridge over tiny Bükkös Brook, this is a neat, well-run establishment on a quiet side street a hop, skip, and jump from the center of town. The narrow staircase and small rooms, with peach bedspreads and overbearing red curtains, give it a genuinely homey feel. Pros:

Friendly service, mostly no-smoking rooms, reasonable rates. Cons: A bit removed from the historic center, small rooms, no Internet access. ⌧*Bükkös part 16, H-2000* ☏*26/312–021* 🖷*26/310–782* ⊕*www.bukkoshotel.hu* ⌁*16 rooms* ⌂*In-room: no a/c, refrigerator. In-hotel: restaurant, laundry service, parking (no fee), no elevator, no-smoking rooms* ▭*DC, MC, V* ⊙|*BP.*

¢ 🖩 **Centrum Panzió.** Szentendre's most pristine B&B has only six rooms, ★ but two are family-sized, and all are pleasantly furnished in shades of blue and gray. Ideally located almost (but not quite) in the center of things, the aptly named Centrum has pleasant Danube views. Service could be a tad friendlier. Pros: Centrally located, reasonable rates. Cons: Touristy area, bland service, few amenities, most rooms with showers only. ⌧*Bogdányi utca 15 (entrance off Rév utca), H-2000* ☏☏*26/302–500* 🖷*26/500–562* ⊕*www.hotelcentrum.hu* ⌁*6 rooms* ⌂*In-hotel: laundry service, parking (no fee), some pets allowed, no elevator* ▭*AE, MC, V* ⊙|*BP.*

NIGHTLIFE & THE ARTS

The annual **Spring Festival,** from mid-March through early April, offers classical concerts in some of Szentendre's churches, as well as jazz, folk, and rock performances in other venues. In July the **Szentendre Summer Days** festival brings open-air theater performances and jazz and classical concerts to Fő tér and the cobblestone courtyard fronting the town hall. Contact Tourinform for schedules and ticket information.

SHOPPING

Flooded with tourists in summer, Szentendre is saturated with the requisite souvenir shops. Among the attractive but overpriced goods sold in every store are dolls dressed in traditional folk costumes, wooden trinkets, pottery, and colorful hand-embroidered tablecloths, doilies, and blouses. The best bargains are the hand-embroidered blankets and bags sold by dozens of elderly women in traditional folk attire, who stand for hours on the town's crowded streets. Many Szentendre stores stay open all day on weekends, unlike those in Budapest.

OFF THE BEATEN PATH

Visegrád. This lovely town 23 km (14 mi) north of Szentendre was the seat of the Hungarian kings during the 14th century, when a hilltop fortress built here by the Angevin kings a century earlier became the royal residence.

Today, the imposing **Fellegvár** *(Citadel)* (⌧*Fellegvár Nagyvillám* ☏*26/398–101* 💳*1,150 HUF* ⊙*Daily 10–6*) towers over the peaceful little town of quiet, tree-lined streets. The forested hills flanking the town offer popular hiking possibilities. You can drive up the winding road to the Citadel in five minutes, but the strenuous climb up the 1,148-foot hill affords great views of the Danube curving through the countryside. Another site worth a look is the separate palace King Matthias had built on the bank of the Danube below the citadel.

Although it was eventually razed by the Turks, nowadays you can see the disheveled ruins of the Királyi palota (Royal Palace) and its Salamon torony (Salamon Tower), which are part of the **Mátyás Király Múzeum** *(King Matthias Museum)* (⌧*Fő utca 29* ☏*26/398–026* ⊕*www.viseg-*

rad.hu/muzeum ✉Free ⊙*Royal Palace Tues.–Sun. 9–6 [entry until 5:30]. Salamon Tower May–Sept., Tues.–Sun. 9–6 [entry until 5:30]).* The Salomon Tower has two small exhibits displaying ancient statues and well structures from the age of King Matthias. Above a ceremonial courtyard rise the palace's various halls; on the left you can still see a few fine original carvings. Inside the palace is a small exhibit on its history, as well as a collection of gravestones dating from Roman times to the 19th century.

Back in the village center, tucked away on a corner down the main street, is the bite-size, powder-yellow **Millennial Chapel** (✉*Fő utca 113*), built in 1896 to celebrate the Magyar Millennium.

ESZTERGOM

21 km (13 mi) north of Visegrád.

Esztergom stands on the site of a Roman fortress, at the westernmost curve of the heart-shape Danube Bend, where the Danube (and a bridge built in 2001 to replace one destroyed in World War II) marks the border between Hungary and Slovakia. St. Stephen, the first Christian king of Hungary and founder of the nation, was crowned here in AD 1000, establishing Esztergom as Hungary's first capital, which it remained for the next 250 years. The majestic Bazilika, Hungary's largest, is Esztergom's main draw, situated on the Vár (Castle) hill, which was home to a series of royal palaces and churches for centuries. Likewise not to be missed is the fine-art collection of the Primate's Palace. If you like strolling, leave yourself a little time to explore the narrow streets of Viziváros (Watertown) below the Bazilika, lined with brightly painted baroque buildings.

Fodor'sChoice Esztergom's **Bazilika** *(Basilica)*, the largest in Hungary, stands on a hill
★   overlooking the town; it is the seat of the cardinal primate of Hungary. Completed in 1856 on the site of a medieval cathedral, this was where the famous anti-communist cleric Cardinal József Mindszenty was finally reburied in 1991 (he was originally buried in Austria), ending decades of religious intolerance by the communists. Its most interesting feature is the Bakócz Chapel (1506), named for a primate of Hungary who only narrowly missed becoming pope. On your left as you enter, the chapel is the most beautiful work of Renaissance architecture in Hungary; note its red marble and magnificent carvings. Other highlights include the sacristy, which contains a valuable collection of medieval ecclesiastical art; the vast crypt, where the cathedral's builders and its key priests are buried; and, for a great view of Esztergom and environs after a steep climb up a long, winding staircase, the observation platform in the cathedral's cupola. The bell tower is also open to the public. ✉*Szent István tér 1, H-2500* ☎*33/311–895 or 33/402–354* ⊕*www.bazilika-esztergom.hu* ✉*Church free, crypt 100 HUF, sacristy 500 HUF, cupola 200 HUF, bell tower 200 HUF* ⊙*Church Mar.–Oct., daily 6–6; Nov.–Feb., daily 6–4. Crypt Mar.–Oct., daily 9–4:30; Nov.–Feb., daily 10–3. Sacristy Mar.–Oct., daily 9–4:30; Nov. and Dec., Tues.–Fri. 11–3:30, weekends 10–5:30. Cupola Apr.–Oct., daily 9–4:30.*

Considered by many to be Hungary's finest art gallery, the **Keresztény Múzeum** *(Museum of Christian Art)*, in the Primate's Palace, has an extensive collection of early Hungarian and Italian paintings (the 14th- and 15th-century Italian collection is unusually large for a museum outside Italy). ⊠ *Primate's Palace, Mindszenty tér 2* ☎ *33/413–880* ⊕ *www.keresztenymuzeum.hu* ⌦ *500 HUF* ⊘ *Apr.–Oct., Tues.–Sun. 10–6; Nov.–Dec. and Mar., Tues.–Sun. 11–3.*

WHERE TO EAT & STAY

$-$$ ✗ **Csülök Csárda.** With its hearty Hungarian fare, cozy rustic atmosphere, and unbeatable location in view of the basilica, the Pork Knuckle Tavern has long been popular with locals and visitors alike. Knuckles are of course the specialty here. Bean soup with knuckle is enough for a small meal but to really fill up, try the "Baking Dish Knuckle," smoked, sliced knuckle fried with potatoes, smothered with a garlicky sour-cream sauce, and served in a baking dish with bits of bacon sprinkled on top. ⊠ *Batthyány utca 9* ☎ *33/412–420* ▭ *AE, DC, MC, V.*

$-$$ ✗ **Padlizsán Étterem.** The elegant Eggplant Restaurant, on a quiet side
★ street at the foot of Castle Hill behind the basilica, is Esztergom's best-kept secret. You might begin with an eggplant salad with balsamic dressing, goat cheese, olives, and pepperoni; and move on to braised venison knuckle with juniper berries, stuffed savoy cabbage, and potato noodles. The wine list is extensive. The soft hues and yellow walls of the two elegant inside rooms are complemented by a rose on every table and jazz music playing softly in the background. ⊠ *Pázmány utca 21* ☎ *33/311–212* ▭ *DC, MC, V.*

¢ ✗☷ **Szalma Csárda & Panzió.** This restaurant and pension is on a tranquil, undeveloped stretch of the Danube a short walk from the town center. The 20-room pension, which resembles a ranch house, has small shower-equipped double rooms that are clean and bright and furnished simply with low, summer-camp-style pine beds. The restaurant ($) is splendidly rustic, complete with a large earthenware stove in the main room and strings of dried red peppers hanging everywhere. Listen to live Gypsy music while enjoying traditional fare such as chicken paprikás with wax beans and dill-spiced dumplings on the side. Pros: Good rates, on the river, excellent restaurant. Cons: Ten-minute walk from town center and basilica, few restaurants nearby, sparse rooms. ⊠ *Prímás-sziget, Nagyduna sétány 2, H-2500* ☎ *33/315–336 or 33/403–838* ⊕ *www.szalmacsarda.hu* ⇴ *19 rooms* ♿ *In-room: no a/ c, no TV (some), Ethernet (some). In-hotel: no elevator* ▭ *No credit cards* ꭍꝈ*BP.*

¢ ☷ **Alabárdos Panzió.** Just downhill from the basilica, this cozy remodeled home provides excellent views of the cathedral and the neighboring Pilis Hills from upstairs. Rooms (doubles and quads) are small but less cramped than at other small pensions. ■**TIP→** **A hearty breakfast including homemade cold cuts is included for 1,000 HUF more per room; if you don't need this, be sure to say so when reserving.** Pros: Near basilica, good rates, nice views from upstairs. Cons: Rooms smallish, along a busy road, breakfast extra. ⊠ *Bajcsy-Zsilinszky út 49, H-2500* ☎ *33/312–640* ⇴ *24 rooms* ♿ *In-room: no a/c. In-hotel: laundry facilities* ▭ *No credit cards* ꭍꝈ*EP.*

7

DANUBE BEND ESSENTIALS

BY BICYCLE

The Danube Bend is a wonderful place to explore by bike; most towns are relatively close together. Some routes have separate bike paths, and others run along the roads. Consult the "Danube Bend Cyclists' Map," available at many tourist offices and Tourinform, for more information.

BY BOAT & FERRY

From April through September, MAHART PassNave operates cruise boats and hydrofoils between Budapest and Esztergom, Visegrád, and Szentendre. It's a wonderfully scenic, if slow, way to make the trip. To save time, many people combine it with a return journey by train or bus.

If you need to cross the river in the Danube Bend, you can take one of several ferries at various points along the shore. The one between Nagymaros and Visegrád affords gorgeous views of Visegrád's citadel and is reached by a beautiful drive through rolling hills on Route 12 south and then west of Nagymaros.

BY BUS

Buses are relatively comfortable (if you get a seat) and run regularly between Budapest's Árpád híd bus station and most towns along both sides of the Danube. The ride to Szentendre takes about half an hour. However, for maximum comfort and convenience—and scenic pleasure—we recommend the HÉV commuter train to Szentendre from Batthány tér in Budapest.

BY CAR

If you don't mind high gas prices and contending with local drivers in the dangerous habit of passing at every opportunity, driving will allow you to see much more in less time than if you try getting around via the somewhat complicated mix of HÉV (commuter train), bus, boat, and/or train that is your other option. Route 11 runs along the western shore of the Danube, connecting Budapest to Szentendre, Visegrád, and Esztergom.

BY TRAIN

Esztergom has frequent daily express and local train service to and from Budapest's Nyugati (West) Station, but there are no direct connections between Szentendre and Esztergom. There is no train service to Visegrád. The HÉV suburban railway runs between Batthyány tér (or Margaret Island, one stop north) in Budapest and Szentendre every 10–20 minutes daily; the trip takes 40 minutes, and a *kiegészítő* (supplementary) ticket—which you need in addition to a Budapest public transport pass or ticket—costs 500 HUF one-way.

VISITOR INFORMATION

The offices below provide a broad range of tourist information and can help arrange private accommodations.

Information Esztergom IBUSZ (⊠ *Kossuth L. u. 5, Esztergom* ☎ *33/520–920*).
Tourinform Szentendre (⊠ *Dumtsa Jenő u. 22, Szentendre* ☎ *26/317–965*).
Visegrád Tours (⊠ *Sirály Restaurant, Rév u. 15, Visegrád* ☎ *26/398–160*).

LAKE BALATON

Lake Balaton, the largest lake in Central Europe, stretches 80 km (50 mi) across western Hungary. Its vast surface conceals modest depths: only 9¾ feet at the center and just 52½ feet at its deepest point, at the Tihany Félsziget (Tihany Peninsula). The Balaton—the most popular playground of this landlocked nation—lies just 90 km (56 mi) southwest of Budapest. On a hot day in July or August, it seems the entire country and half of Germany are packed towel to towel on the lake's grassy public beaches.

On the hilly northern shore, ideal for growing grapes, is Balatonfüred, Hungary's oldest spa town, famed for natural springs that bubble out curative waters. The national park on the Tihany Peninsula lies just to the south, and regular boat service links Tihany and Balatonfüred with Siófok on the southern shore. Flatter and more crowded with resorts and cottages, the southern shore has fewer sights and is not as attractive as the northern one.

Every town along both shores has at least one *strand* (beach). A modest entrance fee is usually charged. If you're interested in exploring beyond the beach you can set out by car, bicycle, or foot, on beautiful village-to-village tours—stopping to view lovely old churches, photograph a stork perched in its nest atop a telephone pole, or climb a vineyard-covered hill for sweeping vistas. Since most vacationers keep close to the shore, a small amount of exploring into the roads and countryside heading away from the lake will reward you with a break from the summer crowds.

BALATONFÜRED

115 km (71 mi) southwest of Budapest.

Fed by 11 medicinal springs, Balatonfüred first gained popularity as a health resort where ailing people with heart conditions and fatigue would come to take or, more accurately, to drink a cure. The waters are still an integral part of the town's identity and consumed voraciously, but only the internationally renowned cardiac hospital has actual bathing facilities. Today Balatonfüred is probably the Balaton's most popular destination, with every amenity to match. Above its busy boat landing, beaches, and promenade lined with plane and poplar trees, the twisting streets of the Old Town climb vineyard-covered hillsides.

A stroll up **Blaha Lujza utca** from Gyógy tér will take you past several landmarks, such as the **Blaha Lujza Ház** (Lujza Blaha House), a neoclassical villa built in 1867 and, later, the summer home of this famous turn-of-the-20th-century actress, humanist, and singer; today, it's a hotel. The sweet little **Kerek templom** (Round Church), consecrated in 1846, was built in a classical style and has a truly rounded interior.

The center of town is **Gyógy tér** *(Spa Square)*, where the bubbling waters from five volcanic springs rise beneath a slim, colonnaded pavilion. In the square's centerpiece, the neoclassical **Well House** of the Kossuth

Spring, you can sample the water, which has a pleasant, refreshing taste despite the sulfurous aroma. All the square's buildings are pillared like Greek temples. On the eastern side of the square is the Állami Kórház (State Hospital), where patients from all over the world are treated. It was here that Rabindranath Tagore, the Nobel Prize–winning Indian poet, recovered from a heart attack in 1926. The tree he planted to commemorate his stay stands in a little grove at the western end of the paths leading from the square down to the lakeside.

Trees, restaurants, and shops line the lakefront **Tagore sétány** *(Tagore Promenade)*, which begins near the boat landing and runs for nearly a kilometer (almost ½ mi).

WHERE TO EAT & STAY

$–$$$ ✕ **Tölgyfa Csárda.** Perched high on a hilltop, the Oak Tree Tavern has breathtaking views over the steeples and rooftops of Balatonfüred and the Tihany Peninsula. The dining room and menu are worthy of a first-class Budapest restaurant, and nightly live Gypsy music keeps things festive. ⊠ *Meleghegy, up the hill at the end of Csárda utca* ☎ *87/343–036* ▤ *MC, V* ⊗ *Closed late Nov.–Apr.*

$–$$ ✕ **Baricska Csárda.** This rambling country-style restaurant has a reed-thatched roof, wood-beamed rooms, vaulted cellars, vine-draped terraces, and views of both vineyards and the lake. The food is hearty yet ambitious: grilled trout, catfish paprikás with spaetzle to soak up the creamy sauce, stuffed cabbage, and staple desserts such as strudels and palacsintas. ⊠ *Baricska dülő, off Rte. 71 (Széchenyi út) behind the Shell station* ☎ *87/580–095* ⌖ *Reservations essential* ▤ *AE, DC, MC, V* ⊗ *Closed Nov.–mid-Mar.*

$ ▥ **Annabella.** The cool, spacious guest quarters in this Miami-style high-rise are especially pleasant in the summer heat. The resort overlooks the lake and Tagore Promenade and has access to excellent swimming and water-sports facilities. Pros: On the lakeshore, excellent views from upper rooms, rooms are big and have balconies, numerous amenities and services. Cons: Bland on the outside, lacking in charm, heavily touristed stretch of lakeshore. ⊠ *Deák Ferenc utca 25, H-8230* ☎ *87/889–400* 🖷 *87/889–412 or 87/889–435* ⊕ *www.danubiushotels.com/annabella* 🖙 *383 rooms, 5 suites* ⌂ *In-hotel: restaurant, bar, pools, bicycles, laundry service, parking (no fee)* ▤ *AE, DC, MC, V* ⊗ *Closed late Oct.–mid-Apr.* ⵧBP.

¢–$ ▥ **Club Imola.** Drive through a metal archway etched with the name "Imola" overhead to find a large square of low-rise buildings surrounded by lush green trees and small gardens—a quiet break from the hustle of the nearby Balatonfüred strand. The main hotel has clean, wooden-furnished rooms that are smallish in size but lower in price. Inside is a huge indoor pool with a Jacuzzi. For longer stays you can rent a gorgeous duplex apartment with a small balcony, skylights, and loft bedroom. Pros: Quiet parklike oasis along busy road, good value, tennis courts and pool. Cons: Lakeshore and attendant attractions a 10-minute walk away, rooms smallish, few restaurants or shops nearby. ⊠ *Petőfi Sándor utca 22, H-8230* ☎ *87/341–722* 🖷 *87/342–602* ⊕ *www.imolanet.hu* 🖙 *18 rooms, 8 apartments* ⌂ *In-hotel: res-*

Fodor'sChoice ★

taurant, bar, tennis courts, pool, laundry service, parking (no fee), no elevator ▭*MC, V* ⚹l*BP.*

SPORTS & THE OUTDOORS

BEACHES

Ⓒ Balatonfüred has three public beaches, most accessibly the **Eszterházy strand** at the end of Liszt Ferenc utca by the Hotel Tagore. It's open 9–7 daily from mid-May to mid-September and costs 500 HUF to enter. Lakeside hotels typically have their own private beaches, with watersports facilities and equipment or special access to them nearby. At most beaches you can rent sailboards, paddleboats, and other water toys.

BICYCLING

Short of jumping in the lake itself, there is nothing like pedaling along the shore, and in particular the roughly hour-long path to Tihany. In Balatonfüred, you can rent for 350 HUF an hour or 2,400 HUF for 24 hours at **Tempo 21** (⊠*Ady Endre utca 52* ☎*87/480–671 or 06– 20/924–3672*). The main office, on Ady Endre utca, is a 10-minute walk from the lake, but you can also rent from the company's stand on Za'konyi Ferenc utca near the main quay.

TIHANY & PENINSULA

★ *11 km (7 mi) southwest of Balatonfüred, 126 km (78 mi) from Budapest.*

The famed town of Tihany, with its twisting, narrow cobblestone streets and hilltop abbey, is at the top of the Tihany Félsziget (Tihany Peninsula), a 12-square-km (less-than-5-square-mile) area joined to the mainland by a narrow neck and jutting 5 km (3 mi) into the lake. The peninsula is not only a major tourist resort—it is, after all, Hungary's closest approximation of an Adriatic experience—but also the most historic part of the Balaton area. In 1952 the entire peninsula was declared a national park, and because of its geological rarities—including smooth Belső Tó (Inner Lake), 82 feet higher than Lake Balaton—it became Hungary's first nature conservation zone. As a result of volcanic activity in the area, there are more than 110 geyser craters.

FodorśChoice On a hilltop overlooking the Old Town is the **Bencés Apátság** *(Benedic-*
★ *tine Abbey)*, whose foundations were laid by King András I (his body lies in the abbey crypt) in 1055. Parts of the abbey were rebuilt in baroque style between 1719 and 1784. The contrast between the simple crypt and the abbey's lavish baroque interior is striking. The altar, abbot's throne, choir parapet, organ case, and pulpit were all the work of Sebestyén Stuhloff, who, according to local legend, immortalized the features of his doomed sweetheart in the face of the angel kneeling on the right-hand side of the altar to the Virgin Mary.

In a baroque house adjoining and entered through the abbey is the **Bencés Apátsági Múzeum** (Benedictine Abbey Museum). The best exhibits are in the basement lapidarium: relics from Roman colonization, including mosaic floors; a relief of David from the 2nd or 3rd century; and 1,200-year-old carved stones. ⊠*Első András tér 1, H-8237* 🏛*87/448–405 abbey, 87/448–650 museum* 🖂*500 HUF for abbey and museum* ☉*May–Sept., daily 9–5:30; Oct.–Mar., Mon.–Sat. 10–3, Sun. 11–3; Apr., daily 10–4:30. Nov.–Mar., church and lapidarium only.*

The **Szabadtéri Múzeum** *(Open-air Museum)*, Tihany's outdoor museum of ethnography, assembles a group of old structures, including an unplastered dwelling house with basalt walls, a thatched roof, verandas, and white-framed windows dating back to the 18th century. Another building is the former house of the Fishermen's Guild, with all kinds of fishing tools on display, including an old boat, parked inside. ⊠*Pisky István sétány 12* 🏛*87/714–960* 🖂*360 HUF* ☉*Apr. 11–June, Tues.–Sun. 10–6; July and Aug., Tues.–Sun. 10–8; Sept.–Oct. 15, Tues.–Sun. 10–6.*

WHERE TO EAT & STAY

$–$$ ✕**Ferenc Pince.** A half-mile walk uphill from the town center, this
★ thatched-roof restaurant and wine cellar has splendid views of the Balaton and surrounding vineyards. The menu is heavy not only on Balaton fish but also beef straight from Hungary's prized gray cattle, as well as poultry, salads, and other national specialties. Wine tastings in the wine cellar, however, are the real draw, allowing you to sample numerous varieties produced by Ferenc Pince. Reservations are required for tastings. ⊠*Cserhegy* 🏛*87/448–575, 20/942–3987 (mobile)* ⊕*www. ferencpince.hu* ▤*No credit cards* ☉*Closed Tues. and Oct.–Apr.*

$ ✕**Pál Csárda.** Two thatched cottages house this simple restaurant right across the street from a modest but attractive outdoor religious site featuring the stations of the cross. The predictable but tasty staples include *gulyás leves* (goulash soup) and *halászlé* (fish stew). You can eat in the garden, which is decorated with gourds and grapevines. ⊠*Visszhang utca 19* 🏛*87/448–605* ▤*AE, DC, MC, V* ☉*Closed Nov.–Mar.*

$ ▦**Club Tihany.** Picture Club Med transposed to late-1980s Central
★ Europe, and you'll have some idea of what to expect at Club Tihany. This 32-acre, parklike lakeside resort stays busy year-round. Accommodations are standard hotel rooms (higher rate for lake views) or individual bungalows with kitchens. The list of activities is impressive—from fishing to thermal bathing in the spa. Pros: Peaceful oasis on tip of peninsula, private beach, lots of amenities and services. Cons: Main hotel less than charming, Tihany center and restaurants a hefty 30-minute walk away, Club Med–look of grounds and bungalows a tad clichéd. ⊠*Rév utca 3, H-8237* 🏛*87/538–564* 🖷*87/448–083* ⊕*www. clubtihany.hu* 🛏*330 rooms, 160 bungalows* 🔧*In-room: kitchen (some), dial-up, refrigerator. In-hotel: 3 restaurants, bars, tennis court, pool, gym, spa, beachfront, bicycles, children's programs (ages 3–17), public Wi-Fi, public Internet* ▤*AE, DC, MC, V* �󠀱⦿*MAP.*

¢ ▦**Adler Inn.** This cozy inn 500 yards above the Balaton shore has a
★ friendly staff and small, clean rooms, each with an outdoor terrace. Outside the inn is a lovely dining area and outdoor pizzeria. Pros: Low rates, small-inn charm, pool, good on-site dining. Cons: Along bland stretch of road, a long walk from Tihany center and to lakeshore, few amenities and services, no credit cards. ⊠*Felsőkopazhegyi út 1/a, H-*

8237 ☎*87/538–000* 📠*87/448–755* ⊕*www.adler-tihany.hu* ⇨*13 rooms, 2 apartments* ⚬*In-hotel: restaurant, pool, parking (no fee), no elevator* ▭*No credit cards* ⊘*Closed Nov.–mid-Mar.* ⦿|*BP.*

BADACSONY

★ *41 km (25 mi) southwest of Tihany, 167 km (104 mi) from Budapest.*

One of the northern shore's most treasured images is of Mt. Badacsony (1,437 feet) rising from the lake. A nature preserve since 1965, the coffinlike basalt peak of the Balaton Highlands is an extinct volcano flanked by smaller cone-shaped hills. The masses of lava that coagulated here created bizarre and beautiful rock formations. Badacsony is an administrative name for the entire area, and includes not just the mountain but also five settlements at its foot. For centuries, the land below the peak has been draped by vineyards, producing many popular white wines. In descending order of dryness, the best-loved Badacsony whites are rizlingszilváni, kéknyelű, and szürkebarát.

Many restaurants and inns have their own wine tastings, as do the numerous smaller, private cellars dotting the hill. Look for signs saying *bor* or *Wein* (wine, in Hungarian and German, respectively) to point the way. Most places are open from mid-May to mid-September.

A good starting point for Badacsony sightseeing is the **Egry József Múzeum** *(József Egry Museum)*, formerly the home and studio of a famous painter of Balaton landscapes whose evocative scenes depict the lake's constantly changing hues, from its angry emerald during storms to its tranquil deep blues. ✉*Egry sétány 12* ☎*87/431–044* ⛃*400 HUF* ⊘*May–Sept., Tues.–Sun. 10–6.*

The steep climb to the **Kisfaludy kilátó** *(Kisfaludy Lookout Tower)* on Mt. Badacsony's summit is an integral part of the Badacsony experience and a rewarding bit of exercise. Serious summitry begins at the Rózsakő (Rose Stone), a flat, smooth basalt slab with many carved inscriptions that can be found behind the Kisfaludy-ház (Kisfaludy House), a restaurant just above the Rózsa Szegedy House. From here a trail marked in yellow leads up to the foot of the columns that stretch to the top. The ascent from Rózsakő should take less than an hour.

Szegedy Róza út, the steep main street climbing the mountain, is flanked by vineyards and villas. This is the place to get acquainted with the writer Sándor Kisfaludy and his beloved bride from Badacsony, Róza Szegedy, to whom he dedicated his love poems. At the summit of her street is **Szegedy Róza Ház** *(Róza Szegedy House)*, a baroque wine-press

GO JUMP IN A LAKE

A veritable national institution that sometimes draws 10,000 participants young and old, healthy and disabled, the *Balatoni átúszás* (Cross-Balaton Swim) is one of Europe's largest swimming events open to the general public. Held on a Saturday in midsummer (usually late July), the 5.2-km (3.3-mi) swim begins on the northern shore, in the village of Révfülöp, and winds up across the lake in Balatonboglár. The registration fee is 3,500 HUF. For details, visit ⊕ *www.balaton-atuszas.com.*

7

house built in 1790 on a grand scale. It was here that the hometown girl met the visiting bard from Budapest. The house now serves as a memorial museum to both of them, furnished much the way it was when Kisfaludy was doing his best work immortalizing his two true loves, Mt. Badacsony and his wife. Szegedy, meanwhile, was heavily involved with wine making, and her homemade vermouth was famous throughout Hungary. ⊠*Szegedy Róza út 87* ☎*87/701–906* 💲*360 HUF* ⊙*May–mid-Oct., Tues.–Sun. 10–6.*

WHERE TO EAT & STAY

$-$$$ ✗**Kisfaludy-ház.** Perched above the Szegedy Róza House is this Badacsony institution, once a wine-press house owned by the poet Sándor Kisfaludy's family. Its wine cellar lies directly over a spring, but the main draw is a vast two-tier terrace that affords a breathtaking view of virtually the entire lake. Naturally, the wines are excellent and are incorporated into some of the cooking, such as creamy cold white-wine soup with dried grapes. ⊠*Szegedy Róza utca 87* ☎*87/431–016* ▤*AE, DC, MC, V* ⊙*Closed Oct.–Apr.*

$-$$ ✗**Halászkert.** The festive Fish Garden has won numerous international awards for its fine Hungarian cuisine. Inside are wooden rafters and tables draped with peachy-pink tablecloths; outside is a large terrace with umbrella-shaded tables. The extensive menu has such fresh-from-the-lake dishes as *halászlé,* and *párolt* (steamed) harcsa drenched with a paprika-dill sauce. There's live Gypsy music several nights a week. ⊠*Park utca 5* ☎*87/431–113 or 87/431–054* ▤*AE, DC, MC, V* ⊙*Closed Nov.–Apr.*

$ ⌂**Club Hotel Badacsony.** A private beach is just a step away from this
Fodor's Choice   hotel right on the shore of Lake Balaton. The Club Hotel is the largest
★   in the area. Rooms are bright and clean, the staff is extremely helpful, and the outdoor swimming pool is heated in cool weather. Pros: Right on the lake, secluded atmosphere, private beach. Cons: Relatively high rates, no a/c, no in-room Internet access. ⊠*Balatoni út 14, Badacsonyomaj, H-8258* ☎*87/471–040 or 87/471–088* 🖶*87/471–059* ⊕*www. badacsonyhotel.hu* 🛏*70 rooms* ⚟*In-room: refrigerator, no a/c. In-hotel: restaurant, bar, tennis court, beachfront, no elevator, public Wi-Fi, public Internet* ▤*AE, DC, MC, V* ⊙*Closed Nov.–Apr.* ⵏ⌶*BP.*

▌OFF THE
BEATEN
PATH

Hévíz. Just 6 km (4 mi) northwest of the charming town of Keszthely at Lake Balaton's southern tip lies one of Hungary's biggest and most famous spa resorts, with the largest natural curative thermal lake in Europe. Lake Hévíz covers nearly 60,000 square yards, with warm water that never grows cooler than 33°C to 35°C (91.4°F–95°F) in summer and 30°C to 32°C (86°F–89.6°F) in winter, allowing year-round bathing. Richly laced with sulfur, alkali, calcium salts, and other curative components, Hévíz water is recommended for various ailments and is guzzled to allay digestive problems and receding gums. Fed by a spring producing 86 million liters (22.7 million gallons) of water a day, the lake cycles through a complete water change every 28 hours. The vast spa park has hospitals, sanatoriums, expensive hotels, and a casino. The **Hévízi Fürdő** *(Hévíz Spa)* (⊠*Dr. Schulhof Vilmos sétány 1* ☎*83/501–700* ⊕*www.spaheviz.hu* 💲*1,500 HUF for 3 hrs, 2,800*

HUFall day)—that is, the public bath facilities—is in a large, turreted medicinal bathing complex.

LAKE BALATON ESSENTIALS

BY AIR

Balaton Airport is in Sármellék, 11 km (7 mi) south of Keszthely, near the western tip of Lake Balaton. Budget airlines Ryanair and German Wings have regular service primarily from the U.K. and Germany. Lufthansa and Malév also operate flights from points in Germany.

AIRPORT
TRANSFERS

Hertz, National, and Fox Autorent car rental agencies have offices at Balaton Airport. Driving distance to Badacsony is 34 km (21 mi), Balatonfüred 73 km (45 mi), Budapest 182 km (113 mi), Héviz 10 km (6 mi), and Tihany 75 km (47 mi; includes a ferry crossing). Without a car, your best bet for getting to Lake Balaton's key towns along the northern shore—or to travel on to Budapest—is to get to the railway station in Keszthely via the Fly-Car shuttle service; the cost is 1,400 HUF. From there, hop any of several daily trains north (transfer in Tapolca) to Badacsony, Balatonfüred, or Budapest. Shuttle service to the spa town of Héviz and Budapest is also available.

Information Fly-Car (✉ *Balaton Airport, Sármellék* ☎ *83/554–056* ⊕ *www. fly-car.hu).*

BY BOAT & FERRY

Ferries are a wonderfully scenic (but slow) way to travel between Lake Balaton's resorts. Schedules are available at tourist offices and from the Balatoni Hajózási Zrt (Balaton Shipping Co.).

BY BUS

Buses headed for the Lake Balaton region depart from Budapest's Népliget station daily. Buses also frequently link Lake Balaton's major resorts. Contact the tourist offices or Volánbusz for schedule and fare information.

BY CAR

Driving is the most convenient way to explore the area, but keep in mind that traffic can be heavy during summer weekends. Expressway E71/M7 is the main artery between Budapest and Lake Balaton and runs along the southern shore almost to the tip of the lake (ongoing construction will see it eventually reach Croatia). From the expressway you can take the two-lane Route 71 along the northern shore to Balatonfüred. The drive from Budapest to Balatonfüred takes about two hours, except on weekends, when traffic can be severe.

BY TRAIN

Daily express trains run from Budapest's Déli (South) Station to Balatonfüred and on to Badacsony, but most routes, once they reach the lake, stop practically everywhere. The two-hour trip to Balatonfüred costs about 2,500 HUF each way. Trains from Budapest serve all resorts on the northern shore; a separate line links resorts on the southern shore. There is no train service to Tihany. Bear in mind that you cannot reserve seats on most Balaton trains—it's first come, first seated.

VISITOR INFORMATION
Lake Balaton's Tourinform offices provide a broad range of tourist information and can help arrange private accommodations.

Information Tourinform Badacsony (⊠ *Park u. 6* 🖼️87/431–046). **Tourinform Balatonfüred** (⊠ *Kisfaludy utca 1* 🖼️87/580–480). **Tourinform Tihany** (⊠ *Kossuth u. 20* 🖼️87/448–804).

TRANSDANUBIA

Western Hungary, often referred to as Transdanubia (*Dunántúl* in Hungarian), is the area south and west of the Danube, stretching to the Slovak and Austrian borders in the west and north and to Slovenia and Croatia in the south. (Although this also includes Lake Balaton, that region is generally thought of separately.) It presents a highly picturesque landscape, including several ranges of hills and small mountains. Most of its surface is covered with farmland, vineyards, and orchards—all nurtured and made verdant by a climate that is noticeably more humid than in the rest of the country.

The Romans called the region Pannonia. For centuries it was a frontier province; today it is far richer in Roman ruins than the rest of Hungary. Centuries later, the 150-year Turkish occupation left its mark on the region, particularly in the south, where it's not uncommon to see a former mosque serving as a Christian church. Austrian influence is clearly visible in the region's baroque buildings, particularly in the magnificent Eszterházy Palace in Fertőd, outside of Sopron. Vienna, after all, is just a few hours' drive away.

SOPRON

★ *211 km (131 mi) northwest of Budapest.*

Sopron, which lies on the Austrian frontier, between Lake Fertő (in German, Neusiedlersee) and the Sopron Hills, is one of Hungary's most picturesque towns. Barely an hour from Vienna by car, it is a bargain shopping center for many Austrians, who flock here for the day. There is much more to Sopron, however, than conspicuous consumption by foreigners. Behind the narrow storefronts along Várkerület, the circular boulevard around Sopron's inner core, and within the city walls (one set built by Romans, the other by medieval Magyars) lies a horseshoe-shape inner city that is a wondrous mix of Gothic, baroque, and Renaissance buildings. In the center of this inner city is Fő tér, the main square of perfectly proportioned Italianate architecture.

Today's city of 60,000 was a small Celtic settlement more than 2,300 years ago. During Roman times, under the name of Scarabantia, it stood on the main European north–south trade route, the Amber Road; it also happened to be near the junction with the east–west route used by Byzantine merchants. In 896 the Magyars conquered the Carpathian basin and later named the city Suprun for a medieval Hungarian warrior. After the Habsburgs took over the territory during the Turkish wars of the 16th and 17th centuries, they renamed the city Ödenburg (Castle on the Ruins) and made it the capital of the rich and fertile Austrian Burgenland. Ferdinand III, later Holy Roman Emperor, was crowned king of Hungary here in 1625, and at a special session of the Hungarian parliament in 1681, Prince Paul Esterházy was elected palatine (ruling deputy) of Hungary. And always, under any name or regime, Sopron was consistently a fine and prosperous place in which to live.

Angyal Patika Múzeum *(Angel Pharmacy Museum)*. A working apothecary between 1642 and 1647, this museum is filled with old Viennese porcelain vessels and papers pertaining to Ignaz Philipp Semmelweis (1815–65), the Hungarian physician whose pioneering work in antiseptics, while he was in Vienna, made childbirth safer. The building itself dates from the 16th century. ⊠*Fő tér 2* ☎*99/311–327* 💲*400 HUF* ☉*Apr.–Sept., Tues.–Sun. 10–6; Oct.–Mar., Tues.–Sun. 2–6.*

Cézár Ház *(Cézár House)*. The Hungarian parliament met in the upstairs rooms here in 1681; the same space now houses a privately endowed museum, created by the widow of József Soproni-Horváth (1891–1961), a remarkable artist. Famous for the wonders he worked with watercolors, Soproni-Horváth used the fragile medium to bring large surfaces to life in a density usually associated with oil paintings while depicting realistic scenes, such as a girl grieving over her drowned sister's body. ⊠*Hátsókapú utca 2* ☎*99/312–326* 💲*Suggested donation of 300 HUF–400 HUF* ☉*Thurs., Fri., and Sun. 10–1, Sat. 10–1 and 3–6.*

Kecske templom *(Goat Church)*. Legend has it that the early Gothic (1280–1300) church takes its name from a medieval billy goat that scratched up a treasure, enabling the Franciscans to build a church on the site (the Benedictines took over in 1802). More likely, however, the name comes from the figures of goats carved into its crests: the coat of arms of the Gutsch family, who financed the church. The Goat Church has a soaring, pointed, 14th-century steeple, three naves, and its original Gothic choir (betraying French influence)—not to mention a Hungarian Gothic-baroque red-marble pulpit, a rococo main altar, baroque altars, and a painting of St. Stephen by a member of the Storno family, one of Sopron's most important dynasties in centuries past. ⊠*Templom utca 1* 💲*Free (donations accepted)* ☉*Daily 10–noon and 2–5.*

Mária szobor *(St. Mary's Column)*. With its finely sculpted biblical reliefs, the column is a superb specimen of baroque design. It was erected in 1745 to mark the former site of the medieval Church of Our Lady, which was destroyed by Sopron citizens in 1632 because they feared the Turks would use its steeple as a strategic firing tower. ⊠*At the Előkapu (Front Gate).*

Ó-zsinagóga *(Old Synagogue)*. Built around 1300, this medieval synagogue is now a religious museum with old Torahs on display and an exhibit about the World War II deportation of the Jews. Restored in 1973, the existing facade dates from 1734. A plaque honors the 1,640 Jews of Sopron who were murdered by the Nazis—the quiet street that is home to this and another old synagogue a few doors away, at No. 11, became the city's Jewish ghetto in May 1944. Only 274 of Sopron's Jews survived. ⊠ *Új utca 22* ☎ *99/311–327* 🖭 *600 HUF* ⊘ *Apr.–Oct., Tues.–Sun. 10–6.*

Rómaikori Kőtár *(Roman Archaeology Museum).* A fine Renaissance courtyard leads to the churchlike vaulted medieval cellar—a perfect setting for the gigantic statues of Jupiter, Juno, and Minerva unearthed beneath the main square during the digging of foundations for the city hall in the late 19th century. On the second floor a separate museum (with identical hours and admission prices) re-creates the living environment of 17th- and 18th-century Sopron apartments. ⊠ *Fő tér 6* ☎ *99/311–327* 🖭 *700 HUF for each museum* ⊘ *Apr.–Sept., Tues.–Sun. 10–6; Oct.–Mar., Tues.–Sun. 10–2.*

Fodor's Choice ★ **Storno Ház** *(Storno House).* On the exquisite main square, this turreted house is the city's finest Renaissance-era building. Downstairs inside its two-story loggia is a restaurant; upstairs, a museum houses a remarkable family collection of furniture, porcelain, sculptures, and paintings. The Stornos were a rags-to-riches dynasty of chimney sweeps originally from Switzerland that, over several generations beginning in the 1870s, bought or just relieved grateful owners of unwanted treasures and evolved into a family of painters and sculptors themselves. On an exterior wall hangs a plaque commemorating visits by King Matthias Corvinus (winter 1482–83) and Liszt Ferenc (1840 and 1881). The museum can be visited by guided tour only, given every half hour. ⊠ *Fő tér 8, H-9400* ☎ *99/311–327* 🖭 *1,000 HUF* ⊘ *Apr.–Sept., Tues.–Sun. 10–6; Oct.–Mar., Tues.–Sun. 2–6, with tours every ½ hr.*

Szent György utca *(St. George Street).* Numerous dragons of religion and architecture coexist in a somewhat harmonious fashion on this street. The **Erdődy Vár** (Erdődy Palace), at No. 16, is Sopron's richest rococo building. Two doors down, at No. 12, stands the **Eggenberg Ház** (Eggenberg House), where the widow of Prince Johann Eggenberg held Protestant services during the harshest days of the Counter-Reformation and beyond. But the street takes its name from **Szent György templom** (St. George's Church), a 14th-century Catholic church so sensitively "baroqued" some 300 years later that its interior is still as soft as whipped cream.

Szentháromság szobor *(Holy Trinity Column).* The centerpiece of Fő tér is a sparkling, spiraling three-tiered monument aswirl with gilded angels. It represents the earliest (1701) and loveliest baroque monument to a plague in all of Hungary—in this case, the country's great plague, which lasted from 1695 to 1701. The kneeling figures carved in the pedestal represent the married couple who ordered the work from the sculptor.

Fodor's Choice ★ **Tűztorony** *(Fire Tower).* The symbol of Sopron's endurance—and entranceway to the Old Town—is 200 feet high, with foundations dating to the days of the Árpád dynasty (9th–13th century) and perhaps back to the Romans. The tower is remarkable for its harmonious blend of architectural styles. The upper portions were rebuilt after most of the earlier Fire Tower was, ironically, destroyed by the Great Fire of 1676. Throughout the centuries the tower bell tolled the alarm for fire or the death of a prominent citizen, and from the loggias musicians trumpeted the approach of an enemy or serenaded the citizenry. Today you can take in good views of the town and surrounding countryside from the top of the tower. ⊠ *Fő tér 8, H-9400* ☎ *99/311–327* 🖾 *700 HUF* ☾ *May–Aug., Tues.–Sun. 10–8; Apr. and Sept.–Oct., Tues.–Sun. 10–6.*

Várkerület. Strolling along the circular boulevard that embraces Sopron's inner core allows you to take in the vibrant harmony of beautifully preserved baroque and rococo architecture and the fashionable shops and cafés of Sopron's thriving downtown business district outside the city walls.

NEED A BREAK?

Red-velvety chairs, an ornate chandelier, a semi-spiraling wooden staircase, and scrumptious pastry are the hallmarks of the cozy little **Dömötöri cukrászda** (⊠ *Széchenyi tér, at the corner of Erszébet utca* ☎ *99/506–623*) on Sopron's second most famous—and largest—square.

OFF THE BEATEN PATH

Eszterházy Palace. The magnificent yellow baroque and rococo palace, built between 1720 and 1760 as a residence for the Hungarian noble family, is prized as one of the country's most exquisite buildings. Though badly damaged in World War II, it was later painstakingly restored, making it clear why in its day the palace was referred to as the Hungarian Versailles. Its 126 rooms include a lavish Hall of Mirrors and a three-story-high concert hall, where classical concerts are held throughout the summer (at irregular intervals). Joseph Haydn, court conductor to the Eszterházy family here for 30 years, is the subject of a small museum inside. The palace lies 27 km (17 mi) southeast of Sopron, in Fertőd. ⊠ *Haydn utca 2, just off Rte. 85, Fertőd* ☎ *99/537–640* 🖾 *1,350 HUF* ☾ *Mid-Mar.–late Oct., Tues.–Sun. 10–6; late Oct.–mid-Mar., Tues.–Sun. 10–4.*

WHERE TO EAT & STAY

$-$$
★

✕ **Perkovátz Ház.** One of Sopron's finest dining options, this is an elegant, plushly carpeted English-style pub-cum-restaurant on spacious Széchenyi tér. You have a choice of such creative, scrumptious fare as pike-perch with rosemary and grilled, honeyed duck with apple salad. ⊠ *Széchenyi tér 12* ☎ *99/316–839* ⊟ *AE, DC, MC, V.*

¢-$$
Fodor's Choice
★

✕ **Soproni Borház.** This 300-year-old wine cellar just off the city's main shopping boulevard offers tastings of 300 different Hungarian wines, including some made in Sopron. Your wine is ordered with a plate of accompanying light fare (all less than 1,000 HUF), which might include goose liver, salami, pork, sausage, and several types of vegetables. You can also order grilled meats for a bit more (priced by weight). Servers are friendly, and will give you an earful along with each glassful of wine you try. ⊠ *Várkerület 15, H-9400* ☎ *99/510–022* ⊟ *MC, V.*

7

¢–$ ✗**Fórum Pizzéria.** Only yards from Fő tér, this is the best bet for pizza in the Old Town and possibly in all of Sopron. At relative bargain prices, here you can choose between some 40 pies and a variety of standard dishes, including grilled meats and fish. ⊠*Szent György utca 3* ☎*99/340–231* ▤*AE, DC, MC, V.*

$ ⊞**Best Western Pannonia Med Hotel.** The 17th-century hotel that once stood here was eventually destroyed in a fire but rebuilt in neoclassical style in 1893—soaring ceilings, dripping chandeliers, and a breakfast room with gilt-edge mirrors and little golden chairs. Standard rooms are comfortable and smart, but they pale in comparison to the handsome suites, which have huge wooden beds and are furnished with antiques. Pros: Grand historic public areas, lots of amenities and services, on main boulevard a short walk from the historic center. Cons: Most rooms a little bland. ⊠*Várkerület 75, H-9400* ☎*99/312–180* 🖷*99/340–766* ⊕*www.pannoniahotel.com* ⇆*48 rooms, 14 suites* ♿*In-room: dial-up, refrigerator, Wi-Fi, Ethernet. In-hotel: restaurant, bar, pool, gym, spa, parking (no fee), public Wi-Fi* ▤*AE, DC, MC, V* ⏐◐⏐*BP.*

$ ⊞**Hotel Sopron.** There's no getting around the Hotel Sopron's outdated
★   1980s-era appearance, so the management wisely emphasizes the panoramic city views and the amenities. This is the only hotel near downtown with an outdoor pool, its own playground, and its own wine cellar (next door). Many, but not all, of the brown-and-beige rooms also have great views of Sopron's Old Town. Pros: Great views, outdoor pool, on-site wine cellar. Cons: 10-minute walk from historic center, few restaurants nearby, anachronistic appearance. ⊠*Fövényverem utca 7, H-9400* ☎*99/512–261* 🖷*99/311–090* ⊕*www.hotelsopron.hu* ⇆*106 rooms, 2 suites* ♿*In-room: refrigerator, no a/c (some), Wi-Fi. In-hotel: restaurant, bar, tennis courts, pool, gym, parking, public Wi-Fi* ▤*AE, MC, V* ⏐◐⏐*BP.*

$ ⊞**Hotel Wollner.** Tucked inside the city center, this charming 18th-cen-
Fodor'sChoice tury peach-colored hotel has been restored to its original splendor.
★   Aside from the exquisite baroque interior, the best thing about the Wollner is its courtyard restaurant, where there is plenty of outdoor seating amid flowers and greenery. Unusual for Hungary, this is a no-smoking hotel—and that goes even for the restaurant. Pros: Historic interior and exterior; right in the center; no-smoking; cozy, charming, and friendly. Cons: No elevator. ⊠*Templom utca 20, H-9400* ☎*99/524–400* 🖷*99/524–401* ⊕*www.wollner.hu* ⇆*18 rooms* ♿*In-room: no a/c, refrigerator, Wi-Fi. In-hotel: restaurant, bars, gym, parking (fee), no elevator, public Wi-Fi* ▤*AE, DC, MC, V* ⏐◐⏐*BP.*

NIGHTLIFE & THE ARTS

From mid- to late March, Sopron's cultural life warms up during the annual **Tavaszi Fesztivál** *(Spring Festival)*, which coincides with Budapest's famous Spring Festival. On hand are classical concerts, folkdance performances, and other events. The peak season for cultural events is from mid-June through mid-July, when the **Sopron Ünnepi Hetek** *(Sopron Festival Weeks)* brings music, dance, and theater performances and art exhibits to churches and venues around town.

PÉCS

390 km (242 mi) southeast of Sopron, 197 km (122 mi) southwest of Budapest.

The southwest's premier city and the fifth largest in Hungary, Pécs (pronounced *paytch*), is a vibrant, cultured, lovely city. Add to this that it is being made even prettier in the run-up to 2010, when it will be "European Capital of Culture" for one year. Pécs has gone through various incarnations in the course of its long history. The Franks called it Quinque Ecclesiae; the Slavs, Pet Cerkve; and the Habsburgs, Fünfkirchen; all three names mean "five churches." Today there are many more churches, plus two mosques and a handsome synagogue. In any language, however, Pécs could just as well be renamed City of Many Museums, for on one square block alone there are seven. A one-day pass covering most of them can be purchased at any participating museum for 1,600 HUF.

Belvárosi plébánia templom *(Inner City Parish Church).* Széchenyi tér is crowned by a delightful 16th-century former Turkish mosque. Dating from the Turkish occupation (1543–1686), the mosque is now a Catholic church. Despite the fierce religious war raging on its walls—Christian statuary and frescoes beneath Turkish arcades and *mihrabs* (prayer niches)—this church, also known as the Gazi Khassim Pasha Jammi, remains the largest and finest relic of Turkish architecture in Hungary. ⊠ *Széchenyi tér* 🕾 *72/321–976* 🖙 *Free* ⊙ *Mid-Apr.–mid-Oct., Mon.–Sat. 10–4, Sun. 11:30–4; mid-Oct.–mid-Apr., Mon.–Sat. 11–noon, Sun. 11:30–2.*

Cella Septichora. This UNESCO World Heritage site in front of Pécs Basilica marks one of Europe's major early Christian cemeteries, complete with crypts and wall paintings. Some of the subterranean crypts and chapels in the **Ókeresztény mauzóleum** *(Early Christian Mausoleum)* date to the 4th century AD; the wall murals (Adam and Eve, Daniel in the Lion's Den, the Resurrection) are in remarkable shape. ⊠ *Szent István tér* 🕾 *72/224–755* 🖙 *Both cemetery and mausoleum 1,500 HUF,; cemetery 1,200 HUF; mausoleum 400 HUF* ⊙ *May–Sept., Tues.–Sun. 10–6; Oct.–Apr., Tues.–Sun. 10–4.*

Fodor'sChoice **Csontváry Múzeum** *(Csontváry Museum).* Mihály Tivadar Csontváry ★ Kosztka (1853–1919) was a pharmacist who worked, as he put it, to "catch up with, let alone surpass, the great masters." An early expressionist and forerunner of surrealism, Csontváry's work even influenced Picasso. His paintings can be seen today almost exclusively here and in a room of the Hungarian National Gallery in Budapest.

The paintings in the five rooms of this museum are arranged in chronological order, to show Csontváry's progression from soulful portraits to seemingly conventional landscapes executed with decidedly unconventional colors to his 1904 *Temple of Zeus in Athens*—about which Csontváry said, "This is the first painting in which the canvas can no longer be seen." After a 1905 tryout in Budapest, Csontváry was ready for a 1907 exhibition in Paris, which turned out to be a huge critical

7

success. Not long after finishing his last great epic painting, *Mary at the Well in Nazareth* (1908), his ego got the best of him and he went a tad mad, too. The magnificent painting of his that Hungarians cherish most, and which has been interpreted as a symbolic self-portrait—*The Solitary Cedar*—is also here. ⊠ *Janus Pannonius utca 11, H-7621* ☎ *72/310–544* 🖃 *700 HUF* ☉ *Tues.–Sun. 10–6.*

★ **Jákovali Hászan Múzeum.** Just beyond the ancient city wall to the west, this 16th-century Turkish mosque is the only Ottoman-era religious building in Hungary with its original minaret and architecture intact. The museum itself has a few artifacts from the Turkish period, plus a few Iznik ceramics. ⊠ *Rákoczi út* ☎ *No phone* 🖃 *500 HUF* ☉ *Tues.– Sun. 10–6.*

Fodor's Choice
★ **Pécs Bazilika** *(Pécs Basilica).* One of Europe's most magnificent cathedrals was promoted from mere cathedral to basilica rank after Pope John Paul II's visit in 1991. At the beginning of the 19th century, Mihály Pollack directed the transformation of the exterior, changing it from baroque to neoclassical; its interior remained Gothic. Near the end of the 19th century, Bishop Nándor Dulánszky decided to restore the cathedral to its original, Árpád-period style—the result is a four-spired monument that has an utterly breathtaking interior frescoed in shimmering golds, silvers, and blues. ⊠ *Szent István tér, H-7621* 🖃 *700 HUF; 2,500 HUF for English-language tour* ☉ *Apr.–Oct., weekdays 9–5, Sat. 9–2, Sun. 1–5; Nov.–Mar., Mon.–Sat. 10–4, Sat. 10–1, Sun. 1–4.*

Vasarely Múzeum *(Vasarely Museum).* The pioneer of Op Art (who left Hungary as a child and spent the rest of his life in Paris) was born Győző Vásárhelyi in 1908 in this house, which has been turned into a museum full of funhouse artistry. The first hall is a corridor of visual tricks devised by his disciples, at the end of which hangs a hypnotic canvas of shifting cubes by Jean-Pierre Yvaral. Upstairs, the illusions grow profound: a zebra gallops by while chess pieces and blood cells seem to come at you. ⊠ *Káptalan utca 3* ☎ *72/514–040* 🖃 *700 HUF* ☉ *Tues.–Sun. 10–6.*

Zsolnay Fountain. At the foot of Széchenyi tér, the grand sloping monumental thoroughfare that is the pride of the city, stands this dainty, petite Art Nouveau majolica temple. The fountain is guarded by shiny ox-head gargoyles made of green eosin porcelain that gush pure drinking water piped into Pécs via Roman aqueducts. It was built in 1912 by the famous Zsolnay family, who developed their unique porcelain art here in Pécs.

★ **Zsolnay Múzeum** *(Zsolnay Museum).* This museum occupies the upper floor of the oldest surviving building in Pécs (1324). A stroll through the rooms is a merry show-and-tell waltz through a revolution in pottery that started in 1851, when Miklós Zsolnay, a local merchant, bought the site of an old kiln and set up a stoneware factory for his son Ignác to run. Ignác's brother, Vilmos, a shopkeeper with an artistic bent, bought the factory from him in 1863, imported experts from Germany, and, with the help of a Pécs pharmacist for chemical-glaze experiments and his daughters for hand-painting, created the distinctive namesake porcelain. ⊠ *Káptalan utca 4* ☎*72/514–040* 🖃*600 HUF* ◷ *Tues.–Sun. 10–6.*

WHERE TO EAT & STAY

$–$$ ✕**All'Elefante Ristorante & Pizzeria.** This bustling Italian pizzeria opens onto a main square in downtown Pécs. The menu includes some 20 kinds of pizza, many pastas, and a wide range of salads, as well as more traditional meat, poultry, and fish dishes. ⊠ *Jókai tér 6* ☎*72/216–055 or 72/532–189* ☰*MC, V.*

$–$$ ✕**Aranykacsa.** The Golden Duck has long been a favorite with duck-loving locals and visitors alike. And yet this elegant restaurant—which has an intimate, pub-like room with dark hues; a more formal, light-hued room decorated with fine Zsolnay porcelain; and courtyard seating, too—offers not just fare such as roast duck with dried prunes and almonds in red-wine sauce, but also wild game and more traditional Hungarian cuisine. ⊠ *Teréz utca 4* ☎*72/211–018* ☰*AE, MC, V.*

$ ⛫**Hotel Millennium Szálló.** Renowned Hungarian architect Sándor Dévényi designed this suburban castle on Kálvária hill, amidst a nature reserve and just outside the Old City wall. The rooms are pleasantly low-key, and four of them look out onto the four spires of the Pécs Basilica. Pros: Unique architecture, peaceful setting with good city views, pool. Cons: Five-minute walk to downtown, few restaurants nearby, relatively few amenities and services. ⊠ *Kálvária utca 58, H-7625* ☎*72/512–222* 📠*72/512–223* ⊕*www.hotelmillennium.hu* ⇆*25 rooms* ⚙*In-room: refrigerator, Wi-Fi. In-hotel: restaurant, pool, laundry service, parking (no fee), no-smoking rooms, some pets allowed, public Wi-Fi* ☰*AE, DC, MC, V* ⋈*BP.*

★

¢–$ ⛫**Hotel Palatinus.** Art Nouveau is found throughout Hungary, but for some pure Art Deco, check out this hotel in downtown Pécs. The grand public areas—lobby, sweeping staircases, restaurant, and ballroom—are all stunning. Rooms are somewhat disappointing after the public areas but are well equipped; most are superiors—around €20 more than the (cramped) standards, but certainly more spacious. Since the ballroom can get noisy during weddings (generally on Saturdays from May through July), request a room on an upper floor. Pros: Right in the center, grand historic building, reasonable rates, popular buffet breakfast on Sundays. Cons: On touristy, sometimes noisy shopping street; most rooms small, lower floors susceptible to noise from ballroom. ⊠ *Király utca 5, H-7621* ☎*72/889–400* 📠*72/889–438* ⊕*www.danubiusgroup.com/palatinus* ⇆*88 rooms, 6 suites* ⚙*In-room: refrigerator, Wi-Fi. In-hotel: 2 restaurants, business center, parking (fee), public Wi-Fi, public Internet* ☰*AE, DC, MC, V* ⋈*BP.*

SHOPPING

Zsolnay Márkabolt. The best place in Hungary to buy Zsolnay porcelain is here in Pécs. At the Zsolnay factory's own outlet, the company offers guaranteed authenticity and the best prices on the full spectrum of pieces—from tea sets profusely painted with colorful, gold-winged butterflies to white-and-night-blue dinner services. ⊠ *Jókai tér 2* ☎*72/310–220.*

TRANSDANUBIA ESSENTIALS

BY BUS

Buses operated by Volanbusz run from Budapest's Népliget station to both Sopron and Pécs several times daily, but trains, in particular Inter-City (IC) service, are faster and more comfortable.

BY CAR

Traveling around Transdanubia is easy by car, allowing you to get between Sopron and Pécs via a lovely rural drive along any of several local routes that take you around Lake Balaton. By car from Budapest, Sopron is around 220 km (138 mi), via the M1 (E75) motorway and then a smaller road, Route 85 and, in the last stretch, Route 84. Pécs and Budapest are directly connected by Route 6, which continues on to the Croatian border.

BY TRAIN

There are good rail connections from Budapest to Sopron and Pécs; the trip—by InterCity (IC) trains, which run several times daily—takes 2½ hours to Sopron, 3 hours to Pécs. Trains to Sopron and Fertőd (home of the Eszterházy Palace) go north through Győr. There are direct connections between Vienna and Sopron. The trip from Sopron to Pécs is long—about 1½ hours from Sopron to Szombathely, where you transfer to the train to Pécs, which takes nearly 4½ hours.

VISITOR INFORMATION

Tourinform offices have loads of information and brochures on Sopron, Pécs, and the surrounding areas. They can also help arrange excursions outside the cities. IBUSZ can help book private rooms in Pécs.

Information IBUSZ (⊠ *Király utca 11, Pécs* ☏ *72/212–157*). **Tourinform Pécs** (⊠ *Széchenyi tér 9, Pécs* ☏ *72/213–315*). **Tourinform Sopron** (⊠ *Liszt Ferenc utca 1, inside the Liszt Ferenc Cultural Center, by Széchenyi tér, Sopron* ☏ *99/517–560*).

EASTERN HUNGARY

One quick look at a map is all that's needed to define eastern Hungary: everything east of the southward-flowing Danube. Although the region is largely made up of—and stereotypically associated with—its sweeping Great Plain, Eastern Hungary also has a hilly and forested stretch up north punctuated by some splendid wine country, bordering Slovakia. Hungarians think of these two major geographic subregions differently.

Hungary's Great Plain—the Nagyalföld—stretches south and east from Budapest to the borders of Croatia and Serbia and as far east as Ukraine and Romania. It covers 51,800 square km (20,000 square mi) and is what many think of as the typical Hungarian landscape. Almost completely flat, it is the home of shepherds and their flocks and, above all, of splendid horses and the csikósok, their riders. The plain's sprawling villages consist mostly of one-story houses, though there are many large farms. Divided into two almost equal parts by the Tisza River, the plain also contains some of Hungary's most historic cities, and although you won't notice during a visit to a larger town like Debrecen, it remains the least developed area of Hungary.

As you near the region, you will soon find yourself driving in a straight line coming from Budapest through the dream landscape of the Hortobágy, a *puszta*, or prairie, marked by vast stretches of dusty grassland interrupted only by stands of trees and distant thatch-roof *tanyák* (ranches). The only detectable movement here comes from the herds of *racka* sheep or cattle drifting lazily across the horizon, guided by shepherds and their trusty *puli* herd dogs. Covering more than 250,000 acres, the Hortobágy became the first of Hungary's four national parks, in 1973.

As for the northern stretch of the east, it runs from the Danube Bend, north of Budapest, along the frontier with Slovakia as far west as Sátoraljaújhely. With its southern edge bordering the Great Plain, it is marked by thickly wooded hills whose highest peaks reach 3,000 feet. Grottoes and caves abound, as well as thermal baths. Historically, the valleys of northern Hungary have always been of considerable strategic importance, as they provided the only access to the Carpathian Mountains. The city of Eger, renowned as one of the historic guardians of these routes, retains its splendor, with many ruins dotting the surrounding hilltops. Last but not least, this is one of the great wine-growing districts of Hungary, with the Eger region contributing the "Magyar nectar" and Tokaj producing the "wine of kings."

Numbers in the margin correspond to numbers on the Eastern Hungary map.

EGER

80 km (50 mi) east of Budapest.

Surrounded by vineyards and with more than 175 of Hungary's historic monuments—a figure surpassed only by Budapest and Sopron—the picture-book baroque city of Eger is ripe for exploration. The city of 60,000, which lies in a fertile valley between the Mátra Mountains and their eastern neighbor, the Bükk Range, has borne witness to much history, heartbreak, and glory. It was settled quite early in the Hungarian conquest of the land, and it was one of five bishoprics created by King Stephen I when he Christianized the country almost a millennium ago.

In 1552 the city was attacked by the Turks, but the commander, István Dobó, and fewer than 2,000 men and women held out for 38 days against 80,000 Turkish soldiers and drove them away. One of Hungary's great legends tells of the women of Eger pouring hot pitch onto the heads of the Turks as they attempted to scale the castle walls. Despite such heroism, Eger fell to the Turks in 1596 and became a key northern outpost of Muslim power until its reconquest in 1687.

Today, restored baroque and rococo buildings line Eger's cobblestone streets, making for excellent strolling and sightseeing. Dobó István utca, which runs right under the castle walls, is not to be missed. The spacious, lovely city park and the adjacent outdoor swimming-and-spa complex make soaking aesthetically as well as physically soothing. Wherever you wander, make a point of peeking into open courtyards, where you may happen upon otherwise hidden architectural gems.

★ The grand, neoclassical **Bazilika**, the second-largest cathedral in Hungary, was built in the center of town early in the 19th century. It is approached by a stunning stairway flanked by statues of Sts. Stephen, László, Peter, and Paul—the work of Italian sculptor Marco Casagrande, who also carved 22 biblical reliefs inside and outside the building. From mid-May through mid-October, organ recitals are held Monday through Saturday at 11:30 AM and Sunday at 12:45 PM. It's best to visit when no masses are taking place—from 9 until 6. ⊠ *Eszterházy tér* ☎ *36/515-725* 💾 *500 HUF for organ recitals, free at other times* ⊙ *Daily 8–8.*

Eger's rococo **Cistercia templom** (*Cistercian Church*) was built during the first half of the 18th century. A splendid statue of St. Francis Borgia kneeling beneath Christ on the cross dominates the main altar, which dates to 1770. ✉*Széchenyi utca 15* 📞*36/511–240* 🎫*Free* ☉*Mass weekdays at 7:15 and 8* AM, *Sun. at 8 and 10* AM *and 7* PM.

Downtown, picturesque **Dobó tér** is a square marked by two intensely animated statues produced in the early 20th century by a father and son: *Dobó the Defender* is by Alajos Stróbl, and the sculpture of a Magyar battling two Turks is by Stróbl's son, Zsigmond Kisfaludi-Stróbl.

Dobó tér's famous statues flank the pale-pink **Minorita templom** (*Minorite Church* 📞*36/516–613* ☉*Daily 10–6*), which with its twin spires and finely carved pulpit, pews, and organ loft is considered one of the finest baroque churches in Central Europe. You can catch an organ recital (350 HUF) here each Thursday at 7 PM from mid-May to mid-September.

☾ **Eger Vár** *(Eger Castle)* was built after the devastating Tatar invasion
Fodor's Choice of 1241–42. When Béla IV returned from exile in Italy, he ordered
★ the erection of mighty fortresses like those he had seen in the West. Within the castle walls an imposing Romanesque cathedral was built and later, during the 15th century, rebuilt in Gothic style; today only its foundations remain. Nearby are catacombs built in the second half of the 16th century by Italian engineers. By racing back and forth through this labyrinth of underground tunnels and appearing at various ends of the castle, the hundreds of defenders tricked the attacking Turks into thinking there were thousands of them. The Gothic-style **Püspök Ház** (Bishop's House) contains the castle history museum and, in the cellar, a numismatics museum. Also here are an art gallery displaying Italian and Dutch Renaissance works; a prison exhibit; and a wax museum, depicting characters from the Hungarian historical novel *Eclipse of the Crescent Moon*, about Hungary's expulsion of the Turks. ✉*Dózsa György tér, H-3300* 📞*36/312–744* 🌐*www.egrivar.hu* 🎫*Castle with castle history museum, art gallery, and prison exhibit 1,200 HUF; numismatics museum 300 HUF; wax museum 350 HUF; castle grounds only 500 HUF* ☉*Castle grounds Apr.–Oct., daily 6* AM*–8* PM; *Nov.–Mar., daily 6–5. Museums Apr.–Sept., Tues.– Sun. 9–5; Oct.–Mar., Tues.–Sun. 9–3. Prison exhibit and catacombs Apr.–Sept., Tues.–Sun. 9–5 (catacombs remain open on Mon.). Wax museum daily 9–6.*

☾ The massive baroque building opposite the basilica is a former lyceum, now the **Eszterházy Károly főiskola** *(Károly Eszterházy Teachers College).* The handsome library on the second floor has a fine trompe-l'oeil ceiling fresco that provides an intoxicating illusion of depth. The fifth floor houses an observatory, now an astronomical museum: here the noonday sun, shining through a tiny aperture, makes a palm-size silvery spot on the meridian line on the marble floor. Climb higher to the grand finale, a "Specula Periscope," or Camera Obscura, on the 10th floor: in a darkened room, a man manipulates three rods of a periscope—in operation since 1776—to project panoramic views of Eger onto a round table. Children squeal with delight as real people and cars hurry and scurry across the table like hyperactive Legos. Tickets can be purchased at the porter's office as you enter. ✉*Eszterházy tér 1*

☎36/520–400 📚*Library 700 HUF, astronomical museum and camera obscura 700 HUF* ⊙*Apr.–Sept., Tues.–Sun. 9:30–3; Oct.–Mar., weekends 9:30–1:30.*

A bridge over the Eger stream leads to an early-17th-century Turkish **minaret**, from the top of which Muslims were called to prayer. After the Turks were driven out of Hungary in the late 1600s, an effort was made to topple the minaret using 400 oxen. The venture failed, and it became Europe's northernmost surviving Turkish structure. Climb to the top for a great view. ✉*Knézich K. utca* ☎36/410–233 or 70/202–4353 📚*200 HUF* ⊙*Apr.–Oct., daily 10–6.*

The **Nagypréposti palota** *(Provost's House)* is a small rococo palace still considered one of Hungary's finest mansions. It serves as the European headquarters of the International Committee of Historic Towns (ICOMOS), but is not open to the public. ✉*Kossuth Lajos utca 4.*

The lovely, dove-gray 18th-century **Rác templom** *(Serbian Orthodox Church)* contains more than 100 icon paintings on wood that look as though they were fashioned from gold and marble. The church occupies a hilltop north of the city center. ✉*Vitkovits utca 30* ☎36/320–129 📚*300 HUF* ⊙*Tues.–Sun. 10–4.*

Eger wine is renowned beyond Hungary. The best-known—but not necessarily the best—variety is *Egri Bikavér* (Bull's Blood of Eger), a full-bodied red wine. Other outstanding vintages are the Medoc Noir, a dark red dessert wine; Leányka, a delightful dry white; and the sweeter white Muskotály. The place to sample them is the **Szépasszony-völgy** *(Lovely Lady Valley)*, a vineyard area a 30-minute walk southwest of the town center; ask **Tourinform** for directions or for information on a tourist bus that can also get you there. More than 200 small wine cellars stand open and inviting in warm weather, and some are open in winter, too. Wines are tapped from the barrel into your glass by the vintners themselves at modest cost (but do inquire politely how much before imbibing). You may also be given a tour of the cellar.

OFF THE BEATEN PATH

Tokaj. Some 120 km (75 mi) east of Eger and 190 km (125 mi) northeast of Budapest, this charming but out-of-the-way village is the center of Hungary's most famous wine region. It is home to the legendary Aszú, a dessert wine made in part from grapes allowed to shrivel on the vine. Aszú is produced to varying degrees of sweetness, based on how many bushels of sweet paste from the shriveled grapes are mixed into regular Tokaj wine; the scale goes from two *puttonyos* (bushels) to nectar-rich six puttonyos. The region's famed wines, dubbed (allegedly by Louis XV) the "wine of kings and king of wines," are typically golden yellow with slightly brownish tints. They've been admired outside of Hungary since Polish merchants first became hooked in the Middle Ages. Other countries have tried with little success to produce the wine from Tokaj grapes. The surrounding countryside is beautiful, especially in October, when the grapes hang from the vines in thick clusters. Before or after descending into the wine cellars for some epic tasting, be sure to pause while the bells toll at the lovely baroque Roman Catholic church (1770) on the main square and wend your way along some of the narrow side streets winding up into the vineyard-covered hills. Tokaj's most famous wine cellar, the more-than-500-year-old **Rákóczi-pince** *(Rákóczi Cellar)* (⊠ *Kossuth tér 15* ☎ *47/352–408* ⊘ *Mid-Mar.–early Oct., daily 11– 7, sometimes later; early Oct.–mid-Mar., by reservation only)*, is also Europe's largest, comprising some 1½ km (1 mi) of branching tunnels extending into the hills (today, about 1,312 feet are still in use). Standard tours (available in English), which include tastings of six different wines, are usually given every hour on the hour (but best to confirm 24 hours in advance) and cost 2,450 HUF. When to visit? There's wine in the cellars any time of year, but Tokaj's best festival is naturally the annual **Szüreti Napok** *(Harvest Days)* on the first weekend of October, celebrating the autumn grape harvest with a parade, a street ball, folk-art markets, and a plethora of wine tastings from the local vintners' stands erected on and around the main square.

WHERE TO EAT & STAY

$–$$$ ✕**Fehér Szarvas.** The name of this homey rustic cellar, a longtime Eger
★ dining landmark, means "white stag," and game is the uncontested specialty. Favorites include venison fillet with goose liver and herb butter, and rosemary-spiced mutton with green-pepper sauce. The many antlers, skulls, skins, and mounted birds hanging from rafters and walls—not to mention the two little stuffed goats by the entrance—make the inn look like Archduke Franz Ferdinand's trophy room. ⊠ *Klapka György utca 8* ☎ *36/411–129* ▤ *AE, DC, MC, V.*

$–$$$ ✕**HBH Bajor Sörház.** For substantial Hungarian (and Bavarian) fare, it's impossible to beat another longtime Eger landmark—the popular HBH Bavarian Beer Tavern, which has a great location on Dobó tér. The cuisine ranges from traditional Hungarian favorites such as veal paprikás to Bavarian-style pork knuckle. Any of these will go down smoothly with a glass of Bull's Blood—or perhaps a Munich Hofbräuhaus, the beer that gives the restaurant its initials. ⊠ *Bajcsy Zsilinszky utca 19, at Dobó tér* ☎ *36/515–516* ▤ *AE, MC, V.*

$ ⊡**Imola Udvarház.** Apartments at the most upmarket small hotel in
★ Eger are pricey for this town, but the location—practically on the steps to the castle—facilities, and pleasant, spacious self-catering quarters justify the rate. The oak- and wicker-furnished apartments are spotless yet homey; the smaller ones have balconies, some with nice views of the main square. The hotel restaurant offers a hundred different wines. Pros: Close to the castle, excellent restaurant, sparkling and modern. Cons: apartments a bit spare, limited Internet access, a five-minute walk to the main square. ⊠ *Dózsa György tér 4, H-3300* ☎ *36/516– 180* ⊕ *www.imolanet.hu* ⤳ *6 apartments* ⚲ *In-room: kitchen, Ethernet. In-hotel: restaurant, bar, parking (fee), no elevator* ▤ *AE, DC, MC, V* ⋈*EP.*

$ ⊡**Hotel Senator Ház.** This little inn, a lovely 18th-century town house,
Fodor's Choice sits on Eger's main square. Whimsical paintings by Budapest artist
★ András Győrffy hang in all the guest rooms—which are decidedly more modern than the small, historical-bric-a-brac-filled lobby might have you believe—and are tastefully decorated in pale tans and whites. Rooms 14 and 15 have the nicest views of the main square. Pros: Right on the main square, cozy and historic, good rates, friendly service.

7

Cons: Modern rooms clash slightly with historic atmosphere, no Internet access. ✉ *Dobó tér 11, H-3300* ☎*36/320–466* 📠*36/411–711* ⊕*www.senatorhaz.hu* ☎*11 rooms* ♿*In-room: refrigerator. In-hotel: restaurant, parking (no fee), no elevator* ⊟*MC, V* 🍽*BP.*

NIGHTLIFE & THE ARTS

From June to mid-September live bands sometimes play folk music for free out on Kis Dobó tér, part of Eger's main square. The **Agria Nyári Játékok** *(Agria Summer Festival)*, which runs from July to early September in various locations, includes folk-dance and theater performances as well as concerts of everything from Renaissance music to jazz to laser karaoke. In early September, the three- to four-day **Szüreti Napok Egerben** *(Eger Harvest Festival)* celebrates the grape harvest with a traditional harvest parade through the town center, wine tastings on the main squares, appearances by the crowned Wine Queen, and an outdoor Harvest Ball on Dobó tér.

DEBRECEN

123 km (77 mi) east of Eger, 226 km (140 mi) east of Budapest.

With a population of just over 200,000, Debrecen is Hungary's second-largest city. Though it has much less clout than Budapest, Debrecen was Hungary's capital twice. In 1849 it was here that Lajos Kossuth declared Hungarian independence from the Habsburgs; in 1944 the Red Army liberated Debrecen from the Nazis and made the city the provisional capital until Budapest was taken.

Debrecen was already a sizable village by the end of the 12th century, and by the 14th century it was an important market town. It takes its name from a Slavonic term for "good earth," and, indeed, much of the country's wheat, produce, meat, and poultry has been produced in this area for centuries. The Puszta starts here at the city's western edge, and its key attraction, Hortobágy, is just under 40 km (25 mi) beyond.

Today Debrecen is a vibrant, friendly city, with thousands attending its esteemed universities. There's only one tram line (number 1), but it runs frequently in a nearly straight line from the train station along downtown's main thoroughfare—the broad, and partly pedestrian, Piac utca—and out to the Nagyerdő (Great Forest), a giant city park. All in all, Debrecen is a good place to spend a day before heading out to the puszta—or, as in the case of many travelers, on the way to or from a journey farther east to Transylvania.

The **Déri Múzeum** *(Déri Museum)* was founded in 1930 to house the art and antiquities of a wealthy Hungarian silk manufacturer living in Vienna. Its two floors are devoted to local history, archaeology, and weapons as well as to Egyptian, Greek, Roman, Etruscan, and Far Eastern art. On the top floor are Hungarian and foreign fine art from the 15th to the 20th century, including the striking (and huge) *Ecce Homo* by the famous 19th-century Hungarian artist Mihály Munkácsy. In front of the museum are allegorical bronze statues by Ferenc Medgyessy, grand prize winner at the 1937 Paris World Exhibition. ✉*Déri tér 1* ☎*52/417–561* 🎫*800 HUF* 🕐*Apr.–Oct., Tues.–Sun. 10–6; Nov.–Mar., Tues.–Sun. 10–4.*

At the corner of Széchenyi utca, the **Kistemplom** *(Small Church)* —Debrecen's oldest surviving church, which was built in 1720—looks like a rococo chess-piece castle on the outside. The three-aisle baroque interior, with a pleasant wood aroma, is well worth a look. This Calvinist venue is known to locals as the *csonka templom* (truncated church), because its onion dome blew down in a gale in 1907. ✉*Révész tér 2* ☎*52/342–872* 🕐*Tues.–Sat. 10–6, Sun. 8:30–11* AM.

Debrecen's one tram line runs out to the **Nagyerdő** *(Great Forest),* a huge city park with a zoo, a sports stadium, swimming pools, an artificial rowing lake, a thermal-spa-cum-luxury-hotel (the Termál Hotel Debrecen), an amusement park, restaurants, and an open-air theater. Also here is the photogenic Kossuth Lajos University, its handsome neo-baroque facade fronted by a large pool and fountain around which six bronze nudes pose in the sun; it would be a shame to visit Debrecen and not see this. The university is one of the few in Central Europe with a real campus.

Fodor'sChoice Because the Oratory in the Reformed College was too small for a large
★ crowd, Lajos Kossuth reread his declaration of independence by popular demand to a cheering public in 1849 in the twin-turreted, orange-yellow **Nagytemplom** *(Great Church).* The most famous building in Debrecen, the Great Church opened its doors in 1821 after more than a decade of construction on the design of Mihály Pécsi; it was built on the site of a 14th-century church that burned down in 1802. As befits Calvinism, the church is not teeming with decoration—but with all the baroque architecture throughout Hungary, you may welcome the contrast. The church's massive organ was made in Vienna in 1838. ✉*Kálvin tér 4, H-4025* ☎*52/412–694* 🎫*300 HUF* 🕐*Jan.–Mar., Mon.–Sat. 10–noon, Sun. 11–1; Apr.–Oct., weekdays 9–4, Sat. 9–1, Sun. after 10* AM *worship–4; Nov. and Dec., Mon.–Sat. 10–noon, Sun. after 10* AM *worship–1.*

Debrecen's main artery, **Piac utca** *(Market Street),* is a wide, long boulevard that runs from the Great Forest to the railroad station. Its history goes back to the Middle Ages, when handfuls of outdoor vegetable and meat markets lined the road here. However, its architectural face began to take shape only in the first decades of the 19th century, under the impact of classicism. The majority of the existing buildings date from the beginning of 20th century, and you'll see several examples of the influence of Secessionism and eclecticism.

For almost 500 years Debrecen has been the stronghold of Hungarian Protestantism—its residents have called it "the Calvinist Rome." Calvinism began to replace Roman Catholicism here in 1536, and two years later the **Református Kollégium** *(Reformed College)* was founded on what is now Kálvin tér (Calvin Square). Early in the 19th century the college's medieval building was replaced by a pillared structure. Inside, the main staircase is lined with frescoes of student life and significant moments in the college's history (all painted during the 1930s). At the

CLOSE UP

A Legendary Little Tree

A weedy-looking but flowering, willow-like little tree stands by a low, wrought-iron fence behind the left rear corner of Debrecen's Nagytemplom. You'd be forgiven for passing this leafy weakling by, but know that you'd be passing by one of this famously Protestant city's most treasured historic relics. According to local tradition, sometime back in the 18th century a Calvinist minister named Bálint got into a scrap at this site over religion with a Catholic priest called Ambrosius. All riled up, the latter broke a branch off a nearby tree, stuck it into the ground, and declared, "Something will come of your religion only when this grows into a tree!" That branch did grow into a tree. Unlike mostly Catholic Hungary, Calvinism flowered in Debrecen, which—along with Transylvania to the east—became a stronghold of Hungary's version of this doctrine. According to locals, during Hungary's October 1956 revolution a Russian tank ran right over this legendary little tree, but the tree survived.

top of the stairs is the **Oratory,** which has twice been the setting for provisional parliaments, in 1849 and 1944. Also worth seeing are the college's **library,** which rotates exhibitions of illuminated manuscripts and rare Bibles, and two **museums.** The Student History Museum commemorates Hungarian intellectuals who studied at the college, and the Religious History Museum showcases jewelry, embroidered clothes, and painted furniture. ⊠ *Kálvin tér 16* ☎ *52/414–744 Ext. 1923* 🖃 *500 HUF* ⊘ *Tues.–Sat. 10–4, Sun. 10–1.*

OFF THE BEATEN PATH

Hortobágy National Park. An easy drive or bus ride 39 km (24 mi) west of Debrecen (187 km [116 mi] east of Budapest) lies the village of Hortobágy, the most famous settlement on the puszta and the main gateway to Hortobágy National Park. At 196,800 acres, the park encompasses the largest continuous grassland in Europe. A major part of the area is formed by natural habitats, meadows, and marshes. Natural wetlands occupy one-third of the park, although artificial wetlands, called fishponds, were created on 14,400 acres in the last century on the worst-quality grazing lands and former marshes. These fishponds are vital to the 342 types of birds registered in Hortobágy National Park, of which 152 exclusively nest there. The park has three different types of terrain: forest, marshland, and grassland. Although you can wander around most of the park for free, three official trails, one in each type of terrain, can be accessed for 900 HUF. Trail tickets and general information are available at the **Hortobágyi Nemzeti Park Látogató és Oktató Központ** *(National Park Visitors and Educational Center)* (⊠ *Petőfi tér 13, Hortobágy* ☎ *52/589–321* ⊕ *www.hnp.hu*), which also has a natural history exhibit and arts and crafts demonstrations.

While you're here, take a stroll through Hortobágy village. Built in 1699, the **Hortobágyi Csárda** *(Hortobágy Inn)* (⊠ *Petőfi tér 2* ☎ *52/589–339* ⊘ *Closed Oct.–mid-Feb.*) is a traditional white stone building that has been a regional institution for most of the last three centuries. Its restaurant is very popular. The **Pásztormúzeum** *(Shepherd Museum)*

(⊠ *Petőfi tér 1* ☏ *52/369–040* ⬛ *500 HUF* ☉ *May–Sept., daily 9–6; Oct. and Apr., daily 10–4; mid-Mar. and Nov., daily 10–2; Dec.–mid-Mar., by appointment only*) exhibits traditional costumes and tools, such as the shepherds' heavy embroidered cloaks and carved sticks. Crossing the Hortobágy River is the puszta's most famous symbol: the curving, white-stone **Kilenc-lyukú híd** *(Nine-Hole Bridge)*. It was built in the early 19th century and is the longest stone bridge in Hungary. Traveling from Debrecen, you'll reach the village of Hortobágy just before you cross the Hortobágy River. There's no train service, but there are around seven buses daily from Debrecen; it's a comfortable, 45-minute ride.

WHERE TO EAT & STAY

$–$$
★
✗ Serpince a Flaskához. Once you've managed to find this very popular pub just yards from Piac utca—-there's only a menu by the door, no sign—you will find yourself in a rustic cellar with vaulted ceilings that's tastefully decorated in an unpretentious manner befitting the Great Plains. For a light meal, try a *palócleves,* a thick, piquantly sourish meat-and-potatoes soup with tarragon and caraway. For something heavier, perhaps the *birka* (lamb) paprikás is the way to go. ⊠ *Miklós utca 4* ☏ *52/414–582* ▭ *AE, DC, MC, V.*

¢–$
★
⊡ Cívis Grand Hotel Aranybika. Art Nouveau classic on the outside, inside the Hotel Golden Bull is a bit of a patchwork quilt. Designed by Hungary's first Olympic champion, Alfréd Hajós, it is the oldest hotel in Hungary (the original was built in the 17th century). Parts of the lobby, like the neo-baroque doorway to the cocktail bar, are gorgeous, as is the airy and elegant restaurant. Brown and beige renovations left over from the 1970s spoil the effect a bit. Pros: Right in the city center, historic architecture, large-hotel amenities and services. Cons: A bit frayed on the inside, relatively high rates, drab rooms. ⊠ *Piac utca 11–15, H-4025* ☏ *52/508–600* ▤ *52/421–834* ⊕ *www.civishotels.hu* ⇔ *201 rooms, 4 suites* ⚲ *In-room: no a/c (some), refrigerator (some), Wi-Fi. In-hotel: restaurant, pool, gym, spa, parking (fee), no-smoking rooms, public Wi-Fi, public Internet* ⦿| *BP* ▭ *AE, DC, MC, V.*

¢
★
⊡ Korona Panzió. This cheery little inn is just down the street from the Great Church. The immaculate rooms are a great value and have contemporary furnishings and terraces. Breakfast costs an extra 1,000 HUF. Pros: Good rates, cozy, no-smoking rooms. Cons: Not quite in the city center or near restaurants, few amenities and services, breakfast extra. ⊠ *Péterfia utca 54, H-4026* ☏ *52/535–260* ▤ *52/535–261* ⊕ *www.hotels.hu/koronapanzio1* ⇔ *16 rooms, 1 suite* ⚲ *In-room: no a/c, VCR, Ethernet, Wi-Fi (some). In-hotel: public Internet, no-smoking rooms* ⦿| *EP* ▭ *No credit cards.*

NIGHTLIFE & THE ARTS

Debrecen Tavaszi Fesztivál *(Debrecen Spring Festival)*, the city's biggest annual event, runs from around mid-March at various venues, packing in some three weeks of concerts, dance, and theater performances, as well as special art exhibits. Jazz fans can hear local ensembles as well as groups from around Hungary and abroad during the **Debreceni Jazz Napok** *(Debrecen Jazz Days)* around mid-September. One of the city's

7

favorite occasions is the **Debreceni Virágkarnevál** *(Flower Carnival)* on St. Stephen's Day (August 20), Hungary's national holiday, when a festive parade of flower-encrusted floats and carriages makes its way down Piac utca along the tram line all the way to the Nagyerdő.

KECSKEMÉT

183 km (114 mi) southwest of Debrecen, 85 km (53 mi) southeast of Budapest.

With a name roughly translating as "Goat Walk," this sprawling town smack in the middle of the country—closer to Budapest than the two larger towns on the Great Plain, Debrecen and Szeged—never fails to surprise first-time visitors with its elegant landmark buildings and interesting museums. Its splendid main square, Szabadság tér (Liberty Square), is marred only by two faceless concrete-block buildings, one of which houses the city's McDonald's. Home of the elite Kodály Institute, where famous composer and pedagogue Zoltán Kodály's methods are taught, the city also maintains an active cultural life. The Kecskemét area, fruit center of the Great Plain, produces *barack pálinka*, a smooth yet tangy apricot brandy that can warm the heart and blur the mind in just one shot.

A short drive from town takes you into Bugac puszta, the expansive sandy grasslands of Kiskunság National Park, the smaller of the two protected areas (the other is Hortobágy National Park) of the Great Plain. You can watch a traditional horse show, do some riding, or immerse yourself in the experience by spending a night or two at one of the inns out on the prairie.

Fodor's Choice   Kecskemét's most famous building is the **Cifrapalota** *(Ornamental Pal-
★   ace)*, a unique and remarkable Hungarian-style Art Nouveau build-ing built in 1902. A three-story cream-colored structure studded with folksy lilac, blue, red, and yellow Zsolnay majolica flowers and hearts, it stands on Liberty Square's corner like a cheerful cream pastry. Once a residential building, it now houses the **Kecskeméti képtár** (Kecske-mét Gallery), with an excellent display of artwork by Hungarian fine artists as well as occasional international exhibits. ⊠ *Rákóczi út 1, H-6000* ☎*76/480–776* ☄*320 HUF Tues.–Sat., free on Sun.* ☉ *Tues.– Sun. 10–5.*

★   The **Magyar Fotográfia Múzeum** *(Hungarian Photography Museum)* is one of the few museums in Hungary dedicated to photography. With a growing collection of more than 500,000 photos, documents, and pieces of equipment, it is the country's most important photography center. ⊠ *Katona József tér 12* ☎*76/483–221 or 76/508–258* ⊕*www. photomuzeum.hu* ☄*400 HUF* ☉ *Wed.–Sun. 10–5.*

The city's oldest church is the **Szent Miklós templom** *(Church of St. Nicho-las)*, known also as the Barátság templom (Friendship Church) because of St. Nick's role as the saint of friendship. Built in Gothic style in either the 13th or 15th century (a subject of debate), it was rebuilt in baroque style during the 18th century. Note the interior's apricot hues, which are typical of many a Kecskemét edifice. ✉ *Kossuth tér 5* ⊙ *Mon.–Sat. 7:30–6, Sun. 7:30–6:30.*

ⓒ The one-of-a-kind **Szórakoténusz Játékmúzeum és Műhely** *(Szórakoténusz Toy Museum and Workshop)* chronicles the history of Hungarian toys with almost 18,000 archaeological pieces such as stone figures and clay figurines from medieval guilds. In the workshop, artisans create traditional toys and invite you to try to make them yourself. ✉ *Gáspár András utca 11* ☎ *76/481–469* 💰 *450 HUF* ⊙ *Tues.–Sun. 10–12:30; toy workshop alternate Sat. 10–noon and 2:30–5, alternate Sun. 10–noon.*

★ Built between 1892 and 1896 by Ödön Lechner in the Hungarian Art Nouveau style that he created, the **Városház** *(Town Hall)* is one of its finest examples. Window frames are arched here, pointed there, and the roof, peppered with tiny copper- and gold-color tiles, looks as if it has been rained on by pennies from heaven. In typical Lechner style, the outlines of the central facade make a curving line to a pointed top. ✉ *Kossuth tér 1* ☎ *76/513–513 Ext. 2263.*

**OFF THE
BEATEN
PATH**

Bugac puszta *(Bugac prairie).* Declared a bioreserve by UNESCO for its unique flora and fauna, this is the central and most-visited section of the 127,200-acre Kiskunsági Nemzeti Park (Kiskunság National Park)—the smaller sister of Hortobágy National Park (to the northeast). This sandy, flat grassland 46 km (29 mi) south of Kecskemét has provided Hungarian poets and artists with inexhaustible material over the centuries. Although it may seem uniform to the casual eye, the Bugac's fragile ecosystem is the most varied of the entire park; its primeval juniper trees are the area's most protected and treasured flora. Today Bugac continues to inspire visitors for both its nature and equestrian traditions. The park's half-hour traditional horse show takes place twice daily; tickets, sold by Bugac Tours at the park entrance, also cover the entrance to the **Pásztor Museum** (Shepherd Museum), which has exhibits about traditional life on the prairie. Bugac Tours also has maps of various marked trails, as does the Kiskunság National Park Management Center in Kecskemét. Areas of the park outside of Bugac can be accessed for free. ✉ *Park entrance: off Rte. 54, by the 21-km marker, Bugac* ☎ *Bugac Tours: 76/575–112 or 76/575–113* ⊕ *www.knp.hu* 💰 *1,500 HUF: entry by carriage plus horse show and admission to the Shepherd Museum; 700 HUF: entry on foot with admission to museum but no horse show (25-min walk to the museum)* ⊙ *May–Oct., weekdays 8–4, weekends 8–1.*

WHERE TO EAT & STAY

$ ✕**Kisbugaci Étterem.** This cozy, csárda-style eatery tucked away on a
★ side street a 10-minute walk from the main square is warm and bright. The inner area has wood paneling and upholstered booths; the outer section has simple wooden tables covered with locally embroidered tablecloths and matching curtains. Food is heavy, ample, and tasty, whether it's "outlaw" paprikás with barley-shape, egg-based pasta; tripe stew with crushed potatoes; turkey breast; or goose liver. Request

7

a plate of dried paprikas—usually crumbled into soup—if you really want to spice things up. ⊠ *Munkácsy utca 10* ☎ *76/322–722* ⊟ *MC, V* ⊗ *No dinner Sun.*

¢ ⊞ **Fábián Panzió.** It's hard to miss this positively pink villa a few blocks ★ from the main square. Once inside, the pink (though muted) continues, mixing with white, turquoise, and lavender. The friendly owners keep their pension immaculate. Rooms are in the main house and (larger ones) in a comely one-story motel-like building in the garden. Pros: Good price, cozy and friendly, pleasant garden. Cons: 10-minute walk from center, few amenities and services, a/c 1,000 HUF extra per day. ⊠ *Kápolna utca 14, H-6000* ☎ *76/477–677* 🖷 *76/477–175* ⊕ *www.hotels.hu/fabian* ⇨ *10 rooms* ﹠ *In-room: refrigerator, Wi-Fi. In-hotel: bicycles, laundry service, public Wi-Fi, no elevator* ⦿|*BP* ⊟ *No credit cards.*

SZEGED

87 km (54 mi) south of Kecskemét, 173 km (107 mi) south of Budapest.

This city of 165,000 at the junction of the Tisza and Maros rivers is the largest and liveliest in southern Hungary. Although Szeged owes its origin to the Tisza River, the river has also been its ruin. In 1879 a disastrous flood destroyed the old Szeged in just one night. Some 150 people died and only 265 houses remained standing—5,458 were destroyed. With international assistance the city was rebuilt.

Historical excavations suggest that Szeged was once the seat of Atilla, the king of the Huns, in the 5th century. Under Turkish rule, which commenced in 1543, the city continued to develop and became a center for trade in southern Hungary. In 1686, with help from Austrian forces, Szeged was liberated from the Turks. But in 1704 Hungarians tried, unsuccessfully, to take back the city. Under continued Austrian rule Szeged served as a military outpost.

Szeged has long been famous for two scrumptious commodities: paprika and salami. Local biochemist Albert Szentgyörgyi won the Nobel Prize in 1937 for his discoveries about vitamin C, extracted from his hometown's ground-up red peppers. World-famous Pick salami also comes from here.

Szeged's large town center—rich with turn-of-the-20th-century buildings and attractive old squares—makes for a bustling atmosphere that is the closest thing in Hungary to Budapest outside of Budapest.

☪ **Anna Spa.** Anna Spa was the site of the Turkish-style Városi Gőzfürdő
Fodor's Choice (City Steam Bath) built in 1896, which operated for decades. Reopened
★ in 2004 after immaculate restoration, this palatial-looking building includes thermal pools, a sauna, a steam room, and more. ⊠ *Tisza Lajos körút 24, H-6725* ☎ *62/425–721* ☞ *1,400 HUF* ⊗ *Weekdays 6 AM–8 PM, weekends 8 AM–8 PM; Mon., Wed., Fri., also 9 PM–midnight.*

★ Szeged's most striking building is the **Fogadalmi templom** *(Votive Church)*, an imposing neo-Romanesque, twin-steepled brick edifice built between 1912 and 1929. More commonly called the Dóm (Cathedral), it seats 6,000 and has a splendid organ with 9,040 pipes, one of the biggest in Europe. ⊠ *Dóm tér* ☎ *62/429–379* ⊠ *Church 400 HUF, steeple 600 HUF, crypt 150 HUF* ☉ *Church Mon. –Sat. 9–6, Sun. 12:30–6. Crypt with advance arrangement only.*

Szeged's neoclassical **Régi Zsinagóga** *(Old Synagogue)* was built in 1839. On its outside wall a marker written in Hungarian and Hebrew shows the height of the floodwaters in 1879, an estimated 3.8 meters (12.4 feet) high. It is open only rarely, for special events. ⊠ *Hajnóczi utca 12.*

The heart of the city center is made up of capacious **Széchenyi tér,** shaded with plane trees, and the adjacent **Klauzál tér,** which is not as green but much more bustling with people and surrounded by imposing buildings.

The most notable of Szeged's structures is the bright yellow, neo-baroque **Városház** *(Town Hall* ⊠ *Széchenyi tér 10)*, built at the turn of the 19th century and, after suffering major damage during the 1879 flood, reconstructed by well-known, eclectic Art Nouveau architect Ödön Lechner. Its spectacular clock tower with a terrace and a roof of colored tiles is visible from afar.

★ The **Új Zsinagóga** *(New Synagogue)*, finished in 1905 near the smaller Old Synagogue, is Szeged's purest and finest representation of the Art Nouveau style. Its wood and stone carvings, wrought iron, stained-glass windows, and spectacular dome are all the work of locals. A memorial in the entrance hall honors Szeged's victims of the Holocaust. ⊠ *Gutenberg utca 20, at Jósika utca* ☎ *62/423–849* ⊠ *300 HUF* ☉ *Apr.–Oct., Sun. and Mon. 9–noon and 1–5; Nov.–Mar., Sun. and Mon. 9–2.*

WHERE TO EAT & STAY

$–$$ ✕ **John Bull Pub.** It's neither typically nor stereotypically Hungarian,
★ but this branch of Hungary's British-style pub chain is popular with locals—with good reason. Szeged's John Bull serves up a whole host of delicious dishes from fish, steak, and Wiener schnitzel to the elaborate Pittsburgh veal ribs with panfried potato wedges. It's on a bustling side street between Széchenyi tér and the cathedral. ⊠ *Oroszlán utca 6, H-6725* ☎ *62/484–217* ⊟ *AE, DC, MC, V.*

¢–$$ ✕ **Öreg Kőrössy Halászkert Vendéglő.** This thatched-roof fisherman's inn on the Tisza River opened in 1930. The menu still includes original house staples such as rich-red *Öreg Kőrössy halászlé* (Old Kőrös fish soup). It's not easy to find; take a car or bus, as it's a long walk north of the city center along the river. We recommend that you check with **Tourinform** for specific directions. ⊠ *Sárga üdülőtelep 262* ☎ *62/495–481* ⊟ *MC, V.*

$ 🖵 **Dóm Hotel.** Just a block from the cathedral on the way to Szeged's bustling squares, this small hotel has mostly bright rooms with silky, apricot bedspreads, standard modern furnishings, and yellow and

7

blood-orange walls. Pros: Right in the center, restaurants nearby, all rooms but one no-smoking. Cons: High rates, some rooms are dark. ⊠*Bajza utca 6, H-6725* ☎*62/423–750* ⊕*www.domhotel.hu* ☞*15 rooms, 2 suites* ⚭*In-room: Ethernet, refrigerator, no-smoking rooms(some). In-hotel: restaurant, laundry service, parking (no fee), no elevator* ☰*AE, DC, MC, V* ⦿*BP.*

¢ ⊞**Marika Panzió.** This friendly inn sits on a historic street in the Alsóváros (Lower Town), a five-minute drive from the city center. Cozy rooms have light-wood paneling and larger-hotel amenities, including color TVs, minibars, and air-conditioning. Pros: Good price, outdoor pool, cozy inn. Cons: 30-minute walk from center, few restaurants nearby, few services. ⊠*Nyíl utca 45, H-6725* ☎*62/443–861* ⊕*www.kronikaspark.hu* ☞*9 rooms* ⚭*In-room: dial-up, refrigerator. In-hotel: pool, laundry service, parking (no fee), no elevator* ☰*AE, DC, MC, V* ⦿*BP.*

NIGHTLIFE & THE ARTS

Szegedi Szabadtéri Játékok *(Szeged Open-Air Festival)*, the city's most important annual event, draws crowds from around the country from mid-July through mid-September. The gala series of dramas, operas, operettas, classical concerts, and folk-dance performances by Hungarian and international artists is held outdoors on the vast cobblestone Dóm tér.

EASTERN HUNGARY ESSENTIALS

BY BUS

Volánbusz has frequent daily service between Budapest's Stadion terminal and Eger (two-hour trip). Getting to Tokaj by bus is a bit of a hassle (time-consuming and sometimes requiring more than one transfer); if you're not driving, go by train (one transfer, in Miskolc). Volánbusz also serves towns throughout the Great Plain from Budapest's Stadion terminal. Local buses connect most towns within the region. Hajduvolán, the regional branch of Volánbusz, has three direct, four-hour routes daily between Debrecen and Szeged (around 3,000 HUF).

BY CAR

Having a car isn't imperative for exploring the region, but it gives you much more flexibility. The flat expanses of the Great Plain region make for easy, if eventually numbing, driving.

The M3 expressway is the main link between Budapest and northern Hungary, cutting toward the northeast and Ukraine. To get to Eger, take the exit near Füzesabony and drive north about 20 km (13 mi). To go on to Tokaj, take the M30 expressway to the smaller, older Route 3 north toward Miskolc, then go east on Route 37 toward Tokaj. An alternate route to Tokaj (shorter on the map but a bit longer in fact): continue on the M3 past the Tisza River, then take secondary roads northeast toward Tokaj.

From Budapest, Route 4 goes straight to Debrecen, but it's faster to take the M3 expressway and switch to Route 33 midway there; the

M5 goes to Kecskemét and Szeged. Secondary Route 47 runs along the eastern edge of the country, connecting Debrecen and Szeged. It's easy to drive between Debrecen and Kecskemét via Route 4 through Szolnok before you drop south in Cegléd. The puszta regions of Bugac and Hortobágy are accessible from Kecskemét and Debrecen by well-marked roads.

BY TRAIN

Trains between Eger and Budapest make the two-hour trip several times daily from Keleti Station, with a transfer in Füzesabony. Direct trains run frequently all day between Budapest and Miskolc (or else Szerencs, a half hour farther east); the travel time to Miskolc on the Intercity (IC) route is around two hours—and from either Miskolc or Szerencs you can transfer to a train to Tokaj. You can also travel between Tokaj and Debrecen by train several times a day in roughly 1½ hours, with a transfer in Nyiregyháza.

Frequent service to the Great Plain from Budapest is available from Nyugati (West) and Keleti (East) stations. Intercity (IC) trains, the fastest choice, run between Budapest and Debrecen (3 hours), Kecskemét (1 hour), and Szeged (2½ hours); they require seat reservations (printed on separate slips of paper), which should be sold to you automatically if you ask for an IC ticket.

VISITOR INFORMATION

The agencies below provide a broad range of tourist information. Tourinform offices can also help arrange private accommodations.

Information **Hortobágy National Park Visitors and Educational Center** (⊠ *Petőfi tér 13, Hortobágy* ☎ *52/589–321* ⊕ *www.hnp.hu*). **Kiskunság National Park Management Center** (⊠ *Liszt Ferenc utca 19, Kecskemét* ☎ *76/501–596* ⊕ *www.knp.hu*). **Tourinform Debrecen** (⊠ *Piac utca 20, Debrecen* ☎ *52/412–250*). **Tourinform Eger** (⊠ *Bajcsy Zsilinszky út 9, Eger* ☎ *36/517–715*). **Tourinform Kecskemét** (⊠ *Kossuth tér 1, Kecskemét* ☎ *76/481–065*) **Tourinform Szeged** (⊠ *Dugonics tér 2, Szeged* ☎ *62/488–699*). **Tourinform Tokaj** (⊠ *Serház utca 1, Tokaj* ☎ *47/352–259*)

HUNGARY ESSENTIALS

TRANSPORTATION

BY AIR

The most convenient way to fly between Hungary and the United States is with Malév Hungarian Airlines' or Delta's nonstop direct service between JFK International Airport in New York and Budapest's Ferihegy Airport. Several other airlines offer connecting service from North America, including Austrian Airlines (through Vienna), British Airways (through London), Czech Airlines (through Prague), and Lufthansa (through Frankfurt or Munich). From Budapest, budget airlines such as Wizz Air and easyJet have regular service to the U.K. and throughout Europe. Ryanair and German Wings fly between Balaton Airport and points in the U.K. and Germany.

Information Austrian Airlines (☎1/999–4012). British Airways (☎1/777–4747). ČSA (Czech Airlines ☎1/318–3045). Delta (☎1/301–6680). easyJet (☎1/301–6680). German Wings (☎044/870–252–1250 ⊕www.germanwings.com). Lufthansa (☎1/266–4511). Malév (☎1/301–6680). Ryanair (⊕www.ryanair.com). Wizz Air (☎1/470–9499).

AIRPORTS

Ferihegy Repülőtér, Hungary's largest commercial airport, is 24 km (15 mi) southeast of downtown Budapest. Most non-Hungarian airlines operate from Terminal 2B; those of Malév, from Terminal 2A. The older part of the airport, Terminal 1, is the main terminal for budget airlines such as easyJet and Wizz Air, and is typically referred to as Ferihegy 1; Terminal 2 is called Ferihegy 2. Balaton Airport, near the western end of Lake Balaton, is 182 km (113 mi) from Budapest, and is used primarily by people wanting to stay in the Balaton region or those flying on Ryanair, which doesn't fly to Budapest.

Information Ferihegy Repülőtér (☎1/296–9696 [central switchboard], 1/296–7000 flight information). Balaton Airport (✉Sármellék ☎83/554–200 ⊕www.flybalaton.com).

BY BOAT

Hungary is well equipped with nautical transport, and Budapest is situated on a major international waterway, the Danube. From mid-April through late October, a hydrofoil run by MAHART PassNave leaves Vienna daily at 9 AM, and after a 5½-hour journey downriver, with a stop in the Slovak capital, Bratislava (and breathtaking views of the cathedral in Esztergom and Visegrád's hilltop fortress), the boats head into Budapest via its main artery, the Danube. The upriver journey likewise starts at 9 AM, but takes almost an hour longer. The cost is €79 one-way, €99 round-trip.

For travel around the Danube Bend, from April through September, MAHART PassNave makes several morning trips daily by cruise boat or hydrofoil from Budapest. The boat can take around five hours from Budapest to Esztergom (1,690 HUF), three hours to Visegrád (1,490 HUF), and two to Szentendre (1,390 HUF); by hydrofoil, it's about half the time but more expensive. Some prefer taking the train or a bus for a faster return journey. Ferry crossings take about 10 minutes and cost roughly 1,200 HUF per car and driver, 200 HUF per passenger.

On Lake Balaton, you can travel slowly but scenically among the major resorts by ferry, for about 400 HUF per person plus at least 1,000 HUF per car. Schedules for Balatoni Hajózási Zrt (Balaton Shipping Co.) are available from most tourist offices in the region.

Information Balatoni Hajózási Zrt (☎87/342–230 in Balatonfüred, 87/431–240 in Badacsony, 84/310–050 in Siófok ⊕www.balatonihajozas.hu). MAHART PassNave (✉Budapest, District V, docked at Vigadó tér ☎1/484–4010 or 1/484–4000 ✉Handelskai 265, Vienna ☎1/729–2161 or 1/729–2162 ⊕www.mahartpassnave.hu).

BY BUS

Most intercity buses in Hungary are run by the state-owned Volánbusz company, which is in partnership with Eurolines, Europe's main coach line. Buses link Budapest's Népliget bus station with most cities in Hungary as well as major cities in Europe. For international routes, buy your tickets well in advance either at the Downtown Travel Center or at the bus station. On many domestic routes, you can buy a ticket only from the bus driver as you board, so arrive early for a good seat. For all schedule and fare information, contact Volánbusz or a tourist office.

From Budapest, buses to the eastern part of Hungary depart from the Stadion station in eastern Pest; those to western Hungary generally leave from the Népliget station, also in eastern Pest. For the Danube Bend, buses leave from the bus terminal at Árpád Bridge, near the northern end of Margaret Island, also in Pest. Most buses are comfortable and air-conditioned, though some are holdovers from the communist era and can get hot on warm summer days. Domestic routes have no toilets, but make occasional pit stops. Smoking on board is prohibited on all routes.

Information Downtown Travel Center (⊠ *District VIII, Rákóczi út 49/a, Budapest).* **Volánbusz** (☎ *1/382–0888 [national info line, 8* AM*–4* PM*, domestic info Ext. 2, international info Ext. 3]* ⊕ *www.volanbusz.hu).*

Budapest Bus Stations Árpád Bridge bus station (⊠ *District III, Árboc u. 1–3Budapest).* **Népliget bus station** (⊠ *District IX, Üllői út 131, Budapest).*

Stadion bus station (⊠ *District XIV, BudapestHungária krt. 48–52).*

Regional Bus Stations Balatonfüred bus station (⊠ *Bajcsy Zsilinszky utca 53, Balatonfüred).* **Debrecen bus station** (⊠ *Szoboszlói út 4–6, Debrecen).* **Eger bus station** (⊠ *Mátyás király út 134, Eger).* **Esztergom bus station** (⊠ *Simon János tér, Esztergom).* **Pécs bus station** (⊠ *Nagy Lajos Király utca 20, Pécs).* **Sopron bus station** (⊠ *Lackner K. utca 9, Sopron).*

BY CAR

To drive in Hungary, Americans and Canadians need an International Driver's License. If you're from the United Kingdom you may use your domestic license. Hungarian drivers are all too fond of passing, so be careful. Speed traps are numerous, so it's best to observe the speed limit; fines start from the equivalent of roughly $50, but they can easily reach $250. Using a cell phone while driving is an offense. Police are supposed to give accused speeders an invoice payable at post offices. (Remember this should an officer suggest an on-the-spot "discount.") Spot checks are frequent, and police occasionally try to take advantage of foreigners, so have your papers on hand.

Hungary has five toll motorways, referred to as M0, M1, M7, M5, and M3. To drive on these roads, you must first stop at a gasoline station and buy a *matrica* (toll pass), affixing it to the lower inside of your car's windshield. A matrica valid for four days costs about HUF 1,500. Gas stations are plentiful nationwide, and many on the main highways stay open all night, even on holidays.

CAR RENTAL   Rates are high. Daily rates for automatics begin around $55–$60 plus 60¢ per kilometer (½ mi); personal, theft, and accident insurance (not required but recommended) runs an additional $25–$30 per day. Rates tend to be lower if you arrange your rental *from home* through the American offices. Some locally based companies offer lower rates. All of the agencies listed here have representation at Ferihegy Airport, in addition to branches downtown. Hertz, National, and Fox Autorent also have branches at Balaton Airport.

Foreign driver's licenses are often accepted by car rental agencies but, technically speaking, are not legally valid.

Major Agencies Avis (⊠ *District V, Szervita tér 8* 🕾 *1/318–4685* ⊕ *www.avis. hu*). **Budget** (⊠ *District I, Hotel Mercure Buda, Krisztina krt. 41–43* 🕾 *1/214–0420* ⊕ *www.budget.hu*). **Europcar** (*also known in Hungary as EUrent* ⊠ *District V, Deák Ferenc tér 3* 🕾 *1/328–6464* ⊕ *www.europcar.hu*). **Hertz** (*also known in Hungary as Mercure Rent-a-Car* ⊠ *District V, Váci utca 19–21* 🕾 *1/235–6008* ⊕ *www.hertz. com*). **National** (*also known in Hungary as National Alamo Hungary* ⊠ *District VIII, Üllői út 60–62* 🕾 *1/477–1080* ⊕ *www.nationalcar.hu*).

Local Agencies Americana Rent-a-Car (⊠ *District VII, Erzsébet körút 9–11* 🕾 *1/886–6128* ⊕ *www.americanarentacar.com*). **CentRent** (⊠ *District III, Kerék utca 80* 🕾 *20/541–1035 or 20/541–1034* ⊕ *www.centrent.hu*). **Fox Autorent** (⊠ *District XI, Nagytétényi út 48–50* 🕾 *1/382–9000* ⊕ *www.fox-autorent.com*).

PARKING   Smaller towns usually have free parking on the street and some hourly fee lots near main tourist zones. Throughout the country, no-parking zones are marked with the international "No Parking" sign: a white circle with a diagonal line through it.

RULES OF THE   Hungarians drive on the right and observe the usual Continental rules
ROAD   (but they revel in passing). Unless otherwise noted, the speed limit in developed areas is 50 kph (30 mph), on main roads 80–100 kph (50–62 mph), and on highways 120 kph (75 mph). Seat belts are compulsory (front-seat belts in lower speed zones, both front and back in higher speed zones), and drinking alcohol is prohibited—there is a zero-tolerance policy, and the penalties are very severe.

BY TRAIN

International trains are routed to two stations in Budapest. Keleti pályaudvar (East Station) receives most international rail traffic coming in from the west. Nyugati pályaudvar (West Station) handles a combination of international and domestic trains.

Train travel within Hungary is low-cost by Western standards and efficient. If possible, avoid *személyvonat* (local trains), which are slow; instead, take Intercity (IC) trains—which are clean and fast but require a *helyjegy* (seat reservation) for about 500 HUF—or gyorsvonat (express trains). On timetables, tracks (*vágány*) are abbreviated with a "v"; *indul* means "departing," and *érkezik* means "arriving." Trains get crowded during weekend travel in summer; you're more likely to have elbow room if you pay a little extra for first-class tickets. Only Hungarian citizens are entitled to student discounts on domestic train fares; all senior citizens (men over 60, women over 55), however, are eligible for a 20% discount. Snacks and drinks are often unavailable on trains, so pack a lunch; train picnics are a way of life.

For all schedule and fare information, regardless of the station, call MÁV's 24-hour hotline.

Information **MAV Passenger Service** (⊠ *District VI, Andrássy út 35, Budapest* ☎ *322–8082 [customer service, in Budapest], 06–40/49–49–49 [24-hr nationwide fare and schedule info]* ⊕ *www.mav.hu*).

Budapest Train Stations **MÁV Train Information** (☎ *06–40/49–49–49 [local charges nationwide]*).**Déli** *Pályaudvar* (*South Railway Station* ⊠ *District XII, Alkotás u.*). **Keleti** *Pályaudvar* (*East Railway Station* ⊠ *District VIII, Baross tér*). **Nyugati** *Pályaudvar* (*West Railway Station* ⊠ *District V, Nyugati tér*).

Regional Train Stations **Balatonfüred train station** (⊠ *Castricum tér*).**Debrecen train station** (⊠ *Petőfi tér 12, Debrecen*). **Eger train station** (⊠ *Állomás tér 1, Eger*). **Kecskemét train station** (⊠ *Kodály Zoltán tér 7, Kecskemét*). **Pécs train station** (⊠ *Indóhász tér*). **Sopron train station** (⊠ *Állomás utca*). **Szeged train station** (⊠ *Tisza pályaudvar, Indóház tér, Szeged*).

CONTACTS & RESOURCES

BANKS & EXCHANGE SERVICES
Even with inflation and the 25% value-added tax (VAT) in the service industry, enjoyable vacations with all the trimmings still remain less expensive in Hungary than in nearby Western European cities such as Vienna.

CURRENCY
Hungary's unit of currency is the forint (HUF). There are bills of 200, 500, 1,000, 2,000, 5,000, 10,000, and 20,000 forints and coins of 1, 2, 5, 10, 20, 50, and 100 forints. The euro will eventually be adopted, but not before 2012.

At press time the exchange rate was 174 HUF to the U.S. dollar. There is still a bit of a black market in hard currency, but changing money on the street is risky (since the point is to cheat you if possible) and illegal to boot, and the bank rate almost always comes close. Stick with banks and official exchange offices. Better yet, head to the nearest ATM—there are lots of them.

Information **American Express** (⊠ *District V, Deák Ferenc u. 10, Budapest* ☎ *1/235–4330* ☎ *1/267–2028*).

CREDIT CARDS
All major cards are accepted in Hungary, though American Express and Diners Club are sometimes not on the list. That said, don't rely on credit cards in smaller towns or less expensive accommodations and restaurants; instead, you may have to look for the nearest ATM. Some accept Plus-network bank cards and Visa credit cards, others Cirrus and MasterCard. You can withdraw forints only (automatically converted at the bank's official rate) directly from your account. Some levy a 1% or $3 service charge. Instructions are available in English.

EMBASSIES

InformationU.S. **Embassy** (⊠ *District V, Szabadság tér 12, Budapest* ☏ *1/475–4400*).

EMERGENCIES

INTERNET, MAIL & SHIPPING

In Hungary, if you are staying at a hotel rather than a family-owned pension, chances are that you will have some sort of Internet access there. Some hotels don't offer work terminals for guest use but do have Wi-Fi or Ethernet that you can access on your own laptop. Budapest has plenty of Internet cafés (look for "Internet" signs), where rates average 300 HUF an hour. In Buda, there's a clearly marked, tiny Internet café (no name, no phone) on Moszkva tér. Two good options in Pest are CT Trade and Internet & Internet.

Smaller cities often have just one or two easy-to-find Internet cafés, but some local Tourinform offices have public Internet access (usually 300–400 HUF an hour). Also, many town government offices and cultural centers, and sometimes even church offices, have public Internet access at a modest fee. Such places are easy to find: just look for the big metal signs along the road with a large @ sign (in black) on a white and blue background; often there's also an arrow pointing in the right direction.

Airmail letters and postcards generally take seven days to travel between Hungary and the United States, sometimes more than twice as long during the Christmas season. For expedited service and to ship larger parcels home, consider an express service like DHL.

Budapest Internet Cafés CT Trade (⊠ *District VII, Kazinczy utca near Dohány utca, Budapest* ☏ *321–5300*). **Internet & Internet** (⊠ *District VI, Kertész utca 41, Budapest* ☏ *268–0023*).

Regional Internet Cafés Arabesque Net Cafe (⊠ *Fellner J. utca 1, Eger* ☏ *36/515–694*). **Debrecen internet café** (⊠ *Lehel utca 20, Debrecen* ☏ *52/522–470*). **Matrix** (⊠ *Kárász utca 5, Szeged* ☏ *62/423–830*). **Mátrix Internet Kávézó** (⊠ *Király utca 15, Pécs* ☏ *72/214–487*). **NETobább eszpresszó** (⊠ *Horváth Mihály utca 3, Balatonfüred* ☏ *87/342–235*). **Silverblue Internet Café** (⊠ *Dunakanyar körút 14, Szentendre* ☏ *26/505–758 or 30/240–5486*). **Teaház & Kávézó** *(Teahouse & Café)* (⊠ *Széchenyi tér 16, Sopron* ☏ *99/340–767*).

Shipping Companies DHL (⊠ *District XI, Kocsis u. 3, Budapest* ☏ *1/382–3499*).

PASSPORTS & VISAS

Only a valid passport is required of Australian, U.S., Canadian, and New Zealand citizens. Citizens of EU countries, including Britain, may enter with either a passport or a national identity card.

TELEPHONES

Within Hungary, most towns can be dialed directly: dial "06" and wait for the buzzing tone; then dial the local number. Cellular phone numbers are treated like long-distance domestic calls: dial "06" before the number (when giving their cellular phone numbers, most people include the 06 anyway). It is unnecessary to use the city code, "1," when dialing within Budapest. The country code for Hungary is "36." When dialing from outside the country, drop the initial "06" prefix that is used domestically for long-distance and cell calls.

INTERNATIONAL CALLS
To make a direct call abroad from Hungary, dial "00," wait for the international dialing tone, then dial the number. For international calls from pay phones—or from your hotel, to save money—the most economical option is to buy one of many international phone cards available at newsstands; the aptly named *Blabla* card (1,000 HUF or 3,000 HUF) has excellent rates.

LOCAL CALLS
Coin-operated pay phones accept 10-HUF, 20-HUF, 50-HUF, and 100-HUF coins; drop in 40 HUF initially, and have at least four more 20 HUF coins on hand for a short call. If you expect to use pay phones often, it's best to use the silver, card-operated telephones. The cards—available at post offices and most newsstands and kiosks—can be had for 800 HUF or 1,800 HUF, and just need to be inserted into the phone.

Information Local Directory Assistance (☎ *198*). Operators theoretically speak English.

TIPPING
In Hungary, tipping is generally done by making it clear when paying that you don't need the change or else specifying the tip-inclusive amount you want change for. Gratuities are not included on bills at most restaurants; when the waiter arrives with the bill, add 10%–15% tip to the amount. Taxi drivers and hairdressers expect 10%–15% tips; hotel porters should get at least 200 HUF. Coatroom attendants receive 50–100 HUF, as do gas-pump attendants if they wash your windows or check your tires; dressing-room attendants at thermal baths receive at least 100 HUF for opening and closing your locker. If a Gypsy band plays exclusively for your table, leave 500–1,000 HUF on the plate provided for that purpose.

TOUR OPTIONS
BOAT TOURS
MAHART PassNave operates boat excursions on the Danube in and beyond Budapest. In Budapest, from late April through September, its popular one-hour *Duna Corso* tour (2,990 HUF) runs around a dozen times daily starting at 10; boats leave from Vigadó tér. There are only six runs daily in October and early November, starting at 11. Two-hour evening cruises replete with music and dancing head out at 7:30 daily from early May through September, and on Fridays and weekends through most of October. Hour-long evening sightseeing cruises on the *Danube Legend,* run by a different company, depart from Vigadó tér four times nightly from May through August, three times nightly in the low season. Operated by the same company from the same piers, the *Duna-Bella* takes six two-hour, daylight cruises a day, including a walk on Margaret Island.

On Lake Balaton, you can arrange boat trips to vineyards, folk-music evenings, overnight trips to local inns, and other organized tours directly with the hotels in the Balaton area and with the help of Tourinform offices. Balatoni Hajózási Zrt (Balaton Shipping Co.) runs several boat tours on the lake: From the main quay at Balatonfüred, the *Csongor* sets out several times daily between 10 AM and 6 PM in July and August for an hour-long jaunt (1,250 HUF) around the Tihany Peninsula; the "Badacsony Tour" departs from Keszthely, at the southern end of the lake, and goes to Badacsony at 10:30 AM each Thursday. Sailing excursions are also offered.

In Szeged, MAHART PassNave offers one-hour boat rides (900 HUF) along the Tisza River from around the first week of July through the end of August; boats depart at 5 PM on Wednesday, Friday, and Sunday.

Information Balatoni Hajózási Zrt (87/342–230 *in Balatonfüred, 87/431–240 in Badacsony, 84/310–050 in Siófok* ⊕ *www.balatonihajozas.hu). Danube Legend and Duna-Bella (*⊠ *District V, docked at Vigadó tér* 1/317–2203). **MAHART PassNave** (⊠ *District V, Belgrád rakpart, Budapest* 1/484–4013 *or 1/318–1223, 62/425–834 in Szeged* ⊕ *www.mahartpassnave.hu*).

BUS TOURS

IBUSZ Travel and Cityrama arrange bus tours from Budapest to points around the country, from short sightseeing trips within Budapest to traditional pig roasts on the Great Plain. In Budapest, IBUSZ Travel conducts three-hour tours of the city that operate all year and cost about 6,000 HUF. They can also provide English-speaking personal guides on request. Cityrama also offers a three-hour city bus tour (about 7,000 HUF per person). Both have commentary in English.

Both companies offer several full-day bus tours from Budapest to the Danube Bend, each costing around 14,000–16,000 HUF. One-day tours to the Balaton take in major sights and include ferry excursions and wine tasting; prices run around 18,000 HUF. And for those wanting to see the Great Plain but not spend the night, both companies offer various daylong tours several times a week from Budapest; prices range from 11,000 HUF to 18,000 HUF.

Information Cityrama (⊠ *District V, Báthori u. 22, Budapest* 1/302–4382 ⊕ *www.cityrama.hu*). **IBUSZ Travel** (⊠ *District V, Ferenciek tere 10, Budapest* 1/485–2765, 1/485–2766, *or 1/485–2700* ⊕ *www.ibusz.hu*).

SPECIAL-INTEREST TOURS

In Budapest, Absolute Walking Tours offers not only historical and general interest tours but also creatively executed theme tours, such as the "Hammer & Sickle Tour" and a "Budapest Night Stroll." By day, its 3½-hour Budapest walk costs 4,000 HUF; just show up at 10:30 AM on Deák tér in front of the pale-yellow Lutheran church.

Chosen Tours offers several tours, including a three-hour combination bus and walking "Classical Jewish Heritage Tour," highlighting the sights and cultural life of Budapest's Jewish history; call for prices and further details. Tours run daily except Saturday.

Information Absolute Walking Tours (⊠ *District V, Sütő u. 2, Budapest* ☎ *1/211–8861* ⊕ *www.absolutetours.com).* **Chosen Tours** (⊠ *District XII, Pagony u. 40 Budapest* ☎🖨 *1/355–2202 or 06–20/451–4040* ⊕ *chosentours@yahoo.com).*

VISITOR INFORMATION

Tourinform, Hungary's national tourist information service, provides information on anything and everything to do with visiting Hungary, and has offices throughout the country. In Budapest, it will refer you to companies that can arrange accommodation in private apartments and rooms; in the countryside, its offices often arrange such accommodation themselves. IBUSZ (⇨ *see* Bus Tours, *above*), with branches throughout Hungary, provides general tourist information, offers a wide range of group tours, and arranges private accommodations.

Information Tourinform (⊠ *District VI, Liszt Ferenc tér* ☎ *1/322–4098 or 1/438–8080 (24-hr hotline)* ⊕ *www.hungarytourism.hu* ⊠ *District V, Sütő utca 2* ☎ *1/316–9800* ⊠ *District I, Szentháromság tér* ☎ *1/488–0475).*

Montenegro

www.fodors.com/forums

By Jane Foster

AN INDEPENDENT COUNTRY SINCE MAY 2006, tiny Montenegro (about the size of Connecticut) overlooks the Adriatic Sea and lies between Croatia, Bosnia-Herzegovina, Serbia, and Albania. The 650,000 people who live here call it Crna Gora (which, like Montenegro, means "black mountain"), in tribute to the imposing, pine-forested mountains of the interior.

Montenegro's main draw is its unspoiled nature, from the sand and pebble beaches along the coast—which is dotted with delightful Venetian-era fortified port towns and home to some excellent seafood restaurants—to the dramatic Alpine mountains of the interior, where visitors can participate in adventure sports such as rafting, mountain biking, and skiing, in winter. The locals are open and friendly, a proud, handsome, and educated people who are keen to preserve their own customs rather than succumb to globalization.

Montenegro's first known inhabitants were the Illyrians, who were farmers and hunters, and also worked iron and traded with the ancient Greeks. Urbanization began in the 4th century BC when the Greeks founded Budva, on the coast. In AD 9, the Romans annexed the region into the province of Illyricum (which ran down the Adriatic coast from the Istrian peninsula to Albania), calling it Doclea after the dominant local Illyrian tribe. When the Roman Empire was divided between east and west in AD 395, the fault line passed right through Montenegro. Later, this was to be the dividing line between Eastern Orthodox and Roman Catholic lands.

In the 7th century, the Slavs arrived from the region that is now Poland. They mixed with the descendants of the Romanized Illyrians and lived in the mountains, in clans, each ruled by a Župan (chieftain). Originally pagan, they soon adopted Christianity. In 1077, their independent state of Duklja (the Slavicized version of the Roman name, Doclea) was recognized as a kingdom by the pope. Later, Duklja became known as Zeta (derived from the old Slavic word for "harvest") and kept its freedom through paying off the Byzantine Empire, and fighting off the Ottoman Turks. Because of the constant threat of Ottoman invasion and fear of rival clans, courage in combat was emphasized as a major virtue in Zeta.

Meanwhile, most of the Montenegrin coast was under Venetian rule from 1420 to 1797. Due to ties with Italy, Roman Catholicism was the dominant faith here, whereas the Eastern Orthodox Church prevailed in Zeta. In fact, politics and religion became so intertwined in Zeta that from 1550 to 1696 it was governed by bishops. In 1697, the Petrović-Njegoš family took the helm as prince-bishops, initiating the Petrović dynasty, which ruled until 1918.

During both world wars, Montenegro sided with the Allies. In 1945, it became one of the six constituent republics that made up Yugoslavia, governed along communist lines by President Tito. Yugoslavia was not part of the Soviet Bloc, however, Tito having broken off relations with Stalin in 1948. The country was ruled under Tito's own form of communism—far more liberal than that in the former USSR.

During the breakup of Yugoslavia in the 1990s, no fighting took place on Montenegrin soil. However, the region did suffer economic hardship and a degree of political isolation. When Croatia and Slovenia claimed independence from Yugoslavia in 1991, Montenegro remained loyal to Belgrade. However, by May 2006, when all that was left of Yugoslavia was the so-called Union of Serbia and Montenegro, Montenegro held a referendum and voted for independence and became its own democratic republic. Today, tourism is the main force behind the economy, and foreign investors (notably Russian and British) keen to be in on the potential boom are buying up properties fast. There are even rumors that Venus and Serena Williams are planning to set up a tennis school here.

EXPLORING MONTENEGRO

Montenegro can be divided into three main areas: coast, highlands, and plains. Tourism is concentrated along the 293-km (183-mi) coast, the top seaside resort being the delightful walled town of Budva with its "riviera," a 21-km (13-mi) stretch of seaboard dotted with beaches and home to the renowned Sveti Stefan island resort. Also on the coast, Kotor draws many visitors thanks to its dramatic location—at the end of a deep fjord—and its charming Old Town, a UNESCO World Heritage Site. Close by, the village of Perast sits in a bay with two tiny islands, each capped by a picturesque church. Moving inland to the mountains, the town of Kolašin lies on the edge of Biogradska Gora National Park, a wonderland of snowcapped Alpine peaks, primeval forest, and five glacial lakes. Nearby, the Tara River Canyon, another UNESCO World Heritage Site, is a popular venue for white-water rafting. The flat Zeta Plain, which lies inland and runs from capital city Podgorica in the north to Lake Skadar in the south, is the country's most fertile farming region but is of less interest to tourists.

ABOUT THE RESTAURANTS

Along the Montenegrin coast, seafood predominates, with starters including *salata od hobotnice* (octopus salad) and *riblja čorba* (fish soup), followed by risotto dishes—most notably *crni rižot* (black risotto prepared with cuttlefish)—*lignje* (squid), or fresh fish from the Adriatic prepared on a barbecue. The quality is generally excellent, and the prices are slightly lower than in neighboring Croatia. Note that on restaurant menus, fresh fish is priced by the kilogram. Inland, cheeses and meat dishes are more common. Cheeses to try include *sir iz ulje* (cheese preserved in olive oil) and *kožji sir* (goat's cheese), which are generally eaten at the beginning of the meal rather than at the end. Popular meat specialties are *pršut* (prosciutto), *Njeguški stek* (steak stuffed with prosciutto and cheese), and *jagnjece pečenje sa ražnja* (whole lamb roasted on a spit).

Montenegrins are also fond of *Šopska salata* (a chopped salad of tomato, green peppers, cucumber, onion, olives, and feta cheese), similar to Greek salad. When it comes to local wines, Vranac is the most highly esteemed red, and Krstac a reliable white.

Montenegro (Crna Gora)

BOSNIA & HERZEGOVINA

SERBIA

HRVATSKA (CROATIA)

ALBANIA

Goražde

Foča

Drina

Gacko

Pljevlja

Bileći

Žabljak

Tara River Canyon

Tara

Trebinje

E762

18

20

6

Nikšić

Bijelo Polje

E65

E80

Tara

Kolašin

Biogradska Gora N.P.

Morinj

Perast

Kotor Bay

Tivat

Prčanj

Kotor see detail map

Zeta

E762

E65

E80

Ivangrad

E65

E80

9

TO DUBROVNIK

Budva see detail map

Cetinje

2-3

2-3

E65

E80

★ **Podgorica**

E80

E65

18

E762

Sveti Stefan

TO BARI

TO ANCONA

Petrovac

2-4

Bar

L. Skadar

TO BARI

E851

Ulcinj

Adriatic Sea

0 ____ 50 mi

0 ____ 50 km

Budva Riviera

E80

2-3

Slovenska Plaža

Bečići

Rafailovici

Budva

Jaz

Trsteno

Sveti Stefan

Ostrvo Sv Nikola

Mogren Plaža 1 & 2

Budva Gradska Plaža

E65

Petrovac

Adriatic Sea

Kraljeva

ABOUT THE HOTELS

Montenegro's most luxurious and most expensive hotels are in Budva and Sveti Stefan on the coast. The country's socialist-era resort hotels are fast being bought up by foreign investors, renovated, and reopened with stunning minimalist interiors and luxurious wellness centers. In addition, a number of small, family-run hotels have entered the market, many of which are centuries-old stone villas that have been converted into delightful little boutique hotels full of character. However, many visitors still prefer to rent a private room or apartment, which can be arranged through local tourist information offices and travel agencies. This option generally offers good value for the money and direct contact with the locals, and remains your best bet for finding a cozy, romantic hideaway inside the fortified Old Towns of places such as Budva and Kotor. The tourist season runs from Easter to late October and peaks in July and August, when prices rise significantly and when it may be difficult to find a place to sleep if you have not booked in advance.

> ### MONTENEGRO TOP 5
>
> ■ **St. Nicholas' Island.** Spend an afternoon swimming and sunning on this uninhabited isle.
>
> ■ **Biogradska Gora National Park.** Get back to nature: stay at an eco-village in gorgeous pine-forested mountains.
>
> ■ **Kotor.** Climb to St. John's Fortress, following the medieval walls, for postcard views.
>
> ■ **Tara River.** Conquer Class III and IV rapids at one of Europe's top white-water rafting spots.
>
> ■ **Sveti Stefan Aman.** Indulge in a night at this luxurious 40-suite resort on a private island.

WHAT IT COSTS IN EUROS (€)				
	$$$$	$$$	$$	$
RESTAURANTS In euros	over € 15	€10–€15	€5–€10	€5–€10
HOTELS In euros	over €200	€150–€200	€100–€150	under €100

Restaurant prices are per person for a main course at dinner. Hotel prices are for a standard double room with Continental breakfast in high season, including tax.

KOTOR

44 km (28 mi) from Debeli Brijeg on the border between Croatia and Montenegro.

Backed by imposing mountains, tiny Kotor lies hidden from the open sea, tucked into the deepest channel of the Bokor Kotorska (Kotor Bay), which is Europe's most southerly fjord. Listed as a UNESCO World Heritage Site, Kotor's medieval Stari Grad (Old Town) is enclosed within well-preserved defensive walls built between the 9th and 18th century and is presided over by a proud hilltop fortress. Within the walls, a labyrinth of winding cobbled streets leads through a series of splendid paved piazzas, rimmed by centuries-old stone buildings, many

IF YOU LIKE

BEACHES

Montenegro's best beaches lie along the Budvanska Rivijera (Budva Riviera), a glorious 21-km (13-mi) stretch of coast south of Budva. Here, the most popular beach is the 1½-km-long (1-mi-long), sandy Slovenska Plaža (Slovenska Beach), close to Budva Old Town and lined by a string of restaurants and cafés. South of here and the same size, Bečići Plaža (Bečići Beach) is another popular sandy strip, overlooked by some of the country's top hotels. In total contrast, close to Sveti Stefan, Kraljevica Plaža (Queen's Beach) and Kraljeva Plaža (King's Beach) are lower-key pebble beaches lying side by side, each in its own secluded bay backed by pine woods. Beach-goers seeking a more pristine experience away from the mainland can catch a taxi boat from Budva harbor to Ostrvo Sveti Nikola (St. Nicholas's Island), known to locals as "Hawaii."

MOUNTAINS

The name Montenegro comes from Venetian dialect and means "Black Mountain." And indeed, the Montenegrin hinterland is dominated by rugged mountains. If you are a hiking enthusiast or if you are simply exhilarated by fresh mountain air, snow-covered Alpine peaks, and hearty, rustic cuisine, then head for Biogradska Gora National Park. Here, slopes covered with dense pine forests rising to heady heights of more than 6,560 feet are punctuated by meadows and glacial lakes.

HISTORIC BUILDINGS

The Montengrin coast is dotted with delightful seaside towns that date back centuries. Kotor's Old Town is a UNESCO World Heritage Site, with medieval walls forming a tri-angular fortification system around a labyrinth of winding cobbled streets, stone-paved piazzas, elegant churches, and baroque palaces. Moving south, Budva was founded by the ancient Greeks, though its present appearance records the centuries spent under Venetian rule. Farther south still, Sveti Stefan is a former fishing village of stone cottages perched upon a tiny island protected by 15th-century fortifications, the entirety of which is now an exclusive hotel.

ADVENTURE SPORTS

The Tara River Canyon, said to be the longest canyon in the world after the Grand Canyon, is one of Europe's top spots for white-water rafting. Nearby, Biogradska Gora National Park offers dramatic Alpine mountains, pine forests, meadows, and glacial lakes, perfect for hiking, mountain biking, and horseback riding. With a 300-km (200-mi) seaboard, Montenegro is a fantastic destination for sailing and scuba diving. If you are in the Budva area, you might also try paragliding for a bird's-eye view over the water.

8

of which now house trendy cafés and chic boutiques at ground level. In the Middle Ages, as Serbia's chief port, Kotor was an important economic and cultural center with its own highly regarded schools of stonemasonry and iconography. Later, it spent periods under Venetian, Austrian, and French rule, though it was undoubtedly the Venetians who left the strongest impression on the city's architecture. Since the breakup of Yugoslavia, some 70% of the stone buildings in the

CLOSE UP

Živjeli! — Cheers!

A typical Montenegrin welcome involves a glass of the potent, national spirit, *rakija.* The most popular variety is *loza* (made from grapes), though in the mountainous regions *šljivovica* (made from plums) and *kruškovac* (made from pears) are also common. Nearly every family makes their own rakija—a source of immense pride to the head of the house—and it is considered rude to turn down the offer of a glass. Rakija is also often drunk as an aperitif. No meal would be complete without a bottle of vino (wine). The most highly regarded is Vranac, a dark ruby red with a 12% alcohol content and rich in tannin. Top of the range is Vranac pro Corde, produced by the Plantaže vineyards. The national pivo (beer), Nikšićko, has been brewed in the town of Nikšić since 1896. A lager made from barley, mountain water, and aromatic hops, it is served well chilled, either on draft or by the bottle.

romantic Old Town have been snapped up by foreigners, mostly Brits and Russians. And even Hollywood is taking notice of this soon-to-be-trendy town: recent visitors include actors Michael Douglas and Catherine Zeta-Jones.

EXPLORING KOTOR

Numbers in the margin correspond to points of interest on the Kotor Old Town map.

Kotor's Old Town takes approximately half a day to explore. Plan your visit for the morning, when the main sights are open to the public and the afternoon sun has yet to reach peak force.

② Glavna Gradska Vrata (Main Town Gate). The Main Town Gate (also known as the Sea Gate because of its position on the coast), which accesses the Stari Grad (Old Town) via the western facade of the city walls, dates back to the 16th century and comprises Renaissance and baroque details. Originally, the outer gate bore a relief of the Venetian Lion, but in Tito's time this was replaced by the Socialist star and dates recording the liberation of Kotor on November 21, 1944 at the end of WWII. There are two other entrances to the Stari Grad: the Južna Vrata (South Gate) and the Sjeverna Vrata (North Gate). ⊠ *Jadranski put.*

① Gradske Zidine (Town Walls). Especially beautiful at night, when they are illuminated, the well-preserved town walls were built between the 9th and 18th century. They measure almost 5 km (3 mi) in length, and reach up to 66 feet in height and 52 feet in width. They form a triangular defense system around the Old Town, then rise up the hill behind it to Tvrdjava Sv Ivana (St. John's Fortress), 853 feet above sea level. You can walk up to the fortress along the walls. Allow at least one hour to get up and back down. Wear good hiking shoes and don't forget to bring some water. ⊠ *Stari Grad (Old Town).*

GREAT ITINERARIES

Despite being a small country, Montenegro is a land of great contrasts, from the calm blue waters of the Adriatic coast to the soaring Alpine mountains of the interior. You would need months to see it all, but the itineraries below offer a glimpse of the highlights.

IF YOU HAVE 3 DAYS

Devote Day 1 to ⚏**Kotor,** checking out the Old Town and climbing up to the hillside fortress for views over the fjord. On the next day, travel up the coast to **Perast,** by taxi boat from Kotor or by bus or private transport. See Perast's twin islands, each crowned with a church, and have lunch in an old-fashioned *konoba* (tavern), either in Perast or the nearby villages of Dobrota or Morinj. In the afternoon, drive down to ⚏**Budva** and explore the Old Town. Spend the night here, and if the City Theatre Festival is under way, attend an evening performance. On Day 3, hop a taxi boat to **Sveti Stefan** to admire its exclusive island hotel and enjoy its sweeping pebble beaches. On your way back to Budva, make a stop at **St. Nicholas's island** for a swim. Spend the last night in Budva.

IF YOU HAVE 5 DAYS

Spend the first day in ⚏**Kotor,** as above, and visit **Perast** in the morning of Day 2. After lunch, drive to ⚏**Kolašin** in the mountains and settle into the **Bianca Resort and Spa.** Spend Day 3 hiking, mountain biking, or horseback riding in **Biogradska Gora National Park.** Devote the morning of Day 4 to relieving aching muscles and reviving tired skin in the Bianca Spa. Drive down to the coast in the afternoon and spend the last two days in ⚏**Budva** and **Sveti Stefan,** as suggested above.

IF YOU HAVE 7 DAYS

As in the previous itineraries, spend your first day in ⚏**Kotor** and the second morning in **Perast,** then drive to ⚏**Kolašin** and get a hotel room for two nights. Devote Day 3 to exploring **Biogradska Gora National Park,** then take a white-water rafting trip down the **Tara River** on Day 4. If the great outdoors still beckons, spend the night in an eco-village in the mountains. After a spa session on the morning of Day 5, head back toward the coast, visiting **Ostrog Monastery** en route. Spend the last two days exploring and relaxing in the seaside resorts of ⚏**Budva** and **Sveti Stefan.**

4 **Katedrala Sv Tripuna** (St. Tryphon's Cathedral). Undoubtedly Kotor's finest building, the Romanesque cathedral dates back to 1166, though excavation work shows there was already a smaller church here in the 9th century. Due to damage caused by a succession of disastrous earthquakes, the cathedral has been rebuilt several times—the twin baroque bell towers were added in the late 17th century. Inside, the most important feature is the 14th-century Romanesque Gothic ciborium above the main altar. Also look out for fragments of 14th-century frescoes, which would once have covered the entire interior. A collection of gold and silver reliquaries, encasing body parts of various saints and crafted by local masters between the 14th and 18th century, is on display in the

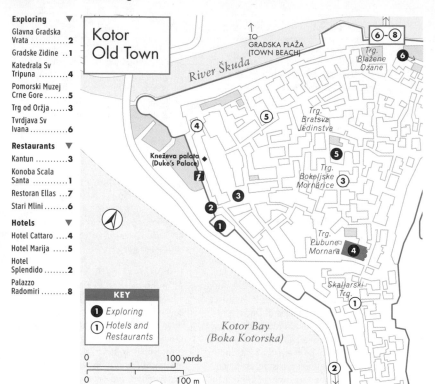

Kotor
Old Town

treasury. ✉ *Trg Ustanka Mornara* ☎*082/322–315* ⊙*May–Oct., daily 9–6; Nov.–Apr., daily 9–2.*

⑤ Pomorski Muzej Crne Gore (Montenegrin Naval Museum). Housed within the 18th-century baroque Grgurina Palace, this museum traces Montenegro's cultural and economic ties to the sea. In the 18th century, tiny Kotor had some 400 ships sailing the world's oceans. The exhibition extends over three floors, and includes model ships; paintings of ships, ship owners, and local naval commanders; navigation equipment; and uniforms worn by Montenegrin admirals and captains. ✉ *Trg Bokeljeske Mornorice* ☎*082/ 325–646* 💶*€2* ⊙ *Weekdays 8–2, weekends 9–noon.*

❸ Trg od Oržja (Square of Arms). The Main Town Gate leads directly into the Square of Arms, Kotor's main square, today a large paved space animated by popular open-air cafés. Under Venice, arms were repaired and stored here, hence the name. Notable buildings on the square include the 17th-century **Toranj za Sat** (Clock Tower), the 19th-century **Napoleonovog Pozorišta** (Napoleon Theatre), and the 18th-century **Kneževa Palata** (Duke's Palace), the latter two now forming part of the upmarket Hotel Cattaro. ✉ *Stari Grad.*

NEED A BREAK? **Café Forza Club** (⊠ *Trg od Oržja bb* ☎ *082/304-352*) With an open-air terrace on Kotor's elegant main square, this popular café is a great place for a refreshing drink or reviving coffee and a slice of calorie-laden gateau. Indoors is a cozy wood-paneled lounge with a small library and several computers with Internet access.

❻ **Tvrdjava Sv Ivana** (St. John's Fortress). On the hill behind Kotor, 853
★ feet above sea level, this fortress is approached via a series of serpentines and some 1,300 steps. The fantastic view from the top makes the climb worthwhile: the terra-cotta-tile rooftops of the Old Town, the meandering fjord, and the pine-clad mountains beyond. On the way up, you will pass the tiny Crkvfa Gospe od Zdravlija (Church of Our Lady of Health), built in the 16th century to protect Kotor against the plague. Be sure to wear good walking shoes and take plenty of water. The route up starts from behind the east side of the city walls. ⊠*Above the Old Town.*

WHERE TO EAT

$$$-$$$$ ✗**Konoba Scala Santa.** The look at this Old Town eatery is rustic but the food sophisticated—with upscale prices to match. If you feel like splashing out on top-notch seafood, this is the place for lobster and fresh fish, such as barbecued *zubatac* (dentex) drizzled with olive oil and served with a wedge of lemon. The candle-lit dining room has exposed stone walls, a wooden beamed ceiling hung with fishing equipment, and a big open fireplace. In summer, extra tables are set outside on the piazza. ⊠*Škaljarska Pjaca bb* ☎*069/299-836* ▤*DC, MC, V* ☉*No lunch Nov.–Apr.*

$$$-$$$$ ✗**Stari Mlini.** This old mill on the Ljuta River dates back to 1670 and is in the neighboring village of Ljuta, 7 km (4 mi) down the coastal road from Perast. It has been authentically restored and made into a rustic but rather expensive restaurant offering excellent food with an emphasis on fish. Try the *crni rižot.* In summer, outdoor tables are set up along the river (which is more of a stream these days). ⊠*Ljuta bb* ☎*082/333-555* ▤*DC, MC, V.*

$$-$$$ ✗**Restoran Ellas.** A popular venue for wedding receptions, Ellas serves local meat and fish specialties on a vine-covered seafront terrace lined with wooden tables and benches. Inside, the cozy stone-walled dining room has an open fireplace and a tile floor. Ellas is in the village of Dobrota, 3 km (2 mi) from Kotor. ⊠*Dobrota bb* ☎*082/335-115* ▤*DC.*

$$ ✗**Kantun.** Locals swear by this friendly, down-to-earth eatery in the Old Town, on a small piazza near the Montenegrin Naval Museum. The menu features a choice of seafood and meat dishes, but ask the waiter to recommend the day's special, which could be anything from *guláš* (Hungarian goulash) to sarma (cabbage leaves stuffed with rice and minced meat). Get a table outside in summer and soak in the Old Town atmosphere. ⊠*Trg od Muzeja bb* ☎*082/325-757* ▤*No credit cards.*

WHERE TO STAY

$$$ ⊞ **Hotel Cattaro.** This elegant, rather formal hotel is as magically central as it gets, occupying the 19th-century Napoleon Theatre, the 18th-century Duke's Palace, and other historic buildings on the Old Town's main square. The spacious rooms and suites have ochre yellow walls, beige curtains and bedspreads, and gray marble en-suite bathrooms. Public spaces are decorated with pictures of seascapes and ships, and portraits of local sea captains. Revelers can hit the in-house nightclub and casino before calling it a night. Pros: In Old Town, plush decor, historic building. Cons: Expensive, slightly lacking in charm, tends to book up. ⊠ *Trg od oružja bb, 85330* ☎ *082/311–000* ⊜ *082/311–080* ⊕ *www.cattarohotel.com* ⤲ *17 rooms, 3 suites* ☖ *Safe, Ethernet, restaurant, bar, no elevator* ⊟ *DC, MC, V.*

$$$ ⊞ **Hotel Splendido.** With splendid views indeed over the fjord, this
Fodor's Choice charming hotel in a stone villa stands on the waterfront in Prčanj, 3 km
★ (2 mi) from Kotor. The villa was built by a wealthy local sea captain in the 18th century and named after the first vessel to circumnavigate the globe from Kotor. The spacious, well-equipped rooms have tile floors, and beds with modern wrought-iron bedsteads. Rooms with sea views cost €10 extra. Excellent facilities include an oval-shape outdoor pool filled with seawater; bicycles, mopeds, and small boats to rent; plus massage and beauty treatments. The hotel's Tramontana restaurant serves Italian cuisine (dinner only) on a seaside terrace and has an adjoining 24-hour bar. Pros: Lovely old building, tastefully furnished, good sports facilities. Cons: Outside Kotor, small bathrooms, tends to book up. ⊠ *Glavati bb, 85331* ☎ *082/301–700* ⊜ *082/336–222* ⊕ *www.hotel-splendido.com* ⤲ *40 rooms, 3 suites* ☖ *Ethernet, restaurant, bar, pool, beachfront, bicycles, no elevator* ⊟ *DC, MC, V.*

$$ ⊞ **Palazzo Radomiri.** This small boutique hotel is in an 18th-century baroque stone building on the seafront in the village of Dobrota, 3 km (2 mi) from Kotor. The rooms and suites, named after local sea captains, are furnished with antiques, and the beds are made up with satin damask linens. Added touches of luxury include en-suite bathrooms stocked with Etro toiletries from Italy and fluffy bath and beach towels. There is a café, but no restaurant. An outdoor pool, sauna, and mini fitness studio round out the offerings. For those arriving by boat, the hotel has its own mooring facilities out front. Pros: Lovely old building, tastefully furnished, good sports facilities. Cons: Outside Kotor, no restaurant, often full in summer. ⊠ *Dobrota bb, 85331* ☎ *082/333–173* ⊜ *082/333–176* ⊕ *www.palazzoradomiri.com* ⤲ *4 rooms, 6 suites* ☖ *Ethernet, bar, pool, gym, beachfront, no elevator, laundry service* ⊟ *DC, V.*

$ ⊞ **Hotel Marija.** Austrian Emperor Franz Joseph stayed in this fine
★ three-story, baroque building in the 19th century, when it was a private home. Today, the hotel offers friendly, spotless, reasonably priced accommodation and a great Old Town location. Each guest room is furnished in its own style, and most have wooden parquet flooring. In good weather, the hotel's ground floor bar and restaurant encompass several outdoor tables on the small piazza. Some guests might find the noise from the surrounding bars excessive; if you prefer, ask for a

room not facing the street. Pros: In Old Town, historic building, helpful staff. Cons: Can be noisy, tends to fill up. ⊠ *Stari Grad 449, 85330* 🕾 *082/325–062* 🖷 *082/325–063* ◆ *17 rooms* ⚅ *Restaurant, bar, no elevator* ☰ *DC, V.*

NIGHTLIFE

Sleepy Kotor is hardly a party destination, its nightlife typically consisting of wining, dining, and people-watching at outdoor cafés and restaurants.

Secondo Porto (⊠ *Škaljari bb* 🕾 *069/087–703*). A major exception to Kotor's otherwise low-key nightlife offerings, this long-standing dance club is known throughout Montenegro and can pack in up to 1,800 revelers in a single night. It's just outside the Old Town walls and is open nightly 10 PM–4 AM in July and August, and just Friday and Saturday nights the rest of the year.

SPORTS & ACTIVITIES

BEACHES
The small pebble Gradska Plaža (Town Beach), just outside the town walls, is fine for a quick dip after a hot day of sightseeing. ■ TIP➔ However, locals prefer the sandy beaches facing the open sea along the Budva Riviera, 21 km (13 mi) down the coast.

SAILING
Several charter companies are based in the protected waters of Kotor Bay. For a one-week trip in August, expect to pay €1,300 for a 33-foot sailboat sleeping six, plus €100 per day for a skipper; prices do not include food, fuel, or mooring fees. Book well in advance—by Easter if you want to sail in July or August. There are also plans to convert the former military shipyard in Tivat, 5 km (3 mi) away, into a 700-berth luxury marina, which would make it the largest yacht marina in the East Mediterranean.

Southsail Charter (🕾 *082/673–418* ⊕ *www.southsail.cg.yu*) has boats based in Kotor marina, as well as in the nearby villages of Prčanj and Morinj. **Montenegro Charter Company** (🕾 *081/202–470* ⊕ *www.montenegrocharter.com*) also sails from Kotor's marina.

KOTOR ESSENTIALS

BY AIR
Tivat Airport is just 8 km (5 mi) from Kotor. Less convenient is the capital's Podgorica Airport, 90 km (56 mi) inland. Alternatively, some visitors fly in to Dubrovnik (Croatia) and drive 60 km (38 mi) down the coast to Kotor.

AIRPORTS & TRANSFERS
From May through October, buses run regularly between Tivat Airport and Kotor; inquire at the airport information desks for schedule and

8

fare information. You can catch a taxi year-round from both Tivat and Podgorica airports.

BY BOAT

From July through September, Azzurraline runs a twice-weekly ferry between Bari (Italy) and Kotor. Also in summer, private taxi boats operate from Kotor's harbor, taking passengers up the coast to the village of Perast.

BY BUS

Regular buses run along the coast, stopping in Kotor en route. There's also a special service between Kotor and Budva.

BY CAR

Having a car in Kotor is not recommended, as the Old Town is pedestrian-only and parking spots can be hard to find, especially in high season.

VISITOR INFORMATION

Kotor's tourist information office gives out free maps and information and can help find private accommodation. You'll find the office in a kiosk just outside the Main Town Gate.

Information Tourist Info Biro–Kotor (⊠ *Jadranski Put, Kotor* ☎ *082/325–950* ⊕ *www.tokotor.com*).

PERAST

15 km (9 mi) from Kotor.

Tiny Perast is a peaceful bay-front village of semi-abandoned baroque stone villas set in gardens filled with fig trees and oleander. It was built by wealthy local sea captains during the 17th and 18th centuries, at a time when it was prosperous enough to have some 100 merchant ships navigating the oceans. In fact, Perast's naval skills were so respected that in the early 18th century, the Russian tsar, Peter the Great, sent his young officers to study at the Perast Maritime Academy.

In the bay in front of Perast lie its main attractions: Sveti Djordje (St. George) and Gospa od Skrpjela (Our Lady of the Rock), a pair of tiny, charming islets, each topped with a church. As Perast has no beach to speak of, it isn't as set up for commercial tourism as its more beach-centric neighbors along the coast. But what it lacks in resort facilities, it amply makes up for with charming small hotels and apartments in tastefully refurbished, elegant old stone villas.

Each year on July 22, Perast celebrates the *fasinada,* a local festival honoring the folkloric origins of Our Lady of the Rock, with a ritual procession of boats carrying stones out to the island at sunset. The stones are dropped into the water around the island, protecting it from erosion by the sea for the coming year. The Fasinada Cup sailing regatta is held on the same day.

Perast can be reached by car or bus, and can also be visited on an organized half-day boat trip from Kotor's harbor.

EXPLORING PERAST

Begin your exploration with a look in the Perast Town Museum, then take a taxi boat from the quayside to visit the island church, Our Lady of the Rock. Head back to town for lunch at one of the area's charming rustic eateries.

★ Unlike its sibling island, St. George, **Gospa od Skrpjela** (Our Lady of the Rock) is man-made. Folklore has it that in 1452, local sailors found an icon depicting the Virgin and Child cast upon a rock jutting up from the water. Taking this as a sign from God, they began placing stones on and around the rock, slowly building an island over it. By 1630 they had erected a church upon the new island. The original icon (which has been attributed to the 15th-century local artist Lovro Dobričević) is displayed on the altar. Over the centuries, locals have paid their respects to it by donating silver votive offerings, some 2,500 of which are now on display. To get here, hop a boat taxi from the waterfront (a five-minute trip). ⊠*Kotor Bay* ☎*082 325–952 Kotor tourist office, for information* 🖃*€2* ⊙*June–Sept., daily 9–7; Oct.–May hours vary.*

In the 17th-century Renaissance-baroque Bujović Palace, on the water's edge, **Muzej Grad Perasta** (Perast Town Museum) displays paintings of local sea captains and their ships, plus a horde of objects connected to Perast's maritime past. ⊠*Obala Marka Martinovića bb* ☎*082/373–519* 🖃*€2* ⊙*June–Sept., Mon.–Sat. 9–9, Sun. 9–2; Oct.–May, daily 9–2.*

Sveti Djordje (St. George), a natural islet, is one of Perast's famous pair of islands. It's ringed by a dozen elegant cypress trees and crowned by the Monastery of St. George, dating back to the 12th century and still inhabited by monks. In the 18th century, the island became a favorite burial place for local sea captains, whose crypts remain today. The island is closed to the public, but you can snap photos from shore or neighboring Our Lady of the Rock to your heart's content. ⊠*Kotor Bay.*

WHERE TO EAT

$$–$$$ ✕**Catovica Mlini.** In the tiny village of Morinj, 10 km (6 mi) from Perast
Fodor'sChoice on the road to Herzeg Novi, this charming, family-run restaurant occu-
★ pies a former water-driven flour mill. You can choose a table either in the stone vaulted dining room or in the lush garden next to the stream. Excellent seafood dishes include *salata od hobotnice, crni rižot,* and *dagnje na buzaru* (mussels cooked in a rich garlic, tomato, wine, and parsley sauce). ⊠*Morinj bb* ☎*082/373–030* 🖃*DC, MC, V.*

$$ ✕**Otok Bronza.** At this restaurant set in a delightful 15th-century stone
★ building, you can eat in the cool flagstone-floor dining room or alfresco at rustic wooden tables and benches under a shady, vine-covered terrace. The house specialties here are *grdoba u bijelom vinu* (sea scorpion in white wine) and *riba pečena u soli* (fish baked in a sea salt crust). But if seafood is beginning to pall, go for *Njeguški stek.* Either way, order a bottle of good local wine, and sit back and enjoy the owner's fine collection of jazz music. ⊠*Perast bb* ☎*069/401–936* 🖃*No credit cards.*

8

WHERE TO STAY

$$–$$$ ⊞ **Hotel Conte.** This 15th-century stone building has been converted to provide seven well-equipped apartments, each with its own kitchen and Jacuzzi. Some units have exposed wooden-beamed ceilings. There is also a pleasant restaurant with a stone-walled dining room and two open-air terraces. Pros: Lovely old building, tastefully furnished, good restaurant. Cons: Tends to fill up. ⊠ *Perast bb, 85336* ☎ *082/373–687* ⊕ *www.hotel-conte.com* ⌨ *7 apartments* ⚘ *Kitchen, Ethernet, restaurant, no elevator* ▤ *DC, V.*

$ ⊞ **Villa Milinović.** This old stone building on Perast's seafront has nine guest rooms with wooden parquet flooring and tasteful wooden furniture. Ask for a room with a sea view. Out front and under the same management, Konoba Milinović serves fresh seafood and barbecued meats on a shady waterside terrace affording views across the bay to the island churches. Pros: Lovely old building, seafront location, good restaurant. Cons: Tends to fill up. ⊠ *Obala Martinovića bb, 85336* ☎ *082/373–556* ⊕ *www.milinovic-perast.com* ⌨ *9 rooms* ⚘ *Restaurant, no elevator* ▤ *DC, V* ⊘ *Closed Nov.–Apr.*

BUDVA

36 km (22 mi) from Perast, 21 km (13 mi) from Kotor.

Montenegro's top seaside resort, Budva has a romantic Old Town, both sand and pebble beaches, a vibrant nightlife, and dozens of hotels. The oldest settlement on the Montenegrin coast, it was founded by the Greeks in the 4th century BC, when what is now the Old Town was an island, which was subsequently joined to the mainland to form a small peninsula. After the Greeks came the Romans—gold and silver jewelry from a Roman necropolis discovered here are on display in the Town Museum. Then, under Byzantine rule (AD 535–841), Budva's earliest churches were built. However, it was under the Venetians (1443–1797) that the Old Town took on its present appearance with the construction of sturdy town walls and the elegant buildings that line its narrow cobbled streets. Budva met near-catastrophe with a dreadful earthquake in 1979. Fortunately, substantial sums of money were invested in its reconstruction, and today many of its old stone buildings host trendy cocktail bars, rustic seafood restaurants, and chic boutiques. South of town, the so-called Budvanska rivijera (Budva Riviera) is a 21-km (13-mi) stretch of coast dotted with some of the country's best beaches. Foreseeing the enormous potential for upmarket tourism, foreign investors (notably Russian and British) are now snapping up socialist-era hotels and converting them into luxurious resorts. Recent high-profile visitors to the Budva area include the Rolling Stones, who played a concert on Jaz Beach, 3 km (2 mi) up the coast, in July 2007.

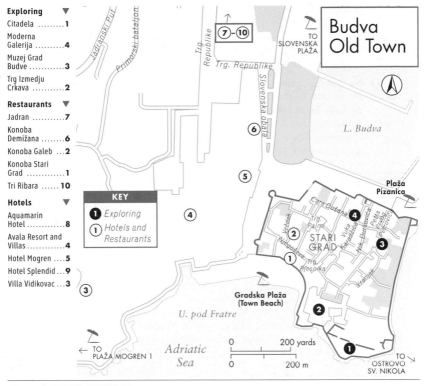

EXPLORING BUDVA

Budva's main cultural attractions lie within the walls of the compact Old Town, which is closed to traffic but can be comfortably explored on foot in a couple of hours.

Numbers in the margin correspond to points of interest on the Budva Old Town map.

❶ **Citadela** (Fortress). On the southern town walls, facing out to sea, this
★ fortress dates back to the 6th century AD. Various alterations and additions were made through the centuries, including the barracks, which were built by the Austrians in 1836. Steps climb to the arched entrance, protected by a cannon, then continue upward to a large terrace offering fine views over the Old Town's terra-cotta rooftops and out to sea. In summer, open-air theater performances are held here. ⊠*Trg Izmedju Crkava* ☞*€2* ⊙*June–Sept., daily 8–midnight; Oct.–May, daily 8–2.*

❹ **Moderna Galerija** (Modern Art Gallery). This pleasant little gallery, in a stone house in the Old Town, exhibits paintings by local artists who have been inspired by Budva. ⊠*Cara Dušana 19* ☎*086/451–343* ☞*€1.50* ⊙*June–Sept., Tues.–Sun. 8–8; Oct.–May, weekdays 8–2.*

Muzej Grad Budve (Budva Town Museum). Combining both archaeological and ethnological exhibits, this museum traces Budva's 2,500-year history. Displays include gold and silver jewelry, ceramics, glassware, and furniture. ⊠*Petra Petrovica bb* ☎*086/453–308* ☜*€1.50* ⊙*June–Sept., Tues.–Sun. 8–8; Oct.–May, Tues.–Fri. 9–8 and weekends 9–5.*

❷ Trg Izmedju Crkava (Square Between the Churches). The largest square in the Old Town is home to three impressive churches from different periods: Sv Marija in Punta (St. Mary in Punta), founded under Byzantine rule in AD 840; Sv Sava (St. Sava), a 12th-century Romanesque church; and Sv Trojice (Holy Trinity), an Orthodox church from 1804. ⊠*Trg Izmedje Crkava.*

WHERE TO EAT

$$$–$$$$
★ ✕**Konoba Galeb.** On a narrow side street in the Old Town, this seafood restaurant has been run by the same family since 1966. The ground-floor dining room has a flagstone floor, whitewashed walls hung with fishing equipment, and a wooden-beamed ceiling. Up top, a lovely roof terrace offers open-air dining through summer. Choose from the day's catch, dentex, bream, or red mullet, and pair it with a good bottle of local wine. ⊠*Vrzdak 11* ☎*086/456–546* ▤*DC, MC, V.*

$$–$$$ ✕**Jadran.** Of the string of eateries lining the mile-long Slovenska Plaža, Jadran is one of the oldest and best known. Blue-and-white tables and chairs are arranged on a large vine-covered terrace, where diners enjoy a large selection of meat and fish dishes. Many people come straight here after a day on the beach. ⊠*Slovenska Obala 10* ☎*086/451–028* ▤*MC.*

$$–$$$
★ ✕**Konoba Demižana.** This esteemed eatery is renowned for excellent fresh seafood. Start with *crni rižot* followed by *jastoži na žaru* (grilled lobster). In the leafy front garden, marked by two towering palm trees, heavy wooden tables and benches are arranged in the shade of a vine-covered terrace and several big green umbrellas. The restaurant is opposite the entrance to the Old Town. ⊠*Slovenska Obala 3* ☎*086/455–028* ▤*DC, MC, V.*

$$–$$$ ✕**Konoba Stari Grad.** If you're looking for literal beachfront dining, this is your spot. Tables are set in the sand near the lapping waves on Gradska Beach. Come for a wide selection of risotto and pasta dishes, salads, and barbecued meat and fish. Or for just a drink, have a seat on one of the lounge-style sofas. ⊠*Njeogoševa 14* ☎*086/454–443* ▤*DC, V.*

$$–$$$
Fodor'sChoice
★ ✕**Tri Ribara.** Overlooking Bečići Beach in the small fishing village of Rafailovici, a 40-minute walk (or 5- to 10-minute drive) from town, the family-run "Three Fishermen" restaurant is widely regarded—by tourists and locals alike—as the best in the Budva area. The look is rustic—an open fireplace indoors, and outside, a terrace filled with heavy wooden tables and benches—and the seafood is exquisite, if pricey. ⊠*Bečićka Plaža 35* ☎*086/471–050* ▤*DC, MC, V.*

WHERE TO STAY

$$$$ 🏨 **Avala Resort and Villas.** Budva's most luxurious hotel is due to open
Fodor'sChoice in mid-2008 with 125 rooms and suites offering gorgeous sea or moun-
★   tain views, 67 villas with their own private pools, a spa and wellness center, and a strikingly sophisticated minimalist look throughout.
Avala is built into the hillside at the end of Gradska Plaža, just outside
the Old Town. Pros: Stunning modern design, seafront location, next
to Old Town. Cons: Construction work might continue past opening,
expensive. ⌂ *Mediteranska 2, 85310* ☎ *086/441–000* 🖷 *086/402–659*
⊕ *www.avalaresort.com* 🛏 *119 rooms, 6 suites, 67 villas* ♿ *Safe, Ethernet, 2 restaurants, bars, pools, gym, spa, beachfront* ▭*DC, MC, V.*

$$$$ 🏨 **Hotel Splendid.** This sophisticated five-star hotel is set among palm
trees in vast grounds overlooking Bečići Plaža, 4 km (2½ mi) from
Budva Old Town. Rooms and suites are decorated in subtle creams and
beiges with splashes of Bordeaux and olive green, and all have en-suite
marble bathrooms and balconies; ask for a room overlooking the sea.
The luxurious spa offers fantastic sea views from its indoor pools—perhaps enjoyed by the Rolling Stones, who stayed here while on tour.
Pros: Smart modern design, seafront location, professional service,
Mick Jagger slept here. Cons: Outside Budva, rather vast and impersonal, expensive. ⌂ *Bečići bb, 85315* ☎ *086/773–777* 🖷 *086/773–757*
⊕ *www.montenegrostars.com* 🛏 *322 rooms, 19 suites* ♿ *Safe, Ethernet, 3 restaurants, bars, pools, gym, spa, beachfront* ▭*DC, MC, V.*

$$ 🏨 **Aquamarin Hotel.** One block in from bustling Slovenska Plaža and a
1½-km (1-mi) walk along the seafront promenade from the Old Town,
this small hotel occupies a white, modern, four-story building set in a
leafy garden. The rooms and suites are simply but smartly decorated
with tile floors and blue-and-white fabrics, and most have balconies.
Request a sea view, if that's your preference. Facilities include a sauna,
small outdoor pool, and a speedboat for hourly hire. Pros: Near beach,
10-minute walk to Old Town, pleasant restaurant terrace. Cons: Rooms
slightly institutional, could be noisy at night due to the proximity of
bars lining Slovenska Plaža. ⌂ *Potkošljun bb, 85310* ☎ *086/460–269*
🖷 *086/460–269* ⊕ *www.aquamarin-hotel.com* 🛏 *6 rooms, 18 suites*
♿ *Restaurant, bar, pool, no elevator* ▭*DC, MC, V.*

$ 🏨 **Hotel Mogren.** A good value in the area, this property offers basic but
comfortable rooms at reasonable prices and a good location—just out-
side the Old Town walls, above Mogren Beach. Ask for a room with a
view of the Old Town. A row of palms fronts the four-story white build-
ing, which dates back to 1935. Pros: Next to Old Town, near beach.
Cons: Dated decor, slow (but friendly) service. ⌂ *85310* ☎ *086/451–102*
🖷 *086/451–102* 🛏 *45 rooms, 4 suites* ♿ *Restaurant, bar* ▭*DC, V.*

$ 🏨 **Villa Vidikovac.** Every room has a sea view at this family-run hotel
above Mogren Beach, a five-minute walk from the Old Town. Rooms are
modern and comfortable, with wooden floors. Facilities include an out-
door pool and Jacuzzi and an indoor mini spa with sauna and Jacuzzi.
Pros: Near Old Town, near beach, great sea views. Cons: Tends to book
up, no restaurant, no bar. ⌂ *Jadranski put bb, 85310* ☎ *086/455–584*
🖷 *086/455–584* ⊕ *www.villavidikovac.com* 🛏 *20 rooms* ♿ *Pool, no
elevator, parking (no fee)* ▭*DC, V* ⊘ *Closed Nov.–Apr.*

8

NIGHTLIFE & THE ARTS

NIGHTLIFE

The most atmospheric bars are in the Old Town, and most stay open until at least 1 AM. For more boisterous activity, try the string of cafés and open-air dance clubs lining the seaside promenade leading onto Slovenska Plaža; as a general rule, the farther they are from the Old Town, the wilder they get. Names and locations change annually, but keep an eye out for long-standing favorite Trocadero, an open-air dance club with occasional live music, mainly by Serbian pop singers.

★ **Kasper** (⊠ *Cara Dušana 10* ☎ *086/442–090*) is a laid-back venue on a small square in the Old Town, with an outdoor bar and tables set up under a big pine tree in summer. The DJ plays a fine mix of jazz, Latino, electro, and house music until at least 2 AM on weekends. **Café Bar Hemingway** (⊠ *Slovenska Obala 11* ☎ *086/452–400*) is a refined spot in a green-shuttered building on the seafront promenade, a short walk from the Old Town. Pick from a good choice of cocktails and bottled wines and chill out in mellow lighting on the leafy terrace out front.

THE ARTS

Summer sees the piazzas in the Old Town transformed into open-air stages with two excellent annual cultural events: Music Festival Budva and the City Theatre Festival.

★ **Music Festival Budva** (⊕ *www.musicfestivalbudva.com*) is a three-day event in late June held at various open-air venues in the Old Town. The "Mediterranean" music menu usually includes a mix of Balkan pop, rock, jazz, and folk. **City Theatre Festival** (⊕ *www.gradtheatar.cg.yu*) stages dramas and classical music concerts at various open-air venues around town, including the upper terrace inside the Citadela and on Trg Izmedju Crkava. The festival runs mid-July through late August.

SPORTS & ACTIVITIES

BEACHES

There are three beaches within comfortable walking distance of Budva's Old Town. Entry to all is free, and inexpensive sun bed and umbrella rentals are available by the day or half day. **Gradska Plaža** (Town Beach), a small pebble beach just outside the Old Town walls, is fine for a quick dip but not somewhere you can really relax, as several cafés and restaurants have tables quite close to the water's edge. The secluded, pebbled **Mogren Beach** is in a small cove that has been awarded the Blue Flag, a worldwide certification recognizing cleanliness and respect for the environment. **Slovenska Plaža** (Slovenska Beach) is a bustling 1½-km (1-mi) stretch of sand lined with bars, restaurants, and hotels. This is Budva's best-known and most commercial beach, complete with water sports facilities, plus bars and clubs working late into the night.

In addition, regular taxi boats depart from Budva harbor taking beachgoers to nearby alternatives such as Sveti Stefan, Kraljeva Plaža (King's Beach), Petrovac, Jaz, Trsteno, and Ostrvo Sv Nikola (St. Nicholas's Island)—a lovely uninhabited isle popular with swimmers.

SCUBA DIVING

With a fine strip of coast offering clean water with good visibility, the Budva Riviera is perfect for scuba diving. Average costs are €20 for a single dive, €80 for a package of five dives, and €30 for a night dive.

Pro Dive Hydrotech (☎ *067/835–538* ⊕ *www.prodive-cg.com*), based at the Queen of Montenegro Hotel in Bečići, 4 km (3 mi) from Budva, offers scuba-diving trips from May to September to various locations along the coast, including coral reefs, underwater caves, and shipwrecks. Training is available for beginners.

PARAGLIDING

Brajici, the 2,490-foot mountain behind Budva, is a popular launching pad for paragliders, offering in-flight views along the coast from Budva Old Town down to the island hotel of Sveti Stefan. Sandy Bečići Plaža is the landing spot. Rates run around €60 per jump, with equipment and instruction provided.

Sokol (☎ *067/557–903*), which means "Eagle," is Budva's main paragliding outfit and operates May–October. Its location changes, but the tourist office can send you in the right direction.

BUDVA ESSENTIALS

BY AIR

The nearest airport to Budva is Tivat Airport, 21 km (13 mi) away. Less convenient options are in Podgorica, 62 km (39 mi) inland, and Dubrovnik, 85 km (53 mi) north, in Croatia.

Airport Transfers In high season (May–October), there is regular bus service between Tivat Airport and Budva; inquire at the airport information desks for schedule and fare information. Taxis operate year-round from both Tivat and Podgorica airports.

BY BOAT

Privately operated taxi boats operate from Budva's waterfront, taking swimmers to nearby beaches.

BY BUS

Many buses travel up and down the coast, stopping in Budva en route. Several companies offer direct routes from Budva to Kotor and Sveti Stefan.

BY CAR

A car is not essential for exploring the coast, which is well served by cheap, if often crowded, buses. In fact, having a car can be a hindrance, as parking is very difficult in popular seaside resorts like Budva and Sveti Stefan. However, if you plan to move inland, a private vehicle is an advantage.

VISITOR INFORMATION

The National Tourism Organization of Montenegro's small information office in the Old Town can answer questions and help book hotels and private accommodations.

Information Tourist Information Service (✉ *Njegoševa 28, Budva* ☎ *086/452–750* ⊕ *www.tob.cg.yu*).

SVETI STEFAN

Fodor's Choice
★ *8 km (5 mi) from Budva.*

Often referred to as the "jewel of the Montenegrin coast," Sveti Stefan is a tiny island protected by 600-year-old defensive walls inside of which nestle several dozen limestone cottages and a small church. The island is actually joined to the mainland by an isthmus, which has a fine pebble beach on each side. Originally a fishing village, it was fortified with sturdy walls in the 15th century to protect it from the Turks and marauding pirates. By the late 19th century, however, many residents had emigrated abroad, due to the poor local economy. In 1955, the few remaining inhabitants were relocated so that the entire village could be renovated and turned into a unique luxury hotel. The resort opened with a splash in 1960, attracting over the years international jet-setters and celebrities, from Richard Burton and Elizabeth Taylor, to Claudia Schiffer and Sylvester Stallone. But when the war hit in the 1990s, tourists stopped coming and the economy took a nosedive, leading Sveti Stefan to fall into total disrepair. Now, after years of exhaustive renovation, it is due to reopen in summer 2008 as the Sveti Stefan Aman, an exclusive resort of luxury suites, each with a private pool.

A modern village has grown up on the mainland facing the island, with small hotels, rental apartments, and restaurants all marketing themselves upon the simple fact that they afford a glimpse of Sveti Stefan's magic. Admiring (and photographing) the island from here is indeed worthwhile, but the best way to experience it is, of course, to book a room at the resort. Once it opens, nonguests might be allowed to visit the complex for a fee; inquire at the tourist office or the hotel for details.

As parking here can be a nightmare, the best way to get to Sveti Stefan is to catch the Olimpia Express mini-bus from Budva, which runs every 30 minutes. Slower but more fun (albeit more expensive), you can also opt for a taxi boat.

WHERE TO EAT & STAY

$$–$$$ ✗ **Villa Drago.** A good place to stop for an informal meal or a drink, this small family-run restaurant is on the mainland hillside overlooking the sea and has a large terrace out front. The staff is friendly and multilingual, and the menu includes both seafood specialties from along the coast and heartier roast meats from the mountains. ✉ *Slobode 32* ☎ *086/468–777* ▭ *No credit cards* ☉ *Closed Nov.–Mar.*

$$$$ ▦ **Sveti Stefan Aman.** Having fallen into complete disrepair during the Yugoslavian war, this magnificent island complex is due to reopen in summer 2008, after years of exhaustive renovation, under the new ownership of Singapore-based Aman Resorts. Nestled within 15th-century defensive walls and laced with cobblestone streets, an entire village of beautifully preserved medieval stone cottages with terra-cotta tile roofs will house 40 luxurious suites, each with a private pool. An additional 10 suites will be in the nearby former Hotel Miločer on the

mainland, originally built as the Montenegrin royal summer residence in the 1930s. Further details were unavailable at press time, but it's safe to say this will be a drop-dead gorgeous property. Pros: Historic buildings, stunning island location, modern interior design. Cons: Renovation work might not be completed to schedule, expensive. ⊠ *Sveti Stefan Island, 85315* ☎ *65/6883–2555 (Singapore)* 🖷 *65/6883–0555 (Singapore)* ⊕ *www.amanresorts.com* ⇥ *50 suites* ▭ *DC, MC, V.*

KOLAŠIN & BIOGRADSKA GORA NATIONAL PARK

138 km (86 mi) from Sveti Stefan.

At an altitude of 3,165 feet, the compact mountain town of Kolašin sits on the edge of Biogradska Gora, Montenegro's oldest national park. Often compared to Switzerland, Biogradska Gora is a hiker's paradise of snowcapped Alpine mountains and dense pine forests interspersed with lush green meadows and glacial lakes, the largest of which is Biogradsko Jezero (Biogradsko Lake).

With an economy formerly based on timber processing, Kolašin has recently entered the field of upscale tourism, thanks primarily to the opening of the luxurious full-service Bianca Resort and Spa. In total contrast, Biogradska Gora National Park is fast becoming a pioneer of sustainable tourism, with several eco-villages offering back-to-basics accommodation in traditional shepherds huts.

Kolašin also makes a good base for white-water rafting on the Tara River, just outside Biogradska Gora National Park. The Tara River Canyon, a UNESCO World Heritage site, is 80 km (50 mi) long and 4,265 feet deep—allegedly the longest canyon in Europe and the second largest in the world after Arizona's Grand Canyon. You can judge for yourself on a rafting trip run by one of several outfitters in town.

Biogradska Gora National Park is open daily 7 AM–3 PM and costs €1 to enter. The park information center (⊠ *Buda Tomovica bb, Kolašin* ☎ *081/865–046*) in Kolašin can set you up with hiking maps and suggested routes.

To get to Kolašin from Budva, either drive down the coast to Petrovac (12 km [8 mi]) and take the E65 to Kolašin, passing through Podgorica en route; or take the scenic (but twisty!) local road inland from Budva to Podgorica, passing through Cetinje, then continue to Kolašin on the E65. A regular bus service covers this route, but you may have to change in Podgorica.

WHERE TO EAT

$–$$ ✕ **Restoran Eko Koliba.** Tucked into a traditional wooden building with a steep-pitched roof, this authentic little eatery near the Tara River offers local goodies such as *kajmak* (a rich, buttery, cream cheese), *pastrmka* (trout), and *jagnjetina u mlijeku* (lamb cooked in milk), all served with delicious homemade bread. ⊠*Trebajevo bb* ☎*067/591–580* ☰*No credit cards.*

$–$$ ✗**Savardak.** This is a great place to try traditional mountain dishes faithfully prepared with old-fashioned recipes. Look for *pršut* (prosciutto), *kačamak* (similar to polenta), and *cicvaru* (a concoction of corn flour, cream cheese, and eggs). The restaurant is hard to miss, as it occupies a traditional (and somewhat bizarre) cone-shape building, called a "Savardak," made of wood and thatch. ⊠*Biocinovice bb* ☎*067/250–087* ☰*No credit cards.*

WHERE TO STAY

$$ ▦**Bianca Resort and Spa.** Commanding magnificent mountain views and
Fodor'sChoice set in 25 acres of pine forests, this luxury hotel resembles a large hunt-
★ ing lodge from the outside. Inside, minimalist modern design combines natural local materials—pinewood and limestone—creating a sophisticated but unpretentious atmosphere. All rooms and suites have modern pine furniture and wall-mounted plasma TVs, and those on the top floor have sloping ceilings with exposed timber beams. The casual-chic public spaces include two restaurants, two bars, and a lounge with a large open fireplace. The Olympic-size indoor pool is housed in a glass-and-wood structure, and the Taiyang Spa offers beauty treatments, massage, solarium, sauna, and Turkish bath. Sports on offer include hiking, mountain biking, horseback riding, skiing, and ice-skating. Pros: Stunning mountain location, modern interior design, professional service. Cons: Out in the boondocks. ⊠*Kolašin bb, 84220* ☎*081/863–000* 🖨*081/863–168* ⊕*www.biancaresort.com* ⇆*102 rooms, 15 suites* ⚴*Safe, Ethernet, 2 restaurants, bars, pools, gym, spa, bicycles* ☰*DC, MC, V.*

$ ▦**Eco Village Jelka.** For a back-to-nature experience, stay at this eco-
☺ village in the mountains above Kolašin at an altitude of 5,740 feet.
★ Accommodation is in 20 traditional wooden shepherds huts, each sleeping two people. Rooms are spotless but extremely basic, just big enough for a double mattress. Bathroom facilities are shared but kept very clean. All the meals are prepared from local organic produce, water is collected from a spring, and tea is made from mountain herbs. From here you can walk to Biogradsko Jezero (Biogradsko Lake), as well as go mountain biking and horseback riding. Transport from the town center can be arranged. Pros: Unique experience, stunning mountain location, the other guests are probably nature-lovers like you. Cons: No private bathrooms, very basic. ⊠*Bjelasica Mountain, 84220* ☎*069/400–094* 🖨*081/860–150* ⊕*www.vilajelka.cg.yu* ⇆*21 huts* ⚴*Restaurant* ☰*No credit cards* ☾*Nov.–May.*

SPORTS & ACTIVITIES

Biogradksa Gora National Park offers a network of marked paths for all levels of hiking amid stunning mountains and lakes. Just outside the park is the Tara River, Montenegro's top destination for white-water rafting. Several Kolašin-based agencies can help you arrange these and other sporting expeditions.

Eco Tours (⌧ *Kolašin bb* ☎ *081/860–700* ⊕ *www.eco-tours.cg.yu*) offers white-water rafting on the Tara River June–September, plus organized hiking tours, Jeep safaris, and horseback riding.

Vila Jelka (☎ *081/860–150* ⊕ *www.vilajelka.cg.yu*) a small hotel and travel agency, can arrange rafting on the Tara River, as well as hiking trips, mountain biking, horseback riding, and photo safaris in Biogradska Gora National Park and the surrounding area.

MONTENEGRO ESSENTIALS

TRANSPORTATION

BY AIR

Montenegro Airlines has service from Podgorcia Airport to Belgrade, Budapest, Frankfurt, Ljubljana, Paris, Rome, Vienna, and Zurich. From Tivat Airport, it flies to Belgrade, Frankfurt, Ljubljana, Paris, and Zurich. The Serbian carrier JAT flies from Belgrade to Podgorica and Tivat, and Slovenia's Adria Airways flies from Ljubljana to Podgorica. Well served by international airlines, Dubrovnik Airport, in Croatia, is a popular alternative gateway to Montenegro, but it's important to note that car rental agencies may charge extra for taking the vehicle across borders.

Airlines Adria Airways (☎ *081/201–201* ⊕ *www.adria.si*). **JAT** (☎ *081/244–248* ⊕ *www.jat.com*).**Montenegro Airlines** (☎ *081/405–501* ⊕ *www.montenegro-airlines.cg.yu*).

Airports Aerodrom Podgorica (☎ *081/243–007* ⊕ *www.montenegroairports. com*). **Aerodrom Tivat** (☎ *082/670–960* ⊕ *www.montenegroairports.com*). **Zračna Luka Dubrovnik** (⌧ *Čilipi bb, Dubrovnik, Croatia* ☎ *385/20–773–377* ⊕ *www. airport-dubrovnik.hr*).

BY BOAT

Montenegro Lines operates regular overnight car ferries year-round to the Montenegrin port of Bar, 38 km (24 mi) south of Budva, from Ancona and Bari in Italy. The Ancona-Bar crossing takes 16 hours; a one-way ticket (interior two-berth cabin with bathroom) costs around €95. The Bari-Bar crossing takes 10 hours and costs about €120. July through September, Azzuraline runs a twice-weekly ferry service from Bari to Kotor. One-way tickets (interior two-berth cabin with sink only) for the nine-hour overnight trip run around €85.

8

Information Azzurraline (✉ *Bari Maritime Station, Bari* ☎ *0039/080/592-84-00* ⊕ *www.azzurraline.com).***Montenegro Lines** (✉ *Obala 13 Jula bb, Bar* ☎ *085/312-366* ⊕ *www.montenegrolines.net*).

BY BUS

Buses are cheap and cover practically the entire country, but many are old and uncomfortable—and if they're full (as is often the case in high season), you might find yourself standing for the duration of your trip. That said, there's no better way to meet the locals and gain insight into Montenegrin life than spending a few hours on a crowded coach. Numerous small bus lines operate regularly along the coast between Herzeg Novi (in the north) and Ulcinj (in the south), stopping at most towns along the way. Autoboka runs buses between Kotor and Budva. Olimpia Express operates minibuses between Budva and Sveti Stefan. For other routes, inquire at the bus station of departure.

Information Autoboka (✉ *Njegoševa 204, Kotor* ☎ *082/322-111* ⊕ *www. autoboka.com*). **Budva Bus Station** (✉ *Ulica Popa Jola Zeca bb, Budva* ☎ *086/456-000*). **Kolašin Bus Station** (✉ *Junaka Mojkovamke Bitke bb, Kolašin* ☎ *081/864-033*). **Kotor Bus Station** (✉ *Škaljari bb, Kotor* ☎ *082/325-089*). **Olimpia Express** (✉ *Trg Sunca 2, Budva* ☎ *086/451-567*).

BY CAR

Although Montenegro's buses have good service along the coast and can get you to most points in the country, renting a car gives you much more flexibility and makes life especially easier when visiting the mountains. The weekly rate for a compact car with unlimited mileage is around €470.

Information Avis (✉ *Podgorica Airport, Podgorica* ☎ *081/622-165* ✉ *Tivat Airport, Tivat* ☎ *082/673-448* ✉ *Slovenska Obbala bb, Budva* ☎ *086/673-448*). **Europcar** (✉ *Podgorica Airport, Podgorica* ☎ *081/606-310* ✉ *Tivat Airport, Tivat* ☎ *082/671-894* ✉ *13 Jula bb, Budva* ☎ *086/401-730*).

BY TRAIN

Due its mountainous nature, Montenegro is poorly served by rail. However, there is a stunningly scenic line connecting the Montenegrin port town of Bar to Belgrade in Serbia, passing through Podgorica and Kolašin en route. From Belgrade, you're well connected to the rest of Europe by train.

Information Bar Train Station (☎ *085/301-623*). **Podgorica Train Station** (✉ *Trg Golo Otočkih Žrtava 13, Podgorica* ☎ *081/441-211*). **Željeznica Crne Gore (Montenegrin Railways)** (☎ *081/441-302* ⊕ *www.zeljeznica.cg.yu*).

CONTACTS & RESOURCES

BANKS & EXCHANGE SERVICES

The official currency has been theeuro since 2002, despite the fact that Montenegro has not yet entered the European Union. At press time the exchange rate was about €1.46 to U.S.$1.

Diners Club, MasterCard, and Visa are widely accepted at the more upmarket hotels, restaurants, shops, and travel agents, but American

Express is not recognized anywhere in Montenegro. In general, banks prefer to exchange foreign currency rather than traveler's checks, even if the checks are in euros. The best banks to approach if you want to exchange traveler's checks are Atlas Mont Bank and Euromarket. ATMs are available in most towns.

EMERGENCIES

Information **Ambulance** (☎ 94). **Fire** (☎ 93). **Police** (☎ 92).

INTERNET, MAIL & SHIPPING

Internet cafés are still rather few and far between. Some set up temporarily for the summer, but few are established on an annual basis. Café Forza Club in Kotor is one exception. However, most decent hotels have Internet connections in the rooms, plus an Internet corner that nonguests are often welcome to use if they ask at the reception desk.

DHL offers reliable international shipping service and is your best bet for sending parcels back home.

Internet Cafés **Café Forza Club** (✉ *Trg od Oržja bb, Kotor* ☎ *082/304–352*).

Post Offices **Budva post office** (✉ *Mediteranska 8, Budva* ☎ *086/452–401*). **Kotor post office** (✉ *Stari Grad bb, Kotor* ☎ *082/322–359*).

Shipping Companies **DHL** (✉ *Trg Palmi 8, Budva* ☎ *086/403–393* ✉ *Marka Miljanova 52, Podgorica* ☎ *081/633–996*).

TELEPHONES

The country code for Montenegro is 382.

TOUR OPTIONS

Many private travel agencies offer tours, with hiking in the mountains and rafting on the Tara River being the most popular. T.A. Meridian runs rafting trips on the Tara River as well as sightseeing excursions to points of interest like Kotor Bay and Dubrovnik. Adriatic Express runs guided tours and excursions out of Budva, including pilgrimages to religious sites and rafting and paragliding trips. Eco Tours, based in Kolašin, specializes in outdoor activities such as rafting, camping, horseback riding, fishing, mountain biking, paragliding, and skiing.

Information **Adriatic Express** (✉ *Popa Jola Zeca bb, Budva* ☎ *086402–600* ⊕ *www.adriaex.com*). **Eco Tours** (✉ *Kolašin bb, Kolašin* ☎ *081/860–700* ⊕ *www.eco-tours.cg.yu*). **T. A. Meridian** (✉ *Stari Grad 436, Kotor* ☎ *082/323–448* ⊕ *www.tameridian.cg.yu*).

VISITOR INFORMATION

Information **National Tourism Organization of Montenegro** (✉ *Rimski Trg 10, Podgorica* ☎ *081/235–155* ⊕ *www.visit-montenegro.org*).

Poland

"Warsaw is filled with the spirit and memories of the uprising during World War II. Kraków is filled with vitality and excitement. Gdańsk is filled with the history of the fight for freedom and the struggle of the shipyard workers."

—Lolo12

"One of Kraków's great charms is its restaurants. Every courtyard and alley provides opportunity for a pleasant café; the cellars are captivating settings for a meal or a jazz performance (or a pool as at Copernicus). Sometimes, when I entered a cellar, my first thought was that it seemed a bit small and dingy, but after about a minute, I realized that the effect was really cozy."

—skatedancer

By Dorota
Wąsik

POLAND SETS QUITE A FEW global records, including the biggest medieval town square, the largest Gothic brick castle, and probably the best vodka in the world—to name just a few. Poland has something for everyone: whether you're into museums or kite-surfing, sleeping in an old palace converted into a hotel or camping by the lake, folk crafts or fine dining, dancing in a bar, or listening to classical music in an ancient church, you will not be disappointed.

The setting for all these activities is impressive indeed: from the belt of silver sands hedged with fragrant pines at the Baltic shore through the zones of countless lakes, vast forests, and picturesque rolling plains, all the way to the sharp granite peaks of the Tatra mountains, Poland's infinite variety of landscapes is arranged in latitudinal strips. Unspoiled nature is the pride of the country, and as much as 18.5% of Poland's area belongs to the "Natura 2000" special protection zones designated by the European Union.

And yet there is much more to Poland than great landscapes: what most attracts visitors is the wealth of culture and history, with important treasures of art and architecture, many of them with UNESCO World Heritage status. It is not just churches and castles either: unique historic sites range from prehistoric settlements to World War II fortifications. In addition to time-weathered monuments and works of art in every style of the last millennium, you will find contemporary art alive and kicking in Poland's beautiful cities. Famous towns with character include dreamlike, medieval Kraków, the old Hanseatic port of Gdańsk, the ever-changing and vibrant capital of Warsaw, and many more dynamic urban centers across the country.

In Poland, you can experience the joy of four distinct seasons: watch ancient Easter traditions celebrated while the world turns green in the spring; slow down during the pleasant summer heat on a café terrace in a medieval town square or at the beach; take to the mountains to watch the colors change in the fall; and enjoy a well-deserved glass of vodka or mulled wine after a day's skiing in the winter.

9

EXPLORING POLAND

The savvy traveler will be enticed by Poland's delightful and wide variety of scenery and architecture. Yet taking it all in takes time, as distances are considerable: the Baltic Sea coast and Mazurian Lakes the north lie 650 km (400 mi) from the towering Tatra Mountains in the south; in between are many historic cities and castles. Driving will give you the freedom to explore the little towns and villages at leisure, and bigger cities and major destinations are reasonably well served by a network of trains and buses. Warsaw is the main transportation hub, and the main international airport, but you can also fly into Gdańsk in the north and work your way south toward Kraków for your return journey, or vice versa.

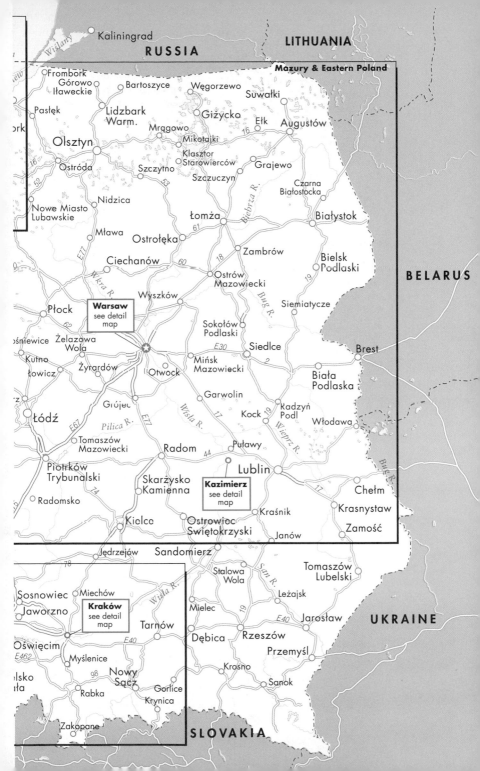

ABOUT THE RESTAURANTS

Although, at a first glance, Polish food may seem somewhat monotonous and heavy, there is much more to it than the stereotypical collation of pork, potatoes, and cabbage. The cuisine reflects Poland's multicultural history. Dishes now considered "typically Polish" are often a mixture of Russian, German, Ukrainian, Italian, Jewish, Lithuanian, Turkish, French, and other cuisines, hence the variety and the unexpected juxtapositions of ingredients. Although the Communist reality tended to "equalize" everything, including the food, the post-Communist era has brought the revival of many of the old traditions of Polish cooking, and finer city restaurants are bringing a nouvelle flair to the tried-and-true favorites. All in all, Polish food can be filling, tasty, and relatively cheap.

> ### POLAND TOP 5
>
> ■ Sip a coffee or a beer in an outdoor café in Kraków's Market Square.
>
> ■ Listen to Chopin's polonaise at his home birthplace, the Żelazowa Wola manor near Warsaw.
>
> ■ Spot the artists with their portable canvases in the streets of Kazimierz Dolny, a Renaissance town at the Vistula River.
>
> ■ Feel the summer vibes at Sopot, an old-fashioned sea resort with a penchant for the latest fashions.
>
> ■ Dance to international klezmer sounds in Kraków's Kazimierz district.

One of the joys of Polish cuisine is the soup, a fundamental part of the daily meal and potentially a meal in itself. Soups are invariably excellent, often thick and nourishing, with lots of peas and beans. Clear beet soup, *barszcz,* is the most traditional, but soured barley soup, *żurek,* should be sampled at least once. Pickled or soused herring is also a favorite Polish appetizer. The Polish chef's greatest love is pork in all its varieties, including suckling pig and wild boar. Traditional sausages, *kabanos,* usually dried and smoked, are delicious, as are the different kinds of *kiełbasa.*

A popular hunter's dish, *bigos,* is made from soured and fresh cabbage, stewed (for several days or weeks) together with many different kinds of meat and sausage. Delicious *gołąbki* (literally "little pigeons" but having nothing to do with their flying namesakes) are cabbage leaves stuffed with rice and meat filling, served with tomato or mushroom cream sauce. *Pierogi* are boiled dumplings with different kinds of fillings. The two most popular kinds are *pierogi ruskie* (the Russian *pierogi*), with potatoes, cottage cheese, onion, salt and pepper, and the *pierogi z kapustą i grzybami,* with cabbage and mushrooms. Dessert remains a major institution in Polish life, and traditional sweets include *pączki* (full and round doughnuts, often filled with wild rose confiture), *nugat* (two wafers with very sweet filling made from honey, nuts, and egg yolks), *piszinger* (many layers of wafer with chocolate filling), *szarlotka* (apple pie), and *sernik* (cheesecake).

The traditional sit-down restaurant is still the main feature of the dining scene in Poland, across all price ranges. But if you are in a hurry

IF YOU LIKE

CASTLES & PALACES

Poland has its fair share of imposing castles and magnificent, aristocratic residences, exemplifying various architectural styles. From royal castles such as Wawel Castle in Kraków and Zamek Królewski in Warsaw to Malbork, the medieval stronghold of the Teutonic Knights, even two world wars and 50 years of Communism haven't erased this heritage.

HIKING

Poland has 23 national parks (8 of them UNESCO Biosphere Reserves) and countless protected areas, spanning an infinite variety of landscapes: from the Baltic shores, the lakes and rivers of northern Poland, and the fertile plains of the interior, to the rolling hills and high mountains in the south. Hiking in the Tatras was a favorite pastime of the late Pope John Paul II, and it appeals to a wide range of travelers.

CAFÉ CULTURE

A café (*kawiarnia*) is part and parcel of everyday culture in any Polish city, as much as in Paris or Vienna. It is a place to socialize, hold a business meeting, have a romantic tryst, read a paper, or just linger. The *cukiernia* is a kind of cafeteria that serves sweets. Every city has its favorite cafés, so seek them out to experience a bit of regular Polish life.

MUSIC

Your travel to Poland is likely to be accompanied with music, played not just in concert halls but also in churches, regional restaurants, and in the streets. Throughout the year, but especially in summer, there are a multitude of music festivals: classical, rock, blues, jazz, folk... you name it. From piano recitals in Żelazowa Wola, the birthplace of Frédéric Chopin, to organ concerts in Gdańsk's Oliwa Cathedral, music is a part of Polish life.

20TH-CENTURY HISTORY

Even though Poland's history is 1,000 years old and counting, the 20th century was particularly tempestuous. Some witnesses to the century's most dramatic events—particularly World War II—are still with us, but with every year there are fewer of them. From the planned socialist community of Nowa Huta in Kraków to the chilling reminders of the Holocaust in Auschwitz-Birkenau to the uplifting story of the Solidarity movement in the Gdańsk Shipyard, the history of the 20th century is waiting to be explored.

CHURCHES

Since Mieszko I embraced Christianity in 966, the church has always been important in the Polish state, and one of the results has been a large outpouring of magnificent religious architecture, be it in the form of modest wooden chapels, austere Romanesque basilicas, exuberant baroque temples, or modern houses of prayer. The Kościół Mariacki in Kraków and Gniezno Cathedral are among the most famous, but in every city and village there are beautiful churches to be found—active centers of worship, where all religious rites and traditions are observed.

9

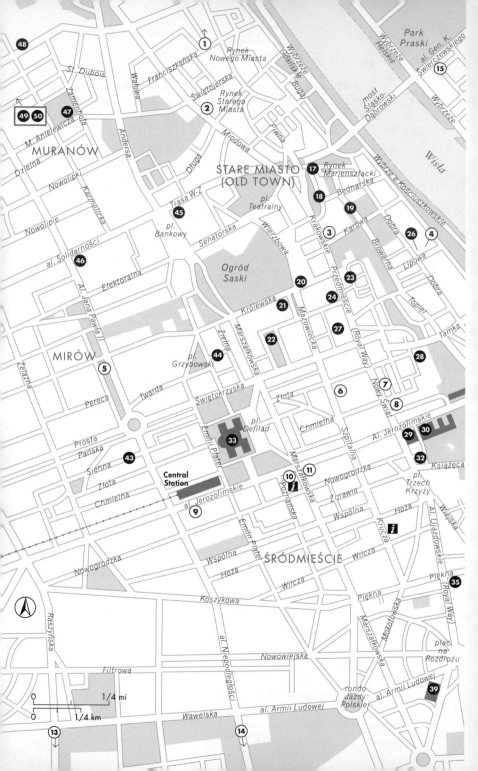

Warsaw

9

there is more variety than ever. Next to the old low-cost, self-service *bar mleczny* (milk bars) and cheap cafeterias, you will find pizza parlors, burger joints, and other fast-food outlets.

Poles traditionally eat their main meal of the day, *obiad* (dinner), between 3 and 5. Many restaurants therefore open at 1 and do not get into full swing until midafternoon. Although in cities there is a growing trend to stay open later ("to the last customer" is a popular new slogan), in smaller towns restaurants still tend to close by 9 PM.

ABOUT THE HOTELS

In general, the quantity, quality, and variety of accommodation choices in Poland have increased over the last 15 years, and most Polish hotels are now on par with those in the rest of the EU. The cities are rich in top-end accommodations, and cheap and comfortable bed-and-breakfast accommodations in private homes or pensions are widely available in the mountains or on the coast.

Service charges are included in the room price, as is a value-added tax (VAT) of 22%. Breakfast is included in most cases. High season is April through October, and prices go down slightly between November and March. Some hotels, especially those in major cities, offer lower weekend rates. Despite an ever-growing number of hotels in top tourist and business destinations—cities such as Kraków, Warsaw, Gdańsk, and Poznań—it is a good idea to book well in advance.

WHAT IT COSTS IN ZŁOTY (Zł) AND EUROS (€)			
$$$$	**$$$**	**$$**	**$**
RESTAURANTS in złoty Over 70	50–70	30–50	Under 30
HOTELS in euros Over €210	€130–€210	€80–€130	Under €80
HOTELS in złoty Over 800	500–800	300–500	Under 300

Restaurant prices are per person for a main course at dinner. Hotel prices are for two people in a double room with a private bath and breakfast in high season.

TIMING

With its characteristically gray, cold weather and short daylight hours, the Polish winter may persuade you to spend your vacation in the Caribbean. Unless you are a skier, spring is a good time for intense, energetic sightseeing. Summers can be hot, especially in southern Poland, but this is still the busiest tourist season. If you are interested in the arts, remember that theaters and concert halls close completely for the months of July and August and often do not get going with the new season's programs until October—on the other hand, there are a number of summer festivals. The fabled Polish Golden Autumn, when the leaves do their thing, lasts until November and can be a good time for touring, although the weather may be a bit unpredictable in transition. The winter sports season is from December to March, when high-season rates are once again in effect in the mountains. In general, central heating is universal and efficient in Poland, but air-conditioning is relatively rare, if increasingly common.

GREAT ITINERARIES

With well over 300,000 square km (116,000 square mi), populated with a variety of natural, and cultural attractions, it is difficult "to do Poland justice" in a trip of a few days. If your time is limited, we strongly recommend selecting just a couple of destinations and seeing them at leisure—otherwise you are running the risk of spending most of your time trying to get from one place to another.

IF YOU HAVE 3 DAYS

Begin in **Warsaw,** where you might want to start with the bird's-eye view from the top of the Palace of Culture and Science, itself a showcase of Communist architecture. You must not miss the city's Stare Miasto (Old Town), which was destroyed during the Second World War and reconstructed during the 1950s. Then, depending on your interests, check out contemporary art at Zachęta or Zamek Ujazdowski, head to Chopin's birthplace at Żelazowa Wola, or hang out in the trendy Praga district. On your second day, head south. If you have a car, take the route via **Kazimierz Dolny,** a Renaissance town on the Vistula River, and get a glimpse of the countryside. You can also catch an express train directly to **Kraków,** Poland's number one destination for a reason: its uniquely intact, medieval Old Town is a treasure trove of art and home to the Jagiellonian University, where Nicolaus Copernicus studied.

IF YOU HAVE 5 DAYS

Begin your stay in **Gdańsk** and explore the historic Old Town, which was originally one of the main Hanseatic ports on the Baltic. Gdańsk is one part of the Trójmiasto (Tri-City); if you have time, check out the old-timer resort of **Sopot** as well. On Day 2, head slowly toward **Warsaw,** taking in **Malbork** to see the vast castle that was the headquarters of the Teutonic Knights (to do this properly, you need at least half a day). Continue on to **Mikołajki** in the Mazury Lake District, and then on to Warsaw. From Day 3, follow the three-day itinerary above.

IF YOU HAVE 7 DAYS OR MORE

If you have more time, there are endless possibilities en route or off the main north–south itinerary described above. From Gdańsk, you may choose to explore the lakes of the Mazury district in more detail, but it may be problematic to rely on public transportation. You could also head southwest toward **Poznań** and **Gniezno,** the cradle of the Polish state. Farther south, Silesia offers roads less traveled but no less exciting, although **Wrocław,** the capital of Lower Silesia, has grown into one of the most fashionable cities in Poland. Closer to Kraków, **Częstochowa** has the 14th-century Pauline Monastery, which contains Poland's holiest relic: the icon of the Black Madonna. Once in Kraków, you are within easy reach of the Tatra mountains: **Zakopane** is only a couple of hours' drive or a bus ride away.

9

WARSAW

Perhaps the only constant quality of Warsaw is change. It is remarkable how often, and how quickly, Poland's capital rebuilds and reinvents itself. Though in the past this reinvention was involuntary—the city having been invaded and destroyed several times over the ages—Warsaw now continues to metamorphose quite well on its own. To today's young Varsovians, and visitors alike, World War II may seem like ancient history, but it is impossible to forget that some 85% of the city was utterly destroyed in the war. The "phoenix from the ashes" label fits no other modern European city more than Warsaw.

In decades immediately after World War II, Poland's capital was often—and rather unjustly—dismissed as a "concrete jungle" or "a life-size model of a city." In the first decade of the 21st century, both these phrases simply no longer apply. Warsaw will consistently surprise you: you may find yourself in a beautiful park wondering whether you are in a city at all; but go just a bit farther, and you will be confronted by a brand-new, tech-and-chic skyscraper you would not necessarily expect in the country from the former Soviet bloc. Warsaw is a modern, thriving metropolis, with everything you'd expect in a bustling urban environment: plush five-star hotels, a thriving arts scene, top-notch contemporary architecture, gourmet restaurants, and upmarket shops. It's worthy of the label "European capital" as much as Berlin, Paris, or Rome.

And yet it is more than a fashionable modern city: it is a city with a memory—or rather with multiple, carefully preserved memories. Within today's Warsaw, you will find the city of Chopin's youth, and also the city that resisted the Nazis in 1944 during the heroic, tragic Warsaw Uprising. Fragments of the city that survived the war acquire a special poignancy in their isolation: odd rows of art nouveau tenements, such as those on the south side of the great square around the Pałac Kultury i Nauki (Palace of Culture and Science) and on ulica Wilcza; the elegant Aleje Ujazdowskie, now the Diplomatic Quarter, leading to the Belvedere Palace; and the Łazienki Palace and Park. The reconstructed areas of the Polish capital—the historic Old Town area, rebuilt brick by brick in the 1950s; the Royal Castle; the Ujazdowski Castle—are moving tributes to the Poles' ability to survive and preserve their history.

There are many areas where the city slows down its pace. The right-bank district of Praga, until recently regarded as an "off-limits" area, is now a fashionable bohemian hangout. The wild, unregulated Vistula River is lined with surprisingly nice city beaches. The city's abundant green space will allow you to walk the length and breadth of town practically from park to park. Warsaw is a city that deserves to be loved; it's definitely a city to enjoy.

EXPLORING WARSAW

Warsaw is an easy city to navigate. The Palace of Culture and Science will certainly provide you with a useful orientation point: to its north lies the Royal Route, the Old Town, and the New Town; to its south, the Diplomatic Quarter and the Łazienki Park. West of the Old Town lie Muranów and Mirów neighborhoods in the former Jewish district. All these sights are on the left bank of the Vistula River.

On the right bank is the Praga District, a poorer quarter of workers and artisans that emerged from the war fairly intact. Today, Praga is becoming increasingly fashionable, and many visitors find its galleries, bars, and unique "provincial" flavor well worth the trip across the Vistula.

Numbers in the text correspond to numbers in the margin and on the Warsaw map.

STARE MIASTO & NOWE MIASTO

The rebuilding of Warsaw's historic Old Town, situated on an escarpment on the left bank of the Vistula, is a real phoenix-risen-from-the-ashes story. Postwar architects, who were determined to get it absolutely as it was before, turned to old prints, photographs in family albums, and paintings, in particular the detailed 18th-century views of Bernardo Bellotto (the nephew of Canaletto). Curiously, they discovered that some of Bellotto's views were painted not from real life but from sketches of projects that were never realized. Whatever your feelings about reproduction architecture—and there's a lot of it in Warsaw—it seems to have worked. The Old Town is closed to traffic, and in its narrow streets you can leave the 21st century behind and relax for a while. Everything here is within easy walking distance. Just a short stroll beyond the Barbakan gate is the New Town, which also has sights well worth seeing.

9

❷ **Archikatedra św. Jana** *(Cathedral of St. John).* Ulica Świętojańska, leading from the Rynek Starego Miasta to the Zamek Królewski, takes its name from this cathedral, which was built at the turn of the 14th century; coronations of the Polish kings took place here from the 16th to 18th century. The crypts contain the tombs of the last two princes of Mazovia, the archbishops of Warsaw, and such famous Poles as the 19th-century novelist Henryk Sienkiewicz, the Nobel Prize–winning author of *Quo Vadis.* ⊠ *Świętojańska 8, Stare Miasto.*

❻ **Barbakan.** The pinnacled Barbakan, the mid-16th-century stronghold in the old city wall on ulica Freta, now marks the boundary between the Old Town and the New Town. From here you can see the partially restored wall that was built to enclose the Old Town. ⊠ *Freta, Stare Miasto.*

❸ **Kościół Jezuitów** *(Jesuit Church).* On the left-hand side of the entrance to the Cathedral of St. John you'll find the early-17th-century Jesuit Church, founded by King Jan III Sobieski. Throughout the postwar years, a visit to this church at Easter was considered a must by Varsovians, and its Gethsemane decorations always contained a hidden political message. (In 1985 the risen Christ had the face of Father Jerzy

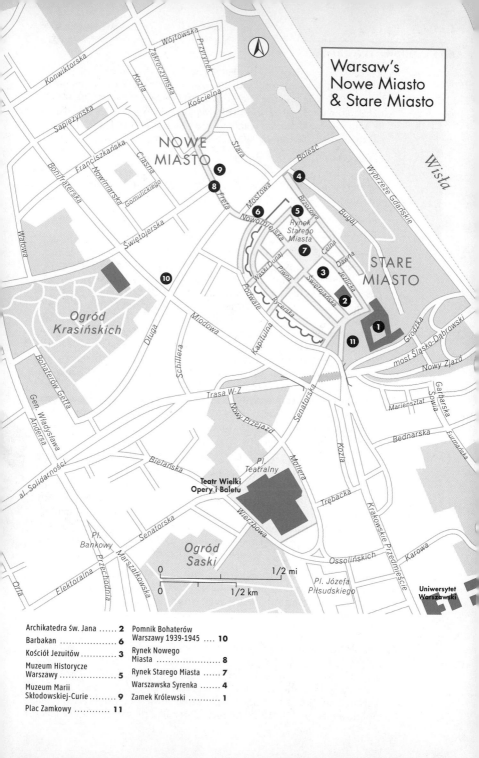

Warsaw's Nowe Miasto & Stare Miasto

NOWE MIASTO

STARE MIASTO

Wisła

Ogród Krasińskich

Rynek Starego Miasta

Trasa W-Z

Pl. Teatralny

Teatr Wielki Opery i Baletu

Ogród Saski

Pl. Bankowy

Pl. Józefa Piłsudskiego

Uniwersytet Warszawski

0   1/2 mi
0   1/2 km

Popiełuszko, the Warsaw priest murdered the previous year by the Polish secret police.) ⊠ *On east side of Świętojańska, 1 block up from Plac Zamkowy, Stare Miasto.*

⑤ Muzeum Historyczne Warszawy *(Warsaw Historical Museum).* Four fine examples of Renaissance mansions can be found on the northern side of the Old Town Square (note the sculpture of a black slave on the facade of No. 34, the **Negro House**). These historical homes, some of which contain Renaissance ceiling paintings, now house the Warsaw Historical Museum. The museum screens a short documentary film on the history of Warsaw daily at noon in English. ⊠ *Rynek Starego Miasta 28–42, Stare Miasto* ☎ *022/635–16–25* ⊕ *www.mhw.pl* ⊡ *zł8* ☉ *Tues. and Thurs. 11–5:30, Wed. and Fri. 11–3:30, weekends 10:30–4.*

⑨ Muzeum Marii Skłodowskiej-Curie *(Marie Curie Museum).* The house in which Marie Curie Skłodowska was born has a small museum inside dedicated to the great physicist, chemist, winner of two Nobel Prizes, and discoverer of radium. ⊠ *Freta 16, Nowe Miasto* ☎ *022/831–80–92* ⊡ *zł6* ☉ *Tues.–Sat. 10–4, Sun. 10–2.*

⑪ Plac Zamkowy *(Castle Square).* Many visitors enter the Old Town through this plaza area on the southern border of the district. You can't miss the **Zygmunt's (Sigismund's) Column,** which honors King Zygmunt III Waza, king of Poland and Sweden, who in the early 17th century moved the capital to Warsaw from Kraków. ⊠ *Stare Miasto.*

⑩ Pomnik Bohaterów Warszawy 1939–1945 *(Monument to the Heroes of Warsaw).* Unveiled in 1989, this monument constitutes a poignant reminder of what World War II meant for the citizens of Warsaw. Massive bronze figures raise defiant fists above the sewer openings used by Polish resistance fighters in Warsaw's Old Town to escape the Nazis in 1944. ⊠ *pl. Krasińskich and Długa, Stare Miasto.*

⑧ Rynek Nowego Miasta *(New Town Square).* Warsaw's so-called "New Town" was actually founded at the turn of the 15th century. This part of the city, however, was rebuilt after World War II following popular 18th- and 19th-century styles and has a more elegant and spacious feel about it than the Old Town. The centerpiece of the district is the leafy New Town Square, slightly more irregular and relaxed than its Old Town counterpart. The houses on the square—and in such nearby streets as ulica Kościelna—have curiously stark and formalized wall paintings. ⊠ *Nowe Miasto.*

★ **⑦ Rynek Starego Miasta** *(Old Town Square).* This is the hub of life in Warsaw's Old Town. The earliest settlers arrived at this spot during the 10th and 11th centuries. Legend has it that a peasant named Wars was directed to the site by a mermaid named Sawa—hence the name of the city in Polish, Warszawa. (Sawa has been immortalized in Warsaw's official emblem.) In the 14th century Warsaw was already a walled city, and in 1413 its citizens obtained a borough charter from the princes of Mazovia. The present layout of the Old Town dates from that time, and traces of the original Gothic buildings still surround the Old Town Square. The appearance of today's square, however, largely dates from

9

the 16th and early 17th centuries, when Warsaw's wealth and importance grew rapidly as a result of the 1569 Polish-Lithuanian union and Warsaw's new status as Poland's capital city.

The Old Town Square is usually very active, even though no traffic is allowed and there is no longer a formal market. Artists and craftspeople of all kinds still sell their wares here in the summer, but don't expect many bargains—tourists are their prime targets. Musical performances are often held here on weekends on a stage erected at the north end of the square. Horse-drawn cabs await visitors. To explore a sample of the square's beautiful and historic houses, visit the **Muzeum Historyczne Warszawy** (⇨ *above)* on the north side. After being almost completely annihilated during World War II, this house like many others was meticulously reconstructed using old prints, plans, and paintings. For some of the best Gothic details, look for No. 31, traditionally known as the House of the Mazovian Dukes. At night the square is lighted up romantically. If you're after good food and atmosphere, this is one of Warsaw's best places to hang out after dark.

Krzywe Koło (Crooked Wheel Street) runs from the Old Town Square to the reconstructed ramparts of the city wall. From this corner you can see out over the Vistula and also over the New Town stretching to the north beyond the city walls. As you look out over the town walls and down the Vistula embankment, you will see the **Stara Prochownia** (Old Powder Tower), now a popular venue for poetry readings, music, and drama. ⊠*Stare Miasto.*

❹ Warszawska Syrenka *(Warsaw Mermaid).* The mermaid is the symbol on the crest of the city of Warsaw. This particular stone statue had been traveling around the city for more than 70 years before finding itself back home in 2000. It had originally been installed in 1855, in the center of a fountain in the Old Town Square. ⊠*Stare Miasto.*

★ ❶ Zamek Królewski *(Royal Castle).* Warsaw's Royal Castle stands on the east side of Castle Square. The princes of Mazovia first built a residence on this spot overlooking the Vistula in the 14th century. Its present Renaissance form dates from the reign of King Zygmunt III Waza, who needed a magnificent palace for his new capital. Reconstructed in the 1970s, it now gleams as it did in its earliest years, with gilt, marble, and wall paintings. It also houses impressive collections of art—including the famous views of Warsaw that were painted by Canaletto's nephew Bernardo Bellotto (also known as Canaletto), which were used as a clue and a model to rebuild the city after the war. Tours in English are available. ⊠*Plac Zamkowy 4, Stare Miasto* ☎*022/657–21–70* 🎟*zł14* ☉*Daily 10–4.*

NEED A BREAK?

Café Bristol (⊠ *Krakowskie Przedmieście 42/44, Stare Miasto* ☎*022/551– 18–28),* with its 1901 décor, is one of the classiest places in town, serving mostly wonderful cakes from the in-house bakery, but also some light savory meals.

THE ROYAL ROUTE

All towns with kings had their "royal routes," and the one in Warsaw stretches south from Castle Square for 4 km (2½ mi), running through busy Krakowskie Przedmieście, along Nowy Świat, and on to the Park Łazienkowski (Łazienki Park). The route is lined with some of Warsaw's finest churches and palaces, but there are also landmarks of some of the city's most famous folk, including Frédéric Chopin. As a child Chopin played in the Kasimir Palace gardens, gave his first concert in the Radziwiłł Palace (now the Pałac Namiestnikowski [Presidential Palace]), then moved with his family to the building that now houses the city's Academy of Fine Arts. Today, the Chopin Society is headquartered in the Pałac Ostrogskich (Ostrogski Palace).

㉖ **Biblioteka Uniwersytetu Warszawskiego** *(Warsaw University Library)*. A
Fodor'sChoice 10-minute walk toward the river from the main campus of Warsaw
★ University is the relatively new (1999) Warsaw University Library, a sight not to be missed, even if you're not on a research trip. You'll find some shops and cafés (including noteworthy restaurant Biblioteka) on the ground floor, but it's the building's roof and its rooftop garden that are truly special and definitely worth the trip. The garden, open to the general public, is both vast and intimate, not to mention one of the most beautiful rooftop spaces in all of Europe. With its nooks, crannies, brooks, paths, lawns, and benches where you can hide with or without a book, the garden provides a perfect space for thought and inspiration. It is also full of surprises: look for various "reinterpretations" of Einstein's theory of relativity. In addition, you'll find a kaleidoscope of vistas of both the city and the library's interior. If you dare, cross the footbridge over the glass library roof—with the sky reflected under your feet, you literally walk among the clouds. ⊠*Dobra 56/66, Powiśle* ☎*22/552–51–78* ⊕*www.buw.uw.edu.pl* ⊠*Garden free* ⊗*Library Mon.–Sat. 9–9, Sun. 3–9; garden daily 9–8.*

㉙ **Former headquarters of the Polish Communist Party.** Anti-Communists love the irony of this once-despised symbol of oppression; for a decade after the Communist fall, until 2001, it was the seat of the Warsaw Stock Exchange (today, it's the Centrum Bankowo-Finansowe). This is not a tourist sight in a strict sense, but it is worth a peek for its monumental—even oppressive—architecture, a remainder of what the fallen system was like. ⊠*Aleje Jerozolimskie and Nowy Świat, Royal Route.*

㉑ **Galeria Zachęta** *(Zachęta Gallery)*. Built at the end of the 19th century by the Society for the Encouragement of the Fine Arts, this gallery has no permanent collection but organizes thought-provoking special exhibitions (primarily modern art) in high-ceilinged, well-lighted halls. It was in this building in 1922 that the first president of the post–World War I Polish Republic, Gabriel Narutowicz, was assassinated by a right-wing fanatic. Admission costs to the exhibits vary. ⊠*pl. Małachowskiego 3, Royal Route* ☎*022/827–69–09* ⊕*www.zacheta. art.pl* ⊠*Most exhibitions zł10* ⊗*Tues.–Sun. 10–6.*

㉚ **Grób Nieznanego Żołnierza** *(Tomb of the Unknown Soldier)*. Built as a memorial after World War I, the Tomb of the Unknown Soldier

9

contains the body of an unidentified Polish soldier brought from the eastern battlefields of the Polish–Soviet war of 1919–20—a war not much mentioned in the 45 years of Communist rule after World War II. Ceremonial changes of the guard take place at noon each Sunday; visitors may be surprised to see the Polish Army still using the goose step on such occasions. The memorial is a surviving fragment of the early-18th-century Saxon Palace, which used to stand here on the west side of plac Piłsudskiego. Behind the tomb are the delightful **Ogród Saski** (Saxon Gardens), which once belonged to the palace and were designed by French and Saxon landscape gardeners. ⊠*pl. Piłsudskiego, Royal Route.*

③② **Kościół świętego Aleksandra** *(St. Alexander's Church).* Built in the early 19th century as a replica of the Roman pantheon, St. Alexander's stands on an island in the middle of **plac Trzech Krzyży**, a name that is notoriously difficult for foreigners to pronounce and means "Three Crosses Square." One of the crosses is on the church itself. ⊠*pl. Trzech Krzyży, Royal Route.*

②⑦ **Kościół świętego Krzyża** *(Holy Cross Church).* The heart of Poland's most famous composer, Frédéric Chopin, is immured in a pillar inside this baroque church. Atop the church steps is a massive, sculpted crucifix. Across from the church is the **statue of Nicolaus Copernicus,** standing in front of the neoclassical Staszic Palace, the headquarters of the Polish Academy of Sciences. Like many other notable Warsaw monuments, this statue is the work of the 19th-century Danish sculptor Bertel Thorvaldsen. ⊠*Krakowskie Przedmieście 3, Royal Route.*

①⑦ **Kościół świętej Anny** *(St. Anne's Church).* Built in 1454 by Anne, princess of Mazovia, the church stands on the south corner of Castle Square. It was rebuilt in high-baroque style after being destroyed during the Swedish invasions of the 17th century, and thanks to 1990s redecoration and regilding, it glows once again. A plaque on the wall outside marks the spot where Pope John Paul II celebrated mass in 1980, during his first visit to Poland after his election to the papacy. ⊠*Krakowskie Przedmieście 68, Royal Route.*

②③ **Kościół Wizytek** *(Church of the Visitation Sisters).* In front of this late-baroque church stands a statue of Cardinal Stefan Wyszyński, primate of Poland from 1948 to 1981. Wyszyński was imprisoned during the 1950s but lived to see a Polish pope and the birth of Solidarity. The fresh flowers always lying at the foot of the statue are evidence of the warmth with which he is remembered. ⊠*Krakowskie Przedmieście 30, Royal Route.*

②② **Muzeum Etnograficzne** *(Ethnographic Museum).* On display here you'll find an interesting collection of Polish folk art, crafts, and costumes from all parts of the country. ⊠*Kredytowa 1, Royal Route* ☎*022/827–76–41* ⊡*zł4, free Wed.* ☉*Tues., Thurs., and Fri. 9–4, Wed. 11–6, weekends 10–5.*

 ③⓪ **Muzeum Narodowe** *(National Museum of Warsaw).* In a functional 1930s building, the National Museum has an impressive collection of contemporary Polish and European paintings, Gothic icons, and works from antiquity. It's usually closed on the day after a major holiday. ✉ *Aleje Jerozolimskie 3, Royal Route* ☎ *022/621–10–31* ⊕ *www. mnw.art.pl* 💲 *zł13, free Wed.* ⊙ *Tues., Wed., and Fri. 10–4, Thurs. noon–5, weekends 10–5.*

■ NEED A BREAK?

Blikle (✉ *Nowy Świat 35, Royal Route*), Warsaw's oldest cake shop, has a black-and-white-tile café that serves savory snacks as well as Blikle's famous doughnuts.

㉔ Pałac Czapskich *(Czapski Palace).* Now the home of the Academy of Fine Arts, the Czapski Palace dates from the late 17th century but was rebuilt in 1740 in the rococo style. Zygmunt Krasiński, the Polish romantic poet, was born here in 1812, and Chopin once lived in the palace mews. ✉ *Krakowskie Przedmieście 5, Royal Route.*

⑱ Pałac Kazanowskich *(Kazanowski Palace).* This 17th-century palace was given a neoclassical front in the 19th century. The courtyard at the rear still contains massive late-Renaissance buttresses and is worth a visit because of its plaque commemorating Zagłoba's fight with the monkeys, from Sienkiewicz's historical novel *The Deluge.* In a small garden in front of the palace stands a **monument to Adam Mickiewicz,** the great Polish romantic poet. It was here that Warsaw University students gathered in March 1968, after a performance of Mickiewicz's hitherto-banned play *Forefathers' Eve,* which set in motion the events that led to the fall of Poland's Communist leader Władysław Gomułka, a wave of student protests, and a regime-sponsored anti-Semitic campaign. Unfortunately, you cannot visit the interior. ✉ *Krakowskie Przedmieście 62, Royal Route.*

★ ☾ ㉝ Pałac Kultury i Nauki *(Palace of Culture and Science).* This massive Stalinist-Gothic structure looks like a wedding cake and is the main landmark in the city. From the 30th floor you can get a panoramic view. The old joke runs that this is Warsaw's best view because it is the only place from which you can't see the palace. To view all of urban Warsaw from 700 feet up, buy tickets at the booth near the east entrance. The building houses a number of facilities, including a swimming pool and the **Museum of Science and Technology.** Also in the palace is the **Teatr Lalek,** a good puppet theater (the entrance is on the north side). ✉ *pl. Defilad 1, Royal Route* ☎ *022/620–02–11, 022/620–49–50 theater* 💲 *zł7.5* ⊙ *Daily 9–6.*

⑲ Pałac Namiestnikowski *(Presidential Palace).* This palace was built in the 17th century by the Radziwiłł family (into which Jackie Kennedy's sister, Lee, later married). In the 19th century it functioned as the administrative office of the czarist occupiers—hence its present name. In 1955 the Warsaw Pact was signed here; later the palace served as the headquarters for the Presidium of the Council of Ministers, and since 1995 it has been the official residence of Poland's president. In the forecourt is an **equestrian statue of Prince Józef Poniatowski,** a nephew of the last king of Poland and one of Napoléon's marshals. He was wounded and drowned in the Elster River during the Battle of Leipzig

40 Million Bricks

One of the most characteristic landmarks of Warsaw, the Palace of Culture and Science produces mixed feelings. Varsovians used to hate this oversize wedding cake, Stalin's "gift" to the city, which meant, "Big Brother is watching you." Adding insult to injury, the Palace landed—not unlike an alien spaceship—in the emptied center of the city, once Warsaw's social and commercial heart, which stopped beating during World War

II. At 762 feet the highest building in Poland, the 40-million-brick edifice turned 50 in 2005. The atmosphere around it—both political and architectural—has changed dramatically, and Varsovians seem to have forgiven and accepted the Palace. Placed atop the Palace in 2001, the (reputedly) largest clock in the world keeps ticking away with the current time in Warsaw, and the viewing platform on the 30th floor still offers the best views of the city.

in 1813, following the disastrous retreat of Napoléon's Grande Armée from Russia. You can't visit the inside, unfortunately. ⊠*Krakowskie Przedmieście 46–48, Royal Route.*

㉘ **Pałac Ostrogskich** *(Ostrogski Palace).* The headquarters of the **Towarzystwo im. Fryderyka Chopina** (Chopin Society) is in this 17th-century palace, which towers above Tamka. The best approach is via the steps from Tamka street. In the 19th century the Warsaw Conservatory was housed here (Ignacy Paderewski was one of its students). Now a venue for Chopin concerts, it is also home to the **Muzeum Fryderyka Chopina** (Frédéric Chopin Museum), a small collection of mementos, including the last piano played by the composer. The works of Chopin (1810–49) took their roots from folk rhythms and melodies of exclusively Polish invention. Thanks to this composer, Poland can fairly claim to have been the fountainhead of popular music in Europe in the mid-19th century, when the composer's polonaises and mazurkas whirled their way around the continent. ⊠*Okólnik 1, Royal Route* ☎*022/827–54–71* ⊕*www.nifc.pl* ✆*Free* ⊙*Mon.–Sat. 10–2, Thurs. noon–6.*

DIPLOMATIC QUARTER PARK ŁAZIENKOWSKI
In the 19th century smart carriages and riders eager to be seen thronged the aleje Ujazdowskie. Today the avenue is a favorite with Sunday strollers. It leads to the beautiful Łazienki Park and the white Pałac Łazienkowski (Łazienki Palace), the private residence of the last king of Poland.

㊱ **Botanical Gardens.** These gardens, covering an area of roughly 3 acres, were laid out in 1818. At the entrance stands the neoclassical **observatory,** now part of Warsaw University. ⊠*Aleje Ujazdowskie 4, Łazienkowski* ☎*No phone* ✆*Free* ⊙*Daily dawn–dusk.*

㊴ **Former Gestapo Headquarters.** The building that currently houses Poland's Ministry of Education was the Gestapo headquarters during World War II. A small museum details the horrors that took place behind its peaceful facade. Because of the subject matter, you must be 14 years or older to visit this museum ⊠*al. Szucha 25, Łazienkowski*

☎022/629–49–19 ☜*Free* ☉ *Wed. 9–5, Thurs. and Sat. 9–4, Fri. 10–5, Sun. 10–4.*

㊶ Pałac Belweder *(Belvedere Palace)*. Built in the early 18th century, the palace was reconstructed in 1818 in neoclassical style by the Russian governor of Poland, the grand duke Constantine. Until 1994 it was the official residence of Poland's president. Now the building is used for some gala state occasions and for some performances during the summer Chopin festival. Belvedere Palace stands just south of the main gates to Łazienki Park. ✉*Belwederska 2, Łazienkowski.*

★ **㊵ Pałac Łazienkowski** *Łazienki Palace)*. This magnificent palace is the focal point of the Park Łazienkowski. This neoclassical summer residence was so faithfully reconstructed after the war that there is still no electricity—be sure to visit when it's sunny, or you won't see anything of the interior. The palace has some splendid 18th-century furniture as well as part of the art collection of King Stanisław August Poniatowski. ✉*Agrykola 1, Łazienkowski* ☎*022/621–62–41* ☜*zł10* ☉*Tues.–Sun. 10–3:15.*

㊷ Pałac Wilanów *(Wilanów Palace)*. A baroque gateway and false moat lead to the wide courtyard that stretches along the front of Wilanów Palace, built between 1681 and 1696 by King Jan III Sobieski. After his death, the palace passed through various hands before it was bought at the end of the 18th century by Stanisław Kostka Potocki, who amassed a major art collection, laid out the gardens, and opened the first public museum here in 1805. Potocki's neo-Gothic tomb can be seen to the left of the driveway as you approach the palace. The palace interiors still hold much of the original furniture; there's also a striking display of 16th- to 18th-century Polish portraits on the first floor. English-speaking guides are available.

OFF THE
BEATEN
PATH

Outside of the Pałac Wilanów, to the left of the main entrance, is a romantic **park** with pagodas, summerhouses, and bridges as well as a lake. Behind the palace is a formal Italian garden from which you can admire the magnificent gilt decoration on the palace walls. There's also a gallery of contemporary Polish art on the grounds. Stables to the right of the entrance now house a poster gallery, the **Muzeum Plakatu** that is well worth visiting—this is a branch of art in which Poles have historically excelled. ✉*Wiertnicza 1, Wilanów* ☎*022/842–81–01* ⊕*www.wilanow-palac.art.pl* ☜*Palace zł15; park zł3, free Thurs.* ☉*Palace Tues.–Sun. 9:30–2:30, Sun. until 6 PM mid-June–mid-Sept. Park daily 9–dusk.*

㊲ Park Łazienkowski *Łazienki Park)*. The 180 acres of this park, commissioned during the late 18th century by King Stanisław August Poniatowski, run along the Vistula escarpment, parallel to the Royal Route. Look for the peacocks that wander through the park and the delicate red squirrels that in Poland answer to the name "Basia," a diminutive of Barbara. Of course, the best way to entice a squirrel to come near is to have some nuts in your hand. In the old coach houses on the east side of the park you'll find the **Muzeum Łowiectwa i Jeździctwa** *(Museum of Hunting* ☎*022/621–62–41)*, which contains a collection of stuffed birds and animals native to Poland. It is open Tuesday through Sunday from 10 to 3; admission is zł5. One of the most beloved sights in Łazienki Park is the **Pomnik Fryderyka Chopina** (Chopin Memorial), a sculpture under a streaming willow tree that shows the composer in a typical romantic pose. In summer, outdoor concerts of Chopin's piano music are held here every Sunday afternoon. ⊠ *Aleje Ujazdowskie, Łazienki.*

☾ ㉟ **Park Ujazdowski** *(Ujazdów Park).* At the entrance to this formal garden, there is a **19th-century weighing booth,** just inside the gate, still in operation. There is also a well-equipped **playground** for small children, with sand, swings, and slides. ⊠ *Corner of Aleje Ujazdowskie and Piękna, Łazienki.*

㉞ **Sejm.** The Polish Houses of the Sejm (parliament) are housed in a round, white debating chamber that was built during the 1920s, after the rebirth of the independent Polish state. ⊠ *Wiejska 6, Diplomatic Quarter.*

NEED A BREAK? | **Modulor Café** (⊠ *pl. Trzech Krzyży 2, Diplomatic Quarter* ☎ *022/627–26–03),* up the street from the Sheraton, has great coffee and a variety of fresh-squeezed juices as well as a hot menu, if you need more substantial fuel.

★ ㉟ **Zamek Ujazdowski** *(Ujazdowski Castle).* If you are interested in modern art, you will find it in the somewhat unlikely setting of this 18th-century castle, reconstructed in the 1980s. Now the home of the **Center for Contemporary Art,** the castle hosts a variety of exhibitions by artists from Poland and all over the world. ⊠ *Aleje Ujazdowskie 6, Łazienki* ☎ *022/628–12–71* 💶 *zł4, free Thurs.* ☉ *Tues.–Thurs. and weekends 11–5, Fri. 11–9.*

JEWISH WARSAW

The quiet streets of Mirów and Muranów, which are now primarily residential neighborhoods, once housed the largest Jewish population in Europe: about 380,000 people in 1939. The Nazis sealed off this area from the rest of the city on November 15, 1940, and the congested ghetto became rapidly less populated as people died from starvation and disease. Between July and September 1942, the Nazis deported about 300,000 Jewish residents to the death camp at Treblinka. On April 19, 1943, the remaining inhabitants began the Warsaw Ghetto Uprising. Children threw homemade bombs at tanks, and men and women fought soldiers hand to hand. In the end, almost all of those remaining died in the uprising or fled through the sewers to the "Aryan side" of Warsaw.

㊻ **Femina Cinema.** Before the war, this area was the heart of Warsaw's Jewish Quarter, which was walled off by the Nazis in November 1940 to isolate the Jewish community from "Aryan" Warsaw. The cinema is one of the few buildings in the district that survived the war. It was here that the ghetto orchestra organized concerts in 1941 and 1942. Many outstanding musicians found themselves behind the ghetto walls and continued to make music despite the dangers. ⊠ *al. Solidarności 115, Muranów.*

㊸ Fragment of ghetto wall. In the courtyard of this building on Sienna Street, through the archway on the left, and just a little farther east, on Złota Street, are the only two surviving fragments of the infamous wall built by the Nazis to close off the Warsaw Ghetto in November 1940. Warsaw's was the largest Jewish ghetto established by the Germans during World War II. Between 300,000 and 400,000 people perished during the three years of its existence, from starvation, diseases (mostly typhoid), and deportation to Nazi death camps. It was the scene of the Warsaw Ghetto Uprising, led by Mordechaj Anielewicz, who died there at the age of 24. Among the hostages of history in the Warsaw Ghetto we find such memorable figures as Władysław Szpilman, "The Pianist" from Polański's movie; and Doctor Janusz Korczak, a pediatrician, pedagogue, and writer who ran an orphanage for Jewish children—and who decided to accompany them all the way to the gas chambers of Treblinka. ✉*Sienna 55, Muranów.*

㊾ Jewish Cemetery. Behind a high brick wall on ulica Okopowa you will find Warsaw's Jewish Cemetery, an island of continuity amid so much destruction of the city's Jewish heritage. The cemetery, which is still in use, survived the war, and although it was neglected and became badly overgrown during the postwar period, it is gradually being restored. Here you will find 19th-century headstones and much that testifies to the Jewish community's role in Polish history and culture. Ludwik Zamenhof, the creator of the artificial language Esperanto, is buried here, as are Henryk Wohl, minister of the treasury in the national government during the 1864 uprising against Russian rule; Szymon Askenazy, the historian and diplomat; Hipolit Wawelberg, the cofounder of Warsaw Polytechnic; and poet Bolesław Leśmian. To reach the cemetery, take Bus 107, 111, or 516 from Plac Bankowy. ✉*Okopowa 49–51, Muranów* 💷*zł4* 🕙*Apr.–Oct., Mon.–Thurs. 10–5, Fri. 9–1, Sun. 11–4; Nov.–Mar., 10–sunset.*

㊺ Jewish Historical Institute & Museum. You'll find the institute behind a glittering new office block on the southeast corner of plac Bankowy—the site of what had been the largest temple in Warsaw, the Tłomackie Synagogue. For those seeking to investigate their family history, the institute houses the **Ronald S. Lauder Foundation Genealogy Project,** which acts as a clearinghouse of information on available archival resources and on the history of towns and villages in which Polish Jews resided. English-speaking staff members are available. The institute also houses a museum that displays a permanent collection of mementos and artifacts and periodically organizes special exhibitions. ✉*Tłomackie 3, Muranów* ☎*022/827–92–21* ⊕*www.jewishinstitute.org.pl* 💷*Free* 🕙*Tues.–Fri. 10–6.*

㊼ Pomnik Bohaterów Getta (*Monument to the Heroes of the Warsaw Ghetto*). On April 19, 1943, the Jewish Fighting Organization began an uprising in a desperate attempt to resist the mass transports to Treblinka that had been taking place since the beginning of that year. Though doomed from the start, the brave ghetto fighters managed to keep up their struggle for a whole month. But by May 16, General Jürgen Stroop could report to his superior officer that the former Jewish District in Warsaw had ceased to exist. The ghetto had become a smoldering ruin, razed by Nazi flamethrowers. A monument marks the location of the house at nearby **ulica Miła 18**, the site of the uprising's command bunker and where its leader, Mordechaj Anielewicz, was killed. ⊠ *Zamenhofa, between Anielewicza and Lewartowskiego, Muranów.*

50 **Powązki Cemetery.** Dating from 1790, Warsaw's oldest cemetery is worth a visit if you are in a reflective mood. Many well-known Polish names appear on the often elaborate headstones and tombs. There is also a recent memorial to the victims of the Katyń Massacre, when 4,000 Polish servicemen, who had been taken prisoner when the Soviets were still aligned with the Nazis, were murdered by the Soviet army on orders from Stalin in 1940 in the Katyń Forest. Enter from ulica Powązkowska. ⊠ *Powązkowska 43–45, next to Jewish Cemetery, Muranów* ⊙ *Sun.–Thurs. 9–3, Fri. 9–1.*

44 **Ulica Próżna.** This is the only street in Jewish Warsaw where tenement buildings have been preserved on both sides of the street. The Lauder Foundation has initiated a plan to restore the street to its original state. No. 9 belonged to Zelman Nożyk, founder of the ghetto synagogue. ⊠ *Muranów.*

48 **Umschlagplatz.** This plaza was the rail terminus from which tens of thousands of the ghetto's inhabitants were shipped in cattle cars to the extermination camp of Treblinka, about 100 km (60 mi) northeast of Warsaw. The school building to the right of the square was used to detain those who had to wait overnight for transport; the beginning of the rail tracks survives on the right. At the entrance to the square is a memorial gateway, erected in 1988 on the 45th anniversary of the uprising. ⊠ *Stawki and Dzika, Muranów.*

OFF THE BEATEN PATH

Warsaw Rising Museum. One of the youngest and certainly one of the best museums in Poland tells the story of the 1944 Uprising by means of interactive displays. The museum features a life-size plane, cobblestone streets, reconstructed sewers (vital transportation and evacuation lines during the battles), photographs, and also video footage and audio recordings. It is a day-by-day account of the heroic struggle of the insurgents, most of them twentysomething years old—often told in their own words. It is impossible not to be involved and moved by it. Allow a minimum of 2½ hours to see the exhibition with a guide. English-language guides are available, but to ensure that you have a guide, you should make a tour reservation on the museum Web site by e-mailing a request to the museum, especially in summer. It is possible to wander around on your own as well. Large groups (11-plus persons) must book their entry in advance. ⊠ *Grzybowska 79, Mirów* ☎ *22/539–79–33* ⊕ *www.1944.pl* ⊠ *zł4, free Sun.* ⊙ *Sept.–June, Wed.–Mon. 8–6 (Thurs. until 8); July and Aug., Wed.–Mon. 10–6 (Thurs. until 8).*

WHERE TO EAT

You'll find a great many restaurants around the Old Town Square and along the Royal Route, but many of these are expensive and priced for tourists and upscale business travelers. There are some great off-the-beaten-path finds in the Diplomatic Quarter, Prwiśle, and Praga neighborhoods.

$$$–$$$$
Fodor'sChoice
★
✗**Biblioteka.** A university library may seem an unlikely location for a gourmet restaurant, but you are in for a delightful surprise. The menu is full of fine cuisine, including an exceptional saddle of deer in calvados sauce served with a layer of eggplant, and *branzino* (sea bass) with Pernod sauce. Good luck trying to decide which excellent dish to choose. The great food is accompanied by fine Italian wines imported directly from the producers. And don't forget dessert: how about a hot chocolate soufflé with mint ice cream? ✉*University of Warsaw Library, Dobra 56/66, Powiśle* ☎*22/620–19–99* ▤*AE, DC, MC, V* ☉*Closed Sun.*

$$–$$$$
✗**Boathouse.** This restaurant away from the city center serves great Mediterranean dishes. "Boathouse sole," a sole fillet stuffed with crabmeat in a crunchy potato crust with saffron sauce and wild-mushroom arancini (fried risotto cakes), served with fresh green asparagus, is really good. Boathouse is popular with expats and families with kids, especially for a Sunday brunch. It is particularly popular in summer. ✉*Wał Miedzeszyński 389a, Praga* ☎*22/616–32–23* ✍*Reservations essential* ▤*AE, DC, MC, V.*

$$–$$$$
Fodor'sChoice
★
✗**Dom Polski.** The "Polish Home" restaurant is more of a manor, with several patrician, yet cozy, rooms and a conservatory. The service is suitably courteous, the food is equally genteel. Although the Polish recipes are traditional Polish recipes, they are not as heavy as much of the country's cuisine and minimize the use of fat. Some good examples from the menu are veal liver with baked apple and caramel sauce and sheatfish (catfish) fillet with green pepper and spinach. ✉*Francuska 11, Śródmieście* ☎*22/616–24–32* ▤*AE, DC, MC, V.*

★ **$$–$$$$**
✗**Kurt Scheller's Restaurant.** The most prominent Swiss chef in Warsaw is still running strong with his signature restaurant in the Rialto Hotel. The food is excellent: interesting reinterpretations of both Polish and international dishes. The menu is always changing, but the cutlet of deer loin roasted in a mushroom crust with blackberry sauce on soft potato pancakes is an excellent example of Kurt Scheller's inspired skill. Both the setting—a beautiful art deco interior—and the service are impeccable. ✉*Rialto Hotel, Wilcza 73, Śródmieście* ☎*22/584–87–71* ✍*Reservations essential* ▤*AE, DC, MC, V.*

$$–$$$$
U Fukiera. This long-established wine bar on the Old Town Square has been turned into a curious—though ultimately inviting—network of elaborately decorated dining rooms. There is a talking parrot in a cage here, and candles adorn all available shelf space (sometimes set dangerously close to diners' elbows). The decor is, admittedly, lovely; the food is okay but overpriced "Light Old Polish." Expect to find such standbys as oven-roasted carp, sautéed veal liver, and crabmeat crepes. As with most places in the Old Town, sadly, you don't really get your

9

money's worth. Nevertheless, there's no denying that this is still one of the most famous and popular restaurants in Warsaw. If you dine here, go in with your eyes open and your pocketbook full. ⊠ *Rynek Starego Miasta 27, Stare Miasto* ☎ *022/831–10–13* ⚓ *Reservations essential* ▤ *AE, DC, MC, V.*

$$–$$$ ✗ **Restauracja Polska.** With a stylish room and some of the best food in the city, this basement restaurant is one of the more popular places to be in Warsaw these days. The tasteful main salon is furnished with antiques and decorated with large bouquets of fresh flowers. You can't go wrong here with the food, especially if you try the homemade pierogi or pike-perch fillet in white-leek sauce. For dessert, the home-made cakes are outstanding. ⊠ *Chocimska 7, Śródmieście* ☎ *022/848– 12–25* ▤ *AE, DC, MC, V.*

★ $–$$$ ✗ **Qchnia Artystyczna.** This artsy place at the back of the Zamek Ujazdowski is not for the impatient. This is a busy restaurant—and deservedly so—and the result can be sometimes hectic, even rude, service. However, all may be forgiven once you dig into your meal, which is always delicious and well prepared. The creative menu, which is freshly prepared and full of flavor, includes everything from potato pancakes to Parma ham to pork in orange sauce. The location is simply unbeatable: in summer, outdoor tables overlook a magnificent view of the park. The best strategy is just to work yourself into a Zenlike state and go with the flow, but make reservations. ⊠ *Zamek Ujazdowski, Aleje Ujazdowskie 6, Łazienki* ☎ *022/625–76–27* ⚓ *Reservations essential* ▤ *AE, DC, MC, V.*

$–$$$ ✗ **Sense.** Its owners claim Sense is the first Asian fusion restaurant in Poland, and that may very well be. Good modern decor complements the East-meets-West cuisine prepared in the open kitchen. The chefs have fun cooking up the names for the dishes, such as "stir crazy," "wok'n'roll," and "hurry curry." You can "go bananas!" for dessert. Of the Asian restaurants in Warsaw, this would have to be near the top of the list. ⊠ *Nowy Świat 19, Śródmieście* ☎ *22/826–65–70* ⚓ *Reservations essential* ▤ *AE, DC, MC, V.*

★ $–$$ ✗ **Biosfeera.** At this fashionable, upscale vegetarian restaurant, you'll find no alcohol, cigarette smoke, or meat. The food is delicious, and the service friendly. Tortillas, pastas, pancakes, and salads are accompanied by freshly squeezed juices, and there is usually a nod to non-veg diners with a fish dish or two; however, most of the menu is vegan. You emerge from the orange glow of Biosfeera refreshed and energized. ⊠ *al. Niepodległości 80, Śródmieście* ☎ *22/898–01–55* ▤ *AE, DC, MC, V.*

$–$$ ✗ **Casa to tu!** "To tu!" means "it's here!" but this casa can be easy to miss: the slightly uninviting entrance is through a courtyard and down steps to a cellar door; you'll see a sign. But once you find the restaurant, you'll be glad for the effort. The gazpacho, paella, and tapas are all excellent, and the setting is very pleasant: calming ambient lighting, warm colors, and wood tables and chairs give the space a comfortable, cozy feel. Plus the service is as good as the prices are reasonable. ⊠ *Nowy Świat 54/56, Śródmieście* ☎ *022/828–00–66* ▤ *AE, MC, V.*

$-$$

Fodor'sChoice

★ ✕**Restauracja Fabryki Trzciny.** You'll find the atmosphere at this restaurant cozy and warm, which is surprising since the modern arts center that houses it was once an industrial warehouse. The cuisine here is classified as "art-industrial cuisine," but the truth is that the food served here is Polish—mostly Varsovian—with influences from the Mediterranean and other European cuisines. Many dishes may recall childhood favorites, such as *leniwe* (sweet cheese raviolis) or *pyzy* (a local version of dumplings). Among the many excellent dishes, don't miss horseradish soup or veal liver in mushroom sauce, both of which are unforgettable. If you feel indecisive, go with the six-course tasting menu and a shot of *Żołądkowa* vodka to wash everything down. ✉*Fabryka Trzciny, Otwocka 14, Praga* ☎*22/619–17–05* ▭*AE, DC, MC, V* ✷*Closed Mon.*

$-$$ ✕**Smaki Warszawy.** You can't go wrong with any of the chef's recommendations, which are usually traditional Polish dishes with a twist. Both the duck breast in a sauce of apples, plums, and apricots and the pappardelle with boletus mushrooms and freshly chopped parsley are truly delicious and among the highlights on the menu. ✉*Żurawia 47, Śródmieście* ☎*022/621–82–68* ▭*AE, DC, MC, V.*

WHERE TO STAY

Warsaw is beginning to deal with its shortage of luxury hotel rooms for business travelers, and you'll now find a good selection of luxury lodgings in the city, including both large international chains and interesting individually owned hotels. However, lower down the price scale, options still remain restricted. Bed-and-breakfast accommodations are difficult to find. In summer there are generally more options because student hostels rent out their spaces. Demand is high, so book well in advance.

$$$$

Fodor'sChoice

★ ▦**Polonia Palace.** When this hotel opened in 1913, it was the best address in Warsaw. Following decades of faded glory—and a two-year-long complete restoration—it reopened in 2005 in a condition that is once again worthy of its name. Corner and front rooms have what is, perhaps, the coolest view in town: the socialist realist Palace of Culture and Science, which is right across the street. The rooms are spacious, although they differ in size and layout, with modern, muted decor and comfortable amenities. The breakfast is an adventure in itself, a full splash featuring caviar and champagne or vodka (yes, we mean *breakfast*); it is served in the grand Ludwikowska restaurant, embellished with crystal chandeliers, mirrors, and some 6 kilos of gold. ✉*Aleje Jerozolimskie 45, 00–692, Śródmieście* ☎*22/318–28–00* ▤*22/318–28–01* ⊕*www.poloniapalace.com* ⤢*198 rooms, 8 suites* ♿*In-room: safe, dial-up, Ethernet. In-hotel: Restaurant, room service, bar, gym, laundry service, concierge, public Internet, public Wi-Fi, parking (fee), no-smoking rooms* ▭*AE, DC, MC, V* ⍥*BP.*

★ $$$$ ▦**Rialto.** Soft jazz plays in the lobby of this boutique hotel, which is completely in tune with its wonderfully consistent and tasteful art deco design, the work of architect Michał Borowski. Original period furniture was hunted down in antiques fairs all over Europe, then lov-

9

ingly restored by Polish artisans and supplemented with quality copies: a Charles Rennie Mackintosh lamp here, a Tamara de Lempicka painting there. Although rooms are a bit on a small side because of the historical building's architectural quirks, their style is large enough that you won't mind. Each room is different, from cool, classy suite No. 65 (with slanted ceilings) to warm, wild African single No. 29. The hotel's fashionable restaurant is run by renowned chef Kurt Scheller. ⊠ *Wilcza 73, 00–670, Śródmieście* ☎22/584–87–00 ⊟22/584–87–01 ⊕*www. rialto.pl* ✒*33 rooms, 11 suites* ⊹*Restaurant, room service, in-room safes, minibars, cable TV, in-room DVD, in-room broadband, gym, hot tub, sauna, bar, library, laundry service, business services, meeting rooms, parking (fee)* ⊟*AE, DC, MC, V* ⊺⊙⟩*BP.*

$$$–$$$$
Fodor's Choice
★

🔳 **Le Regina.** The latest addition to Warsaw's lineup of top-end hotels, this boutique, luxury establishment is an oasis within the busy capital. With a superb location at the north end of the Old Town, the hotel is a remodeled 18th-century palace that's rich in history, including a stint as the quarters of the U.S. Embassy in the 1950s. Rooms are spacious and serene, but the nicest suites are the "deluxe" category, which include private gardens or terraces; the fun and fashionable, black-and-white penthouse suite (No. 303) is stunning. Nice touches include complimentary Internet access—uncommon in this class of hotel—and an umbrella in every closet. However, the sun always shines in Le Regina. ⊠*Kościelna 12, 00–218, Nowe Miasto* ☎022/531–60–00 ⊟022/531–60–01 ⊕*www.leregina.com* ✒*58 rooms, 3 suites* ⊹*Restaurant, room service, in-room safes, minibars, cable TV, Wi-Fi, gym, pool, sauna, bar, laundry service, business services, Internet room, meeting rooms, parking (fee)* ⊟*AE, DC, MC, V* ⊺⊙⟩*BP.*

★ $$$–$$$$ 🔳 **Le Royal Méridien Bristol.** Built in 1901 by a consortium headed by Ignacy Paderewski—the concert pianist who served as Poland's prime minister from 1919 to 1920—the Bristol was long at the center of Warsaw's social life. Impressively situated on the Royal Route, next to the Pałac Namiestnikowski (Presidential Palace), the hotel survived World War II more or less intact. It continues to maintain a long tradition of luxury and elegance under the ownership of Le Méridien. Additionally, the hotel has one of the best cafés in town—no one can resist its pastries. ⊠*Krakowskie Przedmieście 42/44, 00–325, Royal Route* ☎022/625–25–25 ⊟022/625–25–77 ⊕*www.royalmeridienbristolho-tel.com* ✒*163 rooms, 43 suites* ⊹*2 restaurants, café, in-room fax, in-room safes, minibars, cable TV, in-room broadband, indoor pool, gym, massage, sauna, steam room, bar, Internet room, business services, meeting rooms, no-smoking floors* ⊟*AE, DC, MC, V* ⊺⊙⟩*BP.*

$$$ 🔳 **Warsaw Marriott.** Located in the high-rise Lim Center opposite Central Station, the Marriott currently has some of the city's best accommodations, particularly for the price. It's a classy hotel with a well-trained and helpful staff, nearly all of whom speak some English. The views from every room—of central Warsaw and far beyond—are spectacular on a clear day. The Lila Veneda restaurant on the second floor hosts a special Sunday brunch, complete with Dixieland band. ⊠*Aleje Jerozolimskie 65/79, 00–697, Śródmieście* ☎022/630–63–06 ⊟022/620–52–39 ⊕*www.marriott.com* ✒*489 rooms, 34 suites* ⊹*3 restaurants,*

café, room service, in-room data ports, in-room safes, some kitchens, minibars, cable TV, indoor pool, gym, hair salon, hot tub, sauna, 3 bars, casino, nightclub, shop, laundry service, concierge, business services, car rental, parking (fee) ⊟*AE, DC, MC, V* ⦿|*BP.*

$$-$$$ ⊡ **Metropol Hotel.** This 1960s hotel is right on Warsaw's main downtown intersection. Most of the rooms are singles and are large enough to contain a bed, armchairs, and desk without feeling crowded. Bathrooms, though small, are attractively tiled and fitted. Each room has a balcony overlooking busy ulica Marszałkowska, and traffic noise can be very intrusive when the windows are open. There is no air-conditioning, but the hotel's exterior and some interiors received a face-lift recently. ⊠*Marszałkowska 99A, 00–693, Śródmieście* ☏*022/629–40–01* 🖷*022/625–30–14* ⊕*www.syrena.com.pl* ⤢*175 rooms, 16 suites* ⚴*Restaurant, cable TV, business services, meeting room, parking (fee); no a/c* ⊟*AE, DC, MC, V* ⦿|*BP.*

$$-$$$ ⊡ **Novotel Warsaw Airport.** You won't have to worry about getting a good night's sleep if you stay at this Novotel, as it is some distance away from the hustle and bustle of the city center. However, this is far from an ideal location if you are coming to Warsaw to see the sights. If your flight out is early in the morning, though, this is a perfect location for your last night: it's only five minutes from the airport (fortunately, *not* under any flight paths), and it's right across the road from a major area of gardens and parks. Though removed from the heart of the city, the hotel is on the main bus routes; Bus 175 will take you downtown in 15 minutes. The atmosphere is friendly, and the rooms are light, clean, and comfortable. ⊠*1 Sierpnia 1, 02–134, Mokotów* ☏*022/846–40–51* ⊕*www.novotel.com* ⤢*150 rooms* ⚴*Restaurant, minibars, pool, gym, bar, meeting rooms, airport shuttle* ⊟*AE, DC, MC, V* ⦿|*BP.*

★ $$-$$$ ⊡ **Westin Warsaw.** The pleasant, contemporary form of the Westin fits in well with the context of aleja Jana Pawła II, one of the most interesting streets in Warsaw in terms of new architecture. The elevators are fitted within the glass tower, so that you can admire the view while you ride up and down. The lobby, which has a spiral staircase, feels cozy for a big hotel, and you may notice echoes of Mies van de Rohe in the Fusion restaurant, which is so famous for its Sunday brunch that even Varsovians often book in advance. Inside the comfortable rooms, Westin's trademark "Heavenly Bed" is not an empty promise. ⊠*al. Jana Pawła II, 00–854, Śródmieście* ☏*22/450–80–00* 🖷*22/450–81–11* ⊕*westin.com/warsaw* ⤢*345 rooms, 16 suites* ⚴*Restaurant, minibars, cable TV, in-room safe, gym, massage, sauna, bar, in-room broadband, meeting rooms, laundry service* ⊟*AE, DC, MC, V* ⦿|*BP.*

$$ ⊡ **Gromada.** With an excellent location in the center of Warsaw, this white five-story hotel was built during the late 1950s by the Gromada peasants' cooperative and originally had a plant-and-seed store on the ground floor. The hotel, which was renovated in 2003, offers clean and reasonably priced accommodations; rooms are rather small, but the colors are lively, and the bathrooms have been updated. There is no air-conditioning, though. ⊠*pl. Powstańców Warszawy 2, 00–030, Śródmieście* ☏*022/582–99–00* 🖷*022/582–95–27* ⊕*www.gromada.pl*

9

⤳282 rooms ⚄ Restaurant, cable TV, bar, parking (fee); no a/c ▭ AE, DC, MC, V ⍩⊙⍩BP.

$ ⊡ **Logos.** This hotel is situated in Powiśle, across the road from the Vistula River and 10 minutes by foot (admittedly all uphill) from the Royal Route. Traffic noise can be a big problem in front-facing rooms, but courtyard-facing rooms are peaceful. The decor throughout is dull, with plenty of dark-wood paneling and chocolate-brown paint, and there is no air-conditioning. Needless to say, the main draw here is the low price. Only the 10 doubles have private bathrooms. ✉ Wybrzeże Kościuszkowskie 31/33, 00–379, Powiśle ☎022/622–55–61 ⊟022/625–51–85 ⊕ www.hotellogos.pl ⤳137 rooms, 10 with bath ⚄ Restaurant, café, no a/c ▭ AE, DC, MC, V ⍩⊙⍩BP.

NIGHTLIFE & THE ARTS

NIGHTLIFE

Like many large European cities, Warsaw offers a variety of options for activities after dark to meet the growing and changing needs of its population. Some Varsovians still prefer to meet for drinks in the evenings in the old central European style in *kawiarnie* (cafés), where you can linger for as long as you like over a cup of coffee or glass of brandy (well, almost as long as you like, since most cafés are open only until 10 PM). Others head directly to more cosmopolitan pubs, DJ bars, and clubs, many of which stay open until the wee hours. Live music is fairly common, and there is a certain fashion these days for melding art and nightlife into a single multifunctional establishment: you will find more than one concert venue/pub/gallery, or bookshop-cum-café.

BARS & LOUNGES

Harenda (✉ *Krakowskie Przedmieście 4/6, enter from ul. Obożna, Royal Route* ☎022/826–29–00) occasionally hosts some good jazz and has an outdoor terrace that gets crowded in summer. The **John Bull Pub** (✉ *ul. Zielna 37, Śródmieście* ☎022/620–06–56 ✉ *Jezuicka 4, Stare Miasto* ☎022/831–37–62) is open until midnight and serves English draft beers at both its locations. Brilliantly and eccentrically named—the "Bald Penguin" **Łysy Pingwin** (✉ *Ząbkowska 11, Praga* ☎022/628–91–32) is a relaxing pub run by a Swedish Buddhist (*sic!*) who settled in Warsaw's trendy Praga District. **Szpilka** (✉ *pl. Trzech Krzyży 18, Śródmieście* ☎22/628–91–32) is perfect for insomniacs; it opens at 7 PM and stays open until 6 AM. Its sister club Szpulka, which shares the same address, closes as "early" as 3 AM.

CLUBS & DISCOS

The crowd at posh and pricey **Cinnamon** (✉ *pl. Piłsudskiego 1, Śródmieście* ☎022/323–76–00) leans toward businessmen in suits, fashionably dressed models and celebrities, and an international clientele (lots of expats). More of a café-restaurant during the day, it's the hottest club in Warsaw on Thursday through Saturday nights. **Ground Zero** (✉ *al. Wspólna 62, Śródmieście* ☎022/625–43–80), a former bomb shelter, is a large, crowded bi-level disco, probably the most popular in town. An upscale, younger crowd dances to mostly mainstream disco and pop. **Klubokawiarnia** (✉*al. Czackiego 8, Śródmieście*) is relaxed, with funky disco music among plaster busts of Lenin and 1950s propaganda posters. You dance to both DJs and live (mostly rock) music from local bands. House music emporium **Piekarnia** (✉*Młocińska 11, Wola* ☎*022/323–76–00*) might have become too popular for its own good—still, it is one of the uncontested leaders of the Warsaw night scene. Famous international DJs (Roger Sanchez, Barry Ashworth, etc.) are brought in for big events. There is a well-established disco at the student club **Stodoła** (✉*Batorego 10, Ochota* ☎*022/25–86–25*). Though it draws mostly students, it's open to everyone. Music spans from house to techno to R&B to hip-hop, and there are often live bands.

JAZZ CLUBS

Jazz Bistro Gwiazdeczka (✉*Piwna 40, Stare Miasto* ☎*022/887–87–65*) is brighter and more spacious than most smoky jazz clubs in Warsaw and has a glass-covered atrium. **Jazz Café Helicon** (✉*Freta 45/47, Stare Miasto* ☎*022/635–95–05*) is a smoky jazz club, with Latino music on some nights—it has an adjoining specialty record store. **Tygmont** (✉*Mazowiecka 6/8, Śródmieście* ☎*022/828–34–09* ⊕*www.tygmont. com.pl*) is a local legend, frequented by older and younger generations of musicians and audiences.

THE ARTS

You can find out about Warsaw's thriving arts scene in the English-language *Warsaw Insider* or *What's Up*, both of which are available at most major hotels. If you read Polish, the monthly *IKS* (*Informator Kulturalny Stolicy*) and *Activist* and the daily *Gazeta Wyborcza* have the best listings. Tickets for most performances are inexpensive, but if you want to spend even less, most theaters sell general-admission tickets—*wejściówki*—for a few złoty immediately before the performance. Wejściówki are often available for performances for which all standard tickets have been sold. **ZASP** (✉*Aleje Jerozolimskie 25, Śródmieście* ☎*022/621–94–54*), a ticketing agency, is also a good source for information on arts happenings. Tickets for many events can be bought at **EMPiK** (✉*Nowy Świat 15/17, Śródmieście* ☎*022/627–06–50*), a local chain of shops. If you are planning in advance, you can buy tickets for many events from the Web site of **Warsaw Tour** (⊕*www.warsawtour. pl*), which has an English-language option.

MUSIC

☾ In summer, free Chopin concerts are held at the Chopin Memorial in Łazienki Park on Sunday and at Chopin's birthplace, Żelazowa Wola, outside Warsaw. The **Filharmonia Narodowa** (*National Philharmonic* ✉*Sienkiewicza 10, Śródmieście* ☎*022/826–72–81*) hosts an excellent season of concerts, with visits from world-renowned performers and orchestras as well as Polish musicians. Very popular concerts of classical music for children—run for years by Jadwiga Mackiewicz, who is herself almost a national institution—are held here on Sunday at 2; admission begins at zł5. The **Studio Koncertowe Polskiego Radia** (*Polish Radio Concert Studio* ✉*Woronicza 17, Mokotów* ☎*022/645–52–*

52), open since 1992, has excellent acoustics and popular programs of mostly classical and modern classical (and sometimes jazz). The **Royal Castle** (✉ *Plac Zamkowy 4, Stare Miasto* ☎022/657–21–70) has regular concerts in its stunning Great Assembly Hall. The Chopin Society, **Towarzystwo im. Fryderyka Chopina** (✉ *Okólnik 1, Śródmieście* ☎022/827–54–71), organizes recitals and chamber concerts in the Pałac Ostrogskich (Ostrogski Palace).

OPERA & DANCE

Housed in a beautifully restored 19th-century theater, **Opera Kameralna** (✉ *al. Solidarności 76B, Muranów* ☎022/625–75–10), the Warsaw chamber opera, has an ambitious program and a growing reputation for quality performances. **Teatr Wielki** (*Opera House* ✉ *Plac Teatralny 1, Śródmieście* ☎022/826–32–88), Warsaw's grand opera, stages spectacular productions of the classic international opera and ballet repertoire, as well as Polish operas and ballets. The massive neoclassical house, built in the 1820s and reconstructed after the war, has an auditorium with more than 2,000 seats. Stanisław Moniuszko's 1865 opera *Straszny Dwór* (Haunted Manor), a lively piece with folk costumes and dancing, is a good starting point if you want to explore Polish music: the visual aspects will entertain you, even if the music is unfamiliar. Plot summaries in English are available at most performances.

THEATER

The **Globe Theater Group** (✉ *pl. Grzybowski 6/2, Śródmieście* ☎022/620–44–29 ⊕ *www.globetheatre.art.pl*) performs American and British plays at various theater venues. **Teatr Lalek "Guliwer"** (✉ *Różana 16, Śródmieście* ☎022/45–16–76 ⊕ *www.teatrguliwer.waw.pl*) is one of Warsaw's excellent puppet theaters. Warsaw's Jewish Theater, **Teatr Żydowski** (✉ *Plac Grzybowski 12/16, Śródmieście* ☎022/620–70–25 ⊕ *www.teatrzydowski.art.pl*), performs in Yiddish, but most of its productions are colorful costume dramas in which the action speaks as loudly as the words. Translation into English is provided through headphones.

SHOPPING

In terms of shopping, Warsaw has it all—from big, sparkling shopping malls to tiny boutiques and specialty stores, as well as some decent street markets. Shopping hours are usually from 11 AM to 7 PM on weekdays and from 10 AM to 1 PM on Saturday, but shopping malls are open until 8 or even 10 PM. Kiosks, which sell bus and train tickets, newspapers, and cosmetics, are usually open from 7 to 7.

SHOPPING DISTRICTS

Warsaw has four main shopping streets, all in Śródmieście. The larger stores lie on **ulica Marszałkowska** (from ulica Królewska to plac Zbawiciela) and **Aleje Jerozolimskie** (from Central Station to plac Generała de Gaulle'a, in Śródmieście). Smaller stores and more specialized boutiques can be found on **ulica Nowy Świat** and **ulica Chmielna**. Another fashionable shopping street just a bit farther off is **ulica Burakowska,** and some smaller designer shops and ateliers are scattered around town.

SHOPPING MALLS

In the mid-1990s, shopping malls started sprouting like mushrooms in Poland's capital—and new ones continue to appear. One of the most popular shopping malls is **Arkadia** (⊠*al. Jana Pawła II, Muranów* ☎*022/331–34–00* ⊕*www.arkadia.com.pl*), where you can buy almost anything in more than 180 shops, grab a quick bite at a Japanese restaurant, and get your nails done, too. **Galeria Mokotów** (⊠*Wołoska 12, Mokotów* ☎*022/541–30–00* ⊕*www.galeriamokotow.com.pl*) is the big sister among the newer malls. Unceasingly popular, it is still the best destination for designer clothing. Plus it has a good selection of restaurants and snack bars, as well as a multiplex cinema, a play area for children, and a bowling alley.

STREET MARKETS

The largest Warsaw market—known as the Russian market, and composed largely of private sellers hawking everything from antiques to blue jeans—is at the **Tysiąclecia Stadium,** east of the river at Rondo Waszyngtona in Grochów. If you go, watch out for pickpockets. A smaller market (with mostly food vendors) can be found closer to the center—just outside the 19th-century covered markets of **Hala Mirowska.** For treasures among the junk—and the general nostalgic ambience—try one of Warsaw's two flea markets on a Sunday morning: **Olimpia** (⊠*Corner of Górczewska and al. Prymasa Tysiąclecia, Wola*), or **Koło** (⊠*Corner of Obozowa and Ciołka, Wola*).

SPECIALTY STORES

ANTIQUES

For fine antique furniture, art, and china try **Desa** (⊠*Marszałkowska 34/50, Śródmieście* ☎*022/621–66–15*), an auction house and gallery. Remember, however, that most antiques cannot be exported. You will also sometimes find antiques at the Olimpia and Koło flea markets.

ART GALLERIES

There are many galleries in Praga, some seasonal and with "flexible" opening hours, but **Galeria Nizio** (⊠*Inżynierska 3, Praga* ☎*022/618–72–02* ⊕*www.nizio.com.pl*), which moved to Warsaw from New York in 2002, is one of the best established. **Galeria Sztuki Katarzyny Napiórkowskiej** (⊠*Świętokrzyska 32, Śródmieście* ☎*022/652–19–39* ⊕*www.napiorkowska.pl*) holds one of the finest collections of contemporary Polish art in the world. **Raster** (⊠*Hoża 42/8, Śródmieście* ☎*022/869–97–81* ⊕*www.raster.art.pl*) is definitely the most talked-about art gallery in town, showing exhibitions of independent art in a top-floor flat of an old tenement house. It sometimes also has film screenings and live concerts.

CLOTHING FOR CHILDREN

☺ **Endo** (⊠*Mokotowska 51/53, Śródmieście* ☎*022/629–30–65*) sells fun, colorful children's clothing (for ages 2 and up) and has a play area for the young customers.

CLOTHING FOR WOMEN

Warsaw has been blessed with quite a few local talents, and their studios are scattered around town, usually away from the main shopping streets.

The **First Class** (⌧*Jasna 1, Śródmieście* ☎*022/826–88–25*) boutique showcases the designs of Maciej Zień. Designer tandem **Paprocki & Brzozowski** (⌧*Krucza 17, Śródmieście* ☎*048/608–301–120*)—that's Marcin Paprocki and Mariusz Brzozowski—have a shop to sell their fashions. **Pola La** (⌧*Solec 85, Solec* ☎*022/622–89–00*) is the handbag atelier of a talented Polish designer. **Ruta** (⌧*Czerwonego Krzyża 2, entrance from Solec, Solec* ☎*048/601–851–420 bags, 048/501–087–002 hats*) is the shop selling the fantastic hats, bags, and belts designed by Pracownia Kaletnicza and Marta Ruta. Liza Minelli owns one already.

FOLK ART & CRAFTS

Cepelia (⌧*pl. Konstytucji 5, Śródmieście* ☎*022/621–26–18* ⌧*Marszałkowska 99/101, Śródmieście* ☎*022/628–77–57*), which has several branches in Warsaw, sells folk art, including wood carvings and silver and amber jewelry. At **Studio Forma** (⌧*Skorupki 5, Śródmieście* ☎*022/583–68–58*) you can find folk-inspired bright and cheerful wool rugs, made by young Polish artists from Moho Design, which won the owners a prize from *Wallpaper* magazine in 2006.

FOOD

If you are looking for more than just the sweets, **Blikle Delikatesy** (⌧*Nowy Świat 35, Śródmieście* ☎*022/826–45–68*) sells traditional Polish products (such as natural honey or smoked meats) as well as delicious imports (olive oil, cheeses, and much more). Of course, if you *are* looking for sweets, then there is always something for your sweet tooth. After all, Blikle is best known in Poland as the maker of prizewinning *pączki* doughnuts.

GLASS & CRYSTAL

A. Jabłoński (⌧*Nowy Świat 52, Royal Route* ☎*No phone*) sells unique pieces of handblown glass and crystal. **Krosno** (⌧*Arkadia Shopping Mall, al. Jana Pawła II, Muranów* ☎*022/331–25–55*) sells glass from the famous Krosno factory. **Szlifierna szkła** (⌧*Nowomiejska 1/3, Stare Miasto* ☎*022/831–46–43*), next to the Old Town Square, custom engraves all kinds of crystal goods.

JEWELRY

There are many *jubiler* (jewelry) stores clustered around the Old Town and ulica Nowy Świat. **Quadrat–Brodzińska Atelier** (⌧*Marszałkowska 9/15, Śródmieście*) sells jewelry in ultramodern designs. One of the oldest and best-established jewelry stores in Poland is **W. Kruk** (⌧*pl. Konstytucji 6, Śródmieście* ☎*022/628–75–34*). **Zielony Kot** (⌧*Chmielna 26, Śródmieście* ☎*022/826–51–18*), the "green cat" in English, is as fun and funky as the name promises.

LEATHER

JKM (⊠ *Krakowskie Przedmieście 65, Royal Route* ☏022/827–22–62) is a small shop crammed with bags, suitcases, and gloves from the best Polish producers. **Pekar** (⊠ *Aleje Jerozolimskie 29, Śródmieście* ☏022/621–90–82) carries a wide range of bags, gloves, and jackets.

EXCURSION FROM WARSAW

Among day-trip destinations within easy access of Warsaw, Chopin's birthplace at Żelazowa Wola is perhaps the most interesting.

ŻELAZOWA WOLA

30 km (18 mi) west of Warsaw.

★ A mecca for all Frédéric Chopin lovers (his name is Fryderyk in Polish), the composer's birthplace is a small 19th-century manor house, still with its original furnishings and now a museum dedicated to telling the story of the composer's life. When Chopin was born here on February 22 (or March 1), 1810, his father was a live-in tutor for the children of the wealthy Skarbek family. Although the family soon moved to Warsaw, Chopin often returned for holidays, and the house—not to mention the sounds and sights of the Mazovian countryside—is said to have influenced him in his early years.

The manor is surrounded by a beautifully landscaped park that was planted in 1930s and designed by Franciszek Krzywda Polkowski. In summer, from May through September, concerts are held on the house's terrace every Sunday at noon and 3 PM. On weekdays, at noon, there are presentations of young artists and talented students playing Chopin.

If you are driving, take Route 2 (E30) west out of Warsaw, and at Sochaczew, turn north on Route 580. The house is also reachable by PKS bus and by private minibuses running from Warsaw's main bus station *(⇨ By Bus in Warsaw & Mazovia Essentials, below)*, but several companies also offer guided tours that include both Żelazowa Wola and Nieborów, the estate of the Radziwiłł family (and sometimes Arkadia Park as well). *(For information on tour companies, see* ⇨ *Tour Options in Warsaw & Mazovia Essentials, below.)* ⊠ *Żelazowa Wola* ☏046/863–33–00 ☏zł12 ☉ *May–Sept., Tues.–Sun. 9:30–5:30; Oct.– Apr. 9:30–4.*

9

WARSAW ESSENTIALS

BY AIR

If you are flying into Poland from abroad, it's mostly likely that you will fly into Warsaw. The city's Okęcie Airport, also known as Fryderyka Chopina International Airport, is the largest airport in Poland, with about 70% of all the air traffic into and out of the country. In addition, most European airlines connect Warsaw with the United States. The new Etiuda Terminal serves most of the "low-cost" airlines that operate flights within Europe. The flying time from New York to Warsaw is approximately 9 hours, from London approximately 2½ hours.

AIRPORTS & TRANSFERS

Warsaw's Okęcie Airport, also known as Fryderyka Chopina International Airport, is 7 km (4½ mi) south of the city center and has the most international flights into and out of Poland.

The AIRPORT–CITY bus leaves from Platform 4 outside Terminal 1 every 20 minutes and stops at all the major hotels as well as the Central Station. Tickets cost zł6, and the trip takes about 25 minutes. Alternatively, Bus 175 leaves Okęcie about every 10 minutes (at night, Bus 611 is much less frequent). It also runs past most major downtown hotels and is reliable and cheap, but beware of pickpockets. Purchase tickets for zł2.40 at an airport RUCH kiosk. Avoid at all costs the taxi hawkers and unmarked vehicles (which have no number at the top) outside the arrivals hall: not only are these cabs expensive but they can also be dangerous. Your best bet is to call a radio taxi from one of the radio taxi kiosks in the arrivals area, or call your hotel in advance and have them pick you up. A cab ride into the city should cost about zł25 (most hotel taxis have higher, fixed rates, of approximately zł50).

Information Okęcie Airport (⊠ *Żwirki i Wigury 1, Warsaw* ☎ *022/650–42–20* ⊕ *www.polish-airports.com*).

BUS TRAVEL

Warsaw's main bus station, Dworzec PKS Zachodni, 10 minutes from Central Station on Bus 127 or 130, serves most long-distance routes, both domestic and international. Domestic buses headed east leave from Dworzec PKS Stadion on the east bank of the Vistula. The private long-distance bus service Polski Express, which goes to most major destinations within Poland, arrives and departs from Jana Pawła II Station, between Central Station and the Holiday Inn. Polski Express also has a stop at the airport.

Warsaw Buses Dworzec PKS Zachodni (⊠ *Aleje Jerozolimskie 144, Śródmieście, Warsaw* ☎ *022/822–48–11* ⊕ *www.pks.warszawa.pl*). **Dworzec PKS Stadion** (⊠ *Zamoyskiego 1, at Targowa, Praga, Warsaw* ☎ *022/818–15–89* ⊕ *www.pks. warszawa.pl*). **Polski Express** (⊠ *Jana Pawła II, between Central Station and the Holiday Inn, Śródmieście, Warsaw* ☎ *022/620–03–30* ⊕ *www.polskiexpress.pl*).

CAR TRAVEL

Within the city, a car is more of a problem than a convenience. Particularly in Warsaw, traffic jams are frequent and parking is problematic, with a significant threat of theft—of contents, parts, or the entire car—if you leave a Western model unattended. If you do bring your car, park it overnight in a guarded parking garage. A car can be a useful independent means of transportation if you are planning to travel around Mazovia to explore the countryside and off-the-beaten-track sights. Major international car-rental agencies have offices in Warsaw and at the airport.

Information Avis (⊠ *Marriott hotel, Aleje Jerozolimskie 65/79, Śródmieście, Warsaw* ☎ *022/630–73–16)* **Budget** (⊠ *Okęcie Airport, Warsaw* ☎ *022/650–42–62).*

Europcar (✉ *Okęcie Airport, Warsaw* ☎ *022/650-25-64*). **Five** (✉ *Marriott hotel, Aleje Jerozolimskie 65/79, Śródmieście, Warsaw* ☎ *022/629-75-15*). **Hertz** (✉ *Nowogrodzka 27, Śródmieście, Warsaw* ☎ *022/621-13-60* ✉ *Okęcie Airport, Warsaw* ☎ *022/650-28-96*)

EMERGENCIES

Dentists Austria-Dent Center (✉ *Żelazna 54, Śródmieście, Warsaw* ☎ *022/654– 21-16*).

Doctors Damian Medical Center (✉ *Wałbrzyska 46, Warsaw* ✉ *Foksal 3/5, Warsaw* ✉ *Modlińska 310/312, Warsaw* ☎ *022/566-22-22*). **Lux Med Medical Clinics** (✉ *Chmielna 85/87, Warsaw* ✉ *Kopernika 30, Warsaw* ✉ *Aleje Jerozolimskie 162, Warsaw* ☎ *0801/80-08-08*).

Hospitals Dzieciątka Jezus Hospital (✉ *Lindleya 4, Warsaw* ☎ *022/502-16-98*). **Hospital of the Interior Ministry** (✉ *Wołoska 137, Warsaw* ☎ *022/508-20-00*). **Kopernik Hospital** (✉ *Pabianicka 62, Łódź* ☎ *042/689—50-00* ⊕ *www.kopernik. lodz.pl*). **Pulsmed Private Hospital** (✉ *P.O.W. 26, Łódź* ☎ *042/633—32-75* ⊕ *www. pulsmed.com.pl*).

24-Hour Pharmacies Apteka Beata (✉ *al. Solidarności 149, Śródmieście, Warsaw* ☎ *022/620-08-18*). **Apteka Grabowskiego** (✉ *Central Station, 1st fl., Aleje Jerozolimskie 54, Śródmieście, Warsaw* ☎ *022/825-69-86*). **Cito** (✉ *Żeromskiego 39, Łódź* ☎ *042/633-48-29*). **Familia** (✉ *Lutomierska 115a, Łódź* ☎ *042/640-71-27*).

INTERNET

Most hotels in Warsaw offer Internet access (sometimes for a fee). There are also plenty of Internet cafés around, with rates between zł3 and zł30 per hour for high-speed access. In Warsaw, you'll find several hot spots with free Wi-Fi access for those carrying laptops: in Plac Zamkowy, ulica Nowy Świat, ulica Chmielna, Plac Bankowy, Warsaw University Library, the Traffic Club, and even in some restaurants and cafeterias.

Warsaw Internet Cafés Café Casablanca (✉ *Krakowskie Przedmieście 4/6, Warsaw* ☎ *022/828-14-47* ⊕ *www.casablanca.com.pl*). **Courtyard by Marriott Cyber Café** (✉ *Okęcie Airport, Courtyard by Marriott, Żwirki i Wigury 1, Warsaw* ☎ *022/650-650-01-72*). **SImple Internet Café** (✉ *Marszałkowska 99,Warsaw* ☎ *022/628-31-90* ⊕ *www.simpleinternetcafe.com*).

PUBLIC TRANSPORTATION

In Warsaw, a trip on a city bus costs zł2.40. There are also timed tickets: zł3.60 for up to 60 minutes, zł4.50 for up to 90 minutes, and zł6 for up to 120 minutes. A one-day pass is zł7.20, three-day pass, zł12, and a seven-day pass, zł24. There are additional charges for large pieces of luggage. Purchase tickets from RUCH kiosks or directly from bus drivers (zł0.60 surcharge), and validate one in the machine on the bus for each ride. Buses that halt at all stops along their route are numbered 100 and up. Express buses are numbered from E-1 and up. Buses numbered 500–599 stop at selected stops. You can check details on the bus stop's information board. Night buses (numbered 600 and up) operate between 11 PM and 5:30 AM; the fare is three tickets. Buses can be very crowded, and you should beware of pickpockets.

Trams are the fastest means of public transport since they are not affected by traffic holdups, but are also often crowded. Purchase tickets from RUCH kiosks or tram operators, and cancel one ticket in the machine on the tram for each ride. Trams run on a north–south and east–west grid system along most of the main city routes, pulling up automatically at all stops. Each tram has a diagram of the system.

Warsaw's underground opened in spring 1995. Although it has only one line, which connects the southern suburbs (Kabaty) and northern suburbs (Marymont) to the city center, it is clean and fast and costs the same as the tram or bus. Use the same tickets, canceling them at the entrance to the station.

Information ZTM Warszawa (☎ *022/94–84* ⊕ *www.ztm.waw.pl*).

TAXIS

In Warsaw, it is always best to use the services of radio taxis because these are the most reliable and because the operators usually speak English. This is also true in Łódź. The standard charge is about zł5 to zł7 for the first kilometer (½ mi) and zł1.30 to zł2 for each kilometer thereafter (about 50% more at night and during holidays). You do not need to tip taxi drivers, although you can round up the fare to the nearest złoty. Avoid unmarked Mercedes cabs as well as taxis that do not have a number and a name of a company you know on the top. Those "independent" taxis are likely to charge far more than the going rate.

Warsaw Taxi Companies Halo Taxi (☎ *022/96–23*). MPT (☎ *022/91–91*). OK! Taxi (☎ *022/96–28*). Partner Taxi (☎ *022/96–69*). Sawa Taxi (☎ *022/644–44–44*). Super Taxi (☎ *022/96–22*). Tele Taxi (☎ *022/96–27*). Top Taxi (☎ *022/96–64*). Taxi Wawa (☎ *022/96–44*).

TRAIN TRAVEL

As the name implies, Warsaw's Warszawa Centralna (Central Station) is right in the heart of the city, between the Marriott and Holiday Inn hotels, and next to the Palace of Culture. Beware of pickpockets and muggers who prey on passengers as they board or leave trains. Most trains from Warszawa Centralna stop on their way out in Warszawa Wschodnia, Warszawa Zachodnia, Warszawa Gdańska, or Warszawa Wileńska—depending on their direction.

You can purchase train tickets at the train station or at travel agencies, including Orbis. You can also buy tickets on the train (there is a small surcharge), but be warned: old-fashioned regulations require you to notify the train attendant before you actually get on that train if you need to purchase a ticket on board—otherwise, you may have to pay a penalty. Tickets can also be bought online, and the full train timetable (*rozkład jazdy pociągów*) is available on the Web site of Polskie Koleje Państwowe, the Polish national rail company.

Information Polskie Koleje Państwowe (⊕ *www.pkp.pl*). Warszawa Centralna (*Central Station* ⊠ *Aleje Jerozolimskie 54, Śródmieście, Warsaw* ☎ *022/94–36*).

VISITOR INFORMATION

The Warsaw City Information & Promotion Center is open every day from 8 to 8 from May through September, and from 8 to 6 from October through April. There are branches at the arrivals hall of Warsaw's airport and the Central Railway Station.

Information **Warsaw City Information & Promotion Center** (⊠ *Krakowskie Przedmieście 89, Śródmieście, Warsaw* ☏ *022/94–31* ⊕ *www.warsawtour.pl*). **Warsaw Tourist & Cultural Information Center** (⊠ *Palace of Culture & Science, Plac Defilad 1, Śródmieście, Warsaw* ☏ *022/656–68–54* ⊕ *www.e-warsaw. pl*). **Warsaw Tourist Information** (⊠ *Plac Zamkowy 1, Stare Miasto, Warsaw* ☏ *022/635–18–81*).

KRAKÓW

Many first-time visitors to Kraków are surprised at how quickly they feel at home there. Those who fall in love with the city at first sight and claim it as their own are fully justified in their sentiment: since 1978 Kraków has been on the UNESCO World Heritage list, and as such, it "belongs to all the peoples of the world."

Kraków, once the ancient capital of Poland (before finally relinquishing the honor to Warsaw in 1609), has enchanted visitors for thousands of years. It is often called a "magical city" and even the official municipal Web site is proudly called "the Magical Kraków." Krakovian air is composed of hefty doses of oxygen, nitrogen, history, and mystery. Here each stone tells a story, and—be warned!—a song or a sonnet may be lurking around the corner.

Despite Kraków's—and the region's—turbulent past, a wealth of treasures of art and architecture remain almost intact in one of the few Polish cities that escaped devastation by Hitler's armies during World War II. Some will tell you that it is due to Kraków's *chakhra,* a mystic stone that radiates energy from Wawel Hill, thus protecting the city against evil.

9

EXPLORING KRAKÓW

Starting as a market town in the 10th century, Kraków became Poland's capital in 1037. Until as recently as the 19th century walls encircled the Old Town; these were replaced by the Planty, a ring of parkland, in the 1820s. Throughout the 19th and early 20th centuries, the city expanded, and many interesting examples of architecture from that period can be found within the second ring, marked by Aleje and Dietla streets. In late 20th century another phase of the city's development began farther out, and it will most probably continue well into the 21st century.

The best way to explore Kraków is to slow down the pace of your steps in tune with this unhurried city, so reserve some time for just sitting in those wonderful cafés and watching life go by. Remember that most museums are closed on Monday; the synagogues of Kazimierz are closed on Saturday, and in high season, advanced booking is advisable for the Wawel Castle and Wieliczka Salt Mine.

Numbers in the text correspond to numbers in the margin and on the Kraków Stare Miasto and Kazimierz maps.

TIMING

With the arrival of low-cost airlines and continued expansion of the local airport, the number of visitors to Kraków is increasing. Although tourists now arrive in great numbers all year-round, the peak season to visit Kraków is between June and September. In terms of weather, May and September are probably the most pleasant months to visit the city, but Kraków has something to offer for each season.

Temperatures can get very cold in the winter, down to -20°C (-4°F), and summer days are reliably hot, with temperatures of up to 35°C (95°F). The weather is often unpredictable and can turn very rapidly; therefore, it is advisable to bring an umbrella and a jacket even when you are traveling in the summer, just in case.

STARE MIASTO

Kraków's streets are a vast and lovely living museum, and the Stare Miasto (Old Town) in particular is a historical gold mine. Its ancient houses, churches, and palaces can overwhelm visitors with only a few days to see the sights. The heart of it all is Kraków's "drawing room"— the Rynek Główny, or Main Market Square.

WHAT TO SEE

❶ Barbakan. Only one small section of Kraków's city wall still stands, centered on the 15th-century Barbakan, one of the largest strongholds of its kind in Europe. ⊠ *Basztowa, opposite Floriańska, Stare Miasto.*

⓬ Collegium Juridicum. This magnificent Gothic building, built in the early 15th century to house the Jagiellonian University's law students, lies on one of Kraków's oldest streets. ⊠ *Grodzka 53, Stare Miasto.*

★ **❽ Collegium Maius.** Jagiellonian University was another innovation of Kazimierz the Great. Established in 1364, it was the first university in Poland and one of the earliest ones in Europe. The Collegium Maius is the oldest surviving building of the university, though historians are undecided where the very first one stood. Jagiellonian's most famous student, Nicolaus Copernicus, studied here from 1491 to 1495. The first visual delight is the arcaded Gothic courtyard. On the second floor, the **museum** and rooms are a must for all visitors to Kraków. They can be visited only on a guided tour (call in advance for an English guide). On the tour you see the treasury, assembly hall, library, and common room. The museum includes the so-called Jagiellonian globe, the first globe to depict the American continents. ⊠ *ul. Jagiellońska 15, Stare Miasto* ☎ *012/422–05–49* ⊠ *Courtyard free, museum zł8* ⊙ *Museum Mon.–Thurs. 11–3, Sat. 11–1:30.*

★ **⓮ Katedra Wawelska** *(Wawel Cathedral).* Wawel Hill, a 15-acre rocky limestone outcropping on the banks of the Vistula, dominates the old part of the city. The hill was a natural point for fortification on the flat

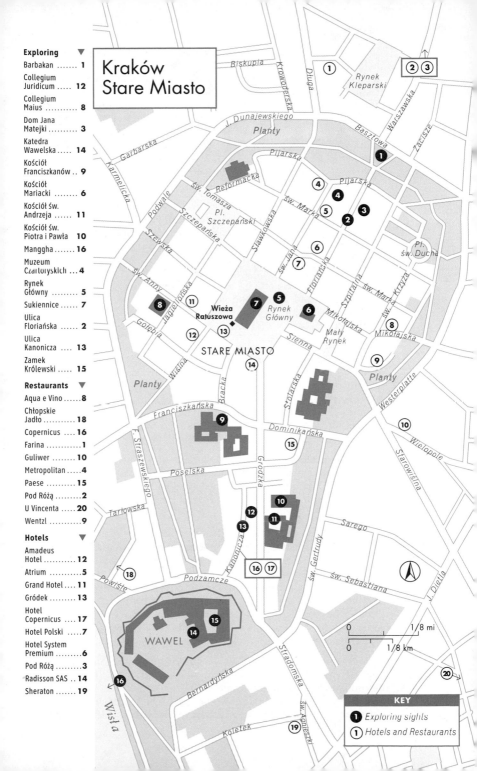

Kraków
Stare Miasto

KEY

1 *Exploring sights*

① *Hotels and Restaurants*

Vistula Plain. During the 8th century it was topped with a tribal stronghold and since the 10th century has held a royal residence and served as the seat of the bishops of Kraków. Construction on the present Wawel Cathedral—the third cathedral in this very place—was begun in 1320, and the structure was consecrated in 1364. Little room for expansion on the hill has meant the preservation of the original austere structure, although a few Renaissance and baroque chapels have been crowded around it. The most notable of these is the **Kaplica Zygmuntowska** (Sigismund Chapel), built in the 1520s by the Florentine architect Bartolomeo Berrecci and widely considered to be the finest Renaissance chapel north of the Alps.

From 1037, when Kraków became the capital of Poland, Polish kings were crowned and buried in the Wawel Cathedral. This tradition continued up to the time of the partitions, even after the capital had been moved to Warsaw. During the 19th century, only great national heroes were honored by a Wawel entombment: Tadeusz Kościuszko was buried here in 1817; Adam Mickiewicz and Juliusz Słowacki, both great romantic poets, were also brought back from exile to the Wawel after their deaths; and Marshal Józef Piłsudski, the hero of independent Poland between the two world wars, was interred in the cathedral crypt in 1935.

The cathedral also has a treasury, archives, library, and museum. Among the showpieces in the library, one of the earliest in Poland, is the 12th-century *Emmeram Gospel* from Regensburg. After touring at ground level, you can climb the wooden staircase of the **Sigismund Tower,** entering through the sacristy. The tower holds the famous Sigismund Bell, which was commissioned in 1520 by King Sigismund the Old and is still tolled on all solemn state and church occasions. ⊠ *Wawel Hill, Stare Miasto* ⊞*Museum zł5* ⊙*Tues.–Sun. 10–5:30.*

⑨ Kościół Franciszkanów *(Franciscan Church & Monastery).* The mid-13th-century church and monastery are among the earliest brick buildings in Kraków. The art nouveau stained-glass windows and wall decorations by Stanisław Wyspiański are true masterpieces. ⊠*pl. Wszystkich Świętych 1, Stare Miasto.*

OFF THE BEATEN PATH

Kopiec Kościuszki *(Kościuszko's Mound).* This mound on the outskirts of Kraków was built in tribute to the memory of Tadeusz Kościuszko in 1820, three years after his death. The earth came from battlefields on which he had fought; soil from the United States was added in 1926. The best place from which to get a panoramic view of the city, the mound presides above a 19th-century Austrian fort. Take Tram 1 or 6 from plac Dominikański to the terminus at Salwator and then walk up aleja Waszyngtona to the mound. ⊠*al. Waszyngtona, Salwator* ⊙*Daily 10–dusk.*

★⑥ Kościół Mariacki *(Church of Our Lady).* Dominating the northeast corner of Rynek Główny is the twin-towered Church of Our Lady, which is also known as St. Mary's Church. The first church was built on this site before the town plan of 1257, which is why it stands slightly askew from the main square; the present church, completed in 1397, was built on the foundations of its predecessor. You'll note that the two towers, added in the early 15th century, are of different heights. Legend has it that they were built by two brothers, one of whom grew jealous of the other's work and slew him with a sword. You can still see the supposed murder weapon, hanging in the gate of the Sukiennice. From the higher tower, a strange bugle call—known as the "Hejnał Mariacki"—rings out to mark each hour. It breaks off on an abrupt sobbing note to commemorate an unknown bugler struck in the throat by a Tartar arrow as he was playing his call to warn the city of imminent attack. The church's main showpiece is the magnificent wooden altarpiece with more than 200 carved figures, the work of the 15th-century artist Wit Stwosz (*Veit Stoss in German*). The panels depict medieval life in detail; the figure in the bottom right-hand corner of the Crucifixion panel is believed to represent Stwosz himself. ⊠*Rynek Główny, entrance from side of plac Mariacki, Stare Miasto* ⌂*Church free, altar zł3* ⊙*Altar Mon.–Sat. 11:30–6, Sun. 2–6.*

⑪ **Kościół świętego Andrzeja** *(Church of St. Andrew).* The finest surviving example of Romanesque architecture in Kraków is this 11th-century fortified church. Local residents took refuge in St. Andrew during Tartar raids. The interior, remodeled during the 18th century, includes a fanciful pulpit resembling a boat. ⊠*At midpoint of ul. Grodzka, on east side, Stare Miasto.*

⑩ **Kościół świętego Piotra i Pawła** *(Church of Saints Peter and Paul).* The first baroque church in Kraków was commissioned for the Jesuit order. It is one of the most faithful and successful examples of transplanting the model of the famous del Gesu Church (the "prototype" Jesuit church in Rome) to foreign soil. At the fence are the figures of the 12 apostles. ⊠*At midpoint of ul. Grodzka, on the east side, next to St. Andrew's Church, Stare Miasto.*

⑯ **Manggha: Centrum Sztuki i Techniki Japońskiej.** The "Manggha" Center for Japanese Art and Technology houses a magnificent collection of woodblock prints, pottery, Samurai armor, netsuke (small sculptures worn on the sash of a kimono), and more. The collection was the gift of an eccentric bohemian named Feliks Jasieński, who became caught up in the fashion of collecting Japanese artifacts in fin de siècle Paris. Jasieński's admiration and obsession with all things Japanese earned him the nickname "Manggha." *Manggha* are picture books containing famous prints of old Japan (not exactly the same as today's manga, which are popular graphic novels). Jasieński actually donated the collection to the Kraków National Museum, but there was no space to properly display it. The present museum opened in late 1994. ⊠*ul. M. Konopnickiej 26, Dębniki* ☎*012/267–27–03* ⊕*www.manggha. krakow.pl* ⌂*zł5, free Wed.* ⊙*Tues.–Sun. 10–6.*

④ **Muzeum Czartoryskich** *(Czartoryski Museum).* The surviving fragment of FodorśChoice Kraków's city wall opposite the Barbakan, where students and amateur ★ artists hang their paintings for sale in the summer, contains the Renaissance Municipal Arsenal, which now houses part of the National Museum's **Czartoryski Collection,** including such celebrated paintings

9

as Rembrandt's *Landscape with the Good Samaritan.* The prize of the collection—and to many observers the most beautiful portrait ever painted—is Leonardo da Vinci's *Cecilia Gallerani,* also known as the *Lady with an Ermine.* ⊠ *św. Jana 19, Stare Miasto* ☏ *012/422–55–66* ⌸ *zł7* ☉ *Tues. and Thurs. 9–3:30, Wed. 11–6, Sat. 10–3:30.*

⑤ **Rynek Główny** *(Main Market Square).* Europe's largest medieval mar-
FodorśChoice ketplace is on a par in size and grandeur with St. Mark's Square in
★ Venice. It even has the same plague of pigeons, although legend tells us the ones here are no ordinary birds: they are allegedly the spirits of the knights of Duke Henry IV Probus, who in the 13th century were cursed and turned into birds. This great square was not always so spacious. In an earlier period it contained—in addition to the present buildings—a Gothic town hall, a Renaissance granary, a large weighing house, a foundry, a pillory, and hundreds of traders' stalls. A few flower sellers under colorful umbrellas and some portable souvenir stalls are all that remain of this bustling commercial activity. Above all, Rynek is Kraków's largest outdoor gathering place, from spring through autumn, with more than 20 cafés scattered around the perimeter of the square.

A pageant of history has passed through this square. From 1320 on, Polish kings came here on the day after their coronation to meet the city's burghers and receive homage and tribute in the name of all the towns of Poland. Albert Hohenzollern, the grand master of the Teutonic Knights, came here in 1525 to pay homage to Sigismund the Old, king of Poland. And in 1794 Tadeusz Kościuszko took a solemn vow to overthrow czarist Russia here.

The square is surrounded by many historic buildings. The **Dom pod Jeleniami** (House at the Sign of the Stag), at No. 36, was once an inn where both Goethe and Czar Nicholas I found shelter. At No. 45 is the **Dom pod Orłem** (House at the Sign of the Eagle), where Tadeusz Kościuszko lived as a young officer in 1777; a little farther down the square, at No. 6, is the **Szara Kamienica** (Gray House), which he made his staff headquarters in 1794. In the house at No. 9, the young Polish noblewoman Maryna Mniszchówna married the False Dymitri, the pretender to the Russian throne, in 1605. (These events are portrayed in Pushkin's play *Boris Godunov* and in Mussorgsky's operatic adaptation of it.) At No. 16 is the **14th-century house** of the Wierzynek merchant family. In 1364, during a "summit" meeting attended by the Holy Roman Emperor, one of the Wierzyneks gave an elaborate feast for the visiting royal dignitaries; today the house is a restaurant.

At the southwest corner of Rynek Square, the **Wieża Ratuszowa** *(Town Hall Tower)* is all that remains of the 16th-century town hall, which was demolished in the early 19th century. The tower houses a branch of the Muzeum Historyczne Miasta Krakowa (Kraków History Museum) and affords a panoramic view of the old city. Although the museum and tower are closed during the winter, it's possible to organize a group visit. ⊠ *Rynek Główny, Stare Miasto* ☏ *012/422–15–04* ⌸ *zł4* ☉ *Apr.–Oct., daily 10–5.*

★ ❼ **Sukiennice** *(Cloth Hall).* A statue of Adam Mickiewicz sits in front of the eastern entrance to the Renaissance Cloth Hall, which stands in the middle of the Main Market Square. The Gothic arches date from the 14th century, but after a fire in 1555 the upper part was rebuilt in Renaissance style. The inner arcades on the ground floor still hold traders' booths, now mainly selling local crafts. On the first floor, in a branch of the National Museum, you can view a collection of 19th-century Polish paintings. The gallery closed in late 2006 for a major renovation and is scheduled to reopen in 2009; until then, part of the collection will be exhibited in the Castle at Niepołomice. ✉*Rynek Główny 1–3, Stare Miasto* ☎*012/422–11–66.*

NEED A BREAK?

One of the oldest cafés in town, **Kawiarnia Noworolski** (✉*Rynek Główny 1, Stare Miasto*), next to the entrance to the National Museum in the Cloth Hall, is a wonderful café where you can sit and watch the goings-on in the square while enjoying a coffee. This is also a good spot from which to observe the hourly trumpet call from the tower of the Church of Our Lady.

In the art nouveau café **Jama Michalikowa** (✉*ul. Floriańska 45, Stare Miasto* ☎*012/422–15–61*), the walls are hung with caricatures by late-19th-century customers, who sometimes paid their bills in kind.

❷ **Ulica Floriańska.** The beautiful **Brama Floriańska** (Florian Gate) was built around 1300 and leads through Kraków's old city walls to this street, which was laid out according to the town plan of 1257. The Gothic houses of the 13th-century burghers still remain, although they were rebuilt and given Renaissance or neoclassical facades. The house at No. 24, decorated with an emblem of three bells, was once the workshop of a bell founder. The chains hanging on the walls of the house at No. 17 barred the streets to invaders when the city was under siege. The **Dom pod Murzynami** (Negroes' House), standing where ulica Floriańska enters the market square, is a 16th-century tenement decorated with two rather fancifully imagined African tribesmen—testimony to the fascination with Africa entertained by Europeans in the Age of Discovery. The house was also once known as Dom pod Etiopy (House under the Ethiopians). ✉*Stare Miasto.*

★ ⓭ **Ulica Kanonicza.** This street, which leads from almost the center of town to the foot of Wawel Hill, is considered by some the most beautiful street in Europe. Most of the houses here date from the 14th and 15th centuries, although they were "modernized" in Renaissance or later styles. The street was named for the many canons of Wawel Cathedral who have lived here, including Pope John Paul II, who lived in the Chapter House at No. 19 and later in the late-16th-century Dean's House at No. 21. "<ASSIGN.SIGHTS TAG="MUSEUM–GAL-LERY"></ASSIGN.SIGHTS>The Chapter House is now the **Muzeum Archidiecezjalne** *(Archdiocesan Museum)* (✉*ul. Kanonicza 19, Stare Miasto* ☎*012/421–89–63*), displaying 13th-century paintings and other art belonging to the archdiocese, not to mention Pope John Paul II's former room. Admission is zł5 and the museum is open Tuesday–Thursday 10–4 and weekends 10–3. ✉*Stare Miasto.*

9

⑮ Zamek Królewski *(Royal Castle).* The castle that now stands here dates
Fodor'sChoice from the early 16th century, when the Romanesque residence that stood
★ on this site was destroyed by fire. King Sigismund the Old brought artists and craftsmen from Italy to create his castle, and despite baroque
reconstruction after another fire in the late 16th century, several parts
of the Renaissance castle remain, including the beautiful arcaded courtyard. After the transfer of the capital to Warsaw at the beginning of the
17th century, the castle was stripped of its fine furnishings, and later in
the century it was devastated by the Swedish wars. In 1905, a volun-
tary Polish society purchased the castle from the Austrian authorities
and began restoration. It narrowly escaped destruction in 1945, when
the Nazis almost demolished it as a parting shot. Today you can visit
the royal chambers, furnished in the style of the 16th and 17th centuries and hung with the 16th-century Arras-style tapestries from the
Low Countries. Counted among the most valuable treasures of the Polish people, the tapestries were evacuated to Canada by Jan Polkowski
(who had been appointed their guardian) during World War II in order
to protect them against the invaders, and returned to Poland in 1961.
The Royal Treasury on the ground floor contains a somewhat depleted
collection of Polish crown jewels; the most fascinating item displayed
here is the *Szczerbiec,* the jagged sword used from the early 14th century onward at the coronation of Polish kings. The Royal Armory
houses a collection of Polish and Eastern arms and armor. The west
wing holds an imposing collection of Turkish embroidered tents.

For many people, the castle's importance extends beyond its history.
Hindu esoteric thinkers claim it is one of the world's mystic energy
centers, a *chakhra.* You may see people leaning against the castle wall
in the courtyard, absorbing the vital, cosmic energy.

☾ Every Polish child knows the legend of the fire-breathing dragon that
once terrorized local residents from his **Smocza Jama** *(Dragon's Den),*
a cave at the foot of Wawel Hill. Follow the signs to the ticket office
opposite the castle, in the direction of the river. The dragon threatened
to destroy the town unless he was fed a damsel a week. The king promised half his kingdom and his daughter's hand in marriage to any man
who could slay the dragon. The usual quota of knights tried and failed.
But finally a crafty cobbler named Skuba tricked the dragon into eating a lambskin filled with salt and sulfur. The dragon went wild with
thirst, rushed into the Vistula River, and drank until it exploded. The
Dragon's Den is still there, however, and in warmer months smoke and
flame belch out of it every 15 minutes to thrill young visitors. A bronze
statue of the dragon itself stands guard at the entrance. The den is open
May–September, Monday–Thursday and weekends 10–3; admission is
zł5. To reach the castle, go to the end of Grodzka or Kanonicza streets,
and then walk up Wawel Hill.

The number of visitors to the royal chambers is limited, and entry tickets are timed; therefore, you should always try to book your tickets in
advance to avoid disappointment. Phone to make the reservation, and
then collect your tickets from the Tourist Service Office (BOT) located
opposite the Sigismund Chapel (the one with the golden dome).

⊠ *Wawel Hill, Wawel* ☎012/422–16–97 ⊠*Royal chambers zł15, royal private apartments zł15, treasury and armory zł15. Free Mon., but portions of the exhibit restricted.* ☉*Royal chambers, treasury, and armory Mon. 9:30–noon, Tues.–Sat. 9:30–3 (Fri. until 4), Sun. 10–3. Closed Mon. Oct.–Mar.*

9

KAZIMIERZ

As Rafael Sharf, founder of London's Jewish Quarterly and himself a Krakovian Jew once remarked, Kraków's Kazimierz is the only place in the world where you will find the street of Corpus Christi crossing the street named after Rabbi Meisels. Kazimierz was founded by King Kazimierz the Great as a separate city in 1335. By the end of the 15th century, it had come to house a growing Jewish district at a time when industrious and enterprising Jews escaping persecution in Western Europe were welcomed by the Polish kings. Thus, Kazimierz became one of the most important centers of the Jewish diaspora in Europe. Here they thrived until World War II.

WHAT TO SEE

㉑ **Kościół Bożego Ciała** *(Corpus Christi Church).* This 15th-century church was used by King Charles Gustavus of Sweden as his headquarters during the Siege of Kraków in 1655. ⊠*Northeast corner of pl. Wolnica, Kazimierz.*

㉓ Kościół na Skałce *(Church on the Rock).* Standing on the Vistula embankment to the south of Wawel Hill, this church is the center of the cult of St. Stanisław. The bishop and martyr was beheaded and dismembered by order of the king in the church that stood on this spot in 1079—a tale of rivalry similar to that of Henry II and Thomas à Becket. The story goes that the saint's body was miraculously reassembled, as a symbol of the restoration of Poland's unity after its years of fragmentation. Beginning in the 19th century, the church also became the last resting place for well-known Polish writers and artists; among those buried here are the composer Karol Szymanowski and the painter and playwright Stanisław Wyspiański. The most recent tomb is that of Nobel Prize–winning poet, Czesław Miłosz. ⊠*Between Paulińska and Skałeczna on the Vistula embankment, Stare Miasto.*

㉒ Muzeum Etnograficzne im. Seweryna Udzieli w Krakowie *(Ethnographic Museum).* Kazimierz's 15th-century Ratusz (Town Hall) stands in the middle of plac Wolnica. It is now the Ethnographic Museum, displaying a well-mounted collection of regional folk art. ⊠*pl. Wolnica 1, Kazimierz* ☎*012/656–28–63* ⊠*zł5* ☉*Mon. 10–6, Wed.–Fri. 10–3, weekends 10–2.*

⑱ Stara Synagoga *(Old Synagogue).* The oldest surviving example of Jewish religious architecture in Poland, this synagogue was built in the 15th century and reconstructed in Renaissance style following a fire in 1557. It was here in 1775 that Tadeusz Kościuszko successfully appealed to the Jewish community to join the national insurrection. Looted and partly destroyed during the Nazi occupation, it has been rebuilt and now houses the **Museum of the History and Culture of Kraków Jews.** It's always closed on the first weekend of the month. ⊠*ul. Szeroka 24, Kazimierz* ☎*012/422–09–62* ⊠*zł5* ☉*Wed., Thurs., and weekends 9–3, Fri. 11–6.*

NEED A BREAK?

Alef Café (⊠*ul. Szeroka 17, Kazimierz* ☎*012/421-38-70*) is as close as you can get to a glimpse of the lost world of Kazimierz. Traditional Eastern European Jewish (but not kosher) dishes are served daily, and musical performances are often given here.

⑲ Synagoga Izaaka. Isaac's Synagogue was named after its founder, Izaak Jakubowicz (reb Ajzyk reb Jekeles). Today the early baroque building with a beautiful, stucco-decorated vault and marvelous arcades in the women's gallery houses an exhibition on the history of Polish Jews. Don't miss the short documentaries (which date between 1936 and 1941) that were created by a German cameraman showing prewar Kazimierz and the deportation to the ghetto. ⊠*ul. Kupa 18, Kazimierz* ☎*12/430–55–77* ⊠*zł7* ☉*Sun.–Fri. 9–7.*

⑰ Synagoga Remuh. This 16th-century synagogue is still used for worship and is named after the son of its founder, Rabbi Moses Isserles, who is buried in the **cemetery** attached to the synagogue. Used by the Jewish community from 1533 to 1799, this is the only well-preserved Renaissance Jewish cemetery in Europe. (The so-called new cemetery on ulica

CLOSE UP

The Bagel Returns Home

In an interesting caprice of culinary history, Bagelmama in Kraków's Kazimierz District is the only bagel shop in Poland. And to think that bagels were probably invented here! The 1610 community regulations of Kraków report that bagels were presented to women in childbirth. Legend has it that the bagel was popularized in Vienna, where it was baked to commemorate the Polish King Sobieski's 1683 triumph over the Turks. It was then named after *beugel* (German for "stirrup"). Around 1900, Polish-Jewish immigrants brought this great bread to New York City, where it continues to thrive. Yet the bakery Pan Beigel ("Mr. Bagel" in English), the original bagel bakery in Kraków's Kazimierz District, which opened in 1915, has long since closed and disappeared. What a coincidence to find that its newly minted successor, Bagelmama—which is owned by Nava, an American expat, musician, and caterer—has opened up in exactly the same location. And so the history of the bagel has come full circle (with a hole in the middle).

Miodowa, which contains many old headstones, was established in 1800.) ⊠ *ul. Szeroka 40, Kazimierz* ⊟ *zł2* ⊙ *Weekdays 9–6.*

㉟ Synagoga Tempel. The 19th-century Reformed Tempel Synagogue has a striking decor complete with stained-glass windows. Today under the care of the local Jewish community, it is the main venue of the famous Jewish Culture Festival. ⊠ *Corner of Miodowa and Podbrzezie, Kazimierz.*

NEED A BREAK?

Bagelmama (⊠ *ul. Podbrzezie 17, Kazimierz* ⊟ *012/431-19-42*) is a cozy little bagel shop.

NOWA HUTA

Fodor'sChoice ★

A story goes that when Fidel Castro visited Kraków, he refused to see the famous royal castle and the largest medieval square in Europe: "Take me to the steelworks," he commanded instead. Although we don't propose to follow the Comandante's example to the letter, a visit to Nowa Huta is definitely worth your while.

Only a 20- to 30-minute tram ride from the city center—take Tram 4 or 15 from Kraków Główny, the city's main railway station—it is quite a different world from the rest of Kraków. You'll feel the change not just in the sweeping scale of urban planning but also in the spirit of the place. A "model socialist town," it was created in the 1950s to house workers at a giant steel factory. Its ideological heritage notwithstanding, Nowa Huta is an interesting example of urban planning and architecture. The Central Square was modeled on that of Versailles, and the buildings that surround it are replete with echoes of the Renaissance and classicism. The street plan of the original residential areas of Nowa Huta is based on an American concept of "neighborhood units" first developed for New York City in the 1920s. Each block of Nowa Huta was equipped with all the necessary facilities to help the neighborhood function—shops, a school, a kindergarten, and so forth.

9

Paradoxically, the "model workers' town" played a key role in the downfall of Communism, and became a stronghold of the Solidarity movement. Wide alleys of Nowa Huta were perfect for more than just May Day parades: in the 1980s, local residents people marched through them in antigovernment demonstrations. It is not easy to cover Nowa Huta sights by walking—it is better to use a bike, tram, or car.

The **Plac Centralny** *(Central Square)* is a good place to start. Take a walk around the square, and check out the showcase Cepelia shop along the way. Then take a stroll through the residential neighborhoods on either side of the wide alleys leading from the square.

Although you won't find the famous statue of Lenin that used to stand on **Aleja Róż** (Boulevard of Roses), some original establishments remain, including Stylowa restaurant and the most authentic milk bar in town.

From plac Centralny, any tram going up aleja Solidarności will take you to **Centrum Administracyjne** *(Central Administration Building)*, the impressive castlelike entrance and offices of the former Lenin Steelworks. Unfortunately, these days it is next to impossible to enter the steelworks as a visitor, but even a peek from outside can give you some idea of the scale of this operation.

A 10-minute drive or ride west of the steelworks is the **Arka Pana** (meaning "The Lord's Ark"), an amazing modern church with facade made of round river stones. These were brought by the people of Nowa Huta to the building site when authorities cut the supplies in yet another effort to stop the church's construction.

Tours by **Crazy Guides** (✉ *Lublańska 22/9* ☎ *048/5000–91–200* ⊕ *www. crazyguides.com*)are great fun, always informal, and private. The highlight has to be the tour of Nowa Huta in a Trabant (the classic Communist-era car), though the company offers many other Kraków tours.

WHERE TO EAT

Kraków's best restaurants can primarily be found in the Old Town, within walking distance of the main tourist sights. Most restaurants are located in the Market Square and the streets around it; some are also in the Kazimierz Quarter. Cheap fast-food joints may be found next door to upmarket establishments. At all but the most touristed restaurants, the custom in Kraków is to make a reservation, even if you do it just a few hours in advance.

$$–$$$$ ✗ **Wentzl.** The owners of this elegant and posh establishment have reincarnated Jan Wentzl's restaurant, which opened in the same building in 1792. On the menu, Old Polish cuisine meets the whole world in the wine list. You'll see saddle of deer marinated in lemongrass with aromatic cinnamon bark and red currant sauce, which you may wish to pair with a Rioja Muga Reserva or a Chianti classico. Not only your taste buds will enjoy this experience, as Wentzl also offers a feast for the eyes: the restaurant is like a small gallery of Ècole de Paris paint-

ings, and there is a great view down to the Market Square. ⊠*Rynek Główny 19, Stare Miasto* ☏*012/429–57–12* ⌕*Reservations essential* ☐*AE, DC, MC, V.*

$–$$$ ✗**Metropolitan.** The smooth and sleek Metropolitan could be mistaken for something straight out of Manhattan. The atmosphere is elegant yet relaxed, and the food would be best summarized as "fusion," from tuna carpaccio served with green apple slices and lime olive oil dressing, to pork tenderloin in plum alcohol. All the dishes are both full of flavor and beautifully presented. ⊠*ul. Sławkowska 3, Stare Miasto* ☏*012/421–98–03* ☐*AE, DC, MC, V.*

$$$ ✗**Copernicus.** This top-class restaurant in one of the city's top hotels is on one of Kraków's loveliest corners, at the foot of Wawel Hill. The imaginative menu is made up of classic Polish dishes—albeit the dishes you might find on the table of a typically aristocratic table—enriched with a cosmopolitan twist. Try the venison pâté with marinated forest mushrooms or sea bass with couscous. In the summer you can dine on the rooftop terrace, with some of the best views in the city. ⊠*Hotel Copernicus, ul. Kanonicza 16, Stare Miasto* ☏*012/431–10–44* ⌕*Reservations essential* ☐*AE, DC, MC, V.*

★ $$–$$$ ✗**Farina.** True to its logo (a sack of flour and a fish), this relatively young restaurant offers consistently good fish, seafood, and homemade pasta. A special selection of seafood is offered Thursday through Sunday. Whatever you order, first you will get Farina's trademark appetizer of an excellent truffle-and-mushroom pâté to spread on scrumptious little rolls. There is a good selection of wines, including a great dry Prosecco that would stand up to any Champagne. ⊠*św. Marka 16, Stare Miasto* ☏*012/422–16–80* ⌕*Reservations essential* ☐*AE, DC, MC, V.*

★ $$–$$$ ✗**Guliwer.** When you step into Guliwer, you may think you've stepped into a French country inn. You're still firmly planted on Polish soil, but the cuisine here is definitively Gallic. The food is simple yet tasty, in tune with the decor. The menu features excellent fish soup, liver Provençale, and crème brûlée. Guliwer has many faithful followers, including poet Wisława Szymborska and film director Andrzej Wajda. ⊠*ul. Bracka 6, Stare Miasto* ☏*012/430–24–66* ☐*AE, DC, MC, V.*

★ $$–$$$ ✗**Pod Różą.** Built in the converted courtyard of a tenement house, "Under the Rose" is airy, spacious, elegant, and contained under a glass roof. A seasonally changing, contemporary menu is matched by impeccable service; there is nightly live piano music. Pheasant with foie gras in a French pastry crust is just one of many mouthwatering options. The chefs make their own pastas, ice cream, and bread. Adjoining sister restaurant Amarone serves slightly cheaper, but no less delicious, Italian cuisine. ⊠*ul. Floriańska 14, Stare Miasto* ☏*012/424–33–81* ⌕*Reservations essential* ☐*AE, DC, MC, V.*

★ $–$$$ ✗**Aqua e Vino.** Venetian owners Roberto and Francesco believe in a hands-on approach to running their restaurant, so they are nearly always present: taking orders, chatting with customers, and checking to make sure that everything is okay. In fact, the homemade pastas, tiramisu, and sgroppino cocktails (made with Prosecco and lemon sorbet) are more than okay—they are excellent. Frequent visitors include

9

Cardinal Dziwisz and conductor John Axelrod, and the Italian community in Kraków call it their second home. ✉*ul. Wiślna 5/10, Stare Miasto* ☎*012/421–25–67* ▭*AE, DC, MC, V.*

$–$$$ ✗**Paese.** The only Corsican restaurant in Poland—and one of the first memorable restaurants of the new post-Communist era—Paese was an immediate success, and it remains just as popular nearly 20 years later. The restaurant consists of a series of pleasant, simple, tavern-like rooms. The menu is extensive enough that you're bound to find something appetizing—perhaps Calvi tenderloin, served in blue-cheese sauce and best accompanied by dumplings. Should you decide to sample the excellent tarte tatin, order it at the beginning of your meal, as it is always freshly prepared from scratch. Despite their essential constancy, both the interior and the menu get subtle face-lifts every now and again. ✉*ul. Poselska 24, Stare Miasto* ☎*012/421–62–73* ⚜*Reservations essential* ▭*AE, DC, MC, V.*

★ **$–$$** ✗**Chłopskie Jadło.** This restaurant's name means "Peasant Kitchen," but this is the most upscale interpretation of that theme imaginable. For a starter try the *żurek* (soured barley soup); then indulge in the very traditional main course of cabbage rolls stuffed with sauerkraut and grits in a mushroom sauce. All meals come with complimentary bread and lard, and the menu is an artery-clogging cross section of traditional Polish peasant cuisine. ✉*św. Agnieszki 1, Stare Miasto* ☎*012/421–85–20* ⚜*Reservations essential* ▭*AE, DC, MC, V.*

$ ✗**U Vincenta.** This is paradise for the connoisseurs of pierogi, the Polish cousins of Italian ravioli and Japanese gyoza. In a tiny interior with no room to twist a cat, young and friendly staff serve your pierogi in some two dozen variations, traditional and novel, savory and sweet. ✉*ul. Józefa 11, Kazimierz* ☎*012/430–68–34* ▭*AE, DC, MC, V.*

WHERE TO STAY

To experience and enjoy Kraków to the fullest, you should try to stay in the Old Town, which will put you within walking distance of most major attractions, cafés, and restaurants. The downside, of course, is that the best places to stay are rather expensive, and the streets surrounding the Market Square can be noisy at night. Cheaper options tend to have a little less character and are farther away from the center.

A viable alternative to a higher-price hotel in Kraków is a short-term apartment rental. Many of these apartment rentals can be made for just a few days' time and are usually considerably cheaper than a hotel room. **P&J Apartments** (✉*ul. Floriańska 39* ☎*48/607–237–647* ⊕*www. apartmentkrakow.pl*) offers 10 simple, no-frills standard, neat apartments in the heart of Kraków's Old Town. Prices range from zł160 to zł220 double. **Orient Express** (✉*ul. Stolarska 13* ☎*12/422–66–72* ⊕*www.pokoje.krakow.pl*) has four types of accommodations: a single for zł150 per night, a double for zł165, and two larger apartments for zł195–zł340 per night. Simple and bright, they are in an excellent location in the Old Town, opposite the Dominican church. All apartments are equipped with satellite TV and a refrigerator (the larger apartments have kitchenettes). The flats are located over a French restaurant; it is possible to get breakfast or dinner for a good price in a package. Prices are negotiable for stays longer than one week.

$$$$ ▦**Radisson SAS.** Across the street from the Kraków's Philharmonic Hall, the Radisson hotel facade mirrors the pattern on the concert hall—although the lines of the former are decidedly more contemporary and sober than those of the latter. The location—at the edge of the leafy Planty, a mere two minutes' walk from the Market Square—is superb. A musical theme continues in the restaurant, which was named Solfeż (as in solfeggio vocal exercises). ✉*ul. Straszewskiego 17, Stare Miasto, 31–101* ☎*012/618–88–88* 🖷*012/618–88–89* ⊕*www.krakow.radissonsas.com* ⤳*196 rooms, 10 suites* ♿*Restaurant, café, room service, minibars, gym, sauna, laundry service, Internet, meeting rooms, business center* ▭*AE, DC, MC, V* ⦿❙*BP.*

$$$$ ▦**Sheraton.** This luxury business hotel is located at the bank of the Wisła River, in the immediate vicinity of the Royal Castle. It seems a popular choice for royals—this is where Earl and Countess of Wessex stayed during their journey to the region (they aptly chose the Wawel Suite). Although Krakovians frown upon the building's not-too-handsome facade, inside the Sheraton offers all the comforts and the quality of service that can be expected of a five-star establishment. ✉*ul. Powiśle 7, Stare Miasto, 31–101* ☎*012/662–10–00* 🖷*012/662–11–00* ⊕*www.starwoodhotels.com* ⤳*224 rooms, 8 suites* ♿*Restaurant, 2 bars, room service, minibars, in-room broadband, Wi-Fi, fitness center, pool, dry cleaning, meeting rooms, business services, babysitting, some pets allowed* ▭*AE, DC, MC, V* ⦿❙*BP.*

★ **$$$–$$$$** ▦**Hotel Copernicus.** Hotel Copernicus is a tastefully adapted medieval tenement house on the oldest and, arguably, the most charming street in Kraków. A story goes that Copernicus himself (a graduate of the Kraków University) stayed here once. Whether that's true or not, traces of history can still be seen throughout the hotel in the Renaissance portals, wall paintings, and floor mosaics. The rooms are happily modern: air-conditioned and equipped with minibars, TVs, and jetted bathtubs. ✉*ul. Kanonicza 16, Stare Miasto, 31–002* ☎*012/424–34–00* 🖷*012/424–34–05* ⊕*www.hotel.com.pl* ⤳*29 rooms, 8 suites* ♿*Restaurant, café, room service, in-room hot tubs, minibars, cable TV, indoor pool, gym, sauna, laundry service, Internet room, meeting room* ▭*AE, DC, MC, V* ⦿❙*BP.*

★ **$$$** ▦**Amadeus Hotel.** A stone's throw from the Rynek, this small hotel is among Kraków's newest. In style and ambience, it claims inspiration from Wolfgang Amadeus Mozart. This cozy and elegant establishment has hosted such celebrities as Mikhail Baryshnikov and Vladimir Putin's wife, Lyudmila. Its international restaurant, in addition to the standard menu, features a selection of dishes from a different country each month. ✉*ul. Mikołajska 20, Stare Miasto, 30-027* ☎*012/429–60–70* 🖷*012/429–60–62* ⊕*www.hotel-amadeus.pl* ⤳*20 rooms, 2 suites* ♿*Restaurant, café, room service, minibars, cable TV, in-room broadband, gym, sauna, bar, laundry service, meeting rooms* ▭*AE, DC, MC, V* ⦿❙*BP.*

★ **$$$** ▦**Grand Hotel.** Without question this hotel around the corner from Kraków's main square is the most elegant address for visitors to the city

9

and the one most accessible to the major sights. The decor is Regency inspired, though most of the furnishings are reproductions. Suite 11 has two large bathrooms, a gilded ceiling, and a bedroom fit for a potentate. The banquet room has its own miniature hall of mirrors. ✉*ul. Sławkowska 5–7, 31–016* ☎*012/421–72–55* 🖷*012/421–83–60* ⊕*www.grand.pl* ⇨*50 rooms, 6 suites* ♿*Restaurant, café, minibars, cable TV, bar* ⊟*AE, DC, MC, V* ¶⊚*BP.*

$$$
Fodor's Choice
★

🖵 **Gródek.**Hidden away from the noise in a cozy cul-de-sac next to the Planty Park and the Dominican convent, this boutique hotel is certainly one of Kraków's finest. Each of the plush and tasteful rooms is furnished in a different style (you can check them out on the Web site), such as the Chinese room (No. 309). Hotel facilities include a library-cum-bar, a winter garden with a gourmet restaurant, and a small but exciting archaeological display. It is a noble and comfortable place with a lot of personality. ✉*ul. Na Gródku 4, Stare Miasto, 31–028* ☎*012/431–90–30* 🖷*012/431–90–40* ⊕*www.donimirski.com* ⇨*21 rooms, 2 suites* ♿*Restaurant, café, room service, minibars, sauna, laundry service, Internet room, meeting rooms* ⊟*AE, DC, MC, V* ¶⊚*BP.*

★ **$$$**
🖵 **Pod Różą.** The management is still proud that both Chopin and Czar Alexander I have slept here. More recently, the hotel has welcomed presidents and royals. Housed in a 14th-century building, the hotel offers guests spacious, high-ceilinged rooms on the fashionable shopping street Floriańska. The first-class Italian restaurant and 15th-century wine cellar add to the hotel's attractions. ✉*ul. Floriańska 14, Stare Miasto, 31–021* ☎*012/424–33–00* 🖷*012/424–33–51* ⊕*www.hotel.com.pl* ⇨*51 rooms, 3 suites* ♿*2 restaurants, café, minibars, cable TV, wine bar, meeting rooms* ⊟*AE, DC, MC, V* ¶⊚*BP.*

$$
🖵 **Hotel Polski Pod Białym Orłem).** Located within the medieval city walls, opposite the open-air art gallery by the Floriańska gate, "Under the White Eagle" is simple and unpretentious. An inn of the same name existed here in the 18th century; today the hotel is again the property of the Czartoryskis, the same family who founded the famous museum next door. Compared with the plush suites pictured on the Web site, the standard rooms are pretty basic, but they remain among the more affordable accommodation options within the Old Town. ✉*ul. Pijarska 17, 31–015* ☎*012/422–11–44* 🖷*012/422–15–29* ⊕*www.podorlem.com.pl* ⇨*50 rooms, 3 suites* ♿*Café, cable TV, some in-room broadband* ⊟*AE, DC, MC, V* ¶⊚*BP.*

$
🖵 **Hotel System Premium.** This solid business hotel is located outside the center, but not too far out, so it's a perfect choice if you are traveling to Kraków by car. The location is also very handy for both the airport and the railway station. A swimming pool, fitness center, and free Internet are thrown into the bargain, making it one of Kraków's best values. ✉*29 Listopada 189, Czerwony Prądnik31–241* ☎*012/614–48–00* 🖷*012/634–05–08* ⊕*www.krakow.hotelsystem.pl* ⇨*159 rooms, 2 suites* ♿*Restaurant, café, room service, cable TV, minibars, in-room broadband, gym, sauna, swimming pool, laundry service, meeting rooms; no a/c* ⊟*AE, DC, MC, V* ¶⊚*EP.*

NIGHTLIFE & THE ARTS

Kraków has a lively tradition in theater and music. You can buy a copy of *Karnet*, which gives detailed cultural information in Polish and English, at most newsstands and most local bookstores. A similar publication called *Miesiąc w Krakowie* (*This Month in Kraków*) is also available on newsstands and in bookstores. Also be on the lookout for a handy, free miniguide with map called *Cracow-life.com* (the publishers run a Web site as well).

NIGHTLIFE

BARS
Many of Kraków's pubs are located in medieval cellars, which make perfect wintertime hangouts. In the summer season, terrace cafés are the best place to sip a cold beer. The highest concentration of drinking establishments will be found in and around the Market Square, in Kazimierz, and in and around plac Nowy. Opening hours are very flexible. Few bars close at midnight, and most stay open while there are customers around, often until 3 or 4 AM.

The mysterious **Alchemia** (⊠*ul. Estery 5, Kazimierz*) is a great bar in the plac Nowy area. Coffee and beer rule the drinks menu, but you can sometimes get decent wines by the glass. **Les Couleurs** (⊠*ul. Estery 10, Kazimierz*) is the address to seek out if you want a Parisian atmosphere along with your drinks. A lazy café during the day, it becomes a frantic bar at night. **O'Morgan's Irish Pub** (⊠*ul. Garncarska 5, Stare Miasto*) is headquarters for Kraków's English-speaking community. There is a good selection of beers—you will find stout and bitter in addition to omnipresent lager. At trendy **Paparazzi** (⊠*ul. Mikołajska 9, Stare Miasto*) you can observe Kraków's beautiful people in action and sip the best cocktails in town: mojitos in the summer, and bloody Marys in the winter. **Singer** (⊠*ul. Estery 20, Kazimierz*) is a good, though smoky, bar in Kazimierz; the first one to open here in the early 1990s. It was named after the famous brand of sewing machines, which are recycled here into coffee tables and candleholders. **Stalowe Magnolie** (*Steel Magnolias* ⊠*ul. św. Jana 15, Stare Miasto*) is an elegant faux fin-de-siècle music club (smart attire required). The selection of cocktails is impressive, but the prices are steep.

CABARET & LIVE MUSIC
Like many restaurants in Kazimierz, **Alef** (⊠*ul. Szeroka 17, Kazimierz*) is a place where klezmer music is on hand every night. **Harris Piano Jazz Bar** (⊠*Rynek Główny 28, Stare Miasto*), in Old Town, is a good spot for jazz.

THE ARTS

CLASSICAL MUSIC
If you're a fan of chamber music, there are occasional performances in the great hall of the Zamek Królewski (Royal Castle) on Wawel Hill, at the Municipal Arsenal, or at the Sukiennice Art Gallery. You can check the schedule in *Karnet* monthly or ask at the Cultural Information Office on św. Jana Street. Smart attire is preferable but not mandatory for classical music concerts.

Kraków's symphony, **Filharmonia im. Karola Szymanowskiego** (⊠*Philharmonic Hall, ul. Zwierzyniecka 1, Stare Miasto* ☎*012/422–94–77 tickets*), gives frequent concerts. Look out for the performances of **Sinfonietta Cracovia** (☎*012/416–70–75 schedule and tickets*); Kraków's young and brilliant city orchestra performs in different venues all over town. Organ recitals can be found in many of Kraków's churches throughout the summer season. The **Summer Organ Concerts** (☎*012/420–49–50*) rate among the best.

OPERA & DANCE

At this writing, Kraków is awaiting the completion of a brand-new opera house in Rondo Mogilskie, though this venue is not expected to be open until at least 2008 or even 2009. For the time being, performances are still held at the Słowacki Theater. Although casual dress will not be frowned upon, this elegant old-timer theater is a perfect excuse to put on your Sunday best, as many Krakovians would, when going to the opera.

The stunning **Teatr im. Juliusza Słowackiego** (*Słowacki Theater* ⊠*pl. św. Ducha 1, Stare Miasto* ☎*012/422–43–22*) hosts traditional opera and ballet favorites as well as dramatic performances. Dance performances are often held at the **Nowohuckie Centrum Kultury** (*Nowa Huta Cultural Center* ⊠*al. Jana Pawła II 232, Nowa Huta* ☎*012/644–02–66*), which is also home to the Kraków Ballet. Near Nowa Huta's Central Square, the Center is a 20- to 30-minute tram ride or a 10-minute taxi ride from Kraków's Old Town.

THEATER

Kraków has a long-standing tradition of classical drama, but most performances are in Polish. English-language performances are advertised in the *Karnet* or at the Cultural Information Office. Every summer in July, Kraków hosts the **Street Theatre Festival** (☎*012/633–89–47*) with performances all around town, but mostly at Kraków's biggest outdoor stage, Rynek Główny.

SHOPPING

Kraków's Old Town is a friendly ground for shoppers—and any time you need to take a break from retail therapy, you can easily find a place to refuel with a cup of coffee, a snack, or a beer. Popular souvenirs to take home include folk crafts such as wooden toys or chess boxes, pottery, and glass, Easter eggs and Christmas ornaments, designer amber jewelry, and Polish-made vodkas and liqueurs. Most shops are open weekdays from 10 to 6, Saturday from 9 to 2.

SHOPPING NEIGHBORHOODS & MALLS

In Kraków's Old Town, you will find a mix of crafts and specialty shops next to department stores and brand-name fashion and leisure-wear stores.

For regionally produced goods, head to the middle of the Rynek Główny, the main Market Square. At the booths in the Sukiennice

(Cloth Hall), you'll find tooled leather goods, wood carvings, regional costumes, amber jewelry, and the embroidered felt slippers made in the Podhale region. Unexpectedly for such a central location, the prices at Cloth Hall are good. Local brands are often disguised behind an English-sounding names, such as a popular fashion chain called **Reserved** (both women's and men's clothing), the more upmarket **Simple** and **Solar** (ladies' attire only), and **5-10-15** for kids.

For a more concentrated shopping experience, head for one of Kraków's shopping malls. **Galeria Kazimierz** (⌧*ul. Podgórska 34, Kazimierz* ☎*012/433–01–01* ⊕*www.galeriakazimierz.pl*) is perhaps the most pleasant shopping mall in the city. It's within walking distance of the heart of Kazimierz and the river and is open seven days a week. Even more centrally located is **Galeria Krakowska** (⌧*Pawia 5* ⊕*www.galeria-krakowska.pl*), right next to Kraków's main railway station and open every day from 9 AM to 10 PM (10 AM to 9 PM on Sundays).

SPECIALTY STORES

ACCESSORIES
Gorseletka (⌧*ul. Szpitalna, Stare Miasto* ☎*012/423–04–37*) specializes in handmade corsets. Old-fashioned and fancy as they are, these tailor-made undergarments can prove surprisingly comfortable. **Pracownia Kapeluszy** (⌧*ul. św. Tomasza, Stare Miasto* ☎*No phone*) is a hatmaker that will take you for a journey back in time to the days when it was unthinkable for a lady not to own a hat—or several hats, for that matter.

ARTS & CRAFTS
The **Galeria Przedmiotu AB** (⌧*Rynek Główny 1/3* ☎*012/429–23–40*), on the northern side of the Cloth Hall, sells beautiful everyday objects and affordable artworks. The **Sukiennice** (⌧*Rynek Główny 1/3, Stare Miasto* ☎*No phone*) is the best place to buy your souvenirs—anything from amber jewelry to leather slippers, Kraków-theme T-shirts to toy dragons, embroidered tablecloths to handcrafted wooden chess sets.

JEWELRY
Mikołajczyni Amber (⌧*Rynek Główny 1/3, Stare Miasto* ☎*012/423–10–81*) is one of the best shops in Kraków for amber jewelry in luxurious settings.

KRAKÓW ESSENTIALS

AIR TRAVEL
Although many people fly into Warsaw from the United States, there are direct air connections on LOT, the Polish airline, between Kraków and Chicago, Newark, and New York (JFK) several times weekly, and the city can be reached by direct flight from most major (and some minor) European cities. With the arrival of low-cost airlines to Kraków, the number of flights is on the increase. *Contact information for all airlines flying into Poland in* ⇨ *Poland Essentials, at the end of this chapter.*

AIRPORTS & TRANSFERS

The Pope John Paul II Kraków–Balice Airport, 11 km (7 mi) west of the city, is the region's only airport. In spring and fall fog can cause frustrating delays.

In summer 2006, a fast train connection finally opened between Balice Airport and Kraków's main railway station. The train stops some 660 feet from the airline terminal; from there you can walk or use the airport shuttle bus, free of charge. The train runs approximately every 40 minutes, the journey takes about 15 minutes, and the tickets (zł3.80) can be bought on board.

Bus 208 runs between the airport and Nowy Kleparz (north from the city center), and Bus 192 between Rondo Mogilskie, the main station, and the airport. The basic fare is zł2.50 with an extra charge for luggage. Tickets can be bought from newspaper kiosks at the terminal, or from the driver (when buying from the driver, there is a surcharge). Taxis are available from outside the terminal, and the fare into the city center is approximately zł60.

Information Pope John Paul II Kraków–Balice Airport (☎ *012/411–19–55* ⊕ *www.lotnisko-balice.pl*).

BUS TRAVEL

Express bus service to Kraków runs regularly to and from most Polish cities. Most buses arrive at the main PKS station, located just to the east of the railway station. From here you can transfer to buses headed for other destinations in the region.

Contacts Kraków Main PKS Station (✉ *pl. Wita Stwosza* ☎ *0300–300–120* ⊕ *www.pks.krakow.pl*).

CAR TRAVEL

A car will not be of much use to you in Kraków, since most of the Old Town is closed to traffic and distances between major sights are short. Elsewhere in the city, traffic jams are frequent and parking space is insufficient; therefore, an automobile may be a bit of a liability. A car will be useful if you set out to explore the region, but even then it is a good idea to consider a train or a bus first. You can approach Kraków either on the E77 highway (from Warsaw and north) or via the E40 (from the area around Katowice). Use the parking facilities at your hotel or one of the attended municipal parking garages (try plac Szczepański or plac świętego Ducha). On the whole, parking space in Kraków is rather scarce and expensive—between zł5 and zł10 per hour.

Car Rentals Avis (✉ *ul. Lubicz 23* ☎ *012/629–61–08* ✉ *Balice Airport* ☎ *012/639–32–89*). **Europcar** (✉ *ul. Szlak 2* ☎ *012/633–21–00* ✉ *Balice Airport* ☎ *012/285–50–45*). **Hertz** (✉ *Balice Airport* ☎ *012/633–21–00*).

EMERGENCIES

Late-night Pharmacies Apteka 24 (✉ *ul. Mogilska 21* ☎ *012/411–01–26*) is open until 10 PM nightly. **Nonstop** (✉ *Dunajewskiego 2* ☎ *012/422–65–04*) is open until 9 PM nightly.

INTERNET

There are a number of Internet hot spots around the Old Town, including in the Market Square and on Szeroka in Kazimierz. Most four- and five-star hotels offer Internet access to their guests free of charge. Internet cafés are in abundance.

TAXIS

There is no shortage of taxis in Kraków, and there are several taxi ranks just outside the Platy Ring—for instance, on plac Szczepański, plac Wszystkich Świętych, or on Sławkowska Street. It is okay to hail a taxi in the street, and it will stop if it is free, but that would be unusual—most people either dial a cab or walk to the taxi rank. Phone rates are slightly cheaper than street rates, and it is definitely cheaper to take a taxi belonging to a reputable radio taxi company than a private taxi. Radio taxi companies are listed below.

Information Mega Taxi (☎ *012/9625*). **Taxi Partner** (☎ *012/9633*). **Taxi Dwójki** (☎ *012/9622*).

TOUR OPTIONS

Orbis, through its subsidiary Cracow Tours, organizes tours by bus, minibus, or limousine—both within Kraków and to neighboring attractions. There are also plenty of smaller operators who provide well-informed, friendly guide services for both individuals and groups.

Emerson Lumico is a friendly and competent travel agency, catering to both groups and individual customers. Clients come from all over the world. The agency's English-speaking staff will help you book a hotel or a vacation apartment; they can also organize a tailor-made tour in Kraków or farther afield.

Jarden Tours specializes in tours of Jewish Kraków. Guides take you around the Kazimierz District, to the former Jewish ghetto in Podgórze, and on a *Schindler's List* tour. There is a specialty bookshop in the Jarden Tours headquarters.

Kraków Bike Tours offers daytime bike tours of Kraków from March through mid-December, as well as nighttime tours from May through October.

From May through September, Żegluga krakowska operates short, one-hour cruises Monday through Saturday on the Wisła River aboard the boat *Nimfa* from the wharf below the Wawel Castle near the Grunwaldzki Bridge; these cruises cost zł10. On Sunday, three-hour round-trip cruises go to Tyniec Abbey at 10, 1, and 4 for zł20.

Information Emmerson Lumico (✉ *ul. Karmelicka 29* ☎ *012/623–40–90 or 048/602–299–800* ⊕ *www.lumico.pl*). **Jarden Tours** (✉ *ul. Szeroka 2* ☎ *012/421–13–74* ⊕ *www.jarden.pl*). **Kraków Bike Tours** (☎ *012/663–731–515* ⊕ *www.krakowbiketour.com*). **Orbis/Cracow Tours** (✉ *Rynek Główny 41* ☎ *012/422–11–57* ⊕ *orbis.krakow.pl*). **Żegluga krakowska** (✉ *Wawel Wharf* ☎ *012/422–08–55*).

9

TRAIN TRAVEL

Nonstop express trains from Warsaw take just under three hours and run throughout the day. All trains arrive at Kraków Główny Station, the city's main railway station, on the edge of the Old Town.

Contacts Kraków Główny Station (✉ *pl. Dworcowy 1* ☎ *012/9436*).

VISITOR INFORMATION

The Cultural Information Center is open weekdays 10–6, Saturday until 4. To check the transportation schedules and purchase air, train, and bus tickets, head to Orbis, which is open weekdays 9–5 and Saturday 9–2. The Tourist Information Point, in the Planty, between the main railway station and Słowacki Theater, is open weekdays 8–8, weekends 9–5.

Information Cultural Information Center (✉ *ul. św. Jana 2* ☎ *012/421–77–87* ⊕ *www.karnet.krakow2000.pl*). **Orbis** (✉ *Rynek Główny 41* ☎ *012/422–11–57*). **Tourist Information Point** (✉ *ul. Szpitalna 25* ☎ *012/432–01–10 or 012/432–00–60*).

MAŁOPOLSKA & THE TATRAS

Just to the south of Kraków, Poland's great plains give way to the gently folding foothills of the Carpathians, building to the High Tatras on the Slovak border. The fine medieval architecture of many towns in the Małopolska (Little Poland) region comes from a period when the area prospered as the intersection of thriving trade routes. In the countryside, wooden homesteads and strip-farmed tracts tell another story: of the hardships and poverty that the peasantry endured before the 20th century brought tourists to the mountains. During the 19th century, when this part of Poland was under Austrian rule as the province of Western Galicia, hundreds of thousands of peasants fled from the grinding toil of farm life to seek their fortune in the United States; it sometimes seems as if every family hereabouts has a cousin in America.

A visit to Kraków and Małopolska is incomplete without trips to at least two nearby destinations: the Wieliczka Salt Mine, where salt has been mined for a thousand years, and Auschwitz and Birkenau, sites of the Nazis' most gruesome and brutal concentration camps. Also within easy reach of Kraków is Zakopane, hiking and winter sports destination, and the self-styled winter capital of Poland.

Małopolska remains intensely Catholic and conservative, and the traditional way of life in the countryside is relatively intact. Folk crafts and customs are still very much alive in the mountains and foothills of *Podhale*. Carved-wood beehives stand in mountain gardens, and worshippers set out for Sunday church in embroidered white-felt trousers.

Numbers in the margin correspond to numbers on the Malopolska map.

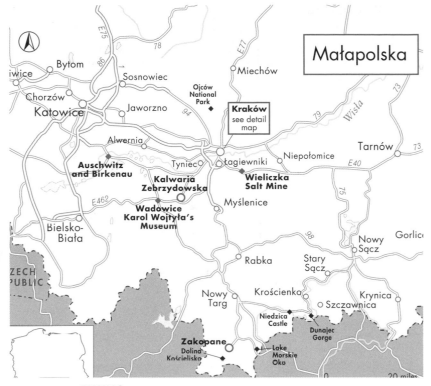

TIMING

For sightseeing and hiking, late spring to early autumn is the best time to visit the Małopolska region. November and March can be rainy and cold, and temperatures will drop to freezing or below during the winter. Most attractions and places of interest, however, remain open year-round. A winter visit to Wieliczka Salt Mine has many advantages: the temperature in the mine is always the same (around 15°C/60°F), making it feel pleasantly warm during the winter months; the mine is also much less crowded in the winter than during the busy summer months. During summer vacations, spa towns, holiday resorts in the mountains, and the hiking trails tend to become crowded, and this is especially true of Zakopane and the Tatra Mountains. Winter is ski season, when mountain resorts again get busy—particularly during weekends. In winter, some hiking trails are closed, and only experienced mountaineers should try to ascend to the upper trails and mountaintops. Nevertheless, many trails remain perfectly accessible to all, especially in the valleys, and the cable-car ride to Gubałówka also runs year-round.

9

AUSCHWITZ & BIRKENAU

60 km (38 mi) west of Kraków.

★ Between 1940 and 1945 more than 1.5 million people, 90% of them Jews from Poland and throughout Europe, died here in the Nazis' largest death-camp complex. The camp in the small town of Oświęcim (better known by its German name, Auschwitz) has come to be seen as the epicenter of the moral collapse of the West, proof of the human capacity for tremendous evil. The gas chambers at nearby Brzezinka (Birkenau) could exterminate thousands in a single day. The first inmates were Polish political prisoners, and the first gas victims were Russian POWs; the dead eventually included Poles, Jews, Romanies (Gypsies), homosexuals, Jehovah's Witnesses, and so-called criminals.

The *Konzentrationslager* (concentration camp) had three parts: Auschwitz, Birkenau, and Monowitz (where a chemical plant was run by prison labor). The barracks at Auschwitz have been completely restored and made into the **Państwowe Muzeum Auschwitz-Birkenau w Oświęcimiu** (Auschwitz-Birkenau State Museum), which has been described by one survivor, the author Primo Levi, as "something static, rearranged, contrived." With that in mind, begin with the heart-rending movie filmed by Soviet troops on January 27, 1945, the day they liberated the few prisoners left behind by the retreating Germans. The English version runs a few times a day, although narration isn't really necessary. Purchase a guidebook in English (most exhibits are in Polish or German), and walk through the notorious gate marked ARBEIT MACHT FREI (Work Brings Freedom). The most provocative exhibits are the huge piles of belongings confiscated from victims, as well as the two tons of human hair intended for use in the German textile industry. The execution wall, the prison block, and the reconstructed crematorium at the end of the tour are harshly sobering.

Far more affecting than the restored Auschwitz are the unaltered barracks, electric fences, and blown-up gas chambers at the enormous **Birkenau** camp, which is 3 km (2 mi) away. More prisoners lived and died here than at Auschwitz, including hundreds of thousands who went directly to the gas chambers from boxcars in which they had been locked up for days. The camp has been preserved to look much the way it did after the Nazis abandoned it. A walk to the back area brings you to the Monument to the Glory of the Victims, designed by Polish and Italian artists and erected in 1967. Behind the trees to the right of the monument lies a farm pond, its banks still murky with human ashes and bone fragments. To hear the tape on the camp's history in English, ask the reception staff in the main guardhouse. There are regularly scheduled, guided tours in English for an additional fee (inquire at the museum). To reach the camps from Kraków, take the E22a or the train or bus from plac Kolejowy. You can park at either camp; from April 15 to October 31 a shuttle bus runs between them once an hour. ⊠ *Więźniów Oświęcimia 20, Oświęcim* ☎ *033/843–20–22* ⊕ *www. auschwitz-muzeum.oswiecim.pl* ▨ *Auschwitz and Birkenau free, film zł2, guided tours in English for up to 10 persons zł210; individual*

tourist joining a guided tour zł26
⊙ *Auschwitz museum daily 8–6, Birkenau daily 9–4.*

WIELICZKA SALT MINE

12 km (7½ mi) southeast of Kraków on the E40.

Fodor'sChoice ★ Visiting the over 700-year-old mines of Wieliczka is a good way to spend half a day, combining the aesthetic pleasure of contemplating these marvelous underground salt chambers with a lesson in history and geology. As an added bonus you can gulp as many breaths of the healthy balsamic air, famous for its medicinal properties, as your lungs can take. Famous fans of the Wieliczka Salt Mine included Polish kings, Nicolaus Copernicus, Johann Wolfgang von Goethe, Tsar Alexander I, and Austro-Hungarian Emperor Franz Josef. If all these arguments were not enough, this first-rate tourist attraction is a Heritage Site recognized by UNESCO. And yes, you are allowed to lick the walls. Be aware that there is a lot of walking on the tour (expect to walk about 2½ km [1½ mi]).

The underground itinerary takes you to several chapels that have been carved from the salt; huge, fantastically shaped multilevel chambers; and salty subterranean lakes that send off fantasmagorical reflections of light. Look especially for the 17th-century **Chapel of St. Anthony's**, with the saints' expressions softened with the moisture coming through the shaft. The colossal **Chapel of the Blessed Kinga** is rather like a cathedral hewn out of salt. After finishing your sightseeing tour, if you are not too tired of walking, you can visit the underground **Museum** that shows the history of salt mining at Wieliczka, as well as the archaeology and geology of the salty region.

You can get to Wieliczka by a slightly rickety suburban train (*przewozy regionalne*): the journey takes only 20 minutes (but you need to walk a little to the mine). There are also minibuses (both tour buses and regular connections by private companies) leaving from the Kraków train station. ⊠*Daniłowicza 10, Wieliczka* ☏*012/278–73–02* ⊕*www. kopalnia.pl* ⊡*zł46* ⊙*Mine Apr.–Oct., daily 7:30–7:30; Nov.–Mar., daily 8–5. Museum daily 8–4.*

THE POPE'S EXPRESS

Wadowice is 48 km (30 mi) southwest of Kraków.

Fodor'sChoice ★ The *Pope's Express*, which commemorates the late John Paul II, is a modern train connecting Kraków—where Karol Wojtyła was a student, a young priest, and then a bishop—with his birthplace in Wadowice.

The train makes stops on the way in places connected with the pope's life and Catholic faith. The most interesting and significant stops are those in Łagiewniki and Kalwaria Zebrzydowska, two very important sanctuaries and pilgrimage sites. The journey between Krakow and Wadowice takes 1 hour 15 minutes, but you can get off at any stop along the way, do some sightseeing, and get back on the next train. Footage from the pope's speeches and his pilgrimages to Poland is shown on screens during the journey. Your best bet is to make this a half-day trip and go back to Kraków for lunch (or bring a picnic to enjoy on the train); there are few good options for lunch in Wadowice.

Once you get off the train in Łagiewniki, one of the trails to the right will take you to the **Sanktuarium Bożego Miłosierdzia** *(Sanctuary of the Divine Mercy)* (⊠ *Łagiewniki* ⊕ *www.milosierdzie.pl*). Between the world wars, in the redbrick nunnery, lived St. Faustyna Kowalska, who started the cult of the Divine Mercy, which, as the faithful believe, was communicated to her by Jesus himself. The modern church was designed by a renowned Polish architect, Witold Cęckiewicz. In the bright church, which accommodates about 5,000 pilgrims, note the beautiful simplicity of the main altar, and the round tabernacle. Take the elevator installed inside the characteristic tower and go up to the viewing platform.

The Pope's Express stops at the major pilgrimage site of **Kalwaria Zebrzydowska** (⊠ *Kalwaria Zebrzydowska* ⊕ *www.kalwaria.eu*) on the UNESCO World Heritage List since 1999. South of the Kalwaria Zebrzydowska town center, atop the Calvary Mount, lies a baroque church and monastery of St. Bernard. The pilgrimage site encompasses also 42 chapels, Stations of the Cross, and Stations of Virgin Mary, scattered to the south and east of the monastery, among rolling hills and picturesque valleys. In front of the temple there is a plaza, called the Paradise Square. On either side it is lined with a 19th-century colonnaded gallery, and enclosed with an iron balustrade incorporating stone pillars and statues. Ascending to the church of St. Mary of the Angels (Portiunculae) is a wide stairway built between 1927 and 1932. Inside, note the frescoes covering the vaults of the nave and the rainbow wall: work of Włodzimierz Tetmajer, a Polish art nouveau artist.

Karol Wojtyła's Museum in Wadowice (⊠ *Kościelna 7, Wadowice* 🕾 *033/823–26–62*) is located in the very house where the Pope from Poland was born, "between five and six in the afternoon" on May 18, 1920. Among the memorabilia, you will find Karol Wojtyła's documents (including school certificates), photographs, and some modest personal objects. When in Wadowice, step into the church: in the chapel of St. Anne is the baptismal font where the future pope was baptized. Admission to the museum is free, but donations are accepted. The museum is open Tuesday through Sunday; from May through September, 9–1 and 2–6, and from October through April, 9–1 and 2–5. ⊠ *Train leaves from Kraków Główny, Kraków* 🕾 *012/393–33–28, 012/393–33–29 in Kraków, 033/823–39–15 Ext. 340 in Wadowice* ⊕ *www.pociagpapieski.pl* 💰 *zł11.50 one-way, zł18 round-trip* ⊙ *Departures from*

Kraków daily at 8:55, 12:55, and 4:55; return from Wadowice daily at 10:30, 2:30, and 6:30.

ZAKOPANE

★ *100 km (62 mi) south of Kraków on Hwy. E95.*

Nestled at the foot of the Tatra Mountains, at 3,281 feet above sea level, Zakopane is the highest town in Poland (it's the southernmost as well). Until the 19th-century Romantic movement started a fashion for mountain scenery, Zakopane was a poor and remote village. During the 1870s, when the Tatra Association was founded, people began coming to the mountains for their health and recreation, and Zakopane developed into Poland's leading mountain resort. At the turn of the 20th century, Zakopane was the place to be. Many artists, scientists, physicians, and politicians frequented this fashionable resort, and some called it home. Of these, the most famous are the composer Karol Szymanowski and the artist and playwright Stanisław Witkiewicz (Witkacy). The father of the latter, also named Stanisław Witkiewicz, was responsible for creating the so-called Zakopane style, inspired by traditional local wooden architecture.

The town is small, and the most important sights can easily be covered on foot. Ulica Krupówki, the main thoroughfare, runs downhill through the town from northwest to southeast. If you begin at the northwest end, you will pass many buildings in the Zakopane style. The street is lined with countless restaurants, bars, and souvenir shops. Ulica Kościuszki runs east to west across Krupówki and links the town with the railway and bus stations. At the bottom of the hill is ulica Kościeliska, another street with a wealth of traditional wooden architecture.

WHAT TO SEE

☘ A cable railway can take you from the center of town up to **Gubałówka**, where on a clear day you will have a fine view of the Tatras and of the town. An alternative to riding the cable car back into town is to walk: take the path along the ridge to Pałkówka and from there back down into town, about 9 km (5½ mi). Children can have their photograph taken on the Gubałówka **terrace** in a carriage drawn by four white mountain sheepdogs and driven by a man dressed in a white bearskin. ✉*Down from corner of ul. Krupówki and ul. Kościeliska, at end of path lined with souvenir stalls* ☎*018/201–48–30* 💰*zł8 one-way, zł14 round-trip* ⏱*8:30–6.*

Kościół świętego Klemensa *(Church of St. Clement)*, at the foot of the hill in town, dates from the mid-19th century. The first church built in Zakopane, it has been decorated by the local artists. The pictures of the Stations of the Cross were painted on glass by Ewelina Pęksowa. The adjoining **Cmentarz na Pęksowym Brzyzku** (Cemetery at Pęksów Bryzek) is the burial place of many famous artists, mountain guides, and other people of the Tatras. This very atmospheric place is also a one-of-a-kind gallery that includes tombstones carved by Władysław

Hasior, Antoni Rząsa, and other local artists who were masters at their art. ⊠*Kościeliska, opposite Kasprusie.*

Muzeum Stylu Zakopiańskiego im. **Stanisława Witkiewicza** *Stanisław Witkiewicz Museum of the Zakopane Style) is devoted to* the "Swiss Alpine" style of architecture, which started to appear in Zakopane during the second half of the 19th century, provoking local architect Stanisław Witkiewicz to create a more appropriate "vernacular" style based on Podhale's folk traditions. His very first project in the so-called Zakopane style was the **Willa Koliba,** which is now this museum dedicated to the architect and his signature style. ⊠*Kościeliska 18* ☎*018/201–36–02* ☜*zł4* ☉ *Wed.–Sun. 9–4.*

A wooden structure in the Zakopane style, **Willa Atma** was home to the great Polish composer Karol Szymanowski in the 1920s and '30s. Szymanowski's best work—including *Harnasie* and *Pieśni kurpiowskie*—was inspired by the local folk music, and he was the first Polish composer after Chopin to receive international recognition. Filled with Szymanowski's music played from the recordings—and sometimes during live recitals—the villa is now a museum dedicated to his life and work. ⊠*Kasprusie 19* ☎*018/201–34–93* ☜*zł5* ☉ *May–Sept., Tues.–Thurs. and weekends 10–4, Fri. 2–8; Oct.–Apr., Tues.–Sun. 10–4.*

Willa pod Jedlami, an elaborate villa and another of Stanisław Witkiewicz's Zakopane buildings, is considered one of his most ambitious works. Since it's still a private home, it is not open to the public, but the outside is worth a look. ⊠*Koziniec 1.*

You can see the work of one of the most original and talented contemporary artists from Zakopane at the **Władysław Hasior Gallery.** Hasior (1928–99) created idiosyncratic assemblages, including very original "banners" such as the Star of the Watering Place. A wide range of examples of his work is on display. ⊠*Jagiellońska 18b* ☎*018/206–88–71* ☜*zł4* ☉ *Wed.–Sat. 11–6, Sun. 9–3.*

WHERE TO EAT

$–$$ **×Bąkowo Zohylina.** Friendly waiters in folk costumes serve hearty
Fodor'sChoice regional dishes while the band plays fiery folk music in the back-
★ ground—rather loudly. This kind of food is designed—and guaranteed—to keep you warm, be it potato pancakes, a "mountaineer's cauldron" (dense, goulashlike soup), or hot oscypek cheese with cranberries. On a chilly day, you can treat yourself to "tea, mountaineer style" (yes, it does include grog); the mirror and the alco-meter in the bathroom will tell you when you've had enough. ⊠*ul. Piłsudskiego 5* ☎*018/206–62–16* ▤*AE, DC, MC, V.*

★ **$–$$** **×Obrochtówka.** This regional restaurant is run by two ladies, Irena Wieczorek and Małgorzata Zawadzka. Most of the time, they can be seen here cooking and supervising the preparation of food, which includes their own home recipes. Lamb dishes and potato pancakes are among the best choices, and if you like participating in the food-preparation process, you can grill your own shish kebab or sausage in the open fireplace. Reputedly, this is a hangout of (harmless) "contemporary mountain robbers," one of whom made it to the finals of the

Polish version of the Big Brother TV show. ⊠*ul. Kraszewskiego 10a* ☎*018/206–62–16* ⊟*AE, DC, MC, V.*

$–$$
Fodor's Choice
★
✗**Sabała.** One of the most popular regional restaurants in Zakopane, Sabała is nearly always full and lively. Given the number of restaurants in Zakopane and the size of this place, that's quite a recommendation indeed. The staff, in regional folk costumes, will bring you well-seasoned grilled meats on wooden plates, and you can select your own fresh and pickled salads from a self-service salad bar. In summer, the elevated terrace, which overlooks the Krupówki promenade, offers perfect people-watching opportunities. You don't need to order food, either: it is fine if you just sip a drink. ⊠*ul. Krupówki 11* ☎*018/201–50–92* ⊟*AE, DC, MC, V.*

★ $–$$
✗**Zbójecka.** One of the nicest traditional Zakopane-style restaurants, Zbójecka is subterranean, reached via stairs leading down to a cozy basement room bathed in light and warmth from a fireplace and an open grill. Diners sink back into wool-upholstered chairs and enjoy a selection of carnivorous delights, including fresh and expertly prepared lamb, beef, pork, and poultry. You'll easily feel you've gone a century back in time and will forget about the nearby bustle of ulica Krupówki. ⊠*ul. Krupówki 28* ☎*018/201–38–54* ⊟*AE, DC, MC, V.*

WHERE TO STAY

In addition to the hotels and pensions in Zakopane itself, there are mountain hostels higher up along the hiking routes in the Tatras. These are, for the most part, fairly modest places that are meant for simple accommodations for skiers and hikers, so don't expect full hotel amenities.

$$$
Fodor's Choice
★
Belvedere Hotel. Close to the center of Zakopane, in a quiet area adjoining the National Park, the Belvedere is probably the most upscale hotel in town. It's also the best. Comfortably furnished rooms come in two variations: "classic" and "wooden" (the latter has slanted ceilings). The hotel has a range of restaurants and bars, as well as great fitness and wellness facilities. At the "Thalgo" Marine Institute of Health and Beauty you can try thalassotherapy. On the whole, Belvedere is a great place to stay, especially if you want to slow down and relax for a few days in the fresh mountain air. ⊠*Droga do Białego 3, 34–500* ☎*018/20–21–200* 🖷*018/20–21–250* ⊕*www.belvederehotel. pl* ➦*130 rooms, 30 suites* ♻*3 restaurants, café, minibars, in-room safes, in-room broadband, cable TV, pool, gym, hot tub, spa, bowling, squash, bowling, 2 bars, business services, meeting rooms, free parking* ⊟*AE, DC, MC, V* ⦿*BP.*

★ $$$
Litwor. This is one of the best hotels in Zakopane. Right on the town's main promenade, it adjoins a quiet, picturesque park. The rooms have all the amenities you might crave, including towel warmers, hair dryers, and heated floors in the plush bathrooms. Plus the hotel's own spa and fitness center has a great enclosed pool, a sauna, solarium, and a gym. Perhaps best of all, the friendly staff seem to enjoy perfecting their English. ⊠*ul. Krupówki 40, 34–500* ☎*018/201–71–89* 🖷*018/201–71–90* ⊕*www.litwor.pl* ➦*58 rooms, 5 suites* ♻*Restaurant, cable TV, indoor pool, in-room safes, gym, hot tub, sauna, steam room, bar, business services, convention center, some pets allowed; no a/c* ⊟*AE, DC, MC, V* ⦿*BP.*

9

$$ ⊡ **Sabała.** This large, historic hotel was built in 1897 in the then-emerging Zakopane style and named after a renowned 19th-century storyteller. The wood-panel rooms are also furnished in beeswax-treated, solid wood furnishings; many have the original fixtures. There's nothing outstanding about this hotel, but the reasonable prices are a draw, as is the excellent restaurant. ⊠*ul. Krupówki 11, 34–500* ☎*018/201–50–92* 🖷*018/201–50–93* ⊕*www.sabala.zakopane.pl* ⇆*50 rooms* ⚘*Restaurant, cable TV, in-room broadband, pool, sauna, some pets allowed; no a/c* ⊟*AE, DC, MC, V* ⏍*BP.*

SHOPPING

Leather and sheepskin products are local specialties, along with hand-knitted socks, sweaters, and caps in white, gray, and black patterns made from rough, undyed wool. The best place to look for local handmade goods is at the **Zakopane market** (⊠*ul. Krupówki*), at the foot of the street on the way to the Gubałówka cable railway. Wednesday is the main market day, but some stalls are here all week. The whole of Krupówki Street is lined with shops and kiosks selling regional products.

SPORTS & THE OUTDOORS

BIKING

Mountain biking has become increasingly popular in the area. Expect to pay around zł50 a day to rent a mountain bike. **Rent a Bike** (⊠*Sienkiewicza 37* ☎*018/201–42–66*) has a small selection of mountain bikes available. You can hire a bike at **Sport & Fun Company Ltd.** (⊠*Rondo 1* ☎*018/201–56–03*).

HIKING

The Gorczański, Pieniński, and Tatrzański (Tatra) national parks all have hiking territory. The routes are well marked, and there are maps at entrance points that give the distances, times, and degrees of difficulty of the trails. On the lower reaches of trails out of major tourist points (such as Zakopane, Szczawnica, and Krynica), walkers crowd the paths, but they thin out as you go higher up. The Tatras are serious mountains: magnificent, but not to be trifled with. Unfortunately, every year, fatal accidents happen. Some trails—notably the so-(aptly)-called **Orla Perć** ("Eagles' Perch") and the last section of the ascent to **Rysy** (the "Rifts"), the Tatra's highest peak—have elements of *via ferrata*, routes where permanent chains are attached to the mountain wall for getting up the steeper slopes. You may have a close encounter with snow in May or even as late as June. Weather can turn rapidly, and you'll definitely find cooler temperatures at the higher elevations, so dress properly, and wear good walking boots or shoes. Even though the trails are well marked, never walk in the Tatras without a detailed map. Pack a bottle of water for proper hydration and a bar of chocolate for an energy boost. You should never walk alone, and always let someone at your hotel know where you are going.

SKIING

Zakopane acquired snow-making machinery in 1990 and is still the region's major center for downhill skiing, although Krynica and Krościenko also have some slopes. You probably will not be traveling with your own skis, but plenty of places rent ski equipment. **Sukces** (⊠*Sienkiewicza 39* ☎*018/206–41–97* ⊕*www.ski-sukces.zakopane.pl*).

A two-person chairlift bring skiers to the peaks of **Butorowy Wierch** (⊠*Powstańców Śląskich* ☎*018/201–39–41*), which has a relatively easy run, suitable even for beginners.

You'll find the most advanced runs at **Kasprowy Wierch** (⊠*Kuźnice* ☎*018/201–45–10 lower station, 018/201–44–05 upper station*). The resort has a gondola cable car, which is very popular, so long lines should be expected (the good news is, you can book a timed ticket in advance, and thus jump the line). Kuźnice, where the cable lift is found, can be reached by a minibus from outside Zakopane's PKS bus station.

NIGHTLIFE & THE ARTS

Zakopane's theatrical and musical performances are often connected with the artists and writers who have made the town their home, particularly Witkiewicz and Karol Szymanowski. Posters on kiosks announce performances. Tourist information will also provide schedules (or you can check them yourself at the tourist office's Web site). Traditional local folk orchestras also perform regularly—often in restaurants to accompany your meal. Every now and then there are jazz concerts and jam sessions. As for nightlife, Zakopane is not the all-night town that Kraków is, but there are some interesting options.

BARS

Ampstrong (⊠*Jagiellońska 18* ☎*018/20–12–904*) used to be called "Pstrąg" ("trout," pronounced p'*strong*) before it wisely changed its name. After all, it is not a fish restaurant, nor do they play Schubert's "Die Forelle." Instead, you can hear fashionable club music: new jazz, funk, reggae, and house. **Caffe Sanacja** (⊠*ul. Krupówki 77* ☎*018/20–13–140*) is a dark, brick-vaulted and wooden enclave for the small but vibrant artistic community. It is an island of rock and jazz, whereas most restaurants and bars around play nothing but local folk music. **Paparazzi** (⊠*Gen. Galicy 8* ☎*018/20–63–251*), the sibling of Kraków's own Paparazzi, is Zakopane's après-ski alternative to folksy traditionalism, offering well-shaken cocktails, a good wine menu, and fusion-style bar food. In summer, garden seating over a shimmering brook is very pleasant.

MUSIC

Every August, Zakopane's International Festival of Highland Folklore takes place, with folk musicians arriving from all over the world. The United Europe Jazz Festival happens at the beginning of May. There is an organ music festival in the summer (June through August). A festival of Szymanowski's music, with concerts all over town, is held each July. The **Kulczycki Gallery** (⊠*Koziniec 8* ☎*018/201–29–36*) occasionally hosts concerts and other events. Concerts are sometimes given at the **Willa Atma** (⊠*Kasprusie 19* ☎*018/206–31–50*).

THEATER

The **Teatr im. Stanisława Ignacego Witkiewicza** (⊠*ul. Chramcówki 15* ☎*018/206–82–97*) has two stages and is considered one of the best theaters in Poland. Some performances are very visual and musical, so it is worth inquiring whether the theater is offering something for which understanding of Polish is not essential.

MAŁOPOLSKA ESSENTIALS

BUS TRAVEL

Zakopane is most easily accessible by bus from Kraków, a two-hour trip by express bus (via Nowy Targ), and seats can be reserved in advance. There are some limited-stop services from Warsaw to Zakopane (five hours). Almost all villages in the region, however isolated, can be reached by PKS bus or a private minibus. The buses themselves can be ancient and slow, so take an express bus if one operates to your destination. The best buses are privately operated; the two biggest companies are Trans-Frej and Szwagropol, both offering regular connections from Kraków to Zakopane via Nowy Targ, and Kraków to Nowy Sącz via Bochnia-Brzesko; both routes take about two hours.

There is regular minibus service from Kraków to Wieliczka. There are also buses to Oświęcim and Wadowice, but both these destinations can be reached faster and more easily by train.

Bus Stations **Zakopane PKS Bus Station** (⊠ *Corner of ul. Kościuszki and ul. Chramcówki, Zakopane* ☎ *018/201–44–53* ⊕ *pks.zakopane.pl*).

Private Bus Companies **Szwagropol** (☎ *018/652—77–80* ⊕ *www.szwagropol. pl*). **Trans-Frej** (☎ *018/288–07–80* ⊕ *www.trans-frej.com.pl*).

CAR TRAVEL

It is not necessary to have a car to explore the southern region. Public transport will take you to even the most remote places—but it will take time and can be uncomfortably crowded. On the other hand, the narrow mountain roads can be trying and dangerous for drivers.

The 7 (E77) highway, which takes you roughly halfway from Kraków to Zakopane, is four-lane all the way. The road that runs the rest of the way, E95, was improved in summer 2006, but some stretches are still single-lane, and horse-drawn carts can cause major delays. Side roads in the region can be very narrow and badly surfaced. In Zakopane and other towns in the region, it is wise to leave your car at a guarded parking lot. If you wish to rent a car, it is most practical to do so in Kraków.

TOUR OPTIONS

Although you will find it easy to travel around Małopolska on your own, for some destinations, you may wish to consider a guided tour. This is especially true of the Tatra mountains, particularly if you would like to go hiking but don't feel experienced enough to do it safely on your own. Klub Przewodników Tatrzańskich and Koło Przewodników Tatrzańskich are associations of experienced mountain guides who know the mountains as only natives can do, and you will definitely be safe in their company. Your visit to Auschwitz will be more valuable if you join one of the English-language guided tours of the camp, or you can book a private tour with a knowledgeable guide. In Wieliczka, you are not allowed to wander on your own, but there are English-language group tours.

Information **Auschwitz-Birkenau Memorial Museum** (✉ *Więźniów Oświęcimia 20, Oświęcim* ☎ *033/843–21–33* ⊕ *www.auschwitz-muzeum.oswiecim.pl*), tours by qualified museum guides. **Klub Przewodników Tatrzańskich PTTK-TPN** (✉ *Chałubińskiego 42a, Zakopane* ☎ *018/206–32–03* ⊕ *www.klub-przew.home. pl*). **Koło Przewodników Tatrzańskich** (✉ *ul. Piłsudskiego 63a, Zakopane* ⊕ *kpt. zakopane.pl*). **Wieliczka Salt Mine Tourist Route** (✉ *Daniłowicza 10, Wieliczka* ☎ *012/278–73–02* ⊕ *www.kopalnia.pl*), guided tours of Wieliczka Salt Mine).

TRAIN TRAVEL

From Kraków, the trip to Zakopane takes a full four to five hours because of the rugged nature of the terrain. Unless you take the overnight sleeper from Warsaw, which arrives in Zakopane at 6 AM, it's better to change to a bus in Kraków.

To visit the Auschwitz memorial, you can take a train to Oświęcim (about 90 minutes from Kraków). Basic regional trains (*przewozy regionalne*) will take you to Wieliczka. The brand-new and shiny Pope's Express from Kraków to Kalwaria Zebrzydowska and Wadowice remains in contrast to most Polish trains (save InterCity express routes), and is a tourist attraction in itself.

Train timetables can be found online at the Web site for Telekomunikacja Kolejowa. (In the English-language version of the site, look for a button on the left for the PKP Train Timetable.)

Information **Pociąg Papieski** (*The Pope's Express* ⊕ *www.pociag-papieski.pl*). **Telekomunikacja Kolejowa** (⊕ *www.tktelekom.pl*). **Zakopane Train Station** (✉ *ul. Chramcówki 23, Zakopane* ☎ *018/201–50–31*).

VISITOR INFORMATION

Information **Orbis Zakopane** (✉ *ul. Krupówki 22, Zakopane* ☎ *018/201– 22–38*). **Zakopane Tourist Information** (*BIT* ✉ *ul. Kościuszki 17, Zakopane* ☎ *018/201–22–11*). **Wadowice Tourist Information** (*BIT* ✉ *Kościelna 4, Wadowice* ☎ *033/873–23–65* ⊕ *www.it.wadowice.pl*).

THE BALTIC COAST & POMERANIA

Poland's Baltic coast stretches for 400 km (249 mi) from the isle of Wolin in the west to the Mierzeja Wiślana (Vistulan Sandbar) in the east. It is mostly a gentle and friendly shore with pine forests leading to sandy beaches, incorporating two national parks and several nature reserves (and farther inland) that are the habitats to many rare species of fish and fowl. The region is also a source of precious amber. But there is more to Pomerania than the Baltic beaches and nature: the bustling city of Gdańsk attracts visitors to the birthplace of the Solidarity movement; it is also perhaps Poland's most attractive historic city after Kraków and a convenient gateway to Poland's castle country.

The Baltic Coast

Until World War II, most of this area of northwestern Poland was included in Prussia and was referred to as "the sandbox of the Holy Roman Empire." It is indeed sandy, but it contains some startling landscapes and magnificent historic sites, such as the fortress of the Teutonic Knights at Malbork (close to and easily accessible by train from Gdańsk) and Frombork, where Copernicus lived and worked, and where he is buried.

Gdańsk, the capital of this region, is linked with two smaller neighboring towns, Gdynia and Sopot, in an urban conglomeration called the Trójmiasto (Tri-City), on the western bank of the Bay of Gdańsk. These cities operate as a single organism (if taken as one, they would make the third-largest city in Poland) and form one of Poland's most exciting and vibrant places. Szczecin, often underrated as a tourist destination, is another interesting city in the region, and a good starting point for further exploration. Malbork, with its historic castle, can be easily seen as a day trip from Gdańsk.

TIMING

If you are planning to spend some time in the beach, July and August are the months to go. This is also when beaches get crowded. (On the other hand, most festivals and other entertainment are concentrated in those two summer months.) June or September can be nice: although it may be cooler, the experience will be no less—and in some places will be considerably more—enjoyable. Tri-City is a year-round destination: its culture and history are not ruled by seasonality.

GDAŃSK

350 km (219 mi) north of Warsaw, 340 km (215 mi) east of Szczecin.

The so-called Trójmiasto (Tri-City) comprises the ancient Hanseatic city of Gdańsk, the historic resort of Sopot, and the much newer town and port of Gdynia, which was created in the 1920s and '30s. You can get a taste of the three cities in two days. They are conveniently joined together by a commuter train: the SKM (Szybka Kolej Miejska, which translates as Fast City Rail).

A stroll down the pristine cobbles of Gdańsk's Old Town is a walk through history, and Sopot is enchanting with the hedonistic atmosphere of a seaside resort filled with neon-lighted bars hidden inside rambling, prewar villas. Gdynia is again different, with a special climate of a 1930s harbor city.

Maybe it's the sea air, or maybe it's the mixture of the city's cultural importance and political tumult. Whatever the reason, Gdańsk is special to Poles—and to Scandinavians and Germans, who visit the

CAUTION

Even in the middle of the summer, good weather may not necessarily be a part of your vacation package. Nights can be cool, and water will never be really warm. Along with swim trunks and sun lotion, you should bring a warm sweater and rain gear. Cool weather does not provide protection from the sun, so don't forget sunblock, whatever the weather!

region in great numbers. From 1308 to 1945, this Baltic port was an independent city-state called Danzig, a majority of whose residents were ethnic Germans. When the Nazis fired the first shots of World War II here on September 1, 1939, they began a process of systematic destruction of Poland that would last for six years and leave millions dead. Nevertheless, in 1997 Gdańsk celebrated its 1,000th year as a Baltic city.

It remains well known as the cradle of the workers' movement that came to be known as Solidarność (Solidarity). Food-price increases in 1970 led to the first strikes at the (former) Lenin Shipyards. The Communist authorities put down the protest quickly and brutally, killing 40 workers in December of that year. Throughout the 1970s, small groups of anti-Communist workers and intellectuals based in Gdańsk continued to organize. By August 1980, they had gained sufficient critical mass to form an organization that the government was forced to recognize eventually as the first independent trade union in the former Soviet bloc. Although the government attempted to destroy Solidarity when it declared martial law in December 1981, union activists continued to keep the objectives of democracy and independence from the Soviet Union alive. After the collapse of the Soviet bloc in 1989, Solidarity leader Lech Wałęsa became president of Poland in the nation's first free elections since World War II.

The historic core of this medieval city can be explored easily on foot. Although Gdańsk was almost entirely destroyed during World War II, the streets of its Główne Miasto (Main Town) have been lovingly restored and still retain their historical and cultural richness. North of the Main Town, the Stare Miasto (Old Town) contains many newer hotels and shops, but several churches and the beautifully reconstructed Old Town Hall justify its name. At the north end of the Old Town sit the shipyards. This site, which captivated world attention during the many clashes between workers and militarized police units during the 1970s and '80s, has now settled back into its daily grind, and the shipyards struggle to make the adjustment to the free market.

9

WHAT TO SEE

Fodor's Choice
★

The largest brick church in the world—and the largest church of any kind in Poland— **Kościół Najświętszej Marii Panny** *(St. Mary's Church)* is on the north side of ulica Piwna. The sanctuary can accommodate 25,000 people. Often referred to by the abbreviated Kościół Mariacki, this enormous 14th-century church underwent major restoration after World War II. Although it originally held 22 altars, 15 of them have been relocated to museums in Gdańsk and Warsaw. The highlight of a visit is the climb up the hundreds of steps to the top of the church tower. Although you must pay zł3 to climb, the cost is significantly cheaper than an aerobics class, and the splendid panorama is spectacular. The church also contains a 500-year-old, 25-foot-high astronomical clock that has only recently been restored to working order after years of neglect. It keeps track of solar and lunar progressions, and it displays the signs of the zodiac, something of an anomaly in a Catholic church. ⊠ *Podkramarska 5, at ul. Piwna, Stare Miasto* ☎ *Tower zł3* ⊙ *Daily 9–5.*

Two blocks west of St. Mary's Church, the **Wielka Zbrojownia** *(Great Armory)* is a good example of 17th-century Dutch Renaissance architecture. The ground floor is now a trade center, and the upper floors house an art school. ⊠ *Piwna, near Targ Węglowy, Stare Miasto.*

Fodor's Choice
★

Three huge and somber crosses perpetually draped with flowers stand outside the gates of the **Stocznia Gdańska** *Gdańsk Shipyard)*, formerly the Lenin Shipyards, which gave birth to the Solidarity Movement. The crosses outside the entrance are the **Monument to Fallen Shipyard Workers** (Pomnik Poległych Stoczniowców), as well as plaques that commemorate the struggle, and a quotation by Pope John Paul II inspired by his visit to the monument in 1987. Formerly inside the shipyard gates (and now a bit farther away), the **Roads to Freedom** exhibition once consisted of a number of symbolic gates, which until recently led to a multimedia exhibition in the historic BPH room on Plac Solidarności, where the Gdańsk Agreements were signed. The BPH room is now closed for renovation but the exhibition itself reopened in July 2007 in a new location at Wały Piastowskie Street (a short walk from the shipyard itself, halfway between the shipyards and the Main Railway Station). The exhibition itself is really interesting, as it traces the beginning and development of the Solidarity movement, taking you on a virtual tour through 1980s Poland. ⊠ *Wały Piastowskie 24, Stare Miasto* ☎ *058/308—47–12* ⊕ *www.fcs.org.pl* ☎ *zł6* ⊙ *Oct.–Apr., Tues.–Sun. 10–4; May–Sept., Tues.–Sun. 10–5.*

The monument in the Gdańsk Shipyards clearly symbolizes the fundamental link in the Polish consciousness between Catholicism and political dissent; another example is **Kościół świętej Brygidy** *(St. Brigitte's Church)*, a few blocks north of the shipyards. After the Communist government declared martial law in 1981 in an attempt to force Solidarity to disband, the union's members began meeting here secretly during celebrations of mass. A statue of Pope John Paul II can be seen in front of the church. ⊠ *ul. Profesorska 17, near Old Town Hall, Stare Miasto.*

Built in 1444, Gdańsk's **Żuraw Gdański** *(Harbor Crane)* was medieval Europe's largest; it's also Europe's oldest crane. It used to play the double role of a port crane and city gate. The structure was given its present shape between 1442 and 1444. Inside, a huge wooden wheel was set in motion by men walking inside it. The crane was used to unload cargo and also to put up ships' masts. Today, it houses the **Muzeum Morskie** (Maritime Museum), with a collection of models of the ships constructed in the Gdańsk Shipyards since 1945. At the museum ticket office, inquire about tickets for tours of the *Sołdek,* a World War II battleship moored nearby on the canal. ✉ *Ołowianka 9–13, Stare Miasto* ☎058/301–86–11 💰*zł8* ⏰ *Oct.–June, Tues.–Sun. 10–4; July–Sept., daily 10–4.*

★ The historic entrance to the Old Town of Gdańsk is marked by the magnificent **Brama Wyżynna** *(High Gate),* which starts the so-called "Royal Route," along which the king passed through the city on his annual visit. The gate is adorned with the flags of Poland, Gdańsk, and the Prussian kingdom. Its builder, Hans Kramer of Saxony, erected it as a link in the chain of modern fortifications put up to frame the western city borders between 1574 and 1576. ✉ *Off Wały Jagiellońskie, at ul. Długa, Stare Miasto.*

Just behind the Brama Wyżynna, the **Brama Złota** *(Golden Gate)* was the second through which the king passed on the Royal Route. This structure dates from 1614 and combines characteristics of both the Italian and Dutch Renaissance. It was built to the design of Abraham van den Blocke. Next to the Golden Gate squats the house of **St. George's Brotherhood** that was erected by Glotau between 1487 and 1494 in the late-Gothic style. ✉ *Off Wały Jagiellońskie, at western end of ul. Długa, Stare Miasto.*

Fodor's Choice ★ One of the city's most distinctive landmarks is the elaborately gilded **Fontanna Neptuna** *(Neptune Fountain)* at the western end of Długi Targ. ⓒ Every day after dusk, it is illuminated, adding a romantic glow to the entire area. Around the fountain, vendors selling amber jewelry and souvenirs maintain a centuries-old tradition of trade at this point. The fountain itself is perhaps the best-known symbol of Gdańsk, emphasizing its bond with the sea. It was sculpted by Peter Husen and Johann Rogge, and the cast, molded in 1615, was commissioned from Augsburg. Between 1757 and 1761 Johann Karl Stender remade the fountain chalice and plinth in the rococo style and added a whole array of sea creatures. ✉*ul. Długa, east of Wały Jagiellońskie, Stare Miasto.*

★ Behind the Fontanna Neptuna on Długi Targ, **Dwór Artusa** *(Artus Mansion) is* one of the more significant of the grand houses that were constructed over a period from the 15th through the 17th century. The mansion was named for mythical King Arthur, who otherwise has no affiliation with the place. This and the other stately mansions on the Długi Targ are reminders of the traders and aristocrats who once resided in this posh district. The elegant interior hides a huge, 40-foot-high Renaissance tiled stove, possibly the world's largest, a mid-16th-century masterpiece by George Stelzener. The mansion's collection

9

also includes Renaissance furnishings, paintings, and holy figures. The building was the meeting place of the Gdańsk city nobles. ✉*Długi Targ 43, Stare Miasto* ☎*058/346–33–58* 🖾*zł5* ⊙*Tues.–Sat. 10–4, Sun. 11–4.*

At the water's edge is the **Brama Zielona** *(Green Gate), the* eastern entrance to the medieval city of Gdańsk. Before this elegant structure was erected, the site had been occupied by the oldest gate in town, the 14th-century Cog Gate. Pulled down in 1564–68, it made room for the current Mannerist building. The construction works, supervised by Regnier of Amsterdam and Hans Kramer from Dresden, lasted from 1568 to 1571. This 16th-century gate killed two birds with one stone, doubling as a royal residence. Unfortunately, the name no longer fits: the gate is now painted brown. ✉*At eastern end of Długi Targ, Stare Miasto.*

On a small island in the canal just north of St. Catherine's Church, the **Wielki Młyn** *(Great Mill) was the* largest mill in medieval Europe from the time of its completion in 1350 until 1945. The structure combined three functions: flour mill, granary, and bakery. It was equipped with 18 overshot waterwheels, each 15 feet in diameter, and the works represented a great technical achievement for the time. Today, it's filled with shops and boutiques, which are open weekdays from 11 to 7, Saturdays from 11 to 3. ✉*Intersection of Podmłyńska and Na Piaskach, Stare Miasto.*

Although Gdańsk's original **Ratusz Główny** *(Old Town Hall)* was completely destroyed during World War II, a careful reconstruction of the exterior and interior now re-creates the glory of Gdańsk's medieval past. Inside, the **Muzeum Historii Miasta Gdańska** (Gdańsk Historical Museum) covers more than five centuries of Gdańsk's history in exhibits that include paintings, sculptures, and weapons. ✉*ul. Długa 47, Stare Miasto* ☎*058/301–48–72* 🖾*Museum zł4* ⊙*Tues.–Sun. 11–4.*

Fodor'sChoice
★ The district of Oliwa, northwest of the Old Town, is worth visiting if only for the magnificent **Katedra w Oliwie** *(Oliwa Cathedral).* Originally part of a Cistercian monastery, the church was erected during the 13th century. Like most other structures in Poland, it has been rebuilt many times, resulting in a hodgepodge of styles from Gothic to Renaissance to rococo. The cathedral houses one of the most impressive rococo organs you're ever likely to hear—and see. It has more than 6,000 pipes, and when a special mechanism is activated, wooden angels ring bells and a wooden star climbs up a wooden sky. Demonstrations of the organ and a brief narrated church history are given almost hourly on weekdays in summer (May through September), less frequently on weekends and the rest of the year. Don't miss a proper full-fledged concert if there is one. The Oliwa District is best reached by train; get off at Gdańsk-Oliwa and walk west up ulica Piastowska to ulica Opacka; or take Tram 2 or 6 toward Sopot. ✉*ul. Cystersów 10, Oliwa.*

Two museums can be found in a beautiful park surrounding the cathedral in Oliwa in the former Abbots' Palace. The **Muzeum Sztuki Współczesnej** *(Modern Art Museum)* has a large collection of works by Polish artists from the inter-war period onward, and not just paintings:

there's a good collection of sculpture, ceramics, fabrics, and tapestry, as well as samples of works for the theater (mise-en-scène). Some names to look out for are Jan Tarasin, Henryk Stażewski, and Jan Sawka. Connected to the Modern Art Museum, administratively and physically, is the **Muzeum Etnograficzne** (*Ethnographic Museum* ⊠*ul. Opacka 12, Oliwa* ☎*058/552–12–71*), in the former Abbots' Granary. The museum displays many fine examples of local crafts from the 19th century and also has an interesting display of amber folk jewelry. It has a separate entrance from the Modern Art Museum and a separate admission fee, but the hours and other contact information are the same for both museums. ⊠*Pałac Opatów, Cystersów 15A, Oliwa* ☎*058/552–12–71* ⊕*www.muzeum.narodowe.gda.pl* ⊠*zł 8 for Modern Art Museum, zł 9 for Ethnographic Museum* ☉*Tues.–Sun. 9–4.*

WHERE TO EAT

Because the parts of the Tri-City (Gdańsk, Sopot, and Gdynia) are linked by good public transit, it's quite easy to dine in any of the three regardless of where you are staying. Be sure to consider restaurants in the other parts of the Tri-City as viable alternatives.

$$-$$$$
Fodor'sChoice
★
✕**Pod Łososiem.** "The Salmon" is certainly the most famous restaurant in Gdańsk, with a long-standing reputation. It is memorable for its elegant baroque-era dining rooms, well-oiled maître d', attentive service, and excellent seafood (the menu also extends to game and fowl dishes). Try the salmon or smoked eel to start, followed by flounder or grilled trout. You may want to try the famous Goldwasser vodka—after all, this is its original source. ⊠*ul. Szeroka 52/53* ☎*058/301–76–52* ⊟*AE, DC, MC, V.*

$$-$$$$
✕**Tawerna.** A scale-model sailing ship outside leads you into a series of wood-paneled dining rooms overlooking the Motława Canal. This is a pleasant place to linger over lunch or dinner. Tawerna's fresh trout is always reliable, but ask the polite, multilingual waitstaff about the fish of the day. The only complaints most diners have regard the price of the meal. Be aware, though, that this is a very touristy spot. ⊠*ul. Powroźnicza 19–20, off Długi Targ* ☎*058/301–41–14* ⊟*AE, DC, MC, V.*

$-$$$
✕**Czerwone Drzwi.** Behind the red door (that's what "Czerwone Drzwi" means in Polish) is a very elegant café-cum-restaurant, a favorite with Gdańsk's fashionable people (with well-stocked wallets). The atmosphere is a little posh but cozy all the same. The menu changes with seasons. Marinated herring is served in a variety of ways, and beefsteak with pepper in brandy is one of the trademark dishes. ⊠*ul. Piwna 52/53. Stare Miasto* ☎*058/301–57–64* ⊟*AE, DC, MC, V.*

★ $-$$
✕**Barracuda.** Although the interior may be rather simple—even a little dull—most people agree that this is one of the best restaurants in Gdańsk. The menu offers a tempting array of seafood dishes, which are the specialties of the house. Examples from the menu include pikeperch in dill sauce, or a sole-salmon duo served with spinach. No matter which you choose, you won't go wrong. Of course, there are also nonfish dishes, but who wants to eat chicken or beef in a fish restaurant in a seaport? ⊠*ul. Piwna 61/63, Stare Miasto* ☎*058/301–49–62* ⊟*AE, DC, MC, V.*

9

WHERE TO STAY

If you do not insist on staying in Gdańsk's Old Town, there are some great options of really classy hotels in beautiful surroundings in Gdańsk-Oliwa, Sopot, or Gdynia-Orłowo. The city transportation system makes it easy enough to travel between the important sights of the three cities, using the combination of convenient commuter trains and fairly inexpensive taxis.

★ $$$$ ⊞ **Hotel Podewils.** This luxurious hotel is located on the edge of the Old Town, opposite the Gdańsk Główny train station. Rooms are stylishly furnished and decorated, the staff are uniformly pleasant, and the facilities are up-to-date; each room includes such extras as a trouser press, a hair dryer, and a DVD player. Each bathroom is equipped with a Jacuzzi tub. ⊠*ul. Szafarnia 2, Stare Miasto, 80–755* ☎*058/300–95–60* 🖷*058/300–95–70* ⊕*www.podewils-hotel.pl* ◤*8 rooms, 2 suites* ⌂*Restaurant, minibars, in-room safes, cable TV, in-room broadband, sauna, bar* ⊟*AE, DC, MC, V* ⦿*BP.*

$$–$$$$ ⊞ **Dwór Oliwski.** This is easily one of the best hotels in Poland. A peace-
Fodor's Choice ful oasis of low, thatched buildings surround a renovated manor and
★ are themselves enveloped by lovely gardens, ponds, and vast woods (ask at the reception for a map of walking trails through Lasy Oliwskie). Large rooms are furnished with luxurious simplicity, and some ground-floor rooms have shuttered windows opening onto the garden. The hotel has its own spa facilities and an excellent French restaurant. ⊠*ul. Bytowska 4, Oliwa, 80–328* ☎*058/554–70–00* 🖷*058/554–70–10* ⊕*www.dwor-oliwski.com.pl* ◤*32 rooms, 8 suites* ⌂*Restaurant, minibars, cable TV, in-room broadband, pool, gym, hot tub, sauna, spa, bar, meeting rooms, free parking* ⊟*AE, DC, MC, V* ⦿*BP.*

★ $$–$$$ ⊞ **Hotel Hanza.** This hotel has the best location in town in a spanking new building set right on the Motława Canal. Though modern, the Hanza blends in with its surroundings nicely. All rooms are air-conditioned for those few weeks in summer when cooling off is really necessary. If you want to stay here, make your reservation as far in advance as possible, especially in peak season. ⊠*ul. Tokarska 6, Stare Miasto, 80–888* ☎*058/305–34–27* 🖷*058/305–33–86* ⊕*www.hanza-hotel.com.pl* ◤*53 rooms, 7 suites* ⌂*Restaurant, minibars, cable TV, in-room data ports, Wi-Fi, gym, hot tub, sauna, bar, laundry service, meeting rooms, free parking* ⊟*AE, DC, MC, V* ⦿*BP.*

NIGHTLIFE & THE ARTS

Although Sopot is where the Tri-City really goes to have fun, there's also good nightlife in Gdańsk. On summer nights, the Old Town teems with street musicians, families, and high-spirited young people. Look for the English-language publication *The Visitor* for information on more timely events. The **Cotton Club** (⊠*al. Złotników 25, Stare Miasto* ☎*058/301–88–13*) draws a mixed crowd to two levels of laid-back drinking and pool tables. The **Jazz Club** (⊠*Długi Targ 39/40, Stare Miasto*) has regular live jazz concerts and the best bar staff in town. **Kamienica** (⊠*ul. Mariacka 23, Stare Miasto*) is a popular bar decorated in murals showing the street outside.

SOPOT

12 km (7½ mi) north of Gdańsk.

Sopot is one of Poland's leading seaside holiday resorts, with miles of sandy beaches—in theory now safe for swimming (efforts are being made to deal with the Baltic's chronic pollution problems). Sopot enjoyed its heyday in the 1920s and '30s, when the wealthy flocked here to gamble and enjoy the town's demure, quiet atmosphere. Once the most elegant seaside resort in Poland, Sopot got a little too popular for its own good in the 1980s, when it began to look more down-at-heels. Today it is restoring its Riviera-like atmosphere. Much of Sopot's life transpires close to the Grand Hotel, which was once—and after the recent restoration, again—*the* place to stay in the area. Sopot's marvelous 19th-century pier is the longest on the Baltic.

The street of Bohaterów Monte Cassino (The Heroes of Monte Cassino), popularly referred to as **Monciak,** which stretches along the main urban axis of Sopot, is one of the most important streets in town. The original German name, Seestrasse (Sea Street), tells you everything you need to know about its purpose. Monciak is lined with numerous pubs, shops, restaurants, cinemas, and galleries as well as countless 19th- and 20th-century houses. In summer, it becomes a venue for itinerant street theaters, musicians, and artists.

When you're walking on Monciak, heading east toward the water, you'll pass through the pleasant **Plac Zdrojowy,** which is filled with outdoor cafés, flowers, fountains, and plenty of places to grab *lody* (ice cream). The **sculpture of a fisherman** is a reminder of Sopot's past as a small fishing village.

WHERE TO EAT

$–$$$ ✕ **Baola II.** The restaurant, which has a blue interior to evoke the sea, is in a former fishing cottage. In summer, the lovely and leafy garden terrace, though small, is very inviting. Duck in raspberry sauce and other excellent dishes are complemented with a decent wine list. ⊠ *ul. Grunwaldzka 27* ☎ *058/550–27–32* ⊟ *AE, MC, V.*

♻ $–$$ ✕ **Tivoli.** This restaurant opened in 2000 in a renovated, 19th-century building. Good Italian food—everything from pizza and pasta to meat and fish—is served in an elegant interior decorated with the colors of Italian flag. There is a special children's menu, and yes, it does include french fries. ⊠ *Bohaterów Monte Cassino 14/16* ☎ *058/555–04–10* ⊟ *AE, MC, V.*

$–$$ ✕ **Złoty Ul.** In the "Golden Beehive," cuisines of many different countries buzz about. You'll find Tex-Mex, Brazilian grilled meats, Mediterranean seafood dishes, and Spanish paella. With so many different cuisines, it comes as a bit of a surprise that the food is actually okay, and often quite a bit more than simply "okay." The great location on the Monciak promenade makes this a particularly attractive place in the summer, when you can sit on the terrace and watch a never-ending show. ⊠ *Bohaterów Monte Cassino 31/35* ☎ *058/555–14–81* ⊟ *AE, MC, V.*

9

WHERE TO STAY

★ $$$–$$$$ 🏨 **Grand Sopot by Sofitel.** The Grand is not only Sopot's best-known hotel, but also one of its best-known landmarks. Designed in the late 1920s, this spectacular neo-baroque structure used to house a casino, which in the mid-war period won the hotel both popularity and ill fame as well. Rumors of gamblers committing suicide both in the hotel itself and outside were willingly—and widely—spread. The hotel was completely renovated from top to bottom in 2006 and has regained much of its prewar splendor. Some renovation work continued at this writing. Rooms are furnished in a combination of modern and period style, but the result is very promising. ⊠*pl. Powstańców Warszawy 8–12, 81–718* ☎*058/551–00–41* 🖷*058/551–61–24* ⊕*www.orbis.pl* ⌑*127 rooms* ⚐*Restaurant, coffee shop, room service, cable TV, gym, hair salon, sauna, steam room, beach, billiards, 2 bars, casino, nightclub, dry cleaning, laundry service, business services, meeting rooms, some pets allowed* ▤*AE, DC, MC, V* ⎅*BP.*

★ $$$–$$$$ 🏨 **Hotel Rezydent.** This classy art nouveau hotel in the heart of Sopot is reminiscent of the grand old days, when Sopot was known as the Riviera of Poland. The rooms have all the expected modern amenities and are beautifully decorated: marble floors, crystal chandeliers, and flower-patterned upholstery on stylish furniture. ⊠*pl. Konstytucji 3 Maja 3, 81–704* ☎*058/555–58–00* 🖷*058/555–58–01* ⊕*www.hotel-rezydent.pl* ⌑*62 rooms, 3 suites* ⚐*Restaurant, café, room service, pub, in-room broadband, Wi-Fi, minibars, in-room safes, laundry service, gym, sauna, spa, meeting rooms, parking (free)* ▤*AE, DC, MC, V* ⎅*BP.*

$$$ 🏨 **Haffner Hotel.** If you like brushing against famous sports champions, movie stars, and models (albeit mostly European ones), the Haffner will be your scene. (Alas, the aura of fame may be in this case contagious—the staff can sometimes be as diffident as the movie stars.) Decor tends toward the rich and heavy (a lot of dark green and dark wood). There is a nice swimming pool, which incidentally does not smell of chlorine. The hotel bar, the Charlie Pub, does smell strongly of cigars, though. The restaurant offers a different, seasonal menu each month. ⊠*ul. Haffnera 59, 81–715, Sopot* ☎*058/550–99–99* 🖷*058/550–98–00* ⊕*www.hotelhaffner.pl* ⌑*100 rooms, 6 suites* ⚐*Restaurant, bar, room service, minibars, cable TV, Internet, gym, pool, hair salon, dry cleaning, laundry service, business services, meeting rooms, parking (fee)* ▤*AE, DC, MC, V* ⎅*BP.*

NIGHTLIFE & THE ARTS

Stroll down ulica Bohaterów Monte Cassino to find the café, pub, or nightclub of your choice. In August, the **Międzynarodowy Festiwal Piosenki** (International Song Festival) is held in the open-air concert hall (Muszla Koncertowa) in Skwer Kuracyjny in the center of town near the pier.

BARS & CLUBS

Sopot has a reputation as a rather extravagant and decadent nightlife scene. Especially in summer, the parties go on long into the night, perhaps until the early morning. The crowds are mostly young, and the parties are mostly cheerfully loud and chaotic (more like a spring-break scene). If this is not your style, then you should avoid the beachside locations in the summer.

Mandarynka (✉ *ul. Bema 6* ☎*058/550–45–63*) is a fashionable bar-cum-club with plenty of comfy sofas where you can simply chill out. Model types tend to congregate at **Number 5** (✉*Bohaterów Monte Cassino 5* ☎*058/550–49–44*). **Viva Club** (✉*al. F. Mamuszki 2* ☎*058/551–53–23*) is a giant, two-level club on the beach with six bars, two dance floors, a stage with catwalk, and a beach terrace for warm weather. It tends to draw a young crowd, particularly for the frequent student parties. **Sfinks** (✉*pl. Powstańców Warszawy 18* ☎*058/550–48–79*) is a modern, avant-garde club. During the summer season there are many live concerts, and when the music is not live, there's always a DJ. It's closed Monday–Wednesday. With a strong Asian theme, the **Siouxie 9** (✉*Bohaterów Monte Cassino 9* ☎*048/508–128–281*) begins the day as a quiet coffee bar, but as night falls, it turns into a popular bohemian hangout.

OPERA

The **Opera Leśna** (*Forest Opera* ✉*Moniuszki 12* ☎*058/555–84–00*) produced a series of famous Wagner concerts during the interwar period, garnering Sopot the title of "Little Bayreuth." The open-air amphitheater (the seating area is partially covered by a roof) is one of the most beautiful outdoor performing arts venues in Europe and has excellent acoustics. The theater complex, which covers nearly 10 acres, can seat 4,400; the orchestra pit alone can accommodate 110 musicians. Both classical and popular music concerts are given throughout the summer, but the theater also hosts many of Sopot's performing arts festivals. This is the venue for the **Sopot Festival**—a fixture on the Sopot summer calendar since the 1960s—and the **Opera Festival,** which was organized to continue the Wagner series. The theater also hosts the International Song Festival.

MALBORK CASTLE

45 km (28 mi) southeast of Gdańsk.

★ One of the most impressive strongholds of the Middle Ages, the huge Zamek w Malborku (Malbork Castle) is the central feature of the quiet town of Malbork (the former German city of Marienburg). In 1230, the Teutonic Knights arrived on the banks of the Vistula River and settled here, aiming to establish their own state on these conquered Prussian lands. The castle passed into Polish hands after the second Toruń Treaty in 1466 concluded the 13-year war between the Poles and the Order of Teutonic Knights. For the next three centuries, Malbork served as the royal residence for Polish kings during their annual visit to Pomerania. The castle was half destroyed during World War II, after which the building underwent a major renovation. Two-hour guided tours offer the best way to see the castle; tours are available in English, and there's an English-language guidebook in the gift shop. You can easily see the castle on a day trip from Gdańsk, but there is a hotel on the castle grounds if you want to spend the night. ⊠*Rte. 50, Malbork* ☎*055/647–09–78* ⊕*www.zamek.malbork.pl* ⚏*zł25* ☉*May–Sept., Tues.–Sun. 9–7; Oct.–Apr., Tues.–Sun. 9–3.*

WHERE TO STAY

$–$$ ⊞ **Hotel Zamek.** The hotel in Malbork's Lower Castle opened in 1993 in a restored medieval building. It's perhaps not as exciting as you might expect given the magnificent surroundings. The decor makes an attempt at re-creating "old-style" rooms, but unfortunately, the faux-medieval look ends up not being very authentic or stylish. Having said that, dark wood and slightly gloomy atmosphere somehow fit in the context, and of course the location is unbeatable. ⊠*ul. Starościńska 14, 82–200* ☎*055/272–33–67* ⊕*www.hotel-zamek.e-tur.com.pl* ⟿*42 rooms* ♿*3 restaurants, café, cable TV, meeting rooms, parking (free).*

BALTIC COAST & POMERANIA ESSENTIALS

AIR TRAVEL

Gdańsk has the main airport in northeastern Poland with regular service, both domestic and international (LOT, Lufthansa, Norwegian, SAS, and Wizzair flights). The airport is expanding, and the number of connections is growing. *For airline contact information, see* ⇨*Poland Essentials, below.*

AIRPORTS

Gdańsk's airport is 16 km (10 mi) out of town in Rębiechowo and can be reached by Bus B (night Bus N3) from the center of Gdańsk, or Bus 510 from Gdynia, or by taxi (about 40 złto Gdańsk, 70 złto Gdynia).

Information **Gdańsk Lech Wałęsa Airport** (⊠ *Słowackiego 200, Gdańsk-Rębiechowo* ☎*058/348–11–63* ⊕ *www.airport.gdansk.pl*). **Interglobus Tour** (☎*091/485–04–22* ⊕*www.interglobus.pl*).

BOAT & FERRY TRAVEL

In summer there are pleasure cruises on the Motława River and the Baltic, and an hourly water-bus service links Gdańsk with Sopot and Gdynia, via Westerplatte and Hel.

Information **Gdańsk Water-Bus Station** (⊠ *Długie Pobrzeże, near Brama Zielona, Gdańsk* ☎*058/301–49–26*). **Gdynia Water-Bus** (⊠ *al. Zjednoczenia 2, Gdynia* ☎*058/620–21–54*). **Polferries** (⊠ *Small Terminal Nowy Port, Przemysłowa 1, Gdańsk* ☎*058/343–00–78* ⊕*www.polferries.pl* ⊠ *Main terminal, Portowa 3, Gdynia* ☎*058/620–87–61*). **Sopot Water-Bus** (⊠ *Sopot Pier, Sopot* ☎*058/551–12–93*). **Stena Line** (⊠ *Kwiatkowskiego 60, Gdynia* ☎*058/665–14–14* ⊕*www.stenaline.pl*).

BUS TRAVEL

Gdańsk is the major gateway for the Baltic coast and northeastern Poland. Gdańsk's PKS bus station is right next to the main train station. Buses may be useful for those who want to venture to small towns off the beaten track since PKS buses link all the small towns of the region; otherwise, trains are more frequent and more comfortable.

A regular service runs throughout the Tri-City area, taking you from Gdańsk through Oliwa and Sopot to Gdynia. The whole trip takes about 1¾ hours. The buses run from 5 AM to 11 PM; after 11 PM there is an hourly night-bus service.

Information Gdańsk PKS Bus Station (✉ *ul. 3 Maja, Gdańsk* ☎ *058/302-15-32* ⊕ *www.pks.gdansk.pl*).

CAR TRAVEL

From Warsaw, Route 7 (E77), a two-lane road for part of its length, goes directly to Gdańsk. From the west, the quickest route to the coast from the border crossing at Frankfurt/Oder is to take Route 2 (E30) to Poznań and then Route 5 (E261) via Gniezno and Bydgoszcz to Świecie, where it becomes Route 1 (E75) and continues via Tczew to the coast.

The road network in this part of Poland is relatively well developed, and there are plenty of gas stations. Although Gdańsk's Stare Miasto (Old Town) and Główne Miasto (Main Town) areas are easily walkable, a car is useful if you wish to visit other parts of the Tri-City region, such as Sopot and the museums and cathedral at Oliwa, or sights farther afield, though all of these are linked by the Gdańsk area transit system.

Information Avis Gdańsk Airport (✉ *ul. Słowackiego 200, Gdańsk-Rębiechowo* ☎ *058/348-12-89* ⊕ *www.avis.pl* ✉ *Gdańsk City Center, ul. Podwale Grodzkie 9, Gdańsk*). **Budget Gdańsk Airport** (✉ *ul. Słowackiego 200, Gdańsk-Rębiechowo* ☎ *058/348-12-98* ⊕ *www.budget.pl*). **Hertz Gdańsk** (✉ *ul. Brygidki 14b, Gdańsk* ☎ *058/301-40-45* ⊕ *www.hertz.com.pl*). **Joka Rent-a-Car** (✉ *Mercure Hevelius Hotel, ul. Heweliusza 22, Gdańsk* ☎ *058/320-56-46* ⊕ *www.joka.com.pl*).

INTERNET

Internet Cafés Crist@l Internet (✉ *ul. Armii Krajowej 13Gdynia* ☎ *048/504-666-993*). **Jazz 'n' Java** (✉ *ul. Tkacka 17/18, Gdańsk* ☎ *058/305-36-16*). **Netcave** (✉ *ul. Pułaskiego 7a, Sopot* ☎ *058/555-11-83*).

TAXIS

Just as in any other Polish city, it is always better to use a network radio taxi—they are cheaper and more reliable. There are few, if any, taxis, in smaller towns and resorts.

Information Taxis in Gdańsk & Vicinity (☎ *058/9624, 058/9686, 058/306-00-00, or 058/9195*).

TOUR OPTIONS

Żegluga Gdańska operates between Tri-City, Westerplatte, and Hel peninsula, and arranges sightseeing trips through the Bay of Gdańsk.

Information Gdańsk Ticket Sales (✉ *Brama Zielona, at eastern end of Długi Targ, Gdańsk* ☎ *058/301-49-26*). **Sopot Ticket Sales and Pier** (✉ *Sopot Pier, Sopot* ☎ *058/551-12-93*). **Żegluga Gdańska** Main Office (✉ *ul. Pończoszników 2, Gdynia* ☎ *058/301-63-35*).

TRAIN TRAVEL

The main station in the Tri-City area is Gdańsk Główny. Many daily trains leave here for Warsaw (four hours), Kraków (eight hours), Poznań (four hours), and Malbork (take the train to Warsaw, which stops in Malbork; local trains can take ages). All the towns of the region can be reached by train. Within the Tri-City area, a fast electric-train service runs every 15 minutes from Gdańsk Główny via Oliwa, Sopot, and Gdynia to Wejherowo. The service operates from 4 AM to 1 AM.

Information Gdańsk Główny (⊠ *ul. Podwale Grodzkie 1, Gdańsk* ☎ *058/94–36*). **Tri-City Fast City Rail** (*PKP Szybka Kolej Miejska w Trójmieście* ☎ *058/721–21–70* ⊕ *www.skm.pkp.pl*).

VISITOR INFORMATION

Information Agencja Infomacji Turystycznej Gdańsk (⊠ *ul. Długa 45, Gdańsk* ☎ *058/301–93–27*).

Malbork Tourist Office (⊠ *ul. Piastowska 15, Malbork* ☎ *091/273–49–90*).

SILESIA

Occupying the southwest corner of Poland, Silesia was an independent duchy ruled by the Polish Piast dynasty in the Middle Ages, but from the 14th century on it was claimed by a succession of monarchs, including rulers of the Holy Roman Empire, Austria, Bohemia, and Prussia. As if this weren't complicated enough, in the 18th century, Prussia and Austria actually fought over the rule of Silesia. Its more contemporary borders—closer approximations of the state as it exists today—were not set until the 20th century, first after World War I and then, finally, after World War II. The new map of Europe—which was finalized by Roosevelt, Churchill, and Stalin—placed most of Silesia within Poland, and Poland's western and eastern Polish borders shifted west. The majority of the prewar ethnic German population was "repatriated" back to German territory. Some parts of southern Silesia were incorporated into Czechoslovakia (now the Czech Republic) and Germany; along the way, some border towns were divided in two and remain living remainders of the region's tumultuous history. Polish Zgorzelec faces the German Görlitz across the river Nysa, and the Olza River divides Polish Cieszyn from Czech Tešin.

The city of Wrocław is the uncontested cultural center of Lower Silesia. It has many attractions of its own and is also a good starting point for day trips into the mountains, smaller towns, and villages. Częstochowa (where you'll find the shrine of Black Madonna), though techically part of Silesia, can also be visited as a day trip from Kraków.

TIMING

The best time to visit Silesia is between May and October, when the weather is most pleasant. This is also when many cultural events and festivals are scheduled. Film fans might want to plan their trip in the last week of July, when Wrocław's "Era New Horizons" Film Festival

takes place. Music fans might want to consider the schedules of the Great Symphony Orchestra of Polish Radio & TV at Katowice, or the Silesian Opera in Wrocław. The latter city offers a seemingly never-ending string of interesting cultural festivals throughout the spring, summer, and early fall. Pilgrims arrive to Częstochowa throughout the year, but the gatherings of the faithful peak in August.

WROCŁAW

350 km (220 mi) southwest of Warsaw, 260 km (165 mi) northwest of Kraków.

Midway between Kraków and Poznań on the Odra River, Wrocław is the capital of Dolny Śląsk (Lower Silesia). The city was founded in the 10th century, when the Ostrów Tumski islet on the Odra became a fortified Slav settlement. There are now some 100 bridges spanning the city's 90-km (56-mi) network of slow-moving canals and tributaries, giving Wrocław its particular charm.

Wrocław—until after World War II known by its German name, Breslau—is an important piece in the jigsaw puzzle of European history. Although postwar Polish Communist authorities tried to erase its past, Wrocław was a German city for much of its existence. The Germanic heritage can still be seen today, notably in the city's architecture and infrastructure.

WHAT TO SEE
Following the destruction that ravaged Wrocław during World War II, many of the city's historic buildings were restored. Wrocław's architectural attractions are its many brick Gothic churches, the majority of which lie in or around the Stare Miasto (Old Town) and Ostrów Tumski, an island in the Odra River. This area is small enough to explore easily on foot. Within a 15-minute drive (or a tram ride) to the east is the famous Centennial Hall by Max Berg and the charming Japanese garden, and the old Jewish cemetery lies within a similar distance, directly south of the old town center.

Fodor'sChoice
★ The **Rynek** *(Market Square) and* the adjoining Plac Solny (Salt Square) form the heart of the Old Town, which stretches between the Fosa Miejska moat and the Odra River. This market square is almost as grand as Kraków's. In the summer it is filled to the brim with sidewalk cafés and street performers. ⊠*Stare Miasto.*

Just off the square to the northwest, the little **Jaś i Małgosia** *(Hansel and Gretel Houses)* are linked by a baroque arcade—holding hands, so to speak. ⊠*Odrzańska and Wita Stwosza, Stare Miasto.*

The magnificently ornate **Ratusz** *(City Hall)* is the highlight of the market square. Mostly Gothic in style, with a dash of Renaissance and baroque thrown in, the town hall was under continuous construction from the 14th to the 16th century as Wrocław grew and prospered. In the center of the spired, pinnacled, and gabled east facade is a Renaissance **astronomical clock** from 1580; the **Gothic portal** was the main entrance of the Ratusz until 1616. The lavish south facade, dating from the 15th and 16th century, swarms with delicately wrought sculptures, friezes, reliefs, and oriels. Today the town hall houses the **Historical Museum of Wrocław**, which is well worth visiting for its interiors. ⊠*Sukiennice 9, Stare Miasto* ☏*071/344–36–38* ⊡*Museum zł6* ☉*Museum Wed.–Fri. 10–4, weekends 10–5.*

★ The massive 14th-century **Kościół świętej Marii Magdaleny** *(St. Mary Magdalene's Church)* has a 12th-century **Romanesque portal** on the south wall that is considered the finest example of Romanesque architecture in Poland. ⊠*Corner of Szewska and Łaciarska, 1 block east of market square, Stare Miasto.*

The 14th-century brick **Kościół świętej Elżbiety** *(Church of St. Elizabeth)* was ravaged by fires in 1975 and 1976 and reopened only in the late 1990s. You can brave the 302-step climb to the top of the **tower** and look inside at the magnificent organ. The church can be reached through the arcade linking the Hansel and Gretel houses. ⊠*Kiełbaśnicza, at św Elżbiety, Stare Miasto.*

Fodor'sChoice
★ **Uniwersytet Wrocławski** *Wrocław University).* Wrocław's university district lies between ulica Uniwersytecka and the river. The university's main building, which dates from the 18th century, was built by Habsburg Emperor Leopold I on the site of the west wing of the former prince's castle. Behind the fountain and up the staircase is the magnificent assembly hall, **Aula Leopoldina**. The Aula is decorated with illusionist frescoes and life-size sculptures of great philosophers and patrons of learning, and allegories of arts and sciences. Climb farther up to the **Mathematical Tower** (sometimes called Astronomers' Tower) for great views of Wrocław's rooftops. ⊠*Plac Uniwersytecki 1, Stare Miasto* ☏*No phone* ⊡*zł4.50* ☉*Oct.–Apr., Thurs.–Tues. 10–3:30; May–Sept., Mon., Tues., Thurs. 10–3:30, Fri.–Sun. 11–5.*

North of the university district, the Most Piaskowy (Sand Bridge) connects the left bank of the Odra with **Wyspa Piasek** *(Sand Island).* On the island directly across from the Sand Bridge is a former Augustinian monastery used as Nazi headquarters during World War II; the building is now the **University Library**. The 14th-century **Kościół Najświętszej Marii Panny** (St. Mary's Church) is in the middle of the island. The church's Gothic interior was restored after World War II; it has a lofty vaulted ceiling and brilliant stained-glass windows. ⊠ *Wyspa Piasek, Stare Miasto.*

★ The 13th-century **Katedra świętego Jana Chrzciciela** *(Cathedral of St. John the Baptist)*, with its two truncated towers, is the focal point of Cathedral Island. Its chancel is the earliest example of Gothic architecture in Poland. The cathedral houses the largest organ in the country, with 10,000 pipes. On the southern side of the cathedral is **St. Elizabeth's Chapel;** a bust of Cardinal Frederick above the entrance, along with numerous other sculptures and frescoes, came from the studio of Gian Lorenzo Bernini. The **Elector's Chapel,** in the northwestern corner of the cathedral, dates from the early 18th century and was designed by the baroque architect Johann Fischer von Erlach of Vienna. As these chapels are often closed, check at the sacristy for an update as well as for admission fees to climb to the top of the towers. ⊠ *Plac Katedralny, Ostrów Tumski* 🖃*zł5 for Tower* ☉*Cathedral daily 10–7; Tower Apr.– Oct., daily 10–5:30.*

★ Behind the cathedral and through a narrow lane to the north is **Ogród Botaniczny** *(Botanical Garden)*, established in the early 19th century. Scattered around the garden among beautiful plants you will find some interesting artworks and monuments—one of them commemorating Brahms, who once visited the garden. (He would be happy to hear that there are classical music concerts in the Botanical Garden every Sunday throughout the summer.) The best time to visit is perhaps late spring: azaleas bloom in the second half of May, peonies and lilies in June. The latter bear fantastic names such as Bacon Gold Nugget, Sometimes Alleluia, or Muscle Man. ⊠ *Sienkiewicza 23, Ostrów Tumski* 🕾*No phone* 🖃*Free* ☉*Apr.–Oct, daily 8–6.*

Racławice Panorama. Today, this panoramic war portrait, 15 meters high and 114 meters long, is the city's biggest and most visited painting, the joint work of Wojciech Kossak and Jan Styka. After World War II the painting came to Wrocław from Lviv, which ceased to be a Polish city and was incorporated into the Soviet Union (now independent Ukraine). For Poles, the Panorama is deeply symbolic in many ways since it depicts the legendary victory of General Tadeusz Kościuszko over the Russians in 1794. With more than 1,500 visitors per day, you have to queue to get in (it would be smart to book your ticket in advance) and admire this circular painting with a crowd of other tourists. ⊠ *Purkyniego 11, Stare Miasto* ⊕*www.panoramaraclawicka.pl* 🖃*zł20* ☉*May–Sept., daily 9–4; Oct.–Apr., Tues.–Sun. 9–4. .*

Fodor's Choice **Hala Ludowa** *(Centennial Hall)*. Featuring prominently in textbooks
★ of architecture students around the world—and now recognized as a UNESCO World Heritage Site—the Centennial Hall was erected between 1911 and 1913 by Max Berg, who was the municipal architect in Breslau. With its amazing reinforced concrete structure, exposed and free from any redundant decorations, the hall is considered a pioneer-

9

ing work of modern engineering and architecture of the early 20th century. This multipurpose recreational building sits in the middle of the Exhibition Grounds. It has a form of a symmetrical quatrefoil with a vast circular central space (215 feet around and 139 feet high) capable of seating 6,000. The dome is topped with a lantern in steel and glass. To improve the acoustics, the walls are covered with an insulating layer of concrete mixed with wood or cork. And the acoustics are amazing indeed. If you cannot take in a concert or another performance here, try it yourself. Stand in the middle of the stage and clap your hands or sing a song. ⊠ *Wystawowa 1, Szczytniki* 🖃*zł5* ☉*Daily 8–7.*

Fodor'sChoice   **Japanese Garden.** Wrocław's Japanese Garden, designed by Fritz von
   ★   Hochberg and Mankichi Arai, opened in 1913 as a part of the Centennial Exhibition—and it was thoroughly restored in 1996 with the aid of Japanese experts. They gave it the name "Hakkōen" ("white and red"), in a reference to the national colors of Poland and Japan. Complete with ponds and waterfalls, a tea ceremony pavilion and arched wooden bridges, it is a lovely place to rest and meditate under the gingko and katsura trees, cedars and cypresses, rare hornbeam maples, and over-100-year-old oaks. ⊠*Park Szczytnicki, Szczytniki* 🖃*zł5* ☉*Daily 9–7.*

▌ NEED A
BREAK?   **Manufaktura Czekolady** (⊠ *Więzienna 31 [corner of Igielna street]* 🖀*mobile only [48] 601–537–255* ☉*Sun.–Tues. noon–8:30, Wed.–Sat. noon–10:30 PM*), the cozy "Chocolate Factory," has chocolate-colored chairs and wallpapers, but more important, excellent homemade chocolates and great coffee.

WHERE TO EAT

Most restaurants in Wrocław, including those listed here, are concentrated in the Market Square or one of the streets immediately surrounding it. Whether you choose Polish or Spanish, Japanese, or French cuisine, you won't have to walk far—different establishments are virtually door-to-door.

$–$$$$ ✕**Casablanca.** The eyes of Humphrey Bogart and Ingrid Bergman follow you from every corner in this film-themed restaurant serving mostly Continental cuisine with several—albeit few and shy—"exotic" additions. On the whole, in Casablanca, it is better to stick to the classics: a carpaccio or a steak is a safer bet than shrimp in coconut. In the summer, the restaurant patio, complete with a fountain in the middle, is one of the most pleasant retreats from the heat in all of Wrocław. The dessert menu features excellent strawberry *granite* with champagne and vanilla ice cream with black pepper. ⊠ *Włodkowica 8a, Stare Miasto* 🖀*071/344–78–17* 🖃*AE, DC, MC, V.*

$–$$$$ ✕**JaDka.** The interior of this elegant restaurant is comfortably luxurious: vaulted ceilings, redbrick walls, tables covered with white linen,
Fodor'sChoice   white candles, and fresh white flowers. The waitstaff are super-atten-
   ★   tive and efficient, so the service is excellent. On the menu is a mix of traditional Polish dishes and their Mediterranean cousins: Spanish gazpacho as well as Polish *barszcz* (borscht) and saddle of deer

with Silesian dumplings, and wonderful homemade *pierogi* alongside typical Italian pasta dishes. This is a good place to sample venison—or anything else that takes your fancy. ⊠*Rzeźnicza 24/25, Stare Miasto* ☎*071/343–64–61* ⊟*AE, DC, MC, V.*

$–$$$ ✕**Gospoda Wrocławska.** This popular, traditional Polish restaurant is right in the heart of Wrocław. The interior is wood-clad and medieval-looking, and although the food is heavy, it is also tasty. At the core of the menu you will find roasts, pork chops, pig's feet, steaks, venison, and other meat dishes. Adjoining the restaurant is a shop where you can buy take-out sandwiches and other products, mostly made on the premises. ⊠*Sukiennice 6, Stare Miasto* ☎*071/342–74–56* ⊟*AE, DC, MC, V.*

WHERE TO STAY

$$
Fodor's Choice
★

☷**Art Hotel.** The charming Art Hotel is true to its name. Located in a carefully restored, furnished, and decorated series of combined 14th- and 15th-century tenement houses, it hides some amazing original pieces: fragments of wall paintings and coats of arms, wooden beams, decorated doors and stairways. The rooms are tasteful and warm, and each is a little different. Nice service touches include homemade cookies as you check in. Works by contemporary Polish artists are displayed in the hallways (in keeping with the theme), and the in-house restaurant is justly considered one of Wrocław's best. ⊠*Kiełbaśnicza 20, 50–110, Stare Miasto* ☎*071/787–71–00* ♨*071/342–39–29* ⊕*www.arthotel. pl* ↘*75 rooms, 3 suites* ⚭*Restaurant, minibars, cable TV, in-room broadband, gym, bar, meeting rooms* ⊟*AE, DC, MC, V* ⊺◎❙*BP.*

★ $–$$
☷**Hotel Tumski.** This hotel has a picturesque location on the island of Wyspa Słodowa, just across the bridge from Ostrów Tumski, another of Wrocław's many islands. Although the rooms are pretty standard, the hotel building itself has a long history; in the 1920s, it was the seat of the Rheno Palatia, the German students' corporation. It's been a hotel only since 2000; still, it draws a wide range of travelers looking for decent accommodations at fair prices. Every year the hotel management and staff organize a truly impressive series of events, including a punting regatta on the Oder and picnics in the Botanical Garden. Hotel Tumski also organizes standard and specialized tours throughout the region. ⊠*Wyspa Słodowa 10, 50–277, Stare Miasto* ☎*071/322–60–88* ♨*071/322–61–13* ⊕*www.hotel-tumski.com.pl* ↘*55 rooms, 2 suites* ⚭*Restaurant, minibars, cable TV, Wi-Fi, bar, meeting rooms, parking (free); no a/c* ⊟*AE, DC, MC, V* ⊺◎❙*BP.*

★ $
☷**Hotel Europeum.** Property of Krzyżowa Foundation for Mutual Understanding in Europe, this modern B&B rises to a very comfortable standard in its 20 rooms, although officially the hotel carries only a modest two stars. Europeum has an excellent location: a five-minute walk from the Market Square and one minute from a nine-screen Helios cinema. Although it is on a busy street, the windows are soundproof, and the a/c (certainly not a given in local hotels) is super efficient. Some rooms overlook a lovely Zen-like terrace covered with river stones. ⊠*Kazimierza Wielkiego 27a, 50–077, Stare Miasto* ☎*071/371–45–00* ♨*071/371–44–01* ⊕*www.europeum.pl* ↘*20 rooms* ⚭*Restaurant,*

9

refrigerators, cable TV, in-room broadband, bar ▤*AE, DC, MC, V* ¶⊚|*BP.*

SHOPPING

Souvenir shops, bookshops, and galleries are scattered around the Old Town, especially in the vicinity of the Market Square and Kiełbaśnicza, Świdnicka, and Oławska streets. Most shops are open Monday through Saturday, from 10 AM to 6 PM. **Galeria Dominikańska** (⊠ *Plac Dominikański 3* ☎ *71/344–95–17*) is a conveniently located department store/mall with a selection of fashion, cosmetics, and food stores, and it is even open on Sunday.

NIGHTLIFE & THE ARTS

Wrocław hosts a great number of festivals, many of them throughout the summer. One of the most renowned of Wrocław's festivals is **Jazz on the Odra** (⊕ *www.jnofestival.pl*), a summertime event that has attracted an international group of performers for more than 40 years. **Wratislavia Cantans** (⊕ *www.wratislavia.art.pl*) is a series of concerts (usually a week in June and a week in September) featuring Gregorian chants, German oratorios, operas, cantatas, and other choral performances. Concerts take place at different points in the city.

If you get tired of the bars around the market square try the **Kalambur** (⊠ *Kuźnicza 29A, Stare Miasto* ☎ *071/343–26–50*). This art nouveau-esque café-bar is attached to a small, well-known theater, where you can sometimes hear live music. The **Pasaż Niepolda** (⊠ *Between Ruska, św. Antoniego, and Kazimierza Wielkiego streets*) is not so much a "passage" as a large and colorful courtyard filled with bars, clubs, and cafés on some 110,000 square feet, situated only 990 feet from the Rynek. This is the place to head in the evening for live music, loud conversation, drinking, or dancing. Most of these clubs open at around 5 or 6 PM and stay open until 2 AM (longer on Saturday nights).

The **Wrocław Philharmonic** (⊠ *Piłsudskiego 19, Stare Miasto* ☎ *071/342–20–01* ⊕ *www.filharmonia.wroclaw.pl*) hosts classical performances several times each week.

Wrocławski Teatr Lalek (⊠ *Plac Teatralny 4, Stare Miasto* ☎ *071/344–12–17*) is widely regarded as the best puppet theater in Poland.

CZĘSTOCHOWA

90 km (56 mi) north of Katowice, 130 km (81 mi) from Kraków.

Częstochowa is known to all Poles as place of residence of the "Queen of Poland," as Virgin Mary has been called since the 18th century. The icon of the Black Madonna is believed to be miraculous, and it attracts thousands of pilgrims every year. The monastery complex, where the painting is kept, is best visited as a day or half-day trip from Kraków or Katowice—just as well, because there's not much to see here otherwise.

Fodor's Choice ★ An estimated 5 million pilgrims a year make their way—some on foot—to the town of Częstochowa. They come to visit the 14th-century

Klasztor Paulinów *(Pauline Monastery)* at the Jasna Góra (Hill of Light). The town itself grew with the monastery, and there is little else to draw visitors here. Although the Communist government planted industry here in the hope of overshadowing the cult, it didn't work. There's still but one reason why masses of people come to this city. Inside the monastery is Poland's holiest shrine, home to the *Black Madonna of Częstochowa,* a wood-pane painting of a dark-skinned Madonna and child, the origins of which are uncertain (legend attributes the work to Luke the Apostle himself, but it may have been painted anytime between the 6th and 14th century, anywhere between Byzantium and Hungary). The Black Madonna has a number of miracles attributed to it, including the repulsion of invading Swedish forces in the 16th century, and its designation as savior of Poland dates from those turbulent days. To see the Black Madonna up close, you have to join the faithful and walk on your knees around the chapel and behind a screen, where the eyes, according to believers, will fix directly on you. There are often times during the day when the icon is veiled, but these are irregular and hard to predict. The monastery was rebuilt in baroque style during the 17th and 18th centuries, as was the interior of the Gothic church. The **Monastery Treasury** holds an important collection of manuscripts and works of art. ⊠*al. Najświętszej Marii Panny 1* ☎*No phone* ⌨*Free* ☉*Basilica daily 5* AM*–9:30* PM *(icon unveiled at 6* AM*). Treasury daily 11–1 and 3–5.*

WHERE TO STAY & EAT

★ $–$$ ✗**Pod Aniołami.** A mere 330 feet down from the main gate of the monastery, "Under the Angels" serves unsophisticated yet tasty traditional Polish dishes in a pleasant wooden interior with a fireplace. Meat with Silesian dumplings accompanied by fresh and pickled salads is a good choice, and the chicken soup with homemade noodles is excellent. ⊠*7 Kamienic 21* ☎*034/322–93–08* ☰*AE, DC, MC, V.*

$–$ ✗**Wiking.** You can take in the local color at this crowded restaurant, which offers Polish, Swedish, and Chinese food—or at least a local version. The specialties are mostly meat dishes, notably the beef with asparagus. ⊠*Nowowiejskiego 10/12* ☎*034/324–57–68* ☰*No credit cards.*

$$ 🏨**Mercure Patria Częstochowa.** This six-story 1980s hotel, which is owned by Accor's Mercure group and managed by Orbis, offers predictable cuisine and accommodations close to the Jasna Góra Monastery. Rooms are brightly furnished and comfortable, and the staff is cheerful and friendly. ⊠*Popiełuszki 2, 42–200* ☎*034/324–70–01* 🖷*034/324–63–32* ⊕*www.mercure.com* ↘*90 rooms, 12 suites* ♤*2 restaurants, Wi-Fi, tennis court, volleyball, bar, meeting rooms; no a/c* ☰*AE, DC, MC, V* ⏲*BP.*

SILESIA ESSENTIALS

AIR TRAVEL

There are two international airports in Silesia. The larger is the Katowice (Pyrzowice) Airport (33 km/20 mi north of the city), the smaller one in Wrocław (approximately 10 km/6 mi west of the city center).

Both serve domestic and international (intra-Europe, but not intercontinental) flights. Some airlines—notably Lufthansa and Wizzair, for whom Katowice is the main Polish base—fly to Katowice year-round; several other airlines offer only seasonal service; and some charter companies also fly into Katowice. Lufthansa, LOT, Norwegian, Ryanair, and Wizzair fly directly into Wrocław.

AIRPORTS & TRANSFERS

There is regularly scheduled bus service between Katowice and its airport via the Lotnisko Airport Bus, which also serves some smaller towns in the area. Regular shuttles operated by Matuszek in coordination with Wizzair go into Kraków.

City Buses 406 and 117—as well as an airport shuttle—operate between the airport and railway station in Wrocław.

Information Katowice-Pyrzowice International Airport (⊠ *Wolności 90, Ożarowice* ☎ *032/392–73–85* ⊕ *www.gtl.com.pl*). **Matuszek** (☎ *032/236–11–11* ⊕ *www.matuszek.com.pl*). **Copernicus Airport Wrocław** (⊠ *Skarżyńskiego 36, Wrocław* ☎ *071/358–10–00* ⊕ *www.airport.wroclaw.pl*).

BUS TRAVEL

Buses are usually slower and less convenient than trains, but they are often indispensable for local travel, especially to smaller towns and villages. The PKS Katowice bus station is about 1,650 feet north of the main railway station and has local, domestic, and international bus connections. The Wrocław Bus Terminal is at the back (south side) of the Main Railway Station.

Information Wrocław Bus Terminal (⊠ *Sucha 1* ☎ *0300–300–122* ⊕ *www.polbus.pl*).

CAR TRAVEL

The A4 motorway connects Kraków with Katowice and Wrocław (via Opole). Most car-rental companies are located at the airports.

Information Avis (☎ *601/354–812 in Katowice, 601/354–811 in Wrocław*). **Budget** (☎ *032/284–50–11 in Katowice, 071/353–77–50 in Wrocław*). **Europcar** (☎ *032/284–50–86 in Katowice, 071/358–12–91 in Wrocław*). **Hertz** (☎ *032/284–51–03 in Katowice, 071/353–77–43 in Wrocław*).

INTERNET

Internet Cafés Cyber Tea Tavern/Pod Kalamburem (⊠ *Kuźnicza 29a, Wrocław* ☎ *071/372–35–71*). **Galaxy** (⊠ *Kazimierza Wielkiego 55, Wrocław* ☎ *071/374–61–14*). **Xtreme Internet Café** (⊠ *Al. NPM 65a, Częstochowa* ☎ *034/368–36–89*).

TAXIS

Calling a taxi is usually cheaper than catching one in the street. Beware of private taxis outside stations and airports; their rates can be exorbitant. It is wise to stick to well-known taxi companies with four-digit phone numbers preceded by the right city code. Be aware that many taxi companies have the same four-digit number in several cities, where the only difference is the city code.

Częstochowa Taxis Echo Taxi (⊠ *Częstochowa* ☎ *34/9625*).

Wrocław Taxis **Radio Taxi Blues** (✉ *Wrocław* ☎ *071/9661*). **Super Taxi** (✉ *Wrocław* ☎ *071/9663*). **City Radio Taxi** (✉ *Wrocław* ☎ *071/9662*).

TRAIN TRAVEL

Several daily trains connect Wrocław and Katowice, and most of these continue to Kraków. From Katowice you can also go up to Częstochowa. Wrocław also has good connections with Warsaw (some via Łódź) and Poznań.

Information Katowice Dworzec Główny (✉ *pl. Szewczyka 1, Katowice* ☎ *032/94-36* ⊕ *www.rozklad.pkp.pl*). **Wrocław Główny** (✉ *Piłsudskiego, Wrocław* ☎ *071/94-36* ⊕ *www.rozklad.pkp.pl*).

VISITOR INFORMATION

Information Częstochowa–Jasna Góra Information Center (✉ *Kordeckiego 2, Częstochowa* ☎ *034/365-38-88* ⊕ *www.jasnagora.pl*). **Wrocław Tourist Information** (✉ *Rynek 14, Wrocław* ☎ *071/344-31-11* ⊕ *www.wroclaw.pl*).

POZNAŃ & WIELKOPOLSKA

Historically, Wielkopolska (Great Poland), which neighbors Dolny Śląsk (Lower Silesia) on the south, and Kujawy and Pomorze on the north, is the oldest part of the Polish state. Gniezno, the first capital of Poland, is worth visiting for its cathedral and, together with the nearby early settlement at Biskupin, could be a day trip from Poznań.

Wielkopolska's capital, Poznań, was the seat of the first Polish bishopric (AD 968), and three of the region's towns—Poznań, Ostrów Lednicki, and Gniezno—each claim that it was in their city that the first Polish ruler, Mieszko, embraced Christianity in 966. Several other historical distinctions are less disputed. In Gniezno, near the tomb of St. Adalbert (Wojciech), the famous Congress of Gniezno took place in the year 1000, during which Holy Roman Emperor Otto III crowned the Polish prince Bolesław Chrobry as King Bolesław I. After Poland's capital was moved from Gniezno to Kraków in 1039, Wielkopolska lost some of its importance but regained it in the period of feudal fragmentation (approximately 1138–1320), when it was the seat of the local line of the Piast Dynasty. The reunification of the Polish lands in the 14th century nurtured further growth of Wielkopolska, and in the 15th century Poznań became an important commercial hub in the trade routes that connected Lithuania with western Europe. During the first and second partition of Poland (1772 and 1793), Wielkopolska was under the rule of Prussia until the successful Wielkopolska Uprising of 1794 made it possible for the region to join Księstwo Warszawskie (the Warsaw Duchy) created by Napoleon Bonaparte. After Napoleon's defeat, Wielkopolska was again under Prussian rule and remained a part of Prussia until Poland regained its independence in 1918.

During Poland's long partition, the people of the region resisted the intensive Germanizing policy; yet the period has left its mark in the architecture of the cities and the specific regional dialect, easily recognizable by Poles from other regions. The Poles of Wielkopolska are

affectionately mocked by their countrymen for having absorbed the archetypal German habits of cleanliness, order, and thrift. The region, which includes both fertile plains and numerous glacial lakes, has a well-developed agricultural base, with large, well-managed farms, which have always driven its prosperous economy.

TIMING

For those who like cheerful commotion and seasonal, outdoor festivals, June will be the best time to visit Poznań. Jarmark Świętojański, which encompasses the feast days of Poznań's patron saints, Peter and Paul, means numerous concerts and festivals (including the Malta International Theatre Festival) that draw thousands of tourists. You may even have difficulty finding accommodations at this time; hotels certainly increase prices for the season. For those who like to relax in the country, summer is the best time to visit. On hot days you can sit by one of many lakes, hike in the Wielkopolski National Park, or go horseback riding in one of several stables in the immediate vicinity of Poznań. Sightseers may wish to wait until September, when the tourist traffic lessens and moderate temperatures are more appropriate for urban exploring. Another reason to wait is that many hotels cut their prices after mid-September by as much as 30%.

POZNAŃ

300 km (186 mi) west of Warsaw, 170 km (105 mi) north of Wrocław.

Halfway between Warsaw and Berlin, in the middle of the monotonously flat Polish lowlands, Poznań has been an east–west trading center for more than 1,000 years. In the Middle Ages, merchants made a great point of bringing their wares here on St. John's Day (June 23), and the annual tradition has continued, though the markets have now been superseded by the International Trade Fairs, which have been held here since 1922. Until the 13th century, Poznań was, on and off, the capital of Poland, and in 968 the first Polish bishopric was founded here by Mieszko I. It still remains the capital of the Wielkopolska (Great Poland) region.

WHAT TO SEE

Despite its somewhat grim industrial outskirts, Poznań has one of the country's most charming Old Towns; consider making a trip through western Poland, if only to visit the city's majestic market square. Poznań may be only the fifth-largest city in Poland, but to a tourist, it may feel larger. The majority of sights are near the Old Town's impressive Stary Rynek (Old Market Square), and other attractions are off in the sprawling maze of ancillary streets. Walking is not recommended here. Invest in some tram tickets and a city map with the transit routes marked; your feet will thank you.

Today's, Poznań's Old Town is a result of the "new" town charter of 1253, which was granted by Prince Przemysł I. Other than the urban layout, not much survived from those days. The present-day **Stary Rynek** *(Old Market Square)* dates primarily from the 16th century and has a somewhat cluttered feeling, since the center is occupied with both 20th-century additions and Renaissance structures. But this is where you'll find the Ratusz, where everyone gathers to watch the famous clock. ⊠*Stare Miasto.*

★ Poznań residents will proudly tell you that the imposing Renaissance **Ratusz** *(Town Hall)* at the center of the Old Market Square is the most splendid building in Poland. The building, which dates to the mid-16th century, was designed by Giovanni Battista Quadro. Every day at noon, hundreds of tourists look up to watch the clock tower, where two billy goats butt heads before disappearing back inside the tower. Legend has it that the clock maker who installed the timepiece planned a party on the occasion. He ordered two goats for the feast, but the goats escaped and started fighting. The mayor was so amused by the event that he ordered the clock maker to construct a mechanism to reenact the goat fight. The town hall now houses a **Muzeum Historii Miasta Poznania** (Museum of City History), which contains a room dedicated to Chopin. ⊠*Stary Rynek 1, Stare Miasto* ☎*061/852–56–13* ⊠*Museum zł5.5* ☉*Mon.–Tues. and Fri. 9–4, Wed. 11–6.*

FodorśChoice **Kościół Farny** *(Parish Church).* A former Jesuit temple, the parish church,
★ which is dedicated to Saints Stanislaus and Mary Magdalene, was consecrated in 1705 (though the construction started as early as 1649). The baroque building—the finest example in the city and one of the best in the entire country—was designed by Bartłomiej Nataniel Wąsowski, the facade by Giovanni Catenacci, and the beautiful archway by Pompeo Ferrari. The interior, in the style of Roman baroque, is decorated with wall paintings by Karol Dankwart, and in the main altar is the painting of St. Stanislaus by Szymon Czechowicz. One of the most valuable objects inside the church is the pipe organ built between 1872 and 1876 by Friedrich Ladegast, the most famous European organ builder of the age. ⊠*At the end of Świętosławska, Stare Miasto.*

The tiny, arcaded shopkeepers' houses in the Old Market Square date to the mid-16th century. Some of them now house the **Muzeum Instru-**

9

mentów Muzycznych *(Museum of Musical Instruments)*, where you can see Chopin's piano and a plaster cast of the maestro's hands. ⊠ *Stary Rynek 45, Stare Miasto* ☎ *061/856–81–78* 💷 *zł6* ⊗ *Tues.–Sat. 11–5, Sun. 10–3.*

A few blocks west of the Old Market Square is the **Muzeum Narodowe w Poznaniu** *(National Museum in Poznań)*, which has a good collection of Polish art (in the new building) and Western European paintings (in the old building; both buildings are connected). You'll see interesting examples of paintings by Dutch masters, in addition to examples of early Polish impressionism, more accurately described as works by artists who were inspired by French impressionism. Represented artists include Wojtkiewicz, Malczewski, and, above all, Pankiewicz; his painting Flower Market, which was painted when Pankiewicz returned from Paris, is considered the first work of Polish impressionism. ⊠ *al. Marcinkowskiego 9, Stare Miasto* ☎ *061/856–80–00* ⊕ *www.mnp.art. pl* 💷 *zł10* ⊗ *Tues. 10–6, Wed. 9–5, Thurs. and Sun. 10–4, Fri. and Sat. 10–5.*

On plac Wolności (Freedom Square) is the beautiful **Biblioteka Raczyńskich** *(Raczyński Library)* built in 1829 by the aristocratic Raczyński family. It remains a working library with a special collection of old manuscripts; otherwise, it's the facade that is remarkable, and you won't be nearly as impressed with the interior. This is a good place to head after visiting the Muzeum Instrumentów Muzycznych and/or Muzeum Narodowe. ⊠ *pl. Wolności 19, Stare Miasto* ☎ *061/852–94–42* 💷 *Free* ⊗ *Daily 9–5.*

Ostrów Tumski *(Cathedral Island), an islet* in the Warta River—about 15 minutes by foot east of the Old Town—is the historic cradle of Poznań. The oldest part of city, it's where the Polanie tribe built their first fortified settlement and their first basilica in the 10th century. During the reign of Poland's first ruler, Mieszko I, the island hosted both the city's lay and ecclesiastical governments. When walking around Ostrów Tumski, you can see the Archbishop's Palace, the tiny, 15th-century church of St. Mary's, and the former Lubrański Academy, a college that was established in 1512 (and which was, until 1991, home to the Archdiocese Museum). ⊠ *Ostrów Tumski.*

★ Poznań's **Katedra św. Piotra i Pawła** *(Cathedral of Saints Peter and Paul)*, which was rebuilt after World War II in pseudo-Gothic style, was originally constructed between the 10th and 11th century. Those remains can be seen in some interior details and in the cellars. The design for the current three-aisle church dates to the 15th century. The Gothic interior reveals, among other treasures, a beautiful late-Gothic **altar** with saints Mary, Catherine, and Barbara, as well as 15th-century **bronze tombstones** from the famous Nuremberg workshops of the Vischers. (These were removed by the Germans during World War II and discovered in the Hermitage in St. Petersburg in the 1990s.) Directly behind the main altar is the heptagonal **Golden Chapel,** worth seeing for the sheer opulence of its romantic Byzantine decor. Within the chapel is the **mau-**

soleum that contains the remains of the first rulers of Poland, Mieszko I and Bolesław the Great. ⊠*ul. Mieszka I, Ostrów Tumski.*

WHERE TO EAT

$$–$$$$ ✕**Bażanciarnia.** You'll find top-notch Old-Polish specialties at Bażanciarnia, which is owned by Magda Gessler, perhaps the best-known Polish restaurateur (or, rather, *restauratress*). In two rooms in a town house on Old Town Square, guests are served in impeccable, high style. The menu includes excellent poultry and venison dishes, which are prepared according to 18th- and 19th-century Polish recipes, some of which are from the collection of the Gessler family. It is one of the most expensive restaurants in Poznań but worth every penny. ⊠*Stary Rynek 94, Stare Miasto* ☎*061/855–33–58* ⊕*www.bazanciarnia.pl* ⚐*Reservations essential* ⊟*AE, MC, V.*

$–$$$ ✕**Kresowa.** On the main town square, this popular restaurant specializes in cuisine from the *kresy* (Poland's former eastern territories of Lithuania, Ukraine, and Belarus). The interior may be a bit unexciting, but the friendly service and tasty food make up for that particular deficiency. Excellent soups include borscht and mushroom, both with a slightly sweet taste. (This can be surprising to the contemporary palate, but it's perfectly proper as far as historical recipes go.) For a main course, try *cepeliny* ("Zeppelin"), potato dumplings stuffed with meat and seasoned with marjoram. ⊠*Stary Rynek 2* ☎*061/853–12–91* ⊟*AE, DC, MC, V* ⊙*No dinner Sun.*

$–$$ ✕**Brovaria.** This hotel restaurant boasts its own microbrewery. Excellent food—a kind of European fusion cuisine—borrows from what is best in various Continental cuisines. The beer is always fresh, having been produced on the spot. The interior is decorated with brewery machinery and utensils. You can pick and choose from a widely varied menu; on offer is everything from beer snacks (such as prunes wrapped in bacon, or Brie rolled in sesame seeds) to full-fledged main courses (such as sirloin steak or lamb chops). There is a separate dining room, for "proper" diners, to supplement the lounge, where you can still get a casual meal. ⊠*Stary Rynek 73–74, Stare Miasto* ☎*061/858–68–68* ⊟*AE, MC, V.*

Fodor's Choice ★

$ ✕**Cocorico.** Mere feet from the facade of the Poznań town church and a one-minute walk from the Old Town Square, this lovely café looks not unlike a traditional Parisian bistro, decorated with French prints on the walls and furnished with cushioned sofas. There's even a pretty garden in the courtyard. It's a perfect stop for coffee and/or cocktails, but you can also get light snacks such as toasts and salads, though the excellent hot cherry sundae is the real treat. ⊠*ul. Świętosławska 9, Stare Miasto* ☎*061/665–84–67* ⚐*Reservations not accepted* ⊟*AE, MC, V.*

Fodor's Choice ★

WHERE TO STAY

$$–$$$ ▣**Hotel Vivaldi.** This pleasant, new hotel not far from the center is surrounded by greenery and perfect for a quiet night's sleep followed by a morning jog. Frequented by business travelers arriving for the trade fairs, it's also a pleasant and reasonably priced option for leisure travelers. The hotel restaurant—named, somewhat predictably, the Four Seasons—serves Polish and Italian cuisine. ⊠*ul. Winogrady 9, 61–663*

9

☎*061/858–81–00* 🖷*061/853–29–77* ⊕*www.vivaldi.pl* ⤳*47 rooms, 1 suite* ♿*Restaurant, minibars, cable TV, in-room broadband, pool, sauna, bar, meeting rooms, parking (fee)* ☰*AE, MC, V* ⏍*BP.*

$$–$$$ ⌗**Sheraton.** This is the newest hotel of the Sheraton network in Poland; it opened in November 2006 as one of the more expensive hotel building projects in this part of the country. Here, you'll find the highest standard of service and plush rooms with all conceivable comforts. The location—across from the Trade Fair grounds and within easy walking distance of the main train station, is a strong selling point. ✉*ul. Bukowska 3/9, 60–813* ☎*061/655–20–00* 🖷*061/655–20–01* ⊕*www.starwoodhotels.com* ⤳*168 rooms, 13 suites* ♿*3 restaurants, minibars, in-room safes, in-room broadband, Wi-Fi, cable TV, indoor pool, sauna, gym, bar, shops, dry cleaning, laundry service, meeting rooms, parking (fee)* ☰*AE, MC, V* ⏍*EP.*

$$ ⌗**Hotel Royal.** On Poznań's main street, this small hotel with just 55 beds in a 19th-century tenement house has a long-standing, if not exactly continuous, tradition of hospitality. The building became a hotel in the 1920s and served in that capacity through much of the 20th century; it was restored to its current status in the late 1990s. The classy interior design—some rooms have wood paneling, some bay windows, some richly patterned fabrics—gives the hotel plenty of character, further enhanced by friendly and efficient service. The restaurant serves breakfast only (included in the room rates). ✉*ul. św. Marcin 71, 61–808* ☎*061/858–23–00* 🖷*061/858–23–06* ⊕*www.hotel-royal. com.pl* ⤳*30 rooms, 1 suite* ♿*Some kitchenettes, some minibars, cable TV, bar, laundry service, Internet room, meeting rooms, parking (free)* ☰*AE, MC, V* ⏍*BP.*

$–$$ ⌗**Brovaria Hotel.** If you want to be near the center of Poznań, it's impossible to get any closer than this small, cozy hotel on the Old Town Square. If one is available, ask for a room overlooking the square. The hotel is located over a great microbrewery restaurant-cum-bar. The rooms are a smooth and happy marriage between classic and contemporary style. ✉*Stary Rynek 73/74, 61–772* ☎*061/858–68–68* 🖷*61/858–68–69* ⊕*www.brovaria.pl* ⤳*16 rooms, 1 suite* ♿*Restaurant, cable TV, in-room broadband, bar* ☰*AE, MC, V* ⏍*BP.*

$–$$ ⌗**Hotel Rzymski.** Prewar traditions combined with modern comforts add up to a true "Poznań bourgeois" atmosphere (in the best sense). What you get are pretty standard hotel rooms—nothing noteworthy, but comfortable nonetheless, though few services or facilities beyond a business center. The hotel has a central location right next to the National Museum, but because of this, rooms in the front can get a bit noisy. Prices can vary considerably, with the cheapest rates being offered on weekends and the highest during one of the many trade fairs. The De Rome restaurant serves Polish and European food. ✉*al. K. Marcinkowskiego 22, 61–827* ☎*061/852–81–21* 🖷*061/852–89–83* ⊕*www.hotelrzymski.pl* ⤳*82 rooms, 5 suites* ♿*2 restaurants, cable TV, in-room broadband, Wi-Fi, bar, business services, meeting rooms, no-smoking rooms, some pets allowed* ☰*AE, MC, V* ⏍*BP.*

$ ⌗**Dom Turysty.** This hotel has only 18 rooms (singles, doubles, and triples), but if you can get in, you'll like its location, right at the center of the Old Town. Expect no luxuries, but the place has character. Rooms are quite spacious and comfortably furnished, with Polish folk touches, and interesting eclectic elements. The staff is friendly and well informed. ✉*Stary Rynek 91, 61–001* ☎*061/852–88–93* ⊕*www.domturysty.naszemiasto.pl* ⤳*18 rooms, 10 with shared bath* ⧠*Restaurant, café, cable TV; no a/c* ⊟*AE, DC, MC, V* ⏐⊙⏐*BP.*

NIGHTLIFE & THE ARTS

If you want to get out for a drink, consider the Brovaria restaurant, which has its own microbrewery *(⇨Brovaria in Where to Eat, above).*

The **Filharmonia Poznańska** (*Poznań Philharmonic* ✉*ul. Św. Marcin 81* ☎*061/852–47–08* ⊕*www.filharmonia.poznan.pl*) holds concerts in Wrocław University's beautifully restored Aula, where the acoustics are excellent.

Stefan Stuligrosz's Boys Choir (✉*Teatr Wielki, ul. Fredry 9* ☎*061/852–82–91*)—the Poznań Nightingales—is one of Poznań's best-known musical attractions.

GNIEZNO

50 km (31 mi) northeast of Poznań on Hwy. 5 (E261).

Lying along the Piast Route—Poland's historic memory lane running from Poznań to Kruszwica—Gniezno is the original capital of Poland and is surrounded by towns whose monuments date as far back as the origins of the Polish state. Legend has it that Lech, the legendary founder of the country, spotted some white eagles nesting on the site; he then named the town Gniezno (Nesting Site) and proclaimed the white eagle the nation's emblem. On a more historical note, in AD 1000, it became the seat of the country's first archbishopric, a couple of years after St. Wojciech (Adalbert) was buried in Gniezno cathedral. In that same year, by St. Adalbert's tomb, the famous conference took place during which Holy Roman Emperor Otto III crowned Bolesław Chrobry as Bolesław I, the ruler of Poland. Since 1419, the archbishop of Gniezno has also been the primate of Poland, making him the head of all Polish Catholic clergy.

★ The town's first cathedral, the **Gniezno Cathedral,** was built by King Mieszko I before AD 977. The present 14th-century building is the most imposing Gothic cathedral in Poland. At the back of the church the 12th-century bronze-cast **Doors of Gniezno** have intricate bas-relief scenes depicting the life of St. Wojciech (Adalbert), a Czech missionary commissioned to bring Christianity to the Prussians in northern Poland. Not everyone appreciated his message: he was killed by pagans. It is said that his body was bought from his murderers by Bolesław I of Poland for its weight in gold, which the Poles paid ungrudgingly. The saint was then laid to rest in the Gniezno church, which was soon promoted to the rank of cathedral. On the altar a silver sarcophagus, supported by four silver pallbearers, bears the remains of St. Wojciech. ✉*Łaskiego 9* 🖭*Doors of Gniezno zł3* ⊙*Mon.–Sat. 10–5, Sun. 1:30–5:30.*

9

Muzeum Archidiecezji Gnieźnieńskiej *(Museum of Gniezno Archdiocese)* is a typical church museum, a bit dusty and old-fashioned. It features a plaster copy of the Doors of Gniezno (but *do* see the real thing), religious art, and some documents. If you have a spare half hour, why not? But if you don't have the time, this can be safely skipped. ✉*ul. Kolegiaty 2* ☎*061/426–37–78* ⊕*www.muzeum.gniezno.net* 💳*zł3* ☉*May–Sept., Mon.–Sat. 9–5:30, Sun. 9–4; Oct.–Apr., Tues.–Sat. 9–4 (Oct. also Sun. 9–4)*.

Housed in a characterless concrete school building in Gniezno, the **Muzeum Początków Państwa Polskiego** *(Museum of the Polish State Origins)* has multimedia exhibitions in five languages, including English, that describe medieval Poland. ✉*Kostrzewskiego 1* ☎*061/426–46–41* 💳*zł3* ☉*Tues.–Sun. 10–5.*

BISKUPIN

30 km (18 mi) north of Gniezno on Rte. E261, toward Bydgoszcz.

Step back in time by wandering along the wood-paved streets and peering into the small wooden huts at the fortified settlement at Biskupin. This 100-acre "Polish Pompeii" is one of the most fascinating archaeological sites in Europe. It was discovered in 1933, when a local school principal and his students noticed some wood stakes protruding from the water during an excursion to Lake Biskupieńskie. The lake was later drained, revealing a settlement largely preserved over the centuries by the lake waters. Dating to 550 BC, the settlement was surrounded by defensive ramparts of oak and clay and a breakwater formed from stakes driven into the ground at a 45-degree angle. A wooden plaque at the entrance shows a plan of the original settlement. The museum holds a yearly festival in the last week of September that includes historic reenactments. ✉*Biskupin* ☎*052/302–50–55* ⊕*www.biskupin.pl* 💳*zł4* ☉*May–Sept., daily 8–6; Oct.–Apr., daily 8–dusk.*

WIELKOPOLSKA ESSENTIALS

AIR TRAVEL

Poznań's Ławica Airport is to the west of the city in the Wola district. Currently the following airlines operate to/from Poznań: Aer Lingus, Ryanair, Wizzair, LOT, Lufthansa, and SAS. Express bus line "L" runs regularly between the airport and the main railway station (also regular Bus 59 and night Bus 242 will take you to the airport); allow about an hour for the journey.

Information Port Lotniczy Poznań–Ławica *(Poznań Airport* ☎*061/84–92–343* ⊕*www.airport-poznan.com.pl)*. **LOT office Poznań** (✉*ul. św. Marcin 69, Poznań* ☎*058/852–28–47)*.

BUS TRAVEL

In Poznań the PKS bus station is a short walk from the train station. Frequent bus service is available to and from Kórnik and Gniezno. Toruń's PKS bus station is east of the Old Town; take local Bus 22 to and from the station.

Information **Dworzec PKS Bus Station Poznań** (✉ *ul. Towarowa 17/19, Poznań* ☎ *061/664–25–25* ⊕ *www.pks.poznan.pl*). **PKS Bus Station Toruń** (✉ *ul. Dąbrowskiego 8–24, Toruń* ☎ *056/655–53–33* ⊕ *www.pks.torun.com*).

CAR TRAVEL

Poznań, on the main east–west route from Berlin to Moscow, is easily accessible by car. Route 2 (E30), which leads from the border at Frankfurt/Oder through Poznań and Warsaw to the eastern border at Terespol/Brest in Belarus, is still mostly a two-lane road and is considered—because of its curves and lack of shoulders—one of the most dangerous roads in Europe.

Car rental in Poland is relatively expensive, particularly with large international car-rental companies. Nevertheless, it's much easier to explore the Wielkopolska with your own vehicle. Prices vary within the range of zł150 to zł500 per day (24 hours), and some companies have a two-day minimum for rentals. Some companies require an additional credit-card deposit of zł1,500 to zł3,000, depending on the class of the rented car. All the major firms have offices in the Poznań city center as well as at Poznań Ławica airport.

Car Rentals **Avis** (✉ *ul. Bukowska 12, Poznań* ☎ *061/849–23–35*). **Budget** (✉ *ul. Roosevelta 18, Poznań* ☎ *061/845–14–89*). **Express Rent a Car** (✉ *ul. Kościuszki 118, near the Ikar Hotel, Poznań* ☎ *61/857–67–07*). **Hertz** (✉ *ul. gen. Andersa 1, Poznań* ☎ *61/868–41–77*).

INTERNET

Internet Cafés **Bajt** (✉ *ul. Zamkowa 5/2, Poznań* ☎ *061/853–18–08*). **Tunel** (✉ *Main Railway Station, ul. Dworcowa 1, Poznań*).

TAXIS

As anywhere else in Poland, using a radio taxi company is recommended; it is both cheaper and safer than a private taxi.

Information **Selected Poznań Radio Taxi Companies** (☎ *061/9661, 061/9667, 061/9622, 061/9623, 061/9624, 061/9625*).

TRAIN TRAVEL

All trains arriving in Poznań stop at Dworzec Główny (Central Station), located in the center, next to the Poznań Trade Fair grounds. Trains run frequently from the modern Poznań Główny to Szczecin (3 hours), Toruń (2½ hours), Wrocław (3 hours), Kraków (8 hours), and Warsaw (4 hours). International destinations include Berlin (4½ hours), Budapest (15 hours), and Paris (20 hours).

Information **Poznań Główny** (✉ *ul. Dworcowa 1, Poznań* ☎ *061/863–38–14* ⊕ *www.pkp.pl*).

VISITOR INFORMATION
Information Gniezno Tourist Information (✉ *Tumska 12* ☎ *061/428–41–00*).
Poznań City TI (✉ *Ratajczaka 44, Poznań* ☎ *061/851–96–45* ⊕ *www.cim.poznan.*
pl). **Wielkopolska Region TI** (✉ *Stary Rynek 59/60, Poznań* ☎ *061/852–61–56*
⊕ *www.city.poznan.pl*).

MAZURY & EASTERN POLAND

Eastern Poland is not a homogenous entity, as it is made up of several very distinct regions, each with its own geographical, historical, and cultural traits. The lands along the Polish eastern border—a border that has shifted several times over the country's long history—have been marked and enriched with the presence of different cultures: Prussians, Lithuanians, Belarusians, Tartars, Jews, and Ukrainians.

All of Eastern Poland is rather "off the beaten path" and most visitors do not get that far. This is not for the lack of attractions—on the contrary, the east has a lot to offer, from the popular Mazury Lake District, through Poland's poorest corner near the Belarusian border, to the virgin forest of Białowieża, to historical towns and villages such as Lublin, Zamość, and Kazimierz Dolny, to the remote and wild Bieszczady mountains. Northeastern Poland has been dubbed the "Green Lungs" of the country. Indeed, the pristine, unspoiled natural environment is the region's main draw; as many as seven national parks and numerous nature reserves have been set aside in the belt of land along the border.

Head for the Mazury lake district in the northeast for kayaking and sailing. To reach the southeast part of the country, the most convenient connection is always via Warsaw, whether you are driving or taking public transportation. South and east of Warsaw you will find many lovely, small cities and towns, including historical and cultural gems such as Kazimierz Dolny and Zamość.

TIMING

Many areas of Eastern Poland—especially destinations like the Mazurian Lakes that are popular for their natural beauty and outdoor activities—are mostly visited during the summer season. Autumn and winter weather usually do nothing but make traveling treacherous, and cold winds do not add to their charms. But in many of the historical towns, including Kazimierz Dolny, Zamość, and Łańcut, you'll find most attractions open year-round and far less crowded streets out of season.

THE MAZURY LAKE DISTRICT

The Mazury Lake District is one of the most famous vacation regions of Poland, particularly popular with those who prefer active leisure, including excellent sailing and kayaking. If you don't like the water, this is the part of Poland to avoid: the area contains some 2,700 large lakes, and countless little "lakelets," connected by a network of riv-

ers, streams, and canals, which splash, spill, and spread through the region's meadows and marshlands. At the center of the region is the area of 1,700 square km (656 square mi) called the Mazurian Great Lakes (Kraina Wielkich Jezior Mazurskich); nearly a third of this area is covered by water. The "great lakes" include two of Poland's largest (Śniardwy and Mamry), as well as the popular resort of Mikołajki, which is more or less in the middle. The Suwalskie Lake District (Pojezierze Suwalskie), which includes Augustów, lies to the east of Mazurian Great Lakes, in the far northeastern corner of Poland.

MIKOŁAJKI
223 km (139 mi) north of Warsaw.

Mikołajki derives its name from the patron saint of the local chapel, St. Nicholas (the name in Polish means "the little Nicks"). Once a medieval fishing hamlet, today it is one of the most popular—if not *the* most popular—resort in the Mazurian Lakes region, referred to as "the Boating Capital of Poland." In fact, in the summer months the small town gets a little too popular for its own good. Mikołajki is situated on the shores of Lake Tałty and Lake Mikołajskie, with Lake Śniardwy nearby. A nature preserve surrounds Lake Łuknajno, 4 km (2½ mi) east of Mikołajki.

Four kilometers (2½ mi) east of Mikołajki lies **Łuknajno Lake**, which covers a little more than 7 square km (2¾ square mi). The lake is a bird sanctuary, with the largest colony of Mute Swan (*Cygnus olor*) in Europe (approximately 1,500 birds), and many other waterbirds: Montagu's harrier (*Circus pygargus*), little bittern (*Ixobrychus minutus minutus*), little crake (*Porzana parva*), common crane (*Grus grus*), and ducks such as wigeon (*Anas penelope*) and northern shoveler (*Anas clypeata*). There are observation towers (*wieża widokowa*) around the lake. Bring your binoculars—or a camera with a good zoom—and indulge in innocent voyeurism, also called bird-watching. Don't forget good walking shoes (or galoshes) because the track can get a little muddy. The reserve's management office is actually in Krutyń, which is 25 km (16 mi) from the reserve. Most tourists skip that and follow the trail marked P1, which follows Spacerowa and Leśna streets in Mikołajki, or the biking route marked R2, which also starts in the center of town on Łabędzia. ⊠ *4 km east of Mikołajki* ☏ *089/742–14–05* 🖼 *Free* ☉ *Daily dawn–dusk.*

WOLF'S LAIR
30 km 19 mi) north of Mikołajki.

Hitler's onetime bunker, at Gierłoż, called Wolfsschanze or Wilczy Szaniec (Wolf's Lair), was built during World War II as his East Prussian military command post. Its massively fortified concrete bunkers were blown up, but you can still climb in and among the remains and get a feel for his megalomania. Wolf's Lair was also where a small group of German patriots tried—and failed—to assassinate Hitler on July 20, 1944. ⊠ *Gierłoż* ☏ *089/752–44–29* ⊕ *www.wolfsschanze.home. pl* 🖼 *zł8, English-language tour zł50* ☉ *Daily 9–sunset.*

KLASZTOR STAROWIERCÓW
Wojnowo is 20 km 12 mi) south of Mikołajki.

The Old Believers Monastery in Wojnowo is on the Krutynia River trail, south/southwest of Mikołajki. The village was founded by the Old Believers (of the Russian Orthodox Church). Also called the Philipons (after Philip the Hermit), Raskolniks, or Schismatics, the Old Believers did not adopt Patriarch Nikon's reforms in the 17th century and were forced to emigrate in order to escape persecution. Initially, they settled in the area around Suwałki, but after refusing military service and the registration of their marriages, they ran afoul of the laws there. They were pardoned and exempt from the military obligation, in return for their help in colonizing the Puszcza Piska forest. In the 1820s and '30s, the Old Believers settled in this area, and Wojnowo is one of several villages they founded. The present monastery was founded in 1836 by a pious elder Ławrientij Rastropin. The hermitage was expanded and turned into a full-fledged monastery, and in the mid-19th century it was changed to a convent. The last nun died in April 2006. Today, the monastery (with its prayer room/chapel) can be visited and remains under the loving care of private owners who want to preserve this place without turning it into a museum; they want to keep it alive. The chapel serves people of every faith, and there are several rooms to rent in the monastery building. ⊠*ul. Wojnowo 76, Ukta, 18 km 11 mi) southwest of Mikołajki* ☏*087/425–70–30* ⊕*www.klasztor.pl* ⊠*Free* ◷*Hours are irregular, but open most days by request.*

WHERE TO STAY & EAT

$ ╳⌨ **Oberźa Pod Psem.** The Under the Dog Auberge, run by artist Krzysz-
Fodor's Choice tof Worobiec and his wife, Danuta, is a very special place, perfect if
★ you want to get away from it all. The owners are set on preserving local traditions, and their hotel is part of a culture park of renovated traditional wooden houses that also includes a private ethnographical museum. The cheeky name should put you on notice to expect a rather remote and relaxed place, with no crisp white tablecloths, but plenty of old wooden furniture and rooms decorated in all the colors of the rainbow. There are few traditional creature comforts, but it's the rusticity that is the draw. Even if you are staying elsewhere, Auberge is worth a trip for a meal, given that it has one of the best restaurants ($–$$) in the entire Mazury region. The owners cook their so-called slow food using regional recipes supplemented by their own imagination. Try *kwaśnica* (a dense soup made with mushrooms and cabbage) or *wereszczaki* (pork in beetroot, served with buckwheat). The hosts make many ingredients, including excellent goat cheese, themselves. They will guide you around their private museum zł5), generally open daily from 11 to 5, which includes a typical Mazurian cottage and a re-created schoolroom of old. ⊠*ul. Kadzidłowo 1, Ukta, 12–20* ☏*048/425–74–74* ⊕*www.oberzapodpsem.com* ⇗*5 rooms* &*Restaurant, sauna* ▭*No credit cards* ⦿*EP.*

$ ⌨ **Klasztor Starowierców** *(Old Believers Monastery).* If you would like to get a small taste of what monastic life might have been like (or rather get a glimpse and then use your imagination), you can rent a cell at this monastery. The rooms are spotlessly clean and cheerful, but very simple, low-key, and modest, and they seem permeated with the mystic aura of the place. This is by no means a typical accommodation, but it is very special and has a definite charm about it. Bathroom facilities are shared, as is a kitchenette, but you can also order prepared meals. Guests can use boats, kayaks, and mountain bikes free of charge. The lakeside location is ideal. ⊠ *Wojnowo 76, Ukta, 12–210, 18 km 11 mi) southwest of Mikołajki* ☏*087/425–70–30* ⇗*5 rooms with shared bath* &*Kitchen, boating, bicycles, parking (free); no room phones, no TV, no a/c* ▭*No credit cards* ⦿*EP.*

SPORTS & THE OUTDOORS

KAYAKING

Fodor's Choice The Krutynia River is considered one of the loveliest lowland kayaking
★ trails in Poland, perhaps even in Europe. It crosses—or rather meanders through—the ancient forest of Puszcza Piska as well as through numerous picturesque lakes. It was the Prussians that gave the river its name: in the old Prussian dialect *Krutina* means "meandering." The infrastructure for tourists (equipment rental, simple dining and lodging establishments) is relatively well developed. The total length of the river is 116.5 km (72 mi), and the entire route takes about seven or eight days. The Krutynia is an easy river to traverse, not too strenuous

for a beginner; however, there are four spots where kayaks have to be carried over land, and 44.5 km (28 mi) of the route is on still water. Trips usually start in the PTTK Marina in Sorkwity (where you can rent a kayak), and then set off for the village of Zyndaki on the northern shore of Zyndackie Lake. The kayak trail ends in Nidzkie Lake, in the PTTK Marina in Ruciane-Nida.

Perkun (⊠*ul. Krutyń 4, Piecki* ☎*089/742–14–30 or 048/600–427–868* ⊕*www.krutynia.com.pl*), which is the popular name for the Perkun Association of Water Guides on Krutynia, organizes boat trips from April through November. The basic rate is zł24 per person per day, but individual tailor-made options may be priced differently. The organization can also put together a short, several-hour kayaking trip for those who don't have time to do the whole route. Boat trips start from the quay next to the bridge in Krutyń, 15 km (9 mi) south of Mikołajki.

Stanica Wodna PTTK-Sorkwity (⊠*ul. Zamkowa 13, Sorkwity* ☎*089/642–81–24* ⊕*www.sorkwity.pttk.pl*) is 30 km (19 mi) west of Mikołajki, near Mrągowo and is open from May through the end of September.

Stanica Wodna PTTK Ruciane-Nida (⊠*al. Wczasów 17, Ruciane-Nida* ☎*087/423–10–12* ⊕*www.uandrzeja.pl*) is about 20 km (12 mi) south of Mikołajki and is open from May through mid-September.

SAILING

There are numerous popular sailing routes along the region's many lakes, and you can easily start in Mikołajki. For instance, the trips from Mikołajki to Ruciane Nida (19 km [12 mi]), Mikołajki to Giżycko (37 km [23 mi], via Lake Niegocin), Mikołajki to Pisz (25 km [16 mi], via Lake Śniardwy), and Mikołajki to Ryn (20 km [12 mi]) are all popular routes. Many variations and circular routes are possible, and it's quite easy to use Mikołajki as your base.

The **Wioska Żeglarska** (*Sailors' Village* ⊠*ul. Kowalska 13* ☎*087/421–60–40* ⊕*www.wioskazeglarskamikolajki.pl*) is a good place to rent a boat. Bareboat yacht charters range from zł130 to zł250 per day, and the marina has full facilities.

If you aren't an experienced sailor, **Żegluga Mazurska** (*Mazurian Sailing Company* ⊠*Port Mikołajki* ☎*097/421–61–02* ⊕*www.zeglugamazurska.com*) offers scheduled pleasure cruises, running between Mikołajki, Ruciane-Nida, and Giżycko, as well as a round-trip itinerary from Mikołajki to Lake Śniardwy. Cruises are scheduled from May through September only and are more frequent in July and August.

KAZIMIERZ DOLNY

★ *40 km (25 mi) west of Lublin, 130 km (80 mi) southeast of Warsaw.*

This small town is so pleasing to the eyes that it has thrived for more than a century as an artists' colony and vacation spot. It sits on a steep, hilly bank of the placid Vistula River, and whitewashed facades and steeply pitched red-tile roofs peek out over the treetops. Although the first settlement existed here in the 12th century, the town was formally founded by King Kazimierz the Great, after whom it was named. This Kazimierz received the nickname Dolny (the Lower) to distinguish it from another newly founded Kazimierz upriver, now part of Kraków. Kazimierz Dolny prospered as a river port during the 16th and 17th centuries, but the partitioning of Poland left it cut off from the grain markets of Gdańsk. Thereafter, the town fell into decline until it was rediscovered by painters and writers during the 19th century. Today, both artistic and nonartistic visitors can still enjoy the Renaissance architecture along the village's dusty cobblestone streets or hike through the nearby hills and gorges.

On the southeast corner of the town's market square lie the **Kamienice Przybyłów** *Przybyła Brothers' Houses)*, left behind by one of the most powerful families in Kazimierz Dolny, the Przybyłas. The ornate houses were built in 1615, and their facades are adorned with the two-story bas-relief figures of St. Nicholas (left) and St. Christopher (right), the brothers' patron saints. ✉*Rynek*.

The **Kamienica Celejowska** *(Celej Family House)*, seat of a powerful Kazimierz clan, stands one block toward the river from the main square, and it is embellished with griffins, dragons, and salamanders. The former residence now houses one of the five sections of the **Muzeum Nadwiślańskie** (Vistula Valley Museum) telling the history of Kazimierz town, and presenting works of the many artists who lived, visited, and worked here, starting from the shaping of the "Kazimierz artists' colony" phenomenon (late 19th century to 1920s), to its flourishing between the world wars, and its postwar and contemporary periods. Some names to look out for include Władysław Ślewiński, Tadeusz Pruszkowski, Antoni Michalak, Teresa Roszkowska, Eugeniusz Arct, Władysław Skoczylas, Jan Cybis, and Artur Nacht-Samborski. ✉*ul. Senatorska 11* 📞*081/881–01–04* 💰*zł5* 🕐*Oct.–Apr., Tues.–Thurs. and Sun. 10–3, Fri. and Sat. 10–5; May–Sept., Tues.–Thurs. and Sun. 10–5, Fri. and Sat. 10–7.*

A covered passageway off ulica Senatorska leads up to the walled courtyard of the **Kościół i klasztor Reformatów** *(Church and Monastery of the Reformati)*, which stands on the southern hill overlooking the town's market square. The Reformati were the reformed Franciscan Order. In the late 18th century an encircling wall was built to protect the monastery's buildings. A plaque inside the passageway memorializes the Nazis' use of the site as a house of torture during World War II. The climb up to the courtyard is worthwhile just for the spectacular view it affords of the town. ✉*ul. Klasztorna, off ul. Senatorska.*

On the north side of the main square is the **Kościół Parafialny** *(Parish Church)*, initially built in Gothic style but remodeled in the so-called Lublin-Renaissance style. The original Gothic structure was badly damaged by fire in 1561, and remained in the state of near-ruin for the next 25 years, just long enough to benefit from the "fashion" for Renaissance architecture in Poland. The result of the combination of styles—Gothic slenderness with Renaissance ornament—is striking. An Italian resident of Poland, Jacob Balin, was the author of the new design for the presbytery. Note the Renaissance stalls, the rococo confessionals, an ornate 17th-century organ and pulpit, and an unusual chandelier made from stags' antlers. ⊠*Rynek, north side.*

The ruins of the 14th-century **Zamek** *(Kazimierz Castle)*, which served as a watchtower to protect the Vistula trade route, stand on a steep hill to the northeast of the town's market square. From here there is a grand view over the town and the Vistula Valley. Good exercise for imagination: try to see the powerful stronghold of Kazimierz Wielki, then an elegant Renaissance palace, in today's romantic ruin left to its own devices. Resident ghosts roam undisturbed most of the time. In the summer, the ruin sometimes becomes illuminated to serve as a backdrop to an open-air concert.

The **Góra Trzech Krzyży** *(Three Crosses Mount)* lies to the east of the market square. The crosses were constructed in 1708 to commemorate the victims of a plague (cholera) that ravaged the town. This vantage point affords perhaps the best view of the town.

OFF THE BEATEN PATH

The village of Janowiec, 6 km (4 mi) west of Kazimierz Dolny, on the other side of the Vistula, is most famous for the ruins of **Firlej Castle.** The castle was built on the high left bank of the Vistula between 1526 and 1537 by Piotr Firlej, and in its time it rivaled the Kazimierz castle across the river. King Sigismundus the Old attended the opening of this magnificent residence, which was built in late-Renaissance style by a renowned Italian architect, Santi Gucci. With Kazimierz Dolny and Janowiec losing their significance, the castle suffered from neglect. Abandoned in 1790, it fell into ruin. It came under the care of the museum authorities in the 1970s, and now the picturesque ruin has been partly restored. A museum displays an architectural and ethnographic exhibition. Summer concerts are the castle's great attraction (May through August; check the program at the tourist information in Kazimierz Dolny). ⊠*ul. Lubelska 10, Janowiec* ☎*081/881–52–29* ⊠*zł8* ☉*Oct.–Apr., Tues.–Fri. 10–3, weekends 10–4; May–Sept., Mon. 10–2, Tues.–Fri. 10–5, weekends 10–7.*

WHERE TO STAY & EAT

In addition to the one recommended below, the hotels Bohema and Król Kazimierz both have good restaurants.

★ **$–$$**   ✕**U Fryzjera.** "At the Barber Shop" commemorates the previous tenant of the house, a barber. The owners' mission is to serve food to the hungry and joy to the sad, and it's a perfect venue to enjoy some excellent klezmer music on Saturday nights (one of the owners is a musician in a klezmer band). Traditional Jewish dishes served here include trout with almonds, *szlajmzupe* soup with chicken livers, buckwheat, and beans), and marinated goose the latter must be ordered in advance, and costs zł130 for the whole goose). The restaurant is also open for breakfast, but it closes at midnight sharp on most days, and at 2 AM on Friday and Saturday. Reservations are not accepted for weekends or holidays. ⊠*ul. Witkiewicza 2* ☎*081/881–04–26* ⊟*AE, DC, MC, V.*

$$$ ⊡**Hotel Król Kazimierz.** The newest and most plush hotel in Kazimierz, which opened in November 2006, is hoping to set a new standard of modern comforts combined with traditional Polish hospitality. The hotel is a converted granary just outside the center of town that has been transformed with a contemporary design. The luxury Kanebo Spa offers holistic body treatments and wellness programs, including yoga and purifying diets. ⊠ *Puławska 86, 24–120* ☎ *081/880–99–99* 🖷 *081/880–98–98* ⊕ *www.krolkazimierz.pl* ⇥ *107 rooms, 8 suites* ⚐ *Restaurant, café, minibars, cable TV, Wi-Fi, pool, spa, bowling, 2 bars, night club, laundry service, meeting rooms, parking (free)* ⊟ *AE, MC, V* ⵙ *BP.*

$$ ▦ **Bohema.** This elegant and comfortable hotel draws visitors not only with its stylish, simple, and chic rooms—which have custom-made furniture—but also with its beauty treatments and massages in its small spa. In tune with the wellness theme, the restaurant offers light and subtle dishes, a departure from traditional Polish cuisine, and gives a much stronger nod toward a sophisticated European menu. ⊠ *Małachowskiego 12, 24–120* ☎ *081/882–10–88* 🖷 *081/881–07–56* ⊕ *www.spakazimierz.pl* ⇥ *15 rooms, 2 suites* ⚐ *Restaurant, minibars, cable TV, in-room broadband, pool, hot tub, sauna, spa, meeting room* ⊟ *AE, DC, MC, V* ⵙ *BP.*

SPORTS & THE OUTDOORS

BOAT TOURS

During the summer season (May through October), you can take boat rides on the Vistula. The most popular, half-hour ride takes you south to Janowiec and its Firlej Castle ruins.

Rejsy po Wiśle (⊠ *ul. Nadwiślańska* ☎ *081/881–01–35* ⊕ *www.rejsys-tatkiem.com.pl*) has six boats, each able to carry from 120 to 240 people. The company offers rides across the river to Janowiec, where you can pick up a 14-km (9-mi) trail to Puławy, and a 50- to 60-minute round-trip cruise on the river for zł12 per person. You can purchase tickets right at the quayside.

Right outside the **Dziunia** (⊠ *ul. Nadwiślańska* ☎ *081/723–50–06*) botel (a boat-hotel), you will find small wooden boats (seating up to 20 people) that sail on itineraries to Janowiec and also on hour-long round-trip river cruises, but these boats specialize in sunset sailing trips for zł10 per person.

HIKING

If you take one of the numerous marked trails, ranging in length from 2 km to 6 km (1 mi to 4 mi), you can easily explore the hilly landscape around Kazimierz (now protected as Kazimierz Landscape Park) on foot. All these walking trails converge on the market square. Tourist tracks lead north (marked red) and south (marked green) along the river from the square, along streets and cart paths, through orchards and quarries. Many of these trails take you through the ravines that are characteristic for this area. In one densely "populated" (or rather, "perforated") section, you'll find 10 km (6 mi) of ravines in every square kilometer.

ZAMOŚĆ

87 km (54 mi) southeast of Lublin, 318 km (198 mi) northeast of Kraków.

Perhaps the most perfect realization of the ideal city—both refined in its beauty and rational in its composition—the fortified town of Zamość has a wonderfully preserved, Renaissance-era central square, wide boulevards, and neat rows of colorful houses with brightly painted facades. The town was conceived in the late 16th century by Hetman Jan Zamoyski as an outpost along the thriving trade route between Lublin and Lwów (now Lviv, Ukraine). He commissioned Italian architect Bernardo Morando, who created a masterpiece of Renaissance urban planning. Zamość became the administrative center of the region and, since 1594, home to Akademia Zamojska, the third Polish university after Kraków and Vilnius (though the Akademia was disbanded in 1784, following the city's decline).

Having welcomed Armenian, Greek, and Jewish settlers (and later also German, Dutch, Scottish, and other merchants and artisans), the town was thriving, and its strong fortifications spared it from destruction during the Cossack invasions, as well as the Swedish onslaught of the 17th century. In the 18th century, as the result of Poland's partitions, Zamość found itself under Austrian rule, and then in the 19th, it passed to the Russians. The Polish victory over the Bolsheviks near Zamość in 1920 kept the way clear for the country's restored independence. World War II saw the town renamed Himmlerstadt, with thousands of its residents (45% of the town was Jewish) deported or exterminated to make way for German settlers. Today the well-preserved city is a UNESCO World Heritage site.

Fodor's Choice
★
Zamość's **Rynek** *(Market Square)* is a breathtaking arcaded plaza of 1,000 square feet, surrounded by the decorative facades of homes built by local merchants during the 16th and 17th centuries. Dominating the square is the impressive baroque **Ratusz** (Town Hall), topped by a 164-foot spire. It is placed unusually: not in the center, but in the corner of the square (to indicate that was less prominent than the palace of the city's founders and owners). The distinctive staircase, which renders the building more imposing, was added later, in the 17th century.

The **Muzeum Zamojskie** *(Zamość Museum)* is housed in four charming town houses next door to the town hall (at the north end of the square). These were called the Armenian houses after their original 16th-century tenants. The interiors themselves—with stucco decorations, wooden ceilings, and arcaded courtyards—are worth a visit, and the collection features paintings of the Zamoyski clan, Polish kings, and a scale model of Zamość. ✉*ul. Ormiańska 24* ☎*084/638–64–94* ⊕*www.muzeum-zamojskie.one.pl* ⚑*zł5* ☉*Oct.–Apr., Tues.–Sun. 9–4; May–Sept., Tues.–Sun. 9–5.*

The Renaissance cathedral, former **Kolegiata** *(St. Thomas Collegiate Church)*, one of Poland's most beautiful Renaissance churches, stands near the southwest corner of the market square. It was built according to the design of Bernardo Morando, just as all other major structures of his "ideal city." In the presbytery are four 17th-century paintings ascribed to Domenico Robusti, Tintoretto's son. The church is also the final resting place of Jan Zamoyski, who is buried in the **Zamoyski Chapel** to the right of the high altar. ✉*ul. Kolegiacka.*

The **Pałac Zamojskich** *(Zamoyski Palace)*, home of the founding family of Zamość, lies in the western, or "top" end of the Old Town, near the Market Square beyond the Collegiate Church. The palace was turned into a military hospital in the 1830s; now it serves as a courthouse. ✉*ul. Zamkowa.*

Behind the Zamoyski Palace is the **Arsenał** *(Arsenal Museum)*, which houses a collection of Turkish armaments and rugs, as well as a model of the original town plan. ✉*ul. Zamkowa 2* ☎*084/638–40–76* 💳*zł5* ☉*Oct.–Apr., Tues.–Sun. 10–4; May–Sept., Tues.–Sun. 10–5.*

Near the northwest corner of the main square, behind Town Hall, is the **Akademia** *(Old Academy)*, a distinguished center of learning during the 17th and 18th centuries and once the third-largest university after those in Kraków and Vilnius. It is now a high school. ✉*ul. Akademicka.*

The old **Synagoga** *(Synagogue)*, east of the Old Academy, was built in 1620 in late-Renaissance style; the two women's galleries were added later. Inside, architectural elements such as the cradle vault with lunettes and stucco decorations are worth noting. It was violated and partly destroyed by the Germans during Word War II, when it housed a carpentry workshop; renovated in the 1960s, it is now a modest museum with plans for further expansion. At the time of this writing, it was recommended that you announce your visit in advance. ✉*ul. Pereca 14* ☎*048/608–409–055 or 048/693–124–572* 💳*zł2* ☉*May–Sept., weekdays 10–3, weekends 10–5; Oct.–Apr., weekends 10–2.*

The oldest entrance to Zamość, the **Brama Lubelska** *(Lublin Gate)* is to the northwest of Market Square, across the road from the Old Academy. In 1588, Jan Zamoyski triumphantly led the Austrian archduke Maximilian into town through this gate after defeating him in his attempt to seize the Polish throne from Sigismund III. He then bricked up the gate to commemorate his victory. ✉*ul. Łukasińskiego.*

What's left of Zamość's fortifications are at the bottom of ulica Staszica. This is the **Bastion i Brama Lwowska** *(Lwów Gate and Bastion)*. With defenses like these—three stories high and 20 feet thick—it is easy to understand why Zamość was one of the few places to escape ruin in the Swedish attack. ✉*ul. Łukasińskiego 2* ☎*084/627–07–48* 💳*zł2* ☉*Weekdays 9–5, weekends 9–3.*

South of the town's marketplace is the **Rotunda,** a monument to a tragic era in Zamość's history. From 1939 to 1944 this fortified emplacement served as an extermination camp, where tens of thousands of Poles, Jews, and Russians were brutally killed, some even burned alive. Now it serves as a memorial to the victims of Nazi brutality in the region. ✉*Droga Męczenników Rotundy* ☎*084/638–52–06 or 048/606–952–*

9

433 📖 *Free* 🕐 *May–Sept., weekdays 7* AM*–8* PM*, Sat. 8–8, Sun. 8* AM*–10* PM*; Oct.–Apr., weekdays 7–3.*

WHERE TO STAY & EAT

$ ✕ **Padwa.** Padwa is two-in-one: a restaurant (in the cellar) and a café (on the ground floor, with an entrance opposite the Zamość Town Hall on the main square). The restaurant offers a tasty and reliable, if not terribly imaginative, menu featuring cutlets and goulashes that is reasonably priced, even almost unreasonably low. At the café, try the hot chocolate. ✉*ul. Staszica 23* ☎*084/638–62–56* 🖃*AE, DC, MC, V.*

$–$$ ⊡ **Hotel Zamojski.** This Orbis hotel is arranged in several historic tenement houses adjoining Market Square. All interiors have been thoroughly renovated, respecting their historical form and style, and the interior decor successfully captures the spirit of the place. The rooms are comfortable and well equipped, and the service is professional. ✉*ul. Kołłątaja 2/4/6, 22–400* ☎*084/639–25–16* 🛏*50 rooms, 4 suites* ♿*2 restaurants, room service, minibars, cable TV, in-room broadband, gym, hair salon, sauna, bar, meeting rooms, parking (free); no a/c* 🖃*AE, DC, MC, V* ⦿*EP.*

$ ⊡ **Hotel Senator.** The hotel's name bears an appendix, "The Romantic Place." Indeed, the location couldn't be more romantic: in a tenement house in the heart of the Old Town, on a small square just off the main square. The decor continues on the romantic note, though the attempt to create an antique (or faux-antique) chivalric theme meets with mixed success and is slightly, well, overdone. Nevertheless, with comfortable rooms and friendly service, the Senator remains one of the best places to stay in town. ✉*Rynek Solny 4, 22–400* ☎*084/638–99–90* 🌐*www.senatorhotel.pl* 🛏*21 rooms, 2 suites* ♿*Restaurant, café, minibars, cable TV, in-room broadband, tennis court, meeting room, parking (free); no a/c* 🖃*AE, DC, MC, V* ⦿*BP.*

MAZURY & EASTERN POLAND ESSENTIALS

AIR TRAVEL

The most convenient international airport for the lakes and northeast Poland would be Gdańsk (⇨ *The Baltic Coast & Pomerania Essentials, above). Kazimierz Dolny can be most easily reached from Warsaw, and Zamość, from either Warsaw or Kraków.

BUS TRAVEL

To travel to Mazury by bus, you must pass through either Olsztyn or Lublin. From Olsztyn (which has a reasonably good connection both with Warsaw and Gdańsk—about four hours each), buses go east toward the lakes—it takes about two hours to get to Mikołajki. Bus services are more frequent in summer, and it's always a good idea to check schedules in advance.

Lublin is the gateway to the southeastern region. Lublin's main station, Dworzec Główny, is just north of the Stare Miasto (Old Town) near the castle and has regular buses to Warsaw (three hours). There are regular buses to Kazimierz Dolny (1½ hours) and Zamość (1¾ hours).

Information Dworzec Główny PKS (✉ *pl. Konstytucji 3 Maja 2a, Olsztyn* ☎ *089/539-17-76* ⊕ *www.pks.olsztyn.pl*). **Dworzec Główny PKS** (✉ *al. Tysiąclecia 4, Lublin* ☎ *081/747-89-22*).

CAR TRAVEL

From Warsaw, you can reach Olsztyn by national Route 7 (E77) to Olsztynek, then national Route 51 (it then continues to Lidzbark Warmiński). Alternatively, Route 61 leads straight north from the capital, and it forks above Pułtusk. Route 61 turns northeast toward Augustów and Wigry, and Route 57 continues straight north to Szczytno. From there, you can turn northwest to Olsztyn (Route 53) or into Route 58 toward the Great Masurian Lakes.

From Warsaw, Route 17 (E372) takes you to Lublin and Zamość (with a convenient detour to Puławy and Kazimierz Dolny if you turn from the main road at Kurów, west into Route 44). From Kraków, the Tarnów–Rzeszów Route 4 (E40) will bring you farther south, close to Łańcut. A car can be useful if you wish to visit some of the smaller towns in this part of Poland and stay independent of bus and railway timetables.

Information Hertz (✉ *ul. Dąbrowszczaków 1, Olsztyn* ☎ *089/552-06-40* ⊕ *www.hertz.com.pl*). **Sixt** (✉ *ul. Unicka 3, Lublin* ☎ *081/743-30-05* ⊕ *www.sixt.pl*).

INTERNET

Internet Cafés Internet Café (✉ *ul. Lubelska 4a, Kazimierz Dolny*). **Internet Café** (✉ *Rynek Wielki 10, Zamość* ☎ *084/639-29-32*). **Piwnica Internetowa** (✉ *ul. Szkolna 3d, Mikołajki*).

TRAIN TRAVEL

Train travel to Mazury requires a transfer in either Olsztyn or Lublin. Olsztyn's main railway station is northeast of the Old Town, and next to the town's bus station. From Olsztyn, it takes about 1¼ hours by train to get to Mrągowo, and another 40 minutes to Mikołajki. Augustów has a direct train connection to Warsaw (4½ hours). There is no convenient train connection between Olsztyn and Augustów.

Lublin's main station, Lublin Główny, is about 4 km (2½ mi) south of the city center; take Bus 13 or 158 between the center and the station. Frequent train service connects Lublin with Warsaw (2½ hours) and Kraków (4½ hours). Trains run regularly between Lublin and Zamość (3 hours). A coach-class ticket costs about the same as the bus.

Information Olsztyn Główny (✉ *pl. Konstytucji 3 Maja 3, Olsztyn* ☎ *089/538-54-53* ⊕ *www.pkp.pl*). **Lublin Główny** (✉ *pl. Dworcowy, Lublin* ☎ *081/531-56-42* ⊕ *www.pkp.pl*).

VISITOR INFORMATION

Information Centrum Informacji Turystycznej w Kazimierzu Dolnym (✉ *Rynek 27, Kazimierz Dolny* ☎ *081/881-00-46* ⊕ *www.kazimierz-dolny.com.pl*). **Mikołajki Tourist Information** (✉ *pl. Wolności 3, Mikołajki* ☎ *087/421-68-50* ⊕ *www.mikolajki.pl*). **Zamojski Ośrodek Informacji Turystycznej** (✉ *Rynek Wielki 13, Zamość* ☎ *084/639-22-92* ⊕ *www.osir.zamosc.pl*).

POLAND ESSENTIALS

TRANSPORTATION

BY AIR

LOT is the Polish national carrier and operates all nonstop flights between the United States and Poland, flying to Warsaw daily and Kraków several times a week from Chicago, New York–JFK, and New York–Newark. There is connecting service from the United States to Poland from most major airports in Europe. European budget airlines can connect you with other destinations in Poland; most of the budget carriers operate online only.

There are relatively few domestic flights in Poland (distances within the country do not justify these). All domestic flights by LOT go via Warsaw (but a new airline, Directfly, may be worth checking if you need to travel across the country, for instance from Kraków to Gdańsk or Wrocław to Gdańsk).

Airline Contacts **Aer Lingus** (☎ 022/626-84-02 in Warsaw ⊕ www.flyaerlingus.com). **Air France** (☎ 022/556-64-00 in Warsaw ⊕ www.airfrance.com). **Alitalia** (☎ 022/962-82-85 in Warsaw, 012/431-06-21 in Kraków). **Austrian Airlines** (☎ 022/627-52-90 in Warsaw, 012/629-66-66 in Kraków ⊕ www.aua.com). **British Airways** (☎ 022/529-90-00 in Warsaw, 012/529-90-00 in Kraków ⊕ www.britishairways.com). **Czech Airlines** (CSA ☎ 022/659-67-99 in Warsaw, 012/639-34-26 in Kraków ⊕ www.csa.cz). **Finnair** (☎ 022/657-01-29 in Warsaw, 012/639-34-23 in Kraków ⊕ www.finnair.com). **Iberia Airlines** (⊕ www.iberia.com). **LOT Polish Airline** (☎ 022/95-7 in Warsaw, 0801-703-703 in Kraków, 058/348-12-60 in Gdańsk ⊕ www.lot.com). **Lufthansa** (☎ 22/338-13-00 in Warsaw ⊕ www.lufthansa.com). **Malév Hungarian Airlines** (☎ 022/697-74-72 in Warsaw ⊕ www.malev.hu). **Northwest/KLM Airlines** (☎ 022/556-64-44 in Warsaw ⊕ www.nwa.com). **SAS Scandinavian Airlines** (☎ 022/850-05-00 in Warsaw, 058/348-12-38 in Gdańsk ⊕ www.flysas.com). **SN Brussels Airlines** (☎ 022/575-71-00 in Warsaw ⊕ www.flysn.com). **Swiss** (☎ 022/697-66-00 in Warsaw, 012/639-34-24 in Kraków ⊕ www.swiss.com). **Virgin Atlantic** (⊕ www.virgin-atlantic.com).

Intra-European Airlines **Aerosvit Airlines** (☎ 022/650-40-60 in Warsaw ⊕ www.aerosvit.com). **Airberlin** (☎ 022/650-11-11 in Warsaw ⊕ www.airberlin.com). **Air Europa** (☎ 022/455-38-40 in Warsaw ⊕ www.air-europa.com). **Belavia** (☎ 022/650-23-14 in Warsaw ⊕ www.belavia.by). **Centralwings** (⊕ www.centralwings.com). **Germanwings** (⊕ www.germanwings.com). **Norwegian** (⊕ www.norwegian.no). **Ryanair** (⊕ www.ryanair.com). **Sky Europe** (☎ 022/433-07-33 in Warsaw ⊕ www.skyeurope.com). **Wizzair** (☎ 022/351-94-99 in Warsaw ⊕ www.wizzair.com).

AIRPORTS

Poland's major international airports are Warsaw's Okęcie Airport, also known as Fryderyka Chopina International Airport, and the Pope John Paul II Kraków–Balice Airport. A few intra-Europe flights land in Gdańsk Lech Wałęsa Airport or one of the other smaller airports around Poland. *For airport contact information, see Essentials in the individual regional sections.*

BY BUS

Buses in Poland are operated mostly by PKS, the former national (state-managed) network that is now being decentralized into regional units. Buses are particularly useful if you need to get to smaller towns and resorts, and they tend to be more convenient for short-distance routes. In mountainous areas of southern Poland, the bus network is better developed than the railway network.

The most recent and reliable timetables can be found in bus stations, and they are usually posted on large boards—departures (*odjazdy*) are usually on a yellow background, and arrivals (*przyjazdy*) on white. Faster express buses (*pośpieszny*) are marked in red to distinguish them from regular, local buses, which are listed in black.

Although you can buy the ticket from the driver, it is better to buy it in advance from the *kasa* (ticket office) in the bus station (*dworzec autobusowy*, which may also be labeled *dworzec PKS* after the name of the national bus line). This guarantees that you have a seat.

BY CAR

If your travel plans include only major cities such as Warsaw, Kraków, Wrocław, and Gdańsk, then you probably do not need to rent a car. You can reach many nearby places by public transit or organized tours. However, if you want to explore off the beaten path or at your own pace, then a car can be a very welcome luxury. Your valid driver's license, issued in any country, will allow you to rent a car in Poland. Be aware that if you are renting outside of Poland and planning to drive into the country, there may be restrictions on border crossings, special insurance requirements, or premiums you must pay. Manual transmissions are the norm, and you may not be able to get a car with an automatic transmission at all; when you can get one, it will often be a luxury car or a larger model. Roads in Poland can be very crowded, and accident rates are significantly higher in Poland than in other parts of Europe, so always drive with care.

Gasoline prices are per liter and are significantly more expensive than in the United States; expect to pay at least $1 per liter, but prices can change. Most major cities and towns have paid parking, but the systems differ.

Seat belts must be worn by all passengers, and the blood-alcohol level indicating drunken driving is quite low. One unusual rule in Poland is that headlights must be used all day from November 1 to March 1.

RENTAL CARS

Car rentals in Poland are relatively expensive, particularly with large international companies. Prices vary within the range of zł150 to zł500 per day (24 hours), and some companies have a two-day minimum for rentals. Some companies require an additional credit-card deposit of between zł1,500 and zł3,000, depending on the class of the rented car.

Many car-rental companies do not allow you to take the car across national borders (especially the eastern border of Poland). For contact information for rental car companies, see F Essentials sections, at the end of each section of this chapter.

BY TRAIN

The Polish railway network is well developed. A full map of railway connections, covering Poland with a dense web, can be seen at the main Web site for PKP State Polish Railways. The State Polish Railways has struggled in the new post-Communist reality, but many improvements have been seen since the early 1990s. Particularly efficient are express trains operated by PKP Intercity, which connect the main cities in the country (including Gdańsk, Kraków, Łódź, Poznań, Warsaw, and Wrocław, among others). These lines tend to have newer carriages and are cleaner and better serviced than some regional trains; they also tend to be very punctual. PKP Intercity has a bilingual Web site (in Polish and English), where you can check timetables and special offers and buy tickets online (but remember that you must print out and keep the confirmation). Regional connections and regular trains (*osobowy*) are more prone to delays, but schedules are fairly accurate. Delays are more likely in winter, when there is heavy snow.

Although you can now purchase tickets for many trains online, most people buy their tickets at the train station or at travel agencies, including Orbis. Look for the *kasa* (ticket office) or *kasy* (ticket offices). You can also buy tickets on the train (there is a small surcharge), but be warned: old-fashioned regulations require you to notify the train attendant that you have no ticket and intend to buy one, *before* you actually board the train—otherwise, you may have to pay a substantial fine.

Information PKP Polish State Railways (⊕ *www.pkp.pl*). **PKP Intercity** (⊕ *www. intercity.pl*). **PKP Polish State Railways Timetable** (⊕ *www.rozklad.pkp.pl*).

CONTACTS & RESOURCES

BANKS & EXCHANGE SERVICES

Credit cards are widespread, but they are not accepted everywhere. Especially for small sums, you would usually be expected to pay in cash (you don't pay with a credit card for your coffee, a newspaper, or a taxi ride). Poland has a good network of ATMs, particularly in the larger cities, where they are numerous and common. You will get the best rate of exchange when you draw money directly from your account using an ATM that is associated with your own bank (so you will not have to pay a fee); even with the typical 2% to 4% currency-conversion charge, the rate of exchange is normally better than when you exchange hard currency or traveler's checks. Currency can be exchanged at either a *kantor* (exchange office) or a bank (usually the former offer better rates than the latter).

Traveler's checks can still be cashed in most—but not all—banks and at a very few kantors; moreover, there is a handling fee and a commission, which probably makes a traveler's check more expensive and definitely more awkward than exchanging or withdrawing cash.

Poland's unit of currency is the złoty. The euro may eventually be adopted, but not before 2012. At this writing the exchange rate was zł2.47 to US$1.

EMBASSIES & CONSULATES

Information **U.S. Embassy** (✉ *Al. Ujazdowskie 29–31, Warsaw* ☎ *022/504–20–00* ⊕ *poland.usembassy.gov*). **U.S. Consulate** (✉ *ul. Stolarska 9, Kraków* ☎ *012/424–51–00* ⊕ *krakow.usconsulate.gov* ✉ *ul. Paderewskiego 8, Poznań* ☎ *061/851–85–16*).

EMERGENCIES

Information **Ambulance** (☎ *999*). **Fire** (☎ *998*). **General Emergencies** (☎ *112*). **Municipal Police** (☎ *986*). **Police** (☎ *997*). **Roadside Assistance** (☎ *981*).

INTERNET, MAIL & SHIPPING

You should have no problems getting online in Poland. Internet service is common in three- to five-star hotels and at freestanding Internet cafés. In hotels, fast Internet connections may be either broadband and/or Wi-Fi—sometimes at an additional fee, but increasingly free of charge. In bigger cities, you will find Internet hot spots (their number is increasing every year). Internet cafés can now be found in some of the smallest villages. Recommended Internet cafés are listed in the Essentials section for each destination covered in this chapter.

Poczta is Polish for "post office." In larger cities, there are many post offices, the *poczta główna* being the main one. Most post offices are usually open 8 AM to 8 PM on weekdays (some smaller post offices close at 4 PM). Some post offices are open also on Saturday (usually until 2 PM). In larger cities there is usually one post office open 24 hours a day (often at or near the city's railways station).

A stamp (*znaczki pocztowe*) to mail a priority letter (up to 50 g) or postcard to the United States (*do Ameryki*) costs zł3.20 at this writing. If your postcard or letter already has stamps, put it in a red mailbox; the transit time is about two weeks.

PASSPORTS & VISAS

Americans traveling to Poland need to have a valid passport, but no visas are required for stays of up to 90 days. Your passport should be valid for at least three months after the time you enter the country. For the latest official policies regarding travel to Poland, you can look at the Web site of the Embassy of Poland in Washington, D.C.

Info **Embassy of Poland** (⊕ *www.polandembassy.org*).

TELEPHONES

Telekomunikacja Polska is the main telecommunications provider, but the competition is gathering pace (with Netia as the main competitor). You will find card-operated phones around in spite of an increasing number of mobile phone users.

CALLING OUTSIDE POLAND

The country code for the United States is 1.

To call internationally, dial "00" followed by the country code.

Access Codes AT&T (☎ *00–800/111–11–11*). **Sprint** (☎ *00–800/111–31–77*). **MCI** (☎ *00–800/111–21–22*)

CALLING CARDS

There are a number of international calling cards available, offering calls at competitive rates. Some of these can be purchased online as a "virtual" phone card. You can also buy them at newsstands and kiosks.

Phone Cards Foncard (⊕ *www.foncard.pl*). **Intrafon** (⊕ *www.intrafon.pl*). **Telerabat** (⊕ *www.telerabat.pl*).

CALLING WITHIN POLAND

All numbers in Poland have nine digits (the first two digits are the area code and must always be dialed). Mobile phone numbers are also nine digits, but they do not have an area code. You must also dial "0" before all numbers.

If you make a call from your hotel, you will be charged a surcharge, which may be quite high—always check before dialing. You can also make a long-distance phone call from any post office.

To reach directory assistance, dial 118–811 to reach the English-language operator for Polish Telecom (Telekomunikacja Polska). This service is available 24 hours a day, seven days a week. The cost of the connection is zł2.44 per minute.

MOBILE PHONES

Renting a mobile phone is uncommon in Poland, but it is easy to buy a Polish SIM card (and, if necessary, an inexpensive phone to go with it). Poland uses the GSM 900/1800 standard. Although these frequencies are different from those used in North America, many tri- and quad-band phones from the United States will be usable in Poland; always check with your carrier to determine the frequencies of your phone and to ensure that your mobile company has a roaming agreement with a company in Poland. In Poland, the main mobile communications providers (at the time of this writing) are Era, Orange, and Plus.

Polish Mobile Companies Era (⊕ *www.era.pl*). **Orange** (⊕ *www.orange.pl*). **Plus** (⊕ *www.plusgsm.pl*).

TIPPING

There are no strict rules when it comes to tipping in Poland; however, it is customary to show your appreciation if you have been served well. In restaurants, cafés, and pubs, you usually just round up the bill to the nearest whole figure. In cheaper places, often you don't leave a tip at all, and in upmarket restaurants, it is customary to tip a bit more (up to 10%). In luxury hotels, tipping the staff (particularly the porters) is more expected than in moderate and inexpensive ones, but it is not mandatory. You don't usually tip taxi drivers in Poland (but again, you may want to round up the bill to the nearest whole złoty, just for convenience), but you might want to tip the driver if he helps with the luggage. It is customary to tip tour guides (often by making a collection among the tour group).

VISITOR INFORMATION

Before you leave, you can get brochures about travel to Poland from the Polish National Tourist Office in the United States.

Contacts Polish National Tourist Office (☎ *201/420–9910* ⊕ *www.polandtour. org*). **Travel Poland** (⊕ *www.travelpoland.com*).

9

Romania

WORD OF MOUTH

"Bucharest was a pleasant surprise, [and] we liked it quite a bit. We had been told to skip it."

—rhkkmk

"One of our most unique Romanian experiences happened as it was getting dark in a small village, which had tons of traffic, including 18-wheel trucks and cement trucks. . . . We encountered about 100 cows returning home from pasture. They were all over this small village road—they own the place, or so you would think. Traffic came to a stop; it took about 15 minutes to go 100 yards. We just laughed and enjoyed it. Each cow knows where they live, and when they reach their gate, they just enter. They were unattended."

—rhkkmk

Updated by
Mark Baker

ROMANIA COULD EASILY BE DESCRIBED as one of those Rodney Dangerfield kinds of countries "that just can't get no respect." Most people's impressions of Romania are limited to outdated notions of children stranded in orphanages or packs of stray dogs roaming the streets, or of vague recollections of the bloody execution of former dictator Nicolae Ceauşescu and his wife, Elena, on Christmas Day 1989. Admittedly, the 40 years the country spent under communism, especially the last decade of Ceauşescu's reign in the 1980s, were brutal, and Romania has had to cope with serious problems. But look beyond the stereotypes and you'll see a totally different side to the story.

It's no stretch to say Romania may be Europe's last great, unspoiled frontier. In the remote areas of Maramureş and Transylvania you'll find vast tracts of pristine wilderness and a traditional way of life that remains untouched by modern civilization. The Carpathian mountains—Europe's second great range after the Alps—cut north–south through the center of the country, affording marvelous hikes through fir-covered forests. Several Transylvanian cities claim intact medieval districts, and fortified churches dominate the villages. To the northeast of the country, the beautiful and intricately painted monasteries of Bucovina are UNESCO World Heritage monuments. In the southeast, you'll find a watery wilderness where the Danube River ends its long journey across Europe and empties into the Black Sea. Even the capital, Bucharest—not normally considered a major tourist draw—seems to sparkle with new energy and vitality these days.

The year 2007 may have marked a turning point in the country's image abroad. On January 1, 2007, Romania achieved its long-term goal of joining the European Union. EU entry is certain to bring with it hundreds of millions of dollars of investment capital and, more important, a renewed sense of pride and confidence. The year 2007 also saw the Transylvanian city of Sibiu chosen as the European Union's rotating cultural capital for the year. And, at the 2007 Cannes Film Festival, for the first time ever, a Romanian director (Cristian Mungiu) walked away with the prize for best picture, the Palme d'Or. It seems Romania has "arrived."

10

Romanian history isn't well known to most visitors, but it's important to understanding Romanians' pride and the country's cultural and ethnic diversity. Romanians trace their heritage to an early tribe, the Dacians, who were conquered by the Romans in the early years of the first millennium AD. The Roman presence lingers to this day in the form of the language (Romanian is a Latin-based tongue, closely related to Italian). Over the centuries, the Romanians found themselves caught in the middle between the Ottoman Turks, Mongol hordes, and Russians to the east, and the Slavs, Hungarians, and later Austrians and Germans to the north and west. Around the turn of the first millennium, the Hungarian kings conquered much of Transylvania, and Hungary (later the Austro-Hungarian Empire) maintained its claim on the territory until long into the modern era. Today, Transylvania still has large pockets of ethnic Hungarians, as well as some ethnic Germans—known locally as "Saxons"—brought here some 800 years ago by the Hungarians to safeguard the land. The two other major Romanian provinces, Moldavia and Wallachia over the years, were engaged in epic battles with the Turks to avoid domination by the Ottoman Empire. By the end of the 19th century, Wallachia and Moldavia had fused into what would become the modern Romanian state. Transylvania joined the new union in 1919 following World War I, when the victorious powers awarded Romania the territory over Hungary.

> ## ROMANIA TOP 5
>
> ■ Stroll the lovely Old Towns of Braşov and Sibiu in Transylvania, and explore the surrounding mountains and castles.
>
> ■ Marvel at the painted monasteries of Bucovina.
>
> ■ Step back in time in remote mountain villages in Maramureş.
>
> ■ Meander the wilderness waterways in the Danube Delta.
>
> ■ Hit the beach at a hopping coastal resort on Romania's Black Sea Coast.

The period between the two World Wars is seen as a short-lived Golden Age. Bucharest, with its then high style and handsome boulevards, even enjoyed the nickname the "Paris of the East." But the rest of the 20th century was an unmitigated disaster. During World War II, Romania for a time sided with Germany, leading to the destruction of much of the country's Jewish population and heritage. After the war, Romania ended up in the Soviet sphere, and 40 years of communist rule brought the country to the brink of collapse. In the 1980s, while much of the country was starving, Ceauşescu ordered a sixth of the city of Bucharest to be knocked down so that he could build a vanity palace—now known as the Palace of Parliament, or *Palatul Parlamentului*. The building is second in size only to the Pentagon near Washington, D.C., and cost an estimated $10 billion to build. Today, most of its oversize rooms stand empty, a testament to the waste and folly of those years.

Ceauşescu's downfall was bloody but brief. Following the anti-communist revolutions throughout Eastern Europe in 1989, it was expected that Ceauşescu's regime would fall, but it wasn't clear how. The first protests against Ceauşescu took place in mid-December that year in the western city of Timişoara. In Bucharest, a week later, Ceauşescu was openly jeered during an address on Revolution Square. He attempted to quiet the crowds, but was forced to retreat from the podium. The square devolved into a riot zone. Hundreds of people were killed. Ceauşescu and his wife attempted to flee, but were later captured, tried, and executed.

Ceauşescu's overthrow initially brought joy to Romanians, but the first decade after 1989 was difficult. Romania was saddled with seemingly intractable problems, mostly a legacy of the former regime. These included the presence of thousands of unwanted children in poorly funded state orphanages. Added to that were rampant hyperinflation, political instability, and even packs of feral dogs roaming city streets throughout the country. Tens of thousands of mostly young people chose to leave the country to seek their fortunes abroad.

Slowly, miraculously, Romania has begun to pull itself together. The European Union imposed strict legal, political, and economic conditions on the country as part of the EU accession process. The political situation—although still fragile—has stabilized. In 2005, the country reformed the currency and inflation has moderated. The icing on the cake came two years later, with the highly coveted entry into the European Union. Nearly 20 years after the 1989 revolution, Romania has not only arrived—it appears poised for prime time.

EXPLORING ROMANIA

Romania is situated in the southeastern corner of Europe, bordered on the east by the Black Sea, and surrounded by the countries of Bulgaria, Serbia, Hungary, Ukraine, and Moldova. Geographically and historically, Romania is divided into three main regions, demarcated by the Carpathians that run down the center of the country. Transylvania, the country's best-known region and home to its most popular tourist attractions, lies to the west of the Carpathians. Here you'll find the lovely restored Saxon towns of Braşov, Sighişoara, and Sibiu. Across the Carpathians to the east is the province of Moldavia and the beautiful painted monasteries of Bucovina. To the south lies Wallachia, mostly flat compared with the rest of the country and home to the capital, Bucharest. Another distinct area, Dobruja, is in the far eastern corner of the country, along the Black Sea. Here you'll find Constanţa and the Danube Delta.

ABOUT THE RESTAURANTS

New restaurants open at a rapid pace, especially in tourist- or business-oriented cities. Although international and ethnic restaurants abound in large cities, expect less variety elsewhere. Menus tend to be meat-oriented, emphasizing pork, though fish, chicken, and beef dishes are also available. Most entrées are fried or grilled. Vegetables appear on menus, but confirmed vegetarians may find choices slim. Salads are abundant and fresh and offer the best option.

Traditional dishes include *mămăligă* (polenta), *sarmale* (cabbage rolls stuffed with meat and rice), *caşcaval pane* (fried sheep's-milk cheese), *ghiveci* (casserole with vegetables), *mititei* (spicy sausages), *ciorbă* (slightly sour soup made with various ingredients), and *clătite* (pancakes filled with cheese, jam, or chocolate).

The familiar alcoholic and nonalcoholic drinks are readily available. In the former category, *ţuică,* a powerful plum brandy, is the national favorite. Romanian wines can be very good and are quite inexpensive. Strong espresso-style coffee is favored, although instant coffee, commonly called *nes,* is also served. Although tap water is generally considered safe, it's a good idea to stick to bottled water, *apă minerală,* which is inexpensive and widely available in restaurants, groceries, and kiosks.

Most restaurants open before noon and continue serving until 10 PM or later. Small-town eateries close earlier. Breakfast places are rare, so it's

10

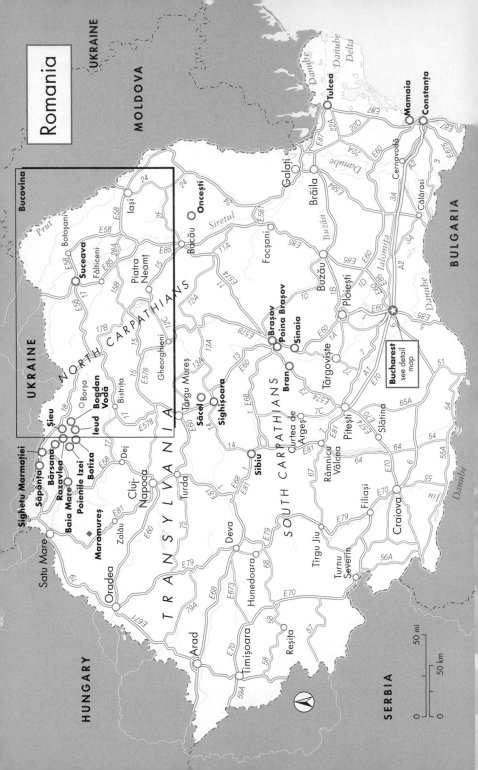

IF YOU LIKE

CHURCHES, MONASTERIES & SYNAGOGUES

Romania, a nation about equal in size to the United Kingdom, has some 2,000 monasteries, countless churches, and about 100 synagogues. Many are active, a fact all the more impressive considering that decades of communist rule actively discouraged religion.

From the multi-gabled roofs and towering spires of Maramureş's exquisite wooden gems to the fortified Saxon-influenced churches of Transylvania and the unique exterior frescoes of Bucovina's monasteries, these religious structures are also temples of history and culture. Many were built centuries ago by ruling princes to commemorate victories, usually against invading Ottoman Turks. Although Romania's extant Jewish population is small, most synagogues are well maintained.

SHOPPING

If you love traditional crafts, pack a spare bag when visiting Roma-

nia, where you'll find variety, fine workmanship, and low prices. Items include handwoven carpets; embroidered blouses, scarves, tablecloths, and bedspreads; painted and beaded eggs; wooden masks; ceramics; icons painted on glass or wood; and leather vests trimmed in fur, tassels, and embroidery. Monastery and museum shops are good places for making such purchases. Although customs officials seldom inspect foreigners' baggage, you should have receipts handy for antiques and art, just in case.

WALKING & HIKING

Romania's Carpathian Mountains afford superb hiking for all levels. A well-organized trail system exists, although many markings are in need of maintenance. Hiking maps are not easy to find, but you can get advice about routes and conditions from Salvamont, an organization that assists hikers. Youll find Salvamont stations in major hiking gateways such as Bran, Braşov, Buşteni, Poiana Braşov, Sinaia, Sibiu, and Zărneşti.

best to grab something in the hotel or pension before setting out for the day. Fast-food chains have proliferated, as have kiosks selling snacks. Along major roads are adequate to good eateries, some with menus in English, and larger gas stations have Western-style convenience stores selling food items.

ABOUT THE HOTELS

Romanian hotels are graded on a star system, with five stars usually reserved for the high-end luxury or corporate chains in Bucharest and other large cities. There's little difference in practice between three- and four-star hotels, with the latter usually having amenities like air-conditioning, hair dryers, and modern key-card door locks. Air-conditioning is a must on the hottest days of summer, but at other times three-star hotels are more than adequate and can run as much as 50–60 RON cheaper a night. One- and two-star properties are not recommended, as these are likely to be older, communist-era places in seedy or outlying areas.

Lodging prices, in general, are reasonable. The main exception is Bucharest, which in spite of a recent influx of nicer three-star hotels remains overpriced. You may have to bite the bullet and pay more than you budgeted for decent accommodation in the capital. As a consolation, prices fall by as much as half outside of Bucharest. You'll see many familiar names in Bucharest and larger cities: Marriott, Hilton, Intercontinental, Howard Johnson's, and others. Prices at these Western chains are usually higher than at home, but it's sometimes possible to arrange special package deals via the Internet before you arrive. Also, hotels will cut rates on slow nights or on weekends, so it always makes sense to ask the reception desk on arrival whether it's possible to get a break on the rack rate. For convenience, some hotels accept and quote their rates in euros, though it is always possible to pay in lei.

In addition to hotels, in smaller tourist towns like Sighişoara, you'll find plenty of privately owned pensions. These are invariably clean and comfortable and offer great value for money. You can also rent rooms in private homes in Bucharest and throughout the country. If you make arrangements through local travel agencies or through ANTREC *(see Visitor Information in Romania Essentials, below)* you can count on a clean, comfortable room and ample meals. Do not expect a private bath or hosts who speak English. Rates run about 50 RON per person per day, including usually one main meal (lunch or dinner).

WHAT IT COSTS IN ROMANIAN LEI (RON) AND EUROS (€)			
	$$$$	$$$	$$	$
RESTAURANTS	over 50 RON	40–50 RON	25–40 RON	under 25 RON
HOTELS in lei	over 500 RON	300–500 RON	150–300 RON	under 150 RON
HOTELS in euros	over €150	€90–€150	€90–€50	under €50

Restaurant prices are per person for a main course at dinner. Hotel prices are for two people in a double room with a private bath and breakfast in high season.

BUCHAREST

Don't come to Bucharest (Bucureşti) looking for a charming Eastern European city like Budapest or Prague. Romania's sprawling capital is grimy, choked with cars and people, and literally falling apart in spots. The city suffered greatly under the Ceauşescu years, when about a sixth of it was bulldozed to make way for the late dictator's megalomaniacal projects, including his gargantuan Palace of Parliament. It was also the scene of heavy fighting in the 1989 revolution that led to Ceauşescu's overthrow. An earlier blow was a devastating earthquake in 1977 that leveled hundreds of buildings and killed more than 1,000 people.

As you walk around the streets, you'll see dozens of buildings still riddled with bullet holes, abandoned historic houses calling out for renovation, and streets and sidewalks upturned and cratered—all but made impassable as cars, buses, and taxis careen around corners from

GREAT ITINERARIES

Generally sunny but mild conditions make May through June and September through October ideal sightseeing months. Winters tend to be cold and snowy, and midsummer days are very hot, except in higher elevations and along the coast. Many hotels at the Black Sea resorts are closed in the off-season. Folkloric festivals take place throughout the year, especially in summer and between Christmas and New Year's.

IF YOU HAVE 3 DAYS

Explore the sights of ⊡ **Bucharest** by strolling along Calea Victoriei to Piaţa Revoluţiei. View at least the exterior of Palatul Parlamentului and then visit Muzeul Ţăranului Român or Muzeul Satului, two museums well worth seeing. On the second day, head north to **Sinaia** to tour Castelul Peleş before continuing to

⊡ **Braşov** and its fine medieval section. Overnight in Braşov or nearby **Poiana Braşov**. On the last day, visit the fortified churches at Prejmer and Hărman, just north of Braşov. Then head southwest on Route 73 to Castle Bran before returning to Bucharest.

IF YOU HAVE 5 DAYS

Follow the itinerary above for the first two days. On the third day, visit Castle Bran before heading northwest to **Sighişoara** and its intact medieval district; continue to ⊡ **Sibiu** to spend the night. On the fourth day, savor Sibiu's Old Town, the Astra outdoor museum, and the Muzeul de Icoane pe Sticlă (Icons on Glass Museum) in nearby Sibiel; overnight again in Sibiu. On the fifth day, return to Bucharest.

all directions. Now that Romania is in the European Union, Bucharest's future looks bright, but for the moment, it's still a work in progress. If you're not a "city" person—the kind of person who thrives on energy and chaos—plan on spending just a day or so in Bucharest to give yourself extra time in the more tranquil and more beautiful towns of Transylvania and farther beyond.

On the other hand—and there definitely is an "other hand"—it would be hard to find a more dynamic city in all of Eastern Europe right now. Bucharest's streets, nightclubs, and restaurants pulsate with life and an infectious energy. EU membership has greatly stoked investor interest, and property values are skyrocketing. Hotels are going up and houses are being rehabbed. Tucked in and amid the ruins, you'll see smart shops and trendy clubs, harbingers of what someday will certainly be a modern, attractive European capital. When that happens, you'll appreciate having seen it as it was.

Bucharest's history goes back several hundred years, but it was only at the end of the 19th century—when modern Romania was formed from pieces of the Austro-Hungarian, Russian, and Ottoman empires—that the city began to take shape. Bucharest takes its name from an ancient legend, according to which a shepherd named Bucur first settled on a site near the Dâmboviţa River, not far from today's city center. Bucharest was first mentioned around the 15th century and grew steadily after that. The city's heyday came in the late 19th and early 20th cen-

10

turies, when it flourished as the capital of the newly formed Romania, proudly referred to as the "Paris of the East." Today that nickname sounds more like the punch line to a bad joke, but Bucharest has clearly got a new lease on life and the future could well see its former luster restored.

EXPLORING BUCHAREST

Sightseeing can best be divided into two segments, to be covered in two days: first from Piața Revoluției north to Parcul Herăstrău, and second from Piața Universității south to the Dâmbovița River, then west to Palatul Parlamentului and Palatul Cotroceni. Plan a full day for each. If time is short, utilize the Metro or taxis for longer stretches such as the trip to Palatul Cotroceni. Ask your hotel about correct taxi fares, and then negotiate.

Bucharest is not laid out in a neat grid, and its many circular *piețe* (plazas) add to the confusion. Street names are not always posted, nor are building numbers. Arm yourself with a good map and don't be shy about asking for assistance. Most Romanians are helpful, and many, especially young, people speak English.

Numbers in the text correspond to numbers in the margin and on the Bucharest map.

6 **Arcul de Triumf** *(Arch of Triumph).* Echoing Bucharest's pretensions as the "Paris of the East," this landmark—built in 1922—commemorates the 1877 War for Independence and those who died in World War I. Climb the stairs for an impressive view out toward the city. ⊠*At the head of Șoseaua Kiseleff.*

2 ★ **Ateneul Român** *(Romanian Athenaeum).* Gorgeous inside and out, this 19th-century concert hall, home of the George Enescu Philharmonic Orchestra, has a neo-baroque dome and classical columns. In theory, there are tours, but the building is often locked. For a look at the inside, it's best to attend a concert. ⊠*Str. Benjamin Franklin 1–3* ☎*021/315–8798.*

3 **Biserica Crețulescu** *(Crețulescu Church).* This 1720s redbrick church next to the former palace has lovely, though faded, interior frescoes and a noted iconostasis (screen separating the altar from the nave in Eastern churches) depicting religious scenes. ⊠*Calea Victoriei 47* ⊙*Daily 6 AM–7 PM.*

9 **Biserica Curtea Veche** *(Old Court Church).* Completed in the mid-16th century, Bucharest's oldest church is an excellent example of that period's Wallachian church architecture, with alternating horizontal bands of brick and plaster moldings. Note the frescoes next to the altar. The church stands opposite the Curtea Veche (the Old Court Palace). ⊠*Str. Franceză* ⊙*Daily 6 AM–7 PM.*

12 ★ **Biserica Stavropoleos** *(Stavropoleos Church).* Lovely wooden and stone carvings and religious paintings adorn the exterior of this church, built between 1724 and 1730. Inside are fresco-covered walls and dome plus an icon-filled gold-leaf iconostasis. In 2007, it was undergoing a long-delayed renovation but was still open to the public. ✉ *Str. Stavropoleos* ⊙ *Daily 6 AM–7 PM.*

NEED A BREAK?

★ **Carul cu Bere** (✉ *Str. Stavropoleos 3,* ☎ *021/313-7560*), Bucharest's oldest surviving beer hall (1880), serves a large selection of beers plus traditional Romanian meals and beer snacks (main courses run 20–30 RON). Ambience is everything here, with stained glass, painted columns, and a winding staircase leading to balcony seats. The beer hall sits across from Stravropoleos Church.

⑩ Curtea Veche *(Old Court).* Dracula buffs can check out the ruins of the palace built by Vlad Ţepeş, the 15th-century prince on whom the fictional count is based. There is a small museum. ✉ *Str. Franceză* ☎ *021/314–0375* ✉ *5 RON* ⊙ *Mon.–Sat. 9–3.*

⑪ Hanul lui Manuc *(Manuc's Inn).* In 1808, a wealthy Armenian built this evocative, timbered inn aimed at traveling merchants. In 2007, it was closed while undergoing an extensive renovation that should see the inn and accompanying restaurant and wine cellar restored to something of its past glory. ✉ *Str. Franceză.*

Lipscani. Developed around 1750, the Lipscani district is one of the oldest in Bucharest. Dirty, confusing, and crying for renovation, it's still of interest, especially the charming **Hanul cu Tei**, a rectangular courtyard between Strada Lipscani and Strada Blănari that houses art and antiques shops.

⑬ Muzeul de Istorie al Comunităţilor Evreieşti din România *(Museum of the History of the Jewish Community in Romania).* Housed in a synagogue dating to 1850, this museum traces the history of Romania's Jewish population—at 750,000, the second largest in Europe prior to World War II. Some 300,000 Romanian Jews perished in the Holocaust, and today's community numbers just over 10,000. ✉ *Str. Mămulari 3* ☎ *021/311–0870* ✉ *Donation* ⊙ *Mon., Wed., and Sun. 9–1; Thurs. 9–4.*

④ Muzeul de Istorie Naturală Grigore Antipa *(Natural History Museum).* Wildlife exhibits from around Romania are displayed in realistic settings, as are dioramas of various ethnic cultures. ✉ *Şos. Kiseleff 1* ☎ *021/312–8826* ✉ *6 RON* ⊙ *Wed.–Sun. 10–7.*

① Muzeul Naţional de Artă *(National Art Museum).* The former royal palace now houses the country's most important art collection, including 15 rooms of paintings and sculptures by European masters and a large collection of Romanian art dating from medieval times to the present. Among the collection are pieces by the sculptor Brâncuşi and marvelous works from the Brueghel school. ✉ *Calea Victoriei 49–53* ☎ *021/313–3030* ✉ *7 RON* ⊙ *Wed.–Sun. 10–6.*

⑧ Muzeul Naţional de Istorie *(National History Museum).* Don't be discouraged by the initial vast emptiness you encounter upon entering this grand neoclassical building: the museum holds a large collection

10

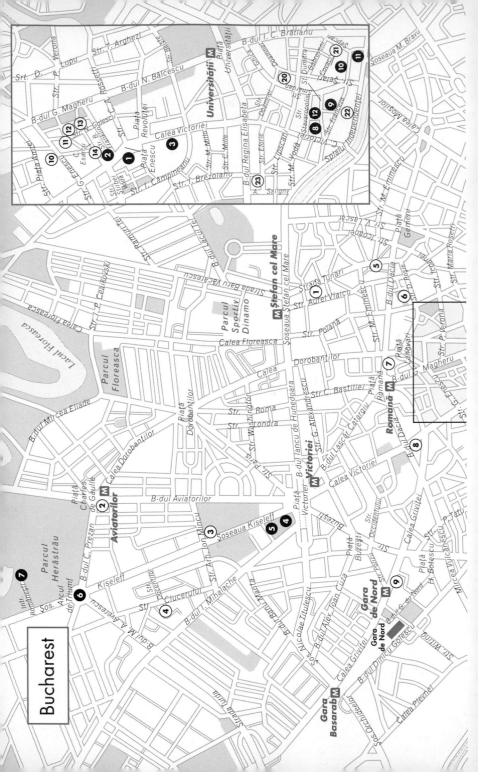

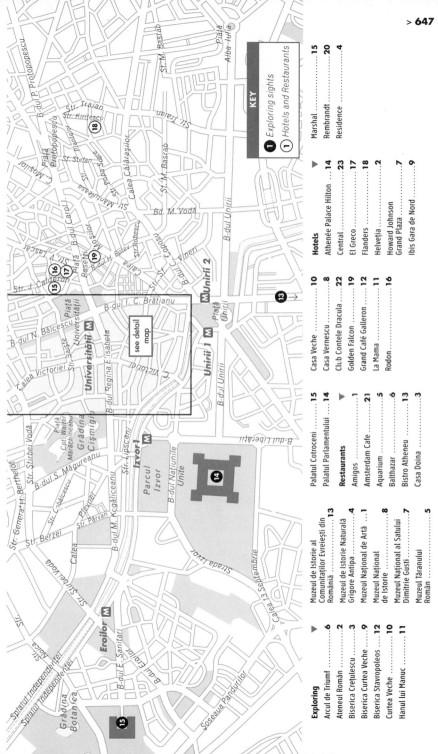

of objects dating from the Neolithic period to the 1920s. Downstairs, the Treasury section contains a mind-boggling assortment of golden objects spanning from Roman days to the present. ⊠ *Calea Victoriei 12* 🕾 *021/315–8207* ☎3 *RON* ⊗ *Tues.–Sun. 10–6.*

7 **Muzeul Naţional al Satului Dimitrie Gusti** *(National Village Museum).* This ★ open-air museum in Herăstrău Park provides the best possible introduction to the myriad architectural styles of Romania's traditional houses, workshops, and churches. The structures, some complete with regional furnishings, have been brought here from around the country. ⊠ *Şos. Kiseleff 28–30* 🕾 *021/222–9106* ⊕ *www.muzeul-satului.ro* ☎5 *RON* ⊗ *Mon. 10–5, Tues.–Sun. 9–7.*

5 **Muzeul Ţaranului Român** *(Romanian Peasant Museum).* Some 90,000
Fodor'sChoice items, ranging from traditional costumes and textiles to ceramics and ★ icons, are on view here, at the first museum in Eastern Europe to receive the European Museum of the Year award (1996). Information in English is available in each room. There's also a highly recommendable exhibition on communist-era statues and posters in the basement. An excellent shop sells traditional crafts. ⊠ *Şos. Kiseleff 3* 🕾 *021/650– 5360* ☎6 *RON* ⊗ *Tues.–Sun. 10–6.*

15 **Palatul Cotroceni** *(Cotroceni Palace).* The Cotroceni, which incorporates ★ French, Romanian, Art Nouveau, and other styles of architecture, was constructed in the late 19th century as the home of Romania's royal family. After a devastating 1977 earthquake, it was rebuilt and now houses the official residence of the Romanian president. The lavish furnishings, art, and personal effects afford a glimpse into the lives of Romania's former royalty. Guides are required (no extra charge) for the one-hour tour, but you must call ahead to reserve a tour. Since the palace is a bit removed from other sights, you might want to take the Metro to the Politehnica station or simply take a taxi. ⊠ *B-dul. Geniului 1* 🕾 *021/317–3107* ☎20 *RON* ⊗ *Tues.–Sun. 10–5.*

14 **Palatul Parlamentului** *(Palace of Parliament).* This mammoth modern
Fodor'sChoice building, one of the largest in the world, stands witness to the megalo-★ mania of the former dictator Ceauşescu. Today, it houses the Romanian parliament. Unlike the royal palaces, every detail is Romanian, from the 24-karat gold on the ceilings to the huge handwoven carpet on the floor. Forty-five-minute tours of the ground-floor rooms depart from an entrance on the northern end of the building (the right-hand side as you stand facing the building from the front). The building also houses the recommended **Museum of Contemporary Art** *(MNAC).* ⊠ *Calea 13 Septembrie 1* 🕾 *021/311–3611* ☎15 *RON, including guided tour* ⊗ *Daily 10–4.*

WHERE TO EAT

New restaurants serving a diversity of cuisines open in Bucharest almost daily, and fast-food chains have invaded the capital. But be sure to sample Romanian cuisine while you're here. Except for at the most upscale places, prices are inexpensive by Western standards. Check your bill for the correct price and number of dishes. No-smoking sections are virtually nonexistent.

$$$–$$$$ ✘**Casa Vernescu.** This elegant French restaurant housed in a magnificent 19th-century mansion serves specialties such as beef and goose liver in red wine sauce and lobster with wild rice. A second, smaller menu highlights Romanian dishes. Dine surrounded by gilded moldings, frescoes, and marble columns or, during warm weather, in the garden. Due to its priciness, Casa Vernescu draws a mostly expense-account crowd. ✉*Calea Victoriei 133* ☎*021/311–9744* 🖃*MC, V.*

$$$ ✘**Aquarium.** Glass on two sides and a cream color scheme create a light, airy interior at this top Italian restaurant. Choose from meat, fish, and pasta dishes such as tagliatelle with seafood and mushrooms. The servers are not particularly friendly, but the food quality is high and the portions are ample. ✉*Str. Alecu Russo 4* ☎*021/211–2820* 🖃*MC, V.*

$$$ ✘**Balthazar.** This refined restaurant brought the fusion cuisine revolu-
★ tion to Bucharest, and although there are now several such places in town, Balthazar is still considered the best of the bunch. The kitchen mixes traditional French preparation techniques and Asian flavors. Try the Peking duck blinis followed by lamb chops served with a cherry sauce. The clientele is a mix of businessmen, the glamor set, and simply foodies out for one of the best meals in town. ✉*Dumbrava Roşie 2* ☎*021/212–1461* ✍*Reservations essential* 🖃*MC, V.*

$$$ ✘**Casa Doina.** An elegant 19th-century villa-turned-restaurant houses two dining salons, one of which is open to the outdoors on three sides in warm weather. The menu combines high-end Continental cuisine and Romanian specialties like *sarmale cu mămăligă* (cabbage rolls with polenta). Tables are mostly filled with tourists, expats, and well-heeled locals out for a special night. ✉*Şos. Kiseleff 4* ☎*021/222–3179* 🖃*AE, DC, MC, V.*

$$ ✘**Amigos.** If you've been traveling around Romania and are growing
☾ weary of cabbage rolls and polenta, the authentic, delicious burritos
★ and fajitas at this Mexican oasis will set you right. In summer, the terrace is packed with Bucharest expats and others who find they can't live without that occasional red hot chili pepper or bite of fresh cilantro. One of the few restaurants in town with a large and centrally located no-smoking section, it's also great for families with children. ✉*Str. Tunari 67–69* ☎*021/610–6218* 🖃*MC, V.*

$$ ✘**Amsterdam Café.** A beacon of civility in the up-and-coming but still-
★ rough-in-spots Lipscani neighborhood, the Amsterdam is popular with students, backpackers, and local residents. It's owned and operated by the people who run the nearby Rembrandt Hotel, and you'll find the same stylish decor and attention to detail. The menu is light, with a range of mostly soups, sandwiches, and tapas-style appetizers. ✉*Str. Covaci 6* ☎*021/313–7581* 🖃*MC, V.*

$$ ✘**Bistro Atheneu.** This popular spot may be reminiscent of a Parisian bistro, but the blackboard's daily listings range from Greek salad to pastas, chicken dishes, and such Romanian favorites as *varza a la Cluj* (layers of chopped meat and cabbage smothered in sour cream). The

10

location is great: just down the street from the Hilton Hotel. ⊠*Str. Episcopiei 3* ☏*021/313–4900* ⊟*MC, V.*

$$ ✕**Club Contele Dracula.** At this unique restaurant, each carefully chosen item—from service plates to wall decorations—somehow relates to the fictional Dracula or the 15th-century prince Vlad Țepeș. Several times each week, the count rises from his cellar coffin to wander, candelabrum in hand, among his guests. The menu highlights well-done Transylvanian and wild game dishes. Not surprisingly, this is a popular spot for visitors. ⊠*Splaiul Independenței 8A* ☏*021/312–1353* ⊟*AE, MC, V* ⊘*No lunxh.*

$$ ✕**Golden Falcon.** Come here for excellent Turkish cooking in an atmo-
★ sphere that's a cross between fine dining and a more casual Turkish eatery. Highlights are the salads that are brought to your table by a rolling cart shortly after you are seated. The creamy hummus may be the best in Eastern Europe, and the yogurt-based salads are divine. Scoop them up with warm Turkish flatbread, which covers half the table. Mains consist mostly grilled kebabs of beef, lamb, and chicken. ⊠*Str. Hristo Botev 18–20* ☏*021/314–2825* ⊟*MC, V.*

$$ ✕**Rodon.** The house restaurant of the spiffy El Greco hotel is so good
★ it's worth a special mention in its own right. The kitchen puts out ultra-fresh seafood as well as traditional Greek mezes and main courses like moussaka, all at prices just slightly higher than at an average, non-boutique-hotel place. A local favorite is the grilled calamari stuffed with feta cheese and diced peppers. The lunch crowd consists of mostly businessmen. Dinner, served on the terrace in nice weather, draws a mix of hotel guests and a smattering of Bucharest society. ⊠*Str. J. L. Calderon 16* ☏*021/315–8141* ⊟*MC, V.*

$–$$ ✕**Casa Veche.** This Italian place in the fashionable quarter near the atheneum first introduced Bucharest residents to pizzas cooked in a wood-burning oven several years ago. And it's still top-notch. The breezy terrace, complete with miniature fountain, might be the most relaxing place in town to kick back for some pizza and a beer. It tends to fill up fast, so come slightly ahead of meal times to secure a table. ⊠*Str. George Enescu 15–17* ☏*021/315–7897* ⊟*MC, V.*

$–$$ ✕**La Mama.** Part of a locally owned chain, La Mama is a great choice for an easy-in, easy-out meal if you're not looking for a big production and are short on time or cash. The menu includes an ample range of pork and chicken staples, Romanian treats like sarmale, and decent soups and salads. Lunches are popular with the local office crowd. ⊠*Str. Barbu Văcărescu 3* ☏*021/212–4086* ⊟*MC, V.*

$ ✕**Grand Café Galleron.** This refurbished 19th-century villa is a perfect
★ stopping off point for a cup of coffee or a light lunch or dinner. Try a French-style croque monsieur or croque madame (grilled cheese with ham or chicken) or pick a salad, served with grilled chicken, tuna, or salmon. While you're here, you can mingle with the Bucharest *fashionistas* and check your e-mail using the free Wi-Fi connection—bring your laptop. ⊠*Str. Nicolae Golescu 18a* ☏*021/312–4565* ⊟*MC, V.*

WHERE TO STAY

Bucharest's hotels are expensive. The city has seen a huge boom in hotel construction in the past few years, but most of the new properties are aimed at business clientele traveling on expenses. For mere mortals, there are a few decently priced three-star options, but these tend to book up fast, so make reservations far in advance. There are, however, a couple of ways to reduce the sticker shock. Many of the hotels empty out on the weekends, so if you arrive on a Friday or Saturday, try bargaining down the rack rate. Also, check hotel Web sites for discounts. Many times you'll find Bucharest weekend packages with rooms priced at less than half the standard rate.

Short-term apartment rentals are also worth considering. Several reliable agencies, such as **Accommodations in Bucharest** (☎0722/627–808 ⊕*www.bucharest-accommodation.com*) and **UNID** (☎0722/245–151 🖷*021/327–5699* ⊕*www.unid.ro*), offer centrally located studios and one-bedroom apartments, usually equipped with a small kitchen. Prices range from about €50–€70 a night—a significant savings over hotels. Be sure to insist on a room near the city center or convenient to public transportation, and try to arrange pickup at the airport or train station, since the apartments are not always easy to find. In summer, make sure the room offers air-conditioning.

$$$$
Fodor's Choice
★

Athenée Palace Hilton. This historic property on Piaţa Revoluţiei continues a tradition of hospitality dating to 1914. The upper lobby's marble columns and the ballroom's stained-glass ceiling recapture this earlier era. Guest rooms are bright and attractive, and the staff is young and enthusiastic. The terrace out back makes a great gathering and drinking spot in summer. Pros: Most prestigious address in the city, perfect central location, historic ambience. Cons: Plain rooms (for the money), central location makes it hard to get to by car, can feel a little impersonal. ⊠*Str. Episcopiei 1–3* ☎*021/303–3777* 🖷*021/315–3813* ⊕*www.hilton.com* ⟲*270 rooms, 15 suites* ⚷*In-room: safe, refrigerator, Ethernet. In-hotel: 3 restaurants, room service, bars, pool, gym, spa, laundry service, concierge, executive floor, public Wi-Fi, airport shuttle, parking (fee), no-smoking rooms* ⊟*AE, DC, MC, V.*

$$$$

El Greco. This spiffy boutique hotel occupies a gorgeous 19th-century manor house in the center of the city on a quiet street not far from the Intercontinental Hotel. The rooms are elegantly proportioned but could use a little more polish at this price level. The reception desk is helpful, and the hotel will go out of its way to help you organize your stay. Pros: Elegant villa setting, central location, excellent restaurant. Cons: Expensive, lacks business amenities, some rooms could use an update. ⊠*Jan Louis Calderon 16* ☎*021/315–8141* 🖷*021/315–8898* ⊕*www.hotelelgreco.ro* ⟲*16 rooms* ⚷*In-room: refrigerator, Ethernet. In-hotel: restaurant, room service, bar, gym, laundry service, public Wi-Fi, parking (fee), no-smoking rooms* ⊟*MC, V.*

$$$$
★

Howard Johnson Grand Plaza. Howard Johnson has come a long way. This is arguably Bucharest's slickest five-star hotel, complete with one of its trendiest sushi bars downstairs. Its amenities set is similar to the Athenée Palace Hilton's, but this hotel feels sleeker and more in

10

touch with the modern world. The rooms have a similarly minimalist and ultrastylish feel, playing right into the hotel's motto: "where the avant-garde checks in at home." Pros: Top business hotel, great central location, excellent in-house restaurants. Cons: Somewhat sterile decor, impersonal feel, expensive, even for this price category. ⊠*Calea Dorobanților 5–7* ☎*021/201–5055* 🖶*021/201–5050* ⊕*www.hojoplaza.ro* 🛏*285 rooms, 20 suites* ☖*In-room: safe, refrigerator, Ethernet. In-hotel: 2 restaurants, room service, bar, pool, gym, spa, laundry service, concierge, executive floor, public Wi-Fi, airport shuttle, parking (fee), no-smoking rooms* ☰*MC, V.*

$$$$ ☷**Marshal.** Opened in 2007 on the site of the former Batistei hotel, the Marshal has a perfect hideaway location on a central yet quiet side street near the U.S. Embassy. The clean rooms are done up in white walls and thick navy carpets, and the cotton bed linens are touted (by the management) to be the best in Bucharest. Pros: Location, still has that brand-new feel, thick mattresses and soft linens. Cons: Should have a fitness center at this price point, slightly sterile, few amenities. ⊠*Str. Dr. Emanoil Bacaloglu 2* ☎*021/314–0880* 🖶*021/314–0888* ⊕*www.hotelmarshal.ro* 🛏*29 rooms* ☖*In-room: refrigerator, Ethernet. In-hotel: restaurant, room service, bar, spa, laundry service, public Wi-Fi, airport shuttle (on request), parking (no fee), no-smoking rooms* ☰*AE, DC, MC, V.*

$$$ ☷**Central.** This renovated 19th-century property is a stones throw from pleasant Cişmigiu Park. Though on the small side, guest rooms are bright and cheery. Baths have a shower but no tub. The reception desk will cut rates on weekends (but not usually in September or October)—be sure to ask. Pros: Central location; clean, modern rooms; excellent value. Cons: Slightly impersonal feel, small rooms, tricky to reach by car because of the small, crowded streets. ⊠*Str. Brezoianu 13* ☎*021/315–5635* 🖶*021/315–5637* ⊕*www.centralhotel.ro* 🛏*61 rooms* ☖*In-room: refrigerator. In-hotel: laundry service, airport shuttle* ☰*MC, V.*

$$$ ☷**Helveția.** No two rooms are alike at this white marble structure near Herăstrău Park. Crystal chandeliers, wall sconces, and serene artwork complement light furnishings and fabrics. Under the same ownership, the even nicer eight-room annex, the Vila Savion, stands directly behind the hotel. The Metro is across the street, providing a one-station hop to the city center. Pros: Near the park, well managed, easy to reach by car. Cons: Metro ride to the center, some of the rooms are small, front rooms can be noisy. ⊠*Piața Charles de Gaulle 13* ☎*021/223–0566* 🖶*021/223–0567* ⊕*helvetia.netvision.net.il* 🛏*40 rooms* ☖*In-room: safe, refrigerator, Wi-Fi. In-hotel: restaurant, bar, laundry service, public Wi-Fi, parking (no fee), no-smoking rooms* ☰*AE, DC, MC, V.*

$$$ ☷**Rembrandt.** This small but nicely renovated business hotel has won
Fodor'sChoice   international recognition for offering beautifully appointed rooms—
★   with authentic Turkish rugs, hardwood floors, and Tiffany lamps—at rates about half of what the chains are asking. The friendly staff will try to accommodate walk-ins, but you're better off booking well in advance since the 16 rooms fill up most nights. Pros: Gorgeous rooms, close to trendy nightlife, friendly reception, lower weekend rates.

Cons: Lipscani location is rough in spots, sometimes hard to book, "tourist" class rooms are small. ⊠*Str. Smârdan 11* ☏*021/313–9315* 🖷*021/313–9316* ⊕*www.rembrandt.ro* ↻*16 rooms* ⚘*In-room: safe (some), DVD, Ethernet (some). In-hotel: restaurant, room service, bar, laundry service, public Wi-Fi, airport shuttle, parking (fee), no-smoking rooms* ▤*MC, V.*

$$$ ⭐ 🖵**Residence Oliviers.** One of the best of the newest crop of three-star hotels, the Oliviers offers some of the most bang for your Bucharest lodging buck. Styled with wicker and white linens, the rooms and public areas incorporate a spare, modern look. The terrace restaurant is popular in summer. Pros: Lovely public areas, friendly reception, excellent restaurant. Cons: A walk from the center, modern style may not be to everyone's liking, may be hard to book in season. ⊠*Str. Clucerului 19* ☏*021/223–1978* 🖷*021/222–9046* ⊕*www.residencehotels.com.ro* ↻*35 rooms* ⚘*In-room: safe, refrigerator, Ethernet. In-hotel: restaurant, bar, gym, laundry service, public Wi-Fi, airport shuttle, parking (fee), no-smoking rooms* ▤*MC, V.*

$$ 🖵**Flanders.** Scandinavian-style furniture fills the uncluttered, spotless guest rooms in this warm and cozy hotel. The location is good: in a quiet neighborhood yet close to the city center. Ask about weekend rate reductions. Pros: Excellent value, in-town location, good restaurant. Cons: Only eight rooms (so book ahead), hard to find by car, only basic amenities. ⊠*Str. Ştefan Mihăileanu 20* ☏*021/327–6572* 🖷*021/327–6573* ↻*8 rooms* ⚘*In-room: safe. In-hotel: restaurant, bar, laundry service, public Wi-Fi, airport shuttle* ▤*MC, V.*

$$ 🖵**Ibis Gara de Nord.** The price is hard to beat for what you get here: decent-size guest rooms in a pleasant rust-and-aqua color scheme. Bathrooms have a stall shower but no tub. By the main railroad station, the location is great if you're traveling by train, but this is not the best part of town. Pros: Convenient to the train station, great value, early breakfasts (4 AM) to accommodate early departures. Pros: Tiny rooms, seedy neighborhood, institutional feel. ⊠*Calea Griviţei 143* ☏*021/300–9100* 🖷*021/300–9098* ⊕*www.ibishotel.com* ↻*230 rooms, 16 suites* ⚘*In-room: Wi-Fi. In-hotel: restaurant, bar, laundry service, public Wi-Fi, parking (fee), no-smoking rooms* ▤*MC, V.*

10

NIGHTLIFE & THE ARTS

To discover what's playing in cinemas, theaters, and concert halls, check the listings in *Şapte Seri* (Seven Evenings), a free weekly mini-magazine available in most hotels and Western-style bars and restaurants. By far the best reference on clubs and bars in English is *Bucharest In Your Pocket,* available at major hotels and some select newsstands for 8 RON.

NIGHTLIFE

Locals and expats alike frequent Bucharest's wealth of bars, clubs, and casinos. Striptease clubs and less reputable bars are part of the scene, so choose your nightspot carefully or it could become an unpleasant, expensive evening. Even in the best places, do not expect a smoke-free environment.

BARS

In Bucharest, as elsewhere, trends change quickly, so check around if your goal is the latest "in" spot. The following are likely to maintain their popularity. **Green Hours** (⊠ *Calea Victoriei 120* ☎ *021/314–5751*) is a nice spot to enjoy live jazz or the occasional classical guitar or drama, but be sure to reserve a seat since the place fills up quickly. The sometimes outrageous **Planter's** (⊠ *Str. Mendeleev 10* ☎ *0723/559–908*) draws a slightly older (late-twenties, thirties), professional crowd to dance on the small dance floor. Not far away from Planter's, **The Office** (⊠ *Str. Tache Ionescu 2* ☎ *021/659–4518*) tends to lure a wealthier and more fashionable crowd. With yellow walls and bright red leather sofas, **Yellow Bar** (⊠ *Str. Edgar Quinet 10* ☎ *021/310–1351*) is a fun place to enjoy a drink and listen to pop and dance tunes.

DISCOS

Locals gyrate and sway on the large, but still crowded, dance floor at **Salsa 3** (⊠ *Str. Mihai Eminescu 89* ☎ *0723/531–841*). **Tunnel Club** (⊠ *Str. Academiei 19–21* ☎ *021/312–6971*) has catacomb-like rooms and good dance music.

THE ARTS

Bucharest has a great many theaters and concert halls. You can purchase tickets for performances directly at the venue's box office. It's usually easy to get tickets without booking ahead.

MUSIC

The **Filarmonica George Enescu** (*George Enescu Philharmonic Orchestra* ⊠ *Str. Benjamin Franklin 1* ☎ *021/315–6875* ⊕ *fge.org.ro*), based in the Romanian Athenaeum, is a top-quality orchestra. Tickets run 10–40 RON. Most performances begin at 7 PM.

Sala Radio (*Radio Hall* ⊠ *Str. Berthelot 60–64* ☎ *021/303–1428*), housed in the National Radio Society building, hosts classical concerts by Romanian and international artists. Performances begin at 7 PM.

OPERA & BALLET

Opera Română (⊠ *B-dul. Kogălniceanu 70–72* ☎ *021/314–6980* ⊕ *www.operanb.ro*) hosts productions by many of the opera world's greatest composers. Ballet performances also take place here. Tickets start around 20 RON. Most performances start at 6:30 PM.

SHOPPING

Bucharest is a good place to buy traditional arts and crafts, as well as antiques. The area around Calea Victoriei is known for fashionable clothing, but prices here tend to be as high as or higher than in Western Europe.

SHOPPING CENTERS & MALLS

The four-story **Bucureşti Mall** (⊠ *Calea Vitan 55–59, near Piaţa Unirii*) houses more than 70 stores, 20 restaurants, a supermarket, a children's play area, an 82-foot-tall fountain, and a 10-screen cinema. The **World Trade Center** (⊠ *Piaţa Montreal 10, next to the Sofitel hotel*) has a small upscale shopping mall. The department store–like **Unirea Shopping Center** (⊠*Piaţa Unirii 1*) can supply all your basic needs.

SPECIALTY STORES

ART & CRAFTS

For traditional handicrafts, such as embroidery and ceramics, check out the *Artizanat* shop at the Unirea Shopping Center (⇨*see Shopping Centers, below*) or, better yet, visit the shops connected to the Romanian Peasant Museum and the Village Museum.

Galateea (⊠*Calea Victoriei 132* ☎*021/659–3814*) carries high-quality paintings, ceramics, glassware, and jewelry. The many galleries and shops in the courtyard at **Hanul cu Tei** (⊠*Off Str. Lipscani*) sell paintings and antiques.

CARPETS

Romania is well known for its handmade carpets; many are woven in monasteries. The shop at the **Romanian Peasant Museum** (⊠*Şos. Kiseleff 3* ☎*021/650–5360*) has an excellent selection of carpets. **Romartizana** (⊠*Piaţa Montreal 10* ☎*021/319–1216*) is also a good spot for carpet shopping.

CRYSTAL & PORCELAIN

Fine-quality Romanian crystal and porcelain are relatively inexpensive. **Sticerom** (⊠*Str. Şelari 9–11* ☎*021/315–9699*) carries a good selection. Glassmakers ply their trade in the store's courtyard weekdays until 6 and Saturday until 3.

ENGLISH-LANGUAGE BOOKS

Libraria Noi (⊠*B-dul Bălcescu 18* ☎*021/311–0700*) has a good selection of English books and videos about Romania and other subjects. Next door, Sala Dalles sells used books.

BUCHAREST ESSENTIALS

AIR TRAVEL

Most international flights, including flights from North America, land at Bucharest's main Henri Coandă International Airport (still often referred to by its former name, "Otopeni"), 16 km (10 mi) north of the city. Domestic flights and a growing number of intra-European budget carriers use the smaller and closer Băneasa Airport, about 10 km (6 mi) from the center. Both airports have basic services, such as restaurants, car rental agencies, and ATMs. Avoid the currency-exchange desks, as rates are not good.

AIRPORT TRANSFERS

From Henri Coandă International Airport: City Bus 783 runs between the airport and several central destinations, including Piată Unirii, every 30 minutes between 6 AM and midnight. Buy tickets (2 RON) at the window near the bus stop. A taxi downtown will cost about 50–60 RON with an honest driver. Avoid the many offers of rides you'll get in the arrivals hall and instead go to the taxis lined up at stands in the parking lot outside. Leave at least an hour to get to the airport during weekdays, and even longer during rush hour. The journey on weekends and in the evening should take about 30-40 minutes.

From Băneasa Airport: To get downtown, take city Bus 131. Bus 205 runs to the main train station, Gara de Nord. A taxi ride downtown with an honest driver will cost about 30 RON and take 30–40 minutes on weekdays, 20 minutes on weekends.

CAR TRAVEL

Driving within Bucharest itself is not recommended. Poor signposting, numerous one-way streets, huge roundabouts from which multiple streets radiate, narrow streets with cars parked on both sides, and a lack of parking spaces are a few of the hazards. Drivers are aggressive and often ignore normal rules and courtesies, and police checks are common. Save the rental car for excursions out of the city.

PUBLIC TRANSPORTATION

Bucharest's surface transit service (RATB) is extensive, and buses and trams are comfortable. However, both are generally crowded and attract pickpockets, and they can be difficult to navigate if you don't speak Romanian. Purchase tickets at kiosks near bus stops; one trip (*una călătorie*) costs about 1 RON. Validate your ticket on board.

The *Metrou* (Metro) is the best way to reach the city center from outlying areas or to visit farther-flung sights like the Arch of Triumph, Cotroceni Palace, and Village Museum. The Metro operates between about 5 AM and 11:30 PM. Purchase a two-ride card in any station (2 RON), place it in the turnstile slot, and retrieve it for the next ride. One-day, 10-trip, and monthly tickets cost 3.5 RON, 7 RON, and 22 RON, respectively.

Stations are marked with a blue-and-white M sign. Metro maps are available in *Bucharest: What, Where, When,* distributed free in most hotels. Within the station you can locate the correct platform by referring to the final stop for your destination's line. Be forewarned, though, that the signage belowground is confusing. If in doubt, don't hesitate to ask someone.

TAXI TRAVEL

■ TIP→Watch taxi drivers in Bucharest very carefully, and refuse any offers inside train stations and airport terminals, or near major hotels. At train stations and airports, it's best to walk outside the terminal to the ranks of ordinary cabs lined up in the parking lot. Officially, at least, taxis represent good value, but there are still plenty of dishonest drivers around waiting to take advantage of unwary visitors.

Drivers are required by law to post their rates on car doors, and this is your best protection against getting ripped off. Look carefully and enter only cabs with posted rates from 1.40 RON to 1.80 RON per kilometer. Hotels and restaurants will happily call a taxi for you if you ask them, but taxis assigned to the major five-star hotels downtown will usually charge more than the street rate. Another strategy is simply to phone for a taxi yourself. There are several reputable companies, and operators usually speak English.

Information **Cris Taxi** (☎ 9461). **Meridian** (☎ 9444). **Prof Taxi** (☎ 9422).

TRAIN TRAVEL
Most international and domestic trains operate from Gara de Nord. Buy tickets at station windows or go to the Agenţia de Voiaj CFR ticket agency.

VISITOR INFORMATION
Bucharest does not have an official tourist information office. Atlantic Tour is a centrally located travel agency that can help with basic information and find hotel rooms. You can also get information from other travel agencies, hotels, and the Romanian Tourist Office in your home country.

Two English-language publications—*Bucharest: What, Where, When,* available free in hotels and travel agencies, and *Bucharest In Your Pocket,* sold in bookstores for 8 RON or often free in major hotels—are filled with information on sights, restaurants, entertainment, and other useful tidbits.

Information **Atlantic Tour** (✉ *Calea Victoriei 202* ☎ *021/312–7757* 🖷 *021/312–6860* ⊕ *www.atlantic.ro*).

THE DANUBE DELTA & THE BLACK SEA COAST

The Delta Dunării (Danube Delta) is Europe's largest wetlands reserve, covering more than 5,000 square km (about 2,000 square mi) of eastern Romania. As the Danube approaches the end of its 2,860-km (1,773-mi) journey to the Black Sea, it divides into three channels. The northernmost branch forms the border with Ukraine, the middle arm leads to the busy port of Sulina, and the southernmost arm meanders toward the little port of Sfintu Gheorghe. From these channels, countless canals widen into tree-fringed lakes, reed islands, and pools covered with water lilies.

The Delta, which is on UNESCO's list of World Heritage Sites, shelters some 300 bird species, including Europe's largest pelican colonies; 160 kinds of fish; 800 plant families; and fishing villages where the Lipoveni people, who immigrated centuries ago from Russia, live in traditional reed cottages. Sign up for a bird-watching tour or boat excursion from Tulcea to penetrate the myriad tiny waterways and villages deep in the Delta.

The area has many small hotels and pensions, but be aware that they seldom respond to individual inquiries and their facilities are limited. Book a room at one of our recommended properties, or let a tour operator in Tulcea, Constanţa, or Bucharest advise you and handle arrangements.

The Black Sea Coast is Romania's favorite escape from the summer heat. Resorts stretch along much of the coast, running both north and

10

south of the main city, Constanţa. Don't come looking for untouched nature and pristine resorts—alas much of the coast is overcrowded and overbuilt. Instead, in July and August come to cool off a bit and relax with what seems to be the rest of the country.

TULCEA

263 km (163 mi) northeast of Bucharest.

The port city of Tulcea is the gateway to the Danube Delta. In addition to being a good starting point for boat excursions into the Delta waterways, it claims some modest Roman remains, a 19th-century mosque, and several museums.

Muzeul Deltei Dunării *(Danube Delta Museum)* provides a good introduction to the flora, fauna, and way of life of the communities in the area. ⊠*Str. Progresului 32* ☎*0240/515–866* ⊠*4 RON* ⊙*June–Aug., daily 8–8; Sept.–May, daily 10–6.*

WHERE TO EAT & STAY

$$ ✗ **Select.** Tulcea is not exactly overrun with excellent restaurants, but
★ the locals swear by this small tavern connected to the Select Hotel, a couple of minutes' walk from the Delta Hotel. The menu offers the standard pork and chicken entrées, but before ordering make sure to ask the waiter if there's any fresh fish in from the Delta. Served lightly breaded and fried, the *solm* (similar to a catfish) is delicious. ⊠*Str. Păcii 6* ☎*0240/506–180* ⊟*No credit cards.*

$$$$ ⊡ **Delta Nature Resort.** This upscale resort is unique in the Delta and all
★ of Romania, offering luxurious, full-service accommodation in beautifully remote surroundings. Guests stay in private bungalows overlooking the river, each sumptuously decorated to reflect local styles and traditions. Guests choose from a variety of daytime activities, including boating, birding, hiking, and fishing. Several day-trip excursions and wine tastings are included. The resort is about 20 km (12 mi) from Tulcea (a taxi costs about 60 RON). For a fee, a pickup service is available from Bucharest's international airport. Pros: Gorgeous remote location, top facilities, structured leisure activities. Cons: Expensive for what's offered, little contact with local people, a bit stuffy. ⊠*Somova-Parches* ☎*021/311–4532* ⊠*021/311–4533* ⊕*www.deltaresort.com* ⇘*30 rooms* △*In-room: safe, refrigerator, Ethernet. In-hotel: restaurant, room service, bar, pool, gym, spa, water sports, no elevator, laundry service, public Internet, airport shuttle (fee), parking (no fee), no-smoking rooms* ⊟*MC, V.*

$$ ⊡ **Delta Hotel.** This boxy communist-era property remains the best choice in Tulcea—primarily because of its convenient location on the river where many excursion boats dock. Ask to see a few different rooms, since various floors are in the process of being renovated. Guest rooms are nothing special but have balconies overlooking the river. Ask about the hotel's Delta cruises. Pros: On the river, clean, good value for money. Cons: Little English spoken, poor restaurant, unattractive building. ⊠*Str. Isaccei 2* ☎*0240/514–720* ⊠*0240/516–260* ⊕*www. deltahotelro.com* ⇘*120 rooms* △*In-room: refrigerator. In-hotel: res-*

taurant, bar, pool, gym, laundry service, parking (no fee), no-smoking rooms ▭*MC, V.*

SPORTS & ACTIVITIES

BOATING & BIRD-WATCHING

May and September are ideal months for bird-watching in the Delta, home to some 300 species. With Tulcea as a starting point, you can travel by boat to villages such as Crişan, Uzlina, Sulina, and Sfântu Gheorghe, all deep in the Delta. From these villages, it's possible to explore countless small waterways with local fisherfolk or in boats arranged by your lodging. Fishing programs can also be arranged. ■**TIP**➡ **Be sure to bring mosquito repellent.**

Danube Delta Tours (✉*Str. Viitorului 13, Tulcea* ☎*0240/536–726* ⊕*www.indanubedelta.ro*) organizes boat trips, bird-watching excursions, and fishing trips for small and large groups.

CONSTANŢA & MAMAIA

123 km (76 mi) south of Tulcea, 266 km (165 mi) east of Bucharest.

Constanţa and Mamaia, though separated by just a couple of miles, couldn't be more different. The former is a gentrifying though still gritty port town—the country's largest harbor and its second- or third-biggest city (depending on who you ask). The latter is sometimes referred to as the "Romanian Riviera," an unbroken chain of seaside hotels and resorts, strung out along an extended sandbar running some 6 km (4 mi) north of Constanţa.

If you're interested in history or cities, or are traveling outside of the main summer season, base yourself in Constanţa, which has an interesting harbor area, a couple of good museums, better restaurants, and more of an urban feel. If you're here to swim at a seaside resort or—like many Romanians who flock here in July and August—want to dance on the beach until dawn, then Mamaia is more of what you're looking for. But don't let the word "Riviera" mislead you. Mamaia was overbuilt in the 1960s and '70s, and though there are a couple of stand-out resorts, it still feels somewhat crowded and tacky.

Though Constanţa grew into a large city only in the past 100 years, its history goes back some 2,500 years to the ancient Greeks. They named the port city "Tomis," and that name continues to pop up on street signs and company names around town. The city was captured by the Romans in 29 BC and was considered at the time such a far-flung holding that the poet Ovid was banished here in AD 8 to die after allegedly insulting Emperor Augustus. Ovid's statue stands in the main square.

Constanţa takes its name from the Roman Emperor Constantine, but the Roman presence did not last long. The city spent most of the late Middle Ages until practically modern times (1878) under the control of the Ottoman Empire. During the communist period, Constanţa was built into the enormous, somewhat blighted seaport you see today. Much of the older city was allowed to slide into ruin.

10

Today, Constanţa is a popular port of call for many Danube River and Black Sea cruises, whose passengers disembark for a few hours to see the sights or swim in Mamaia. City authorities are in the midst of a massive renovation, with hopes eventually to make the place, with its links to ancient Greece and Rome, into a major tourist draw. They're not quite there yet, but it's fun to take at least a couple of hours to poke around the older section's crumbling streets and explore the archaeological sights and museums.

> **PICK YOUR BEACH**
>
> Mamaia is one long stretch of public beach lined with hotels. For convenience, most people set up their towels and umbrellas on the strip in front of their own hotel, but you're free to walk along the shore to find your perfect spot. The beach in front of the Grandhotel Rex is sometimes less crowded, but it's all pretty much the same.

The **Edificiul Roman cu Mozaic** *(Roman Mosaics Building)* houses remains of 4th-century Roman warehouses and shops, plus a mosaic floor more than 21,000 square feet in area. ⊠*Piaţa Ovidiu 12* ☎*0241/618–763* ☜*5 RON* ☉*June–Aug., daily 8–7; Sept.–May, Tues.–Sun. 9–5.*

The **Parcul Arheologic** *(Archaeology Park)* contains 3rd- and 4th-century columns and fragments and a 6th-century tower. ⊠*B-dul. Republicii.*

Traditional-culture buffs shouldn't miss the **Muzeul Artă Populară** *(Ethnographic Museum)*, which displays a fine collection of regional handicrafts and costumes. ⊠*B-dul. Tomis 32* ☎*0241/616–133* ☜*5 RON* ☉*June–Aug., daily 9–7; Sept.–May, daily 9–5.*

An impressive collection of artifacts from Greek, Roman, and Daco-Roman civilizations is on display at the **Muzeul Naţional de Istorie şi Arheologie** *(National History and Archaeological Museum)*, behind Ovid's statue. ⊠*Piaţa Ovidiu 12* ☎*0241/618–763* ☜*10 RON* ☉*June–Aug., daily 9–8; Sept.–May, Tues.–Sun. 9–5.*

WHERE TO EAT

$$ ✗ **El Greco.** This excellent, upscale Greek *taverna* occupies two floors of
★ an older house, a short walk from Constanţa's city center. In summer, get a table on the small terrace and enjoy great salads, grilled meats, and other Greek dishes. El Greco is especially popular with families. ⊠*Str. Decebal 18, Constanţa* ☎*0241/554–032* ▤*MC, V.*

$$ ✗ **Irish Pub.** One of the most popular and fashionable restaurants in Constanţa, the Irish Pub—with little obvious connection to Ireland—attracts a youngish crowd who come here for the good steaks and salads, or just to while away the afternoon over an iced coffee or cold beer. A full breakfast is served well into the afternoon. ⊠*Str. Ştefan cel Mare 1, Constanţa* ☎*0241/550–400* ▤*MC, V.*

WHERE TO STAY

Choose a hotel in Constanţa in off-season (September–June) or if city life and museums are your purpose. Opt for a Mamaia hotel if you're here to swim in July and August, but book far in advance. Many

Mamaia properties (but not those listed here) close October–May. Mamaia hotels do not have street addresses, but all the taxis will know where to go.

$$$ ⊡**Grandhotel Rex.** The undisputed king of the Mamaia resorts is argu-
★ ably the nicest hotel on Romania's Black Sea coast. It dates from that glorious time between the two World Wars when Mamaia really was an exclusive destination. It fell into disrepair during communist times, but is now getting a slow, loving face-lift with new beds and baths for the rooms and a new fitness center and pool. Pros: Beautiful "old school" resort; lovely beach; clean, luxurious rooms. Cons: Most expensive hotel on beach, not as good as the Iaki for water sports. ⊠*Mamaia* ☎*0241/831–520* 🖷*0241/831–690* ⊕*www.grand-hotelrex.ro* ⮌*102 rooms* ♿*In-room: safe, refrigerator, Ethernet. In-hotel: restaurant, room service, bar, pool, gym, spa, beachfront, water sports, laundry service, public Internet, parking (no fee), no-smoking rooms.* ▭*MC, V.*

$$$ ⊡**Iaki.** Similar in age and appearance to the nearby Rex, but a slight step down in terms of out-and-out luxury, the Iaki is nonetheless a bet-ter choice if you're traveling with kids or are here for water sports like snorkeling and paragliding. The indoor pool and fitness club are prob-ably the best in the Constanța area. The lobbies and public areas exude a congenial, old-world feel that extends to the generously sized rooms. Pros: Beautiful old hotel, great spa and fitness club, active water sports programs. Cons: Packed in season, popular with families with children, less than helpful staff. ⊠*Mamaia* ☎*0241/831–025* 🖷*0241/831–169* ⊕*www.iaki.ro* ⮌*98 rooms* ♿*In-room: safe, refrigerator, Ethernet. In-hotel: restaurant, room service, bar, pool(s), gym, spa, beachfront, water sports, laundry service, public Internet, parking (no fee), no-smoking rooms* ▭*MC, V.*

$$ ⊡**Class.** A moderately priced, well-maintained three-star hotel, Class
★ offers excellent value with clean, simple rooms and baths—but not much else. In the center of Constanța, it's close to the port, cultural sights, and museums. Pros: Good value, clean rooms, friendly staff. Cons: Few amenities, no in-room Internet, average restaurant, not close to the beach. ⊠*Str. Rascoala din 1907 Nr. 1, Constanța* ☎*0241/660–766* 🖷*0241/660–909* ⊕*www.hotelclass.ro* ⮌*26 rooms* ♿*In-room: refrigerator. In-hotel: restaurant, laundry service, parking (fee)* ▭*AE, MC, V.*

$$ ⊡**IBIS.** The IBIS formula is simple: a boxy room with all modern con-veniences for a competitive rate. The location is great for strolling the port and museums, less so for the beaches—but transport is available in season. Pros: Great value, good location, modern amenities. Cons: Non-descript rooms, corporate feel, far from Mamaia beaches. ⊠*Str. Mir-cea Cel Bătrân 39–41, Constanța* ☎*0241/508–050* 🖷*0241/508–051* ⊕*www.ibishotel.com* ⮌*154 rooms* ♿*In-hotel: restaurant* ▭*MC, V.*

10

THE BLACK SEA COAST & DANUBE DELTA ESSENTIALS

AIR TRAVEL

Tarom has daily service between Constanţa and Bucharest. The flight takes 45 minutes. The budget carrier Carpatair has flights to Constanţa from the western city of Timişoara. The Constanţa airport lies about 20 km (12 mi) from the center of town and the Mamaia resorts. Taxis are the easiest way in and out. To reach Tulcea from the Constanţa airport, take a taxi to the bus station for onward travel by bus.

BOAT TRAVEL

In Tulcea, you can arrange Danube Delta boat tours through the Tulcea tourist information office or the Delta Hotel. Rates vary depending on the length of the trip.

Constanţa is a popular port of call for many Danube River and Black Sea cruises. The Danube itself does not flow through Constanţa; access to the city is via the 60-km (40-mi) Black Sea Canal. Black Sea cruises put in at the Portul Constanţa, a newly opened passenger terminal in the northern end of the port, close to the old city center and most of the museums.

Information **Portul Constanţa** (☎ No phone ⊕ www.portofconstanta.com).

BUS TRAVEL

There is frequent bus service from Bucharest to Constanţa and Mamaia. Regular buses also link Constanţa and Tulcea.

CAR TRAVEL

You don't need a car to go from Bucharest to Constanţa and Mamaia, since frequent trains and buses ply this route. But if you want to explore other towns along the Black Sea coast, having a car will save time. Regular buses connect Constanţa and Tulcea, but a car is best for reaching other spots on or near the Delta Danube.

The A2 four-lane highway now runs nearly the complete length from Bucharest to Constanţ, allowing you make the nearly 250-km (155-mi) trip in well under three hours. To get from Tulcea to Constanţa, follow the E87 south about 125 km (78 mi).

TRAIN TRAVEL

Several trains leave Bucharest's Gara de Nord each day for the three-hour trip to Constanţa. Book ahead in summer. In Constanţa, purchase tickets at the station or at the Agenţia CFR. Trains do not run between Tulcea and Constanţa.

VISITOR INFORMATION

Tulcea has two helpful organizations, the Information and Ecological Education Center and the Tulcea Tourist Information office, both of which can arrange sightseeing trips. The tourist information office can advise on accommodations in Tulcea and throughout the Delta.

Neither Constanţa nor Mamaia have official tourist information offices, so you'll have to rely on your hotel staff for advice. The Web site of the

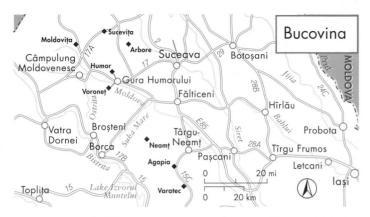

Constanţa city hall (⊕*www.primaria-constanta.ro*) has useful information in its English-language section.

Information Centrul de Informare şi Educaţie Ecologică (*Information and Ecological Education Center* ✉ *Str. Portului 34a, Tulcea* ☎ *0240/518–945* 🖷 *0240/518–975* ⊕ *www.ddbra.ro*). **Tulcea Tourist Information** (✉ *Str. Garii 26, Tulcea* ☎ *0240/519–130*).

BUCOVINA

Moldavia is Romania's northeastern province. During World War II, portions were annexed by the Soviet Union and remain separate to this day. The province claims some of the country's greatest musicians and writers, including Mihai Eminescu, the national poet, and George Enescu, the national composer.

Bucovina, a region within Moldavia that lies west of Suceava and north of Piatra Neamţ, means "beech-covered land," and indeed the area is heavily forested. Here stand Romania's most renowned monasteries. Several were constructed by the 15th-century prince Ştefan cel Mare (Stephen the Great) in gratitude for victories against invading Ottoman Turks. The exterior walls of the "Big Five" painted monasteries (Moldoviţa, Suceviţa, Arbore, Humor, and Voroneţ) are covered eave-to-ground with glorious frescoes. Despite the centuries, many paintings retain their vivid colors. All are UNESCO World Heritage monuments.

More than 15 important monasteries dot this region, so it would be difficult to see them all in one trip. The exceptional Voroneţ, Moldoviţa, and Suceviţa monasteries should be at the top of any list. Though lacking exterior frescoes, the monasteries of Văratec, Agapia, and Neamţ, all situated near the town of Târgu Neamţ, are also well worth seeing. Văratec's shop sells beautiful carpets made by the nuns. Base yourself in Suceava, Gura Humorului (close to the monasteries at Voroneţ and Humor), or a village home. Suceava is a city with museums and a citadel, whereas Gura Humorului is smaller, making it easier to negotiate if you have a car.

10

Monastery entry fees average 4–5 RON, with additional fees for the use of cameras or video equipment. ■TIP→ Be sure to dress appropriately: Both men and women should avoid short pants, and women should wear shirts that cover their shoulders. Always act with discretion and respect. The monasteries are generally open to visitors daily 8 AM–8 PM. If you're lucky, you might chance upon a service where the high voices of nuns sing in response to the chanting of the priest.

Due to the limited public transportation between Bucovina's monasteries, if you don't have a car you might prefer a package tour arranged by an agency in Bucharest. Such tours include an English-speaking guide, lodging, entry fees, and all or some meals, as well as transportation.

VORONEȚ

★ *41 km (25 mi) west of Suceava.*

Often called the "Sistine Chapel of the East," 15th-century Voroneț is renowned for the quality of its frescoes, with their predominant blue hue so deep and penetrating it has been given a name: Voroneț blue. The frescoes depict angels with the faces of Moldavian women playing the shepherd's musical instrument, the *bucium,* while heaven-bound souls are wrapped in traditional embroidered cloths. To get here from Suceava, travel west on E576 until the turnoff for Voroneț. From there, it is about 5 km (3 mi).

WHERE TO STAY

$$ ⚏ **Casa Elena.** This is the nicest guesthouse in the little village of Voroneț.
★ It's within moderate walking distance (about 2 mi) of Voroneț monastery and not far from the larger town of Gura Humorului. Romanian presidents have stayed here, but the owners have kept the property rustic and simple. The nicely proportioned rooms, some in cabins, are basic but clean. The in-house restaurant is easily the best within an hour's drive. Pros: Relatively close to the monastery, excellent restaurant, quiet location. Cons: Need a car to get here, not much to do outside the hotel, indifferent staff and reception. ⊠ *Voroneț 8, Voroneț* ☎ *0230/230–651* 🖷 *0230/235–326* ⊕ *www.casaelena.ro* ⌇ *25 rooms* ⌂ *In-room: kitchen (some), refrigerator, Ethernet. In-hotel: restaurant, bar, gym, spa, laundry service, parking (no fee)* ▭ *MC, V.*

$$ ⚏ **Continental Hotel Suceava.** In a town like Suceava, which lacks satisfactory accommodation, this chain hotel feels like an oasis. The building is a communist-era high-rise, but the owners have worked hard to update the furnishings and provide all the amenities required for a comfortable stay. Pros: Convenient location (close to the bus station), nice rooms, good in-house restaurant (that's open late). Cons: Unattractive modern building, far from the monasteries, not much to do in Suceava. ⊠ *Str. Mihai Viteazul 4–6, Suceava* ☎ *0230/210–944* 🖷 *0230/216–266* ⊕ *www.continentalhotels.ro* ⌇ *25 rooms* ⌂ *In-room: refrigerator, ethernet. In-hotel: restaurant, bar, gym, laundry service, parking (no fee)* ▭ *MC, V.*

HUMOR

8 km (5 mi) northeast of Voroneț, 41 km (25 mi) west of Suceava.

From the 15th century, calligraphers and painters of miniatures perfected their craft at this monastery surrounded by wooden ramparts. Humor is the smallest of the Bucovina monasteries and is known for its deep shades of red. Frescoes depict the stories of the *Last Judgment,* the *Return of the Prodigal Son,* and the *Siege of Constantinople.* Sadly, some paintings have faded. The turnoff for Humor Monastery is off E576, just east of Voroneț.

WHERE TO STAY

$$ 🏨 **Best Western Bucovina.** About 10 km (6 mi) from Voroneț and Humor monasteries, this large, lodge-style hotel makes a good base for sightseeing. The wood-paneled public areas lend a traditional feel, although the impersonal but clean guest rooms are what you'd expect from a large chain. Choose a room on one of the upper floors for dramatic views over the countryside. The reception desk can arrange monastery tours. Pros: Close to two monasteries, international-level services and amenities, in-town location. Cons: Average food, fills up with tour groups, outside of the monasteries there's not much to do in town. ✉ *Gura Humorului* ☎ *0230/207–000* 🖷 *0230/232–115* ⊕ *www.bestwestern.com* ➮ *130 rooms* 🔑 *In-room: safe, refrigerator, Ethernet. In-hotel: restaurant, room service, bar, gym, laundry service, public Internet, parking (no fee)* ⊟ *MC, V.*

MOLDOVIȚA

★ *32 km (20 mi) northwest of Humor, 103 km (64 mi) northwest of Suceava.*

Enclosed by fortification walls, Moldovița was built in 1532 by Prince Petru Rareș to provide refuge to nearby villagers in case of a Turkish attack. An interior painting shows the prince, along with his wife and sons, presenting the monastery to Jesus. Exterior frescoes include the *Liberation of Constantinople,* the *Last Judgment,* and a *Tree of Jesse,* where multiple human figures are gently entwined in leaves and branches. From Suceava, travel west on E576 through the town of Câmpulung Moldovenesc; then, take 17A north to the monastery.

10

SUCEVIȚA

★ *34 km (21 mi) northeast of Moldovița, 50 km (31 mi) northwest of Suceava.*

The powerful stone fortification walls and towers of this late-16th-century structure suggest a bleak medieval castle within. Instead, you'll find wall after wall of magnificent paintings. Sucevița has the greatest number of images—thousands—of all Bucovina's monasteries. Among the most notable are the *Ladder of Virtue,* depicting the 30 steps from Hell to Paradise, and the *Tree of Jesse,* a symbol of continuity between the Old and New Testaments. From Moldovița Monastery, continue on 17A north to the Sucevița turnoff.

BUCOVINA ESSENTIALS

AIR TRAVEL
Tarom flies between Bucharest and Suceava; flights take one hour. The budget carrier Carpatair offers regular flights from its hub in the western Romanian city of Timişoara to Suceava. The Suceava airport, also known as "Ştefan cel Mare" airport, is about 10 km (6 mi) from town. Taxis are relatively cheap and the best way to get to the center of Suceava, from where you can organize your outings to the monasteries or travel onward to Gura Humorului.

BUS TRAVEL
There is regular bus service between Suceava's small main bus station (located in the center, just down the street from the Continental Hotel) and some of the outlying towns such as Gura Humorului.

CAR & TAXI TRAVEL
The best way to travel around this region, if you aren't visiting on a tour, is by car. Driving to the monasteries will allow you to gaze at the frescoes to your heart's content and savor the fir-covered forests of this region in an unrushed manner. The circuit is easy to follow, although sections of road are mountainous and not in the best condition. ■TIP→ You might consider ending, rather than starting, at Voroneţ simply because this monastery inspires such a sense of perfection.

The most direct route from Bucharest to Bucovina takes about eight hours and passes through one of the few nonscenic regions of Romania. From Bucharest take E60 northeast toward Urziceni. This road soon becomes E85; follow it north all the way to Suceava. ■TIP→ For a beautiful but longer and partly mountainous drive, follow E60 north through Braşov and Sighişoara to Târgu Mureş, then 15A to Bistriţa and 17/E576 northeast to Suceava.

For getting to the monasteries that are relatively close to Suceava and Gura Humorului (Voroneţ and Humor), it's also feasible to hire a taxi for the day. You can do this through your hotel or arrange an ad hoc deal directly with the driver.

TRAIN TRAVEL
Trains to Suceava depart regularly from Bucharest's Gara de Nord. *Inter-City* and *Rapid* trains are fastest, making the trip in six to eight hours.

VISITOR INFORMATION
There's not much in the way of visitors' facilities or publicly funded tourist information offices. Consult local travel agencies—APT Bucovina Information Center and Best Travel Bucovina are good—hotel staff, agencies in Bucharest, or the Romanian Tourist Office in your home country for information on visiting Bucovina.

Information APT Bucovina Information Center (⊠ *Str. Universitatii 15–17, Suceava* ☎ *0230/531–977*). **Best Travel Bucovina** (⊠ *Str. Ştefan cel Mare 26, Suceava* ☎ *0230/521–094*).

TRANSYLVANIA

Transylvania, Romania's western province and a favorite with visitors and Romanians alike, is a region of forested mountains, castles, fortified churches, picturesque villages, unspoiled rural landscapes, and cities with historic sections that transport you back to medieval days. And, of course, this is the land of the fictional Count Dracula. The architecture of Sibiu, Braşov, and Sighişoara reflects strong Saxon influence. This ethnic group played a major role here from medieval times until the 1980s when many left to live in Germany. Transylvania was under Austro-Hungarian rule from the end of the 17th century until 1918 and remains home to a large Hungarian minority, as well as to much of Romania's Gypsy population.

Many of the country's most interesting spots are found here. Base yourself in major centers such as Sibiu, Braşov, or Cluj, taking day trips into the countryside, or immerse yourself in village life with occasional overnights in private homes. Look for *camere libere* (rooms available) signs or contact ANTREC.

SINAIA

127 km (79 mi) northwest of Bucharest.

Sinaia is a lovely, ramshackle turn-of-the-century mountain resort, reminiscent of the Tatra resort towns in Slovakia or perhaps a smaller version of Zakopane in Poland. It's situated at the historic border between Wallachia and Transylvania and makes for an easy day trip from either Bucharest or Braşov, or an alternative base if you'd like to mix in some hiking (in summer) or skiing (in winter). Decent high-elevation hiking trails fan out in all directions. Pick up a map from the tourist information office. During winter, the mountains are given over to skiers and snowboarders.

Prior to World War II and the abdication of the royal family, Sinaia was a summer retreat for Romania's aristocracy. It's also home to what some consider to be Romania's most charming castle, Castelul Peleş. A walk up the mountain road Strada Mănăstirii passes grand homes from this period and leads to **Mănăstirea Sinaia** (Sinaia Monastery), dating to 1695, and then farther on to the Castelul Peleş.

If you arrive by train with luggage, take a taxi from the station to your hotel, since it's a steep hike into town. To find the small town area and tourist information office, climb the stairs that start opposite the train station, bearing to the left once you reach the top. To find the Sinaia Monastery and Peleş Castle, bear to the right at the top.

★ **Castelul Peleş** *Peleş Palace)* is one of the best-preserved royal palaces in Europe. Built in the late 19th century in a style called German Renaissance (you might recognize it as mock Tudor), it was King Carol I's attempt to re-create a Bavarian setting in the mountains of Romania. Its 106 rooms are ornately decorated with precious woods, stained glass, *objets d'art,* even scenes from Wagnerian operas. You must join a tour, available in

10

What's All This About Dracula?

Nearly everyone has picked up a copy of Bram Stoker's Gothic horror classic *Dracula* at some point—or at least seen one of the countless movies based on the book. The story is a familiar one: a naïve Englishman travels to faraway Transylvania, meets an evil "Count Dracula," and much neck-biting and bloodsucking ensues. But what does Dracula really have to do with Romania?

The answer, actually, is not much. Though Stoker placed part of the novel in Romania (near the north-central city of Bistriţa), he himself—an Irishman—never set foot in the country.

And as for Dracula? Well, he's entirely fictional, based loosely on a real-life Romanian prince named Vlad Ţepeş, or "Vlad the Impaler." To Romanians, Vlad is something of a hero, having successfully defended his kingdom against an onslaught of Turks in the 15th century. It's true he did have a penchant for impaling the heads of his enemies on stakes, but it's doubtful he ever bit anyone on the neck (or even thought about it). The name "Dracula" was probably borrowed from Vlad Ţepeş's father, who was known as "Vlad II Dracul," or "Vlad the Dragon."

What does this mean for visitors to Romania? Well, first off, take any and all "Dracula" claims with a grain of salt. You'll search in vain for a "Dracula's Castle"—there really isn't one. Vlad Ţepeş was allegedly born in a house in Sighişoara in 1431 that still stands (in fact, it houses a restaurant with pretty good food), but aside from that, real-life "Dracula" monuments are few and far between. Instead, sit back and enjoy the lore. And if you've never read the original novel, take it along with you. It makes a great plane read. Or better yet, save it for one of those spooky castle stays in Transylvania.

English, to see the interior. Photography is not permitted. ⊠ *Str. Peleşului 2, up hill along Str. Mănăstirii* ☎ *0244/312–184* 🎫 *12 RON, including guide* ⊙ *Tues. 11–5, Wed.–Sun. 9–5 (last tour at 4:15).*

Pelişor *Little Peleş)* was the summer home of King Ferdinand, Carol's heir. Though less grand than nearby Peleş Palace, Pelişor has a lovely setting amid trees, flowers, and landscaped lawns. ⊠ *Str. Peleşului* ☎ *0244/312–184* 🎫 *9 RON* ⊙ *Tues. 11–5, Wed.–Sun. 9–5 (last tour at 4:15).*

☺ The **teleferic,** or cable car, takes you up the mountain for panoramic views of the surrounding Carpathian Mountains and the town. Return the same way or hike down the trail, which takes roughly two hours. The cable car is behind Hotel Montana, in the center of town. 🎫 *5 RON one-way* ⊙ *Daily 8–4.*

OFF THE BEATEN PATH

Castle Bran. Looming ominously in the shadow of Mt. Bucegi, Castle Bran is a gloomy though beautifully preserved fortress. Its ramparts, towers, and medieval accoutrements, plus easy accessibility, have led Bran to be hyped as "Dracula's Castle." In reality, Vlad Ţepeş had little if any association with it. Still, Bran is worth a visit. Tours in English are available. ⊠ *Rte. 73, Bran* ✛ *Go north from Sinaia for about 20* *mins, taking the turnoff for Râşnov. At the dead-end, make a left* 📠*12 RON* 🕐*Mon. noon–6, Tues.–Sun. 9–6.*

WHERE TO STAY

Sinaia has several large, modern hotels on its small main drag, but the charms of this town are in the smaller hotels and guesthouses in the surrounding hills.

$$ 🖼 **Casa Teo.** Similar to the Hotel Smart but higher up in the hills and slightly more upmarket, Casa Teo is an older house dating from the 1930s that's been thoroughly remodeled in a strikingly angular, hyper-modern style. The out-of-the-way location is perfect for those seeking peace and quiet, but take a good map before trying to walk up here since the curving roads toward the top of the hill are disorienting. Pros: Quiet location, pretty house, great amenities. Cons: Expensive, may be too far from the action, sleek, modern interiors may not be to everyone's liking. ✉*Str. Calea Codrului 40* ☎*0244/311–062* 🖷*0244/311–157* ⊕*www.casa-teo.ro* 🛏*9 rooms* ♿*In room: safe, refrigerator, Ethernet. In-hotel: restaurant, bar, gym, spa, no elevator, laundry service, parking (no fee)* ▭*MC, V.*

$$ 🖼 **Hotel Smart.** This modern mountain chalet is considered the best
★ of the smaller hotels in town. It's a bit of a hike up from the center, so grab a cab if you're traveling with bags. The white walls and dark brown accents are a little stark, but the rooms are spacious, clean, and well appointed. Six rooms come with a fully equipped kitchen. The sleek dining area—a mix of minimalist modern with exposed beam ceilings—is one of the better places in town to eat. Pros: Rooms have mountain views, quiet location away from the crowds, all modern conveniences. Cons: Plain exterior, rooms could use a splash of color, mattresses a little too firm. ✉*Str. Theodor Aman 16* ☎*0244/312–288* 🖷*0244/312–248* ⊕*www.smarthotel.ro* 🛏*25 rooms* ♿*In-room: kitchen (some), refrigerator, Ethernet. In-hotel: restaurant, bar, gym, spa, laundry service, parking (no fee)* ▭*MC, V.*

BRAŞOV & POIANA BRAŞOV

10

43 km (27 mi) north of Sinaia, 171 km (106 mi) north of Bucharest.

Braşov lies just 2½ hours by train from Bucharest, yet it couldn't be more different. In contrast to the capital's congestion and sprawl, Braşov is clean and compact. Its beautifully preserved historic core was built by the Saxon settlers and much of it remains intact.

That said, you're likely to be disappointed by your first view of Braşov from the train or car window. During the Ceauşescu years, the city was built up into a leading industrial center. The population swelled to the present day 350,000 or so, and many of the new arrivals were housed in the unsightly high-rise apartment blocs that surround the city. But don't despair. Once you've cleared the depressing newer part of the city, you enter the historic core, centered around the main Piaţa Sfatului, and are transported back 500 years in time.

For centuries, Braşov was known by its German name, *Kronstadt,* and was one of the *Siebenbuergen,* the seven fortified Saxon towns of Transylvania. The city retains something of its past ethnic diversity. Although little remains of the former German population (except for the street signs), it's still an important Hungarian city, being the largest town close to two mainly ethnic-Hungarian counties. For several centuries until the early 1800s, ethnic Romanians were barred from living in the center. Their place, just outside the town gates to the immediate north, was called the Şchei. It still exists, so be sure to take in this picturesque neighborhood as well.

Poiana Braşov is a separate ski resort located about 20 minutes away by bus or car. Even if you're not here to ski, you may want to spend part of the day here relaxing in the mountain air. In summer, you can follow hiking trails that wind along the mountainside. There are several traditionally themed restaurants, so plan on having at least one meal here. Phone ahead in summer, though, to avoid disappointment, as things slow down from June through August, and restaurants have been known to close for weeks at a time.

★ The Gothic **Biserica Neagră** *(Black Church),* completed in the 15th century, acquired its name after a 1689 fire left the walls darkened. A superb collection of 119 Turkish carpets, gifts from long-ago merchants, lines the interior. In summer, concerts are presented on a 4,000-pipe organ. The church stands just off Piaţa Sfatului. 🕾*No phone* 📧*4 RON* 🕙*Mon.–Sat. 9–5.*

Strategically overlooking the city, the **Cetate** *(Citadel* ✉*Dealul Cetăţii)* was part of Braşov's early defensive fortifications. Within its stone walls, you'll find shops and a restaurant with medieval decor.

Built in 1420 and once the town hall, the large **Muzeul de Istorie Braşov** *Museum of the History of Braşov)* stands in the center of Piaţa Sfatului. 🕾*0268/472–363* 📧*3 RON* 🕙*Tues.–Sun. 10–6.*

★ Braşov's best sights can be found in and around **Piaţa Sfatului,** a large cobblestone square at the heart of the old Germanic town that still bears traces of its original fortress walls. Shops, cafés, and lively restaurants with outdoor terraces line the square and the pedestrian street, **Strada Republicii,** leading off it.

If time allows, visit the fortified **Saxon churches** in nearby Hărman and Prejmer. Both are UNESCO World Cultural Heritage sites. Regulars buses serve both from Braşov's main bus station. To Hărman, the journey takes about 20 minutes and costs 3 RON. To Prejmer, figure on about 40 minutes and 5 RON.

☾ For a fine view of the city, ride the **Telecabina Tâmpa,** a cable car, to the top of Mount Tâmpa. ✉*Aleea T. Brădiceanu* 🕾*No phone* 📧*5 RON one-way, 8 RON round-trip* 🕙*Tues.–Sun. 9–6 (last trip up at 5:45* PM*).*

WHERE TO EAT

$$ ✕**Bella Muzica.** This deservedly popular cellar restaurant in the his-
★ toric center may be the hardest table to book in the city. The menu
includes traditional staples like Romanian bean soup served in a bowl
of freshly baked bread alongside trendier entrées like Mexican food.
You'll be greeted with a shot of plum brandy on being seated, and the
fun begins from there. One of the many likable oddities of this place is
that you get to choose your own music from a tableside jukebox—so
relax, have a shot of ţuică and a plate of fajitas, and listen to some
Norah Jones. ✉*Piaţa Sfatului 19* ☎*0268/477–946* ✍*Reservations
essential* ▭*MC, V.*

$$ ✕**Casa Hirscher.** Excellent grilled meats and fish and one of the best
wine lists in the city are the main draws of this intimate, tavern-style
Italian restaurant down a small street off the main square. The grilled
salmon, served with a side of spinach, is excellent. Pastas and pizzas are decent. In summer, dine alfresco on the terrace that fronts Str.
Apollonia Hirscher. ✉*Piaţa Sfatului 12–14 (Str. Apollonia Hirscher)*
☎*0268/410–533* ▭*MC, V.*

$$ ✕**Coliba Haiducilor.** This is the nicest of several similar rustic-themed
☯ restaurants that cater mainly to tourists in Poiana Braşov. The name
★ means "Outlaw's Hut," and refers to those romantic Robin Hood fig-
ures of yore who would rob from the rich and give to the poor. The
atmosphere may be touristy, but the food is good—mostly grilled meats
and traditional Romanian fare like sour soups and polenta. Reserve
a table: it's popular in season. Out of season, phone ahead to make
sure it's open. ✉*Poiana Braşov* ☎*0268/262–137* ▭*No credit cards*
☾*Closed Nov. and June.*

$ ✕**Bistro de l'Arte.** Ultracool and arty, this café attracts an arts and the-
FodorśChoice ater crowd that appreciates the excellent food and relaxed atmosphere.
★ The tiny menu—usually offering a couple of soups, salads, and main
dishes—changes daily according to the chef's whims or what's fresh in
the market, and may include regional foods like Hungarian goulash
or international items like pastas and grilled freshwater fish. To find
your way here, walk along the alley that leaves the main square (Piaţa
Sfatului) next to KFC. ✉*Piaţa George Enescu 11B* ☎*0722/219–980*
▭*MC, V.*

WHERE TO STAY

Be sure to get a room as close as possible to Braşov's beautiful and ener-
getic historic core. This is where you'll find most of the main tourist
sights and the best bars and restaurants. Consider Poiana Braşov as a
base only if you're here primarily to ski or hike. A night or two at Count
Kálnoky's Guesthouse, about 45 km (28 mi) north of Braşov, is well
worth the detour if you are spending several days in Transylvania.

$$$ 🏨**ARO Palace.** Braşov's nicest hotel near the historic core attracts a mix
of business types and package tours, and is the best option in town if
you're looking for amenities like a sauna and fitness room. The hotel is
divided into two wings: an older, more evocative Art Deco side dating
from the 1930s that seems to be undergoing constant renovation, and
a newer five-star annex that very much resembles an upmarket interna-

10

tional chain. Ask to see rooms in both sections to see which suits your personal style. Pros: Full-service hotel, knowledgeable staff, fitness room and sauna. Cons: Impersonal, expensive, attracts tour groups. ⌧*B-dul Eroilor 27* ☎*0268/478–800* 🖷*0268/478–889* ⊕*www.aropalace.ro* ⤴*200 rooms* ⌂*In-room: safe, refrigerator, Ethernet. Inhotel: restaurant, room service, bar, gym, spa, no elevator, laundry service, public Wi-Fi, parking (fee), no-smoking rooms* ▤*MC, V.*

$$$
☺
FodorsChoice
★

▣ **Count Kálnoky's Guesthouse.** If you're planning on spending more than a few days in Transylvania, consider staying at least part of the time at this lovingly restored château, in a small, mostly Hungarian village about 45 km 28 mi) north of Braşov. The guesthouse is the dream of owner Count Tibor Kálnoky, who managed to win back some of his noble Hungarian family's property lost to the communists after World War II. The result is an upmarket homestay where guests lodge in the main house or at an annex about 10 minutes' walk through the village. Each room is exquisitely decorated with original furnishings and antiques, creating a nice blend of rustic authenticity and creature comforts, like beautifully tiled modern baths. During the day, you can join a set program of hikes, cultural outings, or horse-cart rides in the forests and villages around the tiny village of Micloşaora. Meals are taken *en groupe*—either outside under the trees or in the wine cellar below the main house. The listed rates are for bed-and-breakfast for two people, though it's expected you'll have lunch and dinner on the premises at an additional cost of €18 per person per meal. Packages are available. Contact the guesthouse to arrange transfers from Braşov or Bucharest, and see the Web site for detailed driving directions. Pros: Beautiful rooms, supervised activities, welcoming staff. Cons: Remote location, add-on expenses can accumulate, lack of modern facilities like in-room TVs and Internet (though many guests prefer it this way). ⌧*Micloşoara nr. 186, Micloşoara* ☎*0267/314–088* 🖷*0267/314–088* ⊕*www.transylvaniancastle.com* ⤴*10 rooms* ⌂*In-room: no TV. Inhotel: spa, laundry service, public Internet, airport shuttle, parking (no fee)* ▤*MC, V (3% charge for credit card).*

$$$ ▣ **Tirol.** This five-story Romanian-Swiss hotel was built in Tyrolean architectural style and has a cozy lobby with a corner fireplace and a glass-wall restaurant overlooking the mountains. Guest rooms, no two alike, are spacious with light wood furnishings. Most have balconies. The price includes complimentary transfers to the ski slopes. Pros: Nicest place in Poiana Braşov, cozy in winter, well-trained staff. Cons: Far from central Braşov, lonely out of season, still a little expensive for what you get. ⌧*Poiana Braşov* ☎*0268/262–460* 🖷*0268/262–439* ⊕*www.hoteltirol.ro* ⤴*54 rooms, 4 suites* ⌂*In-room: safe, refrigerator, Ethernet. In-hotel: restaurant, room service, bar, gym, spa, laundry service, public Wi-Fi, airport shuttle* ▤*MC, V.*

$$ ▣ **Miruna.** With the main ski lift practically at the hotels front door, this Poiana Braşov property is a good choice if you've come to hit the slopes. Otherwise, the Miruna is a cookie-cutter ski chalet, typical of the many neighboring ski hotels built in the 1970s and '80s. The rooms and public areas are clean and well maintained, but basic. The in-house restaurant is good. Book early in winter, since this place fills up fast

when theres snow on the ground. Out of season and in summer, youll likely have the whole place to yourself. Pros: Close to ski lifts, well maintained, good restaurant. Cons: Far from Braşov's historic core, plain rooms, noisy in season. ⊠ *Poiana Braşov 51* ☎ *0268/262–120* 🖷 *0268/262–035* ⊕ *www.mirunahotel.ro* ↺ *3 rooms, 11 suites, 2 villas* ⟳ *In-hotel: restaurant, bar* ═ *MC, V.*

\$\$ ⚏ **Pension Amalfi.** This terrific family-run pension occupies a 17th-cen-
★ tury house on a small side street near the Black Church, in Braşov's historic core. Dante, the Italian owner, will make you feel at home in one of five large rooms, each with its own kitchen. Room No. 5 is a two-floor rooftop apartment with stunning views over the Old Town. Pros: Great location, lovely house, friendly owners. Cons: Lots of stairs, thin mattresses, limited facilities. ⊠ *Str. Paul Richter 7* ☎ *0268/511–883* 🖷 *0268/511–883* ⊕ *www.pensiunea-amalfi.ro* ↺ *5 rooms* ⟳ *In-room: no a/c, kitchen, refrigerator. In-hotel: no elevator, laundry service* ═ *No credit cards.*

\$\$ ⚏ **Pension Curtea Braşoveana.** If the Amalfi is booked, this small, well-maintained pension-motel is an excellent fallback in the same price range. It has a lovely courtyard and small but clean rooms, each tastefully finished with neutral colors and hardwood floors. It's in the older former Romanian enclave of Şchei, not far from the historic core. Pros: Good location, bright rooms, friendly owners. Cons: Few amenities, motel-like look, meager breakfast. ⊠ *Str. Bailor 16* ☎ *0268/472–336* 🖷 *0268/472–145* ⊕ *www.curteabrasoveana.ro* ↺ *14 rooms* ⟳ *In-room: no a/c (some), safe, refrigerator, Wi-Fi (some). In-hotel: no elevator, laundry service* ═ *MC, V.*

SIGHIŞOARA

★ *121 km 75 mi) northwest of Braşov, 248 km (154 mi) northwest of Bucharest.*

As you approach this enchanting place, another creation of Transylvania's Saxons and one of Europe's best-preserved medieval towns, you can see the profile of the towers and spires of Sighişoara's old section rising above the modern town. Each July the Medieval Festival, with people in period costume, re-creates Sighişoara's earlier days. Contact the Romanian Tourist Office in your home country for exact dates.

High above town is the **citadel,** which you enter through a 14th-century **clock tower** that rises 210 feet. Wooden figures symbolizing the days of the week, Peace, Justice, and even an executioner, adorn the tower. A plaque near the tower identifies the house, now a restaurant, where Vlad Ţepeş, the real-life inspiration for Bram Stoker's Dracula, was born.

Within the tower, the **Muzeul de Istorie** (*History Museum* ☎ *0265/771–108*) includes a torture chamber and a medieval arms collection. From the gallery at the top, you can view terra-cotta roofs and the citadel's eight additional remaining towers. The museum is open Monday–Saturday 9–5:30 and Sunday 9–3:30; admission is 5 RON.

10

A narrow, cobbled street within the citadel leads to **Pasajul Scărilor** (Students' Passage), a 175-step covered staircase that in turn leads to **Biserica din Deal** *(Church on the Hill)*, a 14th-century Gothic structure.

WHERE TO EAT

$$ ✕Casa Vlad Dracul. The presumed birthplace of Vlad Ţepeş, the original
☾ Dracula, is a popular spot for a break or a meal. Naturally, any place advertising the Dracula connection will attract tour buses, but the food is genuinely good and the atmosphere fun. You'll find traditional dishes such as pork escalope with brown sauce, and chocolate-filled pancakes. ✉*Str. Cositorarilor 5* ☎*0265/773–304* ▭*No credit cards.*

WHERE TO STAY

Sighişoara has a couple of good hotels and several very nice privately run pensions. The citadel area is quieter and more atmospheric than the rest of town, but is a good distance away from the train and bus stations. Best to take a taxi to your hotel on arrival.

$$ ⛺Casa Cu Cerb. Take the Prince of Wales's advice and stay here.
★ Charles slept at this nicely restored, privately run pension in the heart of the medieval citadel during his visit in 2002. Book early: With only 10 rooms, it fills quickly, but the tasteful furnishings (including lovely hardwood foors) and courteous, professional staff make it worth the effort. Pros: Tastefully appointed rooms, attentive staff, excellent location. Cons: Lots of stairs, few facilities, average breakfast. ✉*Str. Şcolii 1* ☎*0265/774–625* 🖷*0265/777–349* ⊕*www.casacucerb.ro* ⮌*10 rooms* ♿*In-room: no a/c, refrigerator, Ethernet. In-hotel: restaurant, bar, no elevator, laundry service, no-smoking rooms* ▭*MC, V.*

$$ ⛺Casa Epoca. The Casa Epoca is like a page out of *Architectural Digest.*
★ The owners have gone to great lengths to create a highly stylized version of 17th-century life, with beautiful reproduction furniture, some antiques, hardwood flooring, and other period touches. The location, in a quiet part of the citadel, is superb. Pros: Quiet location, beautifully restored interior, relaxed, homey atmosphere. Cons: Few services, lots of stairs, smallish rooms. ✉*Str. Tâmplarilor 4* ☎*0265/773–232* 🖷*0265/772–237* ⊕*www.casaepoca.com* ⮌*10 rooms* ♿*In-room: no a/c, refrigerator, Wi-Fi (some). In-hotel: no elevator, laundry service, some pets allowed, no-smoking rooms* ▭*MC, V.*

$$ ⛺Sighişoara. The restaurant is one of the best in town and the location, at the entrance to the citadel, could not be better, but the Sighişoara's worn, faded guest rooms are a bit of a letdown. The public areas, however, in traditional hunting-lodge style, are cheerier. Pros: Location, good restaurant, full-service hotel. Cons: Plain rooms, feeling the hotel has seen better days, expensive for what you get. ✉*Str. Şcolii 4-6* ☎*0265/771–000* 🖷*0265/777–788* ⮌*32 rooms* ♿*In-room: no a/c (some), refrigerator, Ethernet. In-hotel: restaurant, bar, laundry service, parking (fee), no-smoking rooms* ▭*MC, V.*

Saxons? In Romania?

Though Romania's borders lie far from modern-day Germany, the "Saxon," or German, influence here remains strong. The German presence dates from around 1200, when German settlers from the Rhein and Moselle river valleys were brought in by Hungarian kings to secure the region from the Mongol invaders from the east. The word "Saxon" is actually a misnomer since few if any of the settlers actually came from the part of Germany called Saxony.

The Germans built a series of heavily fortified towns throughout Transylvania, and even today the German word for Transylvania, *Siebenbuergen*, conveys the idea of seven walled castle towns. The Saxon settlements—in effect German enclaves, since the Wallach (Romanian) and Hungarian populations were forbidden to live within the town gates—thrived throughout the Middle Ages. Today,

the town centers of the former Saxon settlements of Braşov and Sibiu, still strongly evocative of their German roots, remain the most beautiful in Transylvania.

The Saxon influence began to wane in the 19th and early 20th centuries. The Saxons were always a minority within Transylvania, and as the local Hungarian and Romanian populations grew, the Saxons could no longer maintain their privileged status. The darkest days came during and after World War II, when many of the Saxon settlers were killed or forcibly expelled. Those who survived the war and stayed suffered at the hands of the postwar Ceauşescu regime, which shamelessly bartered with ethnic Germans wishing to emigrate in exchange for hard currency. By 1989, the German population in cities like Braşov and Sibiu had dwindled to just a few thousand.

SIBIU

92 km 57 mi) southwest of Sighişoara, 271 km (168 mi) northwest of Bucharest.

Sibiu, designated the European cultural capital for the year 2007, is easily Braşov's rival for the most charming town center in Romania. Like Braşov, the city was built up by "Saxon" settlers, brought in during the 12th and 13th centuries by Hungarian kings to fortify the area from the Tartar barbarians from the East. The city—known for centuries by its German name "Hermannstadt"—grew wealthy over the years as it came to dominate local trade. Today, that distinctly German feel remains, and as you walk the beautiful and prosperous-looking Piaţa Mare (Great Square) you'll be forgiven for thinking you're strolling through a beautifully restored German market town like Heidelberg or Ravensburg.

Be sure to leave at least a few hours to explore the narrow alleys and little squares of the historic core. Sections of the medieval walls that successfully repelled the Ottoman invaders still stand as they always have. In addition to the Piaţa Mare, there's the nearby Piaţa Mică, the Small Square, and the Piaţa Huet, with the commanding **Biserica**

10

Evanghelică, (Evangelical Church). Be sure to look up as you pass the steep-roofed 17th-century buildings. Their eyebrow-shape dormer windows are the unofficial symbols of the city.

Sibiu is more than just great architecture. The city's university is home to tens of thousands of students, giving the town a kind of laid-back coffeehouse feel. It's a great place to hang out for a few days and recharge your batteries. The theaters, concerts, and exhibitions are some of the best in the country. The nationally renowned **State Philharmonic Orchestra** (⊠*Str. Cetatii 3–5* ☎*0269/206–507* ⊕*www.filarmonicasibiu.ro*) performs regularly at Thalia Hall. Buy tickets at the box office the day of the performance.

Biserica Evanghelică *(Evangelical Church)* rises just behind Piața Mare in Gothic splendor, its tile-covered spires sparkling in the sun.

Biserica Romano Catolică *(Roman Catholic Church),* a splendid high-baroque structure, stands in Piața Mare.

★ The **Muzeul Brukenthal** *(Brukenthal Museum)* exhibits an impressive collection of silver, paintings, and religious art. Tours are available in English. ⊠*Piața Mare 4–5* ☎*0269/217–691* ⊕*www.brukenthalmuseum. ro* 🎟*6 RON* ⊙*Tues.–Sun. 9–5 (closes at 4 in winter).*

Muzeul Civilzației Populare Tradiționale Astra *(Traditional Folk Civilization Museum),* a short drive from Sibiu, is a 200-acre outdoor exhibit of original dwellings, workshops, and churches from around the country. ⊠*Calea Răşinari* ☎*0269/242–599* ⊕*www.muzeulastra.ro* 🎟*15 RON* ⊙*May–Aug., Tues.–Sun. 10–6; Sept.–Apr., Tues.–Sun. 9–5.*

In the nearby village of **Sibiel,** the **Muzeul de Icoane pe Sticlă** *(The Museum of Painted Glass Icons),* in the courtyard of the Orthodox Church, houses some 700 icons. Returning to Sibiu on the main road from Sibiel, stop at the village of **Cristian** to see its 14th-century fortified church. ⊠*Str. Bisericii 329* ☎*0269/552–536* 🎟*5 RON* ⊙*Daily 8–6.*

WHERE TO EAT

$$ ✕**Crama Sibiul Vechi.** Locals and visitors alike flock to this cellar eatery, where waiters in traditional dress serve such favorites as pork fillet stuffed with ham and mushrooms. Singers render old tunes, embroidered scarves hang from the vaulted brick ceiling, and ceramic plates line the walls. ⊠*Str. Papiu Ilarian 3* ☎*0269/210–461* ▭*No credit cards.*

Fodor'sChoice
★

$$ ✕**La Piazzetta.** This tiny restaurant wins our vote for the best pizza in Romania. The Italian owners have gone to great lengths to re-create an authentic Italian experience, including importing hard-to-find Italian meats and cheeses. The small dining area can get very crowded in the evening, so stop by during the day to reserve a table. ⊠*Str. Piața Mică 15* ☎*0269/230–879* ⚘*Reservations essential* ▭*No credit cards.*
★

WHERE TO STAY

Sibiu has suffered from a shortage of quality hotel rooms, but that was poised to change in 2008 with the opening of several four- and five-star properties, including a new Ramada Inn in the center of town and a project involving the Hilton Hotel group outside the city. Contact the Sibiu Tourist Information office for a status report.

$$$ ⚿ **Împăratul Romanilor.** This 16th-century structure just a block away
★ from Piața Mare has been an inn since 1772. Its name translates into "Roman Emperor," and famous guests have apparently included Emperor Josef II and Johannes Brahms. The lobby is elegant in gold and blue, and guest rooms have antique-style white furniture accented by tufted gold cloth headboards. Some rooms have lofts. The restaurant claims a sliding glass ceiling. Pros: Great location, old-world feel, ornate lobby. Cons: Expensive for what you get, quirky rooms may not be to 'everyone's liking, indifferent staff. ⊠ *Str. Nicolae Bălcescu 2–4* ☎*0269/216–500* 📠*0269/213–278* 🛏*64 rooms, 32 suites* ⟳*In-room: refrigerator, Ethernet. In-hotel: restaurant, room service, bar, laundry service, parking, no-smoking rooms* ☰*MC, V.*

$$ ⚿ **Casa Luxemburg.** A kind of youth hostel for grown-ups, Casa Luxemburg is short on amenities but great on value, with clean, quiet rooms and an unbeatable historic-core location on the Piața Mică. The building itself is a former burgher's residence from the late Middle Ages that now houses the consular offices of the Grand Duchy of Luxembourg. The hotel is managed by the small private travel agency Kultours, which has its office on the ground floor. Pros: Great location, historic atmosphere, low price. Cons: Modest rooms, inedible breakfast, steep staircases. ⊠ *Piața Mică 16* ☎*0269/216–854* 📠*0269/216–854* ⊕*www. kultours.ro* 🛏*12 rooms* ⟳*In-hotel: no elevator* ☰*MC, V.*

$$ ⚿ **Continental.** On the main road into town, this property, part of Romania's biggest chain, is just a 10-minute walk from the historic section. Guest rooms are decorated in blue and white. Geared toward business travelers, the hotel is comfortable and functional. The staff members are helpful, friendly, and professional, and many speak excellent English. Pros: Good location, comfortable rooms, full-service hotel. Cons: Communist-era architecture, thin walls between the room, only "executive" rooms offer air-conditioning. ⊠*Calea Dumbrăvii 2–4* ☎*0269/218–100* 📠*0269/210–125* ⊕*www.continentalhotels.ro* 🛏*169 rooms, 13 suites* ⟳*In-room: no a/c (some), refrigerator, Ethernet. In-hotel: restaurant, room service, bar, laundry service, public Internet, parking (fee), no-smoking rooms* ☰*MC, V.*

10

MARAMUREŞ

324 km (201 mi) north of Sibiu, 595 km (369 mi) northwest of Bucharest.

Tucked away in the mountains of northwestern Romania, Maramureş County seems a region lost in time. Here, in one of the few parts of the country never conquered by the Romans, people claim descent directly from the Dacians. This is a land of homes hiding behind towering wooden gates attached to fences a fraction of their height. Intricately hand-carved in motifs of twisted rope, acorns, crosses, and the sun, these gates have come to symbolize Maramureş. So have the wooden churches—tiny gems from the 13th through 18th century, with multi-gable shingle roofs and soaring, narrow steeples. Many have fine interior frescoes, and several are UNESCO World Cultural Heritage monuments. In late afternoon, when women sit on roadside benches, chatting as they coax wool onto spindles, and red-tasseled horses pull wagons overflowing with hay home from the fields, it's easy to fall under the spell of this special place.

Baia Mare is the largest city in the region, but Maramureş's second city, **Sighetu Marmaţiei** (usually shortened to Sighet), along the Ukrainian border, makes a better base for exploring. It's smaller and friendlier, has a couple of good hotels and dining options, and is closer to the main villages along the picturesque Iza Valley. Be forewarned, though: it's a long haul up to Sighet. The overnight train journey from Bucharest takes about 13 hours (from Braşov, about 10 hours). It's quicker by car, but still a long, 10-hour slog on mainly slow, two-lane roads. There's also not much preparation made for out-of-town visitors. Sighet lacks a tourist information office, and the privately owned travel agencies are more geared to locals going abroad than for visitors wanting to tour Maramureş. You'll also need your own wheels for making the most of your trip here, since bus and train service is sporadic at best.

WHERE TO STAY

Homestays present a great way to experience Maramureş life. Rates run about €20 a night for two including breakfast and often lunch or dinner; baths are usually shared. Look for *camere libere* (rooms available) signs or, more common, Zimmer Frei ("room available" in German) or even "House for Rent" (meaning "room for rent"). Homes that display the green ANTREC logo have been approved by that organization, guaranteeing clean, comfortable accommodations.

$$ ☐ **Casa Iurca de Calineştï.** This tidy, family-run pension is by far the
★ cleanest and coziest accommodation in Sighet. The owners skillfully mix traditional elements like carved wooden furnishings and handwoven rugs with modern touches like super-clean bathrooms and in-room Internet. The back garden restaurant, offering delicious grilled meats and traditional Romanian cooking, might well merit a Michelin star, if Michelin ever got out this far. Even if you're not staying here, book a table for your evening meal. Pros: Excellent restaurant, clean rooms, in-town location. Cons: Indifferent staff, high cost of add-ons like laundry service, some street noise (ask for a room facing the garden). ⊠*Str. Dragoş Vodă 14, Sighetu Marmaţiei* ☎*0262/318–882* 🖷*0262/318– 885* 🖵*10 rooms* ♿*In-room: refrigerator, Ethernet. In-hotel: restaurant, no elevator, laundry service, no-smoking rooms* ▬*MC, V.*

$ ☐ **Bud Mariana.** One of the nicer homestay properties along the Iza River, this large but otherwise ordinary village house has six guest rooms plus a "traditional room" with a display of regional crafts such as embroidered cloths and pillows, handwoven carpets, and painted ceramic plates. You won't get luxury, but the friendly and knowledgeable owners (English-speaking), go out of their way to make you feel welcome. The room rate is for half board breakfast plus lunch or dinner). Its in the village of Onceşti, about 15 km (10 mi) from Sighet and

A GOOD TOUR: VALEA IZEI

Valea Izei Iza Valley) is ideal for observing the traditional life of Maramureş. Follow Route 186 east from Sighetu to Săcel; village after village vies for attention. Onceşti and Bârsana arguably claim the greatest number of impressive gates, and Bârsana's church has a 184-foot steeple. Farther along, admire the wooden churches at Rozavlea and Şieu. The latter is just off Route 186—take the turn for Botiza. Continue on this side road to a fork: left to Botiza, right to Poienile Izei. Both have wonderful churches; vivid frescoes depicting ingenious punishments for sinners cover the interior walls of the latter. Back on the main road, turn right to visit the church at Bogdan Vodă, which also has good frescoes. Near Bogdan Vodă, take the turn for Ieud; this village has fine gates and two wooden churches. If the churches are locked, any passerby will help find the person with the *cheie* pronounced kay-

ă), or key. On Sunday most villagers wear traditional dress.

The town of Sighet, though no beauty spot, has some interesting attractions, including two worthwhile museums: the Memorial to the Victims of Communism, housed in a former prison, and the Muzeul Etnografic al Maramureşului Ethnographic Museum of Maramureş), an outdoor collection of homes and farmsteads from around the county. Another ethnographic museum, displaying regional costumes and artifacts, stands in the town's center. Also here are an impressive synagogue and the childhood home of author Elie Wiesel.

■TIP➔ No trip to Maramureş is complete without a visit to Săpânţa (a 20-minute drive from Sighetu Marmaţiei) and its Cimitirul Vesel (Merry Cemetery). Colorful folk-art paintings and witty words carved into wooden grave markers sum up the deceaseds' lives.

reachable only by car. Pros: In the middle of nowhere, friendly hosts, authentic homestay experience. Cons: Simple rooms with no attached bath, little privacy, in the middle of nowhere. ⊠*Str. Principală 360, Onceşti* ☎*0262/348–448* ☞*6 rooms share 2 baths* ♿*In-room: no a/c, no elevator* ⊟*No credit cards.*

$ 🖫**Perla Sigheteană.** If you are staying in Sighet and the Casa Iurca is full, try getting a room here, the second-best accommodation in town. This chalet-style hotel offers clean, basic rooms with firm mattresses, balconies (some with mountain views), and good-quality linens. Bathrooms are small but well equipped. The hotel draws a 50-50 mix of Romanian families and foreign tourists. Pros: Beautiful back garden, clean rooms, decent restaurant. Cons: Good location (just beyond walking distance to the center of town), impersonal staff, scruffy-looking lobby. ⊠*Str. Avram Iancu 65/A, Sighetu Marmaţiei* ☎*0262/310–613* 🖷*0262/310–268* ☞*8 rooms* ♿*In-room: no a/c, refrigerator, dial-up. In-hotel: restaurant, room service, bar, laundry service, parking (no fee), some pets allowed* ⊟*MC, V.*

10

TRANSYLVANIA ESSENTIALS

AIR TRAVEL

From Bucharest, Tarom maintains regular air service to the cities of Sibiu, Târgu Mureş, and Cluj-Napoca. Tarom flies a couple of times a week from Bucharest to Baia Mare, most convenient for Maramureş. Braşov does not have an airport and is best reached from one of Bucharest's airports. Carpatair flies to Sibiu and Cluj from its hub in Timişoara. Sighişoara can be reached from the Sibiu, Cluj, or Târgu Mureş airports; from there, take a taxi to either the bus or train station (depending on how you're traveling) for your onward journey.

BUS TRAVEL

Trains are better than buses for getting to Transylvania, but consider bus travel to smaller cities and towns that don't lie on the major rail lines. Bus stations are usually located right next to the train station. Inquire locally for timetables.

In Maramureş, regular bus service connects the main cities of Baia Mare and Sighet, but connections to other areas is sporadic at best. As a general rule, don't depend on bus travel to get around Maramureş.

CAR TRAVEL

In Transylvania, you won't need a car if you're going only to main cities like Braşov, Sighişoara, and Sibiu. If you'd like to see some of the other, smaller towns or the countryside, however, you'll see more and save time by driving. Because of the lack of public transportation, a car is essential for exploring Maramureş.

You can rent a car in Braşov or Sibiu, or get your vehicle in Bucharest and drive up. Car rental agencies elsewhere in the region, especially in rural Maramureş, are few and far between.

From Bucharest, E60 passes some lovely scenery as it stretches north through Sinaia to Braşov and Sighişoara. Figure 2½ hours to Braşov. To reach Sibiu, take Route 14 southwest from Sighişoara or E68 west from Braşov.

From Sighişoara to Maramureş, follow Routes 13, 15A, and 17C north to Săcel (passing through the cities of Târgu Mureş and Bistriţa en route), where you turn west, traveling through the Iza Valley along tiny Route 186 to Sighetu Marmaţiei. Roads are generally slow, so figure on a full day of car travel.

TRAIN TRAVEL

Train travel is a viable option for getting around Transylvania if you intend to stick to the main towns. Connections from Bucharest to Braşov are frequent (about one train an hour during the day), and from Braşov, it's relatively straightforward to get to Sibiu, Sighişoara, and points farther afield. Choose *Inter-City* or *Rapid* service to save time.

Train service to and within Maramureş is less frequent. One daily overnight train runs between Bucharest and Sighet, stopping in Braşov en route. The journey from Bucharest to Sighet takes approximately 13 hours.

VISITOR INFORMATION

With the exception of Maramureş, Transylvania is better set up for visitors than other regions of Romania. Tourist information offices in major tourist centers like Braşov, Sibiu, Sinaia, and Sighişoara can arrange tours and provide maps and useful information, including ideas on where to stay, but generally will not book rooms for you. Most tourist offices are closed weekends or work only a half day on Saturday.

In Maramureş, you'll have to do more advance preparation because facilities on the ground are few and far between. Baia Mare has a small tourist information office, but Sighet does not. Nor are the local hotels much help. Try to do as much planning as you can before you arrive.

Information Braşov Tourist Information (⊠ *Piaţa Sfatului 30, Braşov* ☎ *0268/419–078* ⊕ *www.brasovcity.ro*). **Sibiu Tourist Information** (⊠ *Str. Samuel Brukenthal 2, Sibiu* ☎ *0269/208–913* ⊕ *www.sibiu.ro*). **Sighişoara Tourist Information** (⊠ *Str. Octavian Goga 8, Sighişoara* ☎ *0265/770–415*). **Sinaia Tourist Information** (⊠ *47 B-dul Carol 1, Sinaia* ☎ *0244/315–656*). **Baia Mare Tourist Information** (⊠ *Str. Gheorghe Sincai 46, Baia Mare* ☎ *0262/215–543*).

ROMANIA ESSENTIALS

TRANSPORTATION

BY AIR

Bucharest is a major international air destination, with frequent flights from major European cities, and limited direct service from North America. Tarom, the Romanian national carrier, operates an extensive network of European and domestic flights and should be a first point of reference (though the airline's Web site is notoriously difficult to navigate). Delta Airlines has limited nonstop service from Bucharest's Henri Coandă International Airport to New York's JFK Airport. This is currently the only nonstop air service between Romania and the United States.

Many major European carriers, including Lufthansa, Austrian Air, CSA, and British Airways, offer regular service between major cities in their respective countries and Bucharest. Often these can be combined with trans-Atlantic links, allowing for one-stop service between Europe and North America.

In addition, several European and Romanian budget air carriers, including Carpatair, Blue Air, and Wizz Air, now fly regularly between European cities and Romania. The major Romanian entry point for these airlines is Bucharest's Băneasa Airport, but some carriers offer service to other Romanian cities, like Timişoara, Cluj, Târgu-Mureş, Constanţa, Suceava, and Sibiu.

Airlines Austrian Airlines (☎ *021/312-0545* ⊕ *www.aua.com*). **Blue Air** (☎ *021/208-8686* ⊕ *www.blueair-web.com*). **British Airways** (☎ *021/303-2222* ⊕ *www.britishairways.com*). **Carpatair** (☎ *0230/529-559* ⊕ *www.carpatair.ro*). **CSA** (☎ *021/223-3205* ⊕ *www.czechairlines.com*). **Delta** (☎ *021/313-3582*

10

⊕ *www.delta.com*). **Lufthansa** (☎ *021/204–8410* ⊕ *www.lufthansa.ro*). **Tarom** (✉ *Splaiul Independenței 17* ☎ *9361 in Bucharest, 021/317–4444 from outside Bucharest, 0230/214–686 in Suceava, 0269/211–157 in Sibiu, 0262/221–624 in Baia Mare* ⊕ *www.tarom.ro*). **Wizz Air** (☎ *0048/22/351–9499 (to Wizz Air's central call center in Poland)* ⊕ *www.wizzair.com*).

Bucharest Airports Băneasa Airport (✉ *Sos. Bucuresti Ploiesti 40, Băneasa* ☎ *021/232–0020* ⊕ *www.baneasa.aero*). **Henri Coandă International Airport (Otopeni)** (✉ *Calea Bucurestilor 224, Otopeni* ☎ *021/204–1200* ⊕ *www.otp-airport.ro*).

Black Sea & Danube Delta Airport Constanța Airport (✉ *Str. Tudor Vladimirescu 4, Constanța* ☎ *0241/255–100* ⊕ *www.mk-airport.ro*).

Transylvania Airports Baia Mare Airport (✉ *Aeroportul Baia Mare, Baia Mare* ☎ *0262/293–444* ⊕ *www.baiamareairport.go.ro*). **Cluj-Napoca International Airport** (✉ *Str. Traian Vuia 149, Cluj* ☎ *0264/416–702* ⊕ *www.airportcluj.ro*). **Sibiu Airport** (✉ *Sos. Alba Iulia 73, Sibiu* ☎ *0269/229–235* ⊕ *www.sibiuairport.ro*).

BY BUS

Private bus companies operate a dense network of bus connections across the country. Romanians often prefer bus travel to train travel because the connections are more frequent and the departure times more convenient. Buses are often a better option than trains for traveling short distances (up to 150 km/100 mi or so) within a particular region. The quality of the buses varies according to the destination and the bus company. Some are modern and have air-conditioning and other comforts; others are slow and old. Minibuses have replaced standard-size buses on many routes.

Bus stations (*autogara*) are usually located next to train stations, though there are several exceptions (Constanța's bus station, for example, is not close to the train station). Bus stations can be confusing places. Competing companies run buses to the same cities but departing from different gates at different times. Usually there's an information booth somewhere on the premises, but it's rare that that person will speak English. It's best to write down the name of the city you want to travel to and the time you want to leave. The person will then show you what options you have. Getting exact timetable information in advance is difficult, but try the English-language section of ⊕ *www.autogari.ro* to see if buses run between the cities you want to travel to.

Depending on the city and bus company, you can either buy tickets at a ticket window or directly from the driver. If in doubt, simply ask. Try to buy tickets in advance if possible, since buses tend to fill up fast. ATLASSIB, based in Sibiu, runs a modern fleet of minibuses serving destinations around the country.

Information ATLASSIB (✉ *Str. Tractorului 14, Sibiu* ☎ *0269/224–108* ⊕ *www. atlassib.ro*).

BY CAR

If your itinerary includes just Bucharest and a few large towns, like Sibiu, Braşov, or Constanţa, you are better off sticking to trains and buses. If the plan is to go farther afield into Transylvania or Maramureş, or between the painted monasteries of Moldavia where public transportation is lacking, you'll appreciate having your own wheels. The disadvantages of car travel include the high cost of rental and gasoline, not to mention the constant aggravation of driving on crowded and poorly maintained roads. Don't rent a car thinking you're going to save time over long distances. Trains, in general, will be faster.

CAR RENTALS

Car rental prices can be steep. Major international companies, which have offices in Bucharest and other cities, charge about $100 per day (weekly rates average 20% less) for the least expensive vehicle. Car insurance is mandatory. Local rental agencies charge less but may not be dependable.

Information Avis (✉ *Henri Coandă International Airport [Otopeni], Bucharest* ☎ *021/201–4783* ✉ *Băneasa Airport, Bucharest* ☎ *021/230–2482* ✉ *Ştefan cel Mare 15, Constanţa* ☎ *0241/616–733* ✉ *Str. Tribunei 7 [near the entrance to Astra Park], Sibiu* ☎ *0729/800–393* ⊕ *www.avis.ro).* **Econ-Rent** (✉ *Str. 15 Noiembrie 43 ,Braşov* ☎ *0741/773–981).* **Europcar** (✉ *Henri Coandă International Airport [Otopeni], Bucharest* ☎ *021/201–4937* ✉ *Calea Călăraşilor 44, Bucharest* ☎ *021/320–8554* ⊕ *www.europcar.com).* **Hertz** (✉ *Henri Coandă International Airport [Otopeni], Bucharest* ☎ *021/201–4954* ✉ *Băneasa Airport, Bucharest* ☎ *021/549–1460* ✉ *B-dul Tomis 65, Constanţa* ☎ *0241/661–100* ⊕ *www.hertz.com).*

ROAD CONDITIONS

Aside from a very few well-maintained highways, Romanian roads are poor. Four-lane highways are rare, and traffic can be heavy on overcrowded two-lane roads. Obstacles include slow-moving buses and trucks as well as tractors and often horse-drawn carts. Always budget for more hours on the road than it might appear on the map. Watch driving at night, when the situation becomes doubly hazardous because of poorly lighted roads and vehicles.

10

RULES OF THE ROAD

To drive in Romania you will need a valid driver's license from your country of origin and proof of insurance (included with rental cars, but it's best to confirm). For highway travel, your vehicle must also have a special sticker (RoVinieta), available at border crossings, post offices, and large gas stations for around 12 RON for a week's worth of travel, and 20 RON for 30 days. Rental cars should already come with the highway sticker; be sure to ask if in doubt.

Driving is on the right and the rules of the road follow the usual European norms. Speed limits are 50 kph (31 mph) within city limits, 90 kph (about 50 mph) on main roads, and 120 kph (70 mph) on multilane highways. Driving after drinking any amount of alcohol is prohibited. Vehicle spot checks are frequent, but police are generally courteous to foreigners. Officers are no longer allowed to collect on-the-spot fines; he or she will tell you how and where to pay.

BY TRAIN

International trains connect Bucharest to Budapest, Bratislava, Istanbul, Prague, Sofia, and Vienna. Romania's internal rail service, CFR, is decent, though departure times can be inconvenient—often very early or very late. Check departure times in advance at CFR travel offices (Agenţia de Voiaj CFR), found in all major cities, or on the CFR Web site (in English, but you must type in the Romanian names of cities: *Bucureşti*, for example, not Bucharest).

Intercity and Rapid trains are generally good; avoid the very slow-moving Personal (P) trains if possible. You can buy tickets from ticket windows at the train stations or in advance from in-town CFR travel offices. For most trains you'll also have to buy a compulsory seat reservation with your ticket.

Trains are relatively inexpensive. There's little advantage to buying a first-class ticket: the seats are nearly the same, and in some trains the second-class compartments are actually nicer. For night travel, consider booking a *cuşeta*, with bunk beds, or a roomier *vagon de dormit* (sleeper car).

Information Agenţia de Voiaj CFR (⊠ *Str. Domniţa Anastasia 10–14, Bucharest* ☎ *021/313-2643* ⊠ *Str. V. Carnache 4, Constanţa* ☎ *0241/614-960* ⊕ *www.cfr.ro*). **Braşov Train Station** (⊠ *Blvd. Garii 5, Braşov* ☎ *0268/410-233*). **Bucharest Train Station (Gara de Nord)** (⊠ *B-dul. Gării de Nord, Bucharest* ☎ *021/223-0880*). **Constanţa Train Station (Gara)** (⊠ *B-dul Ferdinand 45, Constanţa* ☎ *0241/614-960*). **Sibiu Train Station** (⊠ *Str. Piata 1 Decembrie 1918 nr. 6, Sibiu* ☎ *0269/211-139*). **Sighişoara Train Station** (⊠ *Str. Libertatii 51, Sighişoara* ☎ *0265/771-130*).

CONTACTS & RESOURCES

BANKS & EXCHANGE SERVICES

The best places to obtain local currency is at an ATM, which will be widely available throughout the country. You can also exchange foreign currency at banks and special foreign exchange offices called *casa de schimb valutar*. Rates are posted outside; make sure you're reading *cumpărare* (buying) rates. Most exchange offices do not charge commissions. You may have to show your passport to exchange money, so keep it handy. ■ TIP➔ Never change money on the street, **as you're likely to be cheated.**

CREDIT CARDS & TRAVELER'S CHECKS

Visa and MasterCard are widely accepted in hotels, restaurants, and large or foreign-owned shops. Don't rely on American Express and Diners Club, especially in outlying areas.

Traveler's checks are accepted only at large banks and a few select hotels in Bucharest. Banks charge between 1% and 5% commission.

The American Express representative in Bucharest, Marshal Turism, can issue checks and replace lost ones, but will not cash them.

Information Marshal Turism (⊠ *B-dul. Magheru 43, Bucharest* ☏ *021/319–4455*).

CURRENCY

The unit of currency is the *leu* (usually known by its plural, *lei*) and is designated as RON. Bills come in denominations of 1, 5, 10, 50, 100, and (rarely) 500 RON. One leu is divided into 100 *bani,* with coins of 5, 10, and 50 bani. At this writing, the exchange rate was 2.36 RON to the U.S. dollar. Though Romania is a member of the European Union, the euro is not in circulation. Some larger stores and restaurants (and many hotels) will accept euros, but that is not the norm.

EMERGENCIES

Information Police, ambulance, fire (☏ *112*).

EMBASSIES & CONSULATES

U.S. Embassy (consular section) (⊠ *Str. N. Filipescu 26, Bucharest* ☏ *021/200–3300*).

INTERNET, MAIL & SHIPPING

Internet cafés are hard to find in smaller cities and towns. In Bucharest and Braşov, they're ubiquitous (look for shops with the words "Internet Club" on the front). Nearly all four- and five-star hotels will have at least one public terminal that you can use to check e-mail. If not, the receptionist can point you in the direction of the nearest Internet café. Rates run about 2.50 RON an hour. Many hotels and cafés now offer free Wi-Fi. Like all Wi-Fi spots, however, connections can be spotty.

Post offices (marked "Poşta Romăna") are in the centers of all cities and towns. Standard hours are Monday–Friday 8–7 and Saturday 9–1, though post offices in smaller towns may close earlier or not have weekend service. The main post office in Bucharest has extended hours Monday–Saturday 7:30 AM–8 PM. Cards and letters take 7–10 days to get to North America, and 3–5 days for European destinations. Use an international express service for sending parcels or if you need to send letters quickly. DHL and UPS both operate in Romania.

Internet Cafés Internet Club (⊠ *B-dul Corneliu Coposu 1C, Piaţa Unirii, Bucharest* ☏ *No phone*). **Forte Games** (⊠ *B-dul Tomis 235, Complex Dacia, Constanţa* ☏ *0241/551–251*). **ASSIST** (⊠ *Piaţa 22 Decembrie mezanin, Suceava* ☏ *0230/523–044*). **Cyber Cafe** (⊠ *Str. Apollonia Hirscher 12, Braşov*).

Shipping Companies DHL International (☏ *021/222–1771*). **UPS** (☏ *021/410–0604*).

PASSPORTS & VISAS

U.S. citizens with a valid passport can enter Romania without a visa for stays up to 90 days.

TELEPHONES

COUNTRY
CODE   Romania's country code is 40. When dialing from outside the country, drop any initial "0" from the area code.

To call abroad from Romania, first dial "00" to get an international line and then dial the code of the country you are calling, plus the area code and number. Direct-dial international calls can be made from most hotels and public phones. If you have service with AT&T, MCI, or Sprint, you can place a call by dialing the access numbers below.

Public phones operate with magnetic strip cards (*cartela telefonică*; 10 RON and 20 RON) available at newsstands and tobacco kiosks.

Information International Directory Assistance (☎ *951*). Local Directory Assistance (☎ *931*).AT&T (☎ *021/800–4288*). MCI (☎ *021/800–1800*). Sprint (☎ *021/800–0877*).

TOUR OPTIONS

Travel agencies and tour operators have multiplied in Romania, so choosing carefully is important. Accent Travel & Events, Ad Tour, and Atlantic Tour are well-established firms in Bucharest that arrange local sightseeing trips and package bus excursions around the country. Constanţa travel agencies organize sightseeing bus trips from town and neighboring Black Sea hotels to the Danube Delta; Danubius, Latina, and Mamaia Tours are all good outfits. In Braşov, try DiscoveRomania for adventure tours in Transylvania and special packages for visiting Maramureş.

Information Accent Travel & Events (✉ *Str. Episcopiei 5, Suite 2* ☎ *021/314–1980* 🖷 *021/314–7543* ⊕ *www.accenttravel.ro*). Ad Tour (✉ *Str. Prometeu 31, bl 16G* ☎ *021/233–3949* ⊕ *www.adtour.ro*). Atlantic Tour (✉ *Calea Victoriei 202* ☎ *021/312–7757* 🖷 *021/312–6860* ⊕ *www.atlantic.ro*). Danubius (✉ *B-dul Ferdinand 22-36* ☎ *0241/615–836* 🖷 *0241/618–010* ⊕ *www.danubius.ro*). DiscoveRomania (✉ *Str. Paul Richter 1, Braşov* ☎ *0722/746–262* 🖷 *0268/472–718* ⊕ *www.discoveromania.ro*). Latina (✉ *Primaverii 6, Bl. St. 6* ☎ *0241/639–713*). Mamaia Tours (✉ *Str. Ştefan cel Mare 55* ☎ *0241/664–361*).

VISITOR INFORMATION

The Romanian Tourist Office in your home country can supply maps, brochures, and good information; it also has an informative Web site. Once you arrive in Romania, you'll find decent tourist information offices in several cities, including Braşov, Sighişoara, and Sibiu (though not in Bucharest itself). Private travel agencies, too, can help with excursions, hotels, and restaurants. For renting rooms in private homes, contact ANTREC, a national organization that promotes agrotourism, with branches throughout the country.

Information ANTREC (✉ *Str. Maica Alexandra 7, Bucharest* 🖷 *021/223–7024* ⊕ *www.antrec.ro*). Romanian Tourist Office (⊕ *www.romaniatourism.com*).

Slovakia

WORD OF MOUTH

"We were charmed by Bratislava. Took a great walking tour. Danced at the castle (at a cousin's wedding). Think of Bratislava as a boutique and Prague as a department store, albeit a pretty nice one."

—Dave_in_Paris

"[You'll find n]o horses and carts anymore [in the High Tatras], but [the area is] still nice. The stunning thing is how a rather flat terrain suddenly becomes a high mountain area in only a few km. I went from Krynica via Poprad to Presov, to Kosice this summer. . . . Poprad itself is a rather small place, not very interesting but with quite a number of nice restaurants that are unbelievably inexpensive."

—logos999

Updated by
Diane Naar-
Elphee

SLOVAKIA BECAME AN INDEPENDENT STATE on January 1, 1993, when Czechoslovakia—what is today Slovakia and the Czech Republic—ceased to exist. Except for a brief period during World War II when Slovakia was an independent state under Nazi control, the Czechs and Slovaks had been politically united since the fall of the Austro-Hungarian Empire in 1918. But when 1989's Velvet Revolution ended Communist rule in Czechoslovakia, politicians were quick to exploit it. Slovak nationalist parties won a bit more than 50% of the vote in the crucial 1992 Czechoslovak elections, and once the results were in, the split was decided. Although they speak a language closely related to Czech, the Slovaks had managed to maintain a strong sense of national identity throughout their common statehood. In the end, it was the Slovaks' very different history that split them from the Czechs, and it's this history that makes Slovakia a unique travel destination.

Part of the Great Moravian Empire in the 9th century, the Slovaks were conquered a century later by the Magyars and remained under Hungarian and Habsburg rule. Following the Tartar invasions in the 13th century, many Saxons were invited to resettle the land and develop the economy, including cultivating the region's rich mineral resources. During the 15th and 16th centuries, Romanian shepherds migrated from Walachia through the Carpathian Mountains into Slovakia, and the merging of these varied groups with the resident Slavs bequeathed to the region a rich folk culture and some unique forms of architecture, especially in the east.

Medieval old towns, neatly renovated and filled with color, still exist in Slovakia today, but Communist-era concrete housing projects tend to dominate much of the country. In recent years, however, some of the old gray panel apartment houses have been given lively new facades and crowned with green shrubs, and a crop of modern new shopping malls and megamarts has sprung up.

Slovakia joined the European Union in 2004 and is due to switch to the euro as currency in 2009. Although there is a growing income disparity, you can't tell it by the people on the streets. The Slovaks have leapt from their Communist central-planning past to the global information age, latching onto mobile communication and digital technology. The number of mobile phones per capita has caught up with Western levels. Slovaks adore the Internet, too, and cybercafés have popped up across the big cities. A fast-growing network of ATMs has brought a bank machine to nearly every small town.

Slovakia lies to the east of the Czech Republic and is about one-third as large as its neighbor. Most visitors to Slovakia head first for the great peaks of the Vysoké Tatry (High Tatras), where there is an ample tourist infrastructure, catering especially to hikers and skiers. People who come to admire the peaks, however, often overlook the exquisite medieval towns of Spiš in the plains and valleys below the High Tatras, and the beautiful 18th-century wooden country churches farther east. Removed from main centers, however, these areas are short on tourist amenities. If creature comforts are important to you, stick to the High Tatras.

Forty years of Communism left a clear mark on Slovakia's capital, Bratislava, in the form of hulking concrete structures. But though buildings that were torn down cannot be replaced, there's new life in the old city: Through renovation, the Staré mesto (Old Town) has managed to recapture much of its lost charm, awarding visitors a lovely glimpse of the capital's former glories.

EXPLORING SLOVAKIA

Slovakia can best be divided into four regions of interest: Bratislava and environs, central Slovakia, the High Tatras, and eastern Slovakia. Despite being the capital, Bratislava, in the western part of the country, is probably the least alluring destination. The country's true beauty lies among the peaks of the High Tatras in the north.

SLOVAKIA TOP 5

■ Explore Bratislava's Old Town, a delightful surprise of historic squares.

■ Take advantage of world-class skiing and spectacular hiking in the High Tatras.

■ Visit the sprawling medieval Spišský Hrad, Slovakia's largest castle perched high on a hilltop in eastern Slovakia's Spiš country.

■ Stop off in Levoča, a charming medieval Spiš town that is a fantasy for lovers of Gothic art.

■ Stroll along the enchanting central square of Bardejov—a UNESCO World Heritage site and Slovakia's best-preserved town.

ABOUT THE RESTAURANTS

Slovakia's food is an amalgam of its neighbors' cuisines. As in Bohemia and Moravia, the emphasis is on meat, particularly pork and beef. But the Slovaks, revealing their long link to Hungary, prefer to spice things up a bit, usually with paprika and red peppers. Roast potatoes or french fries are often served, although occasionally you'll find a side dish of tasty *halušky* (dumplings similar to Italian gnocchi or German spaetzle) on the menu. *Bryndzové halušky*, the country's unofficial national dish, is a tasty and filling mix of halušky, soft sheep's cheese, and a little bacon crumbled on top for flavor. Vegetarians don't have many options, though vegetabe salads are normally available. For dessert, the emphasis comes from Vienna: crepes, poppy-seed tortes, and strudel.

Slovaks don't eat out often, particularly since prices have risen markedly in the past few years. As a result, restaurants often cater to foreigners or a business clientele. *Vináreň* (wine bars) specialize in serving wines along with hearty food. Red wines in particular complement the country's cooking; look for *Frankovka*, which is light and slightly acidic. *Vavrinecké* is dark and semisweet and stands up well to red meats.

Many restaurants put out a special luncheon menu (*ponuka dňa* or *špecialita šéfkuchára*). Dinner is usually served from 5:30 until 9 or 10.

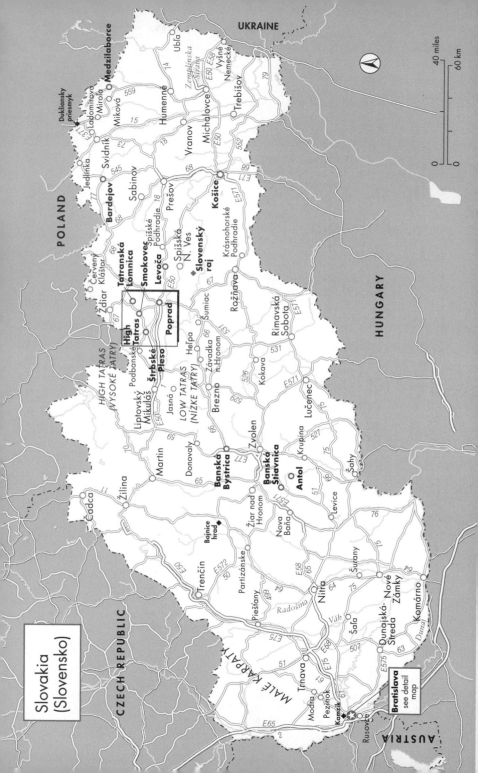

IF YOU LIKE

BICYCLING

There are fantastic bike trails in Slovakia suiting every pedaler's preference, from rugged mountain challenges to comfortable cycling outings. The flatter areas to the south and east of Bratislava and along the Danube are ideal for easy pedaling. For the more adventurous, the Tatras have breathtakingly scenic (and challenging) mountain-biking trails.

HIKING

Slovakia is great for hiking. More than 20,000 km (12,500 mi) of marked trails thread through the mountainous regions and the agricultural countryside. Colored slashes on trees, fences, walls, rocks, and elsewhere mark trails that correspond to the paths shown on the large-scale Súbor turistických maps, which are available at many bookstores and tobacco shops. The best areas for ambitious mountain walkers are the Low Tatras in the center of the country near Banská Bystrica and the High Tatras to the north. ⚠ CAUTION **The weather in the mountains can be unpredictable—snowstorms in summer have been known to occur—so be sure you are fully prepared with warm, waterproof attire.** Make sure your travel and accident insurance covers the cost of mountain rescue, in case of a serious fall. Slovenský raj (Slovak Paradise) national park, in eastern Slovakia, has many waterfalls, caves, and cliffs. An ingenious system of ladders and catwalks makes it possible to see the wild beauty up close.

SHOPPING

The most interesting finds in Slovakia are colorful ceramic pottery (with the colors representing the region of origin), woven textiles, batik-painted Easter eggs, corn-husk dolls, and hand-knit sweaters. These folk-art products are sold from booths in town squares (especially around Christmas), at branches of the ÚL'UV folk-art chain, and folk-art stores in most major towns. Several Dielo folk-art stores sell paintings, wooden toys, great ceramic pieces by Slovak artists, and Slovak folk and classical music at very reasonable prices.

SKIING

Slovakia's High and Low Tatras have some of the region's best—and least expensive—downhill skiing, good for both amateurs and experts. The High Tatras are the best choice, with good snow throughout the winter; superior slopes, ski tows, and chairlifts; and plenty of places to rent equipment. You'll find less rental equipment and fewer ski shops in the Low Tatras. Lifts in both regions generally operate from January through March, but cross-country skiing is a popular alternative in other (still snowy) months.

ABOUT THE HOTELS

Large hotels outside of Bratislava can be somewhat institutional—gray concrete block buildings with drab furnishings—but with a little hunting, it's possible to find more appealing accommodation in historic buildings that date as far back as the 16th century; the decor and the conveniences are usually modern. Other options are private rooms in homes and apartments, which provide an up-close cultural experience; these can be booked through a town's information center or through ⊕ *www.slovakia.com/hotels*.

Slovakia in some places can still be a bargain by Western standards, particularly in the outlying areas, but prices are rising steadily. In Bratislava, hotel rates can be up to 15% higher than in the rest of the country and often meet or exceed U.S. and Western European averages. During festivals and holidays, including Christmas and Easter, hotel rates throughout the country may increase by 15%–25%. Most hotels accept both koruny and euros. Few hotels outside of Bratislava have air-conditioning, but it's not really necessary, especially in the mountains.

WHAT IT COSTS IN KORUNY AND EUROS (€)			
$	**$$**	**$$$**	**$$$$**
RESTAURANTS	under 150 Sk	150 Sk–250 Sk	250 Sk–400 Sk	over 400 Sk
HOTELS in euros	under €60	€60–€100	€100–€160	over €160
HOTELS in koruny	under 2,000 Sk	2,000 Sk– 3,300 Sk	3,300 Sk– 5,300 Sk	over 5,300 Sk

Restaurant prices are for a main course at dinner. Hotel prices are for a double room, including tax and service charges.

BRATISLAVA

Bratislava's Staré mesto (Old Town), on the bank of the Danube, is sporting a bright new coat of paint these days, and many of its buildings have been renovated to former glory. In the pedestrian zone, whimsical bronze statues are frozen walking arm in arm down the street or popping out of imaginary manholes. But though the Old Town is charming, you may get a bit of a sinking feeling when you first enter Bratislava—or "Blava" as its residents affectionately call it—from Vienna. The Communists' blind faith in modernity is evident in the numerous gray concrete high-rise housing projects on the other bank of the Danube and in the Nový most (New Bridge), which resembles a UFO set on sticks.

The jumble of modern Bratislava, however, masks a long and regal history that rivals Prague's in importance and complexity. Settled by Celts and Romans, the city became part of the Great Moravian Empire around the year 860 under Prince Rastislav. After a short period under the Bohemian Přemysl princes, Bratislava was brought into the Hungarian kingdom by Stephen I at the end of the 10th century and given royal privileges in 1217. Following the Tartar invasion in 1241, when many residents were killed, the Hungarian kings brought in German colonists to repopulate the town and ensure a non-Slovak majority. The Hungarians called the town Pozsony, the German settlers called it Pressburg, and the original Slovaks called it Bratislava.

When Pest and Buda were occupied by the Turks in the first half of the 16th century, the Hungarian kings moved their seat to Bratislava, which remained the Hungarian capital until 1784 and the coronation center until 1835. At this time, with a population of almost 27,000, it

GREAT ITINERARIES

Although Slovakia is relatively small, it's difficult to explore in a short period of time without a car because trains are slow and buses are not always user-friendly. Driving from Bratislava to the Tatras will take you a minimum of four hours; the train ride will last at least eight hours, with one connection.

TIMING
The High Tatras are loveliest from January through March, when skiing conditions are at their prime. The summer months in the mountains attract mostly hikers. Because of the snow, many hiking trails, especially those that cross the peaks, are open only between June and October. Temperatures are always much cooler in the mountains; even in summer, bring a sweater or jacket, and don't underestimate the possibility of drastic weather changes.

Bratislava is at its best in the temperate months of spring and autumn. July and August, though not especially crowded, can be quite hot, and winter can bring a fair amount of snow and rain.

Numbers in the text correspond to numbers in the margin and on the Slovakia and Bratislava maps.

IF YOU HAVE 3 DAYS
If you have only a few days to see Slovakia, spend some hours walking through the historic Old Town in ⊞**Bratislava** and spend the night here before heading to the **High Tatras**. Once you get to the mountains, settle down for two nights in a comfortable hotel or a pension in one of the resort towns. ⊞**Smokovec** and ⊞**Tatranská Lomnica** are probably the most convenient places from which to explore the area and go hiking in summer or skiing in winter.

IF YOU HAVE 5 DAYS
Follow the three-day itinerary above and then take an excursion 45 minutes south of the Tatras to the beautiful old Spiš town of ⊞**Levoča**. Spend the night; from here you can also explore the largest castle in Slovakia, Spišský hrad, and the caves and gorges in the area. The following day, head south toward ⊞**Košice**, the capital of the Spiš region, to take in some of the historic sights of the Old Town. From Košice, you can fly back to Bratislava or take a direct day or night train to Bratislava or Prague.

was the largest Hungarian city. Only in 1919, when Bratislava became part of the first Czechoslovak republic, did the city regain its Slovak identity. In 1939, with Germany's assistance, Bratislava infamously exerted its yearnings for independence by becoming the capital of the puppet Slovak state, under the leadership of the controversial Fascist leader Jozef Tiso. In 1945, under Communism, it became the provincial capital of Slovakia, still straining under the powerful hand of Prague (Slovakia's German and Hungarian minorities were either expelled or repressed). Leading up to the 1989 revolution, Bratislava was the site of numerous anti-Communist demonstrations; many of these were carried out by supporters of the Catholic Church, long repressed by the regime then in power. Following the Velvet Revolution in 1989, Bratislava gained importance as the capital of the Slovak Republic within the

Czech and Slovak federal state, but rivalries with Prague persisted. It was only following the breakup of Czechoslovakia on January 1, 1993, that the city once again became a capital in its own right.

EXPLORING BRATISLAVA

To discover Bratislava's charms, travel the city by foot. Imagination is also helpful, as a few of the Old Town's oldest streets are under ongoing reconstruction. If you get an early morning start, you can complete a leisurely walking tour of the Old Town in a day. With the exception of the Slovenská národná galéria, which deserves some time, most of the museums are small and won't detain you long. Avoid touring on Monday, as many sights are closed.

Numbers in the text correspond to numbers in the margin and on the Bratislava map.

WHAT TO SEE

6 **Bratislavsky hrad** *(Bratislava castle).* Bratislava's castle and main landmark has been continually rebuilt since its foundations were laid in the 9th century. The Hungarian kings expanded it into a large royal residence, and the Habsburgs further developed its fortifications, turning it into a very successful defense against the Turks. The existing castle had to be completely rebuilt after a disastrous fire in 1811. The latest in its series of upgrades is currently under way: The entire castle, including the precious collections of the **Slovenské národné múzeum** (Slovak National Museum) inside, is closed for exhaustive restoration work until 2011. ⊠ *Zámocká ul., Starý mesto* ☎ *02/5934–1626* ☉ *Closed for restoration.*

Danubiana. Reminiscent of a Roman galley stuck in the shallows, this modern-art museum sits on the tip of a peninsula that juts into the Danube. World-class exhibitions of sculpture and painting, fabulous views of the river from the café, and the interesting wares of the Artshop are all reasons to find this place on the map. Follow highway E75 6 km (4 mi) south toward Hungary or take Bus 91 from under the Nový most. ⊠ *Vodné dielo, Čunovo* ☎ *02/6252–8501* ⊕ *www.danubiana.sk* ⊠ *80 Sk* ☉ *May–Sept., daily 10–8; Oct.–Apr., daily 10–6.*

4 **Dóm svätého Martina** *(St. Martin's Cathedral).* This massive Gothic church, consecrated in 1452, hosted the coronations of 17 Hungarian royals between the 16th and 19th century. Numerous additions made over the centuries were removed in the 19th century, when the church was "re-Gothicized." Nowadays, the three equal-size naves give an impression of space and light. ⊠ *Rudnayovo nám., Staré mesto* ☎ *02/5443–1359* ⊠ *60 Sk* ☉ *Mon.–Sat. 9–11 and 1–5, Sun. 1–5.*

15 **Františkánsky kostol** *(Franciscan Church).* In this 13th-century church, only the presbytery is still in early-Gothic style. The rest was destroyed in an earthquake in the 17th century and rebuilt in a mixture of baroque and Gothic. Just around the corner, built onto the church, is another quite different and much more stunning Gothic building, the 14th-century **Kaplnka svätého Jána Evangelistu** (Chapel of St. John the

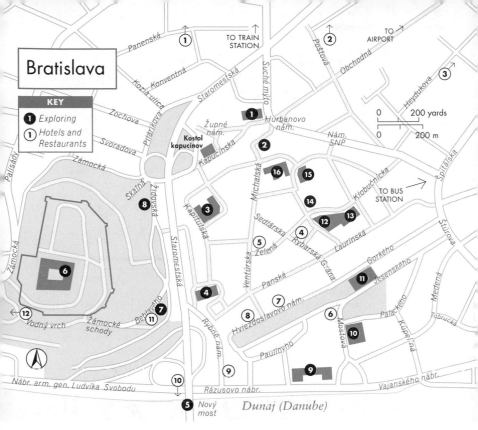

Bratislava

KEY
- **1** Exploring
- **①** Hotels and Restaurants

0 — 200 yards
0 — 200 m

TO TRAIN STATION ↑
TO AIRPORT →
TO BUS STATION →

Kostol kapucínov

Nový most

Dunaj (Danube)

Small Carpathian Wine Route

You'll be hard-pressed to find Slovakian wines in your local liquor store, but it's not for their lack of quality. It's because the Slovaks know a good bottle when they see it—and they've been drinking it all themselves. But this is due to change, as importers become increasingly aware of the topnotch dry varietals coming from the vineyard-covered foothills of the Malé Karpaty (Small Carpathians) in western Slovakia, less than an hour's drive from Bratislava. Among the best are Welschriesling, Riesling, Veltliner, Lemberger, and St. Laurent. Many private vintners now offer wine-tasting visits to their cellars, some complete with meals and accommodation (especially convenient for the over-imbibers). For more information, visit the Small Carpathian Wine Route Association Web site (⊕ *www.mvc.sk*).

Evangelist). Art historians believe that Peter Parler, architect of Prague's Charles Bridge, may have worked on this gem. You can take a look around before or after services (7 AM and 5 PM daily). ⊠*Františkánske nám. 1, Staré mesto* ☏*No phone.*

⓮ Jezuitský kostol *(Jesuit Church).* In 1636 Protestants constructed this church after being granted an imperial concession to build a place of worship on the strict condition that it have no tower. The Jesuits took over the towerless church in 1672 and, to compensate for its external simplicity, went wild with baroque detailing on the inside. ⊠*Kostolna 1, Staré mesto* ☏*No phone.*

Kostol Kapucínov *(Capuchin Chapel).* A pillar of Mary that commemorates the plague stands in front of this small 18th-century chapel. You can sneak a peek inside the chapel before or after the services at 6 AM and 5 PM daily. ⊠*Kapucínska ul. 2, Staré mesto* ☏*02/5930–3800.*

❸ Kostol Klarisiek *(Klariský Church).* This 14th-century church is simple but inspiring, with a wonderfully peaceful early-Gothic interior. The small high-Gothic steeple was added in an unusually secondary position at the back of the church during the 15th century. As a mendicant order, the Poor Clares were forbidden to build a steeple atop the church, so they sidestepped the rules and built it against a side wall. The church is now a concert hall—and usually locked, but you may be able to get in for a concert or during rehearsals. ⊠*Klariská 3, Staré mesto* ☏*No phone.*

❶ Kostol svätej Trojice *(Church of the Holy Trinity).* The ceiling of this golden-yellow baroque church has space-expanding frescoes, the work of Antonio Galli Bibiena from the early 18th century. ⊠*Hurbanovo nám., Staré mesto* ☏*No phone.*

❷ Michalská brána *(Michael's Gate).* The last remaining of the city's three gates was built in two stages. The bottom section of the gate retains its original Gothic design from the 14th century. The copper, onion-dome *veža* (tower) topped with a statue of St. Michael was added in the 18th century. The tower affords a good view over the Old Town, and inside is a display on ancient weapons and town fortifications. ⊠ *Michalská 24, Staré mesto* ☎ *02/5443–3044 or 02/5920–5135* 🖃 *60 Sk* ⊙ *Tues.– Fri. 10–5, weekends 11–6.*

 Mirbachov palác *(Mirbach Palace)*. This rococo palace with original stucco plasterwork was built in 1770. Today it houses the **Galé ria mesta Bratislavy** *(City Gallery of Bratislava)*, which has Gothic paintings and sculptures, a small collection of 18th- and 19th-century Slovak and European art, and changing exhibits of modern art. ⊠ *Františkánske nám. 11, Staré mesto* ☎ *02/5443–1556-8* ⊕ *www. gmb.sk* 🖃 *80 Sk* ⊙ *Tues.–Sun. 11–6.*

⑦ Múzeum umeleckých hodín *(Artistic Clock Museum)*. In the narrowest of rococco-style burgher houses, and one of the few buildings below Bratislava Castle still in its original state, this lovely museum displays a collection of 17th- to 19th-century clocks made mostly by Bratislava clock makers. ⊠ *Židovská 1, Staré mesto* ☎ *02/5441–1940* 🖃 *40 Sk* ⊙ *Tues.–Sun. 10–5.*

⑧ Múzeum židovskej kultúry *(Museum of Jewish Culture in Slovakia)*. This ★ small but stirring museum celebrates the history and culture of the Jews living in the territory of Slovakia since the Great Moravian Empire. There's a collection of religious objects from around the country, many from synagogues in eastern Slovakia. A section is devoted to Slovakia's 71,000 Holocaust victims—out of a total Jewish population of 89,000. Museum staff can help arrange a visit to Slovakia's most important Jewish site, the tomb of Chatam Sofer (1762–1839), one of Europe's leading rabbis of his time; it's just outside the Old Town. ⊠ *Židovská 17, Staré mesto* ☎ *02/5441–8507* ⊕ *www.chatamsofer.com* 🖃 *200 Sk* ⊙ *Sun.–Fri. 11–5.*

Námestie SNP *(SNP Square)*. The square, formerly known as Stalinovo námestie (Stalin Square), was and still remains the center for demonstrations in Slovakia. It's the base from which hundreds of thousands of spectators celebrated independence and the new year on December 31, 1992. SNP stands for "Slovenské národné povstanie" (Slovak National Uprising), an anti-Nazi resistance movement. In the middle of the square are three larger-than-life statues: a dour partisan and two strong, sad women in peasant clothing. ⊠ *Staré mesto.*

⑤ Nový most *(New Bridge)*. Topped by a flying saucer–shaped structure, this futuristic, modern marvel of a bridge—it's sometimes called the UFO bridge (pronounced *ooh-fo*)—would make a splendid site for an alien flick. It's difficult to miss if you're anywhere near the Danube. Speedy glass-face elevators whisk you to the top for views of the city, 262 feet above the Danube River. Also at the top are a bar, a nightclub, and the upscale Taste restaurant. ⊠ *Staré mesto* 🖃 *150 Sk* ⊙ *Daily 10 AM–11 PM.*

⑬ Primaciálny palác *(Primates' Palace)*. This pale pink palace is one of ★ the most valuable architectural monuments in Bratislava. Don't miss the dazzling **Hall of Mirrors,** with its six 17th-century English tapestries depicting the legend of the lovers Hero and Leander. In this room, Napoléon and Habsburg emperor Francis I signed the Bratislava Peace Treaty of 1805, following Napoléon's victory at the Battle of Austerlitz. In the revolutionary year of 1848, when the citizens of the Habsburg lands revolted against the imperial dominance of Vienna, the rebel Hungarians had their headquarters in the palace. Ironically, following the failed uprising, the Habsburg general Hainau signed the rebels' death sentences in the very same room. ⊠ *Primaciálne nám. 1, Staré mesto* ☜40 Sk ⊗ *Tues.–Sun. 10–5.*

⑩ Reduta. The neo-baroque Reduta, which dates to 1914, hosts the Slovak Philharmonic Orchestra. It's well worth attending a concert just to see the gilt elegance of the theater, which is closed to the public until one hour before a performance. Call ahead for ticket reservations; the call center is open Monday, Tuesday, Thursday, Friday 8–2, and Wednesday 1–7. ⊠ *Medená 3, Staré mesto* ☏ *02/5920–8233 or 02/5920–8211* ⊕ *www.filharm.sk.*

⑨ Slovenská národná galéria *(Slovak National Gallery).* A conspicuously modern restoration of old 18th-century barracks houses this gallery. The museum displays an interesting collection of Slovak Gothic, baroque, and contemporary art, along with a small number of European masters and changing exhibits. Guided tours are available in English. ⊠ *Rázusovo nábr. 2, Staré mesto* ☏ *02/5443–2055* ⊕ *www.sng.sk* ☜80 Sk ⊗ *Tues.–Sun. 10–5:30.*

⑪ Slovenské národné divadlo *(SND, Slovak National Theater).* You can see performances of Bratislava's opera, ballet, and theater in this striking baroque building, which was constructed in the 1880s by the famous Central European architectural duo Hermann Helmer and Ferdinand Fellner. ⊠ *Hviezdoslavovo nám. 1, Staré mesto* ☏ *02/5443–3764* ⊕ *www.snd.sk* ⊗ *Open only during performances.*

⑫ Stará radnica *(Old Town Hall).* One of the more interesting buildings in Bratislava, the Old Town Hall developed gradually over the 13th and 14th centuries out of a number of burghers' houses. During the summer brass bands play on a balcony atop the tower; other concerts are given in front of the building on Hlavné námestie in the summer and around Christmas, New Year's, and Easter. After dark, gentle music plays while a light show illuminates the building's facade. You can stop in the **Mestské múzeum** (City Museum) here and learn about Bratislava's storied past. ⊠ *Primaciálne nám. 3, Starý mesto* ☏ *02/5920–5135 or 02/5920–5130* ⊕ *www.muzeum.bratislava.sk* ☜50 Sk ⊗ *Tues.–Sun. 10–5.*

WHERE TO EAT

Prague may have its Slovak rival beat when it comes to architecture, but when it's time to eat, you can thank your lucky stars that you're in Bratislava. The long-shared history with Hungary gives Slovak cuisine an extra flavor that Czech cooking lacks. Prepare for shish kebabs, grilled meats, steaks, and pork dishes. Geographic proximity to Vienna, moreover, has lent some grace and charm to the city's eateries.

★ $$$–$$$$ ╳**Camouflage.** This hip, acclaimed dining spot is set in an 18th-century palace done up with a striking white minimalist interior. A café section puts out light Continental-Asian fusion food in the form of paninis, soups, and salads. The more formal main dining room, elegantly embellished with Andy Warhol reproductions, serves more substantial (and expensive) fare, such as poached salmon served with guacamole, tomato-horseradish relish, and crispy tortilla strips. ⊠ *Ventúrska 1, Staré mesto* ☎ *02/2092–2711* ⊟ *AE, DC, MC, V.*

$$$–$$$$ ╳**Fish Gate.** Conjured up by architect-designer Luigi Bruno, this stylish eatery has a black-and-white interior embellished with rich-red fabrics. The menu features a creative mix of Mediterranean cuisine and offers specials like blue prawn gratin with green curry and noodles, and fried catfish fillet with Bloody Mary sauce. ⊠ *Rybársky brána 8, Staré mesto* ☎ *02/5413–1852* ⊟ *V.*

$$–$$$$ ╳**Slovenská reštaurácia.** This restaurant is one of Bratislava's best. The
Fodor's Choice excellent Slovak specialties include saddle of moufflon (a kind of sheep)
★ with bilberry–wild cherry sauce served with potato croquets cooked with smoked bacon. The attentive waiters dress in rustic rural folk fashion, and the chairs are hand-carved in traditional patterns. Evening meals are accompanied by piano music. ⊠ *Hviezdoslavovo nám. 20, Staré mesto* ☎ *02/5443–4883* ⊕ *www.slovrest.com* ⊟ *AE, MC, V.*

★ $$–$$$ ╳**Modrá hviezda.** Candlelight flickers on the barrel-vaulted ceilings of this intimate family-owned wine cellar in the side of the castle hill. The tasty *Mamičkina špecialita* (Mama's Specialty), beef medallions with a cream sauce and lingonberries, goes well with the *krokety* (fried potato croquettes). ⊠ *Beblavého 14, Starý mesto* ☎ *02/5443–2747* ⊟ *No credit cards* ⊘ *Closed Sun.*

★ ☾ $$–$$$ ╳**Leberfinger.** Rumor has it that Napoléon stopped at this tavern on the Danube across from Old Town, near the New Bridge. The 50-item menu highlights traditional Slovak cuisine. Large appetites will be amply sated by the *Leberfinger:* a gigantic serving of pork Wellington, beef Wellington, and turkey steak served with grilled vegetables, a tiny potato pancake, and three kinds of dressing. Sit indoors beneath murals of old Bratislava, downstairs in a cellar pub, or outside on a patio with a river view. The place is kid-friendly, which is rare in restaurants here. ⊠ *Viedenská cesta 257, Petrzalka* ☎ *02/6231–7590* ⊟ *AE, DC, MC, V.*

★ $$–$$$ ╳**Traja Musketieri.** A swanky cellar restaurant and bar, Three Musketeers is usually overflowing with diplomats, expats, and trendy locals. The menu includes great salmon and trout dishes and a decent house red, all served by period-costume barmaids and stable boys, who tie a giant bib around your neck before you tuck in. ⊠ *Sládkocicova 7, Staré mesto* ☎ *02/5443–0019* ⊟ *AE, MC, V.*

WHERE TO STAY

It hasn't always been the case, but there is now an abundance of good accommodation in Bratislava. Prices may fluctuate around bigger conferences and events, so always double-check current rates. The price of hotel rooms in the Old Town can be disproportionately higher than the cost of accommodation in the rest of the country. To beat the costs—and have a cultural experience to boot—you can arrange to rent a room in a private house, or a whole apartment through a travel agent. The main BKIS office can help with hotel reservations (*see* ⇨ *Visitor Information in Bratislava Essentials, below*).

★ $$$$ ⛶ **Danube.** The design of this French-run hotel on the banks of the Danube echoes the river in its flowing shape and blue accents. Pastels decorate the modern rooms, and the gleaming public areas are everything you'd expect from an international hotel chain. ⊠ *Rybné nám. 1, Staré mesto, 81102* ☎ *02/5934–0000* 🖷 *02/5441–4311* ⊕ *www. hoteldanube.com* ⤳ *264 rooms, 16 suites* ⛾ *In-hotel: 2 restaurants, bar, pool, gym* ☰ *AE, DC, MC, V.*

$$$$ ⛶ **Perugia.** The closest thing to a boutique hotel in Bratislava, the Perugia is a pink postmodern jewel in a renovated building in the center of the pedestrian zone of the Old Town (taxis can get you here, but it's best not to have a car). The clean, colorful rooms open onto an interior courtyard with a large skylight; some have balconies. ⊠ *Zelená 5, Staré mesto, 81101* ☎ *02/5443–1818* 🖷 *02/5443–1821* ⊕ *www.perugia.sk* ⤳ *13 rooms, 1 suite* ⛾ *In-hotel: 2 restaurants* ☰ *AE, DC, MC, V.*

★ $$$$ ⛶ **Radisson SAS Carlton Hotel.** Millions of dollars went into the refurbishment of this 1837 landmark property—and it shows. Everything about this place screams luxury, from the bar with gilt mirrors and mahogany furniture to the three-peppercorn fillet in the restaurant, Brasserie at the Opera. Rooms are traditional, with antique reproductions, plush carpeting, and muted tones, or modern, with blues and reds, and bold furniture. ⊠ *Hviezdoslavovo nám. 3, Starý mesto, 81102* ☎ *02/5939–0000* 🖷 *02/5939–0010* ⊕ *www.carlton.sk* ⤳ *163 rooms, 5 suites* ⛾ *In-room: safe. In-hotel: restaurant, bar, room service, safe, concierge, laundry service* ☰ *AE, DC, MC, V.*

★ $$$–$$$$ ⛶ **Hotel Pension No. 16.** This cozy pension in a quiet residential haven a short drive from the castle is a nice alternative to the big chain hotels—it provides all the conveniences (such as computer terminals with high-speed Internet in every room), but with character. The rooms are inviting, with wooden floors and ceilings. The apartments, which have kitchenettes, are a good deal for families. Breakfast is included. ⊠ *Partizánska 16A, Palisady, 81103* ☎ *02/5441–1672* 🖷 *02/5441–1298* ⊕ *www.hotelno16.sk* ⤳ *11 rooms, 5 apartments* ⛾ *Kitchenettes, Ethernet, no elevator* ☰ *AE, MC, V.*

$$$ ⛶ **Hotel Kamila.** A family-friendly (and car-necessary) place, Hotel Kamila has numerous outdoor activities away from the hubbub of the central city. Take a golf or a horseback-riding lesson before a dip in the pool or a massage. The Slovak actress Kamila Magálová owns this 18th-century château, and rooms reflect her taste, which runs toward light wood and bold patterns. The restaurant serves French and Ger-

man dishes. The hotel lies about 14 km (9 mi) from the Old Town, beyond the airport. A shuttle is available to and from the Bratislava or Vienna airport. ⊠ *Cierna voda 611, Vajnory, 82108* ☎ *02/4594–3611* 📠 *02/4594–3631* ⊕ *www.kamila.sk* ⇆ *21 rooms, 4 apartments* ⬩ *Restaurant, room service, bar, tennis court, pool, gym, spa, bicycles, public Internet, airport shuttle, no elevator* ☰ *MC, V.*

NIGHTLIFE & THE ARTS

Bratislava's nightlife is gaining some energy. It has a decent bar and nightclub scene, with a sufficient number of places to settle in for a few drinks and some music or other entertainment. The pedestrian area of the Old Town is full of cafés and pubs, many with outdoor seating in warm weather. Bratislava hosts an annual jazz festival in October that attracts international talent. In addition, the city has many concerts, dance performances, and operettas to choose from—at reasonable prices (at most 800 Sk). Buy tickets at the venue, or inquire at the main Bratislava Tourist Information office (BKIS; *see* ⇨ *Visitor Information in Bratislava Essentials, below*).

The English-language *Slovak Spectator* (⊕ *www.slovakspectator.sk*), a Bratislava-based weekly newspaper, is a good place to check for weekly listings on the city's cultural life. Also check out ⊕ *www.enjoybratislava.sk*, one of the most informative Web sites about what's on in the city.

NIGHTLIFE

JAZZ & ROCK CLUBS

New clubs open and close quickly. Check the *Slovak Spectator* for the lowdown on the latest hot spots.

The tiny **Jazz Cafe** (⊠ *Ventúrska 5, Starý mesto* ☎ *02/5443–4661*) is one of the few jazz clubs in Bratislava. Catch live performances Thursday through Saturday, but arrive early if you want a table. **The Nu Spirit Bar & Lounge** (⊠ *Medena 16, Staré mesto* ☎ *90/5865–566* ⊕ *www.nuspirit.sk*) serves up live jazz once or twice a week. At other times, DJs spin a mix of soul, jazzy hip-hop, dance-floor jazz, and other grooves to get your feet tapping. The bar serves salads and sandwiches as well as cocktails and other drinks. The **Harley-Davidson Club** (⊠ *Rebarborová 1, Ružinov* ☎ *02/4319–1095*) is an American-style hard-rock club. Take Bus 220 from under the New Bridge to the Ružinovský cintorín (Ružinov Cemetery) stop.

THE ARTS

CONCERTS

The **Slovenská filharmónia** (*Slovak Philharmonic Orchestra* ⊠ *Medená 3, Staré mesto*) plays a full program of Slovak and Czech composers as well as European masters at its home in the Reduta. You can purchase tickets at the box office in person or by phone Wednesdays from 8 to 2, and other weekdays from 1 to 7, as well as one hour before the performance. ⊠ *Medená 3, Staré mesto* ☎ *02/5920–8233 or 02/5920–8211* ⊕ *www.filharm.sk*. **SLUK** (⊠ *Balkanska 31, Rusovce* ☎ *02/6820–9090* *or 02/6820–9011* ⊕*www.sluk.sk*), a folk ensemble, performs unique arrangements of Slovak music and dance.

OPERA & BALLET

The **Slovenské národné divadlo** (*Slovak National Theater* ⊠*Hviezdoslavovo nám.* 1, *Starý mesto* ☎*02/5443–3764* ⊕*www.snd.sk*) is the place for high-quality opera, operettas, and ballet. Buy tickets at the theater office on the corner of Jesenského and Komenské weekdays between 8 AM and 7 PM, Saturdays 9 to 1 (and one hour before show time), and Sundays one hour before the performance.

THEATER

Traditional theater is usually performed in Slovak. Milan Sladek Mime Theater stages world-class wordless performances at the **Divadlo Arena** (⊠*Viedenská cesta 10, Petrzalka* ☎*02/6720–2557 or 02/6224–6875* ⊕*www.divarena.sk*). You can buy tickets at the theater Tuesday–Friday 3–6 and starting one hour before performances.

SHOPPING

Bratislava is an excellent place to purchase Slovak arts and crafts of all kinds. Plenty of folk-art and souvenir shops line Obchodná ulica (Shopping Street), and you'll find booths and stores on Hlavné námestie. Slovak and Czech crystal are also widely available in the Old Town.

Antikvariát Steiner (⊠*Ventúrska ul. 20, Starý mesto* ☎*02/5443–3778* ⊗*Weekdays 10–5*) stocks beautiful old books, maps, graphics, and posters.

For Slovak folk art, try **Folk, Folk** (⊠*Obchodná 10, Staré mesto* ☎*02/5443–4292* ⊠*Rybárska brána 2* ☎*02/5443–0176*), which carries a wide selection of goods, including pottery, handwoven tablecloths, wooden toys, and dolls with Slovak folk costumes. **ÚĽUV** (⊠*Nám. SNP 12, Staré mesto* ☎*02/5292–3802* ⊠*Obchodná 64, Staré mesto* ☎*02/5273–1351/61*), a national chain, has a nice selection of hand-painted table pottery and vases, wooden figures, and village folk clothing. Small corn-husk figures are dirt cheap and can be very beautiful, though not easy to transport.

SPORTS & THE OUTDOORS

For a change of pace, consider spending a few hours pedaling along the popular Danube Trail, which links Bratislava and Vienna, paralleling the Danube for much of its 40-km (25-mi) length. Rentals are available at **Luka** (⊠*Pri Suchom mlyne 84* ☎*907/683–112*) and range from around 80 Sk for an hour to roughly 400 Sk a day. You can also join a three-hour guided bicycle tour along the river starting at the courtyard of the Slovak National Gallery—opposite the Danube's embankment—and pedaling past the Old and New bridges, Devin Castle, the confluence of the Danube and Morava rivers, and former sites of the Iron Curtain and WWII bunkers. It's an easy ride, ending with a relaxing return journey by boat. Tours run twice a day on weekends from

May through September. Tickets cost 950 Sk and include a bicycle, helmet, guide, and boat ticket; buy them at the BKIS office.

BRATISLAVA ESSENTIALS

AIR TRAVEL
ČSA, Sky Europe, and Ryanair have regular service between Bratislava's M.R. Štefánika Airport and an increasing number of major European cities. For better international access, many people fly through Vienna's Schwechat Airport, a mere 60 km (37 mi) west of Bratislava.

AIRPORT TRANSFERS
A taxi ride from the Bratislava airport to the town center should cost no more than 600 Sk. Bus No. 61 runs from the airport to the main train station and takes only 20 minutes; departures are every 10 to 20 minutes from 5 AM to 11 PM. Buses run all day every day between Vienna's airport and Bratislava's main bus station; the journey takes just over an hour and costs about €8–€12. You might also try to make an arrangement with a Slovak cabdriver; a ride to Vienna's airport could cost as little as 2,800 Sk.

Information Bus connection (☎ *02/5557–1312* ⊕ *www.viennaairport.com/ bus*).

BOAT TRAVEL
The Twin City Liner catamaran sails between Vienna and Bratislava (75 minutes) from March to October three to five times daily. The boat is fully air-conditioned and has panoramic windows and a lookout deck for Danube gazing. Boats stop in Bratislava at the Rázusovo nábrižie boat landing, next to Nový sost, and at the landing near Vienna's central Schwedenplatz, accessed via a ramp at Marienbrücke Bridge. Tickets cost €15–€27 (depending on departure time and season) each way.

BUS TRAVEL
Bratislava is well served by international buses, but trains are more comfortable and easier to navigate for non-Slovak speakers. Seven buses a day make the five-hour journey from Prague to Bratislava. From Vienna, there are frequent buses from Autobusbahnhof Wien Mitte, Südtirolerplatz, and Erdberg; the trip takes about an hour from each. One bus a day connects Budapest with Bratislava; the ride takes a little more than four hours.

Bratislava's main bus terminal is roughly 2 km (1 mi) from the city center. To get downtown from the terminal use a taxi or take Trolley 207 or 208 to Mierové námestie or 202 to the Tesco department store.

CAR TRAVEL
A car is not really necessary to explore Bratislava, as the Old Town is compact and many sights can be reached on foot. Buses and trams can take you to attractions outside the city center. If you do decide to drive, keep in mind that city roads are narrow. And don't be surprised to see cars parked halfway on a sidewalk.

PUBLIC TRANSPORTATION

Bratislava's buses and trams run frequently and connect the city center and Old Town with outlying sights. Stops are marked with signs that picture a bus or tram and list the transportation lines served from the stop. Tickets cost 14 Sk for a 10-minute ride, 18 Sk for 30 minutes, and 22 Sk for 60 minutes; you can venture a guess as to how long your ride will take or just buy the 60-minute option to be safe. Tickets are sold at public transportation booths, large hotels, newsstands, and tobacconists; you cannot buy them on board. Starting at 210 Sk, unlimited travel tickets are also available for one, two, three, or seven days. These are sold at public transportation booths (not at newsstands) and at the main train station.

Be sure to validate your ticket in the validating machine as soon as you board. The fine for riding with an unvalidated or expired ticket is 1,400 Sk, paid on the spot. City maps, available at newsstands and at the tourist office, list bus and tram routes. You can also look them up online at ⊕ *www.imhd.sk*.

TAXI TRAVEL

Taxis are easy to hail and are a good option when returning from restaurants or pubs at night. Meters start at 20 Sk–30 Sk and jump 15 Sk–30 Sk per 1 km (½ mi). Some taxi companies have a minimum rate of 100 Sk for one journey. To avoid being ripped off, watch to see that the driver engages the meter. If the meter is broken, negotiate a price with the driver before even getting in the cab. BP Taxi, Fun Taxi, and MB Taxi are reliable.

Information **BP Taxi** (☎ *02/16333 or 02/16000*). **Fun Taxi** (☎ *02/16777*). **MB Taxi** (☎ *02/16916 or 02/4821–2855*).

TRAIN TRAVEL

Reasonably efficient train service regularly connects Prague and Bratislava. Trains depart from Prague's Hlavní nádraží (main station) and from Holešovice station; the journey takes four to five hours. InterCity trains are slightly more expensive but faster (just under four hours). From Vienna Sudbahnhof (south station), trains leave almost every hour on the one-hour trek to Bratislava. The trip from Budapest takes from 2½ to 4 hours, depending on the train. Bratislava's main train station, Hlavná stanica, is about 2 km (1 mi) from the city center. To travel to the center of town from the station, take Tram 1 to Poštová ulica or jump in a taxi.

VISITOR INFORMATION

Bratislavská informačná služba (BKIS; Bratislava Information Service) is a good source for maps and basic information as well as for help finding hotels and private accommodations. The office can also hook you up with a tour guide. It's open weekdays 8:30–7, Saturday 9–7, and Sunday 10–7. There's also a small BKIS office in the Hlavná train station, open weekdays 9–6, weekends 9–2.

If you plan on visiting a number of sights and using public transportation, you might consider purchasing a BCCard (Bratislava City Card), which offers unlimited use of public transport, reduced entry to numerous museums and galleries, a free walking tour of the city, and price reductions in some restaurants and shops. It's available at BKIS in one-, two-, and three-day units and costs €5, €8, and €10, respectively.

Information BKIS (⊠ *Klobučnícka 2, Staré mesto* ☎ *02/16186, 02/5443-3715* ⊕ *www.bkis.sk* ⊠ *Hlavná stanica, Prestanične nám., Staré mesto* ☎ *02/5249-5906*).

CENTRAL SLOVAKIA

Though generally overlooked by tourists, central Slovakia is the country's heart and soul. This is where the nation was born and where Slovak folklore and deep-rooted traditions continue to flourish.

Formerly a medieval mining town, Banská Bystrica lies at the center of the region and is the ideal base from which to explore the towns and villages surrounding it. The region's two other main historical mining towns, Banská Štiavnica and Kremnica, have remained more or less frozen in time since their glory days in the Middle Ages.

The beauty of central Slovakia, however, lies not so much in its architecture as in its inspiring natural landscapes. The region is home to both the High Tatras (covered separately in the next section), the highest mountain range in Slovakia, and the Low Tatras, the country's second-highest range and the largest by area. In the Low Tatras in winter, ski slopes are mostly free from the hordes of tourists that overrun their higher counterparts. Wonderful hiking trails, caves, and scenic valleys make summer an appealing time to visit as well.

BANSKÁ BYSTRICA

205 km (127 mi) northeast of Bratislava on Hwys. D61 and E571 and Rte. 66.

Surrounded by three mountain ranges—the Low Tatras, the Fatras, and the Slovak rudohorie—Banská Bystrica is an ideal starting point for exploring the beauty of the region. Focus on the surrounding woods and hills—the outlying areas are plagued with concrete apartment buildings.

Banská Bystrica has been around since the 13th century, acquiring wealth from the nearby mines. Following the Tartar invasion in 1241, the Hungarian king Béla IV granted special privileges to encourage the immigration of German settlers, who together with the locals developed the prosperous mining of copper and precious metals. During the 19th century, the town was a major focus of Slovak national life, and it was from a school here that the teaching of the Slovak language originated and spread to the rest of the country.

The city is also famous as the center of the Slovak National Uprising (known in Slovak by the initials SNP) during World War II. It was here that the underground Slovak National Council initiated the revolt on

August 29, 1944. For some two months, thousands of Slovaks valiantly rose up against the Slovak puppet regime and their Nazi oppressors, forcing the Germans to divert critically needed troops and equipment from the front lines. Though the Germans quashed the uprising on October 27, the costly operation is credited with accelerating the Allied victory and gaining Slovakia the short-lived appellation of ally.

The **Múzeum Slovenského národného povstania** *(Museum of the Slovak National Uprising)* stands in a large field just outside the center of town, between Horná ulica and Ulica Dukelských hrdinov. It's difficult to miss the tank out front and the monument's massive concrete wings—the effect is particularly striking at night when the monument is lighted up. The museum's focus has been shifting from Communism to more recent national events. ⊠ *Kapitulská 23* ☎ *048/412–3258* ⊕ *www.muzeumsnp.sk* ✆ *50 Sk* ⊘ *May–Sept., Tues.–Sun. 9–6; Oct.– Apr., Tues.–Sun. 9–4.*

A cheery collection of Renaissance and baroque houses lines Námestie SNP; the most impressive is the **Thurzo dom** *(Thurzo House)*, an amalgamation of two late-Gothic structures built in 1495 by the wealthy Thurzo family. The genuine Renaissance sgraffiti decorations on the outside were added during the 16th century, when the family's wealth was at its height. Today the building houses the **Stredoslovenské múzeum** (Central Slovak Museum), which is more interesting for the chance it affords of seeing the inside of the house than for its artifacts. ⊠ *Nám. SNP 4* ☎ *048/412–5897* ✆ *30 Sk* ⊘ *Weekdays 8–noon and 1–4, Sun. 10–noon and 1–5.*

OFF THE BEATEN PATH

Bojnice Hrad. Romantic Bojnice Castle, dating from before 1175, has all the necessary elements of a fairy-tale palace: multilevel turrets with decorative spires, ornate parapets, and a sparkling moat. The interior is beautifully restored and furnished in 12th-century style. Costumed guides lead daytime and candlelight tours (by arrangement), which are available in English. Don't miss the Bojnicky *oltar* (altar), a point of contention between newly formed Czech and Slovak republics in 1993—the Czechs wanted to keep it. During the first weeks of May the castle hosts the International Festival of Ghosts and Spirits. ⊠ *Off Hwys. E572 and 64, 65 km (40 mi) west of Banská Bystrica* ☎ *046/543–0633* ⊕ *www.bojnicecastle.sk* ✆ *Day tour 130 Sk, candlelight tour 200 Sk* ⊘ *Tours July and Aug., 9–5 and at 9 PM; May, June, and Sept., Tues.–Sun. 9–5; Oct.–Apr., Tues.–Sun. 10–3.*

WHERE TO EAT & STAY

★ $–$$ ✕ **Starobystrická pivnica.** Grilled food is the house specialty at this classic wine cellar. The delicious *cesnakova polievka* (garlic soup) is served in a bread bowl. For a main course, try the *Starobystica misa*, a mixed plate with different cuts of grilled pork. ⊠ *Nám. SNP 9* ☎ *048/415–4326* ⊟ *MC, V.*

★ $$ ✕▣ **Arcade Hotel.** This 16th-century building on the main square is an ideal place to stay. The rooms and apartments vary in size, comfort, and cost, but each is equipped with the basic creature comforts. The on-site Italian restaurant ($$–$$$) is set in an old wine cellar with craggy, barrel-vaulted ceilings. ✉ *Nám. SNP 5, 97401* ☎ *048/430–2111* 📠 *048/430–2222* ⊕ *www.arcade.sk* 🛏 *9 rooms, 2 suites, 3 apartments* ♿ *No a/c, safe, no elevator, restaurant, bar* 🚭 *MC, V.*

SPORTS & THE OUTDOORS

The most attractive hiking trails are to the north and west of Banská Bystrica, and there are excellent scenic mountain-biking opportunities in the surrounding area. Popular ski areas in the Low Tatras include Jasenská, 48 km (30 mi) north of Banská Bystrica, and Kubinska Hola, near Dolny Kubin, 71 km (44 mi) north of Banská Bystrica. For hiking maps, suggested bike routes, and more information on all activities, visit the town tourist information office.

BANSKÁ ŠTIAVNICA

48 km (30 mi) south of Banská Bystrica on Hwys. E77 and E571, and Rte. 525.

Since the 11th century, this little town has earned its wealth from mining, and today it's essentially one large mining museum on the UNESCO World Heritage list. German miners arrived here to exploit rich gold and silver deposits, and their success is apparent in some of the town's remaining monuments, such as the golden Trinity column on Trojičné námestie (Trinity Square).

At the **Banské múzeum** *(Open-Air Mining Museum)* you can view some of the town's original mining buildings and machinery—dating to the early 13th century—and take a trip down into a pit mine. The museum is about 2 km (1 mi) from town. ✉ *Štiavnické bane* ☎ *045/691–1541* 💰 *80 Sk* ⊙ *July and Aug., Tues.–Sun. 9–5; Sept.–June, weekdays 8–3.*

The **Nový zámok** *(New Castle)* was built between 1564 and 1571 as part of an effort to strengthen fortification of the town against invasions of the Turks. The six-story Renaissance building was used as a watchtower and later became the town's live clock—the time was announced every quarter hour by a trumpet. Inside are historical exhibits of the Turkish invasions during the 16th and 17th centuries. ✉ *Novozámocká 22* ☎ *045/21543* 💰 *50 Sk* ⊙ *May–Sept., Tues.–Sun. 8–4; Oct.–Apr., weekdays 8–3.*

The **Starý zámok** *(Old Castle)*, built on the rocks above town, dates to the early 13th century, but additions were made in practically every subsequent building style. The castle served as a fortress to protect the wealth of the local bigwigs against the Turkish invaders. ✉ *Starozámocká 11* ☎ *045/691–1543* 💰 *60 Sk* ⊙ *Tues.–Sun. 9–4.*

OFF THE BEATEN PATH

Mansion Saint Anton. Don't miss this charming late-baroque château in the small village of Antol, just outside Banská Štiavnica. The château displays its original furnishings, has an exhibition of hunting arms and game, and is surrounded by French and English gardens. ✉ *Svätý Anton* ☎ *045/691–3932* 💰 *50 Sk* ⊙ *May–Sept., Tues.–Sun. 8–4; Oct.–Apr., Tues.–Sat. 8–3.*

WHERE TO STAY & EAT

$ ✗⊞**Antolský mlyn.** This cheery, family-run pension sits in a tiny village just outside Banská Štiavnica near Mansion Saint Anton. Black lacquer furnishings give the rooms a modern Slovak look. A Continental breakfast is included. The simple whitewashed restaurant ($$) has understated dark wood accents and a Slovak menu of pork, beef, poultry, and fish dishes. ⊠*Svätý Anton, 96972* ☎*045/693–1311* ⊕*www. antolskymlyn.sk* ☛*7 rooms, 1 apartment* ♿*In-room: no a/c. In-hotel: restaurant, bicycles, no elevator* ⊟*DC, MC, V* ⦿*CP.*

★ $ ⊞**Hotel Salamander.** Looking at the freshly painted gray-and-white Hotel Salamander sandwiched along the main square, you'd hardly guess the building actually dates from the 16th century. The rooms have high ceilings with decorative plasterwork, and the public areas are filled with antiques. ⊠*J. Palárika 1, 96901* ☎*045/691–3992* ☎*045/692–1262* ⊕*www.hotelsalamander.sk* ☛*25 rooms, 4 suites* ♿*In-room: no a/c, safe. In-hotel: restaurant, no elevator* ⊟*AE, DC, MC, V.*

CENTRAL SLOVAKIA ESSENTIALS

CAR TRAVEL

The most convenient way to reach Banská Bystrica is by car. From Bratislava, take the D61 and E571 to Zvolen via Nitra, and then follow the 66 to Banská Bystrica; the trip should take roughly 2½ hours. Driving through central Slovakia is relatively quick and hassle-free. Banská Štiavnica is southwest of Zvolen on Route 525; the road is narrow but well marked.

TRAIN TRAVEL

Daily trains connect Bratislava to Banská Bystrica; the journey takes almost three hours. The trip from Košice, in eastern Slovakia, to Banská Bystrica takes about five hours and is one of the most scenic railway trips in the country (take the northern, not the southern, route). Train travel between Banská Bystrica and Banská Štiavnica involves several inconvenient connections and can take up to three hours.

VISITOR INFORMATION

Town tourist information centers can arrange hotels and a variety of English-language tours at a reasonable cost. They also have maps and information about hiking and other outdoor activities in the region and offer tickets to cultural events in Banská Bystrica and Banská Štiavnica. Offices are open May through September, daily 8–5:30, October through April, weekdays 8–4, Saturday 8–2.

Information Banská Bystrica tourist office (⊠*Nám. SNP 14 [main square]* ☎*048/415–5085* ⊕*www.kisbb.sk*). **Banská Štiavnica tourist office** (⊠*Nám. sv. Trojice 3, Banská Štiavnica* ☎*045/694–9653* ⊕*www.banskastiavnica.sk/en/*).

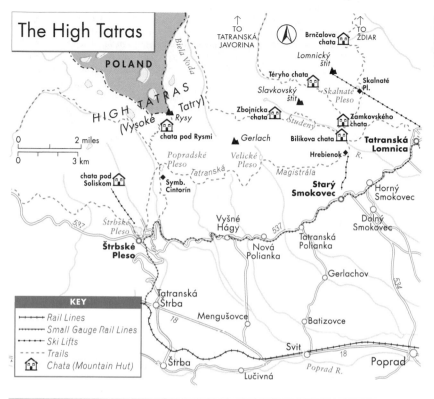

The High Tatras

POLAND

Biela Voda

HIGH TATRAS (Vysoké Tatry)

0 — 2 miles
0 — 3 km

TO TATRANSKÁ JAVORINA ↑

Brnčalova chata

TO ŽDIAR ↑

Lomnický štít

Téryho chata

Slavkovský štít

Skalnaté Pl.

Skalnaté Pleso

Rysy

Zbojnícka chata

Studený

Zamkovského chata

chata pod Rysmi

Gerlach

Bilikova chata

Tatranská Lomnica

Popradské Pleso

Velické Pleso

Hrebienok

R.

Tatranská

Magistrála

chata pod Soliskom

Symb. Cintorín

Starý Smokovec

Horný Smokovec

Štrbské Pleso

Vyšné Hágy

537

Tatranská Polianka

Dolný Smokovec

Štrbské Pleso

Nová Polianka

Gerlachov

534

Tatranská Štrba

Mengušovce

Batizovce

18

Svit

Štrba

Lučivná

Poprad R.

Poprad

18

KEY
- ┝━━━┿ Rail Lines
- ┝━━━━ Small Gauge Rail Lines
- ┝━━━━ Ski Lifts
- ----- Trails
- 🏠 Chata (Mountain Hut)

THE HIGH TATRAS

A visit to the Vysoké Tatry (High Tatras) alone would make a trip to Slovakia worthwhile. Although the range is relatively compact (just 32 km [20 mi] from end to end), its peaks seem wilder and more starkly beautiful than those of the Alps. The highest is Gerlachovský štít, at 8,710 feet; some 20 others exceed 8,000 feet. The 35 mountain lakes are remote and clear, very cold, and sometimes eerily deep. Swimming is not permitted in these glacier lakes. Endemic species of marmot and mountain goat, in addition to the common brown bear, wolf, and lynx, make their home in the High Tatra range.

The best way to see these beautiful mountains is on foot. A reasonably fit person of any age should have little trouble with any of the walks in the area, which take three to five hours each. Even though the trails are well marked, it is very important to buy a walking map of the area—the detailed *Vysoké Tatry, letná turistická mapa* is available for around 55 Sk at newspaper kiosks and some tourist information offices and hotels. If you plan to take any of the higher-level walks, be sure to wear proper shoes with good ankle support. Exercise extreme caution in early spring, when melting snow can turn the trails into icy rivers and cause avalanches. Check with the Horská služba for conditions.

The entire region is crisscrossed with paths ideal for cross-country skiing. You can buy a special ski map at newspaper kiosks as well as at some hotels and tourist offices. The ski season lasts from the end of December through April, though the best months are traditionally January and February. Rental equipment is ubiquitous, and you'll get a complete downhill or Nordic ski set—including skis, boots, and poles—for up to 250 Sk per day. Ždiar, toward the Polish border, has a good downhill and cross-country ski area for all levels of expertise. There are some 20 ski areas in the High Tatras, each offering both cross-country and downhill skiing. Among the most popular are those at Podbanské, Štrbské Pleso, Starý Smokovec, Nový Smokovec, Tatranská Lomnica, Svit–Lopušná, and Dolina.

Most of the tourist facilities in the High Tatras are concentrated in three neighboring resort towns: Štrbské Pleso, to the west; Smokovec, in the middle; and Tatranská Lomnica, to the east. Each town is fairly similar in terms of convenience and atmosphere, and all provide easy passage to the hills, so it makes little difference where you begin your explorations of the mountains.

POPRAD

329 km (204 mi) east of Bratislava along Hwys. D61 and E50.

Poprad, the gateway to the Tatras, is a good place to begin exploring the region. But don't expect a beautiful mountain village. Poprad fell victim to some of the most insensitive Communist planning perpetrated in the country after the war. There's no need to linger here. Instead, drive or take the electric railroad to the superior sights and facilities of the more rugged resorts just over 30 km (19 mi) to the north.

WHERE TO EAT & STAY

★ $–$$ ✕ **Slovenská Reštaurácia.** If you want to spend a few hours in Poprad, having a meal in this charming rustic restaurant is the best way to do so. Try the bryndzové halušky, *strapačky s kapustou* (homemade noodles with sauerkraut), or *pirohy* (potato-dough dumplings stuffed with meat or cheese). ✉ *Ul. 1. mája 216* ☎ *052/772–2870* ☐ *AE, MC, V.*

$ ▥ **Hotel Café Razy.** This newly opened centrally located hotel offers modest but comfortable accommodation in an old town house. The warm, pinewood-furnished rooms, some with a loft under slanting ceilings, are interestingly styled (almost post-modern). ✉ *Námestie sv. Egídia 58, 05801* ☎ *052/776–4101* ⊕ *www.hotelcafecrazy.sk* ☞ *17 rooms* ⚏ *In-room: no a/c, TV. In-hotel: 2 restaurants, bar, no elevator* ☐ *No credit cards.*

SMOKOVEC

12 km (7 mi) north of Poprad on Rte. 534.

The first town you'll reach by road or rail from Poprad is Smokovec, the undisputed center of the Slovak Tatras resorts and a good starting point for mountain excursions. Smokovec is divided into two principal areas, Starý Smokovec (Old Smokovec) and Nový Smokovec (New Smokovec), which are within a stone's throw of each other.

The Tatras seem tailor-made for hikers of all levels. Starý Smokovec is a great starting point for a three-hour trek that parallels a cascading waterfall for much of its 12-km (7-mi) length. From Starý Smokovec, walk out along the main road in the direction of Tatranská Lomnica for roughly 1 km (½ mi). In Tatranská Lesná, follow the yellow-marked path that winds gently uphill through the pines.

Farther along are red markers leading to the funicular at Hrebienok, which brings you back to the relative comforts of Starý Smokovec. However, if you're in good physical shape and there is plenty of daylight left, consider extending your hike by four hours (10 mi [16 km]). (The extension is striking, but avoid it during winter, when you may find yourself neck-deep in snow.) Just before the Bilíkova *chata* (a chata is a mountain hut), turn right along the green path and then follow the blue, red, and then green trails in the direction of windswept Téryho chata, a turn-of-the-20th-century chalet perched amid five lonely alpine lakes. The scenery is a few notches above dazzling. Once you reach the chalet after two strenuous hours of hiking, backtrack to Bilíkova chata. A few steps down from the chata is Studenovodske vopady (Cold-water Waterfalls). Follow the signs from Bilíkova to the funicular at Hrebienok and take it down to Starý Smokovec. It runs at 45-minute intervals (every 10 minutes when busy) beginning at 7:30 AM and ending at 7 PM; the schedule is posted at the Bilíkova chata.

NEED A BREAK?

Don't pass up the chance to take a break with a warm beverage at the Bilíkova chata (☎ *052/442–2439*), a rustic and cozy restaurant and hotel in a little clearing just before you reach Hrebienok. It's open all yearround.

WHERE TO STAY & EAT

★ $–$$ ✕ **Restaurant Svišt.** This restaurant with rustic light-colored wooden furnishings and a welcoming open hearth serves tasty local fare. Try the *kapustová polievka* (sauerkraut soup with mushrooms and sausage). ⊠ *Nový Smokovec 30* ☎ *052/442–2545* ▤ *No credit cards.*

★ $$ ✕▥ **Hotel Smokovec.** This charming hotel near the railway station offers clean, modest rooms with rustic furnishings and good meals in a choice of three different eateries. In the Bistro ($–$$), an open-face grill puts out tasty local fare; try the Tatra trout with cold garnishings. ⊠ *Starý Smokovec 25* ☎ *052/442–5191* ⊕ *www.hotelsmokovec.sk* ⇆ *31 rooms* ⟁ *In-hotel: 3 restaurants, room service, bar, pool* ▤ *MC, V* ⊠ *EP.*

$$$–$$$$ ▥ **Hotel Hubert.** Luxury accommodation is coupled here with a wealth of activities and facilities. You can play chess outdoors, for example, before taking a ride in a horse-drawn carriage or after fishing in the private lake. Guest rooms are tastefully done in modern oak furnishings and pastel hues. The Hubert is on the road between Starý Smokovec and Štrebské Pleso. ⊠ *Gerlachov 302, 05942* ☎ *052/478–0811* ▤ *052/478–0805* ⊕ *www.hotel-hubert.sk* ⇆ *39 rooms* ⟁ *In-hotel: restaurant, room service, bar, tennis court, pool, laundry service, public Internet* ▤ *AE, MC, V.*

★ $$$ ⚅**Grand Hotel.** Along with its sister hotel in Tatranská Lomnica, Grandhotel Praha, this hotel epitomizes Tatra luxury at its turn-of-the-20th-century best. The golden Tudor facade rises majestically over the town, with the peaks of the Tatras looming in the background. In season, skiers and hikers crowd the reception area and hallways (there's ski rental in an adjacent building), but the rooms themselves are quiet. ⊠*Starý Smokovec, 06201* ☎*052/478–0000* 🖷*052/442–2157* ☎*79 rooms, 52 with bath; 5 suites* ⚐*In-hotel: restaurant, bar, pool* ☰*AE, DC, MC, V* ⓘⓞⓘ*BP.*

★ $–$$ ⚅**Villa Dr. Szontagh.** Away from the action in Nový Smokovec, this steepled little chalet provides mostly peace and quiet. The darkly furnished rooms and public areas are well maintained, and the courtly staff goes out of its way to please. The decent restaurant has an extensive wine cellar. ⊠*Nový Smokovec, 06201* ☎*052/442–2061* ⊕*www.szontagh. sk* ☎*9 rooms, 4 apartments, 1 suite* ⚐*In-hotel: restaurant, no elevator* ☰*MC, V* ⊗*Closed Nov.*

SPORTS & THE OUTDOORS
The multipurpose **Tatrasport Adam & Andreas** (⊠*Starý Smokovec* ☎*052/442–5241* ⊕*www.tatry.net/tatrasport*), opposite the bus station, provides numerous all-season sport services—ski lessons and rentals, sleigh rides, mountain guides, bicycle rentals, horseback riding, river rafting, and more.

ŠTRBSKÉ PLESO

18 km (11 mi) west of Smokovec on Rte. 537.

Štrbské Pleso is the main center in the Tatras for active sports. Six ski slopes are close by, and many excellent hiking trails are within easy reach. The town not only has the most modern hotels (and the most jarringly modern hotel architecture), but it also commands the finest panoramas in the Tatras.

WHERE TO STAY
★ $$–$$$ ⚅**Patria.** This modern, slanting pyramid on the shores of a clear mountain lake has two obvious advantages: location and views. Ask for a room on a higher floor; those overlooking the lake have balconies, and the other side opens onto the mountains. Rooms have modern Swedish furniture and crisp white duvets. The hotel is steps from a ski jump, where bungee-jumping can be arranged if you feel the urge for a thrill, and has its own sport shop and ski school. ⊠*Štrbské Pleso, 05985* ☎*052/449–2591* 🖷*052/449–2590* ⊕*www.hotelpatria.sk* ☎*140 rooms, 10 apartments* ⚐*In-hotel: 3 restaurants, bar, pool, children's programs (ages 5–12)* ☰*AE, DC, MC, V.*

SPORTS & THE OUTDOORS
JMG (⊠*Štrbské Pleso* ☎*052/449–2582* ⊕*www.jmg.sk*), at the Hotel Patria, can arrange ski lessons and equipment rental as well as sightseeing flights, paragliding, sleigh rides, and mountain guides. **Jur Sport Agency** (⊠*Hlavná 260, Závažná Poruba* ☎*052/554–7279* ⊕*www. jursport.sk*) arranges two-hour raft trips along the Váh River from

May to September. The starting point is 5 km (3 mi) from Liptovský Mikuláš, west of Štrbské Pleso.

TATRANSKÁ LOMNICA

24 km (15 mi) northeast of Štrbské Pleso on Rte. 537.

Tatranská Lomnica, on the eastern end of the electric rail line, has a near-perfect combination of peace, convenience, and atmosphere. Moreover, the lift behind the Grandhotel Praha brings some of the best walks in the Tatras to within 10 minutes or so of your hotel door.

The Magistrale, a 24-km (15-mi) walking trail that skirts the peaks just above the tree line, affords some of the best views for the least amount of exertion. A particularly stunning stretch of the route—marked by red signposts—begins in Tatranská Lomnica and ends 5 km (3 mi) away in Starý Smokovec. The total walking time is four hours, plus a taxi ride back to where you started.

To start the walk, take the small cable car behind the Grandhotel Praha in Tatranská Lomnica to Skalnaté Pleso (390 Sk round-trip). Here you'll find a food court and bar (*varené víno,* hot spiced wine, is especially good in cold weather). From here you can access the trail immediately. But consider a 30-minute detour via cable car (550 Sk round-trip) to the top of Lomnický štít (8,635 feet), the second-highest peak in the range. Because of the harsh temperatures (be sure to dress warmly even in summer), you're permitted to linger on the limited walkways near the observatory at the top for only 30 minutes, after which you take the cable car back down. Reservations are necessary for the cable car to Lomnický štít, and tickets sell out quickly; if you can't reserve a spot a day in advance, try to get there an hour early to assure a place. For further information, consult the cable car section on ⊕*www.tldtatry.sk,* a local tour operator's Web site.

WHERE TO STAY & EAT

$$–$$$$ ✕**Zbojnícka koliba.** This dark-log mountain cottage restaurant specializes in *kurča* (chicken) cooked on a rotisserie over an open pit. You can order a half or a whole, but either way the wait will be about 55 minutes, as the chicken is prepared fresh. To take the edge off your hunger while you wait, munch on appetizers of bryndza cheese (made from fresh sheep's milk), onions, and pieces of bacon with bread and enjoy the live Gypsy music. ⊠*Toward Grandhotel Praha, Tatranská Lomnica* ☎*052/446–7267* ⊟*No credit cards.*

★ $$$ 🏨**Grandhotel Praha.** In the shadow of Lomnický štít rises a cream-color mansion with red-roof-topped turrets. Built in 1905, Grandhotel Praha is one of the wonders of the Tatras. Public rooms retain a historic elegance: the large lower-level lounge, for example, has huge black easy chairs, intricate crystal chandeliers, and golden-yellow walls characteristic of the time when Maria Theresa ruled the Austro-Hungarian Empire. Guest rooms are spacious, and about half have been renovated. Although the new rooms are crisp, the hyper-modern lines and bright teal fabrics seem a bit out of place. ⊠*Tatranská Lomnica,*

05960 ☎*052/446–7941* 🖷*052/446–7891* ⊕*www.ghpraha.sk* ⟿*83 rooms, 7 suites* ♿*In-hotel: restaurant, bar* ⊟*AE, DC, MC, V.*

$$ ⌗**Villa Beatrice.** Nine apartment suites with at least a bedroom, living room (with pull-out beds), and a kitchen nook make a nice home away from home. Some units also have a fireplace, sauna, or whirlpool; No. 9 is spread over two floors. Contemporary wood furnishings and floral upholstery fill the apartments. Ski rental is available. ⊠*Tatranská Lomnica, 05960* ☎*052/446–7313* 🖷*052/446–7120* ⊕*www.beatrice. sk* ⟿*9 suites* ♿*In-room: no a/c. In-hotel: bicycles* ⊟*MC, V.*

SPORTS & THE OUTDOORS
Skalnaté Pleso, above Tatranská Lomnica, has moderately challenging slopes. You can rent skis at the Grandhotel Praha.

Asociácia horských vodcov (*Mountain Guides Association* ☎*052/442–2066* ⊕*www.tatraguide.com*) provides guides for the more difficult hiking routes for 3,200 Sk–5,500 Sk per day, per person. Individual rates decrease the larger your group. Guides can be hired online via the association's Web site.

HIGH TATRAS ESSENTIALS

AIT TRAVEL
Sky Europe operates regular flights from Prague and London-Stansted to Poprad-Tatry International Airport. From the airport, you can take Bus 12 to downtown Poprad, 5 km (3 mi) away, and connect to the electric rail system to travel on to the resorts.

BUS TRAVEL
Daily bus service connects Bratislava with Poprad (about 6½ hours) and the smaller towns in the area, but trains tend to be quicker and are much more comfortable.

CAR TRAVEL
The High Tatras' efficient electric rail system makes having a car unnecessary if you're staying put in the area. However, if you plan to tour the region's smaller towns and villages or if you are continuing on to eastern Slovakia, a car will prove nearly indispensable. Poprad, the gateway to the Tatras, is 328 km (203 mi) from Bratislava, with a four-lane stretch between the capital and Trenčín and a well-marked, two-lane highway thereafter; the drive takes about 4½ hours.

TRAIN TRAVEL
Regular rail service connects Bratislava with Poprad, but book ahead: the trains are often impossibly crowded in August and during the skiing season. A trip from Bratislava's Hlavná stanica to Poprad's station, Železničná stanica Poprad, takes four hours on an InterCity train, longer on others. To connect to the High Tatras resort towns, you have to switch to the efficient electric railway, which shares the regular train stations but is a smaller gauge. Electric trains run every 30 to 60 minutes. If you're going only to the Tatras, you won't need any other form of transportation.

VISITOR INFORMATION

Tourist information is readily available in the larger resort towns. Tatra Information Board (TIK) in Starý Smokovec provides general tourist information weekdays 8–8, Saturday 8–1. T-Ski Travel can help with accommodations in hotels and *chata*, arrange guides for hikes, organize ski trips, and provide you with rental equipment.

Contacts Tatra Information Board (TIK) (⊠ *Dom Služieb 24, Starý Smokovec* ☎ *052/442–3440* ⊕ *www.tatry.sk.*). **T-Ski Travel** (⊠ *Starý Smokovec 46* ☎ *052/442–3200* ⊕ *www.slovakiatravel.sk*).

EASTERN SLOVAKIA

To the east of the High Tatras lies an expanse of Slovakia that seldom appears on tourist itineraries. However, eastern Slovakia is a hiking wonderland. In addition to the offerings at Slovenský raj national park, trails fan out in all directions in the area known as Spišská Magura, to the north and east of Kežmarok. Good swimming can be found in the lakes in Slovenský raj and in Michalovce, east of Košice.

For 1,000 years, eastern Slovakia was isolated from the West; much of the region was regarded simply as the hinterland of Greater Hungary. Isolation has its advantages, however, and therein may lie the charm of this area. The baroque and Renaissance facades that dominate the towns of Bohemia and Moravia make an appearance in eastern Slovakia as well, but they're often done in local wood instead of stone. Look especially for the wooden altars in Levoča and other towns.

The relative isolation also fostered the development of an entire civilization in medieval times, the Spiš, with no counterpart in the Czech Republic or elsewhere in Slovakia. The territory of the kingdom, which spreads out to the east and south of the High Tatras, was originally settled by Slavonic and later by German immigrants who came here in medieval times to work the mines and defend the western kingdoms against invasion. Some 24 towns eventually came to join the Spiš group, functioning as a miniprincipality within the Hungarian monarchy. The group had its own hierarchies and laws, which were quite different from those brought in by Magyar or Saxon settlers.

Although the last Spiš town lost its independence 100 years ago, much of the group's architectural legacy remains—another by-product of isolation and economic stagnation. Spiš towns are predominantly Gothic beneath their graceful Renaissance overlays. Their steep shingle roofs, high timber-frame gables, and brick-arch doorways have survived in a remarkable state of preservation. Spiš towns are worth seeking out when you see them on a map—look for the prefix *Spišský* preceding a town name.

Farther to the northeast in the foothills of the Carpathian Mountains, the influences of Byzantium are strongly felt, most noticeably in the form of the typically Rusyn (an ethnic minority that speaks its own language related to Ukrainian and Slovak) Greek Catholic and Orthodox wooden churches with onion domes that dominate the villages along the frontier with Poland and Ukraine. This area marks a border in Europe that has stood for a thousand years: the ancient transitional zone between Rome and Constantinople, between Western Christianity and the Eastern Christianity of the Byzantine Empire.

LEVOČA

★ *90 km (56 mi) northwest of Košice on Hwy. E50, 358 km (222 mi) northeast of Bratislava on Hwys. D61 and E50.*

Levoča's Old Town is still partially surrounded by walled fortifications, and you most likely will drive through the medieval Košice Gate to enter the square. This medieval capital of the Spiš region was founded around 1245 and flourished between the 14th and 17th century, when it was an important trade center for art and crafts.

The main architectural sights in town are lined along and in the middle of the main square, **Námestie majstra Pavla**. Note the sgraffiti-decorated house at No. 7, **Thurzov dom** (Thurzov House), named for the powerful mining family. The wonderfully ornate gables date from the 17th century, though the sgraffiti decorations were added in the 19th century. At the top of the square at No. 60 is the **Malý župný dom** (Small County House), the former administrative center of the Spiš region, now used as an archive. Above the doorway is the coat of arms of the Spiš alliance. The monumental classical building next door, the **Veľký župný dom** (Large County House), was built in the early 19th century by Anton Povolný, who was also responsible for the Evangelical Church at the bottom of the square.

★ **Kostol svätého Jakuba** *(St. Jacob's Church)* is a huge Gothic structure begun in the early 14th century but not completed until a century later. The interior is a breathtaking concentration of Gothic religious art. It was here in the early 16th century that the Spiš artist Pavol of Levoča carved his most famous work: the wood high altar, which is said to be the world's largest and incorporates a magnificent limestone relief of the Last Supper. The 12 disciples are in fact portraits of Levoča merchants. A tape recording in an iron post at the back of the church provides detailed information in English. Note: On Saturday afternoons the cathedral is often closed for private wedding ceremonies; it's best to plan a visit before noon. ☒*Nám. majstra Pavla* ☎*053/451–2347* ⊕*www.chramsvjakuba.sk* ☙*60 Sk* ☉*July and Aug., Mon. 11–4, Tues.–Sat. 8:30–4; Sept.–June, Mon. 11:30–4, Tues.–Sat. 8:30–4, Sun. 1–4.*

The **Mestská radnica** *(town hall)*, with its fine whitewashed Renaissance arcades, gables, and clock tower, was built in 1551 after the great fire of 1550 destroyed the old Gothic building along with much of the town. The clock tower now houses a museum, with exhibits of guild flags and a collection of paintings and wood carvings. You can also look at the 18th-century Lady in White, painted on a doorway through which, as legend has it, she let in the enemy for a promise of wealth and a title.

Master Pavol: Wood Carver

11

Little is known about the origin of the great wood-altar carver Master Pavol. He arrived in 1506 to the then very affluent city of Levoča, set up his workshop, and started carving his way into the art history books. He gained a great deal of fame throughout the Spiš region by creating numerous late-Gothic altars. Between 1508 and 1517 he created his best-known and most significant work, the world's largest wooden altar, which soars to a height of 61 feet in St. Jacob's Church, almost completely filling the choir. Master Pavol became a much-respected member of the community and was elected to serve on the city council. He lived out his days at his home and workshop opposite the church, on St. Pavol's Square.

For this act of treason, the 24-year-old beauty's head was chopped off. ⊠*Nám. majstra Pavla* ☎*053/451–2449* 🎫*50 Sk* ☉*Tues.–Sun. 9–5.*

OFF THE BEATEN PATH

Slovenský Raj. A wild and romantic area of cliffs and gorges, caves and waterfalls, Slovak Paradise national park is a dream for adventurous hikers. The gorges are accessible by narrow but secure iron ladders. The main tourist centers are Čingov in the north and Dedinky in the south. To get here from Levoča, head south on Route 533 through Spišská Nová Ves, continuing along the twisting roads to the junction with Route 535. Turn right onto Route 535, following the signs to Mlynky and then for Slovenský Raj, another roughly 30 km (19 mi) through the tiny villages and breathtaking countryside. ⊕ *www.slovenskyraj.info* 🎫*20 Sk.*

Fodor'sChoice

★

This former administrative center of the kingdom is the largest castle in Slovakia—and one of the largest in Europe. Spiš overlords occupied this site starting in 1209. The sprawling fortifications are mostly in ruins, but in the section that has been preserved, a museum houses a collection of torture devices. The hilltop location affords a beautiful view of the surrounding hills and town. From Levoča, it's well worth taking the short 16 km (10 mi) detour east along Route 18 to this striking spot. ⊠*Spišský hrad* ☎*053/454—1336, 053/451-2786 museum* 🎫*120 Sk* ☉*May–Oct., daily 9–7; Nov.–Apr. by appointment only; last entry 1 hr before closing.*

WHERE TO STAY & EAT

$-$$ ✕ **U Janusa.** This family-owned restaurant is the perfect place to get a taste of Slovak culture as well as cuisine. Try one of the local specialties, such as homemade sausage or *zemiakové placky* (potato pancakes). ⊠*Kláštorská 22* ☎*053/451-4592* ▭*No credit cards.*

$$ 🛏 **Hotel Satel.** This beautiful 18th-century mansion is flanked by other historic buildings on the town square. The hotel is arranged around a courtyard that retains its historic flavor, and in summer a fountain flows here. The interior decor, however, can be a bit gaudy—particularly the peach lacquer headboards in the bedrooms and the fuchsia tablecloths

in the restaurant. ⊠*Nám. majstra Pavla 55, 05401* ☎*053/451–2946* 🖷*053/451–4486* ⊕*www.satel-slovakia.sk* 🗩*21 rooms, 2 suites* ⚓*In-hotel: restaurant, bar, no elevator* ☰*DC, MC, V.*

★ $–$$ 🕎**Arkada Hotel.** An interesting history and reasonable prices make this hotel a standout. In the 17th century this 13th-century building became the first printing shop in the Austro-Hungarian Empire. The large, bright rooms—some with arched ceilings—are mostly done in contemporary neutrals. ⊠*Nám. majstra Pavla 26, 05401* ☎☎*053/451–2255* ⊕*www.arkada.sk* 🗩*32 rooms* ⚓*In-hotel: restaurant, bar, no elevator* ☰*MC, V.*

KOŠICE

100 km 62 mi) southeast of Levoča on Hwy. E50 (through Prešov), 402 km (250 mi) east of Bratislava on Hwys. D61 and E571.

In Košice you leave rural Slovakia behind. Though rich historically and with an interesting old town square, Košice is a sprawling, modern city, the second largest in Slovakia after Bratislava. Positioned along the main trade route between Hungary and Poland, the city was the second largest in the Hungarian Empire (after Buda) during the Middle Ages. With the Turkish occupation of the Hungarian homeland during the 16th and 17th centuries, the town became a safe haven for the Hungarian nobility.

You won't see many Westerners strolling Košice's enormous, well-preserved medieval square, Hlavná ulica; most of the tourists in this pedestrian zone are Hungarians on a day trip to shop and sightsee.

On the east side of the town square is the **Dom Košického vládneho programu** *(House of the Košice Government Program)*, where the Košice Program was proclaimed on April 5, 1945, announcing the reunion of the Czech lands and Slovakia into one national state after World War II. ⊠*Hlavná ul.* ⊙*Closed to the public.*

★ The town square is dominated on its southern flank by the huge tower of the Gothic **Dóm svätej Alžbety** *(Cathedral of St. Elizabeth)*. Begun in the 15th century and finally completed in 1508, the cathedral is the largest in Slovakia. Inside the church is one of Europe's largest Gothic altarpieces, a 35-foot-tall medieval wood carving attributed to the master Erhard of Ulm. Most of the great Hungarian leader Francis Rákoczi II's remains were placed in a crypt under the north transept of the cathedral (he left his heart in Paris). ⊠*Hlavná ul.* ☎*No phone.*

Water from the elaborate **Hudobná fontána** *(Music Fountain)*, which lies between the State Theater and the cathedral, springs in harmony with music (generally classical), accompanied by colored lights. It's worth a visit in the evening just to see all the pairs of lovers huddled around the fountain. ⊠*Hlavná ul.*

The **Miklušova väznica** *(Nicholas Prison)*, an old Gothic building used as a prison and torture chamber until 1909, now houses a museum with exhibits on Košice's history. You can even visit the underground

11

premises of the former torture chamber to see replicas of the torture instruments. ⊠*Pri Miklušovej väznici 10* ☎*055/622–2856* 🔁*40 Sk* 🕘*Tues.–Sat. 9–5, Sun. 9–1.*

The **Štátne divadlo** *(State Theater)*, a mishmash of neo-Renaissance and neo-baroque elements built at the end of the 19th century, dominates the center of the town square. The quality of theater, ballet, and opera productions in Košice is top-notch. ⊠*Hlavná. 58* ☎*055/622–1231* 🕘*Weekdays 9–5:30, Sat. 10–1, and 1 hr before performances.*

NEED A BREAK?

Have a cup of coffee and dessert in the Art Nouveau setting of the Café **Slávia** (⊠*Hlavná. 63* ☎*055/622-3190*).

WHERE TO STAY & EAT

★ $–$$ ✗**Sedliacky dvor.** Decorated as an old country cottage, Sedliacky dvor comes complete with wooden tables, a pitchfork, and a picket fence. Expect an enormous plate piled high with various meats and either rice, mushrooms, and cheese or dumplings and red and white cabbage. ⊠*Biela 3* ☎*055/622–0402* ⊟*No credit cards.*

★ $$$ ✗🖼**Hotel Bankov.** Fluffy terry robes and dark-wood reproduction antiques epitomize the luxury of the Bankov—a standard uncommon outside of Bratislava. The thick casement windows on the rear ground level open out onto a summer terrace. The no-smoking restaurant ($$–$$$$) serves upscale meals such as venison and chateaubriand for two, with an extensive wine list including Hungarian varieties. Formerly a 19th-century spa resort, Bankov is now a peaceful respite surrounded by hiking trails in the cool hills a 10-minute drive outside Košice. ⊠*Dolný Bankov 2, 04001* ☎*055/632–4522* 🖨*055/632–4540* ⊕*www.hotelbankov.sk* ⤴*16 rooms, 2 apartments* ♿*In-room: no a/ c. In-hotel: restaurant, bar, pool, laundry service, airport shuttle, no elevator* ⊟*AE, MC, V.*

$ 🖼**Hotel Alessandria.** A few minutes' stroll from Hlavná ulica brings you to this white-and-green hotel in a residential neighborhood. The building was originally constructed in the 19th century, which explains its expansive rooms with antechambers and high ceilings. A lack of coordinating furniture somehow doesn't detract from the overall pleasantness. Breakfast is served in the small restaurant, and in summer a garden terrace is perfect for drinking a beer. Gated parking is a bonus. ⊠*Jiskrova 3, 04001* ☎*055/622–5903* 🖨*055/622–5918* ⤴*10 rooms, 3 apartments* ♿*In-room: no a/c. In-hotel: restaurant, bar, parking (no fee), no elevator* ⊟*AE, DC, MC, V.*

NIGHTLIFE & THE ARTS

Jazz Club (⊠*Kováčska 39* ☎*055/622–4237*), a cozy basement bar, is a popular local hangout. The name is a bit misleading though, as the club has not only live and recorded jazz music but also disco, country, and rap.

The **Štátne divadlo** *(State Theater* ⊠*Hlavná. 58* ☎*055/622–1231*) hosts high-quality theater, ballet, and opera productions. Tickets are reasonably priced and can be bought at the theater box office.

BARDEJOV

80 km (50 mi) north of Košice, 101 km (63 mi) east of Poprad on Rtes. 68 and 77.

Bardejov is a great surprise, tucked away in this remote corner of Slovakia. Recognized as a UNESCO World Heritage Site, it is an exceptionally complete and well-preserved example of a fortified medieval town and possesses one of the nation's most enchanting squares. Indeed, Bardejov owes its splendors to its location astride the ancient trade routes to Poland and Russia. It's hard to put a finger on exactly what makes the square so captivating—it could be the lack of arcades in front of the houses, the high pointed roofs, or the colorful pastels and decorative scenes painted on the facades, which have a light, almost comic effect. Shopping along the pedestrian square is quite pleasant.

The exterior of the Gothic **Kostol svätého Egídia** *(St. Egidius Church)*, built in stages in the 15th century, is undeniably handsome, but take a walk inside for the real treasure. The nave is lined with 11 priceless, purely Gothic side altars, all carved between 1460 and 1510 and perfectly preserved. The most famous of the altars is to the left of the main altar (look for the number 1 on the side). This intricate work of Stefan Tarner depicts the birth of Christ and dates from the 1480s. ⊠*Radničné nám.* ☎*No phone.*

In the center of the town square stands the **radnica** *(town hall)*, a modest building with late-Gothic portals and Renaissance detailing. ⊠*Radničné nám. 17.*

★ The **Šariš** *(Icon Museum)* houses a collection of icons from as early as the 15th century and paintings taken from the area's numerous Greek Catholic and Orthodox churches. Many of the icons depict the story of St. George slaying the dragon (for the key to the princess's chastity belt!). The legend of St. George, which probably originated in pre-Christian mythology, was often used to attract the peasants of the area to the more abstemious stories of Christianity. Pick up the short commentary in English when you buy your ticket; for more detailed information, purchase the Slovak/English book *Ikony* from the reception area. ⊠*Radničné nám. 13* ☎*054/472–2009* ☻*40 Sk* ☻*May–Sept., daily 8–noon and 12:30–4; Oct.–Apr., Tues.–Sun. 8–noon and 12:30–4.*

Four kilometers (2½ mi) north of Bardejov is the historic spa town of **Bardejovské Kupelé.** The tourist information office in Bardejov can help you arrange treatments, which must be reserved ahead of time. The buildings with elaborate decorations and many porches are dormitories for patients. Don't miss the **Múzeum Ludovej Architektúry,** a *skansen* (open-air village museum). Several 19th- and early-20th-century wooden buildings, including a small wooden church from Zboj, have been relocated here to preserve the folk architecture from the Spiš and Rusyn areas. You can see the way villagers lived and in some cases still live today. No cars are allowed, so to visit the museum you must park for a fee at the town's lot and walk up the hill. ⊠*Bardejovské Kupelé* ☎*054/472–2072* 🎟*40 Sk* ⊗*May–Sept., Mon. 12:30–4:30, Tues.–Sun. 9:30–noon, 12:30–4:30; Oct.–Apr., Tues.–Sun. 9:30–noon, 12:30–3.*

This area's great delights are unquestionably the old **Wooden Churches** still in use in their original village settings. For example, in **Jedlinka**, which lies 13 km (8 mi) north of Bardejov, three onion-dome towers from the 18th century rise above the west front of the church. Inside, the north, east, and south walls are painted with biblical scenes; the west wall was reserved for icons, many of which now hang in the Icon Museum in Bardejov. ■**TIP**➔**The churches are usually locked, but if you happen across a villager, ask him or her (with appropriate key-turning gestures) to let you in. More often than not, someone will turn up with a key and you'll have your own guided tour.** The booklet *Wooden Churches Near Bardejov*, available at hotels and bookstores, provides detailed information, pictures, and a rudimentary map. Another good source, the Greek-Catholic Diocese of Presov's Web site (www.grkatpo.sk/drevenecerk) has information about the 27 main wooden churches as well as a map. ⊠*Off Rte. 545 and Rte. 77.*

WHERE TO STAY & EAT

★ $$ 🏨 **Hotel Bellevue.** On a hill outside the center of town, Bellevue affords splendid views of the countryside. The pool, which juts out to the edge of the hill on which it sits and is enclosed by glass, provides one of the best vantage points. In guest rooms, elegant, contemporary cherrywood furnishings are upholstered in botanical prints with deep greens and earth tones. Locals often clog up the bar, but you can grab a table at the adjoining restaurant, whose menu uses an impressive number of vegetables—uncommon in this area—in dishes such as turkey breast stuffed with asparagus. ⊠*Mihalov, 08501* ☎*054/472–8404* 🖷*054/472–8405* ⊕*www.bellevuehotel.sk* ↴*22 rooms, 3 apartments* ♨*In-hotel: restaurant, bar, pool, no elevator* ═MC, V.

MEDZILABORCE

77 km (48 mi) east of Bardejov on Rtes. 77 and 73.

The sleepy border town of Medzilaborce holds an unlikely museum.

★ Here, near the birthplace of Andy Warhol's parents, is the **Múzeum moderného umenia rodiny Warholovcov** *(Warhol Family Museum of Modern Art)*. In all, the museum holds 17 original Warhol silk screens, including two from the famous Campbell's Soup series, and portraits of Lenin and singer Billie Holiday. ⊠*Ul. Andyho Warhola 749* ☎*057/748–0072* 🎟*100 Sk* ⊗*Tues.–Fri. 10–4, weekends noon–4:30.*

EASTERN SLOVAKIA ESSENTIALS

AIR TRAVEL
Sky Europe flies between Bratislava and Košice daily.

BUS TRAVEL
Daily bus service connects Košice with Bratislava and Poprad, but trains tend to be quicker and more comfortable (InterCity trains have air-conditioning, but buses do not). The ride from Bratislava takes about 5 hours (450 Sk); the trip from Poprad lasts 2½ hours (360 Sk).

Once you arrive in eastern Slovakia you can access most of the towns within the region via the extensive, inexpensive local bus network. Schedules are available on ⊕*www.imhd.sk*, which provides comprehensive information on public transportation throughout Slovakia. Slovakia's national bus carrier, Slovenská autobusová doprava (SAD), also has good coverage of the region.

CAR TRAVEL
The drive from Bratislava to Košice takes about six hours; it's best to take the E571 via Nitra, Zvolen, and Rožňava. Poprad is two hours along E50 from Košice.

A car is essential for reaching the smaller towns and wooden churches in this region. The two-lane roads are generally in good condition; some stretches wind past beautiful panoramas, such as Route 547 between Košice and Levoča.

TRAIN TRAVEL
Trains regularly connect Košice to Bratislava (five to six hours, 550 Sk), but book in advance to ensure a seat on these sometimes crowded routes, especially during holidays. The trip from Poprad to Košice takes from 3½ to 4½ hours (460 Sk). You'll have to resort to a rental car or bus to reach smaller villages. Train stations, like Košice's Železničná stanica, are usually in the town center. Further information on train travel is available at ⊕*www.zsr.sk*.

VISITOR INFORMATION
City and town information centers can provide sightseeing information and assist with lodging.

Information **Kosice City Information Center** (⊠ *Hlavná 59, Košice* ☎ *055/625–8888* ⊕ *www.kosice.sk/icmk.asp*). **Levoca Tourist Information Center** (⊠ *Nám. majstra Pavla 58, Levoča* ☎ *053/451–3763* ⊕ *www.levoca.sk/en/english.htm*).

SLOVAKIA ESSENTIALS

11

TRANSPORTATION

BY AIR

Bratislava's Letisko M.R. Štefánika international airport is Slovakia's main airport and one of the fastest-expanding in Europe, with passenger numbers quadrupling between 2004 and 2007. Currently, the primary carriers offering service between major European cities and Bratislava are ČSA, Sky Europe, and Ryanair. Vienna's Schwechat Airport, about 60 km (37 mi) to the west, is served by most international carriers and is a good alternative gateway. Košice's airport sees mostly domestic routes (Sky Europe has regular service to Bratislava) but is adding flights to London, Prague, and Vienna. Poprad-Tatry International Airport also has regular flights from Prague and London-Stansted.

Airlines **ČSA** (☎ *02/5720–0710, 02/5720–0711, 02/5720–0712, 02/5720–0713, 02/5720–0714* ⊕ *www.czech-airlines.com*). **Ryanair** (⊕ *www.ryanair.com*). **Sky Europe** (☎ *02/4850–4850* ⊕ *www.skyeurope.com*).

Airports **Flughafen Wien Schwechat** (✉ *1300 Wien Flughafen, Postfach 1, Vienna Austria* ☎ *431/70070* ⊕ *www.viennaairport.com*). **Kosice International Airport** (✉ *Kosice* ☎ *02/556–8321* ⊕ *www.airportkosice.sk*). **Letisko M.R. Štefánika** (✉ *Ivanská cesta, Letisko, Bratislava* ☎ *02/4857–3353*). **Poprad-Tatry International Airport** (✉ *Na letisko 100, Poprad* ☎ *52/776–3875* ⊕ *www. airport-poprad.sk*).

BY BOAT

The Twin City Liner travels the Danube between Vienna and Bratislava from March to late October.

Information **Twin City Liner** (✉ *Rázusovo nábrižie, Ponton Huma 1, Bratislava* ☎ *09/0361 0716* ✉ *Schwedenplatz, Donauraum Schiffsanlegestelle dock, Vienna, Austria* ☎ *01/58885* ⊕ *www.twincityliner.com*).

BY BUS

Frequent buses connect Vienna, Prague, and Budapest with Bratislava. However, trains are far more comfortable and the stations are easier to navigate if you don't speak Slovak. You can also take a bus between Prague and Poprad, and from Košice into Hungary.

Slovenská autobusová doprava (SAD), the national bus carrier for Slovakia, maintains a comprehensive network in Slovakia. Buy your tickets (*cestovné lístky*) from the ticket window at the bus station (autobusová stanica) or, in smaller stations, directly from the driver on the bus. Long-distance buses can be full on holidays, so you might want to book a seat in advance; any travel agent can help you do this. A drawback to traveling by bus is figuring out the timetables. Beware of the small letters denoting exceptions to the times given.

Information **Bratislava bus station** (✉ *Mylinské nivy 31, Nové Mesto, Bratislava*). **Košice bus station** (✉ *Železničná 1, Košice* ☎ *055/622–5925* ⊕ *www.busy.sk*). **SAD** (☎ *09/7225–0305* ⊕ *www.sad-po.sk*).

BY CAR

Slovakia's motorway network is expanding rapidly, with a route from Bratislava to Košice via Žilina to be completed by 2010 and another to Vienna in the planning stages. Currently the road to Vienna passes through a few small towns, but the trip is still quick (about an hour). Highways link Bratislava with Prague (3½ hours) and Budapest (2½ hours). From Bratislava to Poprad, about half the journey is over multilane highway, and construction continues to complete the link. As you travel east in Slovakia, roads get narrower but are generally in good condition. Though you might find yourself behind a horse cart on a mountain road, a car is still the best way to get around in the far northeast, where traffic is usually light and train connections are scarce.

There are good freeways from Prague to Bratislava via Brno (D1 and D2); the 315-km (195-mi) journey takes about 3½ hours. From Vienna, take the A4 and then Route 50 (or Route 9 via Hainburg) to Bratislava; the 60-km (37-mi) journey takes less than an hour in either case. From Budapest, take the new M1 motorway toward Vienna; the 160-km (99-mi) trip takes roughly 1½ hours.

CAR RENTALS

Rental cars are readily available in Bratislava and Košice at the airports and in town. There are no special requirements for renting a car in Slovakia, but be sure to shop around, as prices can differ greatly. Hertz offers Western makes for as much as $500 per week. Smaller, local companies like Simocar may rent cars for as little as $290 per week for a manual transmission, economy car without air-conditioning and with unlimited mileage. You may buy general accident and theft insurance for around $35 per day. There is a 19% tax on car rentals. Prices are comparable whether or not you arrange for a rental before arriving in Slovakia.

Information **Avis** (✉ *Zadunajská cesta Bratislava* ☎ *02/5341–6111* ✉ *Letisko Košice-Barca, Košice* ☎ *055/643–3099* ⊕ *www.avis.sk*). **Hertz** (✉ *M.R.Stefanik Airport, Bratislava* ☎ *02/5720–1261* ✉ *Letisko Košice-Barca, Košice* ☎ *055/789–6041* ✉ *Poprad-Tatry International Airport* ☎ *911/650–180* ⊕ *www.hertz.sk*). **Simocar** (✉ *Maticna 59, Košice* ☎ *055/685–5283*).

RULES OF THE ROAD

Slovakia follows the usual Continental rules of the road. A right turn on red is permitted only when indicated by a green arrow. On main roads, signposts with yellow diamonds indicate which drivers have the right of way. Signposts with blue circles outlined in red with a single horizontal line in the center indicate a one-way street that you cannot enter. The speed limit is 130 kph (80 mph) on four-lane highways, 90 kph (55 mph) on open roads, 50 kph (37 mph) in built-up areas, and 30 kph (19 mph) in Bratislava's center. The fine for speeding is roughly 1,000 Sk, payable on the spot. To use the highways you need a special label (*diaľničná známka*) displayed on your car window. If you rent a car in Slovakia, the label is provided. Labels cost about 150 Sk for seven days, 300 Sk for a month and are available at border stops and gas stations. Seat belts are compulsory, and drinking before driving is strictly prohibited. Random Breathalyzer checks are not uncommon.

BY TRAIN
Bratislava is the country's international train hub. You can take a direct train from Berlin via Dresden and Prague (en route to Budapest) and from Paris via Frankfurt to Vienna (and connect to another train or bus). One train a day goes to Moscow from Bratislava. Several trains a day link Bratislava with Prague and with Budapest. Vienna has good international connections and numerous trains that make the 70-minute run daily from Vienna's Südbahnhof (South Station) to Bratislava.

Slovakia's state-run rail system, Železnice Slovenskej republiky, is quite extensive. Trains vary in speed, but it's not really worth taking anything other than an "express" train, marked in red on the timetable. Tickets are cheap compared with those in countries farther west. ■ **TIP➡ First class is considerably more spacious and comfortable and well worth the cost (50% more than a standard ticket).** If you don't specify "express" when you buy your ticket, you may have to pay a supplement on the train. If you haven't bought a ticket in advance at the station, it's easy to buy one from the porter on the train for a small extra charge. On timetables, departures appear on a yellow background, arrivals on white. It's possible to book *couchettes* (sleepers) on most overnight trains, but don't expect much in the way of comfort with four to six bunks per room. ■ **TIP➡ The word for "train station" in Slovak is** *železničná stanica.*

Information Železnice Slovenskej republiky (*Railways of the Slovak Republic* ⊕ *www.zsr.sk/english*).

Train Stations Banská Bystrica train station (⊠ *Banská Bystrica*). **Hlavná stanica** (Bratislava's main train station) (⊠ *Prestaničné nám., Staré mesto Bratislava* ☏ *02/5058–7565*). **Košice train station** (⊠ *Železničná 1, Košice* ☏ *055/622–3700*). **Poprad train station** (⊠ *Wolkerova 496, Poprad* ☏ *052/7166–8484*).

CONTACTS & RESOURCES

BANKS & EXCHANGE SERVICES
Bratislava is easily the most expensive area in Slovakia. As a rule, small rural towns are extremely reasonable. Although overcharging foreigners is not a widespread practice, state-subsidized theaters sometimes charge visitors higher prices.

CURRENCY
The unit of currency in Slovakia is the crown, or koruna, written as Sk, and divided into 100 halierov. There are bills of 20, 50, 100, 200, 500, 1,000, and 5,000 Sk, and coins of 10, 20, and 50 halierov and 1, 2, 5, and 10 Sk. The euro will be introduced on January 1, 2009, but it is already accepted by some businesses. At press time, the rate of exchange was 22.51 Sk to the U.S. dollar.

CREDIT CARDS
MasterCard and Visa are more widely accepted than American Express, Discover, or Diners Club. ATMs (called "Bankomats") are widely available and can be found even in small towns, and almost every hotel offers exchange services. Though rates might be a bit better at a bank, hotels have more flexible hours.

EMBASSIES
Information U.S. Embassy (⊠ *Hviezdoslavovo nám. 4, Staré mesto, Bratislava* ☏ *02/5443–3338* ⊕ *www.usembassy.sk*).

EMERGENCIES
Information Ambulance and Police (☏ *112*).

INTERNET, MAIL & SHIPPING
Internet cafés are now abundant in Bratislava and most larger towns. Ask local tourist offices for information and directions. Internet cafés are often located in malls, at larger bus and train stations, and on streets close to town centers. Prices at most Internet cafés run Sk 60–Sk 120 for one hour. Some libraries also provide access to the Web (usually for less than elsewhere).

Most post offices are open weekdays 8–6, Saturdays 8–1; main post offices stay open until 8 PM. Postcards to the United States and Canada cost 12 Sk; letters cost 21 Sk. Use main post offices to ship larger parcels. To rest assured your package gets where it's going, use EMS (Express Mail Service), available at post offices. Prices start from around 650 Sk for parcels weighing half a kilo.

In Bratislava, free Internet access is available at three public terminals in the city center: in the New Town Hall, at the gate to the Archbishop's Palace on Primaciálne námestie, and in the Bratislava Info Centre on Klobucnicka street. There are also five free Wi-Fi zones (you need your own laptop) in the city center: on Primaciálne námestie (Primate's square), Hlavné námestie, Františkánske námestie, Hviezdoslavovo námestie, and in the Front Office of the New Town Hall.

Internet Cafés Internet Cafe Muzeum Bratislava's leading Internet café is behind the Slovak National Museum, on the banks of the Danube near the passenger port. (⊠ *Vajanského nábr. 2* ☏ *02/5934–9196* ⊙ *Weekdays 10–10, weekends 1–10*).

Shipping Companies EMS ☏ *11185* ⊕ *www.ems.com.cn*.

PASSPORTS & VISAS
American, British, and Canadian citizens do not need a visa to enter Slovakia. A valid passport is sufficient for stays of up to 30 days for a U.S. citizen, up to six months for a U.K. citizen, and up to 90 days for a Canadian citizen.

TELEPHONES
The country code for Slovakia is 421. When dialing from outside the country, drop the initial "0" from the area code.

To reach an English-speaking operator for free who can connect your direct, collect, or credit-card call, dial T-Com.

Public pay phones are easily found in town centers. Most public phones take prepaid phone cards, which are available at post offices and some newsstands. A local call starts at 2 Sk. When dialing directory assistance, be aware that not all operators speak English.

Information International Directory Assistance (☏12149). **Local Directory Assistance** (☏1181).

T-Com (☏0800/123–456 or 0800/142–142).

TIPPING

Gratuities are not automatically added to restaurant bills. To reward good service a tip of 10% is considered appropriate in inexpensive restaurants or on group tabs. A 20 Sk tip for porters and room service is usually sufficient. In taxis, round up the bill to the nearest multiple of 10. Give tour guides and helpful concierges 30 Sk.

TOUR OPTIONS

Tatratour is a large, dependable agency that can help arrange sightseeing tours throughout Slovakia. Limba runs trips with a focus on rural Slovakia; the guides are excellent. Slovakia Hiking Tours, based in Central Slovakia, specializes in hiking holidays. IVCO travel, based in western Slovakia, runs several seven-day bike tours throughout the country. Tatra Information Board (TIK) specializes in hiking, skiing, and biking tours in the High Tatras. T-Ski Travel offers tours throughout the country with a sports and outdoors bent.

In Bratislava, Bratislavská informačná služba (BKIS) arranges the best sightseeing tours of the city. One-hour English-language tours are given daily at 2 PM; call at least 90 minutes ahead to reserve a spot and meet at the BKIS office in the Old Town. Tours are free with the BCCard, 560 Sk without.

For a unique alternative, you can take in the Old Town's highlights from the passenger seat of a red vintage automobile-cum-train run on biodiesel. Prešporáčik tours start at Hlavné Námestie (Main Square) and take about 30 minutes, including commentary in English. Tours run from April until October and cost 200 Sk (230 Sk in July and August). Make bookings through BKIS.

If you prefer a more active approach, consider a three-hour guided bicycle tour along the Danube, also arranged through the BKIS office.

Information IVCO travel (✉Nalepkova 2, Piestany92101 ☏033/774–3355 ⊕www.ivcotravel.com). **Limba** (✉Medena 13, Starý mesto, Bratislava ☏02/5441–8601 ⊕www.limba.sk). **Prešporáčik** (✉Hlavné Námestie, Starý mesto, Bratislava ⊕www.presporacik.sk). **Slovakia Hiking Tours** (✉Rybarska 1690/41, Sliac ☏903/542132 ⊕www.slovakiahiking.net). **Tatra Information Board (TIK)** (✉Dom Služieb 24, Starý Smokovec ☏052/442–3440 ⊕www.tatry.sk). **T-Ski Travel** (✉Starý Smokovec 46 ☏052/442–3200 ⊕www.slovakiatravel.sk). **Tatratour** (✉Bajkalská 25, Starý mesto, Bratislava ☏02/5341–1219 or 02/5341–4828 ☏02/5341–2781).

VISITOR INFORMATION

Throughout the country, most cities have good tourist information centers in addition to independent travel agents. Both can help reserve hotels and private rooms as well as arrange tours and provide information. ⇨ *See Visitor Information in individual regional Essentials sections, above, for specific listings within each town.*

The "Come to Slovakia" Web site, operated by the Tourist Office of Slovakia in New York, is one of the best online resources and contains lots of background and practical information about travel in Slovakia geared toward travelers from North America; inquiries may be sent by e-mail or fax. Another good Internet resource is ⊕ *www.slovakiatourism.sk*, run by the Slovak Tourist Board in Slovakia. The Lodging Slovakia and Otels Web sites list many of the country's hotels and provide booking services. The Panorama Web site provides good background information—country news in English, descriptions of tourist attractions, and links related to Slovakia.

Information **Lodging Slovakia** (⊕ *www.lodging.sk*). **Otels** (⊕ *www.slovakiahotels.com*). **Panorama** (⊕ *www.panorama.sk/en*). **Slovak Tourist Board** (⊕ *www. slovakiatourism.sk*). **Tourist and Commercial Office of Slovakia** ✉ *10 E. 40th St., New York, NY 10016* 🖷 *212/679-7045* ✉ *slovakoffice@nyc.rr.com* ⊕ *www. cometoslovakia.com.*

Slovenia

WORD OF MOUTH

"Don't let Slovenia's small size deter you because there are plenty of fun things to do and see. Slovenia has a small coastline on the Adriatic, but we choose to spend our 16 days touring the interior, from bases in the east, center, and west regions of Slovenia. It may sound like a lot of driving, but to cross the whole country on their modern autobahn takes only a few hours."

—LuvToRoam

"We enjoyed our walking tour of the Old Town and were fortunate to go into City Hall and have a private audience with the Mayor of Ljubljana. There was a large Saturday market . . . and the Church of St. Nicholas was worth a visit."

—fun4all4

By Mark Baker
Updated by
Evan Rail

SLOVENIA MAY BE THE BEST-KEPT secret in Europe. Just half the size of Switzerland, the country is often treated as fly-over—or drive-through—territory by travelers heading to better-known places in Croatia or Italy. That's good news for anyone choosing Slovenia as a destination in its own right. It means fewer crowds—even in the peak summer touring months—fewer hassles, and in many ways a more authentic travel experience.

And Slovenia's sights are no less outstanding than those of its neighbors. Admittedly, Slovenia's small Adriatic coastline—not even 30 mi end to end—can't match Croatia for sheer natural beauty. But the coastal towns, especially the intact Venetian jewel of Piran, are lovely in their own right. The Julian Alps northwest of the capital are every bit as spectacular as their sister Alpine ranges in Austria and Switzerland. The electric-blue-turquoise waters of the Soča River, rushing out of the mountains, must be seen—or better, rafted—to be believed. And that's just a start. The extensive cave systems, unspoiled countryside, and even the funky charm of Ljubljana await those with the imagination to choose a destination that is more off the beaten path.

Slovenia's relative obscurity owes much to its history. From Roman times to nearly the present day, Slovenian territory was incorporated into far-larger empires, relegating Slovenia through the ages to the role of rustic, if charming, hinterland.

The territory of Slovenia has been inhabited for tens of thousands of years, but the country's modern history begins with the arrival of the Romans in the 1st century BC. They built villas along the coast and founded the inland urban centers of Emona (Ljubljana) and Poetovio (Ptuj), which today still retain traces of their Roman past. The 6th century AD saw the first influx of Slav migrants, the ancestors of present-day Slovenes, who set up an early Slav state. During the 8th century, the region came under the control of the Franks, and in the 9th century it was passed to the dukes of Bavaria.

In 1335 the Habsburgs took control of inland Slovenia, dividing it into the Austrian crown lands of Carinthia, Carniola, and Styria. Meanwhile, the coastal towns had requested Venetian protection, and they remained under *la serenissima* until 1797, after which they, too, were taken by Austria. During the 15th and 16th centuries, the Turks, eager to extend the Ottoman Empire across the Balkans and north to Vienna, made repeated attacks on the region. However, Slovenia remained under the Habsburgs until 1918, with the exception of a brief period from 1809 to 1813, when it became part of Napoléon's Illyrian Provinces.

In the aftermath of World War I, Italy seized control of the coastal towns, whereas inland Slovenia became part of the Kingdom of Serbs, Croats, and Slovenes; in 1929, the name of the kingdom was changed to Yugoslavia (Land of the Southern Slavs).

Hitler declared war on Yugoslavia in 1941, and shortly afterward Axis forces occupied the country. Slovenia was divided between Germany, Italy, and Hungary. Josip Broz, better known as Tito, set up the anti-Fascist Partisan movement, and many Slovenes took part in resistance activities. When the war ended in 1945, Slovenia became one of the six constituent republics of Yugoslavia, with Tito as president. Slovenes today are proud of their Partisan past, and traveling through the country you see monuments and wall plaques bearing the red star, a symbol of the Partisans and of Communist ideology; many squares and roads are still named after Tito.

12

Half Slovene and half Croat, Tito was undeniably an astute leader. He governed Yugoslavia under Communist ideology, but the system was far more liberal than that of the Soviet-bloc countries: Yugoslavs enjoyed freedom of movement, and foreigners could enter the country without visas. During the cold war, Tito never took sides but dealt cleverly with both East and West, thus procuring massive loans from both.

However, when Tito died in 1980, the system he left behind began to crumble. The false nature of the economy, based on borrowing, became apparent. During the 1980s, an economic crisis set in and inflation soared. Slovenia, accounting for only 8% of Yugoslavia's population, was producing almost a third of the nation's exports. This hard-earned foreign currency ended up in Belgrade and was used in part to subsidize the poorer republics. It was time for change.

In early 1990, buoyed by the recent revolutions across Eastern Europe, Slovenia introduced a multiparty system and elected a non-Communist government. Demands for increased autonomy from Yugoslavia were stepped up, with the threat of secession. A referendum was held, and nearly 90% of the electorate voted for independence. Unlike the other Yugoslav republics, Slovenia was made up almost exclusively of a single ethnic group: Slovenes. Thus, the potential status of ethnic minorities, should the republic secede, was never an issue. Slovenia proclaimed independence on June 25, 1991, and the so-called 10-Day War followed. Yugoslav federal troops moved in, but there was little violence to compare with the heavy fighting in nearby Croatia and Bosnia. Belgrade had already agreed to let Slovenia go.

In 1992, Slovenia gained international recognition as an independent state and began the painstaking process of legal, political, and economic reform needed to join the European Union. That effort bore fruit in May 2004, when Slovenia, along with seven other central and eastern European countries, was admitted into the EU; it adopted the euro as its official currency in 2007. Today, Slovenia's future looks bright. It's simply a matter of time before the country's charms are fully discovered.

EXPLORING SLOVENIA

The principal areas of interest to tourists include the lively and very likable capital Ljubljana, the Julian Alps and Triglav National Park to the northwest, the alpine lakes of Bled and Bohinj, and the Adriatic coast and the Karst region to the southwest. The region to the east, centering on Maribor, Ptuj, and the Haloze Hills, has several vineyards and excellent wine cellars.

ABOUT THE RESTAURANTS

Slovenia's prime contribution to dining has got to be the *gostilna*, essentially an inn or tavern but cleaner, warmer, and more inviting than the English translation suggests. These are frequently family-run, especially in the smaller towns and villages, with Mom in the kitchen and Pop out front pouring beers and taking orders. The staff is usually happy to suggest local or regional specialties. Some of the better ones are situated alongside vineyards or farms.

> ### SLOVENIA TOP 5
>
> ■ Tripping out on the amazing architecture of Ljubljana, courtesy of Jože Plečnik.
>
> ■ Hiking through the forests and trenches at the WWI battleground-cum–nature reserve near Kobarid.
>
> ■ Relaxing on Piran's marble-laden Trg Tartini, just steps from the Adriatic.
>
> ■ Traveling through the rolling hills of the wine country around the old Roman town of Ptuj.
>
> ■ Taking a refreshing dip in Lake Bled, just below the watchful eye of Bled Castle.

Meal times follow the Continental norm for lunch and dinner. Even if a restaurant posts earlier opening times, the kitchen won't normally start operating until noon. Dinners typically start around 7 PM. It can be tough finding a breakfast place, so it's best to take the standard hotel or pension offering of sliced meats and cheeses when available.

Restaurants usually close one day a week. In larger towns like Ljubljana that's likely to be Sunday. In resort areas that cater to a weekend crowd, Monday is the usual day off. If in doubt, phone ahead.

ABOUT THE HOTELS

Don't expect Slovenia to be a cheap option; lodging prices are similar to what you see in Western Europe, and with the euro soaring in value, prices will be particularly painful for Americans. During peak season (July and August), many hotels—particularly those on the coast—are fully booked. Hotels are generally clean, smartly furnished, and well run. Establishments built under Communism are often equipped with extras such as saunas and sports facilities but tend to be gargantuan structures lacking in soul. Hotels dating from the turn of the 20th century are more romantic, as are the castle hotels. Over the last decade many hotels have been refurbished and upgraded.

Private lodgings are a cheaper alternative to hotels, and standards are generally excellent. Prices vary depending on region and season. Look for signs proclaiming *sobe* (room to let) or *apartma* (apartments),

CLOSE UP

Slovenian Cuisine

At first glance, Slovenian cuisine looks a little like fusion food since it melds elements of Italian, Hungarian, Austrian, and Balkan cooking—often to good effect. Italy's contribution stands out most clearly in the full range of pastas and risottos you'll see on many menus. Pizza is ubiquitous and generally of high quality. From Austria come the many pork and other meat dishes and schnitzels, though they are often served with local—and sometimes unusual—sides like spinach *njoki* (gnocchi) or even *ajda* (buckwheat) dumplings. The Balkan influence is seen in the profusion of grilled meats and in one of the most common street foods: *burek,* an oily phyllo pastry stuffed with salty cheese or meat.

Typical local dishes include *krvavice* (black pudding) served with *žganci* (polenta) or Kraški pršut (air-dried Karst ham). Another favorite is *jota,* a filling soup of sauerkraut, beans, and smoked pork. Look too for regional specialties, such as the easier-to-eat-than-pronounce *žlikrofi*—tiny tortellini stuffed with minced potato, onion, and bacon that are the pride of cooks throughout the Idrija region but are nearly impossible to find anywhere else.

With the Adriatic close at hand, you can find excellent seafood. Look for mouthwatering *škampi rižot* (scampi risotto), followed by fresh fish prepared *na žaru* (grilled). Fresh trout with *tržaška* garlic and parsley) sauce is a staple on any menu near the Soča River. The first-rate fish—usually priced on menus per kilogram (2.2 pounds)—are expensive, so don't be surprised when the bill comes.

For an extra boost stop at a *kavarna* (coffee shop) for a scrumptious, calorie-laden *prekmurska gibanica,* a layered cake combining curd cheese, walnuts, and poppy seeds. Another national favorite is *potica,* a rolled cake filled with either walnuts, chocolate, poppy seeds, or raisins.

alongside roads or in towns. Local tourist information centers, or in resorts like Bled or Piran private travel agencies, will often maintain lists of local rooms for rent.

Many hotels will offer better rates for stays of more than three days. Hotel rates frequently include breakfast—usually a mix of breads, cheeses, and cold cuts served buffet-style. Pensions and private rooms may include lunch or dinner—be sure to ask what's included in the price and whether you can opt out if you choose.

Between April and October camping is a reasonable alternative. Most campgrounds are small but well equipped. On the coast, campsites are found at Izola and Ankaran. In Triglav National Park and the Soča Valley there are sites at Bled, Bohinj, Bovec, Kobarid, Soča, and Trenta. Camping outside of organized campsites is not permitted.

To really experience day-to-day life in the countryside you should stay on a working farm. Agrotourism is rapidly growing in popularity, and at most farms you can experience an idyllic rural setting, delicious home cooking, plus a warm family welcome. A brochure, *Tourist*

Farms in Slovenia, is available from the tourist board. More information is available on the board's Web site.

WHAT IT COSTS IN EUROS (€)			
$$$$	**$$$**	**$$**	**$**
RESTAURANTS over €20	€12–€20	€8–€12	under €8
HOTELS over €225	€175–€225	€125–€175	under €125

Restaurant prices are for a main course at dinner. Hotel prices are for two people in a double room in high season, excluding taxes and service charges.

TIMING

The countryside is at its most beautiful in spring and fall, though the best period to visit depends on what you plan to do during your stay. Ljubljana is vibrant the whole year through. Many visitors want to head straight for the coast. Those in search of sea, sun, and all-night parties will find what they're looking for in peak season (July and August), including cultural events, open-air dancing, busy restaurants, and crowded beaches. If you want to avoid the crowds, hit the Adriatic in June or September, when it should be warm enough to swim and easier to find a place to put your beach towel.

In the mountains there are two distinct seasons: winter is dedicated to skiing, summer to hiking and biking. Some hotels close in November and March to mark a break between the two periods. Conditions for more strenuous walking and biking are optimal in April, May, September, and October.

Lovers of fine food and wine should visit Slovenia during fall. The grape harvest concludes with the blessing of the season's young wine on St. Martin's Day, preceded by three weeks of festivities. In rural areas autumn is the time to make provisions for the hard winter ahead: wild mushrooms are gathered, firewood is chopped, and *koline* (sausages and other pork products) areprepared by hand.

Numbers in the margins correspond to numbers on the Slovenia map.

LJUBLJANA

Slovenia's small but exceedingly charming capital is enjoying a tourism renaissance. The advent of low-cost flights from the United Kingdom and increased air service from other European countries have led to a dramatic influx of visitors in recent years and elevated the city's profile abroad. Tourism officials now talk of Ljubljana proudly in the same breath as Prague or Budapest as one of the top urban destinations in Central Europe. That may be wishful thinking, but there's no denying a sense of excitement as new hotels and restaurants open their doors, and each month seems to bring another admiring article in a prestigious newspaper or magazine abroad. Unfortunately, there is still no nonstop service from the United States.

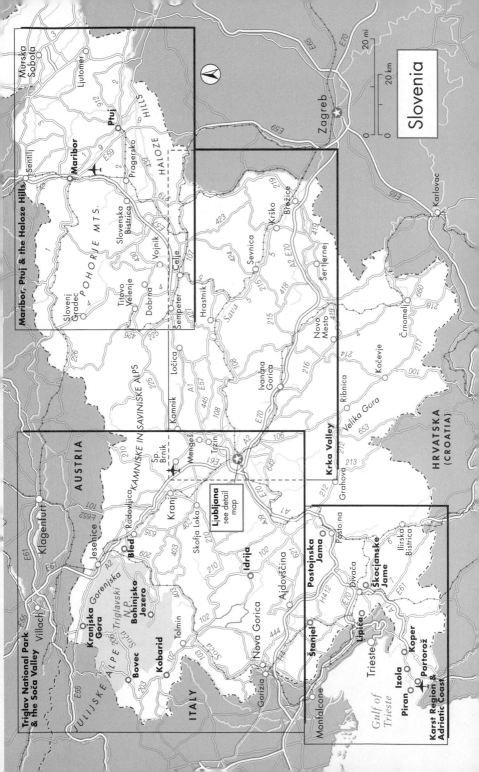

IF YOU LIKE

HIKING

Slovenes love their mountains, and when you reach the northwest of the country you will understand why. The most popular alpine hiking route runs from Maribor, near the Austrian border, to Ankaran on the Adriatic coast. It crosses Triglav National Park and can be walked in 30 days. For less devoted walkers, a day or two of backpacking from one of the alpine resorts is an invigorating way to explore the landscape. Bovec, Bohinj, and Krajnska Gora are all excellent hiking bases. Mountain paths are usually well marked, and mountain lodges have dormitory-style accommodations. Detailed maps are available at local tourist-information centers.

HORSEBACK RIDING

The country's most famous equestrian center is the Lipica Stud Farm, home of the splendid Lipizzaner white stallions. Riding lessons are available, though the farm is geared more toward experienced riders than beginners. It also offers summer riding sessions lasting several days to several weeks. For beginners, a better option might be the Mrcina Ranč at Studor, near Lake Bohinj. Visitors to the Krka Valley can ride at the Struga Equestrian Center at a 12th-century medieval manor near Otočec Castle. The brochure *Riding in Slovenia, Home of the Lipizzaner*, is available from the Slovenian Tourist Board.

KAYAKING, CANOEING & RAFTING

The Soča River has ideal conditions for white-water rafting, kayaking, hydrospeeding (a small board for bodysurfing waves), and canyoning. The season lasts from April to October. The best rapids lie between Bovec and Kobarid. Numerous outfitters in Bovec rent boats and equipment and also offer instruction and guided rafting and kayaking trips. Less exhilarating—though still very fun—river rafting is available near Bled and Bohinj.

WINE & SPIRITS

Slovenes enjoy drinking and produce some excellent wines, but very little of the total output is exported. You can tour the three main wine regions following a series of established "wine roads" (*vinska cesta*). These routes pass through rolling hills, woodlands, and villages and lead directly to vineyards and wine stores. The best white wines, *sivi pinot* (pinot grigio) and *beli pinot* (pinot blanc), are produced in the Podravje region in northeast Slovenia. A notable red is Teran, a varietal made from the refosk grape and produced in the Karst region to the southwest. There has been a recent drive to introduce more sparkling wines: look for the excellent Penina, made using the classic Champagne method from chardonnay and pinot blanc grapes. The favorite national spirit is the potent *rakija*. The base is alcohol distilled from fruit; a variety of wild herbs are added later to give it a more distinct flavor.

The tiny city center is immediately captivating. Part of the charm is doubtless the emerald green Llubljanica River that winds its way slowly through the Old Town, providing a focal point and the perfect back-drop to the cafés and restaurants that line the banks. Partly, too, it's the aesthetic tension between the stately baroque houses along the river and the white neoclassical, modern, and Secessionist set pieces that dot the streets and bridges everywhere. Meticulously designed pillars, orbs, and obelisks lend the city an element of whimsy, a feeling of good cheer that's immediately infectious. And part of the credit goes to the Ljubljaners themselves, who on a warm summer evening can be counted on to come out and party in force. It's a place that's meant to be enjoyed.

In truth, Ljubljana has always viewed itself as something special. Even when it was part of the former Yugoslavia, the city was considered a center of alternative music and arts. This was especially true during the 1980s, when it became the center of the Yugoslav punk movement. The band Laibach, noted for mocking nationalist sentiments, and the absurdist conceptual-art group Neue Slowenische Kunst (NSK) both have their roots here.

The romantic heart of the Old Town dates back centuries. The earliest settlement was founded by the Romans and called Emona. Much of it was destroyed by the Huns under Attila, though a section of the walls and a complex of foundations—complete with mosaics—can still be seen today. In the 12th century, a new settlement, Laibach, was built on the right bank of the river, below Castle Hill, by the dukes of Carniola. In 1335, the Habsburgs gained control of the region, and it was they who constructed the existing castle fortification system.

The 17th century saw a period of baroque building, strongly influenced by currents in Austria and Italy. Walk along the cobblestones of the *Mestni trg* (Town Square) and the *Stari trg* (Old Square) to see Ljubljana at its best, from the colored baroque town houses with their steeply pitched tile roofs to Francesco Robba's delightful *Fountain of the Three Carniolan Rivers*.

For a brief period, from 1809 to 1813, Ljubljana was the capital of Napoléon's Illyrian Provinces. In 1849, once again under the Habsburgs, Ljubljana was linked to Vienna and Trieste by rail. The city developed into a major center of commerce, industry, and culture, and the opera house, national theater, national museum, and the first hotels came into existence.

In 1895 much of the city was devastated by an earthquake. The reconstruction work that followed was carried out in florid Viennese Secessionist style. Many of the palatial four-story buildings that line Miklošičeva, such as the Grand Hotel Union, date from this period.

After World War I, with the birth of the Kingdom of Serbs, Croats, and Slovenes, Ljubljana became the administrative center of Slovenia. Various national cultural institutes were founded, and the University of Ljubljana opened in 1919. If you have been to Prague, you will already

GREAT ITINERARIES

Slovenia's small size can be an advantage. From the centrally located capital, Ljubljana, you can drive to any point in the country in three or four hours.

IF YOU HAVE 3 DAYS
If you have limited time, take one day to discover the Old Town of **Ljubljana**. For the next two days, choose between the mountains or the coast. If you're looking for natural beauty and/or adventure, head for the mountains and lakes of Triglav National Park. Base yourself in **Bled** or **Bohinj**. For the third day, get an early start and head for **Bovec**, via **Kranjska Gora**, for hiking or white-water rafting on the Soča River. If you seek sun and sea instead, go southwest toward the Karst and coast. Stop off at the Škocjan Caves en route, and spend your nights in the beautiful Venetian port of **Piran**.

IF YOU HAVE 5 DAYS
For a longer stay, combine the two optional itineraries listed above. Spend the first day and night exploring Ljubljana's Old Town before making your way northwest to the mountains. After nights in Bled and/or Bohinj and exploring the Soča River valley, continue southwest to the coast. Use Piran as your base for visiting the coastal towns of **Izola** and **Portorož**.

IF YOU HAVE 7 DAYS
If you have a full week, spend a day and night in Ljubljana and then make your way east for a night to the wine-making area around **Maribor** and **Ptuj**. Return to the capital, and then head north for the beauty of the Alps, as outlined in the five-day itinerary. Wrap up the week with a couple of days relaxing on the coast. In hot weather, you can go for a swim at the beaches around Portorož.

have seen some of the work of Jože Plečnik (1872–1957). Born in Ljubljana, Plečnik studied architecture in Vienna under Otto Wagner, then went on to lecture at the Prague School of Applied Arts and served as the chief architect for the renovation of Prague Castle. It was Plečnik who added many of the decorator touches to the city's parks, squares, and bridges. Some of his finest projects include the Triple Bridge, the open-air market on Vodnik Square, and the plans for the Križanke Summer Theater.

The Tito years saw increased industrialization. The population of Ljubljana tripled, and vast factory complexes, high-rise apartments, and modern office buildings extended into the suburbs.

EXPLORING LJUBLJANA

The city center is concentrated within a small area, so you can cover all the sights on foot.

WHAT TO SEE

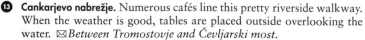 **Cankarjevo nabrežje.** Numerous cafés line this pretty riverside walkway. When the weather is good, tables are placed outside overlooking the water. ⊠ *Between Tromostovje and Čevljarski most.*

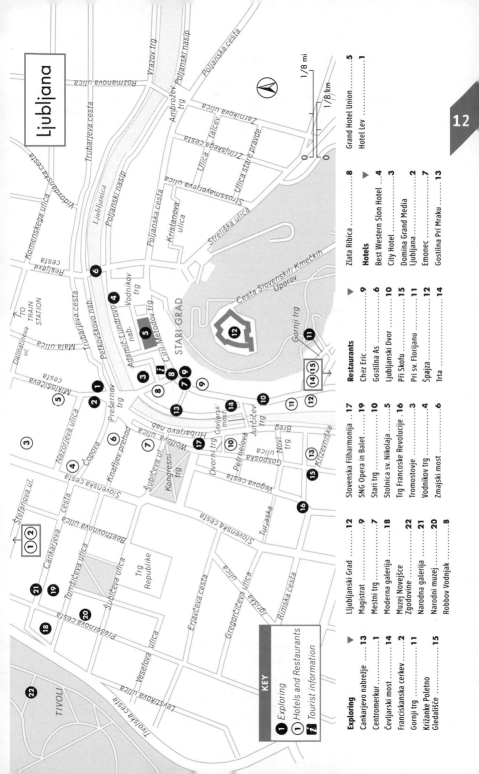

Ljubljana

12

0 1/8 mi
0 1/8 km

① Centromerkur. This magnificent Art Nouveau–style building, dating from 1903, is the oldest department store in town. Most of the structures in Ljubljana built at this time borrowed from the Viennese Secession, making this building—which draws its inspiration more from Paris—a relative rarity. The entrance, off Prešernov trg, bears a flaring iron butterfly wing and is topped by a statue of Mercury. Inside, graceful wrought-iron stairways lead to upper floors. ⊠ *Trubarjeva 1* ☎ *01/426–3170.*

⑭ Čevljarski most *(Cobblers' Bridge).* Linking the old and new sides of town, this romantic pedestrian bridge was built in 1931 according to plans by the architect Jože Plečnik. The name is derived from a wooden structure that once stood here and was lined with shoemakers' huts.

② Franciskanska cerkev *(Franciscan Church).* This massive, pink high-baroque church was built between 1646 and 1660. The main altar, by Francesco Robba (1698–1757), dates from 1736. The three sets of stairs in front are a popular meeting place for students. ⊠ *Prešernov trg 4* ⊙ *Daily 8–6.*

⑪ Gornji trg *(Upper Square).* This cobbled street, just around the corner from Stari trg, is where you'll find some of the capital's finest restaurants and a small but growing collection of design and art studios.

⑮ Križanke Poletno Gledališče *(Križanke Summer Theater).* In the courtyard of an 18th-century monastery, this open-air theater was constructed according to plans drawn up by Jože Plečnik. It was completed in 1976, nearly two decades after the architect's death. The theater seats 1,400, and there's a movable roof in case of rain. ⊠ *Trg Francoske Revolucije.*

Plečnik's House. Architecture enthusiasts will enjoy a visit to architect Jože Plečnik's house, still as he left it, to see his studio, home, and garden. The only drawback is the limited opening times: just four hours a day, two days a week. From the Križanke Summer Theater, cross Zoisova cesta, and then follow Emonska to Karunova. ⊠ *Karunova 4, Trnovo* ☎ *01/280–1600* ☜ *€5* ⊙ *Tues. and Thurs. 10–2.*

⑫ Ljubljanski grad *(Ljubljana Castle).* Ljubljana's hilltop castle affords magnificent views over the river and the Old Town's terra-cotta rooftops, spires, and green cupolas. On a clear day, the distant Julian Alps are a dramatic backdrop. The castle walls date from the early 16th century, although the tower was added in the mid-19th century. The surrounding park was landscaped by Plečnik in the 1930s. ⊠ *Studentovska ul, uphill from Vodnikov trg* ☎ *01/432–7216* ☜ *€3* ⊙ *Apr.– Oct., daily 9 AM–11 PM; Nov.–Mar., daily 10–7.*

The castle ramparts shelter a pleasant café and summer garden. After the steep climb from the Old Town, stop in for a refreshing drink at the Castle Terrace (⊠ *Lljubljanski grad* ☎ *01/439–4140*).

⑨ Magistrat *(Town Hall).* Guarded by an austere 18th-century facade, this building hides delightful secrets within. In the internal courtyard, for example, the walls are animated with murals depicting historic battles

OFF THE
BEATEN
PATH

NEED A
BREAK?

for the city, and a statue of Hercules keeps company with a fountain bearing a figure of Narcissus. ⊠ *Mestni trg 1* ⬚ *Free* ⊘ *Weekdays 9–3, weekends as part of guided tour of city.*

7 **Mestni trg** *(Town Square).* This cobbled square extends into the oldest part of the city. Baroque town houses, now divided into functional apartments, present marvelously ornate facades: carved oak doors with great brass handles are framed within columns, and upper floors are decorated with balustrades, statuary, and intricate ironwork. Narrow passageways connect with inner courtyards in one direction and run to the riverfront in the other. The street-level floors contain boutiques, antiques shops, and art galleries.

12

NEED A BREAK? If you plan to dine in the Old Town, stop first at **Movia** (⊠ *Mestni trg 2* ☎ *01/425–5448*) for an aperitif. This elegant little wine bar stocks a selection of first-rate Slovenian wines, for consumption both on and off the premises. It is closed Sunday.

18 **Moderna galerija** *(Modern Gallery).* The strikingly modern one-story structure contains a selection of paintings, sculpture, and prints by Slovenian 20th-century artists. In odd-number years it also hosts the International Biennial of Graphic Art, an exhibition of prints and installations by artists from around the world. Works by Robert Rauschenberg, Susan Rothenburg, and Max Bill have been shown. The gallery was renovated in 2007. ⊠ *Cankarjeva 15* ☎ *01/241–6800* ⊕ *www. mg-lj.si* ⬚ *Free* ⊘ *Tues.–Sat. 10–6, Sun. 10–1.*

22 **Muzej Novejše Zgodovine** *(Museum of Modern History).* The permanent exhibition on Slovenes in the 20th century takes you from the days of Austria-Hungary, through World War II, the victory of the Partisan liberation movement and the ensuing Tito period, and up to the present day. Relics and memorabilia are combined with a dramatic sound-and-video presentation (scenes from World War II are projected on the walls and ceiling, accompanied by thundering gunfire, screams, and singing). You'll find the museum in a pink-and-white baroque villa in Tivoli Park. ⊠ *Celovška 23* ☎ *01/300–9610* ⊕ *www.muzej-nz.si* ⬚ *€4* ⊘ *Tues.–Sun. 10–6.*

21 **Narodna galerija** *(National Gallery).* This imposing turn-of-the-20th-century building houses the greatest collection of Slovenian art from the 13th through the early 20th century, and a smaller but impressive collection of European paintings. ⊠ *Cankarjeva 20* ☎ *01/241–5418* ⊕ *www.ng-slo.si* ⬚ *€5* ⊘ *Tues.–Sun. 10–6.*

20 **Narodni muzej** *(National Museum).* The centerpiece here is a bronze urn from the 5th century BC known as the Vace Situle. Discovered in Vace, Slovenia, it is a striking example of Illyrian workmanship. ⊠ *Muzejska 1* ☎ *01/241–4400* ⊕ *www.narmuz-lj.si* ⬚ *€3* ⊘ *Tues., Wed., and Fri.–Sun. 10–6, Thurs. 10–8.*

8 **Robbov Vodnjak** *(Robba's Fountain).* When the Slovene sculptor Francesco Robba saw Bernini's *Fountain of the Four Rivers* on Piazza Navona during a visit to Rome, he was inspired to create this allegorical representation of the three main Kranjska rivers—the Sava, the Krka, and the Ljubljanica—that flow through Slovenia. ⊠ *Mestni trg.*

17 **Slovenska Filharmonija** *(Slovenian Philharmonic Hall).* This hall was built in 1891 for one of the oldest music societies in the world, established in 1701. Haydn, Brahms, Beethoven, and Paganini were honorary members of the orchestra, and Mahler was resident conductor for the 1881–82 season. ⊠ *Kongresni trg 10* ☎ *01/241–0800.*

NEED A BREAK? From the Philharmonic Hall, head to the other side of Kongresni trg to find **Zvezda** (⊠ *Kongresni trg 4* ☎ *01/421–9090*). This popular café has comfortable chairs and minimalist lighting, making it a perfect spot for an afternoon *kava smetana* (coffee with whipped cream). The ice cream and cakes are made on the premises and the staff never hurries you.

19 **SNG Opera in Balet** *(Slovenian National Opera and Ballet Theater).* This neo-Renaissance palace, with an ornate facade topped by an allegorical sculpture group, was erected in 1892. When visiting ballet and opera companies come to Ljubljana, they perform here. At this writing, the opera house was closed for a major renovation and was not expected to reopen until mid-2008. ⊠ *Župančičeva 1* ☎ *01/241–1764* ⊕ *www. opera.si* ⊙ *Weekdays 11–1 and one hour before performances.*

10 **Stari trg** *(Old Square).* More a narrow street than a square, the Old Square is lined with cafés and small restaurants. In agreeable weather, tables are set out on the cobblestones.

NEED A BREAK? The best cup of tea in Ljubljana—as well as great coffees—and one of the few breakfast places in town can be found at **Čajna Hiša** (⊠ *Stari trg 3* ☎ *01/439–4140*).

5 **Stolnica sveti Nikolaja** *(Cathedral of St. Nicholas).* This proud baroque cathedral overshadows the daily market on Vodnikov trg. Building took place between 1701 and 1708, and in 1836 the cupola was erected. In 1996, in honor of Pope John Paul II's visit, new bronze doors were added. The main door tells the story of Christianity in Slovenia, whereas the side door shows the history of the Ljubljana diocese. ⊠ *Dolničarjeva 1* ☎ *01/234–2690* ⊕ *lj-stolnica.rkc.si* ⊠ *Free* ⊙ *Daily 7–noon and 3–7.*

16 **Trg Francoske Revolucije** *(French Revolution Square).* When Napoléon took Slovenia, he made Ljubljana the capital of his Illyrian Provinces. This square is dominated by Plečnik's **Ilirski Steber** (Illyrian Column), which was erected in 1929 to commemorate that time.

3 **Tromostovje** *(Triple Bridge).* This striking structure spans the River Ljubljanica from Prešernov trg to the Old Town. The three bridges started as a single span, and in 1931 the two graceful outer arched bridges, designed by Plečnik, were added.

4 **Vodnikov trg** *(Vodnik Square).* This square hosts a big and bustling flower, fruit, and vegetable market. An elegant riverside colonnade designed by Plečnik runs the length of the market, and a bronze statue of the Slovene poet Valentin Vodnik, after whom the square is named, overlooks the scene. ⓥ *Market Mon.–Sat. 7–3.*

❻ **Zmajski most** *(Dragon's Bridge).* Four fire-breathing winged dragons crown the corners of this locally cherished concrete-and-iron structure.

12

**OFF THE
BEATEN
PATH**

Žale. To see one of Plečnik's most dramatic structures, ride bus No. 2, 7, or 22 from the post office out to Žale, a cemetery and memorial designed by the architect in the 1930s. The entrance colonnade and adjoining promenades reflect the Secessionist influence, creating a tranquil resting place inside. ⊠ *Tomačevska cesta, Novo Jarse.*

WHERE TO EAT

Central European food is often considered bland and stodgy, but in Ljubljana you can eat exceptionally well. Fresh fish arrives daily from the Adriatic, and the surrounding hills supply the capital with first-class meat and game, dairy produce, and fruit and vegetables. Ljubljana's relative diversity also affords an opportunity to dabble in international cuisines like Mexican, Japanese, and Chinese if you've already spent some time in the countryside and are looking for a change of pace. At some of the better restaurants the menus may verge on nouvelle cuisine, featuring imaginative and beautifully presented dishes. Complement your meal with a bottle of good Slovenian wine; the waiter can help you choose an appropriate one. For a lunchtime snack visit the market in Vodnik Square. Choose from tasty fried squid and whitebait in the riverside arcade or freshly baked pies and *kròf* (jelly-filled doughnuts) at the square's bakeries.

$$$–$$$$ ╳**Chez Eric.** The cuisine here shows a happy marriage of French and Slovenian cooking. The small number of entrées—four meat and four fish—ensure that each item gets the attention it deserves. Eat on the terrace in warmer months. The restaurant occupies the former site of the Rotovž, next to the town hall on Mestni trg. ⊠ *Mestni trg 3* ☎ *01/251–2839* ▤ *AE, DC, MC, V* ⓥ *Closed Sun.*

★ $$$–$$$$ ╳**Gostilna As.** This refined restaurant—not to be confused with the on-premises beer garden and after-hours club of the same name—is tucked away in a courtyard just off Wolfova ulica. As—or "Ace"—is *the* place to try innovative fish dishes (priced by the dekagram) and pasta specialties, all complemented by a first-rate wine list. The ambience is old-fashioned, but the dishes are creative and modern. ⊠ *Knafljev prehod 5a* ☎ *01/425–8822* ⌕ *Reservations essential* ▤ *AE, DC, MC, V.*

$$$ ╳**Pri sv. Florijanu.** On Gornji trg, on the way to the castle, this upscale eatery serves a new generation of Slovenian cuisine with an international touch, borrowing from French and Asian influences. In every season the chef seems to have the right touch with Slovenia's bounty; porcini mushroom risotto and pumpkin ravioli in the fall, asparagus soup and *motovílec* (lamb's lettuce) salad in the spring. The service is both inviting and discreet. ⊠ *Gornji trg 20* ☎ *01/251–2214* ▤ *AE, DC, MC, V.*

$$$ ✗ **Špajza.** A few doors away from Pri sv. Florijanu, you'll find a restaurant with a series of romantic candlelit rooms and bohemian decor. The menu has local specialties like *Kraški pršut* (Karst air-dried ham) and scampi tails, as well as an inspired selection of salads. They do a great tiramisu. ✉ *Gornji trg 28* ☎ *01/425–3094* ☱ *AE, DC, MC, V* ⊗ *Closed Sun.*

$$$ ✗ **Zlata Ribica.** Although there is a good range of Slovenian and Italian specialties, it's not the food that's the main draw here—it's the riverside location near the Triple Bridge. On a warm summer evening, there's not a better table in town. Despite the name, which translates as "goldfish," there's not much in the way of seafood here—instead the focus is on salads, grilled meats, and game. ✉ *Cankarjevo nab 5* ☎ *01/241–2680* ☱ *AE, DC, MC, V.*

$$–$$$ ✗ **Při Skofu.** This tiny, eclectic neighborhood place serves as a kind of temple for foodies in the suburb of Trnovo. The emphasis is on traditional Slovenian cooking, but not the sort that makes it onto many standard menus. The gnocchi, risotto, and buckwheat dumplings come highly recommended. Most ingredients are purchased daily at Ljubljana's open-air market. The menu changes daily, so ask the server what looks good that day. ✉ *Rečna 8, Trnovo* ☎ *01/426–4508* ☱ *AE, DC, MC, V.*

★ $–$$ ✗ **Trta.** In a country filled with pizza joints, this may be Slovenia's best. It offers supersize pies, fresh and inventive ingredients, and a small garden for warm evenings. Walk south along the river (on the same side as the Old Town), cross over busy Zoisova cesta, and continue along Grudnovo nabrežje. ✉ *Grudnovo nab 23* ☎ *01/426–5066* ☱ *AE, DC, MC, V* ⊗ *Closed Sun.*

WHERE TO STAY

Most of the listed hotels are clustered conveniently around Miklošičeva cesta, the main axis running from the train station down to Tromostovje (Triple Bridge). Ljubljana is expensive by Central and Eastern European standards (comparable to those in Western Europe), but hotel standards are high. In summer you can get better deals through private accommodations or university dorms. Ask about these options at the tourist-information center kiosk in the train station.

★ $$$–$$$$ 🏨 **Grand Hotel Union.** The pricier "Executive" section of this bustling hotel complex in central Ljubljana occupies a magnificent Secessionist-style building; the interior and furnishings remain typically turn-of-the-20th-century Vienna. The "Business" section is in an attached modern building overlooking a pleasant courtyard with a fountain; all the rooms in this section have broadband Internet connections. All hotel facilities are shared by both sections of the hotel and have been modernized with great care. ✉ *Miklošičeva 1–3, 1000* ☎ *01/308–1270* ⊕ *www.gh-union.si* ⊷ *297 rooms, 12 suites* ⊘ *In-room: safe, kitchen (some), Ethernet (some), dial-up (some). In-hotel: 2 restaurants, pool, gym, public Internet, no-smoking rooms,* ☱ *AE, DC, MC, V* ⵣBP.

12

$$–$$$$ ⊞**Hotel Lev.** A series of renovations since 1997 have transformed a nondescript modern building into the country's leading hotel. The Lev makes up for its location—about a 10-minute walk from the city center—with stunning views of Tivoli Park and the Julian Alps outside of Ljubljana. Parking is free, and you'll find easy access to all major highways; soundproof windows keep traffic from spoiling the comfort. Rooms are decorated in soothing pastel tones. Check the Web site for occasional summer discounts. ⊠ *Vošnjakova 1, 1000* ☎*01/433–2155* ⊕*www.hotel-lev.si* ↪*170 rooms* 㐧*In-room: safe (some), dial-up. In-hotel: restaurant, room service, bar, gym, laundry service, public Internet, parking (no fee), no-smoking rooms* ⊟*AE, DC, MC, V* ⊺⊙*BP.*

$$–$$$ ⊞**Best Western Slon Hotel.** Close to the river, this high-rise hotel stands on the site of a famous 16th-century inn and maintains an atmosphere of traditional hospitality. The breakfast is among the finest in the city. The run-of-the-mill rooms are comfortable, and the wood floors are a nice alternative to wall-to-wall carpeting. ⊠*Slovenska 34, 1000* ☎*01/470–1131* ⊕*www.hotelslon.com* ↪*185 rooms* 㐧*In-room: no a/c (some), safe, Ethernet, Wi-Fi. In-hotel: 2 restaurants, room service, no-smoking rooms, parking (no fee)* ⊟*AE, DC, MC, V* ⊺⊙*BP.*

$$–$$$ ⊞**Domina Grand Media Ljubljana.** It's the hotel of the future. At least that's what the owners of this—the city's newest addition to the upscale lodging class—would have us believe. Some of the high-concept amenities include plasma screens in all the rooms, total Internet connectivity, a fully equipped wellness center, and retro-modern furniture straight out of the Jetsons. The location is a bit out of the way, but the hotel offers free shuttle service to the center. ⊠*Dunajska cesta 154* ☎*01/588–2500* ⊕*www.dominagmljubljana.com* ↪*160 rooms, 57 suites* 㐧*In-room: safe, Ethernet, dial-up, Wi-Fi. In-hotel: 2 restaurants, no-smoking rooms* ⊟*AE, DC, MC, V* ⊺⊙*BP.*

$$ ⊞**City Hotel.** The former Turist Hotel has undergone a makeover. The result has been enhanced services, such as wider Internet access for guests, but at a higher price. The basic rooms are clean and the location is excellent. ⊠*Dalmatinova 15, 1000* ☎*01/239–0000* ⊕*www.cityhotel.si* ↪*123 rooms* 㐧*In-room: kitchen (some), Wi-Fi (some). In-hotel: 2 restaurants, bicycles, public Internet* ⊟*AE, DC, MC, V.*

★ $ ⊞**Emonec.** One of the city's newest two-star hotels, Emonec fills a long time gap in the market for a clean, affordable hotel in the center. Don't expect much in the way of frills or services, but the simple modern rooms are tastefully furnished, the breakfast is fine, and the staff is helpful. At this price level in Ljubljana, that's a considerable bargain. ⊠*Wolfova 12* ☎*01/200–1520* ⊕*www.hotel-emonec.com* ↪*26 rooms* 㐧*In-room: no a/c, Ethernet. In-hotel: bicycles, public Internet, parking (no fee), no elevator* ⊟*AE, DC, MC, V* ⊺⊙*BP.*

$ ⊞**Gostilna Pri Mraku.** This friendly pension offers good value with simple but comfortable rooms and a decent restaurant. It is situated on a quiet side street, close to the Križanke Summer Theater. ⊠*Rimska 4, 1000* ☎*01/421–9600* ⊕*www.daj-dam.si* ↪*30 rooms* 㐧*In-room: no a/c (some), safe. In-hotel: restaurant, public Internet, no elevator* ⊟*AE, DC, MC, V.*

NIGHTLIFE & THE ARTS

Although they were considered the workaholics of Yugoslavia, Slovenes do know how to enjoy themselves. One in 10 of the capital's inhabitants is a student, hence the proliferation of trendy cafés and small art galleries. Each year the International Summer Festival breathes new life into the Ljubljana cultural scene, sparking off a lively program of concerts and experimental theater. For information about forthcoming cultural events, check *Events in Ljubljana*, a monthly pamphlet published by the Ljubljana Promotion Center, and the English-language magazine *Ljubljana Life*, both available in major hotels and tourist offices.

NIGHTLIFE

The listed bars and clubs are all situated within walking distance of the center. However, during summer the all-night party scene moves to the Adriatic coast, where open-air dancing and rave parties abound.

CAFÉS

The most idyllic way to close a summer evening is with a nightcap on the terrace of one of the riverside cafés in the Old Town.

Hip **Cafe Galerija** (⊠ *Mestni trg 5* ☎ *01/426–0327*) serves stylish cocktails by candlelight in a North Africa–inspired hideout. With a large terrace and glamorous clientele, **Cafe Maček** (⊠ *Krojaška 5* ☎ *01/425–3791*) is the place to be seen down by the river. **Caffe Boheme** (⊠ *Mestni trg 19* ☎ *01/548–1342*) in the heart of the Old Town is spacious inside and has a terrace with tables and umbrellas outside.

MUSIC

For Latin music or a pick-me-up breakfast in the early hours, visit **Casa del Papa** (⊠ *Celovška 54A* ☎ *01/434–3158*): three floors of exotic food, drinks, and entertainment in tribute to Ernest Hemingway. For live jazz visit **Jazz Club Gajo** (⊠ *Beethovnova 8* ☎ *01/425–3206*), which attracts stars from home and abroad. Clark Terry, Sheila Jordan, and Woody Shaw have all performed here. The student-run club **K4** (⊠ *Kersnikova 4* ☎ *01/431–7010*) hosts visiting DJs and plays a mix of musical styles—house, hip-hop, surf—throughout the week. It attracts a young and alternative crowd; Sunday is gay night.

BARS & CLUBS

If it's rowdy beer-drinking and shot-downing you're looking for, the epicenter for this is the courtyard just off Wolfova ulica 6, or in nice weather just follow the crowds—and the noise—to the Knafljev prehod. **As Lounge** (⊠ *Knafljev prehod* ☎ *01/425–8822*). **Cutty Sark** (⊠ *Knafljev prehod* ☎ *01/425–1477*). For great cocktails, head over to **Salon** (⊠ *Trubarjeva 23* ☎ *01/433–2006*) on a funky street just north of the main Old Town cluster. The gold lamé and leopard-skin interior lends a cool, East Village–like vibe.

THE ARTS

ANNUAL EVENTS

Each year in June, the International Jazz Festival and the Druga Godba (a festival of alternative and ethnic music) are staged at the Križanke Summer Theater. For schedules and tickets contact the box office at Cankarjev dom. Ljubljana's **International Summer Festival** (⊠*Trg Francoske Revolucije 1–2* ☏*01/241–6026* ⊕*www.festival-lj.si*) is held each July and August in the open-air Križanke Summer Theater. Musical, theatrical, and dance performances attract acclaimed artists from all over the world.

GIFT IDEAS

The most interesting gifts to buy in Slovenia are the homemade products you come across in your travels: wine from Ptuj, *rakija* (a potent spirit distilled from fruit) from Pleterje Monastery, herbal teas from Stična Monastery, and honey from Radovljica. The Slovenian products best known abroad are connected with outdoor sports. If you'd like some Planika walking boots or Elan skis, you can get a good deal on them here.

12

PERFORMANCE HALLS

Cankarjev dom (*Cankar House* ⊠*Prešernova 10* ☏*01/241–7100* ⊕*www.cd-cc.si*), opened in 1980 as a modern, rather characterless venue. As a cultural center, however, it is the driving force behind the city's artistic activities, offering up-to-date general information and tickets. A progressive film festival takes place here every November.

CLASSICAL MUSIC

Ljubljana has plenty of events for classical-music lovers. The season, which runs from September through June, includes weekly concerts by the Slovenian Philharmonic Orchestra and the RTV Slovenia Orchestra, as well as performances by guest soloists, chamber musicians, and foreign symphony orchestras. The 19th-century performance hall housing concerts by the **Slovenska Filharmonija** (*Slovenian Philharmonic* ⊠*Kongresni trg 10* ☏*01/241–0800* ⊕*www.filharmonija.si*) is a traditional classical-music venue. The orchestra dates to 1908, but its predecessors have roots in the early 18th century.

THEATER, DANCE & OPERA

From September through June the **SNG Opera in Balet** (*Slovene National Opera & Ballet Theater* ⊠*Župančičeva 1* ☏*01/241–1764* ⊕*www.opera.si*) stages everything from classical to modern and alternative productions.

SHOPPING

Although you wouldn't come to Slovenia to do much serious shopping, fashionable shoe stores abound in Ljubljana; for the latest selection head to shops on Stari trg in the Old Town. If you want to do some hiking but have come unprepared, **Anappurna** (⊠*Krakovski Nasip 10* ☏*01/426–3428*) has a good selection of mountaineering equipment. You can pick up antiques and memorabilia at the **Ljubljana Flea Market**

(✉ *Cankarjevo nab*), held near Tromostovje (Triple Bridge) each Sunday morning. The most interesting shopping experience is undoubtedly a visit to the **open-air market** (✉ *Vodnikov trg*), where besides fresh fruit and vegetables you can find dried herbs and locally produced honey. **Skrina** (✉ *Breg 8* ☎ *01/425–5161*) has some unusual local crafts.

SIDE TRIP TO THE KRKA VALLEY

A drive through the Krka Valley makes a perfect day trip from Ljubljana. The monasteries of Stična and Pleterje offer insight into contemporary monastic life, and there are two castles, Otočec and Mokrice, where you can stop for lunch—or a romantic overnight stay in exquisite surroundings.

Take the E70 highway east out of Ljubljana, and then turn right at Ivančna Gorica to follow a secondary road along the Krka Valley. For a more direct journey home, return to the E70 just north of Šentjernej. There are also buses from Ljubljana to Ivančna Gorica and Šentjernej, but these are practical only if you don't mind walking the final stretch to the monasteries.

★   The **Stična Samostan** *Stična Monastery)* lies 2 km (1 mi) north of Ivančna Gorica. Founded by the Cistercians in 1135, the monastery was fortified in the 15th century to protect against Turkish invasion. Today there are only 10 monks, plus 3 nuns who attend to the cooking. The monks produce excellent herbal teas that work (allegedly) against cellulite, insomnia, poor memory, and practically every other problem you can think of, on sale in the monastery shop. The early Gothic cloisters, the baroque church, and the adjoining **Slovenian Religious Museum** are open to the public. The museum's collections include archives dedicated to the work of Bishop Friderik Baraga, a 19th-century missionary to the United States who compiled the first dictionary of the Native American Otchipwe language. Call first to arrange a visit. ✉ *Stična 17, Ivančna Gorica* ☎ *01/787–7100* 💶 *€4* ☉ *Tues.–Sat. 8–11 and 2–5, Sun. 2–5.*

★   The Carthusian monks of **Pleterje Samostan** *(Pleterje Monastery)* aim "to find God in silence and solitude." Therefore, you can't enter the monastery proper, but you are welcome to view the magnificent 15th-century Gothic church and to watch a fascinating audiovisual presentation (in English) about the way the monks live. The walled monastery is nestled in a lonely valley surrounded by woods. Once a week the monks take a 45-minute walk around the perimeter of the complex. The route is marked with a blue circle and yellow cross, so you can follow the trail independently. A small shop sells rakija, honey, wine, and cheese made by the monks. To reach the monastery from Stična Monastery follow the Krka River through Zagradec, Žužemberk, and Novo Mesto. At Šentjernej, turn south and travel for 6 km (4 mi) to reach Pleterje. ✉ *Drča 1, Šentjernej* ☎ *07/308–1225* 💶 *Free* ☉ *Daily 7:30–5:30.*

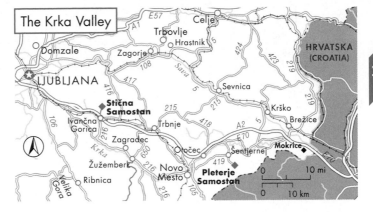

12

WHERE TO STAY

$$ 🏨 **Hotel Grad Otočec.** About 8 km 5 mi) west of Šentjernej, on the road to Novo Mesto, you will find the entrance to the medieval Otočec castle, dating from the 13th century. Now a luxury hotel, complete with period furniture, Otočec sits on an island in the Krka River and is accessible by a wooden bridge. You can also camp on the castle grounds. Nonguests are welcome to dine in the restaurant, where the house specialty is locally caught game. Or just stop by for a drink in the courtyard café. Equestrian and tennis centers are close by. ⊠ *Grajska 1, Otočec ob Krki, 8222* ☎ *07/38–48–900* ⊕ *www.terme-krka.si* ⤵ *16 rooms* ⚘ *In hotel: restaurant* ☰ *AE, DC, MC, V* ⊙|*BP.*

☾ $$ 🏨 **Hotel Toplice.** With 11 springs supplying thermal water, Terme Čatež is the largest natural spa in Slovenia. Hotel Toplice—the newest of the four hotels connected to the spa—is the ultimate destination for recharging your batteries. It houses expansive indoor thermal baths as well as a fully loaded sports center. ⊠ *Topliska 35, Čatež ob Savi, 8251* ☎ *07/493–5023* ⊕ *www.terme-catez.si* ⤵ *140 rooms* ⚘ *In-room: refrigerator, safe. In-hotel: restaurant, tennis courts, pool, gym, spa, public Internet* ☰ *AE, DC, MC, V* ⊙|*BP.*

SPORTS & THE OUTDOORS

For horse lovers the **Struga Equestrian Center** (⊠ *Otočec* ☎ *07/307–5627*), at a 12th-century medieval manor, is a 20-minute walk from Otočec Castle. The center offers riding lessons and rents horses.

MARIBOR, PTUJ & HALOZE HILLS

During the 1st century AD, Poetovio, now known as Ptuj, was the largest Roman settlement in the area that is now Slovenia. Much later, in the 13th century, Maribor was founded. Originally given the German name Marchburg, the city took its Slavic name in 1836. For centuries the two towns competed for economic and cultural prominence within the region, and Maribor finally gained the upper hand in 1846, when a new railway line connected the city to Vienna and Trieste. The area

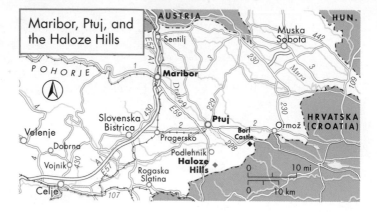

Maribor, Ptuj, and
the Haloze Hills

between Maribor and Ptuj is a flat, fertile flood plain formed by the Drava River. South of Ptuj lie the hills of Haloze, famous for quality white wines.

MARIBOR

128 km (80 mi) northeast of Ljubljana on the E57.

The presence of thousands of university students gives Maribor—Slovenia's second-largest city—a youthful vibe. You'll find plenty of pubs and cafés, especially in the Lent district along the Drava River. The Old Town has retained a core of ornate 18th- and 19th-century town houses, typical of imperial Austria, and much of it is off-limits to cars.

The heart of the Old Town is **Rotovški trg** with the **Kužno Znamenje** (Plague Memorial) at its center and overlooked by the proud 16th-century Renaissance **Rotovž** (town hall).

From Rotovški trg, a number of traffic-free streets lead down to a riverside promenade, known as **Lent.** It is lined with bars, terrace cafés, restaurants, and boutiques.

Below the streets of Maribor lies one of Europe's largest wine cellars. The **Vinag wine cellar** has some 3½ km (2 mi) of underground tunnels, holding almost 6 million liters of wine. Tours and tastings can be arranged in advance by phone. ⊠ *Trg Svobode 3* ☎ *02/220–8111* ⊕ *www.vinag.si.*

The Vodni Stolp (Water Tower), a former defense tower, houses the **Vinoteka Slovenskih Vin** *(Slovenian Wine Shop)*. Here you can sample and purchase more than 500 different Slovenian vintage wines. ⊠ *Usnjarska 10* ☎ *02/251–7743.*

WHERE TO STAY & EAT

In summer, Maribor University dorms are open to visitors, providing a cheap alternative to hotels. For details ask at the Maribor tourist information center.

$–$$ ✕ **Toti Rotovž.** Close to the town hall, this building has been carefully restored to reveal vaulted brick ceilings and terra-cotta floors. The restaurant serves an eclectic mix of Slovene and international dishes, whereas the *klet* (wine cellar) in the basement cooks up barbecued steaks. ✉ *Glavni trg 14* ☎ *02/228–7650* ▤ *AE, DC, MC, V.*

$ ▥ **Hotel Orel.** The modern Orel offers the best accommodations in the city center—an easy stroll down the pedestrian zone to the river. There is a pleasant restaurant at street level, the rooms are comfortable, and the service is friendly. Guests are granted access to the sauna and swimming pools at the Fontana Recreation Center, which is about 220 yards away from the hotel. ✉ *Grajski trg 3A, 2000* ☎ *02/250–6700* ⊕ *www. termemb.si* ⟿ *80 rooms* ⟐ *In room: Ethernet, refrigerator. In-hotel: restaurant, parking (no fee)* ▤ *AE, DC, MC, V* ⦿ *BP.*

SPORTS & THE OUTDOORS

In winter in the Pohorje Mountains, just 6 km (4 mi) southwest of Maribor, you'll find alpine ski runs and cross-country trails. A **cable car** takes you from the south side of town up to the winter resort.

Two well-established bike paths pass through the region. The 95-km (59-mi) **Drava Trail** follows the course of the Drava River through the Kozjak Hills to Maribor and then proceeds to Ptuj. The 56-km (35-mi) **Jantara Trail** runs from Šentilj on the Austrian border to Maribor and continues to Slovenska Bistrica. However, finding a place to rent a bike can be somewhat problematic. Inquire at the Maribor tourist-information center for assistance and information.

PTUJ

25 km (16 mi) southeast of Maribor, 130 km (81 mi) from Ljubljana.

Ptuj, built beside the Drava River and crowned by a hilltop castle, hits the national news each year in February with its extraordinary Carnival celebration, known as Kurentovanje. During the 10-day festival the town's boys and men dress in the bizarre Kurent costume: a horned mask decorated with ribbons and flowers, a sheepskin cloak, and a set of heavy bells around the waist. The task of the Kurent is to drive away the winter and welcome in the spring. You can see Kurent figures on 18th-century building facades in the center of Ptuj, on Jadranska ulica No. 4 and No. 6. It's a charming place and worth an overnight stay.

Ptujski Grad *(Ptuj Castle)* stands at the top of a steep hill in the center of town. Planned around a baroque courtyard, the castle houses a museum that exhibits musical instruments, an armory, 15th-century church paintings, and period furniture. ✉ *Grajska Raven* ☎ *02/787–9230* ⊕ *www.pok-muzej-ptuj.si* 💶 *€4* ⊙ *Mid-Apr.–mid-Oct., daily 9–6; mid-Oct.–mid-Apr., daily 9–4.*

The **Ptuj Regional Museum,** in a former Dominican monastery, has an outstanding collection of ancient artifacts and coins, as well as Roman statuary and tombstones. The museum offers guided tours in English. ⊠*Muzejski trg 1* ☎*02/787–9230* ☜*€4* ☉*Sept.–June, daily 9–6; July and Aug., weekdays 9–6, weekends 9–8.*

Vinska Klet *(Ptuj Wine Cellars)* offers a tasting session with five different wines, bread, and cheese, plus a bottle to take home. You are also given a tour of the underground cellars. A sound-and-video presentation takes you through the seasons of wine making at the vineyards. The wines stocked here come predominantly from the Haloze Hills. One of the best wines is *Šipon*, a dry white that pairs nicely with pork dishes and rich sauces. ⊠*Vinarski trg 1* ☎*02/787–9810* ☜*€6–€8* ☉*Weekdays 7–7, Sat. 7–noon.*

WHERE TO EAT
★ $–$$$ ✕**Ribič.** This lovely riverside restaurant is arguably the city's best. Though the menu offers seafood such as crab and lobster, the real treats here are the river fish, such as trout. The interior is simple, and the walls are hung with fishing nets. In warmer months, sit on the terrace with a view over the Drava. ⊠*Dravska 9* ☎*02/749–0653* ▭*AE, DC, MC, V.*

THE HALOZE HILLS

Borl Castle is 11 km (7 mi) southeast of Ptuj, 140 km (87 mi) from Ljubljana.

The Haloze Hills lie south of Ptuj, close to the Croatian border. Grapes are generally planted on the steeper, south-facing slopes, to take full advantage of the sunshine, whereas the cooler, north-facing slopes are covered with trees and pastures. The best way to explore the region is to pick up the Haloze wine route near **Borl Castle,** through an undulating landscape of vineyards and woodlands. For a map of the route plus a comprehensive list of vineyards and wine stores open to the public, inquire at the Ptuj tourist-information center.

On the road between Podlehnik and Poljčane, keep an eye out for the sign for Štatenberg Castle; you can't stay there, but it has a good restaurant. Built between 1720 and 1740, Štatenberg is a typical example of the baroque style favored by the local aristocracy during the 18th century.

WHERE TO EAT
$ ✕**Štatenberg Castle.** This restaurant serves traditional dishes, such as roast meats, accompanied by excellent local wines. Throughout summer you can sit at tables outside in the courtyard. ⊠*Štatenberg 86, Makole, 8222* ☎*02/803–0216* ▭*No credit cards* ☉*Closed Mon.*

MARIBOR, PTUJ & HALOZE HILLS ESSENTIALS

AIR TRAVEL
In mid-2007, Ryanair became the first low-cost airline with connections to Maribor, flying three times a week from London Stansted.

12

BUS TRAVEL
Regular buses link Maribor and Ptuj to Ljubljana. However, the train is cheaper and more comfortable. An hourly bus service connects Maribor and Ptuj; the 45-minute journey costs around €5.

Information Maribor Bus Station (⊠ *Mlinska 1, Maribor* ☎ *02/235–0212*).

CAR TRAVEL
To reach Maribor from Ljubljana take the E57; for Ptuj turn off at Slovenska Bistrica. A car is almost essential for exploring the Haloze Hills wine route. Some of the country roads are narrow and winding. Although there is snow in winter, it is extremely rare to find roads closed.

TRAIN TRAVEL
Regular train service links Ljubljana and Maribor; several international trains continue to Graz and Vienna. It is also possible to reach Ptuj by train from Ljubljana, though you may have to change at Pragersko. For information contact Ljubljana's train station *(⇨ Train Travel in Ljubljana Essentials)*. Several trains daily connect Maribor and Ptuj, with a change at Pragersko; the 45-minute journey costs around €8.

Information Maribor Train Station (⊠ *Partizanska 50, Maribor* ☎ *02/292–2100*).

VISITOR INFORMATION
Information Maribor Tourist Information (⊠ *Partizanska 47, Maribor* ☎ *02/234–6611* ⊕ *www.maribor-tourism.si*). **Ptuj Tourist Information** (⊠ *Slovenski trg 3, Ptuj* ☎ *02/771–0173* ⊕ *www.ptuj-tourism.si*).

THE ALPS & THE SOČA VALLEY

Northwest of Ljubljana lies an unspoiled region of breathtakingly beautiful mountains, alpine lakes, and fast-running rivers. Much of the region is part of the protected Triglavski Narodni Park (Triglav National Park), and it's the perfect jumping-off spot for adventure pursuits of all sorts. Superior skiing, hiking, rafting, biking, and fly-fishing draw people here from around the world.

Each of the major towns and resorts in the region—Bled, Bohinj, Kranjska Gora, and Bovec—offers something a little different. At Bled the focus is on comfort and excellent facilities, poised against a fairy-tale backdrop of an island church in a green-blue lake. Bohinj's charms are more rustic—a pristine deep-green alpine sea, bordered by mountains on three sides. Kranjska Gora and Bovec offer more immediate access to high-octane adventure. The former is Slovenia's leading ski resort. In summer it opens its lifts to mountain bikers and free-riders seeking the adrenaline rush of a dash down the slopes. Bovec, on the Soča River, offers world-class rafting and canyoning—or gentler floats—down what must be one of the world's most beautiful mountain streams.

These regional centers can be approached individually or, in summer, by car or bus as part of a large loop running northwest from Ljubljana. Proceed first to Bled and on to Bohinj, then push on farther north to Kranjska Gora, over the impossibly high Vršic pass, and down to Bovec. The return to Ljubljana is via the World War I battle town of Kobarid and Idrija.

■ EN ROUTE On the road to Bled from Ljubljana you pass a junction for Radovljica. Turn off here to see the lovingly preserved 17th-century town center and visit the intriguing **Čebelarski muzej** (*Beekeeping Museum* ✉ *Linhartov trg 1, Radovljica* ☎ *04/532–0520*). The museum charges an admission fee of €3.50. It's open from May through August, Tuesday to Sunday from 10 to 1 and 4 to 6; in September and October, it's open Tuesday to Sunday from 10 to noon and 3 to 5; in March, April, November, and December, it's open only on Wednesday and weekends from 10 to noon and 3 to 5.

BLED

50 km (31 mi) northwest of Ljubljana on the E61.

Bled is among the most magnificently situated mountain resorts in Europe. The healing powers of its thermal springs were known during the 17th century. In the early 19th century the aristocracy arrived to bask in Bled's tranquil alpine setting. Even today—when Bled can swell to overflowing in the high season of July and August—it retains something of the refined feel of a *fin-de-siècle* spa town.

Recent years have brought a string of improvements to Bled's tourist facilities. New resorts and wellness centers, arguably the country's best golf course, and a clutch of new adventure-oriented travel agencies mean there is now much more to do than simply stroll the banks of the lake. Bled is also an excellent base for hikes into the eastern half of Triglav National Park.

Blejsko Jezero *(Lake Bled)* is nestled within a rim of mountains and surrounded by forests, with a castle on one side and a promenade beneath stately chestnut trees on the other. Horse-drawn carriages clip-clop along the promenade while swans glide on the water. On a minuscule island in the middle of the lake the lovely **Cerkov svetega Martina** (St. Martin's Pilgrimage Church) stands within a circle of trees. Take a ride over to the island on a *pletna*, an old-fashioned canopied wooden boat similar to a Venetian gondola.

☾ The stately 16th-century **grad** *(castle)* perches above the lake on the summit of a steep cliff, against a backdrop of the Julian Alps and Triglav Peak. You can climb up to the castle for fine views of the lake, the resort, and the surrounding countryside. An exhibition traces the development of the castle through the centuries, with objects from archaeo-

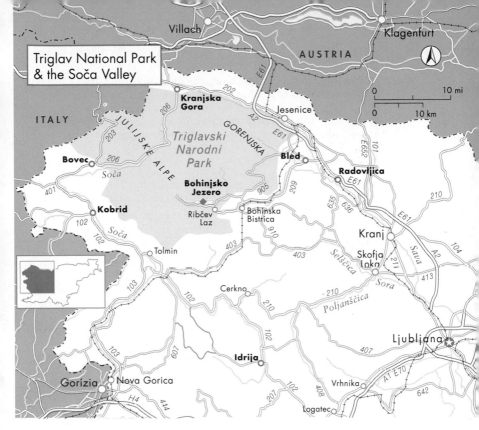

logical finds to period furniture on display. ⊠ *Bled* 🕾 *04/578–0525* 🖼 *€6* 🕐 *May–Sept., daily 8–8; Oct.–Apr., daily 9–5.*

NEED A BREAK?

Even if you're not staying at the illustrious **Grand Hotel Toplice** (⊠ *C. Svobode 12* 🕾 *04/579–1000*), you're welcome to use its sauna and soak in the thermal waters (28°C [83°F]) of the indoor swimming pool. A small admission fee includes a towel and locker. Or try the Toplice's wellness center for various massage treatments, facials, and the tantalizingly labeled "citrus body sensation" (a full-body massage with orange and lemon balm).

♻ The **Soteska Vintgar** *(Vintgar Gorge)* was cut between precipitous cliffs by the clear Radovna River, which flows down numerous waterfalls and through pools and rapids. The marked trail through the gorge leads over bridges and along wooden walkways and galleries. ⊠ *Zgornje Gorje Rd., 5 km (3 mi) northwest of Bled.*

WHERE TO EAT

★ $$$–$$$$ ✕ **Gostilna Lectar.** This warm country-style inn serves an impressive selection of traditional dishes. For a cross section of the local cuisine, try the pumpkin soup, the Peasant's Plate (buckwheat dumplings, mixed smoked meats, potatoes, and fresh steamed vegetables), and the apple strudel. The restaurant is 10 km (6 mi) south of Bled on the

E61 highway. ⊠*Linhartov trg 2, Radovljica* ☎*04/537–4800* ▤*AE, DC, MC, V.*

🕲 $-$$$ ✕**Mlino.** Follow the footpath along the south side of the lake 20 minutes from the center of Bled to reach this informal family restaurant with a lovely garden terrace. Try the Mlino Plate, a mixed platter of barbecued meats served with *djevec* (rice cooked with vegetables). There is a special menu for children, and boats are for hire on the lake. ⊠*C. Svobode 45* ☎*04/574–1404* ▤*AE, DC, MC, V.*

$-$$ ✕**Gostilna pri Planincu.** This friendly place is busy year-round. Locals meet here for morning coffee or a bargain prix-fixe lunch—or just to drink the cheapest beer in town. While rowdy farmers occupy the front bar, lovers share a candlelit supper in the dining room. Portions are "for people who work all day": roast chicken and fries, steak and mushrooms, black pudding, and turnips. For dessert, walnut *štrukli* (dumplings) are served with cream. ⊠*Grajska 8* ☎*04/574–1613* ▤*AE, DC, MC, V.*

WHERE TO STAY

$$$ 🏨**Vila Bled.** Late Yugoslav president Tito was the gracious host to numerous 20th-century statesmen at this former royal residence, amid 13 acres of gardens overlooking the lake. It was converted into a luxurious hotel in 1984 and became part of the Relais & Châteaux group in 1987. After a renovation in 2004, the managers wisely chose to retain many of the original furnishings from the 1950s—giving the rooms and public areas a formal but still retro-chic feel. It's unique. ⊠*C. Svobode 26, 4260* ☎*04/579–1500* ⊕*www.vila-bled.com* ⌁*10 rooms, 20 suites* ⚴*In-hotel: restaurant, bar, tennis court, spa* ▤*AE, DC, MC, V* ⦿*BP.*

★ $$-$$$ 🏨**Grand Hotel Toplice.** This old-fashioned, ivy-covered resort hotel has been favored by British travelers since the 1920s. Directly on the lake, the main building has balconies and big windows from which you can take in dramatic views of the castle and the Julian Alps. The rooms, lounges, and bar are all furnished with antiques and heirloom rugs. It's worth the splurge for a lakeside room. ⊠*C. Svobode 12, 4260* ☎*04/579–1000* ⊕*www.hotel-toplice.com* ⌁*206 rooms* ⚴*In-room: Ethernet. In-hotel: 3 restaurants, bar, pools, gym, spa, public Wi-Fi* ▤*AE, DC, MC, V* ⦿*BP.*

SPORTS & THE OUTDOORS

During summer, the lake turns into a family playground, with swimming, rowing, sailing, and windsurfing. The main swimming area lies below the castle along the northern shore. In winter on Straža Hill, immediately above town, you can ski day and night, thanks to floodlighting. Just 10 km (6 mi) west of Bled, a larger ski area, Zatrnik, has 7 km (4½ mi) of alpine trails. The area's two golf courses—the 18-hole "Kings" course and the 9-hole "Lake" course—are located 4 km (2½ mi) outside of town at the Golf & Country Club Bled. For information on winter and summer sports, contact Bled's tourist-information center or one of the many private travel and activity agencies around town.

BOHINJSKO JEZERO

25 km (16 mi) southwest of Bled, 75 km (47 mi) from Ljubljana.

Bohinjsko Jezero (Lake Bohinj) lies to the south and west of Bled along a crowded two-lane highway that thins out the farther you travel from Bled. If you're driving, follow the signs to "jezero" (lake). The lake area proper begins in the small lakeside village of Ribčev Laz. Lake Bohinj is quieter, wilder and in many ways prettier than Bled, its sister lake to the east.

On the eastern bank of Lake Bohinj in Ribčev Laz, you'll find the 15th-century Gothic church of **Sveti Janez** *(St. John)*. The small church has a fine bell tower and contains a number of notable 15th- and 16th-century frescoes. ⊠ *Ribčev Laz.* At the west end of Lake Bohinj near Ukanc a cable car leads up **Mt. Vogel** to a height of 5,035 feet. From here, you have spectacular views of the Julian Alps massif and the Bohinj valley and lake. From the cable-car base, the road continues 5 km (3 mi) beyond the lake to the point where the Savica River makes a tremendous leap over a 194-foot waterfall. The cable car runs year-round from 8 AM until 6 PM (until 7 PM in July and August). A round-trip ticket costs €8. Gasoline-powered engines are not allowed on Lake Bohinj because of the danger of pollution. The super-quiet **Turistična Ladja** *(Tourist Boat)* runs on electrical power. The boat makes hourly runs during daylight hours from June to mid-September from the boat dock just below Ribčev Laz to Camp Zlatorog on the western side of the lake and back. A ticket costs €6.50 one-way, or €8 round-trip.

WHERE TO STAY

The Bohinj area is the perfect place to bypass the hotels and stay in a private home or pension. The tourist-information center in Ribčev Laz maintains an extensive list. Pensions are usually priced per person and often include lunch or dinner. Some of the nicest properties are in the outlying villages of Ukanc, Stara Fužina, and Srednja Vas—though you'll need your own transportation (bike or car) to get there.

$$ **Hotel Zlatorog.** A very likable, guest-friendly alpine-style hotel stands on the far western edge of the lake. The facilities—including an indoor pool and sauna—and proximity to the ski lifts make it a great winter choice. The large lawn and on-site playground are perfect for families with young children. Even if you're not staying here, you can rent bikes or use the hotel's two tennis courts (€3–€8 an hour). Rooms are divided between the main hotel and an adjoining villa. ⊠ *Ukanc 65, 4265* ☎ *04/572–3381* ⊕ *www.alpinum.net* ↪ *43 rooms, 31 villa rooms* ⬩ *In-room: refrigerator. In-hotel: restaurant, bar, tennis courts, pool, bicycles* ⊟ *AE, DC, MC, V* ⦶*BP.*

$ **Hotel Bellevue.** Off the beaten track, high above Ribčev Laz, this 1930s-era alpine lodge nevertheless affords wonderful views of the lake. Be sure to request a lakeside room. Agatha Christie apparently fell in love with the hotel and stayed here for a month in 1967 on a working holiday. The hotel has set up an Agatha Christie reading room, complete with mini-library and typewriter. ⊠ *Ribčev Laz 65, 4265*

☎04/572–3331 ⊕*www.alpinum.net* ⇨*76 rooms* ⚐*In-hotel: restaurant, bar, tennis court, no elevator* ⊟*AE, DC, MC, V* ⎮⚐⎮*BP.*

$ ⚐ **Pension Stare.** This delightful family-run pension is on the far western end of the lake in the tiny hamlet of Ukanc. To find it, continue beyond the Hotel Zlatorog, down a tiny lane and over a plank bridge. The young couple who own it will greet you with a glass of wine or beer on the terrace. It's very popular, so book in advance. ⊠*Ukanc 128, 4265* ☎04/574–6400 ⊕*www.national-park-hotel.com* ⇨*10 rooms* ⚐*In-room: no a/c, no TV. In-hotel: restaurant, no elevator* ⊟*AE, DC, MC, V* ⎮⚐⎮*BP.*

SPORTS & THE OUTDOORS
Bohinj is a natural base for exploring the trails of the Triglav National Park. Before heading out, pick up a good trail map from the tourist-information center. The cable car to Vogel is an excellent starting point for many of the walks. Just remember to get an early start, wear proper hiking boots, take plenty of water, and protect yourself against the sun. Other popular warm-weather pursuits include swimming, biking, rafting, canyoning, and horseback riding. In winter you can ski at the ski areas of Vogel and Kobla.

☪ **Alpinsport** (⊠*Ribčev Laz 53* ☎04/572–3486 ⊕*www.alpinsport.si*), in the village of Studor, rents mountain bikes and organizes raft, kayak, hydrospeed (a small board for bodysurfing rapids), and canyoning trips. **Perfect Adventure Choice/PAC Sports** (⊠*Ribčev Laz 50* ☎04/574–6511 ⊕*www.pac-sports.com*) is another local outfitter offering river trips and rafting, as well as bike rental and caving expeditions. **Mrcina Ranč** (⊠*Studor, Bohinj* ☎041/790–297 ⊕*www.ranc-mrcina.com*) organizes horseback rides in and around Bohinj and the Triglav National Park to suit all skill levels. It's open year-round.

KRANJSKA GORA

39 km (24 mi) northwest of Bled, 85 km (53 mi) from Ljubljana.

Kranjska Gora, amid Slovenia's highest and most dramatic peaks, is the country's largest ski resort. In summer, the area attracts hiking and mountaineering enthusiasts. It's a pleasant town in any season. The resorts spread out along the perimeter, leaving the surprisingly charming core intact.

WHERE TO STAY
Most of Kranskja Gora's hotels are relatively large and were built during the 1970s and '80s to accommodate ski groups. The tourist-information center can help you find smaller properties, pensions, and private rooms if you are looking for something simpler and cheaper.

$$ ⚐ **Hotel Larix.** A large, modern hotel, similar in price and appearance to the Hotel Kompass across the street, the Larix is cheerier and offers better facilities. These include a large indoor pool, sauna, and wellness center. The location is right next to the main ski lifts on the slopes. Even if you're not staying here, you can pay to use the pool and sauna. ⊠*Borovška 99* ☎04/588–4100 ⊕*www.htp-gorenjka.si*

⤴*120 rooms* ♿*In-hotel: 3 restaurants, bar, pool, gym, spa* ⊟*AE, DC, MC, V* †©†*BP*.

★ $ ⚏ **Hotel Kotnik.** This charming little pastel yellow inn is just a few minutes' stroll from the central square and has a well-informed reception desk. Traditionally furnished rooms are simple but fine for a short stay. Oven-fired pizzas are served in the adjoining restaurant. ⊠*Borovška 75, Kranjska Gora* ☎*04/588–1564* ⊕*www.hotel-kotnik.si* ⤴*15 rooms* ♿*In-hotel: restaurant, room service, no elevator* ⊟*AE, DC, MC, V* †©†*BP*.

SPORTS & THE OUTDOORS

Skiing is the number-one sport in Kranjska Gora. There are more than 30 km (19 mi) of downhill runs, 20 ski lifts, and 40 km (25 mi) of groomed cross-country trails open during the winter ski season, which typically runs from mid-December through mid-March. During summer, from late May through mid-September, mountain biking is big, and you'll find plenty of places to rent bikes, as well as 12 marked trails covering 150 km (93 mi) to take you through scented pine forests and spectacular alpine scenery. An unused railway track, tracing the south edge of the Karavanke Alps, brings hikers and bikers all the way to the village of Jesenice, about 20 km (12 mi) away. The Kranjska Gora Bike Park is oriented more toward experienced free-riders and thrill seekers—those who like to take their bikes to the top of the hill and career back down. There are also numerous hiking trails; you can pick up a good local trail map from the tourist-information center or at kiosks around town.

Fun Bike Park Kranjska Gora (⊠*Borovška 103, Kranjska Gora* ☎*031/ 499–499* ⊕*www.kranjskagora.mtbpark.si*) rents full- and front-suspension mountain bikes for use along downhill mountain and forest trails. The emphasis here is on fast, adrenaline-filled rides. Lifts are open from May through the third week of September.

Kranjska Gora Recreational Ski Center (⊠*Borovška 103, Kranjska Gora* ☎*04/588–1414* ⊕*www.kr-gora.si*) runs the lifts and is the main center for skiing information. The Web site—though mostly in Slovenian—lists prices in English and has a live Web cam so that you can see the conditions.

Sport Bernik (⊠*Borovška 88a, Kranjska Gora* ☎*04/588–1470*) is a full-service sports-equipment rental center, with both skis and mountain bikes in their respective seasons. It's located close to the ski center.

EN ROUTE From Kranjska Gora, head south over the breathtaking **Vršič Pass,** some 5,253 feet above sea level. You'll then descend into the beautiful Soča Valley, winding through the foothills to the west of Triglav Peak and occasionally plunging through tunnels. From Trenta, continue west for about 20 km (12 mi) to reach the mountain adventure resort of Bovec.

In Trenta, you'll find the Triglav National Park Information Center at **Dom Trenta** (⊠*Na Logu v Trenti, Trenta* ☎*05/388–9330*). Here, you can watch a presentation about the history and geography of the region and tour the small museum. It's also a good access point to the 20-km (12-mi) Soča Trail that winds its way along the river's banks. The center is open from April through October, daily from 10 to 6.

BOVEC

35 km (22 mi) south of Kranjska Gora, 124 km (77 mi) from Ljubljana.

Bovec is a friendly, relaxed, youth-oriented town that owes its modern existence largely to the adventure tourism possibilities afforded by the Soča River. The center is filled with private travel agencies, all offering a similar array of white-water rafting, kayaking, canoeing, hydrospeeding, and canyoning trips. The Soča—by the time it reaches Bovec—is a world-class river that regularly plays host to international rafting events. The main tour operators are experienced, and the rafting trips are aimed at all levels of experience. The river is at its best in spring, swelled by the melting snowcaps. But it is raftable throughout the summer. Even if you don't decide to ride, plan a walk along the Soča's banks—the emerald green or electric blue (depending on the glint of the sun) color of the water must be seen to be believed.

WHERE TO STAY

$ **Alp.** This 1970s-era hotel has been modernized and remains in good shape. The rooms are clean and functional. The location is central, just a couple of steps away from the main activities agencies and tourist office. Guests can use the Hotel Kanin swimming pool. ✉ *Trg Golobarskih Žrtev 48* ☎ *05/388–4000* 🌐 *www.alp-chandler.si* *103 rooms* *In-hotel: restaurant, bar, pool* ▭ *AE, DC, MC, V* 🍽 *BP.*

$ **Hotel Dobra Vila.** A welcome high-end addition to the local lodging scene is a lovingly restored, early-20th-century telephone exchange building. The owners added a wine cellar, a top-class restaurant, a reading room, and lovely public areas. The rooms and bath facilities have period fittings. ✉ *Mala vas 112* ☎ *05/389–6400* 🌐 *www.dobra-vila-bovec.com* *12 rooms* *In-hotel: restaurant, bar, laundry service, public Internet, refrigerator* ▭ *AE, DC, MC, V* 🍽 *BP.*

SPORTS & THE OUTDOORS

White-water rafting is not the only game in town. Bovec is a great base for leisurely cycling trips or more aggressive mountain-bike climbs. Private bike outfitters or the tourist-information center can provide maps and advice. It's also a great base for hiking the western regions of the Triglav National Park. The map *Bovec z Okolico* is available at the tourist-information center and kiosks around town; it marks out several good walks and bike trips of varying degrees of difficulty.

Alpe Šport Vančar (✉ *Trg Golobarskih Žrtev 28* ☎ *05/389–6350* 🌐 *www.bovecsport.com*) arranges rafting, kayaking, and canyoning trips of all types, as well as paragliding. It is well regarded locally. **Outdoor Freaks** (✉ *Klanc 9a* ☎ *041/553–675* 🌐 *www.freakoutdoor.com*) rents high-quality Cult mountain bikes and is a good source for local riding and trail information. **Soča Rafting** (✉ *Trg Golobarskih Žrtev*

48 ☎05/389–6200 ⊕*www.socarafting.si*) is one of the better-known rafting and kayaking outfitters.

KOBARID

12

21 km (13 mi) from Bovec, 115 km (71 mi) from Ljubljana.

From Bovec the road follows the Soča River south, running parallel with the Italian border, to pass through the pretty market town of Kobarid.

It's hard to believe now that this idyllic scene was home to some of the bloodiest mountain battles ever fought. In 1917—toward the end of World War I—the combined forces of the Austrian and German armies launched a surprise offensive to try to dislodge Italian forces holding Kobarid and the surrounding Soča Valley. The battle raged on as hundreds of thousands were killed under appalling conditions on both sides. In the end, the Italians retreated and were almost knocked out of the war. "Caporetto"—Kobarid's Italian name—became synonymous throughout Italy with shame and defeat.

Fodor'sChoice ★ In the center of Kobarid, the **Kobariški muzej** *(Kobarid Museum)* has a fascinating exhibition of the fighting, including diaries of the soldiers involved. The museum also gives a 20-minute video presentation—with projections, sound effects, and narration in English. The **Kobarid Historical Walk** takes you on a 5-km (3-mi) hike through lovely countryside, over a hair-raising bridge, and up to a spectacular waterfall. You'll follow the former front line and visit various sites related to World War I along the way. The path is clearly marked, and a self-guiding pamphlet and map are available at the Kobarid Museum. ⊠*Gregorčičeva 10* ☎05/389–0000 ⊕*www.kobariski-muzej.si* ☞€4 ⊗*Daily 9–7.*

WHERE TO STAY & EAT

$–$$$
Fodor'sChoice ★ ⊡**Hotel Hvala.** This delightful family-run hotel is possibly one of the most welcoming places you'll ever stay. The excellent hotel restaurant, Restauracija Topli Val—easily the best in the area—serves local trout and freshwater crayfish, as well as mushrooms and truffles in season. Italians drive over the border just to eat here. ⊠*Trg Svobode 1, 5222* ☎05/389–9300 ⊕*www.topli-val-sp.si* ☞28 *rooms, 4 suites* ⌂*Inhotel: restaurant* ⊟*AE, DC, MC, V* ⦿*BP.*

SPORTS & THE OUTDOORS

The Soča is a prime fishing spot. The river is well stocked with marble trout, rainbow trout, and grayling. However, if you want to fish, bring your own equipment—or be prepared to buy it here—as it is almost impossible to rent. You also need to buy a day permit; for details inquire at Hotel Hvala. The season runs from April through October.

X Point (⊠*Trg Svobode 6* ☎05/388–5308) organizes kayaking, rafting, and canyoning trips and also rents out mountain bikes. In Srpenica, 13 km (8 mi) northwest of Kobarid, **Alpine Action** (⊠*Trnovo ob Soči, Srpenica* ☎05/388–5022) arranges river trips and rents bikes.

There's More to Žlikrofi Than Meets the Eye

Slovenian cooking may seem fairly simple at first, but there's often a lot more work that goes on behind the scenes than you might think. If you travel near the town of Idrija, look out especially for the delicious žlikrofi on many local menus. The pasta dish has been a regional specialty since the mid-1800s, when it was a favorite of hungry miners working the local mercury shafts. But don't be deceived by the relatively simple stuffed tortellini that arrive on your plate; rest assured a lot of effort went on in the kitchen beforehand. In fact, the process is so involved that a couple of years ago the Ministry of Tourism decided to set up a special certification process. Only inns and restaurants that abide by the rules can call their product authentic Idrija žlikrofi. So how to tell the echt from the fake? The ministry sets out the following: the filling must be a mix of potatoes, smoked bacon, onions, spice, and herbs. The filling is then formed into balls the size of a hazelnut and placed on a sheet of thin dough. The dough is folded over and pressed together between the balls so that, to quote, "a sort of ear shape is gained." The ministry also advises not to push the dough down too hard so as to leave the žlikrofi looking like they're wearing a little hat. The ministry doesn't say what the penalty is for the hapless gostilna that breaks the rules. Rest assured, however, that whatever shape your žlikrofi arrive in, they're likely to be delicious—served as a side or as a main course with cheese or mushroom sauce.

IDRIJA

50 km (31 mi) from Kobarid, 60 km (37 mi) from Ljubljana.

Proceed south from Kobarid, passing through the town of Tolmin and on to Idrija, a former mercury-mining town with some interesting sites, excellent food, and one of the country's most beautiful old hotels. Idrija is also known for its handmade lace.

Head to **Anthony's Shaft** to see the oldest part of the mercury mine, the miners' chapel dating back to the 18th century, and a video about the way the miners once lived. ⊠ *Kosovelova 3* ☎ *05/377–1142* ☉ *Tours weekdays at 10 and 4; weekends at 10, 3, and 4.*

WHERE TO STAY & EAT

★ $$ ✕ **Gostilna Kos.** This old-fashioned inn reputedly serves some of the best *Idrija žlikrofi* (tortellini filled with potato, onion, and bacon) around. You can have yours served as a side with roast pork or goulash, or as a main course served plain or topped with sauce. ⊠ *Tomšičeva 4* ☎ *05/372–2030* ⊟ *AE, DC, MC, V.*

$$–$$$$ 🏨 **Kendov Dvorec.** This exclusive 14th-century manor house is in Spod-
Fodor'sChoice nje Idrija, 4 km (2½ mi) from Idrija. Each bedroom is individually dec-
★ orated with 19th-century antiques and details such as bed linens edged with local handmade lace. Reserve a room well in advance because the reputation of this hotel keeps it full. The restaurant is not open to the public, but the owners will prepare a special meal if you phone ahead. ⊠ *Spodnje Idrija, 5280* ☎ *05/372–5100* ⊕ *www.kendov-dvorec.com*

11 rooms ⚒ *In-room: dial-up. In-hotel: restaurant, no elevator* ☰ *AE, DC, MC, V* ⦿|*BP.*

SHOPPING

Numerous boutiques sell *Idrijska čipka* (Idrija lace). For the most original designs try **Studio Irma Vončina** (✉ *Mestni trg 17* ☎ *05/377–1584*). It's open weekdays 10 to noon and 1 to 4, Saturday 10 to noon.

12

ALPS & THE SOČA VALLEY ESSENTIALS

BUS TRAVEL

Hourly buses link Ljubljana to Bled, Bohinj, and Kranjska Gora. There are also several buses daily from Ljubljana through Idrija to Kobarid and on to Bovec. The resorts are linked by local buses; their frequency depends on the season. For schedule and fare information ask at a local tourist-information center.

CAR TRAVEL

From Ljubljana a four-lane highway (E61) runs northwest past Kranj and continues—occasionally reverting to a two-lane highway on some stretches—to the resorts of Bled and Kranjska Gora. Lake Bohinj lies 25 km (16 mi) southwest of Bled along local highway 209. The Vrsic Pass, which connects Kranjska Gora and Bovec, is closed during the winter. If you want to go to Idrija, Kobarid, or Bovec from November to April, you will have to approach them via the south.

TRAIN TRAVEL

In theory it is possible to reach the area from Ljubljana by train, but because Bled Jezero station lies some distance from Lake Bled, and Bohinjska Bistrica station lies even farther from Lake Bohinj, it is simpler and quicker to take the bus.

From mid-June to mid-September ABC Rent-a-Car in Ljubljana arranges trips on an old-fashioned steam locomotive, following the Bohinj line, through the Soča Valley. The trip begins from Jesenice, stops in Bled and Bohinjska Bistrica, and finally brings you to Most na Soči. This is a very family-friendly excursion.

Information ABC Rent-a-Car (✉ *Ulica Jožeta Jame 16, Ljubljana* ☎ *01/510–4320*).

VISITOR INFORMATION

Information Bled Tourist Information (✉ *C. Svobode 15, Bled* ☎ *04/574–1122* ⊕ *www.bled.si*). **Bohinj Tourist Information** (✉ *Ribčev Laz 48, Bohinj* ☎ *04/574–6010* ⊕ *www.bohinj.si*). **Idrija Tourist Information** (✉ *Lapajnetova 7, Idrija* ☎ *05/377–3898* ⊕ *www.rzs-idrija.si*). **Kobarid Tourist Information** (✉ *Gregorčičeva 10, Kobarid* ☎ *05/389–9200* ⊕ *www.kobarid.si*). **Kranjska Gora Tourist Information** (✉ *Tičarjeva 2, Kranjska Gora* ☎ *04/588–1768* ⊕ *www.kranjska-gora.si*).

THE KARST & ADRIATIC COAST

As you move south and west from Ljubljana toward the Adriatic, the breeze feels warmer, the air smells fresher, and the landscape looks less and less like Austria and more and more like Italy.

The word "Karst," or in Slovenian *Kras,* is both a geological and geographic term referring to the large limestone plateau stretching roughly from Nova Gorica in the north to well beyond Divača in the south. It is bordered on the west by the Italian frontier and on the east by the fertile, wine-growing Vipava valley. The Karst is typified by sinkholes, underground caves, and streams. The region is dotted by caves, including two—Postojna and especially Škocjan—of jaw-dropping beauty and size.

To most Slovenians, the word "Karst," conjures up two things: *pršut* (air-dried ham) and blood-red Teran wine. The two pair beautifully, especially with a plate of cheese and a basket of homemade bread, taken at a traditional *osmica,* a small farmhouse restaurant. Teran is a strong wine made from the refosk grape that you will either love or loathe from the first sip. It takes its name from the *terra rossa,* or red soil, that typifies the Karst.

For visitors, the Karst is ideal for low-key exploration. The gentle terrain and the many wine roads (look for the sign that reads *vinska cesta*) are perfect for leisurely walks or bike rides. Several wine roads can be found in the area around the town of Komen and along the main road from Komen to Dutovlje. The pretty towns—with their old stone churches and red-tiled roofs—are a delight. If you have wheels, visit Stanjel to the east of Komen. It's a nearly abandoned hilltop village that's found new life as a haven for artists. The Lipica stud farm—the original breeding ground of the famed Lipizzaner horses of Vienna's Spanish Riding School—is an excellent base.

A little farther on, Slovenia's tiny piece of the Adriatic coast gives tourists a welcome chance to swim and sunbathe. Backed by hills planted with olive groves and vineyards, the small strip is only 47 km (29 mi) long and dominated by the towns of Koper, Izola, Piran, and Portorož.

Following centuries of Venetian rule, the coast remains culturally and spiritually connected to Italy, and Italian is still widely spoken. The medieval port of Piran is a gem and a must-see. Its Venetian core is nearly perfectly preserved. Portorož is a classic fun-and-sun resort. Koper, Slovenia's largest port, and Izola, its biggest fishery, are workaday towns that nevertheless retain a lot of historical charm. For beachgoers the best-equipped beach is at Bernadin, between Piran and Portorož. The most unspoiled stretch of coast is at the Strunjan Nature Reserve—which also has an area reserved for nudists—between Piran and Izola.

Piran and Portorož are very different in character, but either can serve as an excellent base depending on what you plan to do. Choose Portorož if your primary interest is swimming and sunbathing, or if

The Karst Region &
the Adriatic Coast

12

you're seeking a modern hotel with all of the amenities. Pick Piran if you're looking for something quainter, quieter, and more starkly beautiful. Whatever you choose, you can travel easily between the two. Buses make the 10-minute trip at least once an hour in season.

Both Piran and Portorož fill to capacity in July and August, so try to arrange accommodation in advance. If you show up without a room, inquire at one of the privately run travel agencies. Along the coast, these are likely to be more helpful than the local tourist-information centers.

POSTOJNSKA JAMA

44 km (27 mi) from Ljubljana.

☾ **Postojnska Jama** *(Postojna Cave)* conceals one of the largest networks of caves in the world, with 23 km (14 mi) of underground passageways. A miniature train takes you through the first 7 km (4½ mi), to reveal a succession of well-lighted rock formations. This strange underground world is home of the snakelike "human fish" on view in an aquarium in the Great Hall. Eyeless and colorless because of countless millennia of life in total darkness, these amphibians can live for up to 60 years. Temperatures average 8°C (46°F) year-round, so bring a sweater, even in summer. Tours leave every hour on the hour throughout the year. ⊠ *Jamska 30, Postojna* ☎ *05/700–0163* ⊕ *www.postojna-cave. com* 🎟 *€18* ☾ *May–Sept., daily 8:30–6; Apr. and Oct., daily 8:30–5; Nov.–Mar., weekdays 9:30–1:30, weekends 9:30–3.*

ŠKOCJANSKE JAME

26 km (16 mi) from Postojna, 76 km (47 mi) from Ljubljana.

Fodor'sChoice
★
☾
The 11 interconnected chambers that make up the **Škocjan Jama** *(Škocjanske Caves)* stretch for almost 6 km (about 4 mi) through a dramatic, subterranean landscape so unique that UNESCO has named them a World Heritage Site. The 90-minute walking tour of the two

chilly main chambers—the Silent Cave and the Murmuring Cave—winds past otherworldly dripstone sculptures, massive sinkholes, and stalactites and stalagmites that resemble the horns of some mythic creature. The highlight is Europe's largest cave hall, a gorge 479 feet high, 404 feet wide, and 984 feet long, spanned by a narrow bridge lighted with footlights. Far below, the brilliant jade waters of the Reka River rush by on their underground journey. The view is nothing short of mesmerizing. ⊠ *Škocjan 2, Divača* ☎ *05/763–2840* ⊕ *www.park-skocjanske-jame.si* 🎫 *€11* ⊙ *June–Sept., daily at 10, 11:30, and 1–5 (tours leave hourly); Apr., May, and Oct., tours daily at 10, 1, and 3:30; Nov.–Mar., tours at 10 and 1.*

LIPICA

5 km (3 mi) west of Divača, 30 km (19 mi) south of Stanjel, 80 km (50 mi) from Ljubljana.

Lipica is best known as the home of the *Kobilarna Lipica,* the Lipica Stud farm, where the fabled white Lipizzaner horses were first bred. The horse farm is still the primary reason most people come here, though the area has developed into a modern sports complex, with two hotels, a popular casino, an indoor pool, tennis courts, and an excellent 9-hole golf course. It makes a pleasant, hassle-free base for exploring the nearby Škocjan caves and Karst region. The horses, the large areas of green, and the facilities of the Hotel Maestoso—including a pool—are all great for families with children.

🐣 The **Kobilarna Lipica** *(Lipica Stud Farm)* was founded in 1580 by the Austrian archduke Karl II. It's where the white Lipizzaners—the majestic horses of the famed Spanish Riding School in Vienna—originated. Today the farm no longer sends its horses to Vienna, but breeds them for its own performances and riding instruction. The impressive stables and grounds are open to the public. Riding classes are available, but lessons are geared toward experienced riders and must be booked in advance. ⊠ *Lipica 5, Sežana, 6210* ☎ *05/739–1708* ⊕ *www.lipica.org* ⊙ *Dressage performances June–Oct., Tues., Fri., and Sun. at 3. Stable tours July and Aug., daily 9–6; Apr.–June and Sept. and Oct., daily 10–5; Nov.–Mar., daily 11–3.*

WHERE TO EAT

$$–$$$ ✕ **Gostilna Muha.** A friendly, family-run tavern in the village of Lokev is about 4 km (2 mi) from the Lipica stud farm. Sit back and allow the proprietor to suggest the day's specialties. A good starter is *jota,* followed by slow-roasted pork and a green salad topped with a spoonful of beans. ⊠ *Lokev 138, Lokev* ☎ *05/767–0055* ▤ *No credit cards.*

KOPER

50 km 31 mi) southwest of Divača (Lipica), 105 km (65 mi) to Ljubljana.

Today a port town surrounded by industrial suburbs, Koper nevertheless warrants a visit. The Republic of Venice made Koper the regional capital during the 15th and 16th centuries, and the magnificent architecture of the Old Town bears witness to the spirit of those times.

The most important buildings are clustered around **Titov trg**, the central town square. Here stands the **Cathedral,** which can be visited daily from 7 to noon and 3 to 7, with its fine Venetian Gothic facade and bell tower dating back to 1664. Across the square the splendid **Praetor's Palace,** formerly the seat of the Venetian Grand Council, combines Gothic and Renaissance styles. From the west side of Titov trg, the narrow, cobbled **Kidriceva ulica** brings you down to the seafront.

OFF THE BEATEN PATH

Hrastovlje. Hidden behind the 16th-century defensive walls of this small town is the tiny Romanesque **Cerkev sveti Trojice** (Church of the Holy Trinity). The interior is decorated with a remarkable series of frescoes, including the bizarre *Dance Macabre,* completed in 1490. The church is locked, but if you ask in the village the locals will be glad to open it for you. From Koper take the main road toward Ljubljana; then follow the signs for Hrastovlje (22 km [14 mi] from Koper).

WHERE TO EAT

$$$–$$$$ ✕**Skipper.** Noted for its vast summer terrace overlooking the marina, Skipper is popular with the yachting fraternity. The menu includes pasta dishes, risottos, grilled meats, and fish. ⊠*Kopališko nab 3* ☎*05/626–1810* ☲*AE, DC, MC, V.*

IZOLA

6 km (4 mi) from Koper, 112 km (70 mi) from Ljubljana.

Izola is a normally placid fishing town that lets its hair down in summer. DJs decamp from Ljubljana for parties on the coast, artists set up their studios, and the city adopts the relaxed persona of a shaggy beach town. Less industrial than Koper and less self-consciously pretty than Piran, Izola makes a perfect day outing.

It's also a great place to eat. Unlike Piran, where the seafront restaurants cater almost exclusively to tourists, Izola's harbor restaurants are the real deal. The fish is fresh and the customers—many of them local Slovenes—are demanding.

Like that of its immediate neighbor, Koper, the city's history goes back hundreds of years. Izola rose to prominence in the Middle Ages and then declined in the 16th and 17th centuries with the rise of the port of Trieste in present-day Italy. The name "Izola" comes from the Italian word for "island" and describes a time when the walled city in fact was an island. The city walls were knocked down by the French occupation at the start of the 19th century. The bricks were then used to connect the city to the mainland.

WHERE TO EAT

The best restaurants are situated along the marina. The restaurants fill quickly in the evenings, so go early to be assured of a table.

$$–$$$$ ✗**Ribič.** This is the local favorite. The day's catch and prices are listed on a chalkboard out front. If in doubt, ask the server what looks good that day. You can be sure the fish is fresh, but watch the prices. The fish are sold by weight, and you may end up paying more than you intended. ✉ *Veliki trg 3* ☎*05/641–8313* ▤*AE, DC, MC, V.*

NIGHTLIFE

During summer, the Adriatic coast becomes a haven for all-night parties. **Ambasada Gavioli** (✉*Izola* ☎*05/641–8212* ⊕*www.ambasada-gavioli.com*) remains one of the coast's—and the country's—best dance clubs. Gavioli regularly brings in DJs from around the world to play techno, trance, funk, and fusion. You'll find it southwest of the port in the city's industrial area.

PORTOROŽ

7 km (4 mi) from Izola, 124 km (77 mi) from Ljubljana.

Portorož is the most popular of Slovenia's seaside resorts. The name—Port of Roses—recalls the time, a hundred years ago, when it was an exclusive haunt for Austro-Hungarian aristocrats. Those days, however, are long gone. Portorož today definitely caters to the everyman. Here you'll find chock-a-block hotels, restaurants, bars, casinos, and nightclubs—all of the things you associate with a modern package-vacation destination.

Portorož is difficult to grasp at first. The central area is small, although hotels and resorts spread out in all directions along the coast and the surrounding hills. Most of the action takes place along a small stretch of seacoast. Here you'll find the public beaches (which charge a small fee to swim), a pool, and a string of shops and low-priced eateries.

WHERE TO STAY & EAT

Staying in Portorož is expensive, but the hotel standards are high. Many hotels offer cheaper package deals when booked in advance. If you are looking for a cheaper option on accommodations, book a room through **Maona** (✉*Obala 14b, Portorož* ☎*05/674–0363* ⊕*www.maona.si*), a local travel agency.

$$–$$$$ ✗**Ribič.** Enjoy good fresh fish in a relaxed garden setting, 2 km 1 mi) down the coast from Portorož at Seča. ✉*Seča 143, Seča* ☎*05/677–0790* ▤*AE, DC, MC, V* ⊗*Closed Tues.*

$$$$ ⊡ **Grand Hotel Palace.** This modern seaside hotel is connected to the thermal-spa recreation center, which offers massages and medicinal treatments. Rooms are comfortable, and the service is professional. Three other hotels are adjacent in the same complex and interconnected, offering a similar level of service. This is the most expensive of the four. ⊠*Obala 43, 6320* ☏*05/696–1025* ⊕*www.hoteli-palace.si* ⤳*189 rooms, 7 suites* ⚭*In-hotel: 2 restaurants, bar, pools, spa, parking (fee)* ▤*AE, DC, MC, V* †○†*BP.*

PIRAN

12

3 km (2 mi) from Portorož, 126 km (78 mi) from Ljubljana.

The jewel of the Slovenian coast, the medieval walled Venetian town of Piran stands compact on a small peninsula, capped by a neo-Gothic lighthouse and presided over by a hilltop Romanesque cathedral. Narrow, winding, cobbled streets lead to the main square, Trg Tartini, which in turn opens out onto a charming harbor. Historically, Piran's wealth was based on salt making. Culturally, the town is known as the birthplace of the 17th-century violinist and composer Giuseppe Tartini.

If you are arriving by car, don't even try to negotiate the tiny lanes around the harbor. Instead leave the car in the lot outside of town, the lot farthest out has the cheapest long-term rates. A shuttle bus will then take you into town.

ᘓ The **Sergej Mašera Pomorski muzej** *(Sergej Mašera Maritime Museum)* tells the story of Piran's connections with the sea. There is a beautiful collection of model ships, sailors' uniforms, and shipping instruments, and a fascinating historical section on the town's changing affiliations over the centuries. ⊠*Cankarjevo nab 3* ☏*05/671–0040* 🎫*€3.50* ⊗*Maritime Museum Apr.–June and Nov.–Mar., Tues.–Sun. 9–noon and 3–6; July and Aug., Tues.–Sun. 9–noon and 6–9.*

WHERE TO STAY & EAT

Piran's waterfront is filled with romantic, open-air restaurants. The quality of the food and the relatively high prices are pretty much uniform. The best advice is to stroll the walk and see which one appeals. Better food at better prices can be found away from the shore, although then you sacrifice the view.

Piran has only a small number of hotels, and most visitors opt to stay in private rooms or pensions. In season, it's easiest and cheapest to book through the centrally located private travel agency **Maona** (⊠*Cankarjevo nab 7, Piran* ☏*05/673–4520* ⊕*www.maona.si*), which offers doubles in private homes starting at around €50–€60 a night. The rate will be higher for stays of fewer than three nights. Ask for something central and look at the room before accepting; some rooms can be charming, but others are just basic.

$$–$$$ ✕**Gostilnica.** The most intimate of the seafront restaurants is situated toward the end of the promenade. It's a good place to try the *škampi rižot* (scampi risotto), or another favorite, *njoki s skampi in gorgonzola* (shrimp gnocchi with Gorgonzola sauce). ⊠*Prepernovo nab* ☏*05/673–2226* ▤*AE, DC, MC, V.*

★ $$–$$$ ✕**Neptun.** Highly regarded by the locals, this tiny, family-run place focuses on all manner of fish, grilled or fried. Try the grilled shrimp or calamari. In summer you can dine at tables along the quiet street. ✉*Župančičeva 7* ☏*05/673–4111* ▭*No credit cards.*

$–$$ ⊞**Hotel Piran.** A modern building on a quiet patch of coastline close to the seaside restaurants, Hotel Piran is the best place to stay if a sea view is what you're after. Breakfast is served on a rooftop terrace, where you can enjoy stunning views of the Adriatic. ✉*Kidričevo nab 4, 6330* ☏*05/676–2502* ⊕*www.hoteli-piran.si* ⇗*80 rooms, 10 suites* ⚙*In-room: no a/c, refrigerator (some). In-hotel: bar, public Internet, some pets allowed* ▭*AE, MC, V* ⎸⊙⎹*BP.*

★ $ ⊞**Hotel Tartini.** An old facade hides a modern interior with a spacious central atrium. Most rooms have terraces that open out to views of the surrounding red-tiled roofs or the harbor. The location, overlooking Trg Tartini, is out of this world. If you can live without being on the seafront, this is your best option in town. ✉*Trg Tartini 15, 6330* ☏*05/671–1000* ⊕*www.hotel-tartini-piran.com* ⇗*43 rooms, 2 suites* ⚙*In-room: refrigerator. In-hotel: restaurant* ▭*AE, DC, MC, V* ⎸⊙⎹*BP.*

THE ARTS

Piran Musical Evenings are held in the cloisters of the Minorite Monastery every Friday in July and August. The **Primorski Summer Festival** of open-air theater and dance is staged in Piran, Koper, Portorož, and Izola.

THE KARST & ADRIATIC COAST ESSENTIALS

BOAT TRAVEL

During summer, it is possible to reach the Slovenian coast by regularly scheduled ferry service from Italy.

BUS TRAVEL

Several buses a day connect Ljubljana to Koper, Piran, and Portorož, passing through Postojna and Divača on the way. There is also a daily service connecting the coastal towns to Trieste, Italy.

A network of local buses connects all listed sights, with the exception of those in Štanjel and Lipica. Schedules vary depending on the time of year, so contact a local bus station for information.

CAR TRAVEL

A car is advisable for touring the Karst region. However, parking can be a problem along the coast during summer, when town centers are closed to traffic. The E63 highway connects Ljubljana to the coast, passing through the Karst region en route.

TRAIN TRAVEL

Four trains daily link Ljubljana and Koper, passing through Postojna and Divača en route.

VISITOR INFORMATION
Information Štanjel Tourist Information (⊠ *Štanjel Grad, Štanjel* ☎ *05/769–0056* ⊕ *www.komen.si*). **Koper Tourist Information** (⊠ *Ukmarjev trg 7, Koper* ☎ *05/664–6230* ⊕ *www.koper.si*). **Izola Tourist Information** (⊠ *Sončno nab. 4; Izola* ☎ *05/640–1050* ⊕ *www.izola.si*). **Lipica Tourist Information** (⊠ *Lipica 5, Lipica* ☎ *05/739–1580* ⊕ *www.lipica.org*). **Piran Tourist Information** (⊠ *Trg Tartini 2, Piran* ☎ *05/673–4440* ⊕ *www.piran.com*). **Portorož Tourist Information** (⊠ *Obala 16, Portorož* ☎ *05/674–0220* ⊕ *www.portoroz.si*). **Postojna Tourist Information** (⊠ *Jamska 30, Postojna* ☎ *05/700–0100* ⊕ *www.postojna-cave.com*).

SLOVENIA ESSENTIALS

To research prices, get advice from other travelers, and book travel arrangements, visit www.fodors.com.

TRANSPORTATION

BY AIR
There are no direct flights between the United States and Slovenia. The Slovenian national carrier, Adria Airways, flies from many Western European cities to Ljubljana Airport. Adria also has flights to the capitals of other ex-Yugoslav republics from Ljubljana. Adria is a regional carrier of the Star Alliance, linking it with the extensive networks of Austrian Airways, United Airlines, Lufthansa, Air Canada, and LOT, among others. In Slovenia, tickets can be purchased by phone and delivered anywhere in the country in 24 hours.

Aeroflot, Air France, Austrian Airways, Finnair, Hungary's Malev, Serbia's JAT, Turkish Airlines, Ukraine Airlines, Czech Airlines, and Poland's LOT all now offer regular connections to Ljubljana from their respective capital cities. Low-cost airlines have added flights from London's Stansted airport (easyJet, flying to Ljubljana, and Ryanair, flying to Maribor) and Brussels (Wizz Air).

Information Adria Airways (⊠ *Kuzmičeva 7, Ljubljana* ☎ *01/369–1010* ⊕ *www.adria-airways.com*). **Aeroflot** (⊠ *Dunajska cesta 21, Ljubljana* ☎ *01/230–7560* ⊕ *www.aeroflot.ru*). **Air France** (⊠ *Kuzmičeva 5, Ljubljana* ☎ *01/244–3447* ⊕ *www.airfrance.com*). **Austrian Airlines** (⊠ *Čopova 11, Ljubljana* ☎ *01/244–3060* ⊕ *www.aua.com*). **Czech Airlines/CSA** (⊠ *Brnik Airport Terminal, Brnik* ☎ *04/206–1750* ⊕ *www.czechairlines.cz*). **EasyJet** (☎ *04/206–1677* ⊕ *www.easyjet.com*). **Finnair** (☎ *08/01300* ⊕ *www.finnair.com*). **JAT** (⊠ *Slomškova 1, Ljubljana* ☎ *01/231–4340* ⊕ *www.jat.com*). **LOT** (⊠ *Brnik airport terminal, Brnik* ☎ *04/259–4252* ⊕ *www.lot.com*). **Lufthansa** (⊠ *Gosposvetska 6, Ljubljana* ☎ *01/239–1900* ⊕ *www.lufthansa.com*). **Malev** (⊠ *Brnik airport terminal, Brnik* ☎ *04/206–1665* ⊕ *www.malev.hu*). **Ryanair** (⊕ *www.ryanair.com*). **Turkish Airlines** (☎ *04/206–1680* ⊕ *www.turkishairlines.com*). **Ukraine International Airlines** (⊕ *www.flyuia.com*).

AIRPORTS & TRANSFERS
The Ljubljana Airport is at Brnik, 25 km (16 mi) north of the city. The Maribor airport is at Slivnica, 9 km (6 mi) to the south.

Information Ljubljana Airport (✉ *Brnik* ☎ *04/206–1981* ⊕ *www.lju-airport.si*).
Maribor Airport (✉ *Slivnica* ☎ *02/629–1553* ⊕ *www.maribor-airport.si*).

TRANSFERS

Public bus service runs regularly between the airport and Ljubljana's main bus station in the city center. Buses depart from the airport every hour on the hour weekdays and slightly less frequently on weekends. Tickets cost around €4. A private airport shuttle makes the same run in slightly less time. Departures average every 90 minutes or so and the cost is €20. A taxi costs approximately €30. The ride takes about 30 minutes.

Information Ljubljana Airport Shuttle (☎ *040/887–766*).

BY BOAT & FERRY

From early March to late October the *Prince of Venice* high-speed catamaran makes regularly scheduled trips between Venice and Izola, with connecting bus service to Piran and Potorož. Kompas Travel in Potorož can make the booking. The trip takes 2½ hours.

Venezia Lines offers similar runs between Venice and Piran in season, and offers overnight hotel packages in Venice. Maona Travel in Piran can arrange this.

Information **Kompas** (✉ *Obala 41, Portorož* ☎ *05/617–8000* ⊕ *www.kompas-on-line.net*). **Maona** (✉ *Cankarjevo nab 7, Piran* ☎ *05/673–4520* ⊕ *www.maona.si*).

BY BUS

International and domestic bus lines and the Ljubljana municipal bus service all operate conveniently from the city's main bus terminal, not far from the center.

Private coach companies operate to and from Trieste in Italy and Zagreb in Croatia, as well as other European destinations farther afield. Domestic bus service is frequent from the capital to most Slovenian cities and towns (including most of the destinations in this guide). Outside of a car, the bus remains the only practical option to Bled and Bohinj and mountain destinations west and north of the capital. Except during peak travel periods, you can simply buy your ticket on the bus when you board. Otherwise, purchase tickets a day in advance with a reserved seat. Many buses do not run on Sunday.

Within Ljubljana, the municipal bus network is extensive, and service is frequent during weekdays. Service continues but is less frequent on Saturday, Sunday, and holidays. Buses on most lines stop running around 11 PM. To ride the bus, buy plastic bus tokens (*žetoni*) at kiosks and post offices, or simply pay the fare €1 in exact change to the driver.

Information Llubljana Bus Station (✉ *Trg OF 5, Ljubljana* ☎ *01/090–4230* ⊕ *www.ap-ljubljana.si*).

BY CAR

From Budapest and Vienna the Slovenian border is no more than a two-hour drive; from Prague it's eight hours. A tunnel speeds traffic through the Karavanke Alps between Slovenia and Austria. From Vienna the passage is by way of Maribor to Ljubljana, with a four-lane highway most of the way. Slovenia's roads also connect with Italy's *autostrada*.

You don't need a car if you are not planning to leave Ljubljana; however, traveling by car undoubtedly gives you the chance to reach remote areas of the country when and as you wish. Main roads between large towns are comparable to those in Western Europe. Toll plazas are frequent, so have small bills and change handy.

12

Gas stations on border crossings and main roads leading to larger towns are open 24 hours a day; others are open Monday through Saturday from 7 AM to 8 PM.

To rent a car you must have a license that is valid in the issuing country. A midsize car costs about €100 for 24 hours, with unlimited mileage—but much better rates are available for longer periods or if the car is booked in advance over the Internet. You'll also need a valid credit card. Rental agencies can be found in all major towns and at the Ljubljana Airport. *See Car Rentals in Llubljana Essentials.*

Information AMZS-Hertz (⊠ *Dunajska 122, Ljubljana* ☎ *01/530–5380* ⊕ *www. hertz.si*). **Avis** (⊠ *Čufarjeva 2, Ljubljana* ☎ *01/430–8010* ⊕ *www.avis.si*). **Budget** (⊠ *Miklošičeva 3, Ljubljana* ☎ *01/421–7340* ⊕ *www.budget.si*). **Dollar/Thrifty Car Rental** (⊠ *Brnik air terminal, Brnik* ☎ *04/236–5750* ⊕ *www.subrosa.hr*). **National Rent a Car** (⊠ *Baragova 5, Ljubljana* ☎ *01/588–4450* ⊕ *www.nationalcar-slovenia.com*).

RULES OF THE ROAD

Slovenes drive on the right and are obliged to keep their headlights on at all times. Speed limits are 50 kph (31 mph) in urban areas and 130 kph (81 mph) on highways. Local drivers are courteous by European standards. The permitted blood alcohol level is 0.05%; drivers caught exceeding this level can expect penalties similar to those of other European countries.

BY TAXI

Private taxis operate 24 hours a day. Phone from your hotel or hail one in the street. Drivers are bound by law to display and run a meter.

BY TRAIN

There are several trains daily to Venice (five hours), Vienna (six hours), and Budapest (eight hours). There is an overnight service to Prague (12 hours) and a rapid daytime EuroCity connection to Berlin (15 hours). The train station is just north of the city center.

Information Ljubljana Train station (⊠ *Trg OF 6, Ljubljana* ☎ *01/291–3332* ⊕ *www.slo-zeleznice.si*).

CONTACTS & RESOURCES

BANKS & EXCHANGE SERVICES

In major cities banks and ATMs are easy to find. Since Slovenia has adopted the euro as its official currency, you don't need to change money again if you are coming from another euro-zone country. Still, you may see that many prices are still listed in the former currency, the tolar (SIT), which traded at a rate of about 240 to the euro. Prices quoted in this chapter are in euros, unless otherwise noted.

EMBASSIES & CONSULATES
Information U.S. Embassy (⊠ *Prešernova 31, Ljubljana* ☎ *01/200–5500* ⊞ *01/200–5555*).

EMERGENCIES
Information Ambulance & Fire (☎ *112*). **Emergency Road Assistance** (☎ *987*). **Police** (☎ *113*). **Lekarna Miklošič Pharmacy** (⊠ *Miklošičeva 24, Ljubljana* ☎ *01/231–4558*). **Ljubljana Emergency Medical Services** (☎ *01/232–3060*).

INTERNET, MAIL & SHIPPING
Many hotels now set aside at least one terminal for guests to access the Internet—and some of the better places are now adding wireless Wi-Fi networks. Ljubljana has several Internet cafés (known locally as cybercafés), though these are harder to find in outlying cities and towns. Frequently cafés and bars will maintain a computer terminal or two and allow access for a fee—usually around €5 an hour.

Postage is assessed according to weight. The standard international letter rate, including airmail, is €.70 for very light letters, and €1.17 for standard size. Postcards sent abroad cost €.60. Post offices are open weekdays from 8 to 6 and Saturday from 8 to noon. Stamps are also sold at hotels, newsstands, and kiosks.

Information Xplorer CyberCafe (⊠ *Petkovškovo nab 23, Ljubljana* ☎ *01/430–1991*) is the best in town, centrally located and with long opening hours. **Val Hostel** (⊠ *Gregorčičeva 38a, Piran* ☎ *05/673–2555*), a charming hostel in the center of Piran, offers Internet access to nonguests for a nominal fee.

LANGUAGE
Slovene is the country's chief language. In the east, signs are posted in Slovene and Hungarian; on the Adriatic coast both Slovene and Italian are officially used. English, German, and Italian are spoken in many places. In Slovene the words for street (*ulica*) and drive (*cesta*) are abbreviated to ul and c. *Nabrežje* (abbreviated to nab) means "embankment." The word for square is *trg*.

PASSPORTS & VISAS
Valid passport holders from the United States do not need visas for stays of 30 days or less. Citizens of other countries must apply in advance for a 90-day visa from a Slovenian embassy or consulate.

TAXES
Visitors who buy goods worth more than €50 (about $70) at any one store on a single day are entitled to a refund of taxes, which can be as much as 16.67% in Slovenia. When you make a purchase, ask for a Request for V.A.T. Refund form, *Zahtevek za vracilo DDV*. A customs officer will certify the form when you leave the country. To obtain the refund, go to the Global Refund office at the border crossing point or the airport. Exporting historic artifacts is forbidden.

TELEPHONES

COUNTRY CODE

The country code for Slovenia is 386. When dialing from outside the country, drop any initial "0" from the area code.

12

INTERNATIONAL CALLS

To make international calls, dial "00" and then the appropriate country code (calls to the United States and Canada, for example, are preceded by "001"). International calls can be made from local telephones or post offices. For collect calls dial the operator. For international inquiries, dial international directory assistance.

Information International Directory Assistance (☎ *1180*). Operator (☎ *115*).

LOCAL CALLS

Pay phones take magnetic telephone cards, available from post offices and kiosks. Lower rates apply from 10 PM to 7 AM and all day Sunday.

Information Local Directory Assistance (☎ *1188*).

TIPPING

Although tax is already included in listed prices, tips are not included in restaurant bills, and a 10% tip is considered customary. If the service is especially good, tip 15%.

TOUR OPTIONS

Informative and amusing sightseeing walks, organized by the Ljubljana Promotion Center, depart from the Magistrat on Mestni trg daily, June through September. From October through May tours are on Sunday and can be booked through Ljubljana's Turistično Informacijski Center (⇨ *Visitor Information, below*).

TRAVEL AGENCIES

Local travel agencies often supplement the work of the official tourist information centers and can frequently help in booking excursions and finding rooms. In Bled and on the Adriatic coast, the local private agencies are the main source for finding private accommodation.

Information Emona Globtour (✉ *Baragova 5, Ljubljana* ☎ *01/588–4400* 🖷 *01/588–4455*). Kompas Turizem Ljubljana (✉ *Pražakova 4, Ljubljana* ☎ *01/200–6100* 🖷 *01/200–6434* ⊕ *www.kompas.si*). Promet T & T (✉ *Celovška 23, Ljubljana* ☎ *01/519–3511* 🖷 *01/519–5345*). Tirtur Ljubljana (✉ *Majorja Lavriča 12, Ljubljana* ☎ *01/519–8802* 🖷 *01/519–8809*).

VISITOR INFORMATION

Ljubljana's Turistično Informacijski Center (Tourist Information Center) is next to the Triple Bridge on the Old Town side. It's an excellent resource for maps, brochures, advice, and small souvenirs like postcards and T-shirts. It's open weekdays from 8 to 7, Saturday 9 to 5, and Sunday 10 to 6. If you are arriving by train, the TIC kiosk in the train station can help you find accommodations. It's open daily from

8 AM to 9 PM from June through September and 10 to 6 from October through May.

The Slovenian Tourist Board provides information and produces excellent publications on all kinds of tourist activities throughout the country. Each region also has its own tourist-information center. *For individual centers, see Visitor Information in regional Essentials sections.*

Information Slovenian Tourist Information Center (⊠ *Krekov trg 10, Ljubljana, 1000* ☎ *01/306–4575* ⊕ *www.slovenia.info).* Turistično Informacijski Center (*Tourist Information Center [TIC]* ⊠ *Stritarjeva, Ljubljana* ☎ *01/306–1215* ⊕ *www. ljubljana.si).* TIC kiosk (⊠ *Trg OF 6, Ljubljana* ☎ *01/433–9475).*

Eastern and Central Europe Essentials

PLANNING TOOLS, EXPERT INSIGHT,
GREAT CONTACTS

There are planners and there are those who, excuse the pun, fly by the seat of their pants. We happily place ourselves among the planners. Our writers and editors try to anticipate all the issues you may face before and during any journey, and then they do their research. This section is the product of their efforts. Use it to get excited about your trip to Eastern and Central Europe, to inform your travel planning, or to guide you on the road should the seat of your pants start to feel threadbare.

GETTING STARTED

We're really proud of our Web site: Fodors.com is a great place to begin any journey. Scan Travel Wire for suggested itineraries, travel deals, restaurant and hotel openings, and other up-to-the-minute info. Check out Booking to research prices and book plane tickets, hotel rooms, rental cars, and vacation packages. Head to Talk for on-the-ground pointers from travelers who frequent our message boards. You can also link to loads of other travel-related resources.

■ RESOURCES

ONLINE TRAVEL TOOLS

All About Eastern & Central Europe Austrian National Tourist Office (⊕www.austria. info). **Bulgarian State Agency for Tourism** (⊕www.bulgariatravel.org). **Croatian National Tourist Office** (⊕www.croatia.hr). **Czech Tourism** (⊕www.visitczechia.cz). **German National Tourist Office** (⊕www.ComeTo-Germany.com). **Hungarian National Tourist Office** (⊕www.hungary.com or Tourinform.hu). **National Tourism Organization of Montenegro** (⊕www.visit-montenegro.org). **Polish National Tourist Office** (⊕www.polandtour. org). Romania: **Romania National Tourist Office** (⊕www.romaniatourism.com). **Slovakia Tourist Board** (⊕www.slovakia.travel). **Slovenian Tourist Board** (⊕www.slovenia. info). **Tourism Association of Bosnia & Herzegovina** (⊕www.bhtourism.ba).

Currency Conversion Google (⊕www. google.com) does currency conversion. Just type in the amount you want to convert and an explanation of how you want it converted (e.g., "14 Swiss francs in dollars"), and then voilà. **Oanda.com** (⊕www.oanda.com) also allows you to print out a handy table with the current day's conversion rates. **XE.com** (⊕www.xe.com) is a good currency conversion Web site.

Safety Transportation Security Administration (TSA; ⊕www.tsa.gov).

Time Zones Timeanddate.com (⊕www.timeanddate.com/worldclock) can help you figure out the correct time anywhere.

Weather Accuweather.com (⊕www.accuweather.com) is an independent weather-forecasting service with good coverage of hurricanes. **Weather.com** (⊕www.weather.com) is the Web site for the Weather Channel.

VISITOR INFORMATION

CONTACTS

Austria Austrian National Tourist Office (☎212/944-6880 ⊕www.austria.info).

Bosnia & Herzegovina Tourism Association of Bosnia & Herzegovina (⊕www.bhtourism.ba).

Bulgaria Bulgarian State Agency for Tourism (☎212/573-5530 ⊕www.bulgariatravel.org).

Croatia Croatian National Tourist Office (☎212/279-8672 ⊕www.croatia.hr).

Czech Republic Czech Tourism (☎212/288-0830 ⊕www.visitczechia.cz).

Germany German National Tourist Office (☎212/661-7200 ⊕www.ComeToGermany.com).

Hungary Hungarian National Tourist Office (☎212/355-0240 🖷212/695-1221 ⊕www.hungary.com or Tourinform.hu).

Montenegro National Tourism Organization of Montenegro (⊕www.visit-montenegro.org).

Poland Polish National Tourist Office (☎201/420-9910 🖷212/338-9283 ⊕www.polandtour.org).

Romania Romanian National Tourist Office (☎212/545-8484 ⊕www.romaniatourism.com).

Slovakia Slovakia Tourist Board (⊕www.slovakia.travel).

Slovenia Slovenian Tourist Board (⊕www.slovenia.info).

▌ THINGS TO CONSIDER

GOVERNMENT ADVISORIES

As different countries have different world views, look at travel advisories from a range of governments to get more of a sense of what's going on out there. And be sure to parse the language carefully. For example, a warning to "avoid all travel" carries more weight than one urging you to "avoid nonessential travel," and both are much stronger than a plea to "exercise caution." A U.S. government travel warning is more permanent (though not necessarily more serious) than a so-called public announcement, which carries an expiration date.

▌TIP→ Consider registering online with the State Department (https://travelregistration.state.gov/ibrs/), so the government will know to look for you should a crisis occur in the country you're visiting.

The U.S. Department of State's Web site has more than just travel warnings and advisories. The consular information sheets issued for every country have general safety tips, entry requirements (though be sure to verify these with the country's embassy), and other useful details.

At this writing, the U.S. Department of State has issued no Travel Warnings or Public Announcements regarding any country covered in this guide. The usual cautions about safety and security when traveling in an unfamiliar city or country apply to all these places, but in general crime in Central and Eastern Europe (even in those cities and regions where it's on the upswing) is lower than in the United States. You should always be aware of pickpockets, which can be a problem in busy tourist areas in all the major capitals of Central and Eastern Europe. See ⇨Safety in Essentials in each country chapter for destination-specific issues.

General Information & Warnings Australian Department of Foreign Affairs & Trade (⊕ www.smartraveller.gov.au). **Consular**

> **WORD OF MOUTH**
>
> After your trip, be sure to rate the places you visited and share your experiences and travel tips with us and other Fodorites in Travel Ratings and Talk on www.fodors.com.

Affairs Bureau of Canada (⊕ www.voyage. gc.ca). **U.K. Foreign & Commonwealth Office** (⊕ www.fco.gov.uk/travel). **U.S. Department of State** (⊕ www.travel.state.gov).

PASSPORTS & VISAS

Americans can travel throughout Central and Eastern Europe with a valid passport, though specific requirements about passport validity differ by country. Some of these countries are now members of the EU, but some are not.

See the Essentials section at the end of each country chapter for specific entrance requirements.

U.S. Passport Information U.S. Department of State (☎ 877/487–2778 ⊕ http://travel. state.gov/passport).

U.S. Passport & Visa Expediters A. Briggs Passport & Visa Expeditors (☎ 800/ 806–0581 or 202/338–0111 ⊕ www. abriggs.com). **American Passport Express** (☎ 800/455–5166 or 800/841–6778 ⊕ www.americanpassport.com). **Passport Express** (☎ 800/362–8196 ⊕ www. passportexpress.com). **Travel Document Systems** (☎ 800/874–5100 or 202/638–3800 ⊕ www.traveldocs.com). **Travel the World Visas** (☎ 866/886–8472 or 301/495–7700 ⊕ www.world-visa.com).

SHOTS & MEDICATIONS

No vaccinations are required for entry into any of the Eastern and Central European countries covered in this book, but selective vaccinations are recommended. Those traveling in forested areas of most Eastern and Central European countries should consider vaccinating themselves against Central European, or tick-borne, encephalitis. Avian flu has been reported in several countries in the region, so trav-

Insurance Resources

COMPREHENSIVE TRAVEL INSURERS		
Access America	800/729-6021	www.accessamerica.com
CSA Travel Protection	800/873-9855	www.csatravelprotection.com
HTH Worldwide	610/254-8700 or 888/243-2358	www.hthworldwide.com
Travelex Insurance	800/228-9792	www.travelex-insurance.com
Travel Guard International	715/345-0505 or 800/826-4919	www.travelguard.com
Travel Insured International	800/243-3174	www.travelinsured.com
INSURANCE COMPARISON SITES		
Insure My Trip.com		www.insuremytrip.com
Square Mouth.com		www.quotetravelinsurance.com
MEDICAL-ONLY INSURERS		
International Medical Group	800/628-4664	www.imglobal.com
International SOS		www.internationalsos.com
Wallach & Company	800/237-6615 or 540/687-3166	www.wallach.com

elers should use the typical precaution of frequent hand-washing and other good-hygiene practices to minimize the chance of infection. Tick-borne Lyme disease is also a risk in the Czech Republic. If you plan to travel for an extended period of time in rural Bulgaria, it is a good idea to consider vaccinations for hepatitis A and B, spread through food and water. Schedule vaccinations well in advance of departure because some require several doses, and others may cause uncomfortable side effects.

For more information see Health under On the Ground in Eastern and Central Europe, below.

■TIP→ **If you travel a lot internationally—particularly to developing nations—refer to the CDC's** *Health Information for International Travel* **(aka Traveler's Health Yellow Book). Info from it is posted on the CDC Web site (www.cdc.gov/travel/yb), or you can buy a copy from your local bookstore for $24.95.**

Health Warnings National Centers for Disease Control & Prevention (CDC ☎877/394-8747 international travelers' health line ⊕www.cdc.gov/travel). **World Health Organization** (WHO ⊕www.who.int).

TRIP INSURANCE

What kind of coverage do you honestly need? Do you even need trip insurance at all? Take a deep breath and read on.

We believe that comprehensive trip insurance is especially valuable if you're booking a very expensive or complicated trip (particularly to an isolated region) or if you're booking far in advance. Who knows what could happen six months down the road? But whether or not you get insurance has more to do with how comfortable you are assuming all that risk yourself.

Comprehensive travel policies typically cover trip cancellation and interruption, letting you cancel or cut your trip short because of a personal emergency, illness, or, in some cases, acts of terrorism in your destination. Such policies also cover evacuation and medical care. Some also cover you for trip delays because of bad weather or mechanical problems as well as for lost or delayed baggage. Another type of coverage to look for is financial default—that is, when your trip is disrupted because a tour operator, airline, or cruise line goes out of business. Generally you must buy this when you book your trip or shortly thereafter, and it's available to you only if your operator isn't on a list of excluded companies.

If you're going abroad, consider buying medical-only coverage at the very least. Neither Medicare nor some private insurers cover medical expenses anywhere outside of the United States (including time aboard a cruise ship, even if it leaves from a U.S. port). Medical-only policies typically reimburse you for medical care (excluding that related to preexisting conditions) and hospitalization abroad, and provide for evacuation. You still have to pay the bills and await reimbursement from the insurer, though.

Expect comprehensive travel insurance policies to cost about 4% to 7% or 8% of the total price of your trip (it's more like 8%–12% if you're over age 70). A medical-only policy may or may not be cheaper than a comprehensive policy. Always read the fine print of your policy to make sure that you are covered for the risks that are of most concern to you. Compare several policies to make sure you're getting the best price and range of coverage available.

BOOKING YOUR TRIP

Unless your cousin is a travel agent, you're probably among the millions of people who make most of their travel arrangements online.

But have you ever wondered just what the differences are between an online travel agent (a Web site through which you make reservations instead of going directly to the airline, hotel, or car-rental company), a discounter (a firm that does a high volume of business with a hotel chain or airline and accordingly gets good prices), a wholesaler (one that makes cheap reservations in bulk and then re-sells them to people like you), and an aggregator (one that compares all the offerings so you don't have to)?

Is it truly better to book directly on an airline or hotel Web site? And when does a real live travel agent come in handy?

▮ ONLINE

You really have to shop around. A travel wholesaler such as Hotels.com or Hotel-Club.net can be a source of good rates, as can discounters such as Hotwire or Priceline, particularly if you can bid for your hotel room or airfare. Indeed, such sites sometimes have deals that are unavailable elsewhere. They do, however, tend to work only with hotel chains (which makes them just plain useless for getting hotel reservations outside of major cities) or big airlines (so that often leaves out upstarts like jetBlue and some foreign carriers like Air India).

Also, with discounters and wholesalers you must generally prepay, and everything is nonrefundable. And before you fork over the dough, be sure to check the terms and conditions, so you know what a given company will do for you if there's a problem and what you'll have to deal with on your own.

■TIP➜ To be absolutely sure everything was processed correctly, confirm reservations made through online travel agents, discounters, and wholesalers directly with your hotel before leaving home.

Booking engines like Expedia, Travelocity, and Orbitz are actually travel agents, albeit high-volume, online ones. And airline travel packagers like American Airlines Vacations and Virgin Vacations—well, they're travel agents, too. But they may still not work with all the world's hotels.

An aggregator site will search many sites and pull the best prices for airfares, hotels, and rental cars from them. Most aggregators compare the major travel-booking sites such as Expedia, Travelocity, and Orbitz; some also look at airline Web sites, though rarely the sites of smaller budget airlines. Some aggregators also compare other travel products, including complex packages—a good thing, as you can sometimes get the best overall deal by booking an air-and-hotel package.

▮ WITH A TRAVEL AGENT

If you use an agent—brick-and-mortar or virtual—you'll pay a fee for the service. And know that the service you get from some online agent s isn't comprehensive. For example Expedia and Travelocity don't search for prices on budget airlines like jetBlue, Southwest, or small foreign carriers. That said, some agents (online or not) *do* have access to fares that are difficult to find otherwise, and the savings can more than make up for any surcharge.

A knowledgeable brick-and-mortar travel agent can be a godsend if you're booking a cruise, a package trip that's not available to you directly, an air pass, or a complicated itinerary including several overseas flights. What's more, travel agents who specialize in a destination may have exclusive access to certain deals and insider information on things such as charter flights. Agents who specialize in types of travelers (senior citizens, gays and lesbians, naturists) or types of trips (cruises, luxury travel, safaris) can also be invaluable.

■**TIP→** Remember that Expedia, Travelocity, and Orbitz are travel agents, not just booking engines. To resolve any problems with a reservation made through these companies, contact them first.

A top-notch agent planning your trip to Russia will make sure you get the correct visa application and complete it on time; the one booking your cruise may get you a cabin upgrade or arrange to have bottle of champagne chilling in your cabin when you embark. And complain about the surcharges all you like, but when things don't work out the way you'd hoped, it's nice to have an agent to put things right.

Agent Resources American Society of Travel Agents (☎703/739–2782 ⊕www. travelsense.org).

■ ACCOMMODATIONS

Luxury and business-class hotels are appearing with increasing rapidity throughout Central and Eastern Europe, and in the major capitals such as Prague, Budapest, and Warsaw, you may be pleasantly surprised at the number of upscale choices available to you. There are also baroque mansions-turned-guesthouses and elegant high-rise resorts, not to mention bed-and-breakfast inns presided over by matronly babushkas.

Outside major cities, hotels and inns are more rustic than elegant. Standards of service generally do not suffer, but in most rural areas the definition of "luxury" includes little more than a television and a private bathroom. In some instances, you may have no choice but to stay in one of the concrete high-rise hotels that scar skylines from Poland to the Czech

Republic. Huge, impersonal concrete hotels are part of the Communist legacy, but many of these ubiquitous monsters may surprise you with stylish and elegant interiors, in stark contrast to their exterior drabness. However, even in Bulgaria, where changes are very slow, new, luxurious hotels can be found in most regions of the country, if you're willing to pay Western prices.

In rural Eastern and Central Europe, prices are significantly lower than in the large cities, where you may pay hotel rates that are not so much less than those in Paris or Rome. Reservations are vital if you plan to visit Prague, Budapest, Warsaw, or most other major cities during the summer season. Reservations are a good idea but aren't imperative if you plan to strike out into the countryside.

The lodgings we list are the cream of the crop in each price category. We always list the facilities that are available, but we don't specify whether they cost extra; when pricing accommodations, always ask what's included and what costs extra. Properties are assigned price categories based on the range from their least-expensive standard double room at high season (excluding holidays) to the most expensive. Properties marked ✕▣ are lodging establishments whose restaurants warrant a special trip.

Most hotels and other lodgings require you to give your credit-card details before they will confirm your reservation. If you don't feel comfortable e-mailing this information, ask if you can fax it (some places even prefer faxes). However you book, get confirmation in writing and have a copy of it handy when you check in.

Be sure you understand the hotel's cancellation policy. Some places allow you to cancel without any kind of penalty— even if you prepaid to secure a discounted rate—if you cancel at least 24 hours in advance. Others require you to cancel a

Online Booking Resources

AGGREGATORS

Kayak	www.kayak.com	also looks at cruises and vacation packages.
Mobissimo	www.mobissimo.com	
Qixo	www.qixo.com	also compares cruises, vacation packages, and even travel insurance.
Sidestep	www.sidestep.com	also compares vacation packages and lists travel deals.
Travelgrove	www.travelgrove.com	also compares cruises and packages.

BOOKING ENGINES

Cheap Tickets	www.cheaptickets.com	a discounter.
Expedia	www.expedia.com	a large online agency that charges a booking fee for airline tickets.
Hotwire	www.hotwire.com	a discounter.
lastminute.com	www.lastminute.com	specializes in last-minute travel the main site is for the U.K., but it has a link to a U.S. site.
Luxury Link	www.luxurylink.com	has auctions (surprisingly good deals) as well as offers on the high-end side of travel.
Onetravel.com	www.onetravel.com	a discounter for hotels, car rentals, airfares, and packages.
Orbitz	www.orbitz.com	charges a booking fee for airline tickets, but gives a clear breakdown of fees and taxes before you book.
Priceline.com	www.priceline.com	a discounter that also allows bidding.
Travel.com	www.travel.com	allows you to compare its rates with those of other booking engines.
Travelocity	www.travelocity.com	charges a booking fee for airline tickets, but promises good problem resolution.

ONLINE ACCOMMODATIONS

Hotelbook.com	www.hotelbook.com	focuses on independent hotels worldwide.
Hotel Club	www.hotelclub.net	good for major cities worldwide.
Hotels.com	www.hotels.com	a big Expedia-owned wholesaler that offers rooms in hotels all over the world.
Quikbook	www.quikbook.com	offers "pay when you stay" reservations that let you settle your bill at checkout, not when you book.

OTHER RESOURCES

Bidding For Travel	www.biddingfortravel.com	a good place to figure out what you can get and for how much before you start bidding on, say, Priceline.

week in advance or penalize you the cost of one night. Small inns and B&Bs are most likely to require you to cancel far in advance. Most hotels allow children under a certain age to stay in their parents' room at no extra charge, but others charge for them as extra adults; find out the cutoff age for discounts.

■ TIP➔ Assume that hotels operate on the European Plan (EP, no meals) unless we specify that they use the Breakfast Plan (BP, with full breakfast), Continental Plan (CP, Continental breakfast), Full American Plan (FAP, all meals), Modified American Plan (MAP, breakfast and dinner), or are all-inclusive (AI, all meals and most activities).

APARTMENT & HOUSE RENTALS

You can save tremendously by renting a furnished apartment for a weeklong stay in any major capital in Eastern and Central Europe, but increasingly these are being offered through local agencies. In places like the Dalmatian coast in Croatia, you may still find a little old lady at the ferry dock ready to rent you her spare room for a fraction of what you'd pay to stay in a hotel. Recommendations for local apartment rental agencies are given in individual destination chapters.

ONLINE BOOKING RESOURCES

Contacts Barclay International Group (☎516/364-0064 or 800/845-6636 ⊕www. barclayweb.com). **Drawbridge to Europe** (☎541/482-7778 or 888/268-1148 ⊕www. drawbridgetoeurope.com). **Forgetaway** (⊕www.forgetaway.weather.com) **Home Away** (☎512/493-0382 ⊕www.homeaway.com). **Homes Away** (☎416/920-1873 or 800/374-6637 ⊕www.homesaway.com). **Interhome** (☎954/791-8282 or 800/882-6864 ⊕www. interhome.us). **Villas & Apartments Abroad** (☎212/213-6435 or 800/433-3020 ⊕www.vaanyc.com). **Villas International** (☎415/499-9490 or 800/221-2260 ⊕www. villasintl.com).

HOTELS

Hotels in Eastern and Central Europe have improved notably over the past few years. Many formerly state-run hotels were privatized, much to their benefit. International hotel chains have established a strong presence in the region; although they may not be strong on local character, they do provide a reliably high standard of quality. Be aware that some spa hotels don't allow children under 12.

■ AIRLINE TICKETS

Most domestic airline tickets are electronic; international tickets may be either electronic or paper. With an e-ticket the only thing you receive is an e-mailed receipt citing your itinerary and reservation and ticket numbers.

The greatest advantage of an e-ticket is that if you lose your receipt, you can simply print out another copy or ask the airline to do it for you at check-in. You usually pay a surcharge (up to $50) to get a paper ticket, if you can get one at all.

The sole advantage of a paper ticket is that it may be easier to endorse over to another airline if your flight is canceled and the airline with which you booked can't accommodate you on another flight.

■ TIP➔ Discount air passes that let you travel economically in a country or region must often be purchased before you leave home. In some cases you can get them only through a travel agent.

There has been an explosion in nonstop flights to Eastern and Central Europe, not to mention an increase in the number of budget airlines with inexpensive fares within Europe, making most of the major airports in the region reachable from the United States with only one change of planes.

The least expensive airfares to Eastern and Central Europe are priced for round-trip travel and must usually be

10 WAYS TO SAVE

1. Nonrefundable is best. If saving money is more important than flexibility, then nonrefundable tickets work. That said, you'll pay dearly (as much as $200) if you change your plans.

2. Comparison shop. Web sites and travel agents can have different arrangements with the airlines and offer different prices for exactly the same flights.

3. Beware the listed prices. Many airline Web sites—and most ads—show prices *without* taxes and surcharges. Don't buy until you know the full price.

4. Stay loyal. Stick with one or two frequent-flier programs. You'll rack up free trips faster and you'll accumulate more quickly the perks that make trips easier. On some airlines these include a special reservations number, early boarding, access to upgrades, and roomier economy seats.

5. Watch those ticketing fees. Surcharges are usually added when you buy your ticket anywhere but on an airline Web site. (That includes by phone—even if you call the airline directly—and paper tickets regardless of how you book.)

6. Check often. Start looking for cheap fares from three months out to about one month.

7. Don't work alone. Some Web sites have tracking features that will e-mail you immediately when good deals are posted.

8. Jump on the good deals. Waiting even a few minutes might mean paying more.

9. Be flexible. Look for departures on Tuesday, Wednesday, and Saturday, typically the cheapest days to travel. And check on prices for departures at different times and to and from alternative airports.

10. Weigh your options. What you get can be as important as what you save. A cheaper flight might have a long layover or land at a secondary airport, where your ground transport costs are higher.

purchased in advance. Airlines generally allow you to change your return date for a fee; most low-fare tickets, however, are nonrefundable.

■ RENTAL CARS

When you reserve a car, ask about cancellation penalties, taxes, drop-off charges (if you're planning to pick up the car in one city and leave it in another), and surcharges (for being under or over a certain age, for additional drivers, or for driving across state or country borders or beyond a specific distance from your point of rental). All these things can add substantially to your costs. Request car seats and extras such as GPS when you book.

Rates are sometimes—but not always—better if you book in advance or reserve through a rental agency's Web site. There are other reasons to book ahead, though: for popular destinations, during busy times of the year, or to ensure that you get certain types of cars (vans, SUVs, exotic sports cars).

■TIP➡ **Make sure that a confirmed reservation guarantees you a car. Agencies sometimes overbook, particularly for busy weekends and holiday periods.**

Major rental agencies are represented throughout the region, but don't overlook local firms; they can offer bargains, but driving among various countries in the region can still be restricted because of insurance regulations, so be sure you can drive to all the places you want to go; some countries require additional insurance to protect against theft, which can add to your costs. It's important to make sure that quotes for car-rental prices include all necessary insurance. It can sometimes be impossible to get an automatic transmission in the region. It's also important to remember that cars in Europe are generally much smaller than those in the United States, and this means that there may be much less room for large pieces of luggage. Rates and regulations vary widely from country to country. *For more information (and for local contact information for local and international car-rental firms), see ⇨ Essentials in individual country chapters.*

Your driver's license may not be recognized outside your home country. You may not be able to rent a car without an International Driving Permit (IDP), which can be used only in conjunction with a valid driver's license and which translates your license into 10 languages. Check the AAA Web site for more info as well as for IDPs ($15) themselves.

In most Eastern and Central European countries, visitors need an International Driver's Permit; U.S. citizens can obtain one from the American Automobile Association. In some countries, such as Hungary, many car-rental agencies will accept an international license, but a Hungarian permit is technically required. If you intend to drive across a border, ask about restrictions on driving into other countries. The minimum age required for renting is usually 21 or older, and some companies also have maximum ages; be sure to inquire when making your arrangements.

CAR-RENTAL RESOURCES
Automobile Associations U.S.: American Automobile Association (AAA ☎315/797–5000 ⊕www.aaa.com); most contact with the organization is through state and regional members. **National Automobile Club** (☎650/294–7000 ⊕www.thenac.com); membership is open to California residents only.

Major Agencies Alamo (☎800/522–9696, ⊕www.alamo.com). **Avis** (☎800/331–1084, ⊕www.avis.com). **Budget** (☎800/472–3325, ⊕www.budget.com). **Dollar** (☎800/800–6000 in U.S., ⊕www.dollar.com). **Hertz** (☎800/654–3001, ⊕www.hertz.com). **National Car Rental** (☎800/227–7368, ⊕www.nationalcar.com).

Wholesalers Auto Europe (☎888/223–5555 ⊕www.autoeurope.com). **Europe by Car** (☎212/581–3040 in New York or

800/223–1516 ⊕www.europebycar.com). **Eurovacations** (☎877/471–3876 ⊕www.eurovacations.com). **Kemwel** (☎877/820–0668 ⊕www.kemwel.com).

CAR-RENTAL INSURANCE
Everyone who rents a car wonders whether the insurance that the rental companies offer is worth the expense. No one—including us—has a simple answer. It all depends on how much regular insurance you have, how comfortable you are with risk, and whether or not money is an issue.

If you own a car, your personal auto insurance may cover a rental to some degree, though not all policies protect you abroad; always read your policy's fine print. If you don't have auto insurance, then seriously consider buying the collision- or loss-damage waiver (CDW or LDW) from the car-rental company, which eliminates your liability for damage to the car.

Some credit cards offer CDW coverage, but it's usually supplemental to your own insurance and rarely covers SUVs, minivans, luxury models, and the like. If your coverage is secondary, you may still be liable for loss-of-use costs from the car rental company. But no credit-card insurance is valid unless you use that card for *all* transactions, from reserving to paying the final bill. All companies exclude car rental in some countries, so be sure to find out about the destination to which you are traveling.

■**TIP**➔ Diners Club offers primary CDW coverage on all rentals reserved and paid for with the card. This means that Diners Club's company—not your own car insurance—pays in case of an accident. It *doesn't* mean your car-insurance company won't raise your rates once it discovers you had an accident.

Some rental agencies require you to purchase CDW coverage; many will even include it in quoted rates. All will strongly encourage you to buy CDW—possibly

10 WAYS TO SAVE

1. Beware of cheap rates. Those great rates aren't so great when you add in taxes, surcharges, and insurance. Such extras can double or triple the initial quote.

2. Rent weekly. Weekly rates are usually better than daily ones. Even if you want to rent for only five or six days, ask for the weekly rate; it may very well be cheaper than the daily rate for that period of time.

3. Don't forget the locals. Price local companies as well as the majors.

4. Airport rentals can cost more. Airports often add surcharges, which you can sometimes avoid by renting from an agency whose office is just off airport property.

5. Wholesalers can help. Investigate wholesalers, which don't own fleets but rent in bulk from firms that do, and which frequently offer better rates (note that you must usually pay for such rentals before leaving home).

6. Look for rate guarantees. With your rate locked in, you won't pay more, even if the price goes up in the local currency.

7. Fill up farther away. Avoid hefty refueling fees by filling the tank at a station well away from where you plan to turn in the car.

8. Pump it yourself. Don't prepay for rental car gas. The savings isn't that great, and unless you coast in on empty upon return, you wind up paying for gas you don't use.

9. Get all your discounts. Find out whether a credit card you carry or organization or frequent-renter program to which you belong has a discount program. And confirm that such discounts really are a deal. You can often do better with special weekend or weekly rates offered by a rental agency.

10. Check out packages. Adding a car rental onto your air/hotel vacation package may be cheaper than renting a car separately.

implying that it's required—so be sure to ask about such things before renting. In most cases it's cheaper to add a supplemental CDW plan to your comprehensive travel-insurance policy (⇨ *Trip Insurance under Things to Consider in Getting Started, above*) than to purchase it from a rental company. That said, you don't want to pay for a supplement if you're required to buy insurance from the rental company.

Collision-damage waivers (and often theft insurance) must be purchased in most countries in Central and Eastern Europe, so car rentals are liable to be more expensive than in the West. It is advised to check that any advertised prices apply to visitors and not only locals. Most countries require that you will have held your driver's license for at least a year before you can rent a car.

■ TIP➔ You can decline the insurance from the rental company and purchase it through a third-party provider such as Travel Guard (⊕ www.travelguard.com)—$9 per day for $35,000 of coverage. That's sometimes just under half the price of the CDW offered by some car-rental companies.

■ VACATION PACKAGES

Packages *are not* guided excursions. Packages combine airfare, accommodations, and perhaps a rental car or other extras (theater tickets, guided excursions, boat trips, reserved entry to popular museums, transit passes), but they let you do your own thing. During busy periods packages may be your only option, as flights and rooms may be sold out otherwise.

Packages will definitely save you time. They can also save you money, particularly in peak seasons, but—and this is a really big "but"—you should price each part of the package separately to be sure. And be aware that prices advertised on Web sites and in newspapers rarely include service charges or taxes, which can up your costs by hundreds of dollars.

■TIP➜ Some packages and cruises are sold only through travel agents. Don't always assume that you can get the best deal by booking everything yourself.

Each year consumers are stranded or lose their money when packagers—even large ones with excellent reputations—go out of business. How can you protect yourself?

First, always pay with a credit card; if you have a problem, your credit-card company may help you resolve it. Second, buy trip insurance that covers default. Third, choose a company that belongs to the United States Tour Operators Association, whose members must set aside funds to cover defaults. Finally, choose a company that also participates in the Tour Operator Program of the American Society of Travel Agents (ASTA), which will act as mediator in any disputes.

You can also check on the tour operator's reputation among travelers by posting an inquiry on one of the Fodors.com forums.

Organizations American Society of Travel Agents (ASTA ☎703/739–2782 or 800/965–2782 ⊕www.astanet.com). **United States Tour Operators Association** (USTOA ☎212/599–6599 ⊕www.ustoa.com).

■TIP➜ Local tourism boards can provide information about lesser-known and small-niche operators that sell packages to only a few destinations.

▌GUIDED TOURS

Guided tours are a good option when you don't want to do it all yourself. You travel along with a group (sometimes large, sometimes small), stay in prebooked hotels, eat with your fellow travelers (the cost of meals sometimes included in the price of your tour, sometimes not), and follow a schedule.

But not all guided tours are an if-it's-Tuesday-this-must-be-Belgium experience. A knowledgeable guide can take you places that you might never discover on your own, and you may be pushed to see more than you would have otherwise. Tours aren't for everyone, but they can be just the thing for trips to places where making travel arrangements is difficult or time-consuming (particularly when you don't speak the language).

Whenever you book a guided tour, find out what's included and what isn't. A "land-only" tour includes all your travel (by bus, in most cases) in the destination, but not necessarily your flights to and from or even within it. Also, in most cases prices in tour brochures don't include fees and taxes. And remember that you'll be expected to tip your guide (in cash) at the end of the tour.

TRANSPORTATION

If you are planning a trip to the region and wish to visit several different countries, you need to be aware that train service in this region can be slow and uncomfortable. It's possible to drive around the region, but vehicles with automatic transmissions are rare. For many people, flying may be a better choice, especially when you can use a budget airline. With the introduction of cheap one-way flights, SkyEurope, which is based in Vienna and Bratislava, does a pretty good job of connecting the major cities in the region, with the exception of destinations in Bosnia and Herzegovina, Croatia, Hungary, and Montenegro. Wizzair connects Budapest with most of the region's capitals. Otherwise, flights in the region can be quite expensive.

■**TIP**➔ Ask the local tourist board about hotel and local transportation packages that include tickets to major museum exhibits or other special events.

■ BY AIR

Travel time from the United States to Central Europe can vary greatly depending on whether or not you can get a nonstop flight. A nonstop flight from New York to Prague takes 8 hours; connecting flights to Sofia can make that trip last more than 14 hours. There are now quite a few nonstop flights from New York, including flights to Vienna (7½ hours), Prague (8 hours), Budapest (9 hours), Warsaw (9 hours), and Bucharest (10 hours). There are direct flights from Chicago to Warsaw (9 hours). Most trips from the United States require a change at Frankfurt, London, Paris, Prague, Zurich, Amsterdam, or Vienna and can take up to 15 hours. Direct flights from London to all Central European capitals take between 2 and 3½ hours.

Airlines & Airports Airline and Airport Links.com (⊕www.airlineandairportlinks.com)

has links to many of the world's airlines and airports.

Airline Security Issues Transportation Security Administration (⊕www.tsa.gov) has answers for almost every question that might come up.

AIRPORTS

For more in-depth airport information, and for the best way to get between the airport and your destination, see ➪ *Airports in the Essentials section at the end of each country chapter, or in the Essentials section of the city you are flying into.*

Austria Vienna International Airport (VIE 🕾01/7007-0 ⊕www.viennaairport.com).

Bosnia-Herzegovina Sarajevo International Airport (SJJ 🕾033-289-100 ⊕www.sarajevo-airport.ba).

Bulgaria Sofia International Airport (SOF 🕾02/937-2211 ⊕www.sofia-airport.bg).

Croatia Dubrovnik Airport (DBV 🕾020/773-377 ⊕www.airport-dubrovnik.hr). **Split Airport** (SPU 🕾021/203-171 ⊕www.split-airport.hr). **Zagreb Pleso Airport** (ZAG 🕾01/626-5222 ⊕www.zagreb-airport.hr).

Czech Republic Prague Ruzyně Airport (PRG 🕾220-111-111 ⊕www.prg.aero). **Brno-Turany Airport** (🕾545-521-136 ⊕www.airport-brno.cz).

Germany Berlin Tegel Airport (TXL 🕾49/180-5000-186 ⊕www.berlin-airport.de). **Berlin Schönefeld Airport** (SXF 🕾49/180-5000-186 ⊕www.berlin-airport.de).

Hungary Budapest Ferihegy Repülőtér (BUD 🕾1/296-9696 ⊕www.bud.hu).

Montenegro Aerodrom Podgorica (TGD 🕾081/243-007 ⊕www.montenegroairports.com). **Aerodrom Tivat** (TIV 🕾082/670-960 ⊕www.montenegroairports.com).

Poland Gdańsk Lech Wałęsa Airport (GDN 🕾058/348-11-63 ⊕www.airport.gdansk.

pl). **Pope John Paul II Kraków–Balice** (KRK ☎012/411-19-55 ⊕www.lotnisko-balice.pl). **Warszawa Okęcie** (WAW ☎022/650-42-20 ⊕www.polish-airports.com).

Romania Aurel Vlaicu International Airport **(Băneasa)** (BBU ☎021/232-0020 ⊕www. baneasa.aero). **Henri Coandă International Airport (Otopeni)** (OTP ☎021/204-1200 ⊕www.otp-airport.ro).

Slovakia Letisko M.R. Štefánika (⊕BTS ☎02/4857-3353 ⊕www.letiskobratislava. sk). **Košice International Airport** (⊕KSC ☎02/556-8321 ⊕www.airportkosice.sk).

Slovenia Aerodrome Ljubljana (LJU ☎04/206-1981 ⊕www.lju-airport.si) **Maribor Airport** (MBX ☎02/629-1553 ⊕www. maribor-airport.si).

GROUND TRANSPORTATION

For information on airport transfers, see ⇨Airports & Transfers in the Essentials section for each destination chapter.

FLIGHTS

Many U.S. airlines have a European co-carrier that provides connecting service to Eastern and Central Europe from a gateway in Europe. The major European airlines listed here offer service from North America, with connecting service to Eastern and Central Europe from the country's capital. Several of the national airlines of the countries in Eastern and Central Europe offer nonstop service from the United States; others offer only connecting service from within Europe. At this writing, there is no direct air service between the United States and Bosnia and Herzegovina, Croatia, Montenegro, Slovakia, or Slovenia. Slovak Airlines offers service only between Moscow and Bratislava and is not listed here. For Europe-based budget airlines that offer service solely within Europe see ⇨By Air in the Essentials section of each destination chapter; none of these airlines has a U.S. telephone reservations number, and most allow bookings only online.

Airline Contacts Air France (☎800/237-2747 ⊕www.airfrance.us). **Alitalia** (☎800/223-5730 ⊕ www.airfrance.us). **American Airlines** (☎800/433-7300 ⊕www.aa.com). **Austrian Airlines** (☎800/843-0002 ⊕www.aua.com). **British Airways** (☎800/247-9297 ⊕www. britishairways.com). **Continental Airlines** (☎800/231-0856 ⊕www.continental.com). **Delta Airlines** (☎800/241-4141 ⊕www. delta.com). **Finnair** (☎800/950-5000 ⊕www. finnair.com). **KLM Royal Dutch Airlines** (☎800/225-2525 ⊕www.nwa.com). **Lufthansa** (☎800/399-5838 ⊕www.lufthansa. com). **Northwest Airlines** (☎800/225-2525 ⊕www.nwa.com). **SAS Scandinavian Airlines** (☎800/221-2350 ⊕www.flysas.com). **Swiss International Airlines** (☎877/359-7947 ⊕www.swiss.com). **United Airlines** (☎800/538-2929 ⊕www.united.com). **USAirways** (☎800/622-1015 ⊕www. usairways.com).

National Airlines with Service from Both the U.S. & Europe Czech Airlines (CSA ☎800/223-2365 ⊕www.csa.cz). **LOT Polish Airlines** (☎212/789-0970 ⊕www.lot.com). **Malév Hungarian Airlines** (☎800/223-6884 ⊕www.malev.hu). **Tarom Romanian Airlines** (☎877/359-8276 ⊕www.tarom.ro).

National Airlines with Service Only Within Europe Adria Airways (☎(44) 020/7734-4630 in U.K., (386) 1/369-1010 in Slovenia ⊕www.adria.si). **BH Airlines** (☎(387) 33/218-605 in Bosnia and Herzegovina ⊕www.airbosna.ba). **Bulgaria Air** (☎888/462-8542 in U.S., (359) 2/402-04-00 in Bulgaria ⊕www.air.bg). **Croatia Airlines** (☎973/884-3401 in U.S., (385) 1/487-2727 in Croatia ⊕www.croatiaairlines.hr). **Montenegro Airlines** (☎(381) 081/405-501 in Montenegro ⊕www.montenegro-airlines.cg.yu).

▌ BY BOAT & FERRY

Ferries offer a pleasant and cheap mode of transportation to Eastern and Central Europe, although you have to be fairly close to your destination already to hop a Europe-bound ferry or hydrofoil. Flying into the appropriate hub, however, is an option. Water bookings connect Copenhagen, Denmark, to Świnoujście and Gdańsk, Poland. A hydrofoil shuttles visitors from Vienna to Bratislava, Slovakia, or Budapest, Hungary. There is ferry service between Venice and the Slovenian coast. *For country-specific information, see By Boat & Ferry in the Essentials section of the individual destination chapters.*

Traveling by boat or ferry is a possibility up and down the coast in Croatia. Cabins must be booked in advance, but regular seats are readily available. Ferries between Ancona, Trieste, Bari, and Venice in Italy and Croatia operate daily during the summer season. Journeys along the Croatian coast are more expensive than buses but more comfortable.

▌BY BUS

In some countries, especially where trains are largely local (and stop seemingly every 100 feet), buses are actually speedier than rail travel. Comfort and fares vary drastically by nation. *See By Bus in the Essentials section at the end of each country chapter.* Unless you latch on to a real deal on airfare, a bus ticket from London's Victoria Terminal on Eurolines is probably the cheapest transit from the United Kingdom to Eastern and Central Europe, with regularly scheduled service to Budapest, Kraków, Prague, and Warsaw.

Bus Information from the U.K. Eurolines (☎08717/818–181 in U.K. (extra charge for this call) ⊕www.eurolines.com).

▌BY CAR

The positive side of driving is an itinerary free from the constraints of bus and train schedules and lots of trunk room for extra baggage. The negatives are many, however, not the least of which are shabbily maintained secondary roads, the risk of theft and vandalism, and difficulty finding gas. Crowded roads and fast and/or careless drivers add to the danger element, particularly in Poland. However, car travel does make it much easier to get to out-of-the-way monasteries and other sights not easily accessible by public transportation. Good road maps are usually available.

A word of caution: if you have drunk any alcohol whatsoever, do not drive. Penalties are substantial, and the blood-alcohol limit is practically zero. (In the Czech Republic and Hungary, it *is* zero.)

GASOLINE

Gas stations are easy to come by on major thoroughfares and near large cities. Many are open around the clock, particularly in the Czech Republic and Hungary. At least two grades of gasoline are sold in Eastern and Central European countries, usually 90–93 octane (regular) and 94–98 octane (super). Lead-free gasoline is now available in most gas stations.

For additional country-specific information relating to roads, gasoline, and insurance, see By Car in the Essentials section at the end of each country chapter.

ROAD CONDITIONS

Eastern and Central Europe's main roads are built to a fairly high standard. There are now quite substantial stretches of highway on main routes, and a lot of rebuilding is being done in many countries, especially in Poland.

RULES OF THE ROAD

Throughout Eastern and Central Europe, driving is on the right and the same basic rules of the road practiced in the United States and the rest of Europe apply. *For further information see By Car in the Essentials section at the end of each country chapter.*

▌ BY TRAIN

Although standards have improved, on the whole they are far short of what is acceptable in the West. Trains are very busy, and it is rare to find one running less than full or almost so. All countries operate their own dining, buffet, and refreshment services. Always crowded, they tend to open and close at the whim of the staff. In Bulgaria and Hungary, couchette cars are second-class only and can be little more than a hard bunk without springs and adequate bed linen. In Romania, there are first-class couchettes (though they are comparable to second- or third-class compartments in Western Europe); these have room for two people and are relatively safe and clean. First-class couchettes are also available on Czech and Slovak trains, and there are two types of second-class couchettes. The cheaper have six hard beds per compartment; the slightly more expensive have three beds and a sink and are sex-segregated. Some of the most comfortable trains are the express trains in Croatia, the Czech Republic, Hungary, Poland, Slovakia, and Slovenia—they're normally less crowded and more comfortable. (You should make a reservation.)

Although trains in Eastern and Central Europe can mean hours of sitting on a hard seat in a smoky car, traveling by rail is very inexpensive. Rail networks in all the Eastern and Central European countries are very extensive, though trains can be infuriatingly slow. You'll invariably enjoy interesting and friendly traveling company, however; most Eastern and Central Europeans are eager to hear about the West and to discuss the enormous changes in their own countries.

For information about fares and schedules and other country-specific train information, see By Train in the Essentials section at the end of each country chapter.

Rail passes are available for Austria, Croatia, the Czech Republic, Germany, Hungary, Montenegro, Poland, Romania, and Slovenia. Various Eurail and Rail Europe passes can include several groups of countries, among those listed above. Eurail passes are not sold in Europe but must be purchased in the United States. Other country-specific passes may be available in Europe.

Many travelers assume that rail passes guarantee them seats on the trains they wish to ride. Not so. You need to book seats ahead even if you are using a rail pass; seat reservations are required on some European trains, particularly high-speed trains, and are a good idea on trains that may be crowded—particularly in summer on popular routes. You will also need a reservation if you purchase sleeping accommodations.

Information Rail Europe (☎888/382–7245 ⊕www.raileurope.com).

ON THE GROUND

■ COMMUNICATIONS

INTERNET

Internet cafés are increasingly available throughout Eastern and Central Europe. For specific recommendations, see ⇨Internet, Mail & Shipping in the Essentials section at the end of each destination chapter.

Bring an adapter for your laptop plug. Adapters are inexpensive, and some models have several plugs suitable for different systems throughout the world. Some hotels lend adapters to guests for use during their stay.

Contacts Cybercafés (⊕ www.cybercafes. com) lists more than 4,000 Internet cafés worldwide.

PHONES

The good news is that you can now make a direct-dial telephone call from virtually any point on earth. The bad news? You can't always do so cheaply. Calling from a hotel is almost always the most expensive option; hotels usually add huge surcharges to all calls, particularly international ones. In some countries you can phone from call centers or even the post office. Calling cards usually keep costs to a minimum, but only if you purchase them locally. And then there are mobile phones (⇨ *below*), which are sometimes more prevalent—particularly in the developing world—than land lines; as expensive as mobile phone calls can be, they are still usually a much cheaper option than calling from your hotel.

Country codes are as follows: Austria (43), Bosnia and Herzegovina (387), Bulgaria (359), Croatia (385), Czech Republic (420), Germany (49), Hungary (36), Montenegro (382), Poland (48), Romania (40), Slovakia (421), Slovenia (386).

When dialing an Eastern or Central European number from abroad, drop the initial 0 from the local area code. The country code for the United States and Canada is 1; it's 61 for Australia, 64 for New Zealand, and 44 for the United Kingdom.

For additional country-specific telephone information, see Telephones in the Essentials section at the end of each country chapter.

MOBILE PHONES

If you have a multiband phone (some countries use different frequencies from what's used in the United States) and your service provider uses the world-standard GSM network (as do T-Mobile, Cingular, and Verizon), you can probably use your phone abroad. Roaming fees can be steep, however: 99¢ a minute is considered reasonable. And overseas you normally pay the toll charges for incoming calls. It's almost always cheaper to send a text message than to make a call, since text messages have a very low set fee (often less than 5¢).

If you just want to make local calls, consider buying a new SIM card (note that your provider may have to unlock your phone for you to use a different SIM card) and a prepaid service plan in the destination. You'll then have a local number and can make local calls at local rates. If your trip is extensive, you could also simply buy a new cell phone in your destination, as the initial cost will be offset over time.

■TIP➜If you travel internationally frequently, save one of your old mobile phones or buy a cheap one on the Internet; ask your cell phone company to unlock it for you, and take it with you as a travel phone, buying a new SIM card with pay-as-you-go service in each destination.

All the countries of Eastern and Central Europe support the GSM mobile standard. For more specific information, see

⇨Telephones in the Essentials section at the end of each destination chapter.

Contacts Cellular Abroad (☎800/287–5072 ⊕www.cellularabroad.com) rents and sells GMS phones and sells SIM cards that work in many countries. **Mobal** (☎888/888–9162 ⊕www.mobalrental.com) rents mobiles and sells GSM phones (starting at $49) that will operate in 140 countries. Per-call rates vary throughout the world. **Planet Fone** (☎888/988–4777 ⊕www.planetfone.com) rents cell phones, but the per-minute rates are expensive.

▮ CUSTOMS & DUTIES

You're always allowed to bring goods of a certain value back home without having to pay any duty or import tax. But there's a limit on the amount of tobacco and liquor you can bring back duty-free, and some countries have separate limits for perfumes; for exact figures, check with your customs department. The values of so-called "duty-free" goods are included in these amounts. When you shop abroad, save all your receipts, as customs inspectors may ask to see them as well as the items you purchased. If the total value of your goods is more than the duty-free limit, you'll have to pay a tax (most often a flat percentage) on the value of everything beyond that limit.

When traveling to Bulgaria, you should declare video cameras, personal computers, and expensive jewelry upon arrival. Be aware that leaving the country without expensive items declared upon entering can present a huge hassle with airport police.

U.S. Information U.S. Customs and Border Protection (⊕www.cbp.gov).

▮ ELECTRICITY

The electrical current in Eastern and Central Europe is 220 volts, 50 cycles alternating current (AC); wall outlets generally take plugs with two round prongs.

Consider making a small investme[nt] universal adapter, which has severa[l] of plugs in one lightweight, compact unit. Most laptops and mobile phone chargers are dual voltage (i.e., they operate equally well on 110 and 220 volts), so require only an adapter. These days the same is true of small appliances such as hair dryers. Always check labels and manufacturer instructions to be sure. Don't use 110-volt outlets marked FOR SHAVERS ONLY for high-wattage appliances such as hair dryers.

Contacts Steve Kropla's Help for World Travelers (⊕www.kropla.com) has information on electrical and telephone plugs around the world. **Walkabout Travel Gear** (⊕www.walkabouttravelgear.com) has a good coverage of electricity under "adapters."

▮ EMERGENCIES

For country-specific emergency numbers, see Emergencies in the Essentials section at the end of each country chapter.

For U.S. embassy and consulate contact information, see Embassies & Consulates in the Essentials section at the end of each country chapter.

▮ HEALTH

The most common types of illnesses are caused by contaminated food and water. Especially in developing countries, drink only bottled, boiled, or purified water and drinks; don't drink from public fountains or use ice. You should even consider using bottled water to brush your teeth. Make sure food has been thoroughly cooked and is served to you fresh and hot; avoid vegetables and fruits that you haven't washed (in bottled or purified water) or peeled yourself. If you have problems, mild cases of traveler's diarrhea may respond to Imodium (known generically as loperamide) or Pepto-Bismol. Be sure to drink plenty of fluids; if you can't keep fluids down, seek medical help immediately.

Infectious diseases can be airborne or passed via mosquitoes and ticks and through direct or indirect physical contact with animals or people. Some, including Norwalk-like viruses that affect your digestive tract, can be passed along through contaminated food. If you are traveling in an area where malaria is prevalent, use a repellent containing DEET and take malaria-prevention medication before, during, and after your trip as directed by your physician. Condoms can help prevent most sexually transmitted diseases, but they aren't absolutely reliable and their quality varies from country to country. Speak with your physician and/or check the CDC or World Health Organization Web sites for health alerts, particularly if you're pregnant, traveling with children, or have a chronic illness.

For information on travel insurance, shots and medications, and medical-assistance companies, see Shots & Medications under Things to Consider in Before You Go, above.

SPECIFIC ISSUES IN EASTERN AND CENTRAL EUROPE

You may gain weight, but there are few other serious health hazards for the traveler in Eastern and Central Europe. Tap water may taste bad but is generally drinkable; when it runs rusty out of the tap or the aroma of chlorine is overpowering, it might help to have some iodine tablets or bottled water handy. If in doubt, always drink bottled water.

Vegetarians and those on special diets may have a problem with the heavy local cuisine, which is based largely on pork and beef. To prevent your vitamin intake from dropping to danger levels, buy fresh fruits and vegetables at seasonal street markets—regular grocery stores often don't sell them. In Romania, unrefrigerated milk sold in outdoor markets or in villages may not be pasteurized and can make Westerners sick. In Bulgaria, mayonnaise-based fillings are very common in "sandvitchee"—the ubiquitous toasted sandwiches sold at many street kiosks; avoid them.

To avoid problems clearing customs, diabetic travelers carrying needles and syringes should have on hand a letter from their physician confirming their need for insulin injections.

■ MAIL

For country-specific mail information, see Internet, Mail & Shipping in the Essentials section at the end of each country chapter.

■ MONEY

Although several countries in Eastern and Central Europe have already joined the EU, only Austria, Slovenia, and Germany use the euro as their official currency. You may find that many hotels (particularly large business and luxury chain hotels) quote rates in euros even if charges on your final statement appear in local currency.

For country-specific money information, see Money Matters in the Essentials section at the end of each country chapter.

Prices throughout this guide are given for adults. Substantially reduced fees are almost always available for children, students, and senior citizens.

■TIP→ Banks never have every foreign currency on hand, and it may take as long as a week to order. If you're planning to exchange funds before leaving home, don't wait until the last minute.

ATMS & BANKS

Your own bank will probably charge a fee for using ATMs abroad; the foreign bank you use may also charge a withdrawal fee, and your bank may also charge a percentage fee for the currency exchange as well. Nevertheless, you'll usually get a better rate of exchange at an ATM than you will at a currency-exchange office or even when changing money in a bank. And extracting funds as you need them is a safer option than carrying around a large amount of cash.

■TIP➔ PIN numbers with more than four digits are not recognized at ATMs in many countries. If yours has five or more, remember to change it before you leave.

ATMs are common in large and midsize cities throughout the region and more often than not are part of the Cirrus and Plus networks; outside of urban areas, machines are scarce and you should plan to carry enough cash to meet your needs.

CREDIT CARDS

Throughout this guide, the following abbreviations are used: **AE**, American Express; **DC**, Diners Club; **MC**, Master-Card; and **V**, Visa.

It's a good idea to inform your credit-card company before you travel, especially if you're going abroad and don't travel internationally very often. Otherwise, the credit-card company might put a hold on your card owing to unusual activity—not a good thing halfway through your trip. Record all your credit-card numbers—as well as the phone numbers to call if your cards are lost or stolen—in a safe place, so you're prepared should something go wrong. Both MasterCard and Visa have general numbers you can call (collect if you're abroad) if your card is lost, but you're better off calling the number of your issuing bank, since MasterCard and Visa usually just transfer you to your bank; your bank's number is usually printed on your card.

If you plan to use your credit card for cash advances, you'll need to apply for a PIN at least two weeks before your trip. Although it's usually cheaper (and safer) to use a credit card abroad for large purchases (so you can cancel payments or

be reimbursed if there's a problem), note that some credit-card companies *and* the banks that issue them add substantial percentages to all foreign transactions, whether they're in a foreign currency or not. Check on these fees before leaving home, so there won't be any surprises when you get the bill.

■TIP➔ Before you charge something, ask the merchant whether or not he or she plans to do a dynamic currency conversion (DCC). In such a transaction the credit-card *processor* (shop, restaurant, or hotel, not Visa or MasterCard) converts the currency and charges you in dollars. In most cases you'll pay the merchant a 3% fee for this service In addition to any credit-card company and issuing-bank foreign-transaction surcharges.

Dynamic currency conversion programs are becoming increasingly widespread. Merchants who participate in them are supposed to ask whether you want to be charged in dollars or the local currency, but they don't always do so. And even if they do offer you a choice, they may well avoid mentioning the additional surcharges. The good news is that you *do* have a choice. And if this practice really gets your goat, you can avoid it entirely thanks to American Express; with its cards, DCC simply isn't an option.

Credit cards are accepted in places that cater regularly to foreign tourists and business travelers: hotels, restaurants, and shops, particularly in major urban centers. When you leave the beaten path, be prepared to pay cash. Always inquire about credit-card policies when booking hotel rooms. Visa and MasterCard are the most commonly accepted credit cards in the region.

It's smart to write down (and keep separate) the number of each credit card you're carrying along with the international service phone number that usually appears on the back of the card.

Reporting Lost Cards American Express (☎800/528–4800 in the U.S. or 336/393–1111 collect from abroad ⊕www.americanexpress.com). **Diners Club** (☎800/234–6377 in the U.S. or 303/799–1504 collect from abroad ⊕www.dinersclub.com). **MasterCard** (☎800/627–8372 in the U.S. or 636/722–7111 collect from abroad ⊕www.mastercard.com). **Visa** (☎800/847–2911 in the U.S. or 410/581–9994 collect from abroad ⊕www.visa.com).

CURRENCY & EXCHANGE

For the most favorable rates, change money through banks. Although ATM transaction fees may be higher abroad than at home, ATM rates are excellent because they are based on wholesale rates offered only by major banks. You won't do as well at exchange booths in airports or rail and bus stations, in hotels, in restaurants, or in stores. Romania is an exception; exchange bureaus have the best rates, especially in Bucharest and other large cities. To avoid lines at airport exchange booths, get a bit of local currency before you leave home.

■TIP→ Even if a currency-exchange booth has a sign promising no commission, rest assured that there's some kind of huge, hidden fee. (Oh . . . that's right. The sign didn't say no *fee*.) And as for rates, you're almost always better off getting foreign currency at an ATM or exchanging money at a bank.

TRAVELER'S CHECKS

Some consider this the currency of the cave man, and it's true that fewer establishments accept traveler's checks these days. Nevertheless, they're a cheap and secure way to carry extra money, particularly on trips to urban areas. Both Citibank (under the Visa brand) and American Express issue traveler's checks in the United States, but Amex is better known and more widely accepted; you can also avoid hefty surcharges by cashing Amex checks at Amex offices. Whatever you do, keep track of all the serial numbers in case the checks are lost or stolen.

Traveler's checks are increasingly difficult to cash in Eastern and Central Europe. If you are limiting your travel to major cities, your best bet is to take American Express traveler's checks and cash them at an American Express office. But you will generally get a better exchange rate by taking money directly from a local ATM.

Contacts American Express (☎888/412–6945 in U.S., 801/945–9450 collect outside the U.S. to add value or speak to customer service ⊕www.americanexpress.com).

■ SAFETY

Crime rates are rising in Eastern and Central Europe but are still relatively low compared with destinations in Western Europe and the United States, but travelers should beware of pickpockets, which can be a particular concern in crowded areas, especially on public transportation, at railway stations, and in big hotels. In general, always keep your valuables with you—in open bars and restaurants, purses hung on or placed next to chairs are easy targets. Make sure your wallet is safe in a buttoned pocket, or watch your handbag.

Be very careful with your passport through Eastern and Central Europe. It is more highly prized than cash. (The black market price for an American or Canadian passport is around $1,000.) In general, although many countries legally require you to keep your passport on your person at all times, it is usually safer to deposit it in your hotel's safe and to carry a color photocopy.

Car theft is an ongoing concern throughout the region, and many car-rental firms require renters to carry additional insurance for rental cars, particularly if they are renting so-called "luxury" cars such as a Mercedes-Benz or BMW (most cars with automatic transmission will be larger luxury vehicles, if they are available at all). A notorious scam in some cities involves men in plain clothes flashing fake police badges and accusing you of exchanging currency illegally. Do not hand over your passport or money; instead, offer to accompany them (on foot) to your hotel or a police station. If you spot a uniformed policeman, summon him. On trains and buses, groups sometimes cause distractions, then make off with your valuables.

It isn't wise for a woman to go alone to a bar or nightclub or to wander the streets late at night. When traveling by train at night, seek out compartments that are well populated.

For country-specific safety issues, see ⇨ Safety in the Essentials section at the end of each destination chapter.

■ TIP➔ Distribute your cash, credit cards, IDs, and other valuables between a deep front pocket, an inside jacket or vest pocket, and a hidden money pouch. Don't reach for the money pouch once you're in public.

■ TAXES

Most Eastern and Central European countries have some form of value-added tax (V.A.T.); rebate rules vary by country and seem to be in an ongoing state of evolution. One thing you can depend on—you'll need to present your receipts on departure.

When making a purchase, ask for a V.A.T. refund form and find out whether the merchant gives refunds—not all stores do, nor are they required to. Have the form stamped like any customs form by customs officials when you leave the country or, if you're visiting several European Union countries, when you leave the EU. After you're through passport control, take the form to a refund-service counter for an on-the-spot refund (which is usually the quickest and easiest option), or mail it to the address on the form (or the envelope with it) after you arrive home. You receive the total refund stated on the form, but the processing time can be long, especially if you request a credit-card adjustment.

Global Refund is a Europe-wide service with 225,000 affiliated stores and more than 700 refund counters at major airports and border crossings. Its refund form, called a Tax Free Check, is the most common across the European continent. The service issues refunds in the form of cash, check, or credit-card adjustment.

V.A.T. Refunds Global Refund (☎800/566–9828 ⊕www.globalrefund.com).

■ TIME

Austria, Bosnia and Herzegovina, Croatia, the Czech Republic, Hungary, Germany, Montenegro, Poland, Slovakia, and Slovenia are on Central European Time (CET), one hour ahead of Greenwich Mean Time and six hours ahead of the Eastern time zone of the United States. Bulgaria and Romania are two hours ahead of Greenwich Mean Time.

■ TIPPING

For country-specific tipping guidelines, *see Tipping in the Essentials section at the end of each chapter.*

BULGARIAN VOCABULARY

Bulgarian is written in Cyrillic. The following chart lists only pronunciations written in Roman letters.

ENGLISH	PRONUNCIATION

BASICS

Yes/no	da/ne
Please	**mol**ya
Thank you (very much)	blago**dar**ya
Excuse me	iz**ven**ete
I'm sorry.	sa**zhal**yavam
Hello, how do you do	**do**bar den
Do you speak English?	go**vor**ite li an**gliy**ski?
I don't speak Bulgarian.	ne go**vor**ya bul**gar**ski
I don't understand.	ne raz**bir**am.
Please speak slowly.	**mol**ya, govo**rete bav**no
Please write it down.	**mol**ya vi se, na**pish**ete go
Please show me.	**mol**ya vi se, po**kazh**ete mi
I am American (m/f)	as sum ameri**kan**ets/ameri**kan**ka
I am English (m/f)	as sum angli**chan**in/angli**chan**ka
My name is . . .	**kaz**vam se
Right/left	**dya**sno/**ly**avo
Open/closed	oto**vor**eno/zat**vor**eno
Arrival/departure	pristigane/**za**mina**va**ne
Where is . . . ?	**ka**de e
. . . the station?	. . . **gar**ata
. . . the railroad/train?	. . . zhelez**nitsa**/**vla**ku
. . . the bus/tram?	. . . af**to**bus/**tram**vai
. . . the airport?	. . . le**tish**teto
. . . the post office?	. . . **posh**tata?
. . . the bank?	. . . **ban**ka
Stop here	**spre**te tuk
I would like (m/f). . .	bikh **zhel**al/bikh **zhel**ala
How much does it cost?	**kol**ko **stru**va
Letter/postcard	**pis**mo/**posh**tenska **kar**tichka
By airmail	vaz**dush**na **posh**ta
Help!	**po**mosht

NUMBERS

One	edin
Two	dva
Three	ri
Four	chetiri
Five	pet
Six	shest
Seven	sedem
Eight	osem
Nine	devet
Ten	deset
One hundred	sto
One thousand	hilyada

DAYS OF THE WEEK

Sunday	nedelya
Monday	ponedelnik
Tuesday	ftornik
Wednesday	sryada
Thursday	chetvartak
Friday	petak
Saturday	sabota

WHERE TO SLEEP

A room	staya
The key	klyucha
With bath/shower	sus banya/dush

FOOD

A restaurant	restorant
The menu	kartata, menyuto
The check, please.	smetkata
I'd like to order this	oshte malko
Breakfast	zakuska

Lunch	obed
Dinner	vecherya
Bread	hlyab
Butter	maslo
Salt/pepper	sol/piper
Bottle	butika
Red/white wine	cherveno/byalo vino
Beer	bira
(Mineral) Water	(mineralna) voda
Milk	miyako
Coffee	kafe
Tea (with lemon)	chay (s limon)
Chocolate	zahar
Plum brandy	slivova

CROATIAN VOCABULARY

ENGLISH	CROATIAN	PRONUNCIATION

BASICS

Yes/no	Da/ne	dah/neh
Please	Molim (vas)	**moh**-leem (vahs)
Thank you (very much)	Hvala (lijepo)	**hvah**-lah (lyeh-poh)
Excuse me	Oprostite	oh-proh-stee-teh
Hello	Zdravo	**zdrah**-voh
I'm sorry.	Žao mi je.	**zhah**-oh mee yeh
Do you speak English?	Da li govorite engleski?	Dah lee **goh**-voh-ree-teh **ehn**-glehs-kee
I don't understand.	Ne razumijem.	neh rah-**zoo**-myehm
Please show me . . .	Molim vas, pokažite mi . . .	moh-leem vahs, **poh**-kah-zhee-teh mee
I am American (m/f).	Ja sam Amerikanac (Amerikanka).	yah sahm **ah**-meh-ree-kah-nahts **ah**-meh-ree-kahn-kah
My name is . . .	Zovem se . . .	**zoh**-vehm seh
Right/left	Desno/Lijevo	**dehs**-noh/**lyeh**-voh
Open/closed	Otvoreno/zatvoreno	**oh**-tvoh-reh-noh/ **zah**-tvoh-reh-noh
Where is . . . ? . . . the train station?	Gdje je . . . ? . . . železnička? stanica/kolodvor	gdyeh yeh **zheh**-lehz-neech-kah **stah**-neet-sah/**koh**-loh-dvohr
. . . the bus stop?	. . . autobusna stanica?	**ahoo**-toh-boos-nah **stah**-nee-tsah
. . . the airport?	. . . aerodrom?	**ah**-eh-roh-drohm
. . . the post office?	. . . pošta?	**posh**-tah
. . . the bank?	. . . banka?	**bahn**-kah
Here/there	Ovdje/tamo	**ohv**-dyeh/**tah**-moh
I would like. . .	Molim (vas). . . / Htio/htjela bih. . . (m/f)	**moh**-leem (vahs)/ hteeoh/htyeh-lah beeh
How much does it cost?	Koliko košta?	**koh**-lee-koh **kosh**-tah
Postcard	Razglednica	**rahz**-gleh-dnee-tsah
Help!	Upomoć!	**oo**-poh-moch

NUMBERS

One	Jedan	**yeh**-dahn
Two	Dva	dvah
Three	Tri	tree
Four	Četiri	**cheh**-tee-ree
Five	Pet	peht
Six	Šest	shest
Seven	Sedam	**seh**-dahm
Eight	Osam	**oh**-sahm
Nine	Devet	**deh**-veht
Ten	Deset	**deh**-seht
One hundred	Sto	stoh
One thousand	Tisuća	**tee**-soo-chah

DAYS OF THE WEEK

Sunday	Nedjelja	**neh**-dyeh-lyah
Monday	Ponedjeljak	**poh**-neh-dyeh-lyahk
Tuesday	Utorak	**oo**-toh-rahk
Wednesday	Srijeda	**sryeh**-dah
Thursday	Četvrtak	**cheht**-vruh-tahk
Friday	Petak	**peh**-tahk
Saturday	Subota	**soo**-boh-tah

WHERE TO SLEEP

A room	Soba	**soh**-bah
The key	Ključ	klyooch
With bath/shower	S kupaonicom/tušem	suh koo-pah-**oh**-nee-tsohm/**too**-shehm

FOOD

A restaurant	Restoran	rehs-**toh**-rahn
The menu	Jelovnik	yeh-**lohv**-neek
The check, please.	Molim, račun.	**moh**-leem, **rah**-choon
Can I order, please?	Mogu li naručiti, molim vas?	**moh**-goo lee nah-**roo**-chee tee, **moh**-leem vahs

Breakfast	Doručak	**doh**-roo-chahk
Lunch	Ručak	**roo**-chahk
Dinner	Večera	**veh**-cheh-rah
Bread	Kruh	krooh
Butter	Putar/maslac	**poo**-tahr/mahs-lahts
Salt/pepper	Sol/papar	sohl/**pah**-pahr
Wine	Vino	**vee**-noh
Beer	Pivo	**pee**-voh
Water/mineral water	Voda/mineralna voda	**voh**-dah/**mee**-neh-rahl-nah **voh**-dah
Milk	Mlijeko	**mlyeh**-koh
Coffee	Kava	**kah**-vah
Tea	Čaj	chay

CZECH VOCABULARY

Czech is considered a difficult language, but it is pronounced phonetically.

Consonants

c = a "ts" sound, as in *its*
c = a "ch" sound, as in *chair*
ch = a hard "ch" sound, as in *loch*
j = a "y" sound, as in *yes*
ň = an "ny" sound, as in *canyon*

r = a combination of "r" and "z," as in *Dvorak*
š = an "sh" sound, as in *shine*
z = a "z" sound, as in *zero*
ž = a "zh" sound, as in *pleasure*

Vowels

a = a short sound, as in *lamb*
e = a short sound, as in *best*
ě = a short "ye," as in *yes*
i, y = a short sound, as "i" in *city*
o = a short sound, as in *book*
u = pronounced as "oo" in *book*

á = a long sound, as in *father*
é = pronounced as "ai" in *air*
í, ý = as a long "e" sound, as in *meet*
ó = pronounced as "o" in *more*
ú, ů = prounced as "oo" in *boom*

ENGLISH	CZECH	PRONUNCIATION

BASICS

ENGLISH	CZECH	PRONUNCIATION
Yes/no	Ano/ne	**ah**-no/neh
Please	Prosím	**pro**-seem
Thank you	Děkuji	**dyek**-oo-yee
Excuse me	Pardon	**par**-don
Sorry [for doing something]	Promiňte	**proh**-meen-yteh
Hello [during the day]	Dobry den	**dohb**-ree den
Good evening	Dobry vecer	**dohb**-ree veh-chehr
Goodbye [formal]	Na shledanou	**nas**-khleh-dah-noh-oo
Goodbye [informal]	Ahoj	**ah**-hoy
Do you speak English?	Mluvíte anglicky?	**mloo**-vit-eh ahng-**glit**-ski?
I don't understand.	Nerozumím	**neh**-rohz-oom-eem
Please speak slowly.	Prosím, mluvte pomalu.	**pro**-seem, **mloov**-teh **poh**-mah-lo
Please write it down.	Prosím napište to.	**pro**-seem nah-**peesh**-teh toh
Please show me.	Ukažte mně	oo-**kazh**-te mnye
I am American (m/f).	Jsem Američan/ Američanka	sem ah-**mer**-i-chan/ ah-**mer**-i-chan-ka

Right/left	Vlevo/ vpravo	**vleh**-voh/ **vprah**-voh
Open/closed	Otevřeno/ Zavřeno	**Oh**-tev-rzh-ehn-oh/ **zav**-rzh-ehn-oh
Arrival/departure	Příjezd/ Odjezd	**przhee**-yeezhd/ **oh**-dy eezhd
Where is . . . ? . . . the train station? . . . the bus station? . . . the bus stop? . . . the airport?	Kde je . . .? . . . Nádraži? . . . Autobus? . . . Autobus? . . . Letiště?	g-deh yeh nah-**drah**-zee **au**-toh-boos **au**-toh-boos **leh**-tish-tyeh
Stop here.	Zastavte tady.	**zah**-stahv-teh **tah**-dee
I would like . . .	Chtěl bych . . .	kh-tyel bihk
How much does it cost?	Kolik to stojí?	ko-**lik** toh **stoy**-ee
Letter/postcard	Dopis/pohlednice	doh-**pis**-ee/ **poh**-hled-nit-seh
By airmail	Letecky	**leh**-tet-skee
Help!	Pomoc!	**po**-motz

NUMBERS

One	Jeden	ye-**den**
Two	Dva	dvah
Three	Tři	tshree
Four	čryři	ch'**ti**-zhee
Five	Pět	pyet
Six	šest	shest
Seven	Sedm	**sed**-oom
Eight	Osm	**oh**-soom
Nine	Devět	**deh**-vyet
Ten	Deset	**deh**-set
Eleven	Jedenáct	yeh-**deh**-nahtst
Twelve	Dvanáct	**dvah**-nahtst
Thirteen	Třináct	trzhee-**nahtst**
Fourteen	čtrnáct	chtihr-**nahtst**
Fifteen	Patnáct	pat-**nahtst**
Sixteen	šestnáct	shest-**nahtst**

Seventeen	Sedmnáct	sedm-**nahtst**
Eighteen	Osmnáct	ohsm-**nahtst**
Nineteen	Devatenáct	deh-vah-teh-**nahtst**
Twenty	Dvacet	**dvah**-tset
Thirty	Třicet	**trzhee**-tset
Fourty	čtyřicet	**chtee**-rzhee-tset
Fifty	Padesát	**pah**-deh-saht
Sixty	šedesát	**sheh**-deh-saht
Seventy	Sedmdesát	**sedm**-deh-saht
Eighty	Osmdesát	**ohsm**-deh-saht
Ninety	Devadesát	**deh**-vah-deh-saht
One hundred	Sto	stoh
One thousand	Tisíc	**tee**-seets

DAYS OF THE WEEK

Sunday	Neděle	**neh**-dyeh-leh
Monday	Pondělí	**pon**-dye-lee
Tuesday	Útery	**oo**-teh-ree
Wednesday	Středa	**stshreh**-da
Thursday	čtvrek	ch't'v'r-tek
Friday	Pátek	**pah**-tek
Saturday	Sobota	**so**-boh-ta

WHERE TO SLEEP

A room	Pokoj	**poh**-koy
The key	Klíč	kleech
With a bath/a shower	S koupelnou/sprchou	s'**ko**-pel-noh/**sp'r**-khoh

FOOD

A restaurant	Restaurace	**reh**-stau-rah-tseh
The menu	Jídelní lístek	**yee**-dell-nee **lis**-tek
The check, please.	Úcet, prosím.	**oo**-chet **pro**-seem
I'd like to order this.	Chtěl bych tohle	khteel bikh **toh**-leh
Breakfast	Snídaně	**snyee**-dan-ye

Lunch	Oběd	**ob**-yed
Dinner	Večeře	**ve**-cher-zhe
Bread	Chléb	khleb
Butter	Máslo	**mah**-slo
Salt/pepper	Sůl/pepř	sool/pepsh
Bottle	Láhev	**lah**-hev
Red/white wine	Cervené/bílé víno	**cher**-ven-eh/**bee**-leh vee-no
Beer	Pivo	**piv**-oh
(Tap) water	Voda	**vo**-da
Sparkling water	Sodovka	**soh**-dohv-ka
Mineral water	Minerálka	min-eh-**rahl**-ka **vo**-da
Milk	Mléko	**mleh**-koh
Coffee	Káva	**kah**-va
Tea (with lemon)	čaj (s citrónem)	tchai (se tsi-**tro**-nem)
Chocolate	čokoláda	cho-koh-**lah**-da

GERMAN VOCABULARY

ENGLISH	GERMAN	PRONUNCIATION
BASICS		
Yes/no	Ja/nein	yah/nine
Please	Bitte	**bit**-uh
Thank you (very much)	Danke (vielen Dank)	**dahn**-kuh (**fee**-lun-dahnk)
Excuse me	Entschuldigen Sie	ent-**shool**-de-gen zee
I'm sorry.	Es tut mir leid.	es toot meer lite
Good day	Guten Tag	**goo**-ten tahk
Good bye	Auf Wiedersehen	auf **vee**-der-zane
Mr./Mrs.	Herr/Frau	hair/frau
Miss	Fräulein	**froy**-line

NUMBERS

1	ein(s)	eint(s)
2	zwei	tsvai
3	drei	dry
4	vier	fear
5	fünf	fumph
6	sechs	zex
7	sieben	**zee**-ben
8	acht	ahkt
9	neun	noyn
10	zehn	tsane

DAYS OF THE WEEK

Sunday	Sonntag	**zone**-tahk
Monday	Montag	**moan**-tahk
Tuesday	Dienstag	**deens**-tahk
Wednesday	Mittwoch	**mit**-voah
Thursday	Donnerstag	**doe**-ners-tahk
Friday	Freitag	fry-tahk
Saturday	Samstag/ Sonnabend	**zahm**-stakh/ **zonn**-a-bent

USEFUL PHRASES

Do you speak English?	Sprechen Sie Englisch?	**shprek**-hun zee **eng**-glish?
I don't speak German.	Ich spreche kein Deutsch.	ich **shprek**-uh kine doych
Please speak slowly.	Bitte sprechen Sie langsam.	**bit**-uh **shprek**-en- zee **lahng**-zahm
I am American/ British	Ich bin Amerikaner(in)/ Engländer(in)	ich bin a-mer-i-**kahn**-er(in)/ **eng**-glan-der(in)
My name is . . .	Ich heiße . . .	ich **hi**-suh
Where are the restrooms?	Wo ist die Toilette?	vo ist dee twah-**let**-uh
Left/right	links/rechts	links/rechts
Open/closed	offen/geschlossen	O-fen/geh-**shloss**-en
Where is . . .	Wo ist . . .	**vo** ist
the train station?	der Bahnhof?	dare **bahn**-hof
the bus stop?	die Bushaltestelle?	dee booss-**hahlt**-uh- shtel-uh
the subway station?	die U-Bahn- Station?	dee oo-bahn-**staht**- sion
the airport?	der Flugplatz?	dare **floog**-plats
the post office?	die Post?	dee **post**
the bank?	die Bank?	dee **banhk**
the police station?	die Polizeistation?	dee po-lee-tsai-**staht**- sion
the Hospital?	das Krankenhaus?	dahs **krahnk**-en-house
the telephone	das Telefon	dahs te-le-**fone**
I'd like . . .	Ich hätte gerne . . .	ich **het**-uh gairn . . .
a room	ein Zimmer	ein **tsim**-er
the key	den Schlüssel	den **shluh**-sul
a map	eine Stadtplan	I-nuh **staht**-plahn
a ticket	eine Karte	I-nuh **cart**-uh
How much is it?	Wieviel kostet das?	vee-feel **cost**-et dahs?
I am ill/sick	Ich bin krank	ich bin **krahnk**
I need . . .	Ich brauche . . .	ich **brow**-khuh
a doctor	einen Arzt	I-nen **artst**
the police	die Polizei	dee po-li-**tsai**
help	Hilfe	**hilf**-uh
Stop!	Halt!	hahlt
Fire!	Feuer!	**foy**-er
Look out/Caution!	Achtung!/Vorsicht!	**ahk**-tung/for-zicht

DINING OUT

A bottle of . . .	eine Flasche . . .	I-nuh **flash**-uh
A cup of . . .	eine Tasse . . .	I-nuh **tahs**-uh
A glass of . . .	ein Glas . . .	ein glahss
Ashtray	der Aschenbecher	dare **Ahsh**-en-bekh-er
Bill/check	die Rechnung	dee **rekh**-nung
Do you have . . .?	Haben Sie . . .?	**hah**-ben zee
I am a vegetarian.	Ich bin Vegetarier(in)	ich bin ve-guh-**tah**-re-er
I'd like to order . . .	Ich möchte . . . bestellen	ich **mohr**-shtuh . . . buh-**shtel**-en
Menu	die Speisekarte	dee **shpie**-zeh-car-tuh
Napkin	die Serviette	dee zair-vee-**eh**-tuh

MENU GUIDE

ENGLISH	GERMAN

GENERAL DINING

Side dishes	Beilagen
Extra charge	Extraaufschlag
When available	Falls verfügbar
Entrées	Hauptspeisen
(not) included	. . .(nicht) inbegriffen
Depending on the season	je nach Saison
Lunch menu	Mittagskarte
Desserts	Nachspeisen
at your choice	. . . nach Wahl
at your request	. . . nach Wunsch
Prices are . . .	Preise sind . . .
Service included	inklusive Bedienung
Value added tax included	inklusive Mehrwertsteuer (Mwst.)
Specialty of the house	Spezialität des Hauses
Soup of the day	Tagessuppe
Appetizers	Vorspeisen
Is served from . . . to . . .	Wird von . . . bis . . . serviert

BREAKFAST

Bread	Brot
Roll(s)	Brötchen
Eggs	Eier
Hot	heiß
Cold	kalt
Jam	Konfitüre
Milk	Milch
Orange juice	Orangensaft
Scrambled eggs	Rühreier
Bacon	Speck
Fried eggs	Spiegeleier
Lemon	Zitrone
Sugar	Zucker

SOUPS

Stew	Eintopf
Chicken soup	Hühnersuppe
Potato soup	Kartoffelsuppe
Liver dumpling soup	Leberknödelsuppe
Onion soup	Zwiebelsuppe

METHODS OF PREPARATION

Blue (boiled in salt and vinegar)	Blau
Baked	Gebacken
Fried	Gebraten
Steamed	Gedämpft
Grilled (broiled)	Gegrillt
Boiled	Gekocht
Sauteed	In Butter geschwenkt
Breaded	Paniert
Raw	Roh

When ordering steak, the English words "rare, medium, (well) done" are used and understood in German.

FISH AND SEAFOOD

Eel	Aal
Oysters	Austern
Trout	Forelle
Flounder	Flunder
Prawns	Garnelen
Halibut	Heilbutt
Herring	Hering
Lobster	Hummer
Scallops	Jakobsmuscheln
Cod	Kabeljau
Crab	Krabbe
Salmon	Lachs
Mackerel	Makrele
Mussels	Muscheln
Squid	Tintenfisch
Tuna	Thunfisch

MEATS

Veal	Kalb(s)
Lamb	Lamm
Beef	Rind(er)
Pork	Schwein(e)
Ham	Schinken

CUTS OF MEAT

Example: For "Lammkeule" see "Lamm" (above) + ". . . keule" (below)

breast	. . . brust
leg	. . . keule
liver	. . . leber
tenderloin	. . . lende
kidney	. . . niere
rib	. . . rippe

Meat patty	Frikadelle
Meat loaf	Hackbraten

GAME AND POULTRY

Duck	Ente
Pheasant	Fasan
Chicken	Hähnchen (Huhn)
Deer	Hirsch
Rabbit	Kaninchen
Venison	Reh
Pigeon	Taube
Turkey	Truthahn
Quail	Wachtel

VEGETABLES

Eggplant	Aubergine
Cauliflower	Blumenkohl
Beans	Bohnen
green	grüne
white	weiße
Peas	Erbsen
Cucumber	Gurke
Cabbage	Kohl
Lettuce	Kopfsalat
Asparagus, peas and carrots	Leipziger Allerlei
Corn	Mais
Carrots	Mohrrüben
Peppers	Paprika
Mushrooms	Pilze
Celery	Sellerie
Asparagus (tips)	Spargel(spitzen)
Tomatoes	Tomaten
Onions	Zwiebeln

CONDIMENTS

Vinegar	Essig
Garlic	Knoblauch
Horseradish	Meerettich
Oil	Öl
Mustard	Senf
Artificial sweetener	Süßstoff
Cinnamon	Zimt
Sugar	Zucker
Salt	Salz

CHEESE

Mild	Allgäuer Käse, Altenburger (goat cheese), Appenzeller, Greyerzer, Hüttenkäse (cottage cheese), Quark, Räucherkäse (smoked cheese), Sahnekäse (creamy), Tilsiter, Ziegekäse (goat cheese).
Sharp	Handkäse, Harzer Käse, Limburger.
curd	frisch
hard	hart
mild	mild

FRUITS

Apple	Apfel
Orange	Apfelsine
Apricot	Aprikose
Blueberry	Blaubeere
Strawberry	Erdbeere
Raspberry	Himbeere
Cherry	Kirsche
Grapefruit	Pampelmuse
Raisin	Rosine
Grape	Weintraube

Banana	Banane
Pear	Birne

DRINKS

with/without ice	mit/ohne Eis
with/without water	mit/ohne Wasser
straight	pur
brandy	. . . geist
liqueur	. . . likör
Mulled claret	Glühwein
Caraway-flavored liquor	Kümmel
Fruit brandy	Obstler

When ordering a Martini, you have to specify "gin (vodka) and vermouth," otherwise you will be given a vermouth (Martini & Rossi).

BEER AND WINE

non-alcoholic	Alkoholfrei
A dark beer	Ein Dunkles
A light beer	Ein Helles
A mug (one quart)	Eine Maß
Draught	Vom Faß
Dark, bitter, high hops content	Altbier
Strong, high alcohol content	Bockbier (Doppelbock, Märzen)
Wheat beer with yeast	Hefeweizen
Light beer, strong hops aroma	Pils(ener)
Wheat beer	Weizen(bier)
Light beer and lemonade	Radlermaß
Wines	Wein
Rosé wine	Rosëwein
Red wine	Rotwein
White wine and mineral water	Schorle
Sparkling wine	Sekt

White wine	Weißwein
dry	herb
light	leicht
sweet	süß
dry	trocken
full-bodied	vollmundig

NON-ALCOHOLIC DRINKS

Coffee	Kaffee
decaffeinated	koffeinfrei
with cream/sugar	mit Milch/Zucker
black	schwarz
Mineral water	Mineralwasser
carbonated/non-carbonated	mit/ohne Kohlensäure
juice	... saft
(hot) Chocolate	(heiße) Schokolade
Tea	Tee
iced tea	Eistee
herb tea	Kräutertee
with cream/lemon	mit Milch/Zitrone

HUNGARIAN VOCABULARY

Tricky double consonants (with English equivalents as they appear in the pronunciation guide below):

gy = a one-syllable "dy" sound (a quick dya—indicated in the pronunciation guide below as dy)

ly = y (as in "yard")

ny = a one-syllable "ny" (a quick nya—indicated below as ny)

ty = a one-syllable "ty" (a quick tya—indicated below as ty)

Tricky vowels:

ö = the "i" in a short, snapped out "Sir!" (pronounced with slightly rounded lips)

ő = the "i" in a long "siiiir" (pronounced with very rounded lips)

ü = no clear English equivalent; like the "ü" in the German expression "über alles" (pronounced with slightly rounded lips)

ű = a longer form of the "ü" (pronounced with very rounded lips)

ENGLISH	HUNGARIAN	PRONUNCIATION

BASICS

ENGLISH	HUNGARIAN	PRONUNCIATION
Yes/no	Igen/nem	**ee**-gen/nem
Please [when asking for something]	Kérem (szépen)	**kay**-rem (**say**-pen)
Please [to get the attention of someone; e.g., a waiter]	Legyen szives	**le**-dyen **see**-vesh
Thank you (kindly)	Köszöszöm (szépen)	**kuh**-suh-nuhm (**say**-pen)
Excuse me	Elnézést	**el**-nay-zaysht
Sorry [for doing something]	Bocsánat	**boh**-chah-nut
Hello [not too formal]	Szervusz	**ser**-voose
Hi [informal, chummy; commonly used]	Szia	**see**-ya
Good evening	Jó estét	**yo**-esh-tate
Goodbye [formal]	Viszontlátásra	**vees**-ohnt-lot-osh-ruh
Goodbye [informal]	Viszlát	vees-**lot**
Do you speak English?	Beszél angolul?	**bess**-ale un-goal-ool

I don't understand.	Nem értem.	**nem** air-tem
I would like . . .	Szeretnék . . .	**ser**-et-nake
How much does it cost?	Mennyibe kerül?	**men**-yee-beh kair-uhl
Help!	Segitség!	**sheh**-geet-shaig
My name is . . .	[stress on name] . . . a nevem.	uh ne-vem
What is your name?	Mi a neve?	**me** uh ne-ve
Where are you from?	Honnan van?	**hone**-un-vun
What is your occupation?	Mi a foglalkozása?	**me** uh foge-lull-koze-ahsh-uh
Let's have a coffee.	Kávézunk egyet.	**kah**-vaze-oonk e-dyet

NUMBERS

One	egy	edy
Two	kettő	**ket**-tuh
Three	három	**hah**-rome
Four	négy	nay-**dy**
Five	öt	uht
Six	hat	hut
Seven	hét	hate
Eight	nyolc	**ny**-olts
Nine	kilenc	**kee**-lents
Ten	tíz	teez
One hundred	száz	sahz
One thousand	ezer	**ez**-zer

DAYS OF THE WEEK

Sunday	vasárnap	**vuh**-shahr-nup
Monday	hétfő	**hate**-fuh
Tuesday	kedd	ked
Wednesday	szerda	**ser**-duh
Thursday	csütörtök	**chit**-ir-tik
Friday	péntek	**pain**-tek
Saturday	szombat	**soam**-but

FOOD

A restaurant	az étterem	uhz **eht**-teh-rem
The menu	az étlap	uhz **ate**-lup
The check, please.	a számlát kérem.	uh **sahm**-lot **kay**-rem
Breakfast	reggeli	**reg**-ell-ee

POLISH VOCABULARY

ENGLISH	POLISH	PRONUNCIATION

BASICS

ENGLISH	POLISH	PRONUNCIATION
Yes/no	Tak/nie	tahk/nye
Please	Proszę	**pro**-sheh
Thank you	Dziękuję	dzhen-**koo**-yeh
Excuse me	Przepraszam	psheh-**prah**-shahm
Hello	Dzien dobry	dzhehn **dohb**-ry
Do you (m/f) speak English?	Czy pan (pani) mówi po angielsku?	chee **pahn** (**pahn**-ee) moovie poh ahn-**gyel**-skuu?
I don't speak Polish.	Nie mówię po Polsku.	nyeh **moohv**-yeh po-**pohl**-skoo
I don't understand.	Nie rozumiem.	nyeh rohz-**oo**-myehm
Please speak slowly.	Proszę mówić wolniej.	proh-sheh **moo**-veech **vohl**-nyah
Please write it down.	Proszę napisać.	**proh**-sheh nah-pee-sahtch
I am American (m/f)	Jestem Amerykani-nem/Amerykanką	**yest**-em ah-mer-i-**kahn**-in-em/ ah-mer-i-**kahn**-ka
My name is . . .	Nazywam się . . .	nah-**ziv**-ahm sheh
On the right/left	Na prawo/lewo	nah-**prah**-vo/**lyeh**-vo
Where is . . . ?	Gdzie jest . . . ?	gdzhyeh yest
. . . the station?	. . . Dworzec kolejowy?	**dvoh**-zhets koh-lay-oh-vee
. . . the train?	. . . Pociąg?	**poh**-chohnk
. . . the bus?	. . . Autobus?	a'oo-**toh**-boos
. . . the airport?	. . . Lotnisko?	loht-**nees**-koh
. . . the post office?	. . . Poczta?	**poch**-tah
. . . the bank?	. . . Bank?	bahnk
Stop here, please.	Proszę się tu zatrzymać.	**proh**-sheh sheh too zah-**tchee**-mahch
I would like (m/f). . .	Chciałbym . . . / Chciałabym . . .	**kh'chow**-beem/ kh'chow-**ah**-beem
How much?	Ile?	**ee**-leh
Letters/postcards	Listy/kartki	**lees**-tee/**kahrt**-kee

By airmail	Lotniczy	loht-**nee**-chee
Help!	Na pomoc!	na **po**-motz

NUMBERS

One	Jeden	**yeh**-den
Two	Dwa	dvah
Three	Trzy	tchee
Four	Cztery	**chteh**-ree
Five	Pięć	pyehnch
Six	Sze{ć	shsyshch
Seven	Siedem	**shyeh**-dem
Eight	Osiem	**oh**-shyem
Nine	Dziewięć	**dzhyeh**-vyehnch
Ten	Dziesięć	**dzhyeh**-shehnch
One hundred	Sto	stoh
One thousand	Tysiąc	**tee**-shonts

DAYS OF THE WEEK

Sunday	Niedziela	nyeh-**dzhy'e**-la
Monday	Poniedziałek	poh-nyeh-**dzhya**-wek
Tuesday	Wtorek	**ftohr**-ek
Wednesday	Środa	**shroh**-da
Thursday	Czwartek	**chvahr**-tek
Friday	Piątek	**pyohn**-tek
Saturday	Sobota	soh-**boh**-ta

WHERE TO SLEEP

A room	Pokój	**poh**-kooy
The key	Klucz	klyuch
With bath/shower	Z łazienką/ prysznicem	zwah-**zhen**-koh/ spree-**shnee**-tsem

FOOD

The menu	Menu	**men**-yoo
The check, please.	Proszę rachunek	**proh**-sheh rah-**kh'oon**-ehk
Breakfast	Śniadanie	shnya-**dahn**-iyeh
Lunch	Obiad	**oh**-byat
Dinner	Kolacja	koh-**lah**-ts'yah
Beef	Wołowina	voh-woh-**veen**-a
Bread and butter	Chleb i masło	kh'lyep ee **mahs**-woh
Vegetables	Jarzyny	yah-**zhin**-ee
Salt/pepper	Sól/pieprz	sool/pyehpsh
Bottle of wine	Butelkę wina	boo-**tehl**-keh **vee**-na
Beer	Piwo	**pee**-voh
(Mineral) Water	Wodę (mineralną)	**voh**-deh (**mee-nehr**-ahl-nohn
Coffee with milk	Kawę z mliekem	**kah**-veh **zmlehk**-yem
Tea with lemon	Herbatę z cytryną	kh'ehr-**bah**-teh **ststrin**-ohn

ROMANIAN VOCABULARY

	ENGLISH	ROMANIAN	PRONUNCIATION
BASICS			
	Yes/no	Da/nu	dah/noo
	Please	Vă rog	vuh **rohg**
	Thank you	Vă mulţumesc	vuh **mull**-tsoo-mesk
	Excuse me	Scuzaţi-mă	skoo-**zatz**-see-muh
	I'm sorry.	Îmi pare rău.	uhm pah-ray **ruh**-oo
	Hello/how do you do	Bună ziua	boo-nuh **zee**-wah
	Do you speak English?	Vorbiţî engleză?	vor-**beetz** ehn-**glehz**-uh
	I don't speak Romanian.	Nu vorbesc româ neşte.	noo vor-**besk** roh-muh-**nesh**-tay
	I don't understand.	Nu înţeleg.	noo uhn-tseh-**lehgah**
	Please speak slowly.	Vorbiţi rar.	vor-**beetz** rahr
	Please write it down.	Scrieţi, vă rog.	skree-ets vuh **rohg**
	Please show me.	Indicaţi-mi, vă rog.	een-dee-**caht**-zee-mee, vuh **rohg**
	I am American (m/f)	Sunt american/ americană	suhnt ah-mehr-ee-**cahn**/ah-mer-ee-**cahn**-nah
	My name is . . .	Mă numesc	muh noo-**mesk**
	Right/left	Dreapta/stânga	**dryahp**-tah/**stuhn**-gah
	Open/closed	Deschis/închis	deh-**skees**/uhn-**kees**
	Arrivals/departures	Sosiri/plecări	soh-**seer**-ih/pleh-**cuhr**-ih
	Where is . . . ?	Unde este . . . ?	**uhn**-day **ehs**-tay
	. . . the station?	. . . gara/staţie?	**gah**-ruh/**staht**-zee-ay
	. . . the train?	. . . trenul?	**treh**-nul
	. . . the bus/tram?	. . . autobuz/tramvai?	ahu-to-**booz**/ trahm-**viy**
	. . . the airport?	. . . aeroportul?	air-oh-**por**-tull
	. . . the post office?	. . . pos̗tˇa?	**pahsh**-tah
	. . . a bank?	. . . o bancă?	oh **bahn**-kuh
	Stop here.	Opriţi aici.	oh-**preetz** ah-**eech**
	I would like . . .	Aş doresc . . .	ahsh dor-**rehsk**

How much does it cost?	Cît costă?	cuht **cohs**-tuh
a letter/postcard	o scrisoare/carte poştală	oh scree-**swahr**-ray/**kahr**-tay pohsh-**tah**-luh
By airmail	par avion	par ah-vee-**ohn**
Help!	Ajutor!	ah-**zhoo**-tore

NUMBERS

One	Unu	**uh**-nuh
Two	Doi	doy
Three	Trei	tray
Four	Patru	**paht**-ruh
Five	Cinci	cheench
Six	Ωase	**shah**-say
Seven	Ωapte	**shahp**-tay
Eight	Opt	ohpt
Nine	Nouă	**noh**-oo-uh
Ten	Zece	**zeh**-chay
One hundred	O sută	oh **soo**-tuh
One thousand	O mie	oh **mee**-ay

DAYS OF THE WEEK

Sunday	Duminică	duh-**mih**-nih-kuh
Monday	Luni	**luh**-nih
Tuesday	Marţi	mahrts
Wednesday	Miercuri	**meer**-kurih
Thursday	Joi	zhoy
Friday	Vineri	**vee**-nehrih
Saturday	Sîmbătă	**suhm**-buh-tuh

WHERE TO SLEEP

A room	O cameră	oh **kah**-meh-ruh
The key	Cheia	**kay**-ah
With bath/with shower	Cu baie/duş	koo **bah**-yeh/**doosh**

FOOD

A restaurant	Un restaurant	uhn rehs-tau-**rahnt**
The menu	Meniul, lista	**meh**-nee-ool/ **lees**-tah
The check, please.	Plata, vă rog.	**plah**-tah, **vuh** rahg
I'd like to order this.	Aş vrea să comand acesta.	ahsh **vryah** suh coh-**mahnd** ah-**ches**-tah
Breakfast	Micul dejun	**mee**-kuhl deh-**zhoon**
Lunch	Dejun, prînz	deh-**zhoon**/ prunz
Dinner	cina	**chee**-nuh
Bread	pâine	**puhee**-nuh
Butter	Unt	uhnt
Salt/pepper	Sare/piper	**sah**-ray/**pih**-pair
a bottle	O sticlă	oh **steek**-luh
Red/white wine	Vin roşu/alb	veen **roh**-shoo/**ahlb**
Beer	bere	**bare**-ay
(Mineral) Water	Apă (minerală)	**ah**-puh (meen-eh-**rahl**-uh)
Milk	Lapte	**lahp**-tay
coffee (with milk)	cafea (cu lapte)	**cah**-fyah(koo **lahp**-tay)
tea (with lemon)	Ceai (cu lămîie)	**chiy**-ih (koo luh-**muh**-yeh)
Chocolate	Cacao	kah-**cah**-oh
plum brandy	Ţuică	tsooee-kuh

SLOVAK VOCABULARY

	ENGLISH	SLOVAK	PRONUNCIATION
BASICS			
	Yes/No	Ano/Nie	ah-no/nee-ay
	Please	Prosím	**pro**-seem
	Thank you (very much)	Dakujem	**dyak**-we-em
	Pardon me	Pardon	**par**-don
	Hello	Dobry deň	**dob**-ree den
	Do you speak English?	Hovorite anglicky?	ho-vor-**ee**-teh **an**-glits-kay
	I don't speak Slovak.	Nehovorim po slovensky.	**nay**-ho-vor-eem po **sloh**-ven-skee
	I don't understand.	Nerozumiem.	**nay**-roz-ooh-me-em
	Please, speak slowly.	Hovorte prosím pomaly.	ho-vor-**ee**-teh **pro**-seem po-mal-**ee**
	Please, write it down.	Napište mi to prosím.	nah-**peesh**-tay mee toh **pro**-seem
	Show me . . .	Ukažte mi . . .	**ooh**-kazh-tay mee
	I am American (m/f).	Som Američan/ Američanka.	sum ah-**mer**-ee-chan/ ah-**mer**-ee-chan-ka
	My name is . . .	Volam sa .	vo-**lam** sah
	On the right/left	Napravo/nalavo	na-**prah**-vo/ na-**lahv**-oh
	Arrivals	Prichody (trains, buses), Prilety (planes)	pree-ho-dee, **pree**-let-ee
	Where is . . . ?	Kde je . . .	g'deh yeh
	. . . the station?	. . . stanica?	**stan**-eet-sa
	. . . the train?	. . . vlak?	vlahk
	. . . he tram?	. . . električka?	ee-lek-**treech**-ka
	. . . the airport?	. . . letisko?	let-**ee**-sko
	. . . the post office?	. . . poš	**o**-shta
	. . . the bank?	. . . banka?	**bahn**-ka
	Stop here.	Zastavte tu.	zah-**stahv**-teh too
	I would like (m/f). . .	Chcel by som/ Chcela by som	huh'cell bee sum/ huh'cel-la bee sum
	How much does it cost?	Koľko to stoji?	koal-**koh** toh **stoy**-ee

Letter/postcard	List/pohľadnica	eest/poh-lahd-neet-sa
By airmail	Letecky	**leh**-tet-skee
Help!	Pomoc!	**po**-mots

NUMBERS

One	Jeden	**ye**-den
Two	Dva	dvah
Three	Tri	tree
Four	štyri	**shteer**-ee
Five	Peť	pet
Six	šesť	shest
Seven	Sedem	**sed**-em
Eight	Osem	**oh**-sem
Nine	Deveť	**dehv**-et
Ten	Desať	**deh**-saht
One hundred	Sto	stoh
One thousand	Tisíc	**tee**-seets

DAYS OF THE WEEK

Sunday	Nedeľa	**neyd**-yel-ha
Monday	Pondelok	**pahn**-dyel-ahk
Tuesday	Utorok	**ooh**-tehr-ahk
Wednesday	Streda	**strey**-dah
Thursday	štvrtok	**shťver**-tahk
Friday	Piatok	**pee**-ah-tahk
Saturday	Sobota	**so**-boh-ta

WHERE TO SLEEP

A room	Izba	**eez**-bah
The key	Kľuč	klooh'ch
With bath/shower	S kupeľňou	s'kooh-pel-**nyu**

FOOD

Menu	Jedálny listok	ye-**dahl**-nee **lees**-tahk
The check, please.	Učet, prosím.	**oo**-chet **pro**-seem
Breakfast	Raňajky	rah-**nyike**-ee
Lunch	Obed	oh-bed
Dinner	Večera	**vah**'chair-a
Bread	Chlieb	huh'lee'eb
Butter	Máslo	**mah**-slo
Salt/pepper	Soľ/Korenie	sol/**kor**-en-yee
Bottle	Flaša	**flah**-sha
Red/white wine	červené/biele vino	**cher**-ven-eh/**bee**-al-ee **vee**-no
Beer	Pivo	**piv**-oh
Mineral water	Minerálka voda	min-eh-**rahl**-ka **vo**-da
Milk	Mlieko	**m'lee'eck**-oh
Coffee	Káva	**kah**-va
Tea (with lemon)	čaj (s citrónem)	tchai (se tsi-tro-nem)

SLOVENIAN VOCABULARY

ENGLISH	SLOVENIAN	PRONUNCIATION
BASICS		
Yes/no	Da/ne	dah/nay
Please	Prosim	**proh**-seem
Thank you (very much)	Hvala (lepa)	**hvah**-lah (**lay**-pah)
Excuse me	Oprostite	oh-pros-**tee**-tay
I'm sorry	Žal mi je	zh-**ow** mee yay
Hello/how do you do	Dober dan	**doh**-boo dan
Do you speak English?	Govorite angleško?	goh-vor-**ee**-tay ang-**lay**-shkoh
I don't speak Slovenian.	Ne govorim slovensko.	nay goh-vor-**eem** sloh-**ven**-skoh
I don't understand.	Ne razumem.	nay raz-**oom**-em
Please speak slowly.	Prosim, govorite počasi.	**proh**-seem, goh-vor-ee-tay poh-**chah**-see
Please write it down.	Prosim, napišite.	**proh**-seem, nah-**pee**-shee-tay
Please show me.	Prosim, pokažite.	**proh**-seem, poh-**kah**-zhee-tay
I am American	Jaz sem američan	yoo sum ah-mer-ee-**chan**
I am English	Jaz sem anglež	yoo sum ang-**lezh**
My name is . . .	Ime mi je . . .	ee-**may** mee yay . . .
Right/left	Desno/levo	**des**-noh/ **lee**-voh
Open/closed	Odprt/zaprt	**od**-prt/ **za**-prt
Arrival/departure	Prihod/odhod	pree-**hod**/ od-**hod**
Where is . . . ?	Kje je . . . ?	k-**yay** yay . . . ?
. . . the train station?	. . . železniška postaja?	zheh-**lay**-zneesh-kah post-**ay**-ah
. . . the bus stop?	. . . avtobusna postaja?	aw-toh-**boos**-nah post-**ay**-ah
. . . the airport?	. . . letališče?	let-al-**ee**-shuh-cheh
. . . the post office?	. . . pošta?	**poh**-shtah
. . . the bank?	. . . banka?	**ban**-kah
Stop here	Vstavi tukaj	uh-**stah**-vee **took**-ay
I would like . . .	Hotel bi . . .	hot-**ay**-oo bee . . .

How much does it cost?	Koliko stane?	**koh**-lee-koh **stah**-nay
Letter/postcard	Pismo/dopisnica	**pee**-smoh/doh-**pee**-snee-tsah
By airmail	Zračna pošta	**zrah**-chnah **poh**-shtah
Help!	Na pomoč!	nah poh-**moch**

NUMBERS

One	Ena	enah
Two	Dva	dvah
Three	Tri	tree
Four	Štiri	**shtee**-ree
Five	Pet	pit
Six	Šest	shest
Seven	Sedem	**sed**-em
Eight	Osem	**oh**-sem
Nine	Devet	deh-**vit**
Ten	Deset	deh-**sit**
One hundred	Sto	stoh
Two hundred	Dve sto	dvee stoh

DAYS OF THE WEEK

Monday	Ponedeljek	poh-neh-**dee**-lyek
Tuesday	Torek	**tor**-ek
Wednesday	Sreda	**sree**-dah
Thursday	Četrtek	**chet**-rtek
Friday	Petek	**pee**-tek
Saturday	Sobota	soh-**boh**-tah
Sunday	Nedelja	nay-**dee**-lyah

WHERE TO SLEEP

A room	Soba	**soh**-bah
The key	Ključ	kluh-**yooch**
With bath/a shower	s kopanicu/s prho	skoh-pan-**ee**-tsoo/**spruh**-hoh

FOOD

Restaurant	Restavracija	rest-aw-**rats**-ee-yah
The menu	Jedilnik	yed-**eel**-nik
The check, please.	Prosim, račun.	**proh**-seem, rach-**oon**
Breakfast	Zajtrk	**zay**-trik
Lunch	Kosilo	kos-**eel**-oh
Dinner	Obed	oh-**bed**
Bread	Kruh	kroo
Butter	Maslo	**mas**-loh
Salt/pepper	Sol/poper	sol/**poh**-per
Bottle	Steklenica	stek-len-**ee**-tsah
Red/white wine	Črno/belo vino	chur-noh/bel-oh **vee**-noh
Beer	Pivo	**pee**-voh
Water/mineral water	Voda/mineralna voda	**voh**-dah/min-er-**al**-nah **voh**-dah
Milk	Mleko	**mlih**-koh
Coffee (with milk)	Kava z mlekom	**kah**-vah **zmlih**-kom
Tea (with lemon)	Čaj z limono	chay zlcem-**on**-oh

INDEX

ABOUT OUR AUTHORS

Although there's no substitute for travel advice from a good friend who knows your style, our contributors are the next best thing—the kind of people you would poll for travel advice if you knew them.

Mark Baker is a freelance journalist and travel writer residing in Prague, though he spent five years living and working in Vienna as an editor for Economist Intelligence Unit. He's a frequent traveler throughout Eastern and Central Europe. Mark updated the Bulgaria and Romania chapters for this guide.

Jane Foster is a freelance writer who hails from the Yorkshire Dales in the United Kingdom. She studied for a degree in architecture before moving to Rome in 1990, where travel, art, and culture became her main interests. She lived in Split for six years, where she learned to speak Croatian and cook Dalmatian-style, and also fell prey to the pleasures of sailing and nudism. Although she is now based in Athens, she makes frequent trips back to Croatia for both work and pleasure. Jane updated portions of the chapter on Croatia and wrote the new Montenegro chapter for this guide.

Betsy Maury, a former senior editor at Bantam Doubleday Dell, lived in Slovenia for four years, traveling widely in that country and in neighboring Croatia. Since 1999 she has made her home in Budapest. Her enthusiasm for Hungarian cuisine keeps her busy exploring the cosmopolitan city in search of interesting restaurants, and her love of wine has brought her to Croatia on several occasions. She has traveled widely throughout Central Europe, working as a freelance writer. Betsy wrote a new chapter on Bosnia and Herzegovina for this guide, as well as updating portions of the Croatia chapter.

A contributor to previous Fodor's guides to Eastern and Central Europe and Budapest, **Paul Olchváry** lived in Hungary from 1990 to 2000 and has thoroughly explored not only that country but also neighboring Croatia. Translator of nine books from the Hungarian and a writer of short stories and novels, he was a copy writer at Princeton University Press from 2000 to 2005, when he absconded with his wife, Dorottya, to a cabin in the woods of Kismaros, Hungary, to pursue his own writing. Paul updated the chapter on Hungary and portions of the Croatia chapter for this guide.

"Life in Vienna is just wonderful," says Yorkshire-born **Diane Naar-Elphee.** After living in the capital city for 30 years, Diane has become an authority on its art, history, and nightlife. She has worked for many years as a guide-lecturer, and she has traveled the whole country. "Austria can become addictive," she warns. Diane updated the Austria and Slovakia chapters for this guide.

Evan Rail moved to Prague in 2000 and stayed there primarily because of the kvasnicové pivo. For many years, he reviewed restaurants and covered food and drink for the Prague Post until he left to write the *Good Beer Guide to Prague and the Czech Republic* for CAMRA, a U.K. beer consumers' organization. His stories have been included in *Best Food Writing* and *Travelers' Tales* anthologies and appear frequently in *The New York Times* travel section. Evan updated the Czech Republic and Slovenia chapters for this guide.

Dorota Wąsik has been fond of museums and trips to the Polish seaside since her early years. No wonder she grew up to become a travel addict. But all roads take her back to her native Kraków. With a degree in English literature from Jagiellonian University, including a term at Oxford, she works as a writer and translator, a part-time teacher, and an accidental tour guide. She updated the Poland chapter for this guide.